THE COMPLETE HISTORY OF
CRICKET TOURS
AT HOME AND ABROAD

THE COMPLETE HISTORY OF
CRICKET TOURS
AT HOME AND ABROAD

PETER WYNNE-THOMAS

GUILD PUBLISHING
London

This edition published in 1989 by
Guild Publishing
by arrangement with
The Hamlyn Publishing Group Limited
a division of The Octopus Publishing Group
Michelin House, 81 Fulham Road, London SW3 6RB

CN 1570

Contents

ENGLAND ON TOUR

◆

A Record of All England Cricket Tours Overseas,
with Accounts, Results and Statistics,
from the 1859 Trip to North America
to the Tour of Australia
and New Zealand in 1987-8

Introduction

The first tour by English cricketers overseas should have taken place in 1789 to Paris. The visit was arranged in conjunction with the Duke of Dorset, Britain's ambassador in Paris, and the Duke of Leeds, who was the Foreign Secretary. The team travelled to Dover to board the cross Channel ferry, but before they could begin the voyage, they were met by the Duke of Dorset, fleeing from the French Revolution.

Politics had clashed with cricket and the former, not for the last time, had won the day! This first tour has intrigued and baffled historians ever since records of it were unearthed. The question, which should rank among the world's great mysteries, is: who were the English cricketers going to play when they arrived in Paris? If this present volume does nothing more than prompt historians to delve for the answer, the author, at least, will be satisfied.

The story of the adventures and misadventures of English cricketers on tour is in essence the history of the development of the game outside the British Isles. It traces the steady improvement in cricketers overseas and sadly in a few instances the decline of those cricketers. The latter fact is immediately apparent from the first tour which did actually take place. In the late summer of 1859, the pick of England's cricketers crossed the Atlantic to play in the United States and Canada, for North America was regarded as the strongest home of the game outside England – the first cricket international, Canada versus the United States, had been staged as early as 1844. The 1859 English cricketers were overwhelmingly successful, but no more so than they proved to be on their initial visits to other countries. The slow collapse of cricket in North America can be seen as the teams sent from England got progressively weaker.

English cricketers first travelled to Australia in 1861-62, but it was not until 1876-77 that an Australian team was capable of challenging the tourists on even terms – before this the local sides had fielded anything up to 22 players against the English Eleven. The fact that the Australian team actually beat the English cricketers on even terms in 1876-77 meant that the 'Test Match' was born, though it was some years before the 'statisticians' and pressmen concocted the 'Test Match Records', with which everyone is familiar, and at the same time acclaimed England's defeat in 1876-77 as the 'First Test'.

The English tourists who went to Australia in the early days also visited New Zealand on several occasions, but the opposition there was much too weak to challenge the tourists on even terms.

In 1888-89 Major Warton, who had been stationed in South Africa for several years, pioneered the first English tour of that country and his team played South Africa on even terms in two matches, both of which are now described as 'Test Matches', though in reality they have no right to that august title. In the first instance, the English team beat the South Africans with ease, and in the second the English team was not even intended to be representative of England at full strength. To make the position of these Tests even more ludicrous, when the might of South Africa came to England in 1894, the visitors were not considered good enough to feature in the first-class averages. Cricket in South Africa however made great strides in the next few years and soon remedied this slight.

Six years after Major Warton's venture, R. S. Lucas took the first English team to the West Indies. The team were all amateurs and the visit was as much a social one as a cricketing tour, but it did serve to encourage cricket in the West Indies, as G. F. Vernon's adventure had done in India in 1888-89. The important factor of the visits to both India and West Indies was that the native populations were becoming fascinated by the game. In so many other countries where English teams toured, cricket was confined to expatriates. The supreme example of this is in South America. Lord Hawke took a side there in 1911-12 and tours have

gone out quite regularly since, but in Argentina, Brazil, Chile and Peru cricket has remained the game of the English, and the decline of the English community in those countries parallels the decline of cricket also. A similar decline occurred in Egypt, where the large presence of English soldiers, sailors and civil servants created a team which was of first-class standard between the wars. Here at least a native Egyptian side was created but it has since fallen on hard times.

The improvement of the game in India, the West Indies and New Zealand and indeed in Pakistan and Sri Lanka has created its own problems. As late as 1929-30, the M.C.C. were content to leave the best English cricketers at home for the winter and still send out simultaneously 'representative' teams to both West Indies and New Zealand – by some historical quirk both these tours had 'Test Matches'. In the 1950s it became obvious that England could not continue to dispatch the second best to everywhere except Australia and South Africa. The opponents not only beat the weak English team, but were insulted by it.

The solution has yet to be found and politics which cancelled that very first tour very rarely stay in the background. Air travel and the development of one-day matches are two other influences that are changing the traditional pattern of major tours abroad, and the trials of George Parr and his companions on the tour of 1859 are at once completely different yet somehow the same as those met by English cricketers today – the problems of travel, of an alien climate and of opponents whose love of the game is as strong as the tourists.

Scope of Work

This book contains every English overseas tour involving first-class matches and a few other tours by good class English cricketers which the author considers worthy of note.

Tours which are made by 'Commonwealth' or 'International' teams, even though in some instances the majority of the players are from England, are not included, except for the 1967-68 'International' team to Africa and Asia, since this was entirely composed of English County cricketers.

When southern hemisphere countries are toured, the years given to the tour in the headings and elsewhere relate to the season in which the tour is considered to have taken place. Thus tours of Australia and the West Indies will be described by a winter date, e.g. 1970-71, even though the entire tour might have taken place within one calendar year.

Definition of a First-class Match

There is not, nor has there ever been, an authority with powers to rule on the status of matches on a world-wide basis. Dealing with the matches given in this work, there are broadly two areas in which there is no clearly defined ruling on the status of matches. The first involves the early tours to each of the major cricketing countries, prior to those countries having competent 'Boards of Control' to rule on matches. The second involves the non-Test playing countries – the United States, Canada, Argentina, East Africa, Egypt, Malaya, etc. – in which first-class English sides have played three-day 11-a-side matches against representative teams.

The Association of Cricket Statisticians has been working on the problem of first-class status for the last ten years and is in the process of issuing 'Guides' to first-class matches in each country. At the present time 'Guides' to matches in the British Isles, Australia, South Africa and New Zealand have been published and this present book adheres to the rulings given in these Guides. So far as the other countries' matches are concerned, the status allotted to each is the considered opinion of the author.

In the summaries of results for each tour, Test Match results are printed in **bold type**, first-class matches are in ordinary Roman type, and other matches are in *italic type*.

Acknowledgements
The books used in the research for this work are so numerous that a bibliography is impractical. Apart from Wisden's Cricketers' Almanack, the two Lillywhite annuals, the magazines *Cricket, The Cricketer, Wisden Cricket Monthly, Playfair Cricket Monthly* and the various overseas annuals, extensive use has been made of the principal tour books and players' biographies.

The author is indebted to Philip Bailey for providing the first-class averages, to Philip Thorn and Keith Warsop for checking through the manuscript, to Dennis Lambert for providing scores of 1974-75 West Indian tours, to Peter Arnold for his advice and assistance throughout, and also to the various publications of the Association of Cricket Statisticians.

Summary of tours

t Denotes tied match included in draws   * Tours with Test matches
Matches with no play at all are not included

	To	Organiser	Captain	Results All matches				First class			
				P	W	L	D	P	W	L	D
1859	North America	W. P. Pickering	G. Parr	5	5	0	0	Nil			
1861-62	Australia	Spiers and Pond	H. H. Stephenson	12	6	2	4	Nil			
1863-64	Australia and New Zealand	Melbourne C.C.	G. Parr	16	10	0	6	Nil			
1868	North America	North American Cricket	E. Willsher	6	5	0	1	Nil			
1872	North America	M.C.C.	R. A. Fitzgerald	8	7	0	1	Nil			
1873-74	Australia	Melbourne C.C.	W. G. Grace	15	10	3	2	Nil			
*1876-77	Australia and New Zealand	J. Lillywhite	J. Lillywhite	23	11	4	8	3	1	1	1
*1878-79	Australia, New Zealand and USA	Melbourne C.C.	Lord Harris	15	6	3	6	5	2	3	0
1879	North America	J. P. Ford	R. Daft	12	9	0	3	Nil			
*1881-82	USA, Australia and New Zealand	Lillywhite/Shaw/Shrewsbury	A. Shaw	30	15	3	12	7	3	2	2
*1882-83	Ceylon, Australia	Melbourne C.C.	Hon Ivo Bligh	18	9	3	6	7	4	3	0
*1884-85	Egypt, Australia	Lillywhite/Shaw/Shrewsbury	A. Shrewsbury	34	16	2	16	8	6	2	0
1885	North America	E. J. Sanders	R. T. Thornton	8	6	1	1	4	3	1	0
1886	North America	E. J. Sanders	W. E. Roller	9	8	0	1	3	3	0	0
*1886-87	Australia	Lillywhite/Shaw/Shrewsbury	A. Shrewsbury	29	12	2	15	10	6	2	2
1887-88	Australia	Melbourne C.C. (known as G. F. Vernon's Team)	Lord Hawke	26	11	1	14	8	6	1	1
1887-88	Australia and New Zealand	Lillywhite/Shaw/Shrewsbury	C. A. Smith	25	14	2	9	7	5	2	0
*1887-88	Australia	Combined Teams	W. W. Read	1	1	0	0	1	1	0	0
*1888-89	South Africa	Major R. G. Warton	C. A. Smith	19	13	4	2	2	2	0	0
1889-90	Ceylon, India	G. F. Vernon	G. F. Vernon	13	10	1	2	Nil			
1891	North America	Lord Hawke	Lord Hawke	8	6	1	1	2	1	1	0
*1891-92	Malta, Ceylon, Australia	Lord Sheffield	W. G. Grace	29	12	2	15	8	6	2	0
*1891-92	South Africa	W. W. Read	W. W. Read	21	14	0	7	1	1	0	0
1892-93	Ceylon, India	Lord Hawke	Lord Hawke	23	15	2	6	8	4	2	2
1894	North America	Philadelphia	Lord Hawke	5	3	0	2	3	2	0	1
*1894-95	Ceylon, Australia	Australia	A. E. Stoddart	24	10	4	10	12	8	4	0
1894-95	West Indies	Lord Stamford	R. S. Lucas	16	10	4	2	7	3	3	1
1895	North America	Philadelphia	F. Mitchell	5	2	2	1	4	2	2	0
1895-96	South Africa	South Africa	Lord Hawke	18	7	3	8	4	3	0	1
1896-97	West Indies	West Indies	Lord Hawke	14	9	2	3	7	3	2	2
1896-97	West Indies	Jamaica	A. Priestley	16	10	5	1	9	4	5	0
1897	USA	Philadelphia	P. F. Warner	6	2	1	3	3	2	1	0
*1897-98	Australia	Australia	A. E. Stoddart	22	6	5	11	12	4	5	3
1898	North America	Philadelphia	P. F. Warner	8	6	0	2	3	3	0	0
*1898-99	South Africa	J. D. Logan	Lord Hawke	17	15	0	2	5	5	0	0
1899	North America	Philadelphia	K. S. Ranjitsinhji	5	3	0	2	2	2	0	0
1901	North America	Philadelphia	B. J. T. Bosanquet	5	3	2	0	2	1	1	0
*1901-02	Australia	Australia	A. C. MacLaren	22	8	6	8	11	5	6	0
1901-02	West Indies	West Indies	R. A. Bennett	19	13	5	1	13	8	5	0
1902-03	USA, New Zealand and Australia	New Zealand C.C. (known as Lord Hawke's Team)	P. F. Warner	22	19	2	1	10	7	2	1

	To	Organiser	Captain	All matches				First class			
				P	W	L	D	P	W	L	D
1902-03	India	OUA and Calcutta	K. J. Key	19	12	2	5	6	2	2	2
1903	USA	Kent C.C.C.	J. R. Mason	4	4	0	0	2	2	0	0
*1903-04	Australia	M.C.C.	P. F. Warner	20	10	2	8	14	9	2	3
1904-05	West Indies	Lord Brackley	Lord Brackley	20	11	3	6	10	6	3	1
1905	North America	M.C.C.	E. W. Mann	8	5	1	2	2	1	1	0
*1905-06	South Africa	M.C.C.	P. F. Warner	26	17	5	4	12	7	5	0
1906-07	South Africa, New Zealand	M.C.C.	E. G. Wynyard	17	11	2	4	11	6	2	3
1907	North America	M.C.C.	H. K. Hesketh-Prichard	5	1	0	4	2	0	0	2
*1907-08	Australia	M.C.C.	A. O. Jones	19	7	4	8	18	7	4	7
1909	Egypt	M.C.C.	G. H. Simpson-Hayward	8	7	1	0	Nil			
*1909-10	South Africa	M.C.C.	H. D. G. Leveson-Gower	18	9	4	5	13	7	4	2
1910-11	West Indies	M.C.C.	A. W. F. Somerset	12	4	4	4t	11	3	4	4t
*1911-12	Ceylon, Australia	M.C.C.	P. F. Warner	19	13	1	5	14	11	1	2
1911-12	Argentine	M.C.C.	Lord Hawke	9	6	1	2	3	2	1	0
1912-13	West Indies	M.C.C.	A. W. F. Somerset	9	5	3	1	9	5	3	1
1913	USA	Incogniti	C. E. Greenway	6	4	1	1	2	1	1	0
*1913-14	South Africa	M.C.C.	J. W. H. T. Douglas	22	12	1	9	18	9	1	8
1920	North America	Incogniti	E. J. Metcalfe	9	7	0	2	Nil			
*1920-21	Ceylon, Australia	M.C.C.	J. W. H. T. Douglas	23	9	6	8	13	5	6	2
*1922-23	South Africa	M.C.C.	F. T. Mann	22	14	1	7	14	10	1	3
1922-23	Ceylon, Australia and New Zealand	M.C.C.	A. C. MacLaren	23	11	3	9	15	6	3	6
1923	Canada	Free Foresters	E. G. Wynyard	7	6	0	1	Nil			
1924	USA	Incogniti	E. J. Metcalfe	7	2	0	5	Nil			
*1924-25	Ceylon, Australia	M.C.C.	A. E. R. Gilligan	24	8	6	10	17	7	6	4
1924-25	South Africa	S. B. Joel	Hon L. H. Tennyson	21	8	2	11	14	5	2	7
1925-26	West Indies	M.C.C.	Hon F. S. Gough-Calthorpe	13	2	1	10	12	2	1	9
1926-27	India, Burma, Ceylon	M.C.C.	A. E. R. Gilligan	34	11	0	23	30	10	0	20
1926-27	South America	M.C.C.	P. F. Warner	10	6	1	3	5	3	1	1
1926-27	Jamaica	Hon L. H. Tennyson	Hon L. H. Tennyson	7	1	0	6	3	0	0	3
*1927-28	South Africa	M.C.C.	R. T. Stanyforth	18	7	2	9	16	7	2	7
1927-28	Jamaica	Hon L. H. Tennyson	Hon L. H. Tennyson	5	1	2	2	3	0	2	1
*1928-29	Ceylon, Australia	M.C.C.	A. P. F. Chapman	25	11	1	13	17	8	1	8
1928-29	Jamaica	J. Cahn	J. Cahn	6	1	2	3	3	0	2	1
1929	Egypt	H. M. Martineau	H. M. Martineau	5	1	0	4	2	1	0	1
*1929-30	Ceylon, Australia and New Zealand	M.C.C.	A. H. H. Gilligan	23	11	2	10	13	4	2	7
*1929-30	West Indies	M.C.C.	Hon F. S. Gough-Calthorpe	13	4	2	7	12	4	2	6
1929-30	Argentine	Sir J. Cahn	Sir J. Cahn	6	2	1	3	3	1	0	2
1930	Egypt	H. M. Martineau	H. M. Martineau	5	1	1	3	2	1	0	1
*1930-31	South Africa	M.C.C.	A. P. F. Chapman	20	7	1	12	16	5	1	10
1931	Egypt	H. M. Martineau	H. M. Martineau	5	3	0	2	2	2	0	0
1931-32	Jamaica	Lord Tennyson	Lord Tennyson	6	1	3	2	3	0	3	0
1932	Egypt	H. M. Martineau	H. M. Martineau	7	3	4	0	2	0	2	0
*1932-33	Ceylon, Australia and New Zealand	M.C.C.	D. R. Jardine	26	10	1	15t	20	10	1	9t
1933	Egypt	H. M. Martineau	H. M. Martineau	8	4	1	3	2	2	0	0
1933	N. America, Bermuda	Sir J. Cahn	Sir J. Cahn	20	16	0	4	Nil			
*1933-34	India, Ceylon	M.C.C.	D. R. Jardine	34	17	1	16	18	10	1	7
1934	Egypt	H. M. Martineau	H. M. Martineau	10	9	1	0	2	2	0	0
*1934-35	West Indies	M.C.C.	R. E. S. Wyatt	12	2	2	8	12	2	2	8
1935	Egypt	H. M. Martineau	H. M. Martineau	10	3	4	3	2	0	2	0
1935-36	Ceylon, Australia and New Zealand	M.C.C.	E. R. T. Holmes	25	8	2	15	14	5	2	7
1935-36	Jamaica	Yorkshire C.C.C.	P. A. Gibb	6	1	0	5	3	1	0	2
1936	Egypt	H. M. Martineau	H. M. Martineau	10	8	1	1	2	2	0	0
*1936-37	Ceylon, Australia and New Zealand	M.C.C.	G. O. B. Allen	29	9	5	15	20	6	5	9
1936-37	Ceylon, Malaya	Sir J. Cahn	Sir J. Cahn	9	3	0	6	1	1	0	0
1937	Egypt	H. M. Martineau	H. M. Martineau	11	6	1	4	2	1	1	0
1937	Canada	M.C.C.	G. C. Newman	19	12	1	6	Nil			
1937-38	India	Lord Tennyson	Lord Tennyson	24	8	5	11	15	4	5	6

	To	Organiser	Captain	Results All matches				First class			
				P	W	L	D	P	W	L	D
1937-38	South America	Sir T. E. W. Brinckman	Sir T. E. W. Brinckman	11	5	1	5	3	1	1	1
1938	Egypt	H. M. Martineau	H. M. Martineau	12	10	1	1	2	2	0	0
1938-39	Jamaica	Universities	E. J. H. Dixon	7	2	1	4	2	0	1	1
*1938-39	South Africa	M.C.C.	W. R. Hammond	18	9	0	9	17	8	0	9
1938-39	New Zealand	Sir J. Cahn	Sir J. Cahn	10	4	0	6	1	0	0	1
1939	Egypt	H. M. Martineau	H. M. Martineau	10	7	0	3	2	2	0	0
*1946-47	Australia and New Zealand	M.C.C.	W. R. Hammond	29	6	3	20	21	3	3	15
*1947-48	West Indies	M.C.C.	G. O. B. Allen	11	0	2	9	11	0	2	9
*1948-49	South Africa	M.C.C.	F. G. Mann	23	11	0	12	20	9	0	11
*1950-51	Ceylon, Australia and New Zealand	M.C.C.	F. R. Brown	30	10	4	16	20	8	4	8
1951	Canada	M.C.C.	R. W. V. Robins	22	18	2	2	1	1	0	0
*1951-52	India, Pakistan, Ceylon	M.C.C.	N. D. Howard	27	10	3	14	23	7	3	13
*1953-54	West Indies, Bermuda	M.C.C.	L. Hutton	17	8	2	7	10	6	2	2
*1954-55	Ceylon, Australia and New Zealand	M.C.C.	L. Hutton	28	17	2	9	21	12	2	7
1955-56	Pakistan	M.C.C.	D. B. Carr	16	7	2	7	14	7	2	5
1955-56	West Indies, Bermuda	E. W. Swanton	M. J. Cowdrey	7	3	2	2	4	1	2	1
*1956-57	South Africa	M.C.C.	P. B. H. May	22	13	3	6	20	11	3	6
1956-57	Jamaica	Duke of Norfolk	E. D. R. Eagar	10	4	0	6	3	2	0	1
1956-57	India	C. G. Howard	W. J. Edrich	2	1	1	0	2	1	1	0
1957-58	Tanganyika, Kenya, Uganda	M.C.C.	F. R. Brown	9	3	1	5	Nil			
*1958-59	Ceylon, Australia and New Zealand	M.C.C.	P. B. H. May	26	10	4	12	22	7	4	11
1958-59	South America	M.C.C.	G. H. G. Doggart	11	9	0	2	Nil			
1959	North America	M.C.C.	D. R. W. Silk	25	21	0	4	Nil			
1959-60	Rhodesia	Surrey C.C.C.	W. S. Surridge	2	0	1	1	2	0	1	1
*1959-60	West Indies, Honduras	M.C.C.	P. B. H. May	17	6	1	10	13	4	1	8
1960-61	New Zealand	M.C.C.	D. R. W. Silk	21	12	1	8	10	4	1	5
1961	Bermuda	Bermuda C.A.	W. S. Surridge	12	5	0	7	Nil			
1961	Tanganyika, Kenya, Uganda	F. R. Brown	F. R. Brown	7	4	0	3	Nil			
*1961-62	Pakistan, India, Ceylon	M.C.C.	E. R. Dexter	24	8	2	14	22	7	2	13
1962	Bermuda	Gloucestershire C.C.C.	C. T. M. Pugh	9	3	3	3	Nil			
*1962-63	Ceylon, Australia and New Zealand	M.C.C.	E. R. Dexter	32	16	3	13	20	8	3	9
1963-64	Tanganyika, Kenya, Uganda	M.C.C.	M. J. K. Smith	11	7	0	4	2	1	0	1
*1963-64	India	M.C.C.	M. J. K. Smith	10	1	0	9	10	1	0	9
1963-64	Jamaica	Cavaliers	D. C. S. Compton	5	3	0	2	3	2	0	1
1964	N. America, Bermuda	Yorkshire	D. B. Close	12	9	0	3	Nil			
1964-65	West Indies	Cavaliers	T. E. Bailey	7	1	1	5	4	0	1	3
1964-65	World Tour	Worcestershire C.C.C.	D. Kenyon	14	8	1	5	2	1	1	0
1964-65	South America	M.C.C.	A. C. Smith	15	14	0	1	Nil			
*1964-65	South Africa	M.C.C.	M. J. K. Smith	19	11	0	8	17	10	0	7
*1965-66	Ceylon, Australia, New Zealand, Hong Kong	M.C.C.	M. J. K. Smith	31	14	2	15	19	5	2	12
1965-66	Jamaica	Worcestershire C.C.C.	D. Kenyon	5	0	0	5	1	0	0	1
1966-67	Pakistan	M.C.C.	J. M. Brearley	8	4	0	4	7	4	0	3
1966-67	Barbados	Arabs C.C.	A. C. D. Ingleby-Mackenzie	9	4	4	1	Nil			
1967	N. America	M.C.C.	D. R. W. Silk	25	21	0	4	Nil			
*1967-68	West Indies	M.C.C.	M. C. Cowdrey	16	4	0	12	12	3	0	9
1967-68	Africa, Asia	International	M. J. Stewart	21	15	0	6	5	4	0	1
1967-68	Kenya, Uganda	Warwickshire C.C.C.	M. J. K. Smith	9	2	0	7	1	0	0	1
*1968-69	Ceylon, Pakistan	M.C.C.	M. C. Cowdrey	10	2	1	7	7	0	0	7
1968-69	South Africa	R. J. McAlpine	R. J. McAlpine	14	4	5	5	Nil			
1969-70	West Indies	Duke of Norfolk	M. C. Cowdrey	9	5	2	2	3	1	1	1
1969-70	West Indies	Glamorgan C.C.C.	A. R. Lewis	6	1	1	4	2	0	0	2
1969-70	Ceylon, Far East	M.C.C.	A. R. Lewis	8	6	0	2	1	1	0	0
*1970-71	Australia and New Zealand	M.C.C.	R. Illingworth	29	13	3	13	16	4	1	11
1971-72	Zambia	Gloucestershire C.C.C.	A. S. Brown	5	3	0	2	Nil			

	To	Organiser	Captain	All matches				First class			
				P	W	L	D	P	W	L	D
1972-73	West Indies	Kent C.C.C.	B. W. Luckhurst	11	4	0	7	Nil			
1972-73	South Africa	D. H. Robins	D. J. Brown	10	4	4	2	6	1	3	2
1972-73	Malaysia, Singapore	Oxford and Cambridge Universities	P. C. H. Jones	10	8	0	2	Nil			
*1972-73	India, Pakistan, Sri Lanka	M.C.C.	A. R. Lewis	17	4	2	11	16	3	2	11
1973-74	South Africa	D. H. Robins	D. B. Close	13	8	1	4	7	2	1	4
1973-74	Kenya, Zambia, Tanzania	M.C.C.	J. M. Brearley	8	5	0	3	1	1	0	0
*1973-74	West Indies	M.C.C.	M. H. Denness	16	3	3	10	12	2	2	8
1973-74	Barbados	Arabs C.C.	A. R. Lewis	9	3	1	5	Nil			
*1974-75	Australia, New Zealand, Hong Kong	M.C.C.	M. H. Denness	30	11	6	13	18	6	5	7
1974-75	West Indies	English Counties	J. H. Hampshire	7	3	0	4	Nil			
1974-75	South Africa	D. H. Robins	D. B. Close	8	2	3	3	5	0	2	3
1974-75	West Indies	D. H. Robins	J. A. Jameson	12	6	4	2	Nil			
1975-76	South Africa	D. H. Robins	D. Lloyd	11	5	3	3	4	2	2	0
1975-76	West Africa	M.C.C.	E. A. Clark	10	8	0	2	Nil			
1976	Canada	D. H. Robins	P. H. Parfitt	15	14	0	1	Nil			
*1976-77	India, Sri Lanka, Australia	M.C.C.	A. W. Greig	19	5	3	11	16	4	2	10
1976-77	Bangladesh	M.C.C.	E. A. Clark	4	1	0	3	Nil			
1977-78	Far East	D. H. Robins	M. H. Denness	13	7	0	6	1	0	0	1
*1977-78	Pakistan, New Zealand	England	J. M. Brearley	21	8	3	10t	15	4	1	10t
1977-78	Kenya	Minor Counties	D. Bailey	6	5	1	0	Nil			
1978-79	Bangladesh	M.C.C.	E. A. Clark	6	2	0	4	Nil			
*1978-79	Australia	England	J. M. Brearley	26	17	4	5	13	8	2	3
1978-79	South America	D. H. Robins	C. S. Cowdrey	13	13	0	0	Nil			
1979-80	Australia, New Zealand	D. H. Robins	C. S. Cowdrey	15	7	2	6	2	0	0	2
*1979-80	Australia, India	England	J. M. Brearley	21	11	7	3	9	4	3	2
*1980-81	West Indies	England	I. T. Botham	14	5	4	5	9	2	2	5
1980-81	Zimbabwe	Middlesex	J. M. Brearley	6	3	1	2t	3	1	1	1
1980-81	Zimbabwe	Leicestershire C.C.C.	R. W. Tolchard	5	1	1	3	3	0	0	3
*1981-82	India, Sri Lanka	England	K. W. R. Fletcher	22	6	5	11	15	3	1	11
1981-82	South Africa	S.A.B.	G. A. Gooch	8	0	4	4	4	0	1	3
1980-81	Bangladesh	M.C.C.	M. D. Mence	6	1	0	5	Nil			
1981-82	Far East	M.C.C.	A. C. D. Ingleby-Mackenzie	7	3	0	4	Nil			
1982	U.S.A.	M.C.C.	A. R. Lewis	10	9	0	1	Nil			
1982-83	East Africa	Minor Counties	M. D. Nurton	10	7	1	2	Nil			
*1982-83	Australia, New Zealand	England	R. G. D. Willis	26	10	12	4	11	4	3	4
*1983-84	Fiji, New Zealand, Pakistan	England	R. G. D. Willis	18	7	4	7	10	1	2	7
*1984-85	Sri Lanka, India, Australia	England	D. I. Gower	21	7	6	8	12	3	2	7
1984-85	Zimbabwe	M. Vockins	M. C. J. Nicholas	12	6	6	0	2	1	1	0
1985	Canada	M.C.C.	N. E. J. Pocock	12	8	0	4	Nil			
1985-86	Sri Lanka	England	M. C. J. Nicholas	12	2	3	7	7	0	0	7
*1985-86	West Indies	England	D. I. Gower	14	2	10	2	10	1	7	2
*1986-87	Australia, Sharjah	England	M. W. Gatting	33	20	9	4	11	5	3	3
1986-87	West Indies	Yorkshire	P. Carrick	9	6	2	1	1	0	01	
1986-87	Jamaica	Lancashire	D. P. Hughes	3	0	3	0	1	0	1	0
1987-88	Pakistan, India, New Zealand, Australia	England	M. W. Gatting	30	13	8	9	13	2	2	9

1859: the first England cricket tour overseas

'Jemmy Grundy declared we should never see land again; poor George Parr was nearly out of his mind; old Jackson dropped to his knees; and indeed our situation was rather a critical one. Our jib-boom was broken and one poor old sailor had both his legs broken while he and some of the crew were endeavouring to set matters right.' That was William Caffyn's description of part of the homeward journey made by the pioneer English tourists of 1859. Apart from the terrible voyages across the Atlantic however, the tour was a tremendous success. The English team consisted of twelve professionals: H. H. Stephenson, Julius Caesar, Tom Lockyer and William Caffyn of Surrey, George Parr, Jemmy Grundy and John Jackson of Notts, Tom Hayward, R. Carpenter and A. J. Diver of Cambridgeshire, John Wisden and John Lillywhite of Sussex. Fred Lillywhite accompanied the team as reporter and took along his printing-press and scoring-tent.

The side was exceedingly strong, Parr, Carpenter and Hayward being the best batsmen in England at the time, whilst in Jackson and Wisden it possessed the best bowlers of the day. Caffyn, Diver, Grundy and Stephenson were all-rounders and Lockyer the main wicket-keeper. Parr, the Notts captain, led the twelve.

It took a little over a fortnight to cross from Liverpool to Quebec and the side were then taken by special train to Montreal for their first game. Despite poor weather several thousands turned out to watch Twenty-two of Lower Canada oppose the English Eleven and it soon became obvious that the home cricketers were no match for the fast bowling of Jackson, as the score fell to 12 for the loss of 6 wickets. Not that the batsmen found George Parr's under-arm lobs any easier, and in fact the captain ended the match with the splendid figures of 16 wickets for 27 runs. It proved to be the start of a triumphant tour, culminating in a final match—again with odds of twenty-two against eleven—versus a combined United States and Canadian side at Rochester.

Off the cricket field the team were royally welcomed and entertained, the only blot on the itinerary being Fred Lillywhite's printing equipment—at one stage George Parr lost his patience with Fred and in very forthright language consigned both Fred and his baggage to an 'unmentionable region'.

The tour was organised by W. P. Pickering, an old Cambridge Blue and an original member of Surrey County Cricket Club, who had emigrated to Montreal. He obtained guarantees amounting to £1,300 from various sponsors in both Canada and the United States and arranged the fixtures for the tour. After paying out all the expenses, each of the twelve cricketers took home about £90. The team had left England on 7 September and landed back in Liverpool on 11 November.

1859: G. Parr's Team to North America

1st Match: v XXII of Lower Canada (Montreal)   Sept 24, 26.
Lower Canada 85 (J. Jackson 7-21, G. Parr 6-8) & 63 (G. Parr 10-19, J. Jackson 6-20) lost to England 117 (G. Parr 24, Fisher 5-53) & 32-2 by 8 wkts.

2nd Match: v U.E.E. v A.E.E. Exhibition Game (Montreal)   Sept 27, 28, 29, 30.
U.E.E. 188 (John Lillywhite 53) beat A.E.E. 90 (W. Caffyn 5-34) & 44 (J. Wisden 5-18) by an inns & 54 runs.

3rd Match: v XXII of U.S.A. (Hoboken)   Oct 3, 4, 5.
U.S.A. 38 (J. Jackson 10-10, G. Parr 9-26) & 54 (W. Caffyn 16-24) lost to England 156 (Hallis 6-45) by an inns & 62 runs.

4th Match: T. Lockyer's XI v H. H. Stephenson's XI. Exhibition Game (Hoboken) Oct 6, 7, 8.
T. Lockyer's XI 163 (J. Caesar 52) & 90 (G. Parr 36, H. H. Stephenson 5-29) beat H. H. Stephenson's XI 93 (R. Carpenter 52, J. Grundy 5-21) & 86 (J. Wisden 8-45) by 74 runs.*

5th Match: v XXII of Philadelphia (Philadelphia)   Oct 10, 12, 13, 14.
Philadelphia 94 (J. Jackson 8-37) & 60 (J. Wisden 8-39) lost to England 126 (T. Hayward 34) & 29-3 by 7 wkts.

6th Match: North v South. Exhibition Game   Oct 14.
South 59 drew with North 120-6 (T. Hayward 60).

7th Match: v XXII of Hamilton (Hamilton)   Oct 17, 18, 19.
Hamilton 66 (H. H. Stephenson 7-19) & 53 (J. Wisden 14-24) lost to England 79 (W. Caffyn 25) & 41-0 by 10 wkts.

8th Match: v XXII of Canada & U.S.A. (Rochester)   Oct 21, 22, 24
Canada & U.S.A. 39 (J. Wisden 16-17) & 64 (J. Wisden 13-43) lost to England 171 (T. Hayward 50) by an inns & 68 runs.

The first cricket tourists from England, George Parr's side to America in 1859, photographed on board ship at Liverpool on 7 September 1859. Back row: R. Carpenter, W. Caffyn, T. Lockyer, J. Wisden, H. H. Stephenson, G. Parr, J. Grundy, J. Caesar, T. Hayward, J. Jackson. Front row: A. J. Diver, John Lillywhite.

1861-62: the first tour to Australia a great success

The success of the trip to North America persuaded the catering firm of Spiers and Pond that a similar tour to Australia would prove financially profitable, and in 1861 they sent their agent, Mr Mallam, to England in an attempt to sign up the best English professionals. He offered each player £150 plus first-class travelling expenses and this proposal was put to the players during the North v South match at Aston Park, Birmingham, in early September. George Parr and the Notts players immediately stated that the offer was not good enough, but after further discussion Mr Mallam persuaded the leading Surrey cricketers to accept, with H. H. Stephenson acting as captain. The party was made up of H. H. Stephenson, W. Mortlock, G. Griffith, Tom Sewell, Charles Lawrence, W. Caffyn and W. Mudie of Surrey, Tom Hearne of Middlesex, 'Tiny' Wells of Sussex, George Bennett of Kent and two Yorkshiremen – Roger Iddison and E. Stephenson. As no less than ten cricketers had refused terms – Daft, Parr, Jackson, Willsher, Lockyer, Hayward, Carpenter, Grundy, Anderson and Caesar – the party was in no way representative of England, but nevertheless was a reasonably strong combination. 'Tiny' Wells, who was accompanied by his wife, left England first, and the other eleven sailed from Liverpool in the *Great Britain* on 20 October. Unlike the 1859 trip, when storms were encountered in the Atlantic, the voyage to Australia met with calm seas, but it took over two months to reach Melbourne and the team found life on shipboard very tedious.

Over 10,000 people gathered to welcome the English cricketers as they came ashore and the coach in which they were conveyed to the restaurant owned by the sponsors was followed by a crowd of well-wishers – so great was the interest in the tour, that the ground selected for practice had to be kept secret.

In the first match, played against Eighteen of Victoria at Melbourne, each of the English eleven was issued with a hat with a ribbon and also a coloured sash, each man having a different colour and these colours were printed against each player's name on the scorecard. About 15,000 spectators watched the opening day's play, which commenced with the playing of the National Anthem as the England team entered the field. As in America the home team – although receiving odds – proved no match for the Tourists, who won by an innings. The second match involved a journey of about 200 miles by a coach drawn by 5 horses, and although the rough road made the travelling very tiring, the English team again won by an innings – the match ended early, so Griffith challenged 11 of the locals single handed. He bowled all eleven out, without a single one of them scoring a run!

The third match was against virtually the best twenty-two cricketers in Australia and proved to be an even draw. Leaving Victoria after a match at Geelong, the side went by ship to Sydney and again vast crowds turned out to greet the team as it landed. Somewhere between 15,000 and 20,000 people watched the game against New South Wales and the players were given a grand banquet attended by the Governor of the Colony.

The team met with its first defeat – by a Combined Twenty-Two of New South Wales and Victoria at Sydney. The English batting failed, possibly due more to the off-the-field activities than to any skill on the part of the Australian bowlers – scarcely a day passed whilst they were in Sydney without the tourists being entertained to champagne breakfasts, luncheons and dinners. Leaving New South Wales, the Englishmen boarded ship for Tasmania, where they again received a wonderful reception. A match was played at Hobart against Twenty-Two locals, followed by an exhibition game, before they sailed back to Melbourne.

The final match was played on 20, 21 and 22 March and proved an even draw, and each member of the English team then planted an elm tree to commemorate the tour. The sponsors offered the cricketers an extra £1,200 to stay another month, but since many of them had engagements to fulfil in England this was declined. Charlie Lawrence however accepted a post with the Albert Club in Sydney and did not return to England.

From every aspect the tour proved successful and both the sponsors and the cricketers made much more money than they had expected. The voyage home was as calm as the outward journey and the team reached England on 12 May. The Surrey Club gave them a complimentary dinner and they also received a benefit at Weston's Music Hall in Holborn.

Opposite *The fifth match of H. H. Stephenson's tour of Australia in 1861-62, against twenty-two of New South Wales. The England eleven won by 49 runs before an attendance on the first day of 15,000 to 20,000 spectators.*

Below *The first tourists to Australia, taken just before their departure in October 1861. From left: W. Mortlock, W. Mudie, G. Bennett, C. Lawrence, H. H. Stephenson, Mr W. B. Mallam (the agent of the Australian sponsors), W. Caffyn, G. Griffith, T. Hearne, R. Iddison, T. Sewell, E. Stephenson.*

1863-64: George Parr's men play twenty-two a time in Australia and New Zealand

The Melbourne Club did not have the same problems as Spiers and Pond when it came to persuading the leading English cricketers to make a second tour to Australia. This time George Parr was appointed captain and asked to select a team to accompany him. Parr chose two other Notts players – J. Jackson and R. C. Tinley, four Surrey men – Julius Caesar, Tom Lockyer, William Mortlock and William Caffyn; the great Cambridgeshire players, T. Hayward, R. Carpenter and G. Tarrant; George Anderson of Yorkshire and a little known Gloucestershire amateur, Dr E. M. Grace. Mortlock, in fact, altered his mind and his place was taken by Alfred Clarke, the son of the man who founded Trent Bridge Cricket Ground.

The Twelve was thoroughly representative of England and far superior to its predecessor of 1861-62, only Caffyn being a member of both parties. The voyage from Liverpool lasted 61 days and Melbourne was reached on 16 December. Although rougher than the outward trip of 1861, it was a pleasant journey, but George Anderson proved a poor sailor and suffered a great deal from sea-sickness. The team had a fortnight's practice in Melbourne before the first match against Twenty-two of Victoria – it was estimated that about 40,000 watched the contest over the four days, the English team needing nine to win with 6 wickets in hand when stumps were drawn. There followed four up-country matches against local Twenty-twos and 'Spider' Tinley totally baffled the home batsmen with his lobs, his tally of wickets for the four matches being 27, 23, 26, 22 – 98 in all!

On 25 January, the tourists left Victoria by ship for New Zealand, arriving at Port Chalmers after six days, here they were presented to the local Maori chief, who took a special liking to George Parr and followed him everywhere, much to the captain's alarm. From Port Chalmers the team travelled in a coach-and-six, driven by a famous coachman, 'Cabbage-Tree Ned', to Dunedin, where the first match was played. As in Australia the tourists proved too good for the home sides and Tinley continued his success as a lob bowler. As well as Dunedin, matches were played at Christchurch and an athletics contest was also staged. Getting back to Australia, the team went to Castlemaine, whom they beat

by an innings, and each cricketer was presented with a scarf-pin as a memento of the game. On their visit to Sydney, the tourists met Charlie Lawrence, who had stayed behind after the 1861 visit—he scored the most runs for the home team in a match which lasted nine days—several of them being lost due to rain. The most exciting contest of the tour was the third against Twenty-two of New South Wales, the English team winning by just one wicket. After this game the side set sail to return to Melbourne, but a few miles out from Sydney the ship collided with another vessel which sank almost at once. George Parr was paralysed with alarm, whilst Tarrant quite lost his head, rushed down to get his valuables and then tried to jump into the life boat which was being lowered to pick up the survivors from the sunken boat. John Jackson, who had done himself extra well at the farewell lunch before they left, slept soundly through all the confusion. The damage to the team's boat was such that the captain was forced to return to Sydney for repairs and this caused the next fixture—against Geelong—to be delayed by a day. After an exhibition game at Maryborough, Dr Grace challenged any six local players—the challenge was accepted, but the locals could not dismiss the Doctor, who was 106 not out at the end of the day.

The final match against Twenty-two of Victoria took place on 21, 22 and 23 April and due to rain had to be drawn. On 26 April, the team, less Dr Grace, who stayed on to visit friends, and Caffyn, who accepted an engagement in Melbourne, boarded the Bombay steamer for home, arriving at Dover on 13 June.

The tour—not a match lost—was even more successful than the 1861 trip and each player cleared about £250 after expenses, double the amount made previously.

Above *The team for the tour of Australia in 1863-64. The players are, back: J. Caesar, A. Clarke, G. Tarrant, G. Parr, E. M. Grace, R. Carpenter, G. Anderson, W. Caffyn. Front: R. C. Tinley, T. Lockyer, T. Hayward, J. Jackson.*

Right *The match at Melbourne between England and Australia in 1864.*

1863-64: G. Parr's Team to Australia and New Zealand

1st Match: v XXII of Victoria (Melbourne)   Jan 1, 2, 4, 5.
Victoria 146 (R. C. Tinley 11-52) & 143 (R. C. Tinley 8-63) drew with England 176 (T. Hayward 61, R. Carpenter 59, J. M. Bryant 6-43) & 105-4.

2nd Match: v XXII of Bendigo (Bendigo)   Jan 7, 8, 9.
England 85 (T. W. S. Wills 6-35) & 178 beat Bendigo 74 (R. C. Tinley 13-35) & 45 (R. C. Tinley 14-22) by 144 runs.

3rd Match: v XXII of Ballarat (Ballarat)   Jan 11, 12, 13.
Ballarat 82 (R. C. Tinley 13-20) & 94 (T. W. S. Wills 32, R. C. Tinley 10-50) lost to England 188 (J. Caesar 40) by an inns & 12 runs.

4th Match: v XXII of Ararat (Ararat)   Jan 14, 15, 16.
England 137 (R. Carpenter 35, T. W. S. Wills 6-57) beat Ararat 35 (R. C. Tinley 14-22) & 34 (R. C. Tinley 12-23) by an inns & 68 runs.

5th Match: v XXII of Maryborough (Maryborough)   Jan 19, 20, 21.
Maryborough 72 (R. C. Tinley 11-24) & 74 (R. C. Tinley 11-48) lost to England 223 (E. M. Grace 44, T. W. S. Wills 5-82) by an inns & 77 runs.

6th Match: v XXII of Otago (Dunedin)   Feb 2, 3, 4.
Otago 71 (T. Hayward 15-34) & 83 (T. Hayward 9-36) lost to England 99 & 58-1 by 9 wkts.

7th Match: v XXII of Canterbury & Otago (Dunedin)   Feb 4, 5.
Canterbury & Otago 91 (R. C. Tinley 13-49) & 66 (R. C. Tinley 13 wkts) drew with England 73 (E. M. Grace 42).

8th Match: v XXII of Canterbury (Christchurch)   Feb 8, 9.
Canterbury 30 (R. C. Tinley 13-18) & 105 (R. C. Tinley 12-68) lost to England 137 (T. W. S. Wills 6-55) by an inns & 2 runs.

9th Match: G. Parr's XI v G. Anderson's XI. Exhibition Game. (Christchurch)   Feb 9, 10.
G. Parr's XI 64 & 89 beat G. Anderson's XI 71 & 75 by 7 runs.

10th Match: v XXII of Otago (Dunedin)   Feb 16, 17, 18.
England 198 (W. Caffyn 43, T. Hayward 40) beat Otago 98 (J. Jackson 10-21) & 49 (R. C. Tinley 11 wkts) by an inns & 51 runs.

11th Match: v XXII of Castlemaine (Campbell's Creek)   March 2, 3, 4.
England 137 beat Castlemaine 54 (R. C. Tinley 9-28) & 46 (R. C. Tinley 12-28) by an inns & 37 runs.

12th Match: G. Parr's XI v G. Anderson's XI. Exhibition Match. (Melbourne)   March 6, 7, 8, 9.
G. Parr's XI 153 (E. M. Grace 5-33) & 129 (W. Caffyn 40) lost to G. Anderson's XI 168 (T. Lockyer 44, R. C. Tinley 7-76) & 115-6 by 4 wkts.

13th Match: v XXII of New South Wales (Sydney)   March 16, 17, 18, 24.
New South Wales 137 & 50 (J. Jackson 9-20) lost to England 128 (W. Caffyn 25) & 60-6 by 4 wkts.

14th Match: v XXII of New South Wales (Sydney)   March 26, 28, 29.
New South Wales 102 (C. Lawrence 25) & 3-1 drew with England 114 (G. H. B. Gilbert 5-58).

15th Match: v XXII of New South Wales (Sydney)   April 2, 4.
New South Wales 68 & 83 (R. C. Tinley 10-33) lost to England 75 (O. H. Lewis 5-14) & 77-9 (C. Lawrence 6-48) by 1 wkt.

16th Match: v XXII of Geelong (Geelong)   April 12, 13.
Geelong 103 (R. C. Tinley 9-38) & 64-9 drew with England 135 (G. Tarrant 41).

17th Match: G. Parr's XI v G. Anderson's XI (Maryborough). Exhibition Game.   April 14, 15.
G. Anderson's XI 164 (G. Tarrant 35) & 74 (T. Hayward 5-34) beat G. Parr's XI 112 (J. Jackson 45, R. C. Tinley 6-59) & 70 (J. Caesar 6-31) by 56 runs.

18th Match: v XXII of Ballarat (Ballarat)   April 18, 19, 20.
England 310 (R. Carpenter 121, G. Parr 65) drew with Ballarat 128 (R. C. Tinley 8-72) & 48-15 (R. C. Tinley 10-28).

19th Match: v XXII of Victoria (Melbourne)   April 21, 22, 23.
Victoria 150 (J. Jackson 10-34) & 83-17 (G. Tarrant 12-29) drew with England 131.

1868: another visit to Canada and the United States

Nine years had elapsed since the first English team crossed the Atlantic, and in the interval the bitter war between the Northern and Southern United States had taken place, also the popularity of baseball had outstripped that of cricket. Still several supporters of the game in North America had invited V. E. Walker, the Middlesex cricketer, to select a team and play a series of six matches. Several of the best English players, including R. Daft, T. Hayward, R. Carpenter and G. Wootton declined to take part and the twelve eventually consisted of Edgar Willsher (captain) from Kent, T. Humphrey, G. Griffith, H. Jupp and E. Pooley from Surrey, James Lillywhite and H. R. J. Charlwood of Sussex, Joseph Rowbotham and George Freeman of Yorkshire, John Smith and George Tarrant of Cambridgeshire and Alfred Shaw of Notts. It was a very fair side, Freeman and Willsher being the leading bowlers, whilst Jupp and Humphrey were the best bats.

After a crossing of ten days, the team arrived at the mouth of the Hudson on 13 September. The first fixture was in New York and the local Twenty-two were bowled out twice by Willsher, Freeman and Shaw, only one man reaching double figures. From New York the cricketers travelled via Niagara Falls to Montreal. The Canadians proved a very poor match for the English side. The whole Twenty-two of 'All Canada' could score but 28 against the bowling of Freeman and Willsher, then the tourists did what they liked with the home bowling, but rain on two of the four days caused the game to be drawn. After the one contest in Canada the

tour continued with a match at Boston on a pitch described as the worst ever encountered. 'The wicket was laid with thick, coarse, grassy turf, with holes in it big enough to lose the ball. In addition, as it had rained almost without stopping for five days previously, the outsides were covered with water and mud.'

The best match of the tour took place at Germantown against Twenty-two of Philadelphia and the English team just won by two wickets – this fine game was almost ruined by the American umpire whose decisions became so bad that he was eventually replaced.

Apart from the six cricket matches the side took part in several baseball matches, all of which were won by the Americans. The party arrived back in Liverpool on 3 November after another ten-day crossing of the Atlantic.

1872: W. G. Grace spreads the gospel in North America

The fifth major tour to leave England was the first one to be composed of amateur cricketers. In 1871, the secretary of the M.C.C., R. A. Fitzgerald, was asked to select an amateur side to visit North America and the following agreed to make the trip: V. E. Walker, R. D. Walker, R. A. H. Mitchell, J. W. Dale, W. G. Grace, W. H. Hadow, A. Appleby, A. N. Hornby, A. Lubbock, W. M. Rose and the Hon G. R. C. Harris. Between selection and departure, Mitchell, Dale and the two Walkers had to drop out and C. J. Ottaway, C. K. Francis, F. P. U. Pickering and E. Lubbock took their places. The side was therefore not really representative of the amateur strength of English cricket, let alone the full strength, but in W. G. Grace it possessed the greatest exponent of the game.

Leaving England about a month earlier than either of the other two tours to America, the team landed at Point Levi on 17 August after a rough passage and the first match took place at Montreal. W. G. Grace opened the tourists' batting and hit the bowling to all parts of the outfield and beyond. The home bowlers despaired of getting his wicket, but Mr Benjamin, a stout fielder with spectacles on his nose and a pipe in his mouth, suddenly received the ball in his abdomen, where it lodged, and the Champion of England was forced to retire caught. The batting of the Canadians was even poorer than their bowling and the match was won with an innings to spare. The second game took place in Ottawa and again W. G. Grace scored heavily and another innings victory resulted. It was here that the team were entertained to a vast

R. A. Fitzgerald's team to Canada in 1872. Back row: A. Lubbock, W. G. Grace, T. C. Patteson, C. J. Ottaway. Centre: E. Lubbock, R. A. Fitzgerald, A. Appleby. Front: F. P. U. Pickering, Hon G. Harris, A. N. Hornby, W. M. Rose, C. K. Francis.

banquet, the main meat dish being leg of bear, which none of them really relished. Toronto was the venue of the third match—another innings victory and century from W. G. Grace. Good crowds watched the Toronto match, about 5,000 attending each day's play: 'each Englishman was as narrowly scanned and felt as the prize beasts at an Agricultural Show. It was honestly meant and as honestly and kindly taken.' From Toronto the team went to a terrible hotel in London, where 'starvation and flies formed the menu', but another victory was attained. Hamilton was the next stop followed by a three-day excursion to the Niagara Falls and then the match in New York against the local Twenty-two—another innings victory. The great match was in Philadelphia, where about 12,000 spectators watched on the first day. Tremendous shouts greeted the dismissal of Grace for only 14 and the match throughout was punctuated with music from the band on the roof of the club house. The English team were surprised at the great interest shown by the ladies in the cricket—much more so than in England.

The final fixture was at Boston. The ground was terrible, resembling a building plot. The English team were dismissed for 51 and the local Twenty-two managed the same total. Everyone was pleased when 6 o'clock arrived and the stumps were drawn.

The party retraced its steps to Quebec and arrived back in Liverpool on 8 October.

It was hoped that the visit gave encouragement to cricket in North America, but the team found the Americans completely absorbed in the materialistic things of life and everything else was pushed aside in consequence.

1873-74: W. G. takes a party to Australia

In the summer of 1872, W. G. Grace was invited to take a team to Australia, but the offer failed to tempt him and plans were abandoned. The following year, however, the Melbourne Club approached Grace with a better offer and he set about trying to gather a team. Alfred Shaw, the leading slow bowler of the day, refused the terms, as did the best Yorkshire all-rounder, Tom Emmett. Of the wicket-keepers, Pooley of Surrey was in disgrace and Pinder of Yorkshire in domestic disarrangement. Several amateurs, including A. N. Hornby, promised and then withdrew.

The team was finally made up of four Gloucester amateurs, W. G. and his brother G. F. Grace, J. A. Bush, the wicket-keeper, and W. R. Gilbert; a young Surrey amateur, F. H. Boult; R. Humphrey and H. Jupp, the leading Surrey batsmen; James Southerton, who played for Surrey and Sussex as a slow bowler; James Lillywhite, the best Sussex bowler; William Oscroft and Martin McIntyre, both Notts professionals and the Yorkshire batsman, A. Greenwood.

The team left Southampton on 23 October, called at Malta, at Alexandria, where the British Consul asked the side to disembark for a day and play a match, the request being declined, and at Galle, where they changed ships. Melbourne was reached after 52 days—the ship broke the record for the journey between Galle and Australia. On arrival the team found that the organisers in Australia had booked rooms in one hotel for the amateurs and in another for the professionals and this arrangement did not do much to foster team spirit.

The first game commenced on Boxing Day against Eighteen of Victoria. B. B. Cooper, formerly of Middlesex and Kent, hit 84 for the home side, the highest individual innings made up to that time against an English side in Australia, then the tourists collapsed twice, only W. G. batting well, and an innings defeat was suffered. From the financial viewpoint the match was a great success, with 40,000 spectators paying half-a-crown each. There followed three games against local Twenty-twos, during the second of which Humphrey was thrown out of a trap and unable to play for some time due to his injuries. The second major game took place at Sydney against Eighteen of New South Wales. Once more the batting failed and the best innings of the match came from the home batsman Pocock, who was a cousin of the Graces. The tourists lost by 8 wickets.

It had been arranged to play the next game at Maitland, but the ground there was under water and the team went to Bathurst instead. The principal contest of the tour took place at Sydney against a Combined Fifteen of New South Wales and Victoria. Owing to some splendid bowling by Lillywhite, backed up by good fielding and wicket-keeping, a win by the large margin of 218 runs was obtained, making up for the previous defeats, at least to an extent.

The tourists sailed from Sydney back to Melbourne, where G. F. Grace owing to quinsy missed the up-country game at Sandhurst—he recovered for the next match, only to be hit on the head by the first ball he received—this was at Castlemaine, where a dreadful wicket had been 'prepared'. Martin McIntyre, the Notts fast bowler, took full advantage of the conditions, according to the report: 'he played merrily about the ribs of those Castlemaniacs and enjoyed himself in a pure and innocent fashion to the full'.

Since the English Team had been easily beaten in the first match against Eighteen of Victoria, in the return fixture the Victorians reduced the odds to Fifteen. The home side were however too optimistic and lost by 7 wickets—B. B. Cooper again made the best score for his side, but this time it was only 20.

From Melbourne the side sailed across to Tasmania—a large crowd gathered to greet the ship at Launceston, but the passage being rough the English cricketers were unable to return the welcome. The Tasmanians made a poor show with both bat and ball—the best of them being J. C. Lord, who was a useful cricketer in Hampshire at one time. From Launceston the team went by coach to Hobart and though the locals batted better, G. F. Grace hit a great innings of 154 and provided another easy victory. Back the team went to Victoria for a third match against that colony—the odds were increased to Eighteen and the game was fairly even on first innings, after which rain washed out any further play. The final fixture was Kadina in South Australia, where the wicket was pebbles and grit, but no grass—McIntyre chuckled distinctly as he inspected it and the locals were dismissed for 42 and 13—McIntyre had seven wickets for one run in the second innings. Though the official programme of matches was now at an end, the team arranged an extra fixture at Adelaide—much to the annoyance of the promoters—and the Twenty-two of South Australia were beaten by 7 wickets.

Sailing from Glenelg, the cricketers had a pleasant voyage back to Galle, where they again changed ships. They ran aground twice in the Suez Canal, spent a day at the Races in Alexandria, stopped briefly at Malta and Gibraltar and arrived back in Southampton on 17 May.

There was little doubt that cricket in Australia had improved immensely since the previous visit and the Victorians—thanks to William Caffyn in a large part—were the best side met on the tour.

The professionals received £150 for the tour plus £20 in spending money. In addition, many of them took out cricketing equipment to sell and made money from this and from betting on the matches—for example the seven professionals put up £50 for a bet that the tourists would beat the Combined Fifteen of New South Wales and Victoria. Another feature of the tour was the side-betting among spectators—which batsman would score most runs, etc. On one occasion a complete stranger came up to Oscroft before he went in to bat and offered him £20 if he beat W. G. Grace's score.

1876-77: Pooley arrested and Australia win 'first Test Match'

The tour of 1873-74 had not been a success from the team viewpoint because of the division between the amateurs and the professionals. In 1876, therefore, it was decided to revert to an all-professional side and for the first time the tour was run as a speculation on the part of the English, rather than being promoted by the Australians.

James Lillywhite, the Sussex cricketer, arranged, managed and captained the tourists. He picked five Yorkshiremen, G. Ulyett, A. Hill, T. Emmett, Andrew Greenwood and T. Armitage; two from Notts, Alfred Shaw and John Selby; three from Surrey, H. Jupp, E. Pooley and James Southerton (vice-capt); and H. R. J. Charlwood from Sussex. In Shaw, Hill, Emmett and Southerton the side possessed arguably the best bowlers in England, Pooley was the best 'keeper, but without Daft, Lockwood and Shrewsbury the batting looked a little thin.

The ship left Southampton on 21 September and stopped at Gibraltar and Malta. A day was spent in Ceylon and although the locals tried to arrange a match it proved impractical. South Australia was reached on 6 November and nine days were spent in practice before the first match—in Adelaide against Twenty-two of South Australia. Southerton spent a week before the game preparing the wicket and in consequence run-getting was much easier than on the previous visit. About 14,000 watched the play and an innings victory plus a profit of £750 augured well for the tour. In the second game at Sydney, the New South Wales side fielded only Fifteen men and the play was fairly even throughout, so that on the fourth morning of the match New South Wales required 26 to win with three wickets in hand. A strong gale was blowing, which made bowling difficult, but one batsman was quickly run out and the English hopes were still high. The home side however knocked off the runs without further loss. Over 30,000 watched the match, which was regarded as the best of the tour, only marred by the way the spectators disagreed with unfavourable umpiring decisions—the twelfth man of the England party stood as umpire in most matches. Following two victories in up-country games, the side met Fifteen of Victoria. Lillywhite won the toss and put the Victorians in, but a terrific storm quickly flooded the ground and ruined this advantage. In another close finish the tourists again lost. There were two more up-country games, before the return match with New South Wales, in which Spofforth and Evans routed the English side, who lost by 13 wickets. New South Wales immediately challenged the team on even terms, but ended with very much the worse of a draw.

From Sydney the side sailed to New Zealand for a series of eight odds matches, five of which were won by an innings. It was whilst in Christchurch that the constant betting which was a feature of all the cricket resulted in most unfortunate consequences. Pooley found a local spectator who was unfamiliar with the dodge whereby the promoter bets that he can forecast correctly the individual scores of each of the Twenty-two batsmen opposed to the English team. Pooley took odds of £1 to 1s on each batsman's total and wrote down a duck for each. As there were a total of 11 ducks, Pooley demanded £11 less 33 shillings for the innings in which runs had been made. The punter refused to pay up, and after the resulting fight Pooley was charged with assault and maliciously damaging property. He was forced to remain behind in New Zealand awaiting trial, when the English team returned to Australia for the rest of the tour. The loss of Pooley —the team's wicket-keeper—was serious enough, but Jupp, who was a useful substitute behind the stumps, had a bout of insanity as well as suffering from inflammation of the eyes and missed several matches in consequence. Whilst in New Zealand the team suffered from some hair-raising journeys between matches—on the way to Christchurch their coach and horses attempted to cross a swollen river only to be stuck in the middle. The cricketers leapt out of the coach and up to their waists in water and somehow dragged the horses to the bank. They reached a roadman's shelter, which boasted the name of the Otira Hotel, and, having no change of clothes, lit a great fire and stood naked in front of it, whilst they dried out. They spent the night on the floor and when they tried to leave in the morning found that a landslide had cut off the road, so they spent another day at the 'Hotel' whilst the way was cleared—the journey took 80 hours with little oppor-

The team to Australia of 1876-77, led by James Lillywhite and photographed in Melbourne. The players are, as numbered : 1 H. Jupp, 2 T. Emmett, 3 H. Charlwood, 4 J. Selby, 5 J. Lillywhite, 6 T. Armitage, 7 J. Southerton, 8 A. Greenwood, 9 G. Ulyett, 10 A. Hill, 11 A. Shaw, 12 E. Pooley. This team played the first official Test match, but E. Pooley, who looks something of a gambler, was absent, being held in New Zealand on an assault charge arising from his not being paid a gambling debt.

tunity to sleep, and at its end the team had immediately to start another match.

The New Zealand part of the tour, owing to bad arrangements, was a financial failure. After a rough voyage back to Melbourne, the tourists began the first eleven-a-side match ever to take place between an England side and a Combined Australian team on the following day. This game is now regarded as 'The First Test Match'. Australia batted first and scored 245, with Charles Bannerman making the celebrated first 'Test' century – the fact of the matter was that the English team were so exhausted after their New Zealand experiences, that not one of them was fit to field. Bannerman was dropped by Armitage, the batsman hitting a simple catch which struck the fielder in the stomach, and the English bowling was poor in the extreme with several deliveries going high over the batsman's head, whilst others rolled along the ground! Needless to say Australia won by a fair margin.

Three up-country odds matches followed before a return game was played against the Australian Eleven. This time, in better fettle, the English team won by 4 wickets – immediately the cry came up from the betting fraternity that the first match had been 'fixed' in order to promote the gate for the return encounter.

Following the victory against Australia, the team travelled to Adelaide where the final match took place against the local

Twenty-two and then the party set sail for Galle, arriving there on 8 May. After sailing to Brindisi, the rest of the journey was by the overland route and London was reached on 2 June, but still the misguided Pooley was absent. In fact, after his trial the New Zealand public thought he had been hard done by and a subscription was raised for him.

Pooley was dogged by misfortune throughout his life, and 20 years later, when interviewed in retirement by a journalist, he stated 'It was the workhouse, sir, or the river'. In fact, he spent most of his declining years in the workhouse in Lambeth crippled with rheumatism.

The English team found that Australian cricket had again improved upon the standard of 1873 and they were most impressed by Spofforth, Bannerman and the wicket-keeper, Murdoch, as well as the other young stumper, Blackham.

Each of the English team was guaranteed £150 plus first-class passage, but they each returned with about £300. It was reported that the profits from the matches in Sydney were £3,000 and in Melbourne £2,500.

1876-77: J. Lillywhite's Team to Australia and New Zealand

1st Match: v XXII of South Australia (Adelaide)   Nov 16, 17, 18.
England 153 (J. Selby 59) beat S. Australia 54 (A. Shaw 14-12) & 53 by an inns & 46 runs.

2nd Match: v XV of New South Wales (Sydney)   Dec 7, 8, 9, 11.
England 122 & 106 (E. Evans 5-37) lost to N.S.W. 81 (A. Shaw 6-24) & 151-12 by 2 wkts.

3rd Match: v XXII of Newcastle (Newcastle)   Dec 12, 13, 14.
England 96 & 77 beat Newcastle 31 & 68 by 74 runs.

4th Match: v XXII of Goulburn (Goulburn)   Dec 20, 21.
England 125 & 81 beat Goulburn 60 & 51 by 95 runs.

5th Match: v XV of Victoria (Melbourne)   Dec 26, 28, 29, 30.
Victoria 190 (A. Shaw 6-43) & 105 (T. Emmett 6-31) beat England 135 (F. E. Allan 5-44) & 129 (W. E. Midwinter 7-54) by 31 runs.

6th Match: v XXII of Ballarat (Ballarat)   Jan 1, 2, 3.
England 123 (E. Figgis 5-74) & 179 (H. R. J. Charlwood 66) drew with Ballarat 146.

7th Match: v XXII of Geelong (Geelong)   Jan 5, 6, 7.
England 264 (H. R. J. Charlwood 56, Kendall 7-92) beat Geelong 74 (A. Shaw 11-41) & 87 (J. Southerton 10-47) by an inns & 103 runs.

8th Match: v XV of New South Wales (Sydney)   Jan 12, 13, 15.
England 35 (F. R. Spofforth 5-20) & 104 (E. Evans 6-49) lost to N.S.W. 124 (A. Shaw 7-32) & 17-1 by 13 wkts.

9th Match: v New South Wales (Sydney)   Jan 15, 16.
England 270 (G. Ulyett 94, E. Evans 5-96) drew with N.S.W. 82 (A. Shaw 5-19) & 140-6.

10th Match: v XXII of Auckland (Auckland)   Jan 29, 30, 31, Feb 1.
England 225 (H. R. J. Charlwood 65, Bennett 6-45) beat Auckland 109 (A. Shaw 13-39) & 94 by an inns & 22 runs.

11th Match: v XXII of Wellington (Wellington)   Feb 5, 6, 7, 8.
Wellington 31 (A. Shaw 13-11) & 38 (J. Lillywhite 13-22) lost to England 190 (H. R. J. Charlwood 56, Cross 5-60) by an inns & 121 runs.

12th Match: v XXII of Taranaki (New Plymouth)   Feb 12, 13.
Taranaki 32 (J. Lillywhite 13-19) & 47 (J. Southerton 13-25) lost to England 80 (Fitzpatrick 6-41) by an inns & 1 run.

13th Match: v XXII of Nelson (Nelson)   Feb 15, 16.
England 258 (J. Selby 82) beat Nelson 56 (A. Shaw 13-24) & 39 (A. Shaw 13-19) by an inns & 163 runs.

14th Match: v XXII of Westland (Greymouth)   Feb 20, 21, 22.
England 119 & 99-4 drew with Westland 50 (J. Southerton 13-33).

15th Match: v XVIII of Canterbury (Christchurch)   Feb 26, 27, 28.
England 70 (C. Frith 6-23) & 102 beat Canterbury 65 & 84 (A. Hill 12-17) by 23 runs.

16th Match: v XVIII of Otago (Dunedin)   March 2, 3, 5.
Otago 76 & 106 (J. Lillywhite 12-45) drew with England 163 (Millington 6-54).

17th Match: v XXII of Southland (Invercargill)   March 6, 7.
England 158 (A. Greenwood 66) beat Southland 47 (A. Hill 12-17) & 46 (J. Southerton 11-24) by an inns & 65 runs.

18th Match: v Australia (Melbourne)   March 15, 16, 17, 19.
Australia 245 (C. Bannerman 165) & 104 (A. Shaw 5-38) beat England 196 (H. Jupp 63, W. E. Midwinter.5-78) & 108 (T. Kendall 7-55) by 45 runs.

19th Match: v XXII of Bendigo (Bendigo)   March 20, 21, 22.
Bendigo 138 (J. Lillywhite 12-68) & 117 drew with England 99 & 67-3.

20th Match: v XXII of Ballarat (Ballarat)   March 23, 24.
England 159 (E. Morey 5-72) drew with Ballarat 67 (A. Shaw 12-23) & 73-13.

21st Match: v XXII of Ararat (Ararat)   March 26, 27.
England 204 (A. Shaw 86) drew with Ararat 38 & 21-8.

22nd Match: v Australia (Melbourne)   March 31, April 2, 3, 4.
England 261 (G. Ulyett 52) & 122-6 (G. Ulyett 63) by 4 wkts.

23rd Match: v XXII of South Australia (Adelaide)   April 14, 16, 17.
England 75 & 138 (G. Ulyett 58) drew with S. Australia 71 (A. Hill 10-9).

1878-79: betting troubles in Australia, and Lord Harris assaulted

In the spring of 1878, the Melbourne Cricket Club asked I. D. Walker, the Middlesex amateur, to collect a team of twelve amateur cricketers for a tour of Australia the following winter. It was found impossible to gather an amateur side of sufficient strength, and in consequence, two Yorkshire professionals, G. Ulyett and T. Emmett, were chosen to complete the side. I. D. Walker was unable to make the trip and Lord Harris was given the captaincy. The other members of the party were F. A. Mackinnon, F. Penn and C. A. Absolom of Kent, A. N. Hornby, V. P. F. A. Royle and S. S. Schultz of Lancashire, A. J. Webbe of Middlesex, A. P. Lucas of Surrey, H. C. Maul and L. Hone—neither of the last two named appeared in County Championship cricket, though the former played for Warwickshire in the county's second-class days and the latter for Ireland.

The team had a fair batting strength, but the bowling relied heavily on Emmett and no specialist wicket-keeper was taken. The tourists were not representative in any way of either England or even the amateur strength of the country, lacking as they did any member of the Gloucester side.

Going on the overland route to Italy and thence through the Suez Canal, the side reached Adelaide on 22 December. In the opening game, the English team fielded twelve men against the Eighteen of South Australia and won by 3 wickets. The second match commenced at Melbourne on Boxing Day with about 10,000 spectators and an even draw was played against Fifteen of Victoria, for whom the old Oxford Blue, Donald Campbell, hit 128. On the same ground a few days later, the first eleven-a-side match was played against a representative Australian team. Excellent bowling by Spofforth was too much for the visitors who suffered defeat by 9 wickets. This match is now designated an official 'Test Match'—but as pointed out previously the tourists at no time claimed to be repr-sentative of English cricket. Lord Harris ascribed the defeat to bad fielding and dreadful light.

The team sailed from Melbourne to Tasmania aboard a very crowded ship. The first match on the island was played at Hobart on a ground shaped like a hog's back—a very tall long-leg might just be able to see a gigantic deep mid-off! Following two matches of little consequence in Tasmania, the party made its way, via Melbourne back to Sydney, where they met the New South Wales side—again bad fielding lost the tourists the match. The return with New South Wales took place with a minor match at

Bathurst intervening. On the first day against N.S.W., the tourists hit an excellent 267, with Hornby, Lucas and Ulyett all making fifties; by stumps N.S.W. were 53 for 2. Murdoch carried his bat through the completed innings on the second day and in the afternoon, being 90 behind, N.S.W. followed on. Murdoch therefore went in again, and had made 10 when the umpire adjudged him run out. At this point the crowd, disagreeing with the decision, rushed on to the field and surrounded the English fielders, Lord Harris was struck across the body with a whip or stick and though the two ringleaders were arrested, the crowd occupied the ground so that no further play took place that day. Rumours were rife that the umpire had laid a large bet on an English victory–there was no foundation for this charge, but it incensed the mob still further. Gregory, the home captain, asked Lord Harris to change the umpire, but his Lordship refused to do so and Gregory therefore refused to let his batsmen continue. Eventually the matter was settled and play continued on Monday, when New South Wales collapsed on a sticky wicket, leaving the tourists victors by an innings.

In the next game against a local amateur club, Penn dislocated his knee and could not play again on the tour, whilst Lucas split his hand fielding a hard return. Victoria beat the visitors by 2 wickets, and once more bad fielding was the reason. There were two up-country matches before the last serious match–an eleven-a-side against Victoria–which provided Lord Harris with a victory by 6 wickets.

The party went home via New Zealand, where they played one match, and the United States, where a match was played in New York. Neither of these games were of any significance.

The failure of the side was due mainly to bad fielding and the lack of a wicket-keeper. Lord Harris criticised the amateur um-

---

1878-79: Lord Harris's Team to Australia, New Zealand and U.S.A.

Batting Averages

	M	I	NO	R	HS	Avge	100	c/s
G. Ulyett (Yorks)	5	9	0	306	71	34.00	0	3
Lord Harris (Kent)	5	9	0	289	67	32.11	0	2
F. Penn (Kent)	2	3	0	87	56	29.00	0	2
V. P. F. A. Royle (Lancs)	5	8	0	214	75	26.75	0	11
A. P. Lucas (Surrey)	5	9	1	158	51	19.75	0	3
A. N. Hornby (Lancs)	5	9	0	167	67	18.55	0	2
T. Emmett (Yorks)	5	8	2	110	41	18.33	0	2
C. A. Absolom (Kent)	5	8	0	128	52	16.00	0	3
A. J. Webbe (Middx)	5	9	1	101	27	12.62	0	7
F. A. Mackinnon (Kent)	3	6	3	37	15*	12.33	0	0
L. Hone	5	8	1	58	22	8.28	0	6/2
S. S. Schultz (Lancs)	5	8	2	46	20	7.66	0	1

Bowling Averages

	O	M	R	W	Avge	BB	5i
T. Emmett	482.1	255	512	44	11.61	8-47	6
A. N. Hornby	79	48	79	4	19.75	2-9	0
A. P. Lucas	239.1	105	347	14	24.78	3-32	0
C. A. Absolom	71	30	98	3	32.66	2-37	0
G. Ulyett	230	104	367	11	33.36	4-13	0
S. S. Schultz	80.3	27	174	4	43.50	2-8	0

Also bowled: V. P. F. A. Royle 4-1-6-0; Lord Harris 3-0-14-0; F. Penn 3-1-3-0.
Played in non-first-class matches only: H. C. Maul (Warwicks).

1878-79: Lord Harris's Team to Australia, New Zealand and U.S.A.

1st Match: v XVIII of South Australia (Adelaide) Dec 12, 13, 14.
South Australia 110 (T. Emmett 9-45) & 137 (G. Ulyett 9-43) lost to England XII 185 (A. N. Hornby 78) & 63-7 by 3 wkts.

2nd Match: v XV of Victoria (Melbourne) Dec 26, 27, 28.
Victoria 313 (D. Campbell 128) & 214 (G. Ulyett 8-78) drew with England 331 (A. P. Lucas 90, V. P. F. A. Royle 78).

3rd Match: v Australia (East Melbourne) Jan 2, 3, 4.
England 113 (C. A. Absolom 52, F. R. Spofforth 6-48) & 160 (F. R. Spofforth 7-62) lost to Australia 256 (A. C. Bannerman 73, T. Emmett 7-68) & 19-0 by 10 wkts.

4th Match: v XVIII of South Tasmania (Hobart) Jan 9, 10, 11.
Tasmania 82 (T. Emmett 9-33) & 144 (G. Ulyett 9-20) lost to England 133 (A. N. Hornby 61*) & 94-4 by 6 wkts.

5th Match: v XVIII of North Tasmania (Launceston) Jan 13.
North Tasmania 49 (T. Emmett 12-20) & 38-7 drew with England 212 (F. Penn 53).

6th Match: v New South Wales (Sydney) Jan 24, 25, 27, 28.
England 248 (F. Penn 56, G. Ulyett 51, Lord Harris 50, E. Tindall 6-89) & 217 (E. Evans 5-82) lost to New South Wales 240 (W. L. Murdoch 70, N. Thompson 50) & 226-5 (H. H. Massie 78, C. Bannerman 60*) by 5 wkts.

7th Match: v XVIII of Bathurst (Bathurst) Jan 31, Feb 1.
Bathurst 47 drew with England 229.

8th Match: v New South Wales (Sydney) Feb 7, 8, 10.
England 267 (A. N. Hornby 67, G. Ulyett 55, A. P. Lucas 51, F. R. Spofforth 5-93, E. Evans 5-62) beat New South Wales 177 (W. L. Murdoch 82*, T. Emmett 8-47) & 49 (T. Emmett 5-21) by an inns & 41 runs.

9th Match: v XV of the Bohemian Club (Yarra Bend) Feb 17, 18.
Bohemian Club 228 (G. P. Robertson 78) & 262-12 drew with England 255 (A. J. Webbe 62, S. S. Schultz 53).

10th Match: v Victoria (Melbourne) Feb 21, 22, 24, 25
England 325 (G. Ulyett 71, V. P. F. A. Royle 57, A. N. Hornby 50, W. H. Cooper 5-79) & 171 lost to Victoria 261 (D. Campbell 51, T. Emmett 5-93) & 236-8 (T. P. Horan 69) by 2 wkts.

11th Match: v XXII of Bendigo (Sandhurst) Feb 26, 27.
Bendigo 141 & 161-20 drew with England 304 (A. N. Hornby 104).

12th Match: v XXII of Ballarat (Ballarat) March 1, 3.
England 311 (Lord Harris 89, A. N. Hornby 86, A. J. Webbe 53) beat Ballarat 140 (T. Emmett 11-54) & 123 by an inns & 48 runs.

13th Match: v Victoria (Melbourne) March 7, 8, 10.
England 248 (V. P. F. A. Royle 75, Lord Harris 67, G. E. Palmer 6-64) & 54-4 beat Victoria 146 (T. Emmett 6-41) & 155 (T. Emmett 5-68) by 6 wkts.

14th Match: v Canterbury (Christchurch).
Match drawn.

15th Match: v U.S.A. (Hoboken).
England beat U.S.A. by inns & 114 runs.

pires in Australia and would have nothing to do with the Australian theory that amateur umpires were more honest than their professional counterparts. He felt that the Australian bowlers were now better than their English rivals and that in a few years the Australian team would be the equal of a representative English one. His final point was that the professional betting element should be removed from Australian cricket.

The tour was financed by the Melbourne Club who paid all the expenses of the English amateurs and each of the professionals received about £200.

1879: Daft's professionals play cricket – and baseball – in America

J. P. Ford, a member of the Nottingham Town Council, who had interests in North America, asked Richard Daft, the Notts captain to select and lead a side of professionals on a tour of North America in the autumn of 1879. Daft picked six other Notts players: Alfred Shaw, John Selby, Arthur Shrewsbury, William Oscroft, William Barnes and Frederick Morley, plus five Yorkshiremen: Tom Emmett, George Ulyett, Ephraim Lockwood, William Bates and George Pinder, to accompany him. The team was very nearly representative of the full strength of English professional cricket, the strength of the Southern first-class counties being mainly amateur.

The Twelve left Liverpool on 28 August and after a rough seven days crossing reached Canada. The programme began with three matches at Toronto. The ground there was well looked after, but the home cricketers showed little skill and Shaw, Emmett and Morley were much too good for their batsmen. After two victories at Hamilton and London, the team moved to Detroit, where two Kentish cricketers, Littlejohn and Dale, tended the local ground. Rain caused the match here to be drawn, but, as in Canada, the home batsmen made a poor showing. From Detroit, the team moved, via the Niagara Falls, to New York for two matches, where the batsmen mainly went in for the cross-batted swipes of baseball players and Alfred Shaw had another field day. The most important fixture of the tour was in Philadelphia against the local Fifteen – about 25,000 attended the three-day game and due to this fixture the tour was a financial success. The strength of the home team lay in the four members of the Newhall family,

but even they could not prevent an English victory. Back to New York went the team for two matches – one of cricket and the other baseball. The English players proved as inexpert at the latter as the New Yorkers were at the former.

The two remaining games were in Philadelphia. In the first the Young America Club actually challenged the tourists on equal terms, but suffered a great defeat as a result. In the second, rain caused a draw. An additional match was then arranged: Nottinghamshire v Yorkshire, the two elevens being made up mainly of English professionals engaged in America. Notts won by 10 wickets. On 25 October the side left by train for New York and the voyage home and on 4 November all were safe back in Liverpool. The tour was successful from all viewpoints and unlike most of its predecessors it was free from any minor disputes or disagreements.

1879: R. Daft's Team to North America

1st Match: v XXII of Canada (Toronto)   Sept 10, 11.
Canada 31 (A. Shaw 11-17, F. Morley 10-12) & 72 (A. Shaw 11-17) lost to England 101 (D. J. Logan 7-35) & 3-0 by 19 wkts.

2nd Match: v XXII Anglo-Canadians (Toronto)   Sept 12, 13.
Anglo-Canadians 76 (F. Morley 12-24) & 69-14 drew with England 209 (A. Shrewsbury 66, W. Barnes 59, Simpson 6-100).

3rd Match: v XXII of Ontario (Toronto)   Sept 15, 16.
Ontario 65 (F. Morley 10-36) & 54 (T. Emmett 14-36) lost to England 122 (W. Bates 49*) by an inns & 3 runs.

4th Match: v XVII of Hamilton (Hamilton)   Sept 18, 19.
England 186 (D. J. Logan 6-39) beat Hamilton 48 (A. Shaw 13-37) & 35 by an inns & 103 runs.

5th Match: v XXII of Western Ontario (London)   Sept 22, 23.
England 71 (Kennedy 5-34) & 139 beat Western Ontario 37 (A. Shaw 13-12) & 38 (A. Shaw 14-24) by 135 runs.

6th Match: v XVIII of Detroit (Detroit)   Sept 25, 26, 27.
England 191 (W. Oscroft 52) drew with Detroit 59 & 5-1.

7th Match: v XXII of Central New York (Syracuse)   Sept 30, Oct 1.
England 163 (J. Selby 44) beat Central New York 43 (A. Shaw 11-15) & 50 (A. Shaw 13-28) by an inns & 70 runs.

8th Match: v XXII of United New York (States Island)   Oct 4, 5, 7.
United New York 67 (A. Shaw 10-29) & 94 (A. Shaw 11-27) lost to England 188 (G. Lane 5-57).

9th Match: v XV of Philadelphia (Nicetown)   Oct 10, 11, 13.
England 149 (W. Oscroft 62, C. Newhall 6-80) & 133 (E. W. Clarke 6-29) beat Philadelphia 70 (A. Shaw 9-18) & 67 (A. Shaw 7-19, F. Morley 7-32) by 145 runs.

10th Match: v XVIII Baseball Players (Brooklyn)   Oct 14, 15.
Baseball Players 62 & 27 lost to England 107 by an inns & 18 runs.

11th Match: v Young America (Germantown)   Oct 18, 20.
Young America 64 (F. Morley 6-30) & 47 (W. Bates 8-20) lost to England 171 (E. Lockwood 60, C. Newhall 8-62) by an inns & 60 runs.

12th Match: v XXII of Merion Club (Ardmore)   Oct 21, 22.
England 162 (E. Lockwood 88, Braithwaite 8-) drew with Merion 67 & 55-13.

13th Match: Notts v Yorkshire. Exhibition Game (Germantown)   Oct 23, 24.
Notts 148 (A. Shrewbury 51) & 22-0 beat Yorkshire 51 (A. Shaw 5-21) & 118 by 10 wkts.

Richard Daft's team which left for America in 1879. Back: G. Pinder, W. Barnes, E. Lockwood, J. P. Ford, R. Daft, Capt Holden, J. Selby. Centre: A. Shrewsbury, G. Ulyett, A. Shaw, W. Oscroft. Front: T. Emmett, W. Bates, F. Morley.

1881-82: England players try to throw a match against Victoria

James Lillywhite, together with the two Notts cricketers, Alfred Shaw (captain) and Arthur Shrewsbury, undertook the most ambitious tour made to date by English cricketers. They decided to go to Australia via America and New Zealand, playing matches in both countries on the way and thus making the trip more profitable. Apart from the three promoters, the party was made up of William Scotton and John Selby of Notts, William Bates, Tom Emmett, Edmund Peate and George Ulyett of Yorkshire, R. G. Barlow and R. Pilling of Lancashire and William Midwinter from Gloucestershire – an all-professional side.

Sailing from England on 17 September, the team (without Shrewsbury, who was ill) played its first match against Twelve of Philadelphia and won by an innings. Four other matches were played in America. All of them proved a financial loss. The train journey across America was painfully slow at times, with the team getting out and jogging alongside the train on some sections. The game in San Francisco was the low point of the tour – the venue resembled a stone quarry and the crowd was less than a hundred. The home team had little idea of the game and one of the few spectators who knew about cricket complained: 'This is a farce; it's like obtaining money by false pretences.' The lack of gate money in America meant that the team had very few dollars, and when they came to the shipping company for passage across the Pacific they found the Company would not accept Bank of England notes, so they had to cable to London for proof of their bona fides. The ship in which they left America also contained the King of the Sandwich Islands and his retinue. The King was impressed by the singing of some of the cricketers, especially Billy Bates. Tom Emmett was invited to sing, but replied: 'I beg your Majesty's pardon, but I make it a rule never to sing out of England.' When the ship reached Honolulu, the cricketers were invited to the King's palace. The fact that 'Thursday' was lost when the ship crossed the international date line, utterly confused most players.

Australia was reached on 16 November – it had been found impractical to play in New Zealand first – and the first five matches played were all against local Twenty-twos. In the last of these Pilling was unable to field due to sunstroke: some ungenerous things were insinuated about the nature of his illness, but they were untrue. The first serious match was against New South Wales – eleven-a-side – on 9 December etc. Despite two good innings by H. H. Massie, N.S.W. were beaten by 68 runs. About 40,000 spectators attended the game. The second eleven-a-side contest came in Melbourne against Victoria, where a brilliant second innings knock by Shrewsbury won the match after the visitors were forced to follow on. 20,000 attended the second day of this game – believed at the time to be a record.

The betting on cricket, which Lord Harris had deplored on his tour, was still very much in evidence during this match. On the final day, when Victoria needed 94 in their second innings, the odds were 30 to 1 against an English victory. Most of the English team wagered £1 and came away with £30. Another more unpleasant aspect of the game was the rumour that two of the English team had been paid £100 to throw the match. This rumour gained credence when the two players involved seemed to be fielding poorly, including the dropping of an easy catch. The press got hold of the story. It came out that the two players had tried to persuade a third – Midwinter – to come in with them, but Midwinter reported the matter to Alfred Shaw and was afterwards beaten up by the two conspirators.

After a match in Adelaide, the tourists returned to Melbourne to face a Combined Australian Eleven. High scoring necessitated the game going into the fourth day and the steamer which was to take the English side to New Zealand delayed its departure, but the match was still drawn.

Seven matches – all against odds – were played in New Zealand. The two matches from which a reasonable financial return was expected proved otherwise. The game at Christchurch was ruined by rain and at Auckland the promoters discovered that the match was arranged on the Domain, which the public could enter free.

1881-82: Lillywhite, Shaw and Shrewsbury's Team to America, New Zealand and Australia

Batting Averages

	M	I	NO	R	HS	Avge	100	c/s
G. Ulyett (Yorks)	7	14	0	549	149	39.21	1	5
A. Shrewsbury (Notts)	7	12	2	382	82	38.20	0	8
R. G. Barlow (Lancs)	7	14	1	391	75	30.07	0	3
W. Bates (Yorks)	7	13	1	349	84	29.08	0	3
J. Selby (Notts)	7	13	1	312	70	26.00	0	1
W. H. Scotton (Notts)	7	12	1	228	50*	20.72	0	3
E. Peate (Yorks)	7	13	7	104	33*	17.33	0	1
W. Midwinter (Glos)	7	12	0	166	48	13.83	0	8
A. Shaw (Notts)	7	12	0	137	40	11.41	0	5
T. Emmett (Yorks)	7	12	0	109	27	9.08	0	9
R. Pilling (Lancs)	7	13	3	87	23	8.70	0	12/6

Bowling Averages

	O	M	R	W	Avge	BB	5i
W. Bates	402.2	205	520	30	17.33	5-17	1
E. Peate	484.3	234	552	30	18.40	6-30	2
A. Shaw	196	120	171	8	21.37	3-5	0
G. Ulyett	138.1	45	257	10	25.70	2-11	0
T. Emmett	180	74	274	10	27.40	3-27	0
W. Midwinter	301	128	435	13	33.46	4-81	0
R. G. Barlow	94.2	36	147	3	49.00	1-4	0

Played in non-first-class matches only: Jas Lillywhite (Sussex).

The tourists returned to Australia for a second game against Australia, this time at Sydney, and lost by 5 wickets, because Shaw, who won the toss, elected to bat on a sticky wicket. As usual a fresh wicket was cut for the Australian innings.

Two other matches were played against Australia, one of which was lost and the other drawn. By way of consolation, the tourists beat Victoria by 8 wickets.

After a final odds match at Ballarat, the side set sail for England on 22 March from Melbourne and arrived in Naples on 2 May, where half the party took the overland route and most of the remainder went by steamer to Plymouth.

It was remarkable that not a single player was injured on the tour; Ulyett was the most successful batsman – his two innings of 149 and 64 in the final game against Australia being outstanding. Shrewsbury also had an excellent tour. Peate and Midwinter did most of the bowling, the former taking over 200 wickets in all.

The tourists found the Australian wickets much improved and the run-getting was therefore that much higher compared with previous visits.

Each player received £300 and the promoters made a considerable profit, despite the problems in America and the United States.

1882-83: England bring back the Ashes

The Melbourne Cricket Club agreed to organise and manage a tour by a mixed side of amateurs and professionals under the captaincy of the Hon Ivo Bligh, the Kent batsman. The composition of the side was as follows: four professionals, F. Morley and W. Barnes of Notts, and W. Bates of Yorkshire and R. G. Barlow of Lancashire; eight amateurs, the captain (Bligh), A. G. Steel of Lancashire, four Middlesex men in C. T. Studd, G. B. Studd, G. F. Vernon and C. F. H. Leslie plus E. F. S. Tylecote of Kent and W. W. Read of Surrey.

The historic significance of the tour was the pledge by the captain to bring back 'The Ashes' of English cricket, following the obituary which had been published when Australia defeated England at the Oval during the 1882 English season. The tour programme included three matches against the returning victorious Australian side of 1882.

The English team set out from home in two groups, meeting up at Suez and from there sailed to Ceylon, where they played a match – the first of its kind – against a local side. Continuing the voyage, the ship was 360 miles out from Colombo when it collided with a sailing vessel. The two ships then limped back to Colombo for repairs and eventually the team arrived ten days late in Adelaide. The most serious result of the accident was the injury to Fred Morley, the team's only fast bowler, who broke a rib. He carried on through the tour very gamely, but was almost useless.

The delay on the journey meant that the team had to play the first match immediately, with no opportunity for practice and without Ivo Bligh, who had injured his hand on the voyage. Rain happily cut short the first day's play and the match was drawn without even the first two innings being completed. The side then returned to the water for the voyage to Melbourne. The first eleven-a-side game v Victoria was an easy win, because the principal Australian players were absent. After two up-country matches, the side went to Sydney, where they beat the New South Wales eleven by an innings – again the principal players were absent from the home side. Three more odds matches came and went before the tourists met the Australian side which had been

A. Shaw's All-England Eleven, which toured America, Australia and New Zealand. Back: G. Ulyett, R. Pilling, J. Lillywhite (umpire), J. Conway (manager), W. Midwinter, W. Bates. Centre: A. Shrewsbury, A. Shaw, T. Emmett, E. Peate. Front: R. G. Barlow, W. H. Scotton, J. Selby.

The team which recovered the Ashes. The Hon Ivo Bligh's side which visited Australia. Standing: W. Barnes, F. Morley, C. T. Studd, G. F. Vernon, C. F. H. Leslie. Seated: G. B. Studd, E. F. S. Tylecote, the Hon Ivo Bligh, A. G. Steel, W. W. Read. Front: R. G. Barlow, W. Bates.

in England in 1882. This meeting at Melbourne commenced on 30 December and though the captain was well enough to play, poor Morley was confined to bed. The public excitement concerning the match built up to fever pitch and some 54,000

attended the three-day game. Brilliant hitting by Bonnor, who made 85, won the match for the Australians and the tourists paid dearly for dropped catches. Two matches were played in Tasmania before the second meeting with the 1882 Australians.

Bligh won the toss for this crucial match and, batting first, the tourists put together a fair total of 294. From then on the match belonged to Bates who took no less than 15 wickets, including the hat-trick, and the game was won by an innings. The third and deciding match followed immediately, with both sides travelling to Sydney. Bligh again won the toss and over 20,000 watched the English team commence batting. Five wickets went for 76, before Read and Tylecote came together and added 115. The total reached 247. Australia replied with 133 for 1 by the end of the second day, but collapsed to 218 all out. The tourists made only 123 in their second innings, leaving the home side 153 to win. Barlow was equal to the task and in taking 7 wickets bowled them out for 83. During the game there was some unpleasantness when the Australians accused Barlow of running on to the wicket, and cutting up the surface with his spikes; the English captain replied that Spofforth did the same when he bowled.

After the tourists had won this game and thus the series of three by two to one, some ladies burnt the bails used in the match, placed the 'Ashes' in a small urn and presented it to Ivo Bligh – he had won back the ashes of English cricket.

Two other eleven-a-side matches were played on the tour, the first against 'Combined Australia' was lost through bad catching and the second against Victoria was lost through bad batting, though the wicket was all against the visitors. The tour ended on 12 March and the team split into three groups for the journey home, the first group reaching England on 25 April.

The visit was a financial success – each professional received £220 and the amateurs their expenses. Without W. G. Grace, Ulyett, Lucas and Hornby the side was perhaps not the full strength of England, and considering the fact that it never fielded its best eleven fully fit – owing to Morley's injury and various mishaps to Bligh, Steel, Leslie and Barnes – the results were better than expected.

One point which surprised the English visitors was the total absence in Australia of bowlers with doubtful actions, this being a problem which was plaguing English County cricket at the time.

1884-85: dust storms and financial squabbles in Australia

James Lillywhite, Alfred Shaw and Arthur Shrewsbury arranged and managed their second speculative venture to Australia in the winter of 1884-85. This time Lillywhite acted purely as an umpire, whilst Alfred Shaw did not play in any major matches and took over the job as manager. Arthur Shrewsbury was chosen as captain. The other ten tourists were William Barnes, W. H. Scotton, William Attewell, and Wilfred Flowers of Notts; J. Hunter, R. Peel, W. Bates and G. Ulyett of Yorkshire, Johnny Briggs of Lancashire and J. Maurice Read of Surrey. The party contained no amateurs and in the estimation of Shaw was the strongest team ever to represent England in Australia. Writing in 1902, Shaw noted: 'A better side than this, alike for defence and attack, could not then, and I am certain cannot now, be chosen from the ranks of English cricketers.' The comment is of interest, since present-day historians tend to claim that the period commencing 1902 was The Golden Age of English Cricket! Shaw obviously was not of that opinion.

The side sailed from Plymouth on 19 September and after an unusually calm run through the Bay of Biscay arrived at Port Said in eleven days – the stop at Naples was omitted owing to an outbreak of cholera in that city. A match was played in Suez against a combined Army and Navy side on a matting wicket. Several members of the side went on a sight-seeing tour of the Pyramids and Cairo, in the company of Thomas Cook, who had come to Egypt to see the Khedive and arrange for tours up the Nile by his travel firm. On returning to the ship after the sight-seeing, Shaw and Ulyett engaged two Arabs to row them across to the anchorage. The Arabs rowed half the distance and then refused to go further without extra payment. Ulyett grabbed one oarsman by the collar and threw him in the sea, then proceeded to row to the ship, whilst the man swam alongside to the accompaniment of some decorated Yorkshire lingo from George.

The tourists arrived at Adelaide on 29 October, only to be greeted by the news that poor Fred Morley – who had never recovered from the injuries he received on the outward voyage of the last tour – had died. This caused depression among the players, all of whom were friends of Fred.

There were only two days practice before the first game against Fifteen of South Australia and after a close struggle the English side won by 3 wickets – the attendance however was very poor. The cricketing knowledge of the Australians though had increased beyond all recognition compared with a few years back – the English wicket-keeper, for example, was criticised for standing too far from the wicket. Not only was the criticism justified, but such a fine point would never have occurred to the spectators in Australia in the mid-70s.

Following a second odds match, the journey was made by sea

The team Shaw and Shrewsbury took to Australia in 1884-85, photographed in Sydney. The players are as numbered: 1 M. Read, 2 G. Ulyett, 3 W. H. Scotton, 4 R. Peel, 5 Joe Hunter, 6 W. Attewell, 7 A. Shrewsbury, 8 A. Shaw, 9 W. Barnes, 10 J. Lillywhite, 11 W. Flowers, 12 J. Briggs, 13 W. Bates. Notice the blazers and caps compared to the similar picture of 1876-77.

to Melbourne where the first eleven-a-side game was played against Victoria. The members of the 1884 Australian team in England however refused to play for Victoria and the visitors won easily. Without any up-country matches, the side went straight to Sydney to play New South Wales and the 1884 Australians once more refused to participate in the match, which provided another win for the English Eleven. The attendance was some 30,000 which was an improvement on the previous matches. Three odds matches followed, the first of which was played on matting laid on concrete, thus providing a much better wicket than normally seen in these matches.

The South Australian Cricket Association arranged a match between the tourists and the 1884 Australians at Adelaide – the first match of such importance ever staged in the city. The locals agreed to pay each team £450 and were therefore taking a great financial risk in promoting the game. A general holiday was proclaimed for the opening day, but with the admission charge at 2 shillings, only 4,000 spectators turned up. On the second day admission was reduced to a shilling and about 10,000 watched the game. It was on this day that a violent dust-storm occurred and the fielders were forced to lie down flat to avoid being suffocated. The forecasters claimed the dust-storm heralded rain, and sure enough the next day – Sunday – the ground was flooded. The English side, despite having the worst of the pitch, won a decisive victory by 8 wickets. Murdoch, the Australian captain, refused to permit either Lillywhite or Shaw to umpire and the result was that a totally inexperienced local man was used – his decisions were quite hopeless, but seemed to be evenly distributed.

The fact that both teams were paid an equal amount for the match was a sore point with the English team. Shaw argued that when in England the Australians had made a handsome profit, whilst the English professionals had been paid £10 per man. Also the Australians were supposed to be amateurs. Murdoch however continued to demand half the profits of each match and though Shaw offered 30 per cent and then £20 per man, both these suggestions were declined. Most of the Australian press and public seemed to side with the English team in this financial squabble, as did the Australian Cricket Associations. The result was that the second match between 'England and Australia' at Melbourne was played without any of the 1884 Australians taking part and the tourists won by 10 wickets. Six up-country games preceded the match with New South Wales, where once again the 1884 Australians refused to play and the English team won easily.

In the third 'England v Australia' match, four of the 1884 Australians agreed to play, and the tourists were beaten by 7 runs. In this game, the most effective English bowler on the tour, William Barnes, did not bowl. According to the reports the captain, Shrewsbury, asked him to bowl, but he refused – there being some friction between the two – undoubtedly this refusal by Barnes lost the match for England.

Of the other two international matches, each side won one, and in spite of the problems with the 1884 Australians, the series proved a popular one with the paying public.

The most serious injuries received on the tour occurred not on the playing field, but on, or rather off, horseback to 'Boy' Briggs. On the first occasion, he dismounted on the wrong side, being left-handed, and the horse kicked him, almost sending the inexperienced rider over a precipice, and on the second occasion he tried to slow down his runaway mount and went flying over its head, falling flat on his face. Unfortunately he was smoking a pipe at the time and the stem was rammed into the roof of his mouth.

Briggs was unconscious for about four hours and in fact it was reported that he had been killed; luckily he survived, but with a face so bruised that on inspecting it in the mirror, he did not recognise the reflection.

The team returned to Adelaide for the last match of the tour, which was marred by another dust-storm and torrential rain. The side left Australia on 4 April and split up in the Mediterranean, half taking the overland route and the rest sailing to Plymouth.

Financially the promoters were well-rewarded and the players, as well as their £300, received numerous prizes for best performances in the up-country matches—in two games some of the players won shares in gold-mines, which they auctioned off at a handsome profit.

1885: Philadelphia beat North American tourists

E. J. Sanders arranged a short tour of North America for September 1885 and gathered a reasonably strong team of amateurs for the trip. The players involved were Rev R. T. Thornton, A. J. Thornton and T. R. Hine-Haycock of Kent, W. E. Roller and C. E. Horner of Surrey, A. E. Newton of Somerset, H. O. Whitby of Warwickshire, J. A. Turner of Leicestershire, A. R. Cobb of Oxford University, H. Bruen of Ireland and W. E. T. Bolitho of Devon. The team left Liverpool on 20 August and on the return left New York for home on 1 October. The most important fixtures were those against Philadelphia, of which one was won and the other lost—unfortunately W. E. Roller injured his arm during the third game of the tour and could not bowl in either of the Philadelphian games. The attendance in Philadelphia was high, with 8,000 or 9,000 present on some days, and the tourists were surprised to see that nearly half the crowd were women. Rev R. T. Thornton captained the side and the leading batsman was W. E. Roller, whilst Bruen and Horner took most wickets.

The victory by Philadelphia in the first match was a significant milestone for cricket in the United States, being the first time that an English team had tasted defeat. On the afternoon of the third day it appeared that the tourists would save the game—only 1¾ hours remained and the brothers A. J. and R. T. Thornton seemed well set. Their partnership realised 47 runs when C. Newhall bowled R. T. Thornton. The other four wickets then fell for 28 runs, Dan Newhall capturing the final wicket with a lob.

1885: E. J. Sanders' Team to United States and Canada

1st Match: v XII of Staten Island (Staten Is)   Sept 1, 2.
Sanders' XII 91 (J. L. Pool 7-43) & 244 (J. A. Turner 52) drew with Staten Island XII 62 (H. Bruen 8-27) & 72-3.

2nd Match: v XV of Peninsular Club (Detroit)   Sept 5, 7.
Sanders' XI 283 beat Peninsular Club 69 (C. E. Horner 8-29) & 49 (H. O. Whitby 5-11) by an inns & 165 runs.

3rd Match: v Canada (Toronto)   Sept 10, 11.
Canada 76 (W. E. Roller 6-32) & 38 lost to Sanders' XI 133 (E. R. Ogden 5-59) by an inns & 20 runs.

4th Match: v XV of Montreal (Montreal)   Sept 14.
Sanders' XI 110 beat XV of Montreal 28 (H. Bruen 9-14) & 42 (A. J. Thornton 11-27) by an inns & 40 runs.

5th Match: v Philadelphia (Nicetown)   Sept 17, 18, 19.
Philadelphia 200 (C. E. Horner 6-61) & 178 beat Sanders' XI 147 (A. J. Thornton 55, W. C. Lowry 5-55) & 122 by 109 runs.

6th Match: v New York (Staten Island)   Sept 21, 22.
New York 66 (H. Bruen 7-25) & 76 lost to Sanders' XI 267 (A. E. Newton 129, J. L. Pool 6-53) by an inns & 125 runs.

7th Match: v Philadelphia (Nicetown)   Sept 24, 25, 26.
Sanders' XI 193 (W. E. Roller 64) & 317 (R. T. Thornton 107, T. R. Hine-Haycock 85, H. McNutt 6-82) beat Philadelphia 147 (J. A. Scott 56*) & 120 (H. Bruen 6-54) by 243 runs.

8th Match: v XV of New England (Longwood)   Sept 28, 29.
Sanders' XI 59 (Chambers 5-34) & 53 (G. Wright 6-25) beat New England 66 & 30 by 16 runs.

1886: revenge against Philadelphia

E. J. Sanders repeated his tour of the previous year. T. R. Hine-Haycock, J. A. Turner, A. R. Cobb, W. E. Roller of 1885 again went with Sanders, together with H. W. Bainbridge (Warwickshire), K. J. Key (Surrey), Rev A. T. Fortescue (Oxford U), E. H. Buckland (Middx), C. E. Cottrell (Middx), H. Rotherham (Warwicks) and F. T. Welman (Middx). Roller captained the side, which left Liverpool on 19 August and arrived in New York on 29 August, after a rough passage. As previously the two major matches were against Philadelphia, this time however the tourists being victorious in both.

The team was perhaps stronger than in 1885, the leading batsman being K. J. Key, whilst Roller and Cottrell both took 50 wickets at a low cost and were the principal bowlers. The final match ended on 4 October.

Soon after the team returned to England A. R. Cobb died of typhoid—a tragic loss to cricket, since he had been in the Winchester side of 1883 and in 1886 hit 50 for Oxford v Cambridge at Lord's.

1886: E. J. Sanders' Team to America

1st Match: v Staten Island (New York)   Sept 1, 2.
Sanders' XII 203 (G. Lane 5-38) beat Staten Island 74 (C. E. Cottrell 7-17) & 80 (H. Rotherham 7-25) by an inns & 49 runs.

2nd Match: v Ontario (Toronto)   Sept 7, 8.
Sanders' XI 169 (A. T. Fortescue 58*, E. H. Buckland 54) & 15-2 beat Ontario 72 (C. E. Cottrell 6-31) & 111 by 8 wkts.

3rd Match: v XVI of Montreal (Montreal)   Sept 11, 13, 14.
Sanders' XII 257 (J. A. Turner 57, K. J. Key 52) beat Montreal 85 & 55 by an inns & 117 runs.

4th Match: v XV of Longwood Club (Boston)   Sept 15, 16, 17.
Longwood 96 (W. E. Roller 11-44) & 43 lost to Sanders' XI 77 & 64-7 by 3 wkts.

5th Match: v XV of New England (Boston)   Sept 17, 18.
Sanders' XI 116 (Dutton 5-41) & 136-6 (A. R. Cobb 52) drew with New England 109 (C. E. Cottrell 6-45).

6th Match: v XVIII of Baltimore (Baltimore)   Sept 21, 22.
Sanders' XI 257 (K. J. Key 96) beat Baltimore 82 & 117 by an inns & 58 runs.

7th Match: v Philadelphia (Philadelphia)   Sept 23, 24, 25.
Philadelphia 168 (E. H. Buckland 6-53) & 139 (E. H. Buckland 6-52) lost to Sanders' XI 323 (K. J. Key 109, W. E. Roller 75, H. I. Brown 5-113) by an inns & 16 runs.

8th Match: v All New York (New York)   Sept 27, 28, 29.
New York 143 (W. E. Roller 5-56) & 41 (C. E. Cottrell 8-21) lost to Sanders' XI 75 & 113-1 (W. E. Roller 55*) by 9 wkts.

9th Match: v Philadelphia (Philadelphia)   Oct 1, 2, 4.
Philadelphia 128 (C. E. Cottrell 5-55) & 146 (E. H. Buckland 7-63) lost to Sanders' XI 235 (E. H. Buckland 82, A. R. Cobb 51) & 40-4 by 6 wkts.

1886-87: the 'strongest all-round team yet' go to Australia

The combination of Lillywhite, Shaw and Shrewsbury took a third side to Australia in the winter of 1886-87. As on the previous trip, Lillywhite acted as umpire, Shaw as manager and Shrewsbury as captain. In addition there were five Notts cricketers, W. Barnes, W. Gunn, W. H. Scotton, W. Flowers and M. Sherwin; G. A. Lohmann and J. M. Read from Surrey; W. Bates from Yorkshire and J. Briggs and R. G. Barlow of Lancashire—so discounting Shaw there were only eleven players, a fact that caused problems later.

The side left Plymouth on 18 September and the only break in the voyage occurred in Aden, where the ship stopped for ten hours. The Indian Ocean was distinctly choppy, Gunn, Bates and Briggs being the worst sufferers. Adelaide was reached on 29 October and the first game—against the local Fifteen—began the following day. A perfect wicket had been produced and Shrewsbury, despite having no practice, had little difficulty in hitting a hundred, and Barnes also scored well. The attendance however was poor, only 1,000 being present on the opening day, which was a half-holiday. The match was drawn, as was the second game against Victoria—here again there was a perfect wicket and the bowlers were ineffective. For the first time the journey between Adelaide and Melbourne was made by train, rather than sea, though the time taken was 28½ hours, including a break of six hours at Border Town—the through trains with sleeping cars which did the journey in 18 hours were introduced the following year. A magnificent new grandstand had been erected on the Melbourne Ground since the previous English visit and this, combined with the scoreboard which showed the batsmen's names, made the facilities at Melbourne unequalled.

The rain which was to dog the party for most of the tour arrived at Parramatta, where in a low scoring affair on a sticky wicket, the first up-country game was staged. Going on to Sydney, Shrewsbury won the toss and decided to bat on a wicket which turned out to be slow and treacherous. Turner and Ferris, the two New South Wales bowlers, completely baffled the Englishmen and the home side won in two days by 6 wickets. Four odds matches in the N.S.W. country districts produced four victories, the most amazing being at Lithgow, where the Twenty-two were dismissed for 18 and 27, which is possibly a record—Briggs took 27 wickets in the match for 20 runs. To be fair however it must be mentioned that it had rained non-stop for four days prior to the match and the square was under water. A strip of matting was laid on some higher ground which made a very short boundary, counting two, on one side, whilst on the other the fielders had to wade through water to retrieve the ball. The report of the match contains the following description of Barnes' innings: 'Barnes only just managed to crack his egg when a noise behind warned him to depart.'

The return game against New South Wales produced revenge for the visitors. This time, on winning the toss, Shrewsbury put the home side in and they were quickly dismissed by Briggs and Barlow. Turner and Ferris were defied by Shrewsbury and although the Australian pair took all the English wickets, sufficient lead was gained on the first innings to enable a nine wickets victory to be obtained.

The team returned to Melbourne where they played the first of three matches against the Australian side which toured England

in 1886—the weather was poor, both rain and dust-storms marring the play and reducing the attendance to little more than 2,000 each day. Being 93 behind on first innings the tourists were forced to follow on, but, led by Shrewsbury, so well did they play in the latter half of the match that victory was achieved by 57 runs—Briggs' bowling and the English field in the final innings was quite excellent.

The tourists drew their game at Geelong, where everyone was football mad, the local side being the Champions of Victoria, and then won at Ballarat, before their second encounter with the 1886 Australians. Three or four dropped catches in the Australian second innings meant that the English side needed 220 to win in 210 minutes, but the loss of three quick wickets caused the game to be drawn. The two teams immediately left the ground for the express train to Sydney, where the third match was arranged to be played. Here Shrewsbury was lucky to win the toss and bat first, for the wicket got progressively worse and the tourists were able to enforce the follow on and won by 9 wickets. On the Saturday—the second day—about 10,000 watched the game, the best attendance so far.

1886-87: Lillywhite, Shaw and Shrewsbury's Team to Australia

Batting Averages

	M	I	NO	R	HS	Avge	100	c/s
A. Shrewsbury (Notts)	10	18	4	485	144	34.64	1	16
W. Barnes (Notts)	7	12	1	319	109	29.00	1	8
W. Bates (Yorks)	10	17	0	379	86	22.29	0	6
W. Gunn (Notts)	10	16	1	323	61*	21.53	0	13
R. G. Barlow (Lancs)	10	18	3	310	86	20.66	0	9/0
W. Flowers (Notts)	10	15	2	192	52	14.77	0	3
J. M. Read (Surrey)	10	16	0	236	53	14.75	0	3
G. A. Lohmann (Surrey)	10	15	2	191	40*	14.69	0	12
M. Sherwin (Notts)	10	16	8	108	25	13.50	0	22/6
J. Briggs (Lancs)	10	15	0	179	69	11.93	0	3
W. H. Scotton (Notts)	10	16	1	163	43*	10.86	0	4/0
R. Wood (Lancs)	3	5	1	26	10*	6.50	0	0

Bowling Averages

	O	M	R	W	Avge	BB	5i
W. Barnes	374.2	224	338	25	13.52	7-51	2
W. Flowers	365.2	204	345	24	14.37	5-21	2
G. A. Lohmann	763.2	373	915	59	15.50	8-35	7
W. Bates	367	162	445	21	21.19	5-72	1
J. Briggs	581.3	305	667	30	22.23	5-42	2
R. G. Barlow	370	183	439	18	24.38	4-43	0
J. M. Read	28	13	33	1	33.00	1-14	0

Also bowled: R. Wood 8-5-8-0.
Played in non-first-class matches only: A. Shaw (Notts), Jas Lillywhite (Sussex), W. Shaw, J. Clarke.

The party which visited Australia in 1886-87, photographed in Melbourne. This was the team led by Shaw, Shrewsbury and Lillywhite. Back: W. Flowers, A. Shrewsbury, G. A. Lohmann, W. Gunn, W. Barnes, J. M. Read. Seated: W. Bates, A. Shaw, J. Lillywhite (umpire), M. Sherwin, W. H. Scotton, R. G. Barlow. Front: J. Briggs.

Four up-country games were all drawn, three due to rain. At Orange, the English batting order was decided by taking names out of a hat, whilst at Bowral, deep puddles were a feature of the outfield—the weather however was so hot after some torrential rain that the fielders found it quite pleasant running through the water. At Bathurst, the gate had been sold to a local publican for £90 and he even tried to force the players to pay an entrance fee.

Following these country diversions, the tourists went to Sydney where a team representing 'Combined Australia' was met. The first day was disastrous: the Sydney morning papers stated that the game had been postponed and therefore few spectators turned up and the English side, batting first, collapsed before Turner and Ferris for a mere 45. Brilliant English fielding plus a stubborn second innings however pulled the game round and victory—the best of the tour—was obtained by 13 runs. The success was marred to some extent by the bitter argument between Barnes and the Australian batsman, Percy McDonnell. The two came to blows and Barnes took a tremendous swipe at his adversary's face, missed and smashed his fist against a wall. The Notts all-rounder missed almost all the remaining matches as a result.

Lillywhite and Shaw took Barnes' place in the next series of up-country matches, nearly all of which suffered from torrential rain, but in the eleven-a-side games, R. Wood, a Lancastrian, engaged on the Melbourne Ground was co-opted. Turner bowled in great form in the first of these—for New South Wales—and provided the home side with an easy win. Shrewsbury was bowled Turner 0 in both his innings and was presented with a small pair of gold spectacles as a result. A second game against 'Combined Australia' came directly after the defeat by New South Wales—Turner and Ferris again were most effective, but Lohmann was even more so and the English team won by 71 runs.

Moving to Melbourne for the final leg of the tour, the tourists found the game against Victoria clashed with an important race meeting, which ruined the attendance. It had been intended to play a third match against 'Combined Australia' at Melbourne, but the best N.S.W. players couldn't come and the curious Smokers v Non-Smokers match was substituted, the English team being divided with the Victorians. The Non-Smokers hit 803, the runs coming at about 100 an hour. Few members of the public however were attracted to the game, only 500 coming on the Saturday and scarcely 100 on the last day, when at the end of play Scotton, who was batting, picked up the ball as a souvenir and was given out 'handled ball'.

Before catching the boat in Adelaide a final odds match was played against the local Fifteen, but again few spectators turned out. The tourists boarded the *Massilia* for home on 26 March. A stoppage was made at Colombo and also at Aden, where Gunn took part in an athletics match and won four events—Briggs, the ship's champion at the potato race, was however disqualified, through failing to pick up a potato.

According to the Australian newspapes the side was ranked as the finest all-round team ever to visit the Southern Hemisphere. The fielding was generally excellent, the side batted right down the order and it had six good bowlers in Barnes, Flowers, Lohmann, Bates, Briggs and Barlow.

The tourists arrived back in England on 8 May. As a footnote it should be pointed out that the English team was invited to go to New Zealand, but apart from the offer from Auckland, the financial terms were so poor that the invitation was declined.

1887-88: a rival tour goes to Australia and New Zealand

Major Wardill, who managed the 1886 Australian team to England, stated before leaving England that the Melbourne Club intended to invite a mixed team of amateurs and professionals to tour Australia in the winter of 1887-88, and that several prominent amateurs had provisionally agreed to go. In January of 1887 – six months after the announcement of the tour sponsored by the Melbourne Club – it was stated that Lillywhite, Shaw and Shrewsbury intended to manage an English team to Australia in conjunction with the New South Wales Association.

Though the professional trio were asked to reconsider their plans, they refused to do so, and both tours went ahead with the inevitably disastrous financial consequences. Alfred Shaw in his reminiscences states: 'The responsibility for the clashing of interests certainly did not rest with us.' It is however difficult to justify this claim.

Both teams travelled on the Orient steamer *Iberia*, the Melbourne side under the Hon M. B. Hawke went on board at Tilbury on 15 September, whereas the other side joined the boat at Plymouth, and the cricketers all landed at Adelaide on 25 October.

The side for the tour arranged by the Melbourne Club consisted of the Hon M. B. Hawke (Yorkshire) (capt), G. F. Vernon, A. E. Stoddart and T. C. O'Brien, all Middlesex, A. E. Newton (Somerset), W. W. Read and M. P. Bowden (Surrey) and the professionals R. Abel and J. Beaumont (Surrey), J. T. Rawlin, W. Bates and R. Peel (Yorkshire) and W. Attewell (Notts).

The first match took place in Adelaide, where, for the first time,

---

1887-88: G. F. Vernon's Team to Australia

Batting Averages

	M	I	NO	R	HS	Avge	100	c/s
W. W. Read (Surrey)	8	13	2	610	183	55.45	3	13
R. Peel (Yorks)	9	15	2	449	55	34.53	0	11
A. E. Stoddart (Middx)	9	15	0	450	94	30.00	0	8
R. Abel (Surrey)	8	14	1	320	95	24.61	0	8
A. E. Newton (Somerset)	8	12	1	264	77	24.00	0	7/2
W. Attewell (Notts)	9	14	3	212	43	19.27	0	9
T. C. O'Brien (Middx)	7	10	0	186	45	18.60	0	7
J. T. Rawlin (Yorks)	8	12	1	193	78*	17.54	0	5
G. F. Vernon (Middx)	6	9	0	155	50	17.22	0	3
Lord Hawke (Yorks)	3	5	0	76	48	15.20	0	1
M. P. Bowden (Surrey)	6	10	3	99	35	14.14	0	6/5
W. Bates (Yorks)	3	5	0	59	28	11.80	0	2
J. Beaumont (Surrey)	8	12	5	40	16	5.71	0	3

Bowling Averages

	O	M	R	W	Avge	BB	5i
W. Attewell	746.2	404	590	54	10.92	7-15	4
R. Peel	747.2	371	822	50	16.44	5-18	3
W. Bates	136.1	55	194	9	21.55	3-36	0
W. W. Read	19	5	52	2	26.00	1-16	0
A. E. Stoddart	113.3	45	187	7	26.71	2-31	0
J. Beaumont	480	248	668	22	30.36	3-34	0
J. T. Rawlin	234.1	134	221	5	44.20	2-87	0
R. Abel	29	9	46	1	46.00	1-23	0

Played in non-first-class matches only: F. H. Walters, F. Williams, J. Phillips, . McArthur.
Note: Records in Test Match by 'Combined' Team included.

1887-88: G. F. Vernon's Team to Australia

1st Match: v South Australia (Adelaide) Oct 28, 29, 31, Nov 1.
G. F. Vernon's XI 104 (G. Giffen 5-32) & 291 (R. Abel 95, A. E. Stoddart 64, J. J. Lyons 5-75) beat S. Australia 118 (R. Peel 5-31) & 206 (G. Giffen 81) by 71 runs.

2nd Match: v Victoria (Melbourne) Nov 9, 10, 11.
Victoria 152 (J. McIlwraith 60) & 126 (J. McC. Blackham 68) lost to G. F. Vernon's XI 296 (A. E. Stoddart 94, R. Peel 55) by an inns & 18 runs.

3rd Match: v XXII of Castlemaine (Castlemaine) Nov 14, 15.
Castlemaine 109 & 134 (A. E. Stoddart 8-27) drew with G. F. Vernon's XI 181 (R. Peel 63).

4th Match: v XVIII of Sandhurst (Sandhurst) Nov 16, 17.
G. F. Vernon's XI 417 (R. Peel 67, W. Attewell 59*, R. Abel 57, W. W. Read 52, A. E. Newton 51) drew with Sandhurst 135-11.

5th Match: v XVIII of Ballarat (Ballarat) Nov 18, 19.
G. F. Vernon's XI 477 (A. E. Stoddart 95, Hon M. B. Hawke 70, W. W. Read 65, R. Peel 65, W. Attewell 50) drew with Ballarat 67 and 51-2.

6th Match: v New South Wales (Sydney) Nov 25, 26, 28, 29, 30.
G. F. Vernon's XI 340 (R. Abel 88, A. E. Stoddart 55, R. Peel 54, C. T. B. Turner 7-106) & 106 (J. J. Ferris 7-49) lost to N.S.W. 408 (P. S. McDonnell 112, H. Moses 77, S. P. Jones 60) & 40-1 by 9 wkts.

7th Match: v XVIII of Parramatta (Parramatta) Dec 2, 3.
Parramatta 144 (W. Attewell 7-55) & 166-6 drew with G. F. Vernon's XI 116 (Thorpe 7-41).

8th Match: v XXII of Hawkesbury (Richmond) Dec 5, 6.
G. F. Vernon's XI 84 & 108 drew with Hawkesbury 52 (W. Attewell 11-25) & 49-15 (W. Attewell 9-17).

9th Match: v XVIII of Manly (Manly) (One Day) Dec 7.
Manly 148 (A. E. Stoddart 7-34) drew with G. F. Vernon's XI 126-5 (W. Bates 54).

10th Match: v XVIII Melbourne Juniors (Melbourne) Dec 10, 12.
G. F. Vernon's XI 556 (A. E. Stoddart 285, R. Peel 95) drew with Juniors 70-15.

11th Match: v XXII of Maryborough (Maryborough) Dec 14, 15.
G. F. Vernon's XI 258 (A. E. Stoddart 81, T. C. O'Brien 75) drew with Maryborough 98 (R. Peel 10-40) & 55-14.

12th Match: v XXII of Gippsland (Sale) Dec 19, 20.
Gippsland 51 (R. Peel 14-16) & 98 (R. Peel 10-36) lost to G. F. Vernon's XI 152 by an inns & 3 runs.

13th Match: v South Australia (Adelaide) Dec 24, 26, 27, 28.
G. F. Vernon's XI 382 (W. W. Read 183, G. Giffen 5-163) & 59-0 drew with S. Australia 143 (A. H. Jarvis 75) & 493 (G. Giffen 203, W. Godfrey 119).

14th Match: v Combined Australia (Melbourne) Dec 31, Jan 2, 3.
G. F. Vernon's XI 292 (J. T. Rawlin 78*, A. E. Newton 77, G. F. Vernon 50) beat Australia 136 & 78 by an inns & 78 runs.

15th Match: v XV of Yarra Bend (Yarra Bend) (One Day) Jan 5.
G. F. Vernon's XI 186 (T. C. O'Brien 66) beat Yarra Bend 57 (A. E. Stoddard 8-36) by 129 runs.

16th Match: v XVIII of Northern Tasmania (Launceston) Jan 13, 14.
G. F. Vernon's XI 195 (A. E. Stoddart 91) & 27-3 drew with N. Tasmania 162.

17th Match: v XXII of North West Coast (Latrobe) Jan 17, 18.
G. F. Vernon's XI 271 (W. Attewell 122) beat North West Coast 66 (J. Beaumont 9-12) & 97 (R. Peel 13-54) by an inns & 108 runs.

18th Match: v XVIII of South Tasmania (Hobart) Jan 20, 21.
S. Tasmania 59 (R. Peel 11-21) & 91-7 drew with G. F. Vernon's XI 146 (R. Peel 51).

19th Match: v XV of Tasmania (Hobart) Jan 26, 27, 28.
G. F. Vernon's XI 297 (R. Peel 119) drew with Tasmania 405 (K. Burn 99, MacLeod 50, R. Peel 6-89).

20th Match: v XVIII of Benalla (Benalla) Feb 2, 3.
G. F. Vernon's XI 271 beat Benalla 126 & 92 by an inns & 53 runs.

21st Match: v XXII of Cootamundra (Cootamundra) Feb 7, 8.
Cootamundra 105 (R. Peel 13-61) & 20-2 drew with G. F. Vernon's XI 243 (R. Abel 92*).

22nd Match: v New South Wales (Sydney) Feb 17, 18, 20, 21.
G. F. Vernon's XI 337 (W. W. Read 119, C. T. B. Turner 5-128) & 109-2 (W. W. Read 53*, R. Peel 52*) beat N.S.W. 193 & 252 (P. S. McDonnell 56) by 8 wkts.

23rd Match: v XXII of Goulburn (Goulburn) Feb 24, 25.
Goulburn 124 (R. Peel 13-43) drew with G. F. Vernon's XI 31 (Knopp 5-12) & 157.

24th Match: v XVIII of Wagga Wagga (Wagga Wagga) Feb 28, 29.
Wagga Wagga 62 & 106 lost to G. F. Vernon's XI 173 by an inns & 5 runs.

25th Match: v 1888 Australians (Melbourne) March 2, 3, 5.
G. F. Vernon's XI 221 (A. E. Newton 54) & 117 (C. T. B. Turner 7-48) beat Australians 219 (T. P. Horan 67, W. Attewell 5-33) & 32 (W. Attewell 7-15) by 87 runs.

26th Match: v Victoria (Melbourne) March 9, 10, 12.
G. F. Vernon's XI 130 & 368 (W. W. Read 142, A. E. Stoddart 75, J. Worrall 5-33) beat Victoria 81 (W. Attewell 6-30) & 135 (W. Attewell 5-28) by 282 runs.

Match by Combined English Teams: v Australia (Sydney) Feb 10, 11, 13, 14, 15.
England 113 (C. T. B. Turner 5-44) & 137 (C. T. B. Turner 7-43) beat Australia 42 (G. A. Lohmann 5-17, R. Peel 5-18) & 82 (R. Peel 5-40) by 126 runs.

G. F. Vernon's party to Australia in 1887-88, photographed in Melbourne. Back: J. T. Rawlin, M. P. Bowden, G. F. Vernon, Sir T. C. O'Brien, J. Beaumont. Centre: A. E. Newton, W. Bates, the Hon M. B. Hawke (captain), W. Attewell, R. Peel. Front: R. Abel, W. W. Read, A. E. Stoddart.

the South Australians met an England touring party on even terms. Unfortunately several of the best locals could not play, but as matters turned out the English side did not have the walk-over they expected, winning by only 71 runs. Neither W. W. Read (sprained ankle) or G. F. Vernon (badly cut ear) could turn out in this game. Poor weather and a poor attendance matched each other for the second game – against Victoria at Melbourne – which resulted in an innings victory for the tourists. Three up-country matches were contested before the side went to Sydney to play New South Wales. After a fairly even first innings, the visitors collapsed against Turner and Ferris and N.S.W. knocked off the runs required for the loss of one wicket. The Saturday was almost rained off, but a crowd of about 5,000 was present on each of two of the other days. Six odd matches were played in succession – in the second of these at Hawkesbury the captain, the Hon M. B. Hawke, learnt of the death of his father, and immediately left the team in order to travel back to England. G. F. Vernon was appointed captain in his place.

The next eleven-a-side match was the return with South Australia. The high scoring match – W. W. Read made 183 and George Giffen 203 – went into the fifth day, and despite an agreement that it would be played out was left drawn so that the team could travel to Melbourne for the scheduled match against 'Combined Australia'. The effort to get the best Australian eleven failed, only five of the side being worthy of a place in such a team. The Englishmen had no difficulty in winning by an innings.

A match at Yarra Bend was followed by a trip to Tasmania, where four matches against odds were played. Of these the best was at Hobart against Eighteen of Combined Tasmania. The locals hit 405 of which J. Burn made 99 – according to some sources he actually reached 100. At any rate a collection was made for him on the ground.

Getting back to the mainland, the side played at Cootamundra and then the two English touring sides selected the best eleven from among themselves and met Australia in what should have been the best match ever played between the two countries. Six of the leading Australians however could not or would not play, and in rotten weather with few spectators, the England side won with ease, aided by the fact that the Australian captain, McDonnell, put them in to bat on a dead wicket. Walter Read led the Combined England Team.

New South Wales were handicapped by the absence of Ferris for their return game with the tourists. A splendid century by Walter Read gave his team a good lead on first innings and the match was won by 8 wkts – the match was played in pleasant weather, but did not attract the crowds.

Of the two remaining eleven-a-side matches one was against the Australian Team due to tour England in 1888, in which match rain caused the wicket to become very nasty in the final innings, and although needing just 120, the Australians were all out for 32,

1887-88: Lillywhite, Shaw and Shrewsbury's Team to Australia and New Zealand

1st Match: v XVIII of Parramatta (Parramatta)   Nov 4, 5.
Parramatta 72 (J. Briggs 9-33) & 241-16 drew with A. Shrewsbury's XI 272 (G. Ulyett 73).

2nd Match: v New South Wales (Sydney)   Nov 11, 12.
A. Shrewsbury's XI 49 (J. J. Ferris 6-24) & 66 (C. T. B. Turner 6-23) lost to N.S.W. 94 (G. A. Lohmann 5-26) & 25-0 by 10 wkts.

3rd Match: v XVIII of Queensland (Brisbane)   Nov 18, 19, 21.
Queensland 79 & 59 (C. A. Smith 10-28) lost to A. Shrewsbury's XI 138 & 2-0 by 10 wkts.

4th Match: v XXII of Maryborough (Maryborough)   Nov 23, 24.
A. Shrewsbury's XI 166 beat Maryborough 41 (J. Briggs 14-25) & 104 (C. A. Smith 11-11, G. A. Lohmann 10-51) by an inns & 21 runs.

5th Match: v XXII of Gympie (Gympie)   Nov 25-26.
Gympie 45 (J. Briggs 13-24) & 79 lost to A. Shrewsbury's XI 269 (L. C. Docker 58) by an inns & 145 runs.

6th Match: v XVIII of Queensland (Brisbane)   Dec 2, 3, 5.
A. Shrewsbury's XI 133 (A. Coningham 5-73) & 185 (G. A. Lohmann 53) beat Queensland 93 (G. A. Lohmann 7-30) & 116 (J. Briggs 12-47) by 114 runs.

7th Match: v New South Wales (Sydney)   Dec 9, 10, 12.
N.S.W. 149 (H. Moses 68) & 165 lost to A. Shrewsbury's XI 279 (C. A. Smith 68, C. T. B. Turner 7-117) & 39-0 by 10 wkts.*

8th Match: v Victoria (Melbourne)   Dec 16, 17, 19.
Victoria 68 & 100 lost to A. Shrewsbury's XI 624 (A. Shrewsbury 232, G. Brann 118, J. Briggs 75) by an inns & 456 runs.

9th Match: v XXII of Ballarat (Ballarat)   Dec 24, 26, 27.
Ballarat 102 & 127 lost to A. Shrewsbury's XI 152 (L. C. Docker 50, J. Duffy 5-37) & 83-2 (J. M. Read 51) by 8 wkts.*

10th Match: v XVIII of Bendigo (Sandhurst)   Dec 31, Jan 2.
A. Shrewsbury's XI 389 (J. M. Preston 78, R. Pilling 67, G. Ulyett 64, G. Brann 56) drew with Bendigo 165 & 6-6.*

11th Match: v XVIII Melbourne Juniors (North Fitzroy)   Jan 6, 7.
A. Shrewsbury's XI 124 (A. Shrewsbury 51) & 131 drew with Juniors 158 (G. A. Lohmann 8-52).

12th Match: v XXII of Bowral (Bowral)   Jan 10, 11.
A. Shrewsbury's XI 126 beat Bowral 42 (J. Briggs 14-20) & 57 (C. A. Smith 9-15) by an inns & 27 runs.

13th Match: v New South Wales (Sydney)   Jan 13, 14, 16, 17.
N.S.W. 153 (H. Moses 58, G. A. Lohmann 7-68) & 216 (H. Moses 109, G. A. Lohmann 7-97) beat A. Shrewsbury's XI 87 (C. T. B. Turner 8-39) & 129 (A. Shrewsbury 56, C. T. B. Turner 8-40) by 153 runs.

14th Match: v XXII of Bourke (Bourke)   Jan 20, 21.
A. Shrewsbury's XI 69 & 157-6 drew with Bourke 104 (J. M. Preston 8-44).

15th Match: v XVIII of Orange (Orange)   Jan 27, 28.
Orange 76 (J. Briggs 12-37) & 52 lost to A. Shrewsbury's XI 208 (J. M. Read 55) by an inns & 80 runs.

16th Match: v Combined Australia (Sydney)   Feb 3, 4, 6, 7.
Australia 262 (P. S. McDonnell 54, G. A. Lohmann 5-83) & 83 (G. A. Lohmann 7-43) lost to A. Shrewsbury's XI 295 (G. Ulyett 72, W. Newham 53, P. G. McShane 5-103) & 51-5 by 5 wkts.

17th Match: v XVIII of Newcastle (Newcastle)   Feb 16, 17, 18.
A. Shrewsbury's XI 226 (J. Briggs 80) & 42-1 drew with Newcastle 107 (G. A. Lohmann 7-37) & 222 (Wooden 51, C. A. Smith 6-13).

18th Match: v XXII of Tamworth (Tamworth)   Feb 21, 22.
Tamworth 104 (J. Briggs 11-45) & 98 (G. A. Lohmann 7-12) lost to A. Shrewsbury's XI 183 & 20-1 by 9 wkts.

19th Match: v 1888 Australians (Sydney)   Feb 24, 25.
A. Shrewsbury's XI 173 (A. Shrewsbury 51, C. T. B. Turner 5-64) beat Australians 75 (J. Briggs 6-40) & 56 (J. Briggs 5-18, G. A. Lohmann 5-37) by an inns & 42 runs.

20th Match: v XVIII Sydney Juniors (Sydney)   March 2, 3, 5.
Juniors 181 (McDowall 58, J. M. Preston 8-45) & 153 drew with A. Shrewsbury's XI 175 & 5-1.

21st Match: v XVIII of Bathurst (Bathurst)   March 6, 7.
Bathurst 57 & 129 lost to A. Shrewsbury's XI 180 & 7-2 by 8 wkts.

22nd Match: v 1888 Australians (Sydney)   March 9, 10, 12, 13.
A. Shrewsbury's XI 212 (C. A. Smith 59, C. T. B. Turner 7-72) & 402 (A. Shrewsbury 206, J. Briggs 54) beat Australians 190 (J. McC. Blackham 97) & 266 (S. P. Jones 134) by 158 runs.

23rd Match: v XVIII of Wellington (Wellington)   March 23, 24.
A. Shrewsbury's XI 207 (J. M. Read 70) & 21-1 drew with Wellington 86 (G. A. Lohmann 13-37) & 222 (Werry 53).*

24th Match: v XVIII of Canterbury (Christchurch)   March 26, 27, 28, 29.
Canterbury 145 & 80 (J. Briggs 9-43) drew with A. Shrewsbury's XI 78 & 31-0.

25th Match: v XVIII of Canterbury (Christchurch)   March 30, 31.
A. Shrewsbury's XI 140 (R. Halley 6-50) & 100 (H. R. Mathias 6-36) drew with Canterbury 64 (J. Briggs 9-26) & 37-9.

The team taken by Shaw and Shrewsbury to Australia in 1887-88. Back: G. Brann, L. C. Docker, J. Lillywhite, J. M. Read, A. D. Pougher. Centre: G. Ulyett, R. Pilling, C. A. Smith (capt), A. Shrewsbury, G. A. Lohmann. Front: J. M. Preston, J. Briggs, W. Newham. The captain, 'Round-the-Corner' Smith, later became the famous film actor, C. Aubrey Smith.

Batting Averages

	M	I	NO	R	HS	Avge	'100	c/s
A. Shrewsbury (Notts)	8	14	1	766	232	58.92	2	14
G. Brann (Sussex)	5	8	2	158	118	26.33	1	3
C. A. Smith (Sussex)	6	8	0	197	69	24.62	0	4
G. Ulyett (Yorks)	6	10	1	201	72	22.33	0	3
J. Briggs (Lancs)	8	13	1	229	75	19.08	0	7
J. M. Read (Surrey)	8	13	0	218	39	16.76	0	3
A. D. Pougher (Leics)	6	9	2	107	25*	15.28	0	5
L. C. Docker (Derbys)	7	11	1	138	48	13.80	0	6
G. A. Lohmann (Surrey)	8	13	0	173	39	13.30	0	10
W. Newham (Sussex)	7	12	0	146	53	12.16	0	6
J. M. Preston (Yorks)	7	10	1	81	27	9.00	0	3
R. Pilling (Lancs)	8	12	5	48	10	6.85	0	16/6

Bowling Averages

	O	M	R	W	Avge	BB	5i
G. A. Lohmann	659.1	354	755	63	11.98	7-43	7
J. Briggs	371.1	215	436	30	14.53	6-40	2
A. D. Pougher	156	79	189	12	15.75	4-40	0
J. M. Preston	216.2	102	307	17	18.05	4-16	0
C. A. Smith	121	57	153	7	21.85	3-11	0
G. Ulyett	22	5	49	1	49.00	1-32	0

Played in non-first-class matches only: McCormick and Charleston (or Clarkson).
Note: Records in Test Match by 'Combined' Team included.

Attewell taking 7 for 15, and the other was against Victoria, when after a low scoring first innings by each team, Walter Read hit 142 not out and victory was obtained by 282 runs.

After this game a One-day match was organised for the benefit of William Bates, who had been hit in the eye whilst at net practice in Melbourne and had missed most of the fixtures as a result. Considering the loss of both Bates and Lord Hawke for most of the tour, the team had an excellent record – it was a pity that attendances were poor and the visit clashed with the rival venture. It was reported that the Melbourne Club lost £2,000 on the speculation. The team arrived back at Plymouth on 28 April, but without Stoddart who remained in Australia.

Turning to the travels of the party under Lillywhite, Shaw and Shrewsbury, the team, which played its first match at Parramatta on 4 November, consisted of C. A. Smith (capt), W. Newham and G. Brann of Sussex; L. C. Docker of Warwickshire and the following professionals: A. Shrewsbury (Notts); G. Ulyett and J. M. Preston (Yorkshire); A. D. Pougher (Leics); J. Briggs and R. Pilling (Lancashire); G. A. Lohmann and J. M. Read (Surrey). Alfred Shaw did not make the trip.

In their second game the side were caught on a sticky wicket at Sydney and Turner and Ferris bowled them out twice for 115, the match – against New South Wales – being lost by 10 wickets. From Sydney, the team went by steamer to Brisbane, where they played Eighteen of Queensland on the new Exhibition Ground. A fair crowd watched the game and saw the visitors win a low-scoring contest.

At Maryborough, the experiment was made of laying the matting wicket on a thick spread of sawdust. This resulted in a very slow pitch, but with the ball doing the unexpected, it was not a success. An eleven-a-side exhibition game preceded the return with Queensland, which was poorly attended – on the Saturday, a beautiful day, only 1,200 turned up and the last day only 50. Crowds were much improved at Sydney for the second game against New South Wales and for once the English batsmen mastered Turner and Ferris to win the match by 10 wickets.

Victoria put out a very poor side against the tourists and suffered mightily; Shrewsbury took the opportunity to make 232 and the total rose to 624 – victory was achieved by an innings and 456 runs. In reporting the game, one journalist noted: 'Cricket in Melbourne is now very dull, in fact, more so than in any other Australian metropolis. The leading cricketers themselves are stupidly lukewarm, and, seeing that that is the case, the apathy of the public is not surprising.' Shrewsbury's score, the team total and the margin of the win were all records for matches between English teams and the colonies.

Four up-country games came after the success at Melbourne and then the side again pitted its strength against Turner and Ferris – Turner took 16 wickets for 79 and only a splendid fifty

by Shrewsbury prevented complete humiliation. As it was the defeat was by a margin of 153 runs – the second and happily last loss of the tour.

The next major fixture was against 'Combined Australia' and the home side was fairly strong, though Ferris (injured) had to stand down. On the first two days some good cricket was seen, then rain ruined the wicket and gave the bowlers an easy time. The tourists however achieved a deserved victory by 5 wickets. The next eleven-a-side match was also against an Australian team. Shrewsbury hit a workmanlike fifty and then Lohmann and Briggs bowled the tourists to an innings victory. Rain kept the attendance down. The return match against the same Australian combination took place a fortnight later on a hard and true wicket. The first two innings were very even, but Shrewsbury then proceeded to hit another double century and the side just topped 400. S. P. Jones went in at the fall of the second wicket for Australia and carried out his bat for an excellent 134, but the English side won by 158 runs. This was the final match in Australia – the tourists travelled to New Zealand, but without L. C. Docker, arriving on 22 March. The programme in New Zealand consisted of three matches only – one at Wellington and two at Christchurch, all against odds. The side returned to England in the *Coptic*, which reached Plymouth on 12 May.

The tour was a success from the playing angle, but financially Shaw and Shrewsbury lost £2,400 – Lillywhite was unable to meet his share of the loss. It was the last speculative venture by the professional trio.

1888-89: C. Aubrey Smith captains the first tour to South Africa

Major R. Gardner Warton, who served in South Africa for five years on the General Staff, retired at the beginning of 1888 and determined to take a party of English cricketers to Southern Africa in the winter of 1888-89. Major Warton had a difficult task when selecting the team, since the strength of cricket in South Africa compared to that in England was an unknown quantity. The team he chose contained seven men who appeared regularly in first-class County cricket in 1888: C. A. Smith (Sussex) (capt), M. P. Bowden (Surrey) and professionals R. Abel (Surrey), J. M. Read (Surrey), H. Wood (Surrey), J. Briggs (Lancs), F. Hearne (Kent). There was one other professional, A. J. Fothergill (Somerset) and five amateurs of good club standard: Hon C. J. Coventry, J. E. P. McMaster, J. H. Roberts, B. A. F. Grieve and A. C. Skinner.

The side left England on 21 November aboard the *Garth Castle*, calling at Lisbon and Madeira before landing at Cape Town on 14 December. The first match was played on the Newlands Ground against Twenty-two of Western Province and after a close finish was lost by 17 runs. After six games had been completed, four of which were lost, the press were critical of the strength of the English side, but this was of course comment made with hindsight. About Christmas time the side lost J. H. Roberts, who was called back to England on account of the death of his mother. Major Warton then decided to acquire the services of George Ulyett, the Yorkshire batsman, but he did not join the team until 6 February. Away from the Cape, the team encountered cricket fields with not a single blade of grass on them. The grounds, being brick coloured clay, were sprinkled with sand to absorb the moisture. The surface of the wicket had been rolled until it was as hard as asphalt and as level as a billiard table. The ball came off the pitch much faster than in England and rose about six inches higher.

Following the poor start the side improved. Twenty-two of

Johannesburg were beaten by 10 wickets, thanks to some extent to the insistence of C. A. Smith that a green matting wicket be used, thus cutting down the glare. Abel hit a chanceless hundred in the next game and Fifteen of Transvaal were beaten by an innings – to the surprise of the tourists no Dutchmen appeared in the opposition team. Several gold mines were visited during the stay in Johannesburg, and on the final day there the public banquet for the team went on so long that no sleep at all was obtained. Two games were played at Pietersmaritzburg, both providing innings victories with Briggs taking most wickets. Travelling to Durban, the side returned to a grass outfield with a matting wicket. The steamy hot weather worried most of the tourists and a very even draw against the local Eighteen resulted. The journey from Durban to East London was made by boat and three successive wins by innings were obtained – two at Kingwilliamstown and one at Grahamstown, all against Twenty-twos.

The most important match of the tour and the first eleven-a-side fixture was staged at Port Elizabeth on a green matting wicket. The opposing team was a representative South African eleven, which except for the absence of Theunissen of Cape Town, was quite the strongest team that could be formed. About 3,000 people were present to witness the start of this game, which is now regarded as the first Test Match between the two countries.

The play however was not very noteworthy, the English team winning by 8 wickets.

C. A. Smith went down with an attack of fever shortly after the match and for the final fixtures, M. P. Bowden took on the role of captain. A return match against South Africa terminated the visit – Abel hit another chanceless hundred and Briggs took 15 wickets for 28 runs to give 'England' victory by an innings.

The side sailed back to England in the *Garth Castle* arriving on 16 April. C. A. Smith and M. P. Bowden remained behind in South Africa.

From the playing viewpoint the visit, after a deceptive start, was a great success, but despite quite good attendances, the receipts did not cover Major Warton's expenses.

1889-90: one defeat for the first tourists to India

In the autumn of 1889 a team of amateurs under the captaincy and management of G. F. Vernon left England for the Indian sub-continent. Although this was the first English tour to that part of the world, two Indian sides had already visited England and demonstrated that the standard of cricket in India was rapidly improving, both in regard to the native Indian sides and to the cricket played by the Europeans in India. The quality of cricket in Ceylon was not so high, but English teams calling there on the way to Australia could be in no doubt as to the enthusiasm of the population for the game.

The main body of the touring party was G. F. Vernon, J. G. Walker and H. Philipson (Middx), E. M. Lawson-Smith, A. E. Leatham, J. H. J. Hornsby, A. E. Gibson, T. K. Tapling and G. H. Goldney, who left Tilbury on 31 October. Lord Hawke, the Yorkshire cricketer, had gone on ahead, and E. R. de Little and F. L. Shand were to join the side in Colombo. It was hoped that C. I. Thornton would play in some matches, since he was also visiting India – in fact he did not. As the side contained only three cricketers who appeared regularly in county matches in 1889 – Vernon, Walker and Lord Hawke – it would be generous to say that as a whole the party was 'first-class' by English standards.

Arriving in Colombo on 26 November, the cricketers found that the Colombo Cricket Club had arranged a large programme of entertainments in honour of the visit, including various balls, dinners and theatricals.

As T. K. Tapling had had to stop over in Naples and neither Shand (playing in Ceylon) or de Little were available, the first match was played with three substitutes, but the tourists still won with an innings to spare. The second – and only other game in Ceylon – was also won by an innings.

From Ceylon the side went to Calcutta and opposed the local Club. Calcutta batted first and C. E. Greenway carried his bat right through the innings for a faultless 130. A. E. Gibson hit a century for the tourists and the game appeared very even. The Calcutta Club however collapsed in its second innings and the tourists won by nine wickets. After five further matches, the team met the Parsis Eleven in Bombay for the most important fixture of the visit. About 10,000 spectators attended on the first day of the three-day game and saw the tourists dismissed for 97. The Parsis in their turn went for only 82 but some excellent bowling by M. E. Pavri put them back in the game – he took 7 for 34 – and the Parsis required only 77 to win the final innings. M. E. Pavri scored a vital 21 and the tourists suffered their only defeat by 4 wickets. The four remaining matches were rather an anti-climax, three being won by large margins and the fourth drawn.

The tour helped to stimulate interest in the game in India and was generally regarded as a success; unfortunately Lord Hawke was taken ill and could play in only four matches, the Hon A. M. Curzon being co-opted into the team. No less than 14 players were included in the team during the tour in emergency!

United States where cricket took pride of place over baseball and this was reflected in the other matches of the tour. In these engagements the opposition was poor and, though enjoyable from the social viewpoint, the matches were almost non-contests. In Boston there were two good bowlers, Chambers and Wright, in Chicago a good all-rounder, Dr Ogden, and Boyd in Toronto and Bristow in Ottawa showed themselves useful batsmen, but the rest were enthusiastic club cricketers.

The only casualty of the tour was G. W. Hillyard who suffered from sunstroke and came home early. The programme of matches ended on 24 October and the team were back in England on 5 November.

1891: Lord Hawke takes a side to the United States and Canada

G. F. Vernon had intended to take a second team to India in the autumn of 1891, but this having been abandoned, C. W. Alcock, the Surrey secretary, began to organise an amateur tour to North America. Alcock, for business reasons, could not complete the arrangements and Lord Hawke, the Yorkshire captain, took over the managing and selecting of the side. The team contained only five who appeared regularly in first-class games in 1891: the captain, H. T. Hewett (Somerset), S. M. J. Woods (Cambridge U and Somerset), K. J. Key (Surrey) and C. W. Wright (Notts). The remainder of the party consisted of Lord Throwley, the Hon H. A. Milles, G. W. Ricketts, C. Wreford-Brown, K. McAlpine, J. H. J. Hornsby and G. W. Hillyard.

The side was a little stronger than Vernon's Team of 1889-90 and might be described as a moderate first-class combination.

Leaving England on 16 September, the team suffered a rough sea passage, and landing in New York went straight to Philadelphia to play the two most important fixtures of the programme. The initial match was on the ground of the Germantown Club, which the visitors regarded as the equal of any in the world, a splendid pavilion having been recently erected. The Philadelphians, though losing the toss, played well, with G. S. Patterson their best bat making 68 and 43 not out, and the visitors were defeated by 8 wickets. In the return fixture S. M. J. Woods, helped by an over-watered wicket, bowled out the Philadelphians cheaply and avenged the defeat. Philadelphia was the only city in the

1891-92: Lord Sheffield's speculative tour to revive Australian interest

Since the disastrous dual tours of 1887-88, cricket in Australia had been falling in popularity. The Australian side which visited England in 1890 had been beaten in both Tests and its predecessor of 1888 had lost the Test series 2 matches to 1. The internal squabbles between Melbourne and Sydney had done nothing to improve the standing of the game. The press were of the opinion that an English tour was required to stimulate the game in Australia, but as no one in Australia cared to finance such a venture, Lord Sheffield, the great patron of Sussex cricket, decided to try and organise a tour. He first stated that he would not finance the side unless W. G. Grace would agree to captain it and when the Grand Old Man assented, this virtually insured the success of the scheme. Both Shrewsbury and Gunn, the Notts batsmen, refused the terms offered, but Lord Sheffield met with no other refusals of consequence and the side was composed of W. G. Grace and O. G. Radcliffe (Gloucestershire), A. E. Stoddart (Middlesex), G. MacGregor (Cambridge U) and H. Philipson (Northumberland) and the professionals G. A. Lohmann, R. Abel, J. M. Read and J. W. Sharpe (Surrey), W. Attewell (Notts), R. Peel (Yorks), J. Briggs (Lancs) and G. Bean (Sussex). Alfred Shaw, who was employed by Lord Sheffield, went as manager.

The team played matches at Malta and Colombo on the outward journey and began the tour proper at Adelaide on 20 November. The team were confident of victory in the three Tests and wins by an innings at Adelaide and then at Melbourne against Victoria seemed to justify this confidence. Peel missed the Victorian match due to an attack of pleurisy, which happily was of brief duration. W. G. Grace carried his bat through the visitors' innings and appropriately the band struck up 'See the Conquering Hero Comes', as the famous old cricketer went to the wicket.

The third game – against New South Wales – had its start delayed by an hour, when the home captain objected to D. Cotter standing as umpire and W. G. Grace refused to replace him; eventually Alfred Shaw agreed to stand to the satisfaction of both parties. The English win in this game was only by 4 wickets, due to their old adversary Turner, who took 11 wickets.

Six up-country matches were played in succession before the tourists met Australia in the First Test at Melbourne. A crowd of 20,110 came to watch the first day's play and the same number on the second, whilst over 10,000 came on both the third and fourth days. England seemed to have the match in hand, but collapsed against Turner in the final innings after 60 runs were on the board with one wicket down. The better side won and both elevens suffered equally from injury – Briggs and Bean had cut hands, Moses strained his leg and Turner was ill in bed on the first day.

Another six up-country fixtures went by before the Second Test at Sydney. The betting opened at 3 to 1 on England – the bookmakers being as common as on previous English visits. Excellent bowling by Lohmann, after Australia won the toss and elected to bat, reduced the home side to 145 all out. Moses, who was injured in the previous Test, again strained his leg, but the request for a substitute fielder when England batted was at first refused by Grace, who then relented, but refused to permit Syd Gregory to act in that capacity – Gregory being a much better fielder than Moses. A determined innings by Abel, who carried out his bat, gave England a lead of 162 and England looked set for an innings victory. Lyons, Bannerman and Giffen however put Australia back in the game and then rain made the wicket difficult. Dropped catches aided Australia's cause still further, so that England needed 230 to win. Abel, Bean and Grace were all out for 11 and good bowling by Turner and Giffen ran through the remainder. The report of the game ends: 'The enthusiasm at the

finish was something to remember. The crowd howled and yelled, and cheered themselves hoarse and it was sometime before they left the ground.'

The next eleven-a-side game was the return with New South Wales. Centuries from Maurice Read and Lohmann, the latter rather lucky, took the score to 414 and from then the result of the game was hardly in doubt. One of the umpires took objection to a remark made by W. G. Grace concerning a decision and the official refused to stand in the remainder of the match. The match against Victoria provided another win for the English team and came directly before the final fixture, the third Test at Adelaide.

1891-92: Lord Sheffield's Team to Australia								
Batting Averages								
	M	I	NO	R	HS	Avge	100	c/s
W. G. Grace (Gloucs)	8	11	1	448	159*	44.80	1	17
R. Abel (Surrey)	8	12	2	388	132*	38.80	1	10
A. E. Stoddart (Middx)	8	12	0	450	134	37.50	1	5
J. M. Read (Surrey)	8	11	0	328	106	29.81	1	3
R. Peel (Yorks)	7	11	2	229	83	25.44	0	8
G. A. Lohmann (Surrey)	8	11	1	222	102	22.20	1	9
J. Briggs (Lancs)	8	13	0	262	91	20.15	0	8
G. Bean (Sussex)	7	11	1	178	50	17.80	0	5
H. Philipson (Middx)	2	2	1	16	15*	16.00	0	2/3
W. Attewell (Notts)	8	11	3	126	43*	15.75	0	7
G. MacGregor (Middx)	7	9	2	101	31	14.42	0	10/2
J. W. Sharpe (Surrey)	7	9	3	63	26	10.50	0	5
O. G. Radcliffe (Gloucs)	2	3	0	31	18	10.33	0	0
Bowling Averages								
	O	M	R	W	Avge	BB	5i	
W. Attewell	497.5	241	573	44	13.02	6-34	4	
J. Briggs	212.4	71	420	32	13.12	6-49	4	
G. A. Lohmann	416.3	178	640	40	16.00	8-58	2	
R. Peel	192.3	83	283	15	18.13	4-50	0	
W. G. Grace	73.1	21	134	5	26.80	3-64	0	
J. W. Sharpe	287	113	508	17	29.88	6-40	2	

Also bowled: A. E. Stoddart 9-3-22-0.
Played in non-first-class matches only: K. McArthur.

Lord Sheffield's team to Australia in 1891-92, photographed in the Botanical Gardens in Adelaide. Back: A. Shaw, A. E. Stoddart, J. M. Read, H. Phillipson, O. G. Radcliffe. Front: R. Abel, G. A. Lohmann, G. MacGregor, J. Briggs, R. Peel, Dr W. G. Grace (captain), W. Attewell, G. Bean, J. Sharpe.

On a splendid wicket, England batted first and with Stoddart hitting a well-judged 134 and Peel making 82, the total realised 499, but Australia must take some 'credit' for this as their fielding was decidedly poor. Rain on the second afternoon transformed the wicket and with Briggs taking full advantage of the conditions, England ended their tour with an innings victory.

The fielding and bowling of the side was fully up to expectations, but the team lacked steady batsmen of the calibre of Gunn and Shrewsbury, and this resulted in the loss of two Tests. Although the attendances were good in the three main centres, the tour lost money, Lord Sheffield being out of pocket to the tune of £2,000 – the total cost of the visit having been £16,000.

1891-92: bowlers too good for South Africans

It was thought that the idea of an English cricket tour to South Africa in the winter of 1891-92 would not be judicious, at least from the financial aspect, as a team of Rugby footballers had been touring South Africa during the summer. This indeed proved the case and the up-country matches were poorly attended. The cricketers were led by W. W. Read of Surrey and the party consisted of W. Brockwell, H. Wood, G. W. Ayres (Surrey), W. L. Murdoch and G. Brann (Sussex), J. J. Ferris (Gloucester), J. T. Hearne (Middx), A. D. Pougher (Leics), A. Hearne, G. G. Hearne, F. Martin and E. Leaney (Kent), W. Chatterton (Derby) and V. A. Barton (Hants). Much stronger than Major Warton's Team, the side had five good bowlers in J. T. Hearne, Alec Hearne, Martin, Pougher and Ferris, the last named being the old Australian Test player.

Sailing in the *Dunottar Castle*, the tourists arrived at Cape Town on 8 December and had 12 days practice before the first match against Eighteen of Western Province; both this and the following game were draws, but the third match provided an easy win. The features of the three games were the bowling of Ferris and the batting of Chatterton and Alec Hearne. Two matches against Fifteen of Cape Colony – at Port Elizabeth and Kimberley – provided two victories by an innings and neither game went into the third day. The point that the tourists were equipped with bowlers who were much too good for the home batsmen was now obvious to all and this fact further reduced public enthusiasm for the visit.

Fifteen of Transvaal were beaten by nine wickets and in their return game fielded Eighteen men and managed to draw.

The principal match of the tour and the only eleven-a-side fixture was also the final official match, being played at Cape Town on 19, 21 and 22 March. This match is now regarded as a 'Test', but at the time 'Wisden' thought so little of it that no details at all were given of the two South African innings. As in so many other games on the tour, Ferris proved too good for the South African batsmen, taking 13 for 91 in all. In their turn the English batsmen hit the bowling all over the field and Wood scored 134 not out – the only century he ever made in a first-class career which encompassed 316 matches. England won the Test by an innings and 189 runs, though it should be stated that the home side were without A. B. Tancred. F. Hearne, the brother of G. G. and Alec, who played for England, played for South Africa, having emigrated there after the previous tour.

The tour closed with an extra game for the benefit of the professionals. Ferris was the outstanding figure for the visitors, his wicket total being 234, whilst both J. T. Hearne and Martin captured over 100 wickets each.

Apart from an unfortunate incident when the team left Cape Town, no unpleasantness marred the tour, which, socially, was a success, but financially not so. The team arrived back in England in mid-April.

1892-93: another successful tour to Ceylon and India

Lord Hawke captained the second team of amateurs to the Indian sub-continent. The side, which contained three of the 1889-90 team, was somewhat stronger than that combination and the equal of the weakest of the first-class county sides. The full team consisted of Lord Hawke (Yorks) (capt), A. J. L. Hill and F. S. Jackson (Cambridge U), C. W. Wright and J. S. Robinson (Notts), M. F. Maclean, J. H. J. Hornsby, G. F. Vernon, H. F. Wright, A. E. Gibson, A. E. Leatham, G. A. Foljambe, C. Heseltine and J. A. Gibbs, most of whom made an odd appearance in English first-class matches in 1892 for M.C.C. or similar elevens.

The side left Tilbury on 14 October, except for J. H. J. Hornsby who was travelling overland to Naples and Lord Hawke who was indisposed. Arriving at Colombo, the team had two days to get rid of their sea-legs before the first fixture. J. H. J. Hornsby showed excellent form with bat and ball in this game (against Colombo) and the tourists were well placed when rain ended the match. In the second game Hornsby hit 41 out of an all out total of 81 to save the side from disaster, but the opposition made only 24 and 44 to give the Englishmen their first win. The final game in Ceylon was also won, after which the team sailed to Madras. Lord Hawke had now joined the side and the three fixtures in Madras were two against European sides, which were even draws, and a win against a native eleven. The two fixtures in Bangalore, the next stopping place, were both victories. Trask and Troup, the former county cricketers, were in the opposition team in Poona and their batting made the game very finely balanced when stumps were drawn. The three major games took place at Bombay, the first being against the Parsis. J. S. Robinson could not play for the tourists, but Hill bowled to excellent effect in the first innings: 5-2-7-5 and the Parsis were all out for 93. Lord Hawke's side could only manage 73 however and the Parsis won by a large margin due to M. E. Pavri's bowling backed up by good field. Lord Harris, the Governor of Bombay and former England cricketer, watched the match. The tourists had their revenge in the return fixture, winning by the narrow margin of 7 runs, with Hornsby taking 15 wickets. The tedious journey was made from Bombay to Calcutta where the local club was beaten by an innings, but the Bengal Presidency, after following on, obtained a well-deserved draw.

The second defeat of the tour was at the hands of the Behar Wanderers. A. E. Gibson, playing against the tourists, was mainly responsible for this, but Lord Hawke and J. S. Robinson could not play and A. E. Leatham had his first game.

In Allahabad the team met 'All India' – the title however was a little misleading and the Englishmen won by an innings. In the last match of the tour, the visitors hit 483, with seven of the side hitting over 40 and a victory by a margin of an innings and 303 runs was obtained at the expense of Peshawar. The tour finished with a visit to the Khyber Pass under an escort of the Bengal Cavalry. The party then split up, Lord Hawke and three others going off to Nepal for some shooting whilst the rest made their various ways home.

Everyone agreed it was a most successful tour both socially and from the cricketing viewpoint.

1894: Philadelphia invites an amateur team to North America

Under the auspices of the two major Philadelphian Cricket Clubs – Merion and Germantown – an amateur team under Lord Hawke made a short tour of North America in the autumn of 1894. The side, which was undoubtedly a first-class one by English standards, consisted of Lord Hawke (Yorks), L. C. V. Bathurst, G. J. Mordaunt and G. R. Bardswell (Oxford U), A. J. L. Hill (Hants), C. E. de Trafford (Leics), R. S. Lucas (Middx), G. W. Hillyard (Leics), J. S. Robinson and C. W. Wright (Notts), W. F. Whitwell (Durham) and K. McAlpine.

The team left Southampton on 8 September in the S.S. *New York* and arrived in New York on 14 September, the boat creating a new record for the crossing. The first match – on the Staten Island Ground – was ruined by rain, though A. J. L. Hill took the opportunity of hitting a faultless 99 before the weather ended the proceedings.

1894: Lord Hawke's Team to North America

1st Match: v New York (Staten Island C.C.)   Sept 17, 18.
Lord Hawke's XII 289 (A. J. L. Hill 99, L. C. V. Bathurst 53, Kelly 5-84) drew with New York XII – did not bat rain.

2nd Match: v Philadelphia (Merion C.C.)   Sept 21, 23.
Lord Hawke's XI 187 (Lord Hawke 78, H. P. Baily 7-65) & 235 (G. J. Mordaunt 62) beat Philadelphia 169 (F. H. Bohen 79) & 122 (L. C. V. Bathurst 8-44) by 131 runs.

3rd Match: v Philadelphia (Germantown C.C.)   Sept 28, 29.
Lord Hawke's XI 211 beat Philadelphia 107 & 64 (W. F. Whitwell 5-25) by an inns & 40 runs.

4th Match: v Gents of Canada (Toronto)   Oct 3, 4.
Lord Hawke's XI 147 drew with Canada 55 (L. C. V. Bathurst 5-22, A. J. L. Hill 5-33) & 125-5.

5th Match: v XV of Massachusetts (Lowell)   Oct 6, 8.
Lord Hawke's XII 176 (C. E. de Trafford 75, J. Chambers 9-77) beat Massachusetts 53 (G. W. Hillyard 9-15) & 104 by an inns & 19 runs.

The two principal fixtures of the tour were against the Gentlemen of Philadelphia. In the first of these, poor fielding by Philadelphia gave the tourists the match; Lord Hawke made a very lucky 78, which was the highest individual innings. In the second match, the home side batted half-heartedly and lost by an innings – the loss of their best player, G. S. Patterson, due to an injured finger did not help their cause.

The fourth game was at Toronto against Canada. The home side were outplayed and again the fielding was poor. In the final match the tourists had no difficulty in beating Fifteen of Massachusetts.

The team were back in Southampton on 14 October – the reason for the short duration of the tour being that the Oxford men had to be back for the new term.

1894-95: the growing importance of Test Matches in Australia

For the first time the authorities in Melbourne and Sydney joined forces to promote an English team to Australia. A. E. Stoddart, the Middlesex batsman, was invited to captain the team and arrangements to select a side were well in hand even before the English season of 1894 was half over. The full team consisted of A. C. MacLaren (Lancashire), F. G. J. Ford (Middlesex), H. Philipson (Middlesex), L. H. Gay (Somerset) and the professionals T. Richardson, W. Brockwell and W. H. Lockwood (Surrey), Albert Ward and J. Briggs (Lancashire), R. Peel and J. T. Brown (Yorkshire) and Walter A. Humphreys (Sussex). In that the side did not contain W. G. Grace, F. S. Jackson, R. Abel, and W. Gunn the batting was not representative of England, but it is believed that the only bowler who declined terms was William Attewell, so the attack was well chosen.

The side left Tilbury on board the *Ophir* on 21 September, except for H. Philipson, who took the overland route to Naples. A match was played at Colombo on 16 October and though the opening game of the Australian visit commenced at Gawler on 3 November, the first serious match was the eleven-a-side at Adelaide. South Australia were much improved compared to previous tours and the English team were happy to see virtually all their batsmen succeed and the first innings total reach 476. Some slovenly fielding allowed the home side to make 383. George Giffen then routed the tourists for 130 and followed this up with some good batting to inflict a decisive defeat on Stoddart's hopefuls. MacLaren hit 228 in the third match – against Victoria – providing his side with a win, and more good batting, this time by Stoddart, Brown and Brockwell, took the visitors to victory over New South Wales. The only other eleven-a-side match prior to the first Test was against Queensland, the first time that side had attempted to meet an English Team even-handed. It provided an easy win for the tourists. The wicket at Sydney looked plumb and when Australia, winning the toss, hit 586, including 200 by Gregory, then England made 325 and were forced to follow on, the game looked over. Some very stout batting in the second innings set Australia needing 177 to win. At the end of the fifth day, the home side were 113 for 2. Rain came and the character of the wicket changed out of all recognition, Peel bowling England to an unexpected win. Interest in the match was tremendous, the receipts of £2,945 indicated that financially the tour would be a success. A bad wicket was met in the second Test, but at the beginning. England were skittled out for 75 and Australia for 123. The ground recovered, Stoddart batted over 5 hours for 173 and Australia needed 428 in the last innings. They made an excellent start – 190 for 1 – but Brockwell broke through and England won by 94 runs. Australia had to win the third Test to save the rubber

1st Match: v XIII of Colombo (Colombo) (One Day) Oct 16.
English XI 76 (A. Raffel 9-48) & 88-8 beat Colombo 58 (J. Briggs 6-6) by 18 runs.

2nd Match: v XVIII of Gawler (Gawler) Nov 3, 5.
English XI 368 (A. Ward 118, J. T. Brown 56) drew with Gawler 153 (J. Briggs 10-94) & 22-5.

3rd Match: v South Australia (Adelaide) Nov 9, 10, 12, 13, 14.
English XI 476 (J. T. Brown 115, A. E. Stoddart 66, F. G. J. Ford 66, G. Giffen 5-174) & 130 (G. Giffen 6-49) lost to S. Australia 383 (J. Darling 117, G. Giffen 64, R. Peel 5-69) & 226-4 (J. Reedman 83, G. Giffen 58*) by 6 wkts.

4th Match: v Victoria (Melbourne) Nov 16, 17, 19, 20.
English XI 416 (A. C. MacLaren 228, A. E. Stoddart 77, A. E. Trott 6-103) & 288 (A. E. Stoddart 78, R. Peel 65) beat Victoria 306 (J. Harry 70, J. Briggs 5-97) & 253 (G. H. S. Trott 63, R. McLeod 62, R. Peel 5-73) by 145 runs.

5th Match: v New South Wales (Sydney) Nov 23, 24, 26, 27.
N.S.W. 293 (F. A. Iredale 133) & 180 (S. E. Gregory 87, R. Peel 5-64) lost to English XI 394 (J. T. Brown 117, A. E. Stoddart 79, W. Brockwell 81, W. P. Howell 5-44) & 81-2 by 8 wkts.

6th Match: v XXII of New England (Armidale) Nov 30, Dec 1.
English XI 67 & 197 (Cooper 5-52) drew with New England 147 (W. A. Humphreys 10-52) & 11-1.

7th Match: v XVIII of Toowoomba (Toowoomba) Dec 5, 6.
Toowoomba 113 (W. A. Humphreys 9-48) & 105 (J. Briggs 9-52) drew with English XI 216.

8th Match: v Queensland (Brisbane) Dec 7, 8, 10.
English XI 494 (A. E. Stoddart 149, A. Ward 107, A. C. MacLaren 74*, H. Philipson 59, A. Coningham 5-152) beat Queensland 121 (T. Richardson 8-52) & 99 by an inns & 274 runs.

9th Match: v Australia (Sydney) Dec 14, 15, 17, 18, 19, 20.
Australia 586 (S. E. Gregory 201, G. Giffen 161, F. A. Iredale 81, T. Richardson 5-181) & 166 (J. Darling 53, R. Peel 6-67) lost to England 325 (A. Ward 75, J. Briggs 57) & 437 (A. Ward 117, J. T. Brown 53) by 10 runs.

10th Match: v XVIII Sydney Juniors (Sydney) Dec 21, 23.
Juniors 442-9 dec (M. A. Noble 152*, V. T. Trumper 67) drew with English XI 151-6.

11th Match: v Australia (Melbourne) Dec 29, 31, Jan 1, 2, 3.
England 75 (C. T. B. Turner 5-32) & 475 (A. E. Stoddart 173, R. Peel 53, G. Giffen 6-155) beat Australia 123 (T. Richardson 5-57) & 333 (G. H. S. Trott 95, F. A. Iredale 68, W. Bruce 54) by 94 runs.

12th Match: v XVIII of Ballarat (Ballarat) Jan 5, 7.
English XI 187 (J. T. Brown 64, Pearce 7-95) & 149-7 drew with Ballarat 103 (W. A. Humphreys 10-51).

13th Match: v Australia (Adelaide) Jan 11, 12, 14, 15.
Australia 238 (G. Giffen 58, T. Richardson 5-75) & 411 (F. A. Iredale 140, W. Bruce 80, A. E. Trott 72*) beat England 124 (G. Giffen 5-76, S. T. Callaway 5-37) & 143 (A. E. Trott 8-43) by 382 runs.

14th Match: v XVIII of Broken Hill (Broken Hill) Jan 18, 19.
Broken Hill 68 (W. A. Humphreys 10-36) & 102 lost to English XI 178 (A. C. MacLaren 56, A. E. Stoddart 55, Ross 5-60) by an inns & 8 runs.

15th Match: v XVIII of Dandenong (Dandenong) Jan 25, 26.
English XI 193 (A. E. Stoddart 81) & 45-2 drew with Dandenong 224 (W. Wauchope 66).

16th Match: v Australia (Sydney) Feb 1, 2, 4.
Australia 284 (H. Graham 105, A. E. Trott 85*) beat England 65 & 72 (G. Giffen 5-26) by an inns & 147 runs.

17th Match: v XVIII of New England (Armidale) Feb 9, 11.
English XI 187 (A. E. Stoddart 88, Mereweather 5-48) & 112-7 drew with New England 111 (R. Peel 11-45).

18th Match: v Combined N.S.W. & Queensland (Brisbane) Feb 15, 16, 18, 19.
English XI 192 & 279 (A. C. MacLaren 107, T. R. McKibbin 5-98) beat Combined XI 107 (T. Richardson 5-42) & 86 by 278 runs.

19th Match: v XVIII of Newcastle (Newcastle) Feb 22, 23.
Newcastle 189 (Giles 58) & 87-5 drew with English XI 241 (W. Brockwell 73, A. Ward 63).

20th Match: v Australia (Melbourne) March 1, 2, 4, 5, 6.
Australia 414 (J. Darling 74, S. E. Gregory 70, G. Giffen 57, J. J. Lyons 55) & 267 (G. Giffen 51, J. Darling 50, T. Richardson 6-104) lost to England 385 (A. C. MacLaren 120, R. Peel 73, A. E. Stoddart 68) & 298-4 (J. T. Brown 140, A. Ward 93) by 6 wkts.

21st Match: v XVIII of N. Tasmania (Launceston) March 9, 11, 12.
N. Tasmania 178 (N. R. Westbrook 51, W. A. Humphreys 10-98) & 219-13 drew with English XI 291 (A. E. Stoddart 73*, W. Brockwell 69, E. A. Windsor 5-117).

22nd Match: v XV of S. Tasmania (Hobart) March 14, 15, 16.
English XI 91 (C. J. Eady 5-60) drew with S. Tasmania 189-13 (J. S. Howe 51*, F. G. J. Ford 9-56).

23rd Match: v Victoria (Melbourne) March 21, 22, 23, 25.
English XI 131 (H. Trott 8-63) & 270 (F. G. J. Ford 85) lost to Victoria 269 (C. L. McLeod 52) & 136-3 (W. Bruce 72*) by 7 wkts.

24th Match: v South Australia (Adelaide) March 28, 29, 30, April 1, 2.
S. Australia 397 (C. Hill 150*, W. F. Giffen 81, T. Richardson 5-148) & 255 (C. Hill 56) lost to English XI 609 (A. Ward 219, F. G. J. Ford 106, J. T. Brown 101, R. Peel 57, G. Giffen 5-309) & 45-0 by 10 wkts.

Batting Averages

	M	I	NO	R	HS	Avge	100	c/s
A. E. Stoddart (Middx)	10	18	1	870	173	51.17	2	7
A. C. MacLaren (Lancs)	11	20	3	804	228	47.29	3	4
J. T. Brown (Yorks)	12	21	2	825	140	43.42	4	10
A. Ward (Lancs)	12	22	0	916	219	41.63	3	6
L. H. Gay (Som)	6	11	5	186	39*	31.00	0	9/5
F. G. J. Ford (Middx)	11	20	1	508	106	26.73	1	6
W. Brockwell (Surrey)	12	22	1	504	81	24.00	0	11
R. Peel (Yorks)	12	21	1	421	73	21.05	0	10
J. Briggs (Lancs)	12	20	1	360	57	18.93	0	6
W. Lockwood (Surrey)	10	14	2	224	39	18.66	0	5
H. Phillipson (Middx)	9	15	1	187	59	13.35	0	15/3
W. A. Humphreys (Sussex)	4	7	3	42	18*	10.50	0	4
T. Richardson (Surrey)	11	19	5	114	20	8.14	0	1

Bowling Averages

	O	M	R	W	Avge	BB	5i
T. Richardson	592.2	148	1616	68	23.76	8-52	7
J. Briggs	376.1	71	1057	44	24.02	5-97	1
R. Peel	641.2	176	1441	57	25.28	6-67	3
A. E. Stoddart	3	0	31	1	31.00	1-31	0
W. Lockwood	284.4	69	791	18	43.94	4-54	0
W. Brockwell	120	38	336	7	48.00	3-33	0
W. A. Humphreys	112	12	314	6	52.33	2-62	0
F. G. J. Ford	44	8	159	1	159.00	1-47	0

and so determined were they, despite the two losses, that the betting started at evens. This time the rain did not affect the wicket, Australia batted with authority, but the English side fell apart—the highest scorer in either innings was Brown with 39— and Albert Trott, making his debut, took 8 for 43 in England's second innings. England lost by 382 runs. In mitigation, it should perhaps be noted that the game was played in intense heat which upset the tourists much more than the Australians. There were two up-country games prior to the fourth Test which was staged at Sydney. Lockwood was injured, but Stoddart still preferred him to Humphreys, the lob bowler, who had failed to find any form in the serious matches. The wicket at the start was described as 'sticky as glue' and England put Australia in. Six wickets went down for 51, then Graham played an excellent innings of 105— though he was dropped three times—and Trott hit 86 unbeaten. The catching and ground fielding of the English team was shocking, and this decided the game, since the wicket remained bad and England's batsmen were all at sea. The series was now level at two each.

The final Test at Melbourne was the vital game and public interest could hardly have been higher. Thankfully the pitch was perfect throughout, so neither side had an unfair advantage. Both first innings saw high scoring and only 29 runs separated the sides when Australia began their second knock. Splendid bowling by Richardson aided by good fielding dismissed Australia for 267 and the betting was even as England began the fifth day at 28 for 1— about 14,000 people came to watch the crucial last innings. A second England wicket—that of Stoddart—fell quickly, but Brown and Ward, particularly the former, batted in great style. Brown reached 140 in 145 minutes and when he was out the match and series were as good as won.

Four matches were played after the fifth Test, and the fitting climax came at Adelaide, where the team had been defeated at the tour's outset. This time they hit 609 and won by 10 wickets.

The tour made a profit of some £7,000 from total receipts of over £18,000. The tourists arrived back in Plymouth on 8 May.

The interest shown in England in the Test Match series was greater than for any other tour, and finally established the domination of the 'Tests' in the programme of English teams in Australia.

Of those who toured Australia, Humphreys was completely ineffective with his underarm lobs and Gay kept wicket so poorly in the early games that Philipson was soon established as the principal keeper. Lockwood for some reason failed both with bat and ball and his county colleague, Brockwell, did not live up to his reputation. The batting of MacLaren, Stoddart, Brown and Ward however was excellent, whilst Richardson, Peel and Briggs formed a good bowling trio.

1894-95: the first England tour to the West Indies

English cricketers broke fresh ground in the winter of 1894-95 when the first tour to the West Indies was undertaken. Lord Stamford, together with N. Lubbock, Dr R. B. Anderson and Lord Hawke, organised the arrangements and selected the team. It was hoped that Lord Hawke would tour as captain, but in his absence, R. S. Lucas the Middlesex amateur led the party, the remainder of whom were R. Leigh-Barratt (Norfolk), R. Berens, F. W. Bush (Ex-Surrey), H. R. Bromley-Davenport (Cambridge U), J. M. Dawson (Cambridge U), A. Priestley (M.C.C.), R. P. Sewell (Essex), H. S. Smith-Turberville (M.C.C.), W. H. Wakefield (Oxford U), J. H. Weatherby (M.C.C.), M. M. Barker (M.C.C.) and R. L. Marshall. The all-amateur side was by no stretch of the imagination first-class by English standards. The trip was mainly a social one and the cricket was not taken too seriously. The team left Southampton on 16 January in the *Medway* and arrived in Bridgetown on 28 January.

There was much interest in the opening match against Barbados and about 6,000 turned up to watch the play. A right-arm medium bowler, C. Goodman, bowled most effectively for the home side, who won the game by 5 wickets. The return against Barbados lasted five days and scoring was very high. The tourists were no less than 214 behind on first innings, but a century from Dawson and 91 from Bromley-Davenport meant that Barbados required 185 in their last innings, when they collapsed for 157, giving the visitors a well-earned victory. Travelling round the islands the team had easy wins over Antigua, St Kitts and St Lucia, but were beaten in a One-day fixture at Vincent on a pitch totally devoid of grass.

In Trinidad large crowds watched both matches, which were low scoring affairs. Trinidad won the second game, due to an innings of 77 by A. Warner, by 8 wickets. Two games were played against Demerara in Georgetown and again fair crowds watched the games, though the home side did not look as good as the Trinidad Eleven. The visit to Demerara was cut by three days when the boat was delayed and the team went on to Jamaica via Barbados. The passage from Barbados to Jamaica took four days.

1894-95 to West Indies

1st Match: v Barbados (Pickwick C.C.) Jan 29, 30.
R. S. Lucas' XI 48 (C. Goodman 6-14) & 168 (R. S. Lucas 64, R. P. Sewell 51, C. Goodman 8-71) lost to Barbados 100 (F. W. Bush 6-38) & 118-5 by 5 wkts.

2nd Match: v United Services (Pickwick C.C.) (13-a-side) Jan 31, Feb 1.
R. S. Lucas's XIII 247 (R. Leigh-Barratt 56, Hughes 6-84) drew with United Services XIII 124 (F. W. Bush 6-50) & 148-5 (Hughes 70).

3rd Match: v Barbados (Pickwick C.C.) Feb 5, 6, 7, 8, 9.
Barbados 517 (G. Learmond 86, W. Alleyne 82, G. Cox 68, H. Cole 67, C. Browne 74, A. Somers-Cocks 62*) & 157 (H. R. B-Davenport 5-42) lost to R. S. Lucas' XI 303 (F. W. Bush 105, C. Goodman 6-104) & 396 (J. M. Dawson 138, H. R. B-Davenport 91, R. Berens 50, A. Somers-Cocks 8-99) by 25 runs.

4th Match: v Antigua (St John's) Feb 14, 15, 16.
Antigua 107 (H. R. B-Davenport 5-43, F. W. Bush 5-44) & 99 lost to R. S. Lucas' XI 275 (J. M. Dawson 54, H. Smith-Turberville 50, E. Samuel 5-74) by an inns & 69 runs.

5th Match: v St Kitts-Nevis (Springfield) Feb 18, 19.
St Kitts 41 (H. R. Bromley-Davenport 6-3) & 93 lost to R. S. Lucas' XI 169 by an inns & 35 runs.

6th Match: v St Lucia (Castries) (12-a-side) Feb 22, 23.
St Lucia 94 (F. W. Bush 7-34) & 94 (H. R. B-Davenport 9-11) lost to R. S. Lucas' XII 148 (A. Burcher 5-43) & 41-1 by 10 wkts.

7th Match: v St Vincent (Kingston) (One Day) Feb 25.
R. S. Lucas' XII 63 (T. Osment 5-26) lost to St Vincent 138-9. (In another account this was a draw.)

8th Match: v Queen's Park C.C. (Queen's Park) Feb 28, Mar 1.
Queen's Park XII 71 (F. W. Bush 9-22) & 181 (H. R. B-Davenport 6-80) lost to R. S. Lucas' XII 164 (A. Tqitt 5-62) & 89-8 by 3 wkts.

9th Match: v All Trinidad (Queen's Park) March 4, 5.
Trinidad 180 (A. Warner 77) & 78-2 beat R. S. Lucas' XI 94 (J. Woods 6-39) & 162 (R. P. Sewell 66, J. H. Weatherby 56) by 8 wkts.

10th Match: v Demerara (Bourda) March 16, 18.
R. S. Lucas' XI 119 (E. F. Wright 5-34) & 1-0 beat Demerara 73 (H. R. B-Davenport 6-22) & 46 (H. R. B-Davenport 7-17) by 10 wkts.

11th Match: v Demerara (Bourda) March 19, 20.
Demerara 184 (E. F. Wright 54) drew with R. S. Lucas' XI 67-4.

12th Match: v All Jamaica (Kingston) (12-a-side) March 30, April 1.
Jamaica 72 (F. W. Bush 7-46) & 47 (F. W. Bush 7-15) lost to R. S. Lucas' XII 215 by an inns & 96 runs.

13th Match: v Jamaica Born (Kingston) April 2, 3.
R. S. Lucas' XI 285 (R. P. Sewell 77) beat Jamaica Born 58 (F. W. Bush 6-24) & 133 H. R. B-Davenport 5-45, F. W. Bush 5-67) by an inns & 94 runs.

14th Match: v Western Jamaica (Montego Bay) April 5, 6.
R. S. Lucas' XI 181 (F. W. Bush 63) beat W. Jamaica 42 (H. R. B-Davenport 6-13) & 77 (R. S. Lucas 7-40) by an inns & 62 runs.

15th Match: v North Jamaica (St Ann's Bay) April 8, 9.
N. Jamaica 61 (H. R. Bromley-Davenport 6-13) & 58 (H. R. B-Davenport 5-25) lost to R. S. Lucas' XI 81 & 39-3 by 7 wkts.

16th Match: v All Jamaica (Sabina Park) April 11, 12.
R. S. Lucas' XI 83 (J. W. Toone 6-29) & 114 (J. W. Toone 6-51) lost to Jamaica 171 (H. R. B-Davenport 7-68) & 28-2 by 8 wkts.

R. S. Lucas's team for one of the matches on the first tour to the West Indies in 1894-95. Back: Mr Barney (umpire), R. Leigh-Barratt, A. Priestley. Centre: R. Berens, R. L. Marshall, F. W. Bush, R. S. Lucas, R. P. Sewell, J. H. Weatherby, M. M. Barker. Front: J. M. Dawson, H. R. Bromley-Davenport.

In the game against All-Jamaica at Kingston, F. W. Bush came into his own, capturing 14 wickets as the tourists won by an innings. Altogether five games were played in Jamaica of which four were won and the final one lost by 8 wickets. The team sailed back to Barbados and left there on 25 April aboard R.M.S. *Atrato*, arriving back in England on 1 May.

H. R. Bromley-Davenport and F. W. Bush were the mainstay of the tourists' bowling and both took over 100 wickets. There was not much to choose between the principal batsmen, though F. W. Bush scored the most runs.

1895: university men tour North America

Frank Mitchell, the Hon Sec of Cambridge University Cricket Club in 1895, led an amateur side to North America in late summer, 1895. The team consisted of nine Cambridge men: F. Mitchell, N. F. Druce, C. D. Robinson, W. McG. Hemingway, R. A. Studd, C. E. M. Wilson, W. W. Lowe, W. Mortimer and H. H. Marriott; three from Oxford: F. A. Phillips, H. A. Arkwright and J. C. Hartley; and two current county amateurs: V. T. Hill (Somerset) and F. W. Milligan (Yorkshire).

The team, which was quite first-class, sailed from Southampton on 24 August in the *St Louis* and played their first match against New York on 3 and 4 September and their second game against Canada in Toronto. Neither of these opponents caused the young team any problems, but they found sterner stuff in Philadelphia. The first of the three matches played there was against Pennsyl-

vania University (Past and Present), where, after the tourists gained a good first innings lead, they collapsed against Patterson and Clark to lose the match by 100 runs. The final two games were against the formidable Philadelphian side. The first was won, due to some stout batting from Wilson, who carried out his bat for 20 after a two-hour stay. The Philadelphians more than had their revenge in the return match. The Englishmen were dismissed for 198 and the home side replied by adding 200 before the first wicket fell—Patterson and Bohlen being the batsmen. Philadelphia from that moment kept their grip on the match and some good bowling by J. B. King brought victory by an innings.

The tour was regarded as a great success and gave a tremendous boost to American cricket. The tourists arrived back in Southampton on 15 October.

Before the tour began, K. McAlpine was also in the process of arranging an English team to visit America, but as soon as it was realised that two separate sides were being raised, the Philadelphian authorities took steps to cancel Mr McAlpine's tentative plans before they got too far.

1895-96: a strong side do well in South Africa

For reasons both political and accidental, the tour to South Africa under the leadership of Lord Hawke and the management of George Lohmann suffered more than its fair share of disruptions. Lord Hawke, Sir T. C. O'Brien and H. T. Hewett, all of whom travelled separately from the main party, were delayed due to an accident to their steamer and missed the first match. The Jameson Raid caused the postponement of the third fixture and seriously affected the gates at some subsequent ones. H. T. Hewett was summoned back to England by important business after only three matches. S. M. J. Woods began the tour with a strained shoulder which prevented him bowling and then suffered a strained leg, whilst Tyler missed several games through ill-health and C. B. Fry strained his ankle late on, missing the last two fixtures. Added to this catalogue of disasters was a fearful explosion in Johannesburg, which caused the abandonment of one game. The miracle was that the tour itself was not a financial failure and in fact a small profit was reported.

The side consisted of Lord Hawke (Yorks) (capt), T. W. Hayward and G. A. Lohmann (Surrey), C. B. Fry and H. R. Butt (Sussex), S. M. J. Woods, H. T. Hewett and E. J. Tyler (Somerset), A. J. L. Hill and C. Heseltine (Hants), Sir T. C. O'Brien and H. R. Bromley-Davenport (Middx), C. W. Wright (Notts) and A. M. Miller (Wilts). With most members playing regular first-class cricket and two or three players worth their place in the England side, the team was the strongest to visit South Africa up to that date and despite the problems only two games were lost.

The main party landed in Cape Town on 22 December and the first game commenced at Newlands on Boxing Day before a crowd of some 6,000. Batting very poorly the tourists lost by 77 runs against Fifteen of Western Province. The Province then challenged the visitors to a One Day match on even terms and won again—by a single wicket. In the third match the visitors found their feet, hit up 405, with Fry 148 and Woods 89, and won by an innings. There was a nine-day break due to the political situation, but a series of seven odds matches were played with one defeat before the team met the South African Eleven at Port Elizabeth. Unfortunately four of the best home players—Innes, Rowe, A. B. Tancred and A. Richards—could not come, and the English players had the advantage of a turf wicket, most South Africans being used to matting. In fact the English batting was moderate enough, but the South Africans were humiliated by Lohmann, who took 15 for 45. In the second 'Test' at Johannesburg, Lohmann again routed the opposition and with the visitors

Lord Hawke's team to South Africa in 1895-96. Back: E. J. Tyler, Sir T. C. O'Brien, A. M. Miller, T. W. Hayward, G. A. Lohmann. Centre: C. B. Fry, J. D. Logan, Lord Hawke, C. W. Wright, C. Heseltine, A. J. L. Hill. Front: S. M. J. Woods, H. R. Bromley-Davenport, H. R. Butt.

hitting 482, victory was by an innings and 197 runs.

The following match against Fifteen at Griqualand West proved a much closer contest. A local bowler, T. B. Samuels, took 7 for 42 and dismissed the tourists for 95. Helped by some dropped catches Hill and Woods put the Eleven back in the match with a second innings of 231, but some stout batting in the final innings meant that the English side won by the fine margin of 13 runs. Rain caused a draw in the match against Western Province and little interest was shown by the public in either this or the third and final 'Test' which followed. South Africa managed to gather a reasonably representative eleven, but once more Lord Hawke's combination proved far too strong, and, apart from an innings of 30 by Frank Hearne, the South African batting collapsed twice for little over a hundred.

In the evening after this match, Lord Hawke announced that the cup which had been presented by the Union Steamship Company to be awarded to the team which gave the best display against the tourists should go to Kimberley.

The outstanding success of the tour was Lohmann, who took three times as many wickets as the next man. Of the batsmen, the three who stood out from the rest were C. B. Fry, A. J. L. Hill and T. W. Hayward.

The main body of the side arrived back in England in the second week of April.

1896-97: Lord Hawke's team to the West Indies

Lord Hawke had been invited to take the 1894-95 team out to the West Indies, but had had to withdraw. It was understood however that he would try to take a side out in 1896-97 and following an invitation from the Governor of British Guiana and from Trinidad, Barbados and Jamaica, Lord Hawke determined to organise a West Indian Tour. Unfortunately his telegram accepting the islands' invitations was never received and another English party under A. Priestley was being arranged, having accepted an invitation from Jamaica. Lord Hawke met Mr Priestley, but the two could not come to an amicable settlement and both decided to go independently to the West Indies. Fortunately both teams were composed of amateurs and therefore the financial considerations were not of paramount importance, thus the disastrous losses of the twin tours to Australia in 1887-88 were not repeated.

Lord Hawke's team, which sailed from Southampton on 13 January, consisted of Lord Hawke (Yorks) (capt), H. D. G. Leveson-Gower (Oxford U and Surrey), P. F. Warner (Oxford U and Middx), G. R. Bardswell (Oxford U), H. R. Bromley-Davenport (Middx), C. Heseltine (Hants), A. E. Leatham (Gloucs), W. H. Wakefield and R. Berens (Oxford U Authentics), J. M. Dawson and R. W. Wickham (Yorks Gents) and A. D. Whatman (Eton Ramblers), with Kirk the Trent Bridge dressing

room attendant. The team was just about first-class by English standards.

Barbados was reached on 25 January and the side were met by Priestley's Team, who had already played three matches. Without playing any fixtures in Barbados, Lord Hawke's Team sailed to

The team which toured the West Indies in 1896-97. Back row: an unnamed umpire, R. W. Wickham, G. R. Bardswell, A. E. Leatham, C. Heseltine, J. M. Dawson. Centre: W. H. Wakefield, A. D. Whatman. Front: P. F. Warner, H. D. G. Leveson-Gower, Lord Hawke (captain), H. R. Bromley-Davenport, R. Berens.

Trinidad and the first game was played there on 29-30 January. This proved to be a draw, but in the second game against All Trinidad the side met with defeat, the home bowlers Cumberbatch and Woods soon removing all except P. F. Warner with little difficulty. The same bowlers inflicted a second defeat on the tourists in the return fixture. There were three easy victories in Grenada and St Vincent before the next serious matches – against Barbados. In the first of these the tourists obtained a good first innings lead, but, following on, Barbados hit 319 and the match was drawn. The return game was won by P. F. Warner, who hit an undefeated 113 in the second innings, for a 4-wicket win.

The other important matches were against British Guiana at the end of the tour. Three games had been arranged at Georgetown. The tourists won the first two, after which they had a week's holiday from cricket when they sailed up the Demerera River. The final game was unfortunately rained off after the first day. About 5,000 spectators had watched each of the first two fixtures, but only 1,000 turned up for the first day of the final match.

The side sailed back to Barbados and there boarded the *Medway* for the voyage to England. P. F. Warner was the success of the tour and hit four centuries. Bromley-Davenport returned the best bowling figures, but missed some matches in the middle of the tour, due to a broken finger.

1896-97: A. Priestley also takes a team to the West Indies

The team invited to the West Indies by Jamaica and under the leadership of Arthur Priestley left Southampton on 30 December. The members of the side were A. E. Stoddart, C. A. Beldam and W. Williams (Middx), S. M. J. Woods, R. C. N. Palairet and H. T. Stanley (Somerset), R. P. Lewis (Oxford U), C. C. Stone (Leics), F. W. Bush, R. Leigh Barratt, J. Leigh, Dr G. Elliott and A. Priestley (capt).

Arriving in Barbados, the team commenced their first game with almost no practice and were soundly beaten by an innings, Clifford Goodman taking 12 wickets for the home side. The tourists won their second game by an innings, but the opposition

Mr Priestley's team in the West Indies in 1896-97, photographed in Barbados, before the Pavilion.

1896-97: A. Priestley's Team to the West Indies

Batting Averages

	M	I	NO	R	HS	Avge	100	c/s
A. E. Stoddart (Middx)	9	15	0	416	143	27.73	2	10
R. C. N. Palairet (Som)	8	14	1	336	65*	25.84	0	8
F. W. Bush	8	13	1	169	45*	14.08	0	6
S. M. J. Woods (Som)	9	14	0	193	28	13.78	0	8
G. Elliott	5	8	2	78	36*	13.00	0	3
C. A. Beldam (Middx)	7	11	2	115	24*	12.77	0	3
J. Leigh	8	13	0	150	26	11.53	0	4
R. Leigh-Barratt	9	15	0	171	38	11.40	0	7
H. T. Stanley (Som)	9	15	0	151	38	10.06	0	6
W. Williams (Middx)	9	15	3	98	40	8.16	0	6
C. C. Stone (Leics)	3	6	1	38	16*	7.60	0	0
R. P. Lewis (Oxford U)	8	12	7	16	7	3.20	0	7/6
A. Priestley	9	15	1	37	9	2.64	0	5

Bowling Averages

	O	M	R	W	Avge	BB	5i
A. E. Stoddart	303.4	128	520	53	9.81	7-67	5
W. Williams	202.3	55	464	43	10.79	7-38	3
S. M. J. Woods	230.2	75	501	35	14.31	6-60	2
H. T. Stanley	9	2	39	2	19.50	2-20	0
G. Elliott	12	3	29	1	29.00	1-13	0
F. W. Bush	102.4	19	245	8	30.62	2-15	0
R. Leigh-Barratt	113	41	225	6	37.50	3-40	0
C. A. Beldam	11	1	54	1	54.00	1-30	0

Also bowled: J. Leigh 3.2-0-14-0; C. C. Stone 4-2-8-0.
Played in non-first-class matches only: G. A. Maclean.

was the less formidable St Vincent XI. There were two other matches against Barbados, and each side won one.

Stoddart began his great run of success in the next game, hitting 107 v Antigua, 133 v St Kitts, 59 v United Services and 108 v Queens Park. The first three of these games were all innings victories, but the fourth was rained off.

The ninth fixture of the tour, at Port of Spain, was the most important game played up to that date in the West Indies, for it was the first time a representative West Indian Eleven had opposed an English touring team. The West Indian team was captained by Aucher Warner, brother of P. F. Warner, and contained players from Trinidad, British Guiana and Barbados. The match proved to be a fitting one for the occasion. The West Indies went in for the final innings requiring 141 to win, but six wickets fell for 41 and the Englishmen seemed sure of victory. Clarke and Constantine then added 75 and turned the tables on the visitors, the home side winning a great contest amid enormous excitement.

Following the defeat at the hands of the West Indies XI, the tourists played Trinidad twice and lost both encounters due to

poor batting. The final fixtures of the tour were all in Jamaica, where all five games were won. In these matches the dominant feature was the all-round performances of Stoddart, who hit two more hundreds and on three occasions took 10 wickets in a match.

The team, except for C. C. Stone who was laid low with typhoid in Antigua, arrived back in England on 14 April. The results achieved by the touring team were disappointing, with five out of nine major fixtures ending in defeat. Stoddart did wonders, being easily top of both batting and bowling tables and without him, things would have been serious indeed.

In the issue of *Cricket* for 8 April 1897 was published the correspondence between Mr Priestley and Lord Hawke, and it would appear from the details set out that Lord Hawke treated Mr Priestley in a rather high-handed manner.

1897: tourists 0 for 4 against Philadelphia

In the summer of 1897, the associated cricket clubs of Philadelphia invited P. F. Warner to take a side out to the United States. According to Warner he had precisely a fortnight to find a suitable team and put them on the boat. The side was composed of P. F. Warner (Middx) (capt), G. L. Jessop (Gloucs), H. D. G. Leveson-Gower and H. B. Chinnery (Surrey), H. H. Marriott and F. W. Stocks (Leics), J. N. Tonge (Kent), F. G. Bull (Essex), R. A. Bennett (Hants), J. R. Head (Middx), W. M. Hemingway (Gloucs) and A. D. Whatman (Eton Ramblers).

As nearly all the team appeared in county cricket in 1897 and several indeed achieved quite distinguished records, this team was probably stronger than the preceding combination under F. Mitchell.

The team left Southampton on the *St Louis* on 4 September and arrived in America on the evening of 10 September. The first game against New York at Staten Island was a convincing win, but the standard of the New York side was much improved on some of the earlier efforts against English touring parties. Two odds matches of not much importance followed and then the tourists took on Philadelphia. The feature of the match was the

P. F. Warner's team to the U.S.A. in 1897. Back: G. L. Jessop, F. W. Stocks, A. D. Whatman, R. A. Bennett, J. R. Head. Centre: W. McG. Hemingway, J. N. Tonge, P. F. Warner, H. D. G. Leveson-Gower, H. B. Chinnery. Front: F. G. Bull, H. H. Marriott.

bowling of J. B. King. On the first evening he reduced the tourists to 4 wickets down without a run on the board, though it must be admitted that the light was poor. The next morning he ended with 9 for 25. Despite a much better second innings the English team could not recover lost ground and were defeated by 4 wickets. Before the return match, the side visited Niagara Falls, but they did not play any matches in Canada. The home team were without J. A. Lester, their highest scorer in the first game, for the return and Warner's XI managed to cope with J. B. King, going on to win by 7 wickets.

The side sailed for Southampton on 6 October, though Jessop and Marriott stayed behind in New York.

1897-98: Clem Hill's great innings for Australia

Following the success which attended A. E. Stoddart and his team in Australia in 1894-95, the authorities in Sydney and Melbourne invited the Middlesex cricketer to take a second side out in 1897-98. He selected the following 12 to accompany him: A. C. MacLaren (Lancs), J. R. Mason (Kent), N. F. Druce (Surrey), K. S. Ranjitsinhji (Sussex) and the professionals T. Richardson and T. W. Hayward (Surrey), J. T. Hearne (Middx), J. Briggs (Lancs), J. H. Board (Gloucs), W. Storer (Derbys), E. Wainwright (Yorks) and G. H. Hirst (Yorks). E. G. Wynyard (Hants) was selected but had to withdraw, whilst F. S. Jackson and W. Attewell declined. Two criticisms were levelled at the side prior to its voyage, the first being that 13 players were not enough and the second that the bowling was weak. The critics however were a little vague as to the cricketers who might strengthen the bowling.

The team sailed from Tilbury on 17 September, except for Ranjitsinhji, who joined the side later. Although the team stopped at Port Said and Colombo no cricket was played at either. They arrived at their destination on 25 October, the first game commencing three days later against South Australia. Clem Hill played a brilliant innings of 200 for the home team to which Ranjitsinhji replied with a lucky 189 and the match was drawn. Owing to 'flu, Stoddart could not bat for the tourists. The second match against Victoria, a side which was not very strong, was won by 2 wickets. The team went straight to Sydney and playing on the easiest wicket so far they relied heavily on two centuries from MacLaren for victory by 8 wickets. A series of odds matches then came to precede the first Test. This initial game between England and Australia began with some controversy. The Sydney ground authorities decided on the eve of the match that play should not commence on the scheduled first day. This decision was taken without consulting either captain and Stoddart made a formal protest, though in fact the postponement (due to the state of the pitch) helped England, since Ranjitsinhji was unwell. Stoddart did not play owing to a family bereavement, but even in his absence England won by the large margin of nine wickets. A fortnight later Australia redressed the balance with an even bigger victory at Melbourne, though England had the worse of the wicket. Only two odds matches separated this defeat from the third Test. Here again the best English bowler–Richardson–failed and the remainder of the attack seemed to lose heart. Joe Darling batted superbly but when England went to the wicket their leading batsmen were soon dismissed. Following on, MacLaren and Ranji looked as if they might save the game, but when Ranji went the batting collapsed to present Australia with

A. E. Stoddart's team in Australia playing the first Test match at Sydney, which the tourists won by 9 wickets.

a second innings victory. This time England could not blame the wicket.

For England the fourth Test was crucial since the rubber depended upon it. The visitors were without Hirst who had been injured at Adelaide and Wainwright played. About 18,000 people watched the start of the game and saw Australia tumble to six for 58. Clem Hill, the 20-year-old Australian, then played what has

been described as one of the greatest innings ever witnessed. Hill relished the fast bowling of Richardson and found little difficulty with the remainder of the attack. In contrast the English batting was wretched and once more the tourists followed on. Stouter resistence was displayed in the second innings – even Storer with a fractured finger played his part – and Australia needed 115 to win in their second innings. They had little difficulty in reaching their goal.

The English side suffered a further defeat at the hands of New South Wales, before meeting Australia in the final Test, at Sydney. For this game Stoddart stood down – he had totally failed with the bat in eleven-a-side matches and indeed had not even hit a fifty. MacLaren led England, as he had in the other Tests when Stoddart was absent. England batted well in their first innings and Richardson, bowling faster than any previous time on the tour, took 8 wickets in the Australian first innings to give his side a substantial lead. The match was then thrown away by careless batting which Trumble exploited and in the final innings Australia required 275 to win. Three catches were dropped and the home side won, taking the rubber by 4 matches to 1.

The two remaining games of the tour were the returns against Victoria and South Australia. The team left Adelaide on 24 March and the professionals arrived back in England by the overland route through France on 23 April. The amateurs chose to continue by sea, arriving a few days later, except for Ranji who left the team at Colombo.

The English public were most disappointed by the lack of success of the team and only MacLaren and Ranjitsinhji among the batsmen really came up to the mark. Of the bowlers, Hearne was the steadiest and Richardson came off a few times, but the rest found the Australian wickets too good for them.

For Australia the two left-handers Darling and Hill were the successes of the Test series; the former averaged 67.12 and the latter 56.50, both having eight completed innings – needless to say both were well ahead of the best English batsman. Noble was decidedly the most outstanding home bowler, his flighting of the ball being too subtle for the touring batsmen; Jones and Tumble were also most effective. In comparison it was surprising how poorly several of the visiting bowlers performed in the Tests – the great Yorkshireman Hirst took only two wickets for 304 runs.

The barracking of the Australian crowds came in for some criticism from the England captain, but apart from this the social aspect of the tour was unclouded.

The problem of 'throwing', which at one time seemed to be absent from Australian cricket, raised its head, and James Phillips, who umpired for the tourists, no-balled E. Jones twice.

1898: Pelham Warner returns to Canada and the United States

The Associated Crickets Clubs of Philadelphia issued a second invitation to P. F. Warner in 1898 to bring out a team of English Amateurs. This second side was in fact stronger than the first and the members were P. F. Warner (Middx) (capt), E. H. Bray (Middx), C. J. Burnup (Kent), C. O. H. Sewell (Gloucs), R. S. A. Warner, G. E. Winter (Cambridge U), F. Mitchell (Yorks), V. T. Hill (Som), E. C. Lee (Hants), B. J. T. Bosanquet (Middx), R. Berens (Oxford Authentics), J. L. Ainsworth (Liverpool) and E. F. Penn (Eton Ramblers). The team set sail from Liverpool on 27 August. Penn missed the boat and sailed in another which was fortunate for him, since the boat carrying the team broke down three times, the third time being in mid-Atlantic in a considerable gale, which resulted in numerous accidents to passengers and crew.

The first match was on a terrible wicket in Montreal and shooters were the order of the day. W. R. Gilbert and F. W. Terry were two old county cricketers among the opposing Fourteen, but neither achieved much. Before the second match began, two of the tourists, Penn and Lee, went down with scarlet fever. Ontario however were rather foolish to attempt an eleven-a-side match and the English team had an easy win.

Travelling to Philadelphia the side played the first game against the Philadelphians. The match was a very low scoring affair, none of the three completed innings reaching 100 and the visitors, due to Ainsworth's bowling, won by 8 wickets.

New York were quickly disposed of in the next match and after two odds matches, the team played the return against Philadelphia. About 9,000 turned out on the first day of this match, which was by far the best of the tour. The batsmen once more had a poor time, Ainsworth and the Philadelphian, J. B. King, taking the honours with their bowling.

The final fixture was in Chicago. The locals were no match for the visitors on even terms and when a thunderstorm ended the match, Chicago were very near defeat.

After a pretty dreadful series of train journeys between Chicago and New York, the team boarded the liner *Majestic* which docked in Liverpool on 19 October. Penn and Lee recovered from their illness and returned to England in mid-November.

1898: P. F. Warner's Team to North America

1st Match: v XIV of Eastern Canada (Montreal) Sept 8, 9.
P. F. Warner's XII 130 (C. B. Godwin 6-33) & 105 beat E. Canada 82 (B. J. T. Bosanquet 5-9) & 65 by 88 runs.

2nd Match: v Ontario (Toronto) Sept 12, 13, 14.
P. F. Warner's XI 437 (F. Mitchell 128, C. O. H. Sewell 122) beat Ontario 133 (J. L. Ainsworth 7-39) & 164 by an inns & 140 runs.

3rd Match: v Philadelphia (Wissahickon) Sept 16, 17.
Philadelphia 94 (J. L. Ainsworth 6-54) & 59 (J. L. Ainsworth 5-14) lost to P. F. Warner's XI 84 & 70-2 by 8 wkts.

4th Match: v New York (Livingston) Sept 21, 22.
New York 49 (B. J. T. Bosanquet 5-22, J. L. Ainsworth 5-25) & 123 lost to P. F. Warner's XI 419 (V. T. Hill 84, E. H. Bray 83, F. Mitchell 66, C. J. Burnup 61) by an inns & 247 runs.

5th Match: v XVIII Colts of Philadelphia (Haverford) Sept 23, 24, 26.
Colts 77 (J. L. Ainsworth 8-31) & 159 (B. J. T. Bosanquet 8-43) drew with P. F. Warner's XI 133 (D. H. Adams 6-27) & 30-1.

6th Match: v XV of Baltimore (Catonsville) Sept 28, 29.
Baltimore 126 (J. L. Ainsworth 7-35) & 30 (B. J. T. Bosanquet 8-13) lost to P. F. Warner's XI 150 & 8-1 by 9 wkts.

7th Match: v Philadelphia (Manheim) Sept 30, Oct 1, 3.
Philadelphia 143 (J. L. Ainsworth 7-61) & 127 (A. M. Wood 53, J. L. Ainsworth 6-55) lost to P. F. Warner's XI 133 (J. B. King 6-32) & 161-6 by 4 wkts.

8th Match: v Chicago (Chicago) (12 a-side) Oct 8, 10.
Chicago 74 & 83-7 (V. T. Hill 5-21) drew with P. F. Warner's XII 298 (B. J. T. Bosanquet 94, V. T. Hill 60).

1898-99: a train crash and a plague of locusts in South Africa

The fourth Tour to South Africa and the second under Lord Hawke was promoted by the Hon J. D. Logan of Matjesfontein. The side was composed of Lord Hawke (Yorks) (capt), A. G. Archer (Shropshire), H. R. Bromley-Davenport (Middx), F. Mitchell (Yorks), F. W. Milligan (Yorks), P. F. Warner (Middx), C. E. M. Wilson (Yorks) and the professionals J. H. Board (Gloucs), W. R. Cuttell (Lancs), S. Haigh (Yorks), A. E. Trott (Middx), J. T. Tyldesley (Lancs). The old Surrey cricketer G. A. Lohmann, who now resided in South Africa, acted as manager, A. A. White came as umpire and H. Kirk, the Trent Bridge dressing room attendant, was general dogsbody.

The team was by no means representative of England, but merely of good county standard. The inclusion of Haigh and Trott however meant that the bowling was in excellent hands.

Sailing from Southampton in the *Scot* on 3 December, the only break in the journey was for coaling at Madeira, and after a good voyage the team landed at Cape Town on 20 December. Following a knock-up match on 22 December, the first serious game was against Thirteen of Western Province, and a crowd of some 8,000 attended on the second day (Boxing Day). The batsmen found it difficult to get used to the matting wicket and only some good bowling by Haigh won the match. The second game was supposed to be against Western Province, with the home team including Brown, Tate, Guttridge and Barnes (four English coaches in South Africa) but there were objections to this arrangement and it was dropped. It was not until the fifth match of the tour that the team were met on even terms. The game should have been against South Africa, but some unpleasantness between Transvaal and Port Elizabeth prevented this, and the opponents were the Cape Colony XI, except that Bisset and Rowe were absent. The game was finely balanced after the first innings, but Mitchell then hit 81 and again Trott and Haigh won the match. A plague of locusts visited the ground on the last afternoon. At Grahamstown, White no-balled a local – Madden – for throwing, but the tourists were not unduly troubled, winning by 10 wickets.

In Johannesburg the second eleven-a-side game was staged, but the opponents, Transvaal, were completely outclassed and the tourists' score of 539 for 6 declared, containing hundreds by Mitchell, Tyldesley and Trott, broke several records. In Pretoria, the locals included Braund, the Surrey professional, who hit the highest score and returned the best bowling figures. Whilst in Pretoria, two of the team visited President Kruger and unsuccessfully tried to persuade him to come to the match.

The first game against South Africa took place at Johannesburg and large crowds turned out to see the match. At the close of play on the second day, the tourists having been 106 behind on first innings were 173 for 7 and South Africa seemed certain to win. Warner however carried out his bat for 132, then Trott, Haigh and Cuttell bowled out the home side for 99. On South Africa's part however the result was a vast improvement compared to the drubbing in the previous 'Tests'.

The team broke fresh ground by travelling to Bulawayo, where two matches were played. The ground there was laid out in three weeks after the rebellion had been quelled, and looked likely to develop into one of the best in Southern Africa. The wicket was matting and the outfield was bare of grass. Best feature of the first game was the left hand bowling of J. Bissett, who took 9 for 59. Lord Hawke could not play in the second match – against Fifteen of Rhodesia – but the home team's batting was very poor, except for Hallward, the old Lancing captain, who made 52.

The proposed match at Mafeking was abandoned as the local club could not raise a team and the tourists went on to Kimberley.

Lord Hawke's team to South Africa in 1898-99. Back: F. Hearne (umpire), A. G. Archer, W. R. Cuttell, F. Mitchell, C. E. M. Wilson, A. A. White (umpire). Centre: H. R. Bromley-Davenport, F. W. Milligan, S. Haigh, Lord Hawke, J. H. Board, A. E. Trott. Front: J. T. Tyldesley, P. F. Warner.

1898-99: Lord Hawke's Team to South Africa

1st Match: v XIII of Western Province (Cape Town) Dec 24, 26, 27.
English XI 141 (J. Middleton 7-54) & 140 (G. A. Rowe 5-54) beat W. Province 149 (A. E. Trott 7-68) & 107 by 25 runs.

2nd Match: v XIII of Western Province (Cape Town) Jan 2, 3.
English XI 186 (J. Middleton 5-70, G. A. Rowe 5-74) & 149 (G. A. Rowe 6-55) beat W. Province 104 (A. E. Trott 7-52) & 125 by 106 runs.

3rd Match: v XXII of Midlands (Graaf Reinet) Jan 6, 7.
English XI 191 (P. Gardiner 5-71, W. Greybe 5-118) & 63-2 beat Midlands 99 (A. E. Trott 12-38) & 154 by 8 wkts.

4th Match: v XV of Port Elizabeth (Port Elizabeth) Jan 10, 11, 12.
English XI 166 (O'Halloran 5-68) & 187 (A. E. Trott 84, O'Halloran 5-72) beat Port Elizabeth 173 & 80 (A. E. Trott 10-45) by 100 runs.

5th Match: v Cape Colony (Port Elizabeth) Jan 14, 16, 17.
English XI 134 (W. R. Cuttell 53, R. Graham 5-54) & 228 (F. Mitchell 81) beat Cape Colony 112 & 149 by 101 runs.

6th Match: v XV of Eastern Province (Grahamstown) Jan 20, 21.
English XI 210 (A. E. Trott 69, J. Martin 6-60) & 11-0 beat E. Province 88 (A. E. Trott 9-19) & 131 (F. W. Milligan 8-17) by 10 wkts.

7th Match: v XV of Border (Kingwilliamstown) Jan 25, 26.
Border 84 (A. E. Trott 8-41) & 147 (N. H. Giddy 66) lost to English XI 294 (S. Haigh 74) by an inns & 63 runs.

8th Match: v XV of Johannesburg (Johannesburg) Feb 1, 2, 3.
Johannesburg 136 (W. R. Solomon 64, F. W. Milligan 10-64) & 221-8 (J. H. Sinclair 56) drew with English XI 309 (J. H. Sinclair 5-81).

9th Match: v Transvaal (Johannesburg) Feb 4, 6, 7.
Transvaal 211 (A. E. Trott 7-74) lost to English XI 537-6 dec (F. Mitchell 162, J. T. Tyldesley 114, A. E. Trott 101*) by an inns & 203 runs.

10th Match: v XV of Transvaal (Pretoria) Feb 9, 10, 11.
English XI 230 (P. F. Warner 92, W. R. Cuttell 62, L. C. Braund 5-72) & 64-1 beat Transvaal 207 & 85 (A. E. Trott 10-29) by 9 wkts.

11th Match: v South Africa (Johannesburg) **Feb 14, 15, 16.**
England 145 & 237 (P. F. Warner 132*, J. Middleton 5-51) beat South Africa 251 (J. H. Sinclair 86) & 99 (A. E. Trott 5-49) by 32 runs.

12th Match: v XV of Griqualand West (Kimberley) Feb 20, 21.
Griqualand West 236 (W. A. Shalders 76) & 106 lost to English XI 367 (F. Mitchell 82, P. F. Warner 75, W. R. Cuttell 65, C. E. M. Wilson 51, J. Backmann 5-40) by an inns & 25 runs.

13th Match: v XVIII of Bulawayo (Bulawayo) March 1, 2, 3.
Bulawayo 123 & 180 (S. Haigh 11-44) lost to English XII 172 (S. Haigh 52, J. T. Tyldesley 51, J. Bissett 9-59) & 135-1 (P. F. Warner 54*) by 10 wkts.

14th Match: v XV of Rhodesia (Bulawayo) March 4, 6, 7.
English XI 275 (P. F. Warner 80, J. T. Tyldesley 71, H. M. Taberer 5-62) beat Rhodesia 121 (H. Hallward 52, S. Haigh 9-36) & 89 by an inns & 65 runs.

15th Match: v XV of Griqualand West (Kimberley) March 11, 12.
English XI 126 & 16-1 drew with Griqualand West 200 (A. W. Powell 72, S. Haigh 9-44).

16th Match: v Cape Colony (Cape Town) March 25, 27, 28.
Cape Colony 110 (S. Haigh 8-34) & 138 (A. E. Trott 6-73) lost to English XI 277 (W. R. Cuttell 98, C. E. M. Wilson 69, R. Graham 6-97) by an inns & 29 runs.

17th Match: v South Africa (Cape Town) **April 1, 3, 4.**
England 92 (J. H. Sinclair 6-26) & 330 (J. T. Tyldesley 112) beat South Africa 177 (J. H. Sinclair 106) & 35 (S. Haigh 6-11).

Batting first, 9 wickets went down for 54, then Milligan and Archer added 72 for the last wicket. The local Fifteen, thanks to a brilliant innings by Powell, gained a lead on first innings, but a heavy thunderstorm abruptly ended the game as the Englishmen stood at 16 for 1 in their second innings. Haigh performed the hat-trick in this game. On the journey from Kimberley the train in which the team were travelling was involved in a collision. The train slid backwards when negotiating an incline and the brakes failed, allowing it to crash into the train behind. Milligan cut his nose and had his eye blacked, whilst Trott's thumb was put out of joint. Many of the windows were smashed, but the journey resumed and the next stop–Matjesfontein–was reached with no further mishap. The two remaining eleven-a-side fixtures were against Cape Colony (an easy win) and the return against South Africa at Newlands. For some inexplicable reason the South African side included two wicket-keepers in Halliwell and Prince and this strange selection was much criticised. There was a record gate for Newlands on the second day (Easter Monday) and excellent all-round cricket by Sinclair gave the home eleven a lead on first innings of 85. The tourists made 330 in their second attempt with Tyldesley hitting 112, but South Africa collapsed when going for the runs and were all out in 45 minutes, Haigh and Trott making the ball fizz off the matting.

1898-99: Lord Hawke's Team to South Africa

Batting Averages

	M	I	NO	R	HS	Avge	100	c/s
F. Mitchell (Yorks)	5	8	0	372	162	46.50	1	4
J. T. Tyldesley (Lancs)	5	8	0	299	114	37.37	2	4
W. R. Cuttell (Lancs)	5	8	0	271	98	33.87	0	4
A. G. Archer	1	2	1	31	24*	31.00	0	0
P. F. Warner (Middx)	5	8	1	214	132*	30.57	1	1
C. E. M. Wilson (Yorks)	5	8	1	178	69	25.42	0	2
A. E. Trott (Middx)	5	8	1	153	101*	21.85	1	6
F. W. Milligan (Yorks)	5	8	0	120	38	15.00	0	3
J. H. Board (Gloucs)	5	7	2	70	29	14.00	0	6/2
Lord Hawke (Yorks)	5	8	2	69	31*	11.50	0	0
S. Haigh (Yorks)	5	7	1	55	25	9.16	0	4
H. R. Bromley-Davenport (Middx)	4	5	0	7	4	1.40	0	1

Bowling Averages

	O	M	R	W	Avge	BB	5i
W. R. Cuttell	108.3	47	174	16	10.87	4-18	0
S. Haigh	199.3	77	419	33	12.69	8-34	2
A. E. Trott	254.1	84	546	42	13.00	7-74	3
F. W. Milligan	60	23	134	4	33.50	2-13	0

Also bowled: H. R. Bromley-Davenport 8-3-17-0; C. E. M. Wilson 5-0-15-0.
Played in non-first-class matches only: Hon E. Fiennes.

Milligan stayed behind when the Englishmen boarded the *Norman* at Cape Town – he was soon embroiled in the South African war. Southampton was reached on 21 April.

The tour was a great success and there was much surprise at the improvement in South African cricket since the initial tour, only ten years before.

1899: K. S. Ranjitsinhji's team in the United States and Canada

The team which sailed from Liverpool bound for New York on 16 September 1899 consisted of K. S. Ranjitsinhji (Sussex) (capt), G. Brann (Sussex), G. L. Jessop and C. L. Townsend (Gloucs), C. Robson and C. B. Llewellyn (Hants), S. M. J. Woods (Somerset), A. C. MacLaren (Lancs), A. E. Stoddart (Middx), B. J. T. Bosanquet (Oxford U), W. P. Robertson (Cambridge U) and A. Priestley (M.C.C.). In addition V. Barton, the Hampshire professional, travelled as baggage man.

It was obvious from the outset that the team was much too strong, despite being composed purely of amateurs, and it was rather foolish of the organiser to take a sledgehammer to a walnut.

Arriving on 20 September, the team went straight to Philadelphia to play a Colts Twenty-two, but rain and cold marred the drawn match. The first match, which was described as a 'Test Match' in some quarters, against Philadelphia, was most one sided. MacLaren hit 149 in 200 minutes and Jessop 64 in 35 minutes. Apart from Wood and Graves the home batsmen could do little.

In the New York game, the first pair of home batsmen added 109 before a wicket fell, but the tourists had it all their own way for the remainder of the game. The return against Philadelphia was very much a repeat of the first match, except that the English fielding was terrible.

As might be expected, Canada could do no better than Philadelphia in the last match of the tour and the team recorded another innings victory. The tour ended on 13 October and it is believed that the Philadelphian clubs were out of pocket on the venture.

1899: K. S. Ranjitsinhji's Team to North America

1st Match: v XXII Colts of Philadelphia (Elmwood)   Sept 25, 26, 27.
Colts 205 (C. B. Llewellyn 7-55) & 95-9 drew with K. S. Ranjitsinhji's XII 185 (B. J. T. Bosanquet 56, W. P. O'Neill 6-70).

2nd Match: v Philadelphia (Haverford)   Sept 29, 30, Oct 2.
Philadelphia 156 (G. L. Jessop 6-52) & 106 lost to K. S. Ranjitsinhji's XI 435 (A. C. MacLaren 149, G. L. Jessop 64, K. S. Ranjitsinhji 57, A. E. Stoddart 56) by an inns & 173 runs.

3rd Match: v XIV of New York (Staten Island)   Oct 4, 5.
New York 149 (M. R. Cobb 77, G. L. Jessop 9-17) & 132-11 drew with K. S. Ranjitsinhji's XI 330-8 dec (G. Brann 137*, G. L. Jessop 51, M. R. Cobb 5-93).

4th Match: v Philadelphia (Germantown C.C.)   Oct 7, 9, 10.
K. S. Ranjitsinhji's XI 363 (A. E. Stoddart 74, K. S. Ranjitsinhji 68, A. C. MacLaren 52, P. H. Clark 5-77) beat Philadelphia 85 & 147 by an inns & 131 runs.

5th Match: v Canada (Toronto)   Oct 12, 13.
Canada 87 (C. L. Townsend 6-33) & 174 lost to K. S. Ranjitsinhji's XI 267-7 dec (G. L. Jessop 66, A. E. Stoddart 63*) by an inns & 6 runs.

1901: Philadelphia still a force in cricket

The team which accompanied B. J. T. Bosanquet to North America in 1901 was a much more realistic one than had been Ranjitsinhji's side of 1899. The 1901 team was still a first-class one in English terms and the equal of one of the lesser County Championship sides. Arriving in New York from Liverpool on 16 September, the full complement was B. J. T. Bosanquet (Middx) (capt), F. Mitchell (Yorks), E. M. Dowson (Surrey), V. F. S. Crawford (Surrey), E. R. Wilson (Cambridge U), R. E. More (Middx), A. M. Hollins (Oxford U), P. R. Johnson (Cambridge U), R. O. Schwarz (Middx), W. E. Harrison, I. U. Parkin and A. Priestley.

In the first match against the Colts, the tourists were tied up by W. G. Graham, a slow left-armer, and lost by 186 runs – all nineteen of the opposition fielded which made matters more difficult. In the first of the two Philadelphian matches, J. A. Lester batted finely, but no one supported him and the Englishmen won a good match. Breaking new ground the team then went to Bayonne and needed 55 to win in an hour on the last afternoon, and they scored the runs in 45 minutes with 7 wickets in hand. Philadelphia played better than for some years in the return match. Brown hit the first hundred against a touring side since 1892 and the Philadelphians achieved a commanding first innings lead. Clark took the last five wickets in the English second innings in 7 balls and the tourists lost by 229 runs. The final game was against Canada. The tourists had little difficulty in winning, despite missing Mitchell, who had to return home, and More who was ill.

The tour was a success and gave a boost to North American cricket.

1901: B. J. T. Bosanquet's Team to North America

1st Match: v XVIII Colts & Captain (Wissahickon)   Sept 20, 21, 23.
Colts 173 & 242 (R. E. More 7-88) beat B. J. T. Bosanquet's XII 131 (W. G. Graham 6-37) & 98 (W. G. Graham 6-26) by 186 runs.

2nd Match: v Philadelphia (Philadelphia)   Sept 27, 28, 30.
B. J. T. Bosanquet's XI 198 (J. B. King 8-78) & 143 (J. B. King 6-57) beat Philadelphia 103 (R. E. More 6-28) & 177 (J. A. Lester 73*, R. E. More 6-73) by 61 runs.

3rd Match: v Knickerbocker A.C. (Bayonne, N.J.)   Oct 2, 3.
Knickerbocker XII 143 (R. E. More 7-44) & 79 (B. J. T. Bosanquet 7-22) lost to B. J. T. Bosanquet's XII 168 (F. F. Kelly 8-56) & 58-4 by 7 wkts.

4th Match: v Philadelphia (Manheim)   Oct 4, 5, 7.
Philadelphia 312 (R. D. Brown 103, F. H. Bohlen 60, C. C. Morris 55, E. R. Wilson 5-100) & 186 (J. A. Lester 69, R. E. More 6-62) beat B. J. T. Bosanquet's XI 166 (J. B. King 6-74) & 103 (P. H. Clark 7-22) by 229 runs.

5th Match: v Canada (Toronto)   Oct 11, 12.
Canada 97 (E. M. Dowson 7-51) & 114 lost to B. J. T. Bosanquet's XI 218 (B. J. T. Bosanquet 97) by an inns & 7 runs.

1901-02: a poor side do badly in Australia

The 1901-02 visit to Australia was possibly as ill-advised as the twin tours of 1887-88. The M.C.C. agreed in the spring of 1901 to make the necessary arrangements in England and select the team for the tour, but on 13 May, the Committee at Lord's announced that it was impossible to recruit a representative English team and withdrew from the venture. A. C. MacLaren, the Lancashire captain, was then persuaded to attempt the task and eventually gathered the following cricketers to his banner: G. L. Jessop (Gloucs), A. O. Jones (Notts), H. G. Garnett (Lancs), C. P. McGahey (Essex), C. Robson (Hants), T. W. Hayward (Surrey), J. T. Tyldesley (Lancs), William Quaife (Warwicks), A. F. A. Lilley (Warwicks), L. C. Braund (Somerset), C. Blythe (Kent), S. F. Barnes (Lancs) and J. R. Gunn (Notts). The Yorkshire Committee refused to allow W. Rhodes and G. H. Hirst – the two outstanding bowlers of the 1901 season – to go. It was then reported that the 1902 Australians would refuse to play Yorkshire, but this proved to be a false rumour. Several well-known amateurs, including the top three in the 1901 averages, Fry, Ranjitsinhji and Palairet, were also absent. The surprise selection of the side was S. F. Barnes, who was totally unknown to the cricket public at large. Most of Barnes' cricket had been in the Lancashire League, for Rishton and latterly for Burnley, though he had played the odd games for Warwickshire and Lancashire.

The team left Tilbury on board the *Omrah* on 27 September, except for Jessop, who took the overland route to Marseilles. The first match of the tour began in Adelaide five days after landing. Clem Hill hit 107 and 80 and George Giffen picked up 13 wickets to provide an easy win for South Australia. Going on to Melbourne, Barnes was too much for the Victorian team and gave the tourists their first victory in a low scoring match. Runs came much more freely at Sydney in the third match. MacLaren hit a century but when the visitors appeared to have the match in hand the late order N.S.W. batsmen completely altered matters and a finely fought game was lost by 53 runs. There were four odds matches before the first Test at Sydney. MacLaren won the toss and batted. He and Hayward put on 154, there was a middle-order collapse, but all the later men played well and the total realised was 464. The expected large reply from Australia never materialised. Barnes, Braund and Blythe ran through the home batting twice and England attained victory by an innings. Another four odds matches came and went before the second Test at Melbourne. MacLaren won the toss and put Australia in on a sticky wicket. Barnes and Blythe had them all out for 112, but England gave a dreadful display against Noble and Trumble to fall for 61. Australia then slid to 48 for 5 by the close of play. On the next day Hill hit a magnificent 99 and then Duff scored a century, which left England needing 405 to win. Only Tyldesley of the English batsmen looked at home and Australia went on to win by 229 runs. The batsmen partially redeemed themselves in the next two odds matches with Braund, McGahey, Hayward and MacLaren scoring centuries.

Injuries to Barnes and Blythe during the match were the reasons for Australia winning the third Test at Adelaide. The home side required 315 for victory when starting the fourth innings of the game, but with Barnes in bed with an injured knee and Blythe useless through an injured finger, the England attack was too weak to control Clem Hill or indeed any of his colleagues.

The tourists were without Barnes and Blythe for the return with New South Wales, but some extraordinary batting by MacLaren, Hayward and Tyldesley produced a total of 769 and with New South Wales getting the worse of the wicket in their second innings, the English team had a massive win. Barnes could still not play in the fourth Test and though MacLaren won the toss for the fourth time and went on to hit a brilliant 92, the batting in the England second innings was appalling and Australia had no difficulty in winning the rubber. Victoria were beaten in the return game and in the final Test it appeared as if England

---

1901-02: A. C. MacLaren's Team to Australia

1st Match: v South Australia (Adelaide)   Nov 9, 11, 12, 13.
S. Australia 230 (C. Hill 107) & 207 (C. Hill 80, C. Blythe 5-45) beat English XI 118 (G. Giffen 7-46) & 86 (G. Giffen 6-47) by 233 runs.

2nd Match: v Victoria (Melbourne)   Nov 15, 16, 17, 18.
English XI 166 (C. E. McLeod 57) & 174 (C. P. McGahey 57, C. E. McLeod 5-57) beat Victoria 133 (S. F. Barnes 5-61) & 89 (S. F. Barnes 7-38) by 118 runs.

3rd Match: v New South Wales (Sydney)   Nov 22, 23, 25, 26, 27.
N.S.W. 288 (V. T. Trumper 67, L. C. Braund 6-109) & 422 (L. O. S. Poidevin 151*, M. A. Noble 74, F. A. Iredale 67, L. C. Braund 6-130) beat English XI 332 (A. C. MacLaren 145) & 325 (A. F. A. Lilley 80, A. C. MacLaren 73, J. T. Tyldesley 57, T. W. Hayward 53, G. C. Clarke 6-133) by 53 runs.

4th Match: v XVIII of West Maitland (West Maitland)   Nov 29, 30.
West Maitland 558-15 dec (E. Capp 114, N. Lindsay 104, McGlinchy 92) drew with English XI 221-5 (T. W. Hayward 66, Wm Quaife 55*).

5th Match: v XVIII of Glen Innes (Glen Innes)   Dec 2, 3.
Glen Innes 141 (C. Blythe 10-61) & 79 (J. R. Gunn 9-37) lost to English XI 309-7 dec (T. W. Hayward 100, J. R. Gunn 97) by an inns & 89 runs.

6th Match: v XVIII of Armidale (Armidale)   Dec 4, 5.
English XI 254 (J. R. Gunn 119*) & 204-7 (L. C. Braund 72) drew with Armidale 111.

7th Match: v XV of Newcastle (Newcastle)   Dec 7, 9.
English XI 315 (C. P. McGahey 52) & 216 (G. L. Jessop 85) drew with Newcastle 241 (Mackay 68) & 73-0.

8th Match: v Australia (Sydney)   Dec 13, 14, 16.
England 464 (A. C. MacLaren 116, A. F. A. Lilley 84, T. W. Hayward 69, L. C. Braund 58) beat Australia 168 (S. F. Barnes 5-65) & 172 (L. C. Braund 5-61) by an inns & 124 runs.

9th Match: v XVIII of Goulburn (Goulburn)   Dec 20, 21.
Goulburn 190 (A. O. Jones 10-49) & 165-16 dec (Newton 52) lost to English XI 192 (C. P. McGahey 55) & 164-4 (H. G. Garnett 54) by 6 wkts.

10th Match: v XVIII of Bendigo (Bendigo)   Dec 26, 27, 28.
English XI 432 (T. W. Hayward 86, Wm Quaife 73, A. O. Jones 66) & 204-5 (J. T. Tyldesley 73) drew with Bendigo 295 (C. Eeles 78).

11th Match: v Australia (Melbourne)   Jan 1, 2, 3, 4.
Australia 112 (S. F. Barnes 6-42) & 353 (R. A. Duff 104, C. Hill 99, S. F. Barnes 7-121) beat England 61 (M. A. Noble 7-17) & 175 (J. T. Tyldesley 66, M. A. Noble 6-60) by 229 runs.

12th Match: v XVIII of Stawell (Stawell)   Jan 8, 9.
English XI 626 (L. C. Braund 127, C. P. McGahey 101, A. O. Jones 95, G. L. Jessop 68, A. C. MacLaren 56) & 164-3 (C. Robson 74, J. R. Gunn 59) drew with Stawell 130 (L. C. Braund 7-42).

13th Match: v XVIII of Ballarat (Ballarat)   Jan 10, 11.
English XI 469 (T. W. Hayward 197, A. C. MacLaren 138) drew with Ballarat 235-10.

14th Match: Australia (Adelaide)   Jan 17, 18, 20, 21, 22, 23.
England 388 (L. C. Braund 103*, T. W. Hayward 90, Wm Quaife 68, A. C. MacLaren 67) & 247 (H. Trumble 6-74) lost to Australia 321 (C. Hill 98, V. T. Trumper 65, S. E. Gregory 55, J. R. Gunn 5-76) & 315-6 (C. Hill 97, J. Darling 69, H. Trumble 62*) by 4 wkts.

15th Match: v XVI of Country (Melbourne)   Jan 25, 27, 28.
English XI 377-6 dec (Wm Quaife 91, C. P. McGahey 79, T. W. Hayward 57) & 2-0 beat Country XVI 111 & 267 (J. Harry 64) by 10 wkts.

16th Match: v New South Wales (Sydney)   Jan 31, Feb 1, 3, 4, 5.
N.S.W. 432 (S. E. Gregory 147, M. A. Noble 56, R. A. Duff 50) & 209 (S. E. Gregory 75, L. C. Braund 6-90) lost to English XI 769 (T. W. Hayward 174, A. C. MacLaren 167, J. T. Tyldesley 142, G. L. Jessop 87, Wm Quaife 62) by an inns & 128 runs.

17th Match: v XVIII of Western District (Bathurst)   Feb 7, 8.
English XI 505 (Wm Quaife 159*, H. G. Garnett 89, A. C. MacLaren 79, C. P. McGahey 71) drew with Western District 177 (L. C. Braund 12-48).

18th Match: v Australia (Sydney)   Feb 14, 15, 17, 18.
England 317 (A. C. MacLaren 92, J. T. Tyldesley 79) & 99 (J. V. Saunders 5-43, M. A. Noble 5-54) lost to Australia 299 (M. A. Noble 56, W. W. Armstrong 55) & 121-3 (R. A. Duff 51*) by 7 wkts.

19th Match: v Victoria (Melbourne)   Feb 22, 24, 25.
Victoria 129 (T. Warne 61*, L. C. Braund 5-67) & 182 (H. Stuckey 54) lost to English XI 298 (A. C. MacLaren 100, F. Collins 5-52) & 14-2 by 8 wkts.

20th Match: v Australia (Melbourne)   Feb 28, March 1, 3, 4.
Australia 144 & 255 (C. Hill 87, L. C. Braund 5-95) beat England 189 (H. Trumble 5-62) & 178 (M. A. Noble 6-98) by 32 runs.

21st Match: v XVIII of Broken Hill (Broken Hill)   March 11, 12.
English XI 173 & 190-7 (J. T. Tyldesley 69, Wm Quaife 50) drew with Broken Hill 221 (Caust 90*).

22nd Match: v South Australia (Adelaide)   March 14, 15, 17, 18.
S. Australia 207 (N. Claxton 61, J. R. Gunn 5-73, L. C. Braund 5-116) & 306 (N. Claxton 83, C. Hill 61) lost to English XI 318 (J. T. Tyldesley 126, T. W. Hayward 57) & 196-4 by 6 wkts.

1901-02: A. C. MacLaren's Team to Australia

Batting Averages

	M	I	NO	R	HS	Avge	100	c/s
A. C. MacLaren (Lancs)	10	16	0	929	167	58.06	4	19
T. W. Hayward (Surrey)	11	19	1	701	174	38.94	1	5
J. T. Tyldesley (Lancs)	11	19	0	696	142	36.63	2	5
L. C. Braund (Som)	11	19	5	404	103*	28.85	1	24
Wm. Quaife (Warks)	11	19	1	440	68	24.44	0	6
C. Robson (Hants)	1	2	1	24	17*	24.00	0	0/3
A. F. A. Lilley (Warks)	11	18	0	406	84	22.55	0	20/6
C. P. McGahey (Essex)	7	12	2	210	57	21.00	0	3
G. L. Jessop (Gloucs)	10	18	0	359	87	19.94	0	5
A. O. Jones (Notts)	11	19	1	229	44	12.72	0	13
S. F. Barnes (Lancs)	6	10	2	90	26*	11.25	0	5
J. R. Gunn (Notts)	9	16	2	154	30	11.00	0	6
H. G. Garnett (Lancs)	4	6	1	41	17	8.20	0	3/1
C. Blythe (Kent)	8	14	6	62	20	7.75	0	3

Bowling Averages

	O	M	R	W	Avge	BB	5i
S. F. Barnes	285.4	51	676	41	16.48	7-38	5
T. W. Hayward	71	28	208	10	20.80	4-22	0
C. Blythe	298.5	51	711	34	20.91	5-45	1
C. P. McGahey	61.4	12	165	7	23.57	3-58	0
J. R. Gunn	307.1	94	769	29	26.51	5-73	2
L. C. Braund	623.5	147	1779	62	28.69	6-90	7
G. L. Jessop	129	30	397	12	33.08	4-68	5
A. O. Jones	49	8	161	3	53.66	1-24	0

Also bowled: Wm. Quaife 5-0-18-0.
Played in non-first-class matches only: S. V. Green, S. M. J. Woods.

might find further consolation. A first innings lead of 45 was achieved and though Clem Hill managed 87 in his second innings, England needed only 211 for victory and were 87 for 3 at the close of the third day. Unfortunately the wicket got more difficult overnight and against Noble the rest of the side disintegrated.

The tour ended at Adelaide with the return against South Australia, which provided a win for the departing team.

The main party of the touring side arrived back in England on 27 April. The side won bouquets for its fielding, Jessop, Braund, MacLaren and Jones being outstanding. Only MacLaren and Hayward of the batsmen came off and Jessop, Jones and Gunn were complete failures. The bowling, which was weak to begin with, could not stand the absence of Barnes. Australia were not regarded as outstanding and the critics were of the opinion that Stoddart's 1897-98 side would have brought home the 'Ashes'.

1901-02: an amateur team tour the West Indies

H. D. G. Leveson-Gower selected the following team of English amateurs to tour the West Indies in 1901-02: R. A. Bennett (capt), R. N. R. Blaker (Kent), B. J. T. Bosanquet (Middx), T. H. K. Dashwood (Herts), E. W. Dillon (Kent), E. M. Dowson (Surrey), F. L. Fane (Essex), F. H. Hollins (Oxford U), E. C. Lee (Hants), A. D. Whatman (Eton Ramblers) and E. R. Wilson (Cambridge U). The all-amateur side, which contained three of the team that had recently returned from the tour to North America, was about the same strength as that combination. Leaving Southampton on 8 January aboard s.s. *Atrato*, the party arrived in Barbados on 20 January and commenced their first match two days later against Barbados. E. R. Wilson, owing to the death of his mother, and E. M. Dowson, who was ill, could not play and the tourists enrolled L. Arbuthnot and J. A. Davenport to make up the side. The ground was under water when play was scheduled to start, but it quickly dried out and on an easy wicket Barbados ran up a large total. Fast bowling by M. L. Horne then skittled the tourists out and Barbados won by an innings. Wilson and Dowson played in the return game and this made all the difference, the tourists winning by 8 wickets. The third game was against a Combined team of Trinidad, British Guiana and Barbados. Although the Combined side had a lead of 89 on the first innings, their eventual victory was due to the rain-affected wicket on which the tourists played their second innings.

From Barbados the Englishmen went to Jamaica where they took the island by storm. Six matches were played and all were victories, five of them by an innings. The standard of cricket in Jamaica was not up to that of Barbados.

The Combined team of Grenada and St Vincent was beaten twice and the tourists travelled on to Trinidad, where they were

<table>
<tr><td colspan="9">1901-02: R. A. Bennett's Team to the West Indies</td></tr>
<tr><td colspan="9">Batting Averages</td></tr>
<tr><td></td><td>M</td><td>I</td><td>NO</td><td>R</td><td>HS</td><td>Avge</td><td>100</td><td>c/s</td></tr>
<tr><td>B. J. T. Bosanquet (Middx)</td><td>13</td><td>22</td><td>4</td><td>623</td><td>69</td><td>34.61</td><td>0</td><td>13</td></tr>
<tr><td>E. R. Wilson (Cambr U)</td><td>12</td><td>17</td><td>1</td><td>402</td><td>81</td><td>26.80</td><td>0</td><td>12</td></tr>
<tr><td>F. H. Hollins (Oxford U)</td><td>12</td><td>20</td><td>4</td><td>382</td><td>74</td><td>23.87</td><td>0</td><td>19</td></tr>
<tr><td>F. L. Fane (Essex)</td><td>13</td><td>22</td><td>2</td><td>456</td><td>56*</td><td>22.80</td><td>0</td><td>7</td></tr>
<tr><td>E. M. Dowson (Surrey)</td><td>12</td><td>17</td><td>1</td><td>342</td><td>112</td><td>21.37</td><td>1</td><td>8</td></tr>
<tr><td>E. W. Dillon (Kent)</td><td>13</td><td>21</td><td>0</td><td>417</td><td>54</td><td>19.85</td><td>0</td><td>6</td></tr>
<tr><td>A. D. Whatman</td><td>13</td><td>18</td><td>4</td><td>200</td><td>60</td><td>14.28</td><td>0</td><td>11/4</td></tr>
<tr><td>R. N. R. Blaker (Kent)</td><td>12</td><td>19</td><td>0</td><td>256</td><td>55</td><td>13.47</td><td>0</td><td>12</td></tr>
<tr><td>R. A. Bennett</td><td>10</td><td>13</td><td>2</td><td>141</td><td>32*</td><td>12.81</td><td>0</td><td>14/17</td></tr>
<tr><td>E. C. Lee (Hants)</td><td>12</td><td>18</td><td>0</td><td>224</td><td>53</td><td>12.44</td><td>0</td><td>13</td></tr>
<tr><td>T. H. K. Dashwood (Herts)</td><td>13</td><td>19</td><td>1</td><td>200</td><td>32</td><td>11.11</td><td>0</td><td>10</td></tr>
<tr><td>L. Arbuthnot</td><td>7</td><td>11</td><td>6</td><td>44</td><td>17*</td><td>8.80</td><td>0</td><td>2</td></tr>
<tr><td>J. A. Davenport</td><td>1</td><td>2</td><td>0</td><td>0</td><td>0</td><td>0.00</td><td>0</td><td>0</td></tr>
<tr><td colspan="9">Bowling Averages</td></tr>
<tr><td></td><td>O</td><td>M</td><td>R</td><td>W</td><td>Avge</td><td>BB</td><td>5i</td><td></td></tr>
<tr><td>E. R. Wilson</td><td>414.1</td><td>144</td><td>767</td><td>67</td><td>11.44</td><td>7-16</td><td>5</td><td></td></tr>
<tr><td>E. M. Dowson</td><td>404.5</td><td>121</td><td>997</td><td>80</td><td>12.46</td><td>8-21</td><td>5</td><td></td></tr>
<tr><td>R. N. R. Blaker</td><td>30</td><td>9</td><td>74</td><td>5</td><td>14.80</td><td>2-1</td><td>0</td><td></td></tr>
<tr><td>E. W. Dillon</td><td>122.1</td><td>24</td><td>325</td><td>20</td><td>16.25</td><td>3-18</td><td>0</td><td></td></tr>
<tr><td>B. J. T. Bosanquet</td><td>338.3</td><td>92</td><td>906</td><td>55</td><td>16.47</td><td>8-30</td><td>5</td><td></td></tr>
<tr><td>F. H. Hollins</td><td>3</td><td>0</td><td>20</td><td>1</td><td>20.00</td><td>1-20</td><td>0</td><td></td></tr>
<tr><td>E. C. Lee</td><td>17</td><td>5</td><td>56</td><td>1</td><td>56.00</td><td>1-41</td><td>0</td><td></td></tr>
</table>

Also bowled: A. D. Whatman 9-3-23-0.
Played in non-first-class matches only: A. G. Robinson.

<table>
<tr><td colspan="2">1901-02: R. A. Bennett's Team to the West Indies</td></tr>
</table>

1st Match: v Barbados (Wanderers C.C.)   Jan 22, 23, 24.
Barbados 317 (V. Challenor 67, G. Cox 58, F. Hinds 55, B. J. T. Bosanquet 6-89) beat R. A. Bennett's XI 97 (M. L. Horne 8-39) & 149 (F. L. Fane 50, Shepherd 5-53, Layne 5-54) by an inns & 71 runs.

2nd Match: v Barbados (Bridgetown)   Jan 27, 28.
Barbados 193 (E. M. Dowson 5-89) & 141 lost to R. A. Bennett's XI 236 (F. H. Hollins 58) & 99-2 by 8 wkts.

3rd Match: v West Indies (Bridgetown)   Jan 29, 30.
R. A. Bennett's XI 147 (Burton 7-54) & 85 (Woods 7-38) lost to West Indies 236 (H. B. G. Austin 68, G. C. Learmond 54) by an inns & 4 runs.

4th Match: v Jamaica (Sabina Park)   Feb 8, 10.
R. A. Bennett's XI 326 (E. R. Wilson 81, F. H. Hollins 54*) beat Jamaica 33 (E. M. Dowson 8-21) & 154 (E. M. Dowson 8-37) by an inns & 139 runs.

5th Match: v XVI Colts (Sabina Park) (One Day)   Feb 11.
R. A. Bennett's XI 227 beat Colts 78 (E. M. Dowson 10-38) & 43-4 by 149 runs.

6th Match: v Jamaica Born (Sabina Park)   Feb 12, 13.
R. A. Bennett's XI 298 (B. J. T. Bosanquet 58*, E. C. Lee 53, F. A. Foster 6-128) & 134-3 dec (F. L. Fane 56*, R. N. R. Blaker 55) beat Jamaica Born 172 (G. C. Linton 60) & 121 (E. M. Dowson 5-48) by 139 runs.

7th Match: v Jamaica (Sabina Park)   Feb 14, 15.
R. A. Bennett's XI 362 (F. H. Hollins 74, F. A. Foster 6-147) beat Jamaica 117 & 177 (S. Snow 54, B. J. T. Bosanquet 5-29) by an inns & 68 runs.

8th Match: v St Elizabeth XII (Black River)   Feb 18, 19.
St Elizabeth XII 92 (B. J. T. Bosanquet 5-78) & 117 (E. M. Dowson 6-26) lost to R. A. Bennett's XII 330 (T. H. K. Dashwood 120*, E. M. Dowson 80, Gooden 5-78) by an inns & 121 runs.

9th Match: v Combined XI (Sabina Park)   Feb 21, 22.
Combined XI 139 (E. R. Wilson 6-39) & 72 (B. J. T. Bosanquet 8-30) lost to R. A. Bennett's XI 293 (E. R. Wilson 71, B. J. T. Bosanquet 63, E. W. Dillon 50, G. H. Withers 5-77) by an inns & 82 runs.

10th Match: v Grenada & St Vincent (Grenada)   March 5, 6.
Grenada & St Vincent 87 (B. J. T. Bosanquet 5-15) & 108 (B. J. T. Bosanquet 5-35) lost to R. A. Bennett's XI 214 (W. H. Mignon 5-70, R. Olliviere 5-37) by an inns & 19 runs.

11th Match: v Grenada & St Vincent (Grenada)   March 6, 7.
R. A. Bennett's XI 140 (R. Olliviere 9-79) & 109 (A. H. Hughes 5-25) beat Grenada & St Vincent 64 (E. M. Dowson 6-33) & 120 (B. J. T. Bosanquet 5-41) by 65 runs.

12th Match: v Trinidad (Oval, Trinidad) (12-a-side)   March 10, 11, 12.
Trinidad 188 (E. R. Wilson 5-64) & 116 lost to R. A. Bennett's XII 178 (B. J. T. Bosanquet 73, S. Smith 8-88) & 127-6 by 5 wkts.

13th Match: v Trinidad (Queen's Park)   March 14, 15.
Trinidad 114 (B. J. T. Bosanquet 5-72) & 104 (E. M. Dowson 7-30) lost to R. A. Bennett's XII 122 (S. Smith 6-56) & 97-2 by 9 wkts.

14th Match: v West Indies (Queen's Park)   March 20, 21.
West Indies 200 (L. S. Constantine 84, W. Weber 59) & 79 (B. J. T. Bosanquet 5-33) beat R. A. Bennett's XI 71 (S. Smith 9-34) & 97 (S. Smith 7-51) by 111 runs.

15th Match: v British Guiana (Georgetown)   March 31, April 1, 2.
R. A. Bennett's XI 131 (Burton 5-30, Woods 5-81) & 89 (Burton 6-37) lost to British Guiana 154 (E. R. D. Moulder 64, E. R. Wilson 6-30) & 69-6 by 4 wkts.

16th Match: v West Indies (Georgetown)   April 4, 5.
West Indies 92 (E. R. Wilson 7-46) & 33 (E. R. Wilson 7-16) lost to R. A. Bennett's XI 455 (E. M. Dowson 112, B. J. T. Bosanquet 69, A. D. Whatman 60) by an inns & 330 runs.

17th Match: v British Guiana (Georgetown)   April 7, 8, 9, 10.
R. A. Bennett's XI 90 (Burton 6-39) & 277 (B. J. T. Bosanquet 57) lost to British Guiana 206 (E. R. D. Moulder 64) & 163-6 (E. R. D. Moulder 94*) by 4 wkts.
Two other matches were played as 'fill-in' games.

18th Match: v United Services (Bridgetown) (One Day)   Jan 25.
R. A. Bennett's XI 162 (E. W. Dillon 71, Whapham 6-27) beat United Services 152 by 10 runs.

19th Match: v W. Bowring's XI (Barbados)   Jan 31, Feb 1.
R. A. Bennett's XI 384-8 dec (R. N. R. Blaker 100, B. J. T. Bosanquet 97, W. Hoad 5-91) drew with W. Bowring's XI 187 & 175-4 (W. Bowring 55).

headed on first innings, due to some excellent bowling by the left-handed S. Smith, but the combination of Bosanquet, Wilson and Dowson proved too much for Trinidad in their second innings and the tourists won by 5 wickets. Two very bad wickets at Queen's Park provided a second win for the tourists over Trinidad, but a loss against All West Indies, when S. Smith took 9 for 34 and 7 for 51.

The three last matches of the tour were in British Guiana, where, curiously, British Guiana beat the tourists twice, but the visitors managed to defeat the All West Indies Eleven by the large margin of an innings and 330 runs. Wilson took 14 wickets in this match and Dowson hit a century.

The tour was a most pleasant one and Wilson, Dowson and Bosanquet were very successful with the ball. The poor wickets told against the batsmen, only Bosanquet being consistently among the runs.

1902-03: the first full tour of New Zealand

The 1902-03 tour of Lord Hawke's team was a new departure for English cricket, since, for the first time, the principal object of the venture was to visit New Zealand, the American and Australian sections being appendages to the main programme.

The tour was undertaken at the request of the New Zealand Cricket Council, who asked Lord Hawke to select and lead the team. Owing to his mother's illness, Lord Hawke was unable to travel with the side and the duties of captaincy devolved on P. F. Warner (Middx). He was accompanied by C. J. Burnup (Kent), T. L. Taylor (Yorks), F. L. Fane (Essex), B. J. T. Bosanquet (Middx), P. R. Johnson (Somerset), E. M. Dowson (Surrey), J. Stanning (Lancs), A. E. Leatham (Gloucs), A. D. Whatman (Eton Ramblers) and two professionals, G. J. Thompson (Northants) and S. Hargreave (Warwicks). The side, except for Taylor, left Liverpool in the s.s. *Majestic* on 12 November. Arriving at New York, they stayed there overnight and then travelled to San Francisco via Chicago. In San Francisco a single innings match was played on a ground totally unsuitable for cricket—the umpires carried brooms and swept the wicket after each over! Having crossed the Pacific, calling at Honolulu, the tourists arrived in New Zealand and commenced their opening match, against Auckland. Bad fielding by the home side, who then had to bat on a difficult wicket, enabled the visitors to claim an innings victory. In the second game neither Whatman or Stanning could play, so an old Etonian, J. W. Williams, was co-opted—that and the next three odds games were won with ease. The second eleven-a-side contest occurred at Wellington, where about 7,000 spectators attended the first day. Wellington played well for the first two innings, but their batting collapsed in their second attempt and Burnup and Warner hit off the runs for victory without loss. Four more odds matches were played prior to meeting Canterbury. Here the left-handed home batsman, Reese, hit a brilliant hundred, and the Australian, Callaway, bowled well, but the tourists won by 128 runs. Otago did not fare as well as Canterbury. Warner hit 211 in 270 minutes and the home side could only manage 243 in their second innings. The two principal tour games—the final two played—were against Combined New Zealand. Neither match really extended Lord Hawke's team. Having ended the tour of New Zealand the team travelled to Australia, where three first-class matches were played.

The difference in the team's results in New Zealand and

1902-03: Lord Hawke's Team to North America, New Zealand and Australia

Batting Averages

	M	I	NO	R	HS	Avge	100	c/s
P. F. Warner (Middx)	10	16	2	771	211	55.07	2	7
F. L. Fane (Essex)	10	14	1	552	124	42.46	1	4
C. J. Burnup (Kent)	10	16	2	562	103	40.14	1	4
P. R. Johnson (Som)	9	12	4	301	88	37.62	0	9
G. J. Thompson (Norths)	10	13	4	305	80*	33.88	0	3
T. L. Taylor (Yorks)	10	14	0	468	105	33.42	2	8/1
E. M. Dowson (Surrey)	9	12	0	383	86	31.91	0	6
J. Stanning (Lancs)	9	12	3	241	38	26.77	0	7
B. J. T. Bosanquet (Middx)	10	14	1	316	82	24.30	0	8
A. E. Leatham (Gloucs)	5	5	1	45	15	11.25	0	3
A. E. Trott (Middx)	3	5	0	34	17	6.80	0	2
A. D. Whatman	6	6	1	29	13	5.80	0	7/5
S. Hargreave (Warks)	9	11	1	43	14	4.30	0	8

Bowling Averages

	O	M	R	W	Avge	BB	5i
G. J. Thompson	439.2	130	1074	76	14.13	9-85	7
C. J. Burnup	143.5	35	412	28	14.71	6-36	3
E. M. Dowson	129.1	22	353	23	15.34	5-19	1
S. Hargreave	312.1	100	641	23	27.86	6-12	1
B. J. T. Bosanquet	190.1	12	749	26	28.80	6-153	1
A. E. Trott	114.5	15	482	12	40.16	6-88	1

Also bowled: P. F. Warner 1-1-0-0.
Played in non-first-class matches only: J. N. Williams, R. H. Raphael, R. A. Williams.

1902-03: Lord Hawke's Team to the United States, Australia and New Zealand

1st Match: v XVIII of California (San Francisco) Nov 26.
California 125 (B. J. T. Bosanquet 11-37) lost to Lord Hawke's XII 155-8 (P. F. Warner 52) by 3 wkts and 30 runs.

2nd Match: v Auckland (Auckland) Dec 19, 20, 22.
Lord Hawke's XI 321 (F. L. Fane 82, W. Stemson 5-111) beat Auckland 120 & 72 (E. M. Dowson 5-19) by an inns & 129 runs.

3rd Match: v XVIII of Taranaki (Hawera) Dec 30, 31.
Taranaki 146 (F. H. Robertson 52) & 38 (S. Hargreave 9-10, G. J. Thompson 8-19) lost to Lord Hawke's XI 157 (Gudgeon 5-36) & 28-1 by 9 wkts.

4th Match: v XVIII of North Taranaki (New Plymouth) Jan 1, 2.
Lord Hawke's XI 320 (B. J. T. Bosanquet 66, T. L. Taylor 62) beat North Taranaki 86 & 131 by an inns & 103 runs.

5th Match: v XV of Wanganui (Wanganui) Jan 3, 5.
Wanganui 120 & 77 lost to Lord Hawke's XII 140 (Howden 5-40) & 59-3 by 8 wkts.

6th Match: v XVIII of Manawatu (Palmerston) Jan 7, 8.
Lord Hawke's XI 307-8 dec (F. L. Fane 76*, P. F. Warner 69) beat Manawatu 105 & 72 by an inns & 130 runs.

7th Match: v XV of Hawke's Bay (Napier) Jan 10, 12, 13.
Lord Hawke's XII 461 (B. J. T. Bosanquet 136, C. J. Burnup 82, G. J. Thompson 67, A. E. Trott 6-225) beat Hawke's Bay 106 (Lusk 56, S. Hargreave 5-31) & 157 (S. Hargreave 6-34) by an inns & 198 runs.

8th Match: v Wellington (Wellington) Jan 15, 16, 17.
Wellington 243 (Tucker 86, C. Hickson 73) & 140 (G. J. Thompson 7-51) lost to Lord Hawke's XI 289 (C. J. Burnup 69) & 97-0 (C. J. Burnup 50*) by 10 wkts.

9th Match: v XXII of Wairarapa (Greytown) Jan 20, 21.
Lord Hawke's XI 405-7 dec (E. M. Dowson 218*) beat Wairarapa 205 (S. Hargreave 12-51) & 119 (G. J. Thompson 9-27) by an inns & 80 runs.

10th Match: v XXII of Marlborough (Blenheim) Jan 23, 24.
Lord Hawke XI 204 (E. M. Dowson 94) & 18-1 beat Marlborough 59 (G. J. Thompson 15-11) & 162 by 9 wkts.

11th Match: v XVIII of Nelson (Nelson) Jan 27, 28.
Lord Hawke's XI 185 (A. D. Whatman 56) beat Nelson 29 (G. J. Thompson 9-7) & 77 (C. J. Burnup 10-14) by an inns & 79 runs.

12th Match: v XXII of Westland (Greymouth) Jan 30, 31, Feb 2.
Westland 111 (S. Hargreave 10-38) & 64 (S. Hargreave 10-28, G. J. Thompson 10-28) lost to Lord Hawke's XI 69 (Ongley 8-36) & 106-5 (C. J. Burnup 53*) by 5 wkts.

13th Match: v Canterbury (Christchurch) Feb 6, 7, 9.
Lord Hawke's XI 352 (G. J. Thompson 80*, C. J. Burnup 65, P. F. Warner 57, T. L. Taylor 54, S. T. Callaway 5-93, F. S. Frankish 5-124) & 159-7 dec (P. F. Warner 52, F. S. Frankish 5-70) beat Canterbury 224 (D. Reese 111, G. J. Thompson 6-76) & 154 (G. J. Thompson 5-54) by 128 runs.

14th Match: v Otago (Dunedin) Feb 13, 14.
Lord Hawke's XI 473 (P. F. Warner 211, F. L. Fane 85, A. Downes 5-161) beat Otago 124 (C. J. Burnup 5-50) & 119 (H. G. Siedeberg 52, G. J. Thompson 5-35) by an inns & 230 runs.

15th Match: v XV of Southland (Invercargill) Feb 18, 19.
Southland 87 & 104 lost to Lord Hawke's XI 107 (Taylor 5-59) & 87-3 by 7 wkts.

16th Match: v South Island (Dunedin) Feb 21, 23.
Lord Hawke's XI 314 (T. L. Taylor 105, B. J. T. Bosanquet 82) beat South Island 51 (S. Hargreave 6-12) & 133 (C. J. Burnup 6-36) by an inns & 130 runs.

17th Match: v XVIII of South Canterbury (Timaru) Feb 25, 26.
Lord Hawke's XI 172 & 121-7 dec (T. L. Taylor 63*) beat South Canterbury 81 (G. J. Thompson 10-23) & 88 by 124 runs.

18th Match: v New Zealand (Christchurch) Feb 27, 28, March 2.
New Zealand 164 (K. Tucker 50, G. J. Thompson 6-38) & 214 (K. Tucker 67) lost to Lord Hawke's XI 304 (F. L. Fane 124, T. L. Taylor 54) & 75-3 by 7 wkts.

19th Match: v New Zealand (Wellington) March 4, 5, 6.
New Zealand 274 (D. Reese 148, G. J. Thompson 8-124) & 84 (C. J. Burnup 5-8) lost to Lord Hawke's XI 380 (P. F. Warner 125, P. R. Johnson 88) by an inns & 22 runs.

20th Match: v Victoria (Melbourne) March 13, 14, 16.
Lord Hawke's XI 350 (E. M. Dowson 51, B. J. T. Bosanquet 51, J. V. Saunders 6-118) & 134 (F. Collins 7-61) lost to Victoria 271 & 217-3 (H. Graham 92) by 7 wkts.

21st Match: v New South Wales (Sydney) March 20, 21, 23, 24.
New South Wales 144 (A. E. Trott 6-88) & 463 (R. A. Duff 194, A. J. Hopkins 133, B. J. T. Bosanquet 6-153) drew with Lord Hawke's XI 282 (E. M. Dowson 86, B. J. T. Bosanquet 52, M. A. Noble 5-78) & 32-0.

22nd Match: v South Australia (Unley Oval) March 27, 28, 30, 31.
Lord Hawke's XI 553 (T. L. Taylor 105, C. J. Burnup 103, E. M. Dowson 66, B. J. T. Bosanquet 57, P. R. Johnson 54) & 108 (H. Hay 9-67) lost to S. Australia 304 (N. Claxton 88, C. Hill 58, C. B. Jennings 52, G. J. Thompson 9-85) & 454 (D. R. A. Gehrs 100, F. T. Hack 90, C. Hill 73) by 97 runs.

Australia clearly illustrated the difference in standard between the two countries and Lord Hawke's team proved that even the full strength of New Zealand was not yet up to the average first-class county standard in England. The tour however gave a great boost to New Zealand cricket and it was pleasing that financially it paid its way.

The team travelled back to England via the Suez Canal in the s.s. *Oroya*. Dowson, Bosanquet, Thompson and Hargreave took the overland route and got back to England on 4 May and the remainder of the side landed a few days later.

1902-03: Oxford University Authentics in India

The first major tour by an English team to India for 10 years was the joint venture of E. Britten-Holmes and F. H. Stewart, respectively secretaries of the Oxford University Authentics and the Calcutta Cricket Club. Led by K. J. Key (Surrey), the remainder of the team were G. H. Simpson-Hayward, F. G. H. Clayton, J. N. Ridley, C. Headlam, J. E. Tomkinson, F. Kershaw, R. H. Raphael, A. H. Hornby, F. H. Hollins, H. B. Chinnery, J. B. Aspinall, R. A. Williams and H. J. Powys-Keck. The side contained five or six first-class county amateurs and in English terms might be described as just about first-class. The team left

Tilbury in the s.s. *Caledonia* on 24 October and played its first match against the Bombay Presidency on 17 November. Captain Greig, the Hampshire cricketer, hit a splendid 204 for the home team in his second innings and completely altered the complexion of the game, for the tourists had a first innings lead of 109. The Presidency won by 46 runs, but probably because Chinnery was absent ill in the Authentics' second innings. The second game in Bombay was a draw, much in favour of the visitors, against the Hindus, but the Parsis beat the tourists by 8 wickets and the team felt quite shattered after these three very hard opening matches.

In the fourth match at Secunderabad, the tourists were set 146 in 40 minutes and made a fair attempt before the wickets began to fall. Three successive victories followed, then only an earlier drawing of stumps prevented another win at Calcutta against the Bengal Presidency. A weak Calcutta Club however were easily overcome as were the Gentlemen of India, who lacked M. R. Jardine, C. T. Studd, J. G. Greig and H. F. Bateman-Champain. In Peshawar Simpson-Hayward hit 203 not out and the Authentics' total reached 696. Simpson-Hayward was again in form against United Provinces, his century coming in 100 minutes. The team were not troubled in the remaining matches.

It was generally thought that the tour gave an impetus to cricket in India, but due to the Durbar many of the best English cricketers were unable to appear against the Authentics, which made the local teams much weaker than usual. The worst part of the tour was the long distances between many matches – the journey between Trichinopoly and Calcutta by train actually took five days due to floods washing away the line. Considering the problems faced by cricketers in India, the tourists were surprised at the enthusiasm and relatively high standard of play. Except at Delhi, the matches were not played on matting, but the grounds generally were not well equipped.

1902-03: Oxford Authentics to India

1st Match: v Bombay Presidency (Gymkhana Maidan)   Nov 17, 18, 19.
Bombay 204 (Capt Lowis 72, F. G. H. Clayton 7-70) & 412 (J. G. Greig 204, R. A. Williams 5-94) beat Authentics 313 (R. A. Williams 105, J. S. Milne 5-61) & 257 (F. G. H. Clayton 59, H. C. John 5-53) by 46 runs.

2nd Match: v Hindus (Bombay)   Nov 21, 22.
Authentics 356 (F. H. Hollins 141, Balu 5-131) drew with Hindus 158 & 227.

3rd Match: v Parsis (Bombay)   Nov 24, 25.
Authentics 311 (R. H. Raphael 111, A. H. Mehta 6-97) & 124 lost to Parsis 406 (D. D. Kanga 116, K. R. Driver 67, H. D. Kanga 66) & 30-2 by 8 wkts.

4th Match: v Secunderabad (Secunderabad)   Nov 28, 29.
Authentics 249 (F. H. Hollins 121, G. H. Simpson-Hayward 53, Milman 6-80) & 79-4 drew with Secunderabad 106 (G. H. Simpson-Hayward 7-39) & 289-9 dec (Capt McEwan 119*, Milman 78).

5th Match: v Mysore State (Bangalore)   Dec 4, 5, 6.
Mysore 105 (R. A. Williams 9-58) & 248 (B. Jayaram 97) lost to Authentics 209 (H. B. Chinnery 88, Kanaakarathnam 5-43) & 146-4 (R. H. Raphael 62) by 6 wkts.

6th Match: v Madras Presidency (Madras)   Dec 8, 9, 10.
Authentics 85 (J. F. Tweedie 8-30) & 373 (F. H. Hollins 185*) beat Madras 149 & 200 (E. E. L. Challenor 62, C. T. Studd 56, R. A. Williams 5-59) by 109 runs.

7th Match: v South India (Trichinopoly)   Dec 12, 13.
Authentics 215 (A. H. Hornby 67, E. Narayan Rao 7-66) beat South India 89 & 31 (R. A. Williams 6-12) by an inns & 95 runs.

8th Match: v Bengal Presidency (Calcutta)   Dec 22, 23, 24.
Authentics 106 & 275-5 dec (F. H. Hollins 62, H. B. Chinnery 57, A. H. Hornby 52) drew with Bengal 85 (H. J. Powys-Keck 5-33) & 139-5 (S. R. Hignell 51).

9th Match: v Calcutta (Calcutta)   Dec 25, 26, 27.
Authentics 494 (A. H. Hornby 111, K. J. Key 95, F. H. Hollins 90) beat Calcutta 66 (R. A. Williams 6-44) & 95 by an inns & 333 runs.

10th Match: v Gents of India (Bombay)   Jan 5, 6, 7.
Gentlemen 118 (R. A. Williams 5-38) & 143 (W. Marsham 68, H. J. Powys-Keck 5-27) lost to Authentics 135 (A. H. Hornby 54, H. G. Hoare 5-51) & 128-4 (A. H. Hornby 70*) by 6 wkts.

11th Match: v Peshawar (Peshawar)   Jan 12, 13, 14.
Authentics 696 (G. H. Simpson-Hayward 203*, F. H. Hollins 120, A. H. Hornby 72, R. H. Raphael 65) beat Peshawar 168 (M. Lannowe 64, G. H. Neale 55) & 202 (G. H. Neale 124*, G. H. Simpson-Hayward 7-31) by an inns & 330 runs.

12th Match: v Northern Punjab (Rawalpindi)   Jan 15, 16.
Authentics 360 (A. H. Hornby 143, K. J. Key 63) beat N. Punjab 49 (R. A. Williams 7-25) & 106 (H. J. Powys-Keck 9-21) by an inns & 205 runs.

13th Match: v Punjab (Lahore)   Jan 19, 20, 21.
Authentics 150 (K. J. Key 52, S. M. Robinson 7-65) & 145 beat Punjab 101 & 94 (G. H. Simpson-Hayward 5-20) by 100 runs.

14th Match: v Aligarh College (Past & Present) (Aligarh)   Jan 23, 24.
Authentics 97 (Ali Hasan 5-43, Shafkat 5-49) & 141 drew with Aligarh College 57 (G. H. Simpson-Hayward 7-34).

15th Match: v Bundelkhand (Jhansi)   Jan 29, 30.
Bundelkhand 154 (Whatford 82, H. J. Powys-Keck 8-58) & 153 (Whatford 55) lost to Authentics 316-8 dec (R. A. Williams 54, R. H. Raphael 53, Fateh Mahomed 5-110) by an inns & 9 runs.

16th Match: v United Provinces (Allahabad)   Jan 31, Feb 2.
Authentics 265 (G. H. Simpson-Hayward 100, H. B. Chinnery 60) beat United Provinces 68 & 157 by an inns & 42 runs.

17th Match: v Behar Wanderers (Mozufferpore)   Feb 5, 6, 7.
Authentics 246 (H. B. Chinnery 89, F. H. Hollins 65*, P. B. Hudson 6-61) & 273-9 dec (H. B. Chinnery 69, S. Lang 7-116) beat Behar Wanderers 128 (G. H. Simpson-Hayward 7-22) & 47 by 345 runs.

18th Match: v Oudh (Lucknow)   Feb 12, 13, 14.
Authentics 390 (F. G. H. Clayton 85, F. H. Hollins 74, A. H. Hornby 70, G. H. Simpson-Hayward 50, McPherson 6-152) beat Oudh 56 (G. H. Simpson-Hayward 8-19) & 107 by an inns & 227 runs.

19th Match: v Northern India (Cawnpore)   Feb 16, 17.
Authentics 482 (K. J. Key 116, G. H. Simpson-Hayward 88, Robinson 7-146) drew with N. India 176 (K. O. Goldie 57, R. A. Williams 5-40) & 223-7 (Beasley 86).

1903: the first county tour

For the first time, a county side undertook a major overseas tour when Kent travelled to the United States in 1903. The team was J. R. Mason (capt), C. J. Burnup, E. W. Dillon, J. Seymour, W. M. Bradley, H. Z. Baker, A. Hearne, H. C. Stewart, K. L. Hutchings, F. H. Huish, C. Blythe and G. J. V. Weigall with T. Pawley as manager. The side was the full 1903 Kent team minus S. H. Day, whose scholastic duties prevented his going.

Sailing from Liverpool in the s.s. *Oceanic* on 9 September, the team played its first match in Philadelphia against Nineteen Colts and on a rain-affected wicket won with ease. The game against Philadelphia was very even on first innings, but as on previous occasions, when the home side batted a second time only J. A. Lester played the bowling with confidence and Kent went on to a 7 wickets victory. The tourists then journeyed to New York, where they had no difficulty in beating the local side, and their final game was the return with Philadelphia which provided another win, on a fiery wicket. The team arrived back in Liverpool on 17 October, but without Burnup, who went to Mexico.

The complete success of the tour came as a surprise, since the Philadelphians had toured England in 1903 and defeated Kent.

1903: Kent to the United States

1st Match: v XIX Colts (Manheim)   Sept 18, 19.
Colts 79 (C. Blythe 6-29) & 114 (A. Hearne 8-25) lost to Kent XII 169 (D. Graham 7-32) & 25-3 by 8 wkts.

2nd Match: v Philadelphia (Wissahickon)   Sept 25, 26, 27.
Philadelphia 128 (W. M. Bradley 5-58) & 194 (J. A. Lester 93*) lost to Kent 132 (J. B. King 7-39) & 192-3 (C. J. Burnup 94*) by 7 wkts.

3rd Match: v New York (Levingston)   Sept 30, Oct 1.
Kent 202 (H. Z. Baker 55) & 76-4 dec beat New York 100 & 54 by 124 runs.

4th Match: v Philadelphia (Merion C.C.)   Oct 2, 3, 5.
Philadelphia 66 (C. Blythe 5-30) & 177 lost to Kent 180 (E. W. Dillon 64, E. M. Cregar 6-53) & 64-3 by 7 wkts.

1903-04: R. E. Foster hits 287 on first M.C.C. tour of Australia

For the first time, an English side went to Australia under the auspices of the M.C.C. in 1903-04. Originally A. C. MacLaren was asked by the Australians to take out a side, but when S. F. Barnes and W. H. Lockwood refused to accompany him, he declined the invitation. It was not until late June 1903, that the M.C.C. announced that they would be responsible for the English team, and at the same time they announced that P. F. Warner (Middx) would lead the team. At the end of July the party was announced as P. F. Warner (Middx) (capt), R. E. Foster (Worcs), B. J. T. Bosanquet (Middx), and the following professionals: G. H. Hirst (Yorks), W. Rhodes (Yorks), T. W. Hayward (Surrey), H. Strudwick (Surrey), E. G. Arnold (Worcs), L. C. Braund (Somerset), A. F. A. Lilley (Warwicks), A. Fielder (Kent), A. E. Relf (Sussex) and J. T. Tyldesley (Lancs). The final place was later given to A. E. Knight (Leics). The following, all amateurs, declined the invitation: C. B. Fry (Sussex), Hon F. S. Jackson (Yorks), A. C. MacLaren (Lancs), G. L. Jessop (Gloucs), L. C. H. Palairet (Somerset), E. M. Dowson (Surrey) and H. Martyn (Somerset). The terms accepted by the tourists were, for the amateurs, all expenses, for the professionals, all expenses plus £300 and a bonus if the tour were financially successful. It is interesting that no mention in the M.C.C. announcements was made of either Barnes or Lockwood.

Three weeks before the team sailed R. H. Spooner (Lancs) was invited to join the tour, but refused, and the tourists left Tilbury on the s.s. *Orontes* on 25 September. J. A. Murdoch, assistant secretary of M.C.C., accompanied the side. Arriving at Fremantle on 29 October, the tourists opened their programme at Adelaide on 7 November with some excellent batting and would have won the match had time permitted. This encouraging start was maintained in Melbourne, where Victoria collapsed twice against Rhodes and provided the M.C.C. with an innings victory. Going on to Sydney to meet the most powerful state, Rhodes again caused the downfall of the home batsmen and another innings victory was achieved. Queensland did much better than expected in the fourth match, but still lost by 6 wickets and after

two odds matches, the tourists arrived at Sydney for the first Test. The game belonged to R. E. Foster, who created a new Test record by hitting 287 – he batted nearly seven hours and played a splendid innings, which gave England a lead of nearly 300 on first innings. Trumper played brilliant cricket for his side, but his innings of 185 not out could not save Australia, who lost by 5 wickets.

In the second Test, Foster had to retire with a severe chill and could not bat in the second innings, but rain on the first evening made the 221 runs England scored on the first day priceless and Australia were utterly destroyed by Rhodes and England won by 185 runs. The fielding on both sides was described as quite dreadful. Only one up-country game separated the second Test from the third, which was played on a hard fast wicket, unlike the first two games. Here Trumper, Hill and Gregory mastered the English attack and then the visiting batsmen found the pace of the ball off the wicket too much for them. Warner and Hirst

---

1903-04: M.C.C. to Australia

Batting Averages

	M	I	NO	R	HS	Avge	100	c/s
T. W. Hayward (Surrey)	11	17	0	785	157	46.17	2	4
R. E. Foster (Worcs)	13	22	4	821	287	45.61	1	14
B. J. T. Bosanquet (Middx)	12	19	3	587	124*	36.81	2	12
J. T. Tyldesley (Lancs)	13	22	2	670	97	33.50	0	7
G. H. Hirst (Yorks)	12	18	1	569	92	33.47	0	7
A. E. Knight (Leics)	10	16	2	444	104	31.71	1	2
P. F. Warner (Middx)	14	24	1	694	79	30.17	0	5
L. C. Braund (Som)	11	17	0	395	102	23.23	1	17
W. Rhodes (Yorks)	14	18	7	239	49*	21.72	0	14
A. F. A. Lilley (Warks)	11	16	3	226	91*	17.38	0	16/13
A. E. Relf (Sussex)	9	12	2	167	31	16.70	0	13
E. G. Arnold (Worcs)	10	15	3	167	34	13.91	0	13
A. Fielder (Kent)	7	8	3	59	23	11.80	0	3
H. Strudwick (Surrey)	6	5	0	53	21	10.60	0	11/9
G. H. Drummond	1	1	0	1	1	1.00	0	0

Bowling Averages

	O	M	R	W	Avge	BB	5i
W. Rhodes	423.3	112	1055	65	16.23	8-68	7
E. G. Arnold	381.1	102	884	46	19.22	4-8	0
L. C. Braund	279	58	729	37	19.70	8-43	3
A. E. Knight	14	2	43	2	21.50	2-34	0
A. Fielder	139.1	42	323	14	23.07	3-35	0
G. H. Hirst	359.5	87	881	36	24.47	5-37	2
B. J. T. Bosanquet	273.4	23	1011	37	27.32	6-45	2
A. E. Relf	129.4	44	302	10	30.20	3-48	0
R. E. Foster	7	2	34	1	34.00	1-34	0

Also bowled: T. W. Hayward 14-5-27-0; P. F. Warner 10-3-28-0; A. F. A. Lilley 8-2-23-0; G. H. Drummond 5-0-21-0; J. T. Tyldesley 8-1-28-0; H. Strudwick 5-2-6-0.
Played in non-first-class matches only: G. S. Whitfield.

The first M.C.C. team to Australia. Led by Pelham Warner, it brought back the Ashes. Back: A. E. Knight, L. C. Braund, B. J. T. Bosanquet, A. E. Relf, W. Rhodes, E. G. Arnold. Front: G. H. Hirst, R. E. Foster, P. F. Warner, T. W. Hayward, A. F. A. Lilley, J. T. Tyldesley. Foster scored a record 287 in the first Test.

batted well, but the rest were all at sea and Australia saved the rubber.

Both Victoria and New South Wales were beaten in the return fixtures and these matches as well as a visit to Tasmania came before the fourth Test. About 30,000 turned up to watch the second day, which was marred by rain—the crowd became restless at the delay in re-starting after the rain and the bottle-throwing and barracking became pretty intense. Rhodes again caused an Australian collapse and though the English batting was none too robust, Australia required 329 to win in the final innings. Bosanquet took 6 for 51 giving England the Ashes. The fifth Test began only two days after the end of the fourth. Trumper batted in splendid form to hit 88 out of 142 and rain then ruined the wicket

—England were shot out for 61, with Cotter picking up 6 wickets. Australia made 133 in their second innings and with Hayward in bed with tonsilitis, the English position was hopeless. Trumble did the hat-trick and took 7 for 28 as England plunged to defeat.

The last game was the return with South Australia which gave the M.C.C. a farewell victory, Warner, Tyldesley and Foster hitting off 184 for the loss of one wicket in the final innings. In terms of matches the tour was the shortest to Australia since 1882-83.

The success of the English team was due to the variety of the attack—on the batting side, in Trumper, Duff, Noble and Hill, Australia had a better quartet than the best four English batsmen, but the Australian bowling was all right-arm medium, or nearly so, until Cotter was introduced. Lilley kept wicket much better than Kelly, and Warner's captaincy was a large factor in the English victory. In fact the tour was a most satisfactory venture, except from the financial angle, the M.C.C. losing £1,500.

The team arrived back in England on 17 April, taking the overland route from Marseilles.

1904-05: Lord Brackley's team find West Indies improving

Lord Brackley captained his own side to the West Indies in the winter of 1904-05. The team, which left England on 31 December, consisted of Lord Brackley, C. P. Foley (Middx), E. G. Wynyard (Hants), T. G. O. Cole (Lancs), R. C. W. Burn (Oxford U), G. H. T. Simpson-Hayward (Worcs), H. V. Hesketh-Prichard (Hants), H. J. Powys-Keck (Worcs), A. W. F. Somerset (Sussex), C. H. M. Ebden (Sussex), G. H. Drummond (M.C.C.), and two professionals, E. G. Hayes (Surrey) and G. J. Thompson (Northants), together with J. Moss as umpire. The Lancashire batsman Hallows was invited but had to withdraw on medical advice.

The team began their tour in Jamaica and were lucky to draw their first fixture against the island side. In the return, however, Wynyard hit 157 and the tourists had an innings victory. Barbados and a weak West Indian team were also beaten, but the tourists lacked Hayes in their return with Barbados and, collapsing for 95 in their second innings, suffered their first defeat.

Three matches in St Lucia all proved easy victories and the Englishmen then moved on to British Guiana, where they achieved two victories over the colony, though the second proved quite a close encounter. In Trinidad, however, the tourists met their match in Cumberbatch who bowled his team to two victories. In between these two games was the return with the West Indies. The visitors were without Wynyard, who injured his leg, and in a very exciting finish won by 4 runs. The batting of Constantine was perhaps the feature of the match.

The outstanding quality of the tourists was their fielding and very few catches were dropped throughout the tour. Hayes proved himself to be undoubtedly the best all-rounder, while Thompson took over a hundred wickets.

Apart from some unpleasantness concerning the umpiring in St Vincent, the tour was most enjoyable and showed that the standard of West Indian cricket was still improving.

1905: M.C.C. make summer tour of the United States and Canada

Departing from the usual arrangements for tours to North America, the team which went in 1905 left England in July and completed its programme by mid-August. The team, under the auspices of the M.C.C., went at the invitation of the cricket clubs in both the United States and Canada.

The team was almost entirely composed of University players. From Cambridge came E. W. Mann (capt), M. W. Payne, G. G. Napier, C. H. Eyre, H. C. McDonell, F. J. V. Hopley, R. T. Godsell and L. J. Moon; and from Oxford F. A. H. Henley, R. C. W. Burn, H. J. Wyld and V. A. S. Stow; K. O. Hunter completed the party.

Arriving in New York, the tourists began the fixtures with the major one against Philadelphia and had the satisfaction of winning by 7 wickets. The home team however got their revenge in the return, when J. A. Lester put in a splendid all-round performance, hitting a century in the second innings and capping this with 7 wickets for 33. The game against New York was much closer than is usual with these encounters and it is reported that the crowd was a record for a cricket match in that city. The tourists proceeded to Canada for a programme of four matches, but the Canadians proved much too weak and rather foolishly met the English team on even terms in three of the fixtures.

The final game ended on 17 August and the tour could be regarded as successful from every standpoint.

1905-06: one-wicket Test win for South Africa

The first M.C.C. tour to South Africa went out under a guarantee against financial loss given by the South African authorities. Sailing in the *Kinfauns Castle*, the tourists arrived in Cape Town on 28 November. The voyage had been a particularly rough one — windows in the smoking room and cabins had been smashed and at times the waves swept right over the boat.

The team consisted of P. F. Warner (Middx) (capt), F. L. Fane

(Essex), J. N. Crawford (Surrey), E. G. Wynyard (Hants), L. J. Moon (Middx), J. C. Hartley (Sussex), H. D. G. Leveson-Gower (Surrey) and the professionals D. Denton (Yorks), S. Haigh (Yorks), E. G. Hayes (Surrey), W. S. Lees (Surrey), C. Blythe (Kent), A. E. Relf (Sussex) and J. H. Board (Gloucs). The team was in no way representative of England's full strength and was regarded when it set out as the equal of the middle range of the first-class counties.

After some net practice and a scratch game, the programme opened with the game against Western Province. A good all-round performance by the visitors allied to some weak, nervous batting on the part of the home team, gave M.C.C. an easy first win. This was followed by a win in an odds match and another win in the return against Western Province. The fourth match at Kimberley provided yet another victory. At Johannesburg, M.C.C. met Transvaal and gained a substantial first innings lead due to a good knock by Denton. Faulkner batted well for the home side and though M.C.C. required less than 200 in their final innings, they never looked like making the runs. Schwarz spun the ball off the mat at a great pace and no one could master him.

Following an odds match at Potchefstroom, the team returned to Johannesburg for the first Test. This game went all in favour of England until the final day. South Africa, who made only 91 in their first innings, required 284 for victory in their second. The score fell to 105 for 6 and an English win looked assured. Nourse and White then added 121. Further wickets fell to take the total to 239 for 9. Nourse, now partnered by Sherwell, went on to take South Africa to an historic victory by a single wicket. As the final runs were made the crowd rushed onto the ground and carried the two batsmen into the pavilion. It should be mentioned that Haigh, the best English bowler, was absent ill on the final day. Three minor games followed the Test and provided three wins by an innings. Natal were then met and beaten twice, though Nourse again proved a problem, hitting a magnificent 100, and a collection on the ground realised £46 for him.

The second and third Tests were played as consecutive fixtures and both were disasters for England. In the second Test the England batting was quite deplorable and good all-round play by the home side gave them a nine-wicket victory. The third Test was a much higher scoring match, but the home side managed matters rather better than the tourists and won by 243 runs; England left out Wynyard and Board due to illness and injury, but the absence of these two did not materially alter the strength

---

1905-06: M.C.C. to South Africa

1st Match: v Western Province (Cape Town) Dec 2, 4, 5.
M.C.C. 365 (D. Denton 78, A. E. Relf 61*, F. L. Fane 60, P. F. Warner 56, Whitehead 6-100) beat W. Province 96 (S. Haigh 5-29) & 142 (J. N. Crawford 5-41) by an inns & 127 runs.

2nd Match: v XVIII of Worcester (Worcester) Dec 6, 7.
Worcester 107 (J. C. Hartley 9-26) & 203 lost to M.C.C. XII 362 (H. D. G. Leveson-Gower 82, D. Denton 68, P. de Villiers 6-76) by an inns & 52 runs.

3rd Match: v Western Province (Cape Town) Dec 9, 11, 12.
W. Province 81 & 233 (S. J. Snooke 80, S. E. Horwood 74, J. N. Crawford 6-79) lost to M.C.C. 272 (S. Haigh 61, A. E. Relf 60, L. J. Moon 57) & 43-0 by 10 wkts.

4th Match: v XV of Griqualand West (Kimberley) Dec 15, 16.
M.C.C. XII 374 (E. G. Hayes 125, E. G. Wynyard 82, G. A. Verheyen 5-82) & 9-0 beat Griqualand West 174 (A. E. Relf 8-36) & 207 by 11 wkts.

5th Match: v XV of Griqualand West (Kimberley) Dec 19, 20, 21.
Griqualand West 233 (J. F. Mitchell 51) & 187 lost to M.C.C. 432-8 dec (J. N. Crawford 98, D. Denton 64, F. L. Fane 62, E. G. Wynyard 62*, A. E. Relf 51) by an inns & 12 runs.

6th Match: v Transvaal (Johannesburg) Dec 26, 27, 28.
Transvaal 135 (W. S. Lees 5-34) & 305 (W. A. Shalders 66, G. A. Faulkner 63*) beat M.C.C. 265 (D. Denton 132*) & 115 (R. O. Schwarz 5-34) by 60 runs.

7th Match: v XVIII of Western Transvaal (Potchefstroom) Dec 29, 30.
W. Transvaal 92 & 115 lost to M.C.C. 317-6 dec (P. F. Warner 125, F. L. Fane 63) by an inns & 110 runs.

8th Match: v South Africa (Johannesburg) Jan 2, 3, 4.
England 184 & 190 (P. F. Warner 51) lost to South Africa 91 (W. S. Lees 5-34) & 287-9 (A. W. Nourse 93*, G. C. White 81) by 1 wkt.

9th Match: v Pretoria (Pretoria) Jan 6, 8.
M.C.C. 338 (J. C. Hartley 77) beat Pretoria 87 (J. N. Crawford 5-6) & 171 (J. N. Crawford 6-54) by an inns & 70 runs.

10th Match: v Middelburg & District XVIII (Middelburg) Jan 10, 11.
M.C.C. 392 (P. F. Warner 128, F. L. Fane 68, J. N. Crawford 56, Barnes 6-121) beat Middelburg 86 & 187 by an inns & 119 runs.

11th Match: v The Army (Roberts' Heights) Jan 12, 13.
M.C.C. 480-7 dec (D. Denton 130, L. J. Moon 80, H. D. G. Leveson-Gower 67*, J. N. Crawford 54) beat The Army 97 (Mitford 65*) & 165 (McFarlane 68) by an inns & 218 runs.

12th Match: v Natal (Durban) Jan 16, 17, 18.
Natal 191 (A. W. Nourse 119) & 159 (C. Blythe 5-41) lost to M.C.C. 175 (D. Denton 53, A. W. Nourse 5-52) & 176-6 (F. L. Fane 77*) by 4 wkts.

13th Match: v Natal (Pietermaritzburg) Jan 20, 22, 23.
Natal 117 & 173 (S. Haigh 7-58) lost to M.C.C. 191 (F. L. Fane 59, C. F. Hime 5-18) & 100-6 by 4 wkts.

14th Match: v XV of East London (East London) Jan 27, 29.
East London 120 & 73 lost to M.C.C. 206 (J. H. Board 57) by an inns & 13 runs.

15th Match: v XV of Kingwilliamstown (Kingwilliamstown) Feb 3, 5.
M.C.C. XII 415-8 dec (D. Denton 147, F. L. Fane 111) beat Kingwilliamstown 75 & 44 (A. E. Relf 8-12) by an inns & 296 runs.

16th Match: v XVIII of Queenstown (Queenstown) Feb 6, 7.
M.C.C. XII 400-8 dec (J. N. Crawford 212*, A. E. Relf 61) beat Queenstown 111 (C. Blythe 9-16) & 113 by an inns & 176 runs.

17th Match: v XXII of Midlands (Cradock) Feb 12, 13.
Midlands 256 (W. Solomon 54, A. E. Relf 8-58) drew with M.C.C. 413-8 (F. L. Fane 67, P. F. Warner 65, J. C. Hartley 58*).

18th Match: v XVIII of Albany (Grahamstown) Feb 14, 15.
Albany 129 (E. Fock 51) & 51-4 drew with M.C.C. XII 241 (J. C. Hartley 59, F. Bayes 5-45).

19th Match: v XV of Port Elizabeth (Port Elizabeth) Feb 16, 17, 19.
Port Elizabeth 72 (S. Haigh 8-14) & 106 lost to M.C.C. 255 (L. J. Moon 98, A. G. Lyons 7-66) by an inns & 77 runs.

20th Match: v Eastern Province (Port Elizabeth) Feb 20, 21, 22.
E. Province 132 (J. C. Hartley 6-32) & 92 (C. Blythe 5-30) lost to M.C.C. 201 (J. N. Crawford 64, E. G. Wynyard 54*, A. E. E. Vogler 6-56) & 24-0 by 10 wkts.

21st Match: v South-Western Districts XXII (Oudtshoorn) Feb 24, 26.
M.C.C. 95 (G. Rogers 5-24) & 152-6 dec drew with S-W Districts 77 (J. N. Crawford 13-33) & 97-9.

22nd Match: v South Africa (Johannesburg) March 6, 7, 8.
England 148 & 160 (F. L. Fane 65) lost to South Africa 277 (J. H. Sinclair 66) & 33-1 by 9 wkts.

23rd Match: v South Africa (Johannesburg) March 10, 12, 13, 14.
South Africa 385 (C. M. H. Hathorn 102, A. W. Nourse 61, W. S. Lees 6-78) & 349-5 dec (G. C. White 147, L. J. Tancred 73, A. W. Nourse 55) beat England 295 (F. L. Fane 143) & 196 (D. Denton 61, S. J. Snooke 8-70) by 243 runs.

24th Match: v XV of Orange River Colony (Bloemfontein) March 17, 19, 20, 21.
Orange River 279 (Weir 76) & 123 drew with M.C.C. 203 (E. G. Hayes 66) & 169-4.

25th Match: v South Africa (Cape Town) March 24, 26, 27.
South Africa 218 (C. Blythe 6-68) & 138 (G. C. White 73, C. Blythe 5-50) lost to England 198 & 160-6 (F. L. Fane 66*) by 4 wkts.

26th Match: v South Africa (Cape Town) March 30, 31, April 2.
England 187 (J. N. Crawford 74) & 130 lost to South Africa 333 (A. E. E. Vogler 62*, S. J. Snooke 60) by an inns & 16 runs.

1905-06: M.C.C. to South Africa

Batting Averages

	M	I	NO	R	HS	Avge	100	c/s
F. L. Fane (Essex)	12	19	3	607	143	37.93	1	3
D. Denton (Yorks)	12	20	1	613	132*	32.26	2	9
J. N. Crawford (Surrey)	11	18	1	531	74	31.23	0	13
A. E. Relf (Sussex)	9	16	1	404	61*	26.93	0	8
L. J. Moon (Middx)	9	15	0	373	80	24.86	0	5/5
Sir G. Lagden	1	1	0	21	21	21.00	0	0
H. D. G. Leveson-Gower (Surrey)	5	6	1	99	67*	19.80	0	2
E. G. Wynyard (Hants)	6	10	2	156	54*	19.50	0	1
P. F. Warner (Middx)	12	22	3	314	56	16.52	0	3
J. H. Board (Gloucs)	8	14	4	145	39	14.50	0	9/5
E. G. Hayes (Surrey)	8	14	1	186	35	14.30	0	8
S. Haigh (Yorks)	12	19	2	212	61	12.47	0	9
W. S. Lees (Surrey)	10	16	5	127	25*	11.54	0	2
C. Blythe (Kent)	11	15	4	94	27	8.54	0	8
J. C. Hartley (Sussex)	6	8	0	49	29	6.12	0	7

Bowling Averages

	O	M	R	W	Avge	BB	5i
F. L. Fane	2.4	0	17	2	8.50	2-17	0
S. Haigh	241.2	63	625	39	16.02	7-58	2
J. C. Hartley	108	16	333	19	17.52	6-32	1
C. Blythe	480.2	168	1046	57	18.33	6-68	4
W. S. Lees	366.3	132	771	42	18.35	6-78	3
J. N. Crawford	230.3	58	627	34	18.44	6-79	2
A. E. Relf	133.1	32	342	12	28.50	3-40	0
P. F. Warner	8	1	36	1	36.00	1-17	0
E. G. Hayes	3	0	123	2	61.50	1-18	0

Also bowled: Sir G. Lagden 1-0-4-0; H. D. G. Leveson-Gower 6-1-26-0; L. J. Moon 1-1-0-0; E. G. Wynyard 4-0-17-0.
Played in non-first-class matches only: I. D. Difford.

59

of the eleven. Nourse had two good innings and such an advantage did the South Africans gain that they were able to declare with 5 wickets down in their second innings and leave the English team needing 440 to win. The fast right-arm bowling of Snooke finished off the tourists.

Only one game—another odds match—was played prior to the fourth Test, which was staged at Newlands. It was assumed that since South Africa had won the rubber, there would be little interest in the fourth match, but in fact a large crowd watched the contest. This time Blythe bowled splendidly, keeping an accurate length, and only White batted well against him. England needed 159 in the final innings and due to Fane won by 4 wickets. The fifth and final Test followed straight on from the fourth. Once more the English batting let the side down and this time the bowlers did not come to the rescue, the tourists having to suffer a last wicket stand of 94 between Sherwell and Vogler—the latter made some tremendous drives and the crowd of some 10,000 made a collection for him. The South Africans won the match with an innings to spare.

The team arrived back in England on 21 April. Wynyard had come home early due to illness and Leveson-Gower and Moon remained behind in South Africa.

The failure of the English team was due to the poor batting on matting wickets against an attack which was largely made up of leg-break bowlers. The lack of form of several Englishmen—Warner, Denton and Hayes for example—in the Tests was inexplicable, though Hayes did suffer from ill-health on part of the tour.

1906-07: M.C.C. tour New Zealand after internal Australian squabbles

Throughout the English summer of 1906, the public were bombarded with reports of the M.C.C. taking a team to Australia. Originally the difficulties concerning such a tour lay in the squabbles between the Australian authorities, but when these had been ironed out, the M.C.C. stated it was too late to raise a team. Influential figures then stepped in to try to change the M.C.C.'s decision and it was not until the second week of September that, at a special Committee Meeting, the M.C.C. decided the tour was

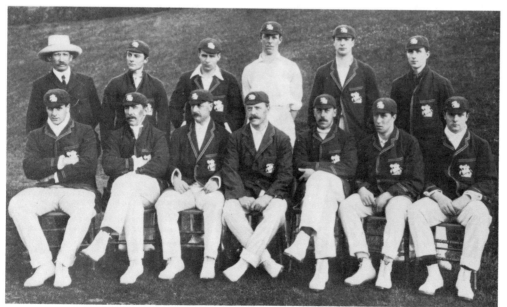

The M.C.C. team photographed in New Zealand in 1906-07. This was an all-amateur side. Back: J. Moss (umpire), W. P. Harrison, P. R. May, W. J. H. Curwen, C. C. Page, N. C. Tufnell. Front: G. T. Branston, A. A. Torrens, C. E. de Trafford, E. G. Wynyard (captain), G. H. Simpson-Hayward, J. W. H. T. Douglas, W. B. Burns.

1906-07: M.C.C. to South Africa and New Zealand

Batting Averages

	M	I	NO	R	HS	Avge	100	c/s
J. W. H. T. Douglas (Essex)	9	14	3	398	67	36.18	0	7
P. R. Johnson (Som)	10	18	1	546	99	32.11	0	7
W. B. Burns (Worcs)	11	20	2	499	59	27.72	0	7
N. C. Tufnell	7	12	4	203	85	25.37	0	5
G. T. Branston (Notts)	10	17	0	424	119	24.94	1	11
W. P. Harrison (Middx)	9	15	0	371	105	24.73	1	3
G. H. T. Simpson-Hayward (Worcs)	9	15	0	369	71	24.60	0	10
C. C. Page (Middx)	11	18	0	439	78	24.38	0	2
R. H. Fox	10	17	3	307	54	21.92	0	12/8
P. R. May (Surrey)	9	16	5	176	32*	16.00	0	3
W. J. H. Curwen (Surrey)	8	14	1	203	76	15.53	0	4
A. A. Torrens	6	9	0	135	87	15.00	0	1
C. E. de Trafford (Leics)	9	16	1	156	28*	10.40	0	4
P. F. C. Williams	1	1	0	3	3	3.00	0	0
E. G. Wynyard (Hants)	3	3	3	86	48*	—	0	1

Bowling Averages

	O	M	R	W	Avge	BB	5i
J. W. H. T. Douglas	239.1	51	663	50	13.26	7-49	5
P. R. May	248.4	46	719	45	15.97	5-37	3
G. H. T. Simpson-Hayward	218.4	31	591	35	16.89	6-39	1
G. T. Branston	250	70	673	36	18.69	5-54	1
W. P. Harrison	26	3	124	6	20.66	4-61	3
R. H. Fox	15	1	51	2	25.50	1-17	0
W. J. H. Curwen	74	23	178	5	35.60	3-47	0
W. B. Burns	18	1	78	2	39.00	1-8	0
A. A. Torrens	99.2	21	250	6	41.66	3-44	0

Also bowled: C. C. Page 3-0-14-0.

definitely off, but would probably go ahead in 1907-08.

This wrangling quite overshadowed the preparations for the M.C.C. tour of New Zealand. The New Zealand Cricket Council invited the M.C.C. to send a team and guaranteed the visit, each major Association contributing £500 and the minor Associations £100 each. The all-amateur team consisted of: E. G. Wynyard (Hants) (capt), C. E. de Trafford (Leics), G. H. T. Simpson-Hayward (Worcs), P. R. Johnson (Somerset), G. T. Branston (Notts), W. J. H. Curwen (Surrey), P. R. May (Surrey), W. B. Burns (Worcs), W. P. Harrison (Middx), R. H. Fox (M.C.C.), C. C. Page (Middx), A. A. Torrens (Kent), N. C. Tufnell, J. W. H. T. Douglas (Essex) and the old Notts player J. Moss as umpire. The New Zealand authorities complained to no avail about the team bringing its own umpire. Sailing from Tilbury in the s.s. *Corinthie*, except for Johnson, who went via Suez, the team travelled to South Africa, where the tour opened with a match against Western Province at Newlands – the one-day game

was won by one wicket.

Before discussing the New Zealand matches, it should be noted that the side contained only five regular 1906 County cricketers plus four 1906 university players, so the team could be described as weak first-class in English terms.

The party reached Wellington on 5 December and travelled straight from there to Auckland for the first match. The home side looked like winning until Branston and Wynyard, in M.C.C.'s second innings, added 119 for the 8th wicket, which forced a draw. The second eleven-a-side game – against Wellington – was also drawn, but was the scene of three injuries – Wynyard broke a tendon in his right leg and missed the rest of the tour, Torrens strained his left leg and Douglas strained his side. It was not surprising therefore that the match against Canterbury, which began only three hours after a rough sea voyage, was lost by 7 wickets. Better fortune awaited the team in Dunedin, where good batting by Page and Simpson-Hayward produced a win. Three odds matches caused the tourists little anxiety, but the return against Auckland was a close thing, two excellent innings by Douglas tipping the balance. The returns against Canterbury and Otago provided the tourists with large victories, though the match at Wellington had to be drawn due to rain.

The most important games of the visit were those against the full strength New Zealand eleven. The first, at Christchurch, was dominated by Johnson who hit 99 and an unbeaten 76, the M.C.C. winning by 9 wickets. For the second game, the tourists were without Simpson-Hayward, the lob bowler having a damaged hand. On a fiery wicket, Douglas took 7 wickets, but Upham retaliated for New Zealand and the home side gained a first innings lead of 5. In the end M.C.C. required 255 to win, but never looked like reaching the target and New Zealand won by 56 runs.

Judged by the results, the M.C.C.'s choice of a suitable team for New Zealand proved entirely satisfactory. The only gap in the side was the lack of a good slow bowler. The batting happily did not rely on one or two men, but had plenty of depth, even without Wynyard – in his absence, de Trafford led the side. The only unfortunate side of the tour was financial. The players did not attract large crowds and the New Zealand Cricket Council lost a considerable sum on the venture.

The team travelled to Sydney after their last match and stayed long enough for some practice with V. T. Trumper at the Cricket Ground, before boarding the s.s. *Ophir* for the voyage home.

1907: South Africans join M.C.C. tour to the United States and Canada

The M.C.C. side which visited North America in the autumn of 1907 differed in one important particular compared with previous English touring sides. The party included the leading two cricketers of the South African tourists to England in the same year. The full side was H. V. Hesketh-Prichard (Hants) (capt), G. T. Branston (Notts), F. H. Browning, L. G. A. Collins (Berks), L. P. Collins (Berks), G. H. Simpson-Hayward (Worcs), G. MacGregor (Middx), E. G. Wynyard (Hants), J. W. H. T. Douglas (Essex), K. O. Goldie (Sussex), R. O. Schwarz (South Africa) and S. J. Snooke (South Africa).

The majority of the team sailed on the *Lucania* from Liverpool on 7 September, but the two South Africans travelled later. The tour opened in New York on 17 September, and as Snooke and Schwarz had not yet arrived. F. H. Bohlen and R. E. Bonner took their places. About 3,000 watched the first day's play, but rain curtailed the remainder of the fixture. Rain then ruined the first match with Philadelphia, which was confined to not much more than one innings each – remarkably 10,000 turned up on the second day, believed to be a record for a match in the United States. The tourists easily beat the Colts, but the return with Philadelphia was most exciting, only five runs separating the teams on first innings and in the final stages the last two home batsmen survived for 13 minutes to save the game.

The last match was against Canada; both teams found batting hard work on a tricky pitch but Canada forced a draw, being 8 wickets down and still 66 in arrears when stumps were drawn.

The only thing that marred the tour was the poor weather, rain interfering with three of the five matches. L. G. A. Collins had the misfortune to crack a rib prior to the first match and appeared just once – in the final game.

1907: M.C.C. to North America

1st Match: v New York (Staten Island)   Sept 17, 18.
M.C.C. 338-4 dec (E. G. Wynyard 145, L. P. Collins 102, J. W. H. T. Douglas 63) drew with New York 66-3.

2nd Match: v Philadelphia (Manheim)   Sept 21, 22, 23.
M.C.C. 162 (G. T. Branston 63, H. V. Hordern 5-41) & 64-3 drew with Philadelphia 157 (R. O. Schwarz 8-55).

3rd Match: v XVII Colts & Captain (St Martin's)   Sept 24, 25.
M.C.C. 329 (K. O. Goldie 147) beat Colts 86 & 70 (G. H. Simpson-Hayward 13-33) by an inns & 173 runs.

4th Match: v Philadelphia (Haverford)   Sept 27, 28, 29, Oct 1.
M.C.C. 222 & 124 (H. V. Hordern 5-38, J. B. King 5-39) drew with Philadelphia 227 & 60-9 (H. V. Hesketh-Prichard 7-20).

5th Match: v Canada (Ottawa)   Oct 2, 3.
M.C.C. 113 & 115-5 dec (R. O. Schwarz 51*) drew with Canada 94 (G. H. Simpson-Hayward 5-25) & 74-8.

1907-08: last wicket stand of 39 wins Test, but Australia retain Ashes

As announced when the M.C.C. declined to tour Australia in 1906-07, the tour was postponed and took place the following winter. The team sailed from Tilbury on 20 October, except for Young, who joined the boat at Plymouth and Hutchings, Fane and Rhodes, who chose the overland route to Marseilles.

The full side was A. O. Jones (Notts) (capt), F. L. Fane (Essex), K. L. Hutchings (Kent), J. N. Crawford (Surrey), R. A. Young (Sussex) and the professionals W. Rhodes (Yorks), L. C. Braund (Somerset), E. G. Hayes (Surrey), J. B. Hobbs (Surrey), C. Blythe (Kent), A. Fielder (Kent), J. Hardstaff (Notts), J. Humphries (Derbys), S. F. Barnes (Staffs). Also on board were George Gunn (Notts), who was going to Australia for his health, but would be available to play if required, and Tarrant of Middlesex. The professionals were paid £300 plus the first-class sea passage, hotel expenses in Australia, travelling expenses etc, and £2 per week for out of pocket expenses. As a matter of interest, the Australian players were each to be paid £25 as an 'honorarium' for each Test.

The M.C.C. team was in no way representative of the full

1907-08: M.C.C. to Australia

1st Match: v Western Australia (Perth)   Oct 26, 28, 29.
M.C.C. 402 (F. L. Fane 133, L. C. Braund 59, A. Christian 5-132) beat W. Australia 152 (T. H. Hogue 60*) & 116 by an inns & 134 runs.

2nd Match: v South Australia (Adelaide)   Nov 9, 11, 12, 13.
S. Australia 343 (C. Hill 104, C. B. Jennings 79, N. H. Claxton 57) & 134 (C. Hill 61, J. N. Crawford 5-40) lost to M.C.C. 660-8 dec (L. C. Braund 160, J. Hardstaff 135, A. O. Jones 119, J. N. Crawford 114) by an inns & 183 runs.

3rd Match: v Victoria (Melbourne)   Nov 15, 16, 18, 19, 20.
Victoria 233 (F. A. Tarrant 65, V. S. Ransford 51, A. Fielder 5-71) & 463 (V. S. Ransford 102, F. A. Tarrant 81, L. P. Vernon 62, C. McKenzie 54, A. Fielder 5-98) drew with M.C.C. 198 (L. C. Braund 62) & 422-9 (J. Hardstaff 95*, A. O. Jones 82, K. L. Hutchings 91).

4th Match: v New South Wales (Sydney)   Nov 22, 23, 25.
M.C.C. 304 (J. Hardstaff 53) & 301 (J. Hardstaff 71, W. Rhodes 50) beat N.S.W. 101 (S. F. Barnes 6-24) & 96 (A. Fielder 6-27) by 408 runs.

5th Match: v Queensland (Brisbane)   Nov 30, Dec 2.
Queensland 78 (C. Blythe 5-35) & 186 (R. J. Hartigan 59, C. Blythe 6-48) lost to M.C.C. 308 (W. Rhodes 70*, A. O. Jones 69, K. L. Hutchings 67, J. W. MacLaren 5-104) by an inns & 44 runs.

6th Match: v An Australian XI (Brisbane)   Dec 6, 7, 9.
An Australian XI 299 (S. J. Redgrave 66, P. A. McAlister 57, L. C. Braund 7-117) & 110-2 (R. J. Hartigan 55*, P. A. McAlister 51*) drew with M.C.C. 223 (K. L. Hutchings 72).

7th Match: v Australia (Sydney)   Dec 13, 14, 16, 17, 18, 19.
England 273 (G. Gunn 119, A. Cotter 6-101) & 300 (G. Gunn 74, J. Hardstaff 63) lost to Australia 300 (C. Hill 87, A. Fielder 6-82) & 275-8 (H. Carter 61) by 2 wkts.

8th Match: v A Victorian XI (South Melbourne)   Dec 21, 23, 24.
M.C.C. 503-9 dec (W. Rhodes 105*, E. G. Hayes 98, J. B. Hobbs 77, A. Fielder 50*) drew with A Victorian XI 488-9 (F. A. Tarrant 159, W. W. Armstrong 117, J. F. Horan 75).

9th Match: v XVIII of Bendigo (Bendigo)   Dec 26, 27, 28.
M.C.C. 213 (J. B. Hobbs 58, E. G. Hayes 53, Anderson 6-26) drew with Bendigo 55.

10th Match: v Australia (Melbourne)   Jan 1, 2, 3, 4, 6, 7.
Australia 266 (M. A. Noble 61, J. N. Crawford 5-79) & 397 (W. W. Armstrong 77, M. A. Noble 64, V. T. Trumper 63, C. G. Macartney 54, H. Carter 53, S. F. Barnes 5-72) lost to England 382 (K. L. Hutchings 126, J. B. Hobbs 83, A. Cotter 5-142) & 282-9 (F. L. Fane 50) by 1 wkt.

11th Match: v Australia (Adelaide)   Jan 10, 11, 13, 14, 15, 16.
Australia 285 (C. G. Macartney 75) & 506 (C. Hill 160, R. J. Hartigan 116, M. A. Noble 65) beat England 363 (G. Gunn 65, J. N. Crawford 62, J. Hardstaff 61) & 183 (J. Hardstaff 72, J. A. O'Connor 5-40, J. V. Saunders 5-65) by 245 runs.

12th Match: v Tasmnia (Launceston)   Jan 18, 20, 21.
M.C.C. 321 (J. B. Hobbs 104, J. Hardstaff 66, W. Richardson 5-87) & 249 (J. Hardstaff 85, J. B. Hobbs 65, E. A. Windsor 5-85) beat Tasmania 276 (T. A. Tabart 57, E. W. Harrison 54) & 174 (E. A. Windsor 75) by 120 runs.

13th Match: v Tasmania (Hobart)   Jan 24, 25, 27.
M.C.C. 455 (W. Rhodes 119, J. Hardstaff 106, F. L. Fane 62, J. B. Hobbs 58, K. L. Hutchings 51) drew with Tasmania 113 (L. C. Braund 5-55) & 317-8 (K. E. Burn 112, C. J. Eady 66, T. A. Tabart 55).

14th Match: v Victoria (Melbourne)   Feb 1, 3, 4.
M.C.C. 338 (J. Hardstaff 122, J. N. Crawford 69, G. H.S. Trott 5-116) & 241-4 dec (J. B. Hobbs 115, K. L. Hutchings 51) beat Victoria 77 (S. F. Barnes 5-32) & 172 (E. V. Carroll 61, S. F. Barnes 5-35) by 330 runs.

15th Match: v Australia (Melbourne)   Feb 7, 8, 10, 11.
Australia 214 (V. S. Ransford 51, J. N. Crawford 5-48) & 385 (W. W. Armstrong 133*, H. Carter 66, V. S. Ransford 54) beat England 105 (J. B. Hobbs 57, J. V. Saunders 5-28) & 186 by 308 runs.

16th Match: v New South Wales (Sydney)   Feb 14, 15, 17, 18, 19, 20.
M.C.C. 298 (K. L. Hutchings 73, R. A. Young 59, A. O. Jones 57*, L. A. Minnett 7-131) & 456 (L. C. Braund 132*, F. L. Fane 101, J. Hardstaff 73, W. Rhodes 58) drew with N.S.W. 368 (E. F. Waddy 107*, C. G. Macartney 96, A. J. Bowden 87, C. Blythe 5-93) & 375-9 (W. Bardsley 108, V. T. Trumper 74, E. F. Waddy 57, W. Rhodes 5-73).

17th Match: v Australia (Sydney)   Feb 21, 22, 24, 25, 26, 27.
Australia 137 (S. F. Barnes 7-60) & 422 (V. T. Trumper 166, S. E. Gregory 56, J. N. Crawford 5-141) beat England 281 (G. Gunn 122*, J. B. Hobbs 72) & 229 (W. Rhodes 69, J. V. Saunders 5-82) by 49 runs.

18th Match: v South Australia (Adelaide)   March 2, 3, 4.
M.C.C. 404 (G. Gunn 102, W. Rhodes 78*, F. L. Fane 59, J. N. Crawford 54, W. A. Hewer 5-149) & 134-4 (J. Hardstaff 63) drew with S. Australia 445 (C. E. Dolling 140, E. R. Mayne 74, L. C. Braund 6-149).

19th Match: v Western Australia (Perth)   March 13, 14, 16.
W. Australia 256 (C. Howard 69) & 265-7 (H. Rowe 105) drew with M.C.C. 362-7 dec (G. Gunn 122*, S. F. Barnes 93).

An M.C.C. selection to tour Australia for the 1907-08 tour. Top: P. A. Perrin, G. H. Hirst, J. W. H. T. Douglas, S. F. Barnes, A. Fielder. Centre: E. G. Arnold, W. Rhodes, A. O. Jones (captain), J. Humphries, T. W. Hayward. Front: C. Blythe, L. C. Braund, J. T. Tyldesley, A. F. A. Lilley, K. L. Hutchings. For one reason or another Hirst, Arnold, Hayward, Tyldesley and Lilley declined the invitations.

Below Three great Yorkshiremen who travelled on cricket tours, but never all together: S. Haigh, G. H. Hirst and W. Rhodes, photographed at a guest house near Huddersfield in 1905.

England strength, Foster, Hayward, Hirst, Tyldesley and Lilley were all asked but refused. For some reason C. B. Fry was not invited.

The *Ophir* arrived in Fremantle on 24 October and the first match took place in Perth, commencing 26 October – there had been a scratch game in Colombo, but since the touring side was composed of only five M.C.C. men, the other seven being passengers from the boat, it is not included as a tour match.

A record attendance welcomed the tourists on the inaugural match against Western Australia, and despite leaving the boat only 48 hours before the start, the M.C.C. found no difficulty in obtaining an innings victory. In Adelaide a second innings victory was achieved, though Rhodes' bowling was affected by an attack of tonsilitis. In the third game, against Victoria, the tourists were lucky to escape defeat, the last man going in with 10 minutes playing time remaining – at the other end Hardstaff batted in great form to carry out his bat for 95. New South Wales were convincingly beaten in the fourth game, the bowling of Barnes and Fielder removing the best state side for 101 and 96. 42,000 watched the

1907-08 : M.C.C. to Ceylon and Australia

Batting Averages

	M	I	NO	R	HS	Avge	100	c/s
G. Gunn (Notts)	11	18	3	817	122*	54.46	4	11
J. Hardstaff (Notts)	17	28	2	1360	135	52.30	3	5
W. Rhodes (Yorks)	17	27	8	929	119	48.89	2	8
J. B. Hobbs (Surrey)	13	22	1	876	115	41.71	2	8
A. O. Jones (Notts)	11	15	1	518	119	37.00	1	18
L. C. Braund (Som)	16	25	3	783	160	35.59	2	25
K. L. Hutchings (Kent)	17	28	0	953	126	34.03	1	23
F. L. Fane (Essex)	16	24	1	774	133	33.65	2	6
J. N. Crawford (Surrey)	16	24	1	610	114	26.52	1	15
S. F. Barnes (Staffs)	12	19	4	342	93	22.80	0	3
R. A. Young (Sussex)	10	15	0	260	59	17.33	0	15/7
A. Fielder (Kent)	10	16	8	134	50*	16.75	0	4
E. G. Hayes (Surrey)	11	14	0	230	98	16.42	0	9/1
C. Blythe (Kent)	11	14	1	145	27*	11.15	0	6
J. Humphries (Derbys)	10	13	1	92	16	7.66	0	18/4

Bowling Averages

	O	M	R	W	Avge	BB	5i
S. F. Barnes	534	145	1185	54	21.95	7-60	5
C. Blythe	393.2	97	935	41	22.80	6-48	3
A. Fielder	418.5	73	1208	50	24.16	6-27	4
J. N. Crawford	566	115	1663	66	25.19	5-40	4
J. B. Hobbs	39	8	128	4	32.00	2-14	8
L. C. Braund	434.5	63	1644	50	32.88	7-117	3
W. Rhodes	427.4	106	1069	31	34.48	5-73	1
E. G. Hayes	46	1	193	5	38.60	2-35	0
J. Hardstaff	29	7	86	2	43.00	1-12	0
G. Gunn	16	5	43	1	43.00	1-16	0
K. L. Hutchings	63.5	11	279	3	93.00	1-3	0

three days' play, 24,000 being present on the second. Queensland proved no match for the M.C.C., Blythe removing them cheaply and M.C.C. having another easy win. After this game A. O. Jones was taken ill and forced to miss the next eight matches, including three Tests. F. L. Fane took over the leadership, but Jones' illness was a bitter blow to the tourists. Rain ruined the match against An Australian Eleven and the side went on to Sydney for the first Test. A very close game was won by Australia by 2 wickets –

George Gunn was co-opted into the England team and hit the highest score in each England innings: 119 and 74. England were condemned for playing a batsman-wicketkeeper, Young, instead of Humphries, and indeed this made the difference between success and failure since Young made numerous wicket-keeping errors and scored only 13 and 3.

The second Test proved even more exciting than the first. England required 73 to win with two wickets remaining. Humphries and Barnes added 34 for the 9th wicket and against all the odds Fielder and Barnes made the other 39—Hazlitt should have run out Fielder as the tail-enders scrambled the winning run. The third Test at Adelaide followed directly on top of the second. England gained a substantial first innings lead, Australian wickets fell quickly in their second innings, but Hartigan and Hill joined forces in a splendid partnership of 243 which altered the whole match—unfortunately for England both batsmen were dropped early in their innings. Set 429 to win, the visitors never looked like making the runs, especially when Hobbs had to retire injured after scoring a single. Hardstaff with 72 put on a brave fight but in vain.

The team went to Tasmania and played two relaxing games on that island. The return against Victoria, which followed, was none too serious and won by 330 runs—the state fielded its second team. The fourth Test was vital for England, who made one change in their eleven; Jones came in as captain. Australia went in to bat on an easy wicket, but were bundled out by Crawford, whose variations of pace were too subtle for the Australian batsmen. Rain however then completely altered the nature of the wicket and England collapsed. When the home team went in a second time, the English bowlers however did not use the pitch to its full advantage and allowed the Australians to survive to continue their innings as the wicket eased. Armstrong hit a well-judged 100 and England required 495 to win—the tourists' batting simply fell apart and Australia won the rubber.

England won the toss in the fifth Test and Jones put Australia in. The decision seemed to pay off as the home side were shot out by Barnes and a first innings lead of 144 attained. Trumper played his best knock of the series in Australia's second innings and England were left requiring 279. The wicket however was not good and although it improved, by that time England's best batsmen had come and gone.

Drawn games with South Australia and Western Australia closed the tour. From England's viewpoint, the tour was a failure, but the difference between the two sides was not very great and one or two blunders by the English side made all the difference. The scoring was very slow and adversely commented upon by many critics, runs coming at only about 50 per hour.

The first of the tourists, Hobbs, Hardstaff and Gunn, arrived back in England on 13 April and most of the remainder the following day.

1909: the first tour to Egypt

The M.C.C. broke fresh ground when they organised a tour to Egypt in the spring of 1909. The main party left Tilbury aboard the R.M.S. *Omrah* on 19 February, whilst the remainder of the side joined the boat at Marseilles. The team, which played its first game on 4 March, consisted of: G. H. Simpson-Hayward (Worcs) (capt), G. T. Branston (Notts), C. H. M. Ebden (Middx); E. G. Wynyard (Hants), E. J. Metcalfe (Herts), R. M. Bell, K. L. Gibson (Essex), A. C. G. Luther (Sussex), Viscount Brackley, B. P. Dobson, A. V. Drummond and H. C. Moorhouse. The all-amateur team was not far below English first-class standard.

Eight matches were played, five of which were one-day games, but the three others against Egypt produced some good cricket, with the tourists winning the series by two to one. Luther was the team's best batsman, whilst Branston was the most effective bowler.

1909-10: Faulkner's performances win Test rubber for South Africa

After the failure of the M.C.C. tour to South Africa in 1905-06, the side chosen to tour in 1909-10 was stronger, but by no means up to the full England team—of the batsmen only Hobbs was worth his place in the best eleven. Several notable amateurs were asked to go but declined, including K. L. Hutchings, A. P. Day and C. B. Fry. The full team was H. D. G. Leveson-Gower (Surrey) (capt), F. L. Fane (Essex), G. H. T. Simpson-Hayward (Worcs), E. G. Wynyard (Hants), M. C. Bird (Surrey), N. C. Tufnell (Cambridge U), and the professionals J. B. Hobbs (Surrey), H. Strudwick (Surrey), F. E. Woolley (Kent), G. J. Thompson (Northants), D. Denton (Yorks), W. Rhodes (Yorks), C. Blythe (Kent) and C. P. Buckenham (Essex). The party left Southampton on R.M.S. *Saxon* on 6 November and arrived in Cape Town on 23 November.

Following a match against Sixteen Colts, the tourists met the current Currie Cup holders, Western Province, and overwhelmed them, Hobbs hitting 114 in 115 minutes and Thompson picking up 7 for 26 in the first innings—he did not bowl in the second. The tour progressed without a hitch until the fifth match at Johannesburg, where over 10,000 watched the first day and where Faulkner's splendid all-round cricket gave Transvaal victory by 308 runs.

This defeat was followed by another brilliant all-round performance by Faulkner to give South Africa victory in the first Test. In the two games Faulkner had innings of 46, 148*, 78 and 123 and bowling figures of 4-49, 5-34, 5-120, 3-40. At the end of the Test, Faulkner was carried shoulder high round the ground. The total attendance was 29,600. The next two games were both against Natal. In the first the home side had to thank two good innings by Nourse for saving the game. In the second Blythe took 7 for 20 to dismiss Natal in the opening innings for 50 and they never recovered.

The second Test provided a second win for the home country. England were set 348 to make in the final innings. Hobbs batted in excellent form, but Faulkner in the end was too good for both the Surrey maestro and most of the other Englishmen and the margin of the victory was 95 runs.

The M.C.C. had three easy games prior to meeting Transvaal. In the first of two matches, Denton hit a century in each innings

1st Match: v XVI Colts (Cape Town)   Dec 1, 2.
M.C.C. XII 320-7 dec (J. B. Hobbs 110, M. C. Bird 67) & 49-3 drew with Colts 223 (F. J. V. Hopley 96).

2nd Match: v Western Province (Cape Town)   Dec 4, 6.
M.C.C. 351 (J. B. Hobbs 114, M. C. Bird 76) beat W. Province 67 (G. J. Thompson 7-26) & 151 by an inns & 133 runs.

3rd Match: v XV of Griqualand West (Kimberley)   Dec 10, 11, 13.
M.C.C. XII 190 (E. G. Wynyard 58, C. P. Buckenham 54, A. Penny 6-65) & 251-6 dec (F. L. Fane 62*) beat Griqualand West 116 & 125 by 200 runs.

4th Match: v XV of Orange Free State (Bloemfontein)   Dec 15, 16, 17.
M.C.C. 231 (M. C. Bird 115, F. J. Wyatt 7-81) & 216-8 dec (J. B. Hobbs 55, F. E. Woolley 50) beat O.F.S. 112 & 135 by 200 runs.

5th Match: v The Reef (Vogelfontein)   Dec 21, 22, 23, 24.
M.C.C. 157 (A. E. E. Vogler 6-58) & 160-3 (W. Rhodes 56*) drew with The Reef 160 (S. J. Snooke 72).

6th Match: v Transvaal (Johannesburg)   Dec 27, 28, 29, 30.
Transvaal 260 (S. J. Snooke 59, R. O. Schwarz 50, G. J. Thompson 5-85) & 421-9 dec (G. A. Faulkner 148*, S. J. Snooke 64, J. W. Zulch 50) beat M.C.C. 196 (M. C. Bird 56) & 177 (D. Denton 63, G. A. Faulkner 5-34) by 308 runs.

7th Match: v South Africa (Johannesburg)   Jan 1, 3, 4, 5.
South Africa 208 (G. A. Faulkner 78, A. W. Nourse 53, G. H. Simpson-Hayward 6-43) & 345 (G. A. Faulkner 123) beat England 310 (J. B. Hobbs 89, W. Rhodes 66, A. E. E Vogler 5-87, G. A. Faulkner 5-120) & 224 (G. J. Thompson 63, A. E. E. Vogler 7-94) by 19 runs.

8th Match: v Natal (Durban)   Jan 8, 10, 11.
Natal 250 (A. W. Nourse 129, H. W. Taylor 55, W. Rhodes 5-43) & 162-8 (A. W. Nourse 54*) drew with M.C.C. 331 (J. B. Hobbs 163, W. Rhodes 64, L. R. Tuckett 7-77).

9th Match: v Natal (Pietermaritzburg)   Jan 14, 15, 17, 18.
Natal 50 (C. Blythe 7-20) & 203 lost to M.C.C. 229 (F. L. Fane 70, H. D. G. Leveson-Gower 56, S. V. Samuelson 5-90) & 26-1 by 9 wkts.

10th Match: v South Africa (Durban)   Jan 21, 22, 24, 25, 26.
South Africa 199 & 347 (G. C. White 118, A. W. Nourse 69, S. J. Snooke 53) beat England 199 (J. B. Hobbs 53, A. E. E. Vogler 5-83) & 252 (J. B. Hobbs 70, G. A. Faulkner 6-87) by 95 runs.

11th Match: v Border (East London)   Jan 29, 31, Feb 1.
Border 144 & 151 lost to M.C.C. 137 & 159-6 (J. B. Hobbs 70) by 4 wkts.

12th Match: v XV of North-Eastern District (Queenstown)   Feb 4, 5.
N-E District 81 & 95 lost to M.C.C. 239 (H. O. Yates 6-75) by an inns & 63 runs.

13th Match: v Eastern Province (Port Elizabeth)   Feb 11, 12.
E. Province 45 (C. Blythe 5-21) & 79 (G. H. Simpson-Hayward 5-14) lost to M.C.C. 263 (J. B. Hobbs 79) by an inns & 139 runs.

14th Match: v Transvaal (Johannesburg)   Feb 18, 19, 21.
M.C.C. 291 (D. Denton 139, G. C. White 5-42) & 271 (D. Denton 138, J. B. Hobbs 55) beat Transvaal 270 (G. C. White 71, J. W. Zulch 53) & 242 (F. le Roux 51*, C. P. Buckenham 6-92) by 50 runs.

15th Match: v Transvaal (Pretoria)   Feb 22, 23, 24.
Transvaal 371-3 (J. W. Zulch 176*, L. Stricker 101, F. le Roux 68*) – rain.

16th Match: v South Africa (Johannesburg)   Feb 26, 28, Mar 1, 2.
South Africa 305 (G. A. Faulkner 76, G. C. White 72, A. E. E. Vogler 65, C. P. Buckenham 5-115) & 237 (S. J. Snooke 52, G. H. Simpson-Hayward 5-69) lost to England 322 (D. Denton 104, F. E. Woolley 58*) & 221-7 (J. B. Hobbs 93*) by 3 wkts.

17th Match: v South Africa (Cape Town)   March 7, 8, 9.
England 203 (F. E. Woolley 69, M. C. Bird 57) & 178 (F. E. Woolley 64, A. E. E. Vogler 5-72) lost to South Africa 207 & 175-6 by 4 wkts.

18th Match: v South Africa (Cape Town)   March 11, 12, 14, 15.
England 417 (J. B. Hobbs 187, W. Rhodes 77, G. J. Thompson 51) & 16-1 beat South Africa 103 (C. Blythe 7-46) & 327 (G. A. Faulkner 99) by 9 wkts.

1909-10: M.C.C. to South Africa

Batting Averages

	M	I	NO	R	HS	Avge	100	c/s
J. B. Hobbs (Surrey)	11	18	1	1124	187	66.17	3	4
D. Denton (Yorks)	12	19	1	650	139	36.11	3	8
W. Rhodes (Yorks)	13	20	1	499	77	26.26	0	12
H. D. G. Leveson-Gower (Surrey)	10	13	2	259	56	23.54	0	4
G. J. Thompson (Northts)	12	18	2	342	63	21.37	0	5
F. L. Fane (Essex)	12	17	0	346	70	20.35	0	5
M. C. Bird (Surrey)	13	21	1	390	76	19.50	0	7
F. E. Woolley (Kent)	12	19	1	343	69	19.05	0	24
G. H. T. Simpson-Hayward (Worcs)	9	14	2	205	37*	17.08	0	4
C. Blythe (Kent)	10	12	8	60	14*	15.00	0	3
C. P. Buckenham (Essex)	8	13	2	75	22	6.81	0	5
E. G. Wynyard (Hants)	4	5	1	25	10*	6.25	0	7
N. C. Tufnell (Cambr U)	6	6	0	37	16	6.16	0	3/3
H. Strudwick (Surrey)	10	14	2	72	15	6.00	0	15/7
Hon R. Ponsonby	1	1	1	3	3*	—	0	0

Bowling Averages

	O	M	R	W	Avge	BB	5i
C. Blythe	382.3	120	783	50	15.66	7-20	3
G. H. T. Simpson-Hayward	262.2	39	714	40	17.85	6-43	2
M. C. Bird	76	16	217	10	21.70	3-11	0
C. P. Buckenham	301	49	839	37	22.67	6-92	2
G. J. Thompson	416	115	1093	48	22.77	7-26	2
W. Rhodes	192.5	47	535	21	25.47	5-43	1
F. E. Woolley	197.2	44	458	15	30.53	3-47	0
J. B. Hobbs	80.2	16	233	7	33.28	2-31	0
E. G. Wynyard	25	1	102	1	102.00	1-93	0

Also bowled: D. Denton 2-1-1-0; H. D. G. Leveson-Gower 4-0-16-0; N. C. Tufnell 3-0-19-0.

The failure to win the rubber was attributed to the batsmen being unaccustomed to matting wickets and the googly bowling with which most of the South Africans exploited these wickets.

The tour was financially a great success and the only problem which caused any headaches was the fact that certain of the tourists were employed as newspaper correspondents and the comments printed under their names during and directly after matches were not always as tactful as they might have been.

When the tour was officially ended Leveson-Gower with Fane, Bird and Simpson-Hayward went with seven South Africans to Rhodesia and played three matches, in Bulawayo, Gwelo and Salisbury.

1910-11: M.C.C. recover from bad start in the West Indies

The team that sailed in the R.M.S.P. *Clyde* on 18 January for the West Indies was a decidedly weak combination. A. C. Johnston, L. H. W. Troughton and G. J. Thompson had all withdrawn from the published side and only eleven players journeyed across the Atlantic in the name of the M.C.C. The press were extremely dubious about the party and a dispute between the shipping company and the Government nearly caused the tour to be abandoned. The team was A. W. F. Somerset (Sussex) (capt), A. P. F. C. Somerset (Sussex), T. A. L. Whittington (Glamorgan), S. G. Smith (Northants), B. H. Holloway (Sussex), D. C. F. Burton (Yorks), H. L. Gaussen and D. S. G. Burton, with the three professionals G. Brown (Hants), J. W. Hearne (Middx) and H. I. Young (Essex). Containing only three regular first-class county men, the team could barely be described as first-class by English standards.

The first three matches of the tour were played in Barbados, two against an island eleven and the third a 'Test Match' against West Indies. The first game, which was delayed by rain, was lost very easily, the tourists falling for 93 and 91. The second match was another massacre and the eleven tourists were reduced to ten by an injury to Holloway–Simpson of Demerera substituted. Owing to quarantine restrictions no Trinidad players could appear in the West Indies team for the 'First Test', but the M.C.C. were

to give M.C.C. a 50-run win. In the second Transvaal made 371 for 3 when rain prevented any further play. England had to win the third Test to save the rubber. The match was evenly balanced throughout, but Hobbs batted soundly after an uncertain start and carrying his bat for 93 not out took England to their first win of the series by 3 wickets.

The fourth Test at Newlands commenced four days after the end of the third. The pattern of the match was similar to its predecessor, but this time South Africa batted last and the irresistible Faulkner took his team to victory in Test and rubber with an undefeated 49–the touring captain, Leveson-Gower, stood down for both this Test and the next, the team being led by Fane.

Unusually the fifth Test followed straight on after the fourth and on the same ground. On a perfect wicket Hobbs and Rhodes gave England a marvellous start with 221 in 157 minutes for the first wicket and from then England remained in charge, though Faulkner hit 99 in the South Africa's second innings.

The last Test was the final match of the tour and the team sailed home on s.s. *Armadale Castle*, landing in Southampton on 2 April.

1910-11 : M.C.C. to West Indies

1st Match: v Barbados (Kensington Oval)   Feb 8, 9.
M.C.C. 93 & 91 (S. Worme 5-40) lost to Barbados 287 (H. B. G. Austin 85, C. A. Browne 66, A. P. F. C. Somerset 5-62) by an inns & 103 runs.

2nd Match: v Barbados (Kensington Oval)   Feb 10, 11.
M.C.C. 139 (C. R. Browne 6-60) & 191 (J. W. Hearne 50) lost to Barbados 352 (L. Archer 63, W. O. Gibbs 56, C. A. Browne 57) by an inns & 22 runs.

3rd Match: v West Indies (Kensington Oval)   Feb 15, 16, 17.
West Indies 271 (G. Challenor 75, H. I. Young 5-61) & 165 lost to M.C.C. 288 (B. H. Holloway 71) & 149-5 (S. G. Smith 54*) by 5 wkts.

4th Match: v British Guiana (Georgetown)   Feb 23, 24, 25.
M.C.C. 225 (T. A. L. Whittington 86) & 333-6 dec (T. A. L. Whittington 154, B. H. Holloway 100) beat British Guiana 190 (J. W. Hearne 5-100) & 133 (S. G. Smith 6-42) by 235 runs.

5th Match: v West Indies (Georgetown)   Feb 27, 28, Mar 1.
West Indies 172 (J. W. Hearne 6-91) & 272 (H. C. Bayley 59, O. Layne 59) lost to M.C.C. 301 (H. I. Young 73, S. G. Smith 59) & 144-6 by 4 wkts.

6th Match: v West Indian XI (Georgetown)   March 2, 3, 4.
West Indian XI 203 (C. V. Hunter 66, J. W. Hearne 6-76) & 224 (C. V. Hunter 58) drew with M.C.C. 332 (H. L. Gaussen 77, A. W. F. Somerset 60, T. A. L. Whittington 58, G. John 5-106, O. Layne 5-104) & 72-5.

7th Match: v Trinidad (St Clair)   March 7, 8, 9.
M.C.C. 90 (J. C. Rogers 5-18) & 127 lost to Trinidad 294 (A. Cipriani 135, J. C. Rogers 67) by an inns & 77 runs.

8th Match: v Trinidad (St Clair)   March 10, 11, 12.
M.C.C. 177 (D. C. F. Burton 57) & 162 (S. G. Smith 52, G. John 5-35) lost to Trinidad 216 (J. C. Rogers 74*, L. S. Constantine 53, J. W. Hearne 7-68) & 126-3 (A. Cipriani 65) by 7 wkts.

9th Match: v Jamaica (Kingston)   March 24, 25, 27.
Jamaica 263 (J. K. Holt 72, J. W. Hearne 6-89) & 310 (F. A. Foster 56, H. C. Duncker 55, J. W. Hearne 5-122) drew with M.C.C. 318 (T. A. L. Whittington 115*, D. C. F. Burton 51) & 51-2.

10th Match: v Jamaica (Kingston)   March 28, 29.
M.C.C. 103 (H. Kennedy 6-47) & 231 (J. W. Hearne 56) drew with Jamaica 153 (S. G. Smith 6-47) & 109-8.

11th Match: v Port Antonio (Port Antonio)   March 31, April 1.
M.C.C. 206 (H. I. Young 54) & 154-5 dec (S. G. Smith 56) beat Port Antonio 124 & 92 (J. W. Hearne 8-32) by 144 runs.*

12th Match: v Jamaica (Kingston)   April 3, 4, 5.
M.C.C. 269 (S. G. Smith 81, B. H. Holloway 59, O. Scott 6-77) & 131 (O. Scott 5-61) tied with Jamaica 173 (S. G. Smith 5-35) & 227.

now without D. C. F. Burton, and a local player substituted for him–happily Holloway had recovered, and in fact a good innings from him probably won the match, though Worme, the best West Indies bowler, had to retire with a broken finger, which aided the visitors' cause.

Moving on to British Guiana, the first match there began after three days of continuous rain. Brilliant batting by Whittington and Holloway however placed the tourists in an invincible position. The pair added 230 for the 1st wicket, a new record for the colony, and the game was won by 235 runs. Smith bowled quite splendidly in this match.

The 'Second Test' provided another victory for the M.C.C., Smith and Hearne bowling out the home side on a perfect wicket for 172, and with Young hitting 73 a substantial first innings lead

1910-11 : M.C.C. to West Indies

Batting Averages

	M	I	NO	R	HS	Avge	100	c/s
T. A. L. Whittington (Glam)	11	20	2	678	154	37.66	2	7
S. G. Smith (Norths)	11	21	3	547	81	30.38	0	6
B. H. Holloway (Sussex)	10	17	0	416	100	24.47	1	7
D. C. F. Burton (Yorks)	10	17	0	334	57	19.64	0	3
J. W. Hearne (Middx)	11	21	2	344	56	18.10	0	11
A. W. F. Somerset (Sussex)	11	17	5	214	60	17.83	0	6/2
G. Brown (Hants)	11	21	1	298	35	14.90	0	9/2
H. L. Gaussen	10	18	0	260	77	14.44	0	0
H. I. Young (Essex)	11	19	2	225	73	13.23	0	5
D. S. G. Burton	10	17	5	138	38*	11.50	0	2
A. P. F. C. Somerset	11	19	5	120	33	8.57	0	5

Also played in one match: L. Heath 15 & 12* (ct 2); C. Simpson 27 & 0 (ct 1); G. Liddlelow 13 & 5; E. L. G. N. Grell 25 & 17 (ct 1).

Bowling Averages

	O	M	R	W	Avge	BB	5i
S. G. Smith	300.2	57	845	47	17.97	6-42	3
H. I. Young	204	41	517	25	20.68	5-61	1
J. W. Hearne	398.4	62	1450	67	21.64	7-68	6
A. P. F. C. Somerset	144.3	15	558	24	23.35	5-62	1
G. Brown	106	15	409	9	45.44	3-26	0

was gained which led to a four-wicket win. Another match against West Indies was arranged in place of the return against British Guiana, but when Archer was dropped from the West Indies team, the two other Barbados players in the squad refused to play. The match was in fact drawn, very much in favour of the tourists.

Travelling to Trinidad, the tourists found themselves coming straight off the boat and on to the cricket field. In these circumstances, it is hardly surprising that they lost the match against Trinidad by an innings. The M.C.C. also lost the return, but having two men injured were forced to recruit two locals as substitutes. The remaining four games were in Jamaica. Rain was the cause for two drawn matches, but the final game ended in a tie.

Considering the difficulties faced by the tourists, the visit could be regarded as a limited success.

1911-12 : Hobbs and Rhodes make 323 for first wicket against Australia

The leading question of 1911 was, would C. B. Fry captain the M.C.C. team to Australia? The fact that Fry did not make up his mind whether he could go until the middle of August put the selectors in some difficulty and it was not until 18 August that it was announced that P. F. Warner (Middx) would lead the tourists. The remainder of the team was: J. W. H. T. Douglas (Essex), F. R. Foster (Warwicks) and the professionals J. B. Hobbs (Surrey), W. Rhodes (Yorks), F. E. Woolley (Kent), S. F. Barnes (Staffs), J. W. Hearne (Middx), G. Gunn (Notts), E. J. Smith (Warwicks), C. P. Mead (Hants), J. W. Hitch (Surrey), H. Strudwick (Surrey), S. Kinneir (Warwicks), J. Vine (Sussex), J. Iremonger (Notts) and T. Pawley (manager). Apart from Fry, only R. H. Spooner and G. L. Jessop declined the M.C.C.'s invitation. The team chosen was as strong as it was possible to obtain and there was little criticism, except perhaps at the absence of Hayward.

The side sailed from Tilbury on the s.s. *Orvieto* on 24 September. A match was played in Colombo and the Australian tour reverted to Adelaide for its opening, rather than Perth. The South Australians were completely outplayed, Warner, Gunn and Foster making hundreds, whilst Foster, Barnes and Douglas swept through the home batting. The match against Victoria was not so easy, but was eventually won by a narrow margin. The most disturbing news on the tour so far however was the illness that kept Warner out of the team. Rain ruined the third match– against New South Wales–and though Queensland did well in the first half of their match, they collapsed to Barnes and Foster in the second innings to provide M.C.C. with another win. The invalid list was however growing. It was stated that Warner could not play for some time, Gunn had a damaged hand and Hitch a strained groin. In the match between the M.C.C. and 'An Australian Eleven', the visitors' batting just folded up and was saved only by a splendid hundred from Douglas. The match, limited to three days was drawn, so that the M.C.C. came to the first Test unbeaten. In a high, but slow, scoring match England were outmanoeuvred from the time they lost the toss–Douglas, who led England in Warner's absence, was taken to task for not giving Barnes the first use of the ball in either innings. The best bat in England's second innings was Gunn, who played with his damaged hand bandaged. For Australia the feature of the play was Trumper's 113, made without a chance.

The second Test was played over the New Year. Barnes this time opened the English bowling and after 5 overs had four wickets for one run. The home team never recovered from this initial shock and though the English batting was a trifle shaky and Australia did much better the second time around, Hobbs played a masterly innings to take England to an unexpected victory. Australia had almost the same unfortunate start to the third Test, but this time the bowler was Foster, and on a perfect wicket only 133 were scored. Hobbs made another excellent hundred in England's first innings and he received support from nearly everyone, so that England built up a lead of colossal proportions. Australia batted very well in their second innings, but Trumper, being injured, could only make a token appearance and this told against the Australians, although England's advantage was so

Below *The M.C.C. party for Australia, 1911-12. Back: E. J. Smith, F. E. Woolley, S. F. Barnes, J. Iremonger, C. P. Mead, J. Vine, H. Strudwick. Centre: W. Rhodes, J. W. H. T. Douglas, P. F. Warner (captain), F. R. Foster, T. Pawley (manager), J. B. Hobbs, G. Gunn. Front: J. W. Hitch, J. W. Hearne. S. Kinneir was in the picture until the glass negative was broken.*
Bottom *Action from the second Test Match in Melbourne, 1911-12. This is Hordern pushing the bowling of England captain J. W. H. T. Douglas into the covers.*

1st Match: v Ceylon (Colombo) (One Day)   October 21.
M.C.C. 213 beat Ceylon 59 by 154 runs.

2nd Match: v South Australia (Adelaide)   Nov 10, 11, 13, 14.
M.C.C. 563 (F. R. Foster 158, P. F. Warner 151, G. Gunn 106) beat S. Australia 141 (C. Hill 51) & 228 (E. R. Mayne 84, J. N. Crawford 63, J. W. H. T. Douglas 5-65) by an inns & 194 runs.

3rd Match: v Victoria (Melbourne)   Nov 17, 18, 20, 21.
M.C.C. 318 (F. R. Foster 101) & 234 (J. B. Hobbs 88, W. Rhodes 66) beat Victoria 274 (H. L. Kortlang 74, D. B. M. Smith 68) & 229 (D. B. M. Smith 84) by 49 runs.

4th Match: v New South Wales (Sydney)   Nov 24, 25, 27, 28.
M.C.C. 238 (G. Gunn 50) drew with N.S.W. 198-8 (S. E. Gregory 66, R. B. Minnett 52*).

5th Match: v Queensland (Brisbane)   Dec 1, 2, 4.
Queensland 290 (C. B. Jennings 91, R. J. Hartigan 59) & 124 (F. R. Foster 6-31) lost to M.C.C. 275 (C. P. Mead 79, W. Rhodes 64*, J. W. Hearne 53) & 140-3 (C. P. Mead 54) by 7 wkts.

6th Match: v Toowoomba (Toowoomba)   Dec 6, 7.
M.C.C. 340-6 dec (F. E. Woolley 99, S. Kinneir 80, J. Iremonger 50*) beat Toowoomba 96 (J. W. H. T. Douglas 5-30) & 110 (A. H. Jones 54) by an inns & 134 runs.

7th Match: v An Australian XI (Brisbane)   Dec 8, 9, 11.
M.C.C. 267 (J. W. H. T. Douglas 101*, S. Kinneir 63) & 279-4 (J. W. Hearne 89*, C. P. Mead 50) drew with Australian XI 347 (J. N. Crawford 110, R. B. Minnett 69, C. Kelleway 66, S. F. Barnes 5-89).

8th Match: v Australia (Sydney)   Dec 15, 16, 18, 19, 20, 21.
Australia 447 (V. T. Trumper 113, R. B. Minnett 90, W. W. Armstrong 60) & 308 (C. Kelleway 70, C. Hill 65, F. R. Foster 5-92) beat England 318 (J. W. Hearne 76, J. B. Hobbs 63, F. R. Foster 56, H. V. Hordern 5-85) & 291 (G. Gunn 62, H. V. Hordern 7-90) by 146 runs.

9th Match: v XV of Bendigo (Bendigo)   Dec 26, 27.
M.C.C. 176 (J. B. Hobbs 67) & 188 (F. E. Woolley 64, W. Rhodes 50) drew with Bendigo 164 (J. W. Hitch 7-47).

10th Match: v Australia (Melbourne)   Dec 30, Jan 1, 2, 3.
Australia 184 (S. F. Barnes 5-44) & 299 (W. W. Armstrong 90, F. R. Foster 6-91) lost to England 265 (J. W. Hearne 114, W. Rhodes 61) & 219-2 (J. B. Hobbs 126*) by 8 wkts.

11th Match: v XV of Geelong (Geelong)   Jan 5, 6.
M.C.C. 285-8 dec (C. P. Mead 65, G. Gunn 51) & 118-4 drew with Geelong 277 (A. E. Liddicut 129).

12th Match: v Australia (Adelaide)   Jan 12, 13, 15, 16, 17.
Australia 133 (F. R. Foster 5-36) & 476 (C. Hill 98, H. Carter 72, W. Bardsley 63, T. J. Matthews 53, S. F. Barnes 5-105) lost to England 501 (J. B. Hobbs 187, F. R. Foster 71, W. Rhodes 59) & 112-3 (W. Rhodes 57*) by 7 wkts.

13th Match: v XV of Ballarat (Ballarat)   Jan 19, 20.
Ballarat 318 (M. Herring 129, E. Herring 55, J. Iremonger 7-66) drew with M.C.C. 349-2 (S. Kinneir 114, J. Vine 112*, J. B. Hobbs 74).

14th Match: v Tasmania (Launceston)   Jan 23, 24, 25.
Tasmania 217 (S. M. McKenzie 59, L. R. Tumilty 56, J. Iremonger 5-52) & 165 lost to M.C.C. 332 (C. P. Mead 98) & 56-2 by 8 wkts.

15th Match: v Tasmania (Hobart)   Jan 26, 27, 29.
Tasmania 124 & 355 (G. D. Paton 112, C. Martin 54, E. T. Boddam 52, J. F. Hudson 51) lost to M.C.C. 574-4 dec (F. E. Woolley 305*, W. Rhodes 102, J. W. Hearne 97) by an inns & 95 runs.

16th Match: v Victoria (Melbourne)   Feb 2, 3, 5, 6.
M.C.C. 467 (J. W. Hearne 143, J. W. H. T. Douglas 140) & 43-2 beat Victoria 195 (W. W. Armstrong 51*) & 314 (W. W. Armstrong 120*, C. McKenzie 78) by 8 wkts.

17th Match: v Australia (Melbourne)   Feb 9, 10, 12, 13.
Australia 191 (R. B. Minnett 56, S. F. Barnes 5-74) & 173 (J. W. H. T. Douglas 5-46) lost to England 589 (J. B. Hobbs 178, G. Gunn 75, F. E. Woolley 56, F. R. Foster 50) by an inns & 225 runs.

18th Match: v New South Wales (Sydney)   Feb 16, 17, 19, 20.
N.S.W. 106 (F. R. Foster 7-36) & 403 (S. E. Gregory 186*, S. H. Emery 65, V. T. Trumper 53) lost to M.C.C. 315 (W. Rhodes 119, G. R. Hazlitt 7-95) & 195-2 (W. Rhodes 109, G. Gunn 56*) by 8 wkts.

19th Match: v Australia (Sydney)   Feb 23, 24, 26, 27, 28, March 1.
England 324 (F. E. Woolley 133*, G. Gunn 52, H. V. Hordern 5-95) & 214 (G. Gunn 61, H. V. Hordern 5-66) beat Australia 176 & 292 (R. B. Minnett 61, V. T. Trumper 50) by 70 runs.

Batting Averages

	M	I	NO	R	HS	Avge	100	c/s
P. F. Warner (Middx)	1	1	0	151	151	151.00	1	0
F. E. Woolley (Kent)	14	18	4	781	305*	55.78	2	14
J. B. Hobbs (Surrey)	11	18	1	943	187	55.47	3	8
W. Rhodes (Yorks)	14	24	4	1098	179	54.90	4	11
G. Gunn (Notts)	9	15	2	665	106	51.15	1	8
J. W. Hearne (Middx)	13	22	4	808	143	44.88	2	5
F. R. Foster (Warks)	13	19	1	641	158	35.61	2	7
J. W. H. T. Douglas (Essex)	12	15	3	416	140	34.66	2	5
C. P. Mead (Hants)	13	18	2	531	98	33.18	0	4
S. Kinneir (Warks)	5	8	0	219	63	27.42	0	1
H. Strudwick (Surrey)	7	7	3	68	28	17.00	0	13/4
E. J. Smith (Warks)	7	9	0	124	47	13.77	0	16/2
S. F. Barnes (Staffs)	13	14	3	126	35	11.45	0	7
J. W. Hitch (Surrey)	8	9	2	79	33*	11.28	0	3
J. Vine (Sussex)	8	9	2	78	36	11.14	0	3
J. Iremonger (Notts)	6	7	0	57	31	8.14	0	4

Bowling Averages

	O	M	R	W	Avge	BB	5i
J. B. Hobbs	18.1	3	62	5	12.40	4-25	0
F. R. Foster	485.1	110	1252	62	20.19	7-36	5
J. W. Hitch	169.4	23	548	27	20.29	4-41	0
S. F. Barnes	472.2	118	1231	59	20.86	5-44	4
J. W. H. T. Douglas	316.5	74	803	37	21.70	5-46	2
F. E. Woolley	156.1	27	503	17	29.58	3-71	0
J. Iremonger	159.5	45	397	12	33.08	5-52	1
J. Vine	38.1	5	182	4	45.50	2-36	0
J. W. Hearne	168.3	12	701	14	50.07	4-66	0

Also bowled: W. Rhodes 62-9-234-0.
Played in non-first-class matches only: W. J. H. Curwen.

crowd had gathered at the railway station to welcome them.

In explaining the success of the England side, P. F. Warner attributed it in some part to internal strife and bitterness in Australian cricket. On the field however the bowling of Barnes and Foster was undoubtedly the great match winner. Douglas gave the leading pair excellent support, but the other bowlers were of little account. Hitch suffered from injury and Hearne could not keep a length, whilst Vine's leg-breaks were easy meat and Iremonger was only of use as a defensive bowler. The fielding was good—Hobbs superb in the covers, Gunn and Woolley safe in the slips, Rhodes useful anywhere and Barnes not as absent-minded as he sometimes looked. Hobbs and Rhodes were the principal batsmen, but Gunn was very sound in his individual manner. The way in which Smith read the bowling of Foster meant that the Warwickshire stumper was preferred to Strudwick.

The Test series was the last in which the great Victor Trumper played, for he refused to tour England with the 1912 Australian team. The season was not a success for him, save for the century in the first Test, and in fact none of the Australian batsmen had much of a record in 1911-12. The best home bowler by a mile was Hordern, who was the only man to average less than 30 runs per wicket.

large that even Trumper could not have altered the result.

The tourists went off to Tasmania leading two to one in the rubber and they came back to clinch the series at Melbourne. Australia were put in on a soft wicket and fell cheaply to Barnes and Foster. Hobbs made yet another hundred and with Rhodes added 323 for the first English wicket. The Australian batting broke down in the second innings, leaving the tourists victors by an innings and 225 runs.

The final Test went into the seventh day due to rain and Australia made some drastic changes in their eleven, but the English team was always in control and thus won the series by four matches to one. There were no other fixtures after the last Test. The team returned home, and taking the overland route from Toulon arrived at Charing Cross on 7 April, where a big

1911-12: M.C.C. play three 'Tests' in the Argentine

At the invitation of the Argentine, the M.C.C. sent over a fairly strong amateur team in the winter of 1911-12. The large English community in the Argentine had developed a good standard of club cricket during the closing years of the 19th century and a body to control cricket in the country was set up. Several cricketers living in the Argentine had had some experience of county cricket in England and the feature of the tour was the series of 'Tests'.

The touring party comprised Lord Hawke (Yorks) (capt), A. C. MacLaren (Lancs), C. E. de Trafford (Leics), A. J. L. Hill (Hants), M. C. Bird (Surrey), W. Findlay (Surrey secretary), E. R. Wilson (Yorks), N. C. Tufnell (Cambridge U), C. E. Hatfeild (Kent), L. H. W. Troughton (Kent), E. J. Fulcher (Norfolk) and Capt H. H. C. Baird (Army). Sailing on the s.s.

A strong amateur side under Lord Hawke went to Argentina in 1912. This team was, back: J. O. Anderson (umpire), Capt H. H. C. Baird, N. C. Tufnell, E. R. Wilson, C. E. Hatfeild, W. Findlay. Front: L. H. W. Troughton, M. C. Bird, C. E. de Trafford, Lord Hawke, A. C. MacLaren, A. J. L. Hill.

Asturias from Southampton on 26 January, the side played its first match on 13 and 14 February. Both this and the second game were drawn due to high scoring, but in the 'First Test', M.C.C. fared badly against Dorning and Foy and some consistent batting by the home team led to an Argentine win by 4 wickets.

The tourists had their revenge in the 'Second Test'. Hill and Bird hit up 106 for the second wicket in the first innings and Bird was again in form in the second innings, and needing 310 to win in the final innings, Argentine collapsed before the bowling of Wilson and were all out for 100.

In the 'Third Test', MacLaren led the M.C.C., due to Lord Hawke being injured. The match was very even throughout, and although M.C.C. only needed 102 to win in the last innings, a determined knock by MacLaren was required to save the day and M.C.C. won by just two wickets.

The nine-match tour, though it created little interest in England, did a great deal to encourage cricket in the Argentine – it was regretted that the tourists did not have time for a brief visit to Chile.

The side arrived back in England on 6 April, except for Lord Hawke, who remained in South America, C. E. de Trafford, who went on to the West Indies and W. Findlay, who had travelled by an earlier boat.

1912-13: Barbados, but not the West Indies, beat M.C.C.

For a second winter A. W. F. Somerset (Sussex) captained the M.C.C. team to West Indies and was accompanied by four of the previous side – his son, A. P. F. C. Somerset (Sussex), S. G. Smith (Northants), T. A. L. Whittington (Glamorgan) and D. C. F. Burton (Yorks). The other members of the side were three professionals, E. Humphreys (Kent), A. E. Relf (Sussex) and W. C. Smith (Surrey), and the amateurs G. A. M. Docker, M. H. C. Doll (Middx), B. P. Dobson, A. Jaques (Hants), S. G. Fairbairn (Bucks). The side was a little stronger than its predecessor, and sailing in the R.M.S. *Magdalena* it reached Barbados on 27 January. The first game, against the island team, commenced three days later. Barbados were without P. A. Goodman, injured, and H. B. G. Austin but still thrashed the tourists, whose bowling was torn apart. The medicine was repeated in the return game – another innings defeat. As however had happened on a previous visit to the West Indies as a whole proved weaker than in part, and the M.C.C. won the 'First Test' by 9 wickets. The representative eleven did not include any Jamaican players, but five from Barbados, three from Trinidad and one each from British Guiana, St Vincent and Grenada. The English side owed their victory to some capital bowling by Humphreys, who took 13 wickets.

Voyaging to Trinidad, the tourists beat the local side by 8 wickets, but were lucky to draw the return, after being dismissed for 87 in their first innings and being forced to follow on 247 in arrears. Many fielding errors led to an English defeat in the

1911-12: M.C.C. to the Argentine

1st Match: v Southern Suburbs (Los Talleres) Feb 13, 14.
M.C.C. 439 (C. E. de Trafford 116, L. H. W. Troughton 71) drew with Southern Suburbs 202 (C. P. Russ 54) & 274-8 (S. A. Cowper 182).

2nd Match: v Combined Camps (Hurlingham) Feb 15, 16.
M.C.C. 109 (C. M. Horsfall 5-21) & 489-7 (L. H. W. Troughton 112*, J. O. Anderson 89, W. Findley 69, Lord Hawke 54) drew with Combined Camps 162 (J. R. Garrod 88).

3rd Match: v Argentine (Hurlingham) Feb 18, 19, 20.
M.C.C. 186 (E. R. Wilson 67*, H. Dorning 6-65) & 157 (L. H. W. Troughton 59*, P. A. Foy 5-49) lost to Argentine 209 & 136-6 by 4 wkts.

4th Match: v Northern Suburbs (Belgrano) Feb 22, 23.
M.C.C. 181 & 300-6 dec (A. J. L. Hill 60, E. R. Wilson 52) beat Northern Suburbs 204 (C. E. Hatfeild 5-42) & 129 (H. H. C. Baird 6-50) by 148 runs.

5th Match: v Argentine (Palermo) Feb 24, 25, 26.
M.C.C. 266 (M. C. Bird 74, E. J. Fulcher 51) & 250 (M. C. Bird 61) beat Argentine 206 & 100 (E. R. Wilson 6-36) by 210 runs.

6th Match: v South (Buenos Aires) Feb 28, 29.
South 137 (N. W. Jackson 51, E. R. Wilson 5-45) & 192 (N. W. Jackson 79, C. E. Hatfeild 5-47) lost to M.C.C. 409-9 dec (E. R. Wilson 105, C. E. Hatfeild 90, C. E. de Trafford 51) by an inns & 80 runs.

7th Match: v Argentine (Lomas) March 2, 3.
Argentine 171 (H. G. Garnett 51*) & 98 lost to M.C.C. 169 (P. A. Foy 7-84) & 102-8 (P. A. Foy 5-42) by 2 wkts.

8th Match: v Argentine-born (Hurlingham) March 6, 7.
Argentine-born 123 (C. E. Hatfeild 7-46) & 167 (C. E. Hatfeild 6-75) lost to M.C.C. 387-4 dec (A. C. MacLaren 172, N. C. Tufnell 163*) by an inns & 97 runs.

9th Match: v North (Rosario) March 9, 10.
North 226 (H. A. Cowes 56, E. R. Wilson 6-66) & 41 (E. R. Wilson 8-10) lost to M.C.C. 209 (A. C. MacLaren 64, P. A. Foy 5-68) & 60-4 by 6 wkts.

'Second Test'. The M.C.C. captain very sportingly allowed Cumberbatch to continue his innings after he had been clean bowled – the batsman's attention had been distracted by leaves blowing across the ground.

A tricky wicket greeted the team in Georgetown, but they won a very low scoring game by 66 runs. In the 'Third Test', the home team was not fully represented and on a docile wicket, the West Indies bowling, which was virtually all fast, suffered greatly. The M.C.C. therefore won the three-match series and the local journalists rather amusingly wrote of 'the Ashes going home'. The tourists ended the tour in splendid style with an innings victory against British Guiana, Humphreys bowling well on an easy pitch. Indeed the all-round performances of Humphreys were the feature of the tour, though Relf ran him a close second.

The captain regretted that the team did not visit Jamaica, but he pointed out that it was a nine-day voyage to that island from the rest of the British West Indies and such a break in the tour programme was impractical.

1913: Incogniti tour the United States

Under the leadership of Col C. E. Greenway, the Incogniti C.C. toured the United States in September 1913. Virtually all the side had experience in first-class county cricket and the team might be regarded as just about 'first-class' by English standards. The full party was Col C. E. Greenway, W. G. M. Sarel (Surrey), the Hon H. G. H. Mulholland (Cambridge U), G. R. R. Colman (Oxford U), M. Falcon (Cambridge U), C. L. St J. Tudor (Sussex), C. E. Hatfeild (Kent), B. G. von B. Melle (Hants), E. J. Metcalfe, D. M. P. Whitcombe, P. Collins and B. P. Dobson.

The tour opened in Philadelphia, where the English team declared in their second innings against Germantown C.C., setting the home side 241 in 120 minutes – the match ended with the total 168 for 5. The second game was against another club side, Merion, who were beaten by an innings, Falcon giving a great all-round display. New York were also defeated by an innings and then came the first of the two important matches of the tour, against Philadelphia. Despite lacking J. B. King and P. H. Clark, the Philadelphians won by 3 wickets. For some reason the Philadelphians made eight changes in the return match, though King and Clark still could not play, and this weakened side lost by 8 wickets. Hatfeild bowled well for the tourists.

The visit ended with a club game against Philadelphia C.C. J. B. King played for the locals and bowled brilliantly taking 12 for 95 in the match. Falcon however improved even on this by skittling out Philadelphia in their second innings for 61 and returning figures of 8 for 14, thus bringing victory by 77 runs.

1913-14: Barnes' haul of wickets in South Africa

The South African authorities raised guarantees worth over £5,000 to enable the M.C.C. tourists to visit them in 1913-14, but, prior to the visit, the home press felt that the South African players would not prove a match for the Englishmen. Rhodesia was again not on the itinerary because the clubs there could not raise the funds to finance the matches.

The M.C.C., after the failure of the team sent in 1909-10, made a great effort to secure the strongest possible side and, apart from refusals by Jessop and P. R. Johnson, the team was as selected. The party was made up of J. W. H. T. Douglas (Essex) (capt), M. C. Bird (Surrey), the Hon L. H. Tennyson (Hants), D. C. Robinson (Gloucs) and the professionals J. B. Hobbs (Surrey), C. P. Mead (Hants), J. W. Hearne (Middx), F. E. Woolley (Kent),

W. Rhodes (Yorks), M. W. Booth (Yorks), H. Strudwick (Surrey), A. E. Relf (Sussex) and S. F. Barnes (Staffs).

On arrival in South Africa, the team suffered a blow when D. C. Robinson, the reserve wicket-keeper fell ill, and as it was unlikely that he would recover in time to play any matches, E. J. Smith (Warwicks) was sent for and arrived in time to appear in the eighth match.

The opening game against Western Province at Newlands saw the tourists still recovering from their voyage. P. T. Lewis hit 151

in 185 minutes for the home side, his innings being the feature of a drawn game. The most important match prior to the first Test was the meeting with Natal. H. W. Taylor played a splendid innings for the Province, carrying out his bat for 83 out of 124. Hobbs also batted in good form, but rain cut the playing time by half and the match was drawn. In the first Test, Taylor repeated his Natal innings, hitting 109 for South Africa out of a total of 182 — no one else could master Barnes. England, aided by several dropped catches, hit 450 and went on to an innings victory. The match against Transvaal followed the same pattern and so did the second Test, though here Barnes' figures created a new record, as he dismissed no less than 17 batsmen — the report of the game noted he bowled with 'great devil'. The English batting collapsed after an excellent start, but this made little difference to the outcome of the match. The third Test began with just a single day separating it from the second, and both were staged at Johannesburg. England won the toss and Hobbs and Rhodes got the visitors off to a fine start, but the later batting failed again, with Blanckenberg bowling very effectively. South Africa's batsmen managed to contain Barnes only to fall to Hearne, who took 5 for 49. England scored more consistently in their second innings and South Africa required 396 in the final innings. Taylor and Zulch made an excellent stand for the first wicket to take the total to 153, but the middle order failed and England won by 91 runs — for South Africa the match was a vast improvement.

A general strike caused problems during the next two games in Transvaal and there was little public interest. Both Griqualand West and Orange Free State were too weak to worry the M.C.C. Transvaal, however, in their return did much better and Barnes, for once, suffered, with Beaumont batting particularly well. The game was drawn. For the local sides, matters improved when Natal, in their return game, beat the M.C.C. by 4 wickets. The defeat was due to two splendid innings from H. W. Taylor — 91 out of 153 and 100 out of 216-6 — and a lack-lustre batting performance by M.C.C., who, without Hobbs, looked rather poor.

Although England had won the rubber, Natal's victory gave South Africa some confidence for the fourth Test, which followed. South Africa went in first and once more collapsed to Barnes, but the South African left-arm bowler, Carter, going round the wicket against a strong wind, completely baffled the English batting, and the home country obtained a first innings lead. A masterly innings by H. W. Taylor then increased the South African advantage and England were set to make 313. Hobbs and Rhodes put on 133

1913-14: M.C.C. to South Africa

1st Match: v Western Province (Cape Town) Nov 8, 9, 11.
W. Province 376 (P. T. Lewis 151, F. D. Conry 53, A. E. Relf 5-67) drew with M.C.C. 199 (J. B. Hobbs 72) & 330 (J. W. Hearne 83, J. B. Hobbs 80, J. W. H. T. Douglas 61, J. M. Blanckenberg 5-91).

2nd Match: v XV of South-Western Districts (Robertson) Nov 14, 15.
M.C.C. 382-7 dec (J. B. Hobbs 107, C. P. Mead 78, M. C. Bird 61) beat S-W Districts 158 (A. de Villiers 74*, F. E. Woolley 5-62) & 136 (W. Rhodes 6-44) by an inns & 88 runs.

3rd Match: v XV of South-Western Districts (Oudtshoorn) Nov 17, 18.
S-W Districts 104 & 93 (S. F. Barnes 7-11) lost to M.C.C. 257 (W. Rhodes 70) by an inns & 60 runs.

4th Match: v Cape Province (Port Elizabeth) Nov 21, 22.
M.C.C. 385 (J. B. Hobbs 170) beat Cape Province 158 & 60 (S. F. Barnes 7-25) by an inns & 167 runs.

5th Match: v XV of Grahamstown & Colleges (Grahamstown) Nov 26, 27.
M.C.C. 321-5 dec (C. P. Mead 84, W. Rhodes 64, A. E. Relf 64*) beat Grahamstown & Colleges 112 & 176 (S. F. Barnes 8-35).

6th Match: v Border (East London) Nov 29, Dec 1, 2.
M.C.C. 356-8 dec (J. W. H. T. Douglas 102*, J. B. Hobbs 57, M. W. Booth 57) beat Border 121 (C. Johnson 51) & 103 (M. W. Booth 5-24) by an inns & 132 runs.

7th Match: v Border (Kingwilliamstown) Dec 3, 4.
M.C.C. 204 (L. H. Tennyson 66) & 163-4 (F. E. Woolley 55) drew with Border 126 & 159-6 (S. G. Fuller 72, R. H. Randall 71).

8th Match: v Natal (Pietermaritzburg) Dec 8, 9, 10.
Natal 124 (H. W. Taylor 83*, F. E. Woolley 5-64) & 69-0 drew with M.C.C. 219-7 dec (J. W. H. T. Douglas 70*, J. B. Hobbs 66, J. L. Cox 6-41).

9th Match: v South Africa (Durban) Dec 13, 15, 16, 17.
South Africa 182 (H. W. Taylor 109, S. F. Barnes 5-57) & 111 (S. F. Barnes 5-48) lost to England 450 (J. W. H. T. Douglas 119, J. B. Hobbs 82, M. C. Bird 61, L. H. Tennyson 52) by an inns & 157 runs.

10th Match: v Transvaal (Johannesburg) Dec 20, 22, 23.
Transvaal 202 (R. Beaumont 62) & 196 (R. Beaumont 52) lost to M.C.C. 427-8 dec (J. B. Hobbs 102, F. E. Woolley 116, M. C. Bird 67) by an inns & 29 runs.

11th Match: v South Africa (Johannesburg) Dec 26, 27, 29, 30.
South Africa 160 (G. P. D. Hartigan 51, S. F. Barnes 8-56) & 231 (A. W. Nourse 56, S. F. Barnes 9-103) lost to England 403 (W. Rhodes 152, C. P. Mead 102, A. E. Relf 63, J. M. Blanckenberg 5-83) by an inns & 12 runs.

12th Match: v South Africa (Johannesburg) Jan 1, 2, 3, 5.
England 238 (J. B. Hobbs 92) & 308 (C. P. Mead 86, J. W. H. T. Douglas 77) beat South Africa 151 (J. W. Hearne 5-49) & 304 (J. W. Zulch 82, H. W. Taylor 70, J. M. Blanckenberg 59, S. F. Barnes 5-102) by 91 runs.

13th Match: v Transvaal (Pretoria) Jan 9, 10, 12.
Transvaal 245 (D. J. Meintjes 87, F. le Roux 69) & 21-2 drew with M.C.C. 330 (C. P. Mead 145, J. W. H. T. Douglas 73, F. le Roux 6-64).

14th Match: v A Transvaal XI (Vogelfontein) Jan 14, 15.
Transvaal XI 170 (L. J. Tancred 68) drew with M.C.C. 350-4 dec. (J. B. Hobbs 137, J. W. Hearne 96, A. E. Relf 55*).

15th Match: v Griqualand West (Kimberley) Jan 17, 19.
M.C.C. 346 (J. B. Hobbs 141, J. W. Hearne 81) beat Griqualand West 75 (S. F. Barnes 5-22, A. E. Relf 5-24) & 170 (W. V. Ling 63, S. F. Barnes 5-22) by an inns & 101 runs.

16th Match: v Orange Free State (Bloemfontein) Jan 23, 24, 25.
M.C.C. 565-8 dec (M. C. Bird 200, J. W. Hearne 108, W. Rhodes 68, J. W. H. T. Douglas 51) beat O.F.S. 117 (S. F. Barnes 7-41) & 74 (S. F. Barnes 6-38) by an inns & 374 runs.

17th Match: v Transvaal (Johannesburg) Jan 30, 31, Feb 1.
M.C.C. 386 (J. W. Hearne 136, W. Rhodes 62) & 211-0 dec (J. B. Hobbs 131*, W. Rhodes 76*) drew with Transvaal 347 (F. le Roux 66, R. Beaumont 65, J. W. Zulch 62, L. J. Tancred 56) & 145-6.

18th Match: v XV of Northern Natal (Ladysmith) Feb 4, 5.
Northern Natal 94 & 141-8 (D. Taylor jun 81) drew with M.C.C. 289-4 dec (A. E. Relf 106, L. H. Tennyson 105).

19th Match: v Natal (Durban) Feb 7, 9, 10.
M.C.C. 132 & 235 (C. P. Carter 6-58) lost to Natal 153 (H. W. Taylor 91, S. F. Barnes 5-44) & 216-6 (H. W. Taylor 100, A. W. Nourse 59) by 4 wkts.

20th Match: v South Africa (Durban) Feb 14, 16, 17, 18.
South Africa 170 (P. A. M. Hands 51, S. F. Barnes 7-56) & 305-9 dec (H. W. Taylor 93, S. F. Barnes 7-88) drew with England 163 (J. B. Hobbs 64, C. P. Carter 6-50) & 154-5 (J. B. Hobbs 97).

21st Match: v South Africa (Port Elizabeth) Feb 27, 28, March 2, 3.
South Africa 193 (P. A. M. Hands 83) & 228 (H. W. Taylor 87, J. W. Zulch 60) lost to England 411 (C. P. Mead 117, F. E. Woolley 54) & 11-0 by 10 wkts.

22nd Match: v Western Province (Cape Town) March 7, 9, 10.
M.C.C. 322 (J. W. H. T. Douglas 93) & 177-4 dec drew with W. Province 210 (M. Commaille 52, J. W. Hearne 7-78) & 178-9 (P. T. Lewis 59).

1913-14: M.C.C. to South Africa

Batting Averages

	M	I	NO	R	HS	Avge	100	c/s
J. B. Hobbs (Surrey)	16	22	2	1489	170	74.75	5	13
J. W. H. T. Douglas (Essex)	18	21	5	827	119	51.68	2	12
J. W. Hearne (Middx)	12	16	1	695	136	46.33	2	9
C. P. Mead (Hants)	16	19	0	745	145	39.21	3	5
W. Rhodes (Yorks)	17	24	3	731	152	34.80	1	29
M. W. Booth (Yorks)	12	14	4	291	57	29.10	0	1
M. C. Bird (Surrey)	17	21	2	551	200	29.00	1	15
F. E. Woolley (Kent)	18	23	1	595	116	27.04	1	29
E. J. Smith (Warks)	8	8	2	146	36	24.33	0	6/1
Hon L. H. Tennyson (Hants)	18	24	0	498	66	20.75	0	10
A. E. Relf (Sussex)	18	21	2	310	55*	16.31	0	22
H. Strudwick (Surrey)	14	13	4	86	26	9.55	0	23/7
S. F. Barnes (Staffs)	12	14	7	49	20*	7.00	0	7
W. H. Crease	1	1	0	2	2	2.00	0	0
R. R. Relf (Sussex)	1	1	1	14	14*	—	0	2

Bowling Averages

	O	M	R	W	Avge	BB	5i
S. F. Barnes	460.2	129	1117	104	10.74	9-103	13
C. P. Mead	8	1	35	2	17.50	2-35	0
J. W. H. T. Douglas	181	31	531	30	17.70	4-14	0
M. C. Bird	53	10	171	9	19.00	3-20	0
M. W. Booth	188	31	530	26	20.38	5-24	1
W. Rhodes	235.1	53	662	31	21.35	4-27	0
A. E. Relf	380.2	109	856	40	21.40	5-24	2
F. E. Woolley	258.3	61	717	33	21.72	6-41	1
J. W. Hearne	209.5	32	724	27	26.81	7-78	2
Hon L. H. Tennyson	14	1	76	1	76.00	1-2	0

Also bowled: J. B. Hobbs 1-0-4-0; E. J. Smith 3-0-21-0; H. Strudwick 3-0-27-0.
Played in non-first-class matches only: I. D. Difford, G. P. Harrison.

before the first English wicket fell and the match faded to a draw. The teams went straight from the fourth Test to Port Elizabeth for the fifth. Barnes was too ill to play and thus South Africa were in a strong position to win this last game. The wicket at Port Elizabeth proved much faster than those for the previous matches and this seemed to upset the South African batsmen, whilst suiting the Englishmen. England won by 10 wickets.

The last match of the tour took place at Cape Town, being the return with Western Province. The home team just managed to bat out time to save the game.

The two outstanding figures of the tour were Hobbs and Barnes. Hobbs was perhaps not as brilliant as on his previous tour to South Africa, but his wicket was probably harder to take, whilst Barnes exploited his wonderful length and variation of spin to its full and it needed exceptional footwork on the part of the batsman to score from him. Rhodes, Relf and Douglas were the other successes of the tour, but Mead, Hearne and Woolley never really lived up to their English reputations. Booth suffered in a motor accident just prior to the first Test and never recovered his form, whilst Bird had few opportunities. The fielding was generally of a high standard, with Hobbs and Tennyson, who disappointed with the bat, brilliant in the out-field.

South Africa missed the great quartette of Schwarz, Vogler, Faulkner and Pegler, all of whom had moved to England. Young Blanckenberg could not make up for the loss of these, but he tried very hard and had some success. The bouquet for batting went to Taylor, whose footwork against Barnes was a revelation. Of the others Zulch and later, P. A. M. Hands, did useful work.

1920: Incogniti unbeaten in the United States and Canada

The following side toured North America in 1920: E. J. Metcalfe (Herts) (capt), T. A. L. Brocklebank, R. C. Brooks, G. H. M. Cartwright, R. St L. Fowler (Hants), D. R. Jardine (Surrey), E. C. Lee (Hants), T. C. Lowry (Cambridge U), J. S. F. Morrison (Somerset), D. Roberts, G. O. Shelmerdine (Cambridge U), E. G. Wynyard (Hants) and M. B. Burrows (Surrey).

Playing nine matches in all, the Incogniti won seven and drew the other two. The two principal matches were against All Philadelphia, over three days each. Both were won.

Fowler was the outstanding player, taking 44 wickets at 10.70 each and scoring 294 runs at an average of 42.00. Jardine hit two centuries, both in New York.

The team sailed to America on the *Mauretania* on 21 August and returned on the same boat on 30 September.

1920: Incogniti to United States and Canada

1st Match: v Frankford (St Martin's)   Aug 31, Sept 1.
Incogniti 282 beat Frankford 147 & 114 by an inns & 21 runs.

2nd Match: v Philadelphia C.C. (St Martin's)   Sept 3, 4.
Philadelphia 255 & 120 lost to Incogniti 406-7 dec (G. O. Shermadine 143) by inns & 31 runs.

3rd Match: v Merion (Haverford)   Sept 6, 7.
Merion 192 & 93-5 drew with Incogniti 317-6 dec.

4th Match: v New York XI (Haverford)   Sept 8, 9.
Incogniti 375-6 dec (D. R. Jardine 157) beat New York XI 150 & 89 by an inns & 136 runs.

5th Match: v All Philadelphia (Haverford)   Sept 10, 11, 13.
Incogniti 326 (R. St L. Fowler 142) & 259-9 dec beat All Philadelphia 308 & 135 by 142 runs.

6th Match: v Germantown (Manheim)   Sept 14, 15.
Germantown 124 & 151 lost to Incogniti 245 & 32-1 by 9 wkts.

7th Match: v All Philadelphia (Manheim)   Sept 17, 18, 20.
Incogniti 219 & 93-5 beat All Philadelphia 86 & 225 by 5 wkts.

8th Match: v All New York (Staten Island)   Sept 22, 23.
Incogniti 377 (D. R. Jardine 133) beat All New York 147 & 89 by an inns & 141 runs.

9th Match: v All Toronto (Toronto) (12 a-side)   Sept 25, 27.
All Toronto 126 & 213 drew with Incogniti 281 & 53-5.

1920-21: Australia win all five Test Matches

The First World War caused a break both in English first-class cricket and in English teams travelling overseas, but within a few months of hostilities ending, the Australian authorities invited the M.C.C. to send out a team. This invitation was declined, but it was impossible to refuse a second for the following winter and, despite some misgivings, the M.C.C. set about organising a party for 1920-21. R. H. Spooner was asked to lead the side, but, having accepted, had to ask to be released for domestic reasons. Jupp also was forced to stand down, but otherwise the selectors met with no major refusals and the team which left Tilbury aboard R.M.S. *Osterley* was: J. W. H. T. Douglas (Essex) (capt), P. G. H. Fender (Surrey), E. R. Wilson (Yorks) and the professionals J. W. Hearne (Middx), E. H. Hendren (Middx), F. E. Woolley (Kent), J. W. H. Makepeace (Lancs), W. Rhodes (Yorks), A. Dolphin (Yorks), A. Waddington (Yorks), H. Howell (Warwicks) and C. A. G. Russell (Essex), with F. C. Toone, Yorkshire's secretary, as manager. J. W. Hitch (Surrey) travelled on a later boat, whilst J. B. Hobbs (Surrey), H. Strudwick (Surrey) and C. H. Parkin (Lancs) joined the boat to Toulon.

Leaving on 18 September, the boat called at Toulon on 25 September, and then continued to Naples, where the team went to view Pompeii. The only other stop was at Port Said before Colombo was reached on 11 October and a one-day game played.

During the run from Colombo to Fremantle, a case of typhoid was reported on the boat and this resulted in the team spending a week in quarantine in Fremantle, and the cancellation of the four-day match in Perth. A one-day match was all that could be managed. The first serious game therefore took place at Adelaide. Parkin bowled splendidly in the first innings and as the M.C.C. found no terrors with the home attack, the game was won by an innings. The second match was a repetition of the first, Victoria also being beaten with an innings to spare. Travelling on from Melbourne to Sydney, the tourists met the strongest state side. The first innings belonged to M.C.C., with Hobbs hitting 112 in 168 minutes and the bowlers dismissing New South Wales cheaply. The home side required 334 to win, which seemed a tall order, but Macartney and Collins tore the M.C.C. bowling to shreds, with an opening stand of 244 in 186 minutes, and Macartney's batting was quite remarkable as New South Wales went to a 6-wicket victory.

After this upset, the visitors played four matches, none of which caused them any sleepless nights, before the first Test in Sydney. To everyone's surprise, Australia won the toss, batted and were dismissed for 267. On the second day, however, before a crowd of some 40,000, England collapsed. Australia seized the initiative and with Collins and Armstrong hitting hundreds in the second innings, they scored 581 in 540 minutes to leave England an impossible fourth innings target.

For the second Test, Australia were without Macartney, but for England worse was in store when Hearne was taken ill so seriously with lumbago on the first day that he could not play again on the tour. Australia again batted first, but this time hit up 499, then rain ruined the wicket and England, apart from Hobbs, who played his best innings of the tour, just folded up, losing by an innings. Only an odds match at Ballarat separated the second and third Tests. The latter was vital for England if the rubber was to be saved. England dismissed Australia for 354 and then, due to Russell, obtained a first innings lead of nearly a hundred. Australia lost 3 second innings wickets for 71 and England appeared on top, but centuries for Kelleway, Armstrong and Pellew quickly reversed the situation. The England fielding left something to be desired, but there were some odd umpiring decisions, which rather depressed the bowlers. Left to make 490, England still looked hopeful – Hobbs played another great innings, but the

1st Match: v Ceylon (Colombo) (One Day)   Oct 11.
Ceylon 122 drew with M.C.C. 108-9.

2nd Match: v Western Australia (Perth) (One Day)   Oct 30.
M.C.C. 276-8 dec (J. W. H. Makepeace 117, J. B. Hobbs 63, E. H. Hendren 60) drew with W. Australia 119-7.

3rd Match: v South Australia (Adelaide)   Nov 5, 6, 8, 9.
S. Australia 118 (C. H. Parkin 8-55) & 339 (A. Richardson 111, P. D. Rundell 75, C. E. Pellew 64) lost to M.C.C. 512-5 dec (J. W. Hearne 182, C. A. G. Russell 156, E. H. Hendren 79, A. Smith 5-120) by an inns & 55 runs.

4th Match: v Victoria (Melbourne)   Nov 12, 13, 15, 16.
Victoria 274 (A. W. Lampard 111) & 85 (W. Rhodes 6-39) lost to M.C.C. 418-3 dec (J. B. Hobbs 131, E. H. Hendren 106*, J. W. Hearne 87) by an inns & 59 runs.

5th Match: v New South Wales (Sydney)   Nov 19, 20, 22.
M.C.C. 236 (J. B. Hobbs 112, E. H. Hendren 67) & 250 (J. W. Hearne 81, P. G. H. Fender 54, J. M. Gregory 5-67) lost to N.S.W. 153 & 335-4 (C. G. Macartney 161, H. L. Collins 106) by 6 wkts.

6th Match: v Queensland (Brisbane)   Nov 27, 29, 30.
Queensland 186 (G. S. Moore 85) & 192 lost to M.C.C. 419 (W. Rhodes 162, J. W. H. T. Douglas 84, C. A. G. Russell 73, S. W. Ayres 5-112) by an inns & 41 runs.

7th Match: v An Australian XI (Brisbane)   Dec 3, 4, 6.
Australian XI 255 (C. G. Macartney 96, W. W. Armstrong 53, C. J. Tozer 51, J. W. H. T. Douglas 5-45) & 182-5 (C. J. Tozer 53, H. Carter 50) drew with M.C.C. 357 (E. H. Hendren 96, C. A. G. Russell 72, E. R. Wilson 56).

8th Match: v Toowoomba (Toowoomba)   Dec 8, 9.
M.C.C. 208-9 dec (W. Rhodes 56) beat Toowoomba 62 (A. Waddington 7-29) & 27 (C. H. Parkin 5-5) by an inns & 119 runs.

9th Match: v N.S.W. Colts XII (Sydney)   Dec 14, 15.
Colts XII 84 (A. Waddington 8-33) & 148-4 drew with M.C.C. 702 (E. H. Hendren 211, J. W. Hearne 144, J. B. Hobbs 64, F. E. Woolley 64).

10th Match: v Australia (Sydney)   Dec 17, 18, 20, 21, 22.
Australia 267 (H. L. Collins 70) & 581 (W. W. Armstrong 158, H. L. Collins 104, C. Kelleway 78, C. G. Macartney 69, W. Bardsley 57, J. M. Taylor 51) beat England 190 (F. E. Woolley 52) & 281 (J. B. Hobbs 59, J. W. Hearne 57, E. H. Hendren 56) by 377 runs.

11th Match: v XV of Bendigo (Bendigo)   Dec 27, 28.
M.C.C. 371 (J. W. H. T. Douglas 119, J. W. H. Makepeace 58, J. B. Hobbs 52) beat Bendigo 65 & 42 by an inns & 264 runs.

12th Match: v Australia (Melbourne)   Dec 31, Jan 1, 3, 4.
Australia 499 (C. E. Pellew 116, J. M. Gregory 100, J. M. Taylor 68, H. L. Collins 64, W. Bardsley 51) beat England 251 (J. B. Hobbs 122, E. H. Hendren 67, J. M. Gregory 7-69) & 157 (F. E. Woolley 50) by an inns & 91 runs.

13th Match: v XV of Ballarat (Ballarat)   Jan 7, 8.
Ballarat 211 (N. Philip 53, W. M. Woodfull 50) & 30 (A. Waddington 8-15) lost to M.C.C. 384-9 dec (F. E. Woolley 159*, P. G. H. Fender 106, C. A. G. Russell 50) by an inns & 143 runs.

14th Match: v Australia (Adelaide)   Jan 14, 15, 17, 18, 19, 20.
Australia 354 (H. L. Collins 162, W. A. S. Oldfield 50, C. H. Parkin 5-60) & 582 (C. Kelleway 147, W. W. Armstrong 121, C. E. Pellew 104, J.M. Gregory 78*) beat England 447 (C. A. G. Russell 135*, F. E. Woolley 79, J. W. H. Makepeace 60, J. W. H. T. Douglas 60, A. A. Mailey 5-160) & 370 (J. B. Hobbs 123, C. A. G. Russell 59, E. H. Hendren 51, A. A. Mailey 5-142) by 119 runs.

15th Match: v XVI of Hamilton (Hamilton)   Jan 25, 26.
M.C.C. 320 (F. E. Woolley 87, J. B. Hobbs 74) drew with Hamilton 98 & 169-13.

16th Match: v XV of Geelong (Geelong)   Jan 28, 29.
M.C.C. 457 (J. B. Hobbs 138, J. W. H. Makepeace 98, W. Rhodes 68, A. Waddington 53) drew with Geelong 261-10 (W. Sharland 102).

17th Match: v Victoria (Melbourne)   Feb 4, 5, 7, 8.
Victoria 268 (G. A. Davies 61, J. Ryder 54) & 295 (J. Ryder 108, H. C. A. Sandford 72) lost to M.C.C. 486 (E. H. Hendren 271, J. W. H. T. Douglas 133*, E. A. McDonald 6-145) & 78-3 by 7 wkts.

18th Match: v Australia (Melbourne)   Feb 11, 12, 14, 15, 16.
England 284 (J. W. H. Makepeace 117, J. W. H. T. Douglas 50) & 315 (W. Rhodes 73, J. W. H. T. Douglas 60, P. G. H. Fender 59, J. W. H. Makepeace 54, A. A. Mailey 9-121) lost to Australia 389 (W. W. Armstrong 123*, J. M. Gregory 77, H. L. Collins 59, W. Bardsley 56, P. G. H. Fender 5-122) & 211-2 (J. M. Gregory 76*, J. Ryder 52*) by 8 wkts.

19th Match: v New South Wales (Sydney)   Feb 18, 19, 21, 22.
M.C.C. 427 (E. H. Hendren 102, J. W. H. Makepeace 73, P. G. H. Fender 60, W. Rhodes 50, A. A. Mailey 7-172) & 381 (F. E. Woolley 138, J. W. H. T. Douglas 82, E. H. Hendren 66) drew with N.S.W. 447 (C. G. Macartney 130, J. M. Taylor 107*, A. Punch 59, T. J. E. Andrews 54, J. M. Gregory 52, J. W. H. T. Douglas 7-98) & 151-2 (H. S. T. L. Hendry 66*, A. Punch 63*).

20th Match: v Australia (Sydney)   Feb 25, 26, 28, Mar 1.
England 204 (F. E. Woolley 53) & 280 (J. W. H. T. Douglas 68, A. A. Mailey 5-119) lost to Australia 392 (C. G. Macartney 170, J. M. Gregory 93, P. G. H. Fender 5-90) & 93-1 (W. Bardsley 50*) by 9 wkts.

21st Match: v XV of Albury (Albury)   March 4, 5.
Albury 146 & 101-10 drew with M.C.C. 326-6 dec (C. A. G. Russell 146, E. R. Wilson 62).

22nd Match: v XVII of Benalla (Benalla)   March 7, 8.
M.C.C. 348-6 dec (P. G. H. Fender 83*, W. Rhodes 71, E. H. Hendren 69, A. Dolphin 58) beat Benalla 69 (A. Waddington 10-31) & 178 by an inns & 101 runs.

23rd Match: v South Australia (Adelaide)   March 11, 12, 14, 15.
S. Australia 195 (P. G. H. Fender 7-75) & 369 (P. D. Rundell 121, G. W. Harris 84, P. G. H. Fender 5-109) lost to M.C.C. 627 (W. Rhodes 210, C. A. G. Russell 201, J. W. H. T. Douglas 106*) by an inns & 63 runs.

Batting Averages

	M	I	NO	R	HS	Avge	100	c/s
J. W. Hearne (Middx)	6	7	0	434	182	62.00	1	3
E. H. Hendren (Middx)	12	20	1	1178	271	62.00	3	10
C. A. G. Russell (Essex)	10	15	1	818	201	58.44	3	7
J. W. H. T. Douglas (Essex)	13	18	4	816	133*	58.28	2	5
J. B. Hobbs (Surrey)	12	19	1	924	131	51.33	4	6
W. Rhodes (Yorks)	12	19	0	730	210	38.42	2	6
F. E. Woolley (Kent)	13	20	2	619	138	34.38	1	13
J. W. H. Makepeace (Lancs)	9	16	1	449	117	29.93	1	0
P. G. H. Fender (Surrey)	9	13	1	325	60	27.08	0	7
E. R. Wilson (Yorks)	7	8	0	124	56	15.50	0	2
A. Waddington (Yorks)	5	8	2	82	51*	13.66	0	2
J. W. Hitch (Surrey)	3	3	0	24	19	8.00	0	1
H. Strudwick (Surrey)	8	13	3	80	24	8.00	0	18/2
C. H. Parkin (Lancs)	11	16	1	134	36	7.88	0	3
H. Howell (Warks)	8	10	5	22	6	4.40	0	1
A. Dolphin (Yorks)	5	5	1	9	6*	2.25	0	8/8

Bowling Averages

	O	M	R	W	Avge	BB	5i
W. Rhodes	183.4	36	479	18	26.61	6-39	1
P. G. H. Fender	233	17	983	32	30.71	7-75	4
C. H. Parkin	404.4	62	1344	43	31.25	8-55	2
F. E. Woolley	424.2	106	1051	31	33.90	4-27	0
J. W. H. T. Douglas	269.2	33	918	27	34.00	7-98	2
J. W. Hitch	47	5	176	5	35.20	4-28	0
E. R. Wilson	135	39	290	8	36.25	2-18	0
J. W. Hearne	147.5	29	407	11	37.00	3-63	0
A. Waddington	122	25	327	7	46.71	3-63	0
H. Howell	248	31	856	17	50.35	4-81	0

Also bowled: J. B. Hobbs 14-3-35-0; E. H. Hendren 3-1-15-0.

other batsmen failed, though they couldn't blame the wicket.

A shipping strike prevented the team going to Tasmania and two odds matches were substituted into the fixture list. M.C.C. then beat Victoria in the return, though the state side were without Armstrong, who had a disagreement with the officials.

In the fourth Test, Russell could not play, but his absence was more than outweighed by the illness of Macartney. Armstrong, though suffering from malaria, hit a century to give Australia a good first innings lead and from then the game ran Australia's way. The margin of victory was 8 wickets. There was a high-scoring draw against New South Wales prior to the fifth Test. Hobbs was lame and should not have played for England, but it was very doubtful if his injury affected the match, since Australia strolled to an easy victory by 9 wickets and thus won all five Tests –the first time this had been achieved.

Three other matches completed the tour, which ended at Adelaide on 15 March. The team returned on the *Osterley* to Toulon, where the journey was continued by train, and Victoria station was reached at 10 p.m. on 17 April.

Of the touring batsmen, only Hobbs and Douglas maintained their reputations. Hendren and Woolley were most disappointing and Russell and Makepeace owed their averages to a few high scores. The less said about the bowling the better. The English fielding also did not bear comparison with the Australian.

The Australians' outstanding bowler was Gregory, but Mailey was very persistent and usually removed the later English batsmen with ease. The home batting was sound throughout, with Macartney, Taylor and Gregory being brilliant.

1922-23: M.C.C. win narrowly in South Africa

The side selected to go to South Africa, though believed to be strong enough to beat the opposition, was not representative of England's full might, since Hobbs, Sutcliffe, Hearne and Parkin all declined invitations. The team which landed at Cape Town on 9 November was: F. T. Mann (Middx) (capt), A. E. R. Gilligan (Sussex), P. G. H. Fender (Surrey), A. W. Carr (Notts), G. T. S. Stevens (Oxford U), V. W. C. Jupp (Sussex) and the following

Some of the M.C.C. team arriving back home at Waterloo from South Africa in March 1923. From left: A. W. Carr, P. G. H. Fender, F. T. Mann, A. E. R. Gilligan and G. T. S. Stevens. The first four all captained England during their careers.

professionals: C. A. G. Russell (Essex), A. Sandham (Surrey), C. P. Mead (Hants), F. E. Woolley (Kent), G. G. Macaulay (Yorks), G. Brown (Hants), A. S. Kennedy (Hants), and W. H. Livsey (Hants).

Despite the fact that the first match began the day after the team's arrival, the M.C.C. found little difficulty in disposing of Western Province and indeed the opposition in the fixtures that followed was scarcely more taxing, until Transvaal were met at Johannesburg and some 14,000 spectators turned up to see the first day's play. Apart from Sandham and Woolley, the M.C.C. batting failed against Nupen and Transvaal gained a first innings

lead – rain however ended the game prematurely.

England were without Russell, injured, for the first Test but looked to have the game well in hand when Kennedy and Jupp dismissed South Africa for 148; Blanckenberg struck back and the English batting crumbled, only the tailenders taking the side into a modest lead. H. W. Taylor then hit a superb 176 and the home team reached 420 in their second innings. Nupen and Blanckenberg made certain that England had no hope of reaching the 387 needed to win and South Africa obtained victory by 168 runs. The second Test followed straight on after this defeat, but the teams travelled to Cape Town. Russell was able to play, but it was a

---

1922-23: M.C.C. to South Africa

1st Match: v Western Province (Cape Town)   Nov 10, 11, 13.
W. Province 145 & 205 lost to M.C.C. 331 (C. P. Mead 97, P. G. H. Fender 96, I. D. Buys 5-121) & 40-4 by 6 wkts.

2nd Match: v South-Western Districts (Oudtshoorn)   Nov 15, 16.
S-W Districts 124 (V. W. C. Jupp 6-23) & 96 (V. W. C. Jupp 6-24) lost to M.C.C. 284 (A. Sandham 75, C. P. Mead 73) by an inns & 64 runs.

3rd Match: v Eastern Province (Port Elizabeth)   Nov 18, 20, 21.
M.C.C. 336-9 dec (P. G. H. Fender 89, F. T. Mann 52, A. W. Carr 50, C. Munro 5-67) beat E. Province 127 (A. E. R. Gilligan 7-75) & 200 (J. Dold 55, W. Brann 52, A. S. Kennedy 5-83) by an inns & 9 runs.

4th Match: v Grahamstown XV (Grahamstown)   Nov 22, 23.
Grahamstown XV 132-9 dec drew with M.C.C. 350-5 (A. Sandham 124, C. P. Mead 93, P. G. H. Fender 60).*

5th Match: v Border (East London)   Nov 25, 27.
Border 70 (A. S. Kennedy 5-7) & 120 (A. L. Wainwright 61, F. E. Woolley 6-43) lost to M.C.C. 271-8 dec (A. Sandham 102) by an inns & 81 runs.

6th Match: v North-Eastern Districts (Queenstown)   Nov 29, 30.
N-E Districts 53 (A. S. Kennedy 6-8) & 44 lost to M.C.C. 242 (V. W. C. Jupp 89) by an inns & 145 runs.

7th Match: v Griqualand West (Kimberley)   Dec 2, 4.
Griqualand West 198 (N. V. Tapscott 57) & 196 lost to M.C.C. 353 (F. E. Woolley 83, C. P. Mead 68, A. Sandham 68, C. M. Francois 7-114) & 42-2 by 8 wkts.

8th Match: v East Rand (Benoni)   Dec 9, 11.
East Rand 196 (S. J. Snooke 76, G. G. Macaulay 5-40) & 46-4 drew with M.C.C. 284 (A. Sandham 128).

9th Match: v Pretoria (Pretoria)   Dec 13, 14.
Pretoria 137 (A. S. Kennedy 6-19) & 116 (G. G. Macaulay 6-18) lost to M.C.C. 300-7 dec (C. A. G. Russell 77, A. W. Carr 63) by an inns & 47 runs.

10th Match: v Transvaal (Johannesburg)   Dec 16, 18, 19.
M.C.C. 240 (F. E. Woolley 76, A. Sandham 75, E. P. Nupen 5-76) & 119-0 (C. A. G. Russell 77) drew with Transvaal 291 (R. H. Catterall 128).*

11th Match: v South Africa (Johannesburg)   Dec 23, 26, 27, 28.
South Africa 148 & 420 (H. W. Taylor 176, W. H. Brann 50) beat England 182 (J. M. Blanckenberg 6-76) & 218 (E. P. Nupen 5-53) by 168 runs.

12th Match: v South Africa (Cape Town)   Jan 1, 2, 3, 4.
South Africa 113 & 242 (R. H. Catterall 76, H. W. Taylor 68, G. G. Macaulay 5-64) lost to England 183 (J. M. Blanckenberg 5-61) & 173-9 (A. E. Hall 7-63) by 1 wkt.

13th Match: v Orange Free State (Bethlehem)   Jan 9, 10.
Northern O.F.S. XV 170 (S. W. Smart 58, V. W. C. Jupp 6-30) & 120 (B. Bourke 52) lost to M.C.C. 325 (C. A. G. Russell 110, A. Sandham 57) by an inns & 35 runs.

14th Match: v Natal (Pietermaritzburg)   Jan 12, 13, 15.
M.C.C. 248 (M. E. Billing 7-95) & 242-6 dec (C. A. G. Russell 86, A. Sandham 76) beat Natal 124 (F. E. Woolley 5-24) & 130 (P. G. H. Fender 5-36) by 236 runs.

15th Match: v South Africa (Durban)   Jan 18, 19, 20, 22.
England 428 (C. P. Mead 181, F. T. Mann 84, P. G. H. Fender 60) & 11-1 drew with South Africa 368 (H. W. Taylor 91, C. M. Francois 72, R. H. Catterall 52, A. W. Nourse 52, A. S. Kennedy 5-88).

16th Match: v Zululand (Eshowe)   Jan 26, 27.
Zululand 105 (G. G. Macaulay 6-19) & 79-3 drew with M.C.C. 206-3 dec (G. Brown 64, A. W. Carr 62).*

17th Match: v Northern Districts (Newcastle)   Jan 30, 31.
N. Districts 137 (A. E. R. Gilligan 5-34) & 67-8 drew with M.C.C. 284-8 dec (F. T. Mann 79, F. E. Woolley 58).

18th Match: v Transvaal (Johannesburg)   Feb 3, 5, 6.
M.C.C. 262 (C. A. G. Russell 81, F. E. Woolley 62, E. P. Nupen 5-48) & 288-4 dec (A. Sandham 114, C. A. G. Russell 58, F. E. Woolley 52) beat Transvaal 171 (R. H. Catterall 68) & 180 by 199 runs.

19th Match: v South Africa (Johannesburg)   Feb 9, 10, 12, 13.
England 244 (A. W. Carr 63, A. E. Hall 6-82) & 376-6 dec (F. E. Woolley 115*, C. A. G. Russell 96, F. T. Mann 59, A. Sandham 58) drew with South Africa 295 (T. A. Ward 64, A. W. Nourse 51, L. E. Tapscott 50) & 247-4 (H. W. Taylor 101, A. W. Nourse 63).

20th Match: v South Africa (Durban)   Feb 16, 17, 19, 20, 21, 22.
England 281 (C. A. G. Russell 140, C. P. Mead 66) & 241 (C. A. G. Russell 111) beat South Africa 179 & 234 (H. W. Taylor 102, A. S. Kennedy 5-76) by 109 runs.

21st Match: v Orange Free State (Bloemfontein)   Feb 24, 26, 27.
M.C.C. 265 (A. Sandham 122, V. W. C. Jupp 55) & 282 (G. B. Street 88, V. W. C. Jupp 55) beat O.F.S. 163 (D. J. de Villiers 59) & 128 (P. G. H. Fender 7-55) by 256 runs.

22nd Match: v Western Province (Cape Town)   March 3, 5, 6.
W. Province 118 & 181 (P. A. M. Hands 94, A. S. Kennedy 5-35) lost to M.C.C. 236 & 64-0 by 10 wkts.

bowler's match. England again began by dismissing South Africa cheaply, but Blanckenberg and a new cap, Hall, kept South Africa in the game and another good innings by Taylor set England 173 to make to win. Hall bowled brilliantly and but for dropped catches would have won the match for South Africa; as it was England scraped home by 1 wicket in a tense finish. Hall was carried shoulder high off the field.

The third Test, which was awaited with great interest, was unfortunately ruined by rain shortly after each side had had an innings. In the fourth Test more good bowling by Hall gave South Africa a first innings lead of 51, but, batting again, England, through Russell and Woolley gained an impregnable position. Mann declared in the hope of bowling South Africa out, but Taylor hit a well-judged century and the match was drawn.

As each team had won one game, it was announced that the fifth Test would be played to a finish. For some unknown reason, South Africa dropped their most formidable bowler, Nupen, replacing him by Conyngham, and this was perhaps the decisive move in the game. Two great innings by Russell, who hit two hundreds in the match, despite feeling unwell, were the backbone of the English batting and indeed the saving of both English innings.

Most unusually for a visiting player, a collection was taken on the ground for Russell, who benefitted by over £90. South Africa required 344 in the final innings and reached 111 for 3 when bad light stopped play at the end of the fourth day. Rain did not allow very much play on the fifth day, but three more wickets went down, while the score rose to 203. Taylor was 76 not out, but on the sixth day even he could not save the match and fell just after reaching his hundred. England thus won the rubber by two to one.

Two more matches – against the Free State and Western Province – brought the tour to a close. The outstanding English batsman was Russell, who adapted himself well to matting wickets. His strength lay in his great defensive powers. The best bowler was Kennedy, though at times Macaulay proved very dangerous. For the South Africans, Taylor remained head and shoulders above the rest, but all the bowlers did good work.

It should be mentioned that Livsey, the reserve wicket-keeper, broke a finger in the sixth match and Street of Sussex was cabled for and appeared in a few games in the latter half of the programme.

When the English side left England it was thought that they would have no difficulty in beating South Africa, so the results, though favourable to England, did nothing to indicate that English cricket was really on the mend after the defeats in 1920-21 and in 1921, at home, against Australia.

1922-23: MacLaren takes an M.C.C. 'A' side to New Zealand

Having selected the leading English team for South Africa, the M.C.C. undertook the arrangements for a second tour to New Zealand. The team chosen was: A. C. MacLaren (Lancs) (capt), A. P. F. Chapman (Berkshire), G. Wilson (Yorks), Hon F. S. Gough-Calthorpe (Warwicks), T. C. Lowry (Cambridge U), C. H. Gibson (Cambridge U), W. W. H. Hill-Wood (Derbys), C. H. Titchmarsh (Herts), J. F. MacLean (Worcs), J. C. Hartley, W. A. C. Wilkinson (Army), Hon D. F. Brand and two professionals, A. P. Freeman (Kent) and H. Tyldesley (Lancs). H. D. Swan was appointed manager. R. St L. Fowler, the Army cricketer, was to have gone, but could not obtain leave.

The standard of the team was perhaps that of one of the weaker county sides and the party sailed from England on 30 September, travelling via the Suez Canal. Over 10,000 came to watch the one-day game in Colombo, despite rain which prevented a start before 1.15. From Colombo the voyage continued on the s.s. *Orvieto* to Australia, where a two-day game was played at Perth, before the first serious match at Adelaide. Here South Australia proved too strong for the visitors. Two good innings from Chapman at Melbourne meant that Victoria only beat the tourists by two wickets and at Sydney Chapman scored a splendid hundred, whilst the veteran captain, MacLaren, hit a fifty and the visitors actually gained a first innings lead over the formidable New South Wales eleven, though later the state side took control and won by five wickets. All in all the weak M.C.C. side had acquitted itself well on the Australian leg of its programme and the team moved from Sydney to New Zealand.

After two two-day matches, the first major game in New Zealand was at Christchurch. Chapman hit a brilliant 183, whilst Gibson took 12 wickets to provide a victory by 8 wickets. Blunt scored a hundred for the home side, but was dropped three times. The M.C.C. were seen to even greater advantage in the 'First Test'. MacLaren hit a double century in 270 minutes, whilst Gibson and Freeman bowled out New Zealand with little difficulty. About 6,500 people watched the first day's play. The

'Second Test' followed directly after the first. The New Zealanders showed much better form and set the M.C.C. 262 to make in 120 minutes – the tourists did not attempt the task. In the 'Third Test', which came six matches later, the M.C.C. were without MacLaren,

1922-23: M.C.C. to Ceylon, Australia and New Zealand

1st Match: v Ceylon (Colombo)   Oct 23.
Ceylon 147-5 dec (E. Kelaart 59*) drew with M.C.C. 100-4.

2nd Match: v Western Australia (Perth)   Nov 3, 4.
M.C.C. 190 (A. P. F. Chapman 75) & 132-3 (A. P. F. Chapman 58, C. H. Titchmarsh 50*) drew with W. Australia 234 (A. Heindricks 91*, A. Evans 53).

3rd Match: v South Australia (Adelaide)   Nov 10, 11, 13.
S. Australia 442 (A. J. Richardson 150, V. Y. Richardson 118, H. Tyldesley 5-100) & 60-4 beat M.C.C. 205 (W. A. C. Wilkinson 64) & 294 (G. Wilson 61, A. P. F. Chapman 53) by 6 wkts.

4th Match: v Victoria (Melbourne)   Nov 17, 18, 20.
M.C.C. 210 (A. P. F. Chapman 73, W. A. C. Wilkinson 62, A. E. V. Hartkopf 5-23) & 231 (C. H. Titchmarsh 82, A. P. F. Chapman 69, A. E. V. Hartkopf 8-105) lost to Victoria 278 (A. E. V. Hartkopf 86, W. M. Woodfull 74) & 164-8 (C. B. Willis 60) by 2 wkts.

5th Match: v New South Wales (Sydney)   Nov 24, 25, 27.
M.C.C. 202 (A. P. F. Chapman 100, C. H. Titchmarsh 79, A. C. MacLaren 54) & 121 lost to N.S.W. (C. G. Macartney 63) & 283-5 (C. G. Macartney 84, T. J. E. Andrews 74) by 5 wkts.

6th Match: v Auckland (Auckland)   Dec 15, 16.
M.C.C. 350 (C. H. Titchmarsh 154, A. C. MacLaren 58, W. A. C. Wilkinson 50, A. Anthony 6-43) drew with Auckland 107-5.

7th Match: v Wanganui (Wanganui)   Dec 19, 20.
Wanganui 129 (H. Lambert 66) & 200 (H. Lambert 63, C. H. Gibson 5-72) lost to M.C.C. 296 (F. S. Gough-Calthorpe 117) & 56-0 by 10 wkts.

8th Match: v Canterbury (Christchurch)   Dec 23, 25, 26.
M.C.C. 454-6 dec (A. P. F. Chapman 183, W. A. C. Wilkinson 102, F. S. Gough-Calthorpe 60) & 23-2 beat Canterbury 181 & 295 (R. C. Blunt 174, R. D. Worker 65, C. H. Gibson 8-57) by 8 wkts.

9th Match: v New Zealand (Wellington)   Dec 30, Jan 1, 2.
M.C.C. 505-8 dec (A. C. MacLaren 200*, J. F. Maclean 84, F. S. Gough-Calthorpe 63) beat New Zealand 222 (A. P. Freeman 5-114) & 127 (C. H. Gibson 5-42, A. P. Freeman 5-72) by an inns & 156 runs.

10th Match: v New Zealand (Christchurch)   Jan 5, 6, 8.
New Zealand 375 (D. C. Collins 102, J. S. Shepherd 66) & 270-8 dec (N. C. Snedden 58, C. C. R. Dacre 58) drew with M.C.C. 384 (A. P. F. Chapman 77, T. C. Lowry 61, J. C. Hartley 60*, W. A. C. Wilkinson 59) & 145-5.

11th Match: v Minor Associations (Temuka)   Jan 9, 10.
Minor Associations 52 (H. Tyldesley 5-19) & 151 lost to M.C.C. 407 (D. F. Brand 85, A. P. F. Chapman 84*, F. S. Gough-Calthorpe 50, G. McWhirter 6-153) by an inns & 204.

12th Match: v Otago (Dunedin)   Jan 12, 13, 15.
Otago 202 (J. Shepherd 52, A. Galland 58) & 129 (J. McMullan 69) lost to M.C.C. 222 (C. H. Titchmarsh 73, A. P. F. Chapman 53) & 112-4 by 6 wkts.

13th Match: v Southland (Invercargill)   Jan 20, 22.
M.C.C. 319 (F. S. Gough-Calthorpe 77) & 101-5 dec beat Southland 153 & 71 (F. S. Gough-Calthorpe 5-17) by 196 runs.

14th Match: v Wellington (Wellington)   Jan 26, 27, 29.
Wellington 104 & 133 lost to M.C.C. 107 (W. S. Brice 5-52) & 131-6 (W. S. Brice 5-45) by 4 wkts.

15th Match: v Minor Associations (Nelson)   Jan 30, 31.
Minor Associations 119 (K. Saxon 60) & 55 (A. P. Freeman 6-27) lost to M.C.C. 249 (A. P. F. Chapman 71*, W. A. C. Wilkinson 52, J. Newman 5-93) by an inns & 75 runs.

16th Match: v New Zealand (Wellington)   Feb 2, 3, 5.
New Zealand 166 (E. H. Bernan 61, F. S. Gough-Calthorpe 6-53) & 215 (D. C. Collins 69, R. C. Blunt 68, C. H. Gibson 5-65) lost to M.C.C. 401 (T. C. Lowry 130, A. P. F. Chapman 71, J. F. Maclean 53) by an inns & 20 runs.

17th Match: v Minor Associations (Palmerston North)   Feb 6, 7.
M.C.C. 306-8 dec (F. S. Gough-Calthorpe 136, C. H. Gibson 58) & 53-6 dec beat Minor Associations 123 & 96 by 140 runs.

18th Match: v East Coast Associations (Napier)   Feb 9, 10.
M.C.C. 140 (Temperton 5-48) & 163-4 dec (C. H. Titchmarsh 63*) drew with East Coast 68 (C. H. Gibson 6-28) & 137-4 (Ellis 54).

19th Match: v Auckland (Auckland)   Feb 17, 19.
M.C.C. 365 (A. P. F. Chapman 108, F. S. Gough-Calthorpe 78, C. H. Titchmarsh 73, W. W. Hill-Wood 52, C. Allcott 6-86) beat Auckland 178 (A. P. Freeman 7-87) & 183 (E. McLeod 50, A. P. Freeman 5-71) by an inns & 4 runs.

20th Match: v New South Wales (Sydney)   March 2, 3, 5.
M.C.C. 275 (A. P. F. Chapman 91, D. F. Brand 60) & 296 (F. S. Gough-Calthorpe 110, H. S. T. L. Hendry 5-118) drew with N.S.W. 314 (W. Bardsley 90, J. M. Taylor 73, A. F. Kippax 59, C. H. Gibson 6-140) & 102-5 (J. M. Taylor 52).

21st Match: v Combined Universities (Melbourne)   March 7, 8.
M.C.C. 258 (W. W. Hill-Wood 84, H. W. Fisher 6-68) & 135-5 drew with Combined Universities 332 (L. F. Freemantle 59, O. E. Nothling 56, W. H. Bailey 51).

22nd Match: v Victoria (Melbourne)   March 9, 10, 12.
M.C.C. 71 (P. Wallace 6-50) & 282-0 (G. Wilson 142*, W. W. Hill-Wood 122*) drew with Victoria 617-8 dec (H. S. Love 192, V. S. Ransford 118*, A. E. Liddicut 102, R. L. Park 101, W. H. Ponsford 62).

23rd Match: v South Australia (Adelaide)   March 15, 16, 17.
S. Australia 495 (A. J. Richardson 280, L. Bowley 76, J. W. Rymill 50, A. P. Freeman 6-176) & 204-4 dec (C. E. Pellew 69) drew with M.C.C. 372 (F. S. Gough-Calthorpe 96, G. Wilson 78, A. P. Freeman 57, H. M. Fisher 5-96) & 248-4 (A. P. F. Chapman 134*).

who had injured his knee, but Lowry hit a century and Chapman 71, whilst most of the New Zealanders struggled, Gough-Calthorpe bowling well, and the visitors went to an innings victory. The match was followed by two minor games and then the return with Auckland, which resulted in another innings victory. Going back to Australia, the M.C.C. played four drawn games to conclude the tour – all were high scoring, except one disastrous first innings against Victoria, when the side collapsed for 71, but made an amazing recovery in their second innings to reach 282 for 0, Hill-Wood and Wilson making hundreds.

Without a doubt the star of the team was Chapman, both his batting and fielding being quite exceptional. C. H. Gibson bowled well. The former was to go on to captain England, but the latter's cricket was mainly to be confined to South America. Brand was another who looked most promising, but was not to be seen in first-class county cricket. After MacLaren's injury, the side was led by J. C. Hartley, who also batted well.

W. Ferguson, the Australian scorer, joined the side in Fremantle and acted as scorer and baggage master through the tour. The only black spot of the visit was on the financial side. The attendances in New Zealand were good on Saturdays, but otherwise poor, with all the up-country games losing money. A strike meant the cancellation of the match with Queensland, which might have improved the situation, and the total loss was £1,929, of which half was borne by the M.C.C.

1923: Free Foresters invited to Canada

Sailing on the s.s. *Montlaurier* from Liverpool on 24 August, the tourists landed at Quebec on 1 September and played their first game at Montreal beginning two days later.

The team consisted of E. G. Wynyard (capt), J. C. Hartley, R. St L. Fowler, F. H. Hollins, O. W. Cornwallis, A. E. L. Hill, J. E. Frazer, D. M. Ritchie, Lord Romilly, J. S. Hughes, J. C. Masterman, M. Patten, G. le Roy Burnham, C. E. Thompson.

The outstanding player of the eight-match tour was R. St L. Fowler, who not only headed the batting averages, but also took 57 wickets at a cost of 7.71 each. The two major matches were against Toronto C.C., in both of which Fowler's bowling proved too much for the opposition, though the tourists' batting did not produce many more runs than Toronto's.

The English side were invited over by the Canadian Cricket Clubs and the leading light in organising the tour was Norman Seagram of Toronto.

1923: Free Foresters to Canada

1st Match: v All Montreal (Montreal)   Sept 3, 4.
Montreal 139 (R. St L. Fowler 7-46) & 98 lost to Free Foresters 128 (J. E. Frazer 82) & 110-6 (R. St L. Fowler 53*) by 4 wkts.

2nd Match: v McGill C.C. (Montreal)   Sept 5, 6.
McGill 76 & 212 lost to Free Foresters 276 (R. St L. Fowler 126) & 14-0 by 10 wkts.

3rd Match: v Toronto C.C. (Toronto) (12 a-side)   Sept 8, 10.
Toronto 92 (R. St L. Fowler 7-21) & 123 (R. St L. Fowler 5-27) lost to Free Foresters 139 (F. H. Hollins 53, H. G. Wookey 5-45) & 78-6 by 5 wkts.

4th Match: v XVIII of Public Schools (Toronto)   Sept 12, 13.
Public Schools 146 (J. S. Hughes 10-38) & 109 drew with Free Foresters 136 (F. Lyon 6-57) & 63-4.

5th Match: v Toronto (Toronto) (12 a-side)   Sept 15, 17.
Toronto 146 & 123 lost to Free Foresters 195 & 78-1 by 10 wkts.

6th Match: v XV of Hamilton (Hamilton)   Sept 17, 18.
Hamilton 124 & 123 lost to Free Foresters 265 (R. St L. Fowler 52, F. H. Hollins 52, D. M. Richie 51, D. Verrier 6-69) by an inns & 18 runs.

7th Match: v Western Ontario (Gault)   Sept 21, 22.
Abandoned.

8th Match: v Ottawa Valley C.C. (Ottawa)   Sept 25, 26.
Ottawa Valley 183 (R. St L. Fowler 6-62) & 61 (D. M. Ritchie 5-17) lost to Free Foresters 437 (C. E. Thompson 85, J. C. Masterman 59, J. S. Hughes 56, O. W. Cornwallis 55) by an inns & 193 runs.

1924: Incogniti tour the United States

Arriving in New York on 8 September, the Incogniti played their first match on matting in Brooklyn, rather than on the grass wicket at Staten Island, as previous teams had done. The Incogs declared in this game to set New York 93 in an hour, but the home side were too surprised by this tactic to take full advantage and the game was drawn. The best match was the first against All Philadelphia. The tourists required 221 to win in their second innings and reached 215 for 8 – some brilliant fielding by the Philadelphians was the feature of the game. Unfortunately the return match was ruined by rain, as were several other of the fixtures.

The touring party were: E. J. Metcalfe (capt), G. F. Earle, T. C. Lowry, T. Arnott, J. J. Thorley, G. B. Cuthbertson, A. H. White, A. H. H. Gilligan, P. H. Irwin, T. A. L. Brocklebank, H. Hargreaves, G. A. S. Hickton, F. B. Landale.

Although the strength of cricket in Philadelphia was still fairly good, there was an almost complete lack of young players and this did not augur well for the future.

1924: Incogniti to United States

1st Match: v New York (Brooklyn)   Sept 12, 13.
Incogniti 234 & 153-6 dec (T. Arnott 50) drew with New York 295 (J. L. Poyer 101) & 63-5.

2nd Match: v Merion C.C. (Philadelphia)   Sept 15, 16.
Merion 204 (J. M. Crosman 50) & 132 (C. C. Morris 52) lost to Incogniti 310-9 dec (T. C. Lowry 105, P. H. Irwin 78) & 33-0.

3rd Match: v All Philadelphia (Philadelphia)   Sept 18, 19, 20.
Philadelphia 315 (J. M. Crosman 91, G. Bottomley 58) & 141 drew with Incogniti 236 & 215-8.

4th Match: v Philadelphia C.C. (St Martin's)   Sept 22, 23.
Philadelphia 192 (E. Hopkinson 58, J. H. Mason 53) drew with Incogniti 279-6 (A. H. White 101, G. B. Cuthbertson 66).*

5th Match: v Frankford (St Martin's)   Sept 25, 26.
Frankford 138 & 119 lost to Incogniti 317 (A. H. H. Gilligan 117, T. C. Lowry 56) by an inns & 60 runs.*

6th Match: v All Philadelphia (Manheim)   Sept 27, 28, 29.
Incogniti 275 (T. Arnott 54) drew with Philadelphia 30-2.

7th Match: v Germantown (Manheim)   Oct 1, 2.
Incogniti 243 drew with Germantown 125 & 75-6.

1924-25: Hobbs and Sutcliffe brilliant, but Australia win

Seven members of the disastrous M.C.C. side of 1920-21, returned to Australia with the 1924-25 side. The full team read: A. E. R. Gilligan (Sussex) (capt), J. L. Bryan (Kent), A. P. F. Chapman (Kent), J. W. H. T. Douglas (Essex) and the professionals J. B. Hobbs (Surrey), H. Sutcliffe (Yorks), E. H. Hendren (Middx), A. Sandham (Surrey), F. E. Woolley (Kent), J. W. Hearne (Middx), W. W. Whysall (Notts), R. Kilner (Yorks), M. W. Tate (Sussex), R. K. Tyldesley (Lancs), A. P. Freeman (Kent), H. Strudwick (Surrey), H. Howell (Warwicks), and as manager F. C. Toone (Yorks secretary).

The only major player to decline an invitation was C. H. Gibson, but his choice raised a storm of controversy, since he did not play in English first-class cricket, so perhaps his withdrawal for business reasons was allied with tact. Originally Hobbs also refused, but changed his mind. It was thought also by the critics that the inclusion of three leg-break bowlers – Tyldesley, Hearne and Freeman – was rather optimistic and that Geary should have travelled instead of Freeman.

The team played the now traditional one-day match in Colombo on the voyage out and landed in Western Australia on 14 October. There were four not very energetic matches, including two against Western Australia, before the side moved to Adelaide for the first important game, which was marked by an uncharacteristic declaration on the part of the home side in their first innings at 346 for 4. This led eventually to an easy M.C.C. win, when South Australia collapsed completely in the second innings to the bowling of Hearne. Against the rather moderate Victorian attack however, the tourists suffered their first defeat, though Hearne with an injured knee could not bat in the second innings. It was a surprise therefore that the visitors went straight from defeat at Melbourne to victory over the much vaunted New South Wales team at Sydney. Tate exploited the damp wicket splendidly and only Bardsley defied him in the first innings, but in the second innings Tyldesley took control. The game was won by 3 wickets. The two games at Brisbane were both drawn and then followed two minor matches, before the first Test at Sydney. Public interest in the game was enormous and about 163,500 people attended the match. Hobbs and Sutcliffe gave England two great starts with partnerships of 157 and 110, and both batsmen made a hundred and a fifty, but the rest of the English batting was nothing like as consistent as Australia's, and though England created a record by making 411 in the final innings, the game was still lost by 195 runs.

The second Test followed the pattern set by its predecessor. Hobbs and Sutcliffe put on 283 for the first wicket and the Yorkshire opener went on to hit a century in each innings, but once more the remaining English batsmen failed. Tate bowled quite splendidly, but he couldn't make up for England's lack of runs, and Australia won by 81 runs. The two major Australian batsmen were Ponsford, who made a century in both Tests and V. Y. Richardson, but A. J. Richardson and Taylor also made

The most famous opening pair in Test history, who performed great deeds, particularly against Australia. Jack Hobbs (left) and Herbert Sutcliffe (right) going out to bat in the second Test match at Melbourne in 1925.

The M.C.C. party which toured Australia in 1924-25. Back: J. L. Bryan, R. K. Tyldesley, M. W. Tate, F. C. Toone (manager), W. W. Whysall, A. P. F. Chapman, A. Sandham. Centre: J. W. Hearne, H. Strudwick, J. W. H. T. Douglas, A. E. R. Gilligan (captain), J. B. Hobbs, F. E. Woolley. Front: R. Kilner, E. H. Hendren, A. P. Freeman, H. Sutcliffe, H. Howell.

notable contributions. No less than 180,605 people watched the game and the receipts were £22,628.

England had to win the third Test to save the rubber. The visitors made a great start by reducing Australia to 22 for 3, but then both Tate and Gilligan had to retire with injuries—in fact Gilligan retired from the match, apart from batting briefly, and Chapman took over the direction. Ryder hit a very sound double century to put Australia back on an even keel and though England's batting was more consistent, the home side obtained a first innings lead of 124. Rain helped England dismiss Australia a second time, which left 375 required. The tourists made a

tremendous fight of it and nearly all the batsmen came off—in the end the margin between the sides was a mere 11 runs.

The team went off to Tasmania for two holiday matches and came back to slaughter Victoria; Hearne and Kilner, making the most of a drying wicket, bowled the State out for 50 in their second innings to bring victory by an innings and 271 runs.

Everything went right for England in the fourth Test—Gilligan at last won the toss; Hobbs and Sutcliffe added 126 and the remaining batsmen all played a part in reaching a total of 548. When Australia batted showers affected the pitch, as did an impatient crowd, and England bowled the home country out

1924-25: M.C.C. to Ceylon and Australia

1st Match: v Ceylon (Colombo)   Oct 4.
M.C.C. 73 (W. T. Greswell 8-38) & 119-4 (A. P. F. Chapman 70*) drew with Ceylon 58.

2nd Match: v Western Australia (Perth)   Oct 17, 18, 20.
M.C.C. 330-7 dec (R. Kilner 103, J. W. H. T. Douglas 62) drew with W. Australia 57 & 157-7 (F. Taafe 71).

3rd Match: v Western Australian Colts (Perth)   Oct 22, 23.
W.A. Colts XV 195 (H. Cantwell 66) drew with M.C.C. 405-7 (W. W. Whysall 90, A. Sandham 79, J. B. Hobbs 74, F. E. Woolley 52).

4th Match: v Western Australia (Perth)   Oct 24, 25, 27, 28.
M.C.C. 397 (A. E. R. Gilligan 138, J. W. Hearne 54, R. Blundell 5-59) beat W. Australia 138 (A. P. Freeman 6-47) & 69 by an inns & 190 runs.

5th Match: v Goldfields Association XV (Kalgoorlie)   Oct 31, Nov 1.
M.C.C. 346-9 dec (F. E. Woolley 67, R. Kilner 63, C. Taylor 5-70) & 111-3 dec drew with Goldfields XV 42 & 52-7.

6th Match: v South Australia (Adelaide)   Nov 7, 8, 10, 11.
S. Australia 346-4 dec (A. J. Richardson 200*, V. Y. Richardson 87) & 103 (J. W. Hearne 5-17) lost to M.C.C. 406 (F. E. Woolley 90, J. W. Hearne 78, H. Sutcliffe 75, J. B. Hobbs 50) & 44-1 by 9 wkts.

7th Match: v Victoria (Melbourne)   Nov 14, 15, 17, 18, 19.
M.C.C. 240 (J. W. H. T. Douglas 59*) & 241 (A. Sandham 66, E. H. Hendren 54) lost to Victoria 229 (H. S. T. L. Hendry 63) & 253-4 (E. R. Mayne 87, W. M. Woodfull 61, A. E. V. Hartkopf 56*) by 6 wkts.

8th Match: v New South Wales (Sydney)   Nov 21, 22, 24, 25.
N.S.W. 271 (W. Bardsley 160, J. M. Taylor 51, M. W. Tate 7-74) & 221 (T. J. E. Andrews 86*, R. K. Tyldesley 6-83) lost to M.C.C. 193 (E. H. Hendren 75*) & 301-7 (J. B. Hobbs 81, A. P. F. Chapman 72) by 3 wkts.

9th Match: v Queensland (Brisbane)   Nov 29, Dec 1, 2.
M.C.C. 522 (E. H. Hendren 168, A. P. F. Chapman 80, A. Sandham 64, J. B. Hobbs 51, P. M. Hornibrook 5-210) drew with Queensland 275 & 131-3 (L. P. D. O'Connor 66*).

10th Match: v An Australian XI (Brisbane)   Dec 4, 5, 6, 8.
Australian XI 526 (F. C. Thompson 114, F. Taafe 86*, W. H. Ponsford 81, L. P. D. O'Connor 50, H. S. T. L. Hendry 68, A. P. Freeman 6-160) & 257 (A. J. Richardson 83, A. F. Kippax 82*) drew with M.C.C. 421 (E. H. Hendren 100, A. P. F. Chapman 92, J. W. H. T. Douglas 54, R. Kilner 52).

11th Match: v Toowoomba (Toowoomba)   Dec 9, 10.
M.C.C. 394-3 dec (J. W. Hearne 174*, M. W. Tate 94, H. Sutcliffe 90) beat Toowoomba XIII 181 (F. Drews 52, A. P. Freeman 6-48) & 87 (R. Kilner 7-36) by an inns & 126 runs.

12th Match: v Australian Juniors XII (Sydney)   Dec 13, 15, 16.
Juniors XII 169 & 93-7 drew with M.C.C. 319-5 dec (J. B. Hobbs 114, H. Sutcliffe 68, E. H. Hendren 54).

13th Match: v Australia (Sydney)   Dec 19, 20, 22, 23, 24, 26, 27.
Australia 450 (H. L. Collins 114, W. H. Ponsford 110, M. W. Tate 6-130) & 452 (J. M. Taylor 108, A. J. Richardson 98, H. L. Collins 60, M. W. Tate 5-98) beat

England 298 (J. B. Hobbs 115, E. H. Hendren 74*, H. Sutcliffe 59, J. M. Gregory 5-111) & 411 (F. E. Woolley 123, H. Sutcliffe 115, J. B. Hobbs 57, A. P. Freeman 50*) by 195 runs.

14th Match: v Australia (Melbourne)   Jan 1, 2, 3, 5, 6, 7, 8.
Australia 600 (V. Y. Richardson 138, W. H. Ponsford 128, A. E. V. Hartkopf 80, J. M. Taylor 72) & 250 (J. M. Taylor 90, M. W. Tate 6-99) beat England 479 (H. Sutcliffe 176, J. B. Hobbs 154) & 290 (H. Sutcliffe 127, F. E. Woolley 50, A. A. Mailey 5-92) by 81 runs.

15th Match: v Ballarat XV (Ballarat)   Jan 10, 12.
Ballarat XV 185 (R. Kilner 6-27) & 154 (H. Austin 64, R. K. Tyldesley 6-37) drew with M.C.C. 299 (J. L. Bryan 83, R. Kilner 64, J. W. Hearne 50).

16th Match: v Australia (Adelaide)   Jan 16, 17, 19, 20, 21, 23.
Australia 489 (J. Ryder 201*, T. J. E. Andrews 72, A. J. Richardson 69) & 250 (J. Ryder 88) beat England 365 (J. B. Hobbs 119, E. H. Hendren 92) & 363 (W. W. Whysall 75, H. Sutcliffe 59, A. P. F. Chapman 58) by 11 runs.

17th Match: v Tasmania (Launceston)   Jan 27, 28, 29.
M.C.C. 218 (A. Sandham 116) & 331-7 dec (E. H. Hendren 101*, A. E. R. Gilligan 60, A. Sandham 51) beat Tasmania 166 (R. Kilner 5-35) & 264 (G. W. Martin 121) by 119 runs.

18th Match: v Tasmania (Hobart)   Jan 30, 31, Feb 2.
Tasmania 89 (M. W. Tate 6-26) & 224 (H. Howell 6-96) lost to M.C.C. 449 (H. Sutcliffe 188, A. Sandham 92, E. H. Hendren 50) by an inns & 136 runs.

19th Match: v Victoria (Melbourne)   Feb 6, 7, 9, 10.
M.C.C. (H. Sutcliffe 193, W. W. Whysall 89, H. Sutcliffe 88, J. L. Bryan 59, H. Ironmonger 5-93) beat Victoria 179 (V. S. Ransford 62, W. M. Woodfull 60, R. Kilner 5-48) & 50 (R. Kilner 5-18, J. W. Hearne 5-30) by an inns & 271 runs.

20th Match: v Australia (Melbourne)   Feb 13, 14, 16, 17, 18.
England 548 (H. Sutcliffe 143, W. W. Whysall 76, R. Kilner 74, J. B. Hobbs 66, E. H. Hendren 65) beat Australia 269 (J. M. Taylor 86) & 250 (J. M. Taylor 68, M. W. Tate 5-75) by an inns & 29 runs.

21st Match: v New South Wales (Sydney)   Feb 21, 23, 24, 25.
M.C.C. 626 (E. H. Hendren 165, F. E. Woolley 149, A. Sandham 137, J. L. Bryan 72) & 296-8 (A. Sandham 104, F. E. Woolley 80) drew with N.S.W. 619 (T. J. E. Andrews 224, H. L. Collins 173, R. Kilner 6-145).

22nd Match: v Australia (Sydney)   Feb 27, 28, March 2, 3, 4.
Australia 295 (W. H. Ponsford 80) & 325 (T. J. E. Andrews 80, C. Kelleway 73, W. A. S. Oldfield 65*, M. W. Tate 5-115) beat England 167 (C. V. Grimmett 5-45) & 146 (C. V. Grimmett 6-37) by 307 runs.

23rd Match: v Northern Districts (West Maitland)   March 6, 7.
N. Districts XV 157 (J. W. Hearne 8-18) & 153-7 (G. Bell 68) drew with M.C.C. 337-7 dec (H. Sutcliffe 136*, R. Kilner 66).

24th Match: v South Australia (Adelaide)   March 13, 14, 15.
M.C.C. 179 (A. Sandham 59, A. J. Richardson 5-52) & 264 (W. W. Whysall 101, A. Sandham 64, E. H. Hendren 59, C. V. Grimmett 7-85) lost to S. Australia 443 (J. W. Rymill 146, P. D. Rundell 90, D. E. Pritchard 87) & 1-0 by 10 wkts.

1924-25: M.C.C. to Ceylon and Australia

Batting Averages

	M	I	NO	R	HS	Avge	100	c/s
H. Sutcliffe (Yorks)	12	18	0	1250	188	69.44	5	6
E. H. Hendren (Middx)	14	22	3	1233	168	64.89	4	12
J. B. Hobbs (Surrey)	10	17	1	865	154	54.01	3	0
A. Sandham (Surrey)	12	19	0	866	137	45.58	3	3
F. E. Woolley (Kent)	10	17	0	737	149	43.35	2	10
A. P. F. Chapman (Kent)	13	19	1	625	92	34.72	0	10
J. L. Bryan (Kent)	8	10	1	300	72	33.33	0	4
W. W. Whysall (Notts)	11	17	0	566	101	33.29	1	16/2
J. W. Hearne (Middx)	11	17	1	513	193	32.06	1	9
J. W. H. T. Douglas (Essex)	8	11	2	239	62	26.55	0	4
R. Kilner (Yorks)	12	19	1	448	103	24.88	1	5
M. W. Tate (Sussex)	14	20	2	339	44	18.83	0	7
A. E. R. Gilligan (Sussex)	15	24	4	357	138	17.85	1	9
A. P. Freeman (Kent)	9	14	4	157	50	15.70	0	9/1
R. K. Tyldesley (Lancs)	10	12	2	150	39	15.00	0	8
H. Strudwick (Surrey)	11	14	4	70	22	7.00	0	22/9
H. Howell (Warks)	7	9	4	28	9	5.60	0	0

Bowling Averages

	O	M	R	W	Avge	BB	5i
H. Strudwick	3	0	9	1	9.00	1-9	0
M. W. Tate	502.2	93	1464	77	19.01	7-74	7
A. P. F. Chapman	21.2	3	82	4	20.50	2-33	0
R. Kilner	375	57	1007	40	25.17	6-145	4
H. Howell	121.4	6	453	15	30.20	6-96	1
A. P. Freeman	325	45	1209	40	30.22	6-47	2
J. W. Hearne	259	30	979	30	32.63	5-17	2
A. E. R. Gilligan	289.7	32	1075	28	38.39	4-12	0
R. K. Tyldesley	246	31	908	22	41.27	6-83	1
F. E. Woolley	169	24	549	13	42.23	4-77	0
E. H. Hendren	9.1	0	61	1	61.00	1-27	0
J. W. H. T. Douglas	100.1	10	393	6	65.50	2-25	0

Also bowled: J. L. Bryan 8-0-57-0; J. B. Hobbs 8-0-37-0; H. Sutcliffe 6-0-25-0; A. Sandham 4.1-0-25-0; W. W. Whysall 2-0-9-0.

twice for under 300 to produce an innings victory–the first by England against Australia since 1912.

This success was however short-lived for in the fifth and final Test, the English batting once more collapsed–even Hobbs and Sutcliffe made a duck each and Australia won by 307 runs. The slow right-arm bowler, Grimmett, on his Test debut, was the cause of England's downfall, taking 11 for 82 in the match.

The last match of the tour was another defeat–at the hands of South Australia by 10 wickets–but the M.C.C. were without Hobbs and Sutcliffe. Those two batsmen were without doubt the outstanding players of the tour and their batting quite outshone that of their colleagues. Woolley and Hendren certainly improved on their efforts of 1920-21 but not to any marked extent. Chapman's impetuosity was his undoing, though he did play some useful innings. Whysall and Kilner also made runs, but Hearne and Sandham had a lean time. The bowling relied too heavily on Tate; Gilligan and Douglas proved of little account and as forecast Freeman was superfluous. It must however be noted that generally England out-fielded Australia, except perhaps in their returns to the wicket.

For Australia Taylor was the principal batsman and a much safer player than hitherto, but Ponsford was only a fraction behind him. Ryder unfortunately missed two Tests due to a bad back but headed the averages with some good innings. In the bowling Grimmett was the discovery of the season, whilst Gregory still remained a powerful force.

Financially the tour was most successful and socially no major upset marred its progress.

1924-25: England 'second team' draw series

Under the auspices of S. B. Joel, a strong English team went out to South Africa in the winter of 1924-25. The side was: the Hon L. H. Tennyson (Hants) (capt), T. O. Jameson (Hants), J. C. W. MacBryan (Somerset), F. W. H. Nicholas (Essex), A. H. H. Gilligan (Sussex), E. L. D. Bartley (Navy), C. S. Marriott (Kent) and the professionals G. E. Tyldesley (Lancs), E. H. Bowley

(Sussex), P. Holmes (Yorks), C. A. G. Russell (Essex), A. S. Kennedy (Hants), C. W. L. Parker (Gloucs), G. Geary (Leics) and W. E. Astill (Leics). F. W. Gilligan of Essex was invited but had to decline.

The fact that South Africa had done so well against the M.C.C. side in 1922-23 caused the critics to wonder if the present team were not attempting too much–with the leading English players being in Australia, this was of necessity the England second team. In view of what happened a few years later, it is interesting to note that there was considerable debate on the subject of the 'Test Matches' which were to be played on the tour. In the end it was generally agreed that these could not be official 'Tests' since

1924-25: S. B. Joel's Team to South Africa

1st Match: v Schools & Colleges XV (Cape Town) (One Day) Nov 13.
Schools XV 34 (C. W. L. Parker 6-1) & 46-11 lost to Joel's XI 133 (A. J. Bell 6-35) by 99 runs on first inns.

2nd Match: v Western Province (Cape Town) Nov 14, 15.
Joel's XI 252-9 dec (A. S. Kennedy 67*, J. Bolton 6-81) drew with W. Province 118 (A. S. Kennedy 5-42) & 82-8.

3rd Match: v Natal (Pietermaritzburg) Nov 19, 20.
Joel's XI 179 (D. P. Conyngham 5-90) & 108-5 drew with Natal 202 (H. W. Taylor 58, A. S. Kennedy 5-67).

4th Match: v Natal (Durban) Nov 21, 22, 24.
Joel's XI 154 (P. Holmes 62, D. P. Conyngham 5-49) & 296-9 dec (J. C. W. MacBryan 120, G. E. Tyldesley 61, D. P. Conyngham 5-101) drew with Natal 116 (C. S. Marriott 6-45) & 172-4.

5th Match: v Pretoria (Berea Park) Nov 26, 27.
Pretoria 255 (L. C. A. Newnham 58) & 50-2 drew with Joel's XI 199 (F. W. H. Nicholas 54).

6th Match: v Griqualand West (Kimberley) Nov 29, Dec 1, 2.
Joel's XI 272 & 362 (G. E. Tyldesley 174, C. A. G. Russell 59, J. C. W. MacBryan 55) drew with Griqualand West 293 (L. E. Tapscott 102, W. V. Ling 91) & 246-8 (C. D. McKay 111*, W. V. Ling 75).

7th Match: v Rhodesia (Bulawayo) Dec 5, 6, 8.
Joel's XI 294 (E. H. Rowley 131, T. O. Jameson 90*) & 42-2 beat Rhodesia 121 & 212 (F. H. Morgan 50, G. Geary 5-70) by 8 wkts.

8th Match: v Transvaal (Johannesburg) Dec 16, 17, 18.
Transvaal 109 (A. S. Kennedy 6-46) & 354 (H. G. Deane 118, M. J. Susskind 88) lost to Joel's XI 349 (G. E. Tyldesley 147, P. Holmes 56) & 117-2 (G. E. Tyldesley 55*) by 8 wkts.

9th Match: v East Rand (Benoi) Dec 19, 20.
Joel's XI 457 (E. H. Bowley 152, C. A. G. Russell 54, W. D. Duff 5-121) & 85-5 drew with East Rand 260 (S. J. Snooke 69).

10th Match: v South Africa (Johannesburg) Dec 23, 24, 26.
Joel's XI 198 (E. H. Bowley 57, L. H. Tennyson 57, E. P. Nupen 5-54) & 149 (E. H. Bowley 54, G. E. Tyldesley 51, E. P. Nupen 5-33) lost to South Africa 295 (V. H. Neser 80, A. W. Nourse 71) & 53-1 by 9 wkts.

11th Match: v South Africa (Durban) Jan 1, 2, 3, 5.
Joel's XI 285 (E. H. Bowley 118, E. P. Nupen 5-65) & 174 (P. Holmes 81, E. P. Nupen 7-46) beat South Africa 211 (H. W. Taylor 112, W. E. Astill 5-82) & 200 (V. H. Neser 52, A. S. Kennedy 5-51) by 48 runs.

12th Match: v Northern Natal (Ladysmith) Jan 6, 7.
Joel's XI 269 (J. Riddell 5-58) drew with N. Natal 124 (T. O. Jameson 7-37) & 147-6 (V. Sparks 52).

13th Match: v Northern Districts XV (Bethlehem) Jan 9, 10.
N. Districts XV 139 (T. O. Jameson 12-37) & 110-8 drew with Joel's XI 267 (C. A. G. Russell 65, D. de Villiers 6-6).

14th Match: v South Africa (Cape Town) Jan 15, 16.
South Africa 113 (G. Geary 6-37) & 150 (R. H. Catterall 50) lost to Joel's XI 224 (C. A. G. Russell 54, G. E. Tyldesley 50, A. E. Hall 6-62) & 40-0 by 10 wkts.

15th Match: v Country Districts (Worcester) Jan 20, 21.
Country Districts 113 (G. Geary 6-40) & 132 (E. Neethling 64) lost to Joel's XI 251 (G. E. Tyldesley 92, T. O. Jameson 64, I. Buys 5-77) by an inns & 6 runs.

16th Match: v S.W. Districts (Mossel Bay) Jan 23, 24.
S.W. Districts 47 (G. Geary 6-26) & 105 lost to Joel's XI 353-9 dec (P. Holmes 104, T. O. Jameson 63*, C. A. G. Russell 56) by an inns & 201 runs.

17th Match: v Eastern Province (Grahamstown) Jan 28, 29.
E. Province 62 (A. S. Kennedy 6-27) & 165 (D. Dold 57) lost to Joel's XI 212 (A. S. Kennedy 58, C. Munro 7-81) & 19-2 by 8 wkts.

18th Match: v Border (East London) Jan 31, Feb 2.
Border 200 (C. W. L. Parker 5-39) & 107-5 drew with Joel's XI 311-4 dec (J. C. W. MacBryan 114, T. O. Jameson 62*, E. H. Bowley 61).

19th Match: v South Africa (Johannesburg) Feb 6, 7, 9, 10.
Joel's XI 239 (C. A. G. Russell 80, T. O. Jameson 53*) & 164 (E. P. Nupen 5-51) drew with South Africa 193 (M. J. Susskind 55) & 16-0.

20th Match: v Orange Free State (Bloemfontein) Feb 13, 14, 16.
Joel's XI 442 (T. O. Jameson 133, G. E. Tyldesley 96, F. W. H. Nicholas 78, E. H. Bowley 67) drew with O.F.S. 384 (S. K. Coen 103, C. Maritz 56, R. Dick 51).

21st Match: v South Africa (Port Elizabeth) Feb 20, 21, 23, 24.
South Africa 183 (I. J. Siedle 52, G. Geary 5-63) & 200 (R. H. Catterall 86) beat Joel's XI 94 & 268 (G. E. Tyldesley 79, P. Holmes 62, A. E. Hall 5-76) by 21 runs.

1924-25: S. B. Joel's Team to South Africa

Batting Averages

	M	I	NO	R	HS	Avge	100	c/s
G. E. Tyldesley (Lancs)	11	19	2	965	174	56.76	2	3
T. O. Jameson (Hants)	10	15	4	430	133	39.09	1	4
E. H. Bowley (Sussex)	14	22	1	732	131	34.85	2	18
P. Holmes (Yorks)	13	20	1	536	81	28.21	0	7
C. A. G. Russell (Essex)	12	19	2	469	80	27.58	0	4
J. C. W. MacBryan (Som)	10	16	0	426	120	26.62	2	8
A. S. Kennedy (Hants)	14	20	2	391	67*	21.72	0	4
Hon L. H. Tennyson (Hants)	14	23	2	342	57	16.28	0	5
F. W. H. Nicholas (Essex)	5	8	2	91	78	15.16	0	0
C. W. L. Parker (Gloucs)	13	18	5	191	51*	14.69	0	2
A. H. H. Gilligan (Sussex)	5	7	1	85	19	14.16	0	2
E. L. D. Bartley (Navy)	12	19	8	117	24	10.63	0	24/8
G. Geary (Leics)	11	16	1	143	37	9.40	0	7
W. E. Astill (Leics)	2	3	0	27	16	9.00	0	2
C. S. Marriott (Kent)	8	9	2	14	4	2.00	0	2

Bowling Averages

	O	M	R	W	Avge	BB	5i
G. Geary	407.5	104	955	59	16.18	6-37	3
C. W. L. Parker	284.1	77	721	44	16.38	5-39	1
A. S. Kennedy	478.5	119	1287	65	19.81	6-27	5
C. A. G. Russell	9	1	21	1	21.00	1-8	0
E. H. Bowley	29	3	112	5	22.40	3-18	0
C. S. Marriott	209	48	563	24	23.45	6-45	1
T. O. Jameson	113	21	343	14	24.50	3-13	0
W. E. Astill	117	40	223	8	27.87	5-82	1

Also bowled: Hon L. H. Tennyson 10-0-56-0.
Played in non-first-class matches only: A. S. Frames.

1925-26: M.C.C. to West Indies

1st Match: v Barbados Colts XV (Bridgetown) Jan 1, 2.
M.C.C. 310-8 dec (F. B. Watson 97, E. J. Smith 59) drew with Colts XV 96 (R. Kilner 7-24) & 116-7.

2nd Match: v Barbados (Bridgetown) Jan 4, 5, 6.
M.C.C. 151 (H. C. Griffith 5-54) & 65 (G. N. Francis 6-21) lost to Barbados 289-7 dec (G. Challenor 124) by an inns & 73 runs.

3rd Match: v West Indies (Bridgetown) Jan 8, 9, 11, 12.
M.C.C. 597-8 dec (W. R. Hammond 238*, T. O. Jameson 98, E. J. Smith 73, W. E. Astill 66, P. Holmes 63) drew with West Indies 147 (G. Challenor 63, P. H. Tarilton 50) & 21-6.

4th Match: v Barbados (Bridgetown) Jan 14, 15, 16.
Barbados 401-5 dec (P. H. Tarilton 178, E. L. G. Hoad 71, L. S. Birkett 62*) drew with M.C.C. 110 (G. N. Francis 7-50) & 184-8.

5th Match: v Trinidad (Port of Spain) Jan 21, 22, 23.
M.C.C. 272 (W. R. Hammond 56, H. L. Dales 50, G. John 5-54) & 198-6 (W. E. Astill 61, W. R. Hammond 52) drew with Trinidad 259 (A. Cipriani 103, W. R. Hammond 6-89).

6th Match: v Trinidad (Port of Spain) Jan 26, 27, 28.
Trinidad 173 (J. A. Small 57, W. R. Hammond 5-39) & 270-7 dec (W. H. St Hill 105, G. Dewhurst 56, R. Kilner 6-83) drew with M.C.C. 143 & 177-3 (P. Holmes 56).

7th Match: v West Indies (Port of Spain) Jan 30, Feb 1, 2.
West Indies 275 (C. R. Browne 74, G. Dewhurst 55) & 281 (C. A. Wiles 75, H. B. G. Austin 69, W. E. Astill 6-67) lost to M.C.C. 319 (F. B. Watson 79, P. Holmes 65) & 240-5 by 5 wkts.

8th Match: v British Guiana (Georgetown) Feb 9, 10, 11.
M.C.C. 350 (F. B. Watson 73, W. E. Astill 69, T. O. Jameson 57) & 46-0 drew with British Guiana 373 (E. A. Phillips 92).

9th Match: v West Indies (Georgetown) Feb 13, 15, 16, 17.
West Indies 462 (C. R. Browne 102*, C. V. Wight 90, G. Challenor 82, W. H. St Hill 72, G. Dewhurst 54) drew with M.C.C. 264 (F. B. Watson 59, P. Holmes 53) & 243-8 (L. H. Tennyson 57*, W. E. Astill 51).

10th Match: v British Guiana (Georgetown) Feb 19, 20, 22.
M.C.C. 385 (W. R. Hammond 111, F. B. Watson 64, F. S. Gough-Calthorpe 64) & 124-2 drew with British Guiana 348 (M. P. Fernandes 120).

11th Match: v Jamaica (Kingston) March 10, 11, 12.
Jamaica 334 (E. A. Rae 75, C. M. Morales 74, F. R. Martin 66) & 128 (O. C. Scott 54, R. Kilner 7-50) lost to M.C.C. 238 (P. Holmes 62) & 227-5 (P. Holmes 62) by 5 wkts.

12th Match: v Jamaica (Kingston) March 13, 15, 16.
Jamaica 255 (O. C. Scott 58) & 277-5 (R. K. Nunes 140*, O. C. Scott 72) drew with M.C.C. 476-9 dec (T. O. Jameson 110, F. B. Watson 103*, L. G. Crawley 85, R. Kilner 54, E. J. Smith 50).

13th Match: v Jamaica (Kingston) March 18, 19, 20.
Jamaica 445-9 dec (R. K. Nunes 83, F. R. Martin 80, O. C. Scott 62, J. K. Holt 57) drew with M.C.C. 510-6 (P. Holmes 244, W. E. Astill 156, E. J. Smith 65).

England could not have a representative eleven in two countries at the same time.

The team left England aboard the *Edinburgh Castle* on 24 October and opened its campaign with a one-day match at Newlands on 13 November. The side more than held its own in the early matches and gained a creditable win over Transvaal, due to two good innings by Tyldesley and Kennedy's bowling. In the 'First Test', the tourists' batting failed badly, though they were without Holmes, who was ill. Nupen bowled well on the matting wicket, but the English bowlers could not use it to the same advantage. Holmes came into the team for the 'Second Test', as did Astill, who was coaching in South Africa. The latter played for Marriott, who was unwell. The addition of these two cricketers made all the difference—Holmes scored 101 runs and Astill took 6 wickets—and victory was obtained by 48 runs.

South Africa were without four of her leading players for the 'Third Test' and most importantly without Nupen. Geary found the wicket—matting over coarse grass—just to his liking, and as Tyldesley and Russell came off with the bat the visitors won the game at a canter. The home side were back at full strength for the 'Fourth Test', but a very even match had to be drawn because of rain on the final day.

The bowling of Nupen and Hall won South Africa the last 'Test', though the tourists fought back splendidly in the final innings and the difference between the sides was only 21 runs.

The tour was felt to be a success. The English side's tail was rather too pronounced. Tyldesley was the best bat, whilst Geary stole the bowling honours. Two of the features of the tour were the wicket-keeping of Bartley and Bowley's efforts at first slip. On the financial side, the venture lost about £4,000.

1925-26: Barbados again beat M.C.C., but 'Test' series won

In the previous winter, the M.C.C. had promised to send a team out to the West Indies and indeed had appointed R. St L. Fowler as captain and obtained promises from several other players. It was not until September that the tour was cancelled, but the M.C.C. then stated that if invited by the West Indian authorities, they would send a team in 1925-26. Unfortunately Fowler died in June 1925, at the early age of 34, and the team which travelled

to the West Indies was: F. S. Gough-Calthorpe (Warwicks) (capt), the Hon L. H. Tennyson (Hants), T. O. Jameson (Hants), C. T. Bennett (Cambridge U), L. G. Crawley (Cambridge U), H. L. Dales (Middx) and the professionals W. E. Astill (Leics), G. C. Collins (Kent), W. R. Hammond (Gloucs), C. F. Root (Worcs), P. Holmes (Yorks), R. Kilner (Yorks), F. B. Watson (Lancs) and E. J. Smith (Warwicks). Capt C. Levick acted as manager and Collins was baggage-master.

The team might be described as of strong county standard, though there was only one fast bowler—Collins—which seemed a little odd, when it is recalled that fast bowlers are the life-blood of West Indian cricket.

The tour opened in Barbados at the beginning of January and, after a looseller against a Colts team, the tourists were totally outplayed by Barbados, the fast bowling of Francis and Griffith being altogether too much for them. In the 'First Test', which came immediately afterwards, the M.C.C. had their team picked for them owing to the indisposition of Watson and Bennett. Hammond and Jameson however batted quite brilliantly, the Gloucester man being in for 5 hours without giving a chance. Then the West Indies had to bat on a sticky wicket and only further rain saved them from a heavy defeat. Positions were reversed for the return against Barbados and time now saved M.C.C. from an innings defeat. Moving on to Trinidad, the tourists played two even draws against the island, before meeting West Indies. In this 'Second Test', the visitors won a match through all-round ability, no one player taking a decisive role.

The three games in British Guiana were all drawn. All were high scoring and with matches restricted to three days each, only in the 'Third Test' did a definite result look a possibility, but here rain flooded the ground on the last afternoon. The last leg of the tour began after the long voyage to Jamaica. The weakest of the four colonies, Jamaica were always behind in the three matches played–even in the final one when they hit 445, the M.C.C. went to 510 for 6 before time ran out.

The best bat on the tour was Holmes and he would have had even better figures but for his sea-sickness. Hammond also batted in good style and was a wonderful fielder. Fourth in the batting was Watson, a difficult man to dislodge. The best bowler was Astill who turned the ball both ways and was effective on matting wickets. The only problem on the tour was in fact the umpiring, which except in British Guiana left much to be desired.

1926-27: first M.C.C. tourists unbeaten in India, Burma and Ceylon

This first M.C.C. tour to India, and indeed the first English tour of the sub-continent since 1902-03, was a much too ambitious venture. To fit in all 34 fixtures and the travelling entailed, many of the games were reduced to two-day matches and thus had little prospect of definite finishes. It was all done with the best of intentions, but to the players it seemed at times like a gruelling marathon that would never end.

The team was A. E. R. Gilligan (Sussex) (capt), P. T. Eckersley (Lancs), M. Ll. Hill (Somerset), G. F. Earle (Somerset), Major R. C. J. Chichester-Constable (Yorks 2nd), R. E. S. Wyatt (Warwicks) and the professionals W. E. Astill (Leics), G. S. Boyes (Hants), G. Brown (Hants), J. H. Parsons (Warwicks), A. Sandham (Surrey), G. Geary (Leics), M. W. Tate (Sussex) and J. Mercer (Glamorgan). Root had been invited but Worcester refused to release him.

Sailing from Tilbury on 24 September in the s.s. *Narcunda*, the team called at Marseilles and Port Said before reaching Bombay, where they stopped for a few hours and then voyaged on to Karachi, where the first four matches were played.

The first three games being only two days each were drawn, though the tourists were well placed in them all. In the three-day match against All Karachi, some hard-hitting batting by Parsons and the all-round cricket of Tate gave the tourists victory by an innings. Both matches at Rawalpindi were drawn, the most noteworthy feature being Tate's century in 120 minutes in the second.

Next stop on the tour was Lahore where four matches were contested and only the one of three-days duration provided the

tourists with another innings victory. Wyatt hit a careful hundred, whilst Geary took 11 wickets. By some misfortune both the tourists' wicket-keepers were injured prior to this game, Hill having a poisoned foot and Brown a hand injury. The team therefore called on A. Dolphin, the Yorkshire stumper, who was in India coaching. After two matches in Ajmere, the side arrived in Bombay for a series of five matches. In the first–against Hindus– some 45,000 attended on the two days and watched Nayudu hit 153 in 100 minutes off the visitors' attack. Victory by an innings was gained over Bombay Presidency, with Sandham and Wyatt giving the team a grand start by reaching 224 before a wicket fell. The 'First Test' followed this game. The Indians proved as good as the tourists and only the first innings of each team were completed. The other 'Test' was played at the team's next venue– Calcutta. Owing to injury and illness, the side were down to ten men and the Maharajah of Patiala made up the team in the two first-class matches in Calcutta, both of which ended in victory–in the second game, which was the 'Test', Wyatt played a brilliant undefeated innings of 97 on a worn pitch to take the M.C.C. to a hard-fought win.

Going on from Calcutta to Burma, the team played two games in Rangoon. Here the wicket was a matting one and the locals were saved in the first game by the old Essex cricketer Hubert Ashton, who scored 48 and an undefeated 60. In the second match, Boyes removed him cheaply twice and the M.C.C. won just in time by 10 wickets. From Rangoon and on to Madras, where three games took place–Wyatt, for a bet, drove round the ground on a motor-cycle with a woman's hat on his head, much to the amusement of the crowd.

In the first game in Ceylon, Tate completed the double of 1,000 runs and 100 wickets for the tour. The matches in Ceylon proved easy ones for the tourists and in the second Wyatt performed the unusual feat of scoring a century and taking a hat-trick.

The team returned to India and the last match was played in Patiala against the Maharajah's side, where the old Australian cricketer who used to play for Middlesex, Tarrant, scored a hard hit 68. The team returned to England in mid-March, having been undefeated in 34 matches. It is not strictly correct to state that the team were undefeated, since they were beaten in a one-day unofficial match against Delhi Ladies! Sandham and Wyatt were the leading run-getters, Tate and Geary shared bowling honours.

The M.C.C. depart from Tilbury on board the s.s. Narcunda *for the first tour of India since 1902-03 on 24 September 1926. On the steps wearing a pullover is R. E. S. Wyatt, later to lead M.C.C. in the West Indies.*

1926-27: M.C.C. to India, Burma and Ceylon

1st Match: v Parsis & Moslems (Karachi)   Oct 19, 20.
M.C.C. 339 (R. E. S. Wyatt 63, A. Sandham 57, M. W. Tate 57, A. E. R. Gilligan 57, Ghulam Mahomed 5-114) & 77-4 drew with Parsis & Moslems 187 (M. J. Mobed 54) & 138-3 dec.

2nd Match: v Hindus & Rest (Karachi)   Oct 23, 24.
Hindus & Rest 335 (D. Jagannath 73, L. Semper 64*, M. A. Gopaldas 62, M. W. Tate 5-61) drew with M.C.C. 249-5 (A. Sandham 129, J. H. Parsons 58).

3rd Match: v Europeans (Karachi)   Oct 26, 27.
M.C.C. 377 (A. Sandham 67, G. Geary 52) & 139-3 drew with Europeans 151.

4th Match: v Karachi (Karachi)   Oct 29, 30, 31.
Karachi 129 & 240 (J. Naomal 83, M. P. Dastur 61, M. W. Tate 5-35) lost to M.C.C. 517 (J. H. Parsons 139, M. W. Tate 77, A. E. R. Gilligan 73, G. F. Earle 51, N. J. O. Carbutt 5-135) by an inns & 148 runs.

5th Match: v Europeans (Rawalpindi)   Nov 3, 4.
M.C.C. 431-8 dec (A. Sandham 150, P. T. Eckersley 86, M. W. Tate 66, G. F. Earle 59, C. B. Barlow 5-93) & 185-5 dec (A. E. R. Gilligan 68) drew with Europeans 145 (F. J. Matthews 57) & 85-1.

6th Match: v Rawalpindi (Rawalpindi)   Nov 5, 6.
Rawalpindi 195 (Feroze Khan 83, G. S. Boyes 6-37) & 108-3 drew with M.C.C. 330-4 dec (R. E. S. Wyatt 125*, M. W. Tate 103).

7th Match: v The Army (Lahore)   Nov 10, 11.
The Army 73 (R. E. S. Wyatt 6-33) & 212-5 (R. E. H. Hudson 94, E. H. P. Mallinson 75) drew with M.C.C. 252-6 dec (A. Sandham 141*).

8th Match: v Southern Punjab (Lahore)   Nov 13, 14.
M.C.C. 285 (P. T. Eckersley 65, Nazir Ali 7-114) drew with S. Punjab 89 (M. W. Tate 5-39) & 148-9.

9th Match: v Northern Punjab (Lahore)   Nov 15, 16.
N. Punjab 169 (S. E. West 73, G. S. Boyes 5-28) drew with M.C.C. 373-8 (M. W. Tate 95, G. F. Earle 82, R. E. S. Wyatt 65, G. Geary 51).

10th Match: v Northern India (Lahore)   Nov 18, 19, 20.
N. India 100 (M. W. Tate 5-48) & 101 (G. Geary 7-34) lost to M.C.C. 333-6 dec (R. E. S. Wyatt 130*, A. Sandham 72) by an inns & 132 runs.

11th Match: v Rajputana & BBCI Railway (Ajmere)   Nov 23, 24.
Rajputana 155 (G. Geary 8-56) & 126-3 drew with M.C.C. 287 (A. Sandham 103).

12th Match: v Rajputana & Central India (Ajmere)   Nov 26, 27.
Rajputana & Central India 123 & 47 (G. Geary 5-14) lost to M.C.C. 337-9 dec (A. Sandham 81, J. H. Parsons 59*, M. Leyland 51) by an inns & 167 runs.

13th Match: v Hindus (Bombay)   Nov 30, Dec 1.
M.C.C. 363 (G. F. Earle 130, A. Sandham 52, M. W. Tate 50) & 74-1 drew with Hindus 356 (C. K. Nayudu 153, S. R. Godambe 58, L. P. Jai 53, W. E. Astill 5-75).

14th Match: v Parsis & Europeans (Bombay)   Dec 4, 5.
M.C.C. 334 (M. W. Tate 133, J. H. Parsons 73, R. J. Jamshedji 6-104) & 135 (R. J. Jamshedji 5-43) drew with Parsis & Europeans 252 (D. K. Kapadia 55, S. H. Colah 51).

15th Match: v Hindu-Mahommadan XI (Bombay)   Dec 7, 8.
Hindu-Mahommadan XI 167 (L. P. Jai 63) & 148-4 (Wazir Ali 67*) drew with M.C.C. 324 (G. Brown 84, A. Sandham 52 (Nazir Ali 6-128).

16th Match: v Bombay Presidency (Bombay)   Dec 10, 12, 13.
M.C.C. 435 (R. E. S. Wyatt 138, A. Sandham 124, W. E. Astill 53) beat Bombay Presidency 115 (G. Geary 5-28) & 203 (B. K. Kalapsi 77) by an inns & 117 runs.

17th Match: v All India (Bombay)   Dec 16, 17, 18.
M.C.C. 362 (R. E. S. Wyatt 83, J. H. Parsons 58) & 97-5 drew with All India 437 (D. B. Deodhar 148, J. G. Navie 74, K. M. Mistri 51).

18th Match: v Anglo-Indians in Bengal (Calcutta) (One Day)   Dec 22.
M.C.C. 222-2 dec (A. Sandham 112*, G. Brown 67) beat Anglo-Indians 103 (M. W. Tate 5-46).

19th Match: v British in Bengal (Calcutta) (One Day)   Dec 24.
British 152-7 dec drew with M.C.C. 102-5 (A. Sandham 53*).

20th Match: v Europeans in the East (Calcutta)   Dec 26, 28, 29.
Europeans 146 & 125 (G. S. Boyes 7-52) lost to M.C.C. 326 (A. Sandham 112, F. A. Tarrant 6-75) by an inns & 55 runs.

21st Match: v All India (Calcutta)   Dec 31, Jan 2, 3.
All India 146 (M. W. Tate 6-42) & 269 (J. L. Guise 91, F. R. R. Brooke 72) lost to M.C.C. 233 (W. E. Astill 66, M. W. Tate 58) & 185-6 (R. E. S. Wyatt 97*) by 4 wkts.

22nd Match: v Rangoon Gymkhana (Rangoon)   Jan 9, 10.
M.C.C. 381-6 dec (J. H. Parsons 160, G. Geary 75*) drew with Rangoon 173 (J. Mercer 6-39) & 211-5 (H. Ashton 60*, W. B. Giles 55).

23rd Match: v All Burma (Rangoon)   Jan 12, 13.
All Burma 144 (M. W. Tate 5-37) & 137 (M. W. Tate 5-35) lost to M.C.C. 276 (R. E. S. Wyatt 78, J. H. Parsons 64, G. Smith 5-94) & 7-0 by 10 wkts.

24th Match: v An Indian XI (Madras)   Jan 18, 19.
An Indian XI 238 (S. Mahomed Hussain 90, C. Ramaswamy 60) drew with M.C.C. 344 (R. E. S. Wyatt 55, W. E. Astill 54*).

25th Match: v Madras Europeans (Madras) (One Day)   Jan 21.
Europeans 201-9 dec drew with M.C.C. 155-8 (M. W. Tate 53).

26th Match: v All Madras (Madras)   Jan 23, 24, 25.
M.C.C. 361 (G. Brown 84, P. T. Eckersley 69*, J. H. Parsons 62, G. P. Ganapathy 5-72) & 233-7 dec (A. Sandham 82, G. Brown 56) beat Madras 256 (C. K. Nayudu 59, R. Nailer 54, C. P. Johnstone 51) & 127 by 211 runs.

27th Match: v Europeans in Ceylon (Colombo)   Jan 28, 29.
Europeans 154 (G. R. Neale 76, W. E. Astill 5-52) & 194-4 (A. E. Blair 95*) drew with M.C.C. 419 (R. E. S. Wyatt 76, J. H. Parsons 67, W. E. Astill 66, A. Sandham 51, E. P. Wedlake-Lewis 5-87).

28th Match: v Ceylonese (Colombo)   Jan 31, Feb 1.
Ceylonese 165 (S. Perinpanayagam 56) & 190-8 (C. T. van Geyzel 66, F. C. W. van Geyzel 59, R. E. S. Wyatt 5-39) drew with M.C.C. 483-8 dec (R. E. S. Wyatt 124, M. W. Tate 121, G. Geary 61*, G. Brown 51).

29th Match: v Up-Country XI (Daruwella)   Feb 3, 4.
M.C.C. 223 (A. Sandham 108, R. L. Kannangara 5-60) & 74-1 drew with Up-Country XI 166 (A. E. Blair 51, M. W. Tate 6-34).

30th Match: v All Ceylon (Colombo)   Feb 5, 7, 8.
M.C.C. 431-8 dec (R. E. S. Wyatt 101, W. E. Astill 65, J. H. Parsons 64, A. Sandham 57) beat Ceylon 105 (M. K. Albert 51, W. E. Astill 7-18) & 235 (F. A. Waldock 61, M. W. Tate 5-23) by an inns & 91 runs.

31st Match: v Aligarh University (Aligarh)   Feb 18, 19.
Aligarh Univ 86 (M. W. Tate 5-31, J. Mercer 5-52) lost to M.C.C. 197 (A. Sandham 52) by an inns & 14 runs.

32nd Match: v Delhi & District (Delhi) (One Day)   Feb 20.
M.C.C. 232-4 dec (G. Brown 98, A. Sandham 56) drew with Delhi 92-9.

33rd Match: v Northern India (Delhi)   Feb 22, 23, 24.
M.C.C. 369-9 dec (R. E. S. Wyatt 96, A. Sandham 74, J. H. Parsons 61, G. F. Earle 58, Nazir Ali 6-156) drew with N. India 185 (R. E. H. Hudson 61, W. E. Astill 5-45) & 260-1 (Wazir Ali 113*, Dilawar Hussain 85).

34th Match: v Patiala (Patiala)   Feb 26, 27.
Patiala 303-4 dec (Wazir Ali 149, F. A. Tarrant 68) drew with M.C.C. 252 (R. E. S. Wyatt 67, M. W. Tate 65).

1926-27: first English tourists to Uruguay, Chile and Peru

It was originally intended that the M.C.C. should send a team of amateurs to Argentine, but the programme was expanded until additional matches had been arranged in Uruguay, Chile and Peru – it was the first time an English side had been seen in any of those three countries.

The party consisted of: P. F. Warner (Middx) (capt), T. O. Jameson (Hants), G. O. B. Allen (Middx), G. R. Jackson (Derbys), G. J. V. Weigall (Kent), L. C. R. Isherwood (Sussex), J. C. White (Som), R. T. Stanyforth (Army), Lord Dunglass (Middx), M. F. S. Jewell (Worcs), H. P. Miles (M.C.C.), T. A. Pilkington.

Sailing on the s.s. *Andes*, the team played their first match in a suburb of Montevideo, before going on to the Argentine. The three major games of the tour were the 'Tests' against Argentina, who were captained by C. H. Gibson. In the 'First Test', Marshal hit a century for the home side, but rain forced a draw. At Belgrano in the 'Second Test', some good bowling by Jameson and White brought victory for M.C.C., but in the 'Third' a thunderstorm caused the wicket to be quite treacherous and Dorning quite unplayable, so that Argentina squared the series. It was then agreed to arrange a fourth and deciding 'Test' at Belgrano and the M.C.C. abandoned their proposed trip to Mar del Plata. Argentina scored 271 in their first innings, but some lively batting by the M.C.C. tail took the visitors' total to 384, at which point Warner declared, leaving just two hours playing time. J. C. White then bowled out the opposition with five minutes to spare and M.C.C. won by an innings.

The tourists crossed the Andes and played both Chile and Peru, before returning to England.

On a political note, it should be mentioned that one of the

'Tests' was watched by the President of the Argentine, whilst Lord Dunglass, who played, became better known as Sir Alec Douglas Home, who was Prime Minister in 1963-64.

The M.C.C. team of amateurs under P. F. Warner leaving London for the tour of Argentina, Uruguay, Chile and Peru in 1926-27. Warner is third from right. On the left is G. O. B. Allen and next to him Lord Dunglass.

1926-27: M.C.C. to South America

1st Match: v Montevideo (Blanqueado)   Dec 24, 25.
M.C.C. 366-7 dec (T. O. Jameson 100, P. F. Warner 81, G. R. Jackson 61) beat Montevideo 64 (J. C. White 7-27) & 98 (T. O. Jameson 5-21) by an inns & 204 runs.

2nd Match: v Northern Suburbs (Saenz Pena)   Dec 28, 29.
M.C.C. 459 (T. O. Jameson 120*, M. F. S. Jewell 88, G. O. B. Allen 87) drew with N. Suburbs 189 (R. A. de C. Lyons 71, G. O. B. Allen 6-29) & 174-6 (W. A. Cowes 67*).

3rd Match: v Argentine (Hurlingham)   Dec 31, Jan 1, 2.
Argentine 327 (H. W. Marshal 105, K. Henderson 70, G. O. B. Allen 5-115) drew with M.C.C. 90-4.

4th Match: v Concordia (Concordia)   Jan 4, 5.
Concordia 78 (H. P. Miles 6-29) & 173 (H. P. Miles 6-60) lost to M.C.C. 365 (L. C. R. Isherwood 101, G. J. V. Weigall 73, J. C. White 73*) by an inns & 114 runs.

5th Match: v Argentine (Belgrano)   Jan 8, 9, 10.
M.C.C. 249 (R. T. Stanyforth 56, F. A. Bryans 5-67) & 193-8 dec beat Argentine 153 (T. O. Jameson 5-27) & 162 (T. O. Jameson 5-29) by 127 runs.

6th Match: v Rosario (Rosario)   Jan 12, 13.
M.C.C. 112-6 dec & 54-5 drew with Rosario 76.

7th Match: v Argentine (Palermo)   Jan 15, 16, 17.
Argentine 134 (J. C. White 5-65) & 63 beat M.C.C. 89 (H. Dorning 7-38) & 79 (D. Ayling 6-32) by 29 runs.

8th Match: v Argentine (Belgrano)   Jan 20, 21, 22.
Argentine 271 (J. Knox 75) & 101 (J. C. White 5-25) lost to M.C.C. 384-9 dec (R. T. Stanyforth 91, G. R. Jackson 73) by an inns & 12 runs.

9th Match: v Chile (Valparaiso)   Jan 26, 27.
Chile 158 (O. H. Bonham-Carter 62) & 149 lost to M.C.C. 221 (G. R. Jackson 52) & 87-3 by 7 wkts.

10th Match: v Lima (Lima)   Feb 6.
Lima 28 (G. O. B. Allen 6-7) & 56 (G. O. B. Allen 6-15) lost to M.C.C. 173 (R. G. Brown 5-50) by an inns & 89 runs.

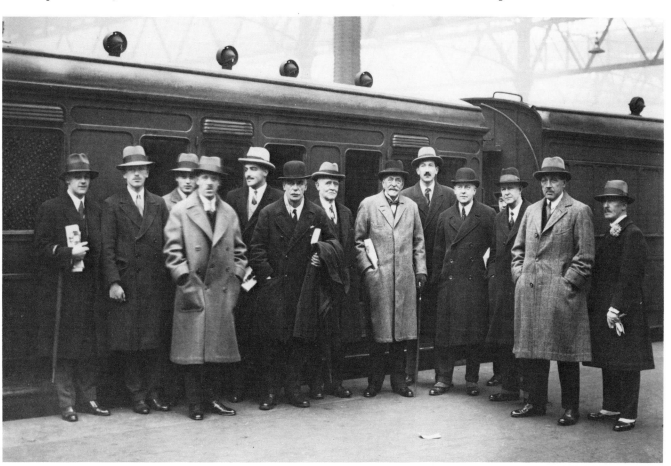

1926-27: draws for Tennyson in Jamaica

In the spring of 1927, the Hampshire captain, the Hon L. H. Tennyson, took a team on a month's tour of Jamaica. The side was the Hon L. H. Tennyson (Hants) (capt), T. Arnott (Glamorgan), L. Green (Lancs), H. M. Morris (Essex), A. L. Hilder (Kent), P. G. H. Fender (Surrey), Rev F. H. Gillingham (Essex), E. R. T. Holmes (Surrey), J. P. Parker (Hants) and four professionals G. E. Tyldesley (Lancs), J. O'Connor (Essex), D. Sullivan (Glamorgan) and H. C. Lock (Surrey).

Although the team was up to first-class county standard, it was very weak on bowlers and this was reflected in the results—six of the seven matches being drawn, including the three important fixtures against Jamaica. The four professionals were involved in a motor accident after the third match of the tour—Tyldesley was unable to play again on the tour and O'Connor and Sullivan missed the next two matches.

1926-27: Hon L. H. Tennyson's Team to Jamaica

1st Match: v XVI Colts (Melbourne Park) Feb 17, 18.
Tennyson's XI 440 (G. E. Tyldesley 106, J. O'Connor 103) drew with XVI Colts 366-10 (H. F. Bicknell 76*, J. O'Connor 6-100).

2nd Match: v Jamaica (Sabina Park) Feb 19, 21, 22.
Jamaica 419-9 dec (R. K. Nunes 200*, E. A. Rae 98) & 77-3 drew with Tennyson's XI 449 (G. E. Tyldesley 101, P. G. H. Fender 68).

3rd Match: v Jamaica (Melbourne Park) Feb 24, 25, 26.
Jamaica 304-5 dec (R. K. Nunes 108) drew with Tennyson's XI 146 (L. G. Hylton 5-34) & 367-9 (G. E. Tyldesley 118, T. Arnott 84).

4th Match: v XV of Cornwall (Montego Bay) March 1, 2.
Cornwall XV 315 drew with Tennyson's XI 389-9 (L. Green 105, E. R. T. Holmes 105).

5th Match: v Middlesex (Port Maria) March 5, 6.
Tennyson's XI 366-9 dec (L. Green 101, A. L. Hilder 92) beat Middlesex 126 (P. G. H. Fender 7-40) & 211 (L. E. Saunders 66) by an inns & 29 runs.

6th Match: v Portland Combination XV (Port Antonio) March 7, 8.
Combination XV 300 (S. Lynch 85) & 41-1 drew with Tennyson's XI 368 (J. O'Connor 147).

7th Match: v Jamaica (Sabina Park) March 9, 10, 11, 12.
Tennyson's XI 443 (J. O'Connor 154, L. H. Tennyson 90) & 280 (T. Arnott 71) drew with Jamaica 519 (F. R. Martin 204*, E. A. Rae 84) & 59-0.

1927-28: South Africa draw with weak M.C.C. side

The team which sailed from Southampton on the liner *Kenilworth Castle* on 21 October bound for Cape Town was as follows: Capt R. T. Stanyforth (Army) (capt), G. T. S. Stevens (Middx), E. W. Dawson (Leics), R. E. S. Wyatt (Warwicks), G. B. Legge (Kent), I. A. R. Peebles, and the professionals W. E. Astill (Leics), G. Geary (Leics), W. R. Hammond (Gloucs), H. Sutcliffe (Yorks), G. E. Tyldesley (Lancs), P. Holmes (Yorks), H. Elliott (Derbys), A. P. Freeman (Kent), S. J. Staples (Notts).

The press were quite critical of the party, stating that the M.C.C. seemed to underestimate the strength of South Africa, as indeed had been the case in the past. The major criticism was levelled at the appointment of Stanyforth, who had never played in county cricket, as captain, though he was only given the leadership after G. R. Jackson, the Derbyshire cricketer, who was originally chosen, had to decline through ill health. Certainly the team was not representative of England's full strength, being without Hobbs, Hendren, Tate, Larwood, Jardine and Chapman.

Arriving in Cape Town on 7 November, the team played their first game at Newlands. This was ruined by rain, though no less than 50 bags of sawdust were scattered on the pitch in a vain attempt to continue the match.

As on previous tours, the M.C.C. did not find the opposition

very taxing until they played Transvaal, and the only two points arising from these early games were the injury to Freeman at Kimberley and the consequent opportunity then afforded to young Peebles in the next game—the unknown bowler took 10 wickets in the match against the Free State. In both the first and second matches against Transvaal, the home side obtained a first innings lead, but stout batting in M.C.C.'s second innings saved the side each time. Holmes hit a century in the first match and Hammond in the second.

The first Test was staged in Johannesburg, and after Geary's spin diddled out the South Africans in the first innings, England remained in charge, though the batting presented a very odd picture—Holmes, Wyatt, Stevens and Legge all failed to score and centuries by Sutcliffe and Tyldesley were responsible for England's lead on first innings. The visitors won the game by 10 wickets. The second Test at Cape Town was played straight after the first. England, batting first, collapsed to Bissett, and South Africa gained a lead on first innings of 117. The English batting

---

1927-28: M.C.C. to South Africa

1st Match: v Western Province (Cape Town) Nov 13, 14, 15.
M.C.C. 138 drew with W. Province 67-6 (A. P. Freeman 5-15).

2nd Match: v Griqualand West (Kimberley) Nov 19, 21, 22.
M.C.C. 366-8 dec (G. E. Tyldesley 143, H. Sutcliffe 100) beat Griqualand West 118 (S. J. Staples 5-25) & 173 (N. V. Tapscott 75) by an inns & 75 runs.

3rd Match: v Orange Free State (Bloemfontein) Nov 25, 26, 28.
O.F.S. 192 (J. M. M. Commaille 77, I. A. R. Peebles 7-54) & 236 (T. E. Holmes 61, J. M. M. Commaille 54) lost to M.C.C. 592-7 dec (P. Holmes 279*, G. B. Legge 120, H. Sutcliffe 73, G. T. S. Stevens 51) by an inns & 164 runs.

4th Match: v Natal (Pietermaritzburg) Nov 30, Dec 1, 2.
Natal 171 (W. E. Astill 5-38) drew with M.C.C. 333 (G. E. Tyldesley 161).

5th Match: v Natal (Durban) Dec 3, 5, 6.
M.C.C. 354-4 dec (H. Sutcliffe 93, G. E. Tyldesley 76, R. E. S. Wyatt 56*, G. B. Legge 50*) drew with Natal 192 (I. J. Siedle 80, W. E. Astill 5-42) & 167-6 (R. H. Catterall 63).

6th Match: v Transvaal (Pretoria) Dec 9, 10, 11.
M.C.C. 205 (H. Sutcliffe 57, C. L. Vincent 6-59) & 328-3 (P. Holmes 184*) drew with Transvaal 382-7 dec (J. P. Duminy 95, A. H. C. Cooper 86).

7th Match: v XV of Transvaal & Natal Schoolboys (Witwatersrand) Dec 13, 14.
M.C.C. 312 (R. E. S. Wyatt 136*, G. T. S. Stevens 70) & 206-4 (W. R. Hammond 65*) drew with XV Schoolboys 199 (G. Geary 7-58).

8th Match: v Transvaal (Johannesburg) Dec 16, 17, 19.
M.C.C. 129 (H. Sutcliffe 59, E. P. Nupen 5-68) & 360-9 dec (W. R. Hammond 132, W. E. Astill 66, H. Sutcliffe 57, C. L. Vintcent 5-78) drew with Transvaal 199 (H. G. Deane 65*, J. P. Duminy 55, G. Geary 6-75) & 183-3 (J. P. Duminy 74*).

9th Match: v A South African XI (Benoni) Dec 20, 21.
A South African XI 86 (W. R. Hammond 6-32) & 305-9 (L. T. H. Trotter 76) drew with M.C.C. 323 (P. Holmes 128, W. R. Hammond 61).

10th Match: v South Africa (Johannesburg) Dec 24, 26, 27.
South Africa 196 (R. H. Catterall 86, G. Geary 7-70) (C. L. Vintcent 53*, W. R. Hammond 5-36, G. Geary 5-60) lost to England 313 (G. E. Tyldesley 122, H. Sutcliffe 102, W. R. Hammond 51, H. L. E. Promnitz 5-58) & 57-0 by 10 wkts.

11th Match: v South Africa (Cape Town) Dec 31, Jan 2, 3, 4.
England 133 (G. F. Bissett 5-37) & 428 (H. Sutcliffe 99, R. E. S. Wyatt 91, P. Holmes 88, G. E. Tyldesley 87) beat South Africa 250 (H. W. Taylor 68) & 224 (H. W. Taylor 71) by 87 runs.

12th Match: v Eastern Province (Port Elizabeth) Jan 7, 9.
E. Province 136 (S. J. Staples 7-38) & 98 lost to M.C.C. 49 (A. L. Ochse 5-31) & 187-0 (R. E. S. Wyatt 101*, H. Sutcliffe 79*) by 10 wkts.

13th Match: v Border (East London) Jan 13, 14.
Border 146 (A. P. Freeman 8-48) & 107 (W. E. Astill 6-23) lost to M.C.C. 362-5 dec (W. R. Hammond 166*, E. W. Dawson 59) by an inns & 109 runs.

14th Match: v South Africa (Durban) Jan 21, 23, 24, 25.
South Africa 246 (H. G. Deane 77, E. P. Nupen 51) & 464-8 dec (J. F. W. Nicolson 78, R. H. Catterall 76, H. G. Deane 73, E. P. Nupen 69, H. W. Taylor 60) drew with England 430 (W. R. Hammond 90, G. E. Tyldesley 78, R. E. S. Wyatt 58, G. T. S. Stevens 69, C. L. Vintcent 6-131) & 132-2 (G. E. Tyldesley 62*, P. Holmes 56).

15th Match: v South Africa (Johannesburg) Jan 28, 30, 31, Feb 1.
England 265 (R. E. S. Wyatt 58, A. E. Hall 6-100) & 215 (P. Holmes 63) lost to South Africa 328 (H. W. Taylor, H. B. Cameron 64) & 156-6 by 4 wkts.

16th Match: v South Africa (Durban) Feb 4, 6, 7, 8.
England 282 (G. E. Tyldesley 100, W. R. Hammond 66, H. Sutcliffe 51, E. P. Nupen 5-83) & 118 (G. F. Bissett 7-29) lost to South Africa 332-7 dec (R. H. Catterall 119, H. B. Cameron 53) & 69-2 by 8 wkts.

17th Match: v Combined South African Schools (Grahamstown) Feb 13, 14.
M.C.C. 222-5 dec (H. Sutcliffe 80, P. Holmes 68) & 204-5 (R. E. S. Wyatt 61*, G. B. Legge 50) drew with S.A. Schools 291 (R. Byron 101, H. Rees 60, H. G. O. Owen-Smith 55, A. P. Freeman 6-53).

18th Match: v Western Province (Cape Town) Feb 18, 20, 21.
M.C.C. 415-8 dec (R. E. S. Wyatt 73, R. T. Stanyforth 71*, W. E. Astill 66, H. Sutcliffe 62) & 87-2 beat W. Province 162 (L. Serrurier 74*, A. P. Freeman 5-49) & 339 (A. W. Palm 71, S. Steyn 51, A. P. Freeman 5-102) by 8 wkts.

1927-28: M.C.C. to South Africa

Batting Averages

	M	I	NO	R	HS	Avge	100	c/s
G. E. Tyldesley (Lancs)	14	21	2	1130	161	59.47	4	1
P. Holmes (Yorks)	14	22	3	1112	279*	58.52	3	3
H. Sutcliffe (Yorks)	14	23	4	1030	102	51.50	2	4
W. R. Hammond (Glos)	14	21	2	908	166*	47.78	2	13
R. E. S. Wyatt (Warks)	15	19	5	592	101*	42.28	1	7
G. B. Legge (Kent)	8	9	1	259	120	32.37	1	5
G. T. S. Stevens (Middx)	13	17	2	335	69	22.33	0	13
W. E. Astill (Leics)	13	15	0	331	66	22.07	0	11
E. W. Dawson (Leics)	8	9	1	129	59	16.12	0	1
S. J. Staples (Notts)	11	12	2	141	39	14.10	0	7
R. T. Stanyforth (Army)	14	14	2	120	71*	10.00	0	19/6
I. A. R. Peebles (Middx)	11	14	7	69	26*	9.85	0	3
A. P. Freeman (Kent)	12	11	3	39	9*	4.87	0	3
G. Geary (Leics)	10	10	1	33	24*	3.66	0	6
H. Elliott (Derbys)	3	3	0	4	3	1.33	0	4/2

Played in one match: J. C. Hubble (Kent) 10 (ct 5); S. K. Coen (Orange Free State) 3.

Bowling Averages

	O	M	R	W	Avge	BB	5i
G. Geary	224.3	61	489	28	17.46	7-70	3
A. P. Freeman	325.3	73	965	50	19.30	8-48	4
I. A. R. Peebles	179.1	37	588	28	21.00	7-54	1
S. J. Staples	413.5	108	842	40	21.05	7-38	2
W. E. Astill	279.2	68	782	35	22.34	6-23	3
W. R. Hammond	250	58	644	27	23.85	6-32	2
R. E. S. Wyatt	197	53	561	19	29.52	3-60	0
G. T. S. Stevens	163.4	22	559	17	32.88	3-31	0

Also bowled: G. B. Legge 3-0-23-3; G. E. Tyldesley 0.3-0-2-0; P. Holmes 2-0-13-0; H. Sutcliffe 1-0-10-0.

1927-28: The Hon L. H. Tennyson's Team to Jamaica

1st Match: v All Jamaica (Sabina Park)   Feb 9, 10, 11, 13.
Jamaica 429 (C. M. Morales 143, N. N. Nethersole 71, F. R. Martin 65*, J. J. Cameron 52) & 253-6 dec (J. K. Holt 74, G. A. Headley 71) beat Tennyson's XI 227 (C. P. Mead 103*) & 237 (T. Arnott 60, O. C. Scott 6-75) by 218 runs.

2nd Match: v Middlesex XV (Port Maria)   Feb 15, 16.
Tennyson's XI 240 (C. P. Mead 107) & 36-0 drew with Middlesex XV 226 (A. L. Hilder 9-49).

3rd Match: v All Jamaica (Melbourne Park)   Feb 18, 20, 21, 22.
Tennyson's XI 252 (C. P. Mead 117) & 259 (G. M. Lee 97, F. J. Seabrook 59, O. C. Scott 8-67) lost to Jamaica 609 (G. A. Headley 211, J. K. Holt 100, C. M. Morales 84, R. K. Nunes 53) by an inns & 98 runs.

4th Match: v Cornwall XV (Montego Bay)   Feb 24, 25.
Cornwall XV 125 & 249 (A. V. Lee 70) lost to Tennyson's XI 347-7 dec (L. H. Tennyson 125, T. Arnott 71, G. D. Kemp-Welch 63) & 29-1 by 9 wkts.

5th Match: v All Jamaica (Sabina Park)   Feb 28, 29, March 1, 2, 3.
Jamaica 438 (J. K. Holt 142, F. R. Martin 83, L. G. Hylton 55, R. K. Nunes 53) & 338-6 dec (F. R. Martin 141*, L. G. Hylton 60, G. A. Headley 71) drew with Tennyson's XI 327 (A. K. Judd 75, L. H. Tennyson 70, M. J. C. Allom 62, T. Arnott 58) & 288-7 (C. P. Mead 151, P. T. Eckersley 50).

---

in the second innings however redressed the balance and Astill and Freeman took their side to victory. In this game Geary injured his elbow and was not able to play in the remaining Tests, which proved unfortunate for England. The success in the two Tests was quickly countered by Eastern Province who dismissed M.C.C. for 49—the lowest innings ever made by the M.C.C. in South Africa until then. Staples and Peebles, however, struck back and sparkling batting from Wyatt won the game.

South Africa, with the rubber at stake, fought hard in the third Test and consistent batting by the home side produced a draw. The two other Tests were played consecutively, with no minor matches intervening. Hall and Bissett—the contrast of a slow left-armer and fast right-arm—dismissed England twice in the fourth Test and without Geary the South African batting flourished to bring England its first defeat. In the last innings, the visitors were handicapped by an injury to Stanyforth and Freeman kept wicket for part of the time.

The fifth Test again showed South Africa to advantage. Once more Bissett and Hall kept the English batsmen within bounds, Bissett being absolutely deadly in the second innings; his pace was assisted by a strong wind and he found the knack of making the ball rear up in an alarming manner. South Africa won by eight wickets and deservedly squared the series.

The Union Castle liner *Saxon* brought the tourists back to Southampton, but without Dawson, who stayed behind, having become engaged to be married whilst on tour, and Tyldesley and Sutcliffe, who left the boat in Madeira for a brief holiday.

The failure of the English side to win the rubber was in part due to Geary's injury but also to the weakness of the later batting. Both the all-rounders, Astill and Stevens, failed to make runs in the Tests and since the tail of Stanyforth, Peebles and Freeman could not be relied upon, it made England very vulnerable should any of the leading batsmen fail. South Africa's batting had much more depth and in Bissett they possessed the bowler of the series.

1927-28: by banana boat to Jamaica

The Hon L. H. Tennyson repeated his venture of 1926-27, by taking a team to Jamaica in the spring of 1928. The team travelled in the banana boat *Changuinola* and had a very rough outward

journey. It was therefore not too surprising that Jamaica won the first match, which began on the second day after the tourists' arrival. The team was: Hon L. H. Tennyson (Hants) (capt), T. Arnott (Glamorgan), A. L. Hilder (Kent), M. J. C. Allom (Surrey), Col D. C. Robinson (Gloucs), G. D. Kemp-Welch (Warwicks), F. J. Seabrook (Gloucs), G. J. V. Weigall (Kent), P. T. Eckersley (Lancs), A. K. Judd (Hants) and the professionals C. P. Mead (Hants), G. M. Lee (Derbys), D. Sullivan (Glamorgan) and E. W. Clark (Northants).

The immediate effect of playing the first game so soon after arrival was not only defeat, but also strains to Allom and Clark, which rendered them useless for the rest of the tour. With these two bowlers out of action, the team were in the same state as the previous year—strong batting but no bowlers—and of the two other meetings with All Jamaica, one was lost and the other drawn.

The feature of the cricket was Mead's batting, but Kemp-Welch also played several good innings. Hilder proved to be the best bowler—a lot was expected of Lee, but he was too slow off the pitch. The fielding in general was good, especially Seabrook in the deep and the stumper, Sullivan.

1928-29: great batting by Hobbs, Sutcliffe and Hammond beats Australia

In choosing the side to visit Australia in 1928-29, the M.C.C. departed from its usual custom and instead of the M.C.C. Committee selecting the players, a team of selectors was appointed for the task—Lord Harris, J. W. H. T. Douglas, P. F. Warner, A. E. R. Gilligan, F. T. Mann and H. D. G. Leveson-Gower. The side they picked came in for considerable press criticism, mainly because only one all-rounder—Tate—was chosen, though the absence of Woolley, Hallows and Holmes was also noted.

The party selected was: A. P. F. Chapman (Kent) (capt), J. C. White (Somerset), D. R. Jardine (Surrey) and the professionals J. B. Hobbs (Surrey), G. E. Tyldesley (Lancs), H. Sutcliffe (Yorks), E. H. Hendren (Middx), C. P. Mead (Hants), M. W. Tate (Sussex), M. Leyland (Lancs), H. Larwood (Notts), S. J. Staples (Notts), G. Duckworth (Lancs), L. E. G. Ames (Kent), G. Geary (Leics), W. R. Hammond (Gloucs) and A. P. Freeman (Kent). F. C. Toone was again the manager.

The side left England in two groups, and joined up at Toulon for the voyage on the s.s. *Otranto*. The now traditional one-day game was played in Colombo and the team arrived at Fremantle two days prior to the match against Western Australia. The tourists gave a satisfactory account of themselves in this game,

The M.C.C. party which toured Australia in 1928-29. Back: G. Duckworth, L. E. G. Ames, C. P. Mead, M. W. Tate, E. H. Hendren. Centre: M. Leyland, S. J. Staples, W. R. Hammond, F. C. Toone (manager), H. Sutcliffe, H. Larwood, A. P. Freeman. Front: G. E. Tyldesley, J. C. White, A. P. F. Chapman (captain), D. R. Jardine, J. B. Hobbs. G. Geary is not in the picture.

Below England's two fast bowlers, Harold Larwood and Maurice Tate, on the cross-channel ferry Invicta on 20 April 1929 after the successful tour of Australia.

Sydney the scoring reached new heights. M.C.C. hit 734 for 7 declared, with Hammond, Hendren and Jardin all in three figures, but a young unknown by the name of Bradman scored 87 and 132 not out and with Kippax also making a hundred the fourth draw was recorded.

Victory came at last against An Australian Eleven, when Larwood, Tate and White managed to dismiss this experimental side for under 300 twice – though Bradman carried out his bat for 58. A second win came against the modest Queensland team, before the first Test at Brisbane. Winning the toss, England hit over 500, with a century by Hendren. Larwood then broke the back of the Australian innings and the home team were all out for 122 – Chapman had a lead of 399, but mindful of the runs still in the pitch, he did not enforce the follow-on, and when eventually Australia began their second innings, they faced a target of 742. Larwood took two quick wickets and then overnight rain did the rest, White picking up 4 wickets for 7 runs on the last day. England therefore won the first Test by 675 runs.

Following a country game, the second Test began at Sydney – by this time it had been decided that Staples was not fit enough to continue the tour and he returned home. Australia won the toss and batted. Some good bowling by Geary and Larwood dismissed the home side for 253, though Australia were most unlucky to lose

but press reports of the mounting casualty list were quite frightening. Geary broke his nose in the match, Staples was struck down with rheumatism, Freeman suffered a stiff neck and Tate a strained arm. Freeman was well enough however to appear in the second game, at Adelaide, where very high scoring was the order of the day, nearly 1,400 runs coming for the loss of 24 wickets. Hammond, Chapman and Leyland all made hundreds for the tourists, whilst V. Y. Richardson replied with a double century.

Larwood showed himself in fine form at Melbourne, taking 7 for 51 and dismissing Victoria for 164. Rain and more high scoring then arrived to produce a third drawn match. Tate made his first appearance in this game, but Staples was still too unwell. In

1928-29: M.C.C. to Ceylon and Australia

Batting Averages

	M	I	NO	R	HS	Avge	100	c/s
W. R. Hammond (Glos)	13	18	1	1553	251	91.35	7	10/3
D. R. Jardine (Surrey)	12	19	1	1168	214	64.88	6	5
E. H. Hendren (Middx)	12	17	1	1033	169	64.56	3	8
L. E. G. Ames (Kent)	8	8	3	295	100*	59.00	1	8/10
J. B. Hobbs (Surrey)	11	18	1	962	142	56.58	2	2
H. Sutcliffe (Yorks)	11	16	0	852	135	53.25	2	4
M. Leyland (Yorks)	12	17	3	614	137	43.85	3	7
C. P. Mead (Hants)	10	14	3	460	106	41.81	1	2
G. E. Tyldesley (Lancs)	12	16	2	509	81	36.35	0	4
A. P. F. Chapman (Kent)	14	17	1	533	145	33.31	1	23
H. Larwood (Notts)	13	14	0	367	79	26.21	0	8
M. W. Tate (Sussex)	13	17	1	322	59	20.12	0	8
G. Geary (Leics)	12	16	3	215	66	16.53	0	7
J. C. White (Som)	15	18	7	137	30	12.45	0	7
G. Duckworth (Lancs)	9	13	6	84	39*	12.00	0	17/4
A. P. Freeman (Kent)	10	7	3	42	17	10.50	0	1

Bowling Averages

	Balls	M	R	W	Avge	BB	5i
J. C. White	5213	223	1471	65	22.63	8-126	5
G. Geary	2757	104	956	37	25.83	5-35	3
M. W. Tate	4072	174	1329	44	30.11	5-35	1
H. Larwood	2726	61	1254	40	31.35	7-51	2
A. P. Freeman	2323	32	1136	35	32.45	5-51	3
W. R. Hammond	1594	50	661	11	60.09	3-53	0
M. Leyland	742	12	357	4	89.25	2-37	0

Also bowled: D. R. Jardine 112-3-67-2; G. Duckworth 8-0-7-0; E. H. Hendren 120-2-57-0; C. P. Mead 8-0-11-0; H. Sutcliffe 32-1-18-0.
S. J. Staples (Notts) was selected for the tour and travelled to Australia, but was taken ill before he played in a match and was sent home.

Some of the 1928-29 touring party to Australia photographed at the Scarborough festival in 1928. Left to right: Macaulay (who did not tour), M. Leyland, G. Geary, A. P. F. Chapman, W. R. Hammond, G. Duckworth, G. E. Tyldesley, H. Sutcliffe, J. B. Hobbs, E. H. Hendren, M. W. Tate.

Ponsford with a broken wrist. On the second day, the crowd numbered 58,456–a new record–and England through Hammond gradually built a commanding lead. Australia did better in their second innings, Woodfull and Hendry making hundreds, but they still lost by 8 wickets.

1928-29: M.C.C. to Ceylon and Australia

1st Match: v Ceylon (Colombo) (One Day)   Oct 6.
Ceylon 96-7 dec lost to M.C.C. 150-6 (A. P. F. Chapman 60, J. B. Hobbs 54) by 10 wkts.

2nd Match: v Western Australia (Perth)   Oct 18, 19, 20.
M.C.C. 406 (D. R. Jardine 109, E. H. Hendren 90, G. E. Tyldesley 66) & 26-0 drew with W. Australia 257 (W. Horrocks 75*, F. Bryant 61).

3rd Match: v South Australia (Adelaide)   Oct 26, 27, 29, 30.
M.C.C. 528 (W. R. Hammond 145, A. P. F. Chapman 145, H. Sutcliffe 76, C. P. Mead 58, C. V. Grimmett 6-109) & 341-4 (M. Leyland 114, H. Sutcliffe 70, J. B. Hobbs 64, C. P. Mead 58*) drew with S. Australia 524 (V. Y. Richardson 231, D. E. Pritchard 119, A. P. Freeman 5-180).

4th Match: v Victoria (Melbourne)   Nov 1, 2, 3, 5.
Victoria 164 (W. M. Woodfull 67*, H. Larwood 7-51) & 135-0 (H. S. T. L. Hendry 74*, W. H. Ponsford 60*) drew with M.C.C. 486 (D. R. Jardine 104, E. H. Hendren 100, H. Larwood 79, A. P. F. Chapman 71, J. B. Hobbs 51).

5th Match: v New South Wales (Sydney)   Nov 9, 10, 12, 13.
M.C.C. 734-7 dec (W. R. Hammond 225, E. H. Hendren 167, D. R. Jardine 140) drew with N.S.W. 349 (C. Kelleway 93*, D. G. Bradman 87, A. F. Kippax 64, A. P. Freeman 5-136) & 364-3 (A. F. Kippax 136*, D. G. Bradman 132*).

6th Match: v An Australian XI (Sydney)   Nov 16, 17, 19, 20.
Australian XI 231 (D. G. Bradman 58*) & 243 (A. Jackson 61, G. W. Harris 56) lost to M.C.C. 357 (G. E. Tyldesley 69, M. W. Tate 59, C. P. Mead 58, J. B. Hobbs 58) & 118-2 (J. B. Hobbs 67*) by 8 wkts.

7th Match: v Queensland (Brisbane)   Nov 24, 26, 27.
Queensland 116 (A. P. Freeman 5-51) & 160 (J. L. Litster 59, G. Geary 5-47) lost to M.C.C. 293 (M. Leyland 114, O. E. Nothling 5-78) by an inns & 17 runs.

8th Match: v Australia (Brisbane)   Nov 30, Dec 1, 3, 4, 5.
England 521 (E. H. Hendren 169, H. Larwood 70, A. P. F. Chapman 50) & 342-8 dec (C. P. Mead 73, D. R. Jardine 65*, C. V. Grimmett 6-131) beat Australia 122 (H. Larwood 6-32) & 66 by 675 runs.

9th Match: v Combined Country XI (Warwick)   Dec 8, 10.
Country XI 128 (A. P. Freeman 8-32) & 213 (A. P. Freeman 7-74) lost to M.C.C. 510 (G. E. Tyldesley 115, W. R. Hammond 110, H. Sutcliffe 77, M. Leyland 67*) by an inns & 169 runs.

10th Match: v Australia (Sydney)   Dec 14, 15, 17, 18, 19, 20.
Australia 253 (W. M. Woodfull 68, G. Geary 5-35) & 397 (H. S. T. L. Hendry 112, W. M. Woodfull 111, J. Ryder 79) lost to England 636 (W. R. Hammond 251, E. H. Hendren 74, G. Geary 66) & 16-2 by 8 wkts.

11th Match: v Newcastle & Hunter District XI (Newcastle)   Dec 21, 22.
District XI 350-9 dec (O. Osland 78, F. Henderson 60, R. H. B. Bettington 53) drew with M.C.C. 281 (H. Larwood 92).

12th Match: v Australia (Melbourne)   Dec 29, 31, Jan 1, 2, 3, 4, 5.
Australia 397 (J. Ryder 112, A. F. Kippax 100, D. G. Bradman 79) & 351 (D. G. Bradman 112, W. M. Woodfull 107, J. C. White 5-107) lost to England 417 (W. R. Hammond 200, D. R. Jardine 62, H. Sutcliffe 58, D. D. Blackie 6-94) & 332-7 (H. Sutcliffe 135) by 3 wkts.

13th Match: v XII of Geelong (Geelong) (One Day)   Jan 7.
M.C.C. 289-7 dec (H. Sutcliffe 56, J. B. Hobbs 50) drew with Geelong 124-6 (A. W. H. Urbahns 51).

14th Match: v XIII of Bendigo (Bendigo)   Jan 9, 10.
M.C.C. 305 (E. H. Hendren 73, G. E. Tyldesley 52) & 255 (D. R. Jardine 83*, W. R. Hammond 73) drew with Bendigo 168 (J. Thomas 63*, H. Larwood 6-20).

15th Match: v Tasmania (Launceston)   Jan 12, 14, 15.
Tasmania 229 (G. F. Martin 92) & 137 (M. W. Tate 5-35) lost to M.C.C. 482-8 dec (D. R. Jardine 214, C. P. Mead 106) by an inns & 116 runs.

16th Match: v Tasmania (Hobart)   Jan 18, 19.
Tasmania 66 & 93 lost to M.C.C. 223 (L. E. G. Ames 100*) by an inns & 64 runs.

17th Match: v South Australia (Adelaide)   Jan 25, 26, 28, 29.
M.C.C. 392 (H. Sutcliffe 122, E. H. Hendren 90, J. B. Hobbs 75, T. A. Carlton 5-64) & 307-5 dec (D. R. Jardine 114, J. B. Hobbs 101, L. E. G. Ames 51*) drew with S. Australia 178 (V. Y. Richardson 82, J. C. White 7-66) & 75-1.

18th Match: v Australia (Adelaide)   Feb 1, 2, 4, 5, 6, 7, 8.
England 334 (W. R. Hammond 119*, J. B. Hobbs 74, H. Sutcliffe 64, C. V. Grimmett 5-102) & 383 (W. R. Hammond 177, D. R. Jardine 98) beat Australia 369 (A. Jackson 164, J. Ryder 63, J. C. White 5-130) & 336 (J. Ryder 87, D. G. Bradman 58, A. F. Kippax 51, J. C. White 8-126) by 12 runs.

19th Match: v XIII of Ballarat (Ballarat)   Feb 9, 11.
M.C.C. 493-9 dec (L. E. G. Ames 127, J. B. Hobbs 82*, M. Leyland 75, G. E. Tyldesley 65, E. H. Hendren 61, G. Bennetts 7-127) drew with Ballarat 77 (A. P. Freeman 7-26) & 176-9.

20th Match: v New South Wales (Sydney)   Feb 15, 16, 18, 19.
N.S.W. 128 (J. C. White 5-48) drew with M.C.C. 144-4 (G. E. Tyldesley 68).

21st Match: v Western Districts (Bathurst)   Feb 21, 22.
M.C.C. 319 (L. E. G. Ames 123, G. E. Tyldesley 50) beat Western Districts 127 (H. Larwood 5-17) & 81 (A. P. Freeman 8-31).

22nd Match: v XIII of Southern Districts (Goulburn)   Feb 25, 26.
M.C.C. 250 (L. E. G. Ames 94, J. B. Hobbs 54, W. Lampe 5-46) & 226-5 dec (D. R. Jardine 85*) drew with Southern Districts 135 (A. P. Freeman 8-66) & 135-4 (A. Allsopp 79*).

23rd Match: v Victoria (Melbourne)   March 1, 2, 4, 5.
Victoria 572-9 dec (W. M. Woodfull 275*, L. S. Darling 87, J. Ryder 60) drew with M.C.C. 303 (W. R. Hammond 114, G. E. Tyldesley 81) & 308-3 (D. R. Jardine 115, G. E. Tyldesley 68*, M. Leyland 54).

24th Match: v Australia (Melbourne)   March 8, 9, 11, 12, 13, 14, 15, 16.
England 519 (J. B. Hobbs 142, M. Leyland 137, E. H. Hendren 95) & 257 (J. B. Hobbs 65, M. W. Tate 54, M. Leyland 53*, T. W. Wall 5-66) lost to Australia 491 (D. G. Bradman 123, W. M. Woodfull 102, A. G. Fairfax 65, G. Geary 5-105) & 287-5 (J. Ryder 57*) by 5 wkts.

25th Match: v An Australian XI (Perth)   March 21, 22, 23.
An Australian XI 310 (A. J. Richardson 101*, H. Rowe 73) & 186-3 (J. Ryder 81*, W. Horrocks 76) drew with M.C.C. 241 (W. R. Hammond 80).

Just over a week later, the third Test began – it was vital for Australia to win. Ryder certainly won the toss and batted, and he and Kippax both hit hundreds, but Hammond replied with a double century, so that the game remained level at the half-way mark. Bradman hit his first Test century in the second innings, leaving England with 332 to get on a wicket damaged by rain – most of the press appeared to believe that the visitors would be lucky to reach 100. Hobbs and Sutcliffe opened the batting and played a dead bat at everything that needed playing, whilst ignoring virtually all the other deliveries. The opening partnership of 105 was in the opinion of many the best piece of batting ever seen in a Test Match – Hobbs was out on 49, Sutcliffe, with the wicket easing all the time went on to 135, and England won the match by 3 wickets and with it the series. The total attendance was 262,467 and the receipts £22,561 18s.

The tourists then played four minor matches and a game against South Australia, before coming to the fourth Test at Adelaide. As can be seen from the four innings totals – 334, 369, 383 and 336 – the game was very finely balanced. England relied heavily on Hammond in their batting, and the Gloucester player hit two hundreds, whilst Australia owed most to Jackson who signalled his debut with a marvellous innings of 164. In the end England won a great match by 12 runs.

In the final Test Australia received some consolation – the scoring was generally very slow and the match dragged on for eight days, but Australia broke down the English batting in the second innings and had little difficulty in winning by 5 wickets. A concluding game was played at Perth and the team sailed home on the *Ormonde*, arriving in Toulon on 20 April and in England the following day.

Although Hammond was perhaps the success of the tour, the innings of Hobbs and Sutcliffe were also of great importance, as were those of Jardine. The surprise of the visit was possibly White, who bowled uncommonly well, his slow left-arm spin keeping all the batsmen quiet. Tate also did magnificent work throughout. Larwood bowled well at the start of the tour, but tired later and Geary also bowled well. Chapman led the side with

flair, but his batting was not very sound. The public interest in the Tests was enormous and so were the profits – £17,968. There was a lot of adverse comment on the barracking, but apart from in one Victorian match, it was not exceptional.

1928-29: Julien Cahn's trip to Jamaica

For the third time in as many years, a privately organised tour went out to Jamaica. On this occasion, the team was that of Julien Cahn, the well-known Nottingham patron of the game.

The team was Lord Tennyson (Hants), E. W. Dawson (Leics), F. W. H. Nicholas (Essex), A. L. Hilder (Kent), F. C. W. Newman (Surrey) and W. H. Vaulkhard and the professionals A. Sandham (Surrey), J. Iddon (Lancs), W. E. Astill (Leics), H. A. Peach (Surrey), W. W. Whysall (Notts), J. O'Connor (Essex), M. S. Nichols (Essex), B. Lilley (Notts), J. Mercer (Glamorgan), F. J. Durston (Middx) and G. Shaw (Trent Bridge pavilion attendant).

The professionals travelled from Avonmouth on the *Comito* sailing direct to Kingston, whilst the amateurs sailed on the *Mauretania* from Southampton to New York, and the two parties joined forces in Jamaica on 14 February.

Julien Cahn, with his wife, as well as Mrs F. W. H. Nicholas also accompanied the tourists.

After an opening odds match, the first game against All Jamaica began on 21 February. In a very high-scoring game, the home

Julien Cahn's privately organised party which toured Jamaica in 1928-29. Back: G. Shaw, W. W. Whysall, J. Iddon, A. L. Hilder, F. J. Durston, M. S. Nichols, J. Mercer, W. E. Astill, H. A. Peach. Front: Unknown, A. Sandham, Lord Tennyson, J. Cahn, E. W. Dawson, F. W. H. Nicholas, B. Lilley, J. O'Connor.

side won by 7 wickets; unfortunately Cahn was injured and unable to play in the remaining matches. The second match against Jamaica was drawn, but in the third the tourists met with another defeat, though Sandham batted splendidly in both innings. The third game was in fact against a West Indies team, since Constantine, Small and Francis reinforced the local side. Judging by the strength of Cahn's team there was little doubt that cricket in Jamaica was making considerable progress. The tourists were most impressed by the batting of George Headley.

The team returned to England on 2 April.

1928-29: Julien Cahn's Team to Jamaica

1st Match: v Jamaica Next XV (Melbourne Pk)   Feb 18, 19.
Next XV 342-8 dec (F. C. Isaacs 71, A. L. Silvera 51*) drew with Cahn's XI 290 (J. O'Connor 114, W. E. Astill 53).

2nd Match: v Jamaica (Melbourne Pk)   Feb 21, 22, 25.
Cahn's XI 217 (J. Iddon 72, L. G. Hylton 5-24) & 336 (H. A. Peach 75, F. W. H. Nicholas 63*, J. O'Connor 63) lost to Jamaica 503 (J. K. Holt 128, R. K. Nunes 112, I. Barrow 61, G. A. Headley 57, J. O'Connor 5-96) & 51-3 by 7 wkts.

3rd Match: v Garrison XIII (Camp St Andrew)   Feb 26.
Garrison XIII 121 (J. Mercer 7-23) lost to Cahn's XI 196-9 (A. L. Hilder 63).

4th Match: v Jamaica (Sabina Pk)   Feb 27, 28, March 1.
Jamaica 462 (E. R. Rae 121, W. Beckford 74, F. R. Martin 64) & 211-9 dec (W. E. Astill 7-60) drew with Cahn's XI 343 (W. W. Whysall 80, Lord Tennyson 78, F. W. H. Nicholas 64, G. C. Scott 6-135) & 226-5 (Lord Tennyson 105*).

5th Match: v M.C.C. XV (Port Maria)   March 5, 6.
Cahn's XI 415 (W. W. Whysall 105, A. Sandham 66, J. O'Connor 56, B. Lilley 54) drew with M.C.C. XV 215-5 (H. B. Young 82, Lee Carr 72*).

6th Match: v West Indian XI (Sabina Park)   March 12, 13, 14, 15, 16.
West Indian XI 317 (J. K. Holt 128, E. A. Rae 64) & 447 (G. A. Headley 143, J. K. Holt 56) beat Cahn's XI 271 (A. Sandham 159*, J. A. Small 7-77) & 349 (W. E. Astill 83, A. Sandham 62, J. Iddon 62) by 144 runs.

1929: Martineau takes a team to Egypt

H. M. Martineau, who was a great supporter of cricket and ran a team based at his country house near Maidenhead, undertook the first of eleven tours to Egypt in the spring of 1929. His team contained a number of well-known amateur cricketers and though perhaps not as strong as the sides fielded by Julien Cahn was certainly on the borderline of 'first-class' by English standards. The touring party was: H. M. Martineau (capt), A. C. Johnston (Hants), L. C. R. Isherwood (Sussex), S. A. Block (Surrey), R. W. Skene (Oxford U), R. S. G. Scott (Oxford U), F. O. G. Lloyd, I. S. Akers-Douglas, C. H. Knott (Kent), C. K. Hill-Wood (Derbys) and G. E. C. Wood (Kent).

The tour consisted of five matches, played during the first two weeks in April, and the two most important fixtures were both three-day games against All Egypt. The first was a draw, but in the second Egypt seemed certain to win, setting the tourists 286 to make in their last innings. Akers-Douglas and Block however added 159 for the second wicket and the tourists won by 4 wickets.

1929: H. M. Martineau's Team to Egypt

1st Match: v Alexandria (Alexandria)   April 2, 3.
Martineau's XI 457-6 dec (C. H. Knott 151*, R. W. Skeyne 116, A. C. Johnston 68) drew with Alexandria 231 (H. W. Grant 66) & 300-3 (M. C. O'Brian 118*, C. I. Thomas 68, J. de V. Biss 67*).

2nd Match: v Gezira Sporting Club (Cairo)   April 5, 6.
Gezira Sporting Club 104 & 319 (J. H. de la Mare 102, H. S. Mitchell 99) drew with Martineau's XI 189 (R. W. Skene 50) & 145-8.

3rd Match: v All Egypt (Cairo)   April 8, 9.
Martineau's XI 310-8 dec (S. A. Block 93, C. H. Knott 90* & 170-5 dec (I. S. Akers-Douglas 67*) drew with All Egypt 194 (J. C. de V. Biss 74) & 151-7 (H. S. Mitchell 50).

4th Match: v The Army (Cairo)   April 11, 12.
Army 283 (Rusbridge 54, Pope 53*) & 223-5 dec (H. S. Mitchell 76, R. C. G. Joy 53*) drew with Martineau's XI 299 (L. C. R. Isherwood 98) & 96-5.

5th Match: v All Egypt (Alexandria)   April 15, 16, 17.
All Egypt 217 (A. R. I. Mellor 75*, R. C. G. Joy 53) & 327 (H. S. Mitchell 68, R. A. Rusbridge 69, G. S. Duckworth 51) lost to Martineau's XI 261 (C. H. Knott 88) & 286-6 (I. S. Akers-Douglas 142, S. A. Block 67) by 4 wkts.

1929-30: Duleepsinhji wins praise in New Zealand

The M.C.C. took the unique step of organising two Test-playing tours in the winter of 1929-30, this one and that which follows, to West Indies. Obviously both teams could not be representative of England's full strength and in fact neither were. Not because the talents were evenly distributed between the two, but because many of the leading English players of 1929 remained aloof from both. The side which travelled to New Zealand was to be led by A. E. R. Gilligan, but because of ill-health he had to stand down and his brother took over the leadership. The party which sailed on 28 September aboard the R.M.S. *Orford* was A. H. H. Gilligan (Sussex) (capt), K. S. Duleepsinhji (Sussex), E. W. Dawson (Leics), G. B. Legge (Kent), M. J. L. Turnbull (Glamorgan), M. J. C. Allom (Surrey), G. F. Earle (Somerset), E. T. Benson (Oxford U), and the professionals F. E. Woolley (Kent), E. H. Bowley (Sussex), M. S. Nichols (Essex), T. S. Worthington (Derbys), F. Barratt (Notts) and W. L. Cornford (Sussex).

After the one-day game in Colombo, the side commenced the first-class section of the tour at Perth on 31 October. In this match and in the following one against South Australia the tourists won with ease, due to some effective bowling. Against the stronger Victorian team, things went well initially, but in the end Woodfull hit a good hundred to provide the state with a win by 7 wickets. As might have been expected the New South Wales side toyed with the tourists' attack, hundreds coming from Bradman, Kippax, Allsopp and Jackson, plus 90 from McCabe, but the M.C.C. were undaunted, Woolley made a double century, and the match was drawn. The visitors suffered a crop of injuries: Barratt had to stop bowling due to a strained arm, Bowley aggravated an old leg injury and also had to retire from bowling, whilst Nichols, suffering from tonsilitis, could not play. Cornford had received a bad cut over the eye in the previous game, but came on the field as a substitute, as indeed did Nichols. In the match against Queensland, Ducat, who was coaching in Australia, was co-opted into the side. There was a twelve-day break in the programme whilst the team made their way to New Zealand and this helped some of the injured to recover, though Bowley was out of action with sciatica until the end of January. The first six matches in New Zealand however caused the tourists few problems. The

---

1929-30: M.C.C. to Ceylon, Australia and New Zealand

Batting Averages

	M	I	NO	R	HS	Avge	100	c/s
K. S. Duleepsinhji (Sussex)	13	22	4	890	117	49.44	1	17
F. E. Woolley (Kent)	12	18	1	780	219	45.88	3	12
E. H. Bowley (Sussex)	6	7	1	256	109	42.66	1	3
M. S. Nichols (Essex)	11	17	5	482	82	40.16	0	11
G. B. Legge (Kent)	9	14	2	453	196	37.75	1	1
A. H. H. Gilligan (Sussex)	13	18	0	523	70	29.05	0	1
E. W. Dawson (Leics)	13	22	1	548	83*	26.09	0	2
T. S. Worthington (Derbys)	13	15	0	370	125	24.66	1	7
M. J. L. Turnbull (Glam)	8	13	2	232	100	21.09	1	6
G. F. Earle (Som)	7	10	0	191	49	19.10	0	4
M. J. C. Allom (Surrey)	12	15	10	82	18*	16.40	0	5
F. Barratt (Notts)	11	14	2	173	46	14.41	0	2
A. Ducat (Surrey)	1	2	0	23	13	11.50	0	0
E. T. Benson (Oxford U)	4	5	0	48	29	9.60	0	4/1
W. L. Cornford (Sussex)	10	13	2	104	29	9.45	0	18/8

Bowling Averages

	Balls	M	R	W	Avge	BB	5i
M. S. Nichols	1871	43	791	43	18.39	8-65	2
G. F. Earle	30	1	20	1	20.00	1-20	0
F. E. Woolley	1863	69	850	36	23.61	7-76	2
M. J. C. Allom	2384	67	961	39	24.64	5-26	2
G. B. Legge	84	0	78	3	26.00	3-24	0
T. S. Worthington	1782	56	806	30	26.86	3-16	0
K. S. Duleepsinhji	158	0	135	5	27.00	4-49	0
E. H. Bowley	626	13	353	12	29.41	5-30	1
F. Barratt	2260	55	887	27	32.85	5-32	2

Also bowled: E. W. Dawson 24-0-30-0; W. L. Cornford 42-3-20-0.

first Test took place at Christchurch. Allom and Nichols proved too much for the home batsmen and any chances New Zealand had of winning the match were thrown away by poor fielding.

The second Test produced much higher scoring. New Zealand began with an opening partnership worth 276 by Mills and Dempster though Woolley tricked out nearly all the others cheaply and England were never in danger of defeat, the match,

restricted to three days, petering out in a draw.

In the match against Auckland, Benson was adjudged out 'handled ball', though the Auckland wicket-keeper declared that the batsman did not even touch the ball!

Rain washed out the third Test, but not before Bowley and Duleepsinhji had hit centuries, Duleepsinhji's innings was described as the best seen in New Zealand in recent years. Because of the waterlogged third Test, an extra Test was staged, but this was just a high-scoring draw and the tour ended with a win at New Plymouth over Taranaki.

The team travelled home via the Panama Canal in the *Rangitane* and landed back in England on 2 April. The success of the tour was Duleepsinhji, whose batting won great praise. Both the veteran Woolley and young Nichols performed good work as allrounders. Allom bowled well, his fast deliveries having plenty of life. Turnbull however was a disappointment, as was Barratt, who did well only in Australia. The fielding was very variable, so was Cornford's wicket-keeping.

The New Zealanders had good batsmen, but the bowling was weak and the fielding generally poor. The umpiring, especially in the minor matches, was very moderate.

1929-30: Sandham's 325 in the West Indies

The second major touring party of 1929-30 set off for the West Indies on 14 December aboard the *Carare* from Avonmouth. The team was the Hon F. S. Gough-Calthorpe (Warwicks) (capt), R. T. Stanyforth (Army), N. E. Haig (Middx), G. T. S. Stevens (Middx), R. E. S. Wyatt (Warwicks) and the professionals W. Rhodes (Yorks), G. Gunn (Notts), E. H. Hendren (Middx), W. E. Astill (Leics), A. Sandham (Surrey), L. E. G. Ames (Kent), J. O'Connor (Essex), L. F. Townsend (Derbys), W. Voce (Notts) and, on the advice of previous tourists, J. Hardstaff (Notts) as umpire. R. H. Mallett also accompanied the team as honorary manager. Although the team was by no means representative of England's full strength, it was probably the best side England had ever sent to the West Indies.

Arriving in Bridgetown on 27 December, the tourists played their first match against Barbados commencing on New Year's Day. Barbados batted and hit 345, with a 17-year-old—J. E. D.

Left *Bill Voce (below signature) and George Gunn (holding pipe and raincoat) being seen off on 14 December 1929 for the tour of the West Indies. Among those wishing them well are fellow Nottinghamshire players S. J. Staples (below signature) and Harold Larwood (to Gunn's left).*

Below *The party for the tour of the West Indies in 1929-30. With the captain, the Hon F. S. Gough-Calthorpe in the centre, the remaining players, clockwise from manager R. H. Mallett on the left are: N. E. Haig, G. Gunn, E. H. Hendren, R. E. S. Wyatt, A. Sandham, L. F. Townsend, G. T. S. Stevens, Capt R. T. Stanyforth, W. Rhodes, W. Voce, J. Hardstaff (umpire), L. E. G. Ames, J. O'Connor, W. E. Astill.*

Sealy—scoring exactly 100. The M.C.C. however were not over-awed by the infant prodigy and Hendren hit 223 not out in 330 minutes as the total reached 513. Rain interfered with play and the match was drawn. Hendren went on to hit another double century in the second match—the return against Barbados—and M.C.C. again exceeded 500 in another drawn match.

The third game played in Bridgetown was the first Test. Wyatt, who injured his foot was not available, but he was hardly required. The match was another high-scoring draw, though England would probably have won if time had allowed. Headley and Roach hit hundreds for the home team, whilst Sandham did likewise for England. Hendren contented himself with 80 and 36 not out. It was Hendren's flair for the hook shot that brought him so many runs. The West Indian fast bowling was just his cup of tea.

Going on to Trinidad, the tourists met matting wickets for the first time and the scoring dropped considerably. In the first game against the Colony, the team met its first defeat, but in the return, again with low scores, they had their revenge. Voce bowled ex-

1st Match: v Barbados (Bridgetown) Jan 1, 2, 3, 4.
Barbados 345 (J. E. D. Sealy 100, G. Challenor 51) drew with M.C.C. 513 (E. H. Hendren 223*, G. Gunn 66, R. E. S. Wyatt 55).

2nd Match: v Barbados (Bridgetown) Jan 6, 7, 8, 9.
Barbados 246 (J. E. D. Sealy 77, L. A. Walcott 73*) & 378-6 (E. L. G. Hoad 147, P. H. Tarilton 105, E. L. Bartlett 67) drew with M.C.C. 560-7 dec (E. H. Hendren 211*, A. Sandham 103, L. F. Townsend 97, R. E. S. Wyatt 81).

3rd Match: v West Indies (Bridgetown) Jan 11, 13, 14, 15, 16.
West Indies 369 (C. A. Roach 122, F. I. de Caires 80, J. E. D. Sealy 58, G. T. S. Stevens 5-105) & 384 (G. A. Headley 176, C. A. Roach 77, F. I. de Caires 70, G. T. S. Stevens 5-90) drew with England 467 (A. Sandham 152, E. H. Hendren 80) & 167-3 (A. Sandham 51).

4th Match: v Trinidad (Port of Spain) Jan 22, 23, 24, 25.
Trinidad 150 & 333 (W. H. St Hill 102, M. G. Grell 54, W. Rhodes 5-76) beat M.C.C. 167 & 214 (E. H. Hendren 96) by 102 runs.

5th Match: v Trinidad (Port of Spain) Jan 27, 28, 29.
M.C.C. 142 & 118 beat Trinidad 108 (W. Voce 6-50) & 130 (W. Voce 6-60) by 22 runs.

6th Match: v West Indies (Port of Spain) Feb 1, 3, 4, 5, 6.
England 208 (E. H. Hendren 77, H. C. Griffith 5-63) & 425-8 dec (E. H. Hendren 205*, L. E. G. Ames 105) beat West Indies 254 (L. N. Constantine 58, E. A. C. Hunte 58) & 212 (W. Voce 7-70) by 167 runs.

7th Match: v British Guiana (Georgetown) Feb 10, 11, 12.
M.C.C. 605-5 dec (E. H. Hendren 254*, A. Sandham 112, J. O'Connor 67, L. F. Townsend 60) beat British Guiana 307 (C. R. Browne 61, C. V. Wright 51) & 288 (K. L. Wishart 88) by an inns & 10 runs.

8th Match: v British Guiana (Georgetown) Feb 15, 17, 18, 19.
British Guiana 264 (K. L. Wishart 77) & 184 (W. Rhodes 5-57) lost to M.C.C. 555-7 dec (E. H. Hendren 171, L. E. G. Ames 107, A. Sandham 65) by an inns & 107 runs.

9th Match: v West Indies (Georgetown) Feb 21, 22, 24, 25, 26.
West Indies 471 (G. A. Headley 114, C. A. Roach 209, E. A. C. Hunte 53) & 290 (G. A. Headley 112, C. R. Browne 70*) beat England 145 (E. H. Hendren 56) & 327 (E. H. Hendren 123, L. N. Constantine 5-87) by 289 runs.

10th Match: v Jamaica Colts XV (Kingston) March 19, 20.
Colts XV 311 (A. L. Silvers 56, N. N. Nethersole 50) drew with M.C.C. 208 (A. Sandham 53) & 135-2 (A. Sandham 68).

11th Match: v Jamaica (Kingston) March 22, 24, 25, 26.
M.C.C. 220 (O. C. Scott 6-118) & 441-6 dec (G. Gunn 178, A. Sandham 155) drew with Jamaica 248 (G. A. Headley 64) & 324-4 (F. R. Martin 106*, O. C. da Costa 84*, G. A. Headley 72).

12th Match: v Jamaica (Kingston) March 28, 29, 31, April 1.
M.C.C. 396 (F. S. Gough-Calthorpe 79, G. Morais 6-142) & 344-6 dec (L. E. G. Ames 142*, N. Haig 72, F. S. Gough-Calthorpe 51) drew with Jamaica 418 (C. C. Passailaigue 183, G. A. Headley 52) & 78-2.

13th Match: v West Indies (Kingston) April 3, 4, 5, 7, 8, 9, 10, 11, 12.
England 849 (A. Sandham 325, L. E. G. Ames 149, G. Gunn 85, E. H. Hendren 61, J. O'Connor 61, R. E. S. Wyatt 58, O. C. Scott 5-266) & 272-9 dec (E. H. Hendren 55, A. Sandham 50) drew with West Indies 286 (R. K. Nunes 66) & 408-5 (G. A. Headley 223, R. K. Nunes 92).

ceptionally well and took 12 wickets, his medium-pace deliveries gathering speed off the wicket.

In the second Test, West Indies gained a first innings lead of 46, but Hendren immediately put the deficit to rights with yet another double century and enabled England to declare, setting West Indies 380 to win. Voce had all the home batsmen in trouble and taking 7 for 70 took England to a fine victory. It was during this Test and the preceding one that 'bodyline' bowling was experienced by the English batsmen, the leading exponent being Constantine, who kept up a continual barrage of bouncers round the batsman's head. The tactics of the England opener, Gunn, were of course designed to infuriate the fast West Indian bowlers. Gunn would start walking down the wicket before the ball was delivered and could play a dead bat shot which left the ball just a few feet in front of him. The West Indian press described Gunn as 'The man who walks about the pitch and tickles the ball where he likes'.

During one of Hendren's innings, when two unsuccessful appeals had been made, a wag in the crowd shouted, 'How much Patsy gib you, Mr Hardstaff?'

After the relatively low scores of Trinidad, the party sailed on to British Guiana – Hendren made another double century in the opening match there and M.C.C. won by an innings. Wyatt had recovered from his injured foot, but Stanyforth was injured and the manager cabled to England for another wicket-keeper. Price of Middlesex was sent out. British Guiana were also beaten by an innings in the return match, though Hendren managed only 171. In the third Test, England's fielding was very poor, numerous catches going down, and as the tourists' batting also failed in the

first innings, West Indies won with ease. Headley hit a century in each innings.

The final leg of the tour was in Jamaica. The first game against the Colony was drawn, with Gunn and Sandham creating a new record by adding 322 for the first wicket in M.C.C.'s second innings. The return was also a high-scoring draw, but when it came to the fourth Test, it was agreed, since each team had won one match so far, the game should be played to a finish. England hit 849 in the opening innings, with Sandham making 325 in ten hours batting. The West Indies scored only 286, but Gough-Calthorpe did not enforce the follow on, a tactic which brought him much criticism at the time. When England declared in their second innings, West Indies required 836 to win. Rain prevented any play for two days and when West Indies were 408 for 5, the match had to end to enable the English team to catch the boat home.

The tourists arrived back in England on 27 April. The matches had been well attended throughout the tour, which had been most successful. The outstanding cricketer was undoubtedly Hendren, but Sandham, Ames and Gunn also could point to good returns. The bowlers had to work hard for their wickets, with Rhodes, Stevens, Voce and Astill the best of the bunch.

1929-30: Sir Julien Cahn's team in the Argentine

For the second successive winter, Sir Julien Cahn took a side across the Atlantic, this time to visit the Argentine. The team sailed from Tilbury on the *Avelona Star* on 20 February, bound for Buenos Aires. The full party was Sir Julien Cahn (capt), F. W. H. Nicholas (Essex), F. C. W. Newman (Surrey), T. Arnott (Glamorgan), L. Green (Lancs), P. T. Eckersley (Lancs), H. R. Munt (Middx), R. W. V. Robins (Middx), H. R. S. Critchley-Salmonson (Somerset), G. F. H. Heane (Notts), S. D. Rhodes (Notts), C. W. Flood, C. A. Rowland and the two old Notts professionals J. R. Gunn and T. L. Richmond. H. D. Swan of Essex also accompanied the team.

Six matches were played in all, but the ones of importance were the three 'Tests' against Argentina. Some good bowling by Robins provided the tourists with victory in the 'First Test'. In the 'Second' they were lucky to scrape a draw and the 'Third' was also drawn, but in favour of the visitors. Owing to a split finger whilst practising before the first match of the tour, Rowland was unable to appear in any of the matches. The tourists found the standard of cricket fairly high in the Argentine and the cricket grounds excellent.

The side returned to England on the *Avila Star*, disembarking at Plymouth on 23 April.

1st Match: v Northern Suburbs (Saenz Pena) March 15, 16.
Northern Suburbs XII 280 (G. P. Brooke-Taylor 75) beat Cahn's XII 99 & 151 (F. W. H. Nicholas 51) by an inns & 30 runs.

2nd Match: v Argentina (Belgrano) March 18, 19.
Argentina 167 (R. W. V. Robins 5-45) & 109 (R. W. V. Robins 6-40) lost to Cahn's XI 244 (L. Green 102) & 34-0 by 10 wkts.

3rd Match: v Argentina (Hurlingham) March 22, 23, 24.
Argentina 190 (K. Henderson 59, T. L. Richmond 5-58) & 203 (K. Henderson 85, R. W. V. Robins 6-65) drew with Cahn's XI 189 (R. W. V. Robins 71) & 116-8.

4th Match: v Southern Suburbs (Lomas) March 26, 27.
Cahn's XI 283 (F. W. H. Nicholas 87) drew with Southern Suburbs 148 & 192-5 (R. de C. Lyons 73).

5th Match: v Argentina (Belgrano) March 29, 30, 31.
Cahn's XI 426 (P. T. Eckersley 88, J. R. Gunn 70, L. Green 66, F. W. H. Nicholas 56, S. D. Rhodes 54) & 155 (D. Ayling 5-62) drew with Argentina 337 (P. A. Foy 71, F. A. Bryans 65, T. L. Richmond 5-134) & 167-7 (G. P. Brooke-Taylor 55).

6th Match: v An Argentina XI (Hurlingham) April 1, 2.
Cahn's XI 164 & 41-2 beat An Argentina XI 56 & 147 (Cecil Ayling 52) by 8 wkts.

1930: Egypt win a 'Test'

Mr Martineau took his second team to Egypt in April 1930 and again the programme was one of five matches, with two 'Tests' against All Egypt. In the 'First' Lloyd and Peebles dismissed Egypt for 77 whilst the tourists hit 400 and went on to win by an innings. The Egyptians however played much better in the return at Alexandria and though Peebles took ten wickets, including a hat-trick, and C. H. Knott hit 123 in a defiant second innings, the tourists were beaten by 62 runs.

The touring team was H. M. Martineau (capt), F. O. G. Lloyd, R. S. G. Scott (Sussex), C. H. Knott (Kent), C. K. Hill-Wood (Derbys), A. C. Johnston (Hants), I. A. R. Peebles (Middx), J. F. N. Mayhew (Oxford U), R. M. Handfield-Jones, W. G. L. F. Lowndes (Hants) and J. C. Masterman.

Knott was the outstanding bat of the tour, whilst Peebles took the bowling honours.

1930: H. M. Martineau's Team to Egypt

1st Match: v Alexandria (Alexandria)   April 1, 2.
Martineau's XI 355 (H. M. Martineau 104, C. K. Hill Wood 58) & 300-3 dec (A. C. Johnston 125*, W. G. Lowndes 74, C. H. Knott 70*) drew with Alexandria 326 (M. E. O'Brian 134, G. S. Duckworth 68*) & 183-5 (M. E. O'Brian 89).

2nd Match: v The Army (Cairo)   April 4, 5.
The Army 275 (R. A. Rusbridge 56, J. D. Radford 50) & 190 (E. S. Cole 57) drew with Martineau's XI 247 & 184-7 (C. H. Knott 62).

3rd Match: v Gezira Sporting Club (Cairo)   April 7, 8.
Gezira Sporting Club 228 (E. S. Cole 95*) & 245 (H. R. Holme 68, E. T. Castagli 57) lost to Martineau's XI 405-7 dec (W. G. Lowndes 180, C. H. Knott 130) & 70-7 by 3 wkts.

4th Match: v All Egypt (Cairo)   April 11, 12, 13.
All Egypt 77 & 183-5 drew with Martineau's XI 400 (R. S. Scott 96, C. K. Hill Wood 91, A. C. Johnston 68).

5th Match: All Egypt (Alexandria)   April 14, 15, 16.
All Egypt 297 (M. E. O'Brian 121, E. S. Cole 59) & 226 (K. F. Miles 54) beat Martineau's XI 182 & 279 (C. H. Knott 123) by 62 runs.

1930-31: South Africa win Test series

The team which went out on the *Edinburgh Castle* on 17 October to tour South Africa had two notable omissions in Sutcliffe and Larwood, and the fact that the Yorkshire batsman was not selected came in for a great deal of criticism, which by the end of the visit was proved justified.

Of those who were originally chosen in mid-July, only Ames was forced to stand down and his place was taken by Farrimond. The full party was: A. P. F. Chapman (Kent) (capt), J. C. White (Somerset), R. E. S. Wyatt (Warwicks), M. J. L. Turnbull (Glamorgan), I. A. R. Peebles (Middx), M. J. C. Allom (Surrey) and the professionals W. R. Hammond (Gloucs), E. H. Hendren (Middx), M. Leyland (Yorks), M. W. Tate (Sussex), T. W. J. Goddard (Gloucs), W. Voce (Notts), G. Duckworth (Lancs), W. Farrimond (Lancs) and A. Sandham (Surrey). The manager who joined the team in South Africa was W. Sewell–apparently the sole applicant for the job!

The arrival in Cape Town was followed by a warm-up game against a Colts Fifteen, before the initial first-class match against Western Province. This game and the two that came after it proved easy ones for the tourists, but at this point Sandham was injured in a motor accident and was unable to play again on the tour.

Meeting the strongest Province, Transvaal, at Johannesburg without Sandham and with Allom developing a chill and unable to bowl in the second innings, M.C.C. were lucky to get away with a draw. Travelling on to Rhodesia, the injury list lengthened. Hendren, Duckworth and Goddard all went down with 'flu, so

---

1930-31: M.C.C. to South Africa

1st Match: v Western Province Schools XV (Cape Town)   Nov 6.
W.P. Schools XV 115 (M. Leyland 7-7) lost to M.C.C. 294-6 (E. H. Hendren 100, R. E. S. Wyatt 58, A. Sandham 53) by 8 wkts.

2nd Match: v Western Province (Cape Town)   Nov 8, 10, 11.
W. Province 113 (M. W. Tate 5-18) & 122 lost to M.C.C. 412-7 dec (R. E. S. Wyatt 138, W. R. Hammond 100, A. Sandham 72, E. H. Hendren 58*) by an inns & 177 runs.

3rd Match: v Griqualand West (Kimberley)   Nov 15, 17, 18.
Griqualand West 310 (X. C. Balaskas 83, F. Nicholson 57) & 156-2 dec drew with M.C.C. 232 (W. Voce 57, W. R. Hammond 53, N. A. Quinn 5-56).

4th Match: v Natal (Durban)   Nov 21, 22, 23.
Natal 288 (J. Easterbrook 64, T. Woods 55, M. W. Tate 5-64) & 114-2 drew with M.C.C. 402 (A. P. F. Chapman 80, W. R. Hammond 75, R. E. S. Wyatt 63, E. H. Hendren 51).

5th Match: v Transvaal (Johannesburg)   Nov 29, Dec 1, 2.
M.C.C. 238 (W. R. Hammond 70, R. E. S. Wyatt 58) & 195 drew with Transvaal 176 (I. A. R. Peebles 5-45) & 206-4 (S. H. Curnow 83*, H. W. Taylor 56).

6th Match: v Rhodesia (Bulawayo)   Dec 6, 8, 9.
M.C.C. 278 (R. E. S. Wyatt 78, D. S. Tomlinson 5-106) & 322 (M. Leyland 169) drew with Rhodesia 248 (Hayward 95, Symington 60, I. A. R. Peebles 6-57).

7th Match: v Northern Rhodesia (Livingstone) (One Day)   Dec 11.
N. Rhodesia 73 lost to M.C.C. 234-9 (M. Leyland 65, M. J. L. Turnbull 63) by 9 wkts.

8th Match: v Transvaal (Johannesburg)   Dec 16, 17, 18.
M.C.C. 317 (A. P. F. Chapman 87, E. H. Hendren 75, C. L. Vincent 6-54) drew with Transvaal 279 (B. Mitchell 56, H. W. Taylor 54, M. W. Tate 5-55).

9th Match: v Transvaal Cricket Union (Berea Pk) (One Day)   Dec 19.
M.C.C. 39-0: rain.

10th Match: v South Africa (Johannesburg)   Dec 24, 25, 26.
South Africa 126 & 306 (B. Mitchell 72, R. H. Catterall 54, H. B. Cameron 51) beat England 193 (E. P. Nupen 5-63) & 211 (W. R. Hammond 63, M. J. L. Turnbull 61, E. P. Nupen 6-87) by 218 runs.

11th Match: v South Africa (Cape Town)   Jan 1, 2, 3, 5.
South Africa 513-8 dec (I. J. Siedle 141, B. Mitchell 123, H. W. Taylor 117, R. H. Catterall 56) drew with England 350 (E. H. Hendren 93, W. R. Hammond 57, M. Leyland 52) & 252 (E. H. Hendren 86, W. R. Hammond 65).

12th Match: v Natal (Durban)   Jan 10, 12.
Natal 107 & 107 (W. Voce 5-31) lost to M.C.C. 284 (E. H. Hendren 79, M. J. L. Turnbull 55, A. Woods 6-83) by an inns & 70 runs.

13th Match: v South Africa (Durban)   Jan 16, 17, 19, 20.
South Africa 177 (W. Voce 5-58) & 145-8 (H. W. Taylor 64*) drew with England 223-1 dec (W. R. Hammond 136*, R. E. S. Wyatt 54).

14th Match: v Cape Province (East London)   Jan 24, 26.
Cape Province 156 (K. G. Viljoen 86) & 131 lost to M.C.C. 336-8 dec (W. R. Hammond 126, M. W. Tate 72) by an inns & 49 runs.

15th Match: v Eastern Province (Port Elizabeth)   Jan 31, Feb 2, 3.
M.C.C. 272 (R. E. S. Wyatt 86, C. Maritz 5-53) & 199-6 dec (W. Farrimond 62) beat E. Province 140 & 105 (I. A. R. Peebles 6-51) by 226 runs.

16th Match: v Orange Free State (Bloemfontein)   Feb 7, 9, 10.
O.F.S. 148 (R. Fox 54) & 127 (I. A. R. Peebles 6-50) lost to M.C.C. 492 (E. H. Hendren 170, M. W. Tate 56, R. E. S. Wyatt 55, W. Farrimond 51*) by an inns & 217 runs.

17th Match: v South Africa (Johannesburg)   Feb 13, 14, 16, 17.
England 442 (M. Leyland 91, W. R. Hammond 75, E. H. Hendren 64) & 169-9 dec (E. P. Nupen 6-46) drew with South Africa 295 (H. W. Taylor 72, B. Mitchell 68, I. J. Siedle 62, I. A. R. Peebles 6-63) & 280-7 (B. Mitchell 74, H. B. Cameron 69*).

18th Match: v South Africa (Durban)   Feb 21, 23, 24, 25.
South Africa 252 (B. Mitchell 73, I. J. Siedle 57) & 219-7 dec drew with England 230 (M. W. Tate 50, C. L. Vincent 6-51) & 72-4.

19th Match: v South African Schools XV (Grahamstown)   March 2, 3.
M.C.C. 180 (E. H. Hendren 73*, Levick 5-43) & 305-9 (M. J. L. Turnbull 89, R. E. S. Wyatt 66) drew with Schools XV 130 (T. W. J. Goddard 5-31).

20th Match: v Western Province (Cape Town).
M.C.C. 254 (M. W. Tate 115*, E. H. Hendren 61) & 335-6 dec (M. J. L. Turnbull 139, M. Leyland 50, E. H. Hendren 50) drew with W. Province 316 (J. Goulden 75*, T. de Klerk 54, M. J. C. Allom 6-42) & 141-2 (G. F. Bond 77*, F. Martin 55).

---

there were only eleven fit players and in Northern Rhodesia, Crisp was co-opted into the team.

The first Test was staged at The Wanderers, Johannesburg, over the Christmas period. Peebles and Voce bowled out South Africa on the first day for 126 and by the close England had already gained a first innings lead and looked favourites to win the game. Over 20,000 came on the second day and saw the home team fight back–the English tail collapsed, then Mitchell and Cameron batted well, but England were without Peebles, who had strained a leg. On the third day the tourists were set 240 to win, but Nupen exploited his skill on the matting wicket to the full and South Africa took the game by 28 runs. Going straight on to Cape Town for the second Test, South Africa began in fine style, Mitchell and Siedle putting on 260 for the first wicket. Taylor also batted finely and England managed to draw the match only through some stubborn batting by Hendren. Again the tourists suffered through

J. C. White, E. H. Hendren and the captain, A. P. F. Chapman, trying to say some last goodbyes from the railway train on 17 October 1930 as the journey to South Africa begins.

injury, since Duckworth hurt his hand and Hammond took over behind the wicket.

For the next game, the M.C.C. co-opted H. W. Lee, the Middlesex cricketer, who was coaching in South Africa, and he appeared in four subsequent matches, including the fourth Test.

In the third Test at Durban, England were very much on top, but rain completely washed out the second day, making a draw inevitable. The three provincial matches that followed caused the tourists few worries and England went into the fourth Test with more confidence. The main problem was finding a good opening pair, but the partnership of Wyatt and Lee in this game did not solve it. There was however some very consistent batting in England's first innings and a total of 442 was reached. Peebles bowled out South Africa for 295 and on the final day England hit some quick runs to enable Chapman to declare, setting South

Africa 316 to win. For a long time it was anybody's match, but in the end South Africa played out for a draw, with Cameron being unbeaten on 69.

In the fifth Test, Chapman won the toss and put South Africa in on a drying pitch, but when the home side had reached 32 without loss, rain ended play for the day. Slow batting by both sides on the second and third days made certain the game would be drawn and the final day's play was of no interest. The team, which had lost the Test series by one match to nil, played two other games before travelling back to England in the *Balmoral Castle*, reaching home on 30 March. Turnbull, Allom and Hammond travelled separately from the main party.

The most impressive bowlers on the tour were Peebles and Voce. The Notts player was distinctly effective on the matting wickets, his break off the wicket coming with a decided nip. Peebles on the other hand adjusted his bowling very well to suit both matting and turf and was much improved on his previous tour. Tate was a model of length and accuracy, as was White, but Goddard and Allom did not live up to their reputations.

Hammond and Hendren were the batsmen of the side, whilst Wyatt and Leyland were most consistent, but the lack of an opening batsman after Sandham's accident was very noticeable. On the South African side, Nupen remained the best bowler and Mitchell, Taylor and Siedle stood out in a good batting line-up.

1931 : Martineau's third trip to Egypt

The following went to Egypt on the third tour arranged by H. M. Martineau: H. M. Martineau (capt), W. O'B. Lindsay (Oxford U), Col E. S. B. Williams (Army), G. D. Kemp-Welch (Warwicks), D. N. Moore (Gloucs), J. C. Masterman, W. G. L. F. Lowndes (Hants), C. H. Knott (Kent), Lord Dalmeny (Middx), H. W. F. Franklin (Essex) and J. H. Nevinson (Oxford U). The tour followed the same pattern as in the previous year, with five matches, of which two were against All Egypt. In the 'First Test' both sides collapsed, Cole taking 7 wickets for Egypt, but in the

1930-31 : M.C.C. to South Africa

Batting Averages

	M	I	NO	R	HS	Avge	100	c/s
W. R. Hammond (Glos)	13	19	2	1045	136*	61.47	3	18
E. H. Hendren (Middx)	14	18	1	914	170	53.76	1	12
W. Farrimond (Lancs)	9	13	5	297	62	37.12	0	6/6
M. Leyland (Yorks)	15	22	1	774	169	36.85	1	1
R. E. S. Wyatt (Warks)	15	23	1	768	138	34.90	1	3
M. W. Tate (Sussex)	12	17	2	516	115*	34.40	1	3
M. J. L. Turnbull (Glam)	14	21	2	541	139	28.47	1	3
A. P. F. Chapman (Kent)	14	17	0	471	87	27.70	0	12
H. W. Lee (Middx)	5	7	0	158	42	22.57	0	1
W. Voce (Notts)	13	18	3	296	57	19.73	0	3
J. C. White (Som)	13	18	2	256	36*	16.00	0	4
T. W. J. Goddard (Glos)	7	6	0	53	25	8.83	0	1
I. A. R. Peebles (Middx)	14	17	4	114	28	8.76	0	9
G. Duckworth (Lancs)	7	7	3	29	14*	7.25	0	11/5
M. J. C. Allom (Surrey)	9	9	2	50	19	7.14	0	1

Also played in two matches: A. Sandham 72, 6.

Bowling Averages

	O	M	R	W	Avge	BB	5i
M. J. C. Allom	184	38	403	22	18.31	6-42	1
M. W. Tate	347	106	621	33	18.81	5-18	3
I. A. R. Peebles	444.4	80	1274	66	19.30	6-50	5
W. Voce	479.5	139	1046	49	21.34	5-31	2
J. C. White	348.4	107	698	29	24.06	3-13	0
T. W. J. Goddard	160.2	40	380	13	29.23	4-43	0
R. E. S. Wyatt	51	11	210	7	30.00	3-33	0
M. Leyland	94	19	283	9	31.44	3-4	0
W. R. Hammond	221.4	51	494	15	32.93	4-63	0

Also bowled: A. P. F. Chapman 1-0-4-0; E. H. Hendren 3-1-7-0; H. W. Lee 7-1-26-1. R. J. Crisp played in one non-first-class match.

visitors' second innings Franklin and Williams batted well to set Egypt to make 410 in the final innings. Capt Rogers hit a fine 84 not out and consistent batting produced a score of 341, but it was not enough.

In the 'Second Test', the Egyptian fielding was very poor and allowed the tourists to reach the mammoth total of 531, with Knott hitting a double century and 256 being added in 110 minutes for the sixth wicket by Knott and Franklin. Egypt subsided to an innings defeat.

1931: H. M. Martineau's Team to Egypt

1st Match: v Alexandria (Alexandria)   March 31, April 1.
Martineau's XI 454-5 dec (D. N. Moore 115, C. H. Knott 93, W. O'B. Lindsay 76, S. B. Williams 56) beat Alexandria 253 (De Biss 85) & 168 (Bassett 51) by an inns & 33 runs.

2nd Match: v United Services (Cairo)   April 3, 4.
Martineau's XI 308 (G. D. Kemp-Welch 103, C. H. Knott 69) & 169 (C. H. Knott 57) drew with United Services 270 (Cole 63, Radford 61) & 140-3.*

3rd Match: v Gezira Sporting Club (Cairo)   April 6, 7.
Martineau's XI 334-9 dec (D. N. Moore 143, S. B. Williams 63, C. H. Knott 50) & 59-2 drew with Gezira Sporting Club 176 & 324-6 dec (Pank 114, Dury 78*, Cole 61).*

4th Match: v All Egypt (Cairo)   April 8, 9, 10.
Martineau's XI 195 (W. G. Lowndes 64) & 347 (H. W. F. Franklin 79, S. B. Williams 71) beat All Egypt 133 & 341 (Pank 95, Rogers 84) by 68 runs.*

5th Match: v All Egypt (Alexandria)   April 14, 15.
Martineau's XI 531 (C. H. Knott 227, H. W. F. Franklin 119, W. O'B. Lindsay 75) beat All Egypt 128 & 132 by an inns & 271 runs.

1931-32: Lord Tennyson in Jamaica

The winter of 1931-32 was a quiet one for English cricketers. The M.C.C. did not send a team abroad – the idea of a tour of India was mooted but nothing more was heard of it. In the spring Lord Tennyson took a party to Jamaica for a series of six matches.

The team was Lord Tennyson (Hants) (capt), A. P. F. Chapman (Kent), G. T. S. Stevens (Middx), B. H. Valentine (Kent), G. D. Kemp-Welch (Warwicks), C. F. Walters (Worcs), G. N. Scott-Chad (Norfolk), H. F. Bagnall (Northants) and the professionals G. Geary (Leics), W. E. Astill (Leics), G. Brown (Hants), E. H. Bowley (Sussex), M. S. Nichols (Essex) and C. C. R. Dacre (Gloucs).

The playing record of the side reflected the lack of bowling, which proved to be totally inadequate in the three matches against All Jamaica – there seemed no possibility of dismissing Headley, who hit 344 not out, 84 and 155 not out, and 140 in the three games. Kemp-Welch batted well for the tourists and most of the team made runs at various times on the tour, but the shadow of Headley loomed over all.

1931-32: Lord Tennyson's Team to Jamaica

1st Match: v Jamaica (Kingston)   Feb 18, 19.
Tennyson's XII 285 (B. H. Valentine 101, G. D. Kemp-Welch 75) & 88-3 drew with Jamaica XII 286-10 dec (J. Groves 89, G. T. S. Stevens 5-104).

2nd Match: v Jamaica (Kingston)   Feb 20, 22, 23, 24.
Jamaica 702-5 dec (G. A. Headley 344, C. C. Passailaigue 261*) beat Tennyson's XI 354 (G. D. Kemp-Welch 105, A. P. F. Chapman 79, O. C. Scott 6-146) & 254 (B. H. Valentine 84) by an inns & 97 runs.*

3rd Match: v Jamaica (Kingston)   Feb 27, 29, March 1, 2.
Tennyson's XI 402 (G. D. Kemp-Welch 186, C. C. R. Dacre 75, O. C. Scott 5-129) & 188 (O. C. Scott 6-91) lost to Jamaica 228 (G. A. Headley 84, G. T. S. Stevens 8-87) & 363-5 (G. A. Headley 155, R. K. Nunes 125) by 5 wkts.*

4th Match: v Cornwall XV (Kingston)   March 5, 6.
Cornwall XV 141 (M. S. Nichols 6-40) & 185-8 drew with Tennyson's XI 244 (E. H. Bowley 130, G. N. Scott-Chad 60).

5th Match: v Port Maria (Port Maria)   March 7, 8.
Tennyson's XI 139-5 dec (C. F. Walters 65) & 151 (Lord Tennyson 50) beat Port Maria 147-7 dec & 107 (M. S. Nichols 8-44) by 36 runs.

6th Match: v Jamaica (Kingston)   March 10, 11, 12, 14.
Tennyson's XI 333 (E. H. Bowley 69, C. F. Walters 50) & 359 (E. H. Bowley 115) lost to Jamaica 561 (I. Barrow 169, G. A. Headley 140, O. C. Da Costa 66) & 133-6 (I. Barrow 58) by 4 wkts.*

1932: Martineau's team lose both 'Tests' to Egypt

H. M. Martineau's team left England on 22 March on its now annual visit. The 1932 side was: H. M. Martineau (capt), E. W. Dawson (Leics), G. S. Wills, G. F. Earle (Somerset), J. V. Hermon, R. T. Stanyforth (Army), C. E. Awdry (Wilts), W. G. L. F. Lowndes (Hants), A. L. Hilder (Kent), I. A. R. Peebles (Middx) and A. E. L. Hill (Hants).

The tour was increased from five matches to seven and as usual the two major fixtures were the 'Tests' against Egypt. In the 'First Test', the tourists were set to make 340 in the last innings, but after 150 had been hit for the loss of only 3 wickets, the tail collapsed – unfortunately Earle was involved in a motor accident on the second day and could not bat. The 'Second Test' was altogether a remarkable game. Egypt were dismissed for 161 by Peebles in their first innings and were forced to follow on 175 in arrears. O'Brian then scored a century and took Egypt to 444. The tourists required only 270 to win, but never looked like making the runs and for the first time Egypt won both 'Tests'.

The tourists batting was inconsistent and the bowling relied heavily on Peebles, but the standard of cricket in Egypt was very high at this time.

1932: H. M. Martineau's Team to Egypt

1st Match: v Alexandria (Alexandria)   March 29, 30.
Martineau's XI 207 (A. L. Hilder 90) & 271 (R. T. Stanyforth 130) beat Alexandria 139 (T. M. Sturgess 62) & 215 (J. C. de V. Biss 56) by 124 runs.*

2nd Match: v United Services (Aboukir)   April 1, 2.
Martineau's XI 277 (A. L. Hilder 121) & 187-6 dec (E. W. Dawson 63, W. G. L. F. Lowndes 52) beat United Services 110 & 199 (Harston 53, Peacock 52) by 155 runs.*

3rd Match: v Gezira Sporting Club (Cairo)   April 4, 5, 6.
Martineau's XI 144 & 302 (A. L. Hilder 107, W. G. L. F. Lowndes 62) lost to Gezira Sporting Club 305 (E. S. Cole 145, H. R. Holme 68) & 142-4 (H. R. Holme 51) by 6 wkts.*

4th Match: v Maadi S.C. (Maadi)   April 8, 9.
Maadi 180 & 65 lost to Martineau's XI 286-7 dec (R. I. Campbell 111, R. T. Stanyforth 66) by an inns & 61 runs.*

5th Match: v United Services (Gezira)   April 11, 12, 13.
Martineau's XI 206 (E. W. Dawson 103) & 222 (W. G. L. F. Lowndes 81, G. F. Earle 50) lost to United Services 190 (F. Ward 60) & 241-9 by 1 wkt.*

6th Match: v All Egypt (Cairo)   April 15, 16, 18.
Egypt 259 (Rogers 57, R. G. W. Melsome 50) & 253 beat Martineau's XI 164 (E. W. Dawson 57) & 211 (E. W. Dawson 53) by 137 runs.

7th Match: v All Egypt (Alexandria)   April 21, 22, 23.
Martineau's XI 336 (W. G. L. F. Lowndes 95, I. A. R. Peebles 54, E. W. Dawson 50) & 140 lost to Egypt 161 & 444 (M. E. O'Brien 177, R. G. W. Melsome 74, F. Ward 64) by 129 runs.

1932-33: Jardine, Larwood and the 'bodyline' tour

Of all the pre-war English tours, the 1932-33 to Australia remains uppermost in the mind. The controversy regarding the policy of the English captain had long lasting repercussions on both Test and County cricket.

Preparations for the tour began in earnest in 1931, when the M.C.C. Committee decided on a selection Committee of three – P. F. Warner, P. A. Perrin and T. A. Higson – to act for two years, rather than the customary one, for the sole purpose of developing an England side to win back the Ashes, which Australia had gained during the 1930 series in England. The Tests in England in 1931 and 1932 against the weak New Zealand and Indian teams were to be used as experiments for the 1932-33 tour – there were no major tours in 1931-32. Prior to selecting the touring team, Lord Hawke was added to the selection committee as chairman. The

first move the committee made was on 4 July 1932, when it was announced that D. R. Jardine would lead the side – the only other candidate for the job was in reality Chapman, but there was no doubt that on his past record he was a liability as a batsman. A few days after Jardine's appointment, P. F. Warner and R. C. N. Palairet were appointed joint-managers. On 15 July the three principal batsmen and the two wicket-keepers for the tour were announced – Hammond, Sutcliffe, Duleepsinhji, Ames and Duckworth – no surprises here. The next group to be selected were G. O. B. Allen, Robins, F. R. Brown, Wyatt, Larwood, Voce and the Nawab of Pataudi – this was at the beginning of August. In mid-August Leyland, Verity and Tate were added to complete the team, but Robins decided to decline the invitation and his place finally went to T. B. Mitchell. At the last moment Duleepsinhji was compelled to stand down and his place went to Paynter, and finally Bowes was added to the side.

The team that sailed on the *Orontes* on 17 September was therefore: D. R. Jardine (Surrey) (capt), R. E. S. Wyatt (Warwicks) (vice-capt), G. O. B. Allen (Middx), F. R. Brown (Surrey), Nawab of Pataudi (Worcs), and the professionals W. R. Hammond (Gloucs), H. Sutcliffe (Yorks), M. Leyland (Yorks), H. Verity (Yorks), W. E. Bowes (Yorks), E. Paynter (Lancs), G. Duckworth (Lancs), L. E. G. Ames (Kent), T. B. Mitchell (Derbys), H. Larwood (Notts), W. Voce (Notts) and M. W. Tate (Sussex). By general consent it was the strongest available English combination, but was criticised for being too large. The fact that there were two managers – Warner and Palairet – was also thought a retrograde step.

Following the usual match in Colombo, the team started the tour in earnest at Perth on 21 October. Neither in this game nor the next three were the tourists greatly extended and indeed both South Australia and Victoria were overwhelmed. All the M.C.C. batsmen made runs in these games, centuries coming from the Nawab, Sutcliffe, Leyland, Jardine, Hammond and two fifties from Wyatt. All the bowlers took wickets, except Larwood, who bowled only 11 overs. The first serious problem occurred at

Above *The M.C.C. party for the famous tour of 1932-33 ready to sail from Tilbury on the Orient liner* Orontes *on 17 September 1932. Harold Larwood is being introduced to Captain O'Sullevan by M.C.C. captain Douglas Jardine. On the left are G. O. B. Allen and L. E. G. Ames. To the right are Duckworth and Hammond, with Leyland and Sutcliffe with their backs to the camera half hiding Mitchell, then Paynter, Verity, Voce and Wyatt.*

Below *The Yorkshiremen on the 1932-33 tour arrive at Kings Cross. From left : Leyland, Sutcliffe, Bowes and Verity.*

Melbourne in the fifth game against An Australian Eleven, when the tourists' batting folded up before the bowling of Nagel and on a reasonable wicket, the team was out for 60. The match was drawn due to rain, but the other interesting point was the cheap dismissal twice of Bradman by Larwood. In the next match, however, the M.C.C. batting recovered and the normally formidable New South Wales team was beaten by an innings.

The first Test commenced at Sydney directly after the victory over the State side. Australia won the toss and batted, but without Bradman, who was too ill to play. The opening day belonged to McCabe and Larwood. The Notts fast bowler quickly dismissed Ponsford, Fingleton and Kippax. Voce removed Woodfull, but McCabe played the innings of a lifetime and was 187 not out when the innings ended at 360. Sutcliffe, Hammond and the Nawab all made hundreds for England, then when Australia batted a second time the home side collapsed against Larwood, who took 5 for 28, and England won by 10 wickets. This was the first Test Match in which the English bowlers used leg-theory bowling, or 'bodyline' as the Australian press quickly tagged it. The idea was not a new one and in the recent past had been employed by certain West Indian fast bowlers, but unless a team possessed a bowler who was both exceptionally fast and at the same time accurate, the theory was more or less useless, and the batsmen would have a field day hooking the mediocre bowling to the boundary. England however had in Larwood a bowler who was both fast and accurate, so that the batsman faced with a fast short-pitched delivery on the leg stump had to attempt some sort of shot and any misjudgement would send the ball into the hands of a ring of short legs. This theory had been tried out to a limited extent in the two matches prior to the Test and had achieved the objective of dismissing Bradman, who had been so phenomenally successful during the 1930 Australian tour in England.

In the second Test, the usually fast Melbourne pitch, which ought to have been ideal for leg-theory bowling – and England included all four of their fast men, in Larwood, Voce, Bowes and Allen – was designed for the spinner. O'Reilly, the Australian leg-break and googly bowler, took ten wickets and England lost by 111 runs. Bradman played, scoring an unbeaten hundred in the second innings.

The great bodyline argument really exploded during the third Test at Adelaide. England, batting first, made a very poor start, but good innings by Leyland, Wyatt and Paynter took the total to 341. When Australia batted Larwood and Allen sent the first four batsmen back for 51 and in the course of this a ball from Larwood hit Woodfull severely on the chest. The crowd continuously barracked the English fast bowlers and the noise of 50,000 spectators roaring themselves hoarse with anger and fury was pretty intimidating – the fact that Jardine, the English captain, was the very personification of the aloof and austere Englishman further incensed the crowd. At close of play on the second day Australia had to some extent recovered to 109 for 4. When the game resumed on Monday, Jardine continued with his tactics of leg-theory, in spite of condemnation in the weekend press and the growing personal bitterness between the two opposing elevens – some remarks between the Australian captain, Woodfull and Pelham Warner had the effect of aggravating the situation still further. The situation became even worse when a ball from Larwood hit Oldfield on the head. The Australian batsman had to retire and was unable to take any further part in the match. From then on, for the remainder of the tour, the Australian players refused to attend any of the usual social functions given for the English team and two days later the Australian Board of Control sent a cable to M.C.C. which read:

'Body-line bowling has assumed such proportions as to menace the best interests of the game, making protection of the body by the batsman the main consideration. This is causing intensely bitter feeling between the players as well as injury. In our opinion it is unsportsmanlike. Unless stopped at once it is likely to upset the friendly relations existing between Australia and England.'

The M.C.C. reply deplored the statements in the cable and stated that the M.C.C. had the fullest confidence in the English captain and his team. It went on to say that the bowler was not to blame for the deliveries which hit Woodfull and Oldfield, but if the Australian authorities felt it wise to cancel the remainder of the tour they should do so.

England won the third Test by a large margin and in the interval of three weeks between the third and fourth Tests, tempers cooled and the Australian Board decided not to end the tour. In the meantime however questions were being asked at Government level, with the British Dominions Secretary involved, and judging by the rumpus in the press both in Australia and England, 'war' was about to be declared at any moment.

Happily there were no serious incidents in the fourth Test at Brisbane, and though Australia lost the match, it was due more to some plucky batting by Paynter, who had been hauled out of hospital by Jardine, than the bowlers. The first two innings of the fifth Test were very even, due to poor catching on both sides. It was estimated that England dropped no less than 14. Larwood hit 98 and was then caught in the deep by Ironmonger, the worst fieldsman on the home side. Australia collapsed, mainly to Verity, in their second innings and the tourists had no difficulty in winning the game by 8 wickets, thus ending a series which generated more ill-feeling between the two sets of players than any other. It also generated more books than any other, the rights and wrongs of bodyline bowling being furiously debated.

The tourists played two more State matches and then travelled to New Zealand where two Tests were played. Both these games were curtailed by rain and just the first innings of each side completed with England obtaining vast leads in each. In the second Hammond hit 336 not out which created a new record for Test cricket. He was at the wicket only 315 minutes. Jardine did not play in this game, England being led by Wyatt, and Larwood, who had injured his foot in the fifth Test against Australia, did not appear in any of the subsequent matches.

Hammond and Sutcliffe were the outstanding batsmen of the tour, but England's weak point was finding a replacement for Hobbs. Wyatt partnered Sutcliffe in the first two Australian Tests, Jardine for the other three. Neither was very successful. Lower down the order Leyland and Paynter both played useful innings. Pataudi however, after making a century in the first Test

1932-33: M.C.C. to Ceylon, Australia and New Zealand

Batting Averages

	M	I	NO	R	HS	Avge	100	c/s
W. R. Hammond (Glos)	15	21	2	1569	336*	82.58	5	16
H. Sutcliffe (Yorks)	16	22	1	1345	194	64.05	5	4
Nawab of Pataudi (Worcs)	10	13	0	623	166	47.92	4	2
M. Leyland (Yorks)	13	21	1	880	152*	44.00	2	3
E. Paynter (Lancs)	14	19	3	626	102	39.12	1	5
R. E. S. Wyatt (Warks)	18	27	2	963	78	38.52	0	9
M. W. Tate (Sussex)	7	10	5	186	94*	37.20	0	2
D. R. Jardine (Surrey)	15	21	2	698	108*	36.74	1	15
L. E. G. Ames (Kent)	18	24	1	736	107	32.00	2	16/8
G. O. B. Allen (Middx)	14	17	0	409	66	24.06	0	14
H. Larwood (Notts)	10	13	2	258	98	23.45	0	3
F. R. Brown (Surrey)	11	15	1	301	74	21.50	0	8
W. Voce (Notts)	12	17	6	225	66	20.45	0	8
H. Verity (Yorks)	15	18	3	300	54*	20.00	0	16
G. Duckworth (Lancs)	9	11	5	108	27*	18.00	0	12/4
W. E. Bowes (Yorks)	12	11	6	49	20	9.80	0	1
T. B. Mitchell (Derbys)	11	8	1	28	10	4.00	0	7

Bowling Averages

	Balls	M	R	W	Avge	BB	5i
E. Paynter	258	7	71	5	14.20	3-40	0
H. Larwood	2127	45	817	49	16.67	6-38	3
H. Verity	2818	128	809	45	17.98	7-37	3
T. B. Mitchell	1158	24	558	26	21.46	6-70	2
G. O. B. Allen	2206	51	965	41	23.54	5-69	1
W. E. Bowes	1864	29	900	37	24.32	6-34	1
W. Voce	2236	39	928	37	25.08	5-85	1
M. W. Tate	1093	38	379	15	25.27	4-53	0
F. R. Brown	1008	27	493	19	25.95	4-81	0
W. R. Hammond	1674	38	597	20	29.85	6-43	1

Also bowled: L. E. G. Ames 128-1-51-1; M. Leyland 101-1-55-1; R. E. S. Wyatt 144-2-74-1; D. R. Jardine 104-3-42-0; H. Sutcliffe 24-0-18-0.

Above *The Ashes-winning M.C.C. party of 1932-33, the 'bodyline' tour. Back: G. Duckworth, T. B. Mitchell, the Nawab of Pataudi, M. Leyland, H. Larwood, E. Paynter, W. Ferguson (scorer). Centre: P. F. Warner (manager), L. E. G. Ames, H. Verity, W. Voce, W. E. Bowes, F. R. Brown, M. W. Tate, R. C. N. Palairet (manager). Front: H. Sutcliffe, R. E. S. Wyatt, D. R. Jardine (capt), G. O. B. Allen, W. R. Hammond.*

Below *The Brisbane Test in 1932-33. Larwood is bowling to the Australian captain, Woodfull, and there is a semi-circle of six short legs waiting for a catch. The ball goes over Woodfull's head.*

was dropped—it was thought he made batting look more difficult than it really was.

Larwood was undoubtedly the man who won the Tests, none of the Australian batsmen, save for McCabe in the first Test, being happy against him and whatever the rights and wrongs of bodyline, Larwood was the ideal man to exploit it. Allen, who refused to use leg-theory, also bowled well and was perhaps the surprise of the tour. Bowes and Voce also bowled well at times, though the latter missed some matches due to illness.

The most disappointed tourist must have been Tate. On his two previous visits to Australia, he had been the backbone of the English attack: this time he was completely surplus to requirements.

The tourists travelled home via Fiji, Honolulu and Vancouver, and then across Canada, where they viewed the Niagara Falls. From the financial viewpoint, the tour was a success, but not on the scale of the 1928-29 tour.

1933: Martineau's team fight back

After the defeats of 1932, H. M. Martineau travelled to Egypt in 1933 with a stronger side: H. M. Martineau (capt), H. D. Read (Essex), G. N. B. Huskinson (Notts), A. W. Tyler (Army), B. H. Valentine (Kent), A. K. Judd (Hants), R. H. J. Brooke (Oxford U), C. E. Awdry (Wilts), E. W. Dawson (Leics), G. F. Earle (Somerset) and C. H. Knott (Kent).

Brooke, Knott and Valentine all returned batting averages over 50 and had a highly successful tour, whilst H. D. Read, the fast bowler who was to play for England a little later proved too good for many of the Egyptian batsmen. Both 'Tests' were won by large margins, but the tourists met with one defeat—against the United Services—when Cole took 8 wickets in 12 overs and bowled them out for 57. The innings of the tour was one of 191 by Knott, hit in about 85 minutes with 15 sixes and 17 fours.

1933: Sir Julien Cahn's team in North America and Bermuda

Sailing on the *Empress of Britain* from Southampton on 12 August, Sir Julien Cahn's team began its tour in Canada with two matches against Montreal, followed by two against Ottawa. There was a slight shock in the initial game, when the tourists were in difficulties on a matting wicket and won by a single wicket, but from then on most of the games provided easy wins for the visitors, until the team arrived in Bermuda and had two very good matches against Somerset C.C., winning one by three runs due to a magnificent catch on the boundary by Heane dismissing the last man. In the final game against Bermuda, an unbroken ninth wicket stand by Blunt and Maxwell saved the day and meant that the English side sailed for home unbeaten.

Cricket in North America remained at a low level and Cahn's team, which was of good first-class standard, found the opposition, with the exception of Bermuda, to be very mediocre in strength.

The tourists were: Sir Julien Cahn (capt), R. C. Blunt (New Zealand), P. A. Gibb (Cambridge U), S. D. Rhodes (Notts), D. P. B. Morkel (South Africa), G. F. H. Heane (Notts), G. F. Summers, E. W. Swanton, E. P. Solbe, F. C. W. Newman (Surrey), C. R. N. Maxwell, I. A. R. Peebles (Middx), R. W. V. Robins (Middx), T. B. Reddick (Middx) and H. R. Munt (Middx).

1933: Sir Julien Cahn's Team to North America and Bermuda

1st Match: v XV of Montreal (Montreal)   Aug 19.
Montreal 103 lost to Cahn's XI 122-9 by 1 wkt.

2nd Match: v XV of Montreal (Montreal)   Aug 21.
Cahn's XI 224 (D. P. B. Morkel 123) beat Montreal 66 by 158 runs.

3rd Match: v Ottawa XII (Ottawa)   Aug 22.
Cahn's XI 217-1 dec (P. A. Gibb 100*, G. F. Summers 72*) drew with Ottawa XII 121-9.

4th Match: v Ottawa XII (Ottawa)   Aug 23.
Ottawa XII 111 lost to Cahn's XI 225 (E. W. Swanton 57, I. A. R. Peebles 56) by 4 wkts.

5th Match: v Toronto Council (Toronto)   Aug 24.
Toronto Council 86 lost to Cahn's XI 252-7 (S. D. Rhodes 80, I. A. R. Peebles 57) by 7 wkts.

6th Match: v All Toronto (Armour Heights)   Aug 25.
Cahn's XI 304-8 dec (D. P. B. Morkel 64, R. C. Blunt 58, G. F. Parkinson 51) beat All Toronto 77 by 227 runs.

7th Match: v Toronto C.C. (Toronto)   Aug 26.
Toronto C.C. 142 lost to Cahn's XI 143-6 (G. F. H. Heane 67*) by 4 wkts.

8th Match: v Hamilton XV (Hamilton)   Aug 28.
Hamilton XV 72 lost to Cahn's XI 211 (P. A. Gibb 61, R. C. Blunt 53*) by 5 wkts.

9th Match: v Ridley College XV (St Catherine's)   Aug 29.
Ridley College XV 123 lost to Cahn's XI 127-5 by 5 wkts.

10th Match: v London XV (London)   Aug 30.
Cahn's XI 280-4 dec (G. F. Summers 80*, S. D. Rhodes 70) beat London XV 128 by 152 runs.

11th Match: XIV of Chicago (Chicago)   Sept 2.
Chicago XIV 62 lost to Cahn's XI 247 (E. W. Swanton 51, D. P. B. Morkel 51) by 10 wkts.

12th Match: v XV of Chicago (Chicago)   Sept 3.
Chicago XV 119 lost to Cahn's XI 133-5 (R. C. Blunt 74*) by 5 wkts.

13th Match: v New York XV (Livingstone)   Sept 6.
New York XV 136 lost to Cahn's XI 166-2 (R. C. Blunt 92*, S. D. Rhodes 62*) by 8 wkts.

14th Match: v New York XV (Staten Island)   Sept 7.
Cahn's XI 275-5 dec (D. P. B. Morkel 126, G. F. H. Heane 78) drew with New York XV 82-12.

15th Match: v Crescent Athletic Club XVI (Long Island)   Sept 8.
Crescent A.C. XVI 90 lost to Cahn's XI 200 by 4 wkts.

16th Match: v B.C.A. Colts XI (Prospect, Bermuda)   Sept 11.
Cahn's XI 196-4 dec (F. C. W. Newman 104) drew with Colts 71-7.

17th Match: v St Ged C.C. (Prospect)   Sept 12.
Cahn's XI 209 (G. F. Summers 82) beat St Ged C.C. 107 by 102 runs.

18th Match: v B.C.A. XI (Prospect)   Sept 13.
B.C.A. XI 134 (J. Benevides 51) lost to Cahn's XI 172-5 (S. D. Rhodes 90) by 8 wkts.

19th Match: v Somerset C.C. (Prospect)   Sept 14.
Cahn's XI 85 beat Somerset C.C. 82 by 3 runs.

20th Match: v All Bermuda (Prospect)   Sept 15.
All Bermuda 147 drew with Cahn's XI 91-8.

1933-34: strong England team beat India

The problems connected with bodyline bowling carried on through the 1933 English season and leg-theory was employed by the West Indian bowlers during the Tests of that summer. Jardine continued to lead England and in fact hit a century in the second Test against the leg-theory of Martindale and Constantine. Larwood missed almost the whole season through injury and did not appear in the Test series. The M.C.C. and the Australian Board of Control continued their discussions of the problem, which in reality boiled down to the question of whether leg-theory bowling was in the best interests of the game.

The original party chosen to tour India was Jardine, Walters, Valentine, Wyatt, Levett, Jas Langridge, Nichols, Verity, Townsend, Bakewell, E. W. Clark, Gregory, Paynter, Barnett, Ames and A. N. Other. Sutcliffe and Hammond both declined to go. Later Wyatt withdrew and so did Ames. The final team which sailed on 22 September was: D. R. Jardine (Surrey) (capt), C. F. Walters (Worcs), B. H. Valentine (Kent), C. S. Marriott (Kent), W. H. V. Levett (Kent), J. H. Human (Cambridge U), and the professionals A. Mitchell (Yorks), A. H. Bakewell (Northants), C. J. Barnett (Gloucs), R. J. Gregory (Surrey), Jas Langridge (Sussex), L. F. Townsend (Derbys), M. S. Nichols (Essex), H. Verity (Yorks), H. Elliott (Derbys) and E. W. Clark (Northants) with Major E. Ricketts as manager.

The tour opened in Karachi on 15 October, but it was not until the eighth match at Patiala that the tourists were seriously extended, Wazir Ali scoring a very sound 156 and giving a local side first innings lead for the first time on the tour – Tarrant, the old Middlesex all-rounder, also appeared in this match and his bowling worried several of the M.C.C. team.

The first Test was played in Bombay and a crowd of some 50,000 attended the first day's play – similar sized crowds also appeared on the other three days and the overall total was estimated at 250,000. Valentine hit a forceful hundred for England, though he was dropped twice, and good bowling by Nichols gave the visitors victory with 9 wickets in hand. India made five changes for the second Test, but only a splendid rearguard innings by C. K. Nayudu prevented a second England victory. The Test however was followed by the tourists' sole defeat of the programme. In a

---

1933-34: M.C.C. to India and Ceylon

Batting Averages

		M	I	NO	R	HS	Avge	100	c/s
D. R. Jardine	(Surrey)	14	19	3	835	102	52.18	2	20
C. F. Walters	(Worcs)	11	18	2	689	102	43.06	1	5
B. H. Valentine	(Kent)	14	22	1	834	145	39.71	2	10
C. J. Barnett	(Glos)	16	25	1	880	140	36.67	3	22
L. F. Townsend	(Derbys)	15	22	4	566	93*	31.44	0	8
Jas Langridge	(Sussex)	14	19	3	487	70	30.43	0	5
A. H. Bakewell	(Northts)	11	18	2	479	158	29.93	1	6
A. Mitchell	(Yorks)	13	21	0	616	161	29.33	1	18
H. Verity	(Yorks)	14	18	4	384	91*	27.42	0	e8
R. J. Gregory	(Surrey)	10	15	2	349	148	26.84	1	13
H. Elliott	(Derbys)	7	5	1	89	37*	22.25	0	9/6
M. S. Nichols	(Essex)	14	22	3	404	79	21.26	0	17
J. H. Human	(Cambr U)	10	14	2	186	48	15.50	0	4
W. H. V. Levett	(Kent)	12	18	6	144	25	12.00	0	18/9
E. W. Clark	(Northts)	14	14	8	62	11	10.33	0	0
C. S. Marriott	(Kent)	9	9	1	26	8	3.25	0	2

Bowling Averages

	O	M	R	W	Avge	BB	5i
L. F. Townsend	242.3	72	608	43	14.13	7-16	4
H. Verity	482.2	179	1180	78	15.12	7-37	5
E. W. Clark	381.1	111	890	56	15.89	6-24	2
M. S. Nichols	344.2	70	989	55	17.98	5-14	2
Jas Langridge	262.5	97	585	31	18.87	5-63	1
C. S. Marriott	288.4	103	669	32	20.90	6-35	2
J. H. Human	51.3	5	220	7	31.42	2-11	0
C. J. Barnett	80	20	211	3	70.33	1-22	0

Also bowled: R. J. Gregory 16-3-51-1; D. R. Jardine 2-0-6-0; A. Mitchell 9-1-32-2; B. H. Valentine 13-2-48-1; C. F. Walters 2-1-8-0.
The Maharajah of Patiala played in one non-first-class match.

After the controversy of the 'bodyline' tour of Australia, D. R. Jardine was also captain of the party to India in 1933-34. Here he is, with pipe, beginning the journey at St Pancras station on 22 September 1933, accompanied by some of his team.

1933-34: M.C.C. to India and Ceylon

1st Match: v C. B. Rubie's XI (Karachi) Oct 15, 16.
M.C.C. 292 (C. F. Walters 71, C. J. Barnett 62, B. H. Valentine 59, J. Harris 5-89) & 70-4 dec drew with Rubie's XI 99 & 103-6.

2nd Match: v Karachi XI (Karachi) Oct 18, 19.
M.C.C. 362-8 dec (C. F. Walters 101, A. H. Bakewell 96, B. H. Valentine 59, A. Mitchell 53) drew with Karachi XI 89 & 112-4.

3rd Match: v Sind (Karachi) Oct 21, 22, 23.
M.C.C. 307-5 dec (C. J. Barnett 122, D. R. Jardine 101*) & 140-8 dec (C. J. Barnett 54) beat Sind 189 (H. Verity 6-46) & 167 (M. J. Mobed 60) by 91 runs.

4th Match: v N.W. Frontier Province (Peshawar) Oct 28, 29.
N.W. Frontier 94 (M. S. Nichols 5-28) & 121 lost to M.C.C. 350-7 dec (L. F. Townsend 94, A. Mitchell 84, D. R. Jardine 67) by an inns & 135 runs.

5th Match: v Punjab Governor's XI (Lahore) Nov 1, 2.
M.C.C. 402-7 dec (A. Mitchell 184, Jas Langridge 52, B. H. Valentine 51, L. F. Townsend 50) drew with Governor's XI 253-8 (C. K. Nayudu 116).

6th Match: v Northern India (Lahore) Nov 4, 5.
N. India 53 & 58 lost to M.C.C. 246-7 dec (A. Mitchell 54, L. F. Townsend 50) by an inns & 135 runs.

7th Match: v Southern Punjab (Amritsar) Nov 9, 10, 11.
S. Punjab 264 (N. B. Amarnath 109, Yuvaraj of Patiala 66) & 103-1 (S. Wazir Ali 63) drew with M.C.C. 450-7 dec (L. F. Townsend 93*, C. F. Walters 86, B. H. Valentine 75, M. S. Nichols 55).

8th Match: v Patiala (Patiala) Nov 12, 13, 14, 15.
M.C.C. 330 (D. R. Jardine 80, A. Mitchell 59) drew with Patiala 335-6 (S. Wazir Ali 156, N. B. Amarnath 53).

9th Match: v Delhi & District (New Delhi) Nov 18, 19.
Delhi 98 (H. Verity 5-40) & 102 lost to M.C.C. 333 (A. Mitchell 109, Maharajah of Patiala 54, C. J. Barnett 52) by an inns & 133 runs.

10th Match: v The Viceroy's XI (New Delhi) Nov 21, 22, 23.
Viceroy's XI 160 (H. Verity 7-37) & 63 (M. S. Nichols 5-14) lost to M.C.C. 431-8 dec (B. H. Valentine 145, D. R. Jardine 93, C. F. Walters 65, A. Mitchell 59) by an inns & 208 runs.

11th Match: v Rajputana (Ajmer) Nov 25, 26.
M.C.C. 213 (C. J. Barnett 75) beat Rajputana 32 (E. W. Clark 5-10, L. F. Townsend 5-16) & 74 (L. F. Townsend 7-22) by an inns & 107 runs.

12th Match: v Western India States (Rajkot) Nov 29, 30, Dec 1.
W. India States 104 (L. F. Townsend 7-16) & 249 (Dr. Gurtu 61, H. Verity 6-83) lost to M.C.C. 254-5 dec (C. J. Barnett 84, M. S. Nichols 52) & 60-6 by 4 wkts.

13th Match: v Jamnagar XI (Jamnagar) Dec 3, 4.
Jamnagar 90 (Jas Langridge 5-18) & 45-6 drew with M.C.C. 151-8 dec (C. F. Walters 60).

14th Match: v Bombay Presidency (Bombay) Dec 8, 9, 10.
Bombay 87 & 191-5 (V. M. Merchant 67*) drew with M.C.C. 481-8 dec (R. J. Gregory 148, D. R. Jardine 102, Jas Langridge 66, C. F. Walters 54).

15th Match: v Bombay City (Bombay) Dec 12, 13.
Bombay 140 & 26-2 drew with M.C.C. 319-8 dec (A. H. Bakewell 107, R. J. Gregory 53*).

16th Match: v India (Bombay)   Dec 15, 16, 17, 18.
India 219 & 258 (N. B. Amarnath 118, C. K. Nayudu 67, M. S. Nichols 5-55) lost to England 438 (B. H. Valentine 136, C. F. Walters 78, D. R. Jardine 60, Mahomed Nissar 5-90) & 40-1 by 9 wkts.

17th Match: v Poona XI (Poona) Dec 20, 21.
M.C.C. 161-5 dec (C. F. Walters 84) drew with Poona 83 (S. Nazir Ali 57, H. Verity 8-37) & 39-2.

18th Match: v British in Bengal (Calcutta) (One Day) Dec 27.
M.C.C. 187-5 dec (C. J. Barnett 94) drew with British in Bengal 121-8.

19th Match: v Indians & Anglo-Indians (Calcutta) (One Day) Dec 28.
Indians & Anglo-Indians 123 lost to M.C.C. 179-6 (A. H. Bakewell 54) by 8 wkts.

20th Match: v An Indian XI (Calcutta) Dec 30, 31, Jan 1.
M.C.C. 331 (H. Verity 91*, L. F. Townsend 69, C. F. Walters 67) & 279-5 dec (M. S. Nichols 79, B. H. Valentine 74) drew with An Indian XI 168 & 152-1 (H. P. Ward 77*, C. P. Johnstone 69*).

21st Match: v India (Calcutta)   Jan 5, 6, 7, 8.
England 403 (Jas Langridge 70, D. R. Jardine 61, H. Verity 55*) & 7-2 drew with India 247 (M. Dilawar Hussain 59, V. M. Merchant 54) & 237 (M. Dilawar Hussain 57).

22nd Match: v Vizianagram's XI (Benares) Jan 11, 12, 13.
Vizianagram's XI 124 & 140 (L. F. Townsend 5-30) beat M.C.C. 111 (B. H. Valentine 53, Mahomed Nissar 6-60) & 139 by 14 runs.

23rd Match: v Central India (Indore) Jan 16, 17.
M.C.C. 157 (C. F. Walters 54, C. K. Nayudu 6-36) & 52-0 drew with Central India 157.

24th Match: v Central Provinces & Berar (Nagpur) Jan 19, 20, 21.
Central Provinces 195 (C. K. Nayudu 107, C. S. Marriott 6-35) & 188 (C. S. Nayudu 61*) lost to M.C.C. 261 (C. J. Barnett 140, C. K. Nayudu 5-87) & 129-4 (B. H. Valentine 50*) by 6 wkts.

25th Match: v Moin-ud-Dowlah XI (Secunderabad) Jan 23, 24, 25.
M.C.C. 112 (S. Mushtaq Ali 5-37) & 303 (M. S. Nichols 55, L. Amar Singh 5-82) drew with Moin-ud-Dowlah XI 194 (L. Amar Singh 58, H. Verity 5-63) & 188-9 (C. K. Nayudu 79).

26th Match: v Mysore (Mysore) Jan 28, 29.
M.C.C. 451-7 dec (C. F. Walters 155, Jas Langridge 104, D. R. Jardine 66*) beat Mysore 107 (E. W. Clark 7-8) & 56 (E. W. Clark 5-19, C. J. Barnett 5-21) by an inns & 288 runs.

27th Match: v Madras (Madras) Feb 3, 4, 5.
M.C.C. 603 (A. Mitchell 161, A. H. Bakewell 158, R. J. Gregory 66, L. F. Townsend 53*) beat Madras 106 & 145 (C. P. Johnstone 69, C. S. Marriott 5-43) by an inns & 352 runs.

28th Match: v Indian Cricket Federation (Madras) (One Day) Feb 7.
M.C.C. 268-6 dec (M. S. Nichols 67, Jas Langridge 61, C. F. Walters 56) beat Indian Cricket Federation 81 by 187 runs.

29th Match: v India (Madras)   Feb 10, 11, 12, 13.
England 335 (A. H. Bakewell 85, D. R. Jardine 65, C. F. Walters 59, L. Amar Singh 7-86) & 261-7 dec (C. F. Walters 102) beat India 145 (H. Verity 7-49) & 249 (Yuvaraj of Patiala 60, Jas Langridge 5-63) by 202 runs.

30th Match: v All Ceylon (Colombo) Feb 16, 17, 18.
All Ceylon 106 (E. W. Clark 6-24) & 189 (N. S. Joseph 78) lost to M.C.C. 272 (C. J. Barnett 116, W. T. Brindley 5-40) & 25-0 by 10 wkts.

31st Match: v Galle (Galle) (One Day) Feb 20.
Galle 79-7 dec drew with M.C.C. 59-2.

32nd Match: v India & Ceylon (Colombo) Feb 22, 23, 24.
M.C.C. 155 (L. F. Townsend 56, L. Amar Singh 6-62) & 78 (E. Kelaart 5-17) beat India & Ceylon 104 & 121 by 8 runs.

33rd Match: v Up Country XI (Darrawella) Feb 26.
M.C.C. 228-2 dec (A. H. Bakewell 101*, A. Mitchell 66, C. J. Barnett 53) & 53-1 dec beat Up Country XI 72 & 100-2 on 1st inns by 156 runs.

34th Match: v An Indian XI (Bombay) March 4, 5, 6.
M.C.C. 224 (A. Mitchell 91) & 215 (A. H. Bakewell 56, L. Amar Singh 5-109) drew with An Indian XI 238 (V. M. Merchant 89*) & 112-4.

low-scoring match at Benares, some fast bowling by Mohammad Nissar swept through the M.C.C. batting and the local side won by 14 runs, in spite of a gallant attempt by Jardine to save the game. It was most unfortunate for India that Nissar, through illness, could not play in the third and final Test at Madras. In addition Nazir Ali could not bowl in England's first innings and these two factors made all the difference, England winning by 202 runs. After the third Test, the team travelled to Ceylon, where two games were played, and then a final match took place at Bombay for the Indian Earthquake Fund. The Indian team might well have won this match, but, when set 202 to win, the batsmen went on the defensive, Jamshedji actually being at the wicket 150 minutes for 17 runs, and the stumps were drawn with the Indians 112 for 4. Spectators barracked their own players.

Compared with the previous M.C.C. tour of 1926-27, the Indian grounds had greatly improved, as had the accommodation for the players. The attendances at the matches were also much larger. The Indian fielding in the first half of the tour however was of a low standard and Jardine was very much the superior captain when it came to bowling and fielding changes.

Of the tourists, Jardine, Walters and Valentine were the best batsmen, whilst Verity was the most feared of the bowlers. Marriott did not come off and Human suffered from malaria.

1934: Martineau returns to Egypt

The programme of matches was increased to ten for Martineau's sixth tour of Egypt and the touring party was also increased in strength. The team was: H. M. Martineau (capt), D. F. Mendl, G. E. Livock (Middx), C. G. Ford, W. E. Harbord (Yorks), D. R. Wilcox (Essex), J. L. Guise (Middx), E. Cawston (Sussex), C. H. Knott (Kent), G. F. Earle (Somerset) and F. R. Brown (Surrey).

The two matches against Egypt were both won, but the second was very close and although Brown took 10 wickets for the tourists, Cole obtained some cheap wickets for the home side and Martineau's team won by just 2 wickets.

Brown was the all-rounder of the side, but J. L. Guise hit 661 runs in all with an average of 73.44, and Knott again did well.

1934: H. M. Martineau's Team to Egypt

1st Match: v Alexandria (Alexandria)
Alexandria 295 (F. R. Brown 6-72) & 151 (C. H. Knott 5-25) lost to H. M. Martineau's XI 442 (C. G. Ford 100, J. L. Guise 83, B. de Botton 6-102) & 5-0 by 10 wkts.

2nd Match: v R.A.F. Depot (Abukir)
H. M. Martineau's XI 316-6 dec (F. R. Brown 117, E. Cawston 65) beat R.A.F. Depot 104 (F. R. Brown 8-34) by 212 runs.*

3rd Match: v United Services (Gezira)
United Services 71 (J. L. Guise 5-26) & 217 (E. S. Cole 52, F. R. Brown 5-97) lost to H. M. Martineau's XI 271 (D. R. Wilcox 73, G. F. Earle 63) & 18-2 by 8 wkts.*

4th Match: v Gezira S.C. (Gezira)
H. M. Martineau's XI 352-7 dec (J. L. Guise 145) & 105-1 (D. F. Mendl 74) beat Gezira S.C. 245 & 211 by 9 wkts.

5th Match: v Other Ranks XII (Abbassia).
H. M. Martineau's XI 326-7 dec (C. H. Knott 129) beat Other Ranks XII 137 by 189 runs.*

6th Match: v Maadi S.C. (Maadi).
Maadi S.C. 217 beat H. M. Martineau's XI 127 (R. M. Bradley 5-33) by 90 runs.

7th Match: v Y.M.C.A. (Willcocks Recreation Grd).
H. M. Martineau's XI 297-7 dec (E. Cawston 82, J. L. Guise 76) beat Y.M.C.A. 127 (C. H. Knott 6-33) by 170 runs.

8th Match: v All Egypt (Gezira) April 19, 20, 21.
Egypt 179 (I. J. Kilgour 74) & 282 (R. M. Bradley 69, Partridge 59) lost to H. M. Martineau's XI 588-5 dec (J. L. Guise 217, C. H. Knott 171, F. R. Brown 121) by an innings & 127 runs.*

9th Match: v Victoria College XII (Victoria Coll)
H. M. Martineau's XI 261-8 dec (G. F. Earle 121) beat Victoria College 61 by 200 runs.

10th Match: v All Egypt (Alexandria) April 25, 26, 27.
All Egypt 181 (F. R. Brown 5-58) & 146 (F. R. Brown 5-45) lost to H. M. Martineau's XI 218 (E. Cawston 113, E. S. Cole 6-46) & 110-8 by 2 wkts.

1934-35: England captain's jaw fractured in the West Indies

As was usual with tours other than those to Australia, the English team was in no way representative of the full strength of the country. On the batting side, Sutcliffe was absent, but on the bowling, Verity and Bowes—two of the three main bowlers of the 1934 series in England against Australia—were elsewhere. The team which sailed was: R. E. S. Wyatt (Warwicks) (capt), E. R. T. Holmes (Surrey) (vice-capt), D. C. H. Townsend (Oxford U), K. Farnes (Essex), W. E. Harbord (Yorks), W. R. Hammond (Gloucs), E. H. Hendren (Middx), M. Leyland (Yorks), L. E. G. Ames (Kent), J. Iddon (Lancs), G. A. E. Paine (Warwicks), C. I. J. Smith (Middx), W. E. Hollies (Warwicks), W. Farrimond (Lancs) and the manager T. H. Carlton Levick.

The party had a very rough crossing of the Atlantic, most of the side being very sea-sick and quite unfit for cricket when they arrived in Barbados. In the opening match against the colony, the home team had much the better of a drawn game, only Hendren with a defensive second innings fifty saving the team from defeat. Things went much better in the return fixture. Hammond hit a glorious double century and with Smith had a tenth wicket stand of 122—rain prevented M.C.C. from winning on the final day.

The first Test was quite sensational. Wyatt put the West Indies in on a damp wicket and Farnes' fast bowling dismissed the formidable West Indian batting for 102. England struggled to 81 for 7, but rain had made the wicket even worse and Wyatt declared at this modest total. The West Indies then collapsed to 51 for 6 and Grant had the audacity to declare also, though leaving England a day and a half to make just 73! Wyatt then reversed the England batting order in the hope that the tail might survive long enough to let the wicket improve. Six England wickets dis-

---

1934-35: M.C.C. to West Indies

1st Match: v Barbados (Bridgetown) Dec 29, 31, Jan 1.
Barbados 382 (J. E. D. Sealey 87, E. L. G. Hoad 69, W. E. Hollies 5-81) & 149-7 dec drew with M.C.C. 170 & 221-5 (E. H. Hendren 54, R. E. S. Wyatt 51).

2nd Match: v Barbados (Bridgetown) Jan 3, 4, 5.
M.C.C. 601 (W. R. Hammond 281, C. I. J. Smith 83, R. E. S. Wyatt 65) drew with Barbados 177 (G. M. Carew 68) & 8-1.

3rd Match: v West Indies (Bridgetown) Jan 8, 9, 10.
West Indies 102 & 51-6 dec (C. I. J. Smith 5-15) lost to England 81-7 dec & 75-6 (E. A. Martindale 5-22) by 4 wkts.

4th Match: v Trinidad (Port of Spain) Jan 15, 16, 17.
M.C.C. 348 (W. R. Hammond 116, L. E. G. Ames 69, C. I. J. Smith 54) & 200-6 dec (M. Leyland 77*) drew with Trinidad 371-7 dec (A. Maynard 200*, G. A. E. Paine 5-68) & 159-8.*

5th Match : v Trinidad (Port of Spain) Jan 19, 21, 22.
M.C.C. 226 (L. E. G. Ames 67) & 103 (M. Leyland 59, B. J. Sealey 5-26) drew with Trinidad 230-9 dec (L. N. Constantine 68, R. E. S. Wyatt 5-10) & 86-6.

6th Match: v West Indies (Port of Spain) Jan 24, 25, 26, 28.
West Indies 302 (J. E. D. Sealey 92, L. N. Constantine 90) & 280-6 dec (G. A. Headley 93) beat England 258 (E. R. T. Holmes 85*, J. Iddon 73) & 107 by 217 runs.

7th Match: v British Guiana (Georgetown) Feb 5, 6, 7.
British Guiana 258 (W. E. Hollies 5-29) & 284-2 (F. I. de Caires 80, C. Jones 72*, C. de Freitas 71) drew with M.C.C. 421 (E. H. Hendren 148, J. Iddon 68).*

8th Match: v British Guiana (Georgetown) Feb 10, 11, 12.
British Guiana 188-8 dec (K. L. Wishart 56, G. A. E. Paine 6-67) & 57 lost to M.C.C. 41-5 dec & 205-1 (W. R. Hammond 106, D. C. H. Townsend 93*) by 9 wkts.*

9th Match: v West Indies (Georgetown) Feb 14, 15, 16, 18.
England 226 & 160-6 dec (R. E. S. Wyatt 71) drew with West Indies 184 (G. A. Headley 53, K. L. Wishart 52, W. E. Hollies 7-50) & 104-5.

10th Match: v Jamaica (Kingston) March 5, 6, 7.
Jamaica 305 (I. Barrow 108, C. H. Moodie 94) & 146-3 dec drew with M.C.C. 289 (E. H. Hendren 118, E. R. T. Holmes 72) & 75-1.

11th Match: v Jamaica (Kingston) March 9, 11, 12.
M.C.C. 321 (L. E. G. Ames 89, J. Iddon 58, E. H. Hendren 54, H. H. H. Johnson 5-71, D. P. Beckford 5-90) & 109-3 drew with Jamaica 452-6 dec (G. A. Headley 127, R. L. Fuller 113, C. H. Moodie 60*, I. Barrow 59).*

12th Match: v West Indies (Kingston) March 14, 15, 16, 18.
West Indies 535-7 dec (G. A. Headley 270*, J. E. D. Sealey 91, R. S. Grant 77, G. A. E. Paine 5-168) beat England 271 (L. E. G. Ames 126, J. Iddon 54) & 103 by an inns & 161 runs.

appeared for 49 and it appeared as if Grant's bold move would pay off, but Wyatt then joined Hammond and the pair took England to a remarkable win. Hammond, who made 43 and 29, stated later that they were the hardest innings he had ever played.

Moving on to Trinidad, the island had the best of both matches against the tourists and then came the second Test. Wyatt gambled and put the West Indies in. The ploy didn't work. Constantine hit a brilliant 90 and Sealy 92. England failed to gain a first innings lead and were eventually left with 325 to get. Wyatt baffled everyone by reversing the batting order again and England staggered to 75 for 5 – his theory was that England couldn't win, but that West Indies only stood a chance if they dismissed the major batsmen with the new ball. At any rate the theory failed and so did England.

There was yet another odd match at Georgetown. British

The M.C.C. team to tour the West Indies at Paddington station on 15 December 1934. Left to right: D. C. H. Townsend, E. R. T. Holmes, Sir Stanley Jackson, Maurice Leyland, R. E. S. Wyatt (captain), K. Farnes, J. Iddon, W. Farrimond, C. I. J. Smith, W. E. Hollies.

Guiana declared when they had made 188 for 8, then M.C.C. declared at 41 for 5 and proceeded to dismiss the colony for 57 in their second innings. Hammond knocked up a century on an easy wicket on the third day and the match was won. The third Test proved a dull affair.

The final leg of the tour was in Jamaica, which was reached via Panama. In the first game against Jamaica both Hollies and Farrimond were injured – Wyatt acted as wicket-keeper – and in the second match the tourists co-opted T. Arnott (Glamorgan), who was in Kingston on holiday, into the side. Both matches were drawn. The result of the rubber depended on the fourth Test. Headley scored a marvellous double century, none of the English bowlers causing him the least worry, and West Indies declared at 535 for 7. When England batted, Wyatt was hit by a ball from Martindale which fractured his jaw and the England captain was out of the match – he was taken unconscious to hospital. Oddly enough, Grant, the West Indies captain was injured later in the game, so that the match ended with two new captains – Holmes and Constantine. The fast bowling of Martindale and Constantine proved too much for the England batsmen and West Indies won the match with an innings to spare.

During the tour the M.C.C. in England solved the bodyline problem by amicable means, though there were great upheavals at Trent Bridge.

Neither Martindale or Constantine used leg-theory on this tour and the only complaints came from some weird umpiring decisions. Leyland suffered from a very strange leg before wicket dismissal, and he came into the dressing room without a word, slowly sat down and glanced round, then muttered: 'I've never seen owt like it.'

England lacked fast bowlers on this tour, and an injury to Farnes which kept him out of several games was a serious blow. Headley was without a doubt the batsman of the series – none of the English players being very consistent. Once more England had underestimated the strength of the West Indians.

1934-35: M.C.C. to the West Indies

Batting Averages

	M	I	NO	*R	HS	Avge	100	c/s
W. R. Hammond (Glos)	10	17	3	789	281*	56.35	3	15
L. E. G. Ames (Kent)	11	18	5	566	126	43.53	1	12/3
E. H. Hendren (Middx)	11	18	1	673	148	39.58	2	4
J. Iddon (Lancs)	11	15	3	351	73	29.25	0	7
R. E. S. Wyatt (Warks)	12	19	3	386	71	24.12	0	7/1
E. R. T. Holmes (Surrey)	12	17	5	285	85*	23.75	0	9
D. C. H. Townsend (Oxf U)	11	19	1	424	93*	23.55	0	2
M. Leyland (Yorks)	11	18	2	347	77*	21.68	0	5
C. I. J. Smith (Middx)	9	13	0	240	83	18.46	0	2
W. E. Harbord (Yorks)	4	6	0	81	32	13.50	0	2
W. Farrimond (Lancs)	4	5	1	52	24*	13.00	0	6/4
G. A. E. Paine (Warks)	10	15	3	125	49	10.41	0	13
W. E. Hollies (Warks)	8	8	3	49	20	9.80	0	1
K. Farnes (Essex)	7	8	1	56	22	8.00	0	4

Also played in one match: T. Arnott (Glam) 1 (ct 1).

Bowling Averages

	O	M	R	W	Avge	BB	5i
R. E. S. Wyatt	96	25	307	18	17.05	5-10	1
W. E. Hollies	206.4	58	498	26	19.15	7-50	3
T. Arnott	29	4	88	4	22.00	4-88	0
G. A. E. Paine	369	103	957	40	23.92	6-67	3
J. Iddon	69.5	13	207	7	29.57	4-14	0
K. Farnes	184	34	550	18	30.55	4-40	0
C. I. J. Smith	238	48	705	21	33.57	5-15	1
M. Leyland	166.5	48	453	11	41.18	4-54	0
W. R. Hammond	57	11	161	2	80.50	1-10	0
E. R. T. Holmes	113	16	458	5	91.60	1-10	0

Also bowled: W. E. Harbord 1-0-1-0; E. H. Hendren 1-0-11-0; D. C. H. Townsend 5-1-22-0.

1935: Martineau's team to Egypt

Perhaps in view of the success attained in 1934, Martineau took a slightly weaker team out in 1935, but found he had under-estimated the opposition and suffered no less than four defeats, including both 'Test Matches'.

The touring party were: H. M. Martineau (capt), D. R. Wilcox (Essex), A. W. G. Hadingham (Surrey), C. G. Ford, D. A. M. Rome, A. K. Judd (Hants), A. G. Hazlerigg (Leics), R. Page (Army), A. R. Legard (Oxford U), E. L. Armitage (Hants) and B. H. Valentine (Kent). In the 'First Test', running commentaries were broadcast by the Egyptian State Broadcasting Service and this must have inspired the home team who won by an innings. For the first time, the tourists met a team composed entirely of native-born Egyptians and only just won the single innings match. In the game against Other Ranks, the whole touring party fell ill with food poisoning – the doctor's remedy being half a tin of Eno's per man, which rather upset the batting order.

D. R. Wilcox and B. H. Valentine were the best batsmen, whilst Judd and Legard had almost identical bowling returns – averaging 19.90 and 19.91 respectively.

1935: H. M. Martineau's Team to Egypt

1st Match: v Alexandria (Alexandria).
Alexandria 341 & 144-2 drew with H. M. Martineau's XI 334-9 dec (E. L. Armitage 77, D. R. Wilcox 71) & 49-0.

2nd Match: v Quails (Alexandria).
Quails 170 (P. C. Organ 85, A. K. Judd 6-54) lost to H. M. Martineau's XI 174-4 (B. H. Valentine 89) by 6 wkts.

3rd Match: v Gezira (Gezira).
H. M. Martineau's XI 210 (D. R. Wilcox 78) & 217-6 dec (D. A. M. Rome 76) drew with Gezira S.C. 184 & 211-6 (Thomas 76).

4th Match: v United Services (Gezira).
H. M. Martineau's XI 275 (D. R. Wilcox 115*, A. W. G. Hadingham 72, Booker 8-68) & 97 (F. Rawson 5-45, Booker 5-50) lost to United Services 167 (Booker 50*) & 206-5 (M. J. Lindsay 80) by 5 wkts.

5th Match: v All Egypt (Gezira).
All Egypt 507 (Thomas 139, Musson 97, F. Rawson 81) beat H. M. Martineau's XI 141 (E. S. Cole 5-37) & 201 (A. W. G. Hadingham 70, C. G. Ford 51) by an inns & 165 runs.

6th Match: v Maadi S.C. (Maadi).
H. M. Martineau's XI 361-3 dec (D. R. Wilcox 154, A. G. Hazlerigg 79) beat Maadi S.C. 129 (A. K. Judd 5-38) by 232 runs.

7th Match: v Egyptian C.C. (Gezira).
H. M. Martineau's XI 141-8 dec (Abdou 8-51) beat Egyptian C.C. 122 (Z. Taker 72) by 19 runs.

8th Match: v Other Ranks (Abbassia).
H. M. Martineau's XI 187 (D. A. M. Rome 62) lost to Other Ranks 188-9 (Ward 78) by 1 wkt.

9th Match: v Victoria College (Victoria Coll).
H. M. Martineau's XI 256-6 dec (A. K. Judd 80, D. A. M. Rome 73) drew with Victoria College 142-7 (G. G. Edwards 81*).

10th Match: v All Egypt (Alexandria).
All Egypt 264 (B. de Botton 115, A. R. Legard 6-99) & 167 (R. G. Musson 55) beat H. M. Martineau's XI 196 (Booker 9-92) & 130 (Booker 7-43) by 105 runs.

1935-36: young M.C.C. party tour New Zealand

The team which represented M.C.C. on the tour of 1935-36 was essentially a side of up and coming young players – the eldest being 34 and no less than 10 of the 14 being under 30. Apart from giving New Zealand the chance of entertaining a full tour from England, rather than a brief visit after a major tour in Australia, the object of the venture was to give experience to the young players in the hope that several of them would be suitable for the tour to Australia in 1936-37.

The M.C.C. originally asked Wyatt to captain the side, but he

---

1935-36: M.C.C. to Ceylon, Australia and New Zealand

1st Match: v Ceylon (Colombo).
Ceylon 107 drew with M.C.C. 27-3.

2nd Match: v W. Australia (Perth)   Oct 31, Nov 1, 2.
M.C.C. 344 (D. Smith 83, Jas Langridge 59, N. S. Mitchell-Innes 58) & 266 J. Hardstaff jun 55, J. H. Parks 51, E. R. T. Holmes 51) drew with W. Australia 232 (F. A. Taafe 76, J. M. Sims 7-95) & 23-1.

3rd Match: v South Australia (Adelaide)   Nov 8, 9, 11, 12.
M.C.C. 371 (J. Hardstaff jun 90, J. H. Human 87, J. H. Parks 67, D. Smith 52, M. G. Waite 5-42) & 174 beat S. Australia 322 (C. W. Walker 65*, M. G. Waite 58) & 187 (D. G. Bradman 50) by 36 runs.

4th Match: v Victoria (Melbourne)   Nov 15, 16, 18, 19.
Victoria 332-9 dec (K. E. Rigg 112, H. J. Plant 64, J. W. Scaife 60) & 122-1 dec (K. E. Rigg 59*) drew with M.C.C. 252 (J. H. Parks 72, R. G. Gregory 5-69) & 46-3.

5th Match: v New South Wales (Sydney)   Nov 22, 23, 25.
M.C.C. 260 (J. Hardstaff jun 77, J. H. Parks 55) & 163 lost to N.S.W. 385 (A. E. Marks 88, F. A. Easton 77, A. D. McGilvray 66, J. M. Sims 6-125) & 39-0 by 10 wkts.

6th Match: v Queensland (Brisbane)   Nov 29, 30, Dec 2, 3.
Queensland 203 (E. C. Bensted 64) & 249 (R. M. Levy 76, J. A. J. Christy 66*, A. D. Baxter 5-61) lost to M.C.C. 558 (J. H. Human 118, D. Smith 109, W. Barber 91, E. R. T. Holmes 80, T. Allen 5-108) by an inns & 106 runs.

7th Match: v An Australian XI (Sydney)   Dec 6, 7, 9, 10.
M.C.C. 411-9 dec (J. Hardstaff jun 230*, Jas Langridge 53, H. I. Ebeling 5-101) & 207-9 dec (J. Hardstaff jun 63, H. I. Ebeling 6-58) beat An Australian XI 227 (A. E. Marks 64) & 188 by 203 runs.

8th Match: v Wellington (Wellington)   Dec 20, 21, 23.
Wellington 164 (J. R. Lamason 62, J. M. Sims 8-53) & 146 (J. Ell 61) beat M.C.C. 166 & 130 (E. D. Blundell 5-50) by 14 runs.

9th Match: v Canterbury (Christchurch)   Dec 24, 25, 26.
Canterbury 243 (J. L. Kerr 146*) & 172 (J. L. Kerr 71, H. D. Read 6-61) lost to M.C.C. 364 (W. Barber 116, Hon. C. J. Lyttelton 80, N. S. Mitchell-Innes 50, I. B. Cromb 5-52) & 52-0 by 10 wkts.

10th Match: v South Canterbury (Timaru)   Dec 27, 28.
M.C.C. 182 (E. R. T. Holmes 61) & 278-6 (N. S. Mitchell-Innes 90*, J. H. Parks 58, W. Barber 50) drew with S. Canterbury 219 (C. Allcott 74).

11th Match: v Otago (Dunedin)   Dec 31, Jan 1, 2.
Otago 78 & 357 (V. G. Cavenagh 66, D. Smith 52) lost to M.C.C. 550 (D. Smith 165, J. H. Parks 103, N. S. Mitchell-Innes 87, J. Hardstaff jun 86, J. H. Human 57) by an inns & 115 runs).

12th Match: v Southland (Invercargill)   Jan 4, 6.
M.C.C. 489 (J. H. Parks 201, E. R. T. Holmes 100, Jas Langridge 118, N. McGowan 5-96) drew with Southland 53-4: rain.

13th Match: v New Zealand (Dunedin)   Jan 10, 11, 13.
New Zealand 81 (H. D. Read 6-26) & 205-7 (H. G. Vivian 87*, H. D. Read 5-74) drew with M.C.C. 653-5 dec (W. Barber 173, Jas Langridge 106*, J. H. Parks 100, J. H. Human 97, J. Hardstaff jun 76, E. R. T. Holmes 54*).

14th Match: v New Zealand (Wellington)   Jan 17, 18, 20.
New Zealand 242 (A. W. Roberts 75*) & 229-3 dec (J. L. Kerr 105*, H. G. Vivian 96) drew with M.C.C. 156 (N. S. Mitchell-Innes 57) & 130-7 (Jas Langridge 61*).

15th Match: v Wanganui (Wanganui)   Jan 24, 25.
M.C.C. 202-2 dec (J. H. Parks 113*) & 198-8 dec (J. Hardstaff jun 60, F. Warnes 5-71) beat Wanganui 130 & 75 (J. M. Sims 5-40) by 195 runs.

16th Match: v Taranaki (New Plymouth)   Jan 27, 29.
M.C.C. 221 (J. M. Sims 51) & 214-5 dec (J. Hardstaff jun 109*) drew with Taranaki 66 (J. M. Sims 5-19) & 138-9 (A. D. Baxter 5-34).

17th Match: v Rangitikei (Marton)   Jan 31, Feb 1.
M.C.C. 248 (Jas Langridge 77, H. Marshall 7-102) & 186-4 dec (N. S. Mitchell-Innes 104*) drew with Rangitikei 47 (A. D. Baxter 6-20) & 18-1.

18th Match: v Manawatu (Palmerston)   Feb 5, 6.
M.C.C. 176 (J. Hardstaff jun 75, J. Murchison 6-51) drew with Manawatu 85-7: rain.

19th Match: v Hawke's Bay (Napier)   Feb 7, 8.
Hawke's Bay 88 (Jas Langridge 8-25) & 97-6 drew with M.C.C. 171-8 dec.

20th Match: v Poverty Bay (Gisborne)   Feb 11, 12.
M.C.C. 296-5 dec (J. H. Human 50*) & 158-9 dec beat Poverty Bay 105 (S. D. Reeves 51) & 67 by 192 runs.

21st Match: v Bay of Plenty (Rotorua)   Feb 15.
Bay of Plenty 99 (J. M. Sims 5-26) lost to M.C.C. 291-6 (J. H. Human 107) by 9 wkts.

22nd Match: v Piako (Matamata)   Feb 18, 19.
Piako 140 drew with M.C.C. 100-4: rain.

23rd Match: v Auckland (Auckland)   Feb 21, 22, 24.
Auckland 306-6 dec (W. M. Wallace 113, P. E. Whitelaw 73, L. F. Townsend 53) drew with M.C.C. 329 (J. H. Parks 88, W. Barber 72, C. J. Lyttelton 60, J. M. Sims 52).

24th Match: v New Zealand (Auckland)   Feb 28, 29, March 2.
New Zealand 368 (C. J. Elmes 99, I. B. Cromb 74) & 128-3 (A. M. Matheson 50*) drew with M.C.C. 435 (J. Hardstaff jun 147*, W. Barber 93, J. H. Parks 65).

25th Match: v New Zealand (Christchurch)   March 6, 7, 9.
M.C.C. 195 (W. Barber 60) & 142-2 drew with New Zealand 334 (J. L. Kerr 132, H. D. Read 5-72).

---

declined and the position was filled by Holmes. The full team was: E. R. T. Holmes (Surrey) (capt), J. H. Human (Middx), Hon C. J. Lyttelton (Worcs), N. S. Mitchell-Innes (Somerset), S. C. Griffith (Surrey), A. G. Powell (Essex), A. D. Baxter (Lancs), H. D. Read (Essex) and the professionals W. Barber (Yorks),

Above *An M.C.C. party with some young new faces for the tour of New Zealand in 1935-36. Back: J. H. Parks, S. C. Griffith, A. G. Powell, D. Smith, J. M. Sims, J. Hardstaff, jun, James Langridge. Front: W. Barber, H. D. Read, the Hon C. J. Lyttelton, E. R. T. Holmes, A. D. Baxter, N. S. Mitchell-Innes, J. H. Human.*
Right *One of the greatest foes England faced on the cricket field, either at home or on tour, was Australia's captain, Don Bradman. Here he is getting a ball away through the slips, watched by England's wicket-keeper batsman, Leslie Ames.*

J. Hardstaff jun (Notts), Jas Langridge (Sussex), J. H. Parks (Sussex), J. M. Sims (Middx) and D. Smith (Derbys).

The team played the usual one-day match in Colombo and then began the tour in earnest at Perth, where they had the best of a drawn game. At Adelaide, they met South Australia captained by Bradman and with a good team performance won by 36 runs. Rain spoilt the game at Melbourne, where the State had the better of a draw and then the tourists were defeated at Sydney due to poor batting. Queensland however lost by an innings, with Barber and Smith giving the M.C.C.'s innings a good start by adding 201 before being parted; Holmes and Human also batted in style.

The last match in Australia proved a triumph for Hardstaff, who hit an unbeaten 230 against An Australian XI.

In New Zealand the first match was lost by 14 runs, when the M.C.C. were caught on a tricky wicket, but after that the batsmen flourished and when it came to the first 'Unofficial Test', the visitors hit 653 for 5 declared in reply to New Zealand's 81 all out; Vivian batted stubbornly in the second innings to save the home side from defeat. The second 'Unofficial Test' was played directly after the first and in this the positions were reversed, with the M.C.C., through James Langridge struggling for a draw.

The other two 'Tests' were played at the end of the tour. In the match at Auckland, Hardstaff hit a good hundred, but high scoring throughout meant a drawn game, whilst at Christchurch rain washed out the final day.

The success of the tour was Hardstaff, who easily headed the batting averages and alone completed 1,000 in the first-class games. The Sussex pair of Parks and Langridge showed good all-round form, but a tendency to feel for deliveries outside the off-stump led to the downfall of Smith on too many occasions. Sims' slows proved most effective, but Read was a disappointment. Socially the tour was a success, but the New Zealand Cricket Council reported a financial loss of £3,400.

1935-36: M.C.C. to Ceylon, Australia and New Zealand

Batting Averages

	M	I	NO	R	HS	Avge	100	c/s
J. Hardstaff jun (Notts)	13	21	4	1044	230*	61.41	2	2
D. Smith (Derbys)	11	18	3	711	165	47.40	2	10
Jas Langridge (Sussex)	12	18	5	554	106*	42.61	1	6
W. Barber (Yorks)	13	19	0	797	173	41.94	2	12
J. H. Parks (Sussex)	13	21	1	808	103	40.40	2	9
J. H. Human (Middx)	12	17	0	519	118	30.52	1	5
Hon C. J. Lyttelton (Worcs)	9	15	0	371	80	24.73	0	2
J. M. Sims (Middx)	14	19	3	388	52	24.25	0	11
N. S. Mitchell-Innes (Som)	10	15	0	335	87	22.33	0	9
E. R. T. Holmes (Surrey)	12	17	1	333	80	20.81	0	3
S. C. Griffith (Cambr U)	11	13	4	152	35	16.88	0	11/2
A. G. Powell (Essex)	4	7	1	40	32	6.66	0	6/1
H. D. Read (Essex)	10	12	4	47	25*	5.87	0	3
A. D. Baxter (Lancs)	10	11	2	48	10*	5.33	0	1

Bowling Averages

	Balls	M	R	W	Avge	BB	5i
J. M. Sims	3144	59	1563	70	22.32	8-53	3
H. D. Read	1897	30	1053	44	23.93	6-26	4
A. D. Baxter	1941	47	864	31	27.87	5-61	1
Jas Langridge	1413	46	488	16	30.50	4-53	0
J. H. Parks	1964	81	751	24	31.29	4-46	0
J. H. Human	432	9	221	7	31.57	2-27	0
E. R. T. Holmes	558	13	253	7	36.14	1-2	0

Also bowled: Hon C. J. Lyttelton 104-1-49-0; J. Hardstaff jun 28-0-6-0; N. S. Mitchell-Innes 20-0-13-0; D. Smith 5-0-5-1.

1935-36: Yorkshire tour Jamaica

Following the precedent of Kent, who went to the U.S.A. some thirty years before, Yorkshire took their County side to Jamaica in the early months of 1936. The team sailed on the s.s. *Ariguani* on 30 January and played the first match against a team of Fifteen Schoolboys on 15 February.

The members of the touring party were: P. A. Gibb (capt), A. Mitchell, A. Wood, M. Leyland, H. Verity, E. P. Robinson, H. Fisher, L. Hutton, C. Turner, H. Sutcliffe, T. F. Smailes and W. E. Bowes. G. H. Hirst went as umpire. The County captain, A. B. Sellers, was unable to go.

The three important matches were against All Jamaica. In the first, Jamaica were dismissed relatively cheaply after winning the toss and batting. Yorkshire, through Mitchell, obtained a first innings lead and then managed to dismiss Jamaica a second time for under 300, Verity bowling very well. Mitchell hit an unbeaten hundred as Yorkshire obtained a 5-wicket win, with two minutes playing time in hand. The other two matches fell into the category of high-scoring draws, with neither side having an advantage, though Yorkshire enforced the follow on in the second match.

Mitchell was certainly the batsman of the tour, and the bowling honours were shared between Verity, Robinson and Bowes.

1935-36: Yorkshire to Jamaica

1st Match: v Schoolboys XV (Sabina Pk)   Feb 15, 17.
Schoolboys XV 194 (R. C. Humphries 57) & 61-5 drew with Yorkshire 222 (P. A. Gibb 50*).

2nd Match: v Jamaica Next XII (Sabina Pk)   Feb 19, 20.
Next XII 185 & 116-1 (V. A. Valentine 53*) drew with Yorkshire 214 (P. A. Gibb 74, V. A. Valentine 5-54).

3rd Match: v Jamaica (Melbourne Pk)   Feb 22, 24, 25, 26.
Jamaica 280 (W. G. Beckford 65, G. A. Headley 62, I. Barrow 59, L. G. Hylton 52, H. Verity 5-34) & 257 (G. A. Headley 74, W. G. Beckford 54, H. Verity 5-62) lost to Yorkshire 325 (E. P. Robinson 68, A. Mitchell 66) & 214-5 (A. Mitchell 101*, E. P. Robinson 63) by 5 wkts.

4th Match: v Cornwall (Montego Bay)   Feb 28, 29.
Yorkshire 295-6 dec (H. Sutcliffe 151, J. R. S. Raper 62) & 220-3 (L. Hutton 107*) drew with Cornwall 156 (Russell 55*).

5th Match: v Jamaica (Melbourne Pk)   March 4, 5, 6, 7, 9.
Yorkshire 465 (M. Leyland 115, A. Wood 94, P. A. Gibb 58) & 60-0 drew with Jamaica 314 (O. C. Stephenson 76) & 349-8 dec (D. P. Beckford 114, E. A. Rae 56).

6th Match: v Jamaica (Sabina Pk)   March 11, 12, 13, 14, 16.
Yorkshire 556-8 dec (H. Verity 101, A. Mitchell 77, A. Wood 77, M. Leyland 75, C. Turner 65, L. Hutton 59) & 68-1 drew with Jamaica 592 (C. Boy 139, G. A. Headley 118, C. C. Passailaigue 82, L. G. Hylton 80).

1936: F. R. Brown helps Martineau in Egypt

The annual April visit of H. M. Martineau's team to Egypt contained the same programme of fixtures as in the previous year, but the touring sides results were greatly improved, due in the main to some splendid bowling by F. R. Brown, who captured 64 wickets at 14 runs apiece. The touring party was H. M. Martineau (capt), D. R. Wilcox (Essex), C. H. Knott (Kent), F. R. Brown (Surrey), D. A. M. Rome, D. C. H. Townsend (Oxford U), R. E. S. Wyatt (Warwicks), K. A. Sellar (Sussex), A. W. Childs-Clarke (Middx), W. M. Welch, J. C. Atkinson-Clark (Middx) and F. S. Buckley (Berks).

Both the 'Tests' were won by Brown's bowling and in the second, Egypt had reached 119 for 3—needing 151 to win—when the last 7 wickets went down for 20 runs. Wyatt was the outstanding bat of the tour and hit two centuries, but Sellar was unlucky in that he hit a beautiful hundred against the United Services and

then wrenched his knee. The fielding of Wyatt, Knott and Wilcox was superb.

The only defeat of the tour was against the Gezira Sporting Club and in this game the ninth tourists' wicket fell just five minutes from time—unfortunately Wilcox could not bat due to sunstroke.

1936: H. M. Martineau's Team to Egypt

1st Match: v Alexandria XII (Alexandria)   April 1, 2.
Alexandria XII 220 (A. J. Fletcher 113, F. R. Brown 6-31) & 89 (R. E. S. Wyatt 6-36) lost to Martineau's XII 239-8 dec (R. E. S. Wyatt 59, M. L. Eggar 6-80) & 72-1 by 10 wkts.

2nd Match: v Royal Navy (Alexandria)   April 3, 4.
Martineau's XI 276 (R. E. S. Wyatt 120*) beat Royal Navy 82 & 103 (Robson 51) by an inns & 93 runs.

3rd Match: v Gezira Sporting Club (Gezira)   April 6, 7.
Gezira 248 (R. G. Musson 113) & 222-9 dec (R. G. Musson 101) beat Martineau's XI 234 (D. C. H. Townsend 59) & 126 by 110 runs.

4th Match: v United Services (Gezira)   April 8, 9.
United Services 305 (R. G. Musson 50) & 144 (F. R. Brown 5-26) lost to Martineau's XI 371-9 dec (K. A. Sellar 108, D. A. M. Rome 69, F. R. Brown 61) & 79-6 by 4 wkts.

5th Match: v Army Other Ranks (Abbassia) (One Day)   April 11.
Martineau's XI 259-6 dec (W. M. Welch 67) drew with Army Other Ranks 191-7 (Hegele 71*, Moxley 51).

6th Match: v Egyptian C.C. (Gezira) (One Day)   April 13.
Martineau's XI 210-9 dec (K. A. Sellar 53) beat Egyptian C.C. 51 (J. C. Atkinson-Clark 5-24) by 159 runs.

7th Match: v R.A.F. (Gezira)   April 15, 16.
Martineau's XI 159 (R. E. S. Wyatt 51) & 358-8 dec (R. E. S. Wyatt 112, D. C. H. Townsend 79, C. H. Knott 65) beat R.A.F. 105 (F. R. Brown 8-33) & 219 (Cruikshanks 64) by 193 runs.

8th Match: v All Egypt (Gezira)   April 18, 20, 21.
All Egypt 166 (F. R. Brown 7-55) & 369 (Hegele 82*, Joy 84, Cruikshanks 59, F. R. Brown 8-126) lost to Martineau's XI 266 (D. R. Wilcox 135, R. E. S. Wyatt 56) & 271-2 (D. R. Wilcox 127, D. C. H. Townsend 119) by 8 wkts.

9th Match: v All Egypt (Alexandria)   April 23, 24, 25.
Martineau's XI 243 (C. H. Knott 79) & 246 (D. A. M. Rome 72, E. Cawston 6-67) beat All Egypt 339 (Halsey 107, Scott 62, Booker 56, Whitmarsh 51, R. E. S. Wyatt 7-78) & 139 (F. R. Brown 8-81) by 11 runs.

10th Match: v Victoria College XV (Victoria Coll) (One Day)   April 27.
Martineau's XI 251-5 dec (A. W. Childs-Clarke 108, F. R. Brown 68) beat Victoria Coll 103 (D. A. M. Rome 5-8) by 148 runs.

1936-37: Bradman brilliant in 3-2 Ashes victory for Australia

The bodyline controversy had been happily settled by the time the 1936-37 M.C.C. touring party left Southampton aboard the R.M.S. *Orion* on 12 September 1936. The team was G. O. B. Allen (Middx) (capt), R. W. V. Robins (Middx), R. E. S. Wyatt (Warwicks), K. Farnes (Essex), and the professionals W. R. Hammond (Gloucs), H. Verity (Yorks), M. Leyland (Yorks), L. E. G. Ames (Kent), W. Voce (Notts), C. J. Barnett (Gloucs), J. Hardstaff (Notts), T. S. Worthington (Derbys), W. H. Copson (Derbys), J. M. Sims (Middx), A. E. Fagg (Kent), L. B. Fishlock (Surrey), G. Duckworth (Lancs) and Capt R. Howard as the manager.

Only E. R. T. Holmes, who had been in the original party, had had to decline—his place was taken by Wyatt, who had been superseded as England captain by Allen in the 1936 series at home to India. Both Voce and Larwood had stated, after the bodyline controversy, that they did not wish to be picked for England, but in the summer of 1936, Voce had stated he would be available for selection if required. The surprise omission was Paynter, who had done so well in 1932-33.

The tourists played the usual one-day game in Colombo and arrived at Fremantle on 13 October, commencing their first match at Perth three days later. In this game an easy victory was obtained with centuries from Wyatt and Hammond. Unfortunately the injuries which were to dog the tourists also commenced. Duckworth fractured a finger and in practice after the game Robins also broke a finger. Before the second match, Ames had back

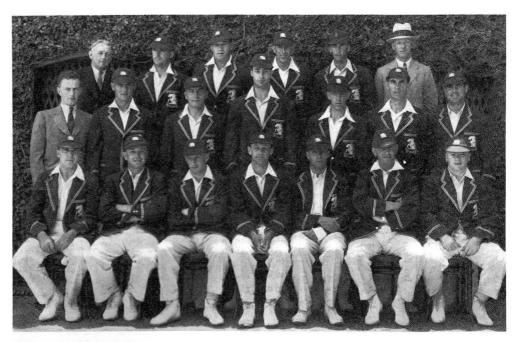

Right *The party for the full tour of Australia of 1936-37, the tour which followed the bodyline series. Back: W. Ferguson (scorer), L. B. Fishlock, T. S. Worthington, A. E. Fagg, J. Hardstaff, R. Howard (manager). Centre: T. H. Wade, H. Verity, C. J. Barnett, K. Farnes, W. H. Copson, J. M. Sims, W. Voce. Front: L. E. G. Ames, W. R. Hammond, R. W. V. Robins, G. O. B. Allen (captain), R. E. S. Wyatt, M. Leyland, G. Duckworth.*

Below *The captain, G. O. B. Allen, and R. E. S. Wyatt on the initial part of the journey to Australia in 1936, leaving Waterloo station.*

trouble, so that the team, after one first-class game, were without both wicket-keepers. The match was a high-scoring draw.

In the third Australian game—an up-country affair—Wyatt broke his wrist, and the M.C.C. therefore had to call on a substitute to complete the eleven for the match against South Australia. Two brilliant innings by Hammond saved the batting and Allen's bowling then won the game.

The team met its first defeat at the hands of New South Wales, when O'Reilly and Mudge took advantage of a wearing wicket and the middle batting as well as the tail just folded up.

A gallant hundred by Leyland aided by some poor catching saved the M.C.C. from defeat at the hands of An Australian Eleven and after a drawn game against Queensland, the first Test was staged at Brisbane. England went into the match very much as under-dogs. The batting up to now had been most unreliable, the fielding indifferent and the injury list appalling. On the day however, the home side were outplayed from start to finish—Voce, who had done nothing as yet on the tour, bowled splendidly and took 10 wickets for 57, Leyland saved the English batting in the

first innings, whilst in the second Allen made the highest score with 68. It is true that Australia were forced to bat in the final innings on a sticky wicket, but this did not affect the result, which went in England's favour to the tune of 322 runs. It was Bradman's first Test as Australia's captain.

An up-country game alone separated the first Test from the second. In this England were fortunate to win the toss. Batting first, the tourists reached 100 for 1 by lunch and 279 for 3 by the close of the first day—the total rose to 426 for 6 by the end of a rain interrupted second day, at which point Allen declared and put Australia in on another sticky wicket. They were all out for 80, Voce having 4 wickets for 10 runs. The pitch improved and Australia, following on, also improved, but still lost the match by an innings.

England had all the luck, but for a team that was written off in many quarters to win the first two Tests by vast margins required

1936-37: M.C.C. to Ceylon, Australia and New Zealand

Batting Averages

	M	I	NO	R	HS	Avge	100	c/s
W. R. Hammond (Glos)	14	23	2	1242	231*	59.14	5	11
C. J. Barnett (Glos)	15	25	0	1375	259	55.00	5	6
R. E. S. Wyatt (Warks)	12	18	1	785	144	46.17	3	4
M. Leyland (Yorks)	15	27	5	972	126	44.18	3	3
L. E. G. Ames (Kent)	14	23	0	811	109	35.26	1	25/4
J. Hardstaff jun (Notts)	18	31	3	929	110	33.17	1	7
G. O. B. Allen (Middx)	14	20	3	472	88	27.67	0	13
A. E. Fagg (Kent)	10	17	1	399	112	24.93	1	6
T. S. Worthington (Derby)	14	25	1	571	89	23.79	0	10
L. B. Fishlock (Surrey)	13	22	3	363	91	19.10	0	7
R. W. V. Robins (Middx)	12	16	0	297	61	18.56	0	4
W. H. Copson (Derby)	8	10	5	52	12	10.40	0	4
J. M. Sims (Middx)	13	16	1	147	43	9.80	0	12
W. Voce (Notts)	14	21	10	101	24*	9.18	0	8
H. Verity (Yorks)	13	22	2	180	31	9.00	0	10
G. Duckworth (Lancs)	7	8	2	46	15*	7.66	0	11/4
K. Farnes (Essex)	12	15	6	21	8*	2.33	0	7

Also played in two matches: T. H. Wade (Essex) 10,0, 0 (st 1).

Bowling Averages

	Balls	M	R	W	Avge	BB	5i
W. H. Copson	1253	23	535	27	19.81	4-32	0
K. Farnes	2033	30	928	44	21.09	6-96	1
W. R. Hammond	1507	27	577	27	21.37	5-39	2
J. M. Sims	2298	32	1125	47	23.93	5-37	2
G. O. B. Allen	2153	26	1085	43	25.23	6-53	2
W. Voce	2619	37	1164	43	27.06	6-41	1
H. Verity	3343	118	1043	38	27.44	5-42	2
R. W. V. Robins	1235	8	638	16	39.87	4-63	0
M. Leyland	211	1	130	2	65.00	1-1	0
T. S. Worthington	648	8	346	4	86.50	1-8	0

Also bowled: L. E. G. Ames 28-1-16-1; C. J. Barnett 80-1-24-2; L. B. Fishlock 6-0-8-0; J. Hardstaff jun 34-2-27-0; R. E. S. Wyatt 72-0-71-1.
Capt R. Howard (Lancs) played in 2 non-first-class matches.

1936-37: M.C.C. to Ceylon, Australia and New Zealand

1st Match: v All Ceylon (Colombo) (One Day) Oct 3.
Ceylon 149-4 dec lost to M.C.C. 232-5 (G. O. B. Allen 82*, J. Hardstaff jun 65*) by 5 wkts.

2nd Match: v Western Australia (Perth) Oct 16, 17, 18.
W. Australia 142 & 147 (J. M. Sims 5-37) lost to M.C.C. 469-4 dec (W. R. Hammond 141, R. E. S. Wyatt 106, J. Hardstaff jun 87*, C. J. Barnett 54) by an inns & 180 runs.

3rd Match: v Combined Western Australia XI (Perth) Oct 22, 23, 24.
M.C.C. 497 (W. R. Hammond 107, L. B. Fishlock 91, T. S. Worthington 89, G. O. B. Allen 65) & 120-4 drew with Combined XI 436 (C. L. Badcock 167, W. Horrocks 140).

4th Match: v Clare County XI (Clare) (One Day) Oct 28.
Clare County 62-4 dec lost to M.C.C. 141-6 by 9 wkts.

5th Match: v South Australia (Adelaide) Oct 30, 31, Nov 2, 3.
M.C.C. 233 (W. R. Hammond 104, F. A. Ward 5-79) & 236 (W. R. Hammond 136, F. A. Ward 5-98) beat S. Australia 162 (G. O. B. Allen 6-53) & 202 (V. Y. Richardson 55) by 105 runs.

6th Match: v Victoria (Melbourne) Nov 6, 7, 9, 10.
M.C.C. 344 (C. J. Barnett 131, J. Hardstaff jun 85, J. Frederick 6-65) & 36-3 drew with Victoria 384 (I. S. Lee 160, R. G. Gregory 128).

7th Match: v New South Wales (Sydney) Nov 13, 14, 16, 17.
N.S.W. 273 (R. H. Robinson 91, S. J. McCabe 83, W. R. Hammond 5-39) & 326 (A. G. Chipperfield 97*) beat M.C.C. 153 (C. J. Barnett 70, H. Mudge 6-42) & 311 (W. R. Hammond 91, M. Leyland 79, W. J. O'Reilly 5-67) by 135 runs.

8th Match: v An Australian XI (Sydney) Nov 20, 21, 23, 24.
M.C.C. 288 (M. Leyland 80, L. E. G. Ames 76, R. W. V. Robins 53, A. G. Chipperfield 8-66) & 245-8 (M. Leyland 118*) drew with An Australian XI 544-8 dec (C. L. Badcock 182, W. A. Brown 71, D. G. Bradman 63, J. H. W. Fingleton 56).

9th Match: v Queensland (Brisbane) Nov 27, 28, 30, Dec 1.
M.C.C. 215 (M. Leyland 98) & 528-8 dec (C. J. Barnett 259, A. E. Fagg 112, L. E. G. Ames 60) drew with Queensland 243 (W. A. Brown 74, R. E. Rogers 62) & 227-9 (G. G. Baker 63).

10th Match: v Australia (Brisbane) Dec 4, 5, 7, 8, 9.
England 358 (M. Leyland 126, C. J. Barnett 69, W. J. O'Reilly 5-102) & 256 (G. O. B. Allen 68, F. A. Ward 6-102) beat Australia 234 (J. H. W. Fingleton 100, S. J. McCabe 51, W. Voce 6-41) & 58 (G. O. B. Allen 5-46) by 322 runs.

11th Match: v Queensland Country XI (Ipswich) Dec 12, 14.
Country XI 300 (T. Allen 118, J. G. Maddern 62) & 124 drew with M.C.C. 406 (W. R. Hammond 109, T. S. Worthington 72).

12th Match: v Australia (Sydney) Dec 18, 19, 21, 22.
England 426-6 dec (W. R. Hammond 231*, C. J. Barnett 57) beat Australia 80 & 324 (S. J. McCabe 93, D. G. Bradman 82, J. H. W. Findleton 73) by an inns & 22 runs.

13th Match: v New South Wales Country XI (Newcastle) Dec 26, 28.
Country XI 188-4 dec (R. G. Beattie 124*) drew with M.C.C. 178-4 (A. E. Fagg 67).

14th Match: v Australia (Melbourne) Jan 1, 2, 4, 5, 6, 7.
Australia 200-9 dec (S. J. McCabe 63) & 564 (D. G. Bradman 270, J. H. W. Fingleton 136) beat England 76-9 dec (M. W. Sievers 5-21) & 323 (M. Leyland 111*, R. W. V. Robins 61, W. R. Hammond 51, L. O'B. Fleetwood-Smith 5-124) by 365 runs.

15th Match: v Tasmania (Launceston) Jan 9, 11.
Tasmania 104 & 209 (S. W. L. Putman 77, J. M. Sims 5-39) lost to M.C.C. 317 (L. E. G. Ames 109, A. E. Fagg 60, J. Hardstaff jun 55, T. S. Worthington 50, S. W. L. Putman 5-87) by an inns & 4 runs.

16th Match: v Tasmania (Launceston) (One Day) Jan 12.
M.C.C. 250 (D. Thollar 5-67) drew with Tasmania 145-5.

17th Match: v Tasmania Combined XI (Hobart) Jan 15, 16, 18.
M.C.C. 418 (C. J. Barnett 129, J. Hardstaff jun 110, G. O. B. Allen 55) & 111-1 (R. E. S. Wyatt 68*) drew with Combined XI 134 (W. A. S. Oldfield 60*).

18th Match: v South Australia (Adelaide) Jan 22, 23, 25, 26.
M.C.C. 301 (C. J. Barnett 78, G. O. B. Allen 60, R. E. S. Wyatt 53) drew with S. Australia 194-4 (A. J. Ryan 71): rain.

19th Match: v Australia (Adelaide) Jan 29, 30, Feb 1, 2, 3, 4.
Australia 288 (S. J. McCabe 88) & 433 (D. G. Bradman 212, S. J. McCabe 55, R. G. Gregory 50, W. R. Hammond 5-57) beat England 330 (C. J. Barnett 129, L. E. G. Ames 52) & 243 (R. E. S.Wyatt 50, L. O'B. Fleetwood-Smith 6-110) by 148 runs.

20th Match: v Victorian Country XI (Geelong) Feb 6, 8.
M.C.C. 282 (J. Hardstaff jun 94, L. E. G. Ames 51, J. Collins 5-48) & 251 (M. Leyland 53) drew with Country XI 161 (R. W. V. Robins 5-36).

21st Match: v Southern New South Wales (Canberra) Feb 10, 11.
M.C.C. 380 (L. E. G. Ames 82, J. Hardstaff jun 67, M. Leyland 67, R. E. S. Wyatt 51, C. V. Jackson 5-143) beat Southern N.S.W. 162 & 78 (W. H. Copson 7-16) by an inns & 140 runs.

22nd Match: v New South Wales (Sydney) Feb 13, 15, 16, 17.
N.S.W. 231 & 246 (S. J. McCabe 93, J. H. W. Fingleton 60) beat M.C.C. 73 (J. G. Lush 6-43) & 299 (C. J. Barnett 117, J. Hardstaff jun 64, L. E. G. Ames 60, J. G. Lush 7-72) by 105 runs.

23rd Match: v Victoria (Melbourne) Feb 19, 20, 22, 23.
M.C.C. 187 (L. E. G. Ames 64) & 132-3 (J. Hardstaff jun 60*, W. R. Hammond 56) drew with Victoria 292 (R. G. Gregory 86, A. L. Hassett 54).

24th Match: v Australia (Melbourne) Feb 26, 27, March 1, 2, 3.
Australia 604 (D. G. Bradman 169, C. L. Badcock 118, S. J. McCabe 112, K. Farnes 6-96) beat England 239 (J. Hardstaff jun 83, W. J. O'Reilly 5-51) & 165 (W. R. Hammond 56) by an inns & 200 runs.

25th Match: v Victorian Country XII (Benalla) March 5, 6.
M.C.C. XII 344 (L. B. Fishlock 104, W. R. Hammond 53, W. Voce 53*) & 118-6 drew with Country XII 147-8 dec (A. Davidson 52).

26th Match: v Combined Universities (Sydney) March 8, 9.
M.C.C. 212-9 dec (W. R. Hammond 103) drew with Universities XII 169-7 (A. Chapman 57).

27th Match: v Canterbury & Otago (Christchurch) March 19, 20, 22.
M.C.C. 217 (R. E. S. Wyatt 63) & 250-8 (R. E. S. Wyatt 100, T. S. Worthington 79) drew with Canterbury & Otago 157.

28th Match: v A New Zealand XI (Wellington) March 24, 25, 27.
M.C.C. 427 (R. E. S. Wyatt 144, L. E. G. Ames 97, G. O. B. Allen 88) drew with New Zealand XI 265 (H. G. Vivian 88, M. L. Page 50) & 163 (W. A. Hadlee 82).

29th Match: v Auckland & Wellington (Auckland) April 1, 2, 3.
Auckland & Wellington 183 (P. E. Whitelaw 99*) & 123 (H. Verity 5-42) lost to M.C.C. 205 (R. E. S. Wyatt 56, J. Hardstaff jun 51) & 192-3 by 7 wkts.

---

a trifle more than luck, and the team played very well.

Again only an up-country game came before the third Test, which Australia had to win to save the rubber. Interest in the game was tremendous – 350,534 attended, a new record. Bradman won the toss, but Australia collapsed to 200 for 9. Due to rain however the wicket was getting progressively worse and Bradman declared. England wickets fell with alarming rapidity, so that Allen also declared at 76 for 9 – he was roundly criticised for this on the grounds that he ought to have closed the innings earlier. Australia, through a double hundred by Bradman and a century by Fingleton, went on to a total of 564 and England lost.

The trip to Tasmania and a rain-ruined fixture against South Australia preceded the fourth Test. Bradman hit a second double hundred and the England batting was very patchy on a plumb wicket. Australia levelled the series.

The deciding Test was held at Melbourne. Australia built up the huge total of 604 in the first innings, assisted by dropped catches and some indifferent ground fielding. The England batting however failed, apart from Hardstaff, who played his best innings of the tour, and following on the visitors faced a spinners' wicket. Australia won the 'Ashes' with little difficulty.

The tourists went on to New Zealand, playing three matches there, but no Test. From New Zealand the side sailed to Honolulu and Los Angeles, spending a few days in Hollywood, then across America to New York and home on the *Queen Mary*.

Financially the tour had been a great success, the total gross English share being £40,000. The professionals received a minimum £400 for the tour.

England's failure can be attributed to a combination of poor batting and brilliance on the part of Bradman. Of the England batsmen, only Hammond, Leyland and Barnett maintained their reputations. Fagg unfortunately contracted rheumatic fever and returned home early. Voce was the bowler of the tour, but was better in the first three Tests than the last two, which told against England, since Allen, with a strained leg muscle, was not really fit for the final Test.

1936-37: Cahn's team to Ceylon and Malaya

In the spring of 1937, Sir Julien Cahn took his team on a nine-match tour of Ceylon and Malaya. The side, which arrived in Colombo on 4 March, consisted of Sir Julien Cahn (capt), C. S. Dempster (Leics), R. J. Crisp (South Africa), I. A. R. Peebles (Middx), D. P. B. Morkel (South Africa), C. R. N. Maxwell (Notts), R. E. C. Butterworth (Middx), B. H. Lyon (Gloucs), S. D. Rhodes (Notts), T. B. Reddick (Middx), J. B. Hall (Notts), C. C. Goodway (Staffs), G. F. Summers and two New South Wales bowlers, who joined the team in Ceylon, H. Mudge and J. E. Walsh. E. G. Wolfe, Sir Julien's brother-in-law, acted as manager.

Of the five games played in Ceylon, the most important was

Sir Julien Cahn's party to Ceylon and Malaya in 1936-37.
Back: J. E. Walsh, H. Mudge, S. D. Rhodes, G. F. Summers,
T. B. Reddick, E. G. Wolfe, J. B. Hall, R. E. C. Butterworth.
Front: I. A. R. Peebles, B. H. Lyon, C. R. Maxwell, Sir Julien
Cahn, D. P. B. Morkel, C. S. Dempster.

that against All Ceylon, which was won by 6 wickets. Mudge and
Dempster hit hundreds; Crisp made 43 in 14 minutes. Peebles,
who suffered from shoulder trouble, had to drop out after the first
two matches.

In Malaya, a three-day game was played against All Malaya,
but was drawn due to rain. There were three country matches, in
which the local sides proved very inferior to the tourists, who were
well on top in every game, winning one by an innings. Cahn's
team however was an exceptionally strong one, well above average
first-class county standard.

1936-37: Sir Julien Cahn's Team to Ceylon and Malaya

1st Match: v Ceylon Cricket Association (Colombo)
Ceylon C.A. 345 (J. Pulle 88, H. Roberts 85, M. Spittel 58, J. E. Walsh 5-89) drew with
Cahn's XI 190 (C. S. Dempster 58) & 190-6 (C. R. N. Maxwell 56).

2nd Match: v D. A. Wright's XI (Colombo).
Cahn's XI 288 (R. C. Butterworth 78, C. R. N. Maxwell 64, C. Allen 5-89) & 206-9 dec
(B. H. Lyon 52) drew with D. A. Wright's XI 189 & 244-5 (T. Kelaart 90*).

3rd March: v Ceylonese XI (Colombo).
Cahn's XI 388 (C. S. Dempster 97, T. B. Reddick 92, C. R. N. Maxwell 81, H. Mudge 57)
drew with Ceylonese XI 362 (F. C. de Saram 102, A. Gooneratne 64*).

4th Match: v Combined Colleges (Colombo).
Combined Colleges 158 (R. J. Crisp 7-28) lost to Cahn's XI 203 (T. B. Reddick 57,
P. Pereira 6-33).

5th Match: v All Ceylon (Colombo) March 18, 19, 20.
All Ceylon 207 (H. Roberts 70, G. S. Hubert 66) & 334 (F. C. Saram 66, M. Spittel 59,
J. E. Walsh 5-96) lost to Cahn's XI 478 (H. Mudge 118, C. S. Dempster 112, R. C.
Butterworth 76, C. R. N. Maxwell 58, G. Pereira 7-158) & 66-4 by 6 wkts.

6th Match: v All Malaya (Singapore) March 27, 28, 29.
All Malaya 161 (J. E. Walsh 5-42) & 206-7 dec (H. O. Hopkins 78) drew with Cahn's XI
193 & 122-5 (C. S. Dempster 50*).

7th Match: v Selangor (Kuala Lumpur).
Selangor 81 & 56 (J. E. Walsh 5-21) lost to Cahn's XI 372 (H. Mudge 110, C. R. N.
Maxwell 86, B. Mayo 5-88) by an inns & 235 runs.

8th Match: v Perak (Ipoh).
Perak 63 & 81-6 drew with Cahn's XI 293 (R. C. Butterworth 70, C. S. Dempster 68).

9th Match: v Penang (Penang).
Penang 134 (J. E. Walsh 5-41) & 137-6 (H. O. Hopkins 50*) drew with Cahn's XI 281
(R. C. Butterworth 69, C. R. N. Maxwell 50).

1937: Martineau continues Egyptian tours

The team which H. M. Martineau took to Egypt in the spring of
1937 was not as strong as the previous year. The side was H. M.
Martineau (capt), D. R. Wilcox (Essex), N. Vere-Hodge (Essex),

1937: H. M. Martineau's Team to Egypt

1st Match: v Alexandria (Alexandria) March 30, 31.
Martineau's XII 408-9 dec (A. G. Powell 115, N. Vere-Hodge 74, D. Roberts 59) beat
Alexandria XII 83 & 318 (R. H. Werner 109) by an inns & 7 runs.

2nd Match: v R.A.F. Depot (Abukir) April 2, 3.
R.A.F. Depot 131 (Taylor 62*, J. H. Nevinson 5-45) & 223-9 (Taylor 57, A. W. Childs-
Clarke 7-112) drew with Martineau's XI 388-6 dec (D. R. Wilcox 179. J. Gillespie 94*).

3rd Match: v Gezira Sporting Club (Gezira) April 5, 6.
Gezira 146 & 264-7 (G. A. Thomas 127*, I. J. Kilgour 56, S. Enderby 54) drew with
Martineau's XI 171-9 dec (R. M. Munro 5-39) & 119-7 (D. R. Wilcox 60*).

4th Match: v R.A.F. (Heliopolis) April 7.
R.A.F. 249-9 dec (A. C. Howie 64, A. W. Childs-Clarke 5-52) drew with Martineau's XI
192-4 (J. Gillespie 71*).

5th Match: v United Services (Gezira) April 9, 10, 13.
Martineau's XI 345 (N. Vere-Hodge 127) & 132-4 dec (D. R. Wilcox 91*) drew with
United Services 196 (I. J. Kilgour 54, Cruikshanks 52, N. Turner 5-74) & 158-7 (Lawson
62, A. C. Howie 58*).

6th Match: v Maadi Sporting Club (Maadi) (One Day) April 12.
Martineau's XI 271-6 dec (D. R. Wilcox 102) beat Maadi 63 by 208 runs.

7th Match: v Army Other Ranks (Abbassie) (One Day) April 14.
Martineau's XI 192 (J. A. Deed 56, J. Gillespie 53) beat Other Ranks 174 (Brown 57,
W. Isaacs 5-69) by 18 runs.

8th Match: v Egyptian C.C. (Cairo) (One Day) April 15.
Martineau's XI 91 (Abdou 5-25) beat Egyptian C.C. 72 (J. H. Nevinson 5-24) by 19 runs.

9th Match: v All Egypt (Gezira) April 17, 19, 20.
All Egypt 277 (I. J. Kilgour 86, G. A. Thomas 55) & 170 (J. H. Nevinson 5-44) beat
Martineau's XI 237 (D. R. Wilcox 70, N. Vere-Hodge 66, T. E. Clarke 5-16) & 136 (J.
Gillespie 72, Abdou 9-60) by 74 runs.

10th Match: v All Egypt (Alexandria) April 22, 23
All Egypt 224 (R. H. Werner 85, Cruikshanks 62, J. H. Nevinson 5-69, N. Turner 5-76) &
122 (A. W. Childs-Clarke 5-48, J. H. Nevinson 5-58) lost to Martineau's XI 374 (D. R.
Wilcox 126, A. G. Powell 76, A. W. Childs-Clarke 59) by an inns & 28 runs.

11th Match: v Victoria College (Victoria Coll) April 26.
Martineau's XI 271-9 dec (J. Gillespie 96, N. Vere-Hodge 57, L. Bolton 6-66) beat
Victoria College 147 by 124 runs.

J. V. Gillespie, W. J. H. Isaacs, J. A. Deed (Kent), N. F. Turner, D. Roberts, A. G. Powell (Essex), A. W. Childs-Clarke (Middx), D. A. M. Rome and J. H. Nevinson (Middx).

Despite the rather weak nature of the team, the 'Tests' with Egypt were drawn one each. In the first of these, the first native Egyptian to appear on the home side, Abdou, bowled splendidly and took 9 wickets for 60 in the first innings. In the second match good bowling by Nevinson won the game for the tourists. The native Egyptian team in their single innings game against the Englishmen lost a close contest by just 19 runs, Abdou again bowling well.

As expected, the results of the tour did not compare favourably with 1936.

1937: an exhausting M.C.C. tour of Canada

A tour of Canadian cricketers had taken place in England in the summer of 1936 and as it proved a successful venture, the Canadian cricket authorities invited M.C.C. to send an English team to Canada in 1937. The all-amateur side was composed of G. C. Newman (Middx) (capt), H. J. Enthoven (Middx), A. G. Powell

---

1937: M.C.C. to Canada

1st Match: v All Toronto (Toronto) Aug 2.
M.C.C. 251-4 dec (H. J. Enthoven 101*, K. A. Sellar 56) drew with All Toronto 189-7 (L. A. Percival 78).

2nd Match: v Toronto C.C. (Toronto) Aug 3.
Toronto C.C. 209 (P. F. Seagram 66, D. W. Forbes 6-54) drew with M.C.C. 119-9 (N. G. Wykes 56, E. Carlton 5-42).

3rd Match: v United Colleges (Ridley) Aug 4.
M.C.C. 238-6 dec (N. G. Wykes 89) drew with United Colleges 133-8 (L. C. Bell 56, J. T. Neve 5-37).

4th Match: v Waterloo C.C. (Waterloo) Aug 5.
Waterloo 145 lost to M.C.C. 192-7 (N. G. Wykes 72) by 4 wkts.

5th Match: v R. C. Matthews' XI (Toronto) Aug 6, 7
R. C. Matthews' XI 288 (L. C. Bell 93) & 7-0 beat M.C.C. 157 (E. Jemmott 6-39) & 137 (K. A. Sellar 111) by 10 wkts.

6th Match: v Royal Society of St George (Winnipeg) Aug 10
St George 81 (D. Forbes 6-31) & 17-7 (G. C. Newman 5-7) lost to M.C.C. 124 (C. Bligh 5-53) by 3 wkts.

7th Match: v Royal Society of St George (Winnipeg) Aug 11.
St George 46 & 39-3 lost to M.C.C. 139-9 dec (C. Bligh 5-71) by 9 wkts.

8th Match: v Regina (Regina) Aug 12.
M.C.C. 202 (R. H. Foster 5-88) & 116-3 beat Regina 50 (J. M. Brocklebank 5-22) by 152 runs.

9th Match: v Alberta (Calgary) Aug 13.
Alberta 129 (J. M. Brocklebank 6-30) lost to M.C.C. 185-6 (N. G. Wykes 58) by 7 wkts.

10th Match: v Alberta (Calgary) Aug 14.
Alberta 98 (J. M. Brocklebank 5-54) lost to M.C.C. 159 (G. Pain 5-32) by 4 wkts.

11th Match: v Mainland League (Brockton Point) Aug 17.
Mainland League 184 lost to M.C.C. 231-6 (K. A. Sellar 92*) by 5 wkts.

12th Match: v Victoria (Victoria) Aug 18.
Victoria 87 (J. M. Brocklebank 5-21, A. P. Singleton 5-12) & 94-5 dec lost to M.C.C. 97 (J. Payne 5-23) & 94-3 by 1 wkt.

13th Match: v Cowichan (Duncan) Aug 19.
Cowichan 61 (J. T. Neve 5-19) & 50-7 lost to M.C.C. 135 by 5 wkts.

14th Match: v Vancouver Colts XV (Brockton Point) Aug 20.
Colts XV 162 (A. P. Singleton 6-58) lost to M.C.C. 195-7 (K. A. Sellar 70, N. G. Wykes 52) by 8 wkts.

15th Match: v British Colombia (Brockton Point) Aug 21.
M.C.C. 119-1 (C. H. Taylor 62*): rain.

16th Match: v Eastern Canada XI (Westmount) Aug 28, 29.
M.C.C. 221 (A. G. Powell 68, E. F. Loney 5-63) & 274-6 dec (N. G. Wykes 83, A. G. Powell 59) drew with E. Canada 216 (K. Ross 85) & 154-5.

17th Match: v Ottawa Valley (Ottawa) Aug 31.
Ottawa Valley 199-6 dec (J. Seager 70, G. Dicker 60) drew with M.C.C. 141-3 (J. F. Mendl 50*).

18th Match: v Montreal XV (Montreal) Sept 1.
Montreal XV 121 (J. M. Brocklebank 10-27) lost to M.C.C. 161-1 (N. G. Wykes 74*) by 9 wkts.

19th Match: v All Montreal (Montreal) Sept 2.
M.C.C. 255-7 dec (C. H. Taylor 118) beat All Montreal 214 (M. Davies 118*) by 41 runs.

(Essex), N. G. Wykes (Essex), K. A. Sellar (Sussex), A. P. Singleton (Worcs), J. M. Brocklebank (Cambridge U), N. M. Ford (Middx), D. F. Mendl, J. C. Masterman, C. H. Taylor (Leics), D. W. Forbes and J. T. Neve.

The team found the great heat and the vast distances to be travelled more formidable than the opposition and were described after the only defeat—against Hon R. C. Matthews' team—as in an advanced state of exhaustion and decrepitude. Nearly everywhere matches were played on matting wickets, which took the shine off the ball after about three overs and thus put the burden of the attack on the spinners, Brocklebank and Singleton. The former headed the averages with 52 wickets at 10 runs each. Wykes and Sellar were the leading batsmen.

1937-38: Lord Tennyson wins rubber in India

Lord Tennyson was unable to obtain the best possible team for his tour of India. The side that left Victoria Station for the journey overland to Marseilles and thence on board the *Viceroy of India* to Bombay was Lord Tennyson (Hants) (capt), T. O. Jameson (Hants), I. A. R. Peebles (Middx), N. W. D. Yardley (Yorks), P. A. Gibb (Yorks), T. S. Worthington (Derbys), A. W. Wellard (Somerset), A. R. Gover (Surrey), J. H. Parks (Sussex), Jas Langridge (Sussex), J. Hardstaff (Notts), G. H. Pope (Derbys), W. J. Edrich (Middx), T. P. B. Smith (Essex) and N. McCorkell (Hants). A. P. F. Chapman, W. R. Hammond and T. W. J. Goddard declined invitations, whilst Yorkshire refused to allow Leyland to go.

The team arrived in Bombay on 25 October and went to Baroda for a two-day game before travelling by ship to Karachi for the first first-class match. This was a high scoring draw against Sind. There were two minor games before the 'First Test', which the tourists won, with Yardley making the highest score of the match, 96. A severe earthquake held up play on the second day. Switching from turf to matting the team then suffered its first defeat by 2 wickets against Rajputana. However the 'Second Test' brought another victory, with Gover taking ten wickets and Edrich

---

1937-38: Lord Tennyson's Team to India

Batting Averages

	M	I	NO	R	HS	Avge	100	c/s
W. J. Edrich (Middx)	14	24	5	876	140*	46.10	2	11
J. Hardstaff jun (Notts)	12	21	3	706	213	39.22	1	0
Jas Langridge (Sussex)	13	20	1	650	144	34.21	1	11
T. S. Worthington (Derby)	11	18	2	530	82	33.12	0	7
A. W. Wellard (Som)	10	16	1	433	90	28.86	0	16
N. W. D. Yardley (Yorks)	12	20	0	519	96	25.95	0	4
G. H. Pope (Derby)	13	20	2	441	89	24.50	0	15
J. H. Parks (Sussex)	12	20	0	480	89	24.00	0	9
P. A. Gibb (Yorks)	12	18	3	349	136*	23.26	1	21/1
I. A. R. Peebles (Middx)	8	9	4	93	37*	18.60	0	6
N. T. McCorkell (Hants)	10	16	3	241	58	18.53	0	16/5
Lord Tennyson (Hants)	12	18	2	263	118	16.43	1	6
Capt T. O. Jameson (Hants)	6	7	0	83	47	11.85	0	1
T. P. B. Smith (Essex)	10	15	5	83	25*	8.30	0	4
A. R. Gover (Surrey)	9	13	3	72	18*	7.20	0	2

Also played in one match: A. L. Hosie (Hants) 11.

Bowling Averages

	O	M	R	W	Avge	BB	5i
G. H. Pope	341.4	71	924	58	15.93	5-27	6
J. H. Parks	60.4	22	123	7	17.57	2-12	0
Jas Langridge	120.3	17	354	20	17.70	6-41	1
A. R. Gover	257.5	38	876	47	18.63	5-40	3
A. W. Wellard	321.2	40	1022	47	21.74	6-46	2
T. S. Worthington	140.1	20	426	18	23.67	4-46	0
W. J. Edrich	97.5	9	318	13	24.46	4-25	0
T. P. B. Smith	199	24	675	23	29.34	4-61	0
Capt T. O. Jameson	38	3	109	3	36.33	1-5	0
I. A. R. Peebles	104.5	7	404	6	67.33	2-72	0

Also bowled: J. Hardstaff jun 4-0-18-1; N. W. D. Yardley 10-1-40-1; Lord Tennyson 2-1-4-0.

---

batting well on a worn wicket to make the necessary runs in the final innings.

With Mushtaq Ali and Amarnath hitting hundreds in the 'Third Test', India won by 93 runs and the home country did even better in the 'Fourth', winning by an innings, the swing

bowling of Amar Singh proving too good for the visitors after Mankad had hit an impressive hundred. The 'Fifth Test' followed directly after the 'Fourth' and on its result depended the rubber. Amar Singh again proved too much for the English batsmen who were dismissed for 130. Pope and Wellard struck back and removed India for 131. In the second innings the tourists did much better and since Wellard and Pope again destroyed India, Lord Tennyson's side won the rubber.

The players nearly all suffered ailments or injury at some time on the tour and rarely could Lord Tennyson put his best eleven into the field—even he went down with dysentry at Porbandar. Langridge strained his right thigh and Gover his right knee.

Wellard was probably the best bowler but he suffered a vast number of dropped catches. Pope also bowled well and hit many useful runs. The outfielding of Yardley, Edrich and Hardstaff was much applauded throughout the tour. The visit was socially a great success, but the cricketers discovered that the travelling was very arduous.

The great discovery in the opposition camp was Vinoo Mankad, whose all-round cricket impressed everybody.

1937-38: Sir T. E. W. Brinckman's tour to South America

The following team left Southampton aboard the s.s. *Arlanza* on 27 November 1937 bound for South America: Sir T. E. W. Brinckman (capt), R. E. S. Wyatt (Warwicks), A. Sandham (Surrey), L. C. Eastman (Essex), F. E. Covington (Middx), M. W. Tate (Sussex), W. F. F. Price (Middx), F. J. Durston (Middx), A. Wood (Yorks), W. R. Skinner (M.C.C.), F. R. Santall (Warwicks), E. A. Watts (Surrey), H. W. Dods (Lincs) and W. R. Albertini (Berks), with E. W. S. Thompson as manager and F. Chester as umpire. In addition J. M. Sims, who was coaching in the Argentine, would join the party on arrival.

During a stop in Lisbon on the way out, Tate got a poisoned foot and as a result did not play in a single match. The boat was 30 hours late arriving in Montevideo, so the proposed match there was postponed and the tourists pressed onward to Buenos Aires. There were two two-day fixtures, both drawn in favour of the home teams before the 'First Test' at Belgrano. Wyatt hit a brilliant 162 out of a total of 298 and the tourists won by just 2 wickets. In the 'Second Test' however the English side were caught on a crumbling wicket and D. Ayling, bowling his off-spinners round the wicket, was quite unplayable. In the deciding 'Test', the tourists' batting proved more solid. Dods hit a hundred and a total of 417 was realised. Argentina then collapsed to Watts, but following on the home side made 384 and the tourists required 132 in 70 minutes to win – the score was 91 for 6 at stumps.

The team sailed for home on the *Highland Brigade* and reached England on 10 February. The tour was most successful, but the matches were not well attended, there being little interest in cricket outside the British community.

1938: Martineau's annual trip to Egypt

The team which H. M. Martineau took to Egypt in 1938 was back to the standard of 1936, if not higher. Ten matches were won and the only loss was against the Gezira Sporting Club, when Sumner played two good innings and Cripps bowled well. The tourists were however handicapped in their second innings since Powell was absent ill. In the 'First Test' a violent sandstorm prevented any play on the first day. Wilcox hit his hundred in 90 minutes

and on the last day Egypt were set to make 358 in under three hours. Hamilton and Sumner actually put on 138 for the first wicket in 52 minutes, and 268 were scored in 160 minutes, but Egypt lost with 15 minutes remaining.

Clever spin bowling by Benka dismissed Egypt for 208 in the first innings of the 'Second Test', and the tourists replied with 532, Ball making 196. Hamilton hit the only century of the tour against the tourists in Egypt's second innings, but it was a vain attempt and the home team only just avoided an innings defeat.

The side that toured was: H. M. Martineau (capt), A. P. F. Chapman (Kent), B. H. Valentine (Kent), D. R. Wilcox (Essex), A. G. Powell (Essex), A. W. Childs-Clarke (Middx), H. F. Benka (Middx), D. C. Rought-Rought (Cambridge U), F. St G. Unwin (Essex), R. E. Evans (Kent 2nd), D. C. S. Ball, A. E. C. Smith (Middx). R. E. S. Wyatt was forced to decline his invitation at the last moment due to a family bereavement.

1938-39: Combined Oxford and Cambridge tour of Jamaica

To celebrate the 75th anniversary of Kingston Cricket Club, the Club invited a team of University players to tour Jamaica in July and August 1938. The object of the tour was to play both cricket and football and to this end no less than 21 players went out. The members who played in the seven cricket matches were: E. J. H. Dixon (capt), R. C. M. Kimpton, W. Murray-Wood, M. M. Walford, G. R. J. de Soysa, R. E. Whetherly, B. H. Belle, M. D. P. Magill (all Oxford) and J. H. Cameron, A. H. Brodhurst, A. H. Fabian, R. G. Sturdy, N. W. Beeson, M. A. C. P. Kaye, D. C. Wilson (all Cambridge). The others, who confined their efforts to the football field, were J. W. Naylor, J. Allen, I. D. McIntosh, R. M. Hollis, E. Hirst, J. H. Binch and J. C. N. Burrowe. (J. H. Cameron did not travel with the tourists, but played in the two matches against All Jamaica.)

The feature of the tourists' cricket was their fielding, which, even on the rough outfields, was excellent. In the first important match against Jamaica, the island required 25 to win with two wickets in hand when the game ended and the Universities had misfortune to bat on wet wickets in both this game and the return, which was won by Jamaica. The wet weather also affected the attendances at these matches and the Kingston Club suffered a financial loss on the venture. The outstanding batsman of the tour was Kimpton, who hit the best hundred of his career against Jamaica. Murray-Wood did well in the club games, but failed in the two important ones. Walford batted consistently and discovered he could bowl. Wilson was the most effective bowler after the captain had worked out the best field placings for him.

1938: H. M. Martineau's Team to Egypt

1st Match: v Alexandria C.C. (Alexandria)   March 29, 30.
Alexandria 158 (R. G. Dyson 54) & 231 (R. G. Dyson 58, L. G. Irvine 53) lost to Martineau's XI 427-3 dec (D. R. Wilcox 195, B. H. Valentine 119, R. E. Evans 78) by an inns & 38 runs.

2nd Match: v R.A.F. Depot (Abukir)   April 1, 2.
Martineau's XI 107 (Cook 6-14) & 401-6 dec (B. H. Valentine 194, F. St. G. Unwin 58) beat R.A.F. Depot 192 (H. F. Benka 5-67) & 143 (H. F. Benka 5-48) by 173 runs.*

3rd Match: v Army Other Ranks (Abbassia) (One Day)   April 4.
Martineau's XI 253 (A. P. F. Chapman 74) beat Army Other Ranks 129 (H. F. Benka 5-37) by 124 runs.

4th Match: v Gezira Sporting Club (Gezira)   April 5, 6.
Martineau's XI 146 & 217 (A. P. F. Chapman 68, V. Cripps 5-26) lost to Gezira 187 (W. A. R. Sumner 88, D. C. Rought-Rought 5-40, H. F. Benka 5-66) & 177-6 (W. A. R. Sumner 95) by 4 wkts.

5th Match: v R.A.F. (Heliopolis) (One Day)   April 8.
R.A.F. 236-7 dec (Cook 72) drew with Martineau's XI 182-6 (D. C. S. Ball 88*).*

6th Match: v Egyptian C.C. (Gezira) (One Day)   April 9.
Martineau's XI 189-0 dec (D. R. Wilcox 109, R. E. Evans 76*) beat Egyptian C.C. 97 (A. E. C. Smith 5-15) by 92 runs.*

7th Match: v United Services (Gezira)   April 11, 12, 13.
Martineau's XI 319 (H. F. Benka 75, A. P. F. Chapman 57, D. C. S. Ball 54) & 191 beat United Services 201 (S. Enderby 52, H. F. Benka 5-50) & 278 (W. A. R. Sumner 64, H. F. Benka 5-109) by 31 runs.

8th Match: v Willcocks S.C. (Gezira) (One Day)   April 14.
Willcocks S.C. 176 (J. S. Dawson 51, H. F. Benka 6-73) lost to Martineau's XI 178-8 by 2 wkts.

9th Match: v All Egypt (Gezira)   April 17, 18, 19, 20.
Martineau's XI 399 (D. R. Wilcox 136, H. F. Benka 58) & 248-8 dec (H. F. Benka 77) beat All Egypt 290 (C. P. Hamilton 51, R. E. S. Yeldham 55) & 268 (C. P. Hamilton 80, W. A. R. Sumner 57) by 89 runs.*

10th Match: v R.A.F. (Alexandria) (One Day)   April 21.
Martineau's XI 284-7 dec (A. E. C. Smith 74, Cook 5-56) beat R.A.F. 68 (H. F. Benka 5-22) by 216 runs.

11th Match: v All Egypt (Alexandria)   April 22, 23, 25.
All Egypt 208 (H. F. Benka 9-81) & 367 (C. P. Hamilton 130, A. Cook 98) lost to Martineau's XI 532 (D. C. S. Ball 196, A. P. F. Chapman 88, B. H. Valentine 72) & 45-1 by 9 wkts.

12th Match: v Victoria College (Victoria Coll) (One Day)   April 26.
Martineau's XI 373-4 dec (D. R. Wilcox 120, F. St. Unwin 82, A. W. Childs-Clarke 69) beat Victoria College 45 (Unwin 5-7) by 330 runs.

1938-39: Combined Oxford and Cambridge Team to Jamaica

1st Match: v Kingston C.C. Minor XI (Dunoon Pk) (One Day)   July 31.
Oxf/Cambr XI 284 (W. Murray-Wood 128, M. M. Walford 56) drew with Kingston 81-3.

2nd Match: v Melbourne C.C. (Melbourne Pk) (One Day)   Aug 2.
Oxf/Cambr XI 180-7 dec (G. R. de Soysa 75) drew with Melbourne 159-2 (O. Stephenson 74, I. Barrow 51).*

3rd Match: v Kensington (Kensington Oval) (One Day)   Aug 4.
Oxf/Cambr XI 223-7 dec (W. Murray-Wood 55) drew with Kensington 131-9.

4th Match: v Kingston C.C. (Sabina Pk)   Aug 5, 6.
Kingston 250 (R. C. Marley 78) & 125 lost to Oxf/Cambr XI 273-5 dec (M. M. Walford 124, G. R. de Soysa 61) & 105-4 by 6 wkts.

5th Match: v Jamaica (Sabina Pk)   Aug 10, 11, 13.
Oxf/Cambr XI 355 (R. C. M. Kimpton 113, J. H. Cameron 62, M. M. Walford 51) & 99 (G. H. Moodie 5-32) drew with Jamaica 227 (O. C. Stephenson 76, M. M. Walford 6-49) & 204-8 (K. H. Weekes 106).

6th Match: v Lucas C.C. (Sabina Pk)   Aug 16, 18.
Lucas 255-6 dec (K. H. Weekes 126) lost to Oxf/Cambr XI 257-9 (W. Murray-Wood 66, R. C. M. Kimpton 65) by 2 wkts.*

7th Match: v Jamaica (Sabina Pk)   Aug 20, 22, 23, 24.
Oxf/Cambr XI 128 & 141 (G. H. Moodie 5-63) lost to Jamaica 343 (S. M. Abrahams 110, I. Barrow 65, K. H. Weekes 58, D. C. Wilson 5-81) by an inns & 74 runs.

1938-39: ten-day 'timeless' Test in South Africa

The tour to South Africa in 1938-39 will always be remembered for its last match – the timeless Test, which ended in a draw after ten days, only because the tourists had to catch the ship back to England. Many records were broken in this game, but the fact that no Test had ever lasted so long will be its lasting memorial.

Hammond, who had changed his status from professional to amateur, captained England in the 1938 Tests against Australia and was the automatic choice as captain of the touring team to South Africa. The full party, which sailed on the *Athlone Castle* on 21 October, was W. R. Hammond (Gloucs), (capt), H. T. Bartlett (Sussex), K. Farnes (Essex), P. A. Gibb (Yorks), B. H. Valentine (Kent), N. W. D. Yardley (Yorks) and the professionals L. E. G. Ames (Kent), W. J. Edrich (Middx), T. W. J. Goddard (Gloucs), L. Hutton (Yorks), E. Paynter (Lancs), R. T. D. Perks (Worcs), H. Verity (Yorks), L. L. Wilkinson (Lancs), D. V. P. Wright (Kent) and A. J. Holmes as manager. In the rough seas of the Bay of Biscay, Yardley fell, cracking a rib, and was unable to play in the first few matches. D. C. S. Compton had declined the invitation to tour due to his commitments to Arsenal Football Club.

The programme opened with a Country match on 8 November and as in previous visits to South Africa the M.C.C. had few problems in the initial matches, winning five of the first six. In Johannesburg however the Transvaal side found the English attack posed few problems. Mitchell and Viljoen both played excellent innings and the Provincial side declared at 428 for 8. The M.C.C. were unfortunate to have Hutton injured in the first over, struck on the head by a ball from Davies, and this prevented him playing in the first Test. Transvaal gained a large first innings lead, but rain marred the closing stages of the game, which was drawn.

The first Test began on the same ground six days later. Gibb was included in place of Hutton and had innings of 93 and 106 – even this great effort was surpassed by Paynter who hit a century in each innings. Goddard knocked out the middle of the home batting with a hat-trick, but Dalton, coming in at No. 8, hit a century and the match went on to a predictable draw. There was a record attendance of 22,000 on the second day (Boxing Day).

Travelling straight on to Cape Town for the second Test, the tourists found rain preventing a start before 3.30 on the first day, but the wicket had been covered and played easily. Hammond, Ames and Valentine hit hundreds for England, whilst Nourse, son of the old Test cricketer, hit a hundred for South Africa and another draw was completed.

When Hammond won the toss in the third Test and England strolled to 469 for 4, with Paynter making a double century and the captain 120, another draw looked likely, but Farnes somehow extracted a little life from the docile pitch and South Africa collapsed for 103. Following on, they recovered their poise; the deficit was however too great and England just won by an innings.

Both matches in Rhodesia were ruined by rain, though Goddard had time to perform a second hat-trick in the game at Salisbury.

Hammond won the toss again in the fourth Test – his eighth

1938-39: M.C.C. to South Africa

Batting Averages

	M	I	NO	R	HS	Avge	100	c/s
E. Paynter (Lancs)	12	14	0	1072	243	76.57	5	5
L. Hutton (Yorks)	14	19	1	1168	202	64.88	5	7
W. J. Edrich (Middx)	15	20	5	914	219	60.93	4	12
W. R. Hammond (Glos)	15	18	1	1025	181	60.29	4	15
N. W. D. Yardley (Yorks)	11	12	2	577	182*	57.70	3	2
L. E. G. Ames (Kent)	13	16	3	683	115	52.53	2	14/7
H. T. Bartlett (Sussex)	10	10	3	358	100	51.14	1	5
B. H. Valentine (Kent)	13	16	3	590	112	45.38	2	6
P. A. Gibb (Yorks)	12	17	0	738	120	43.41	2	10/1
D. V. P. Wright (Kent)	13	10	2	248	61	31.00	0	6
H. Verity (Yorks)	12	12	2	245	39	24.50	0	7
K. Farnes (Essex)	14	11	4	146	33*	20.85	0	5
R. T. D. Perks (Worcs)	10	7	3	57	22	14.25	0	2
T. W. J. Goddard (Glos)	10	8	2	76	33	12.66	0	2
L. L. Wilkinson (Lancs)	12	6	2	25	13*	6.25	0	4

Also played in one match: Ft-Lieut A. J. Holmes (Sussex) 3*.

Bowling Averages

	O	M	R	W	Avge	BB	5i
L. L. Wilkinson	231.3	31	830	44	18.86	5-10	2
H. Verity	428	132	937	47	19.93	7-22	3
T. W. J. Goddard	311	72	817	31	26.35	6-38	1
K. Farnes	384.7	59	1207	44	27.43	7-38	2
D. V. P. Wright	343.4	35	1453	51	28.49	6-55	2
R. T. D. Perks	244.5	29	788	25	31.52	5-100	1
W. J. Edrich	143	16	458	13	35.23	4-10	0
W. R. Hammond	97	23	260	7	37.14	1-3	0
L. Hutton	24	1	108	2	54.00	1-20	0

Also bowled: B. H. Valentine 3-1-12-0; N. W. D. Yardley 3-0-15-0; E. Paynter 2-0-7-0.

1938-39: M.C.C. to South Africa

1st Match: v Western Province Country XI (Cape Town)   Nov 8, 9.
M.C.C. 589-8 dec (E. Paynter 193, W. R. Hammond 106, B. H. Valentine 69, L. Hutton 68, H. Verity 66*, P. Sleigh 5-161) beat Country XI 140 & 107 by an inns & 342 runs.

2nd Match: v Western Province (Cape Town)   Nov 12, 14, 15.
W. Province 174 & 169 (A. Ralph 61, K. Farnes 7-38) lost to M.C.C. 276 (H. T. Bartlett 91*) & 69-2 by 8 wkts.

3rd Match: v Griqualand West (Kimberley)   Nov 19, 21, 22.
M.C.C. 676 (E. Paynter 158, L. Hutton 149, N. W. D. Yardley 142, W. J. Edrich 109, J. P. McNally 5-154, E. V. Franz 5-105) beat Griqualand West 114 (H. Verity 7-22) & 273 (A. P. Steyn 65, F. Nicholson 61) by an inns & 289 runs.

4th Match: v Orange Free State (Bloemfontein)   Nov 26, 28.
O.F.S. 128 (L. L. Wilkinson 5-10, D. V. P. Wright 5-81) & 260 (S. K. Coen 61, H. Verity 7-75) lost to M.C.C. 412-6 dec (N. W. D. Yardley 182*, H. T. Bartlett 100) by an inns & 24 runs.

5th Match: v Natal (Durban)   Dec 3, 5, 6.
Natal 307 (R. L. Harvey 92, W. W. Wade 56) & 30-0 drew with M.C.C. 458 (W. R. Hammond 122, L. Hutton 108, W. J. Edrich 98, E. L. Dalton 6-116).

6th Match: v North-Eastern Transvaal (Pretoria)   Dec 10, 12, 13.
N-E Transvaal 161 (L. Brown 75, L. L. Wilkinson 5-24) & 142 lost to M.C.C. 379-6 dec (E. Paynter 102, B. H. Valentine 100, L. Hutton 66).

7th Match: v Transvaal (Johannesburg)   Dec 16, 18, 19.
Transvaal 428-8 dec (B. Mitchell 133, K. G. Viljoen 97, A. B. C. Langton 58) & 174-2 (S. H. Curnow 91) drew with M.C.C. 268 (L. E. G. Ames 109, E. Q. Davies 6-82).

8th Match: v South Africa (Johannesburg)   Dec 24, 26, 27, 28.
England 422 (E. Paynter 117, B. H. Valentine 97, P. A. Gibb 93, N. Gordon 5-103) & 291-4 dec (P. A. Gibb 106, E. Paynter 100, W. R. Hammond 58) drew with South Africa 390 (E. L. Dalton 102, B. Mitchell 73, A. D. Nourse 73, A. B. C. Langton 64*, K. G. Viljoen 50) & 108-1.

9th Match: v South Africa (Cape Town)   Dec 31, Jan 2, 3, 4.
England 559-9 dec (W. R. Hammond 181, L. E. G. Ames 115, B. H. Valentine 112, P. A. Gibb 58, N. Gordon 5-157) drew with South Africa 286 (A. D. Nourse 120, H. Verity 5-70) & 201-2 (E. A. B. Rowan 89*, P. G. V. van der Bijl 87).

10th Match: v Eastern Province (Port Elizabeth)   Jan 7, 9.
E. Province 172 (A. H. Coy 54*, K. Farnes 5-58) & 111 lost to M.C.C. 518-6 dec (L. Hutton 202, E. Paynter 99, W. R. Hammond 52, P. A. Gibb 51) by an inns & 235 runs.

11th Match: v Border (East London)   Jan 13, 14, 16.
Border 121 & 275 (R. J. Evans 88, D. Dowling 61) lost to M.C.C. 320 (N. W. D. Yardley 126, D. V. P. Wright 61) & 79-1 (W. J. Edrich 50*) by 9 wkts.

12th Match: v South Africa (Durban)   Jan 20, 21, 23.
England 469-4 dec (E. Paynter 243, W. R. Hammond 120) beat South Africa 103 & 353 (B. Mitchell 109, E. A. B. Rowan 67, K. G. Viljoen 61) by an inns & 13 runs.

13th Match: v Combined Transvaal XI (Johannesburg)   Jan 27, 28, 30.
Combined Transvaal 304 (B. Mitchell 83, K. G. Viljoen 76) & 220-2 (A. Melville 107, E. A. B. Rowan 67*) drew with M.C.C. 434 (L. Hutton 148, W. R. Hammond 79, B. H. Valentine 71, S. F. Viljoen 6-91).

14th Match: v Rhodesia (Bulawayo)   Feb 4, 6, 7.
M.C.C. 307-5 dec (L. Hutton 145, E. Paynter 53) drew with Rhodesia 242 (P. N. F. Mansell 62).

15th Match: v Rhodesia (Salisbury)   Feb 10, 11, 13.
M.C.C. 180 (J. H. Charsley 6-58) & 174-2 dec (W. J. Edrich 101*) drew with Rhodesia 96 (T. W. J. Goddard 6-38) & 95-6.

16th Match: v South Africa (Johannesburg)   Feb 18, 20, 21, 22.
England 215 (L. Hutton 92, A. B. C. Langton 5-58) & 203-4 (W. R. Hammond 61*) drew with South Africa 349-8 dec (E. A. B. Rowan 85, A. Melville 67, B. Mitchell 63).

17th Match: v Natal (Pietermaritzburg)   Feb 25, 27, 28.
Natal 295 (E. L. Dalton 110, A. D. Nourse 67) & 219 (D. V. P. Wright 6-55) lost to M.C.C. 407 (W. J. Edrich 150, L. E. G. Ames 62) & 110-1 (L. Hutton 53*) by 9 wkts.

18th Match: v South Africa (Durban)   March 3, 4, 6, 7, 8, 9, 10, 11, 13, 14
South Africa 530 (P. G. V. van der Bijl 125, A. D. Nourse 103, A. Melville 78, R. E. Grieveson 75, E. L. Dalton 57, R. T. D. Perks 5-100) & 481 (A. Melville 103, P. G. V. van der Bijl 97, B. Mitchell 89, K. G. Viljoen 74) drew with England 316 (L. E. G. Ames 84, E. Paynter 62) & 654-5 (W. J. Edrich 219, W. R. Hammond 140, P. A. Gibb 120, E. Paynter 75, L. Hutton 55).

Two members of the touring party to South Africa in 1938-39 return home in March 1939, Ken Farnes (left) and Hedley Verity (right). They are being greeted by Farnes' father (centre). This is a particularly poignant picture, as these two were the best-known English cricketers killed in the Second World War.

successive correct call in Test Matches – and England batted first, but showers soon came to assist the bowlers and for the only time in this Test series South Africa dismissed England cheaply. The home team went on to achieve a first innings lead of 134, but their slow scoring allied to more rain which washed out the third day produced a third drawn match.

The fifth Test followed a win over Natal. South Africa won the toss and batted for the first two and a half days to total 530. England fared poorly on the fourth day and were 268 by the close for the loss of 7 wickets. South Africa gained a lead of 214 on first innings, but did not enforce the follow on and when their second innings ended shortly before stumps on the sixth day, England required 696 to win. Hutton, Gibb and Edrich made a determined effort on the seventh day and by its close England had moved to 253 for 1, Gibb 78 not out, Edrich 107 not out. Rain prevented any play on the eighth day (Saturday) and on the Monday England went on to 496 for 3, needing only 200 more for victory. On the tenth day, South Africa bowled and fielded very tightly – only 39 runs came in the first hour – but then England, seeing rain in the air, began to hit out. The score reached 654 for 5, only 42 needed, when a thunderstorm just before 4 o'clock ended the game, the tourists having to travel back to Cape Town – a distance of about 1,000 miles – to catch the *Athlone Castle* for home. The match was therefore drawn and England won the series one match to nil.

Hammond was criticised for his over-cautious approach in the Test Matches, delaying declarations on several occasions until all hope of a win had gone. The batting was also very slow. The tourists' batsmen had a tremendous time, and scarcely anyone failed, but the bowlers struggled, the perfect pitches being the problem. Everywhere, except in Rhodesia, the matches were played on turf rather than matting, quite a change from the earlier tours, and the excessive care with which the groundsmen prepared these relatively new turf wickets can take the blame for the dullness of the big matches.

1938-39: Sir Julien Cahn's last tour to New Zealand

At the invitation of the New Zealand Cricket Council, Sir Julien Cahn took his team out there in the early months of 1939. The team, which left England on 6 January, was Sir Julien Cahn (capt), C. S. Dempster (Leics), A. H. Dyson (Glamorgan), C. C.

Goodway (Warwicks), J. Hardstaff (Notts), G. F. H. Heane (Notts), V. E. Jackson (Leics), J. G. Lush (New South Wales), C. R. N. Maxwell (Notts), H. Mudge (New South Wales), N. Oldfield (Lancs), W. E. Phillipson (Lancs), T. P. B. Smith (Essex), E. A. Watts (Surrey), J. E. Walsh (Leics) and W. E. Astill (Leics) acting as scorer.

After four minor games, the side met Canterbury at Lancaster Park, where a determined innings of 180 by Hardstaff prevented the tourists collapsing and the game was drawn. Large crowds watched the match, the receipts being £510. In the second important match, Otago were beaten by an innings. Dempster batted 337 minutes for his double century and Smith's spin dismissed Otago twice for under 200. The 'Test Match' was completly ruined by rain, but about 5,000 watched the only day's play. The last important game was staged in Auckland, where Cahn's side hit 456 and gained a large first innings lead but could not force a win when Auckland followed on.

The tour was a great success and despite some bad weather a profit of £155 was made, which Sir Julien gave to the New Zealand Cricket Council. Owing to a shipping strike, the return voyage to England was delayed and the county players only just arrived back for the start of the English season.

This was the last overseas tour undertaken by Sir Julien Cahn – he died on 26 September 1944.

1938-39: Sir Julien Cahn's Team to New Zealand

1st Match: v Secondary Schools (Auckland) (One Day)   Feb 13.
Schools 85 (J. E. Walsh 7-24) lost to Cahn's XI 286-8 (J. Hardstaff jun 56).

2nd Match: v Waikato (Hamilton)   Feb 15, 16.
Waikato 131 drew with Cahn's XI 304-8 (C. S. Dempster 64, W. E. Phillipson 52).*

3rd Match: v Wanganui (Wanganui) (One Day)   Feb 18.
Wanganui 121 (H. Cuming 57, J. G. Lush 5-16) lost to Cahn's XI 291-3 (A. H. Dyson 103, H. Mudge 72, C. S. Dempster 52).*

4th Match: v Minor Associations (Palmerston North)   Feb 21, 22.
Minor Associations XII 206 (Evans 72, J. E. Walsh 8-37) & 119-10 (E. A. Watts 5-37) drew with Cahn's XII 418 (J. Hardstaff jun 160, E. A. Watts 80).*

5th Match: v Canterbury (Christchurch)   Feb 24, 25, 27.
Canterbury XII 464 (J. L. Kerr 124, R. E. J. Menzies 77, I. B. Cromb 66) & 233 (M. P. Donnelly 56) drew with Cahn's XII 410 (J. Hardstaff jun 180, G. F. H. Heane 67, A. W. Roberts 5-107).

6th Match: v Secondary Schools (Oamaru)   March 1, 2.
Cahn's XI 380-6 dec (V. E. Jackson 135, N. Oldfield 104, C. S. Dempster 65) beat Secondary Schools 84 (T. P. B. Smith 7-4) & 87 (J. E. Walsh 5-33) by an inns & 209 runs.*

7th Match: v Otago (Dunedin)   March 3, 4, 6
Otago XII 184 (A. R. Knight 53, T. P. B. Smith 5-56) & 108 lost to Cahn's XII 437 (C. S. Dempster 200, E. A. Watts 84) by an inns & 142 runs.

8th Match: v New Zealand (Wellington)   March 10, 11, 13.
New Zealand 170-5 dec (W. M. Wallace 54) drew with Cahn's XI 163-7: rain.*

9th Match: v Bay of Plenty (Rotorua) (One Day)   March 15.
Bay of Plenty 233 (N. W. Bayley 76, R. Barlow 51, J. E. Walsh 5-69) drew with Cahn's XI 126-8 (H. Mudge 60).*

10th Match: v Auckland (Auckland)   March 17, 18, 20.
Cahn's XII 456 (J. Hardstaff jun 84, N. Oldfield 70, V. E. Jackson 59, C. S. Dempster 56) drew with Auckland XII 270 (H. T. Pearson 76, J. E. Walsh 5-91) & 305-3 (P. E. Whitelaw 100, G. L. Weir 96).

1939: the last cricket tour to Egypt

For his eleventh annual tour to Egypt, H. M. Martineau took with him R. E. S. Wyatt (Warwicks), F. R. Brown (Surrey), T. N. Pearce (Essex), A. W. Childs-Clarke (Middx), A. P. Singleton (Worcs), D. F. Walker (Oxford), C. H. Taylor (Leics), H. R. Crouch (Surrey 2nd), R. de W. K. Winlaw (Surrey), A. G. Powell (Essex) and B. Stevens.

It is believed that this tour created a new vogue by being the first to travel by air from England. The side flew from Croydon on 31 March in an Imperial Airways Frobisher air liner. The flight to Marseilles took four hours and from there the team transferred on to a flying boat which flew via Rome and Athens, touching down at Alexandria in time for dinner. Several county players, who normally would have refused Martineau's invitation, accepted because the flight considerably reduced the time spent away from England.

Of the two important matches, the 'First Test' was a very exciting match throughout. The tourists won in the final over with three wickets in hand, Walker hitting his 60 in under 50 minutes. The 'Second Test' was quite astonishing. Egypt gained a first innings lead of 154, through a century by Hamilton, and in the end required 176 in their second innings in two hours to win – the home team sank to 50 all out, Childs-Clarke taking 4 for 15. In the other games Wyatt batted splendidly, as did Walker, and of the newcomers Singleton bowled and batted well – a most cheerful cricketer.

The team flew back to England on 29 April. It was to prove the last important English cricket tour to Egypt, though many first-class cricketers were destined to play there during the Second World War.

1939: H. M. Martineau's Team to Egypt

1st Match: v Alexandria (Alexandria)   April 3, 4.
Martineau's XI 284 (D. F. Walker 116, R. E. S. Wyatt 68) & 149-5 dec (T. N. Pearce 53) drew with Alexandria 195 (B. de Botton 70) & 106-8.

2nd Match: v R.A.F. Depot (Abuqir)   April 5, 6.
Martineau's XI 256 (D. F. Walker 100, R. E. S. Wyatt 62*) & 177-2 dec (R. E. S. Wyatt 84*) beat R.A.F. Depot 112 (Moody 51, A. P. Singleton 6-30) & 111 by 210 runs.

3rd Match: v Alexandria Area XI (Alexandria) (One Day)   April 8.
Area XI 42 (H. R. Crouch 8-20) & 115-6 lost on first innings to Martineau's XI 163-9 dec.

4th Match: v Gexira (Gezira)   April 10, 11, 12.
Martineau's XI 495 (C. H. Taylor 112, D. F. Walker 100, T. N. Pearce 57, F. R. Brown 52, J. H. Whitehead 6-109) & 219-2 dec (C. H. Taylor 114*, R. E. S. Wyatt 76) drew with Gezira 434 (R. J. Parkhouse 121, M. St. J. Packe 109, R. E. S. Yeldham 62) & 131-2 (C. P. Hamilton 51*).

5th Match: v R.A.F. Egypt (Gezira) (One Day)   April 13.
Martineau's XI 351-9 dec (R. E. S. Wyatt 113, F. R. Brown 77, B. Stevens 59) beat R.A.F. 116 (D. F. Walker 5-15) by 235 runs.

6th Match: v Army Other Ranks (Helmieh Camp) (One Day) April 14.
Martineau's XI 297-8 dec (R. E. S. Wyatt 100*, T. N. Pearce 84) drew with Army Other Ranks 210-9 (Warwick 57).

7th Match: v United Services (Gezira)   April 15, 17.
United Services 157 (C. P. Hamilton 59, A. P. Singleton 6-21) & 172 (R. E. S. Yeldham 86, F. R. Brown 5-86) lost to Martineau's XI 380 (R. de W. K. Winlaw 101, C. H. Taylor 71, A. P. Singleton 61*) by an inns & 51 runs.

8th Match: v All Egypt (Gezira)   April 20, 21, 22.
Egypt 319 (R. J. Parkhouse 110, J. E. S. Walford 75, W. A. R. Sumner 52, F. R. Brown 8-117) & 255 (C. P. Hamilton 56) lost to Martineau's XI 363 (F. R. Brown 79, D. F. Walker 59) & 209-7 (T. N. Pearce 75*, D. F. Walker 60) by 3 wkts.

9th Match: v Victoria College (Victoria)   April 24.
Martineau's XI 304-4 dec (D. F. Walker 100, H. R. Crouch 84*, A. G. Powell 51) beat Victoria College 122 by 182 runs.

10th Match: v All Egypt (Alexandria)   April 25, 26, 27.
Martineau's XI 241 (F. R. Brown 87*, D. F. Walker 69) & 329 (C. H. Taylor 99, T. N. Pearce 76, J. E. S. Walford 5-93) beat Egypt 395 (C. P. Hamilton 113, J. K. Luard 78, W. G. Tailyour 58, H. M. Martineau 5-133) & 50 by 125 runs.

1939-40: abortive M.C.C. tour of India

In the summer of 1939, the M.C.C. selected the following team to tour India for 1939-40: A. J. Holmes (Sussex) (capt), H. T. Bartlett (Sussex), J. M. Brocklebank (Lancs), S. C. Griffith (Sussex), R. H. C. Human (Worcs), R. E. S. Wyatt (Warwicks) and the professionals Emrys Davies (Glam), H. E. Dollery (Warwicks), H. Gimblett (Som), G. H. Pope (Derbys), John Langridge (Sussex), G. S. Mobey (Surrey), M. S. Nichols (Essex), J. F. Parker (Surrey), T. P. B. Smith (Essex) and A. W. Wellard (Somerset) with Lieut-Col C. B. Rubie as manager.

The side was very much an England second team squad and probably not as strong as Lord Tennyson's team of 1937-38. War broke out before the M.C.C. party could leave England, and the tour was cancelled.

1946-47: England well beaten in first post-war tour of Australia

Within a few weeks of V.J. Day, the Australian Board of Cricket Control put out an invitation to the M.C.C. for a visit by the English team to Australia in the winter of 1946-47. Dr Evatt, a member of the Australian Government, supported this invitation in the strongest terms during a speech in London on 1 October 1945 and on 9 October the M.C.C. promised to send a team. No doubt the success of the Victory 'Tests' which were played in England between the Australian Services and England in the summer of 1945 had a lot to do with the speedy way M.C.C. agreed to make the tour. The discussion regarding the selection of the team began before Christmas 1945. The first problems seemed to involve the bowling strength, since both Farnes and Verity had died in the War. The Tests played against India in the summer of 1946 were used to a large extent as trials for the Australian visit. The eventual team was: W. R. Hammond (Gloucs) (capt), N. W. D. Yardley (Yorks) (vice-capt) and P. A. Gibb (Yorks) as the only amateurs, and A. V. Bedser (Surrey), D. C. S. Compton (Middx), W. J. Edrich (Middx), T. G. Evans (Kent), L. B. Fishlock (Surrey), J. Hardstaff (Notts), L. Hutton (Yorks), J. T. Ikin (Lancs), James Langridge (Sussex), R. Pollard (Lancs), T. P. B. Smith (Essex), W. Voce (Notts), C. Washbrook (Lancs) and D. V. P. Wright (Kent). Major R. Howard was manager and W. Ferguson acted as scorer. E. A. Bedser also travelled with the team.

The team sailed from Southampton on the R.M.S. *Stirling Castle* on 31 August. The main criticism of the team by the press was that it was too old and the names of Gimblett, Dollery, Brookes and Robertson were noted as omissions, but in retrospect it is doubtful if any or all of this quartet would have altered the outcome of the tour.

Unlike the pre-war voyages the ship did not stop, except overnight at Port Said, and the journey was accomplished in 24 days. This took the organisers by surprise and two minor additional matches were hastily added before the 'official' start of the tour at

---

1946-47: M.C.C. to Australia and New Zealand

Batting Averages

	M	I	NO	R	HS	Avge	100	c/s
L. Hutton (Yorks)	14	21	3	1267	151*	70.38	3	5
Jas Langridge (Sussex)	4	3	1	130	100	65.00	1	2
D. C. S. Compton (Middx)	19	31	4	1660	163	61.48	5	11
W. R. Hammond (Glos)	13	19	0	781	208	41.10	2	12
W. J. Edrich (Middx)	18	27	2	998	119	39.92	1	15
J. Hardstaff jun (Notts)	8	13	1	471	155	39.25	1	3
C. Washbrook (Lancs)	18	29	0	1129	133	38.93	4	6
N. W. D. Yardley (Yorks)	19	27	4	814	126	35.39	1	11
J. T. Ikin (Lancs)	20	30	6	822	102*	34.25	1	24
T. G. Evans (Kent)	16	22	6	438	101	27.37	1	29/5
L. B. Fishlock (Surrey)	10	17	1	329	57	20.56	0	5
T. P. B. Smith (Essex)	10	12	1	186	46	16.90	0	5
A. V. Bedser (Surrey)	15	22	5	264	51	15.52	0	8
P. A. Gibb (Yorks)	9	14	1	199	37*	15.30	0	10/1
W. Voce (Notts)	10	11	1	131	28	13.10	0	3
R. Pollard (Lancs)	13	9	4	49	12*	9.80	0	6
D. V. P. Wright (Kent)	15	18	5	84	20	6.46	0	5

Bowling Averages

	Balls	M	R	W	Avge	BB	5i
J. Hardstaff jun	112	1	50	3	16.66	3-24	0
D. C. S. Compton	812	18	364	17	21.41	7-36	1
N. W. D. Yardley	1859	17	477	16	29.81	3-19	0
T. P. B. Smith	2012	18	1087	32	33.96	9-121	2
D. V. P. Wright	3458	47	1916	54	35.48	7-105	3
A. V. Bedser	4040	87	1667	47	35.46	4-21	0
R. Pollard	2558	73	1021	28	36.46	4-19	0
J. T. Ikin	857	9	488	13	37.53	4-51	0
W. Voce	1781	45	801	21	38.14	6-38	1
W. J. Edrich	2072	33	1032	26	39.69	4-26	0
Jas Langridge	800	15	297	7	42.42	3-60	0

Also bowled: W. R. Hammond 24-0-8-0; B. Fishlock 8-0-3-0; P. A. Gibb 8-0-14-0; L. Hutton 168-1-132-2.

The first M.C.C. party to tour after the Second World War was the team to Australia and New Zealand in 1946-47. Here are the players as an Australian cartoonist saw them, left to right, from top: N. W. D. Yardley, T. G. Evans, T. P. B. Smith, L. Hutton, A. V. Bedser, J. Hardstaff, W. Voce, R. Pollard, W. R. Hammond, J. T. Ikin, W. J. Edrich, James Langridge, P. A. Gibb, Major R. Howard (manager), L. B. Fishlock, C. Washbrook, D. V. P. Wright, D. C. S. Compton.

Opposite *Denis Compton batting during his innings of 98 in the match against the Combined XI at Perth. G. Kessey is the wicket-keeper.*

Below *The two greatest batsmen of the 1930s were the captains of England and Australia in the first post-war Test series. Photographers gather round as Australia's Bradman (with bat) and England's Hammond inspect the Test wicket at Adelaide.*

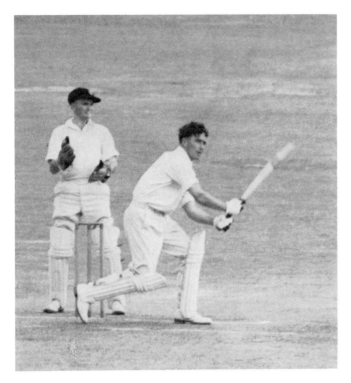

Perth. In the two opening first-class games the bat dominated and high scoring draws were the result. M.C.C. however bowled to much greater effect in the next two important matches, very nearly winning the first and easily beating Victoria in the second. The bowling of Wright in this match raised English hopes. The matches against An Australian Eleven and New South Wales were both rained off, and after a draw with Queensland, the first Test began at Brisbane. The great debate earlier on was whether Bradman would play–the fact that he did and that he scored 187 had something to do with England's downfall, but the visitors also had the misfortune of batting twice on a rain-affected wicket, their batting collapsing in each innings, and Gibb made one or two bad blunders behind the wicket.

There was a brief respite at Gympie before the second Test at Sydney. Hammond won the toss, and though Australia were without Lindwall–ill with chicken pox–the tourists' batting was very inept against the spin of McCool and Johnson. Barnes and Bradman both hit 234 and England faced an impossible task in their innings. Edrich hit a century and most of the other English batsmen managed something, but the result was still an innings defeat. In the third Test, England gave a good account of themselves in the first innings. It was not until Tallon and Lindwall came together in Australia's second innings and added 154 for the 8th wicket that the match slipped from England's grasp and from then on it was all they could do to hang on for a draw. 343,675 people watched the game and the receipts of £44,063 were a record. There was little to choose between the two sides after each

1946-47: M.C.C. to Australia and New Zealand

1st Match: v Northam & Country Districts (Northam)   Oct 2, 3.
Northam 123 (T. P. B. Smith 5-55) & 71 (W. J. Edrich 6-20) lost to M.C.C. 409-6 dec (W. R. Hammond 131, D. C. S. Compton 84, L. Hutton 51) by an inns & 215 runs.

2nd Match: v Western Australian Colts (Freemantle)   Oct 7.
M.C.C. 197-4 dec (P. A. Gibb 51, L. B. Fishlock 50) drew with Colts 138-6.

3rd Match: v Western Australia (Perth)   Oct 11, 12, 14.
W. Australia 366 (D. Watt 85, M. Herbert 53) & 48-1 drew with M.C.C. 477 (W. R. Hammond 208, J. T. Ikin 66, J. Hardstaff jun 52, C. Puckett 5-126).

4th Match: v Combined XI (Perth)   Oct 17, 18, 19.
Combined XI 462 (D. Watt 157, I. W. Johnson 87) drew with M.C.C. 302 (D. C. S. Compton 98, C. Washbrook 80, N. W. D. Yardley 56).

5th Match: v South Australian Country XI (Port Pirie)   Oct 22, 23.
M.C.C. 487-6 dec (L. Hutton 164, D. C. S. Compton 100, L. B. Fishlock 98, J. Hardstaff jun 67) beat S.A. Country XI 87 (T. P. B. Smith 5-16, D. V. P. Wright 5-40) & 92 by an inns & 308 runs.*

6th Match: v South Australia (Adelaide)   Oct 25, 26, 27, 28.
M.C.C. 506-5 dec (L. Hutton 136, C. Washbrook 113, W. J. Edrich 71, D. C. S. Compton 71, N. W. D. Yardley 54) drew with S. Australia 266 (D. G. Bradman 76, R. James 58, P. L. Ridings 57, T. P. B. Smith 5-93) & 276-8 (R. J. Craig 111, J. Mann 62*).*

7th Match: v Victoria (Melbourne)   Oct 31, Nov 1, 2, 4.
M.C.C. 358 (D. C. S. Compton 143, N. W. D. Yardley 70) & 279-7 dec (L. Hutton 151) beat Victoria 189 (A. L. Hassett 57, D. V. P. Wright 6-48) & 204 (A. L. Hassett 57, M. R. Harvey 57) by 244 runs.*

8th Match: v An Australian XI (Melbourne)   Nov 8, 9, 11, 12, 13.
M.C.C. 314 (L. Hutton 71, C. Washbrook 57, W. R. Hammond 51, C. L. McCool 7-106) drew with An Australian XI 327-5 (A. R. Morris 115, D. G. Bradman 106).

9th Match: v New South Wales (Sydney)   Nov 15, 16, 18, 19.
N.S.W. 165-4 dec (A. R. Morris 81) drew with M.C.C. 156-2 (L. Hutton 97): rain.*

10th Match: v Queensland (Brisbane)   Nov 22, 23, 25, 26.
Queensland 400 (G. G. Cook 169, R. E. Rogers 66, A. S. Young 53) & 230-6 dec (L. J. Johnson 75) drew with M.C.C. 310 (W. J. Edrich 64*, D. C. S. Compton 55, C. L. McCool 6-105) & 238-6 (C. Washbrook 124, W. J. Edrich 71).*

11th Match: v Australia (Brisbane)   Nov 29, 30, Dec 2, 3, 4, 5.
Australia 645 (D. G. Bradman 187, A. L. Hassett 128, C. L.McCool 95, K. R. Miller 79, D. V. P. Wright 5-167) beat England 141 (K. R. Miller 7-60) & 172 (E. R. H. Toshack 6-82) by an inns & 332 runs.

12th Match: v Queensland Country XI (Gympie)   Dec 7, 9.
Country XI 208 (T. Allen 53, T. P. B. Smith 5-80) & 311-9 (C. G. R. Stibe 75, K. Gartrell 52) drew with M.C.C. 282 (J. Hardstaff jun 64, L. B. Fishlock 62, T. E. Ball 5-69).*

13th Match: v Australia (Sydney)   Dec 13, 14, 16, 17, 18, 19.
England 255 (W. J. Edrich 71, J. T. Ikin 60, I. W. Johnson 6-42) & 371 (W. J. Edrich 119, D. C. S. Compton 54, C. L. McCool 5-109) lost to Australia 659-8 dec (S. G. Barnes 234, D. G. Bradman 234) by an inns & 33 runs.

14th Match: v New South Wales Country XI (Newcastle)   Dec 21, 23.
M.C.C. 395 (W. R. Hammond 142, L. B. Fishlock 110, W. J. Edrich 59, M. Hinman 5-92) & 146-6 (D. C. S. Compton 75*) drew with N.S.W. Country XI 202.*

15th Match: v New South Wales Southern Districts (Canberra)   Dec 27, 28.
M.C.C. 465-8 dec (L. Hutton 133, C. Washbrook 115, D. C. S. Compton 76) drew with N.S.W. Southern Districts 11-4.

16th Match: v Victorian Country Team (Bendigo)   Dec 30.
Victorian Country 156 (T. P. B. Smith 6-43) lost to M.C.C. 200-4 (W. J. Edrich 62).

17th March: v Australia (Melbourne)   Jan 1, 2, 3, 4, 6, 7.
Australia 365 (C. L. McCool 104*, D. G. Bradman 79) & 536 (A. R. Morris 155, R. R. Lindwall 100, D. Tallon 92) drew with England 351 (W. J. Edrich 89, C. Washbrook 62, N. W. D. Yardley 61) & 310-7 (C. Washbrook 112, N. W. D. Yardley 53*).

18th Match: v Combined XI (Hobart)   Jan 10, 11, 13.
M.C.C. 278 (W. J. Edrich 82, L. B. Fishlock 52, A. V. Bedser 51) & 353-9 dec (D. C. S. Compton 124, J. Hardstaff jun 60, J. T. Ikin 50, J. Laver 5-26) drew with Combined XI 374 (K. R. Miller 70, J. Gardiner 94, S. G. Barnes 57) & 145-2 (I. W. Johnson 80*).*

19th Match: v Tasmania (Launceston)   Jan 15, 16, 17.
M.C.C. 467-5 dec (D. C. S. Compton 163, J. Hardstaff jun 155, L. Hutton 51) drew with Tasmania 103 & 129-6.

20th Match: v South Australia (Adelaide)   Jan 24, 25, 27, 28.
M.C.C. 577 (W. R. Hammond 188, Jas Langridge 100, L. Hutton 88, L. B. Fishlock 57) & 152-2 (L. Hutton 77) drew with S. Australia 443 (R. A. Hamence 145, R. James 85, P. L. Ridings 77).*

21st Match: v Australia (Adelaide)   Jan 31, Feb 1, 3, 4, 5, 6.
England 460 (D. C. S. Compton 147, L. Hutton 94, J. Hardstaff jun 67, C. Washbrook 65) & 340-8 dec (D. C. S. Compton 103*, L. Hutton 76) drew with Australia 487 (K. R. Miller 141*, A. R. Morris 122, A. L. Hassett 78, I. W. Johnson 52) & 215-1 (A. R. Morris 124*, D. G. Bradman 56*).

22nd Match: v Victoria Country XI (Ballarat)   Feb 11, 12.
Country XI 268 (D. Brown 62) & 70-5 drew with M.C.C. 288 (P. A. Gibb 69, T. G. Evans 82, D. C. S. Compton 61).

23rd Match: v Victoria (Melbourne)   Feb 14, 15, 17, 18.
M.C.C. 355 (D. C. S. Compton 93, J. T. Ikin 71, L. B. Fishlock 51) & 118 (G. E. Tribe 6-49) drew with Victoria 327 (A. L. Hassett 126, R. N. Harvey 69, G. E. Tribe 60).

24th Match: v New South Wales (Sydney)   Feb 21, 22, 24, 25.
N.S.W. 342 (E. W. Lukeman 70, D. K. Carmody 65, T. P. B. Smith 9-121) & 262-6 dec (R. K. Kissell 80) drew with M.C.C. 266 (D. C. S. Compton 75) & 205-3 (D. C. S. Compton 74*, L. Hutton 72).*

25th Match: v Australia (Sydney)   Feb 28, March 1, 3, 4, 5.
England 280 (L. Hutton 122*, W. J. Edrich 60, R. R. Lindwall 7-63) & 186 (D. C. S. Compton 76, C. L. McCool 5-44) lost to Australia 253 (S. G. Barnes 71, A. R. Morris 57, D. V. P.Wright 7-105) & 214-5 (D. G. Bradman 63) by 5 wkts.

26th Match: v Wellington (Wellington)   March 10, 11, 12.
M.C.C. 176 (C. Washbrook 68) & 271-6 dec (C. Washbrook 133, R. McK. Murray 5-85) beat Wellington 160 (F. R. Crawford 50, W. Voce 6-38) & 73 by 214 runs.

27th Match: v Otago (Dunedin)   March 15, 17, 18.
Otago 340 (B. Sutcliffe 197) & 262-7 dec (B. Sutcliffe 128) drew with M.C.C. 385-6 dec (N. W. D. Yardley 126, J. T. Ikin 102, T. G. Evans 101) & 216-9 (T. G. Evans 64).*

28th Match: v New Zealand (Christchurch)   March 21, 22, 24, 25.
New Zealand 345-9 dec (W. A. Hadles 116, B. Sutcliffe 58) drew with England 265-7 dec (W. R. Hammond 79, J. Cowie 6-83).

29th Match: v Auckland (Auckland)   March 28, 29.
M.C.C. 240 (D. C. S. Compton 97) beat Auckland 85 (D. C. S. Compton 7-36) & 90 by an inns & 65 runs.*

Bruce Dooland takes a low catch to dismiss Hammond off his own bowling in the third Test at Melbourne in 1946-47.

had completed an innings in the fourth Test at Adelaide, and with Compton going on to complete a century in both innings, Hammond was able to declare setting Australia 314 in 195 minutes – Bradman declined the challenge.

Fibrositis kept Hammond out of the fifth Test, Yardley leading England. Some splendid bowling by Wright gave England a first innings lead, but England were unable to press home their advantage due to the illness of Hutton, who had had to retire in the first innings. Australia won a well-fought match by five wickets and the Ashes by three matches to nil.

The M.C.C. went by flying boat to New Zealand, where four matches, including a rain-soaked Test were played. The team flew back to England calling at Bowen, Darwin, Surabaya, Singapore, Rangoon, Calcutta, Karachi, Bahrein, Basra, Cairo, Marseilles and finally Poole Harbour – the whole journey taking seven and a half days. The heavy baggage and three of the team travelled in the *Largs Castle* and did not participate in the New Zealand part of the tour.

Financially the tour was a great success with a profit of some £50,000. Each professional received £550 plus bonus, which in most cases exceeded £200.

Weak bowling and some poor fielding was the main cause of England's failure, but Hammond failed as a batsman and his captaincy came in for much adverse criticism. The two serious injuries of the tour were to Fishlock and Langridge. Hutton, Compton (after a poor start), Edrich and Washbrook were all successful batsmen – but it is only necessary to state that Yardley's 10 wickets at 37.20 runs each put him at the top of the bowling

averages, to show how the attack fared. Lindwall, Miller, Toshack and McCool all had bowling averages under 30 for Australia. Bradman easily topped the Australian batting, though Miller, Barnes and Morris each averaged over 70. All round Australia were much stronger than the English team expected and thoroughly deserved their victory.

1947-48: M.C.C. fail to win a match in West Indies

The M.C.C. sent a weak team out to the West Indies in 1947-48 and the slim chance it had of success vanished under an epidemic of illness and injury. Compton, Edrich, Hutton and Washbrook, the four principal English batsmen of the 1947 series against South Africa, declined to go, as did Bedser and Wright and indeed the England captain, Yardley.

G. O. B. Allen was brought out of virtual retirement (he had two County Championship innings for Middlesex in 1947) to lead the side, who were S. C. Griffith (Sussex), K. Cranston (Lancs), D. Brookes (Northants), H. J. Butler (Notts), T. G. Evans (Kent), J. Hardstaff (Notts), R. Howorth (Worcs), J. T. Ikin (Lancs), J. C. Laker (Surrey), W. Place (Lancs), J. D. B. Robertson (Middx), G. A. Smithson (Yorks), M. F. Tremlett (Som) and J. H. Wardle (Yorks).

The side left England aboard the s.s. *Tettela* on 23 December 1947. The voyage was a rough one and the ship docked in Bridgetown, Barbados three days late, which meant that the side had only two days in find their landlegs before the first match. Allen had strained a leg whilst on board ship and had to miss the first three games—starting an injury list that never ended. Both matches against Barbados were high scoring draws, though rain prevented a possible M.C.C. win in the second. Butler pulled a leg muscle in the first game, so for the third match, which was the first Test, England were without their captain and their principal fast bowler. West Indies reached 244 for 3 on the opening day, then rain and a brilliant spell from Laker whipped the rest out for 52. Hardstaff with 98 kept England in the game, but in their second innings West Indies greatly improved, setting England to make 395 to win on a sticky wicket—more rain arrived and the match was drawn.

Travelling on to Trinidad, the team played another high-scoring draw, the only point to note being that Hardstaff, who was again the highest scorer, tore a hamstring while fielding and was out of the side for the next month. In the return against Trinidad, Butler returned and bowled out the locals for 185, then went down with malaria. Place also joined the injury list and the team went into the second Test with only 12 fit men. Griffith, the reserve wicket-keeper, was brought into the team as a batsman and hit the first first-class hundred of his career, saving the side from collapse. West Indies found few terrors in the English bowling and in England's second innings Robertson batted grimly to prevent a home win.

Because of the injury problem, Allen cabled to England and Hutton arrived as a reinforcement for the first match against British Guiana—it was just as well, since the side was down to ten

1947-48: M.C.C. to the West Indies

Batting Averages

	M	I	NO	R	HS	Avge	100	c/s
L. Hutton (Yorks)	5	10	1	578	138	64.22	2	6
S. C. Griffith (Sussex)	6	9	2	314	140	44.85	1	5/1
J. Hardstaff jun (Notts)	8	14	0	619	105	44.21	1	4
D. Brookes (Northts)	3	5	0	182	108	36.40	1	1
W. Place (Lancs)	8	15	3	423	120*	35.25	2	1
K. Cranston (Lancs)	10	18	1	549	84	32.29	0	3
J. D. B. Robertson (Middx)	11	21	1	625	133	31.25	1	9
G. O. B. Allen (Middx)	6	11	2	262	77	29.11	0	5
R. Howorth (Worcs)	11	18	4	380	67*	27.14	0	1
J. T. Ikin (Lancs)	10	15	1	303	65	21.64	0	8
T. G. Evans (Kent)	9	15	1	300	53	21.42	0	14/3
J. C. Laker (Surrey)	8	12	2	212	55	21.20	0	4
G. A. Smithson (Yorks)	7	12	1	186	42	16.90	0	0
H. J. Butler (Notts)	4	5	3	33	15*	16.50	0	1
J. H. Wardle (Yorks)	6	8	1	77	35	11.00	0	2
M. F. Tremlett (Som)	9	13	3	80	36	8.00	0	1

Bowling Averages

	O	M	R	W	Avge	BB	5i
J. C. Laker	388.5	116	973	36	27.02	7-103	3
H. J. Butler	91	19	281	10	28.10	3-32	0
R. Howorth	518.3	149	1169	30	38.96	6-124	1
G. O. B. Allen	66	7	280	6	46.67	2-82	0
K. Cranston	247	67	651	12	54.25	4-78	0
M. F. Tremlett	281	70	700	10	70.00	3-62	0
J. H. Wardle	171.5	34	441	6	73.50	3-65	0
J. T. Ikin	231	39	685	8	85.62	3-55	0

Also bowled: J. Hardstaff jun 16-2-73-1; J. D. B. Robertson 15-3-47-0; L. Hutton 5-1-20-0; T. G. Evans 3-1-8-0; G. A. Smithson 2-0-11-0.

fit men. Hutton hit 138 in his first innings and was 62 not out when Cranston declared in the second.

For the third Test, Goddard, the West Indies captain, bowled brilliantly to dismiss England for 111 and took his side to an easy win by 7 wickets.

The final section of the tour was in Jamaica. There were two drawn matches against the colony before the fourth Test. Allen won the toss. Hutton and Robertson began with an opening stand of 129, but the rest were unable to muster another hundred and as Weekes made a splendid hundred to give West Indies a lead of 263, England had little hope of even a draw. In the event the match was lost by 10 wickets. So the tour ended without a win.

Only Laker of the M.C.C. bowlers came out of the tour with much credit, and in the Tests Robertson, Hutton and Hardstaff were the ones who really offered England much hope. For the West Indies, the emergence of Worrell and Weekes was the prime factor of the Test series.

1947-48: M.C.C. to West Indies

1st Match: v Barbados (Bridgetown) Jan 9, 10, 12, 13.
M.C.C. 334 (R. Howorth 67*, J. D. B. Robertson 51, D. Brookes 50, E. A. V. Williams 5-73) & 260-6 (J. D. B. Robertson 90, W. Place 55) drew with Barbados 514-4 dec (A. M. Taylor 161, C. L. Walcott 120, E. D. Weekes 118*, J. D. C. Goddard 52).

2nd Match: v Barbados (Bridgetown) Jan 15, 16, 17, 19.
Barbados 243-6 dec (G. M. Carew 81, J. Lucas 56) & 182-8 (J. C. Laker 5-76) drew with M.C.C. 358 (D. Brookes 108, J. Hardstaff jun 105).

3rd Match: v West Indies (Bridgetown) Jan 21, 22, 23, 24, 26.
West Indies 296 (G. E. Gomez 86, J. B. Stollmeyer 78, J. C. Laker 7-103) & 351-9 dec (R. J. Christiani 99, E. A. V. Williams 72, W. Ferguson 56, R. Howorth 6-124) drew with England 253 (J. Hardstaff jun 98, J. D. B. Robertson 80) & 86-4 (J. D. B. Robertson 51*).

4th Match: v Trinidad (Port of Spain) Jan 29, 30, 31, Feb 2.
Trinidad 481-4 dec (G. E. Gomez 178*, R. Tang Choon 103, A. G. Genteaume 101) & 101-0 dec (K. Trestrail 53*) drew with M.C.C. 418 (J. Hardstaff jun 92, K. Cranston 82, J. T. Ikin 65, T. G. Evans 53) & 80-3.

5th Match: v Trinidad (Port of Spain) Feb 4, 5, 6, 7.
M.C.C. 305 (G. O. B. Allen 77, K. Cranston 53) & 252-6 dec (W. Place 120*) drew with Trinidad 185 & 322-7 (A. G. Ganteaume 90, D. St. E. Atkinson 83*).

6th Match: v West Indies (Port of Spain) Feb 11, 12, 13, 14, 16.
England 362 (S. C. Griffith 140, J. C. Laker 55, W. Ferguson 5-137) & 275 (J. D. B. Robertson 133, W. Ferguson 6-92) drew with West Indies 497 (A. G. Ganteaume 112, G. M. Carew 107, F. M. M. Worrall 97, G. E. Gomez 62) & 72-3.

7th Match: v British Guiana (Georgetown) Feb 19, 20, 21, 23.
M.C.C. 332 (L. Hutton 138, K. Cranston 73) & 191-6 dec (L. Hutton 62*, J. Trim 5-36) drew with British Guiana 296 (H. P. Bayley 113, J. C. Laker 5-74) & 76-1.

8th Match: v British Guiana (Georgetown) Feb 25, 26, 27, 28.
No play due to rain.

9th Match: v West Indies (Georgetown) March 3, 4, 5, 6.
West Indies 297-8 dec (F. M. M. Worrell 131*, R. J. Christiani 51) & 78-3 beat England 111 (J. D. C. Goddard 5-31) & 263 (J. Hardstaff jun 63, W. Ferguson 5-116) by 7 wkts.

10th Match: v Jamaica (Sabina Pk, Kingston) March 15, 16, 17, 18.
Jamaica 344-7 dec (K. R. Rickards 112*, G. A. Headley 65, O. Cunningham 57, A. E. McKenzie 51) & 233-4 dec (C. Bonitto 100, J. K. Holt 87) drew with M.C.C. 278 (K. Cranston 84, J. Hardstaff jun 69) & 88-3.

11th Match: v Jamaica (Melbourne Pk, Kingston) March 20, 22, 23, 24.
M.C.C. 313 (L. Hutton 128, S. C. Griffiths 51, I. Iffla 5-90) & 221-7 dec (J. Hardstaff jun 68) drew with Jamaica 258 (C. Bonitto 57, F. M. M. Worrell 52) & 178-3 (F. M. M. Worrell 106*).

12th Match: v West Indies (Sabina Pk, Kingston) March 27, 29, 30, 31, April 1.
England 227 (J. D. B. Robertson 64, L. Hutton 56, H. H. H. Johnson 5-41) & 336 (W. Place 107, J. Hardstaff jun 64, L. Hutton 60, H. H. H. Johnson 5-55) lost to West Indies 490 (E. D. Weekes 141, W. Ferguson 75, K. R. Rickards 67) & 76-0 by 10 wkts.

1948-49: last man Gladwin wins Test with leg-bye in South Africa

Following the disastrous tour of 1947-48, the M.C.C. Selection and Planning Sub-Committee deliberated on the future policy regarding International tours and in August 1948 issued a report. The M.C.C. stated that they could only accept responsibility for overseas tours if the County Committees gave their whole-hearted support, if the M.C.C. were allowed to decide whether or not the status of the tour was sufficient to permit Test Matches, if the remuneration to professionals was increased to allow for the loss of possible winter earnings and if in South Africa, West Indies and India, the host country guaranteed the M.C.C. against financial loss. It was also maintained that official tours should not take place every year and to this end the proposed 1949-50 tour to India was cancelled.

For the tour to South Africa in 1948-49, the M.C.C. were able to select England's strongest side. The two major absentees were the England captain, Yardley, and Edrich. The team which left England on 7 October aboard the *Durban Castle* was F. G. Mann

1948-49: M.C.C. to South Africa

1st Match: v Western Province (Cape Town)   Oct 29, 30, Nov 1.
W. Province 386-4 dec (O. E. Wynne 108, O. Newton-Thompson 78, J. E. Cheetham 68*, H. G. Owen-Smith 65*) & 88-4 dec lost to M.C.C. 357-5 dec (F. G. Mann 112, J. F. Crapp 83, T. G. Evans*) & 118-1 (C. Washbrook 50*) by 9 wkts.

2nd Match: v Country Districts XI (Robertson)   Nov 3, 4.
Country Districts 115 & 95 (R. O. Jenkins 6-47) lost to M.C.C. 310-5 dec (L. Hutton 81, C. H. Palmer 76*) by an inns & 100 runs.

3rd Match: v Cape Province (Cape Town)   Nov 6, 8, 9.
Cape Province 225 (O. E. Wynne 105) & 323 (J. E. Cheetham 94, R. G. Draper 56, R. O. Jenkins 5-87) lost to M.C.C. 456 (L. Hutton 125, D. C. S. Compton 121, R. O. Jenkins 75*) & 93-0 (L. Hutton 62*) by 10 wkts.

4th Match: v Griqualand West (Kimberley)   Nov 13, 15, 16.
M.C.C. 542-4 dec (C. Washbrook 86, D. C. S. Compton 150*, R. T. Simpson 91, A. J. Watkins 55, F. G. Mann 50) beat Griqualand West 258 (C. Helfrich 71, R. O. Jenkins 5-88) & 212 (D. V. P. Wright 5-61) by an inns & 72 runs.

5th Match: v Orange Free State (Bloemfontein)   Nov 19, 20, 22.
M.C.C. 449-7 dec (L. Hutton 134, J. F. Crapp 127*, A. V. Bedser 77*) & 41-1 beat O.F.S. 251 (E. Warner 55, R. O. Jenkins 5-76) & 238 (R. O. Jenkins 7-94) by 9 wkts.

6th Match: v Natal (Durban)   Nov 26, 27, 28.
M.C.C. 391-9 dec (D. C. S. Compton 106, J. F. Crapp 62, L. Hutton 61, C. N. McCarthy 5-110) & 129-6 (L. Hutton 78) drew with Natal 373 (O. C. Dawson 83, L. W. Payn 82, A. D. Nourse 72).

7th Match: v N-E. Transvaal (Benoni)   Dec 3, 4.
N-E. Transvaal 168 (K. J. Funston 65) & 113 (R. O. Jenkins 7-55) lost to M.C.C. 484-4 dec (D. C. S. Compton 300, R. T. Simpson 130*) by an inns & 203 runs.

8th Match: v Combined Transvaal XI (Pretoria)   Dec 7, 8.
M.C.C. 483-4 dec (R. T. Simpson 145, C. Washbrook 144, C. H. Palmer 69*. R. O. Jenkins 55*) drew with Combined Transvaal 151 (L. Sadler 53, R. O. Jenkins 5-71) & 140-5.

9th Match: v (Johannesburg)   Dec 10, 11, 13.
M.C.C. 513-7 dec (L. Hutton 174, D. C. S. Compton 84, T. G. Evans 77*, A. J. Watkins 61, R. T. Simpson 57) drew with Transvaal 560 (D. W. Begbie 154, A. Melville 92, T. A. Harris 98).

10th Match: v South Africa (Durban)   Dec 16, 17, 18, 20.
South Africa 161 & 219 (W. W. Wade 63) lost to England 253 (L. Hutton 83, D. C. S. Compton 72, N. B. F. Mann 6-59) & 128-8 (C. N. McCarthy 6-43) by 2 wkts.

11th Match: v Natal Country Districts (Ladysmith)   Dec 22, 23.
Country Districts 131 & 202 (M. F. Tremlett 108*) & 56-4 by 6 wkts.
278-7 dec (M. F. Tremlett 108*) & 56-4 by 6 wkts.

12th Match: v South Africa (Johannesburg)   Dec 27, 28, 29, 30.
England 608 (C. Washbrook 195, L. Hutton 158, D. C. S. Compton 114, J. F. Crapp 56) drew with South Africa 315 (B. Mitchell 86, W. W. Wade 85) & 270-2 (E. A. B. Rowan 156*, A. D. Nourse 56*).

13th Match: v South Africa (Cape Town)   Jan 1, 3, 4, 5.
England 308 (C. Washbrook 74, A. M. B. Rowan 5-80) & 276-3 dec (L. Hutton 87, A. J. Watkins 64*, J. F. Crapp 54, D. C. S. Compton 51*) drew with South Africa (B. Mitchell 120, A. D. Nourse 112, O. E. Wynne 50, D. C. S. Compton 5-70) & 142-4.

14th Match: v Eastern Province (Port Elizabeth)   Jan 8, 10, 11.
M.C.C. 450-9 dec (C. H. Palmer 116, D. C. S. Compton 108, A. J. Watkins 83) & 353-3 (J. F. Crapp 103*, F. G. Mann 80, R. T. Simpson 67, C. H. Palmer 57) drew with E. Province 397 (D. Dimbleby 87, J. H. B. Waite 80, K. G. Dimbleby 61).

15th Match: v Border (East London)   Jan 16, 17, 18.
Border 156 (R. O. Jenkins 5-60) & 89 (J. A. Young 6-38) lost to M.C.C. 272-9 dec (J. F. Crapp 86, C. H. Palmer 65) by an inns & 27 runs.

16th Match: v Transvaal (Johannesburg)   Jan 21, 22, 23.
M.C.C. 244-9 dec (L. Hutton 84, R. T. Simpson 54) & 40-0 drew with Transvaal 254 (B. Mitchell 60).

17th Match: v Rhodesia (Bulawayo)   Jan 30, 31, Feb 1.
Rhodesia 174 & 166 drew with M.C.C. 193 (D. C. S. Compton 60, E. S. Newson 5-54) & 117-2.

18th Match: v Rhodesia (Salisbury)   Feb 4, 5, 7.
M.C.C. 228 (L. Hutton 79, S. H. Martin 6-49) drew with Rhodesia 61 (A. V. Bedser 6-17) & 191-5 (C. Pretorius 75).

19th Match: v South Africa (Johannesburg)   Feb 13, 14, 15, 16.
England 379 (A. J. Watkins 111, C. Washbrook 97, J. F. Crapp 51, C. N.McCarthy 5-114) & 253-7 dec (L. Hutton 123) drew with South Africa 257-9 dec (A. D. Nourse 129*, W. W. Wade 54) & 194-4 (E. A. B. Rowan 86*, K. G. Viljoen 63).

20th Match: v A Natal XI (Pietermaritzburg)   Feb 19, 21, 22.
Natal XI 288 (A. D. Nourse 117, I. de Gersigny 77) & 257-6 dec (A. D. Nourse 76) drew with M.C.C. 276 (M. F. Tremlett 105, C. H. Palmer 80, D. Dinkleman 5-113) & 260-4 (D. C. S. Compton 141, M. F. Tremlett 63*).

21st Match: v Natal (Durban)   Feb 25, 26, 28.
Natal 217 (J. A. Young 5-25) & 166 (D. Dowling 50, D. V. P. Wright 7-54) drew with M.C.C. 237 (R. T. Simpson 119*, L. W. Payn 5-59) & 6-0.

22nd Match: v South Africa (Port Elizabeth)   March 5, 7, 8, 9.
South Africa 379 (W. W. Wade 125, B. Mitchell 99, A. D. Nourse 73) & 187-3 dec (B. Mitchell 56) lost to England 395 (F. G. Mann 136*, A. M. B. Rowan 5-167) & 174-7 by 3 wkts.

23rd Match: v Combined Universities (Cape Town)   March 12, 14, 15.
M.C.C. 477 (C. Washbrook 153, D. C. S. Compton 125, M. F. Tremlett 56) beat Universities 274 (B. Crews 104, H. Birrell 56, L. Wiley 50) & 151 (D. C. S. Compton 6-62) by an inns & 52 runs.

(Middx) (capt), C. H. Palmer (Worcs), R. T. Simpson (Notts), S. C. Griffith (Sussex) and the professionals J. A. Young (Middx), R. O. Jenkins (Worcs), J. F. Crapp (Gloucs), A. J. Watkins (Glam), T. G. Evans (Kent), D. V. P. Wright (Kent), C. Gladwin (Derbys), A. V. Bedser (Surrey), M. F. Tremlett (Somerset), C. Washbrook (Lancs), L. Hutton (Yorks) and D. C. S. Compton (Middx) with Col M. A. Green as manager.

The M.C.C. did not have its customary easy start to the tour, for Western Province hit 386 for 4 and then declared. M.C.C. matched this and in the second innings Cheetham generously declared again to set M.C.C. 118 in 55 minutes, a challenge the tourists readily accepted. Natal and Transvaal also provided strong opposition and both games were high scoring draws. In between them, Compton hit his record 300 in 181 minutes at Benoni, but the bowling was exceedingly weak and not up to first-class standard.

After all the high scoring, the first Test provided a great contrast, with no individual hundreds and the bowlers generally in command. The game came to a tremendous climax when England needed two to win with two wickets left and three deliveries of the final over remaining. Gladwin actually obtained the winning run off the final ball with a leg-bye.

The second Test, at Johannesburg, was watched on the first day by a record crowd of 35,000 and they saw Hutton and Washbrook put on 359 for the first English wicket – another record. It was soon obvious however that the pitch was too easy to produce anything but a draw, so the bowlers had a thankless task. Moving straight back to Cape Town for the third Test, England batted first on an unexpectedly tricky wicket, but the home bowlers failed to exploit it to the full and though South Africa gained a lead on first innings, the absence of the left-arm spinner, N. B. F. Mann, through injury, allowed England to build a good second innings score and draw the game.

The team went up to play two matches against Rhodesia and also make a trip to the Victoria Falls, prior to the fourth Test. Although the pitch at Johannesburg had been improved a little in favour of the bowlers since the second Test, the result was another draw. The England captain declared to set South Africa 376 in 270 minutes, but the home side made no attempt to hit off the runs.

The final Test at Port Elizabeth proved the reverse of the previous game. This time Nourse declared to set England 172 in 95 minutes. England went for the runs, despite wickets falling fast and took the match with three wickets in hand.

Sailing home in the *Stirling Castle*, the team landed at South-

1948-49: M.C.C. to South Africa

Batting Averages

	M	I	NO	R	HS	Avge	100	c/s
D. C. S. Compton (Middx)	17	26	5	1781	300	84.80	8	25
L. Hutton (Yorks)	14	21	1	1477	174	73.85	5	8
R. T. Simpson (Notts)	12	19	5	788	130*	56.28	2	5
C. Washbrook (Lancs)	15	23	2	1124	195	53.52	3	4
J. F. Crapp (Glos)	14	19	3	820	127*	51.25	2	7
C. H. Palmer (Worcs)	11	18	4	478	116	34.14	1	1
C. Gladwin (Derbys)	16	16	7	289	52*	32.11	0	4
M. F. Tremlett (Som)	10	10	1	286	105	31.77	1	5
F. G. Mann (Middx)	19	24	2	673	136*	30.59	2	10
A. J. Watkins (Glam)	15	18	2	474	111	29.62	1	18
T. G. Evans (Kent)	11	14	4	288	77*	28.80	0	13/11
R. O. Jenkins (Worcs)	13	12	2	268	75*	26.80	0	6
A. V. Bedser (Surrey)	14	17	3	271	77*	19.35	0	8
J. A. Young (Middx)	14	8	4	53	22*	13.25	0	5
D. V. P. Wright (Kent)	15	11	4	91	25*	13.00	0	3
S. C. Griffith (Sussex)	10	10	2	47	13	5.87	0	21/5

Bowling Averages

	O	M	R	W	Avge	BB	5i
C. H. Palmer	30	7	64	5	12.80	3-7	0
R. O. Jenkins	408.7	65	1508	71	21.24	7-55	6
C. Gladwin	437.1	131	945	42	22.50	4-27	0
J. A. Young	430.1	123	1014	41	24.73	6-38	2
M. F. Tremlett	103	16	287	11	26.09	2-7	0
A. V. Bedser	475.1	97	1273	45	28.28	6-17	1
D. V. P. Wright	378.1	53	1544	51	30.27	7-54	2
D. C. S. Compton	275.4	40	1051	30	35.03	6-62	2
A. J. Watkins	96	12	352	4	88.00	2-16	0

Also bowled: L. Hutton 1-0-7-0; F. G. Mann 1-0-8-0.

Newlands cricket ground, Cape Town, 29 October 1948 and captain F. G. Mann leads out a strong M.C.C. side to play Western Province in the first match of the tour of South Africa, 1948-49. From left: C. Washbrook, L. Hutton, C. Gladwin, F. G. Mann, R. T. Simpson, T. G. Evans and D. C. S. Compton.

ampton on 1 April. Although the side had been undefeated on tour and won the rubber by two matches to nil, the difference between the two teams was marginal – victory by a hair's breadth by England in the first Test put South Africa at a disadvantage and Nourse took a tremendous gamble in the fifth Test, which did not pay off. The most noteworthy point on the tour was the fact that several of the Provincial teams put up great fights against the tourists – in most previous tours, only Transvaal were worthy opponents.

Hutton, Washbrook and Compton all had good records, but the surprise of the visit was the bowling of Jenkins, whose leg breaks proved most effective.

1950-51: Australia still on top in post-war Tests

The major problem which faced both the M.C.C. and the press selectors concerning the proposed visit to Australia in 1950-51 was that of the captaincy. Both Yardley and Mann declined the invitation and after much speculation F. R. Brown was chosen – he had led England in two Tests against New Zealand in the summer of 1949, but Yardley had resumed the leadership in the initial Tests against West Indies in 1950. The other two difficulties concerned Compton, whose knee injury was making him doubtful, and Washbrook, who declined the original invitation.

The team that sailed on the *Stratheden* from Tilbury on 14 September was F. R. Brown (Northants) (capt), D. C. S. Compton (Middx), R. T. Simpson (Notts), T. E. Bailey (Essex), J. G. Dewes (Middx), D. S. Sheppard (Sussex), J. J. Warr (Middx), L. Hutton (Yorks), D. B. Close (Yorks), A. V. Bedser (Surrey), W. E. Hollies (Warwicks), D. V. P. Wright (Kent), A. J. W. McIntyre (Surrey), T. G. Evans (Kent), R. Berry (Lancs) and W. G. A. Parkhouse (Glamorgan) with Brig M. A. Green and

Brian Close, seen here bowling at Lord's in 1949, was the surprise choice for the tour to Australia in 1950-51. He was only 19 years old and already England's youngest Test player.

J. A. Nash as joint-managers. By a special arrangement C. Washbrook (Lancs) was allowed to fly out later and join the side in Australia. The two notable omissions were Edrich and Tattersall, but the press also took the selectors to task for sending so many young and inexperienced players.

Right *Freddie Brown, M.C.C.'s captain, making a farewell speech aboard the Stratheden at Tilbury on 14 September 1950, as the team left to tour Australia. From the left, T. E. Bailey is talking to J. G. Dewes, then come D. S. Sheppard, J. J. Warr and L. Hutton, with D. B. Close on Brown's left.*

Below *Cyril Washbrook was allowed to fly out later to join the 1950-51 tour of Australia. Here he hits Colin McCool to the fence for four in the match with Queensland at Brisbane.*

Below right *On the last day of the first Test of the 1950-51 tour at Brisbane, D. V. P. Wright snicked a ball from Iverson into his pad, and wicket-keeper Don Tallon comes round to try to take the catch.*

The match against Ceylon, which had had to be omitted in 1946-47, was played again, but unfortunately Hutton damaged a finger while batting and missed the first three games in Australia as a result. The team landed in Fremantle on 9 October and after two warm up games met the Western Australian team on 20 October. The match was drawn very much in favour of the visitors. A sporting declaration led to a win against South Australia, then the match against Victoria was ended by rain with the sides fairly even – the M.C.C. were captained by Compton in this match, Brown being injured, the first time an official M.C.C. team abroad had had a professional at its head. Miller hit a double century and Morris 168 for New South Wales as their score reached 509 for 3 and the M.C.C. bowling looked distinctly thin. The match however was drawn, as was the Queensland game which preceded the first Test. Hasset won the toss and batted – the luck and decision were to govern the match result, for, although England bowled quite brilliantly – Bailey, Brown,

Bedser and Wright all taking credit – and dismissed Australia on a good pitch for 228, the rains then arrived and for the rest of the match the wicket was unplayable. Brown declared at 68 for 7 and Australia collapsed to 32 for 7 in their second innings. England required 193 to win in the final innings. Hutton played a magnificent unbeaten innings of 62, but no one could stay with him and Australia won by 70 runs.

Compton was unable to play in the second Test due to his damaged knee and his absence possibly made the difference between victory and defeat.

For the second time England began by bowling out Australia cheaply, due to the efforts of Bailey and Bedser, though they had assistance from the pitch. England's batting however crumbled and only determination by Brown, Bailey and Evans produced a small first innings lead. Brown, Bailey and Bedser then dismissed Australia for 181, which left England requiring 179 to win. With three days to make the runs, England adopted the 'get them in singles' policy, which immediately gave the bowlers a psychological advantage, and apart from Hutton's 40 in 160 minutes, the English batting gradually faded away.

The return against New South Wales produced a high-scoring draw with Simpson hitting 259 and looking more like the batsman English spectators knew.

The third Test belonged to Iverson. He was an off-spin bowler, with a freakish grip, which meant that the batsman found it very difficult to tell at the moment of delivery what his intentions were. He had arrived in first-class cricket only in the previous season at the age of 34. Although playing in the first two Tests, his real worth was shown in the third. England batted first on a perfect pitch, but Miller produced an exceptional burst of fast bowling and only a moderate score of 290 was attained. Miller then went on to hit 145 not out and place Australia 136 runs in the lead. In England's second innings the wicket was taking spin and Iverson with an analysis of 19.4-8-27-6 won the match and the Ashes for Australia.

On the final day of the Test, Brown telephoned to England for two bowlers, on the grounds that Bailey and Wright were injured – Bailey had fractured his right thumb in the game and Wright tore a groin muscle. J. B. Statham and R. Tattersall, both of Lancashire, were flown out to join the side in time to play in an up-country game on 24 January.

Tattersall was drafted into the team for the fourth Test which began ten days later. Australia batted first and a double century by Morris gave them a total of 371 on a good wicket. England's batting, except for Hutton, who remained unbeaten on 156, collapsed and when Australia piled up 403 in their second innings, England needed an impossible 503 to win. Simpson made the highest score of 61, but the visitors never looked like approaching the target.

The fifth Test provided England with their first post-war victory. Brown and Bedser began by dismissing Australia for 217, then England, through Hutton and Simpson, gained a lead of 103 – a last wicket stand of 74 between Simpson and Tattersall giving England an unexpected bonus. Bedser and Wright bowled out Australia cheaply in the second innings, leaving only 95 for victory, of which Hutton made 60 – it was an appropriate end for the splendid batting the Yorkshireman had displayed throughout the tour.

The four matches in New Zealand produced three wins and were a somewhat light-hearted anti-climax to the battle against Australia.

The team flew home via Fiji, Honolulu, San Francisco and New York, the whole journey from Auckland to London Airport taking four and a half days.

England lost the series against Australia due to the lack of experienced middle order batsmen, a fact magnified by Compton's complete failure. Hutton was the best batsman on either side and Bedser the best bowler. Australia felt the lack of Bradman and relied very much on Hassett and Miller. Lindwall was not quite the menace he had been in England in 1948, but now he and Miller had Iverson to baffle any surviving batsmen.

1950-51: M.C.C. to Ceylon, Australia and New Zealand

1st Match: v Ceylon (Colombo) (One Day) Oct 1.
M.C.C. 279-6 dec (A. J. W. McIntyre 104) drew with Ceylon 99-5.

2nd Match: v Western Australian Country XI (Northam) (One Day) Oct 14.
M.C.C. 329-5 dec (D. S. Sheppard 117, W. G. A. Parkhouse 86) drew with W. A. Country XI 113-7.

3rd Match: v Western Australian Colts XI (Perth) Oct 16, 17.
W. A. Colts XI 103 & 117 lost to M.C.C. 369-4 dec (R. T. Simpson 109, W. G. A. Parkhouse 79, D. C. S. Compton 76, D. S. Sheppard 57) by an inns & 149 runs.*

4th Match: v Western Australia (Perth) Oct 20, 21, 23, 24.
M.C.C. 434-9 dec (D. B. Close 108, D. C. S. Compton 106, J. G. Dewes 94) & 121-3 dec drew with W. Australia 236 (W. Langdon 60, D. K. Carmody 59, D. V. P. Wright 7-60) & 207-4 (T. Outridge 92).*

5th Match: v South Australia (Adelaide) Oct 27, 28, 30, 31.
S. Australia 350 (R. A. Hamence 114) & 185-3 dec (L. Duldig 70, N. Dansie 64) lost to M.C.C. 351-9 dec (L. Hutton 126, R. T. Simpson 119) & 186-3 (R. T. Simpson 69, C. Washbrook 63) by 7 wkts.*

6th Match: v Victoria (Melbourne) Nov 3, 4, 6, 8.
M.C.C. 306-9 dec (D. C. S. Compton 107) & 79-4 drew with Victoria 331 (R. Howard 139, D. T. Ring 75, T. E. Bailey 5-84).

7th Match: v New South Wales (Sydney) Nov 10, 11, 13, 14.
N.S.W. 509-3 dec (K. R. Miller 214, A. R. Morris 168, J. W. Burke 80) & 140-2 dec (J. K. Burke 60*, J. R. Moroney 53) drew with M.C.C. 339 (L. Hutton 112, D. C. S. Compton 92, C. Washbrook 50, F. F. Johnston 6-100) & 143-2 (C. Washbrook 53*).*

8th Match: v New South Wales Country XI (Newcastle) Nov 17, 18.
N.S.W. Country XI 169 (R. G. Beattie 69, W. E. Hollies 5-39) drew with M.C.C. 142 (J. G. Dewes 71, J. Bull 6-24).

9th Match: v New South Wales Northern Districts (Lismore) Nov 20, 21.
M.C.C. 274 (R. T. Simpson 66, D. S. Sheppard 52, J. G. Dewes 50) drew with Northern Districts 156 & 55-2.

10th Match: v Queensland (Brisbane) Nov 24, 25, 27, 28.
Queensland 305 (A. H. Carrigan 100, K. A. Archer 63, E. A. Toovey 58) & 5-1 drew with M.C.C. 291 (J. G. Dewes 117, C. Washbrook 81, L. J. Johnson 6-66).*

11th Match: v Australia (Brisbane) Dec 1, 2, 4, 5.
Australia 228 (R. N. Harvey 74) & 32-7 dec beat England 68-7 dec (W. A. Johnston 5-35) & 122 (L. Hutton 62*) by 70 runs.

12th Match: v Queensland Country XI (Toowoomba) Dec 8, 9.
M.C.C. 428-6 dec (R. T. Simpson 98, T. G. Evans 94, D. C. S. Compton 92, D. S. Sheppard 72, W. G. A. Parkhouse 57) & 294-7 dec (T. E. Bailey 63, W. G. A. Parkhouse 58) drew with Country XI 220 (T. Allen 85, D. V. P. Wright 5-52).*

13th Match: v Southern Districts of New South Wales (Canberra) Dec 12, 13.
M. C. C. 180 (J. Robinson 5-40) & 281-3 (D. S. Sheppard 105, D. B. Close 105*, L. Hutton 54) drew with Southern Districts 164 (W. Hedditch 52*).*

14th Match: v An Australian XI (Sydney) Dec 15, 16, 18, 19.
Australian XI 526-9 dec (J. W. Burke 128, A. R. Morris 100, K. A. Archer 81, K. R. Miller 62) drew with M.C.C. 321 (D. C. S. Compton 115, W. G. A. Parkhouse 58, A. K. Walker 5-60) & 173-3 (J. G. Dewes 66).*

15th Match: v Australia (Melbourne) Dec 22, 23, 26, 27.
Australia 194 (A. L. Hassett 52) & 181 beat England 197 (F. R. Brown 62) & 150 by 28 runs.

16th Match: v New South Wales (Sydney) Dec 30, Jan 1, 2, 3.
N.S.W. 333 (A. R. Morris 105, K. R. Miller 98, J. H. de Courcy 72) & 130-6 (J. R. Moroney 51*) drew with M.C.C. 553-8 dec (R. T. Simpson 259, L. Hutton 150, W. G. A. Parkhouse 92).*

17th Match: v Australia (Sydney) Jan 5, 6, 8, 9.
England 290 (F. R. Brown 79, L. Hutton 62) & 123 (J. B. Iverson 6-27) lost to Australia 426 (K. R. Miller 145*, I. W. Johnson 77, A. L. Hassett 70) by an inns & 13 runs.

18th Match: v Tasmania (Hobart) Jan 13, 15, 16.
Tasmania 192 & 229 (E. Rodwell 60) lost to M.C.C. 234 (C. Washbrook 61) & 188-1 (D. C. S. Compton 77, D. S. Sheppard 67*) by 9 wkts.*

19th Match: v Combined XI (Launceston) Jan 19, 20, 22.
Combined XI 289 (G. B. Hole 105, J. Laver 59, A. V. Bedser 5-57) & 103 lost to M.C.C. 382-7 dec (D. C. S. Compton 142, C. Washbrook 112) & 13-0 by 10 wkts.

20th Match: v South Australian Country XI (Renmark) Jan 24, 25.
S.A. Country XI 84 (R. Berry 6-36) & 124 lost to M.C.C. 233 (F. R. Brown 77, L. D. Curtiss 9-60) by an inns & 25 runs.

21st Match: v South Australia (Adelaide) Jan 27, 29, 30, 31.
M.C.C. 211 (G. Noblet 5-56) & 220 (L. Hutton 66, S. McLean 5-68) beat S. Australia 126 & 153 (D. V. P. Wright 5-57) by 152 runs.

22nd Match: v Australia (Adelaide) Feb 2, 3, 5, 6, 7, 8.
Australia 371 (A. R. Morris 206) & 403-8 dec (J. W. Burke 101*, K. R. Miller 99, R. N. Harvey 68) beat England 272 (L. Hutton 156*) & 228 (R. T. Simpson 61) by 274 runs.

23rd Match: v Victoria (Melbourne) Feb 10, 12, 13, 14.
Victoria 441 (A. L. Hassett 232, D. T. Ring 74) & 234 (R. N. Harvey 56) drew with M.C.C. 414 (L. Hutton 128, T. E. Bailey 125, D. T. Ring 5-134) & 36-1.

24th Match: v Victorian Country XI (Geelong) Feb 16, 17.
Country XI 217-7 dec (H. Heard 84) drew with M.C.C. did not bat: rain.

25th Match: v Victoria Country Districts (Euroa) Feb 19, 20.
Country Districts 97 drew with M.C.C. 64-0: rain.

26th Match: v Australia (Melbourne) Feb 23, 24, 26, 27, 28.
Australia 217 (A. L. Hassett 92, A. R. Morris 50, A. V. Bedser 5-46, F. R. Brown 5-49) & 197 (G. B. Hole 63, R. N. Harvey 52, A. V. Bedser 5-59) lost to England 320 (R. T. Simpson 156*, L. Hutton 79) & 95-2 (L. Hutton 60*) by 8 wkts.

27th Match: v Auckland (Auckland) March 6, 7, 8.
Auckland 146 (D. V. P. Wright 5-54) & 168 (W. M. Wallace 68, R. Tattersall 5-33) lost to M.C.C. 298-7 dec (D. C. S. Compton 78, L. Hutton 69, J. G. Dewes 61) & 20-0 by 10 wkts.*

28th Match: v Otago (Dunedin) March 10, 12.
M.C.C. 381-8 dec (C. Washbrook 147, D. S. Sheppard 75) beat Otago 83 (R. Tattersall 6-29) & 137 by an inns & 161 runs.

29th Match: v New Zealand (Christchurch) March 17, 19, 20, 21.
New Zealand 417-8 dec (B. Sutcliffe 116, W. M. Wallace 66, J. R. Reid 50, W. A. Hadlee 50) & 46-3 drew with England 550 (T. E. Bailey 134*, R. T. Simpson 81, D. C. S. Compton 79, F. R. Brown 62, C. Washbrook 58, A. M. Moir 6-155).

30th Match: v New Zealand (Wellington) March 24, 26, 27, 28.
New Zealand 125 (D. V. P. Wright 5-48) & 189 (V. J. Scott 60, R. Tattersall 6-44) lost to England 227 (L. Hutton 57) & 91-4 by 6 wkts.

Financially the tour was nothing like as successful as previous M.C.C. visits and the profit amounted to only £3,842–a tenth of that produced in 1946-7–but the rather strained atmosphere between the two sides, which had never really disappeared following the bodyline tour, seemed at last to have gone.

1951: M.C.C. amateur team to Canada

The Canadian Cricket Association invited the M.C.C. to send an amateur team out to Canada in the summer of 1951, the hosts to pay all expenses. The object was to encourage the game, which had suffered a set-back in the 14 years since the previous visit.

The side which sailed from Liverpool on 24 July was R. W. V. Robins (Middx) (capt), M. M. Walford (Somerset), I. P. Campbell (Kent), J. R. Thompson (Warwicks), A. W. H. Mallett (Kent), A. G. Powell (Essex), G. H. Chesterton (Worcs), J. J. Warr (Middx), W. G. Keighley (Yorks), J. N. Bartlett (Sussex), A. McCorquodale (Middx), C. R. D. Rudd (Oxford U), A. H. Brodhurst (Gloucs) and Dr E. K. Scott.

All the matches were played on matting wickets, which were rather against the faster bowlers, but certainly meant that no really appalling pitches were met. The sun shone, and despite the popularity of baseball, the local press gave good coverage.

The two important fixtures were the 'Tests'. In the first at Vancouver some all-round cricket by Robins completely demolished the opposition–the captain took 9 wickets for 34 and scored 64. In the 'Second Test', Canada, due to good batting by T. L. Brierley, the pre-war Glamorgan player, were only just behind on first innings, but fell cheaply when batting a second time.

Robins returned the best bowling figures of the tour and Keighley headed the batting. The side left Canada on the *Empress of France* on 14 September.

1951-52: M.C.C. tour India and Pakistan

Only two of the nineteen cricketers who represented M.C.C. in Australia the previous winter arrived in Bombay aboard the *Chusan* for the tour of the Indian sub-continent. On paper therefore the party hardly represented England's second team, let alone the first. The side was N. D. Howard (Lancs) (capt), D. B. Carr (Derbys), D. V. Brennan (Yorks), R. T. Spooner (Warwicks) and the professionals T. W. Graveney (Gloucs), F. A. Lowson (Yorks), J. D. B. Robertson (Middx), A. J. Watkins (Glam), D. Kenyon (Worcs), A. E. G. Rhodes (Derbys), D. Shackleton (Hants), J. B. Statham (Lancs), M. J. Hilton (Lancs), F. Ridgway (Kent), R. Tattersall (Lancs), C. J. Poole (Notts)–the last named replaced J. T. Ikin, who was not fit enough to make the tour.

Despite the lack of famous players, the team were given a tremendous reception on landing and crowds lined the route from the docks to the Brabourne Stadium, where the team went for practice, prior to the first match. Unfortunately Poole broke a finger whilst in the nets and could not play until December.

After a high-scoring draw against a Universities XI, the team beat Western India by two wickets–a notable victory since the local side was regarded as the strongest in the country.

The first Test was staged in Delhi, where a splendid hundred by Watkins saved the team from defeat, but the tourists were without Graveney, who was ill, and Rhodes. The latter's injury proved so serious that he was sent home and E. Leadbeater of Yorkshire was flown out as a replacement.

The team moved on to Pakistan, where after a drawn match with Punjab, they met Pakistan in the first 'Unofficial Test'. Scoring was painfully slow and it was soon obvious that there would be no definite outcome to the match. A promising 16-year-old, Hanif Mohammad, opened the batting for the home eleven. In the second 'Unofficial Test', England collapsed on coir matting, Fazal Mahmood taking 6 for 40, and though Statham and Shackleton bowled exceptionally well and Graveney bolstered up the second innings with a century, Pakistan won by 4 wickets. The party returned to India for the second Test against that country and after two first innings each of which easily exceeded 400, Ridgway and Watkins suddenly surprised themselves by dismissing India for 208 in the second innings. Time however did not allow England to get the reward they deserved.

In the third Test, England were without Lowson, who damaged a finger, and Poole was brought into the side. The batting was depressingly slow–about 35 runs per hour–and the match was drawn, long before the end. Hilton and Tattersall bowled out India on the first day of the fourth Test for 121–the only time in Tests that the Lancashire spinners really proved their worth. Watkins batted well and when India went cheaply in the second innings, England won by 8 wickets.

Both Central Zone and South Zone were beaten with ease, so

The end of England's first innings in the third Test match in Calcutta on the M.C.C. tour of India, Pakistan and Ceylon in 1951-52. Leadbeater is run out attempting a second run off Mankad. Leadbeater had been flown out as a replacement.

England came to the fifth Test with more confidence than for the previous internationals. The captain however went down with pleurisy and Carr led England for the first time. The tourists made a fair start, reaching 224 for 5 at the close of the first day. The death of George VI meant the cancellation of the second day,

---

1951-52: M.C.C. to India, Pakistan and Ceylon

1st Match: v University of India (Bombay)   Oct 5, 6, 7.
M.C.C. 340 (T. W. Graveney 101, J. D. B. Robertson 58, H. T. Dani 5-79) & 40-0 drew with University 375 (P. Roy 89, R. B. Kenny 86*, H. T. Dani 66).

2nd Match: v Western India (Ahmedabed)   Oct 9, 10, 11.
W. India 164 (G. Kishenchand 65) & 139 (D. K. Gaekwad 66*) lost to M.C.C. 192 (T. W. Graveney 62, J. M. Patel 5-40) & 112-8 (S. Nyalchand 5-36) by 2 wkts.

3rd Match: v Holkar (Indore)   Oct 13, 14, 15.
Holkar 291 (B. B. Nimbalkar 63, H. G. Gaekwad 62*, C. T. Sarwate 59) & 142-5 (C. T. Sarwate 56*) drew with M.C.C. 329 (J. D. B. Robertson 131, F. A. Lowson 70).

4th Match: v Northern India (Amritsar)   Oct 20, 21, 22.
M.C.C. 340 (F. A. Lowson 138, T. W. Graveney 79, M. K. Rajdhan 6-72) & 173-4 (J. D. B. Robertson 105) drew with N. India 209 (L. Amarnath 97*, D. Shackleton 5-36).

5th Match: v National Defence Academy (Dehra Dun) (One Day)   Oct 26.
N.D.A. 80 (A. E. G. Rhodes 5-22) lost to M.C.C. 87-1 (A. J. Watkins 59) by 9 wkts.*

6th Match: v Services XI (Dehra Dun)   Oct 28, 29, 30.
Services XI 167 & 175 (H. R. Adhikari 64) drew with M.C.C. 338-4 dec (T. W. Graveney 101, R. T. Spooner 90, N. D. Howard 51) & 4-0.

7th Match: v India (New Delhi)   Nov 2, 3, 4, 6, 7.
England 203 (J. D. B. Robertson 50, S. G. Shinde 6-91) & 368-6 (A. J. Watkins 137*, D. B. Carr 76, F. A. Lowson 68) drew with India 418-6 dec (V. S. Hazare 164*, V. M. Merchant 154).

8th Match: v Punjab C.A. (Sialkot)   Nov 10, 11, 12.
Punjab C.A. 364 (Nazar Mohammad 140, Agha Ahmad Raza 52) & 114-6 dec drew with M.C.C. 229 (D. B. Carr 63, Fazal Mahmood 5-58) & 50-1.

9th Match: v Pakistan (Lahore)   Nov 15, 16, 17, 18.
M.C.C. 254 (J. D. B. Robertson 61, Khan Mohammad 5-84) & 368-1 (R. T. Spooner 168*, T. W. Graveney 109*, J. D. B. Robertson 70) drew with Pakistan 428-8 dec (Maqsood Ahmad 137*, M. E. Z. Ghazali 86, Nazar Mohammad 66).

10th Match: v Universities XI (Lahore)   Nov 20, 21.
Universities 88 & 245-2 dec (Shakoor Ahmad 104, Shujayuddin 112*) drew with M.C.C. 133-3 dec (D. Kenyon 70*) & 54-1.*

11th Match: v Bahawalpur-Karachi (Bahawalpur)   Nov 24, 25, 26.
Bahawalpur 348-9 dec (Imtiaz Ahmed 99, Hanif Mohammad 71, Wazir Mohammad 67) drew with M.C.C. 123 & 131-3 (J. D. B. Robertson 50*).

12th Match: v Pakistan (Karachi)   Nov 29, 30, Dec 1, 2.
M.C.C. 123 (Fazal Mahmood 6-40) & 291 (T. W. Graveney 123, Khan Mohammad 5-88) lost to Pakistan 130 & 288-6 (Hanif Mohammad 64, A. H. Kardar 50*) by 4 wkts.

13th Match: v Bombay (Bombay)   Dec 8, 9, 10.
M.C.C. 338 (D. Kenyon 95, F. A. Lowson 84, R. V. Divecha 6-74) & 126-3 (F. A. Lowson 71*) drew with Bombay C.A. 291 (R. S. Modi 86, S. W. Sohoni 58*).

14th Match: v India (Bombay)   Dec 14, 15, 16, 18, 19.
India 485-9 dec (V. S. Hazare 155, P. Roy 140, C. D. Gopinath 50*) & 208 drew with England 456 (T. W. Graveney 175, A. J. Watkins 80) & 55-2.

15th Match: v Maharashtra (Poona)   Dec 21, 22, 23.
Maharashtra 249 (M. R. Rege 133) & 124-2 (H. T. Dani 72*) drew with M.C.C. 410 (F. A. Lowson 76, D. Kenyon 76, D. V. Brennan 67*, D. Shackleton 66, C. J. Poole 50, D. G. Chowdhury 5-124).

16th Match: v Bengal (Calcutta)   Dec 26, 27, 28.
Bengal 188 (C. S. Nayudu 57, R. Tattersall 7-58) & 134 (N. Chatterjee 59) lost to M.C.C. 342-8 dec (A. J. Watkins 113*) by an inns & 20 runs.

17th Match: v India (Calcutta)   Dec 30, 31, Jan 1, 3, 4.
England 342 (A. J. Watkins 68, C. J. Poole 55, R. T. Spooner 71) & 252-5 dec (R. T. Spooner 92, C. J. Poole 69*) drew with India 344 (D. G. Phadkar 115, M. H. Mankad 59) & 103-0 (M. H. Mankad 71*).

18th Match: v East Zone (Jamshedpur)   Jan 6, 7, 8.
M.C.C. 370-5 dec (J. D. B. Robertson 183, D. B. Carr 66*, A. J. Watkins 63) & 20-1 beat East Zone 158 (B. Frank 98*, D. Shackleton 5-64) & 228 (B. Frank 75) by 9 wkts.

19th Match: v India (Kanpur)   Jan 12, 13, 14.
India 121 (R. Tattersall 6-48) & 157 (H. R. Adhikari 60, M. J. Hilton 5-61) lost to England 203 (A. J. Watkins 66, Ghulam Ahmed 5-70) & 76-2 by 8 wkts.

20th Match: v Central Zone (Nagpur)   Jan 20, 21, 22.
Central Zone 134 & 196 (C. T. Sarwate 54) lost to M.C.C. 296 (C. J. Poole 87, D. Kenyon 59, C. T. Sarwate 6-107) & 38-1 by 9 wkts.

21st Match: v Hyderabad (Hyderabad)   Jan 26, 27, 28.
Hyderabad 320 (Ali Hussain 95, E. B. Aibara 76, M. V. Bobjee 66) & 82-3 drew with M.C.C. 441-8 dec (D. Kenyon 112, T. W. Graveney 96, C. J. Poole 79, E. Leadbeater 63*, Ghulam Ahmed 5-123).

22nd Match: v South Zone (Bangalore)   Feb 1, 2, 3.
South Zone 217 (L. T. Adisesh 69) & 221 (M. Kannaiyaram 56*, M. J. Hilton 5-44) lost to M.C.C. 335-9 dec (F. A. Lowson 98, R. T. Spooner 63, D. B. Carr 56, T. D. Krishna 5-93) & 104-1 (F. A. Lowson 57*) by 9 wkts.

23rd Match: v India (Madras)   Feb 6, 8, 9, 10.
England 266 (J. D. B. Robertson 77, R. T. Spooner 66, M. H.Mankad 8-55) & 183 (J. D. B. Robertson 56) lost to India 457-9 dec (P. R. Umrigar 130*, P. Roy 111, D. G. Phadkar 61) by an inns & 8 runs.

24th Match: v Commonwealth XI (Colombo)   Feb 16, 17, 18.
Commonwealth XI 517 (C. I. Gunesekara 135, K. R. Miller 106, R. N. Harvey 74) beat M.C.C. 103 & 155 by an inns & 259 runs.

25th Match: v Ceylon (Colombo)   Feb 22, 23, 24.
Ceylon 58 & 179 (E. Leadbeater 5-41) lost to M.C.C. 270-4 dec (T. W. Graveney 102*, R. T. Spooner 83, D. Kenyon 52) by an inns & 33 runs.

26th Match: v Central Province XI (Kandy)   Feb 27, 28.
Central Province 165 (T. B. Werapitiya 57) & 106 (E. Leadbeater 6-35) lost to M.C.C. 300 (T. W. Graveney 120) by an inns & 29 runs.

27th Match: v Galle Gymkhana Club (Galle)   March 2, 3.
M.C.C. 187 (R. B. Wijesinghe 5-72) & 106-4 beat Galle 75 (M. J. Hilton 6-28) & 217 (B. R. Heyn 61) by 6 wkts.

1951-52: M.C.C. to India, Pakistan and Ceylon

Batting Averages

		M	I	NO	R	HS	Avge	100	c/s
T. W. Graveney	(Glos)	19	32	7	1393	175	55.72	6	4
C. J. Poole	(Notts)	11	13	2	491	87	44.63	0	4
F. A. Lowson	(Yorks)	16	28	5	1016	138	44.17	1	5
J. D. B. Robertson (Middx)		19	31	3	1173	183	41.89	3	12
A. J. Watkins	(Glam)	19	25	2	872	137*	37.91	2	19
R. T. Spooner	(Warks)	17	26	2	886	168*	36.91	1	20/4
E. Leadbeater	(Yorks)	8	7	2	176	63*	35.20	0	5
D. B. Carr	(Derby)	18	22	3	579	76	30.47	0	18
D. Kenyon	(Worcs)	17	29	4	733	112	29.32	1	2
A. E. G. Rhodes	(Derby)	3	3	1	55	45	27.50	0	0
D. Shackleton	(Hants)	16	20	3	306	66	18.00	0	4
N. D. Howard	(Lancs)	15	21	1	335	51	16.75	0	11
J. B. Statham	(Lancs)	15	16	4	162	27	13.50	0	5
M. J. Hilton	(Lancs)	15	14	1	173	47	13.30	0	9
F. Ridgway	(Kent)	16	17	8	114	24	12.66	0	14
R. Tattersall	(Lancs)	16	18	11	82	32*	11.71	0	6

Bowling Averages

	O	M	R	W	Avge	BB	5i
J. D. B. Robertson	106	31	263	14	18.78	3-9	0
J. B. Statham	369.5	106	807	40	20.17	4-9	0
M. J. Hilton	412.5	159	906	41	22.09	5-44	2
D. Shackleton	484.1	125	1184	51	23.21	5-36	2
F. Ridgway	409	87	1068	41	26.04	4-20	0
R. Tattersall	546.3	157	1284	49	26.20	7-58	2
A. E. G. Rhodes	73.2	17	225	8	28.12	4-100	0
T. W. Graveney	42.4	7	182	6	30.33	4-67	0
D. B. Carr	246.3	43	819	23	35.60	4-37	0
E. Leadbeater	198.1	45	692	20	34.60	5-41	1
C. J. Poole	23	4	72	2	36.00	1-8	0
A. J. Watkins	425.2	111	969	25	38.76	3-20	0

Also bowled: R. T. Spooner 3-0-17-0; N. D. Howard 6-0-29-1; D. Kenyon 1-0-9-0; F. A. Lowson 2-0-16-0.

but on the third Mankad removed the last five batsmen for 42 runs. Umrigar and Roy hit hundreds for India and though England did better in their second innings, the match was won by India with an innings to spare.

The team travelled from Madras to Colombo for a four-match visit to Ceylon. In the first match they met a strong Commonwealth Eleven, which included the Australians Harvey and Miller. The tourists were completely outplayed. The umpiring in the matches in Ceylon was not all that could be desired and Statham, after having many appeals turned down, clean bowled the last batsman, breaking the leg-stump in the process. 'That was bloody close, wasn't it?' he asked the umpire.

The batsman of the tour was Graveney, but in the Tests Watkins did remarkably well. Lowson scored runs in the ordinary games but did not appear to have the temperament for Test cricket, whilst Kenyon had a very poor time. Ridgway and Statham were the best of the faster bowlers—for some reason Howard neglected Shackleton—Tattersall worked hard, but Hilton disappointed.

Mankad had a great series and was the outstanding figure of the Tests.

1953-54: Hutton the first professional to captain M.C.C. touring party

For the home series against India in 1952, the selectors broke with tradition and appointed a professional–Len Hutton–as captain of England. There was no M.C.C. tour overseas in the winter of 1952-53, but in 1953-54, after Hutton had won back the Ashes in the summer, he was the automatic choice to lead the M.C.C. in the West Indies.

The tour ended as the most controversial and unhappy venture since the Bodyline Tour, but it began amicably enough, the team flying out to Bermuda for three preliminary matches. The side

which left England on 14 December was L. Hutton (Yorks) (capt), T. E. Bailey (Essex), D. C. S. Compton (Middx), P. B. H. May (Surrey), T. W. Graveney (Gloucs), T. G. Evans (Kent), W. Watson (Yorks), J. H. Wardle (Yorks), F. S. Trueman (Yorks), J. C. Laker (Surrey), G. A. R. Lock (Surrey), A. E. Moss (Middx), R. T. Spooner (Warwicks), K. G. Suttle (Sussex), J. B. Statham (Lancs) and C. H. Palmer (Leics), as a player-manager. This was the first time the full strength of England had toured West Indies and the only absentee of note was A. V. Bedser.

Leaving the tranquility of Bermuda, the M.C.C. travelled to Jamaica, trouncing the island team by an innings. Watson hit an excellent hundred, but the main reason for the success was the fast bowling of Statham and Trueman, who made the ball lift alarmingly on the hard wicket. In the return, Jamaica batted poorly in their first innings, but Holt made 152 in the second innings and the game was drawn.

England picked four fast bowlers for the first Test at Sabina Park and then found the pitch was a docile one. West Indies hit

1953-54: M.C.C. to the West Indies

1st Match: v Combined Bermuda XI (Hamilton)   Dec 16, 17.
Combined XI 73 & 104 (J. C. Laker 5-35) lost to M.C.C. 205 (J. C. Laker 67, T. W. Graveney 52) by an inns & 28 runs.

2nd Match: v All Bermuda (Hamilton)   Dec 20, 21, 22.
M.C.C. 148 (E. Woods 5-49) & 166-6 dec drew with Bermuda 133 (G. A. R. Lock 8-54) & 90-6.

3rd Match: v Bermuda (Hamilton)   Dec 23, 24, 26.
Bermuda 133 (G. A. R. Lock 7-35) drew with M.C.C. 135-1 (L. Hutton 67, W. Watson 55*).

4th Match: v Combined Parishes (Innswood, Jam.)   Dec 30, 31.
Parishes 168 (M. C. Frederick 85) & 89-3 drew with M.C.C. 275-4 dec (T. E. Bailey 78, D. C. S. Compton 73).

5th Match: v Jamaica (Kingston)   Jan 2, 3, 5, 6.
Jamaica 266 (K. R. Rickards 75, M. C. Frederick 60) & 170 (F. S. Trueman 5-45) lost to M.C.C. 457-7 dec (W. Watson 161, T. W. Graveney 82, D. C. S. Compton 56) by an inns & 21 runs.

6th Match: v Jamaica (Melbourne Pk, Kingston)   Jan 8, 9, 11, 12.
Jamaica 187 (M. C. Fredericks 58) & 328-4 dec (J. K. Holt 152, A. F. Rae 53, G. A. Headley 53*) drew with M.C.C. 286 (P. B. H. May 124) & 34-1.

7th Match: v West Indies (Sabina Pk, Kingston)   Jan 15, 16, 18, 19, 20, 21.
West Indies 417 (J. K. Holt 95, C. L. Walcott 65, J. B. Stollmeyer 60, E. D. Weekes 55, C. A. McWatt 54) & 209-6 dec (E. D. Weekes 90*) beat England 170 & 316 (W. Watson 116, P. B. H. May 69, L. Hutton 56, E. S. M. Kentish 5-49) by 140 runs.

8th Match: v Leeward Is (Antigua)   Jan 25, 26.
Leewards 38 (J. H. Wardle 5-7) & 167 (D. C. S. Compton 5-50) lost to M.C.C. 261 (L. Hutton 82, T. W. Graveney 50) by an inns & 56 runs.

9th Match: v Barbados (Bridgetown)   Jan 29, 30, Feb 1, 2, 3.
Barbados 389 (D. St. E. Atkinson 151) & 179 (G. A. R. Lock 5-57) lost to M.C.C. 373 (K. G. Suttle 96, L. Hutton 59*, P. B. H. May 57, W. Watson 53) & 196-9 (K. G. Suttle 62, J. D. C. Goddard 5-43) by 1 wkt.

10th Match: v West Indies (Bridgetown)   Feb 6, 8, 9, 10, 11, 12.
West Indies 383 dec (C. L. Walcott 220, B. H. Pairaudeau 71, D. St. E. Atkinson 53) & 292-2 dec (J. K. Holt 166, F. M. M. Worrell 76*) beat England 181 (L. Hutton 72) & 313 (D. C. S. Compton 93, L. Hutton 77, T. W. Graveney 64*, P. B. H. May 62) by 181 runs.

11th Match: v British Guiana (Georgetown)   Feb 17, 18, 19, 20.
M.C.C. 607 (W. Watson 257, T. W. Graveney 231) beat British Guiana 262 (R. J. Christiani 75, J. H. Wardle 6-77) & 247 (R. J. Christiani 82) by an inns & 98 runs.

12th Match: v West Indies (Georgetown)   Feb 24, 25, 26, 27, March 1, 2.
England 435 (L. Hutton 169, D. C. S. Compton 64, S. Ramadhin 6-113) & 75-1 beat West Indies 251 (E. D. Weekes 94, C. A. McWatt 54) & 256 (J. K. Holt 64) by 9 wkts.

13th Match: v Windward Is (St George's, Grenada)   March 6, 8.
M.C.C. 205-7 dec (L. Hutton 82) & 177-3 (P. B. H. May 93*, J. H. Wardle 66) drew with Windwards 194 (I. Neverson 90*, F. S. Trueman 7-69).

14th Match: v Trinidad (Port of Spain)   March 10, 11, 12, 13, 15.
Trinidad 329 (G. E. Gomez 91, J. B. Stollmeyer 89) & 232 (N. Asgarali 65) lost to M.C.C. 331-8 dec (W. Watson 141, C. H. Palmer 87) & 233-3 (D. C. S. Compton 90*, T. E. Bailey 90) by 7 wkts.

15th Match: v West Indies (Port of Spain)   March 17, 18, 19, 20, 22, 23.
West Indies 681-8 dec (E. D. Weekes 206, F. M. M. Worrell 167, C. L. Walcott 124, D. St. E. Atkinson 74) & 212-4 dec (F. M. M. Worrell 56, D. St. E. Atkinson 53, C. L. Walcott 51*) drew with England 537 (P. B. H. May 135, D. C. S. Compton 133, T. W. Graveney 92) & 98-3.

16th Match v Jamaica Colts & Country XI (Montego Bay)   March 26, 27.
M.C.C. 135 (T. E. Bailey 55) drew with Combined XI 97-6: rain.

17th Match: v West Indies (Sabina Pk, Kingston)   March 30, 31, Apr 1, 2, 3.
West Indies 139 (C. L. Walcott 50, T. E. Bailey 7-34) & 346 (C. L. Walcott 116, J. B. Stollmeyer 64) lost to England 414 (L. Hutton 205, J. H. Wardle 66) & 72-1 by 9 wkts.

The four Yorkshiremen on the 1953-54 M.C.C. tour of the West Indies. From left: Willie Watson, Fred Trueman, Johnny Wardle and the captain, Len Hutton.

Left *The second Test match on the 1953-54 tour, and the second won by the West Indies. Tom Graveney, on-driving Sonny Ramadhin at the Kensington Oval, Barbados, scored 64 not out.*

Below *The England team being presented to the Governor, Sir Alfred Savage, before the start of the third Test against the West Indies in 1953-54. The players are L. Hutton, T. E. Bailey, D. C. S. Compton, J. C. Laker, J. H. Wardle, G. A. R. Lock, W. Watson, J. B. Statham, P. B. H. May, T. G. Evans, T. W. Graveney, K. C. Suttle.*

1953-54: M.C.C. to the West Indies

Batting Averages

	M	I	NO	R	HS	Avge	100	c/s
L. Hutton (Yorks)	8	12	2	780	205	78.00	2	3
W. Watson (Yorks)	9	16	3	892	257	68.61	4	4
T. W. Graveney (Glos)	8	14	3	617	231	56.09	1	14
T. E. Bailey (Essex)	8	11	4	346	90	49.42	0	3
D. C. S. Compton (Middx)	10	14	1	630	133	48.46	1	7
K. G. Suttle (Sussex)	4	7	1	251	96	41.83	0	3
P. B. H. May (Surrey)	10	18	2	630	135	39.37	2	0
C. H. Palmer (Leics)	3	4	0	142	87	35.50	0	0
J. H. Wardle (Yorks)	5	5	0	130	66	26.00	0	5
J. C. Laker (Surrey)	7	9	1	123	33	15.37	0	4
F. S. Trueman (Yorks)	8	9	3	81	20	13.50	0	7
R. T. Spooner (Warks)	5	8	1	93	28	13.28	0	4/3
G. A. R. Lock (Surrey)	9	12	2	105	40*	10.50	0	6
A. E. Moss (Middx)	5	6	2	39	16	9.75	0	2
T. G. Evans (Kent)	6	8	0	72	28	9.00	0	9/1
J. B. Statham (Lancs)	5	6	2	28	10*	7.00	0	2

Bowling Averages

	O	M	R	W	Avge	BB	5i
J. B. Statham	194.5	35	541	22	24.59	4-35	0
A. E. Moss	161.5	38	490	18	27.22	4-47	0
T. E. Bailey	251.5	79	611	22	27.77	7-34	1
J. H. Wardle	240.3	77	569	18	31.61	6-77	1
F. S. Trueman	319.4	81	909	27	33.66	5-45	1
J. C. Laker	330.5	113	756	22	34.36	4-47	0
G. A. R. Lock	486.1	157	1178	28	42.07	5-57	1
D. C. S. Compton	81.4	16	325	6	54.16	2-40	0

Also bowled: C. H. Palmer 22-13-33-0; T. W. Graveney 16-6-71-0; L. Hutton 6-0-43-0.

417, whereas the tourists were muddled by Ramadhin and Valentine, falling for 170. Stollmeyer did not enforce the follow on, an action that produced some ugly demonstrations by the crowd. When West Indies batted a second time Lock was no-balled for throwing, which upset some of the English players. England were eventually set 457 to make in 570 minutes. By the close on the fifth day, the total had reached 233 for 2. The crowd was becoming more and more critical of Stollmeyer and the umpires were also under extreme pressure—attacks, though not of a serious nature, were made on the wife and son of one umpire. As it was England collapsed on the sixth day and West Indies won by a large margin.

A two-day game was played in the Leewards, before the team moved to Barbados. England won a dramatic game against the island team, but the umpires again no-balled Lock for throwing. West Indies outplayed England in the second Test; Hutton's concentration was upset by the crowd's barracking. The English batting in fact was quite dreadful in the first innings and the tourists reached the low point of their travels.

Beating British Guiana with ease gave England some confidence for the third Test, which had to be won. Hutton called correctly and he played a masterly innings to give England a total of 435. The West Indies' first innings was marred by the riot which erupted when McWatt was run out. Suddenly the air was filled with flying bottles and broken beer crates. The English outfielders ran into the centre of the pitch and mounted police arrived. It was suggested that Hutton call the team in, but he refused and gradually calm was restored—Wardle helped to break the tension with some of his clowning. A police cordon was required around the umpire's house for the rest of the game. England enforced the follow on and won the game by 9 wickets.

Injuries kept Valentine, Gomez and Evans out of the fourth Test, also Statham pulled a rib muscle after nine overs and was out for the rest of the tour. None of this had much bearing on the match which was a very high-scoring draw. It seemed impossible to complete games on the jute-matting of Port of Spain. The only disagreements in the match were the English players' complaints on several umpiring decisions. Hutton also had a few words to say to Trueman regarding his behaviour on the field.

The deciding Test took place at Sabina Park. West Indies elected to bat and on what seemed a perfect wicket suddenly found themselves all out for 139, Bailey produced the bowling performance of his career, taking 7 for 34. Hutton then played another incredible innings, being at the wicket just under nine hours and making 205. West Indies did better in their second innings, but

the tourists won by 9 wickets and managed to draw the series.

The M.C.C. team came in for a lot of criticism for not hiding their displeasure at some of the umpiring decisions and dramatic gestures together with untactful remarks by the players did not help to calm the volatile crowds, but despite all the uproar, which the press in some cases blew up out of all proportion, the relations between the two teams were fairly harmonious, which certainly helped matters.

The two batsmen of the side were Hutton and Compton, whilst Statham and Bailey stood out as the best bowlers. Trueman was much too erratic.

Walcott, Weekes and Worrell remained the best home batsmen, though a 17-year-old Sobers looked a promising all-rounder.

1954-55: the speed of Tyson shatters Australia

Hutton, who had won the Ashes for England in 1953 at home, led the M.C.C. to Australia in 1954-55, with the task of retaining them.

The team, which was selected on 27 July was L. Hutton (Yorks) (capt), P. B. H. May (Surrey) (vice-capt), R. T. Simpson (Notts), W. J. Edrich (Middx), T. E. Bailey (Essex), M. C. Cowdrey (Kent), D. C. S. Compton (Middx), A. V. Bedser (Surrey), T. G. Evans (Kent), J. H. Wardle (Yorks), J. B. Statham (Lancs), T. W. Graveney (Gloucs), R. Appleyard (Yorks), J. McConnon (Glam), P. J. Loader (Surrey), F. H. Tyson (Northants) and K. V. Andrew (Northants). The manager was C. G. Howard and the baggage-master G. Duckworth, the old Lancashire wicket-keeper. The players omitted most noted by the press were Trueman, Lock and Laker.

Of this original selection the only doubt was Compton. In the end he travelled later by air, and J. V. Wilson (Yorks) was added to the party. Also included was H. W. Dalton as masseur, the first time such an official had been sent.

Leaving Tilbury on the s.s. *Orsova*, the side arrived at Perth

1954-55: M.C.C. to Ceylon, Australia and New Zealand

Batting Averages

	M	I	NO	R	HS	Avge	100	c/s
D. C. S. Compton (Middx)	11	16	2	799	182	57.07	3	3
L. Hutton (Yorks)	15	25	2	1059	145*	46.04	2	6
T. W. Graveney (Glos)	15	22	3	855	134	45.00	4	20
P. B. H. May (Surrey)	18	29	3	1096	129	42.15	4	16
M. C. Cowdrey (Kent)	17	31	1	1019	110	33.96	3	13
T. E. Bailey (Essex)	15	21	2	551	88	29.00	0	7
R. T. Simpson (Notts)	16	27	3	644	136	26.83	1	5
F. H. Tyson (Northts)	14	20	4	286	62*	17.87	0	3
J. V. Wilson (Yorks)	11	19	2	301	72	17.70	0	10
J. H. Wardle (Yorks)	18	23	3	341	63	17.05	0	9
W. J. Edrich (Middx)	11	18	0	293	88	16.27	0	5
J. McConnon (Glam)	5	7	1	85	22	14.16	0	2
T. G. Evans (Kent)	13	20	2	244	40	13.55	0	34/7
J. B. Statham (Lancs)	13	14	4	132	25	13.20	0	6
R. Appleyard (Yorks)	13	17	9	82	19*	10.25	0	8
A. V. Bedser (Surrey)	7	11	2	85	30	9.44	0	3
P. J. Loader (Surrey)	11	13	2	90	22	8.18	0	6
K. V. Andrew (Northts)	8	11	2	71	28*	7.88	0	16/2

Bowling Averages

	Balls	M	R	W	Avge	BB	5i
R. Appleyard	1962	82	656	44	14.90	6-21	2
J. B. Statham	2445	69	916	54	16.96	6-23	2
F. H. Tyson	2764	65	1140	64	17.81	7-27	4
P. J. Loader	1902	42	817	41	19.92	6-21	1
J. V. Wilson	183	0	100	5	20.00	2-1	0
J. H. Wardle	3153	135	1166	57	20.45	5-42	3
T. E. Bailey	1898	49	769	36	21.36	4-53	0
A. V. Bedser	1655	33	659	24	27.45	5-57	1
J. McConnon	601	18	267	8	33.37	2-37	0
D. C. S. Compton	128	1	101	2	50.50	1-21	0

Also bowled: T. W. Graveney 102-3-47-1; M. C. Cowdrey 68-1-71-1; W. J. Edrich 64-2-53-0; L. Hutton 6-0-2-1; R. T. Simpson 28-1-5-2.
C. G. Howard played in one non-first-class match.

Above *Trevor Bailey in typical obdurate mood quietly playing a ball from Ray Lindwall during the second Test in Sydney of the 1954-55 tour of Australia.*

Left *England wicket-keeper Keith Andrew runs out Australia's Graeme Hole in the first Test of the 1954-55 Australian tour at Brisbane.*

on 7 October – there had been the usual one-day game in Colombo.

The team won the first three first-class matches, though only a bright knock by Compton, who had just arrived, saved the side at Adelaide. The three wins were followed by three draws.

The first Test was lost because Hutton gambled and put in Australia. The home side replied to this impudence by hitting 601 for 8 and then declaring. Hutton had thought the battery of four fast bowlers – Statham, Tyson, Bailey and Bedser – would break through. The problem was that about ten catches were dropped and Morris and Harvey both hit centuries. The England batting, which lacked Compton, who was injured fielding, collapsed twice to Lindwall, Miller and later the spin of Benaud and Johnson. Australia won by an innings with a day to spare.

In the second Test Morris won the toss and put England in. Splendid bowling all round dismissed the tourists for 154, but Bailey and Tyson made certain that Australia did not obtain a commanding lead and May hit a century in England's second innings, so that the home side required 223 for victory. It was not an unreasonable target, but Statham and Tyson bowled in great style, making the ball get up nastily, and with only Harvey really defying them, the English pacemen won the game by 38 runs. One interesting note on the match was the dropping of Bedser. This caused quite a stir, but was justified.

After an up-country game, the teams met at Melbourne for the third Test. Hutton decided to bat on winning the toss, only to see Cowdrey play a lone role in the England innings. Miller, who had missed the previous Test through injury, bowled with great fire,

dismissing Hutton, Edrich and Compton for 14 runs. Statham and Tyson retaliated and Australia had a first innings lead of only 40. England's batting was stronger in the second innings, with May playing a good innings of 91, and Australia required 240 to win. As in the second Test Tyson and Statham swept right through them. This time even Harvey did not survive. The receipts for the match were a record £47,933.

On the holiday trip to Tasmania McConnon broke the little finger of his right hand and returned to England. Back on the mainland, South Australia were beaten by an innings and 143 runs, which was a pleasant prelude to the fourth Test. Australia were without Lindwall, but on the first day it was so hot, no one was keen to field. Australia batted and England wilted. The home team hit 323 and the tourists methodically plodded to 341 in 541 minutes, so it looked a certain draw. Hutton however brought on Appleyard after Statham had bowled two overs in Australia's second innings and this unexpected move produced three quick wickets, after which Tyson and Statham dealt with the remainder and England, though Miller grabbed three wickets, won at a canter. Thus the Ashes were retained.

The worst storms in fifty years ruined the fifth Test and it was drawn, though England were well on top.

The four matches in New Zealand included two Tests, both of which England won and in the second, the home side were dismissed for a record low of 26. The tourists flew home via the United States arriving in London on 5 April.

The Australian critics berated their team, describing it as worse than the 1912 side which went to England, when most of the best players of the day refused to go.

Tyson and Statham were the cricketers of the tour – Tyson was regarded as the fastest Englishman to visit Australia since Larwood. Hutton led the team ably and managed his bowlers well, but his batting was much more defensive than previously. Cowdrey and May were the two young successes in the batting line-up, though Graveney also made a big impression.

One of the problems Australia faced was that of the captaincy, and many felt that Miller ought to have been preferred to Johnson, but Australia also suffered from a large crop of injuries, which must be taken into account.

1954-55: M.C.C. to Ceylon, Australia and New Zealand

1st Match: v Ceylon (Colombo) (One Day) Sept 30.
M.C.C. 178-8 dec (M. C. Cowdrey 66*) drew with Ceylon 101-4.

2nd Match: v Western Australian Country XI (Bunbury) Oct 11, 12.
M.C.C. 344-5 dec (W. J. Edrich 129, L. Hutton 59, T. W. Graveney 58) drew with Country XI 116 (J. McConnon 5-30) & 128-6.

3rd Match: v Western Australia (Perth) Oct 15, 16, 18, 19.
W. Australia 103 (J. B. Statham 6-23) & 255 (K. D. Meuleman 109, D. K. Carmody 75) lost to M.C.C. 321 (L. Hutton 145*) & 40-3 by 7 wkts.

4th Match: v Combined XI (Perth) Oct 22, 23, 25.
Combined XI 86 & 163 lost to M.C.C. 311 (P. B. H. May 129) by an inns & 62 runs.

5th Match: v South Australia (Adelaide) Oct 29, 30, Nov 1, 2.
M.C.C. 246 (D. C. S. Compton 113, J. W. Wilson 5-81) & 181 (L. Hutton 98) beat S. Australia 254 (L. E. Favell 84, F. H. Tyson 5-62) & 152 (R. Appleyard 5-46) by 21 runs.

6th Match: v An Australian XI Nov 5, 6, 8, 9, 10.
M.C.C. 205 (R. T. Simpson 74, I. W. Johnson 6-66) drew with Australian XI 167-7.

7th Match: v New South Wales (Sydney) Nov 12, 13, 15, 16.
M.C.C. 252 (M. C. Cowdrey 110, L. Hutton 102) & 327 (M. C. Cowdrey 103, L. Hutton 87) drew with N.S.W. 382 (W. J. Watson 155, K. R. Miller 86) & 78-2.

8th Match: v Queensland (Brisbane) Nov 19, 20, 22, 23.
M.C.C. 304 (R. T. Simpson 136, D. C. S. Compton 110) & 288 (P. B. H. May 77, D. C. S. Compton 69, T. E. Bailey 51*) drew with Queensland 288 & 25-2.

9th Match: v Australia (Brisbane) Nov 26, 27, 29, 30, Dec 1.
Australia 601-8 dec (R. N. Harvey 162, A. R.Morris 153, R. R. Lindwall 64*, G. B. Hole 57) beat England 190 (T. E. Bailey 88) & 257 (W. J. Edrich 88) by an inns & 154 runs.

10th Match: v Queensland Country XI (Rockingham) Dec 4, 6.
M.C.C. 317 (W. J. Edrich 129, J. V. Wilson 61, D. Watt 5-56) beat Qld Country XI 95 & 210 (W. M. Brown 78, R. Appleyard 7-51) by an inns & 12 runs.

11th Match: v Prime Minister's XI (Canberra) (One Day) Dec 8
M.C.C. 278-7 dec (P. B. H. May 101, T. W. Graveney 56) beat Prime Minister's XI 247 (R. Benaud 113) by 31 runs.

12th Match: v Victoria (Melbourne) Dec 10, 11, 13, 14.
M.C.C. 312 (M. C. Cowdrey 79, T. E. Bailey 60) & 236-5 dec (P. B. H. May 105*, M. C. Cowdrey 54) drew with Victoria 277 (R. N. Harvey 59, F. H. Tyson 6-68) & 88-3.

13th Match: v Australia (Sydney) Dec 17, 18, 20, 21, 22.
England 154 & 296 (M. C. Cowdrey 54) beat Australia 228 & 184 (R. N. Harvey 92*, F. H. Tyson 6-85) by 38 runs.

14th Match: v N.S.W. Northern Districts XI (Newcastle) Dec 27, 28, 29.
Districts XI 211 (R. McDonald 63, J. H. Wardle 6-36) & 246 (R. Wotton 52, R. Appleyard 5-59) lost to M.C.C. 438 (P. B. H. May 157, T. G. Evans 69, D. C. S. Compton 60, J. Bull 5-80) & 20-1 by 9 wkts.

15th Match: v Australia (Melbourne) Dec 31, Jan 1, 3, 4, 5.
England 191 (M. C. Cowdrey 102) & 279 (P. B. H. May 91, W. A. Johnston 5-85) beat Australia 231 (J. B. Statham 5-60) & 111 (F. H. Tyson 7-27) by 128 runs.

16th Match: v Combined XI (Hobart) Jan 8, 10, 11.
Combined XI 221 (R. N. Harvey 82, E. Rodwell 70) & 184-6 dec (R. Benaud 68*) drew with M.C.C. 242 (T. E. Bailey 53) & 99-2.

17th Match: v Tasmania (Launceston) Jan 13, 14, 15.
M.C.C. 317 (T. W. Graveney 134, J. H. Wardle 63, J. V. Wilson 62*, L. Hutton 61) & 133-6 dec beat Tasmania 117 (P. J. Loader 6-22) & 200 (J. Maddox 62*) by 243 runs.

18th Match: v South Australian Country XI (Mount Gambier) Jan 18, 19.
M.C.C. 328 (R. T. Simpson 68, P. B. H. May 62, D. C. S. Compton 53) beat S.A. Country XI 106 (R. Appleyard 6-26) & 45 (J. B. Statham 6-3) by an inns & 177 runs.

19th Match: v South Australia (Adelaide) Jan 21, 22, 24.
S. Australia 185 (G. R. Langley 53) & 123 lost to M.C.C. 451 (D. C. S. Compton 182, P. B. H. May 114, M. C. Cowdrey 64) by an inns & 143 runs.

20th Match: v Australia (Adelaide) Jan 28, 29, 31, Feb 1, 2.
Australia 323 (L. V. Maddocks 69) & 111 lost to England 341 (L. Hutton 80, M. C. Cowdrey 79) & 97-5 by 5 wkts.

21st Match: v Victoria Country XI (Yallourn) Feb 5, 7.
Country XI 182 (W. Young 56, J. H. Wardle 5-46) & 99 (J. H. Wardle 7-45) lost to M.C.C. 307-8 dec (L. Hutton 75, R. T. Simpson 59, T. W. Graveney 50) by an inns & 26.

22nd Match: v Victoria (Melbourne) Feb 11, 12, 14, 15.
Victoria 113 drew with M.C.C. 90-1: rain.

23rd Match: v New South Wales (Sydney) Feb 18, 19, 21, 22.
N.S.W. 172 (B. C. Booth 74*, A. V. Bedser 5-57) & 314-8 dec (R. B. Simpson 98, K. R. Miller 71, J. W. Burke 62, R. Benaud 57, J. H. Wardle 5-118) beat M.C.C. 172 & 269 (L. Hutton) by 45 runs.

24th Match: v Australia (Sydney) Feb 25, 26, 28, March 1, 2, 3.
England 371-7 dec (T. W. Graveney 111, D. C. S. Compton 84, P. B. H. May 79, T. E. Bailey 72) drew with Australia 221 (C. C. McDonald 72, J. H. Wardle 5-79) & 118-6.

25th Match: v Canterbury (Christchurch) March 5, 7, 8.
Canterbury 140 & 206 (J. G. Leggat 99) lost to M.C.C. 302 (T. W. Graveney 101, F. H. Tyson 62*) & 45-3 by 7 wkts.

26th Match: v New Zealand (Dunedin) March 11, 12, 14, 15, 16.
New Zealand 125 (B. Sutcliffe 74) & 132 lost to England 209-8 dec & 49-2 by 8 wkts.

27th Match: v Wellington (Wellington) March 19, 21, 22.
M.C.C. 207 (T. W. Graveney 102) & 201 (J. R. Reid 5-56) beat Wellington 127 (J. H. Wardle 5-42) & 94 (R. Appleyard 6-21) by 187 runs.

28th Match: v New Zealand (Auckland) March 25, 26, 28.
New Zealand 200 (J. R. Reid 73) & 26 (R. Appleyard 4-7) lost to England 246 (L. Hutton 53, A. M. Moir 5-62) by an inns & 20 runs.

1955-56: umpiring decisions provoke 'incident' in Pakistan

The M.C.C. dispatched what was described as an 'A' team to Pakistan for a series of sixteen matches in the winter of 1955-56. The party which sailed from Liverpool on 3 December aboard the s.s. *Circassia* was D. B. Carr (Derbys) (capt), W. H. H. Sutcliffe (Yorks), P. E. Richardson (Worcs), A. J. Watkins (Glam), K. F. Barrington (Surrey), G. A. R. Lock (Surrey), D. B. Close (Yorks), M. J. Cowan (Yorks), A. E. Moss (Middx), J. M. Parks (Sussex), P. J. Sainsbury (Hants), H. W. Stephenson (Somerset), R. Swetman (Surrey), F. J. Titmus (Middx), M. Tompkin (Leics) and the manager C. G. Howard. P. J. Loader had to withdraw due to unfitness and Lock took his place.

The side was a very young one, only Watkins, Stephenson and Tompkin being over 20, but no official Test Matches were in the programme, which was designed to assist in the growth of cricket in Pakistan.

The tour opened in Karachi on 26 December and the team performed well in both matches played in that city, winning one and having the best of a draw. Rain ruined the match at Hyderabad, but the tourists beat the Amir of Bahawalpur's Eleven by an innings. Both victories were the results of good bowling by Lock. A dull draw against the Universities preceded the first 'Unofficial Test', which was remarkably boring – about 30,000 watched the third day's play, when in 5½ hours just 107 runs were scored. M.C.C. dropped several catches which did not improve the remote possibility of a definite finish. Travelling to East Pakistan, the team were beaten in the second 'Unofficial Test' by an innings, Fazal Mahmood and Khan Mohammad using the matting wicket to full advantage and the visitors' batting disintegrating twice. Cowan, the M.C.C. fast bowler, strained his back just before the game and was flown home a few days later – N. I. Thomson of Sussex came as a replacement. After the defeat, two successive innings' victories were achieved, Lock taking 20 wickets in the two matches.

The M.C.C. needed to win the third 'Unofficial Test' to save the series, but despite an injury to Fazal, Pakistan won by seven wickets, with the slow left-arm spin of Kardar causing the batsmen much anguish.

An incident in this match caused much upset at the time and

1955-56: M.C.C. to Pakistan

Batting Averages

	M	I	NO	R	HS	Avge	100	c/s
P. E. Richardson (Worcs)	11	16	1	650	105	43.33	2	5
K. F. Barrington (Surrey)	12	17	2	586	87	39.06	0	6
D. B. Close (Yorks)	12	20	1	684	92	36.00	0	12
F. J. Titmus (Middx)	11	16	1	457	72	30.46	0	8
M. Tompkin (Leics)	11	16	1	334	85	22.26	0	2
R. Swetman (Surrey)	8	11	2	197	45	21.88	0	16/5
P. J. Sainsbury (Hants)	9	11	5	130	32	21.66	0	5
D. B. Carr (Derbys)	11	17	2	310	61	20.66	0	7
A. J. Watkins (Glam)	11	15	1	256	59	18.28	0	10
G. A. R. Lock (Surrey)	11	15	2	237	62*	18.23	0	9
H. W. Stephenson (Som)	8	10	2	122	39	15.25	0	13
W. H. H. Sutcliffe (Yorks)	10	14	1	173	58	13.30	0	5
J. M. Parks (Sussex)	10	15	0	198	52	13.20	0	3
M. J. Cowan (Yorks)	4	3	2	8	6	8.00	0	1
A. E. Moss (Middx)	11	13	4	41	14	4.55	0	1
N. I. Thomson (Sussex)	4	5	1	9	7	2.25	0	2

Bowling Averages

	O	M	R	W	Avge	BB	5i
G. A. R. Lock	557	296	869	81	10.72	8-17	10
P. J. Sainsbury	184.4	90	268	16	16.75	3-10	0
A. E. Moss	318	92	717	41	17.48	5-25	1
N. I. Thomson	88.5	25	215	11	19.54	4-59	0
F. J. Titmus	323.2	124	651	28	23.25	4-50	0
M. J. Cowan	71.5	19	133	5	26.60	3-76	0
D. B. Close	145	58	313	11	28.45	2-40	0
D. B. Carr	32	16	86	3	28.66	2-19	0
K. F. Barrington	28.1	9	69	2	34.50	1-3	0
A. J. Watkins	145	62	282	7	40.28	2-30	0

Also bowled: J. M. Parks 6-1-39-1; P. E. Richardson 4-1-19-1; W. H. H. Sutcliffe 12.4-4-26-3; R. Swetman 2-0-10-1.

The M.C.C. 'A' team which toured Pakistan in 1955-56. The captain D. B. Carr is seated centre, with the manager C. G. Howard on his left and W. H. H. Sutcliffe on his right. Behind are M. Tompkin, P. J. Sainsbury, M. J. Cowan, D. B. Close, H. W. Stephenson, F. J. Titmus, G. A. R. Lock, J. M. Parks, R. Swetman, A. E. Moss, K. F. Barrington, A. J. Watkins, P. E. Richardson.

the stage was reached where M.C.C. offered to recall the team. On the first day there were four lbw decisions against M.C.C. batsmen and some undiplomatic comments by the tourists. On the evening of the third day of the match, some of the M.C.C. team proceeded to pour cold water over Idris Begh, one of the umpires, in the way students might act on a Rag Night. The press naturally went to town on the story. The President of M.C.C., Lord Alexander, cabled the Pakistan cricket authorities and offered to cancel the rest of the tour, at the same time paying Pakistan compensation for any lost revenue. The incident however was papered over and the three remaining games completed, though in the final 'Unofficial Test', which M.C.C. won by 2 wickets, Imtiaz Ahmed accused the M.C.C. players of abusing the umpires and the tour ended on rather a sour note.

The team flew home to London on 16 March and on 20 March M.C.C. at Lord's issued a prepared statement on the incidents. The M.C.C. laid the blame for throwing a bucket of water over the umpire directly on D. B. Carr, the captain, who was present at the incident.

The feature of the tour was the splendid bowling of Lock. Richardson and Close dominated the disappointing batting.

1955-56: Swanton takes team to the West Indies and Bermuda

The first major tour since the Second World War not under the auspices of the M.C.C., left Heathrow Airport on 5 March 1956 under the managership of E. W. Swanton. The team was M. C.

Cowdrey (Kent) (capt), G. H. G. Doggart (Sussex), J. J. Warr (Middx), T. W. Graveney (Gloucs), F. H. Tyson (Northants), D. E. Blake (Hants), A. C. D. Ingleby-Mackenzie (Hants), G. Goonesena (Notts), A. S. M. Oakman (Sussex), M. J. Stewart (Surrey), Swaranjit Singh (Warwicks) and R. G. Marlar (Sussex), and R. C. M. Kimpton (Worcs) joined the side in Barbados.

Although the tourists lost the first match against Barbados, in the second game Graveney hit a century, and due to the bowling of Warr and Goonesena, the tourists enforced the follow on. Walcott then made a hundred which ensured a draw.

Going on to Trinidad, the tourists beat the island side – Graveney hit another century – but were defeated by a West Indies XI. Ramadhin bowled with great skill and Sobers hit a splendid 71.

The tour ended in Bermuda with a one-day match against the local side. Graveney was the star of the batting, though Stewart also performed well and Goonesena was the leading all-rounder. Tyson headed the bowling with 26 wickets at 15.65 runs each.

1956-57: South Africa's Endean out 'handled ball' in Test

The sixteen players under the managership of F. R. Brown who left England bound for South Africa aboard the *Edinburgh Castle* were P. B. H. May (Surrey) (capt), D. J. Insole (Essex), T. E. Bailey (Essex), P. E. Richardson (Worcs), M. C. Cowdrey (Kent), A. S. M. Oakman (Sussex), D. C. S. Compton (Middx), J. M. Parks (Sussex), T. G. Evans (Kent), B. Taylor (Essex), J. H. Wardle (Yorks), J. B. Statham (Lancs), F. H. Tyson (Northants), P. J. Loader (Surrey), G. A. R. Lock (Surrey) and J. C. Laker (Surrey). The two notable omissions were Graveney and Trueman, otherwise the team was as strong as could be collected.

The tourists began the visit in a blaze of glory, Boland, Western Province, Eastern Province, Orange Free State, Rhodesia (twice) providing six consecutive innings victories. Wardle, who played in four of the six matches took 33 wickets, while May hit four centuries.

As had happened on previous tours, Transvaal provided the M.C.C. with stiffer opposition. Heine and Adcock put the visitors' batting in perspective and a win was achieved by just 3 wickets. The M.C.C. then met Tayfield at Pretoria and collapsed twice. Wardle bowled well, but could not prevent the first defeat of an M.C.C. side in South Africa since 1930-31. Two drawn matches brought the team to Johannesburg for the first Test. There was tremendous interest in the match, over 100,000 attending the five days – a new record – but the batting was dread-

fully slow. The bowlers received some help from the wicket; England, batting first plodded to 45 in the 2½ hours before lunch on the first day and the tempo never increased. England won the game due to some great bowling by Bailey and Statham in the final innings, when South Africa, needing 204 to win, fell for 72.

The second Test began directly after the first and followed the same slow tempo and the same result, when by coincidence England bowled out South Africa in their final innings for 72 yet again – Wardle took 7 for 36. Endean was adjudged out 'handled ball' in this match, the first instance in Test cricket.

Above *The M.C.C. party arrive at Cape Town for the 1956-57 tour. From the left: P. B. H. May, D. C. S. Compton, unknown, M. C. Cowdrey, J. M. Parks, A. S. M. Oakman, T. E. Bailey, D. J. Insole, J. C. Laker, P. E. Richardson, unknown, G. Duckworth, J. B. Statham, F. H. Tyson, J. H. Wardle, T. G. Evans, P. J. Loader, B. Taylor, F. R. Brown, G. A. R. Lock.*

Left *Action from the second Test match of the 1956-57 tour, the match in which South Africa's Russell Endean was out 'handled ball'. This ball from Statham was snicked by Tayfield but fell short of Insole at second slip. Cowdrey, Bailey and Evans are the other fielders.*

Some more pedestrian batting was featured in the third Test. This time South Africa required 190 to win in the fourth innings with 250 minutes left – when the final hour arrived 83 were needed, but it was all too much.

Cautious batting remained the order of the day in the fourth Test, but for the first time South Africa won the toss and batted first. McLean hit a lucky 93 and a total of 340 was reached. The home team kept a firm grip on the match from then on and the bowling of Tayfield, who was chaired off the field at the end of play, won the game for South Africa.

South Africa needed to win the fifth Test to square the rubber. England were unfortunate in that their two best bowlers, Statham and Wardle, could not play due to injury. The most controversial feature of the match was the pitch, which had been relaid only three months before. This provided a great many shooters, especially as the match wore on, and Tyson had easily his best return of the tour. England, though, batted very feebly and it was the lack of runs in the end that lost them the match, rather than the absence of Statham and Wardle. Heine and Adcock proved the tourists' downfall in the first innings, then Tayfield delivered

1956-57: M.C.C. to South Africa

Batting Averages

	M	I	NO	R	HS	Avge	100	c/s
P. B. H. May (Surrey)	16	24	1	1270	206	55.21	6	4
D. J. Insole (Essex)	18	25	4	996	192	47.42	4	24
M. C. Cowdrey (Kent)	18	27	1	1035	173	39.80	2	28
D. C. S. Compton (Middx)	14	22	1	792	131	37.71	2	7
T. E. Bailey (Essex)	16	25	2	703	162	30.56	2	10
P. E. Richardson (Worcs)	17	26	0	789	117	30.34	2	2
A. S. M. Oakman (Sussex)	14	19	0	534	150	28.10	1	16
F. H. Tyson (Northts)	13	17	5	294	55*	24.50	0	4
T. G. Evans (Kent)	12	19	1	354	80	19.67	0	31/9
B. Taylor (Essex)	11	13	0	249	65	19.15	0	12/6
G. A. R. Lock (Surrey)	14	18	4	229	39	16.35	0	11
J. H. Wardle (Yorks)	14	18	3	207	37	13.80	0	11
J. C. Laker (Surrey)	14	16	6	79	17	7.90	0	3
J. B. Statham (Lancs)	12	14	6	42	12*	7.00	0	5
P. J. Loader (Surrey)	15	16	2	81	13	5.78	0	5

Also played in one match: F. R. Brown (Northants) 0; J. M. Parks (Sussex) 4.

Bowling Averages

	O	M	R	W	Avge	BB	5i
J. H. Wardle	380.3	94	1103	90	12.25	8-80	8
G. A. R. Lock	352.7	120	833	56	14.87	6-14	4
T. E. Bailey	254.5	76	461	29	15.89	5-20	1
P. J. Loader	316	76	751	46	16.32	7-28	1
J. B. Statham	233.2	40	607	36	16.86	5-26	1
F. H. Tyson	254.3	65	636	37	17.18	6-40	1
J. C. Laker	387.7	122	875	50	17.50	6-47	2
D. C. S. Compton	16.2	1	73	3	24.33	2-43	0

Also bowled: A. S. M. Oakman 15-4-48-0; F. R. Brown 9-2-26-0; T. G. Evans 1-0-8-0.

the *coup de grace*. The run-rate reached a new all-time low for Test cricket, with 122 being hit on the third day in 290 minutes.

South Africa therefore drew the series and deserved to do so. Of the English batsmen, Insole proved what rugged determination can do and headed the Test averages. Richardson also did well, but the rest did nothing to improve their reputations – May was brilliant in the ordinary matches, but failed in the Tests, as did Compton. Cowdrey found Tayfield too much for him. Parks developed eye trouble and was sent home – it was not felt necessary to send a replacement, though, with hindsight, Graveney ought to have gone.

Wardle's left-handed off-breaks and googlies were the basis of the English attack, Laker however disappointed. Tyson was not the fast bowler he had been in Australia and Statham, except at the end, was the best of the quicker bowlers.

South Africa suffered from the injury which kept McGlew out of four Tests, but Goddard batted well and Tayfield bowled in tremendous form.

Record crowds watched the tourists' matches. The M.C.C. share of the receipts from the matches was about £60,000, which meant a profit of £26,500.

1956-57: silver jubilee visit to India

The purpose of the visit to India with its two matches was to celebrate the silver jubilee of the Bengal Cricket Association and the team flew out from London on Boxing Day 1956 and returned by air on 11 January. The party was W. J. Edrich (Middx) (capt), R. T. Simpson (Notts), W. Watson (Yorks), A. V. Bedser (Surrey), T. W. Graveney (Gloucs), C. L. McCool (Somerset), F. S. Trueman (Yorks), A. E. Moss (Middx), A. Wharton (Lancs), B. Dooland (Notts), G. E. Tribe (Northants) and T. L. Livingston (Northants) with C. G. Howard as manager.

The team played two matches, losing one and winning one. Graveney's hundreds in the second match came in fine style as the batting of the official England side struggled in South Africa.

The spin of Ghulam Ahmed and Mankad proved decisive in the first game, whilst Tribe was the most effective visiting bowler.

1956-57: C. G. Howard's Team to India

1st Match: v Chief Minister's XI (Calcutta) Dec 30, 31, Jan 1, 2.
Chief Minister's XI 149 and 378-8 dec (N. Contractor 157, V. S. Hazare 60, L. Armanath 59) beat Howard's Team 227-9 dec (W. J. Edrich 58) and 158 by 142 runs.

2nd Match: v President's XI (Bombay) Jan 5, 6, 7, 8.
Howard's Team 319 (T. W. Graveney 153) and 313-7 dec (T. W. Graveney 120, W. J. Edrich 58) beat President's XI 171 (P. R. Umrigar 57) and 309 (P. R. Umrigar 100) by 152 runs.

1956-57: Duke of Norfolk's team to Jamaica

At the invitation of the Jamaican Cricket Association, the Duke of Norfolk took a team out to the island in the early months of 1957.

The side consisted of E. D. R. Eagar (Hants) (capt), J. J. Warr (Middx), D. E. Blake (Hants), T. W. Graveney (Gloucs), T. Greenhough (Lancs), A. C. D. Ingleby-Mackenzie (Hants), R. E. Marshall (Hants), A. E. Moss (Middx), D. V. Smith (Sussex), G. E. Tribe (Northants), W. Watson (Yorks), D. V. P. Wright (Kent), D. Barrick (Northants) and Lord Cobham (Worcs).

The three major matches were against the Jamaica team and the tourists won two, with the other drawn. Tribe was the best bowler of the side and took 45 wickets at a cost of 17.91 runs each. The batting laurels went to Marshall and Watson. Smith also played some impressive innings. Blake, the wicket-keeper, broke an arm and Ingleby-Mackenzie took over the stumping duty in the second half of the tour.

The best batting for Jamaica came from O. G. Smith who hit two centuries and a 50 in the first-class matches. Kentish was the most effective of the home bowlers but only appeared in one match.

The team returned home on 7 April. The Jamaican authorities had guaranteed the necessary £10,000 required to pay for the tour – happily the receipts from the matches, which proved most popular, just about covered this sum.

1956-57: Duke of Norfolk's Team to Jamaica

1st Match: v St Mary (Prospect St Mary) Feb 22, 23.
Norfolk's XI 168 (W. Watson 77) & 214-1 dec (R. E. Marshall 106*, D. V. Smith 60) beat St Mary 98 & 187 (Pottinger 61, D. V. P. Wright 7-31) by 97 runs.

2nd Match: v Country Districts (Chedwyn Park) Feb 25, 26.
Country Districts 232-9 dec drew with Norfolk's XI 363-8 (R. E. Marshall 87, W. Watson 76, G. E. Tribe 66).

3rd Match: v Jamaica Next XI (Sabina Park) Feb 27, 28, March 1.
Norfolk's XI 334-5 dec (R. E. Marshall 95, T. W. Graveney 90, W. Watson 55*) & 185-7 dec (D. V. Smith 72) drew with Jamaica Next XI 222-9 dec & 185-5 (G. Smith 64).

4th Match: v All Jamaica (Sabina Park) March 2, 4, 5.
Jamaica 327 (N. L. Bonitto 129, J. K. Holt jun 71, G. E. Tribe 5-95) & 326-5 dec (E. D. McMorris 114) drew with Norfolk's XI 379 (T. W. Graveney 92, D. E. Blake 62, R. Gilchrist 5-110) & 222-7.

5th Match: v St Elizabeth (Monymusk) March 7, 8.
St Elizabeth 121 & 134-5 drew with Norfolk's XI 248-8 dec (R. E. Marshall 128).

6th Match: v Cornwall XVI (Montego Bay) March 9, 11.
Cornwall 116-13 dec (A. E. Moss 6-36) & 94-10 drew with Norfolk's XI 232 (D. V. Smith 55, A. C. D. Ingleby-Mackenzie 50, Lord Cobham 50).

7th Match: v Combined Estates (Frome) March 12, 13.
Combined Estates 127 (G. E. Tribe 6-41) & 110 (G. E. Tribe 5-48) lost to Norfolk's XI 258-9 dec (R. E. Marshall 100, D. V. Smith 62) by an inns & 21 runs.

8th Match: v Jamaica (Malbourne Park) March 15, 16, 18, 19.
Jamaica 330-9 dec (O. G. Smith 118, A. E. Moss 5-84) (J. K. Holt jun 93*) lost to Norfolk's XI 218 (W. Watson 71*, T. W. Graveney 51, E. S. Kentish 5-36) & 291-7 (R. E. Marshall 97, D. Barrick 66) by 3 wkts.

9th Match: v Jamaica (Sabina Park) March 21, 22, 23, 25, 26.
Jamaica 261 (O. G. Smith 118, E. D. McMorris 58) & 321 (O. G. Smith 82, A. F. Rae 74, J. K. Holt jun 55, G. E. Tribe 6-83) lost to Norfolk's XI 235 (D. T. Dewdney 7-55) & 348-3 (T. W. Graveney 83*, R. E. Marshall 82, D. V. Smith 68, W. Watson 54*) by 7 wkts.

10th Match: v Combined Parishes (St Antonio) March 28.
Norfolk's XI 267 (R. E. Marshall 69) drew with Combined Parishes 93-4.

1957-58: first tour of Tanganyika, Kenya and Uganda

Due to the enthusiasm of Mr A. Davies of the Kenya Kongonis Club, the M.C.C. were persuaded to take a team out to East Africa for the first time in 1957-58.

The party flew from England on Boxing Day 1957 and went direct to Dar-es-Salaam, where the first match was staged on 28 December. The team was F. R. Brown (Northants) (capt), S. C. Griffith (Sussex) (vice-capt/manager), J. A. Bailey (Essex), G. W. Cook (Kent), G. H. G. Doggart (Sussex), A. C. D. Ingleby-Mackenzie (Hants), C. J. M. Kenny (Essex), P. E. Richardson (Worcs), R. V. C. Robins (Middx), D. R. W. Silk (Somerset), M. J. K. Smith (Warwicks), J. J. Warr (Middx) and W. R. Watkins (Middx) as baggage master.

Tanganyika held the tourists to a close draw, but the English side was still recovering from the journey. After the single game in Dar-es-Salaam, the side went to Mombasa and then on to Nairobi, where the Kongonis managed to inflict the sole defeat on the M.C.C., after Brown had set them 212 to win at 80 per hour. Prodger hit an excellent unbeaten hundred.

The final leg of the tour was in Kampala against Uganda, where the tourists proved too good for the locals.

The tour was a great success and just reward for those who organised it. Doggart found he could make runs on the matting wickets and was the best bat; Robins just headed the bowling, but Brown, Bailey and Warr were also most useful.

The team returned to England by air on 21 January.

1957-58: M.C.C. to East Africa

1st Match: v Tanganyika (Dar-es-Salaam)   Dec 28, 29. . .
Tanganyika 167-7 dec (R. D. Patel 56) & 91-7 dec drew with M.C.C. 95 (Mohmedhussein 5-17) & 146-7.

2nd Match: v Coast XI (Mombasa)   Dec 31, Jan 1.
Coast XI 120 & 80 lost to M.C.C. 164 & 37-0 by 10 wkts.

3rd Match: v Kenya Kongonis (Nairobi)   Jan 4, 5.
M.C.C. 340-7 dec (M. J. K. Smith 80, A. C. D. Ingleby-Mackenzie 76) & 115-5 dec (G. W. Cook 53) lost to Kenya Kongonis 245 (P. R. Morris 73, P. Prodger 52, G. L. Krauss 50*) & 212-3 (P. Prodger 115, D. W. Dawson 62*) by 7 wkts.

4th Match: v Kongonis' President's XI (Nyeri) (One Day)   Jan 8.
M.C.C. 195 (F. R. Brown 87) beat President's XI 87 by 108 runs.

5th Match: v H. L. Hunter's XI (Rift Valley) (One Day)   Jan 10.
M.C.C. 291-3 dec (G. H. G. Doggart 110*) drew with H. L. Hunter's XI 173-5.

6th Match: v Kenya C.A. (Nairobi)   Jan 11, 12.
M.C.C. 219 (G. H. G. Doggart 103, D. R. W. Silk 51) & 161-3 dec (D. R. Silk 62) drew with Kenya C.A. 131 & 151-5 (Gursaran Singh 59).

7th Match: v C. O. Oates' XI (Eldoret) (One Day)   Jan 14.
M.C.C. 263-9 dec (M. J. K. Smith 89) drew with C. O. Oates' XI 181-6 (D. W. Dawson 54).

8th Match: v Kongonis Festival XII (Nairobi) (One Day) Jan 16.
M.C.C. 302-9 dec (P. E. Richardson 131) drew with Festival XII 194-8 (D. Lee 59).

9th Match: v Uganda (Kampala)   Jan 18, 19.
Uganda 122 & 143 (J. A. Boucher 51) lost to M.C.C. 263 (M. J. K. Smith 63, A. C. D. Ingleby-Mackenzie 57) & 6-0 by 10 wkts.

1958-59: May's side disappoints against Australian 'throwers'

The team selected to visit Australia for 1958-59 was announced at the end of July: P. B. H. May (Surrey) (capt), T. E. Bailey (Essex), M. C. Cowdrey (Kent), T. G. Evans (Kent), T. W. Graveney (Gloucs), J. C. Laker (Surrey), P. J. Loader (Surrey), G. A. R. Lock (Surrey), C. A. Milton (Gloucs), P. E. Richardson (Worcs), J. B. Statham (Lancs), R. Subba Row (Northants), R. Swetman (Surrey), F. S. Trueman (Yorks), F. H. Tyson

---

1958-59: M.C.C. to Ceylon, Australia and New Zealand

1st Match: v Ceylon (Colombo) (One Day)   Oct 5.
Ceylon 47-6; rain stopped play.

2nd Match: v Board of Control President's XI (Colombo)   Oct 6.
No play due to rain.

3rd Match: v Western Australia (Perth)   Oct 17, 18, 20, 21.
M.C.C. 351 (T. W. Graveney 177*, P. B. H. May 60) & 146-4 dec (M. C. Cowdrey 65*) drew with W. Australia 221 (R. B. Simpson 60) & 124-3 (J. W. Rutherford 77*).

4th Match: v Combined XI (Perth)   Oct 24, 25, 27, 28.
M.C.C. 349 (P. B. H. May 113, M. C. Cowdrey 78, T. G. Evans 55, B. Strauss 5-99) & 257-4 (M. C. Cowdrey 100*, T. E. Bailey 71*, F. S. Trueman 53) drew with Combined XI 260 (N. C. O'Neill 104).

5th Match: v South Australia (Adelaide)   Oct 31, Nov 2, 3.
S. Australia 165 (J. C. Laker 5-31) & 194 (J. C. Laker 5-70) lost to M.C.C. 245 (P. E. Richardson 88, J. W. Martin 7-110) & 115-1 (C. A. Milton 63*) by 9 wkts.

6th Match: v Victoria (Melbourne)   Nov 7, 8, 10, 11.
M.C.C. 396 (C. A. Milton 116, R. Subba Row 83) & 149-3 dec (T. W. Graveney 78*) beat Victoria 252 (I. R. Huntington 73, C. C. McDonald 54, J. B. Statham 7-47) & 206 (C. C. McDonald 62, G. A. R. Lock 6-74) by 87 runs.

7th Match: v New South Wales (Sydney)   Nov 14, 15, 17, 18.
N.S.W. 391-7 dec (R. N. Harvey 149, J. W. Burke 104, N. C. O'Neill 84) drew with M.C.C. 177 (R. Benaud 5-48) & 356-6 (P. E. Richardson 87, C. A. Milton 81, T. W. Graveney 59, R. Swetman 52).

8th Match: v Australian XI (Sydney)   Nov 21, 22, 24, 25.
M.C.C. 319 (P. B. H. May 140, T. W. Graveney 80) & 257-3 dec (P. B. H. May 114, R. Subba Row 68*, P. E. Richardson 52) beat Australian XI 128 & 103 (G. A. R. Lock 6-29) by 345 runs.

9th Match: v Queensland (Brisbane)   Nov 28, 29, Dec 1, 2.
M.C.C. 151 (R. Subba Row 51, R. R. Lindwall 5-57) & 71-4 drew with Queensland 210.

10th Match: v Australia (Brisbane)   Dec 5, 6, 8, 9, 10.
England 134 & 198 (T. E. Bailey 68) lost to Australia 186 & 147-2 (N. C. O'Neill 71*) by 8 wkts.

11th Match: v Tasmania (Hobart)   Dec 13, 15, 16.
M.C.C. 229-7 dec (P. B. H. May 80, P. E. Richardson 56) drew with Tasmania 94-4 (R. Stokes 54*).

12th Match: v Combined XI (Launceston)   Dec 18, 19, 20.
M.C.C. 384-9 dec (C. A. Milton 85, P. B. H. May 80, M. C. Cowdrey 72, T. Cowley 5-92) & 162-4 (T. W. Graveney 52) drew with Combined XI 241 (C. C. McDonald 104).

13th Match: v South Australia (Adelaide)   Dec 24, 26, 27, 29.
M.C.C. 276 (T. W. Graveney 54) & 195-9 dec (R. Swetman 76, B. Hurn 5-62) drew with S. Australia 223 (J. Lill 86, F. S. Trueman 5-46) & 138-9 (L. E. Favell 52).

14th Match: v Australia (Melbourne)   Dec 31, Jan 1, 2, 4, 5.
England 259 (P. B. H. May 113, A. K. Davidson 6-64) & 87 (I. Meckiff 6-38) lost to Australia 308 (R. N. Harvey 167, J. B. Statham 7-57) & 42-2 by 8 wkts.

15th Match: v Australia (Sydney)   Jan 9, 10, 12, 13, 14, 15.
England 219 (R. Benaud 5-83) & 287-7 dec (M. C. Cowdrey 100*, P. B. H. May 92) drew with Australia 357 (N. C. O'Neill 77, A. K. Davidson 71, K. D. Mackay 57, L. E. Favell 54, J. C. Laker 5-107) & 54-2.

16th Match: v Victoria (Melbourne)   Jan 17, 19, 20, 21.
Victoria 286 (J. H. Shaw 94, C. N. Crompton 73, F. S. Trueman 5-42) & 180 (C. N. Crompton 64) lost to M.C.C. 313 (W. Watson 141, M. C. Cowdrey 85) & 156-1 (P. E. Richardson 65) by 9 wkts.

17th Match: v New South Wales (Sydney)   Jan 23, 24, 26, 27.
N.S.W. 215 (R. N. Harvey 92) & 44-0 drew with M.C.C. 303 (P. B. H. May 136, T. E. Bailey 54, R. Benaud 5-83).

18th Match: v Australia (Adelaide)   Jan 30, 31, Feb 2, 3, 4, 5.
Australia 476 (C. C. McDonald 170, J. W. Burke 66, N. C. O'Neill 56) & 36-0 beat England 240 (M. C. Cowdrey 84, R. Benaud 5-91) & 270 (P. B. H. May 59, T. W. Graveney 53*) by 10 wkts.

19th Match: v Victorian Country XI (Wangaratta) (One Day)   Feb 7.
Country XI 31 (P. J. Loader 5-17) lost to M.C.C. 308-8 (P. B. H. May 56, T. W. Graveney 50, J. B. Mortimore 50*) by 9 wkts.

20th Match: v Southern New South Wales (Wagga Wagga) (One Day)   Feb 9.
Southern N.S.W. 117 lost to M.C.C. 260-8 (P. E. Richardson 77, W. Watson 63) by 7 wkts.

21st Match: v Prime Minister's XI (Canberra) (One Day)   Feb 10.
Prime Minister's XI 288-7 dec (A. R. Morris 79, B. James 88) lost to M.C.C. 332 (M. C. Cowdrey 101, E. R. Dexter 76) by 4 wkts.

22nd Match: v Australia (Melbourne)   Feb 13, 14, 15, 17, 18.
England 205 (P. E. Richardson 68) & 214 (T. W. Graveney 54) lost to Australia 351 (C. C. McDonald 133, A. T. W. Grout 74, R. Benaud 64) & 69-1 (C. C. Mc-Donald 51*) by 9 wkts.

23rd Match: v Otago (Dunedin)   Feb 21, 23, 24.
Otago 70 (F. S. Trueman 5-34) & 157 (F. S. Trueman 8-45) lost to M.C.C. 321 (M. C. Cowdrey 115, P. B. H. May 97) by an inns & 94 runs.

24th Match: v New Zealand (Christchurch)   Feb 27, 28, March 2.
England 374 (E. R. Dexter 141, P. B. H. May 71) beat New Zealand 142 (G. A. R. Lock 5-31) & 133 (J. W. Guy 56, G. A. R. Lock 6-53) by an inns & 99 runs.

25th Match: v Wellington (Wellington)   March 6, 7.
M.C.C. 511-9 dec (M. C. Cowdrey 117, P. E. Richardson 111, W. Watson 106, T. W. Graveney 91) beat Wellington 127 & 173 (R. A. Vance 53) by an inns & 211 runs.

26th Match: v Northern & Central Districts (Hamilton)   March 10, 11, 12.
M.C.C. 198 (T. W. Graveney 108, D. D. Beard 6-34) & 73-0 drew with Districts 185.

27th Match: v New Zealand (Auckland)   March 14, 16, 17, 18.
New Zealand 181 (B. Sutcliffe 61) drew with England 311-7 (P. B. H. May 124*, P. E. Richardson 67).

(Northants), J. H. Wardle (Yorks) and W. Watson (Leics), with F. R. Brown as manager, E. D. R. Eagar as assistant manaager and G. Duckworth as baggage-master. Prior to the announcement of the side, Wardle and Laker had stated that they did not wish to tour, but amid a lot of press comment, both altered their minds.

The newspapers were well pleased with the final composition of the squad and could only bemoan the omission of Dexter. Soon after the team had been made public however, the Yorkshire Committee sacked Wardle due to his being at loggerheads with the county captain. Wardle wrote a series of articles in the *Daily Mail* which served to add fuel to the explosive situation and the M.C.C. withdrew his invitation.

The team of 16 players instead of 17 therefore sailed off on the s.s. *Iberia* bound for Fremantle. The traditional match in Colombo was ruined by rain. Watson, who had injured a knee on shipboard, was flown to Perth for treatment.

After drawing both matches in Perth, the side went to Adelaide, where South Australia were beaten due to the spin of Laker and Lock, and then to Melbourne where Statham and Lock removed the opposition. When An Australian Eleven was convincingly beaten at Sydney, May hitting a hundred in each innings, England looked favourites to win the first Test. Trueman could not play owing to back trouble, but it was feeble batting that let England down.

Bailey batted 458 minutes to make 68 to try to save England but it was a vain attempt as O'Neill hit a splendid not out 71 to bring Australia victory by 8 wickets. Owing to an injury to Subba Row, Mortimore was flown out to reinforce the team. Watson was given a full trial in the two Tasmanian matches which followed the first Test and seemed fit.

The second Test was fairly even on the first innings, due to a century from May, but the left-arm fast bowler Meckiff shattered the English second innings with 6 for 38 and Australia won by 8 wickets. The success of Meckiff increased the already large press campaign against his bowling action and indeed against that of J. W. Burke, the Australian opening bat and occasional bowler, and Slater of Western Australia, who played in the third Test. England had to stop Australia winning this game and with Meckiff breaking down allied to some better batting by May and Cowdrey, the game was drawn. May took the unusual step of playing E. R. Dexter in the match, despite the fact that he had not played in a match and had just flown in from England.

In the fourth Test, knowing England had to win, May put Australia in and saw McDonald and Burke put on 171 before the first wicket fell. Laker could not play and England had the fast trio of Tyson, Truman and Statham, but they made little impression. When the tourists batted, Benaud's spin proved to be the key to the Ashes and England, after being forced to follow on,

Above *The third Test match at Sydney on the 1958-59 M.C.C. tour of Australia. Roy Swetman is caught by 'Slasher' Mackay at forward short leg for 41 off Richie Benaud. The other fielders are Neil Harvey, Wally Grout and Alan Davidson.*

Left *Another victim for Benaud's leg trap. England opener Arthur Milton caught by Alan Davidson for 8 in the second innings of the third Test at Sydney in 1958-59. Grout and Mackay are the other fielders.*

1958-59: M.C.C. to Ceylon, Australia and New Zealand

Batting Averages

	M	I	NO	R	HS	Avge	100	c/s
P. B. H. May (Surrey)	17	26	2	1512	140	63.00	6	5
T. W. Graveney (Gloucs)	19	30	4	1229	177*	47.26	2	18
M. C. Cowdrey (Kent)	20	31	5	1209	117	46.50	4	23
R. Subba Row (Northts)	10	15	3	414	83	34.50	0	2
W. Watson (Leics)	12	18	1	554	141	32.58	2	4
C. A. Milton (Gloucs)	12	24	3	658	116	31.33	1	11
P. E. Richardson (Worcs)	18	30	0	886	111	29.53	1	4
T. E. Bailey (Essex)	13	22	3	501	71*	26.36	0	5
R. Swetman (Surrey)	15	21	5	415	76	25.93	0	24/3
E. R. Dexter (Sussex)	12	17	1	330	141	20.62	1	1
J. B. Statham (Lancs)	9	12	5	131	36*	18.71	0	4
F. S. Trueman (Yorks)	17	21	2	312	53	16.42	0	16
J. B. Mortimore (Gloucs)	12	12	2	151	44*	15.10	0	4
T. G. Evans (Kent)	7	10	0	124	55	12.40	0	8/3
G. A. R. Lock (Surrey)	15	18	1	191	44	11.23	0	9
J. C. Laker (Surrey)	10	13	3	107	22*	10.70	0	1
P. J. Loader (Surrey)	8	10	7	31	11*	10.33	0	1
F. H. Tyson (Northts)	16	17	2	149	33	9.93	0	2

Bowling Averages

	Balls	M	R	W	Avge	BB	5i
J. C. Laker	2257	63	655	38	17.23	5-31	3
F. S. Trueman	2723	61	1067	57	18.71	8-45	4
P. J. Loader	1359	30	507	26	19.50	4-23	0
J. B. Statham	1665	30	549	28	19.60	7-47	2
G. A. R. Lock	3682	118	1328	57	23.29	6-29	4
F. H. Tyson	2490	70	934	37	25.24	4-40	0
J. B. Mortimore	1643	62	537	20	26.85	4-30	0
E. R. Dexter	653	17	265	9	29.44	3-11	0
T. E. Bailey	1448	31	516	10	51.60	3-35	0
T. W. Graveney	162	1	107	1	107.00	1-39	0

Also bowled: M. C. Cowdrey 51-0-42-1; C. A. Milton 32-1-33-0; R. Subba Row 12-1-7-0.

only just avoided the ignominy of an innings defeat.

A car accident involving Loader and Statham prevented either playing in the fifth Test. Watson was also injured, so England entered the match with little prospect of saving their self-respect. The batting again fell to pieces and Australia gained a first innings lead of 146. Lindwall created a new record in the second innings by taking his 217th Test wicket and beating the 216 taken by Grimmett. England managed to avoid an innings defeat, but not by very much.

The team went off to New Zealand, where life was much simpler, and after beating Otago by an innings, they won by the same margin in the first Test against New Zealand and against Wellington. Rain marred the remaining two matches. The team then flew back to England via the United States.

With England losing the series against Australia by four matches to nil, it was difficult to find the individual successes of the tour. It was quite apparent that Tyson was 'over the hill' and that Bailey and Evans were no longer the players of old. Statham and Laker were the only bowlers to command much respect in the Tests. The batting was very poor, the contrast between the Test averages of the two sides being very marked. Australia had seven batsmen averaging over 25, England had three.

In mitigation, it must be admitted that the tourists suffered from more than the usual crop of injuries and there was the continued controversy over Australia's bowlers with 'throwing' actions – but the two leading Australian wicket-takers were Benaud and Davidson, about whose action there was no debate.

1958-59: M.C.C. tour of Brazil and Argentina

The team which arrived by air in Rio de Janeiro on 21 December 1958 was G. H. G. Doggart (Sussex) (capt), D. B. Carr (Derbys) (vice-capt), J. A. Bailey (Essex), P. I. Bedford (Middx), M. H. Bushby (Kent), C. B. Howland (Cambridge U), A. C. D. Ingleby-Mackenzie (Hants), R. V. C. Robins (Middx), D. M. Sayer (Kent), D. R. W. Silk (Somerset), M. J. K. Smith (Warwicks) and O. S. Wheatley (Warwicks). Originally E. R. Dexter was selected, but he was sent to reinforce M.C.C. in Australia and Sayer took

his place. M. J. Bear joined the team in the Argentine, where he was coaching.

Four matches were played in Brazil, two being against the Brazil C.A., but the opposition proved rather weak and even the fact that the games were played on matting made little difference.

In the Argentine the two important three-day matches were the 'Tests'. At Hurlingham in the 'First Test', Argentine showed some fight and batting first reached 120 for 1, but Wheatley then took control. In the 'Second Test' Ingleby-Mackenzie broke a finger and Argentine made a good start, before a double century by Mike Smith put the visitors in a strong position.

The speed of Sayer and spin of Bedford were too good for the home sides, whose field placings and general tactics were not very sophisticated. It was hoped however that the tour would help to improve cricket in both Brazil and the Argentine.

1958-59: M.C.C. to South America

1st Match: v Brazil (Niteroi) (One Day) Dec 23.
M.C.C. 20-2: rain stopped play.

2nd Match: v Brazil C.A. (Niteroi) Dec 24, 26.
M.C.C. 223-4 dec (M. J. K. Smith 81) & 239-8 dec (A. C. D. Ingleby-Mackenzie 109, M. J. K. Smith 61) beat Brazil C.A. 72 & 66 by 324 runs.

3rd Match: v Brazil C.A. (Pirituba) Dec 27, 28.
M.C.C. 338-6 dec (G. H. G. Doggart 97, D. R. W. Silk 93, A. C. D. Ingleby-Mackenzie 60, M. H. Bushby 52) & 56-1 dec beat Brazil C.A. 125 (T. M. Spitteler 62) & 74 by 195 runs.

4th Match: v Sao Paulo (Pirituba) Dec 30.
Sao Paulo 41 lost to M.C.C. 42-2.

5th Match: v Argentine C.A. Colts XVI (Hurlingham) One Day Jan 2.
M.C.C. 290-4 dec (G. H. G. Doggart 81, M. H. Bushby 56, D. R. W. Silk 53, A. C. D. Ingleby-Mackenzie 52) drew with Colts XVI 42-13 (J. A. Bailey 6-14).

6th Match: v Argentine C.A. (Lomas) Jan 3, 4.
M.C.C. 145-7 dec (D. R. W. Silk 56) & 170-2 dec (M. J. K. Smith 56, G. H. G. Doggart 53*) beat Argentine C.A. 16 (J. A. Bailey 5-11) & 136 by 163 runs.

7th Match: v Argentine C.A. (Belgrano) Jan 6, 7.
M.C.C. 423-7 dec (D. R. W. Silk 150, M. H. Bushby 84, G. H. G. Doggart 79, D. B. Carr 66) beat Argentine C.A. 203 (E. McCrea-Steele 59, P. I. Bedford 7-64) & 119.

8th Match: v Argentine C.A. (Hurlingham) Jan 9, 10, 11.
Argentine C.A. 188 (C. D. Ayling 86, O. S. Wheatley 5-39) & 195 (P. I. Bedford 5-73) lost to M.C.C. 363 (D. B. Carr 144, M. H. Bushby 70) & 21-0 by 10 wkts.

9th Match: v Northern Camps XV (Venado Tuerto) (One Day) Jan 13.
M.C.C. 235 (G. H. G. Doggart 141) beat Northern Camps XV 89 (J. A. Bailey 6-16, R. V. C. Robins 5-31) by 146 runs.

10th Match: v Argentine C.A. (Belgrano) Jan 15, 16, 17.
M.C.C. 410-6 dec (M. J. K. Smith 216, D. B. Carr 91) beat Argentine C.A. 81 & 112 (P. I. Bedford 5-25) by an inns & 217 runs.

11th Match: v Argentine C.A. (Belgrano) (One Day) Jan 17.
M.C.C. 270-1 dec (M. J. Bear 115*, D. R. W. Silk 100*) beat Argentine C.A. 103 by 167 runs.

1959: M.C.C. find Philadelphia in sad decline

In the second half of the 1959 summer, a team of amateurs made a 25-match tour of North America under the auspices of the M.C.C. The team was D. R. W. Silk (Somerset) (capt), J. R. Thompson (Warwicks) (vice-capt/manager), J. F. Pretlove (Kent), J. A. Bailey (Essex), D. J. Mordaunt (Sussex), P. I. Bedford (Middx), M. H. Bushby (Kent), D. J. Green (Derbys), A. C. Smith (Warwicks), J. D. Piachaud (Hants), R. M. Prideaux (Cambridge U), C. B. Howland (Cambridge U) and R. W. Barber (Lancs).

Most of the matches on the tour were of one-day duration, and having got used to the matting wickets in the first few fixtures, the tourists soon settled down.

The most important match of the visit was the three-day game with Canada – the 'Test Match'. In this game Prideaux hit a well-judged century and some devastating bowling by Piachaud ended any hopes the Canadians might have entertained.

The final matches were played in the United States, but the M.C.C. found the former famous centre of Philadelphia was only a shadow of the days before 1914.

1st Match: v Montreal District XI (Montreal)   July 31.
M.C.C. 192 beat Montreal District 106 (P. I. Bedford 6-32) by 86 runs.

2nd Match: v Montreal District League XI (Montreal)   Aug 1.
M.C.C. 145 beat Montreal League 75 (D. J. Mordaunt 6-29) by 70 runs.

3rd Match: v Eastern Canada (Ottawa)   Aug 2, 3.
M.C.C. 133 (R. W. Barber 55, B. Christen 8-64) & 168-6 dec drew with Eastern Canada 123 (J. D. Piachaud 5-15) & 139-5 (Iles 58*).

4th Match: v Ottawa Valley C.C. (Ottawa)   Aug 4.
M.C.C. 347-7 dec (R. M. Prideaux 91, M. H. Bushby 71, D. J. Green 56) drew with Ottawa Valley 60-1.

5th Match: v Hamilton & District (Hamilton)   Aug 7.
M.C.C. 228-4 dec (D. R. W. Silk 128) beat Hamilton & Distr 157 by 71 runs.

6th Match: v Toronto (Toronto)   Aug 8.
M.C.C. 205-8 dec drew with Toronto 199-7 (D. Trowse 87*, R. W. Barber 6-73).

7th Match: v Toronto & Districts XI (Toronto)   Aug 10.
M.C.C. 252-8 dec (M. H. Bushby 61, R. W. Barber 54) beat Toronto & District 157 (P. I. Bedford 8-60).

8th Match: v Ontario All Star XI (St Catherines)   Aug 11.
M.C.C. 195 (D. R. W. Silk 60*, B. Christen 6-46) beat All Star XI 112 (P. I. Bedford 5-21) by 83 runs.

9th Match: v British Columbia Mainland League All Stars (Vancouver)   Aug 13.
M.C.C. 249-5 dec (R. M. Prideaux 60, A. C. Smith 53*) beat All Stars 134 by 115 runs.

10th Match: v Western Canada All Stars (Vancouver)   Aug 14, 15.
All Stars 111 & 160 (J. D. Piachaud 5-29) lost to M.C.C. 211-9 dec & 61-4 by 6 wkts.

11th Match: v Victoria (Victoria, B.C.)   Aug 16.
M.C.C. 193 beat Victoria 75 (J. A. Bailey 5-22) by 118 runs.

12th Match: v British Columbia Colts XI (Vancouver)   Aug 18.
M.C.C. 246-9 dec (R. M. Prideaux 60, A. C. Smith 53) beat Colts XI 48 (J. D. Piachaud 8-17) by 198 runs.

13th Match: v British Columbia C.A. (Vancouver)   Aug 19.
M.C.C. 159 (J. F. Pretlove 73) beat British Columbia C.A. 103 (J. D. Piachaud 6-41).

14th Match: v Kootenary-Okanagan XI (British Columbia)   Aug 22.
M.C.C. 161-6 dec beat Kootenary-Okanagan XI 20 (J. A. Bailey 5-9).

15th Match: v Calgary All Stars (Calgary)   Aug 26.
M.C.C. 260-4 dec (R. M. Prideaux 140, J. F. Pretlove 58) beat Calgary All Stars 79 by 181

16th Match: v Edmonton Representative XI (Edmonton)   Aug 28.
M.C.C. 208-6 dec (J. R. Thompson 80) beat Edmonton 41 by 167 runs.

17th Match: v Alberta All Stars   Aug 29.
M.C.C. 242-6 dec (R. W. Barber 73) beat Alberta All Stars 64 (P. I. Bedford 5-24) by 178 runs.

18th Match: v Alberta All Stars   Aug 30.
M.C.C. 251-4 dec (R. M. Prideaux 87) beat Alberta All Stars 54 (P. I. Bedford 5-6) by 197 runs.

19th Match: v Manitoba (Winnipeg)   Sept 2.
M.C.C. 168-7 dec (D. R. W. Silk 60*) drew with Manitoba 24-4.

20th Match: v Canada (Toronto)   Sept 5, 6, 7.
M.C.C. 350 (R. M. Prideaux 106, J. R. Thompson 73, R. W. Barber 54, B. Christen 6-115) & 13-0 beat Canada 184 (V. Walker 55, P. I. Bedford 5-54) & 178 (Trowse 59, J. D. Piachaud 7-32) by 10 wkts.

21st Match: v Toronto Colts (Toronto)   Sept 8.
M.C.C. 160-5 dec beat Colts 73 by 87 runs.

22nd Match: v Western Ontario (Guelph)   Sept 9.
M.C.C. 176-4 dec (M. H. Bushby 54, D. J. Green 66*) beat Western Ontario 46 (J. D. Piachaud 6-20) by 130 runs.

23rd Match: v South-Western Ontario Cricket League (London)   Sept 10.
M.C.C. 217-5 dec (R. M. Prideaux 131) beat S-W Ontario 57 (J. D. Piachaud 7-25) by 160 runs.

24th Match: v Philadelphia (Philadelphia)   Sept 12.
M.C.C. 280-5 dec (D. J. Mordaunt 134) beat Philadelphia 63 (A. C. Smith 7-30) by 217

25th Match: v British Commonwealth C.C. (Washington)   Sept 14.
M.C.C. 302-5 dec (J. F. Pretlove 100*, R. M. Prideaux 61) beat Commonwealth 88 (P. I. Bedford 5-28) by 214 runs.

1st Match: v Rhodesia (Salisbury)   Oct 10, 11, 12.
Rhodesia 246 (R. Gripper 73, P. N. F. Mansell 66*, G. A. R. Lock 6-76) & 160 (G. A. R. Lock 5-44) beat Surrey 297 (K. F. Barrington 111, P. N. F. Mansell 6-77) & 107 (P. N. F. Mansell 7-43) by 2 runs.

2nd Match: v Rhodesia (Bulawayo)   Oct 17, 18, 19.
Surrey 75 (J. Partridge 6-27) & 380 (J. H. Edrich 151, D. G. W. Fletcher 91, P. N. F. Mansell 6-158) drew with Rhodesia 321 (D. Lewis 118) & 53-3.

1959-60: successful tour of the West Indies and Honduras

The team which the M.C.C. selected for the West Indies surprised many of the press by its youthful appearance. Evans, the principal English wicket-keeper since the war, had retired. Neither Lock nor Laker was included and Bailey was also dropped. The team which sailed on the *Camito* on 8 December 1959 was P. B. H. May (Surrey) (capt), F. S. Trueman (Yorks), J. B. Statham (Lancs), A. E. Moss (Middx), M. C. Cowdrey (Kent), D. A. Allen (Gloucs), K. V. Andrew (Northants), K. F. Barrington (Surrey), E. R. Dexter (Sussex), T. Greenhough (Lancs), R. Illingworth (Yorks), G. Pullar (Lancs), M. J. K. Smith (Warwicks), R. Subba Row (Northants) and R. Swetman (Surrey), with R. W. V. Robins as manager.

The critics raised few queries, except that Close and Parks might have been included and possibly Taylor of Yorkshire. The failure in Australia and the number of new faces meant that the press did not give the team much hope of beating the West Indies.

The tour commenced at Grenada with a 10-wicket win over the Windwards, but any hopes raised by this victory were soon dashed in Bridgetown where Barbados hit 533 for 5 and declared, then dismissed M.C.C. cheaply, forcing them to follow on and eventually defeating them by 10 wickets. Nurse hit a double century and Sobers 154. The formidable fast bowler Griffith caused the visiting batsmen most trouble.

The first Test followed four days later. Statham could not play due to an injury received in the previous match. The wicket was absolutely plumb and when May won the toss, England batted stoutly—only May of the batsmen failed, while Barrington and Dexter hit hundreds. West Indies did not begin their innings until lunch on the third day and England reduced them to 114 for 3. At this point Worrell joined Sobers in a partnership which lasted from 4.50 on Friday to 11.40 on Tuesday and added 399 runs—a record for West Indies in Test Matches. Needless to say the match was drawn.

Moving on to Trinidad, where the Port of Spain wicket was now turf for the first time, England beat the local side twice, before tackling West Indies in the second Test. May won the toss and somehow England survived a barrage of bumpers and short-pitched deliveries from Hall and Watson to reach 382—Barrington and Smith hit hundreds, but May again failed. Both Hall and Watson were cautioned by the umpires for excessive use of the short-pitched delivery. On the third day West Indies collapsed in a quite unexpected fashion in the face of Trueman and Statham. Eight wickets went down for 98, at which point the crowd—a record 29,000—erupted. Bottles began to fly, followed by beer cans and a vast assortment of missiles. The playing area was filled with a seething mass—the players marooned on the pitch. Eventually the combined efforts of the fire brigade, mounted police and riot squad restored order. No further play was possible that day, but after a break on Sunday, the match resumed on Monday and continued in comparative peace. Kanhai scored a great century in West Indies second innings, but England's commanding lead was too much and the tourists won by 256 runs. The total attendance for the match was a record 98,000.

The third Test played at Sabina Park, Kingston, was most exciting, in that the initiative swung from one side to the other

1959-60: Surrey tour Rhodesia

Shortly after the close of the 1959 English season, a party of Surrey cricketers travelled to Rhodesia for a two-match tour. Some fine leg-spin bowling by Mansell gave Rhodesia a victory by 2 runs in the first game and in the second Surrey, batting first, collapsed to the opening bowler, Partridge. Edrich hit a century in the second innings, but the tourists were lucky to avoid a second defeat. The team which went out was W. S. Surridge (capt), J. H. Edrich, K. F. Barrington, D. G. W. Fletcher, A. V. Bedser, R. Swetman, G. A. R. Lock, M. J. Stewart, T. H. Clark, E. A. Bedser, A. J. W. McIntyre, P. J. Loader and B. Constable.

Above *The two captains, F. C. M. 'Gerry' Alexander of the West Indies and Peter May of England going out to toss up before the second Test at Port of Spain, West Indies, in 1959-60.*

Above left *Clearing up the mess at the Queen's Park Oval, Port of Spain, Trinidad, after the bottle-throwing riot on 30 January 1960, during the second Test between the West Indies and England. A record 29,000 crowd erupted when the West Indies collapsed.*

and the outcome was in doubt almost to the last. May again won the toss and batted, but Hall's fast deliveries proved too much for everyone but Cowdrey, who made 114 and played one of the best innings of his long career. West Indies began strongly, with a Sobers century and fifties by McMorris and Nurse, but England fought back to remove the last seven wickets for 24 runs. Cowdrey again played magnificently in England's second innings to make the highest score of 97. West Indies were set 230 to win in 245 minutes, on a wicket that helped the bowlers. The home team went for the runs, but gave up finally when six wickets had gone and the match was drawn. May refused to permit Kanhai to use a runner in this last innings – which produced some controversy, but in the end it was discovered that May was in the wrong.

Georgetown, British Guiana, was the scene of the fourth Test. A week before it, May's health broke down and it was announced that he had been unwell for some time, not having recovered from an operation in the summer. He was flown back to England and Cowdrey took over the leadership. Hall once more caused problems in England's first innings, but slow batting by West Indies allied to very defensive tactics on the part of Cowdrey made a draw almost certain before the home innings had progressed far – Sobers spent 420 minutes on his 145. Subba Row, who had come into the England team for May, chipped a knuckle bone in England's second innings, but the game gradually petered out. Statham received the news that his son was dangerously ill and he left for home directly after the game. Parks, the Sussex batsman, came out as a reinforcement and hit 183 against Berbice in the match following the Test.

England only required to draw the fifth Test to win the series and this they managed to do, Cowdrey making a century in the first innings and Parks one in the second.

The tour ended with two one-day matches in Honduras—about 4,000 turned out to watch each game, which were of an exhibition nature.

Despite the riot in Trinidad and the problems of bouncers, the visit was most successful, the relationship between the two sides amicable and record crowds with record receipts and profits were the order of the day.

The problem of throwing, which had been so evident in Australia, was now common in the West Indies but the umpires were reluctant to enforce the law, though in general the standard of umpiring was much better than on the previous visit.

Cowdrey was the outstanding bat and opened the England innings with Pullar, who was most consistent. Dexter played well, but Barrington suffered very much from the bouncers. Trueman and Statham proved an outstanding partnership, but the spinners had a poor time. Sobers stood head and shoulders above the rest of the West Indies batsmen.

1960-61: young M.C.C. party fly out to New Zealand

The M.C.C. sent a young team out to New Zealand in the winter of 1960-61 under the captaincy of D. R. W. Silk (Somerset), the rest of the side being W. Watson (Leics) (vice-capt), D. A. Allen (Gloucs), R. W. Barber (Lancs), J. D. F. Larter (Northants), J. T. Murray (Middx), D. E. V. Padgett (Yorks), J. M. Parks (Sussex), R. M. Prideaux (Kent), W. E. Russell (Middx), D. M. Sayer (Kent), D. R. Smith (Gloucs), W. J. Stewart (Warwicks) and D. Wilson (Yorks). The manager was a New Zealander, J. H. Phillipps, who had managed two New Zealand teams in England. The object of the tour was to visit as many centres as possible and this made the travelling quite a major feature of the tour. In addition the team were billeted out with various families at each stop for economic reasons, which tended to go against the building up of team spirit.

The team travelled from England by air, the first major M.C.C. side to do so on the outward journey, though several had flown home.

Prior to the first 'Unofficial Test', the only difficulty the side faced was at Christchurch, where the M.C.C. were required to make 190 in 215 minutes. Watson hit a brilliant 106 in 161 minutes, but the rest of the batting failed and the tourists won by only one wicket.

In the 'First Test', both sides declared their first innings closed, before Barber and Allen dismissed New Zealand cheaply in the second innings, leaving M.C.C. 145 minutes to make 206. 100 came in 77 minutes, but after Prideaux went, wickets fell and the team opted for a draw. Watson led the M.C.C. side in this and in the 'Second Test', which was won by New Zealand due to

Alabaster exploiting the worn wicket with his leg breaks in the final innings.

The great match of the tour was against the Governor-General's Eleven, led by Lord Cobham – a record 27,000 watched the second day's play. The M.C.C. won, thanks to the leg-breaks of Barber, who took 7 for 89 in the last innings. The 'Third Test' was the final match of the tour. Larter, the tourists' fast bowler, could not play owing to appendicitis after the first day, but in fact rain cut short the game, which was drawn.

The team suffered from a large number of injuries. Silk injured his hand early on, whilst Stewart was hampered by a troublesome knee injury.

Prideaux was the outstanding batsman, though Padgett did well in the later matches and Watson was a tower of strength. The batting of Russell, Parks and Barber disappointed. The bowling was not as good as hoped. Larter did not really look hostile and Sayer was mediocre. Allen easily headed the bowling table in all matches, but in the first-class games, the variable Barber was more successful if more expensive.

Financially the tour produced a deficit of £1,527.

1961: Surridge takes a team to Bermuda

Under the sponsorship of the Bermuda Cricket Association, the following team left England by air on 8 July 1961 for a three-week tour of the colony: W. S. Surridge (Surrey) (capt), K. C. Bates, K. Cranston (Lancs), M. P. Murray (Middx), J. K. Hall (Surrey), J. K. E. Slack (Cambridge U), W. Murray Wood (Kent), J. C. L. Gover, G. P. S. Delisle (Middx), C. B. R. Fetherstonhaugh (Devon), I. R. Lomax (Wilts), T. W. Graveney (Worcs), A. C. Revill (Leics) and M. J. Osborne.

The innings of the tour was by Graveney, who hit 205 not out in under 300 minutes against Bermuda in the 'First Test' – he also hit 104 in 150 minutes in the 'Second Test' and ended the tour with an average of 86.75. The other batsmen found the matting on concrete wickets a bit of a problem.

The best bowler was Hall, whose fast bowling picked up 33 wickets at 12.66. Surridge split a finger in the second match and was not very effective.

Fetherstonhaugh proved an excellent wicket keeper and also batted with confidence. The best of the home players was Sheridan Raynor who scored a splendid century off the tourists' attack.

1961-62: F. R. Brown's tour of East Africa

Under the leadership of F. R. Brown (Northants), the following went on a four-week tour of East Africa in the autumn of 1961: R. E. Marshall (Hants), R. A. Gale (Middx), W. E. Alley (Somerset), P. M. Walker (Glam), J. B. Mortimore (Gloucs), A. C. D. Ingleby-Mackenzie (Hants), D. J. Shepherd (Glam), L. A. Johnson (Northants), J. K. Hall (Surrey), P. J. Loader (Surrey), R. I. Jefferson (Surrey), P. B. Wight (Somerset) and D. W. Dawson.

The three important matches were those against Kenya, Tanganyika and Uganda. Each of these was won, the closest being that in Nairobi, where Brown's bowling proved very effective and a good innings by Alley took the tourists to a four-wicket victory.

1961-62: England beat Pakistan and lose to India

The M.C.C. followed a pattern which had been established for two or three previous major tours by announcing the names of a list of possibles (this time numbering 29) for the visit to the Indian sub-continent. No less than eight of those asked stated they were not available and as seven of the eight were certainties if England wished to field the strongest possible team in the Tests, this meant that the eventual side was little better than M.C.C. 'A'. The eight who declined were D. B. Close, M. C. Cowdrey, J. H. Edrich, J. A. Flavell, P. B. H. May, J. B. Statham, R. Subba Row and F. S. Trueman. Among those who refused were the two most likely captains, May and Cowdrey. The team which left England by air on 8 October was E. R. Dexter (Sussex) (capt), M. J. K. Smith (Warwicks) (vice-capt), D. A. Allen (Gloucs), R. W. Barber (Lancs), K. F. Barrington (Surrey), A. Brown (Kent), B. R. Knight (Essex), G. A. R. Lock (Surrey), G. Millman (Notts), J. T. Murray (Middx), P. H. Parfitt (Middx), G. Pullar (Lancs), P. E. Richardson (Kent), W. E. Russell (Middx), D. R. Smith (Gloucs) and D. W. White (Hants), with T. N. Pearce (manager) and H. W. Dalton (masseur). The only omission commented upon in the press was that of Titmus.

Since India arranged to tour West Indies in February, March and April, the original tour programme had to be changed, which caused some oddities.

After two matches at Rawalpindi and Lyallpur, the first Test v Pakistan took place at Lahore. England were without Lock, but

1961-62: M.C.C. to India, Pakistan and Ceylon

1st Match: v President's XI (Rawalpindi)   Oct 13, 14, 15.
President's XI 208 & 195-8 dec (Mushtaq Mohammad 102*, G. A. R. Lock 5-53) drew with M.C.C. 197 (Javed Akhtar 7-56) & 154-7 (W. E. Russell 72).

2nd Match: v Governor's XI (Lyallpur)   Oct 17, 18, 19.
M.C.C. 252 (K. F. Barrington 55, Afaq Hussain 6-89) & 106 (G. Pullar 53, A. D'Souza 7-33) beat Governor's XI 119 & 210 (Shakoor Ahmed 60, Mahmood Hussain 50, D. A. Allen 7-67) by 29 runs.

3rd Match: v Pakistan (Lahore)   Oct 21, 22, 24, 25, 26.
Pakistan 387-9 dec (Javed Burki 138, Mushtaq Mohammad 76, Saeed Ahmed 74) & 200 lost to England 380 (K. F. Barrington 139, M. J. K. Smith 99) & 209-5 (E. R. Dexter 66*) by 5 wkts.

4th Match: v Combined Universities (Poona)   Oct 28, 29, 30.
Universities 346-9 dec (A. G. Milkha Singh 74, H. Gore 54, S. P. Gaekwad 53) & 67-3 drew with M.C.C. 417 (K. F. Barrington 149*, J. T. Murray 74, G. Pullar 64, N. Vishwanath 6-161).

5th Match: v West Zone (Ahmedabad)   Nov 3, 4, 5.
M.C.C. 272-7 dec (G. Pullar 104) & 167-5 dec (P. H. Parfitt 58) drew with West Zone 211 (V. H. Bhosle 62*, D. R. Smith 5-58) & 159-5 (R. F. Surti 51*).

6th Match: v Bombay (Bombay)   Nov 7, 8, 9.
M.C.C. 286-5 dec (R. W. Barber 71, M. J. K. Smith 56, J. T. Murray 51*) & 125-1 dec drew with Bombay 224 (S. G. Adhikari 87) & 137-7.

7th Match: v India (Bombay)   Nov 11, 12, 14, 15, 16.
England 500-8 dec (K. F. Barrington 151*, E. R. Dexter 85, G. Pullar 83, P. E. Richardson 71) & 184-5 dec (K. F. Barrington 52*) drew with India 390 (S. A. Durani 71, C. G. Borde 69, V. L. Manjrekar 68, M. L. Jaisimha 56) & 180-5 (V. L. Manjrekar 84, M. L. Jaisimha 51).

8th Match: v President's XI (Hyderabad)   Nov 18, 19, 20.
President's XI 281-5 dec (Nawab of Pataudi 70, R. F. Surti 69, P. Roy 65) & 163-5 dec (A. L. Apte 76*) lost to M.C.C. 261 (M. J. K. Smith 89, R. W. Barber 54) & 184-6 (P. H. Parfitt 84) by 4 wkts.

9th Match: v Rajasthan (Jaipur)   Nov 22, 23, 24.
Rajasthan 268 (S. A. Durani 124, D. R. Smith 6-47) & 155-6 dec drew with M.C.C. 222-6 dec (K. F. Barrington 91) & 86-2.

10th Match: v Central Zone (Nagpur)   Nov 26, 27, 28.
M.C.C. 405-3 dec (P. H. Parfitt 166*, W. E. Russell 101, P. E. Richardson 58) & 58-3 drew with Central Zone 234 (M. Sharma 68, K. Rungta 52) & 235-6 dec (Suryavir Singh 112).

11th Match: v India (Kanpur)   Dec 1, 2, 3, 5, 6.
India 467-8 dec (P. R. Umrigar 147*, V. L. Manjrekar 96, M. L. Jaisimha 70) drew with England 244 (R. W. Barber 69*, S. P. Gupte 5-90) & 497-5 (K. F. Barrington 172, E. R. Dexter 126*, G. Pullar 119).

12th Match: v North Zone (Jullundur)   Dec 8, 9, 10.
North Zone 152 (V. L. Mehra 56) & 145 (V. L. Mehra 53) lost to M.C.C. 256-9 dec (E. R. Dexter 72, V. M. Muddiah 6-71) & 42-1 by 9 wkts.

13th Match: v India (New Delhi)   Dec 13, 14, 16, 17, 18.
India 466 (V. L. Manjrekar 189*, M. L. Jaisimha 127) drew with England 256-3 (K. F. Barrington 113*, G. Pullar 89).

14th Match: v East Zone (Cuttack)   Dec 22, 23, 24.
M.C.C. 261-4 dec (K. F. Barrington 80*, P. E. Richardson 59) & 277-5 (P. E. Richardson 147) drew with East Zone 263-8 dec (R. B. Kenny 70, M. P. Barua 66).

15th Match: v Services XI (Calcutta)   Dec 26, 27, 28.
M.C.C. 339-9 dec (P. H. Parfitt 112, R. W. Barber 58, E. R. Dexter 58) beat Services XI 172 (V. K. Dandekar 69, D. W. White 5-42) & 130 by an inns & 37 runs.

16th Match: v India (Calcutta)   Dec 30, 31, Jan 1, 3, 4.
India 380 (C. G. Borde 68, Nawab of Pataudi 64, V. L. Mehra 62, D. A. Allen 5-67) & 252 (C. G. Borde 61) beat England 212 (P. E. Richardson 62, E. R. Dexter 57, S. A. Durani 5-47) & 233 (E. R. Dexter 62) by 187 runs.

17th Match: v South Zone (Bangalore)   Jan 6, 7, 8.
M.C.C. 193 (M. J. K. Smith 57, E. A. S. Prasanna 5-66) & 192-2 dec (M. J. K. Smith 67*, G. Pullar 52) beat South Zone 132 & 216 (S. Nazareth 65, A. V. Jaganath 52).

18th Match: v India (Madras)   Jan 10, 11, 13, 14, 15.
India 428 (Nawab of Pataudi 103, N. J. Contractor 86, F. M. Engineer 65, R. G. Nadkarni 63) & 190 (V. L. Manjrekar 85, G. A. R. Lock 6-65) beat England 281 (M. J. K. Smith 73, S. A. Durani 6-105) & 209 by 128 runs.

19th Match: v Pakistan (Dacca)   Jan 19, 20, 21, 23, 24.
Pakistan 393-7 dec (Javed Burki 140, Hanif Mohammad 111, Saeed Ahmed 69) & 216 (Hanif Mohammad 104, Alim-ud-Din 50, D. A. Allen 5-30) drew with England 439 (G. Pullar 165, R. W. Barber 86, K. F. Barrington 84) & 38-0.

20th Match: v Combined XI (Bahawalpur)   Jan 26, 27, 28.
M.C.C. 114 (Fazal Mahmood 6-28) & 69-0 drew with Combined XI 162 (Asif Ahmed 58).

21st Match: v Pakistan (Karachi)   Feb 2, 3, 4, 6, 7.
Pakistan 253 (Alim-ud-Din 109, Hanif Mohammad 67) & 404-8 (Hanif Mohammad 89, Imtiaz Ahmed 86, Alim-ud-Din 53) drew with England 507 (E. R. Dexter 205, P. H. Parfitt 111, G. Pullar 60, A. D'Souza 5-112).

22nd Match: v Ceylon C.A. (Colombo)   Feb 10, 11.
M.C.C. 257 (E. R. Dexter 74, P. H. Parfitt 73, P. E. Richardson 52, I. Gunasekera 5-61) & 159 (N. Chanmugam 5-43) drew with Ceylon C.A. 235 (H. I. K. Fernando 79, E. R. Dexter 5-112) & 20-0.

23rd Match: v Up-Country XI (Radella)   Feb 13, 14.
Up-Country XI 204 (G. Goonesena 68, A. S. Brown 6-38) & 93 (G. A. R. Lock 5-22) lost to M.C.C. 290 (M. J. K. Smith 85, G. A. R. Lock 74) & 10-0 by 10 wkts.

24th Match: v Ceylon (Colombo)   Feb 16, 17, 18.
Ceylon 210 (C. N. Lafir 84) & 144 (E. R. Dexter 5-51) lost to M.C.C. 284 (K. F. Barrington 93, P. H. Parfitt 50) & 72-2 by 8 wkts.

Brown, Barber and Allen managed to dismiss Pakistan cheaply in their second innings to leave England 250 minutes to make 208 – a fine display by Dexter, in his first Test as captain, won the game.

Three drawn matches were played before England switched opponents and met India. England piled up 500 before Dexter declared and as India made 390, a draw became the obvious outcome, though Dexter made a sporting declaration which was ignored.

In the second Test against India progress was slow due in part to the unruly crowd, who flashed mirrors in the eyes of the batsmen and threw missiles at the fieldsmen. Fires and fights kept breaking out. This was all to India's disadvantage, since the home side bowled England out cheaply and enforced the follow on. In the second innings however Pullar, Barrington and Dexter made hundreds and the game was drawn. Rain ruined the third Test, the final two days being washed out. The batting was slow however and without the rain the match would probably have been drawn anyway. The Nawab of Pataudi (son of the old England and India Test player) made his debut for India in this game.

India won the toss and the game in the fourth Test at Calcutta. Solid batting gave the home side 380 on the first innings, then England fell to Durani and Borde. Allen and Lock struck back, but on a spinners' wicket England never looked like making the 421 needed for victory and a succession of nine England v India draws was broken.

In complete contrast to the usual method set by Test captains when leading in the series with one match to go, Contractor in the fifth Test won the toss and scored freely, his example was followed by the Nawab, whose hundred came in 155 minutes. India scored their total of 428 at not much under a run per minute, but dropped catches helped their cause. The English batsmen were not so fluent and battled against the spin of Durani and Borde. The match was won by India just after lunch on the fifth day.

Travelling to East Pakistan, England played the second Test against Pakistan at Dacca. The home team were not inspired by India and the Test was probably the most boring on record – Hanif batted about 15 hours for 215 runs in his two innings. England were somewhat quicker, but with about two days to go a draw seemed the only result conceivable.

Barrington could not play in the third Test at Karachi and White had to retire after opening the English bowling, due to a pulled muscle. Neither problem had much bearing on the out-

1961-62: M.C.C. to India, Pakistan and Ceylon

Batting Averages

	M	I	NO	R	HS	Avge	100	c/s
K. F. Barrington (Surrey)	17	26	7	1329	172	69.94	5	12
E. R. Dexter (Sussex)	17	27	5	1053	205	47.86	2	15
G. Pullar (Lancs)	17	25	1	1046	165	43.58	3	5
P. H. Parfitt (Middx)	17	29	4	1043	166*	41.72	3	23
P. E. Richardson (Kent)	17	30	3	1003	147	37.14	1	11
M. J. K. Smith (Warks)	17	29	6	789	99	34.30	0	12
R. W. Barber (Lancs)	18	23	4	637	86	33.52	0	9
W. E. Russell (Middx)	12	21	3	603	101	33.50	1	6
J. T. Murray (Middx)	11	15	3	278	74	23.16	0	14/3
B. R. Knight (Essex)	16	20	3	380	39*	22.35	0	11
A. Brown (Kent)	11	7	5	39	12*	19.50	0	7
D. A. Allen (Gloucs)	16	15	2	233	40	17.92	0	6
G. A. R. Lock (Surrey)	15	17	5	182	49	15.16	0	20
G. Millman (Notts)	14	18	6	177	36*	14.75	0	23/8
D. R. Smith (Gloucs)	13	11	3	114	34	14.25	0	6
D. W. White (Hants)	12	9	1	54	15	6.75	0	3

Also played in two matches: J. G. Binks (Yorks) 12, 0 (ct 7, st 1).

Bowling Averages

	O	M	R	W	Avge	BB	5i
D. W. White	225	52	635	32	19.84	5-42	1
A. Brown	237	61	586	25	23.44	4-13	0
G. A. R. Lock	695.3	287	1406	59	23.83	6-65	2
D. R. Smith	348	81	859	36	23.86	6-47	2
B. R. Knight	365	95	1024	39	26.25	4-7	0
W. E. Russell	79	30	165	6	27.50	3-25	0
D. A. Allen	719.3	272	1427	50	28.54	7-67	3
P. H. Parfitt	114	30	340	11	30.90	3-60	0
E. R. Dexter	327	89	805	24	33.54	5-51	1
K. F. Barrington	112	27	323	9	35.88	2-3	0
R. W. Barber	438.1	92	1384	35	39.54	4-66	0

Also bowled: J. T. Murray 7-2-18-2; G. Pullar 14-6-37-1; P. E. Richardson 20-9-48-3; M. J. K. Smith 12-4-17-2.

come of the game which England would have won if dropped catches had not occurred – the immobile Hanif was missed twice. Dexter hit a double century, but even he took 500 minutes over the task.

The tour ended with a three-match visit to Ceylon.

With England fielding almost a second team, the results of the tour were much as expected. Dexter and Barrington were the best batsmen, and of the younger players, Parfitt proved the most effective. Lock and Allen were the hardest worked and most deserving of the bowlers – England really missed a pair of fast bowlers.

Murray, the wicket-keeper, was taken ill and went home. Binks was flown out as a replacement, but with Millman keeping well was not required very much.

The tour proved very popular and about 1,200,000 watched the eight Tests.

1962 : Gloucestershire tour Bermuda

In April 1962, the Gloucestershire County Team made a three-week tour of Bermuda. The team was: C. T. M. Pugh (capt), D. R. Smith, J. B. Mortimore, A. S. Brown, D. M. Young, C. A. Milton, D. A. Allen, B. J. Meyer, A. Dindar, F. J. Andrews, D. Carpenter, C. Cook and D. G. A'Court.

The most important game against 'Pick of Bermuda' was drawn after three declarations – it was limited to two days. Brown was the most effective bowler on the tour, whilst Pugh and Mortimore were the best batsmen.

1962: Gloucestershire to Bermuda

1st Match: v Devonshire R.C. (Devonshire R.C.)   April 10.
Gloucs 253 (D. R. Smith 86*, D. M. Young 69, C. Ford 6-63) lost to Devonshire 256-7 (C. Dill 76) by 3 wkts.

2nd Match: v Western Counties (Somerset C.C.)   April 12.
Western Counties 196 (W. Wilson 77) beat Gloucs 124 by 72 runs.

3rd Match: v Bermuda C.A. (National Sports Club)   April 17.
Gloucs 204-5 dec (D. M. Young 61, C. T. M. Pugh 51) beat Bermuda C.A. 56 (A. S Brown 8-32) by 148 runs.

4th Match: v Pond Hill Stars (Somerset C.C.)   April 19.
Pond Hill Stars 114 (A. S. Brown 6-48) beat Gloucs 89 by 25 runs.

5th Match: v Somers Isles Cricket League (Devonshire R.C.)   April 21.
Somers Isles 264-8 dec (F. Nisbett 87, E. Pitcher 69) drew with Gloucs 205-3 (C. T. M. Pugh 125*).

6th Match: v Somerset C.C. (Somerset C.C.)   April 22.
Somerset C.C. 250-5 dec (N. L. Hazel 85, A. S. Bean 79) drew with Gloucs 134-6 (C. A. Milton 56*, J. B. Mortimore 53).

7th Match: v National Sports Club (National S.C.)   April 24.
Gloucs 256-7 dec (J. B. Mortimore 69, A. S. Brown 54) beat National S.C. 81 by 175 runs.

8th Match: v Eastern Counties (National S.C.)   April 26.
Gloucs 258-6 dec (J. B. Mortimore 111, A. Dindar 56) beat Eastern Counties 89 by 169 runs.

9th Match: v Pick of Bermuda (Devonshire R.C.)   April 28, 29.
Pick of Bermuda 271-6 dec & 222-5 dec (C. W. Smith 63) drew with Gloucs 278-8 dec (D. A. Allen 96) & 159-5.

1962-63 : Dexter's side draw series with Australia

The team to tour Australia in 1962-63 was E. R. Dexter (Sussex) (capt), M. C. Cowdrey (Kent) (vice-capt), D. A. Allen (Gloucs), K. F. Barrington (Surrey), L. J. Coldwell (Worcs), T. W. Graveney (Gloucs), R. Illingworth (Yorks), B. R. Knight (Essex), J. D. F. Larter (Northants), J. T. Murray (Middx), P. H. Parfitt (Middx), G. Pullar (Lancs), the Rev D. S. Sheppard (Sussex),

A. C. Smith (Warwicks), J. B. Statham (Lancs), F. J. Titmus (Middx) and F. S. Trueman (Yorks), with the Duke of Norfolk as manager, A. V. Bedser as his assistant, W. R. Watkins as scorer, and S. Cowan as masseur. Announced in August, there were no alterations when the side flew to Aden on 27 September and then sailed on the *Canberra*, via Colombo to Fremantle.

The press were on the whole unable to improve on the selectors' choice, but wondered if the side could bowl out Australia as Trueman and Statham were moving into the veteran class for effective fast bowlers.

Although the team beat Western Australia in the first first-class match, the batting failed in the second game and a Combined Eleven won by 10 wickets. R. B. Simpson hit 109 and 66 not out for the victors. After a series of draws, New South Wales inflicted an innings defeat on the tourists. R. B. Simpson made another hundred and Benaud took 7 for 18 in the M.C.C.'s second innings. The prospects for England were now looking decidedly nasty.

Australia had all the best of the first Test and Benaud was happy to declare with only 4 second innings wickets down to set England 378 in 360 minutes. Dexter batted exceptionally well, as he had in the first innings, but England were fighting to save the game when stumps were drawn. The second Test proved a tremendous tussle – Dexter again batted in good form and Trueman and Statham managed to dismiss Australia twice for reasonable totals. England required 234 to win in the final innings and a century from Sheppard produced a win by 7 wickets, Australia dropping some vital catches.

The team went to Tasmania for the break between the second and third Tests and overwhelmed the Combined Eleven at Launceston, who were dismissed for 77 and 57. The third Test took place at Sydney. Graveney was too ill to play and Parfitt re-appeared, having taken Graveney's place in the first Test. The difference between the two teams on first innings was minimal, but Davidson produced a great opening spell at the start of England's second innings and the tourists never recovered, leaving Australia the simple task of making 65 to win, which they did with a day and a half to spare.

Australia decided to play safe in the fourth Test and both sides seemed too frightened of losing to make a real attempt to win, though Australia were handicapped when Davidson broke down early in the England first innings. As it was England needed 356 to win at 89 an hour when the final innings began. Barrington

---

1962-63: M.C.C. to Ceylon, Australia and New Zealand

Batting Averages

	M	I	NO	R	HS	Avge	100	c/s
K. F. Barrington (Surrey)	17	27	5	1763	219*	80.13	6	17
M. C. Cowdrey (Kent)	16	29	5	1380	307	57.50	3	10
T. W. Graveney (Worcs)	11	18	4	737	185	52.64	2	13
B. R. Knight (Essex)	12	19	5	675	125	48.21	2	4
E. R. Dexter (Sussex)	16	27	1	1107	102	42.57	1	14
F. J. Titmus (Middx)	16	21	6	595	137*	39.66	1	10
Rev D. S. Sheppard (Sussex)	16	28	0	1074	113	38.35	1	11
G. Pullar (Lancs)	10	19	1	564	132	31.33	1	0
A. C. Smith (Warks)	13	16	5	330	69*	30.00	0	37/1
P. H. Parfitt (Middx)	14	22	2	525	131*	26.25	1	14
R. Illingworth (Yorks)	12	16	3	329	65*	25.30	0	10
D. A. Allen (Gloucs)	9	9	3	119	32*	19.83	0	5
F. S. Trueman (Yorks)	12	14	0	194	38	13.85	0	9
J. T. Murray (Middx)	7	9	4	69	24*	13.80	0	11/1
J. B. Statham (Lancs)	9	11	2	96	30	10.66	0	6
L. J. Coldwell (Worcs)	9	8	4	14	4	3.50	0	6
J. D. F. Larter (Northts)	10	3	1	6	4*	3.00	0	3

Bowling Averages

	Balls	M	R	W	Avge	BB	5i
F. S. Trueman	2563	54	1020	55	18.54	7-75	4
D. A. Allen	2322	89	690	29	23.79	5-43	2
J. D. F. Larter	2123	49	938	39	24.05	4-24	0
F. J. Titmus	3939	134	1399	49	28.55	7-79	2
J. B. Statham	2325	34	1043	33	31.60	4-49	0
B. R. Knight	1558	38	691	20	34.55	3-32	0
K. F. Barrington	1212	27	653	17	38.41	3-32	0
L. J. Coldwell	1979	48	821	21	39.09	6-49	1
R. Illingworth	1793	56	709	17	41.70	4-34	0
E. R. Dexter	1656	26	759	18	42.16	4-8	0

Also bowled: T. W. Graveney 72-2-36-2; G. Pullar 72-0-38-0.

Above *The M.C.C. party after their arrival at Fremantle on board the liner* Canberra *for the Australian tour of 1962-63. Back: P. H. Parfitt, A. C. Smith, F. J. Titmus, J. D. F. Larter, B. R. Knight, T. W. Graveney, L. J. Coldwell, the Rev D. S. Sheppard, A. V. Bedser (assistant manager). Front: J. T. Murray, G. Pullar, D. A. Allen, E. R. Dexter (captain), J. B. Statham, the Duke of Norfolk, R. Illingworth, F. S. Trueman, M. C. Cowdrey, K. F. Barrington.*

Left *The first day of the first Test at Brisbane on the 1962-63 tour. Bill Lawry caught for 5 by Alan Smith off Fred Trueman. The other batsman is Bobby Simpson.*

Below *England captain Ted Dexter caught by Simpson for 47 from the bowling of Norman O'Neill in the final Test of the 1962-63 tour. Barrington is the non-striker.*

1st Match: v Ceylon (Colombo)   Oct 3.
M.C.C. 181-8 dec (D. S. Shephard 73) drew with Ceylon 152-8 (C. I. Gunesekara 76, R. Illingworth 5-59).

2nd Match: v Western Australia Country XI (Kalgoorlie)   Oct 16, 17.
M.C.C. 247-7 dec (G. Pullar 102) & 314-8 (J. T. Murray 102, D. S. Sheppard 59) drew with W.A. Country XI 212 (L. Campbell 66).

3rd Match: v Western Australia (Perth)   Oct 19, 20, 22.
M.C.C. 303 (F. J. Titmus 88, E. R. Dexter 76) & 49-0 beat W. Australia 77 & 274 (K. Gartrell 72, M. Vernon 68) by 10 wkts.

4th Match: v Combined XI (Perth)   Oct 26, 27, 29, 30.
M.C.C. 157 (B. R. Knight 65*) & 270 (D. S. Sheppard 92, E. R. Dexter 60, D. E. Hoare 5-60) lost to Combined XI 317 (R. B. Simpson 109, J. Parker 55, W. M. Lawry 52, D. A. Allen 5-76) & 115-0 (R. B. Simpson 66*) by 10 wkts.

5th Match: v South Australia (Adelaide)   Nov 2, 3, 5, 6.
S. Australia 335 (J. Lill 87, I. M. McLachlan 53) & 283-7 dec (G. St. A. Sobers 99) drew with M.C.C. 508-9 dec (F. J. Titmus 137, K. F. Barrington 104, T. W. Graveney 99, B. R. Knight 55, A. C. Smith 55, N. J. N. Hawke 6-130) & 95-1 (G. Pullar 56).

6th Match: v Australian XI (Melbourne)   Nov 9, 10, 12, 13.
M.C.C. 633-7 dec (K. F. Barrington 219*, B. R. Knight 108, E. R. Dexter 102, M. C. Cowdrey 88) & 68-5 dec drew with Australian XI 451 (R. B. Simpson 130, B. K. Shepherd 114, I. M. McLachlan 55, R. N. Harvey 51) & 201-4 (B. K. Shepherd 91*, I. M. McLachlan 68).

7th Match: v New South Wales Country XI (Griffith)   Nov 14.
N.S.W. Country XI 186-6 dec (M. Rudd 82) lost to M.C.C. 187-3 (G. Pullar 77*, E. R. Dexter 76*) by 7 wkts.

8th Match: v New South Wales (Sydney)   Nov 16, 17, 19.
M.C.C. 348 (G. Pullar 132, M. C. Cowdrey 50) & 104 (R. Benaud 7-18) lost to N.S.W. 532-6 dec (N. C. O'Neill 143, R. B. Simpson 110, R. N. Harvey 63, R. G. Flockton 62*, A. K. Davidson 55) by an inns & 80 runs.

9th Match: v Queensland (Brisbane)   Nov 23, 24, 26, 27.
Queensland 433-7 dec (K. D. Mackay 105*, S. C. Trimble 95, G. M. Bizzell 59, A. T. W. Grout 56) & 94-7 drew with M.C.C. 581-6 dec (K. F. Barrington 183*, D. S. Sheppard 94, B. R. Knight 81, E. R. Dexter 80, T. W. Graveney 52).

10th Match: v Queensland Country XI (Toowoomba)   Nov 28.
Qld Country XI 202-4 dec (I. B. Oxenford 66, W. Brown 56*) lost to M.C.C. 204-3 (P. H. Parfitt 128*) by 7 wkts.

11th Match: v Australia (Brisbane)   Nov 30, Dec 1, 3, 4, 5.
Australia 404 (B. C. Booth 112, K. D. Mackay 86*, R. Benaud 51, R. B. Simpson 50) & 362-4 dec (W. M. Lawry 98, R. B. Simpson 71, R. N. Harvey 57, N. C. O'Neill 56) drew with England 389 (P. H. Parfitt 80, K. F. Barrington 78, E. R. Dexter 70, R. Benaud 6-115) & 278-6 (E. R. Dexter 99, G. Pullar 56, D. S. Sheppard 53).

12th Match: v Queensland Country XI (Townsville)   Dec 7, 8.
Qld Country XI 165 & 138 (D. A. Allen 5-57) lost to M.C.C. 423-9 dec (T. W. Graveney 118, P. H. Parfitt 98, D. S. Sheppard 67, R. Illingworth 58) by an inns & 120 runs.

13th Match: v Victorian Country XII (Bendigo)   Dec 10, 11.
Victorian Country XII 110 & 159-4 (F. Watts 63) drew with M.C.C. 360-8 dec (M. C. Cowdrey 111, K. F. Barrington 90, T. W. Graveney 59*).

14th Match: v Victorian Country XII (Shepparton)   Dec 12.
Victorian Country XII 191-6 dec lost to M.C.C. 196-5 (G. Pullar 51) by 6 wkts.

15th Match: v Victoria (Melbourne)   Dec 14, 15, 17, 18.
Victoria 340 (W. M. Lawry 177, N. L. West 70) & 175 (L. J. Caldwell 6-49) lost to M.C.C. 336 (G. Pullar 91, R. Illingworth 50) & 180-5 (M. C. Cowdrey 63, D. S. Sheppard 50) by 5 wkts.

16th Match: v South Australian Country XI (Port Lincoln)   Dec 20.
S.A. Country XI 55 lost to M.C.C. 56-0 by 10 wkts.

17th Match: v South Australia (Adelaide)   Dec 23, 24, 26, 27.
M.C.C. 586-5 dec (M. C. Cowdrey 307, T. W. Graveney 122*, D. S. Sheppard 81, K. F. Barrington 52) & 167-6 dec (K. F. Barrington 52*) drew with S. Australia 450 (L. E. Favell 120, G. St. A. Sobers 89, H. N. Dansie 64, I. M. McLachlan 62, J. C. Lill 55) & 113-4 (G. St. A. Sobers 75*).

18th Match: v Australia (Melbourne)   Dec 29, 31, Jan 1, 2, 3.
Australia 316 (W. M. Lawry 52) & 248 (B. C. Booth 103, W. M. Lawry 57, F. S. Trueman 5-62) lost to England 331 (M. C. Cowdrey 113, E. R. Dexter 93, A. K. Davidson 6-75) & 237-3 (D. S. Sheppard 113, M. C. Cowdrey 58*, E. R. Dexter 52) by 7 wkts.

19th Match: v Combined XI (Launceston)   Jan 4, 5, 7.
M.C.C. 331-7 dec (D. S. Sheppard 82, K. F. Barrington 73, B. R. Knight 68, R. Illingworth 65*) & 116-1 (D. S. Sheppard 67) beat Combined XI 77 & 57 by 313 runs.

20th Match: v Tasmania (Hobart)   Jan 8, 9.
Tasmania 203 (R. Stokes 82) & 181-6 (R. Stokes 76*) drew with M.C.C. 324 (P. H. Parfitt 121, G. Pullar 63, J. O'Brien 7-73).

21st Match: v Australia (Sydney)   Jan 11, 12, 14, 15.
England 279 (M. C. Cowdrey 85, G. Pullar 53, R. B. Simpson 5-57) & 104 (A. K. Davidson 5-25) lost to Australia 319 (R. B. Simpson 91, B. K. Shepherd 71*, R. N. Harvey 64, F. J. Titmus 7-79) & 67-2 by 8 wkts.

22nd Match: v New South Country XI (Newcastle)   Jan 18, 19, 20.
M.C.C. 319 (B. R. Knight 73, G. Pullar 53 & 190-4 dec (E. R. Dexter 71*) beat N.S.W. Country XI 203 (D. Dives 71) ? 161 (D. A. Allen 5-38) by 145 runs.

23rd Match: v Australia (Adelaide)   Jan 25, 26, 28, 29, 30.
Australia 393 (R. N. Harvey 154, N. C. O'Neill 110) & 293 (B. C. Booth 77, R. B. Simpson 71) drew with England 331 (K. F. Barrington 63, E. R. Dexter 61, F. J. Titmus 59*, G. D. McKenzie 5-89) & 223-4 (K. F. Barrington 132*).

24th Match: v Victoria (Melbourne)   Feb 1, 2, 4, 5.
M.C.C. 375 (T. W. Graveney 185, I. Meckiff 5-93) & 218-5 dec (E. R. Dexter 70, K. F. Barrington 66) drew with Victoria 307 (J. Potter 106, D. A. Allen 5-43) & 188-9 (R. M. Cowper 51).

25th Match: v Prime Minister's XI (Canberra) (One Day)   Feb 6.
M.C.C. 253-7 dec (D. S. Sheppard 72) beat Prime Minister's XI 250 (R. Benaud 68, D. A. Allen 5-68) by 3 runs.

26th Match: v New South Wales Country XI (Dubbo)   Feb 8, 9.
N.S.W. Country XI 137 & 227-5 (I. Drake 101) drew with M.C.C. 451-8 dec (T. W. Graveney 106, M. C. Cowdrey 97, D. S. Sheppard 93, B. R. Knight 70).

27th Match: v New South Wales Country XI (Tamworth)   Feb 11, 12.
N.S.W. Country XI 109 (B. Weissel 51) & 222 lost to M.C.C. 322-6 dec (E. R. Dexter 87, B. R. Knight 62, R. Illingworth 62*) & 10-0 by 10 wkts.

28th Match: v Australia (Sydney)   Feb 15, 16, 18, 19, 20.
England 321 (K. F. Barrington 101) & 268-8 dec (K. F. Barrington 94, D. S. Sheppard 68, M. C. Cowdrey 53) drew with Australia 349 (P. J. P. Burge 103, N. C. O'Neill 73, R. Benaud 57, F. J. Titmus 5-103) & 152-4 (P. J. P. Burge 52*).

29th Match: v New Zealand (Auckland)   Feb 22, 23, 25, 26.
England 562-7 dec (P. H. Parfitt 131*, K. F. Barrington 126, B. R. Knight 125, M. C. Cowdrey 86) beat New Zealand 258 (B. W. Yuile 64, R. C. Motz 60, J. R. Reid 59) & 89 by an inns & 215 runs.

30th Match: v New Zealand (Wellington)   March 1, 2, 4.
New Zealand 194 (R. W. Blair 64*) & 187 (W. R. Playle 65) lost to England 428-8 dec (M. C. Cowdrey 128*, K. F. Barrington 76, A. C. Smith 69*) by an inns & 47 runs.

31st Match: v Otago Invitation XI (Dunedin)   March 8, 9, 11.
Otago 116 (F. S. Trueman 5-19) & 170 (F. S. Trueman 6-64) lost to M.C.C. 296-9 dec (D. S. Sheppard 76, M. C. Cowdrey 60, P. H. Parfitt 54) by an inns & 10 runs.

32nd Match: v New Zealand (Christchurch)   March 15, 16, 18, 19.
New Zealand 266 (J. R. Reid 74, F. S. Trueman 7-75) & 159 (J. R. Reid 100) lost to England 253 & 173-3 by 7 wkts.

made certain that England could not lose, hitting an excellent hundred.

The fifth and last Test, which ought to have been the climax of the tour, with each side having won one match so far, turned out to be a very poor affair and the crowd could not be blamed for their barracking. Dexter won the toss and England spent the first day making 195 for 5. Australia gained a small lead on first innings and later, with Sheppard, Cowdrey and Barrington all making runs, Dexter declared to set Australia 241 in 240 minutes. Four wickets went down for 70 when Lawry took control and amid slow hand clapping and boos batted out time.

Going on to New Zealand, the tourists played two Tests straight away and won both by an innings. The third and final Test was won by 7 wickets and the side flew home with at least some credit.

The chief memory of the tour was the poor English fielding. The best English batting came from Barrington, Dexter and Cowdrey. In the bowling Titmus proved well worth his place, which was surprising, since he was expected to play second fiddle to Allen when the tour began. Trueman bowled much better than his critics forecast, but Statham was not so good as previously. Larter was too inaccurate to make much of a contribution and little was seen of Coldwell or Knight in the important games. Murray lost the wicket-keeping position to Smith.

Simpson was the dominant Australian batsman, neither Lawry nor O'Neill being quite as good as feared. Davidson and McKenzie led the Australian attack – Benaud, after a brilliant start, falling away.

1963-64: M.C.C. tour of Tanganyika, Kenya, Uganda

Following the path of F. R. Brown's tour two years before, the M.C.C. sent the following side to East Africa in the autumn of 1963: M. J. K. Smith (Warwicks) (capt), W. Watson (Leics) (player-manager), P. H. Parfitt (Middx), M. J. Stewart (Surrey), C. Milburn (Northants), J. B. Mortimore (Gloucs), R. J. Langridge (Sussex), R. N. S. Hobbs (Essex), T. W. Cartwright (Warwicks), L. A. Johnson (Northants), J. D. F. Larter (Northants) and I. J. Jones (Glamorgan).

The team, which was of good first-class county standard, was obviously too strong for the opposition. All the matches were played on jute matting rather than coir, which meant that life was easier for the batsmen. The most important match of the tour was against an East African Invitation Eleven at Kampala, but the tourists found little difficulty in winning by an innings. The only game that was at all close was the match against the Kenya Kongonis. Smith set the locals 298 to win. Shuttleworth and Giles put on 83 for the last wicket and were within 11 of victory, when Shuttleworth was run out.

A young local batsman who impressed the tourists was Basharat – better known now as the Notts cricketer, B. Hassan.

The tour was not a financial success, the attendances in Nairobi being much lower than expected.

1963-64: all five Tests drawn in India

Following the complaints regarding the over-long tour to the Indian sub-continent in 1961-62, the M.C.C. experimented with an eight-week tour to India alone, consisting of ten matches only, five of which were Tests.

Before selecting the team, the M.C.C. drew up a list of no less than 36 possible players and asked each if he were available. The team eventually announced was M. C. Cowdrey (Kent) (capt), M. J. K. Smith (Warwicks) (vice-capt), K. F. Barrington (Surrey), J. G. Binks (Yorks), J. B. Bolus (Notts), J. H. Edrich (Surrey), I. J. Jones (Glamorgan), B. R. Knight (Essex), J. D. F. Larter (Northants), J. B. Mortimore (Gloucs), J. M. Parks (Sussex), J. S. E. Price (Middx), P. J. Sharpe (Yorks), F. J. Titmus (Middx) and D. Wilson (Yorks) with D. G. Clark as manager. The side was much better than the one of 1961-62, though lacking Dexter, Trueman and Close, a trio which had featured strongly in the home Tests of 1963.

A few weeks after the team had been announced, Cowdrey stated he was not fit, owing to an arm injury and M. J. Stewart of Surrey was included, with M. J. K. Smith taking over as captain.

Flying to India, the tour began at Bangalore, where a high-scoring draw was played. In the second game however the local side – South Zone – proved very vulnerable to spin and a combination of Titmus, Wilson and Barrington was too much for them.

India scored 457 for seven in the first Test and the only effective English bowler was Titmus, but slow scoring after a bright first day made a draw certain. England had four players who were taken ill during the match, which did not help the tourists' cause.

In the match after the first Test, Barrington had the misfortune to break a finger, and Smith cabled home for some reinforcements – M. C. Cowdrey and P. H. Parfitt were dispatched but did not arrive in time for the second Test. England went into the game in dire straits, since Edrich, Sharpe and Mortimore were all on the sick list, so both wicket-keepers had to be played. At tea-time on the first day Stewart fell ill and the match continued with only ten men in the English camp. India totally failed to take advantage of the situation and some splendid all-round cricket by the English ten easily saved the day.

England had twelve fit men for the third Test, Cowdrey and Parfitt having arrived. Price produced his best performance to dismiss India for 241, but England in reply struggled. Cowdrey with a slow hundred managed to get a small first innings lead, but loss of time due to rain put any question of a definite decision out of court.

Cowdrey hit another century in the fourth Test and England gained a lead of over a hundred. Kunderan however insured India against defeat and on the last day the Nawab hit a double century, but it was purely academic.

The pitch for the last Test at Kanpur was completely dead and the twenty-two players merely went through the motions for the statutory five days. Knight and Parfitt hit hundreds for England and Nadkarni gave an exhibition display on the final day. The

1963-64: M.C.C. to India

Batting Averages

	M	I	NO	R	HS	Avge	100	c/s
K. F. Barrington (Surrey)	4	4	1	336	108	112.00	1	2
M. C. Cowdrey (Kent)	4	5	2	315	151	105.00	2	5
P. H. Parfitt (Middx)	5	7	3	351	121	87.75	1	2
J. H. Edrich (Surrey)	6	8	1	386	150	55.14	1	1
P. J. Sharpe (Yorks)	6	10	2	434	86	54.25	0	4
M. J. K. Smith (Warks)	8	11	4	376	75*	53.71	0	4
J. B. Bolus (Notts)	9	15	0	752	113	50.13	1	4
M. J. Stewart (Surrey)	5	5	0	223	119	44.60	1	3
J. M. Parks (Sussex)	8	10	3	271	52	38.71	0	11/2
D. Wilson (Yorks)	9	8	2	203	112	33.83	1	1
F. J. Titmus (Middx)	7	8	3	164	84*	32.80	0	5
B. R. Knight (Essex)	8	10	1	276	127	30.66	1	1
J. B. Mortimore (Gloucs)	6	6	1	143	73*	28.60	0	7
J. G. Binks (Yorks)	6	5	0	121	55	24.20	0	13/1
J. S. E. Price (Middx)	7	4	1	34	32	11.33	0	3
J. D. F. Larter (Northts)	7	4	1	12	10	4.00	0	2

Also played in 5 matches: I. J. Jones (Glam) 5.

Bowling Averages

	O	M	R	W	Avge	BB	5i
K. F. Barrington	39.3	8	131	7	18.71	3-11	0
F. J. Titmus	474.5	178	1000	36	27.77	6-73	2
J. S. E. Price	184.1	34	569	17	33.47	5-73	1
J. D. F. Larter	151.3	27	477	14	34.07	2-22	0
J. B. Mortimore	308.2	123	603	16	37.68	5-75	1
D. Wilson	302	117	569	13	43.76	4-28	0
B. R. Knight	147.2	27	493	11	44.81	3-24	0
I. J. Jones	124	19	417	9	46.33	3-59	0
P. H. Parfitt	145	51	402	8	50.25	2-71	0

Also bowled: J. B. Bolus 17-4-63-2; J. M. Parks 14-1-95-1; M. J. K. Smith 14-0-60-0; M. J. Stewart 7-0-42-0; J. H. Edrich 5-1-27-0; M. C. Cowdrey 5-0-34-0; P. J. Sharpe 2-1-4-0; J. G. Binks 2-0-16-0.

(Kent), T. E. Bailey (Essex), E. R. Dexter (Sussex), F. S. Trueman (Yorks), T. W. Graveney (Worcs), P. E. Richardson (Kent), J. T. Murray (Middx), R. E. Marshall (Hants), A. C. D. Ingleby-Mackenzie (Hants), A. T. Castell (Hants), K. E. Palmer (Somerset) and R. N. S. Hobbs (Essex).

The tour commenced with two minor games and then the three matches against Jamaica followed. Compton celebrated his return to first-class cricket with a century in the first match against Jamaica, but the tourists' bowling was none too effective and Jamaica declared in both innings with only 5 and 4 wickets lost.

In the second match Worrell, the Jamaican captain, declared to set the visitors 377 in 420 minutes. Dexter hit a brilliant hundred in 67 minutes and Graveney also reached a hundred to bring the Cavaliers victory by 4 wickets. Some good leg-break bowling by Hobbs dismissed the home team twice in the third match and with another hundred from Dexter, the Cavaliers won by 5 wickets.

The tour was most enjoyable, but was of little interest to the public, less than 1,000 watching each day's play.

1964: Yorkshire tour North America and Bermuda

After the 1964 English season, the Yorkshire side travelled to North America for a three-week tour. Sponsored by various organisations and guaranteed by the cricket authorities in Canada, United States and Bermuda, the team, under the management of R. A. Roberts, flew from London on 18 September to New York. The side was D. B. Close (capt), J. H. Hampshire, D. E. V. Padgett, R. A. Hutton, P. J. Sharpe, R. Illingworth, J. G. Binks, F. S. Trueman, D. Wilson and M. Ryan–because of illness A. G. Nicholson could not go and G. St. A. Sobers, the West Indies Test cricketer, was co-opted for the latter matches.

The first two matches in New York were in fact against West Indian elevens who played cricket to a fairly high standard. Visits were made to Toronto and British Columbia, then down to

---

last match was one of three declarations against North Zone, but the result was another draw and the England party flew home.

All five Tests had been drawn and to some extent England deserve credit for achieving this, for the side was decimated by injury and illness. The best English bowler was Titmus, whose off-spin proved the one really effective weapon in the attack, though Price improved as the tour went on. Cowdrey's technique was too good for the Indian bowlers and Smith batted well, but most of the younger element did little to improve their standing, though Bolus played some determined knocks.

On the Indian wickets however it was very difficult to assess a player's true value and even from the Indian press came cries that the pitches must be altered if Indian cricket was to survive.

1963-64: Compton takes Cavaliers to Jamaica

Whilst the M.C.C. team struggled against doped pitches and illness in India, the 'International Cavaliers Cricket Club' travelled to Jamaica for a five-match tour of that island. The team which was entirely composed of English county cricketers was: D. C. S. Compton (Middx) (capt), J. C. Laker (Essex), T. G. Evans

1963-64: Cavaliers to Jamaica

1st Match: v Combined Parishes (Montego Bay) (One Day) Jan 6.
Combined Parishes 164 lost to Cavaliers 166-6 (E. R. Dexter 55) by 4 wkts.

2nd Match: v Colts & Country XI (Monymusk) Jan 7, 8.
Cavaliers 211 (R. E. Marshall 51, R. G. Scarlett 6-59) & 102-2 drew with Colts & Country XI 239 (G. Robinson 57, R. Grandison 56).

3rd Match: v Jamaica (Kingston) Jan 9, 10, 11.
Jamaica 254-5 dec (E. Griffith 146) & 202-4 dec (H. Reid 101*, E. D. McMorris 60) drew with Cavaliers 238-7 dec (D. C. S. Compton 103) & 216-8 (J. T. Murray 60, E. R. Dexter 58).

4th Match: v Jamaica (Kingston) Jan 15, 16, 17, 18.
Jamaica 279 (L. A. King 75, R. N. S. Hobbs 5-69) & 260-6 dec (M. L. C. Foster 136*) lost to Cavaliers 163 (T. E. Bailey 76) & 377-6 (E. R. Dexter 176, T. W. Graveney 108*) by 4 wkts.

5th Match: v Jamaica (Kingston) Jan 22, 23, 24, 25.
Jamaica 185 (E. D. McMorris 103*) & 246 (E. Griffith 63) lost to Cavaliers 297-6 dec (E. R. Dexter 120, J. T. Murray 68) & 135-5 (P. E. Richardson 84) by 5 wkts.

1964: Yorkshire to North America and Bermuda

1st Match: v New York Combined Leagues (Mount Vernon) Sept 19
Yorkshire 217-8 dec (D. B. Close 76) drew with Combined Leagues 176-4 (King 56).

2nd Match: v New York Combined Leagues (Randall's Island) Sept 20.
Yorkshire 125 (Larrier 6-41) beat Combined Leagues 56 (F. S. Trueman 6-21) by 69 runs.

3rd Match: v British Commonwealth C.C. (Washington) Sept 21.
Yorkshire 350 (R. Illingworth 103, J. G. Binks 69, D. Wilson 62) beat British Commonwealth C.C. 46 by 304 runs.

4th Match: v Toronto C.C. (Toronto) Sept 23.
Yorkshire 251-6 dec (D. E. V. Padgett 77, G. Boycott 75) drew with Toronto 94-5.

5th Match: v Ontario XI (Toronto) Sept 24.
Yorkshire 189-6 dec (J. H. Hampshire 54, R. Illingworth 51) drew with Ontario 114-2 (A. Khan 52*).

6th Match: Alberta (Calgary) Sept 25.
No play due to rain.

7th Match: v British Columbia (Vancouver) Sept 26.
Yorkshire 246 (J. H. Hampshire 76) beat British Columbia 88 by 158 runs.

8th Match: v Southern California (Hollywood) Sept 27.
Yorkshire 251 (D. E. V. Padgett 50) beat Southern California 77 (R. Illingworth 4-17) by 174 runs.

9th Match: v Southern California (Hollywood) Sept 28.
Yorkshire 326-9 dec (R. Illingworth 144) beat Southern California 65 (D. Wilson 6-11)

10th Match: v St George's C.C. (Hamilton) Oct 1.
St George 48 lost to Yorkshire 322-8 (G. St. A. Sobers 117, G. Boycott 108) by 5 wkts.

11th Match: v Somerset C.C. (Hamilton) Oct 3.
Yorkshire 172 beat Somerset C.C. 141 by 31 runs.

12th Match: v Bermuda (Hamilton) Oct 4.
Yorkshire 255 (P. J. Sharpe 114*) beat Bermuda 65 by 190 runs.

13th Match: v Pick of the Leagues (Hamilton) Oct 6.
Pick of the Leagues 69 lost to Yorkshire 167 (G. St. A. Sobers 77).

Hollywood, before the major matches played in Bermuda. Here the bowling of Trueman and Sobers was too much for the locals, but the matches were well attended, at least 10,000 watching each day.

The team arrived back in England on 8 October.

1964-65: Cavaliers visit the West Indies

Having toured Jamaica the previous winter, the Cavaliers repeated the visit in 1964-65, but included Barbados on the itinerary. The team was: T. E. Bailey (Essex) (capt), M. C. Cowdrey (Kent), T. G. Evans (Kent), K. W. R. Fletcher (Essex), G. Goonesena (Notts), J. H. Hampshire (Yorks), R. G. A. Headley (Worcs), A. C. D. Ingleby-Mackenzie (Hants), B. R. Knight (Essex), A. P. E. Knott (Kent), J. C. Laker (Essex), R. E. Marshall (Hants), P. E. Richardson (Kent), F. S. Trueman (Yorks) and D. W. White (Hants).

Jamaica were dismissed by Laker for 214 in the first innings of the initial first-class match and though the Cavaliers declared soon after getting a first innings lead, the match was drawn. The Cavaliers fell cheaply to Hall and Sobers in the return game and were easily beaten.

Both matches in Barbados were drawn, though in the first the Cavaliers were forced to follow on and had to rely on some good batting by Richardson and Cowdrey for their second innings recovery.

1964-65: Cavaliers to West Indies

1st Match: v Eastern Zone (St Mary, Jamaica) (One Day)   Jan 27.
Cavaliers 295-6 dec (R. G. A. Headley 69, J. H. Hampshire 52, P. E. Richardson 51) drew with Eastern Zone 132-3.

2nd Match: v Jamaica Colts (St Ann's Bay)   Jan 29, 30.
Cavaliers 312-8 dec (B. R. Knight 133, K. W. R. Fletcher 75) & 132-5 (R. E. Marshall 66) drew with Colts 241 (L. Chambers 65).

3rd Match: v Jamaica (Montego Bay)   Feb 4, 5, 6.
Jamaica 214 (H. Bennett 64, J. C. Laker 5-54) & 249-4 dec (R. Pinnock 67*, M. L. C. Foster 61) drew with Cavaliers 250-4 dec (M. C. Cowdrey 77*, R. G. A. Headley 76, P. E. Richardson 54) & 122-3 (R. G. A. Headley 74*).

4th Match: v Central Zone (Mandeville)   Feb 10, 11.
Central Zone 144 (R. G. A. Headley 6-38) & 112 (G. Goonesena 6-38) lost to Cavaliers 237-9 dec & 22-1.

5th Match: v Jamaica (Kingston)   Feb 13, 15, 16.
Jamaica 332 (G. St. A. Sobers 129, E. D. A. McMorris 61, F. S. Trueman 5-78) & 242-6 dec (C. C. Hunte 78, E. H. C. Griffith 61) beat Cavaliers 189 (J. H. Hampshire 55) & 176 (K. W. R. Fletcher 78) by 209 runs.

6th Match: v Barbados (Bridgetown)   Feb 20, 22, 23.
Barbados 333-4 dec (M. R. Bynoe 110, S. M. Nurse 100, G. St. A. Sobers 52) & 222-4 (P. D. Lashley 90) drew with Cavaliers 152 & 326-4 dec (P. E. Richardson 114, M. C. Cowdrey 95).

7th Match: v Barbados (Bridgetown)   Feb 25, 26, 27.
Cavaliers 264-5 dec (P. E. Richardson 73*, B. R. Knight 68) & 266-9 dec (B. R. Knight 110, A. P. E. Knott 66) drew with Barbados 270-3 dec (R. Brancker 125*, P. D. Lashley 113*) & 241-7 (R. Bradshaw 57, K. D. Boyce 55).

1964-65: champions Worcestershire go on world tour

The Champion County of 1964, Worcestershire, undertook a tour of 15 matches, commencing in Kenya and ending in Los Angeles, which involved a journey round the world. Under the managership of J. Lister, the players were D. Kenyon (capt), T. W. Graveney, B. L. d'Oliveira, R. G. A. Headley, M. J. Horton, D. N. F. Slade, D. W. Richardson, R. Booth, N. Gifford, J. A.

1964-65: Worcestershire to Africa, Asia and N. America

1st Match: v Kenya (Nairobi)   Feb 13, 14, 15.
Worcestershire 353 (B. L. d'Oliveira 162) & 282-8 dec (T. W. Graveney 92, D. Kenyon 82, B. L. d'Oliveira 53) drew with Kenya 354-4 dec (Narendra Patel 127, Akhil Lakhani 122) & 139-5 (Charanjive 50).

2nd Match: v Rhodesia (Bulawayo)   Feb 20, 21, 22.
Worcestershire 277 (B. L. d'Oliveira 73, D. N. F. Slade 64*, G. B. Lawrence 6-61) & 161-5 dec (D. Kenyon 63) beat Rhodesia 82 (L. J. Coldwell 5-18) & 160 (G. B. Lawrence 60*, L. J. Coldwell 5-26) by 196 runs.

3rd Match: v Country Districts (Que Que)   Feb 24, 25.
Worcestershire 348-6 dec (R. G. A. Headley 178, B. L. d'Oliveira 51) & 56-3 dec beat Country Districts 169-6 dec (E. Butcher 51) & 150 (N. Gifford 5-54) by 85 runs.

4th Match: v Rhodesia (Salisbury)   Feb 27, 28, March 1, 2.
Rhodesia 235 (A. J. Pithey 98) & 344-4 dec (R. A. Gripper 116, A. J. Pithey 68*, K. C. Bland 62, J. D. McPhun 61) beat Worcestershire 308-6 dec (T. W. Graveney 136*, D. N. F. Slade 58) & 115 (V. E. J. Dickinson 5-44, J. H. du Preez 5-36) by 156 runs.

5th Match: v Calcutta (Ballygunge)   March 5, 6.
Calcutta 166 (C. V. Gadkari 90) & 188-6 (J. M. Wilson 68) drew with Worcestershire 445-6 dec (T. W. Graveney 104, B. L. d'Oliveira 104, R. G. A. Headley 102, D. W. Richardson 58).

6th Match: v Chief Minister's XI (Eden Gardens, Calcutta)   March 9, 10.
Chief Minister's XI 240-9 dec (P. Roy 58) & 127-5 dec (R. Saxsena 69) drew with Worcestershire 215.

7th Match: v Malaysia (Singapore)   March 13, 14.
Worcestershire 254-9 dec (T. W. Graveney 161, Way 5-57) & 131-3 dec beat Malaysia 101 (B. L. d'Oliveira 7-31) & 135 (J. Jeremiah 54, N. Gifford 7-38) by 149 runs.

8th Match: v Singapore (Singapore) (One Day)   March 15.
Worcestershire 252-4 dec (T. W. Graveney 92, M. J. Horton 69) drew with Singapore 71-2.

9th Match: v Selangor State XI (Kuala Lumpur) (One Day)   March 19.
Worcestershire 296-3 dec (M. J. Horton 127*, R. G. A. Headley 107) drew with Selangor 69-4.

10th Match: v Malaysia (Kuala Lumpur)   March 20, 21.
Worcestershire 310-7 dec (T. W. Graveney 58, B. L. d'Oliveira 55, D. Kenyon 54) beat Malaysia 119 (N. Gifford 7-56) & 74 (L. J. Coldwell 6-46) by an inns & 117 runs.

11th Match: v Royal Bangkok Sports Club (Bangkok) (One Day)   March 24.
Worcestershire 242-8 dec (B. L. d'Oliveira 117) beat Royal Bangkok S.C. 62 (L. J. Coldwell 5-24) by 180 runs.

12th Match: v Hong Kong League President's XI (Hong Kong)   March 26.
Worcestershire 282 (T. W. Graveney 116) beat President's XI 102 by 180 runs.

13th Match: v Hong Kong (Kowloon)   March 27, 28.
Hong Kong 150 (J. Fawcett 58, B. L. d'Oliveira 5-51) & 108 (B. L. d'Oliveira 5-21) lost to Worcestershire 359 (T. W. Graveney 132, D. N. F. Slade 51, Daniels 5-90) by an inns & 101 runs.

14th Match: v Honolulu (Honolulu)   March 30.
Worcestershire 184-5 dec (T. W. Graveney 85*) beat Honolulu 48 by 136 runs.

15th Match: v South California C.A. (Hollywood).   April 3.
No play due to rain.

Flavell, B. M. Brain and L. J. Coldwell. Although only twelve players were taken, happily there were no serious injuries and no need to co-opt any additional men.

Kenya batted very well in the opening match and were able to declare with four wickets down, after obtaining a lead on first innings, but in the end the target of 282 in 180 minutes was too large for the home side and the game was drawn.

Each side won one match in the two games against Rhodesia. Coldwell dismissed Rhodesia quickly in the first game, but in the second Worcester collapsed before the spinners in their second innings.

Two minor matches were played in India—both draws—before the team went on to Singapore and Malaysia. Rain unfortunately marred several matches as it did the final match in Hollywood, which was completely washed out.

Graveney hit well over 1,000 runs on the tour, easily the best record, and Coldwell returned the best bowling figures.

1964-65: M.C.C. tour of South America

A Committee under the chairmanship of Lord Luke raised the funds to finance the 1964-65 M.C.C. team to South America where it was felt that some additional stimulus to the game was required, following the M.C.C. tour of 1958-59. As the M.C.C.

Graeme Pollock out and a wicket for John Price in the final Test of the 1964-65 tour of South Africa. Jim Parks took the diving catch behind the wicket.

had not intended to make another tour before 1968, private finance was required for this additional visit.

The team which left England by air on 7 December was: A. C. Smith (Warwicks) (capt), P. I. Bedford (Middx), A. R. Duff (Worcs), R. A. Gale (Middx), C. Gibson (M.C.C.), M. G. Griffith (Sussex), R. A. Hutton (Yorks), R. I. Jefferson (Surrey), R. C. Kerslake (Somerset), A. R. Lewis (Glamorgan), D. J. Mordaunt (Sussex), R. C. White (Gloucs) and J. D. Martin (Somerset).

The first four matches were played in Brazil, where cricket seemed to be gradually dying, no new players coming along to replace the old stagers. Cricket was also very limited in Chile where three matches took place and the major games were reserved for the Argentine. The three 'Tests' however provided the M.C.C. with three large victories, but there was no doubt that the Argentine had some good young players, who needed more coaching to improve their standard.

The M.C.C. left South America on 12 January. Gale headed the batting table, but Mordaunt, Hutton and Lewis were not far behind. The two spinners Duff and Bedford captured most wickets.

1964-65: M.C.C. undefeated in South Africa

With E. R. Dexter announcing that he was intending to stand as a candidate in the forthcoming General Election and M. C. Cowdrey stating he was not available, the M.C.C. chose M. J. K. Smith (Warwickshire) to lead the side to South Africa. The remainder of the team was K. F. Barrington (Surrey), G. Boycott (Yorks), T. W. Cartwright (Warwicks), R. W. Barber (Warwicks), J. M. Parks (Sussex), P. H. Parfitt (Middx), J. T. Murray (Middx), J. M. Brearley (Middx), N. I. Thomson (Sussex), D. J. Brown (Warwicks), F. J. Titmus (Middx), R. N. S. Hobbs (Essex), D. A. Allen (Gloucs), J. S. E. Price (Middx) and E. R. Dexter, who failed in his attempt to get into Parliament and joined the side as vice-captain.

The critics were worried about the batting in the absence of Cowdrey, Russell, Graveney and Stewart. The selection of Brearley in preference to the last three noted was bitterly criticised.

Travelling to South Africa by air for the first time, the M.C.C. began the tour with two matches in Rhodesia. The early matches all produced wins, or draws in the tourists' favour – even the usually formidable Transvaal side was beaten by an innings.

In the first Test at Durban, Smith was fortunate to win the toss and see his team reach 485 for 5 declared, for the wicket soon began to take spin and the South Africans were bemused by Allen and Titmus. England won by an innings.

Following two more innings victories, Smith again won the toss in the second Test. Barber, Dexter and Barrington mastered the home bowling and a total of 531 was reached. South Africa still could not tackle Titmus and Allen with any certainty and were forced to follow on. A great century by Bland, who used his feet to the spinners prevented England going two up in the series.

It was South Africa's turn to bat first and exceed 500 in the third Test. Slow scoring however meant that England had no chance of winning, even before they began to bat, and the game meandered to a tame draw. There was a great hullabaloo in this game on the subject of batsmen 'walking' if they thought a catch had been taken and the umpire seemed uncertain. In this match Barlow of South Africa stood his ground, while Barrington 'walked'. The former went on to 138.

The match against Border, which was won by 9 wickets, saw a

1st Match: v Matabeleland XI (Bulawayo) Oct 21, 22.
Matabeleland 133 & 144 (F. J. Titmus 7-58) lost to M.C.C. 253-9 dec (M. J. K. Smith 60, P. H. Parfitt 55) & 28-0 by 10 wkts.

2nd Match: v Rhodesia (Salisbury) Oct 24, 25, 26, 27.
Rhodesia 281 (K. C. Bland 66, A. J. Pithey 65) & 225 (N. Frangos 82) lost to M.C.C. 298 (P. H. Parfitt 82, K. F. Barrington 74) & 209-5 (R. W. Barber 108) by 5 wkts.

3rd Match: v South African Colts (Benoni) Oct 30, 31, Nov 2.
Colts 398 (N. Rosendorff 83, B. A. Richards 63, N. S. Crookes 60, J. T. Botten 57, M. J. Macaulay 55) & 161 (F. J. Titmus 5-71) drew with M.C.C. 267 (J. M. Brearley 68) & 241-8 (G. Boycott 53, E. R. Dexter 50, N. S. Crookes 5-102).*

4th Match: v Transvaal Country Districts (Vereeniging) Nov 3, 4.
M.C.C. 337-5 dec (J. M. Brearley 102, M. J. K. Smith 102) drew with Transvaal 107 & 271 (P. S. Heine 108, R. N. S. Hobbs 5-146).

5th Match: v Transvaal (Johannesburg) Nov 6, 7, 9.
Transvaal 125 & 257 (I. R. Fullerton 92) lost to M.C.C. 464-9 dec (K. F. Barrington 169, M. J. K. Smith 124, R. W. Barber 59, P. S. Heine 5-110) by an inns & 82 runs.

6th Match: v Natal (Durban) Nov 13, 14, 16, 17.
Natal 360-9 dec (G. D. Varnals 111, R. Dumbrill 68, N. I. Thompson 5-58) & 102 lost to M.C.C. 445 (J. M. Parks 80, P. H. Parfitt 74, D. J. Brown 69, E. R. Dexter 59) & 19-0 by 10 wkts.*

7th Match: v Eastern Province (Port Elizabeth) Nov 20, 21, 23.
M.C.C. 447-7 dec (G. Boycott 193, M. J. K. Smith 153) beat E. Province 133 (F. J. Titmus 5-32) & 164 (F. J. Titmus 5-38).*

8th Match: v Western Province (Cape Town) Nov 27, 28, 30, Dec 1.
M.C.C. 441 (K. F. Barrington 169, G. Boycott 106) & 228-6 dec (K. F. Barrington 82, J. M. Brearley 64) drew with W. Province 357 (P. L. van der Merwe 121, L. J. Weinstein 53) & 158-8.*

9th Match: v South Africa (Durban) Dec 4, 5, 7, 8.
England 485-5 dec (K. F. Barrington 148*, J. M. Parks 108*, R. W. Barber 74, G. Boycott 73) beat South Africa 155 (D. A. Allen 5-41) & 226 (K. C. Bland 68, F. J. Titmus 5-66) by an inns & 104 runs.

10th Match: v South African Universities (Pietermaritzburg) Dec 12, 14, 15.
Universities 114 (K. F. Barrington 5-29) & 130 (E. V. Chatterton 54) lost to M.C.C. 356 (G. Boycott 81, J. T. Murray 81, M. J. K. Smith 76, P. H. Parfitt 50, R. S. Steyn 5-84) by an inns & 112 runs.

11th Match: v North-Eastern Transvaal (Pretoria) Dec 18, 19, 21.
N.E. Transvaal 204 & 135 lost to M.C.C. 350 (J. T. Murray 142, F. J. Titmus 65, G. G. Hall 6-145) by an inns & 11 runs.

12th Match: v South Africa (Johannesburg) Dec 23, 24, 26, 28, 29.
England 531 (E. R. Dexter 172, K. F. Barrington 121, R. W. Barber 97, P. H. Parfitt 52, P. M. Pollock 5-129) drew with South Africa 317 (A. J. Pithey 85, E. J. Barlow 71) & 336-6 (K. C. Bland 144*, R. G. Pollock 55, T. L. Goddard 50).

13th Match: v South Africa (Cape Town) Jan 1, 2, 4, 5, 6.
South Africa 501-7 dec (A. J. Pithey 154, E. J. Barlow 138, K. C. Bland 78) & 346 (E. J. Barlow 78, R. G. Pollock 73, K. C. Bland 64, D. T. Lindsay 50) drew with England 442 (M. J. K. Smith 121, E. R. Dexter 61, J. M. Parks 59, R. W. Barber 58, H. D. Bromfield 5-88) and 15-0.

14th Match: v Border (East London) Jan 9, 11, 12.
Border 215 (W. S. Farrer 66, R. W. Barber 6-67) & 244 (H. M. Ackerman 108, C. P. Wilkins 65) lost to M.C.C. 407-5 dec (T. W. Cartwright 111, E. R. Dexter 110, G. Boycott 56) & 54-1 by 9 wkts.*

15th Match: v Orange Free State (Bloemfontein) Jan 15, 16, 18.
O.F.S. 170 & 171-9 dec (R. van der Poll 92) lost to M.C.C. 199-7 dec (J. M. Parks 89, G. Boycott 73, M. J. Macaulay 7-58) & 143-3 by 7 wkts.

16th Match: v South Africa (Johannesburg) Jan 22, 23, 25, 26, 27.
South Africa 390-6 dec (E. J. Barlow 96, A. J. Pithey 95, J. H. B. Waite 64, T. L. Goddard 60, K. C. Bland 55) & 307-3 dec (T. L. Goddard 112, R. G. Pollock 65*) drew with England 384 (P. H. Parfitt 122*, K. F. Barrington 93, R. W. Barber 61) & 153-6 (G. Boycott 76*).

17th Match: v Griqualand West (Kimberley) Jan 29, 30, Feb 1.
Griqualand West 140 (C. W. Symcox 62) & 107 (K. F. Barrington 7-40) lost to M.C.C. 226 & 24-0 by 10 wkts.

18th Match: v Invitation XI (Cape Town) Feb 5, 6, 8, 9.
Invitation XI 437 (K. C. Bland 116, D. Gamsy 88, R. K. Muzzell 70, J. T. Botten 53, P. L. van der Merwe 50, T. W. Cartwright 5-107) & 316-7 dec (R. G. Pollock 91, K. C. Bland 67, D. Gamsy 55, R. K. Muzzell 52) drew with M.C.C. 326 (G. Boycott 114, T. W. Cartwright 53) & 205-7 (M. J. K. Smith 78*).*

19th Match: v South Africa (Port Elizabeth) Feb 12, 13, 15, 16, 17.
South Africa 502 (R. G. Pollock 138, E. J. Barlow 69, P. L. van der Merwe 66, T. L. Goddard 61) & 178-4 dec (R. G. Pollock 77*) drew with England 435 (G. Boycott 117, K. F. Barrington 72) & 29-1.

Batting Averages

		M	I	NO	R	HS	Avge	100	c/s
K. F. Barrington	(Surrey)	13	18	5	1128	169*	86.76	4	7
M. J. K. Smith	(Warks)	14	17	2	877	153	58.46	3	21
G. Boycott	(Yorks)	15	25	5	1135	193*	56.75	4	7
T. W. Cartwright	(Warks)	8	10	4	293	111*	48.83	1	6
E. R. Dexter	(Sussex)	13	19	2	791	172	46.52	2	11
R. W. Barber	(Warks)	11	14	1	595	108	45.76	1	14
J. M. Parks	(Sussex)	12	17	3	524	108*	37.42	1	21/3
P. H. Parfitt	(Middx)	15	20	1	708	122*	37.26	1	22
J. T. Murray	(Middx)	10	14	3	398	142	36.18	1	23/8
J. M. Brearley	(Middx)	12	19	3	406	68	25.37	0	12
N. I. Thomson	(Sussex)	13	13	5	167	39	20.87	0	7
D. J. Brown	(Warks)	10	9	2	141	69	20.14	0	2
F. J. Titmus	(Middx)	10	12	3	156	65	17.33	0	6
R. N. S. Hobbs	(Essex)	9	7	2	72	36	14.40	0	6
D. A. Allen	(Gloucs)	11	11	1	95	38*	9.50	0	4
J. S. E. Price	(Middx)	10	8	2	26	10	4.33	0	2

Played in one match: K. E. Palmer (Som) 10.

Bowling Averages

	O	M	R	W	Avge	BB	5i
K. F. Barrington	73.1	23	174	24	7.25	7-40	2
D. A. Allen	506.4	182	921	38	24.23	5-41	1
F. J. Titmus	593.1	188	1240	51	24.31	5-32	4
D. J. Brown	256.1	67	637	23	27.69	4-42	0
R. W. Barber	187	44	605	21	28.80	6-67	1
J. S. E. Price	287	71	789	27	29.22	4-42	0
R. N. S. Hobbs	316	103	796	27	29.48	3-24	0
N. I. Thomson	492.2	170	1034	35	29.54	5-58	1
T. W. Cartwright	366.3	141	817	25	32.68	5-107	1
G. Boycott	94	24	262	8	32.75	3-47	0
E. R. Dexter	91	14	307	4	76.75	1-32	0
P. H. Parfitt	83	25	198	2	99.00	1-9	0
K. E. Palmer	63	8	189	1	189.00	1-113	0

Also bowled: M. J. K. Smith 11-1-43-0.

bowlers however and the game was another draw—in an attempt at the impossible, South Africa made a sporting declaration in their second innings, but rain ended the match.

The touring team therefore ended the campaign undefeated, which surprised many of their detractors. In the closing stages they were also handicapped by injuries to Price, Cartwright and Brown, so their performance was certainly meritorious. Dexter batted better for not being captain and Barrington performed well throughout. Boycott came good in the last two Tests, but Brearley failed sadly. The faster bowlers achieved little and most of the work of prising out the opposition rested with Titmus and Allen.

Both the attendance figures and match receipts showed a drop compared with the previous M.C.C. visit.

1965-66: England and Australia draw Test series

The party selected to go to Australia in 1965-66 was: M. J. K. Smith (Warwicks) (capt), M. C. Cowdrey (Kent) (vice-capt), D. A. Allen (Gloucs), R. W. Barber (Warwicks), K. F. Barrington (Surrey), G. Boycott (Yorks), D. J. Brown (Warwicks), J. H. Edrich (Surrey), K. Higgs (Lancs), I. J. Jones (Glamorgan), J. D. F. Larter (Northants), J. T. Murray (Middx), P. H. Parfitt (Middx), J. M. Parks (Sussex), W. E. Russell (Middx), F. J. Titmus (Middx), S. C. Griffith (manager), J. T. Ikin (manager's assistant), J. Jennings (physiotherapist). The obvious absentees were Dexter and Statham and in fact the fast bowling department looked weak, since both Larter and Jones were unlikely to withstand the rigours of the tour.

For the first time the M.C.C. team flew all the way to Australia by jet, though with a stopover in Colombo.

The first two major matches of the tour were in Perth. In the first game, after declarations, a nine-run win was achieved, but the bowling on both sides was rather thin. The bowling again struggled in the second game. Higgs and Jones were very wayward and three declarations still resulted in a draw. In Adelaide

young batsman—Ackerman—hit a brilliant hundred. He later played for Northants. South Africa had all the best of the fourth Test, but failed to win. For some unknown reason Smith put the home team in to bat, but he was saved from the consequences of his folly by, first, three expensive blunders on the part of wicket-keeper Waite, second, by rain which cut over three hours off the playing time and third, by Boycott who defied the bowlers in the final innings.

South Africa needed to win the fifth Test to save the series and they began quite splendidly with 502 in just under two days. Dour batting by Boycott and Barrington frustrated the home

Cowdrey put South Australia in on a damp pitch and, appreciating this, Larter, Allen and Brown shot out the opposition for 103. Although batting better in the second innings, South Australia lost by 6 wickets and things were looking up for the tourists. The match against Victoria provided that State with its first victory against M.C.C. since the war. Both the tourists' bowling and batting failed in the first innings and though improving in the second, due to Barrington who hit 158 and took 4 for 24, it was too late. Some very consistent batting—no less than seven of the team made fifties, produced victory over New South Wales and there was more high scoring in the drawn game with Queensland, though the sick list was mounting, both Cowdrey and Barber being indisposed.

Rain decided the first Test, half of the first day and all of the second disappearing, and it was not until the fourth day that Australia declared the first innings of the match closed at 443 for 6. The match headed gently for a draw.

A generous declaration by State captain Favell gave the M.C.C. a win over South Australia. The bat dominated the second Test—England's attack was suspect in the absence of both Brown and Higgs and though Jones, Knight and Allen removed Australia for 358, they struggled in the second innings and another draw emerged. England won the toss in the third Test and Barber and Boycott gave the tourists a great start with a partnership of 234. The second wicket did not fall until 303 and on a pitch which was worsening Brown bowled splendidly to dismiss Australia; the follow on was enforced and this time Titmus and Allen went straight through the home batting to bring England an innings victory. The holiday matches in Tasmania were played prior to the fourth Test, in which England were completely outplayed. McKenzie and Hawke demolished the English batting, then Simpson and Lawry opened with a partnership of 244.

The fifth Test ought to have been an exciting struggle, each side having won one game. England batted, and though both openers fell quickly, Barrington hit a sparkling hundred, which seemed to set the tempo for the match, but somehow the lower order English batsmen dragged their feet and when Australia batted, the over rate was so painfully slow that the game wound methodically down. It was a feeble end to what was, on the whole, a good tour.

The first New Zealand Test gave England a bit of a jolt, but at the close the home team were fighting to save themselves. Rain ruined the second Test, but the third was just plain dull—England required 204 to win in 270 minutes but never looked likely to approach the modest target. The team flew home via Hong Kong, where two one-day matches were played.

1965-66: M.C.C. to Australia and New Zealand and Ceylon and Hong Kong

1st Match: v Ceylon C.S. President's XI (Colombo) (One Day) Oct 19.
M.C.C. 198-6 dec (R. W. Barber 64) drew with President's XI 156-6.*

2nd Match: v Ceylon (Colombo) (One Day) Oct 20.
M.C.C. 127 (N. Chanmugam 5-26) drew with Ceylon 77-1 (R. Reid 54): rain.*

3rd Match: v Western Australia Country XI (Moora) (One Day) Oct 27.
M.C.C. 252-7 dec (J. H. Edrich 66) beat W.A. Country XI 150 (J. McCormack 64, R. W. Barber 5-64) by 82 runs.

4th Match: v Western Australia (Perth) Oct 29, 30, Nov 1, 2.
M.C.C. 447-5 dec (R. W. Barber 126, J. M. Parks 107, W. E. Russell 81, M. J. K. Smith 67*) & 156-5 dec beat W. Australia 303-9 dec (P. C. Kelly 119, D. Chadwick 52*, I. J. Jones 5-59) & 291 (M. Vernon 118, P. C. Kelly 108*) by 9 runs.*

5th Match: v Combined XI (Perth) Nov 5, 6, 8, 9.
M.C.C. 379-7 dec (M. J. K. Smith 112, J. H. Edrich 92, F. J. Titmus 69) & 205-4 dec (R. W. Barber 113) drew with Combined XI 231-5 dec (R. M. Cowper 89, P. J. P. Burge 52) & 322-6 (R. M. Cowper 122*, P. J. P. Burge 50).*

6th Match: v South Australia (Adelaide) Nov 12, 13, 15, 16.
S. Australia 103 & 364 (L. E. Favell 96, A. B. Shiell 83, L. Marks 67, B. N. Jarman 61) lost to M.C.C. 310 (G. Boycott 94, K. F. Barrington 69, J. H. Edrich 61, D. J. Sincock 5-113) & 158-4 (K. F. Barrington 51) by 6 wkts.

7th Match: v Victoria Country Districts (Hamilton) (One Day) Nov 17.
Country Districts 167-6 (J. Kerr 50) lost to M.C.C. 264 (J. M. Parks 75, W. E. Russell 50) by 6 wkts.*

8th Match: v Victoria (Melbourne) Nov 19, 20, 22, 23.
Victoria 384-7 dec (W. M. Lawry 153, D. R. Cowper 60, G. D. Watson 59*, I. R. Redpath 53) & 165 (W. M. Lawry 61) beat M.C.C. 211 & 306 (K. F. Barrington 158, M. C. Cowdrey 52) by 32 runs.*

9th Match: v Victoria Country XI (Euroa) Nov 24.
No play due to rain.

10th Match: v New South Wales (Sydney) Nov 26, 27, 29, 30.
M.C.C. 527-6 dec (W. E. Russell 93, R. W. Barber 90, F. J. Titmus 80, M. C. Cowdrey 63, J. M. Parks 63, D. A. Allen 54*) & 2-1 beat New South Wales 288 (K. D. Walters 129, B. C. Booth 80) & 240 (G. Thomas 56, F. J. Titmus 5-45) by 9 wkts.*

11th Match: v Queensland (Brisbane) Dec 3, 4, 6, 7.
M.C.C. 452-5 dec (J. H. Edrich 133, W. E. Russell 110, K. F. Barrington 80, F. J. Titmus 51*) & 123-2 dec (J. H. Edrich 68*) drew with Queensland 222 (P. J. P. Burge 114*) & 315-8 (T. R. Veivers 74, D. Bull 64, P. J. P. Burge 60).*

12th Match: v Queensland Country Districts XI (Beaudesert) (One Day) Dec 8.
Country Districts 152-7 dec (G. Jennings 77) lost to M.C.C. 159-3 by 7 wkts.

13th Match: v Australia (Brisbane) Dec 10, 11, 13, 14, 15.
Australia 443-6 dec (W. M. Lawry 166, K. D. Walters 155, T. R. Veivers 56) drew with England 280 (F. J. Titmus 60, K. F. Barrington 53, J. M. Parks 52, P. I. Philpott 5-90) & 186-3 (G. Boycott 63*).*

14th Match: v Prime Minister's XI (Canberra) (One Day) Dec 17.
Prime Minister's XI 288-7 dec (A. P. Sheahan 79, J. W. Burke 60) lost to M.C.C. 289-8 (G. Boycott 95, M. C. Cowdrey 52, M. J. K. Smith 51) by 2 wkts.*

15th Match: v N.S.W. Country Districts XI (Bathurst) (One Day) Dec 18
Country Districts XI 221 (K. F. Barrington 6-92) lost to M.C.C. 256-6 (J. H. Edrich 67, K. F. Barrington 61) by 5 wkts.*

16th Match: v N.S.W. Country Districts XI (Albury) (One Day) Dec 20.
Country Districts XI 190 (G. Stacey 56) lost to M.C.C. 253-5 (M. J. K. Smith 81, J. H. Edrich 76) by 6 wkts.*

17th Match: v South Australia Country Districts XI (Mount Gambier) (One Day) Dec 22
Country Districts XI 176-6 dec lost to M.C.C. 223-2 (G. Boycott 99, P. H. Parfitt 52) by 8 wkts.*

18th Match: v South Australia (Adelaide) Dec 23, 24, 27, 28.
S. Australia 459-7 dec (A. B. Shiell 202*, B. N. Jarman 70, I. M. Chappell 59) & 253-4 dec (I. M. Chappell 113*) lost to M.C.C. 444 (J. T. Murray 110, M. J. K. Smith 108, B. R. Knight 79, K. F. Barrington 63) & 270-4 (R. W. Barber 77, M. C. Cowdrey 63*, G. Boycott 58) by 6 wkts.

19th Match: v Australia (Melbourne) Dec 30, 31, Jan 1, 3, 4.
Australia 358 (R. M. Cowper 99, W. M. Lawry 88, R. B. Simpson 59) & 426 (P. J. P. Burge 120, K. D. Walters 115, W. M. Lawry 78, R. B. Simpson 67) drew with England 558 (J. H. Edrich 109, M. C. Cowdrey 104, K. F. Barrington 63, J. M. Parks 71, F. J. Titmus 56*, G. Boycott 51, G. D. McKenzie 5-134) & 5-0.

20th Match: v Australia (Sydney) Jan 7, 8, 10, 11, 12.
England 488 (R. W. Barber 185, J. H. Edrich 103, G. Boycott 84, D. A. Allen 50*, N. J. Hawke 7-105) beat Australia 221 (R. M. Cowper 60, G. Thomas 51, D. J. Brown 5-63) & 174 by an inns & 93 runs.

21st Match: v Northern N.S.W. Country Districts XI (Newcastle) Jan 14, 15, 17.
Country Districts XI 334 (C. Baker 101, K. M. Hill 98) & 126 lost to M.C.C. 449 (M. J. K. Smith 164, F. J. Titmus 114) & 13-0 by 10 wkts.

22nd Match: v Tasmania (Launceston) Jan 19, 20, 21.
M.C.C. 371-9 dec (M. J. K. Smith 96, J. M. Parks 91, M. C. Cowdrey 63) & 289-7 (M. C. Cowdrey 108, J. M. Parks 58, B. R. Knight 51) drew with Tasmania 322 (B. Richardson 112, B. Patterson 67*).*

23rd Match: v Combined XI (Hobart) Jan 22, 24, 25.
Combined XI 199 (R. M. Cowper 53, F. J. Titmus 6-65) & 271-1 (R. M. Cowper 143, W. M. Lawry 126*) drew with M.C.C. 471-9 dec (G. Boycott 156, J. T. Murray 83, M. C. Cowdrey 70, K. Hooper 5-106).*

24th Match: v Australia (Adelaide) Jan 28, 29, 31, Feb 1.
England 241 (K. F. Barrington 60, G. D. McKenzie 6-48) & 266 (K. F. Barrington 102, F. J. Titmus 53, N. J. N. Hawke 5-54) lost to Australia 516 (R. B. Simpson 225, W. M. Lawry 119, I. J. Jones 6-118) by an inns & 9 runs.

25th Match: v New South Wales (Sydney) Feb 4, 5, 7, 8.
New South Wales 488 (G. Thomas 129, R. B. Simpson 123, K. D. Walters 57) drew with M.C.C. 329 (P. H. Parfitt 87) & 472-6 (W. E. Russell 101*, B. R. Knight 94, G. Boycott 77, R. W. Barber 75, M. J. K. Smith 64).

26th Match: v Australia (Melbourne) Feb 11, 12, 14, 15, 16.
England 485-9 dec (K. F. Barrington 115, J. M. Parks 89, J. H. Edrich 85, M. C. Cowdrey 79) & 69-3 drew with Australia 543-8 dec (R. M. Cowper 307, W. M. Lawry 108, K. D. Walters 60).

27th Match: v President's XI (Wellington) Feb 19, 21, 22.
President's XI 237 (R. W. Morgan 72, M. J. F. Shrimpton 58, D. A. Allen 5-96) & 188-7 drew with M.C.C. 359-6 dec (P. H. Parfitt 121, M. J. K. Smith 78, G. Boycott 51).*

28th Match: v New Zealand (Christchurch) Feb 25, 26, 28, March 1.
England 342 (D. A. Allen 88, P. H. Parfitt 54, M. J. K. Smith 54) & 201-5 dec (M. J. K. Smith 87) drew with New Zealand 347 (B. E. Congdon 104, R. C. Motz 58, E. C. Petrie 55) & 48-8.

29th Match: v New Zealand (Dunedin) March 4, 5, 7, 8.
New Zealand 192 (R. C. Motz 57) & 147-9 drew with England 254-8 dec (M. C. Cowdrey 89*, J. T. Murray 50).

30th Match: v New Zealand (Auckland) March 11, 12, 14, 15.
New Zealand 296 (B. W. Sinclair 114, B. E. Congdon 64, D. A. Allen 5-123) & 129 drew with England 222 (M. C. Cowdrey 59, W. E. Russell 56) & 159-4.

31st Match: v President's XI (Hong Kong) (One Day) March 18.
M.C.C. 149-7 (C. Metcalfe 5-41): rain stopped play.

32nd Match: v Hong Kong (Kowloon) (One Day) March 19.
M.C.C. 266-6 dec (G. Boycott 108, W. E. Russell 59) beat Hong Kong 193 (D. Coffey 88) by 73 runs.

1965-66: M.C.C. to Ceylon, Australia and New Zealand

Batting Averages

	M	I	NO	R	HS	Avge	100	c/s
K. F. Barrington (Surrey)	11	17	3	946	158	67.57	3	10
F. J. Titmus (Middx)	10	12	4	528	80*	66.00	0	7
J. M. Parks (Sussex)	12	18	6	771	107*	64.25	1	32/6
M. C. Cowdrey (Kent)	16	26	6	1076	108	53.80	2	12
R. W. Barber (Warks)	13	22	2	1001	185	50.05	3	10
M. J. K. Smith (Warks)	17	28	5	1079	112*	46.91	2	28
W. E. Russell (Middx)	12	20	4	709	110	44.31	2	7
J. H. Edrich (Surrey)	16	25	1	1060	133	44.16	3	6
B. R. Knight (Essex)	9	13	3	426	94	42.60	0	6
G. Boycott (Yorks)	13	21	2	784	156	41.26	1	6
D. A. Allen (Gloucs)	15	15	6	285	88	31.66	0	9
J. T. Murray (Middx)	9	11	1	305	110	30.50	1	17/3
P. H. Parfitt (Middx)	12	21	2	565	121	29.73	1	12
D. J. Brown (Warks)	11	13	1	157	44	13.08	0	1
K. Higgs (Lancs)	14	10	6	38	12*	9.50	0	5
I. J. Jones (Glam)	14	10	2	30	16	3.75	0	4
J. D. F. Larter (Northts)	5	3	0	7	4	2.33	0	4

Bowling Averages

	Balls	M	R	W	Avge	BB	5i
W. E. Russell	56	1	36	3	12.00	3-20	0
K. F. Barrington	260	1	149	6	24.83	4-24	0
K. Higgs	3279	100	1214	44	27.39	4-5	0
D. J. Brown	2134	49	1026	35	29.31	5-63	1
I. J. Jones	3093	74	1473	48	30.68	6-118	2
F. J. Titmus	3363	90	1109	36	30.81	6-65	2
D. A. Allen	4546	186	1594	47	33.91	5-96	2
J. D. F. Larter	794	12	411	12	34.25	4-49	0
B. R. Knight	1728	55	658	19	34.63	4-84	0
P. H. Parfitt	662	20	325	7	46.42	2-5	0
G. Boycott	594	25	285	4	71.25	2-32	0
R. W. Barber	1409	8	873	10	87.30	2-33	0

Also bowled: M. C. Cowdrey 8-0-7-0; J. H. Edrich 6-0-6-0; J. T. Murray 24-0-19-0; J. M. Parks 48-4-17-1; M. J. K. Smith 24-0-9-0.

Above *A vociferous Australian appeal for leg before wicket against England skipper Mike Smith in the first Test of the 1965-66 Australian tour at Brisbane. Bob Cowper and Wally Grout seem confident but the verdict was no.*

Below *Bob Barber out at last. A tired Barber bowled by Neil Hawke after scoring 185 in the third Test at Sydney, an innings which was the basis of an innings victory for the tourists.*

The main problem, which was forecast by the critics, was the fitness of the fast bowlers. In the event Larter spent most of his time recovering from strains, Brown was also injury prone and B. R. Knight (Essex) was in fact flown in to make good the party just before the first Test. The third fast man, Jones, improved as the tour progressed, but his habit of running on to the wicket was frowned on by the umpires and he was actually barred from further bowling in one match. Higgs, also, suffered illness which lost him many opportunities.

Boycott and Barber prospered as opening partners to some extent, but Boycott had the unfortunate habit of making the bowling look twice what it was. Barrington and Edrich both did well, as did Cowdrey. Parks should have been played just as a batsman, since he was worth a place in the Test side, but his keeping left something to be desired.

Smith refused to give Barber's leg spin a proper chance and this left the slow bowling very poor, since Titmus was right out of sorts.

For Australia Simpson and Lawry were absolute reliability and Walters was very promising. Hawke and McKenzie, the two principal bowlers, both suffered injuries which was inconsiderate, since Australia had no replacements.

1965-66: champions Worcestershire go to Jamaica

Sponsored by Carreras of Jamaica Ltd, Worcestershire, the 1965 County Champions, made a short tour of Jamaica in the spring of 1966. Unfortunately all the matches were drawn, as they were arranged for two days only, except for the one first-class game. The team flew to Jamaica via New York and the first game commenced on 18 March on the West Indies Sugar Company ground, but rain cut into the match.

In the first-class game, Sobers captained the local side and hit a scintillating century to save his side from defeat.

The touring party was D. Kenyon (capt), M. J. Horton, R. G. A. Headley, B. L. d'Oliveira, D. W. Richardson, J. A.

Ormrod, R. Booth, D. N. F. Slade, B. M. Brain, L. J. Coldwell, J. A. Flavell, N. Gifford. T. W. Graveney had to stand down at the last minute owing to his wife's illness.

1966-67: first M.C.C. under-25 tour goes to Pakistan

The side which M.C.C. sent to Pakistan in 1966-67 was a new experiment for English cricket, in that selection was confined to players under 25. In format the programme followed that of the 1963-64 tour to India, with a heavy list of fixtures crammed into a few weeks. This imposed a severe strain on cricketers unused to living in Pakistan.

The team was J. M. Brearley (Middx) (capt), D. J. Brown (Warwicks) (vice-capt), R. N. Abberley (Warwicks), D. L. Amiss (Warwicks), G. G. Arnold (Surrey), M. Bissex (Gloucs), K. W. R. Fletcher (Essex), R. N. S. Hobbs (Essex), R. A. Hutton (Yorks), A. P. E. Knott (Kent), J. A. Ormrod (Worcs), P. I. Pocock (Surrey), D. L. Underwood (Kent) and A. R. Windows (Gloucs) with L. E. G. Ames as manager.

Playing their opening match at Hyderabad, the M.C.C. began with a win against Southern Zone. Brown bowled splendidly and Brearley and Amiss carried the batting. Victory was also achieved in the second game, but Abberley, who hit 92, damaged a finger and as he would be unable to play in the next few weeks was flown home, M. A. Buss taking his place.

The 'First Test' at Lahore was a high-scoring draw. Pakistan made little effort to make runs, Mushtaq taking 323 minutes over his hundred, whilst Majid spent 190 minutes over reaching fifty. Fletcher batted well and relatively quickly for M.C.C., but there was never even a remote possibility of a definite outcome to the game, after Pakistan's first innings had been declared closed at 429 for 6.

The match against Northern Zone was noteworthy for Brearley's triple century – M.C.C. hit 514 for 4 on the first day in 5½ hours play and in terms of speed both the total and Brearley's 312 not out were new records in Pakistan. Hobbs, Hutton and Fletcher then bowled the opposition out twice to provide an innings victory. The next game produced another win with a hundred from Amiss, but some of the M.C.C. batsmen were unable to fathom Intikhab Alam, the young leg-spinner who later played many years with Surrey.

Brearley hit a double century in the 'Second Test', but his chief partner Amiss was lucky to reach three figures, being dropped several times. The match was interrupted by rain and though Brearley enforced the follow on and Mushtaq was injured, Asif Iqbal hit a marvellous hundred to save the match for Pakistan.

The 'Third Test' followed immediately. The M.C.C. were hit by illness and injury and not at their best. Pakistan gained a first innings lead of 37, but three run outs in their second innings together with a series of bumpers meant that they were unable to capitalise on their advantage and M.C.C. were set 255 in 220 minutes. Brearley decided not to attempt to win and the game was drawn.

Brearley, Amiss and Fletcher all batted well on the tour – England made a great discovery in Knott, and Hobbs and Pocock showed much promise in the spin department, so the tour was certainly successful from England's future. For Pakistan Asif was a great captain and Majid a most promising bat. Wasim Bari as a wicket-keeper batsman also impressed.

1966-67: Arabs tour Barbados

A strong side of Arabs made a seven-match tour of Barbados in January 1967. The party consisted of A. C. D. Ingleby-Mackenzie (Hants) (capt), C. A. Fry (Northants), A. H. Barker (Oxford U), H. C. Blofeld (Cambridge U), A. R. Duff (Worcs), G. P. S. Delisle (Middx), I. R. Lomax, S. G. Metcalfe (Oxford U),

1966-67: Arabs to Barbados

1st Match: v Pickwick (Kensington Oval)   Jan 7.
Arabs 227-9 dec (S. G. Metcalfe 73, A. R. Duff 56*) beat Pickwick 178 (A. Taylor 65) by 49 runs.

2nd Match: v E. De C. Weekes' XI (Kensington Oval)   Jan 8.
E. De C. Weekes' XI 114 (J. D. Piachaud 5-40) & 104-5 lost to Arabs 239 (H. C. Blofeld 50) by 8 wkts.

3rd Match: v Combined Barbados Schools (Harrison College)   Jan 10, 11.
Schools 180 (J. D. Piachaud 6-56) & 156-9 dec drew with Arabs 198 (A. H. Barker 65) & 66-7.

4th Match: v Lodge School Past & Present (St John)   Jan 12.
Arabs 225-9 dec (G. P. S. Delisle 62) lost to Lodge School 260-8 (G. Hutchinson 82, A. Bethell 67) by 5 wkts.

5th Match: v Carlton-Maple (Black Rock)   Jan 13.
Arabs 136 (G. Sealy 5-37) lost to Carlton-Maple 182-9 (C. Burnham 60) by 5 wkts.

6th Match: v Wanderers (Bridgetown)   Jan 15.
Wanderers 191 (J. D. Piachaud 5-60) beat Arabs 80 (R. Edwards 7-33) by 111 runs.

7th Match: v Police (Queen's Park)   Jan 16.
Police 206-7 dec lost to Arabs 220-7 (C. A. Fry 67) by 3 wkts.

8th Match: v Empire-Spartan (Queen's Park)   Jan 18.
Arabs 78 (A. Howard 5-26) lost to Empire-Spartan 91-7 by 4 wkts.

9th Match: v President's XI (Kensington Oval)   Jan 20, 21, 22.
Arabs 97-9 dec & 143 beat President's XI 133 (J. D. Piachaud 6-45) & 81 (K. E. Walters 7-27) by 26 runs.

J. D. Piachaud (Hants), P. D. Hill-Wood, S. H. Parker-Bowles, D. Perrett, P. Wigan and K. E. Walters (Barbados). The last-named played due to some last minute withdrawals from the original side.

The outstanding player of the tour was Piachaud and his off-breaks captured 38 wickets at 12.7 each. Metcalfe was the most successful bat, though Duff also played well. Ingleby-Mackenzie was taken ill and missed three games.

The major match of the tour was the three-day game against a President's XI, which included Gordon Greenidge, P. D. Lashley and other West Indian cricketers of note. Rain badly affected the wicket and the Arabs won a low scoring match by 26 runs.

1967: M.C.C. visit North America for Canadian Centenniel

On 21 July 1967 the M.C.C. side left London for Canada to help celebrate the Canadian Centenniel Year. The team was D. R. W. Silk (Somerset) (capt), R. A. Gale (Middx), R. C. Kerslake (Somerset), D. Bennett (Middx), J. P. Fellows-Smith (Northants), G. N. S. Ridley (Kent), E. A. Clark (Middx), J. D. Piachaud (Kent), D. J. Mordaunt (Sussex), A. R. Duff (Worcs), R. Aldridge, C. J. Saunders (Oxford U), A. E. Moss (Middx) and the old West Indian batsman, Everton Weekes.

The most serious cricket was played in the first ten days in Ottawa, when six one-day games were followed by the 'Test Match' against Canada. The spin of Piachaud and Ridley proved too much for the home side in this match and a century from Gale together with 99 by Fellows-Smith produced an innings victory for the tourists.

After visiting the West Coast of Canada the side went, via Toronto, to the United States for five matches and had a hard fight in the match against Staten Island, but most of the games were more in the nature of exhibition matches and no defeats were met.

Bennett had an outstanding tour with the bat and all the bowlers returned good figures, Weekes played some innings reminiscent of his best days. In addition the old West Indian Test player acted as wicket keeper when injury early on the tour meant that Saunders was forced to miss some of the matches. Bennett easily topped the batting averages whilst Moss was the leading bowler.

1967: M.C.C. to North America

1st Match: v Manitoba (Ottawa)   July 22.
M.C.C. 223-6 dec (R. A. Gale 103, J. P. Fellows-Smith 52*) beat Manitoba 36 by 187 runs.

2nd Match: v Ontario (Ottawa)   July 23.
M.C.C. 178-7 dec drew with Ontario 98-7.

3rd Match: v British Columbia (Ottawa)   July 24.
M.C.C. 200-5 dec (D. Bennett 69*, R. C. Kerslake 69) beat British Columbia 53 (G. N. S. Ridley 5-15) by 147 runs.

4th Match: v Saskatchewan (Ottawa)   July 25.
M.C.C. 203-4 dec (D. J. Mordaunt 72, R. A. Gale 64) beat Saskatchewan 74 (J. D. Piachaud 5-32) by 129 runs.

5th Match: v Quebec (Ottawa)   July 26.
Quebec 55 lost to M.C.C. 56-2 by 8 wkts.

6th Match: v Alberta (Ottawa)   July 27.
M.C.C. 185-7 dec (D. R. W. Silk 67) beat Alberta 58 by 127 runs.

7th Match: v Canada (Ottawa)   July 29, 30, 31.
Canada 161 (V. K. Taylor 50, J. D. Piachaud 5-22) & 172 (J. D. Piachaud 8-86) lost to M.C.C. 355 (R. A. Gale 102, J. P. Fellows-Smith 99, D. Bennett 51) by an inns & 22 runs.

8th Match: v Saskatchewan (Regina)   Aug 5.
M.C.C. 178-5 dec beat Saskatchewan 58 by 120 runs.

9th Match: v Alberta (Edmonton)   Aug 7.
Alberta 92 lost to M.C.C. 94-1 (E. D. Weekes 54*) by 9 wkts.

10th Match: v British Columbia Mainland League (Vancouver)   Aug 10.
B.C. Mainland League 51 (D. J. Mordaunt 5-11) lost to M.C.C. 52-0 by 10 wkts.

11th Match: v British Columbia Mainland League (Vancouver)   Aug 11.
M.C.C. 215-6 dec (D. Bennett 117*) beat B.C. Mainland League 82 by 133 runs.

12th Match: v British Columbia C.A. (Vancouver)   Aug 12.
M.C.C. 209-7 dec (R. A. Gale 112) beat British Columbia C.A. 137 by 72 runs.

13th Match: v Victoria (Vancouver)   Aug 13.
M.C.C. 233-6 dec (G. N. S. Ridley 82, R. C. Kerslake 58) beat Victoria 115 (D. J. Mordaunt 6-36) by 118 runs.

14th Match: v Quebec C.A. (Montreal)   Aug 18.
M.C.C. 189-1 dec (R. A. Gale 112*, D. R. W. Silk 51) drew with Quebec C.A. 32-1.

15th Match: v Quebec C.A. (Montreal)   Aug 19.
Quebec C.A. 158 (E. Braithwaite 56, J. D. Piachaud 5-63) lost to M.C.C. 162-6 (R. A. Gale 56) by 4 wkts.

16th Match: v Hamilton & District League (Toronto)   Aug 20.
M.C.C. 177-7 dec (D. Bennett 61, E. A. Clark 52) beat Hamilton 86 (A. E. Moss 5-6) by 91 runs.

17th Match: v South Ontario C.A. (London)   Aug 23.
M.C.C. 216-3 dec (D. Bennett 103*, E. A. Clark 66) beat South Ontario 77 (A. R. Duff 5-33) by 139 runs.

18th Match: v J. Benson's XI (Toronto)   Aug 25.
M.C.C. 155-5 dec beat J. Benson's XI 60 by 95 runs.

19th Match: v Toronto (Toronto)   Aug 26.
M.C.C. 240-3 dec (E. A. Clark 90, E. D. Weekes 53*) beat Toronto 128 by 112 runs.

20th Match: v Toronto & District C.C. (Toronto)   Aug 27.
Toronto 10-1: rain stopped play.

21st Match: v British Commonwealth in Washington (Washington)   Aug 30.
M.C.C. 182-7 dec (D. Bennett 71) beat British Commonwealth 115 (J. D. Piachaud 5-5) by 67 runs.

22nd Match: v U.S.C.A. Southern Zone (Washington)   Aug 31.
M.C.C. 177-5 dec (G. N. S. Ridley 66, E. A. Clark 50) beat Southern Zone 34 (A. E. Moss 5-9, J. D. Piachaud 5-10) by 143 runs.

23rd Match: v Philadelphia C.C. (Philadelphia)   Sept 2.
M.C.C. 211-6 dec (D. J. Mordaunt 59*, E. A. Clark 59) beat Philadelphia 77 by 134 runs.

24th Match: v Staten Island C.C. (Staten Island)   Sept 3.
M.C.C. 184-9 dec (L. Mullings 5-32) drew with Staten Island 125-8.

25th Match: v New York Inter-state League (New York)   Sept 4.
M.C.C. 140-8 dec beat New York League 53 (A. E. Moss 6-14) by 87 runs.

1967-68: England win despite another riot in the West Indies

On the eve of the final Test against Pakistan at the Oval in August 1967, Brian Close, the England captain for all six home Tests of that summer, was censured for alleged unfair play, whilst leading Yorkshire against Warwickshire. This led to him being sacked as captain of the M.C.C. team to West Indies–an appointment which had been made by the selectors some time previously. The controversy divided cricket followers into two camps and was described as 'one of the unhappiest ten days in the game's history'. Close's crime was that of 'time-wasting' on the final afternoon of the Warwickshire match to prevent Yorkshire being defeated.

Close's replacement as captain was Colin Cowdrey, who had therefore at last been promoted to the captaincy, after years as vice-captain, in most unpleasant circumstances.

The full touring party was M. C. Cowdrey (Kent) (capt), F. J. Titmus (Middx) (vice-capt), K. F. Barrington (Surrey), G. Boycott (Yorks), D. J. Brown (Warwicks), B. L. d'Oliveira (Worcs), J. H. Edrich (Surrey), T. W. Graveney (Worcs), K. Higgs (Lancs), R. N. S. Hobbs (Essex), I. J. Jones (Glamorgan), A. P. E. Knott (Kent), C. Milburn (Northants), J. M. Parks (Sussex), P. I. Pocock (Surrey), J. A. Snow (Sussex) and

L. E. G. Ames as manager. Aside from the absence of Close, the main criticism was the absence of Lock and Underwood and the fact that Brown was preferred to Arnold. In passing it should be mentioned that M. J. K. Smith had announced his retirement and was not in the running for the captaincy.

The tour opened in Barbados and after a Colts game a high scoring match against the island side was played. The team then went straight on to Trinidad and were outplayed by the locals, being lucky to draw the game. The first Test was held at Port of Spain where England's solid batting hit 568 – Barrington and Graveney made hundreds. West Indies however had to rely on Lloyd and were unable to avoid the follow on. In the final session of play Sobers and Hall managed to save the side from an innings defeat.

Jamaica was the scene of M.C.C.'s first victory, when on a difficult wicket Snow shattered the Jamaican batting in their first innings and just managed to bring M.C.C. a win in extra time by taking the final wicket when the tailenders proved troublesome.

England had all the best of the second Test. Cowdrey batted in splendid form and assisted by Edrich and Barrington gave England a substantial first innings total, which looked larger when Snow put the West Indies batting to rout with figures of 7 for 49. West Indies followed on. Again the batting failed and the score stood at 204 for 5 when the umpire gave Butcher out caught at the wicket. This correct decision was not acceptable to the crowd and a bottle-throwing riot commenced. This upset the English players and West Indies, through Sobers, saved the match. The third Test also ended in a draw. Although West Indies batted first, England still achieved a first innings lead, with Edrich and Boycott giving the side an opening partnership of 172, but Lloyd hit a hundred in the West Indian second innings and there was no hope of a definite finish.

A fatal declaration by Sobers, made on the strength of some good bowling in the first innings by Butcher, gave England victory with three minutes to spare in the fourth Test.

West Indies had all the best of the fifth Test. Kanhai and Sobers hit centuries and England had Lock to thank for reaching a satisfactory total. The spin bowler batted 150 minutes to make 89, his highest score in first-class cricket. On the final day, England needed 308 to win, but collapsed to 41 for 5 against the spin bowling of Gibbs. All seemed lost, but Cowdrey and Knott shared in a partnership of 127 that saved the game, England having one wicket to fall when the stumps were drawn.

The tour was a huge success from England's viewpoint and from the viewpoint of diplomacy, since several problems which might have got out of hand were kept in perspective. England returned home undefeated.

Cowdrey and Boycott took the honours in the batting and Snow was the leading bowler – England now had a fast bowler who was better than his West Indian counterpart and the home side were therefore reluctant to indulge in a bumper war.

The sad note in the tour was the injury to Titmus, who lost four toes in a boating accident shortly before the third Test. Lock was flown in as a replacement, being dispatched from Western Australia, where he was wintering.

For the West Indies, Hall and Griffiths, the famous fast bowlers, were no longer to be feared and the bowling revolved around Sobers and Gibbs. The most promising of the younger element was a bespectacled left-hander – Clive Lloyd.

1967-68: International Eleven tour Africa and Asia

Though entitled an International Eleven, the side which toured parts of Africa and Asia in the early months of 1968 was composed entirely of English County cricketers, so presumably the title was describing the extent of the tour rather than its individuals. The team, managed by J. Lister, was M. J. Stewart (Surrey) (capt), D. L. Amiss (Warwicks), G. G. Arnold (Surrey), J. Birkinshaw (Leics), M. H. Denness (Kent), K. W. R. Fletcher (Essex), G. Goonesena (Notts), A. W. Greig (Sussex), Khalid Ibadulla (Warwicks), H. Latchman (Middx), H. J. Rhodes (Derbys), K. G. Suttle (Sussex), R. W. Tolchard (Leics) and D. L. Underwood (Kent).

1967-68: International XI to Africa and Asia

1st Match: v Sir Ernest Beoku-Betts' XI (Freetown)   Jan 19, 20.
Beoku-Betts XI 63 (G. Goonesena 6-23) & 102 lost to International XI 379-5 dec (D. L. Amiss 120, M. H. Denness 110, K. Ibadulla 55) by an inns & 214 runs.

2nd Match: v Sierra Leone Selection Trust Ltd (Yengema) (One Day)   Jan 21.
Sierra Leone 50 (H. C. Latchman 5-9) lost to International XI 51-1 by 9 wkts.

3rd Match: v University of Sierra Leone (Njala) (One Day)   Jan 24.
International XI 275-5 dec (M. J. Stewart 73, M. H. Denness 63, A. W. Greig 63) beat University 29 by 246 runs.

4th Match: v Sierra Leone (Freetown)   Jan 26, 27.
Sierra Leone 117 (M. Turay 53) & 100 (A. W. Greig 6-36) lost to International XI 335-8 dec (D. L. Amiss 118) by an inns & 118 runs.

5th Match: v Uganda (Kampala)   Feb 3, 4, 5.
Uganda 228 (Davda 55, Mushtaq 53) & 115 lost to International XI 325 (K. Ibadulla 88, J. Birkenshaw 69, K. W. R. Fletcher 67, R. W. Tolchard 54) & 22-2 by 8 wkts.

6th Match: v Rift Valley Invitation XI (Nakura) (One Day)   Feb 7.
International XI 275-8 dec (M. H. Denness 107) drew with Rift Valley 147-8.

7th Match: v East African Conference XI (Nairobi)   Feb 9, 10, 11.
International XI 306 (J. Birkenshaw 97, D. Pringle 5-97) & 187 (K. W. R. Fletcher 50, J. Birkenshaw 50, D. Pringle 5-67) drew with East African XI 231 (P. Upendra 79) & 206-9 (V. Noordin 56).

8th Match: v Pakistan Board of Control XI (Karachi)   Feb 16, 17, 18, 19.
International XI 182 (K. G. Suttle 79, Saeed Ahmed 5-39) & 351-7 dec (K. W. R. Fletcher 108*, J. Birkenshaw 59, A. W. Greig 54) beat Board of Control XI 246 (Javed Burki 58) & 244 (Saeed Ahmed 97, Mohammed Ilyas 50) by 43 runs.

9th Match: v Indian XI (Bombay)   Feb 23, 24, 25, 26.
International XI 255 (D. L. Amiss 109) & 314-7 dec (K. W. R. Fletcher 107*, K. G. Suttle 66, K. Ibadulla 55, S. Venkataraghavan 5-80) beat Indian XI 138 & 249 (V. Bhosle 69) by 182 runs.

10th Match: v Chief Minister's XI (Madras)   Feb 29, March 1, 2, 3.
International XI 360 (K. Ibadulla 107, A. W. Greig 106, D. L. Amiss 67, V. V. Kumar 5-113) & 205-5 dec beat Chief Minister's XI 164 (D. L. Underwood 6-41) & 111 by 290 runs.

11th Match: v Ceylon President's XI (Colombo)   March 5, 6, 7.
International XI 179 (K. G. Suttle 63, Abu Fuard 6-31) & 155-2 dec (K. W. R. Fletcher 82*, K. G. Suttle 59) beat President's XI 42 (D. L. Underwood 8-10) & 98 (D. L. Underwood 7-33) by 194 runs.

12th Match: v Ceylon Government Service C.A. (Kandy)   March 9, 10.
Ceylon G.S.C.A. 200 (D. P. de Silva 50*) drew with International XI 322-9 (H. C. Latchman 62*, H. J. Rhodes 54, T. B. Kehelgamuwa 6-67).

13th Match: v Singapore (Singapore)   March 17, 18.
International XI 307-7 dec (M. J. Stewart 66, G. Goohesena 55) beat Singapore 67 (D. L. Underwood 7-30) & 35 by an inns & 205 runs.

14th Match: v Combined Services (Singapore) (One Day)   March 19.
International XI 190 beat Combined Services 81 by 109 runs.

15th Match: v Malacca C.A. (Malacca)   March 21, 22.
Malacca C.A. 67 & 23-7 drew with International XI 211 (M. H. Denness 57).

16th Match: v Negri Sembilan H.H. Invitation XI (Seremban)   March 23, 24.
Invitation XI 85 (D. L. Underwood 8-19) drew with International XI 122-1 (K. G. Suttle 54*).

17th Match: v M.C.A. Patron's XI (Penang)   March 26, 27.
Patron's XI 101 & 41 (G. G. Arnold 6-7) lost to International XI 235-3 dec (K. W. R. Fletcher 121*) by inns & 93 runs.

18th Match: v M.C.A. President's XI (Kuala Lumpur)   March 30, 31.
President's XI 54 (D. L. Underwood 6-12) & 83 (D. L. Underwood 5-28) lost to International XI 225 (Dr A. E. Delikan 7-71) by an inns & 88 runs.

19th Match: v Royal Bangkok Sports Club (Bangkok) (One Day)   April 3.
International XI 267-5 dec (D. L. Amiss 82, M. J. Stewart 51) drew with Royal Bangkok S.C. 117-7.

20th Match: v Hong Kong C.A. President's XI (Hong Kong) (One Day)   April 5.
International XI 233-8 dec (K. G. Suttle 61, M. J. Stewart 57, K. Ibadulla 56) beat President's XI 74 (H. J. Rhodes 5-16) by 159 runs.

21st Match: v Hong Kong League XI (Kowloon)   April 6, 7.
International XI 353 (K. Ibadulla 70, M. H. Denness 52, J. Murphy 5-65) beat Hong Kong League XI 66 & 73 by an inns & 214 runs.

The tour began in Sierra Leone, which was new ground for an English touring side of any importance. The four matches played there did not tax the tourists too much, for though cricket seemed to flourish in Freetown the standard was not very high. In Kenya however the tourists had to struggle to prevent defeat at the hands of an East African XI, and the last pair survived for 12 minutes to save the game. In Pakistan Fletcher hit a century which enabled a declaration to take place, setting the local side 288 to make at 52 per hour. The spin of Goonesena however proved too much for them and victory was obtained by 43 runs.

In India another victory was obtained after Stewart declared at Bombay and again at Madras. Brilliant bowling by Underwood, who used a damp wicket to its best advantage, gave the tourists an easy win in Colombo. The team travelled on to Singapore and Malaysia, before stops in Thailand and finally Hong Kong.

The party arrived back in England on 10 April. The most impressive young player on the tour was R. W. Tolchard, the wicket-keeper.

1967-68: champions Warwickshire visit Kenya and Uganda

The Warwickshire county cricketers, complete with a plane load of supporters, toured East Africa in the autumn of 1967, playing eight matches. The team was M. J. K. Smith (capt), T. W. Cartwright, D. L. Amiss, J. A. Jameson, Khalid Ibadulla, R. N. Abberley, A. C. Smith, R. B. Edmonds, L. R. Gibbs, D. J. Brown and J. M. Allan.

The most important match was against an Invitation Eleven at Mombasa. Warwickshire obtained a large lead on the first innings, but rain and a not out innings of 86 by R. D. Patel saved the local side. The two other three-day matches were against Uganda and Kenya. In both these games rain prevented a completion.

C. S. Elliott, the old Derbyshire cricketer, travelled with the team as umpire.

1967-68: Warwickshire to Uganda and Kenya

1st Match: v Kampala C.C. (Kampala)   Sept 28.
Warwickshire 232-4 dec (J. A. Jameson 102) drew with Kampala C.C. 178-5 (Bowles 52, de Souza 52).

2nd Match: v African XI (Logogo Stadium)   Sept 29.
African XI 133-8 dec drew with Warwickshire 86-3.

3rd Match: v Uganda (Kampala)   Sept 30, Oct 1, 2.
Uganda 205 (Lawrence 67, Bhasker 66) drew with Warwickshire 342-6 (D. L. Amiss 126, T. W. Cartwright 93*).

4th Match: v Invitation XI (Eldoret)   Oct 4.
Warwickshire 216 (D. L. Amiss 67, M. J. K. Smith 57, Patel 6-61) beat Invitation XI 91 (R. B. Edmonds 5-21) by 125 runs.

5th Match: v Rift Valley (Nakuru)   Oct 6.
Warwickshire 233-6 dec (R. N. Abberley 85, D. L. Amiss 59) drew with Rift Valley 182-8.

6th Match: v Kenya Kongonis (Nairobi)   Oct 7, 8, 9.
Kongonis 156 (T. W. Cartwright 6-55) & 302 (Tongue 137, M. J. K. Smith 81) drew with Warwickshire 199 (D. L. Amiss 61, R. N. Abberley 56) & 214-7 (J. A. Jameson 96, Khalid Ibadulla 74).

7th Match: v Invitation XI (Mombasa)   Oct 14, 15, 16.
Invitation XI 116 (Babla 56) & 206-8 (R. D. Patel 86*, A. C. Smith 5-37) drew with Warwickshire 413-7 dec (J. A. Jameson 76, M. J. K. Smith 73, Khalid Ibadulla 62, T. W. Cartwright 57*, W. J. Stewart 52).

8th Match: v Nyeri (Nyeri)   Oct 19.
Warwickshire 149-9 dec (M. J. K. Smith 54) beat Nyeri 107 by 42 runs.

9th Match: v Kenya (Nairobi)   Oct 21, 22, 23.
Warwickshire 368-9 dec (T. W. Cartwright 123, Khalid Ibadulla 79, M. J. K. Smith 63) & 58-1 drew with Kenya 255-9 dec (Virendra 82, Jawahirshah 74, A. C. Smith 5-66).

1968-69: the d'Oliveira affair – then riots in Pakistan

The d'Oliveira affair was the dominant feature of the sporting press in the last weeks of the 1968 summer. The M.C.C. were programmed to tour South Africa in the winter of 1968-69 and announced the following team: M. C. Cowdrey (Kent) (capt), T. W. Graveney (Gloucs) (vice-capt), K. F. Barrington (Surrey), G. Boycott (Yorks), D. J. Brown (Warwicks), T. W. Cartwright (Warwicks), R. M. H. Cottam (Hants), J. H. Edrich (Surrey), K. W. R. Fletcher (Essex), A. P. E. Knott (Kent), J. T. Murray (Middx), R. M. Prideaux (Northants), P. I. Pocock (Surrey), J. A. Snow (Sussex), D. L. Underwood (Kent). The main criticism was the absence of Milburn. Cartwright was pronounced unfit after the selection was made public and d'Oliveira was chosen to replace him. The South African Government stated that they could not accept d'Oliveira, a Cape Coloured, as a member of the touring party and the M.C.C. therefore cancelled the tour. The South African Government blamed 'political forces' for the selection of d'Oliveira on the grounds that Cartwright was picked as a bowler and had been replaced by d'Oliveira, who was primarily a batsman.

It was proposed that the M.C.C. should make a tour of India, Pakistan and Ceylon, but on financial grounds the visit to India had to be cancelled – Mrs Gandhi refused to release the £20,000 foreign exchange that the tour required.

The party eventually left London on 21 January 1969. The team showed two more alterations to the original, Barrington and Boycott being replaced by C. Milburn (Northants) and R. N. S. Hobbs (Essex). The four initial matches were played in Ceylon, the major one being the three-day game against Ceylon, which was drawn on a placid wicket. The contrast between Ceylon and Pakistan was alarming. The latter country was in a state of political upheaval. The first Test in Lahore was played in or around a continuous riot. Somehow Cowdrey managed to score a century amid the general confusion and but for Asif, Pakistan would have been in a very parlous condition – he hit 70 out of 206. Cowdrey set Pakistan 300 minutes to make 323 but they fell well short. The match over-rate was deplorable.

Going straight to Dacca for the second Test, the M.C.C. found the city's law and order had completely broken down. Police and military had withdrawn leaving the city in the hands of the left-wing students, who tended to use the match as a focal point for their grievances. As can be imagined this did not make for a very pleasant atmosphere for any cricket match. Snow and Brown dismissed Pakistan for 246 and then a great innings from d'Oliveira saved England. On a difficult pitch Pakistan were in danger of collapsing in their second innings, but Mushtaq, Saeed and Majid held fast and the game was drawn. The third Test began three days later in Karachi, but before the England first innings could be completed rioting ended the match and the tourists hurriedly left for England. The credit for surviving so long in such chaotic conditions belongs to Ames, the manager, who through all the problems remained calm.

The M.C.C. party leave London airport in January 1969 for the tour of Ceylon and Pakistan. This tour was arranged after the cancellation of the South African tour due to the inclusion in the party of Basil d'Oliveira (seen at the foot of the steps behind captain Cowdrey). In the event the tour of Pakistan was truncated by rioting.

1968-69: weak side tours South Africa

R. J. McAlpine captained the following side which made a 3½-week tour of South Africa in February and March 1969: R. A. Gale (Middx), R. V. C. Robins (Middx), M. O. C. Sturt (Middx), A. E. Moss (Middx), I. R. Lomax (Wilts), E. J. Lane-Fox (Oxon), A. R. B. Neame (M.C.C.), S. G. Metcalfe (Oxford U), P. L. B. Stoddart (Bucks), B. C. G. Wilenkin (Cambridge U), T. B. L. Coghlan (Cambridge U), E. Arundel (M.C.C.), J. Hurn (Wilts), N. Style and D. C. Wing.

The first two games were in Salisbury and in both the tourists were lucky to get away with draws. The Rhodesian Currie Cup players took the English bowling apart in both games.

There followed five matches in Johannesburg, with the tourists decisively beaten in three. Moss provided the team with its first victory at White River in N.E. Transvaal, when he returned the curious bowling analysis of 19-12-15-2.

Of the two games played in Swaziland, one was rained off entirely and the other drawn in an interesting state.

In the final match Robins took 5 for 56, whilst Lomax hit 59 and victory was obtained by 3 wickets. Syd Buller accompanied the side as umpire.

1968-69: R. J. McAlpine's Team to South Africa

1st Match: v President's XI (Salisbury)   Feb 16.
President's XI 333-6 dec (S. Robertson 108, A. J. Pithy 92, K. C. Bland 42) drew with McAlpine's XI 184-8 (S. G. Metcalfe 60).

2nd Match: v Stragglers C.C. (Salisbury)   Feb 17.
McAlpine's XI 247-7 dec (R. A. Gale 101, E. Lane Fox 59, M. Shacklock 5-97) lost to Stragglers C.C. 251-3 (J. Clarke 127*, P. R. Carlstein 64) by 7 wkts.

3rd Match: v Staggerers C.C. (Johannesburg)   Feb 19, 20.
Staggerers 182 (B. Pfaff 77) & 170-6 dec beat McAlpine's XI 155-8 dec & 103 by 94 runs.

4th Match: v Country Club (Johannesburg)   Feb 22.
McAlpine's XI 177-9 dec lost to Country Club 180-4 by 6 wkts.

5th Match: v Vagabonds (Johannesburg)   Feb 23.
McAlpine's XI 203-9 dec (N. Style 71) drew with Vagabonds 171-9 (W. Kerr 73).

6th Match: v Wanderers (Johannesburg)   Feb 24.
McAlpine's XI 169 (E. Lane Fox 67) lost to Wanderers 173-5 (W. Kerr 62) by 5 wkts.

7th Match: v Wilfred Isaac's XI (Johannesburg)   Feb 25.
Isaac's XI 168-4 dec drew with McAlpine's XI 112-8 (E. Lane Fox 60).

8th Match: v White River (White River)   Feb 26.
McAlpine's XI 127 (B. C. G. Wilenkin 74) beat White River 88 (A. R. B. Neame 7-51) by 39 runs.

9th Match: v Swaziland (Usutu)   March 1.
McAlpine's XI 202-5 dec (R. A. Gale 91) drew with Swaziland 169-6.

10th Match: v Swaziland (Usutu)   March 2.
No play due to rain.

11th Match: v Hilton College (Hilton)   March 4.
McAlpine's XI 218-2 dec (I. R. Lomax 116*, B. C. G. Wilenkin 73) beat Hilton College 100 (R. V. C. Robins 7-45) by 118 runs.

12th Match: v Grasshoppers (Pietermaritzburg)   March 5.
Grasshoppers 215-7 dec (L. Lund 82) lost to McAlpine's XI 217-5 (S. G. Metcalfe 84, A. R. B. Neame 71) by 5 wkts.

13th Match: v Kookaburras (Mount Egdecombe)   March 7.
McAlpine's XI 95 lost to Kookaburras 101-2 (A. McLeod 53*) by 8 wkts.

14th Match: v Crickets (Kloof)   March 8.
Crickets 146 (A. R. B. Neame 5-35) drew with McAlpine's XI 128-9 (R. A. Gale 50).

15th Match: v Inanda (Johannesburg)   March 9.
Inanda 161 (R. V. C. Robins 5-56) lost to McAlpine's XI 163-7 (I. R. Lomax 59) by 3 wkts.

1969-70: Duke of Norfolk's team to the West Indies

Sponsored partly by Gillette Industries, the Duke of Norfolk managed a team to the West Indies in February and March 1970. The full side was M. C. Cowdrey (Kent) (capt), J. Birkenshaw (Leics), the Earl of Cottenham, M. H. Denness (Kent), M. J. Edwards (Surrey), A. W. Greig (Sussex), M. G. Griffith (Sussex), R. N. S. Hobbs (Essex), B. Leadbeater (Yorks), C. M. Old (Yorks), P. J. Sharpe (Yorks), D. L. Underwood (Kent), A. Ward (Derbyshire). The Duke of Norfolk accompanied the side as did E. W. Swanton and C. S. Elliott (umpire).

The team flew straight to Barbados and after a few days acclimatisation, went on to St Lucia for a series of three matches. The major game, a three-day fixture with the Windward Islands, was rained off on the last day but saw Cowdrey in fine form and Underwood return figures of 18-10-19-3. A crowd of some 6,000 turned out in Dominica for the next game, which the visitors won by 8 runs. Going on to Trinidad via St Vincent, the tourists were beaten by Trinidad, for whom Inshan Ali took 12 for 153. The final leg of the tour was in Barbados, where the island fielded a young side and lost by an innings. The tour was a success and particularly appreciated in the various Windward Islands.

1969-70: Duke of Norfolk's XI to West Indies

1st Match: v St Lucia (St Lucia) (One Day)   Feb 25.
Norfolk's XI 185-4 dec (A. W. Greig 55*, B. Leadbeater 53*) drew with St Lucia 98-7.

2nd Match: v St Lucia (St Lucia) (Limited Over)   Feb 26.
Norfolk's XI 163-7 beat St Lucia 131-8 by 32 runs.

3rd Match: v Windward Islands (St Lucia)   Feb 27, 28, March 1.
Norfolk's XI 220 (M. C. Cowdrey 81, P. J. Sharpe 64) & 116-1 (M. H. Denness 53*) drew with Windward Is 193 (H. Williams 54, R. N. S. Hobbs 6-82).

4th Match: v Dominica (Roseau) (Limited Over)   March 2.
Norfolk's XI 191 beat Dominica 183 (I. Shillingford 57, G. C. Shillingford 53) by 8 runs.

5th Match: v St Vincent (St Vincent) (Limited Over)   March 3.
Norfolk's XI 251-8 (M. H. Denness 58) beat St Vincent 106.

6th Match: v Trinidad (Port of Spain)   March 6, 7, 8, 9.
Norfolk's XI 150 (Inshan Ali 8-58) & 297 (J. Birkenshaw 64, M. C. Cowdrey 57*) lost to Trinidad 252 (H. Ramoutar 56) & 199-2 (C. A. Davis 96*, O. Durity 60) by 8 wkts.

7th Match: v Tobago (Shaw Park) (Limited Over)   March 11.
Norfolk's XI 206 (M. H. Denness 83, M. J. Edwards 55) beat Tobago 106 by 100 runs.

8th Match: v Barbados (Bridgetown)   March 14, 15, 16.
Barbados 208 (D. A. J. Holford 67, N. Clarke 51) & 192 lost to Norfolk's XI 452 (P. J. Sharpe 84, M. C. Cowdrey 83, J. Birkenshaw 78, A. W. Greig 65) by an inns & 52 runs.

9th Match: v Barbados (Bridgetown) (Limited Over)   March 18.
Norfolk's XI 172-8 (B. Leadbetter 80*, A. W. Greig 54) lost to Barbados 175-2 (P. D. Lashley 102*) by 8 wkts.

1969-70: champions Glamorgan tour Bermuda and West Indies

To celebrate the winning of the 1969 County Championship, Glamorgan, sponsored by Rizla Ltd, made a six-match tour of the West Indies in April 1970. The team was managed by P. B. Clift, the county coach, and the party consisted of A. R. Lewis (capt), A. Jones, R. C. Davis, K. J. Lyons, B. A. Davis, P. M. Walker, E. W. Jones, M. A. Nash, A. E. Cordle, D. L. Williams, D. J. Shepherd, G. C. Kingston, O. S. Wheatley and D. W. Lewis. The County found the West Indian opposition stronger than

---

1969-70: Glamorgan to West Indies

1st Match: v St George's C.C. (Bermuda)   April 1, 2.
St George's 163 (W. Pitcher 55) and 175 beat Glamorgan 142 (W. Pitcher 5-28) & 164 by 32 runs.

2nd Match: v St Kitts (Basseterre)   April 4, 5, 6.
Glamorgan 279 (A. Jones 86, R. C. Davis 61) & 158-3 dec (B. A. Davis 88*) drew with St Kitts 181 (P. M. Walker 5-43) & 220-9 (L. Sargeant 105).

3rd Match: v Windward Islands (Roseau)   April 7, 8, 9.
Windward Is 302 (N. Phillip 96, T. M. Findlay 51) & 173-4 dec (V. Elwin 59) drew with Glamorgan 268-8 dec (E. W. Jones 64) & 125-3.

4th Match: v Grenada (St George's, Grenada)   April 11, 12.
Glamorgan 153-5 dec & 103-1 dec (A. Jones 53) drew with Grenada 152-7 dec & 88-8.

5th Match: v Trinidad Colts (Brechin Castle) (Limited Over)   April 15.
Glamorgan 156-7 beat Colts 131-9 by 25 runs.

6th Match: v Trinidad (Port of Spain)   April 17, 18, 19.
Glamorgan 272 (A. Jones 114, Inshan Ali 5-44) & 96 lost to Trinidad 242 & 127-5 by 5 wkts.

expected and the only victory came against the Colts in Trinidad – the attendances of the two matches played on this island were badly affected by the Black Power movement, which was causing much political unrest. As with the Duke of Norfolk's side, the left-arm spinner Inshan Ali worried the Welshmen, who were easily beaten by Trinidad. The other first-class match was drawn, though Phillip for the Windward Islands hit 96 very quick runs and E. W. Jones also batted well.

1969-70: M.C.C. tour Ceylon and Far East

It was intended to tour Uganda, Zambia and Kenya, but these three countries all took umbrage at the proposed visit of South Africa to England and cancelled the arrangements. The M.C.C. therefore, for the second successive winter, were forced to replan and the team were welcomed in Ceylon, Malaysia, Singapore, Thailand and Hong Kong instead. The tourists were A. R. Lewis (Glamorgan) (capt), A. C. Smith (Warwicks) (player-manager), G. G. Arnold (Surrey), W. Blenkiron (Warwicks), G. Boycott (Yorks), K. W. R. Fletcher (Essex), R. M. C. Gilliat (Hants), J. H. Hampshire (Yorks), A. Jones (Glamorgan), P. I. Pocock (Surrey), G. R. J. Roope (Surrey), D. J. Shepherd (Glamorgan), R. W. Taylor (Derbys), D. Wilson (Yorks) and J. S. Buller as umpire.

About 10,000 attended the first day of the opening match in Colombo and saw Ceylon take a first innings lead against the tourists, but a century by Alan Jones redressed the balance and Wilson's left-arm spin did the rest. The tourists combined coaching with playing in matches and found an unexpected enthusiasm for the game in Malaysia and Singapore. The team went to Bangkok, where the game was kept alive by a group of dedicated cricketers, and to Hong Kong.

The team flew back home after the final game on 15 March.

1969-70: M.C.C. to Ceylon and Far East

1st Match: v Ceylon (Colombo)   Feb 20, 21, 22, 23.
M.C.C. 132 & 302-7 dec (A. Jones, Sahabandu 5-86) beat Ceylon 134 (D. Wilson 6-35) & 127 (D. Wilson 8-36) by 173 runs.

2nd Match: v Yang Di Pertuan Besar's XI (Seremban)   Feb 26, 27.
M.C.C. 305-8 dec (J. H. Hampshire 67, R. M. C. Gilliat 66, G. Boycott 60, C. Navaratnam 5-90) drew with Besar's XI 110 & 163-7.

3rd Match: v Singapore (Singapore)   Feb 28, March 1.
M.C.C. 315-3 dec (G. Boycott 149*, K. W. R. Fletcher 96*, A. Jones 67) beat Singapore 178 (W. Dougan 5-38) & 122 (D. Wilson 6-45) by 121 runs.

4th Match: v Malaysian President's XI (Ipoh)   March 3, 4.
M.C.C. 272-6 dec (G. Boycott 147*, J. H. Hampshire 55*, A. Jones 53) & 25-1 dec beat President's XI 61 & 73 by 163 runs.

5th Match: v Malaysia (Kuala Lumpur)   March 7, 8.
M.C.C. 345-4 dec (R. M. C. Gilliat 109, A. R. Lewis 74, G. Boycott 66*) & 110-2 dec (K. W. R. Fletcher 50*) beat Malaysia 102 & 113 by 240 runs.

6th Match: v Royal Bangkok Sports Club (Bangkok)   March 11.
M.C.C. 223-1 dec (G. Boycott 116, A. Jones 102*) beat Royal Bangkok S.C. 52 (D. J. Shepherd 5-16) by 171 runs.

7th Match: v Hong Kong President's XI (Hong Kong)   March 14.
M.C.C. 204 (D. Wilson 57) beat President's XI 140 (D. Wilson 6-58) by 64 runs.

8th Match: v Hong Kong (Kowloon)   March 15.
M.C.C. 190-0 dec (A. Jones 104*, G. Boycott 79*) drew with Hong Kong 125-5.

1970-71: Illingworth's team regain the Ashes

Following the cancellation of the South African visit to England in the summer of 1970, a series was arranged against a Rest of the World Team. In so far as the M.C.C. proposed to visit Australia

in the winter of 1970-71, the major point in these matches was that Illingworth led the English side in place of Cowdrey, who had been injured. During the 1970 season the press, when not occupied with the South African 'Ban the Tour' news, concerned itself about the prospective captaincy of M.C.C. in Australia – the lobbies were divided between Cowdrey as captain and Illingworth as his number two, or vice-versa. The first announcement from Lord's however was that D. G. Clark would manage the side. Later the M.C.C. announced that Illingworth would be captain and the full team was: R. Illingworth (Leics) (capt), M. C. Cowdrey (Kent) (vice-capt), G. Boycott (Yorks), B. L. d'Oliveira (Worcs), J. H. Edrich (Surrey), K. W. R. Fletcher (Essex), J. H. Hampshire (Yorks), B. W. Luckhurst (Kent), P. Lever (Lancs), J. A. Snow (Sussex), K. Shuttleworth (Lancs), A. Ward (Derbys), D. Wilson (Yorks), D. L. Underwood (Kent), A. P. E. Knott (Kent) and R. W. Taylor (Derbys), with B. Thomas as assistant to D. G. Clark.

The critics questioned the absence of A. W. Greig, R. N. S. Hobbs and M. H. Denness, and were worried about the lack of good fielders.

The team flew from London on 18 October, but in view of complaints of 'jet-lag' by some recent tour managers, the first game did not commence until the 28 October, when a one-day affair was won by 10 wickets. The feature of the matches prior to the first Test was the inability of the tourists to dismiss the opposition cheaply. South Australia hit 649 for 9 declared, in the initial first-class match, but they were much aided by a double century from the South African Barry Richards. Against Victoria the M.C.C. collapsed in front of A. L. Thomson, a relatively unknown fast bowler, and then Victoria scored over 300 before declaring. New South Wales declared with 410 on the board, whilst Queensland hit 360. The M.C.C. attack was not helped by a foot injury to Ward, which ended the tour for him after the fifth match. R. G. D. Willis, the young Surrey fast bowler, was flown out as a replacement.

The team therefore began the first Test rather on the defensive. Australia batted first and with Stackpole making a double century the home team reached 433. England however batted with remarkable consistency to obtain a lead of 31 and Australia struggled in their second innings; in fact England might have forced a win if the over rate had not been so slow.

Western Australia, led by Lock, had all the best of a drawn match before the second Test, the first England had ever played

---

1970-71: M.C.C. to Australia and New Zealand

Batting Averages

	M	I	NO	R	HS	Avge	100	c/s
G. Boycott (Yorks)	12	22	6	1535	173	95.93	6	6
J. H. Edrich (Surrey)	14	25	5	1136	130	56.80	3	8
B. W. Luckhurst (Kent)	11	20	3	954	135	56.11	4	11
B. L. d'Oliveira (Worcs)	13	20	3	870	162*	51.17	4	6
A. P. E. Knott (Kent)	12	17	5	539	101	44.91	1	24/4
J. H. Hampshire (Yorks)	10	17	3	463	156*	33.07	1	6
R. Illingworth (Leics)	14	21	4	537	53	31.58	0	6
K. W. R. Fletcher (Essex)	12	21	1	602	80	30.10	0	10
M. C. Cowdrey (Kent)	11	18	1	511	101	30.05	1	3
J. A. Snow (Sussex)	10	10	1	150	38	16.66	0	2
R. W. Taylor (Derbys)	5	6	0	98	31	16.33	0	14/5
P. Lever (Lancs)	13	13	1	188	64	15.66	0	6
R. G. D. Willis (Surrey)	9	8	3	74	27	14.80	0	4
D. Wilson (Yorks)	6	3	0	35	19	11.66	0	3
K. Shuttleworth (Lancs)	9	10	2	88	24	11.00	0	3
A. Ward (Derbys)	2	3	1	15	8*	7.50	0	0
D. L. Underwood (Kent)	13	14	7	41	13*	5.85	0	11

Bowling Averages

	O	M	R	W	Avge	BB	5i
D. L. Underwood	422	110	1123	43	26.11	6-12	3
J. A. Snow	306.5	57	1021	38	26.86	7-40	2
R. G. D. Willis	182	29	738	23	32.08	4-81	0
K. Shuttleworth	188.5	23	662	17	38.94	5-47	1
P. Lever	311.2	48	951	23	41.34	4-17	0
A. Ward	38.5	3	166	4	41.50	2-25	0
M. C. Cowdrey	24	0	127	3	42.33	2-46	0
R. Illingworth	284	71	883	20	44.15	3-39	0
K. W. R. Fletcher	40.3	2	232	5	46.40	3-43	0
B. L. d'Oliveira	192	34	569	12	47.41	2-15	0
D. Wilson	120.7	19	406	8	50.75	3-32	0

Also bowled: G. Boycott 4.4-0-31-1; J. H. Hampshire 9-0-53-0; B. W. Luckhurst 2-0-6-0.

at Perth. This match, which saw a maiden hundred by Greg Chappell, was another draw. Illingworth set Australia 245 to make in 145 minutes on the final day and it was a challenge completely ignored by Lawry, who spent an hour making six runs.

Another match of declarations and ultimately a draw was played against South Australia, after which the tourists went to Tasmania before the third Test at Melbourne. Three days of almost continuous rain caused this to be the first Test in Australia between the two countries to be abandoned entirely due to the weather, but the Australian Board and the English officials in Australia agreed to play a one-day game on what should have been the last day of the Test and to reschedule the remaining fixtures to insert an additional Test.

The fourth Test at Sydney began four days after the hastily arranged one-day international. England batted first and after making a modest 332 went on to dominate the game completely. Snow bowled brilliantly, when no other fast bowler could get anything out of the wicket and Boycott batted in his best form to make the highest score in both England innings—77 and 142 not out. Of the Australians only Lawry mastered the tourists' attack and with grim determination remained unbeaten after 255 minutes, seeing all ten wickets fall. England won by the large margin of 299 runs. Aside from the victory over Tasmania, it was the first first-class win of the tour.

Bad behaviour by the crowd marred the fifth Test, which was drawn in Australia's favour due to poor English catching, Cowdrey being the main culprit. Both Thomson and Snow bowled bouncers, but only the latter was warned by the umpires. Play on the last day was rather pointless, but made even more so by more unruly demonstrations by the spectators, who booed and slow hand-clapped. Luckhurst, who hit a century in England's first innings, broke a finger.

The sixth Test followed directly after the fifth and though Illingworth was in a position to enforce Australia to follow on, he did not do so as the pitch eased in the later stages of the match—the last day was pretty pointless. The seventh Test began after an interval of nine days and two one-day games. Australia gained an 80-run lead on first innings, but Snow was again warned against bowling bumpers. The crowd became restive and Illingworth actually led the England team off the field, only resuming when the umpires threatened to award the match to Australia by default. The English batting in the second innings improved greatly on the first and Australia needed 223 on a pitch which aided the bowlers. Stackpole put up a lone fight and England won by 62 runs, thus taking the series two matches to nil.

The tour ended with five matches in New Zealand, including two Tests, one of which was won by England and the other drawn.

Illingworth thoroughly deserved the success he achieved, for he welded the team into a very competent unit. England's bowling relied very much on Snow, and the batting laurels went to Boycott, Edrich and Luckhurst. Illingworth and d'Oliveira also had good tours, but Underwood should have done better in the Tests. Cowdrey was a shadow of his former self, the loss of the leadership seeming too much for him.

Australia had a poor time, only Lawry really living up to his reputation, though Lillee and O'Keeffe looked good prospects.

1970-71 : M.C.C. to Australia and New Zealand

1st Match: v South Australia Country XI (Port Pirie)   Oct 28.
Country XI 146-9 dec (J. Kernahan 54) lost to M.C.C. 148-0 (B. W. Luckhurst 82*, G. Boycott 64*) by 10 wkts.*

2nd Match: v South Australia (Adelaide)   Oct 30, 31, Nov 1, 2.
M.C.C. 451-9 dec (G. Boycott 173, K. W. R. Fletcher 70, J. H. Edrich 63, J. H. Hampshire 52) & 235-4 (B. L. d'Oliveira 103*, K. W. R. Fletcher 80) drew with S. Australia 649-9 dec (B. A. Richards 224, I. M. Chappell 93, J. P. Causby 68, K. G. Cunningham 65, G. S. Chappell 57).

3rd Match: v Victoria Country XI (Horsham)   Nov 4.
Country XI 152-8 dec lost to M.C.C. 153-3 (J. H. Edrich 57) by 7 wkts.

4th Match: v Victoria (Melbourne)   Nov 6, 7, 8, 9.
M.C.C. 142 (A. L. Thomson 6-80) & 341 (M. C. Cowdrey 101) lost to Victoria 304-8 dec (A. P. Sheahan 71, I. R. Redpath 68) & 180-4 (A. P. Sheahan 58*, I. R. Redpath 57) by 6 wkts.

5th Match: v New South Wales (Sydney)   Nov 13, 14, 15, 16.
N.S.W. 410-5 dec (K. D. Walters 201*, G. R. Davies 57, K. J. O'Keeffe 55*, A. J. Turner 50) drew with M.C.C. 204 (K. J. O'Keeffe 6-69) & 325-1 (B. W. Luckhurst 135, G. Boycott 129*, K. W. R. Fletcher 51*).

6th Match: v Queensland Country XI (Warwick)   Nov 18.
Country XI 89 lost to M.C.C. 300 (B. L. d'Oliveira 105, M. C. Cowdrey 53) on first innings.

7th Match: v Queensland (Brisbane)   Nov 21, 22, 23, 24.
Queensland 360 (S. C. Trimble 177, R. F. Surti 83) drew with M.C.C. 418-4 (G. Boycott 124*, J. H. Edrich 120, K. W. R. Fletcher 77).

8th Match: v Queensland Country XI (Redlands Bay)   Nov 25.
Country XI 142 lost to M.C.C. 155-3 (R. Illingworth 52) by 7 wkts.*

9th Match: v Australia (Brisbane)   Nov 27, 28, 29, Dec 1, 2.
Australia 433 (K. R. Stackpole 207, K. D. Walters 112, J. A. Snow 6-114) & 214 (W. M. Lawry 84, K. Shuttleworth 5-47) drew with England 464 (J. H. Edrich 79, B. W. Luckhurst 74, A. P. E. Knott 73, B. L. d'Oliveira 57) & 39-1.

10th Match: v Western Australia (Perth)   Dec 5, 6, 7, 8.
W. Australia 257-5 dec (R. J. Inverarity 93, R. Edwards 56) & 285 (A. L. Mann 110) drew with M.C.C. 258-3 dec (G. Boycott 126, B. W. Luckhurst 111) & 256-6 (J. H. Edrich 70, B. W. Luckhurst 60).

11th Match: v Western Australia Country XI (Narrogin)   Dec 9.
Country XI 150-2 dec (T. Waldron 58, P. Silinger 50) lost to M.C.C. 163-5 (K. W. R. Fletcher 66) by 5 wkts.*

12th Match: v Australia (Perth)   Dec 11, 12, 13, 15, 16.
England 397 (B. W. Luckhurst 131, G. Boycott 70) & 287-6 dec (J. H. Edrich 115*, G. Boycott 50) drew with Australia 440 (I. R. Redpath 171, G. S. Chappell 108, I. M. Chappell 50) & 100-3.

13th Match: v South Australia (Adelaide)   Dec 18, 19, 20, 21.
S. Australia 297-2 dec (B. A. Richards 146, A. J. Woodcock 119*) & 338-7 dec (G. S. Chappell 102, K. G. Cunningham 60, A. J. Woodcock 52) drew with M.C.C. 238 (M. C. Cowdrey 57) & 336-8 (B. L. d'Oliveira 162*, G. Boycott 92).

14th Match: v Tasmania (Hobart)   Dec 23, 24, 26.
M.C.C. 316-4 dec (J. H. Hampshire 156*, J. H. Edrich 52) & 72-1 beat Tasmania 164 (P. Roberts 77) & 223 (K. Ibadulla 51) by 9 wkts.

15th Match: v Combined XI (Launceston)   Dec 27, 28, 29.
M.C.C. 184-4 (G. Boycott 74, M. C. Cowdrey 66) drew Combined XI did not bat: rain.

16th Match: v Australia (Melbourne)   Dec 31, Jan 1, 2.
No play due to rain.

17th Match: v Australians (Melbourne) (Limited Over)   Jan 5.
M.C.C. 190 (J. H. Edrich 82) lost to Australians 191-5 (I. M. Chappell 60) by 5 wkts.

18th Match: v New South Wales Country XI (Wagga Wagga)   Jan 7.
Country XI 117 lost to M.C.C. 241-4 (G. Boycott 76, B. W. Luckhurst 62) by 9 wkts.

19th Match: v Australia (Sydney)   Jan 9, 10, 12, 13, 14.
England 332 (G. Boycott 77, J. H. Edrich 55) & 319-5 dec (G. Boycott 142*, B. L. d'Oliveira 56, R. Illingworth 53) beat Australia 236 (I. R. Redpath 64, K. D. Walters 55) & 116 (W. M. Lawry 60*, J. A. Snow 7-40) by 299 runs.

20th Match: v Northern New South Wales (Newcastle)   Jan 16, 17, 18.
M.C.C. 355-4 dec (B. W. Luckhurst 124, K. W. R. Fletcher 122, R. Illingworth 55*) & 322-4 (J. H. Hampshire 122, M. C. Cowdrey 70) drew with Northern N.S.W. 171 (D. Wilson 7-62).

21st Match: v Australia (Melbourne)   Jan 21, 22, 23, 25, 26.
Australia 493-9 dec (I. M. Chappell 111, R. W. Marsh 92*, I. R. Redpath 72, W. M. Lawry 56, K. D. Walters 55) drew with England 392 (B. L. d'Oliveira 117, B. W. Luckhurst 109) & 161-0 (G. Boycott 76*, J. H. Edrich 74*).

22nd Match: v Australia (Adelaide)   Jan 29, 30, Feb 1, 2, 3.
England 470 (J. H. Edrich 130, K. W. R. Fletcher 80, G. Boycott 58, J. H. Hampshire 55, D. K. Lillee 5-84) & 233-4 dec (G. Boycott 119*) drew with Australia 235 (K. R. Stackpole 87) & 328-3 (K. R. Stackpole 136, I. M. Chappell 104).

23td Match: v Southern New South Wales (Canberra)   Feb 6.
No play due to rain.

24th Match: v Western Australia (Sydney) (Limited Over)   Feb 8.
M.C.C. 152 (B. L. d'Oliveira 54) drew with W. Australia 24-2.

25th Match: v New South Wales Country XI (Parkes)   Feb 9.
Country XI 116 (D. Wilson 5-50) lost to M.C.C. 184-7 (R. W. Taylor 77) by 7 wkts.

26th Match: v Australia (Sydney)   Feb 12, 13, 14, 16, 17.
England 184 & 302 (B. W. Luckhurst 59, J. H. Edrich 57) beat Australia 264 (G. S. Chappell 65, I. R. Redpath 59) & 160 (K. R. Stackpole 67) by 62 runs.

27th Match: v Wellington (Wellington) (Limited Over)   Feb 20.
Wellington 188 beat M.C.C. 165 by 23 runs.

28th Match: v Otago (Dunedin) (Limited Over)   Feb 21.
M.C.C. 167 beat Otago 144-7 by 23 runs.

29th Match: v New Zealand (Christchurch)   Feb 25, 26, 27, March 1.
New Zealand 65 (D. L. Underwood 6-12) & 254 (G. M. Turner 76, B. E. Congdon 55, D. L. Underwood 6-85) lost to England 231 (B. L. d'Oliveira 100) & 89-2 (J. H. Hampshire 51*) by 8 wkts.

30th Match: v Central Districts (Palmerston North) (Limited Over)   March 3.
Central Districts 208-6 lost to M.C.C. 209-6 (B. W. Luckhurst 85) by 4 wkts.

31st Match: v New Zealand (Auckland)   March 6, 7, 8, 9.
England 321 (A. P. E. Knott 101, P. Lever 64, B. L. d'Oliveira 58, M. C. Cowdrey 54, R. S. Cunis 6-76) & 237 (A. P. E. Knott 96) drew with New Zealand 313-7 dec (M. G. Burgess 104, G. M. Turner 65, G. T. Dowling 53, D. L. Underwood 5-108) & 40-0.

1971-72: Gloucestershire win 'Tests' in Zambia

The Gloucestershire County side at the invitation of the Zambia Cricket Union undertook a three-week tour of that country in October 1971. The team which flew from Heathrow on 5 October was A. S. Brown (capt), C. A. Milton, G. G. M. Wiltshire, D. R. Shepherd, J. Davey, J. H. Shackleton, J. C. Foat, J. P. Sullivan, R. B. Nicholls, Sadiq Mohammad, Zaheer Abbas and two Glamorgan players, D. J. Shepherd and R. C. Davis, together with G. W. Parker as manager.

The 'First Test' against Zambia began on 8 October and the local side hit up 355 in their first innings, but Milton, Zaheer and Davis all scored heavily to put Gloucester in the lead and Don Shepherd bowled the Zambians out cheaply in the second innings, in time to allow the tourists to win by 5 wickets. Unfortunately Brown was taken ill after this match and Don Shepherd led the team for the rest of the visit.

In the 'Second Test' two innings of note by Zaheer made certain of victory, whilst in the 'Third' Sadiq held the batting together with 124 out of a total of 250.

Cricket did not appear to be played in Zambian schools and was kept going by expatriates and Asians.

1971-72: Gloucestershire in Zambia

1st Match: v Zambia (Lusaka)   Oct 8, 9, 10.
Zambia 355 (B. Ellis 87, D. C. Patel 58) & 145 lost to Gloucs 335 (Zaheer Abbas 117, R. C. Davis 73, C. A. Milton 70) & 169-5 by 5 wkts.

2nd Match: v Livingstone (Bharat Grd) (Limited Over)   Oct 14.
Gloucs 238-4 (Zaheer Abbas 88*, Sadiq Mohammad 67) drew with Livingstone 130-7.

3rd Match: v Zambia (Kitwe)   Oct 16, 17, 18.
Zambia 123 (R. C. Davis 6-27) & 169 (R. C. Davis 5-62) lost to Gloucs 225-6 dec (Zaheer Abbas 60) & 68-2 (Zaheer Abbas 55*) by 8 wkts.

4th Match: v Copperbelt XI (Kitwe)   Oct 20, 21.
Gloucs 218 (J. C. Foat 64, R. B. Nicholls 55) & 204-2 dec drew with Copperbelt XI 196-9 dec (R. Goodchild 71) & 187-1.

5th Match: v Zambia (Lusaka)   Oct 23, 24, 25.
Zambia 203 & 122 lost to Gloucs 250 (Sadiq Mohammad 124, G. Rees 5-93, P. G. Nana 5-102) & 70-4 by 6 wkts.

1972-73: Kent lose one-day matches in West Indies

The John Player League Champions of 1972, Kent, were invited to tour the West Indies with the object of playing a series of one-day matches based on the John Player Rules.

The team flew from London on 4 January and after a single day's recovery period, were beaten by Jamaica by 33 runs. Boyce hit a splendid 72 in the return match the following day, but again Jamaica proved the winners.

Flying on to Trinidad, the county side beat the Under-25s, but failed against the full island side.

Barbados also beat Kent twice and the tour ended in Guyana where two more defeats were suffered.

The touring party was B. W. Luckhurst (capt), G. W. Johnson, R. B. Elms, D. A. Laycock, J. N. Graham, R. A. Woolmer, D. Nicholls, A. G. E. Ealham and J. N. Shepherd; B. Dudleston (Leics), K. D. Boyce (Essex) and J. M. Brearley (Middx) as guest players; and C. Lewis, county coach, L. E. G. Ames, county manager, and M. C. Cowdrey, who joined the side in Trinidad.

The games in Guyana and the smaller islands were watched by large crowds and in every way except the actual results the tour was successful. It was really expecting too much of the visitors to produce their best form against strong opposition in so short a time—the whole trip only lasted 18 days.

1972-73: Kent to West Indies

1st Match: v Jamaica (Kingston) (Limited Over)   Jan 6.
Jamaica 181-7 (M. L. C. Foster 67*) beat Kent 149 by 32 runs.

2nd Match: v Jamaica (Kingston) (Limited Over)   Jan 7.
Kent 193-9 (K. D. Boyce 72) lost to Jamaica 195-6 by 4 wkts.

3rd Match: v Trinidad Under 25 XI (Brechin Castle) (Limited Over)   Jan 9.
Kent 167 beat Under 25 XI 131 by 36 runs.

4th Match: v Trinidad (Port of Spain) (Limited Over)   Jan 11.
Kent 143 lost to Trinidad 144-6 by 4 wkts.

5th Match: v Tobago (Tobago) (Limited Over)   Jan 12.
Kent 182 beat Tobago 115 by 67 runs.

6th Match: v Barbados (Bridgetown) (Limited Over)   Jan 13.
Barbados 173-8 (G. A. Greenidge 97) beat Kent 160 by 13 runs.

7th Match: v Barbados (Bridgetown) (Limited Over)   Jan 14.
Barbados 169-8 beat Kent 132 by 37 runs.

8th Match: v St Lucia (St Lucia) (Limited Over)   Jan 15.
Kent 187 beat St Lucia 100 by 87 runs.

9th Match: v Antigua (Antigua) (Limited Over)   Jan 16.
Kent 235-6 (J. M. Brearley 82, K. D. Boyce 52*) beat Antigua 205 (I. V. A. Richards 63, B. D. Julien 5-20) by 30 runs.

10th Match: v Guyana (Berbice) (Limited Over)   Jan 18.
Guyana 197-9 beat Kent 160 (J. N. Shepherd 57*) by 37 runs.

11th Match: v Guyana (Georgetown) (Limited Over)   Jan 20.
Guyana 226-6 (A. I. Kallicharran 67, C. H. Lloyd 51) beat Kent 164-8 by 62 runs.

1972-73: D. H. Robins' tour of South Africa

The problems of flying straight from England and playing cricket against first-class players without any preliminary practice or warm-up games were quite apparent on this tour, in which the team organised by D. H. Robins, the old Warwickshire cricketer, played Eastern Province and Western Province in two first-class games within a week of arrival and lost both.

The full touring party was: D. J. Brown (Warwicks) (capt), C. T. Radley (Middx), J. T. Murray (Middx), R. G. D. Willis (Warwicks), F. C. Hayes (Lancs), M. J. Smith (Middx), J. H. Hampshire (Yorks), R. D. V. Knight (Gloucs), D. P. Hughes (Lancs), R. N. S. Hobbs (Essex), D. R. Turner (Hants), J. K.

1972-73: Derrick Robins' Team to South Africa

1st Match: v Eastern Province (Port Elizabeth)   Jan 1, 2, 3.
Robins XI 306-4 dec (C. T. Radley 125, M. J. Smith 116) & 135 (J. T. Murray 58, R. Hanley 6-34) lost to E. Province 218 (S. J. Bezuidenhout 54) & 224-4 (S. J. Bezuidenhout 97, C. P. Wilkins 58) by 6 wkts.

2nd Match: v Western Province (Cape Town)   Jan 5, 6, 8.
W. Province 371-2 dec (E. J. Barlow 147, O. J. A. Snyman 133*, J. R. Cheetham 54) & 175-2 dec (O. J. A. Snyman 70, C. A. Gie 62*) beat Robins XI 234 (J. H. Hampshire 65, F. C. Hayes 50, M. H. Bowditch 5-31) & 191 (F. C. Hayes 59) by 121 runs.

3rd Match: v O.F.S. & Griqualand West (Bloemfontein) (Limited Over)   Jan 10.
Robins XI 312-6 (J. H. Hampshire 105*, D. R. Turner 88) beat Combined XI 269-7 (M. J. Doherty 68, S. D. Bruce 52) by 43 runs.

4th Match: v Transvaal (Johannesburg)   Jan 12, 13, 14.
Robins XI 344-9 dec (M. J. Smith 113, F. C. Hayes 75) & 199-4 dec (C. T. Radley 102) drew with Transvaal 275-6 dec (A. Bacher 147, S. J. Cook 64) & 188-8.

5th Match: v Northern Transvaal (Pretoria) (Limited Over)   Jan 17.
Robins XI 241-9 (F. C. Hayes 66, M. J. Smith 53) beat N. Transvaal 220 (D. Lindsay 92) by 21 runs.

6th Match: v Natal (Durban)   Jan 19, 20, 21.
Natal 180-8 dec (R. G. D. Willis 6-26) & 227-8 dec (A. Bruyns 65, H. R. Fotheringham 61) lost to Robins XI 250-9 dec (M. J. Smith 62, C. T. Radley 59) & 160-6 (C. T. Radley 53) by 4 wkts.

7th Match: v Border (East London) (Limited Over)   Jan 24.
Robins XI 213 (J. H. Hampshire 67) beat Border 106 (R. N. S. Hobbs 5-28) by 107 runs.

8th Match: v Combined B Section XI (Pretoria)   Jan 26, 27, 28.
Robins XI 237 (C. T. Radley 80, J. T. Murray 64) & 200-5 dec (J. T. Murray 63*, J. H. Hampshire 56*) drew with Combined XI 208-8 dec (A. A. During 66*, H. R. Fotheringham 51) & 85-4.

9th Match: v Invitation XI (Johannesburg)   Feb 2, 3, 5, 6.
Invitation XI 387-9 dec (B. A. Richards 100, A. Bruyns 97, B. L. Irvine 53) beat Robins XI 118 & 152 by an inns & 117 runs.

10th Match: v Invitation XI (Johannesburg) (Limited Over)   Feb 6.
Robins XI 146 lost to Invitation XI 147-9 (M. J. Procter 58) by 1 wkt.

1972-73: D. H. Robins' Team to South Africa

Batting Averages

	M	I	NO	R	HS	Avge	100	c/s
C. T. Radley (Middx)	6	12	0	554	125	46.16	2	7
J. T. Murray (Middx)	5	8	1	245	64	35.00	0	14
R. G. D. Willis (Warks)	5	5	3	69	34	34.50	0	2
F. C. Hayes (Lancs)	6	11	2	304	75	33.77	0	1
M. J. Smith (Middx)	6	12	0	380	116	31.66	2	1
J. H. Hampshire (Yorks)	6	12	2	258	65	25.80	0	2
A. Long (Surrey)	1	2	0	44	29	22.00	0	1
R. D. V. Knight (Gloucs)	5	10	0	188	44	18.80	0	5
D. P. Hughes (Lancs)	5	9	0	159	44	17.66	0	0
R. N. S. Hobbs (Essex)	3	3	1	30	17*	15.00	0	3
D. R. Turner (Hants)	3	5	0	70	24	14.00	0	0
J. K. Lever (Essex)	5	8	3	39	13	7.80	0	2
A. S. Brown (Gloucs)	2	4	0	29	18	7.25	0	1
P. J. Lewington (Warks)	3	3	2	7	5*	7.00	0	1
D. J. Brown (Warks)	3	4	0	13	8	3.25	0	1
R. D. Jackman (Surrey)	1	2	0	5	5	2.50	0	1
P. Willey (Northnts)	1	1	0	2	2	2.00	0	0

Bowling Averages

	O	M	R	W	Avge	BB	5i
P. Willey	15	5	36	4	9.00	4-36	0
J. H. Hampshire	6	4	13	1	13.00	1-13	0
J. K. Lever	147	41	348	16	21.75	3-20	0
R. N. S. Hobbs	98.2	18	325	10	32.50	4-55	0
R. G. D. Willis	131.2	31	358	11	32.54	6-26	1
D. P. Hughes	103.1	27	393	10	39.30	3-34	0
D. J. Brown	68.4	16	209	4	52.25	2-45	0
A. S. Brown	44	6	176	3	58.66	2-72	0
R. D. Jackman	17	3	66	1	66.00	1-66	0
P. J. Lewington	76	13	279	4	69.75	2-56	0
R. D. V. Knight	59	12	194	2	97.00	1-14	0

1972-73: Oxford and Cambridge Universities to Malaysia and Singapore

1st Match: v Singapore C.C. (Singapore).
Oxbridge 268-8 dec (P. D. Johnson 67) beat Singapore C.C. 122 by 146 runs.

2nd Match: v Civil Service (Singapore).
Oxbridge 251-8 dec (A. K. C. Jones 79, H. K. Steele 50) beat Civil Service 69 (R. J. Hadley 5-21) by 182 runs.

3rd Match: v Singapore C.A. (Singapore).
Singapore C.A. 251-8 dec (Chaturvedi 82, Tessensohn 59) & 156-9 dec (Jaya 61) drew with Oxbirdge 182-5 dec (M. J. J. Faber 52) & 187-8 (P. Hodson 50).

4th Match: v ANZUK Forces (Singapore).
Oxbridge 241 (P. C. H. Jones 50, Casey 6-88) beat ANZUK Forces 115 by 126 runs.

5th Match: v Johore (Johore).
Oxbridge 244 (H. K. Steele 56, de Silva 5-72) & 152-2 dec (M. J. J. Faber 62, P. D. Johnson 55*) drew with Johore 157 & 154-6 (Toh Choo Beng 59).

6th Match: v Malacca (Malacca).
Malacca 78 (C. B. Hamblin 5-32) & 85 (P. H. Edmonds 6-8) lost to Oxbridge 192-8 dec by an inns & 29 runs.

7th Match: v Perak (Perak).
Perak 33 (R. J. Hadley 5-3) & 70 (P. H. Edmonds 5-7) lost to Oxbridge 171-6 dec (J. M. Ward 52*) by an inns & 68 runs.

8th Match: v Penang (Penang).
Penang 105 & 79 lost to Oxbridge 224-3 dec (M. J. Heal 64, P. D. Johnson 60*, A. K. C. Jones 56) by an inns & 40 runs.

9th Match: v Negri Sembilan (Negri Sembilan).
Negri Sembilan 189 (Bala Kandjah 60, H. K. Steele 6-63) & 113 lost to Oxbridge 130 (Navaratnam 5-24) & 173-4 by 6 wkts.

10th Match: v Malaysia C.A. (Kuala Lumpur).
Oxbridge 257 (P. D. Johnson 74) & 276-9 dec (M. G. Heal 90, H. K. Steele 51) beat Malaysia C.A. 217 (Koo Kim Kuang 57, Ranjit Singh 50) & 86 (P. H. Edmonds 5-33) by 230 runs.

Lever (Essex), P. J. Lewington (Warwicks), P. Willey (Northants) and A. Long (Surrey). A. S. Brown was sent for after the second match when Willey was injured. J. D. Bannister travelled as manager, J. Jennings as physiotherapist and Brian Johnston as press officer.

After the initial defeats, the tourists almost beat Transvaal and then obtained their first first-class victory over Natal, winning off the last ball.

The most important match was virtually a 'Test Match' at Johannesburg and because of injuries, the tourists called in R. D. Jackman, the Rhodesian and Surrey cricketer, but even so South Africa (styled Invitation Section A XI) won by an innings. B. A. Richards hit a brilliant hundred and with Procter and Barlow in the attack, the tourists' batting crumbled. Over 16,000 watched the second day's play.

Radley headed the first-class averages, whilst Lever was easily the best bowler.

1972-73: Oxford and Cambridge tour Malaysia

Professor J. W. Linnett arranged a ten-match tour of Malaysia and Singapore by a combined team of 14 cricketers who represented Oxford or Cambridge University in 1972. The side was P. C. H. Jones (capt), A. K. C. Jones, S. C. Corlett, M. J. J. Faber, C. B. Hamelin, M. G. Heal and J. M. Ward of Oxford; and from Cambridge P. H. Edmonds, R. J. Hadley, P. Hodson, P. D. Johnson, M. P. Kendall, H. K. Steele and C. R. V. Taylor. Peter Wheatley acted as manager.

The pace attack of Hadley and Corlett proved too good for most of the opposition and against Perak Hadley returned figures of 5-3-3-5. The leading batsman was Johnson who hit three memorable fifties.

The reason for the tour was to try and improve cricket in Malaysia, but only in Johore was any coaching done. The tour which took place in July and August lasted four weeks and involved 10 matches, none of which was lost.

The hospitality received throughout the tour was almost overwhelming and the grateful players found they were hard put to keep match fit.

1972-73: the M.C.C. tour to India, Pakistan and Sri Lanka

The problem of the captaincy of major M.C.C. tours continued to tax the selectors in the summer of 1972; Illingworth who led England against Australia through that season declined the leadership of the winter tour. M. J. K. Smith was then offered the post and declined. In the end the captaincy was given to A. R. Lewis, the only other contender of any standing being J. M. Brearley. The full side, announced in September, was A. R. Lewis (Glamorgan) (capt), M. H. Denness (Kent) (vice-capt), D. L. Amiss (Warwicks), G. G. Arnold (Surrey), J. Birkenshaw (Leics), R. M. H. Cottam (Northants), K. W. R. Fletcher (Essex), N. Gifford (Worcs), A. W. Greig (Sussex), A. P. E. Knott (Kent), C. M. Old (Yorks), P. I. Pocock (Surrey), G. R. J. Roope (Surrey), R. W. Tolchard (Leics), D. L. Underwood (Kent) and B. Wood (Lancs), with D. B. Carr as manager. Both G. Boycott and J. A. Snow refused invitations to tour.

The team flew into Bombay on 30 November and after a rest travelled on to Hyderabad for the opening match. Arnold, Pocock and Wood were already indisposed with stomach upsets, but the game was a tame draw. Another draw was played at Indore, after Central Zone had decided not to attempt the sporting chance of 216 in 140 minutes. A third game of declarations was acted out before the first Test in Delhi. Some great bowling by Arnold dismissed India for 173. Only Greig of the English batsmen could however master Chandrasekhar and England's lead amounted to just 27 runs. The English spinners, Underwood and Pocock, ran through the Indian second innings, which left the tourists needing 207 for victory. Lewis and Greig, though kept in check by the spin of Bedi, took England to a 7-wicket win. The second Test followed directly after. Again the scoring was low, but this time the Indian bowlers, Chandrasekhar and Bedi, held the upper hand and evened the series to one match each.

Away from the excitement of the Tests, the tourists played another drawn match of declarations – the Nawab of Pataudi (now playing as M. A. Khan) hit a hundred, as did Knott and Fletcher.

Fletcher continued to bat well in the third Test and was unlucky to be 97 not out when the English innings ended, Chandrasekhar once more caused the damage. M. A. Khan hit the

1972-73: M.C.C. to Pakistan, India and Sri Lanka

1st Match: v Board President's XI (Hyderabad)   Dec 5, 6, 7.
President's XI 317-5 dec (S. M. Gavaskar 86, A. V. Mankad 60*, R. D. Parkar 59, C. P. S. Chauhan 53) & 84-2 (C. P. S. Chauhan 56*) drew with M.C.C. 321-7 dec (M. H. Denness 95, D. L. Amiss 81).

2nd Match: v Central Zone (Indore)   Dec 9, 10, 11.
M.C.C. 261-9 dec (B. Wood 117) & 209-4 dec (K. W. R. Fletcher 56, G. R. J. Roope 50) drew with Central Zone 255-3 dec (Suryaveer Singh 102, S. A. Durani 81*) & 114-4 (P. Sharma 51*).

3rd Match: v North Zone (Amritsar)   Dec 15, 16, 17.
M.C.C. 285-3 dec (K. W. R. Fletcher 120*, G. R. J. Roope 68, B. Wood 54) & 123-4 dec (A. W. Greig 54) drew with North Zone 166-7 dec (Madan Lal 66, M. Amarnath 51, R. M. H. Cottam 5-19) & 147-8.

4th Match: v India (New Delhi)   Dec 20, 21, 23, 24, 25.
India 173 (S. Abid Ali 58, G. G. Arnold 6-45) & 233 (E. D. Solkar 75, F. M. Engineer 63) lost to England 200 (A. W. Greig 68*, B. S. Chandrasekhar 8-79) & 208-4 (A. R. Lewis 70*) by 6 wkts.

5th Match: v India (Calcutta)   Dec 30, 31, Jan 1, 3, 4.
India 210 (F. M. Engineer 75) & 155 (S. A. Durani 53, A. W. Greig 5-24) beat England 174 (B. S. Chandrasekhar 5-65) & 163 (A. W. Greig 67, B. S. Bedi 5-63) by 28 runs.

6th Match: v South Zone (Bangalore)   Jan 6, 7, 8.
South Zone 274-5 dec (M. A. K. Pataudi 100*, B. P. Patel 93) & 214-7 dec (K. Jayantilal 103*) drew with M.C.C. 299-5 dec (A. P. E. Knott 156, K. W. R. Fletcher 100*) & 104-1.

7th Match: v India (Madras)   Jan 12, 13, 14, 15, 16.
England 242 (K. W. R. Fletcher 97*, B. S. Chandrasekhar 6-90) & 159 (M. H. Denness 76) lost to India 316 (M. A. K. Pataudi 73) & 86-6 by 4 wkts.

8th Match: v East Zone (Jamshedpur)   Jan 20, 21, 22.
M.C.C. 306-5 dec (G. R. J. Roope 125, R. W. Tolchard 70) & 99-4 dec drew with East Zone 148 (A. Roy 70, R. M. H. Cottam 5-25) & 176-8.

9th Match: v India (Kanpur)   Jan 25, 27, 28, 29, 30.
India 357 (A. L. Wadekar 90, S. M. Gavaskar 69, M. A. K. Pataudi 54) & 186-6 (G. R. Viswanath 75*) drew with England 397 (A. R. Lewis 125, J. Birkenshaw 64, K. W. R. Fletcher 58).

10th Match: v West Zone (Ahmedabad)   Feb 2, 3, 4.
M.C.C. 279-5 dec (G. R. J. Roope 130, D. L. Amiss 63) & 208-9 dec (R. W. Tolchard 51*, P. K. Shivalkar 6-77) drew with West Zone 218-4 dec (A. V. Mankad 54, H. S. Kanitkar 53*, C. P. S. Chauhan 51) & 194-4 (K. D. Ghavri 79*, H. S. Kanitkar 72*).

11th Match: v India (Bombay)   Feb 6, 7, 8, 10, 11.
India 448 (F. M. Engineer 121, G. R. Viswanath 113, A. L. Wadekar 87, S. A. Durani 73) & 244-5 dec (S. M. Gavaskar 67, F. M. Engineer 66) drew with England 480 (A. W. Greig 148, K. W. R. Fletcher 113, A. P. E. Knott 56, B. S. Chandrasekhar 5-135) & 67-2.

12th Match: v Central Province (Kandy) (Limited Over)   Feb 14.
M.C.C. 273-8 (D. L. Amiss 55, M. H. Denness 53, A. W. Greig 63) beat Central Province 107 by 166 runs.

13th Match: v Sri Lanka (Colombo)   Feb 16, 17, 18.
Sri Lanka 86 & 200 lost to M.C.C. 163 (A. W. Greig 61, D. S. de Silva 5-40) & 127-3 (D. L. Amiss 51*) by 7 wkts.

14th Match: v Governor's XI (Peshawar)   Feb 24, 25, 26.
No play: rain.

15th Match: v Pakistan (Lahore)   March 2, 3, 4, 6, 7.
England 355 (D. L. Amiss 112, K. W. R. Fletcher 55, M. H. Denness 50) & 306-7 dec (A. R. Lewis 74, M. H. Denness 68, A. W. Greig 72) drew with Pakistan 422 (Sadiq Mohammad 119, Asif Iqbal 102, Mushtaq Mohammad 66) & 124-3 (Talat Ali 57).

16th Match: v President's XI (Rawalpindi)   March 9, 10, 11, 12, 13.
President's XI 216-8 dec (Aftab Baluch 50) & 88 (N. Gifford 6-30) lost to M.C.C. 147 (Mohammad Nazir 5-49) & 158-6 (D. L. Amiss 62*) by 4 wkts.

17th Match: v Pakistan (Hyderabad)   March 16, 17, 18, 20, 21.
England 487 (D. L. Amiss 158, K. W. R. Fletcher 78, A. P. E. Knott 71) & 218-6 (A. W. Greig 64, A. P. E. Knott 63*) drew with Pakistan 569-9 dec (Mushtaq Mohammad 157, Intikhab Alam 138, Asif Iqbal 68, P. I. Pocock 5-169).

18th Match: v Pakistan (Karachi)   March 24, 25, 27, 28, 29.
Pakistan 445-6 dec (Majid Khan 99, Mushtaq Mohammad 99, Sadiq Mohammad 89, Intikhab Alam 61) & 199 (N. Gifford 5-55, J. Birkenshaw 5-57) drew with England 386 (D. L. Amiss 99, A. R. Lewis 88, K. W. R. Fletcher 54) & 30-1.

highest score for India, who batted much more solidly than the visitors and gained a useful first innings lead. England collapsed to the spinners in their second innings, but they made India struggle for the 86 required in the final innings and six wickets went down before India won.

The fourth Test saw higher scoring. India, now leading 2 to 1 in the series, were interested only in a draw and the two first innings were not completed until the final morning of the match.

The same pattern was evident in the fifth Test. Engineer and Viswanath made hundreds for India, as did Fletcher and Greig for England and the game slid to a draw.

The defeated England side went on to Sri Lanka for two matches before commencing the series against Pakistan. The one first-class match before the first Test was totally washed out. In the Test itself, England began with a century partnership from Amiss and Denness, but the batting fell away at the end with the last five wickets going for 25 runs. Asif Iqbal and Sadiq hit hundreds to give Pakistan a lead and though England had a few hiccups in their second innings, the match was drawn.

Pakistan had a chance of winning the second Test, but stout batting by Greig and Knott in the second innings after 5 wickets had gone down for 77, saved the visitors.

The M.C.C. party leaving for the tour to India, Pakistan and Sri Lanka in 1972-73. From left at front: K. W. R. Fletcher, A. P. E. Knott, D. B. Carr (manager), A. R. Lewis (captain), B. Wood, D. L. Amiss, D. L. Underwood, M. H. Denness, R. W. Tolchard. On the steps is B. W. Thomas and behind G. G. Arnold and J. Birkenshaw, P. I. Pocock and G. R. J. Roope, C. M. Old and R. M. H. Cottam, A. W. Greig and N. Gifford.

Batting Averages

	M	I	NO	R	HS	Avge	100	*c/s
K. W. R. Fletcher (Essex)	14	22	5	881	120*	51.82	3	15
A. W. Greig (Sussex)	13	21	3	826	148	45.88	1	16
D. L. Amiss (Warks)	12	23	4	861	158	45.31	2	5
R. W. Tolchard (Leics)	7	9	4	221	70	44.20	0	15
A. P. E. Knott (Kent)	13	20	3	666	156	39.17	1	23/2
M. H. Denness (Kent)	14	23	1	706	95	32.09	0	9
J. Birkenshaw (Leics)	10	15	2	393	64	30.23	0	8
A. R. Lewis (Glam)	12	18	2	483	125	30.18	1	1
G. R. J. Roope (Surrey)	12	20	2	532	130	29.55	2	16
C. M. Old (Yorks)	8	13	5	208	42	26.00	0	6
B. Wood (Lancs)	11	20	2	465	117	25.83	1	4
N. Gifford (Worcs)	7	6	3	71	24	23.66	0	4
G. G. Arnold (Surrey)	12	13	2	176	45	16.00	0	0
D. L. Underwood (Kent)	10	8	4	55	20*	13.75	0	4
R. M. H. Cottam (Northts)	9	5	1	25	13	6.25	0	0
P. I. Pocock (Surrey)	12	14	3	60	33	5.45	0	5

Bowling Averages

	O	M	R	W	Avge	BB	5i
B. Wood	20	5	49	3	16.33	2-10	0
R. M. H. Cottam	212	61	508	28	18.14	5-19	2
N. Gifford	290.4	106	568	24	23.67	6-30	2
A. W. Greig	329.1	89	759	29	26.17	5-24	1
G. G. Arnold	341.3	87	842	29	29.03	6-45	1
C. M. Old	206.2	47	555	17	32.64	4-43	0
P. I. Pocock	471.2	117	1234	37	33.35	5-169	1
D. L. Underwood	442.5	164	934	26	35.92	4-56	0
J. Birkenshaw	347.1	75	1032	25	41.28	5-57	1
K. W. R. Fletcher	29	4	125	2	62.50	1-12	0
G. R. J. Roope	48	15	110	1	110.00	1-10	0

Also bowled: D. L. Amiss 3-0-13-0; M. H. Denness 1-0-7-0; A. P. E. Knott 4-0-29-0.

Rioting and crowds invading the pitch were the feature of the third Test, which like its predecessors ended in a draw. The bowling of Gifford and Birkenshaw, whose spin dismissed Pakistan for 199 on the last day was outstanding.

The great successes of the tour were Greig and Fletcher. Greig really mastered the Indian spinners and his bowling and fielding combined to make him the best all-rounder in the English team. Lewis also came out of his ordeal well, both as batsman and captain. Old looked most promising, even on the slow wickets, and learnt a lot from Arnold. Amiss did well in Pakistan, but struggled in India. Knott was rather disappointing.

In India the great players were the spinners Chandrasekhar and Bedi, but Pakistan had five really notable men: Majid, Asif Iqbal, Sadiq, Mushtaq and Intikhab.

1973-74: D. H. Robins' second tour to South Africa

D. H. Robins took a second team to South Africa in the autumn of 1973. Mindful of the previous year's record, he recruited a stronger side: D. B. Close (Somerset) (capt), Younis Ahmed (Surrey), J. H. Edrich (Surrey), B. C. Francis (Essex), R. A. Woolmer (Kent), G. R. J. Roope (Surrey), M. J. Smith (Middx), J. T. Murray (Middx), J. N. Shepherd (Kent), J. K. Lever (Essex), G. W. Johnson (Kent), P. G. Lee (Lancs), J. W. Gleeson (Australia), J. A. Snow (Sussex), R. W. Tolchard (Leics) and R. E. East (Essex). L. E. G. Ames travelled as manager and J. Jennings as physiotherapist.

The team flew from London on 15 October and created history in the first match of the tour by playing against an African XI in Soweto. The three major games of the tour however were the 'Tests' against the South African Invitation XI. The 'First Test' took place at Cape Town and the tourists arrived there with a good record, having beaten two Provincial sides and drawn with two more. In the 'Test' the visitors gained a first innings lead and came close to winning, but the task of making 238 in 180 minutes proved a little too steep, especially when rain interrupted.

The 'Second Test' was a high-scoring draw. Edrich hit 170, but Richards for South Africa managed 180 — any hopes of a

1st Match: v African XI (Soweto) (One Day) Oct 20.
Robins XI 359 (G. R. J. Roope 110, J. H. Edrich 108) beat African XI 137 (J. W. Gleeson 7-33) by 222 runs.

2nd Match: v Orange Free State (Bloemfontein) (Limited Over) Oct 23.
Robins XI 243-9 (J. H. Edrich 79, J. N. Shepherd 54) beat O.F.S. 120-7 (R. East 52*) on faster scoring rate.

3rd Match: v Griqualand West (Kimberley) (Limited Over) Oct 24.
Robins XI 197-6 (G. W. Johnson 65, B. C. Francis 65) beat Griqualand West 112-7 by 85 runs.

4th Match: v Western Province (Cape Town) Oct 26, 27, 28.
W. Province 286-4 dec (H. M. Ackerman 179*, F. S. Goldstein 54) & 149-5 drew with Robins XI 375-4 dec (B. C. Francis 194, J. H. Edrich 118).

5th Match: v Border (East London) (Limited Over) Oct 31.
Robins XI 274-4 (D. B. Close 72, Younis Ahmed 61, M. J. Smith 56) beat Border 152 (J. W. Gleeson 5-32) by 122 runs.

6th Match: v Natal (Durban) Nov 2, 3, 5.
Robins XI 222-8 dec (G. W. Johnson 57) & 98-2 dec drew with Natal 134-7 dec & 32-0.

7th Match: v Northern Transvaal (Pretoria) (Limited Over) Nov 7.
N. Transvaal 202-8 (K. D. Verdoorn 80) lost to Robins XI 203-4 (B. C. Francis 106, M. J. Smith 54) by 6 wkts.

8th Match: v Transvaal (Johannesburg) Nov 9, 10, 12.
Transvaal 217-9 dec & 199 lost to Robins XI 303-6 dec (Younis Ahmed 123) & 116-2 by 8 wkts.

9th Match: v Eastern Province (Port Elizabeth) Nov 16, 17, 19.
E. Province 123 (A. M. Short 58) & 206 (C. P. Wilkins 51) lost to Robins XI 261 (R. A. Woolmer 83, Younis Ahmed 80) & 69-2 by 8 wkts.

10th Match: v African XI (New Brighton) Nov 22.
No play due to rain.

11th Match: v South African Invitation XI (Cape Town) Nov 23, 24, 26, 27.
Invitation XI 278 (H. M. Ackerman 76, E. J. Barlow 61) & 287-8 dec (B. A. Richards 81, H. M. Ackerman 56, E. J. Barlow 54, J. K. Lever 5-62) drew with Robins XI 329 (B. C. Francis 87, G. R. J. Roope 65) & 142-5.

12th Match: v South African Invitation XI (Durban) Nov 30, Dec 1, 3, 4.
Robins XI 383-9 dec (J. H. Edrich 170, J. T. Murray 59, D. B. Close 50) & 39-0 drew with Invitation XI 454 (B. A. Richards 180, A. J. S. Smith 81, V. A. P. van der Bijl 50*).

13th Match: v South African Invitation XI (Johannesburg) Dec 7, 8, 10, 11.
Robins XI 227-9 dec (G. R. J. Roope 53, J. N. Shepherd 53) & 218 lost to Invitation XI 528-8 dec (E. J. Barlow 211, B. L. Irvine 125, M. J. Procter 54, J. K. Lever 6-117) by an inns & 83 runs.

14th Match: v South African Invitation XI (Johannesburg) (Limited Over) Dec 12.
Robins XI 201-9 beat Invitation XI 198 (H. M. Ackerman 65) by 3 runs.

definite finish were removed by a four-hour stoppage for rain.

In the 'Third Test' South Africa dominated throughout and won by an innings. Gleeson was unfit, which was a serious blow to the tourists and Barlow, after being dropped, went on to make 211. Snow was not selected for this 'Test' for disciplinary reasons.

Younis Ahmed and Edrich headed the batting averages, whilst Gleeson topped the bowling table. The tour was regarded as a major breakthrough in sport, since both Younis of Pakistan and Shepherd of the West Indies were among the visiting team.

Batting Averages

	M	I	NO	R	HS	Avge	100	c/s
Younis Ahmed (Surrey)	6	10	3	351	123	50.14	1	3
J. H. Edrich (Surrey)	6	10	1	441	170	49.00	2	1
B. C. Francis (Essex)	6	11	2	411	194	45.66	1	2
R. A. Woolmer (Kent)	6	7	1	229	83	38.16	0	5
G. R. J. Roope (Surrey)	7	10	1	293	75	32.55	0	6
M. J. Smith (Middx)	3	5	0	149	44	29.80	0	1
J. T. Murray (Middx)	4	5	0	146	59	29.20	0	9
D. B. Close (Som)	7	11	3	200	50	25.00	0	8
J. N. Shepherd (Kent)	7	7	0	169	53	24.14	0	4
J. K. Lever (Essex)	6	4	3	20	9*	20.00	0	2
G. W. Johnson (Kent)	3	6	1	96	57	19.20	0	3
P. G. Lee (Lancs)	3	3	2	19	11	19.00	0	0
J. W. Gleeson (NSW)	4	2	0	10	7	5.00	0	3
J. A. Snow (Sussex)	5	3	0	6	6	2.00	0	0
R. W. Tolchard (Leics)	3	3	3	75	40*	—	0	6/1
R. E. East (Essex)	1	1	1	15	15*	—	0	0

Bowling Averages

	O	M	R	W	Avge	BB	5i
J. W. Gleeson	134	47	361	18	20.05	4-59	0
J. A. Snow	168.1	38	411	18	22.83	4-52	0
J. K. Lever	197.2	41	528	20	26.40	6-117	2
J. N. Shepherd	208	45	566	15	37.73	4-54	0
R. A. Woolmer	106	22	315	9	35.00	3-60	0
P. G. Lee	69.2	13	244	5	48.80	2-17	0
G. R. J. Roope	14	0	56	1	56.00	1-21	0
D. B. Close	47	9	184	2	92.00	1-0	0

Also bowled: G. W. Johnson 23-10-36-0; Younis Ahmed 8-1-33-0; R. E. East 9-2-13-0; M. J. Smith 3-1-7-0.

1973-74: M.C.C. tour of Kenya, Zambia and Tanzania

Under the managership of J. A. Bailey, the following team toured East Africa in January 1974: J. M. Brearley (Middx) (capt), J. A. Bailey (Essex) (vice-capt), D. L. Acfield (Essex), R. W. Barber (Warwicks), T. W. Cartwright (Somerset), L. J. Champniss (Bucks), E. A. Clark (Middx), N. J. Cosh (Surrey), A. L. Dixon (Kent), M. G. Griffith (Sussex), J. L. Hutton, R. D. V. Knight (Gloucs), D. R. Owen-Thomas (Surrey) and P. H. Parfitt (Middx).

The programme on the visit was too tightly arranged, which meant that the players could not give of their best, but the party went through without defeat.

The important match of the tour was against East Africa, when some good bowling by Cartwright proved too much for the local side. Knight was the best batsman in this match as indeed he was throughout the tour, except on two wet wickets. Barber suffered an injured hand, but batted well on occasion, as did Parfitt. Cartwright was easily the best bowler, his 35 wickets costing 11.20 each.

The best of the local players were almost without exception Asians, Jawahir Shah being the most notable figure.

It was to be hoped that the tour helped to boost cricket in the three countries visited.

1973-74: M.C.C. to East Africa

1st Match: v Zambia (Lusaka)   Dec 29, 30.
M.C.C. 118 (M. Pardor 5-45) & 166-7 dec (E. A. Clark 53*) drew with Zambia 153 & 62-8.

2nd Match: v Zambia (Kitwe)   Dec 31, Jan 1.
Zambia 158 & 95 lost to M.C.C. 136-6 dec (R. W. Barber 50) & 118-5 by 5 wkts.

3rd Match: v Tanzania (Dar-es-Salaam)   Jan 4, 6.
M.C.C. 275 (P. H. Parfitt 53) & 216-6 dec (J. M. Brearley 66) drew with Tanzania 306 (Pranlal 69, Tapu 64) & 103-2.

4th Match: v Moshi (Moshi) (Limited Over)   Jan 7.
M.C.C. 306-7 (M. G. Griffith 96, R. W. Barber 64, P. H. Parfitt 64) beat Moshi 123-6 by 183 runs.

5th Match: v Kenya Coast XI (Mombasa) (Limited over)   Jan 10.
M.C.C. 272-2 (R. D. V. Knight 137*, E. A. Clark 56*) beat Kenya 236-7 by 36 runs.

6th Match: v Kenya (Mombasa)   Jan 11, 12, 13.
Kenya 276 (Narendra 95, Jahawir 64) & 218-6 dec (Jagoo 72) drew with M.C.C. 221 (R. W. Barber 99, Mehmood 6-33) & 133-4.

7th Match: v Kenya & Uganda XI (Nairobi)   Jan 15, 16.
Combined XI 101 (D. L. Acfield 5-22) & 112 lost to M.C.C. 177-6 dec (E. A. Clark 63) & 37-1 by 9 wkts.

8th Match: v East Africa (Nairobi)   Jan 18, 19, 20.
M.C.C. 300 (P. H. Parfitt 83, R. D. V. Knight 78) & 208-7 dec (R. D. V. Knight 51*) beat East Africa 169 (Jagoo Shah 53, T. W. Cartwright 5-53) & 102 (T. W. Cartwright 5-30) by 237 runs.

1973-74: England draw Test series in West Indies

The saga of the English captaincy continued to be a subject of debate through 1973. The defeat of England by West Indies in England in the summer of 1973 signalled the end of Illingworth as England's leader. Lewis, who had led M.C.C. to India the previous winter, had retired due to injury and the succession therefore fell to Denness, the vice-captain in India. The full touring party was M. H. Denness (Kent) (capt), A. W. Greig (Sussex) (vice-capt), D. L. Amiss (Warwicks), G. G. Arnold (Surrey), J. Birkenshaw (Leics), G. Boycott (Yorks), K. W. R. Fletcher (Essex), F. C. Hayes (Lancs), M. Hendrick (Derbys), J. A. Jameson (Warwicks), A. P. E. Knott (Kent), C. M. Old (Yorks), P. I. Pocock (Surrey), R. W. Taylor (Derbys), D. L. Underwood (Kent), R. G. D. Willis (Warwicks) and the manager D. B. Carr. The outstanding omission was that of Snow, but he had had a great deal of injury in the last year or so and it was felt not worth risking him. In Old, Hendrick and Willis the team had three 24-year-old players who looked to be capable of taxing the opposition.

1973-74: M.C.C. to the West Indies

Batting Averages

	M	I	NO	R	HS	Avge	100	c/s
D. L. Amiss (Warks)	9	16	1	1120	262*	74.66	5	3
G. Boycott (Yorks)	10	16	3	960	261*	73.84	3	3
A. W. Greig (Sussex)	9	14	1	665	148	51.15	3	12
K. W. R. Fletcher (Essex)	10	16	3	564	129*	43.38	2	9
M. H. Denness (Kent)	10	17	2	504	67	33.60	0	5
J. Birkenshaw (Leics)	5	6	2	127	53*	31.75	0	2
F. C. Hayes (Lancs)	9	16	2	444	88	31.71	0	8
R. G. D. Willis (Warks)	6	6	5	30	10*	30.00	0	8
A. P. E. Knott (Kent)	10	17	1	474	87	29.62	0	14
J. A. Jameson (Warks)	7	13	0	325	91	25.00	0	6
R. W. Taylor (Derby)	3	3	0	69	65	23.00	0	5/1
M. Hendrick (Derby)	5	5	3	29	16	14.50	0	2
D. L. Underwood (Kent)	7	10	3	100	24	14.28	0	5
G. G. Arnold (Surrey)	8	10	2	101	25	12.62	0	2
C. M. Old (Yorks)	6	10	0	122	53	12.20	0	2
P. I. Pocock (Surrey)	7	11	0	77	23	7.00	0	3

Bowling Averages

	O	M	R	W	Avge	BB	5i
J. A. Jameson	35	10	74	4	18.50	2-25	0
K. W. R. Fletcher	20.5	4	63	3	21.00	2-25	0
A. W. Greig	277.1	57	766	30	25.53	8-86	3
M. Hendrick	108.2	21	320	12	26.66	4-38	0
J. Birkenshaw	165.5	35	467	16	29.18	6-101	1
R. G. D. Willis	140	27	526	15	35.06	4-91	0
P. I. Pocock	326.3	79	844	19	44.42	5-110	1
D. L. Underwood	263.5	88	573	12	47.75	2-48	0
G. G. Arnold	174.3	40	611	12	50.91	5-44	1
C. M. Old	135.4	28	459	9	51.00	3-56	0

Also bowled: G. Boycott 9-1-33-1; F. C. Hayes 0.2-0-4-0.

The M.C.C. party for the West Indies reporting at Lord's on the last day of 1973-74. From the front: M. H. Denness (captain), A. P. E. Knott, R. W. Taylor, K. W. R. Fletcher, J. Birkenshaw, D. L. Amiss, F. C. Hayes, D. L. Underwood, J. A. Jameson, G. G. Arnold, P. I. Pocock, C. M. Old, M. Hendrick, R. G. D. Willis, A. W. Greig.

The team flew from London on 11 January direct to Barbados and opened the tour with two minor matches in St Lucia, before taking on the President's XI. A great opening partnership of 252 by Boycott and Amiss, the former going on to 261 not out, gave the tourists a bright start. Arnold then took five wickets to dismiss the opposition for 164, but from then on matters did not go right and the game was drawn. On a very slow pitch, the match against Trinidad, which came next in the programme, was a very dull affair.

The first Test began at Port of Spain on 2 February and England had a terrible time for the first half as West Indies swept to a first innings lead of 261. Boycott and Amiss however began the second innings with a stand of 209 and the score rose to 315 for 1, but Gibbs then took a hand and the score tumbled to 392 all out. West Indies had no problem in knocking off the 132 required to win.

Amiss saved the second Test when all seemed lost. Again England had an enormous deficit on first innings – 230 – and going in again lost their 7th wicket at 271. Amiss however would not be moved and aided by the tail enders, notably Old, held out. The Warwickshire batsman made 262 not out.

M.C.C. however suffered a humiliating defeat at the hands of Barbados, just before the third Test, which was a repeat of the second, except that Fletcher and Knott were England's savours,

though it must be admitted that Gibbs the off-spinner could not bowl in the second England innings. No less than 99 no-balls were called in this match. On the third day a record crowd watched the game and so many clamoured for admittance that security broke down outside the ground. Happily the spectators behaved splendidly in the circumstances and play was hardly disrupted at all.

England got off to a good start in the fourth Test, making 448 in their first innings, with a century by Greig, but rain then washed out most of the remaining time. Sobers, although chosen, did not turn up for the match, and his place was given to Foster.

England had to win the final Test to save the series, but they failed to gain a lead on first innings, despite some magnificent bowling by Greig who reduced West Indies from 224 for 2 to 305 all out. Boycott then held England together in the second innings, as indeed he had done in the first, so that West Indies required 226 to win and over a day to make the runs. Greig actually opened the bowling with off-breaks and the West Indian batsmen seemed to lose their nerve as the game edged on with either team able to win – in the end it was England's by 26 runs.

England therefore, perhaps unjustly, drew the series one match each. Greig was the player of the series, but he was also responsible for the one major incident of the tour, when he fielded the final ball of the day in the first Test and ran out Kallicharran, who thought play was over and was walking to the pavilion. The authorities in fact over-ruled the umpire and allowed Kallicharran to continue on the next day, which resulted in vast press lectures on the authority of the umpires and the Laws.

Denness did not have a very good tour, seeming to be out of his depth, both as captain and batsman. Amiss played well and looked much better than in England. The fast bowlers were of no consequence and for what wickets they could get England relied on the spinners – at least in the Tests.

Rowe and Fredericks were the outstanding home batsmen, and the days of Sobers, Kanhai and Lloyd appeared over.

1973-74: Arabs' second tour to Barbados

In January 1974, the Arabs made a second major tour to Barbados. The team, which contained mainly first-class cricketers, was A. R. Lewis (Glamorgan) (capt), R. C. Kinkead-Weekes (Oxford U), S. G. Metcalfe (Oxford U), Earl of Cottenham, C. A. Fry (Northants), R. C. Daniels, M. J. J. Faber (Oxford U), R. J. Priestley, J. R. T. Barclay (Sussex), J. W. O. Allerton (Oxford U), T. J. Mottram (Hants), R. A. Hutton (Yorks), J. M. M. Hooper (Surrey), J. O. Trumper and I. A. Balding.

The tour began with an easy win over the Windward Islands, but were quickly brought down to earth by Clyde Walcott's XI in the second game. The highest innings was 121 by Daniels, made on a difficult wicket against the Wanderers in a match which was won in the penultimate over – Faber had the misfortune to break a finger whilst batting.

The only three-day game was against the President's XI. Lewis scored two innings of 80 and 85, but was unable to prevent defeat by 7 wickets. The best bowler on the tour was Mottram, and Lewis was the leading batsman. Daniels broke a finger, which got in the way of a quicker ball from Griffith in the sixth match.

1974-75: Lillee and Thomson destroy England in Australia

The team selected to go to Australia in 1974-75 was M. H. Denness (Kent) (capt), J. H. Edrich (Surrey) (vice-capt), D. L. Amiss (Warwicks), G. G. Arnold (Surrey), G. Boycott (Yorks), K. W. R. Fletcher (Essex), A. W. Greig (Sussex), M. Hendrick (Derbys), A. P. E. Knott (Kent), P. Lever (Lancs), D. Lloyd (Lancs), C. M. Old (Yorks), R. W. Taylor (Derbys), F. J. Titmus (Middx), D. L. Underwood (Kent) and R. G. D. Willis (Warwicks), with A. V. Bedser as manager, A. C. Smith as his assistant and B. W. Thomas as physiotherapist. For the first time for several years, the captaincy remained unchanged for two successive major tours. The critics attacked the inclusion of five faster bowlers and felt a batsman should have replaced Hendrick.

In fact the emergence of a great pair of Australian fast bowlers – Lillee and Thomson – governed the destiny of the Ashes, but of course in August 1974, the English selectors were not to know that, though it was forcefully pointed out that of the six selectors only two were really familiar with cricket in Australia. The team did not leave England however before controversy enveloped it. Boycott withdrew on the ground that he was not yet fit enough mentally to return to Test cricket. The England captain deposed in favour of Denness two years previously, Illingworth, then leapt into print with the headline BOYCOTT QUITS FRED KARNO'S ARMY. Illingworth attacked Denness's captaincy and the non-selection of Snow. Greig also criticised the selection

1974-75: M.C.C. to Australia and New Zealand

Batting Averages

	M	I	NO	R	HS	Avge	100	c/s
M. H. Denness (Kent)	15	25	4	1136	188	54.09	3	10
K. W. R. Fletcher (Essex)	16	22	3	919	216	48.36	2	18
D. L. Amiss (Warks)	15	23	2	983	164*	46.80	3	12
A. W. Greig (Sussex)	14	22	2	934	167*	46.70	2	19
A. P. E. Knott (Kent)	14	21	4	723	106*	42.52	1	44/2
J. H. Edrich (Surrey)	13	19	4	576	70	38.40	0	9
D. Lloyd (Lancs)	11	18	1	534	80	31.41	0	9
R. W. Taylor (Derby)	6	5	2	89	27*	29.66	0	11/1
B. W. Luckhurst (Kent)	10	17	1	415	116	25.93	1	13
M. C. Cowdrey (Kent)	7	12	1	284	78	25.81	0	4
C. M. Old (Yorks)	12	15	3	286	48	23.83	0	e8
D. L. Underwood (Kent)	14	14	3	209	33	19.00	0	2
F. J. Titmus (Middx)	9	13	1	174	61	14.50	0	4
M. Hendrick (Derby)	8	9	4	62	24*	12.40	0	7
R. G. D. Willis (Warks)	9	15	6	108	21	12.00	0	5
P. Lever (Lancs)	10	4	1	35	14	11.66	0	6
G. G. Arnold (Surrey)	12	12	2	34	14	4.25	0	3

Also played in two matches B. Wood (Lancs) 0, 33 (ct 3); in one match A. C. Smith (Warks) 15.

Bowling Averages

	O	M	R	W	Avge	BB	5i
D. L. Underwood	412.3	102	1214	48	25.29	7-113	2
C. M. Old	206.7	25	871	33	26.39	7-59	1
A. W. Greig	367.2	63	1421	50	28.42	5-51	3
M. Hendrick	160.3	26	582	19	30.63	5-68	1
R. G. D. Willis	223.7	29	811	26	31.19	5-61	1
P. Lever	228.4	21	923	27	34.18	6-38	1
F. J. Titmus	258.3	50	771	21	36.71	3-61	0
G. G. Arnold	331.3	51	1136	30	37.86	5-86	1

Also bowled: M. C. Cowdrey 4-0-27-2; K. W. R. Fletcher 6-0-45-0; D. Lloyd 6.6-2-25-2; B. W. Luckhurst 1-0-1-1; B. Wood 4-0-19-0.

in an interview. B. W. Luckhurst was chosen by the selectors to fill Boycott's place.

The tour opened with a one-day game at Port Lincoln, before the first first-class match against South Australia, when M.C.C. had the better of a draw and were handicapped by Old straining his knee. The tourists had all the best of a draw against Victoria, and might have won if Titmus had been allowed to bowl earlier. Some good off-spin bowling by Greig won the game against New South Wales and an all-round performance produced a victory in the next first-class match against Queensland. So to the first Test. Australia won the toss and batted, but on a moderate wicket had to thank Ian Chappell for a total of 309. Then the fast but erratic Thomson rattled all the England batsmen except Greig, who fought through to the only century of the match. England were 44 behind on first innings. Ian Chappell declared in the second innings to set the visitors 333 in 400 minutes, but it was really a

The M.C.C. party for Australia in 1974-75 at London airport. Back: K. W. R. Fletcher, B. W. Luckhurst, G. G. Arnold, D. L. Amiss, D. Lloyd, R. W. Taylor. Centre: F. J. Titmus, D. L. Underwood, C. M. Old, A. W. Greig, R. G. D. Willis, M. Hendrick, P. Lever. Front: B. W. Thomas (physiotherapist), A. V. Bedser (manager), M. H. Denness (captain), J. H. Edrich, A. P. E. Knott, A. C. Smith (assistant manager).

question of survival – and England failed. Thomson took 6 for 46. Amiss batted with a broken thumb, Edrich with a broken hand. The weakened batting collapsed against Western Australia when set 298 to win in 245 minutes. The selectors flew out Cowdrey as reinforcement.

The second Test was a disaster for England, who disintegrated when put into bat on the first day and lost the match by 9 wickets. Thomson again proved the destroyer, though England's injury list was frightening – Amiss and Edrich were joined by Lever and Hendrick.

The third Test proved a great contrast to the two previous defeats. The England batting was no better, but the bowling, despite the absence of Hendrick, who played but retired after 2½ overs, kept the Australian batting very much in check. It was a nail-biting draw, with Australia wanting 8 to win with 2 wickets in hand when time was called.

Between the third and fourth Tests, a One-day International was played, but proved of little interest, only 18,977 attending the game, which England won with ease.

The first headline of the fourth Test was that the England captain stood down, due to lack of form; Edrich took over. This did not, however, have the desired effect on the batting and as England's bowlers failed miserably, the match and the Ashes were lost. A Sydney record of 178,027 people attended the match.

M.C.C. went off to Tasmania to recuperate and came back to beat New South Wales, but this improvement did not last as far as the fifth Test. Denness, who returned to the side, put Australia in on a damp pitch and Underwood got England off to a great start, as the home side floundered to 84 for 5, but the tail wagged furiously and the total rose to 304. England were shot out by Lillee and Thomson for 172 and although Thomson was absent injured in the second innings only a determined Knott put up much resistance. Australia won by 163 runs.

Against all the odds England fought back in the sixth Test, in which nearly everything went right for the tourists. Lever bowled Australia out for 152, Denness and Fletcher hit centuries and despite Greg Chappell's hundred in the second innings, England did not need to bat twice. It should be stated that Thomson was unfit for the match.

In New Zealand England played two Tests, winning the first by an innings but having the second rained off. The tourists ended their programme with two pleasant matches in Hong Kong.

The series belonged to Lillee and Thomson, the latter a new-comer to English players, but the former known in England in 1972. It was the combination of the two that was lethal.

On the England side Greig and Knott were the batting successes – going in at 6 and 7! Of the bowlers Willis was the best but went rapidly downhill after the third Test, due to injury. Underwood also did well, having matured. The England fielding was far poorer than the Australian and though Denness's captaincy had improved on his West Indian performance, it still left something to be desired.

1st Match: v South Australia Country XI (Port Lincoln) (One Day)   Oct 30.
Country XI 7-1 drew with M.C.C. – rain.

2nd Match: v South Australia (Adelaide)   Nov 1, 2, 3, 4.
S. Australia 247 (J. Nash 67, M. Hendricks 57) & 320 (I. M. Chappell 78, G. J. Cosier 65, M. Hendrick 5-68) drew with M.C.C. 349-9 dec (J. H. Edrich 58, A. W. Greig 54, T. J. Jenner 5-110) & 82-3.

3rd Match: v Victoria Country XI (Warrnambool) (One Day)   Nov 6.
M.C.C. 158-4 dec (B. W. Luckhurst 94) drew with Country XI 83-5.

4th Match: v Victoria (Melbourne)   Nov 8, 9, 10, 11.
Victoria 293-8 dec (W. L. Stillman 61, R. J. Bight 53) & 174-8 drew with M.C.C. 392-9 dec (D. L. Amiss 152, B. W. Luckhurst 116).

5th Match: v Capital Territory Country XI (Canberra) (One Day)   Nov 13.
M.C.C. 159-2 dec (D. Lloyd 66, J. H. Edrich 51 ret) drew with Country XI 58-1.

6th Match: v New South Wales (Sydney)   Nov 15, 16, 17, 18.
N.S.W. 338 (I. C. Davis 91, A. Turner 72, G. J. Gilmour 59*, R. B. McCosker 52) & 174 (R. B. McCosker 56, Greig 5-55) lost to M.C.C. 332-7 dec (K. W. R. Fletcher 79, A. W. Greig 70) & 181-4 (D. Lloyd 80, K. W. R. Fletcher 57*) by 6 wkts.

7th Match: v Queensland Country XI (Nambour)   Nov 20.
No play due to rain.

8th Match: v Queensland (Brisbane)   Nov 22, 23, 24, 25.
M.C.C. 258 & 175 (G. Dymock 5-48) beat Queensland 226 (G. S. Chappell 122) & 161 (G. S. Chappell 51) by 46 runs.

9th Match: v South-East Queensland (Southport) (One Day)   Nov 26.
S-E Queensland 52 (A. W. Greig 5-1) lost to M.C.C. 53-0 by 10 wkts.

10th Match: v Australia (Brisbane)   Nov 29, 30, Dec 1, 3, 4.
Australia 309 (I. M. Chappell 90, G. S. Chappell 58) & 288-5 dec (G. S. Chappell 71, K. D. Walters 62*, R. Edwards 53) beat England 265 (A. W. Greig 110) & 166 (J. R. Thomson 6-46) by 166 runs.

11th Match: v Western Australia (Perth)   Dec 7, 8, 9, 10.
W. Australia 265-8 dec (W. J. Edwards 50) & 346-5 dec (R. J. Inverarity 99, G. D. Watson 86*, R. S. Langer 62*) beat M.C.C. 314-5 dec (A. W. Greig 167*, A. P. E. Knott 62) & 177 (A. W. Greig 57, R. G. Paulsen 7-41) by 120 runs.

12th Match: v Western Australia Country XI (Geraldton) (One Day)   Dec 11.
M.C.C. 214-6 dec (B. W. Luckhurst 76) drew with Country XI 153-9.*

13th Match: v Australia (Perth)   Dec 13, 14, 15, 17.
England 208 (A. P. E. Knott 51) & 293 (F. J. Titmus 61, J. R. Thomson 5-93) lost to Australia 481 (R. Edwards 115, K. D. Walters 103, G. S. Chappell 62) & 23-1 by 9 wkts.

14th Match: v South Australia (Adelaide)   Dec 21, 22, 23.
S. Australia 270-6 dec (G. J. Cosier 70, J. A. Woodcock 62, D. L. Underwood 5-58) & 222-6 dec (R. Drewer 61) drew with M.C.C. 277-2 dec (M. H. Denness 88*, M. C. Cowdrey 78, D. L. Amiss 73) & 210-6 (D. L. Amiss 57).

15th Match: v Australia (Melbourne)   Dec 26, 27, 28, 30, 31.
England 242 (A. P. E. Knott 52) & 244 (D. L. Amiss 90, A. W. Greig 60) drew with Australia 241 (I. R. Redpath 55, R. G. D. Willis 5-61) & 238-8 (G. S. Chappell 61).

16th Match: v Australia (Melbourne) (Limited Over)   Jan 1.
Australia 190 lost to England 191-7.

17th Match: v Australia (Sydney)   Jan 4, 5, 6, 8, 9.
Australia 405 (G. S. Chappell 84, R. B. McCosker 80, G. G. Arnold 5-86) & 289-4 dec (G. S. Chappell 144, I. R. Redpath 105) beat England 295 (A. P. E. Knott 82, J. H. Edrich 50) & 228 (A. W. Greig 54) by 171 runs.

18th Match: v Tasmania (Hobart)   Jan 11, 12, 13.
M.C.C. 204-4 dec (B. W. Luckhurst 59) drew with Tasmania 189-5 (J. S. Wilkinson 79, S. J. Howard 69).

19th Match: v Tasmania (Launceston)   Jan 14, 15, 16.
Tasmania 164 & 105 lost to M.C.C. 341-4 dec (M. H. Denness 157*, B. W. Luckhurst 74) by an inns & 72 runs.

20th Match: v New South Wales (Sydney)   Jan 18, 19, 20.
M.C.C. 315-5 dec (M. H. Denness 99, K. W. R. Fletcher 85, D. Lloyd 51, D. L. Amiss 52) & 266-7 dec (D. L. Amiss 124, A. P. E. Knott 79) beat N.S.W. 157 (Old 7-59) & 237 (D. J. Colley 90) by 187 runs.

21st Match: v Australia (Adelaide)   Jan 25, 26, 27, 29, 30.
Australia 304 (T. J. Jenner 74, K. D. Walters 55, D. L. Underwood 7-113) & 272-5 dec (K. D. Walters 71*, R. W. Marsh 55, I. R. Redpath 52) beat England 172 (M. H. Denness 51) & 241 (A. P. E. Knott 106*, K. W. R. Fletcher 63) by 163 runs.

22nd Match: v Northern New South Wales (Newcastle)   Feb 1, 2, 3.
Northern N.S.W. 251-5 dec (C. Baker 73, O. Bush 63) & 270-6 dec (G. R. Davies 82, R. Haworth 65*, O. Bush 50) lost to M.C.C. 221-5 dec (D. L. Amiss 74, J. H. Edrich 66*, B. W. Luckhurst 50) & 242-6 (M. C. Cowdrey 85, B. W. Luckhurst 58) by 4 wkts.*

23rd Match: v New Zealand (Melbourne) (Limited Over)   Feb 5.
New Zealand 262-8 beat M.C.C. 196 (A. W. Greig 79) by 66 runs.

24th Match: v Australia (Melbourne)   Feb 8, 9, 10, 12, 13.
Australia 152 (I. M. Chappell 65, P. Lever 6-38) & 373 (G. S. Chappell 102, I. R. Redpath 83, R. B. McCosker 76, I. M. Chappell 50) lost to England 529 (M. H. Denness 188, K. W. R. Fletcher 146, A. W. Greig 89, J. H. Edrich 70, M. H. N. Walker 8-143) by an inns & 4 runs.

25th Match: v Wellington (Wellington)   Feb 15, 16, 17.
M.C.C. 218 (A. P. E. Knott 56) & 52-1 drew with Wellington 188-6 dec (J. F. M. Morrison 80, G. A. Newdick 57).

26th Match: v New Zealand (Auckland)   Feb 20, 21, 22, 23, 25.
England 593-6 dec (K. W. R. Fletcher 216, M. H. Denness 181, J. H. Edrich 64, A. W. Greig 51) beat New Zealand 326 (J. M. Parker 121, J. F. M. Morrison 58, K. J. Wadsworth 58, A. W. Greig 5-98) & 184 (J. F. M. Morrison 58, G. P. Howarth 51*, A. W. Greig 5-51) by an inns & 83 runs.

27th Match: v New Zealand (Christchurch)   Feb 28, March 1, 2, 3, 4, 5.
New Zealand 342 (G. M. Turner 98, K. J. Wadsworth 58) drew with England 272-2 (D. L. Amiss 164*, M. H. Denness 59*).

28th Match: v New Zealand (Dunedin) Limited Over)   March 8.
M.C.C. 136 drew with New Zealand 15-0.

29th Match: v New Zealand (Wellington) (Limited Over)   March 9.
New Zealand 227 (B. E. Congdon 101) drew with M.C.C. 35-1.

30th Match: v Hong Kong President's XI (Hong Kong) (One Day)   March 12.
M.C.C. 239-3 dec (K. W. R. Fletcher 103) beat President's XI 155 by 84 runs.

31st Match: v Hong Kong (Hong Kong) (One Day)   March 13.
M.C.C. 234-3 dec (D. L. Amiss 101, B. Wood 68) beat Hong Kong 132 by 102 runs.

1974-75: English Counties XI tour of the West Indies

The following side visited Trinidad and Barbados in February 1975: J. H. Hampshire (Yorks) (capt), J. Birkenshaw (Leics), R. O. Butcher (Middx), R. E. East (Essex), F. C. Hayes (Lancs), D. P. Hughes (Lancs), P. G. Lee (Lancs), J. K. Lever (Essex),

A. G. Nicholson (Yorks), D. W. Randall (Notts), G. Sharp (Northants), B. Wood (Lancs) and R. C. S. Titchener-Barratt (player-manager), with T. W. Spencer (umpire) and E. Solomon (scorer). Unfortunately Hughes had to return home due to a family bereavement and Wood was summoned to New Zealand to assist the M.C.C. team, so the team was unexpectedly depleted, S. A. Gomes was co-opted as a replacement.

The side drew all their important matches, but won all three one-day games. The batting and fielding was good, but the attack was not strong enough to overcome the opposition. The matches were poorly attended and there was little interest in the visit.

1st Match: v Trinidad Under 23 (Queen's Park)   Feb 5, 6.
English XI 181-9 dec (J. H. Hampshire 52) & 173-4 dec (B. Wood 54) drew with Trinidad 133 & 72-4.*

2nd Match: v Trinidad (Queen's Park)   Feb 8, 9, 10.
Trinidad 274-5 dec (L. Gomes 103, S. A. Gomes 56) & 161 drew with English XI 240 (B. Wood 77) & 74-3.*

3rd Match: v Barbados (Bridgetown)   Feb 14, 15, 16.
English XI 222 (D. W. Randall 60) & 149-6 dec drew with Barbados 140-5 dec & 76-2.

4th Match: v Barbados   Feb 18, 19, 20.
Barbados 131 (W. Ashby 52, R. E. East 5-25) & 174 (R. C. S. Titchener-Barratt 5-25) drew with English XI 216-8 dec (S. A. Gomes 104) & 15-1.*

5th Match: v British High Commission XI (Bridgetown) (Limited Over)   Feb 21.
English XI 251-3 (J. H. Hampshire 134, D. W. Randall 92) beat High Commission XI 174-8 (C. L. King 53) by 77 runs.

6th Match: v Texaco (Brighton St Michael) (Limited Over)
English XI 175-6 (J. H. Hampshire 50) beat Texaco 92 by 83 runs.*

7th Match: v St Catherines (East Pt, St Phillip) (Limited Over)
English XI 164-9 beat St Catherines 160-9 by 4 runs.

1974-75: D. H. Robins' third tour to South Africa

The combination taken out by D. H. Robins in 1974-75 was not as powerful as the 1973-74 team and failed to win any of the first-class matches, but was more successful in the one-day games.

The team was D. B. Close (Somerset) (capt), B. C. Francis (Essex), J. F. Steele (Leics), F. C. Hayes (Lancs), J. H. Hampshire (Yorks), R. W. Tolchard (Leics), J. N. Shepherd (Kent), S. Turner (Essex), E. E. Hemmings (Warwicks), S. J. Rouse (Warwicks), G. A. Greenidge (Sussex), C. T. Radley (Middx), Younis Ahmed (Surrey), J. Lyon (Lancs), T. J. Jenner (Australia), M. H. N. Walker (Australia), F. M. Francke (Sri Lanka) and

A. W. Greig (Sussex) – Greig joined the team after being with the M.C.C. in Australia.

The most important match was against the President's XI at Cape Town, when two excellent innings by Barlow and R. G. Pollock combined with the bowling of Van der Bijl to defeat the tourists by 260 runs. R. G. Pollock was also in fine form for Eastern Province, scoring centuries in both innings. As on the previous visit the tourists played one-day matches against African sides.

1974-75: D. H. Robins' tour to the West Indies

The following team made a short tour of the West Indies in 1974-75: J. A. Jameson (Warwicks) (capt), D. L. Bairstow (Yorks), R. M. H. Cottam (Northants), B. Dudleston (Leics), P. H. Edmonds (Middx), M. J. Harris (Notts), G. W. Johnson (Kent), Mushtaq Mohammad (Northants), P. I. Pocock (Surrey),

S. J. Rouse (Warwicks), P. J. Sainsbury (Hants), J. N. Shepherd (Kent), M. J. Smith (Middx), R. W. Tolchard (Leics) and S. Turner (Essex), with L. E. G. Ames as manager, D. Bennett as assistant manager and J. A. Jennings as physiotherapist.

Three weeks before the team left England the governments of Guyana and Trinidad & Tobago announced that the side would not be permitted to tour those countries due to Mr Robins connections with South Africa; it was also incorrectly reported that Mushtaq had been barred from joining the tour by the Pakistan Cricket Board for the same reasons. Mr Robins wrote to the two governments explaining his views, but neither would reverse its decision and the team, which flew out on 16 October, confined its matches to the Leeward Islands and Barbados.

The major match of the tour – a three-day game against Barbados was not started because of rain and two limited overs games were played there. Rain also marred several other fixtures. Mushtaq and G. W. Johnson played well on the tour.

1975-76: D. H. Robins' fourth tour to South Africa

In taking his fourth team to South Africa in successive years, D. H. Robins originally intended to include only players under the age of 25, but it was not possible to produce a strong enough side with this limitation and some more experienced players were added to the party. The full team was D. Lloyd (Lancs) (capt), G. A. Cope (Yorks), P. Carrick (Yorks), P. G. Lee (Lancs), D. W. Randall (Notts), P. A. Slocombe (Somerset), D. S. Steele (Northants), F. C. Hayes (Lancs), M. Hendrick (Derby), R. W. Tolchard (Leics), G. P. Howarth (Surrey), T. M. Chappell (Australia), J. R. Douglas (Australia), D. F. Whatmore (Australia) and G. B. Troup (New Zealand). F. J. Titmus joined the team later, when both Hendrick and Cope dropped out with injuries.

The war in Angola overshadowed the tour, as did the internal cricketing events in South Africa, when the three bodies governing white, black and coloured cricket in the country merged into one – unfortunately a selected 'mixed' team which was to have played the tourists never materialised due to squabbles.

The visitors played four first-class matches, winning two and losing two, though the game against Natal was desperately close and the tourists, set 164 to win on a spinners' wicket, failed by only 3 runs. Steele batted well, averaging 60 in all matches.

The team was managed by K. F. Barrington, whose guidance proved invaluable to the younger members.

1975-76: the first M.C.C. tour to West Africa

At the invitation of the West Africa Cricket Conference and with financial assistance from various businesses in the area, the M.C.C. sent for the first time a team to West Africa in the winter

of 1975-76. The side was: E. A. Clark (Middx) (capt), R. W. Barber (Warwicks) (vice-capt), J. G. Lofting (player-manager), J. R. T. Barclay (Sussex), L. J. Champniss (Bucks), T. M. Cordaroy (Middx), G. F. Goddard (Scotland), A. J. Good (Lancs), J. M. M. Hooper (Surrey), R. Julian (Leics), R. D. V. Knight (Gloucs), M. D. Mence (Berks), D. Nicholls (Kent) and D. C. Wing. M. C. Cowdrey agreed to join the tour halfway through, as Knight had to return to England.

The tour began in Gambia, where both matches were won. The tourists flew on to Sierra Leone where the first three-day game was played against West Africa. It was a fairly even match until the home side, requiring 241 to win in the final innings, collapsed to the fast bowling of Good. There were two matches in Ghana before the 'Second Test' against West Africa was played in Nigeria. Wing completely demolished the West Africans in their first innings and the tourists won with ease.

1976: tourists find standard in Canada dropping

The tour which D. H. Robins made to Canada in September and October 1976 played 15 one-day matches. The tourists found that the standard of cricket in the country had fallen compared with that of 1967 when the last major English side visited Canada.

The team was P. H. Parfitt (Middx) (capt), P. J. Sainsbury (Hants) (vice-capt), C. W. J. Athey (Yorks), J. R. T. Barclay (Sussex), P. R. Downton (Kent), M. W. Gatting (Middx), I. J. Gould (Middx), D. I. Gower (Leics), D. R. Gurr (Somerset), G. W. Humpage (Warwicks), V. J. Marks (Somerset), A. S. Patel (Middx), S. P. Perryman (Warwicks), R. L. Savage (Warwicks) and C. J. Tavare (Kent), with D. Bennett as manager.

The visit was marred by demonstrations against the team, organised under the impression that the side was from South Africa—in fact few if any of the tourists had been with D. H. Robins on tours there, so the demonstrators were confused.

The best match was against Edmonton, where the tourists just managed to win by 10 runs, but generally they were too strong.

1976-77: successful tour of India and the Centenary Test

The leading English cricketers had a rest in the winter of 1975-76 and after the mauling by Thomson and Lillee in the 1974-75 series under Denness, which was followed by an innings defeat at the hands of Australia in England in the First Test of 1975, the captaincy was given to A. W. Greig—not that this improved the English record, for they went down 3 matches to nil in the 1976 home series against the West Indies. The selectors however kept their faith in Greig and the full party to go to India in 1976-77 was A. W. Greig (Sussex) (capt), J. M. Brearley (Middx) (vice-capt),

Below The M.C.C. party for the tour of India and Sri Lanka in 1976-77, which culminated in the Centenary Test in Melbourne on the way home. Back: R. W. Tolchard, G. D. Barlow, R. A. Woolmer, G. Mill, C. M. Old, R. G. D. Willis, M. W. W. Selvey, J. K. Lever, D. L. Amiss, G. A. Cope, D. W. Randall. Front: B. W. Thomas (physiotherapist), K. W. R. Fletcher, A. P. E. Knott, A. W. Greig (captain), J. M. Brearley, D. L. Underwood, K. F. Barrington (manager).

Bottom left John Lever bowling in the second Test in Calcutta. Lever figured in the dispute about his use of Vaseline, allegedly to keep the shine on the ball.

Bottom right Tony Greig is chaired by his team after the third Test in Madras which ensured an England win in the series. He and Brearley have their stumps.

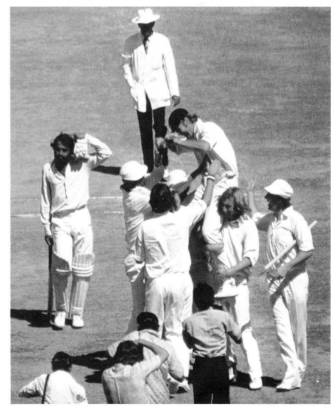

Above *The two teams for the Centenary Test, Melbourne, 1977. Back: D. L. Amiss, D. W. Hookes, R. A. Woolmer, G. J. Gilmour, J. K. Lever, R. G. D. Willis, G. J. Cosier, C. M. Old, R. D. Robinson, D. G. Barlow, R. J. Bright, I. C. Davis, D. W. Randall. Front: K. W. R. Fletcher, M. H. N. Walker, A. P. E. Knott, R. W. Marsh, A. W. Greig, G. S. Chappell, J. M. Brearley, K. D. Walters, D. L. Underwood, D. K. Lillee.*

Left *Action from the Centenary Test, Melbourne, 1977. Brearley about to be caught by Hookes in the gully off Lillee.*

Below *The hero of the Centenary Test, Derek Randall, hooking for four. He scored a brilliant 174.*

D. L. Amiss (Warwicks), G. D. Barlow (Middx), G. A. Cope (Yorks), K. W. R. Fletcher (Essex), A. P. E. Knott (Kent), J. K. Lever (Essex), G. Miller (Derbys), C. M. Old (Yorks), D. W. Randall (Notts), M. W. W. Selvey (Middx), R. W. Tolchard (Leics), D. L. Underwood (Kent), R. G. D. Willis (Warwicks) and R. A. Woolmer (Kent) with K. F. Barrington as manager. Those who were not included were Boycott, who still shunned Test cricket, Snow, whose fitness had caused him to miss two of the five Tests in 1976, Steele, who was most unlucky not to get a place and Willey, Hendrick and Gooch, who also just missed selection.

The tour was basically to India, but in order to celebrate the centenary of the first Test in 1877, the team were to go to Australia at the end of the programme and play a 'Centenary Test'.

Flying to India, the tourists began their fixtures with a drawn match against West Zone, in which Brearley, Fletcher and Greig all made hundreds. In the draw against Central Zone Barlow and Knott hit centuries, and the high scoring continued through all the early matches; the bowlers did not quite do enough to remove the opposition, but all the games ended with M.C.C. on top.

In the first Test, England began painfully, losing 4 for 65, but Amiss, Knott and Lever came to the rescue to build a reasonable total. Lever then celebrated his Test debut by bowling India out and the home team followed on 259 in arrears. Underwood did the rest and England unexpectedly won by an innings. The second Test was played on a difficult wicket, with the bowlers in charge. Hard fought innings by Tolchard and Greig, who batted with a high temperature, put England over 150 ahead on the first

innings and India could do little in their second attempt, so that the tourists went two up in the series.

India's batting failed again in the third Test and England won a low scoring game by 200 runs. This match was the scene of the 'Vaseline' incident. Lever used strips of gauze coated with vaseline to prevent sweat running into his eyes, but the umpires maintained that the vaseline was used to keep the shine on the ball.

India batted better in the fourth Test and as Chandrasekhar exploited the wearing pitch to its full in England's first innings and Bedi continued the treatment in the second England innings, the home side won by 140 runs.

set 463 to win. It seemed an impossible task, but an inspired performance by Randall, who hit 174, took England to within 45 runs of Australia and thus gave the supporters of both teams something about which to enthuse.

The tour of India was a great success for Greig, not only as a batsman but as a captain, and for once the English visitors managed to conquer the irritating ailments which usually sink most of the team. The English bowling of Underwood, who was at last really effective away from home, Willis, in short spells, and Lever, caused the Indian batsmen to struggle nearly all the time. The English batting was however unreliable and Knott was often required to make up for the deficiencies higher up. The fielding was very good, except in the last Test. The Indian spinners were not as destructive as expected, but perhaps this was due to the fact that India played three Tests against New Zealand immediately before the England series.

The moves to set up the World Series 'Super Tests' were being made in the spring of 1977, but it was not until May that the general public in England realised the extent of the plans.

1976-77: M.C.C. tour of Bangladesh

At the invitation of the Bangladesh Cricket Control Board, M.C.C. sent out a team for a brief tour in the winter of 1976-77. The side, which arrived by air on 29 December, was E. A. Clark (Middx) (capt), J. R. T. Barclay (Sussex), A. R. Duff (Worcs), J. M. M. Hooper (Surrey), M. D. Mence (Berks), M. E. J. C. Norman (Leics), J. D. Piachaud (Oxford), N. F. M. Popplewell (Hants), B. Taylor (Essex), D. R. Owen-Thomas (Surrey), M. J. Vernon (Gloucs), R. C. Kinkead-Weekes (Middx), D. C. Wing (Cambs) and J. G. Lofting as player-manager.

There were three two-day matches, two of which were drawn and one three-day 'Test' against Bangladesh. The home team won the toss and batted very slowly to reach 266 for 9 declared. M.C.C. attacked from the start of their innings, with Barclay making a splendid 65, but the only hope of a definite result was for M.C.C. to dismiss Bangladesh cheaply in their second innings. This they failed to do and the game was drawn. The attendance for the three days was about 90,000.

The fifth Test was very even. India ought to have scored more since the tourists dropped a number of catches, but these second lives were not used to the full. England began their last innings 214 in 245 minutes, but could only reach 152 for 7.

Having finished the tour of India, the team flew to Sri Lanka where four matches were played and then on to Australia for the Centenary Test. They had one game in Perth against Western Australia, in which the home side had the best of a draw, but because of travel difficulties, the M.C.C. arrived only the day before the match.

The Centenary Test, which was played in Melbourne before a gathering of most of the old England-Australia Test cricketers and in the presence of the Queen, commenced on 12 March. The first two innings went entirely the way of the bowlers, with Australia dismissed for 138 and England for only 95. Australia fell to 187 for 5 in their second innings, but Marsh hit a hundred and with fifties from Davis, Hookes and Walters, England were

1977-78: D. H. Robins' tour of the Far East

Rain affected many of the matches on this tour to Malaysia, Singapore, Hong Kong and Sri Lanka. The team was M. H. Denness (Essex) (capt), M. J. Smith (Middx), P. Carrick (Yorks), C. S. Cowdrey (Kent), J. E. Emburey (Middx), D. I. Gower (Leics), D. R. Gurr (Somerset), G. P. Howarth (Surrey), Intikhab Alam (Surrey), K. B. S. Jarvis (Kent), J. K. Lever (Essex), H. Pilling (Lancs), R. W. Tolchard (Leics), P. Willey (Northants) and J. G. Wright (Derbys), with J. Lister as manager.

The team flew to Singapore and had two days in which to get acclimatised before going to Seremban for the first match. The tourists were well in control when at lunch on the second day rain flooded the ground and ended the game. The tourists were too good for most of the opposition and it was a pity that both the matches that might have extended them – in Sri Lanka – were drawn because of rain. Spin bowling reigned supreme throughout the tour, with Intikhab, Emburey and Willey prospering.

Gower batted in tremendous form in Hong Kong and in his innings of 114 v Combined Services hit no fewer than 10 fours and 5 sixes. The matches in Sri Lanka were watched by large crowds – in the first match there the gates were closed with 15,000 present, and it was a pity that such enthusiasm was not rewarded by better weather in the three-day matches.

1977-78: England tour of Pakistan and New Zealand

The Kerry Packer saga ran unabated through the English summer of 1977 and England, led by Brearley, had little difficulty in crushing an Australian side preoccupied by other matters. Boycott announced that he was now available for Test Matches and the England selectors put him back in the team. The England team (the T.C.C.B. had suggested that Test Match tours should be sent out under the title 'England', rather than 'M.C.C.') for the tour of Pakistan and New Zealand was selected as follows: J. M. Brearley (Middx) (capt), G. Boycott (Yorks) (vice-capt), I. T. Botham (Somerset), G. A. Cope (Yorks), P. R. Downton

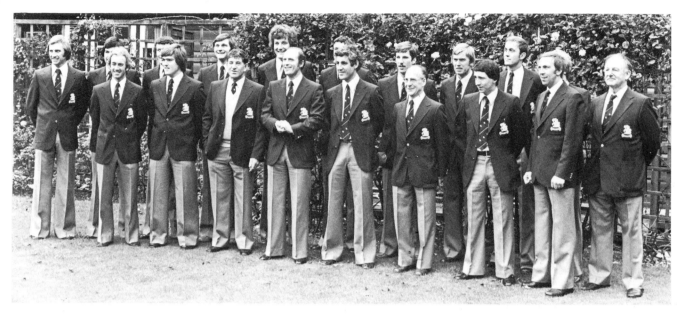

The England party for Pakistan in 1977-78. From left : J. K. Lever, G. Miller (partly obscured), R. W. Taylor, G. R. J. Roope (half-hidden), M. W. Gatting, C. M. Old, K. F. Barrington (manager), R. G. D. Willis, G. Boycott, M. Hendrick (almost hidden), J. M. Brearley, I. T. Botham, B. W. Thomas (physiotherapist), B. C. Rose, D. W. Randall, P. H. Edmonds, G. A. Cope, P. R. Downton (completely hidden), G. Saulez (scorer).

(Kent), P. H. Edmonds (Middx), M. W. Gatting (Middx), M. Hendrick (Derbys), J. K. Lever (Essex), G. Miller (Derbys), C. M. Old (Yorks), D. W. Randall (Notts), G. R. J. Roope (Surrey), B. C. Rose (Somerset), R. W. Taylor (Derbys) and R. G. D. Willis (Warwicks), with K. F. Barrington as Manager and B. W. Thomas as physiotherapist.

The players who had signed contracts for the Kerry Packer organisation, A. W. Greig, A. P. E. Knott, R. A. Woolmer, J. A. Snow, D. L. Underwood and D. L. Amiss, were not considered, which in effect meant that the English First Eleven lost four or five of its members.

It is worth nothing that each member of the England touring

party was paid £5,000, plus £100 for each previous M.C.C. tour. The payment for the 1976-77 tour had been £3,000.

The team flew from England on 24 November and the initial first-class match was begun on 30 November. After two draws, victory was achieved at Peshawar, immediately prior to the first Test. Like England, Pakistan were badly affected by players signing for the Packer organisation – Asif, Mushtaq, Imran, Majid and Zaheer were all playing in Australia – and the home team were fortunate that two young players, Mudassar and Haroon, hit hundreds for them. Pakistan had the better of a drawn game, but politically motivated riots on the second and third days marred the match. England won two one-day Internationals, before the second Test at Hyderabad. Pakistan again had much the better of a draw, and might have won, but Wasim Bari did not risk declaring until it was too late to dangle a carrot in front of the visiting batsmen.

Pakistan managed to win the last one-day International. In a minor game directly after it Brearley broke his arm and thus Boycott led England into the third Test. C. T. Radley (Middx) joined the team to replace Brearley. Kerry Packer released Mushtaq, Zaheer and Imran prior to the game and they arrived ready to represent Pakistan, but if they had been selected for the Pakistan side, England would have refused to play and thus ended the series. So Pakistan did without the three and a very dull plodding match was painfully enacted. The umpires pulled up stumps an hour before the end to save any further misery. That was therefore the end of the three-match series against Pakistan – three draws, and the England team flew off to New Zealand for a Test Match series of three.

The tour opened in Auckland too soon after the England arrival and the tourists had the worse of a draw. There was an exciting tie against Central Districts. With the scores level the last home batsman attempted a wild swipe at Willis and was bowled.

The first Test took place at Wellington and New Zealand created history by beating England for the first time – after 47 previous matches. The end of the first two innings left New Zealand with a 13-run advantage, but Willis then dismissed the home team for 123, leaving England requiring only 137 to win. The tourists capitulated before Richard Hadlee, who took 6 for 26, and New Zealand won by 72 runs.

The defeat was avenged in the second Test. Botham hit his maiden Test hundred and then returned the best bowling figures of the New Zealand first innings with 5 for 73 as England gained a handsome lead of 183. England went on to win by 174 runs.

The third Test was a high-scoring draw on an excellent wicket. In general the batting was too slow, neither side being too keen on losing the series, which was as a result drawn one match each.

1977-78: England to Pakistan and New Zealand

Batting Averages

	M	I	NO	R	HS	Avge	100	c/s
G. Boycott (Yorks)	13	20	3	867	123*	51.00	3	4
I. T. Botham (Som)	9	12	4	397	126*	49.62	2	7
G. R. J. Roope (Surrey)	14	19	4	725	102*	48.33	1	19
J. M. Brearley (Middx)	6	9	3	252	74	42.00	0	6
G. Miller (Derby)	13	17	3	468	98*	33.42	0	11
B. C. Rose (Som)	12	19	3	508	110*	31.75	2	8
C. T. Radley (Middx)	7	11	0	312	158	28.36	1	4
D. W. Randall (Notts)	14	21	0	589	104	28.04	1	7
R. W. Taylor (Derby)	11	13	2	236	45	21.45	0	20/1
M. W. Gatting (Middx)	8	12	2	177	66	17.70	0	7
C. M. Old (Yorks)	10	12	1	191	55	17.36	0	6
G. A. Cope (Yorks)	6	5	1	60	22	15.00	0	1
J. K. Lever (Essex)	8	8	2	65	33*	10.83	0	4
R. G. D. Willis (Warks)	11	11	6	50	14	10.00	0	3
P. H. Edmonds (Middx)	12	11	0	104	50	9.45	0	23
M. Hendrick (Derby)	7	6	2	33	15*	8.25	0	1
P. R. Downton (Kent)	4	2	0	9	9	4.50	0	11

Bowling Averages

	O	M	R	W	Avge	BB	5i
R. G. D. Willis	241.6	58	658	39	16.87	5-32	1
C. M. Old	176.3	56	488	28	17.42	6-54	1
I. T. Botham	210.4	41	691	35	19.74	7-58	3
J. K. Lever	192.3	40	576	29	19.86	5-59	1
G. Miller	249.2	51	880	38	23.15	6-62	2
P. H. Edmonds	337	85	834	33	25.27	7-66	1
M. Hendrick	128.5	28	288	10	28.80	2-20	0
G. A. Cope	161	40	455	14	32.50	3-102	0
M. W. Gatting	20.7	3	71	2	35.50	1-0	0

Also bowled: G. Boycott 4-0-5-0; D. W. Randall 2-0-3-0; G. R. J. Roope 3-0-19-0.

The twin tour could not be regarded as a success for England. The batting was too brittle. The one real bonus of the visit was the form of Botham, who made a great impact as both batsman and bowler. Roope and Randall were great fieldsmen, but hardly worth their places as batsmen. Rose was another failure and lost his Test place. Willis was the best bowler, though Old also could point to some good performances.

1977-78: the Minor Counties tour to Kenya

A representative team of the Minor Counties made their first overseas tour to Kenya, flying from London on 9 January 1978 to Nairobi. The team was D. Bailey (Ches) (capt), M. J. Ikin (Staffs), M. D. Nurton (Oxfords), N. A. Riddell (Durham), B. G. Collins (Herts), K. V. Jones (Beds), G. Wallen (Devon), P. H. Jones (Suffolk), M. Beaty (Cumberland), P. J. Kippax (Northumberland), P. N. Gill (Staffs), J. S. Wilkinson (Durham), D. I. Yeabsley (Devon) and R. Entwistle (Cumberland), with C. G. Howard as manager.

The first match was lost, but the side quickly learnt from this, and adapting well to the matting wickets won the other five matches. Unfortunately the three-day game with East African C.C. was washed out without a ball being bowled.

The tour was entirely successful and most enjoyable, the standard of cricket being very fair, but almost wholly confined to the Asian community.

1977-78: Minor Counties Team to Kenya

1st Match: v Kenya C.A. Chairman's XI (Nairobi)   Jan 11.
Minor Counties 241-6 dec (R. Entwistle 66) lost to Kenya C.A. 242-5 (Rehman 139, Jawahir 52) by 5 wkts.*

2nd Match: v Kenya C.A. (Nairobi)   Jan 13, 14, 15.
Minor Counties 344-7 dec (M. D. Nurton 83, P. J. Kippax 89, D. Bailey 59) & 153-3 dec (R. Entwistle 64) beat Kenya C.A. 178 (Jawahir 75, B. G. Collins 5-52) & 226 (Charantive 67, Nasoor 59) by 93 runs.

3rd Match: v Rift Valley (Nakuru)   Jan 17.
Minor Counties 221-7 dec (M. J. Ikin 94, K. V. Jones 66) beat Rift Valley 118 (Shah 67) by 103 runs.

4th Match: v East African C.C. (Impala Gymkhana)   Jan 19.
East African C.C. 121-7 lost to Minor Counties 125-2 (D. Bailey 58) by 8 wkts.*

5th Match: v East Africa C.C.   Jan 20, 21, 22.
No play: Rain.

6th Match: v Mombasa Sports (Mombasa)   Jan 28.
Minor Counties 311-9 (R. Entwistle 62, M. J. Ikin 67, P. N. Gill 67, N. A. Riddell 53) beat Mombasa Sports 141-9 by 170 runs.

7th Match: v Kenya Kongonis (Nairobi)   Jan 29.
Minor Counties 247-7 (P. J. Kippax 76, R. Entwistle 54) beat Kenya Kongonis 97 (M. J. Ikin 5-27) by 150 runs.

1978-79: second M.C.C. tour of Bangladesh

The M.C.C. made their second tour to Bangladesh in December 1978 and January 1979. The team was: E. A. Clark (Middx) (capt), B. L. Reed (Hants), A. R. Duff (Worcs), S. Dyson (M.C.C.), C. A. Fry (Hants), C. B. Hamblin (Oxford U), C. C. Hunte (West Indies), J. A. Jameson (Warwicks), P. J. Levington (Berks), W. G. Merry (Herts), H. K. More (Scotland), N. J. W. Stewart (Berks), K. Taylor (Yorks) and C. L. Toole. B. L. Reed acted as manager.

The three 'Tests' against Bangladesh were all drawn, two of them in favour of the tourists. The visitors received an enthusiastic welcome everywhere and it was estimated that 200,000 people watched 13 days of cricket.

1978-79: M.C.C. to Bangladesh

1st Match: v C.C.B. President's XI (Jessore)   Dec 29, 30.
President's XI 210-8 dec (Shafiqul 51) & 52-3 dec drew with M.C.C. 166 & 5-2.

2nd Match: v Bangladesh (Mymensingh)   Jan 1.
Bangladesh 104-9 lost to M.C.C. 106-0 (J. A. Jameson 61) by 10 wkts.*

3rd Match: v Bangladesh (Rajshahi) (Limited Over)   Jan 3, 4, 5.
M.C.C. 247 (J. A. Jameson 59, Nazrul 5-70) & 114-1 dec (C. C. Hunte 55) drew with Bangladesh 173 & 104-2.*

4th Match: v Bangladesh (Chittagong)   Jan 7, 8, 9.
M.C.C. 303-8 dec (C. C. Hunte 89, H. K. More 60) & 105-3 dec (C. C. Hunte 53) drew with Bangladesh 192 (Shafiqul 73, W. G. Merry 5-45) & 97-7.

5th Match: v Bangladesh (Dacca) (Limited Over)   Jan 10.
M.C.C 155-7 beat Bangladesh 84 (C. L. Toole 5-6) by 71 runs.

6th Match: v Bangladesh (Dacca)   Jan 11, 12, 13.
M.C.C. 210 (E. A. Clark 71) & 172-4 dec (C. C. Hunte 60) drew with Bangladesh 152 (N. J. W. Stewart 5-44) & 147-8.

1978-79: England easily beat Australia in 'Packer' tour

The 1978-79 series against Australia was played in competition with the World Series Cricket matches organised by Kerry Packer's companies. The English team therefore lacked Underwood, Knott, Amiss and Greig, but for the Australians matters were much more serious – of the seventeen who toured England in the summer of 1977, only two played in the 1978-79 series against England. The press, which was in the main anti-Packer, maintained that the 1977 Australians were second rate and most would have been discarded anyway. This theory, however, was totally demolished a year later when the opposing factions sank their differences and all the major pro-Packer Australians resumed their places in the official Test team.

Returning however to the summer of 1978, when the English selectors were picking the side to go to Australia, the problem initially was yet again the captaincy. Brearley had proved himself the ideal captain, but his performance as a batsman was not up to Test standard, so the newspapers had a field day on the old question of whether a captain is worth his place on his leadership alone. With all the disasters attributed to captains in the past, the selectors thought the answer was 'Yes'. The full team was J. M. Brearley (Middx) (capt), R. G. D. Willis (Warwicks) (vice-capt), I. T. Botham (Somerset), G. Boycott (Yorks),

---

1978-79: England to Australia

Batting Averages

	M	I	NO	R	HS	Avge	100	c/s
D. W. Randall (Notts)	10	18	2	763	150	47.68	2	6
R. W. Tolchard (Leics)	3	5	1	142	72	35.50	0	13
J. M. Brearley (Middx)	11	21	5	538	116*	33.62	1	11
D. I. Gower (Leics)	12	20	1	623	102	32.78	1	7
G. Boycott (Yorks)	12	23	3	533	90*	26.65	0	5
G. Miller (Derby)	11	18	3	398	68*	26.53	0	5
I. T. Botham (Som)	9	14	0	361	74	25.78	0	14
G. A. Gooch (Essex)	13	23	1	514	74	23.36	0	13
R. W. Taylor (Derby)	10	15	2	230	97	17.69	0	35/6
P. H. Edmonds (Middx)	7	9	2	115	38*	16.42	0	8
C. M. Old (Yorks)	6	6	1	81	40	16.20	0	2
C. T. Radley (Middx)	6	9	0	138	60	15.33	0	2
R. G. D. Willis (Warks)	10	13	4	115	21*	12.77	0	3
J. E. Emburey (Middx)	9	12	2	101	42	10.10	0	9
J. K. Lever (Essex)	6	7	0	67	28	9.57	0	0
M. Hendrick (Derby)	8	12	4	68	20	8.50	0	6

Bowling Averages

	O	M	R	W	Avge	BB	5i
M. Hendrick	185.4	40	399	28	14.25	5-11	1
G. Miller	277.1	74	607	36	16.86	6-56	2
J. E. Emburey	261.1	73	563	31	18.16	5-67	1
I. T. Botham	239.3	44	848	44	19.27	5-51	2
R. G. D. Willis	210.3	34	696	34	20.47	5-44	1
C. M. Old	138	24	452	21	21.52	6-42	1
J. K. Lever	119.1	18	377	13	29.00	4-28	0
P. H. Edmonds	147	34	397	11	36.09	5-52	1
G. A. Gooch	26	2	80	1	80.00	1-16	0

Also bowled: G. Boycott 3-0-11-0; D. W. Randall 2-0-9-0; C. T. Radley 1-0-4-0.

Above *England in Australia, 1978-79, taken before the fourth Test at Sydney. Back: D. W. Randall, C. T. Radley, J. K. Lever, G. Miller, I. T. Botham, P. H. Edmonds, M. Hendrick, J. E. Emburey, G. A. Gooch, D. I. Gower, R. W. Tolchard, G. Saulez (scorer). Front: B. W. Thomas (physiotherapist), G. Boycott, R. G. D. Willis, J. M. Brearley (captain), D. J. Insole (manager), R. W. Taylor, C. M. Old, K. F. Barrington (assistant manager).*

Right *The second Test of the 1978-79 Australian tour. Maclean about to be caught by Gooch off Miller.*

P. H. Edmonds (Middx), J. E. Emburey (Middx), G. A. Gooch (Essex), D. I. Gower (Leics), M. Hendrick (Derbys), J. K. Lever (Essex), G. Miller (Derbys), C. M. Old (Yorks), C. T. Radley (Middx), D. W. Randall (Notts), R. W. Taylor (Derbys) and R. W. Tolchard (Leics) with D. J. Insole as manager, K. F. Barrington as his assistant and B. W. Thomas as physiotherapist. The critics, apart from wondering if Tavare might have been picked, or Bairstow as reserve wicket-keeper, agreed with the selectors, and the team flew out on 24 October. The only query was Botham, who had injured himself at a farewell party, but he was expected to be fit before the first Test.

England had a surprise start to the tour when the batting collapsed twice against South Australia and the visitors were beaten, a young fast bowler, R. M. Hogg, causing the downfall. No other cloud however disturbed the party's progress to the first Test, when Australia had a terrible first two days – England obtaining a first innings lead of 170 – and though the home side

made a much better fight in their second attempt, England won by 7 wickets.

Boycott and Gower in contrasting styles saved the England batting in the second Test. Willis dismissed Australia cheaply and England went on to win by 166 runs. Against all the predictions, Australia won the third Test. Hogg bowled exceptionally well to remove England twice and Wood and Darling produced the runs for Australia. The home team looked like squaring the rubber in the fourth Test, when they again brushed aside the English batting and, through Darling and Border, obtained a first innings advantage of 142. Randall and Brearley happily returned to form in the England second innings and Australia required 205 to win in 265 minutes. The spinners, Miller and Emburey, took command, bringing England victory by 93 runs.

The trip to Tasmania and two one-day Internationals took place before the fifth Test, when the teams were even on first innings, but after Australia had taken six England second innings

wickets for 132, Miller and Taylor more than doubled the score, then Australia fell to Willis and Hendrick and lost by 205 runs.

Australia had some consolation in winning two one-day Internationals, but England found little difficulty in crowning the tour with victory in the sixth Test Match.

Owing to the counter-attractions of World Series Cricket, the interest in the 'official' Tests was much lower than usual and attendances at most games were very low. With Australia fielding virtually a second eleven, it was impossible to make any sound judgements on the performances of the English players. Gower and Randall easily topped the Test batting averages, but only

because of the moderate achievements of the rest–Boycott and Brearley averaged 21.91 and 16.72 respectively and the other specialist batsman, Gooch, managed 22.36. The arguments over the Yorkshire captaincy obviously distracted Boycott from his run-making. The batting survived because of the strength of the all-rounders, Botham and Miller. Hendrick and Miller led the bowling table, but the outstanding man of the series was Hogg for Australia who took 41 wickets at 12.85 each.

The team were fortunate regarding injuries, the only serious one being to Tolchard–Bairstow was flown out to replace him, but scarcely played.

1978-79: England to Australia

1st Match: v South Australia Country XI (Renmark) (One Day)   Nov 1.
England 199-4 dec (C. T. Radley 64) drew with S.A. Country XI 137-6.

2nd Match: v South Australia (Adelaide)   Nov 3, 4, 5, 6.
S. Australia 311 (J. E. Nash 124) & 149 (I. R. McLean 52, P. H. Edmonds 5-52) beat England 232 (D. I. Gower 73, G. Boycott 62) & 196 (D. I. Gower 50) by 32 runs.

3rd Match: v Victoria Country XI (Leongatha) (One Day)   Nov 8.
England 130-8 dec beat Victoria Country XI 59 (J. E. Emburey 5-10) by 71 runs.

4th Match: v Victoria (Melbourne)   Nov 10, 11, 12, 13.
Victoria 254 (J. K. Moss 73) & 33-0 drew with England 241-8 dec (J. M. Brearley 116, D. W. Randall 63).

5th Match: v Capital Territory XI (Canberra) (Limited Over)   Nov 15.
England 255-2 (G. Boycott 123, R. W. Tolchard 108) beat Capital Territory 76 by 179 runs.*

6th Match: v New South Wales (Sydney)   Nov 17, 18, 19, 20.
England 374 (D. W. Randall 110, G. A. Gooch 66, I. T. Botham 56) & 4-0 beat N.S.W. 165 (J. Dyson 67, G. Miller 6-56) & 210 (A. M. Hilditch 93, I. T. Botham 5-51) by 10 wkts.

7th Match: v Queensland Country XI (Bundaberg) (Limited Over)   Nov 22.
England 259-5 (R. W. Tolchard 74, J. M. Brearley 59) beat Qld Country XI 127 by 132 runs.

8th Match: v Queensland (Brisbane)   Nov 24, 25, 26, 27.
Queensland 172 & 289 (J. A. Maclean 94, I. T. Botham 5-70) lost to England 254 (J. M. Brearley 75*, D. W. Randall 66) & 208-4 (G. Boycott 60) by 6 wkts.

9th Match: v Australia   Dec 1, 2, 3, 5, 6.
Australia 116 & 339 (K. J. Hughes 129, G. N. Yallop 102) lost to England 286 (D. W. Randall 75, R. M. Hogg 6-74) & 170-3 (D. W. Randall 74*) by 7 wkts.

10th Match: v Western Australia (Perth)   Dec 9, 10, 11.
England 144 (R. W. Tolchard 61*) & 126 (B. Yardley 5-54) beat W. Australia 52 (M. Hendrick 5-11) & 78 by 140 runs.

11th Match: v Western Australia Country XI (Albany) (Limited Over)   Dec 13.
England 208-4 (G. A. Gooch 112) beat W.A. Country XI 139 (R. Miguel 51, P. H. Edmonds 6-53) by 69 runs.

12th Match: v Australia (Perth)   Dec 15, 16, 17, 19, 20.
England 309 (D. I. Gower 102, G. Boycott 77, R. M. Hogg 5-65) & 208 (R. M. Hogg 5-57) beat Australia 190 (P. M. Toohey 81*, R. G. D. Willis 5-44) & 161 (G. M. Wood 64) by 166 runs.

13th Match: v South Australia (Adelaide)   Dec 22, 23, 24.
S. Australia 241-7 dec (B. L. Causby 87, R. J. Parker 51) & 231-6 dec (R. K. Blewett 51) drew with England 234-5 dec (R. W. Tolchard 72, C. T. Radley 60) & 238-9 (G. Miller 68*, G. A. Gooch 64).

14th Match: v Australia (Melbourne)   Dec 29, 30, Jan 1, 2, 3.
Australia 258 (G. M. Wood 100) & 167 beat England 143 (R. M. Hogg 5-30) & 179 (R. M. Hogg 5-36) by 103 runs.

15th Match: v Australia (Sydney)   Jan 6, 7, 8, 10, 11.
England 152 (I. T. Botham 59, A. G. Hurst 5-28) & 346 (D. W. Randall 150, J. M. Brearley 53, J. D. Higgs 5-148) beat Australia 294 (W. M. Darling 91, A. R. Border 60*) & 111 by 93 runs.

16th Match: v Australia (Sydney) (Limited Over)   Jan 13.
Australia 17-1 drew with England did not bat.

17th Match: v Northern New South Wales (Newcastle)   Jan 14, 15, 16.
Northern N.S.W. 223-9 dec (J. Gardner 59, C. Beatty 62) & 166 (C. Evans 64) lost to England 163 & 230-1 (G. Boycott 117*, C. T. Radley 55*, J. M. Brearley 50) by 9 wkts.

18th Match: v Tasmania (Launceston) (Limited Over)   Jan 18.
England 240-8 (I. T. Botham 61, D. W. Randall 60) beat Tasmania 77 by 163 runs.

19th Match: v Tasmania (Hobart)   Jan 19, 20, 21.
Tasmania 105 (C. M. Old 6-42) & 118-4 drew with England 210-5 dec (G. Boycott 90*).

20th Match: v Australia (Melbourne) (Limited Over)   Jan 24.
Australia 101 lost to England 102-3 by 7 wkts.

21st Match: v Australia (Adelaide)   Jan 27, 28, 29, 31, Feb 1.
England 169 (I. T. Botham 74) & 360 (R. W. Taylor 97, G. Miller 64) beat Australia 164 & 160 by 205 runs.

22nd Match: v Tasmania (Melbourne) (Limited Over)   Feb 3.
Tasmania 131-6 lost to England 134-7 by 3 wkts.

23rd Match: v Australia (Melbourne) (Limited Over)   Feb 4.
England 212-6 (D. I. Gower 101) lost to Australia 215-6 (P. M. Toohey 54*, K. J. Hughes 50) by 4 wkts.*

24th Match: v Geelong & District (Geelong) (Limited Over)   Feb 6.
England 165-9 beat Geelong 100-9 by 48 runs.

25th Match: v Australia (Melbourne) (Limited Over)   Feb 7.
England 94 lost to Australia 95-4 by 6 wkts.

26th Match: v Australia (Sydney)   Feb 10, 11, 12, 14.
Australia 198 (G. N. Yallop 121) & 143 (B. Yardley 61*, G. Miller 5-44) lost to England 308 (G. A. Gooch 74, D. I. Gower 65) & 35-1 by 9 wkts.

1978-79: D. H. Robins' tour to South America, including Colombia

In February and March 1979, D. H. Robins took his team to South America and broke new ground in visiting Colombia as well as Peru, Brazil, Chile and Argentina.

The team was C. S. Cowdrey (Kent) (capt), C. W. J. Athey (Yorks), N. E. Briers (Leics), R. G. L. Cheatle (Sussex), I. J. Gould (Middx), T. A. Lloyd (Warwicks), D. N. Patel (Worcs), S. P. Perryman (Warwicks), G. B. Stevenson (Yorks), L. B. Taylor (Leics), K. P. Tomlins (Middx) and J. P. Whiteley (Yorks).

All thirteen of the matches played were won, including the most important, which was the single 'Test' match played against Argentina.

P. H. Parfitt travelled as manager and H. Blofeld as assistant manager.

The full results of the tour have not been published.

1979-80: D. H. Robins' under-23 team to Australia and New Zealand

D. H. Robins confined his team to players under 23 for his six-week tour of Australia and New Zealand in February and March 1980. The team was C. S. Cowdrey (Kent) (capt), C. W. J. Athey (Yorks), K. J. Barnett (Derbys), N. G. B. Cook (Leics), K. E. Cooper (Notts), A. L. Jones (Glamorgan), C. Maynard (Warwicks), W. G. Merry (Middx), G. J. Parsons (Leics), D. N. Patel (Worcs), A. C. S. Pigott (Sussex), C. J. Richards (Surrey), G. C. Small (Warwicks), K. Sharp (Yorks) and R. G. Williams (Northants). B. Simmons travelled as manager, H. C. Blofeld as P.R.O. and L. E. G. Ames as 'vice-chairman'.

The strength of the team was in its spin attack of Patel, Williams and Cook, which coped successfully with most opposition batsmen, the two defeats being against North Tasmania, when the batting failed, and against Otago Minor Association, who were bowled out for 85 by Cooper in their first innings, but came back to win by 7 wickets through a century from Blakely. Both first-class matches were drawn – rain prematurely ended the first and in the second against Young New Zealand, Cowdrey declared to set the opposition 223 at about 5 runs an over.

1979-80: Derrick Robins' Team to Australia and New Zealand

1st Match: v New South Wales Colts (Sydney) (Limited Over)   Feb 17.
N.S.W. Colts 98-9 (C. W. J. Athey 5-14) lost to Robins XI 100-5 by 5 wkts.

2nd Match: v New South Wales Colts (Sydney)   Feb 18, 19.
Robins XI 169 (D. N. Patel 52) & 155-7 dec drew with N.S.W. Colts 93-8 dec (N. G. B. Cook 5-17) & 220-8.

3rd Match: v North-Western Tasmania (Devonport)   Feb 24, 25.
N.W. Tasmania 223-6 dec & 125-4 dec drew with Robins XI 129-7 dec & 125-8.

4th Match: v North Tasmania (Launceston) (Limited Over)   Feb 27.
Robins XI 241 (C. W. J. Athey 56) beat N. Tasmania 146 by 95 runs.

5th Match: v North Tasmania (Launceston) (Limited Over)   Feb 28.
Robins XI 102 lost to N. Tasmania 104-1 by 9 wkts.

6th Match: v Tasmanian C.A. (Hobart)   March 4, 5.
Robins XI 256-5 dec (K. Sharp 102*, K. J. Barnet 61) & 140-4 dec (C. S. Cowdrey 50*) drew with Tasmanian C.A. 163-7 dec & 136-6 (B. F. Davison 87*).

7th Match: v Otago Minor Association (Alexandra)   March 8, 9.
Robins XI 171-9 dec & 146-5 dec lost to Otago M.A. 85 (K. E. Cooper 6-32) & 234-3 (J. Blakely 124*) by 7 wkts.

8th Match: v Canterbury Minor Association (Ashburton)   March 11, 12.
Robins XI 173 (C. S. Cowdrey 60*) drew with Canterbury M.A. 88-1.

9th Match: v Marlborough (Blenheim) (One Day)   March 14.
Robins XI 181-8 dec beat Marlborough 138 by 43 runs.

10th Match: v Nelson (Nelson)   March 15, 16.
Nelson 147-9 dec & 274-5 dec (G. N. Edwards 144*, M. H. Toynbee 65) lost to Robins XI 184-7 dec (C. W. J. Athey 69) & 238-5 (C. W. J. Athey 73) by 5 wkts.

11th Match: v Manawatu (Palmerston North) (Limited Over)   March 18.
Manawatu 122 lost to Robins XI 123-0 (K. Sharp 69*, C. W. J. Athey 49*) by 10 wkts.

12th Match: v Hawke's Bay & Wairarapa (Napier)   March 19, 20.
Robins XI 232-5 dec (K. J. Barnett 81, R. G. Williams 52*) & 106-4 beat Hawke's Bay & W. 108 & 228 (Thompson 77) by 6 wkts.

13th Match: v Northern Districts (Hamilton)   March 22, 23, 24.
N. Districts 218-9 dec (D. N. Patel 5-69) & 226-3 (J. G. Gibson 65, J. M. Parker 60*, C. M. Kuggeleijn 50) drew with Robins XI 318-8 dec (K. Sharp 106, C. Maynard 57*).

14th Match: v Thames Valley Invitation XI (Ngatea)   March 25, 26.
Thames Valley 172 (K. Puna 77*) & 95 (R. G. Williams 5-34) lost to Robins XI 321-8 dec (R. G. Williams 157*, C. Maynard 50*) by an inns & 54 runs.

15th Match: v Young New Zealand (Auckland)   March 28, 29, 30.
Robins XI 223 (D. N. Patel 105, M. C. Snedden 5-41) & 300-4 dec (C. W. J. Athey 116, K. Sharp 82, D. N. Patel 54) drew with Young N.Z. 301-8 dec (I. D. Smith 72, M. C. Snedden 69) & 160-6 (J. A. Rutherford 75).

1979-80: England tour Australia with the West Indies

On 30 May 1979, the World Series Cricket organisation announced that agreement had been reached with the Australian Board of Control and that as a result the W.S.C. cricket programme would cease and the players contracted to that programme paid off. The result of this agreement was a hastily arranged tournament of one-day Internationals and Test Matches in Australia for the winter of 1979-80, with both England and West Indies touring there. The English schedule was a total of 20 matches in Australia of which nine were one-day Internationals and three were Test Matches.

England selected the following for the tour: J. M. Brearley (Middx) (capt), D. L. Bairstow (Yorks), I. T. Botham (Somerset), G. Boycott (Yorks), G. R. Dilley (Kent), G. A. Gooch (Essex), D. I. Gower (Leics), M. Hendrick (Derbys), W. Larkins (Northants), J. K. Lever (Essex), G. Miller (Derbys), D. W. Randall (Notts), R. W. Taylor (Derbys), D. L. Underwood (Kent), P. Willey (Northants), R. G. D. Willis (Warwicks). A. V. Bedser

The England party for the 1979-80 tour of Australia, in which a triangular one-day tournament took place with the West Indies as the third team. Back: G. B. Stevenson, P. Willey, J. E. Emburey, G. Saulez (scorer), G. R. Dilley, I. T. Botham, J. K. Lever. Centre: D. W. Randall, D. L. Bairstow, D. I. Gower, G. A. Gooch, W. Larkins, R. W. Taylor. Front: B. W. Thomas (physiotherapist), D. L. Underwood, R. G. D. Willis, A. V. Bedser (manager), J. M. Brearley, G. Boycott, K. F. Barrington (assistant manager).

went as manager. Old declined the invitation on medical grounds and the only omission of any note was Edmonds. Underwood was the sole W.S.C. player to be selected.

The side flew from London on 4 November and their arrival in Australia was greeted with cat-calls from the local press. The English authorities were unhappy about quite a number of points regarding the one-day rules and also the proposed floodlit matches: questions such as the proposed fines for slow over-rates, the use of a white ball, the number of bumpers to be allowed per over, whether the tourists would have to pay the cost of organising practice sessions under floodlight and a number of others. These problems were built on by the Australian press and Brearley, in particular, came in for heavy attack, which spilt over from the press into the crowds at the matches. The bitter rivalry between W.S.C. and the I.C.C. could not be eradicated overnight.

Of the three Tests played in this confused fixture list, the first, at Perth, which was staged a month after the tour began, will always be remembered for Lillee's aluminium bat, which he attempted to use in the first innings – the argument held up play for ten minutes, after which he reverted to a traditional type. England held their own for the first half of the game, but in the final innings only Boycott held out as his colleagues were dismissed cheaply and Australia won by 138 runs. In the second Test, both sides struggled in their first innings on a damp wicket, but again England's second innings was a one-man-band – Gower – and though Underwood took three Australian wickets cheaply when the home side needed 216 to win Greg Chappell and Hughes steered them to victory.

With the series of three already decided, England went to Melbourne for the third Test. Brearley won the toss and Gooch and Boycott gave the tourists a great start with a partnership of 116, then the middle batting surrendered with a squeak. Australia built up a lead of 171 and although Botham hit a marvellous hundred, Australia wanted a mere 103 to win – the final margin was 8 wickets. The contrast between the five to one Test series in 1978-79 and the three to nil defeat was sharp indeed. The English authorities cried that the series was not 'for the Ashes', a statement which ranked with the famous remark that W.S.C. matches would be granted 'first-class' status if Mr Packer had played ball.

The other section of the tour concerned the one-day Internationals between Australia, England and West Indies. In the preliminary matches, England performed the best, winning 5 out of 8. West Indies came second and thus the final was between those two, which was a terrible blow to the organisers, since the

absence of Australia badly affected the attendance. Three dropped catches lost England the first match of the three to decide the champion country and as West Indies won the second with ease – Greenidge and Richards batting in top form – a third game was not required and West Indies took the crown.

The English side's batting was never very satisfactory. Randall was tried as an opener, but this experiment failed. Gower, who had looked so good the previous year, was not at all sound in the middle order, save for his 98 at Sydney. Willey, who performed well in one-day games, failed miserably in the Tests with 35 runs in 6 innings. Even Botham failed, except in the final Test, and later in India.

From Australia England flew to India for a special Test to celebrate the Golden Jubilee of the Indian Board of Cricket Control. The game was Botham's. He took 13 wickets and hit the only hundred of the match winning the game for England single-

1979-80: England to Australia and India								
Batting Averages								
	M	I	NO	R	HS	Avge	100	c/s
G. A. Gooch (Essex)	7	14	3	639	115	58.09	1	9
G. Boycott (Yorks)	8	15	4	599	110	54.45	2	3
G. Miller (Derby)	4	6	2	203	71	50.75	0	3
I. T. Botham (Som)	6	10	1	331	119*	36.77	2	5
G. R. Dilley (Kent)	5	6	3	101	38*	33.66	0	2
G. B. Stevenson (Yorks)	4	5	2	91	33	30.33	0	0
J. M. Brearley (Middx)	7	11	1	302	81	30.20	0	5
P. Willey (Northts)	8	12	3	269	101*	29.88	1	3
D. I. Gower (Leics)	9	15	2	354	98*	27.23	0	6
D. W. Randall (Notts)	6	10	0	250	97	25.00	0	3
R. W. Taylor (Derby)	8	11	1	227	47*	22.70	0	29/1
W. Larkins (Northts)	6	10	1	190	90	21.11	0	3
J. E. Emburey (Middx)	3	4	0	71	50	17.75	0	2
J. K. Lever (Essex)	7	7	2	75	22	15.00	0	4
D. L. Underwood (Kent)	6	8	0	88	43	11.00	0	5
D. L. Bairstow (Yorks)	2	2	0	13	12	6.50	0	2
R. G. D. Willis (Warks)	4	6	0	21	11	3.50	0	0
M. Hendrick (Derby)	1	1	0	1	1	1.00	0	0
Bowling Averages								
	O	M	R	W	Avge	BB	5i	
I. T. Botham	242	81	532	34	15.64	7-48	4	
D. L. Underwood	260	81	609	25	24.36	7-66	1	
G. B. Stevenson	87	13	307	11	27.90	4-44	0	
G. R. Dilley	88.1	11	243	7	34.71	3-40	0	
G. A. Gooch	43	13	113	3	37.66	2-16	0	
J. K. Lever	235.5	55	622	16	38.87	4-111	0	
J. E. Emburey	111.2	25	282	7	40.28	3-80	0	
P. Willey	111	18	332	7	47.42	3-68	3	
G. Miller	106	20	268	5	53.60	2-47	0	
R. G. D. Willis	113	30	252	3	84.00	1-26	0	
Also bowled: G. Boycott 4-0-19-0; M. Hendrick 4-1-14-0; W. Larkins 6-0-15-0.								

Above *England players (Brearley and Taylor facing) make a concerted but unsuccessful appeal for leg before wicket against McCosker in the second Test match at Sydney on the 1979-80 tour.*

Above right *The one-day grand final at Melbourne between England and the West Indies at Melbourne. Bairstow survives a run-out attempt as Holding dives for the ball and wicket-keeper Deryck Murray watches.*

Right *The England party went from Australia to India to play a Golden Jubilee Test match against the home country in February 1980. The Indian captain Sunil Gavaskar caught behind by Taylor off Botham in the second innings.*

Right *One-day evening matches were a feature of the 1979-80 Australian tour. The sunset, clouds and floodlights make a dramatic backdrop for this match at Sydney.*

Far right *The Golden Jubilee Test match in India was a personal triumph for Ian Botham, who produced the greatest all-round performance in Test history—an innings of 114 and bowling analyses of 6-58 and 7-48.*

handed. The rest of the team were still shell-shocked from the junketings in Australia.

The whole tour was best forgotten. Botham enhanced his reputation and Gooch improved. Miller and Hendrick were both injured, which adversely affected the bowling, Emburey and G. B. Stevenson (Yorkshire) being flown out as replacements. Willis had a lean time and ended the tour by only being first change, instead of opening the bowling.

For Australia, Greg Chappell was outstanding. Lillee worried England most, but Dymock headed the Test bowling table. Hogg was slain by the West Indians and Thomson was of little account.

1979-80: M.C.C. to Australia and India

1st Match: v Queensland (Brisbane) Nov 12, 13, 14.
England 176 (D. W. Randall 97, C. G. Rackemann 5-25) & 226-5 dec (G. Miller 57*, P. Willey 57*, D. I. Gower 50) drew with Queensland 219-9 dec (T. V. Hohns 62, M. F. Kent 58) & 97-1.

2nd Match: v Northern New South Wales (Newcastle) (Limited Over) Nov 17.
Northern N.S.W. 133 (C. Beatty 67) lost to England 136-1 (G. Boycott 78) by 9 wkts.

3rd Match: v Northern New South Wales (Newcastle) (Limited Over) Nov 18.
England 213-7 (J. M. Brearley 67, W. Larkins 51) beat Northern N.S.W. 181-7 (G. G. Geise 58*) by 32 runs.

4th Match: v Combined Universities (Adelaide) Nov 22, 23, 24, 25.
England 179 (D. W. Randall 61, G. Kirkwood 5-52) & 411-8 dec (G. A. Gooch 124, I. T. Botham 76, R. W. Taylor 57*) drew with Universities 168 (C. Beatty 53, D. L. Underwood 8-41) & 227-5 (D. M. Wellham 95, P. J. Davies 57).

5th Match: v West Indies (Sydney) (Limited Over) Nov 28.
England 211-8 (P. Willey 58*) beat West Indies 196 (L. G. Rowe 60) by 2 runs.

6th Match: v Tasmania (Hobart) Nov 30, Dec 1, 2.
England 214-3 dec (G. A. Gooch 101*) & 135-1 dec (G. A. Gooch 70*, D. I. Gower 53) beat Tasmania 71-3 dec & 178 (R. L. Knight 74, D. L. Underwood 7-66).

7th Match: v South Australia (Adelaide) Dec 4, 5, 6.
England 252-2 dec (G. Boycott 110, J. M. Brearley 81) & 227-7 dec (G. Miller 71, G. Boycott 63*) drew with South Australia 226-4 dec (J. J. Crowe 78*) & 181-3 (W. M. Darling 75*, J. J. Crowe 55).

8th Match: v Australia (Melbourne) (Limited Over) Dec 8.
Australia 207-9 (G. S. Chappell 92) lost to England 209-7 (G. Boycott 68) by 3 wkts.

9th Match: v Australia (Sydney) (Limited Over) Dec 11.
England 264-7 (G. Boycott 105, P. Willey 64) beat Australia 192 (T. J. Laughlin 74) by 72 runs.

10th Match: v Australia (Perth) Dec 14, 15, 16, 18, 19.
Australia 244 (K. J. Hughes 99, I. T. Botham 6-78) & 337 (A. R. Border 115, J. M. Wiener 58, I. T. Botham 5-98) beat England 228 (J. M. Brearley 64) & 215 (G. Boycott 99*, G. Dymock 6-34) by 138 runs.

11th Match: v West Indies (Brisbane) (Limited Over) Dec 23.
England 217-8 (G. Boycott 68, D. I. Gower 59) lost to West Indies 218-1 (C. G. Greenidge 85*, I. V. A. Richards 85*) by 9 wkts.

12th Match: v Australia (Sydney) (Limited Over) Dec 26.
Australia 194-6 (I. M. Chappell 60*, G. S. Chappell 52) lost to England 195-6 (G. Boycott 86*, P. Willey 51) by 4 wkts.

13th Match: v Queensland (Brisbane) Dec 28, 29, 30, 31.
England 324 (G. A. Gooch 115, J. E. Emburey 50) & 274-8 dec (P. Willey 101*, G. A. Gooch 53) beat Queensland 237 (W. R. Broad 53, A. D. Parker 52*, M. G. Morgan 50) & 223 by 138 runs.

14th Match: v Australia (Sydney) Jan 4, 5, 6, 8.
England 123 & 237 (D. I. Gower 98*) lost to Australia 145 & 219-4 (G. S. Chappell 98*) by 6 wkts.

15th Match: v West Indies (Melbourne) Jan 12.
No play: rain.

16th Match: v Australia (Sydney) (Limited Over) Jan 14.
Australia 163 lost to England 164-8 (G. A. Gooch 69) by 2 wkts.

17th Match: v West Indies (Adelaide) (Limited Over) Jan 16.
West Indies 246-5 (I. V. A. Richards 88, A. I. Kallicharran 57, C. G. Greenidge 50) beat England 139 (A. M. E. Roberts 5-22) by 107 runs.

18th Match: v West Indies (Melbourne) (Limited Over) Jan 20.
West Indies 215-8 (C. G. Greenidge 80) beat England 213-7 (P. Willey 51) by 2 runs.

19th Match: v West Indies (Limited Over) Jan 22.
England 208-8 (G. Boycott 63) lost to West Indies 209-2 (C. G. Greenidge 98*, I. V. A. Richards 65) by 8 wkts.

20th Match: v New South Wales (Canberra) Jan 27, 28, 29.
New South Wales 212-7 dec (K. D. Walters 62) & 243-2 dec (A. M. J. Hilditch 78, T. M. Chappell 70*) lost to England 203 & 254-2 (W. Larkins 90, G. A. Gooch 73*, G. Boycott 51) by 8 wkts.

21st Match: v Australia (Melbourne) Feb 1, 2, 3, 5, 6.
England 306 (G. A. Gooch 99, J. M. Brearley 60*, D. K. Lillee 6-60) & 273 (I. T. Botham 119*, G. A. Gooch 51, D. K. Lillee 5-78) lost to Australia 477 (G. S. Chappell 114, I. M. Chappell 75, B. M. Laird 74, A. R. Border 63) & 103-2 by 8 wkts.

22nd Match: v India (Bombay) Feb 15, 17, 18, 19.
India 242 (I. T. Botham 6-58) & 149 (I. T. Botham 7-48) lost to England 296 (I. T. Botham 114, K. D. Ghavri 5-52) & 98-0 by 10 wkts.

1980-81: England well beaten in tour of the West Indies

The selectors delayed announcing the English team for West Indies until 15 September, due to a small extent to the injuries of Willey, Dilley, Edmonds and Botham, though whether anyone could forecast the fitness of those four three months ahead—the tour did not commence until January—seemed unlikely. The team was I. T. Botham (Somerset) (capt), R. G. D. Willis (Warwicks) (vice-capt), D. L. Bairstow (Yorks), G. Boycott (Yorks), R. O. Butcher (Middx), G. R. Dilley (Kent), P. R. Downton (Middx), J. E. Emburey (Middx), M. W. Gatting (Middx), G. A. Gooch (Essex), D. I. Gower (Leics), G. Miller (Derbys), C. M. Old (Yorks), B. C. Rose (Somerset), G. B. Stevenson (Yorks), P. Willey (Northants). A. C. Smith was appointed manager with K. F. Barrington as his assistant, and B. W. Thomas as physiotherapist.

The team left England on 15 January and the tour opened in Trinidad on 23 January, where England had little difficulty in beating a Young West Indian XI. The four-day game against the Windwards was washed out by rain and replaced by two one-day matches, both of which England won, but they were unlucky to lose the first one-day International by just two runs. Rain ruined the first-class game at Port of Spain, just prior to the first Test. In this England were completely outplayed; the fast brigade of Roberts, Holding, Croft and Garner blasted their way through the English batting—Boycott alone achieved a fifty—but the England attack without Willis's old power was soon blunted and the West Indies made a big score.

The Warwickshire bowler had broken down in Trinidad and Jackman was sent as a replacement. The arrival of Jackman coincided with the Guyanan section of the tour. Politics then took over and on 26 February the Guyana Government decided to expel Jackman on the grounds that he had played cricket in South Africa. The authorities at Lord's countered by refusing to play the second Test, due to commence on 28 February. The English team flew to Barbados as the various West Indian Governments took stock of the situation. The tour was in the balance. On 4 March, the Governments concerned agreed that the tour should continue and the scheduled one-day match against Barbados began as planned the next day. In the meanwhile, Rose, who had eye trouble, was flown home and Athey of Yorkshire arrived to take his place.

England won the one-day game, but drew with Barbados, prior to the third Test at Bridgetown. Once more the tourists were outplayed. Clive Lloyd hit a century in the first innings and Richards one in the second—the English batting wilted before the fast bowlers, except that Gooch fought splendidly in the second innings. The defeat was by 298 runs.

The match was marred by the sudden death of Barrington, the assistant manager, on the second evening.

The fourth Test was the first staged at St John's, Antigua. England saved the game due to rain and an unbeaten hundred from Boycott in the second innings, after they had been nearly 200 behind on the first innings.

The last leg of the tour took the team to Jamaica where they first met the island side. The game was drawn, but the team did well enough to obtain a first innings lead—if they had played two spinners, there might have been a chance of victory.

The final game of the visit was the fifth Test. Lloyd put England in but his gamble only half worked, as Boycott and Gooch gave their team a good start—the other batsmen failed miserably however and West Indies gained their customary large first innings lead. The England second innings slumped to 32 for 3 and a loss seemed likely, but Gower and Willey put on a hundred for the fourth wicket and the match was drawn. England thus fought back well in the last two Tests, to save some honour.

West Indies won the series by two matches to nil and there could be no doubt that they were the better team. The idea of saddling Botham with the captaincy was obvious madness and the great all-rounder proved it by his performances – his Test batting average was 10.42.

The advocates of Botham as captain were quick to point out that the atmosphere between the teams, in the English team itself and even in the crowds – for once there were no riots – was excellent and Botham deserved his credit for this. It did not seem to occur to these advocates that the serene atmosphere was due to the fact that the West Indies were never even remotely in danger of losing a single Test.

The successes in the English side were Gooch and Gower and for West Indies Holding and Croft, though Richards did all that was expected of him and the old maestro, Lloyd, flourished once more.

Below *The England party in Barbados for the third Test of the tour of the West Indies, 1980-81. Back: D. L. Bairstow, R. D. Jackman, M. W. Gatting, C. W. J. Athey, G. B. Stevenson, G. R. Dilley, J. E. Emburey, P. Willey, D. I. Gower, P. R. Downton, R. O. Butcher, G. Saulez (scorer). Front: B. W. Thomas (physiotherapist), G. A. Gooch, G. Miller, I. T. Botham, A. C. Smith (manager), G. Boycott, C. M. Old, K. F. Barrington (assistant manager). It was during this match that Ken Barrington died.*

Bottom left *Colin Croft was one of the most successful in a battery of fast bowlers which the West Indies used to destroy the English batting in the 1980-81 tour of the West Indies.*

Bottom right *David Gower was one of the few English batsmen on the 1980-81 tour of the West Indies to return with his reputation undiminished. He appears to be enjoying this sweep to fine leg.*

1980-81: England to West Indies

1st Match: v Young West Indies (Pointe-a-Pierre) Jan 23, 24, 25, 26.
England 483-6 dec (D. I. Gower 187, M. W. Gatting 94, G. Boycott 87, R. A. Harper 5-142) & 208-5 dec (G. Boycott 87) beat Young West Indies 320 (P. J. Dujon 105*) & 181 (G. Miller 6-70) by 190 runs.

2nd Match: v Windward Is (Arnos Vale) Jan 30, 31, Feb 1, 2.
No play.

3rd Match: v Windward Is (Arnos Vale) (Limited Over) Feb 1.
England 165-9 beat Windward Is 150-9 by 15 runs.

4th Match: v Windward Is (Arnos Vale) (Limited Over) Feb 2.
Windward Is 183 (L. John 56) lost to England 184-4 (G. Boycott 85, G. A. Gooch 50) by 6 wkts.*

5th Match: v West Indies (Arnos Vale) (Limited Over) Feb 4.
West Indies 127 (E. H. Mattis 62) beat England 125 (I. T. Botham 60) by 2 runs.

6th Match: v Trinidad & Tobago (Port of Spain) Feb 7, 8, 9, 10.
England 355 (G. A. Gooch 117, D. I. Gower 77, G. Boycott 70) drew with Trinidad & Tobago 392-8 (H. A. Gomes 75, D. L. Murray 75, T. Cuffy 61, R. Nanaan 66*).

7th Match: v West Indies (Port of Spain) Feb 13, 14, 16, 17, 18.
West Indies 426-9 dec (D. L. Haynes 96, C. G. Greenidge 84, C. H. Lloyd 64, A. M. E. Roberts 50*, J. E. Emburey 5-124) beat England 178 (C. E. H. Croft 5-40) & 169 (G. Boycott 70) by an inns & 79 runs.

8th Match: v Guyana (Georgetown) Feb 21, 22, 23, 24.
No play.

9th Match: v Guyana (Georgetown) Feb 24.
No play.

10th Match: v Guyana (Georgetown) Feb 25.
No play.

11th Match: v West Indies (Berbice) (Limited Over) Feb 26.
England 137 lost to West Indies 138-4 by 6 wkts.

12th Match: v West Indies (Georgetown) Feb 28, March 1, 2, 4, 5.
Cancelled.

13th Match: v Barbados (Bridgetown) (Limited Over) March 5.
England 207-6 (G. A. Gooch 84) beat Barbados 196 (G. N. Reifer 55) by 11 runs.

14th Match: v Barbados (Bridgetown) March 7, 8, 9, 10.
England 298 (G. Boycott 77) & 219-6 drew with Barbados 334 (C. L. King 76, J. E. Emburey 5-92).

15th Match: v West Indies (Bridgetown) March 13, 14, 15, 17, 18.
West Indies 265 (C. H. Lloyd 100, H. A. Gomes 58) & 379-7 dec (I. V. A. Richards 182*, C. H. Lloyd 66) beat England 122 & 224 (G. A. Gooch 116, D. I. Gower 54) by 298 runs.

16th Match: v Leeward Is (Plymouth) March 21, 22, 23, 24.
Leeward Is 161 (A. L. Kelly 72, G. R. Dilly 5-48, G. B. Stevenson 5-50) & 263 (S. I. Williams 62, V. A. Amory 56) lost to England 251 (G. Miller 91*, G. Boycott 72) & 174-5 (R. O. Butcher 77*) by 5 wkts.

17th Match: v West Indies (St Johns) March 27, 28, 29, 31, April 1.
England 271 (P. Willey 102, C. E. H. Croft 6-74) & 234-3 (G. Boycott 104*, G. A. Gooch 83) drew with West Indies 468-9 dec (I. V. A. Richards 114, C. G. Greenidge 63, C. H. Lloyd 58, M. A. Holding 58*).

18th Match: v Jamaica (Kingston) April 4, 5, 6, 7.
England 413 (G. Boycott 98, M. W. Gatting 93) & 294-8 dec (G. A. Gooch 122, R. O. Butcher 51) drew with Jamaica 368 (L. G. Rowe 116, M. C. Neita 67, R. A. Austin 62, J. E. Emburey 6-92).

19th Match: v West Indies (Kingston) April 10, 11, 12, 14, 15.
England 285 (G. A. Gooch 153, M. A. Holding 5-56) & 302-6 dec (D. I. Gower 154*, P. Willey 67) drew with West Indies 442 (C. H. Lloyd 95, H. A. Gomes 90*, D. L. Haynes 84, C. G. Greenidge 62).

1980-81: England to the West Indies

Batting Averages

	M	I	NO	R	HS	Avge	100	c/s
G. A. Gooch (Essex)	7	13	0	777	153	59.76	4	4
D. I. Gower (Leics)	8	14	1	726	187	55.84	2	4
G. Boycott (Yorks)	9	17	2	818	104*	54.53	1	2
P. Willey (Northts)	7	13	5	383	102*	47.87	1	0
G. Miller (Derby)	4	7	3	151	91*	37.75	0	4
R. O. Butcher (Middx)	7	13	2	385	77*	35.00	0	7
M. W. Gatting (Middx)	5	9	0	268	94	29.77	0	3
C. W. J. Athey (Yorks)	4	8	0	121	41	15.12	0	1
I. T. Botham (Som)	8	14	0	197	40	14.07	0	8
B. C. Rose (Som)	3	5	0	69	43	13.80	0	1
D. L. Bairstow (Yorks)	4	7	2	64	26*	12.80	0	9/1
R. D. Jackman (Surrey)	5	7	2	47	17	9.40	0	0
J. E. Emburey (Middx)	7	10	2	74	34	9.25	0	3
P. R. Downton (Middx)	6	9	1	67	26*	8.37	0	11/3
G. R. Dilley (Kent)	7	8	4	26	15*	6.50	0	0
C. M. Old (Yorks)	4	4	0	13	8	3.25	0	5
G. B. Stevenson (Yorks)	4	4	0	6	3	1.50	0	0

Bowling Averages

	O	M	R	W	Avge	BB	5i
G. Miller	109.2	29	299	14	21.35	6-70	1
R. D. Jackman	136.2	29	380	12	31.66	4-68	0
I. T. Botham	224.2	43	790	23	34.34	4-77	0
G. R. Dilley	212.2	44	733	20	36.65	5-48	1
G. B. Stevenson	88	16	337	9	37.44	5-50	1
J. E. Emburey	300.4	95	675	18	37.50	6-92	3
P. Willey	110	28	269	7	38.42	3-29	0
C. M. Old	62.3	14	208	5	41.60	3-60	0

Also bowled: G. Boycott 3-2-5-0; M. W. Gatting 3-1-10-0; G. A. Gooch 42-14-108-1.

In the first game the visitors declared to set Zimbabwe 282 to win, but after losing some quick wickets, they settled for a draw. In the victory by Zimbabwe, Heron defied the bowlers with an excellent 66. In the final match, the highest innings was the fourth, but Zimbabwe's total of 333 fell 83 short of victory.

1980-81: Middlesex to Zimbabwe

1st Match: v Zimbabwe (Salisbury) (Limited Over) Sept 25.
Middlesex 237-4 (W. N. Slack 84, M. W. Gatting 51) tied with Zimbabwe 237-4 (D. A. G. Fletcher 108, J. G. Heron 58).

2nd Match: v Zimbabwe (Salisbury) Sept 27, 28, 29.
Middlesex 316-7 dec (J. M. Brearley 76, M. W. Gatting 63, W. N. Slack 60, R. H. Kaschula 5-97) & 310-8 dec (M. W. Gatting 79, J. E. Emburey 79) drew with Zimbabwe 345-4 dec (R. D. Brown 108, T. W. Dunk 106) & 181-6 (A. J. Pycroft 61*).

3rd Match: v Zimbabwe (Umtali) (Limited Over) Sept 30.
Zimbabwe 129 lost to Middlesex 133-0 (J. M. Brearley 77, P. R. Downton 53*) by 10 wkts.*

4th Match: v Zimbabwe (Bulawayo) Oct 4, 5, 6.
Middlesex 231 (M. W. Gatting 71, M. W. W. Selvey 67, R. H. Kaschula 6-68) & 211 (M. W. Gatting 54) lost to Zimbabwe 231 (J. E. Emburey 5-76) & 213-6 (J. G. Heron 66, J. E. Emburey 5-70) by 4 wkts.

5th Match: v Zimbabwe (Gwelo) (Limited Over) Oct 8.
Middlesex 253-6 (P. R. Downton 100, C. T. Radley 71) beat Zimbabwe 167-7 by 88 runs.

6th Match: v Zimbabwe (Salisbury) Oct 11, 12, 13.
Middlesex 289 (M. W. Gatting 99, R. O. Butcher 50, D. A. G. Fletcher 5-48) & 244 (W. N. Slack 94, I. J. Gould 57) beat Zimbabwe 118 (R. M. Bentley 65, M. W. W. Selvey 7-45) & 333 (R. D. Brown 78, A. J. Pycroft 76, J. G. Heron 53, S. P. Hughes 6-78) by 82 runs.

1980-81: Middlesex tour of Zimbabwe

The Middlesex team went on a six-match tour of Zimbabwe in September and October 1980 with the following side: J. M. Brearley (capt), R. O. Butcher, N. G. Cowans, P. R. Downton, J. E. Emburey, M. W. Gatting, I. J. Gould, S. P. Hughes, R. J. Maru, W. G. Merry, C. T. Radley, M. W. W. Selvey, W. N. Slack and K. P. Tomlins, with as manager, D. Bennett.

The County had the better of the three limited overs games, but the three first-class fixtures were very even. Gatting had a splendid time with the bat and never failed, but the bowlers found things more difficult.

1980-81: M.C.C. to Bangladesh

A party of 14 players under the captaincy of M. D. Mence (Berks) toured Bangladesh, playing six matches including three 'Tests'. The rest of the team were M. Asif Din (Warwicks), J. H. Hampshire (Yorks), R. A. Hutton (Yorks), J. A. Jameson (Warwicks), R. V. Lewis (Dorset), J. D. Monteith (Ireland), A. Needham (Surrey), M. C. J. Nicholas (Hants), S. G. Plumb (Norfolk), S. S. Surridge (Surrey), P. H. L. E. Wilson (Surrey) and N. J. W. Stewart. The manager was J. R. Stephenson. All three 'Tests' were drawn, but M.C.C. won the single one-day International. Nicholas proved the outstanding batsman and Monteith the best bowler.

1980-81: Leicestershire tour of Zimbabwe

In March 1981, Leicester followed Middlesex's footsteps and played a series of matches in Zimbabwe. Owing to the fact that Gower was with England in the West Indies and Davison and Clift were absent, the county co-opted two non-Leicester men. The full team was R. W. Tolchard (capt), J. P. Agnew, J. C. Balderstone, T. J. Boon, P. Booth, N. E. Briers, R. A. Cobb, N. G. B. Cook, G. Forster, J. H. Hampshire (Yorks), G. J. Parsons, D. S. Steele (Derbys), L. B. Taylor and D. A. Wenlock, with D. Tebbitt as manager.

The chief point of interest was the third first-class game which was drawn with the scores level, Cook being run out on the last ball. Rain seriously affected the first three-day match.

The best innings of the tour belonged to J. H. Hampshire, who scored 112 in the final match.

1981-82: England lose to India — and the first Test for Sri Lanka

The problem of the captaincy continued to exercise the minds of the selectors at the beginning of the 1981 English season and eventually Botham resigned to allow Brearley to be re-appointed, but the latter made it clear that he did not wish to go to India. The critics were divided between Fletcher of Essex or Barclay of Sussex as tour captain. On 30 August Fletcher was appointed.

The full team was announced on 8 September as K. W. R. Fletcher (Essex) (capt), R. G. D. Willis (Warwicks) (vice-capt), P. J. W. Allott (Lancs), I. T. Botham (Somerset), G. Boycott (Yorks), G. Cook (Northants), G. R. Dilley (Kent), J. E. Emburey (Middx), M. W. Gatting (Middx), G. A. Gooch (Essex), D. I. Gower (Leics), J. K. Lever (Essex), C. J. Richards (Surrey), C. J. Tavare (Kent), R. W. Taylor (Derbys) and D. L. Underwood (Kent), with R. Subba Row as manager and B. W. Thomas as physiotherapist. There were no outstanding omissions.

Above *The England party to tour India in 1981-82, photographed at Lord's before their departure. Back: M. W. Gatting, G. Cook, D. I. Gower, J. E. Emburey, G. R. Dilley, P. J. W. Allot, C. J. Tavare, C. J. Richards, G. Saulez (scorer). Front: B. M. Thomas (physiotherapist), J. K. Lever, R. W. Taylor, D. L. Underwood, K. W. R. Fletcher (captain), R. G. D. Willis, I. T. Botham, G. A. Gooch, R. Subba Row (manager).*

Right *The first Test in Bombay of the 1981-82 tour of India. Vengsarkar snicks Dilley and Botham juggles with the ball at second slip. It was eventually held by Tavare at first slip.*

Within a few weeks, the anti-South African lobby were attacking the inclusion of Boycott and Cook on the tour and the stage was reached where the Indian Government appeared to be adamant that unless these two withdrew, the tour was off. The T.C.C.B. refused to omit the two players and the bargaining and posturing continued for about three weeks. Less than a week before the team was scheduled to depart, the Indian Government allowed the tour to go ahead and the party set out on 5 November.

Even when the side landed, the Communist Party in India called for a boycott of the Tests, but the anti-tour faction soon evaporated.

Following a warm-up match in Bombay, the tourists played a high-scoring match at Pune, which looked like a draw until Botham hit 98 in 73 minutes and gave England victory by 6 wickets. Scoring was much harder in the second match with spin predominating. Underwood had a field day and the tourists won a second match. There was a draw in Baroda, but a victory in the first one-day International.

The first Test was staged at Bombay. India struggled to 179 in their first innings, but Doshi dismissed England for 166. In the final innings the tourists required 241 to win – against all predictions, the batting surrendered to the Indian seamers and the home

country won by the large margin of 138 runs. The English officials complained about the umpiring.

In the second Test England batted with care and with Gavaskar also being careful for 708 minutes, the match drifted to a draw. The game was marred by a breach of etiquette on the part of the English captain, who showed his disgust at being dismissed by knocking over the stumps. England were without Willis in this match, due to a stomach upset. The tourists batting collapsed in the match against the North Zone, but redeemed itself in the second innings.

A splendid 88 by Vengsarkar gave India her first win in a limited-overs match, played just prior to the third Test. England objected to one of the umpires appointed for this game and the appointment was altered.

With Boycott intent on beating the record for the most runs in Test cricket, England crawled to 190 for 1 on the first day of the third Test. The Indian batsmen also broke records by adding century partnerships for the 8th and 9th wickets – the game staggered to a draw. Fletcher then made some pointed remarks about England's slow scoring: Boycott took umbrage. The scoring however did not improve in the fourth Test, though wickets fell faster and Fletcher declared to set India 306 in 360 minutes – bad

1981-82: England to India and Sri Lanka

Batting Averages

	M	I	NO	R	HS	Avge	100	c/s
G. Boycott (Yorks)	8	14	5	701	105	77.88	2	3
I. T. Botham (Som)	11	15	1	760	142	54.28	2	7
G. A. Gooch (Essex)	13	21	3	967	127	53.72	2	10
D. I. Gower (Leics)	13	18	3	755	94	50.33	0	7
C. J. Richards (Surrey)	6	6	4	97	46	48.50	0	11/1
K. W. R. Fletcher (Essex)	13	18	6	581	108	48.41	1	9
G. Cook (Northts)	7	10	1	372	104*	41.33	2	5
C. J. Tavare (Kent)	13	19	0	761	149	40.05	1	10
M. W. Gatting (Middx)	12	14	1	509	127	39.15	2	5
G. R. Dilley (Kent)	10	11	2	204	52	22.66	0	3
R. W. Taylor (Derbys)	11	10	2	132	40	16.50	0	27/1
D. L. Underwood (Kent)	11	10	5	74	22*	14.80	0	3
R. G. D. Willis (Warks)	10	6	3	26	13	8.66	0	3
J. E. Emburey (Middx)	12	12	2	79	33	7.90	0	5
J. K. Lever (Essex)	8	5	0	36	16	7.20	0	2
P. J. W. Allott (Lancs)	7	5	1	22	9*	5.50	0	3

Bowling Averages

	O	M	R	W	Avge	BB	5i
D. I. Gower	5	2	6	1	6.00	1-1	0
G. Cook	6.5	1	21	2	10.50	2-18	0
D. L. Underwood	385.3	150	784	34	23.05	6-64	3
J. E. Emburey	380.1	98	1063	42	25.30	6-33	1
R. G. D. Willis	242.1	63	687	24	28.62	4-35	0
J. K. Lever	214	45	664	20	33.20	5-100	1
I. T. Botham	317.2	64	928	25	37.12	5-61	1
M. W. Gatting	11	1	40	1	40.00	1-16	0
P. J. W. Allott	181.4	39	601	15	40.06	5-54	2
G. R. Dilley	210.2	29	767	15	51.13	3-93	0
K. W. R. Fletcher	29	2	121	2	60.50	1-6	0
G. A. Gooch	58.1	14	150	2	75.00	2-12	0

Also bowled: C. J. Richards 2-1-5-0; C. J. Tavare 4-0-18-0; R. W. Taylor 2-0-6-0.

light cut 70 minutes off this and Gavaskar took care of the rest.

Following the match Boycott flew home. He complained of stomach trouble and felt it impossible to continue. News of the forthcoming pirate tour to South Africa had not yet leaked out.

Dropped catches assisted India in the Madras Test, on the first day, and on the second India actually continued throughout the day without losing a wicket. Viswanath and Yashpal added 217. Botham for several overs kept up a barrage of derisive gestures and remarks at the batsmen – totally uncalled-for behaviour. The match was drawn.

England again complained about an umpire appointed for the deciding one-day International – but India went on to win the match and the series.

Rain interrupted the final Test, and though Botham hit a well-judged hundred, there was never a great deal of hope that a definite decision would occur, so India won the rubber one match to nil.

The better side won and England could not really lay all the blame on the umpires. Botham and Gower had a good tour, whilst Gooch improved after a tentative start. Allott also looked a better bowler, but his partner Dilley was a disappointment. In the spin department Doshi and Shastri had the edge on Underwood and Emburey.

The tourists went on to Sri Lanka, where, after a drawn three-day game, they played two limited-overs matches and then the inaugural Test against Sri Lanka. The newcomers did well up to the halfway stage, but Emburey bowled them out cheaply in the second innings and Tavare delivered the final punch with an innings of 85. There was a final game for the benefit of the baggage-man and the side arrived back in England on 24 February.

1981-82: S.A.B. English team in South Africa

The official England team landed at Gatwick airport from their tour of India and Sri Lanka. Four days later twelve England cricketers arrived at Johannesburg and the news of the English tour to South Africa hit the headlines.

The team was G. A. Gooch (Essex) (capt), J. E. Emburey (Middx), J. K. Lever (Essex), D. L. Underwood (Kent), G. Boycott (Yorks), D. L. Amiss (Warwicks), A. P. E. Knott (Kent), M. Hendrick (Derbys), W. Larkins (Northants), P. Willey (Northants), C. M. Old (Yorks) and L. B. Taylor (Leics) – three players already playing in South Africa, G. W. Humpage (Warwicks), R. A. Woolmer (Kent) and A. Sidebottom (Yorks), joined the side in the following week or so. Only the absence of Botham and Willis deprived the side of being as strong as any which could be fielded by the official England eleven.

The first reaction to the tour came from India, who threatened to cancel their proposed visit to England if any of the tourists were chosen for England. Northants allegedly demanded the withdrawal of the players' county registrations and Michael Foot, the leader of the Labour Party, demanded that the Government condemn the tourists and their action – the government refused to do this.

The fixtures began with a two-day warm-up game which was drawn. In the first one-day International Gooch hit a superb hundred, but the combination of Richards, Cook and Pollock proved too much for the tourists' attack and South Africa won fairly comfortably.

The three-day match against Western Province proved a disastrous one for the visitors – Lever broke down in his first over and then Emburey fractured his thumb, putting himself out of the rest of the tour and worse seriously weakening the tourists' spin attack. The tourists were set 249 in 240 minutes, but reached 225 for 8 when stumps were drawn.

In the 'First Test', South Africa got off to a good start, making 277 for 1 on the opening day. The English side collapsed before van der Bijl and though Gooch hit a good century when they followed on, South Africa won the game.

In the second one-day International about 14,000 watched South Africa win – van der Bijl was too accurate for the visiting batsmen and their attack was weak, since Old could not play.

The 'Second Test' saw some excellent bowling from Lever, only Kirsten showing much resistance to him, but rain reduced play and the game drifted to a draw. Procter could not captain South Africa, who were led by Richards. Rain also interferred with the third one-day International, producing an exciting finish with the tourists needing 4 off the last over – they could make only two. Rain also ruined the last match, the 'Third Test', but the English team had all the better of a draw. The T.C.C.B. announced prior to this game that the tourists would be banned from Test cricket for three years.

Although they did not win a match, the team was not outclassed and if the tour had been prolonged might well have beaten South Africa.

1981-82: S.A.B. Team to South Africa

1st Match: v S.A. Under 25 (Pretoria)   March 3, 4.
S.A.B. XI 152-7 dec (A. P. Kuiper 5-22) & 32-2 drew with S.A. Under 25 XI 170-8 dec.

2nd Match: v South Africa (Port Elizabeth) (Limited Over)   March 6.
S.A.B. XI 240-5 (G. A. Gooch 114, D. L. Amiss 71*) lost to South Africa 244-3 (S. J. Cook 82, B. A. Richards 62, R. G. Pollock 57*) by 7 wkts.

3rd Match: v Western Province (Cape Town)   March 8, 9, 10.
W. Province 263-8 dec (A. P. Kuiper 90) & 204-7 dec (P. N. Kirsten 67*) drew with S.A.B. XI 219 (G. A. Gooch 58, D. L. Amiss 52) & 225-8 (G. Boycott 95).

4th Match: v South Africa (Johannesburg)   March 12, 13, 14, 15.
South Africa 400-7 dec (S. J. Cook 114, P. N. Kirsten 88, B. A. Richards 66, R. G. Pollock 64*) & 37-2 beat S.A.B. XI 150 (D. L. Amiss 66*, V. A. P. van der Bijl 5-25) & 283 (G. A. Gooch 109, V. A. P. van der Bijl 5-79) by 8 wkts.

5th Match: v South Africa (Durban) (Limited Over)   March 17.
South Africa 231-6 beat S.A.B. XI 152 by 79 runs.

6th Match: v South Africa (Cape Town)   March 19, 20, 21, 22.
S.A.B. XI 223 (G. A. Gooch 83) & 249-3 dec (W. Larkins 95, D. L. Amiss 73*, G. A. Gooch 68) drew with South Africa 235 (P. N. Kirsten 114, J. K. Lever 6-86) & 38-0.

7th Match: v South Africa (Johannesburg) (Limited Over)   March 24.
South Africa 243-5 (S. J. Cook 62, C. E. B. Rice 58*, A. P. Kuiper 54) beat S.A.B. XI 111-7 on faster scoring rate.

8th Match: v South Africa (Durban)   March 26, 27, 28, 29.
South Africa 181-9 dec (A. J. Kourie 50*, L. B. Taylor 5-61) & 143-2 (S. J. Cook 50*) drew with S.A.B. XI 311-8 dec (R. A. Woolmer 100, D. L. Amiss 50, V. A. P. van der Bijl 5-97).

Kapil Dev batting in the 1981 Bombay Test against England, a low-scoring match comfortably won by India.

W. Millet (Ches) (Manager), N. G. B. Cook (Leics), S. J. Dennis (Yorks), C. F. E. Goldie (Cambr U), S. P. Henderson (Cambr U), R. P. Hodgson (Yorks), J. A. Jameson (Warwicks), W. G. Merry (Middx) and Mushtaq Mohammad (Northants), N. E. J. Pocock (Hants), N. P. D. Ross (Middx), F. J. Titmus (Middx). Nine of the ten matches ended in victory for M.C.C., including the single 'Test' against the United States. Jameson scored most runs and Mushtaq took most wickets, easily topping the bowling with 30 at an average of 7.30 each.

1982: M.C.C. to U.S.A.

1st Match: v American Cricket Society (Overpec Park)   Sept 18.
*M.C.C. 170 (Mushtaq 53, R. Etwaroo 7-59) *at American C.S. 125 (N. G.B. Cook 5-35) by 45 runs.*

2nd Match: v New Jersey (Elizabeth)   Sept 19.
M.C.C. 185-4 dec (J. A. Jameson 81) beat New Jersey 35 by 150 runs.

3rd Match: v Washington Cricket League (West Potomac Park)   Sept 21
M.C.C. 138-8 dec (Mushtaq 34) beat Washington C.L. 125 (H. J. Cummins 57) by 13 runs.

4th Match: v United States (Prior C.C.)   Sept 25, 26.
M.C.C. 168-9 dec (Mushtaq 58, N. E. J. Pocock 54, E. Grant 5-41) & 144-6 dec (R. P. Hodgson 65) beat United States 151 (S. J. Dennis 5-48) & 77 (Mushtaq 7-15) by 84 runs.

5th Match: v U.S.C.A. (Central Zone) (Chicago)   Sept 28.
M.C.C. 133 beat Central Zone 126 (Mushtaq 5-49) by 7 runs.

6th Match: U.S.C.A. (Central Zone) (Chicago)   Sept 29.
M.C.C. 193-4 dec (Mushtaq 59) beat Central Zone 110 by 84 runs.*

7th Match: v S. California President's XI (Los Angeles)   Oct 2.
M.C.C. 186-2 dec (S. P. Henderson 100, R. P. Hodgson 74) beat President's XI 149 (N. G. B. Cook 5-48) by 37 runs.*

8th Match: v S. California (Los Angeles)   Oct 3.
M.C.C. 206-9 dec (Mushtaq 58, B. Brown 5-69) beat S. California 142 (Mushtaq 6-33) by 64 runs.

9th Match: v N. California (San Francisco)   Oct 5.
N. California 157-8 dec (P. Muspratt 64) drew with M.C.C. 121-7.

10th Match: v N. California President's XI (Larkspur)   Oct 6.
M.C.C. 159-2 dec (J. A. Jameson 103) beat N. California President's XI 62 by 97 runs.*

1981-82: M.C.C. to Far East

The M.C.C. arranged a seven-match tour of Hong Kong, Thailand and Singapore in October 1981. The team was of almost first-class standard and consisted of M. H. Denness, E. A. Clark, F. J. Titmus, M. D. Mence, N. E. Briers, N. E. J. Pocock, A. C. D. Ingleby-Mackenzie (capt), N. G. B. Cook, M. O. C. Sturt, P. J. Kippax, D. C. Wing, J. A. Bailey (manager) and H. J. Rhodes.

The tourists won three matches, including the only two-day game; Denness scored the most runs—408, average 58.28, and Titmus took most wickets—21, average 11.76.

1981-82: M.C.C. to Far East

1st Match: v Hong Kong C.A. (Hong Kong)   Oct 17.
M.C.C. 190-8 dec (P. J. Kippax 52) drew with Hong Kong C.A. 163-9.*

2nd Match: v Hong Kong President's XI (Hong Kong)   Oct 18.
M.C.C 209-5 dec (M. H. Denness 83, N. E. Briers 52) drew with President's XI 152-9.

3rd Match: Hong Kong Island Select XI (Hong Kong)   Oct 20.
M.C.C. 122-8 dec (B. Wigley 5-30) drew with Select XI 70-7.

4th Match: v Hong Kong Mainland XI (Hong Kong)   Oct 22.
M.C.C. 216-2 dec (M. H. Denness 78, M. D. Mence 50) drew with Mainland XI 156-9 (B. Catton 51, F. J. Titmus 6-48).*

5th Match: v Royal Bangkok S.C. (Bangkok)   Oct 27.
M.C.C. 175-2 dec (M. H. Denness 95, N. E. Briers 70) beat Royal Bangkok S.C. 71 (P. J. Kippax 5-22) by 104 runs.

6th Match: v Singapore C.A. (Singapore)   Oct 30.
M.C.C. 201-2 dec (N. E. J. Pocock 86 N. E. Briers 66) beat Singapore C.A. 120 (A. Taylor 58) by 81 runs.*

7th Match: v Singapore President's XI (Singapore)   Oct 31, Nov 1.
M.C.C. 213-6 dec (M. H. Denness 106, M. D. Mence 51) beat President's XI 56 & 87 by an inns and 70 runs.

1982: M.C.C. to U.S.A.

The following team undertook a ten-match tour of the United States in September-October 1982: A. R. Lewis (capt) (Glam), F.

1982-83: Minor Counties to East Africa

Under C. G. Howard as manager, the following represented the Minor Counties C.A. on their 10-match tour of East Africa: M. D. Nurton (capt) (Oxon), M. S. A. McEvoy (Cambs), F. L. Q. Handley (Norfolk), P. D. Johnson (Lincs), S. R. Porter (Oxon), A. Griffiths (Staffs), R. D. P. Huggins (Norfolk), S. Lines (Beds), R. F. Howlett (Suffolk), D. Nicholls (Staffs), J. Smith (Shrops), I. Gemmell (Ches), R. W. Flower (Staffs), A. W. Lyon (Bucks), with J. Oliver as assistant manager. The tour was highly successful with only one match lost; McEvoy, Handley, and Johnson all made plenty of runs, while Flower with 43 wickets at 13 runs each was the outstanding bowler.

1982-83: Minor Counties to East Africa

1st Match: v Kenya XI (Nairobi) (Limited Overs)   Oct 8.
M.C.C.A. 164 lost to Kenya 166-5 (S. Khan 71) by 5 wkts.

2nd Match: v Kenya (Nairobi)   Oct 9, 10, 11.
Kenya 362-6 dec & 185 drew with M.C.C.A. 255 & 256-7 (M. D. Nurton 89).

3rd Match: v Malawi (Blantyre)   Oct 16, 17, 18.
M.C.C.A. 297 & 159-2 (F. L. Q. Handley 83) dec beat Malawi 201 & 113 (R. W. Flower 7-55) by 142 runs.

4th Match: v Malawi Chairman's XI (Mpingwe)   Oct 19.
Malawi Chairman's XI 147 lost to M.C.C.A. 149-2 by 8 wkts.

5th Match: v Malawi Select XI (Blantyre)   Oct 20 (Limited Overs).
M.C.C.A. 362 beat Malawi Select XI 172-8 by 190 runs.

6th Match: v Zambia President's XI (Mufulira)   Oct 22.
M.C.C.A. 216-8 drew with Zambia President's XI 24-1–rain.

7th Match: v Zambia (Kitwe)   Oct 24, 25.
M.C.C.A. 206-8 dec & 151-5 dec beat Zambia 110 & 150 by 97 runs.

8th Match: v Tanzania CA Chairman's XI (Dar-es-Salaam)   Oct 28.
Tanzania C.A. Chairman's XI 189 lost to M.C.C.A. 191-0 (F. L. Q. Handley 116) by 10 wkts.*

9th Match: v Tanzania (Dar-es-Salaam)   Oct 30, 31.
Tanzania 171 & 116 lost to M.C.C.A. 204-5 dec & 84-4 by 6 wkts.

10th Match: v Dar-es-Salaam C.A. (Dar-es-Salaam)   Nov 2
Dar-es-Salaam C.A. 170 lost to M.C.C.A. 171-6 by 4 wkts.

1982-83: England to Australia and New Zealand

The players who had toured South Africa the previous winter were banned from selection and thus the England team for this tour was only half strength. Without Gooch there was no settled pair of opening batsmen and rarely did England get off to a sound start.

The team which flew to Brisbane on 13 October was R. G. D. Willis (captain), D. I. Gower, G. Cook, G. Fowler, A. J. Lamb, D. W. Randall, C. J. Tavare, I. T. Botham, G. Miller, E. E. Hemmings, V. J. Marks, N. G. Cowans, R. D. Jackman, D. R. Pringle, I. J. Gould, R. W. Taylor, with D. J. Insole as manager and N. Gifford as his assistant.

Australia won the Test series by two matches to one, England's victory coming in the fourth match by the narrow margin of three runs. Australia were handicapped throughout the series by an injury to Lillee in the first Test which kept him out of the remainder. The major disappointment of the tour was the failure of Botham, his major asset in fact being his brilliant fielding.

Three England batsmen came out of the visit with credit, Gower, Lamb and Randall, but Tavare found the pace of the wickets too much for him. The side included three off-spinners, Hemmings, Miller and Marks, which was one too many, but when Randall was injured, T. E. Jesty (Hampshire) was flown out and appeared in one-day matches.

As well as the Test series England were involved in the Benson & Hedges World Cup Series, in which New Zealand also participated. England won only four of their ten matches and were thus not included in the finals. In New Zealand the team played only three one-day internationals, which proved a dismal end to the tour, as New Zealand won all three—only Gower came out of them with an untarnished reputation.

Above *Geoff Miller catches Jeff Thomson off Ian Botham to give England victory by 3 runs in the Melbourne Test.*

Below *The England party in 1982-83. Back: Jesty, Lamb, Marks, Fowler, Cook, Pringle, Cowans, Tavare, Hemmings, Gould, Jackman. Front: Miller, Botham, Gower, Willis, Taylor, Randall.*

1st Match: v Queensland (Brisbane) Oct 23, 24, 25.
Queensland 297-9 dec (H. Frei 57, R. B. Phillips 55*, A. B. Henschell 50) & 435-5 dec (G. S. Chappell 126, K. C. Wessels 103, R. B. Kerr 65, A. B. Henschell 54) beat England 372 (A. J. Lamb 117, D. I. Gower 100) & 189 (A. B. Henschell 5-60) by 171 runs.

2nd Match: v Northern New South Wales (Newcastle) Oct 27, 28, 29.
Northern N.S.W. 163 (R. B. McCosker 53, E. E. Hemmings 5-38) & 166 (G. Arms 53) lost to England 305 (C. J. Tavare 157, D. I. Gower 56, S. Hathersall 5-37) & 27-0 by 10 wkts.

3rd Match: v South Australia (Adelaide) Oct 31, Nov 1, 2, 3.
England 492-9 dec (G. Miller 83, A. J. Lamb 78, E. E. Hemmings 60*, G. Cook 58, R. D. Jackman 50*) & 226-8 dec drew with S. Australia 344 (D. W. Hookes 74, K. J. Wright 65*, P. R. Sleep 51) & 271-8 (A. M. J. Hilditch 79).

4th Match: v Western Australia (Perth) Nov 5, 6, 7, 8.
W. Australia 167 & 197 lost to England 156 (I. T. Botham 65, T. M. Alderman 5-63) & 209-9 (D. W. Randall 92, T. M. Alderman 5-67) by 1 wkt.

5th Match: v Australia (Perth) Nov 12, 13, 14, 16, 17.
England 411 (C. J. Tavare 89, D. W. Randall 78, D. I. Gower 72, B. Yardley 5-107) & 358 (D. W. Randall 115, A. J. Lamb 56, G. F. Lawson 5-108) drew with Australia 424-9 dec (G. S. Chappell 117, K. J. Hughes 62, D. W. Hookes 56, J. Dyson 52, G. F. Lawson 50) & 73/2.

6th Match: v New South Wales (Sydney) Nov 20, 21, 22, 23.
England 240 (G. Cook 99, I. J. Gould 73) & 342 (C. J. Tavare 147, G. Cook 77, M. J. Bennett 5-123) beat N.S.W. 250-9 dec (S. J. Rixon 57*, S. B. Smith 50) & 306 (P. M. Toohey 69, T. M. Chappell 61, J. Dyson 59, E. E. Hemmings 5-101). by 26 runs.

7th Match: v Australia (Brisbane) Nov 26, 27, 28, 30, Dec 1.
England 219 (A. J. Lamb 72, G. F. Lawson 6-47) & 309 (G. Fowler 83, G. Miller 60, J. R. Thomson 5-73, G. F. Lawson 5-87) lost to Australia 341 (K. C. Wessels 162, G. S. Chappell 53, B. Yardley 53, R. G. D. Willis 5-66) and 190-3 (D. W. Hookes 66*) by 7 wkts.

8th Match: v Victoria (Melbourne) Dec 4, 5, 6, 7.
England 275 (D. I. Gower 88, R. J. Bright 5-81) & 324-7 dec (A. J. Lamb 108, D. I. Gower 88) drew with Victoria 295 (G. N. Yallop 69) and 122-4 (M. D. Taylor 56*).

9th Match: v Australia (Adelaide) Dec 10, 11, 12, 14, 15.
Australia 438 (G. S. Chappell 115, K. J. Hughes 88) & 83-2 beat England 216 (A. J. Lamb 82, D. I. Gower 60) & 304 (D. I. Gower 114, I. T. Botham 58, G. F. Lawson 5-66) by 8 wkts.

10th Match: v Tasmania (Hobart) Dec 18, 19, 20.
Tasmania 273 (S. J. Reid 79, S. L. Saunders 53) & 131-5 dec (D. A. Smith 52*) lost to England 141-1 dec (G. Cook 73*, G. Fowler 63) & 264-4 (D. W. Randall 90*, G. Fowler 66, D. I. Gower 50*) by 6 wkts.

11th Match: v Tasmania (Launceston) (Limited Over) Dec 22.
Tasmania 112 lost to England 113-6 (I. T. Botham 56) by 4 wkts.

12th Match: v Australia (Melbourne) Dec 26, 27, 28, 29, 30.
England 284 (C. J. Tavare 89, A. J. Lamb 83) & 294 (G. Fowler 65) beat Australia 287 (K. J. Hughes 66, D. W. Hookes 53, R. W. Marsh 53) & 288 (D. W. Hookes 68, A. R. Border 62*, N. G. Cowans 6-77) by 3 runs.

13th Match: v Australia (Sydney) Jan 2, 3, 4, 6, 7.
Australia 314 (A. R. Border 89, J. Dyson 79) & 382 (K. J. Hughes 137, A. R. Border 83, K. C. Wessels 53) drew with England 237 (D. I. Gower 70, D. W. Randall 70, J. R. Thomson 5-50) and 314-7 (E. E. Hemmings 95).

14th Match: v Australia (Sydney) (Limited Over) Jan 11.
Australia 180 beat England 149 by 31 runs.

15th Match: v New Zealand (Melbourne) (Limited Over) Jan 13.
New Zealand 239-8 (J. G. Wright 55) beat England 237-8 (D. I. Gower 122) by 2 runs.

16th Match: v New Zealand (Brisbane) (Limited Over) Jan 15.
England 267-6 (D. I. Gower 158) beat New Zealand 213 by 54 runs.

17th Match: v Australia (Brisbane) (Limited Over) Jan 16.
England 182 (D. W. Randall 57) lost to Australia 184-3 (D. W. Hookes 54*) by 7 wkts.

18th Match: v New Zealand (Sydney) (Limited Over) Jan 20.
New Zealand 199 (B. A. Edgar 74) lost to England 200-2 (A. J. Lamb 108*, C. J. Tavare 83*) by 8 wkts.

19th Match: v Australia (Melbourne) (Limited Over) Jan 23.
England 213-5 (A. J. Lamb 94, D. W. Randall 51*) lost to Australia 217-5 (A. R. Border 54, J. Dyson 54, D. W. Hookes 50) by 5 wkts.

20th Match: v Australia (Sydney) (Limited Over) Jan 26.
England 207 beat Australia 109 by 98 runs.

21st Match: v New Zealand (Adelaide) (Limited Over) Jan 29.
England 296-5 (D. I. Gower 109, I. T. Botham 65, T. E. Jesty 52*) lost to New Zealand 297-6 (R. J. Hadlee 79, J. J. Crowe 50) by 4 wkts.

22nd Match: v Australia (Adelaide) (Limited Over) Jan 30.
England 228-6 (D. I. Gower 77) beat Australia 214-7 (D. W. Hookes 76) by 14 runs.

23rd Match: v New Zealand (Perth) (Limited Over) Feb 5.
England 88-7 lost to New Zealand 89-3 by 7 wkts.

24th Match: v New Zealand (Auckland) (Limited Over) Feb 19.
England 184-9 (D. I. Gower 84) lost to New Zealand 187-4 (G. M. Turner 88) by 6 wkts.

25th Match: New Zealand (Wellington) (Limited Over) Feb 23.
New Zealand 295-6 (G. M. Turner 94, B. A. Edgar 60) beat England 192 by 103 runs.

26th Match: v New Zealand (Christchurch) (Limited Over) Feb 26.
New Zealand 211-8 beat England 127 (D. I. Gower 53) by 84 runs.

Batting Averages		M	I	NO	R	HS	Avge	100	c/s
A. J. Lamb	(Northts)	9	18	0	852	117	47.33	2	6
D. W. Randall	(Notts)	9	17	1	732	115	45.75	1	11
D. I. Gower	(Leics)	10	19	1	821	114	45.61	2	9
E. E. Hemmings	(Notts)	9	9	3	228	95	38.00	0	3
G. Cook	(Northts)	7	14	1	428	99	32.92	0	4
I. J. Gould	(Sussex)	4	5	0	164	73	32.80	0	9/1
G. Miller	(Derby)	10	19	4	465	83	31.00	0	5
R. D. Jackman	(Surrey)	4	5	2	88	50*	29.33	0	2
C. J. Tavare	(Kent)	10	19	0	489	147	25.73	1	4
G. Fowler	(Lancs)	9	18	0	445	83	24.72	0	6
I. T. Botham	(Som)	9	18	0	434	65	24.11	0	17
R. W. Taylor	(Derby)	7	14	5	188	37	20.88	0	17/1
D. R. Pringle	(Essex)	9	16	5	207	47*	18.81	0	6
R. G. D. Willis	(Warks)	7	13	5	65	26	8.12	0	7
V. J. Marks	(Som)	4	6	0	41	13	6.83	0	5
N. G. Cowans	(Middx)	8	13	2	70	36	6.36	0	5

Bowling Averages	O	M	R	W	Avge	BB	5i
G. Cook	56	12	178	8	22.25	3-47	0
R. G. D. Willis	225	41	656	28	23.42	5-66	1
G. Miller	325	96	761	27	28.18	4-63	0
N. G. Cowans	223.4	38	745	26	28.65	6-77	1
D. R. Pringle	263.3	53	739	22	33.59	4-66	0
E. E. Hemmings	323	84	789	23	34.30	5-101	1
I. T. Botham	319.4	63	1033	29	35.62	4-43	0
R. D. Jackman	88.5	15	272	3	90.66	2-37	0
V. J. Marks	107	26	351	3	117.00	1-39	0

Also bowled: G. Fowler 6-0-43-2; A. J. Lamb 1-1-0-0

1983-84: England to Fiji, New Zealand and Pakistan

With the contingent who toured South Africa still banned from official England touring parties the team, which did not leave England until after Christmas, had a disastrous tour. Apparently at the request of the senior players the fixtures for the three-country tour were reduced to the minimum and as a result only 15 players were included: R. G. D. Willis (capt), D. I. Gower, D. W. Randall, V. J. Marks, C. L. Smith, I. T. Botham, G. Fowler, M. W. Gatting, G. R. Dilley, A. J. Lamb, C. J. Tavare, R. W. Taylor, N. A. Foster, N. G. Cowans and N. G. B. Cook, with A. C. S. Pigott co-opted for one Test. The manager was A. C. Smith, assistant N. Gifford.

The start of the tour was in Fiji with two one-day games played in most uncomfortable weather, January being quite the wrong month for cricket there. England were defeated in a Test series in New Zealand for the first time, though they did win the one-day

1st Match: v Fiji Cricket Association President's XI (Lautoka) Jan 2.
England 274-6 (M. W. Gatting 142) beat F.C.A.P. XI 76 by 198 runs.

2nd Match: v Fiji Cricket Association President's XI (Suva) Jan 3.
England 146-9 beat F.C.A.P. XI 128 by 18 runs.

3rd Match: v Auckland (Auckland) Jan 7, 8, 9.
England 220 (D. I. Gower 84, M. W. Gatting 56, M. C. Snedden 6-70) & 321 (R. W. Taylor 86, I. T. Botham 64) drew with Auckland 283-8 dec (J. G. Bracewell 104*) & 58-1.

4th Match: v Central Districts (Palmerston North) Jan 11, 12, 13.
England 294-6 dec (C. J. Tavare 89, G. Fowler 83, A. J. Lamb 51) & 300-6 dec (G. Fowler 104, I. T. Botham 80, D. W. Randall 66) drew with C. Districts 168 (V. J. Marks 5-66) & 163-2 (R. T. Hart 67, P. S. Briasco 65*).

5th Match: v Northern Districts (Hamilton) Jan 14, 15, 16.
England 287-3 dec (C. L. Smith 138*, D. I. Gower 69) & 194-2 dec (D. W. Randall 101*, C. L. Smith 50) beat Northern Districts 111 (N. A. Foster 6-30) & 293 (C. M. Presland 58, A. D. G. Roberts 58, G. P. Howarth 55) by 77 runs.

6th Match: v New Zealand (Wellington) Jan 20, 21, 22, 23, 24.
New Zealand 219 (J. J. Crowe 52, I. T. Botham 5-59) & 537 (J. V. Coney 174*, M. D. Crowe 100, B. L. Cairns 64) drew with England 463 (D. W. Randall 164, I. T. Botham 138, B. L. Cairns 7-143) and 69-0.

7th Match: v Otago (Dunedin) Jan 27, 28, 29.
England 194-8 dec (V. J. Marks 50) & 118-4 drew with Otago 152-9 dec (V. J. Marks 5-52).

8th Match: v Otago (Alexandra) Jan 30. (Limited Over)
England 297-4 (C. J. Tavare 126, A. J. Lamb 106*) beat Otago 185-8 (S. J. McCullum 97*, B. R. Blair 53) by 112 runs.

9th Match: v New Zealand (Christchurch) Feb 3, 4, 5.
New Zealand 307 (R. J. Hadlee 99) beat England 82 & 93 (R. J. Hadlee 5-28) by an innings and 132 runs.

international series. The Pakistan leg of the tour began with a Test, and a jet-lagged England side lost by 3 wickets. In the next match Botham was injured and returned home, while Willis had to withdraw from the second Test with food poisoning and Gower took over the leadership. Willis also missed the third Test and as both were drawn, Pakistan won the series one match to nil.

In some quarters the tour was regarded as the unhappiest ever undertaken by England and the newspaper allegations of drug-taking among the team in New Zealand, though not proved, did little to engender a pleasant atmosphere.

1984-85: England to Sri Lanka, India and Australia

The England team arrived in New Delhi on 31 October just before the assassination of Mrs Gandhi. This tragedy led to a rescheduling of the first fortnight. The team flew to Colombo, cancelling the first three matches in India, and played two hastily arranged games in Sri Lanka before returning to India, where the

fixture list had been adjusted and the matches began on 13 November. There was a second political tragedy, when the Deputy British High Commissioner, Percy Norris, was murdered on the eve of the first Test. It was suggested that the tour should be abandoned, but it continued and without any further political problems.

The team was D. I. Gower (captain), M. W. Gatting, R. T. Robinson, G. Fowler, M. D. Moxon, A. J. Lamb, C. S. Cowdrey, R. M. Ellison, V. J. Marks, P. J. W. Allott, N. A. Foster, N. G. Cowans, P. H. Edmonds, P. I. Pocock, P. R. Downton, B. N. French with A. S. Brown and N. Gifford as manager and assistant. The most notable omission was Botham, though the South African contingent were still banned.

The tour proved a success, with England winning the Test series by two matches to one. Gatting at last fulfilled his potential. Robinson and Fowler also had good tours with the bat, but the bowling relied heavily on Foster. Agnew was co-opted, but played in only one first-class game.

The team travelled from India to take part in the Benson & Hedges World Championship in Australia, but lost all three of their matches.

Top *Mike Gatting tucks a ball to leg in the Second Test against India at Delhi.*

Above *David Gower prepares to drive in the First Test at Bombay.*

1984-85: England to Sri Lanka, India and Australia

1st Match: v Sri Lanka Cricket Board President's XI (Colombo) Nov 7, 8, 9.
S.L.C.B.P. XI 298-9 dec (P. A. DeSilva 105) & 134-7 (D. M. Vonhagt 53) drew with England 273-9 dec (M. W. Gatting 97, D. I. Gower 86, A. J. Lamb 53).

2nd Match: v Sri Lankan XI (Colombo) (Limited Over) Nov 10.
Sri Lankan XI 178–No Result: rain.

3rd Match: v Indian Cricket Board President's XI (Jaipur) Nov 13, 14, 15.
I.C.B.P. XI 195-5 dec (A. O. Malhotra 102*) & 117-3 (M. Azharuddin 52*) drew with England 444-8 dec (R. M. Ellison 83*, D. I. Gower 82, R. T. Robinson 81, V. J. Marks 66).

4th Match: v Indian Under-25 XI (Gujarat) Nov 17, 18, 19.
England 216 (M. W. Gatting 52) & 117 lost to Indian U-25 XI 392-6 dec (M. Azharuddin 151, R. Madhavan 103*, K. Srikkanth 92) by an innings and 59 runs.

5th Match: v West Zone (Rajkot) Nov 21, 22, 23, 24.
England 458-3 dec (M. W. Gatting 136*, G. Fowler 116, R. T. Robinson 103, D. I. Gower 57) & 138-7 dec (A. Patel 5-42) drew with West Zone 393-7 dec (D. B. Vengsarkar 200*, L. S. Rajput 79).

6th Match: v India (Bombay) Nov 28, 29, Dec 1, 2, 3.
England 195 (L. Sivaramarkrishnan 6-64) & 317 (M. W. Gatting 136, P. R. Downton 62, G. Fowler 55, L. Sivaramakrishnan 6-117) lost to India 465-8 dec (R. J. Shastri 142, S. M. H. Kirmani 102) & 51-2 by 8 wkts.

7th Match: India (Pune) (Limited Over) Dec 5.
India 214-6 (D. B. Vengsarkar 105, K. Srikkanth 50) lost to England 215-6 (M. W. Gatting 115) by 4 wkts.*

8th Match: v North Zone (Bombay) Dec 7, 8, 9.
North Zone 186 & 176-3 (Gursharan Singh 50*) drew with England 377 (R. T. Robinson 138, C. S. Cowdrey 70, R. S. Ghai 7-110).

9th Match: v India (Delhi) Dec 12, 13, 15, 16, 17.
India 307 (R. N. Kapil Dev 60) & 235 (S. M. Gavaskar 65, M. B. Armanath 64) lost to England 418 (R. T. Robinson 160, P. R. Downton 74, A. J. Lamb 52, L. Sivaramakrishnan 6-99) & 127-2 by 8 wkts.

10th Match: v East Zone (Gauhati) Dec 19, 20, 21.
England 290 (G. Fowler 114, A. Kumar 5-81) beat East Zone 117 & 52 by an innings and 121 runs.

11th Match: v India (Cuttack) (Limited Over) Dec 27.
India 252-5 (R. J. Shastri 102, K. Srikkanth 99) lost to England 241-6 (M. W. Gatting 59) on scoring rate.

12th Match: v India (Calcutta) Dec 31, Jan 1, 3, 4, 5.
India 437-7 dec (R. J. Shastri 111, M. Azharuddin 110) & 29-1 drew with England 276 (A. J. Lamb 67).

13th Match: v South Zone (Secunderabad) Jan 7, 8, 9, 10.
South Zone 306 (K. Srikkanth 90, Arshad Ayub 58, J. P. Agnew 5-102) & 259-8 dec (M. Azharuddin 52) drew with England 334 (M. D. Moxon 153, M. W. Gatting 50, W. V. Raman 5-59) & 132-5.

14th Match: v India (Madras) Jan 13, 14, 15, 17, 18.
India 272 (M. B. Armanath 78, R. N. Kapil Dev 53, N. A. Foster 6-104) & 412 (M. Azharuddin 105, M. B. Armanath 95, S. M. H. Kirmani 75, N. A. Foster 5-59) lost to England 652-7 dec (M. W. Gatting 207, G. Fowler 201, R. T. Robinson 74, A. J. Lamb 62) & 35-1 by 9 wkts.

15th Match: v India (Bangalore) (Limited Over) Jan 20.
India 205-6 lost to England 206-7 (A. J. Lamb 59) by 3 wkts.*

16th Match: v India (Nagpur) (Limited Over) Jan 23.
England 240-7 (M. D. Moxon 70) lost to India 241-7 (R. N. Kapil Dev 54, S. M. Gavaskar 52) by 3 wkts.

17th Match: v India (Chandigarh) (Limited Over) Jan 27.
England 121-6 beat India 114-5 (R. J. Shastri 53) by 7 runs.

18th Match: v India (Kanpur) Jan 31, Feb 1, 3, 4, 5.
India 553-8 dec (D. B. Vengsarkar 137, M. Azharuddin 122, K. Srikkanth 84, R. J. Shastri 59) & 97-1 dec (M. Azharuddin 54*) drew with England 417 (R. T. Robinson 96, D. I. Gower 78, G. Fowler 69, M. W. Gatting 62) & 91-0.

19th Match: v Australia (Melbourne) (Limited Over) Feb 17. (day/night).
England 214-8 (A. J. Lamb 53) lost to Australia 215-3 (R. B. Kerr 87, D. M. Jones 78*) by 7 wkts.*

20th Match: v India (Sydney) (Limited Over) Feb 26. (day/night).
India 235-9 (K. Srikkanth 57) beat England 149 by 86 runs.

21st Match: v Pakistan (Melbourne) (Limited Over) Mar 2. (day/night).
Pakistan 213-8 (Mudassar Nazar 77) beat England 146 (A. J. Lamb 81) by 67 runs.

1984-85: England to Sri Lanka, India and Australia

Batting Averages

	M	I	NO	R	HS	Avge	100	c/s
M. W. Gatting (Middx)	11	17	5	1029	207	85.75	3	10
M. D. Moxon (Yorks)	3	4	0	231	153	57.75	1	2
R. T. Robinson (Notts)	11	18	3	861	160	57.40	3	1
G. Fowler (Lancs)	10	15	0	727	201	48.46	3	3
A. J. Lamb (Northts)	10	14	2	441	67	36.75	0	13
D. I. Gower (Leics)	11	15	1	482	86	34.42	0	10
N. A. Foster (Essex)	7	8	4	128	29	32.00	0	2
P. R. Downton (Middx)	9	11	3	238	74	29.75	0	20/3
C. S. Cowdrey (Kent)	9	11	1	211	70	21.10	0	9
V. J. Marks (Som)	6	8	1	142	66	20.28	0	1
P. H. Edmonds (Middx)	11	12	0	241	49	20.08	0	5
R. M. Ellison (Kent)	8	10	1	152	83*	16.88	0	2
P. J. W. Allott (Lancs)	3	3	1	29	14	14.50	0	0
B. N. French (Notts)	4	5	0	63	19	12.60	0	12/2
P. I. Pocock (Surrey)	8	9	3	48	22*	8.00	0	2
N. G. Cowans (Middx)	10	8	1	21	10	3.00	0	3

Played in one match: J. P. Agnew (Leics) 12*

Bowling Averages

	O	M	R	W	Avge	BB	5i
N. A. Foster	230.1	58	655	29	22.58	6-104	1
J. P. Agnew	45	4	205	7	29.28	5-102	1
P. H. Edmonds	498.1	184	1019	32	31.84	4-13	0
N. G. Cowans	267.5	60	916	25	36.64	3-59	0
P. I. Pocock	321.1	73	932	23	40.52	4-57	0
V. J. Marks	121	28	321	7	45.85	4-48	0
C. S. Cowdrey	114	12	442	9	49.11	3-61	0
R. M. Ellison	210.1	57	550	11	50.00	4-66	0

Also bowled: P. J. W. Allott 62.1-11-209-2; G. Fowler 1-1-0-0; M. W. Gatting 34-2-90-1; D. I. Gower 3-0-13-0; A. J. Lamb 2-1-6-1; R. T. Robinson 1-1-0-0.

1984-85: England to Sharjah

A four-nations tournament was staged in Sharjah between England, India, Pakistan and Australia. The following represented England: N. Gifford (captain), D. W. Randall, C. M. Wells, D. R. Pringle, P. H. Edmonds, B. N. French, R. M. Ellison, N. A. Foster, R. J. Bailey, P. I. Pocock, R. T. Robinson, G. Fowler, D. M. Moxon. India beat Australia in the final.

1984-85 England to Sharjah

1st Match: v Australia (Sharjah) (Limited Over) Mar 24.
England 177-8 lost to Australia 178-3 by 2 wkts.

2nd Match: v Pakistan (Sharjah) (Limited Over) Mar 26.
Pakistan 175-7 (Javed Miandad 71) beat England 132 by 43 runs.

1984-85: English Counties to Zimbabwe

Under the management of Michael Vockins, the Worcestershire secretary, the following team left England on 9 February for a 12-match tour of Zimbabwe: M. C. J. Nicholas (captain) (Hants), T. A. Lloyd (Warwicks), P. Bainbridge (Gloucs), B. C. Broad (Notts), N. G. B. Cook (Leics), M. R. Davis (Som), D. B. d'Oliveira (Worcs), G. Monkhouse (Surrey), P. G. Newman

1984-85: English Counties XI to Zimbabwe

1st Match: v Zimbabwe Country Districts (Harare) (Limited Over) Feb 13.
English Counties XI 211-6 (B. C. Broad 111) beat Zimbabwe Country Districts 162 (G. A. Hick 53) by 49 runs.*

2nd Match: v Zimbabwe (Harare) Feb 15, 16, 18.
English Counties XI 295 (B. C. Broad 64, N. F. Williams 62*) & 178-4 dec (V. P. Terry 80*, T. A. Lloyd 50) beat Zimbabwe 219-7 dec (A. C. Waller 60*) & 137 (D. L. Houghton 55, N. G. B. Cook 5-41) by 117 runs.

3rd Match: v Zimbabwe (Harare) (Limited Over) Feb 17.
Zimbabwe 232-8 beat English Counties XI 176-9 (B. C. Broad 52, I. P. Butchart 5-31) by 56 runs.

4th Match: v Zimbabwe B (Kwekwe) (Limited Over) Feb 20.
English Counties XI 214-5 (B. C. Broad 78) beat Zimbabwe B 177 by 37 runs.

5th Match: v Zimbabwe B (Bulawayo) Feb 22, 23, 25.
English Counties XI 338 (P. Bainbridge 147*, M. C. J. Nicholas 91) & 260-5 dec (V. P. Terry 135*, D. B. d'Oliveira 50) beat Zimbabwe B 331 (M. P. Jarvis 58, E. A. Brandes 56, K. G. Walton 54, A. H. Omarshah 50) & 138 (R. G. Williams 7-49) by 129 runs.

6th Match: v Zimbabwe (Bulawayo) (Limited Over) Feb 24.
English Counties XI 252-8 (V. P. Terry 77, M. C. J. Nicholas 73) lost to Zimbabwe 258-6 (R. D. Brown 80, A. C. Waller 56) by 4 wkts.*

7th Match: v Zimbabwe B (Hwange) (Limited Over) Feb 27.
Zimbabwe B 184-8 (G. Monkhouse 5-44) lost to English Counties XI 186-3 (B. C. Broad 115) by 7 wkts.

8th Match: v Zimbabwe (Harare) Mar 1, 2, 4.
English Counties XI 288 (V. P. Terry 129, B. C. Broad 59) & 174-5 dec (M. C. J. Nicholas 95, V. P. Terry 53) lost to Zimbabwe 178 (G. A. Paterson 76, N. F. Williams 7-55) & 288-7 (D. L. Houghton 84, A. C. Waller 75) by 3 wkts.

9th Match: v Zimbabwe (Harare) (Limited Over) Mar 3.
English Counties XI 149-8 (D. B. d'Oliveira 63, P. W. E. Rawson 5-33) lost to Zimbabwe 150-3 (R. D. Brown 75) by 7 wkts.

10th Match: v Zimbabwe B (Mutare) (Limited Over) Mar 6.
English Counties XI 259-9 (B. C. Broad 76, M. C. J. Nicholas 56) beat Zimbabwe B 184 (C. A. T. Hodgson 68) by 71 runs.

11th Match: v Zimbabwe (Harare) (Limited Over) Mar 9.
Zimbabwe 202-6 (G. A. Hick 61) beat English Counties XI 173-9 by 29 runs.*

12th Match: v Zimbabwe (Harare) (Limited Over) Mar 10.
Zimbabwe 243-9 (D. L. Houghton 76, A. J. Pycroft 53) beat English Counties XI 167 by 76 runs.

(Derbys), R. J. Parks (Hants), V. P. Terry (Hants), T. M. Tremlett (Hants), N. F. Williams (Middx), R. G. Williams (Northants).

Zimbabwe won all four of the one-day Internationals. The most successful of the tourists' batsmen were Terry, Broad and Nicholas, while the two Williamses and Cook proved the most effective bowlers.

1985: M.C.C. to Canada

The M.C.C. team, managed by J. R. Stephenson, was N. E. J. Pocock (captain), R. W. Tolchard, J. Cumbes, F. L. Q. Handley, S. P. Henderson, T. J. Hopper, N. J. Kemp, P. J. Kippax, R. J. Lanchbury, P. J. Lewington, R. V. Lewis, W. G. Merry and D. Wilson. Henderson topped the batting averages and Lanchbury also scored heavily. The spin bowling of Wilson, Kippax and Lewington was generally beyond the Canadians, though in the three-day match Canada fared much better than on the previous visit in 1967.

1985: M.C.C. to Canada

1st Match: v Victoria & District (Victoria) Sept 11
M.C.C. 219-5 dec (R. V. Lewis 103, R. J. Lanchbury 61) beat Victoria 110 (P. J. Kippax 5-23) by 109 runs.

2nd Match: v British Columbia League (Vancouver) Sept 13.
M.C.C. 204-2 dec (F. L. Q. Handley 121, R. W. Tolchard 52) beat British Columbia League 106 (D. Wilson 5-14) by 98 runs.*

3rd Match: v British Columbia C.A. (Vancouver) Sept 14.
M.C.C. 124 (N. J. Kemp 59) drew with British Columbia C.A. 123-9.

4th Match: v Calgary & District (Calgary) Sept 15.
Calgary 124 lost to M.C.C. 125-2 (R. V. Lewis 60) by 8 wkts.

5th Match: v Edmonton & District (Edmonton) Sept 17.
M.C.C. 241 (R. J. Lanchbury 100, S. P. Henderson 52, J. Hussein 5-38) beat Edmonton 136 (P. J. Lewington 5-50) by 105 runs.

6th Match: v Manitoba Cricket League (Winnipeg) Sept 18 (Limited Overs).
M.C.C. 271-6 (N. J. Kemp 115, S. P. Henderson 81) beat Manitoba 164-9 (G. Boodoo 66, O. Dipchand 53) by 107 runs.

7th Match: v Canada (Toronto) M.C.C. 336-2 dec (R. V. Lewis 131, S. P. Henderson 100*, R. J. Lanchbury 59) & 300-3 dec (R. J. Lanchbury 160, R. V. Lewis 64) drew with Canada 337-6 dec (E. Jack 86, R. S. A. Jayasekera 65, D. Bagot 59, B. Singh 54) & 169-4 (F. Kirmani 93*).*

8th Match: v Quebec & Ottawa (Ottawa) Sept 24.
M.C.C. 156 (C. Henry 5-42) drew with Quebec & Ottawa 73-9.

9th Match: v Toronto C.C. (Toronto) Sept 26.
M.C.C. 24-0–rain stopped play.

10th Match: v Ontario Under 25 (Toronto) Sept 27 (Limited Overs).
M.C.C. 175-8 (S. P. Henderson 65) beat Ontario Under 25 132-7 by 43 runs.

11th Match: v Hamilton & District (Cambridge) Sept 28.
Hamilton 74 lost to M.C.C. 75-1 by 9 wkts.

12th Match: v Toronto & District (Toronto) Sept 29 (Limited Overs).
M.C.C. 230-6 (N. J. Kemp 59) beat Toronto 190-9 (C. Neblett 58) by 40 runs.

1985-86: England B to Sri Lanka

This tour was originally intended to encompass three countries, but Bangladesh and Zimbabwe refused entry to players with South African connections and the tour was then rescheduled with a single longer visit to Sri Lanka. The selectors chose a blend of youth and experience, but the main reason behind the visit was to blood new players for future Test tours.

The team was M. C. J. Nicholas (capt), C. L. Smith, S. J. Rhodes, C. W. J. Athey, W. N. Slack, D. W. Randall, K. J. Barnett, M. D. Moxon, D. R. Pringle, D. V. Lawrence, N. G. B. Cook, T. M. Tremlett, J. P. Agnew and N. G. Cowans; the assistant manager N. Gifford played in the third 'Test', and the manager was P. Lush.

All five 'Tests' were drawn, the wickets not being suitable for the batch of seam bowlers sent by England and none of them improved his reputation. Slack and Smith were the best batsmen, Athey owing his average to one innings, while Barnett was laid low by a virus and went home early.

The selection of only one spinner, Cook, was foolhardy and this was proved when Gifford played in the third Test. The experiment of sending out a second team was expensive and as yet has not been repeated at this level.

1985-86: England B to Sri Lanka

1st Match: v Sri Lanka Colts (Colombo) Jan 12, 13, 14.
Sri Lanka Colts 247 (A. Ranatunga 120) & 102-2 dec drew with England B 112 (S. D. Anurasiri 5-38) & 96-3 (C. W. J. Athey 53).*

2nd Match: v Sri Lanka Board President's XI (Colombo) Jan 16, 17, 18.
S.L.B. President's XI 331-5 dec (S. Warnakulasuriya 93, A. P. Gurusinha 82, S. Wettimuny 57) & 106-1 (S. M. S. Kaluperuma 50) drew with England B 288 (C. L. Smith 116, E. A. R. DeSilva 5-85).

3rd Match: v Sri Lanka XI (Colombo) Jan 20, 21, 22, 23.
England B 363 (W. N. Slack 96, S. J. Rhodes 77, C. L. Smith 62) & 121-5 dec (S. J. Rhodes 57) drew with Sri Lanka XI 245 (A. P. Gurusinha 111, N. G. B. Cook 6-69) & 111-4.*

4th Match: Sri Lanka XI (Colombo) Jan 26, 27, 28, 29.
Sri Lanka XI 428-8 dec (S. Wettimuny 138, S. M. S. Kaluperuma 70, R. S. Mahanama 58, A. Ranatunga 52) & 127-3 drew with England B 365 (C. L. Smith 76, M. D. Moxon 52, K. J. Barnett 51 ret ill, W. N. Slack 50).

5th Match: Sri Lanka XI (Colombo) (Limited Over) Feb 1.
England B 162-8 lost to Sri Lanka XI 163-6 (D. S. B. P. Kuruppu 80) by 4 wkts.

6th Match: v Sri Lanka XI (Colombo) (Limited Over) Feb 2.
England B 178-9 (C. W. J. Athey 70) lost to Sri Lanka XI 182-6 by 4 wkts.

7th Match: v Sri Lanka XI (Kandy) (Limited Over) Feb 4.
England B 194-9 (M. C. J. Nicholas 50) beat Sri Lanka XI 190 (S. A. R. Silva 53) by 4 runs.

8th Match: v Sri Lanka XI (Kandy) Feb 6, 7, 8, 9.
Sri Lanka XI 271 (P. A. DeSilva 81, A. P. Gurusinha 67) & 180-9 dec (S. K. Ranasinghe 68) drew with England B 160 (C. D. U. S. Weerasinghe 5-49, K. P. J. Warnaweera 5-72) & 221-5 (W. N. Slack 67).

9th Match: v Sri Lanka XI (Colombo) (Limited Over) Feb 11.
Sri Lanka XI 185-8 (R. S. Mahanama 111) beat England B 177-9 (C. L. Smith 67) by 8 runs.*

10th Match: v Sri Lanka XI (Colombo) (Limited Over) Feb 13.
Sri Lanka XI 204-5 (M. A. R. Samarasekera 68, H. P. Tillekeratne 59) lost to England B 207-3 (W. N. Slack 122*, C. L. Smith 60*) by 7 wkts.*

11th Match: v Sri Lanka XI (Colombo) Feb 16, 17, 18, 19.
England B 369-8 dec (D. W. Randall 92, W. N. Slack 85, C. L. Smith 51) & 167-3 (D. W. Randall 60) drew with Sri Lanka XI 390-6 dec (M. A. R. Samarasekera 110, R. S. Mahanama 67, R. S. Madugalle 57 ret hurt, T. L. Fernando 56).*

12th Match: v Sri Lanka XI (Galle) Feb 22, 23, 24, 25.
Sri Lanka XI 231 (D. C. Wickremasinghe 87, N. G. Cowans 6-50) & 272 (H. P. Tillekeratne 105, S. Warnakulasuriya 50) drew with England B 335-6 dec (C. W. J. Athey 184, C. L. Smith 70*).*

1985-86: England B to Sri Lanka

Batting Averages	M	I	NO	R	HS	Avge	100	c/s
C. L. Smith (Hants)	6	9	1	419	116	52.37	1	1
S. J. Rhodes (Worcs)	7	10	4	292	77*	48.66	0	9/3
C. W. J. Athey (Gloucs)	7	11	1	451	184	45.10	1	13
W. N. Slack (Middx)	6	10	0	431	96	43.10	0	0
D. W. Randall (Notts)	5	8	1	212	92	30.28	0	5
K. J. Barnett (Derbys)	4	6	2	112	51*	28.00	0	1
M. C. J. Nicholas (Hants)	6	8	1	172	49	24.57	0	5
M. D. Moxon (Yorks)	4	5	0	110	52	22.00	0	5
D. R. Pringle (Essex)	5	8	3	105	38*	21.00	0	2
D. V. Lawrence (Gloucs)	5	5	1	63	27	15.75	0	1
N. G. B. Cook (Leics)	7	7	2	68	39	13.60	0	4
T. M. Tremlett (Hants)	5	5	1	27	21	6.75	0	3
J. P. Agnew (Leics)	6	4	0	10	9	2.50	0	0

Played in 3 matches: N. G. Cowans 2*, 0*; in 1 match: N. Gifford 4*.

Bowling Averages	O	M	R	W	Avge	BB	5i
N. Gifford	53	14	128	7	18.28	4-81	0
D. R. Pringle	129.5	37	273	12	22.75	4-23	0
J. P. Agnew	185.3	36	458	17	26.94	3-57	0
N. G. B. Cook	340.5	121	739	24	30.79	6-69	1
N. G. Cowans	83	22	229	7	32.71	6-50	1
D. V. Lawrence	145	22	525	7	75.00	3-50	0

Also bowled: C. W. J. Athey 12-2-51-2; K. J. Barnett 11-2-52-2; M. D. Moxon 5-1-15-0; M. C. J. Nicholas 18-5-45-1; D. W. Randall 0.4-0-7-1; W. N. Slack 8-1-15-0; C. L. Smith 23.5-6-72-1; T. M. Tremlett 123-35-302-3

1985-86: England to West Indies

The South African rebels—Gooch, Emburey, Willey and Taylor—resumed their international careers after a three-year ban, but were unable to prevent England being totally out-played: every Test was lost, the only crumb of comfort being a win in the one-day international at Port of Spain, when Gooch hit a brilliant 129 not out. In the first-class matches the averages clearly show the inability of England's batsmen.

The team was D. I. Gower (capt), M. W. Gatting, A. J. Lamb,

G. A. Gooch, I. T. Botham, D. M. Smith, R. T. Robinson, P. Willey, R. M. Ellison, J. E. Emburey, P. H. Edmonds, P. R. Downton, J. G. Thomas, N. A. Foster, L. B. Taylor and B. N. French. A. S. Brown acted as manager and R. G. D. Willis as his assistant, the latter coming in for criticism for the way he organised practice sessions.

Gatting had his nose broken in the first one-day international and W. N. Slack was flown out to replace him.

Emburey was one of the few players to come back with his reputation intact, the faster bowlers, except Thomas and the under-used Taylor, being largely ineffectual. Botham's bowling fell away badly and he set a poor example for the less seasoned players to follow; unfortunately Gower's character was not strong enough to give the right amount of encouragement which so many of the tourists needed.

1985-86: England to West Indies

1st Match: v Windward Islands (St. Vincent)   Feb 1, 2, 3, 4.
England 186 (M. W. Gatting 77, D. J. Collymore 5-34) & 94 (S. J. Hinds 5-21) lost to Windward Islands 168 & 113-3 by 7 wkts.

2nd Match: v Leeward Islands (Antigua)   Feb 7, 8, 9, 10.
Leeward Islands 236 (R. M. Otto 55, N. C. Guishard 54) & 288 (R. M. Otto 92) drew with England 409 (M. W. Gatting 71, R. T. Robinson 68, A. J. Lamb 64, G. A. Gooch 53) & 94-8 (R. B. Richardson 5-40).

3rd Match: v Jamaica (Kingston)   Feb 13, 14, 15, 16.
England 371 (M. W. Gatting 80, A. J. Lamb 78) & 177-5 dec (A. J. Lamb 60*) beat Jamaica 222 (M. C. Neita 66) & 168 by 158 runs.

4th Match: v West Indies (Kingston) (Limited Over)   Feb 18.
England 145-8 lost to West Indies 146-4 by 6 wkts.

5th Match: v West Indies (Kingston)   Feb 21, 22, 23.
England 159 (G. A. Gooch 51) & 152 (P. Willey 71) lost to West Indies 307 (C. G. Greenidge 58, H. A. Gomes 56, P. J. L. Dujon 54, R. M. Ellison 5-78) & 5-0 by 10 wkts.

6th Match: v Trinidad and Tobago (Port-of-Spain)   Feb 28, Mar 1, 2.
England 229 (R. T. Robinson 76, A. H. Gray 5-50) & 101-4 dec drew with T & B 109 (N. A. Foster 6-54) & 116-4 (A. Rajah 55*).

7th Match: v West Indies (Port-of-Spain) (Limited Over)   Mar 4.
West Indies 229-3 (I. V. A. Richards 82, R. B. Richardson 79, D. L. Haynes 53) lost to England 230-5 (G. A. Gooch 129*) by 5 wkts.*

8th Match: v West Indies (Port-of-Spain)   Mar 7, 8, 9, 11, 12.
England 176 (D. I. Gower 66, A. J. Lamb 62) & 315 lost to West Indies 399 (R. B. Richardson 102, D. L. Haynes 67, M. D. Marshall 62*, J. E. Emburey 5-78) & 95-3 by 7 wkts.

9th Match: v Barbados (Bridgetown)   Mar 14, 15, 16, 17.
England 171 (V. S. Greene 5-72) & 312 (I. T. Botham 70, P. Willey 60) lost to Barbados 217 (A. S. Gilkes 52) & 268-7 (L. N. Reifer 59*, N. Johnson 56) by 3 wkts.

10th Match: v West Indies (Bridgetown) (Limited Over)   Mar 19.
West Indies 249-7 (I. V. A. Richards 62, R. B. Richardson 62) beat England 114 by 135 runs.

11th Match: v West Indies (Bridgetown)   Mar 21, 22, 23, 25.
West Indies 418 (R. B. Richardson 160, D. L. Haynes 84, I. V. A. Richards 51) beat England 189 (D. I. Gower 66, G. A. Gooch 53) & 199 by an innings and 30 runs.

12th Match: v West Indies (Port-of-Spain) (Limited Over)   Mar 31.
England 165-9 (R. T. Robinson 55) lost to West Indies 166-2 (D. L. Haynes 77, I. V. A. Richards 50*) by 8 wkts.*

13th Match: v West Indies (Port-of-Spain)   Apr 3, 4, 5.
England 200 & 150 lost to West Indies 312 (I. V. A. Richards 87, I. T. Botham 5-71) & 39-0 by 10 wkts.

14th Match: v West Indies (Antigua)   Apr 11, 12, 13, 15, 16.
West Indies 474 (D. L. Haynes 131, M. D. Marshall 76, M. A. Holding 73, R. A. Harper 60) & 246-2 dec (I. V. A. Richards 110*, D. L. Haynes 70) beat England 310 (D. I. Gower 90, W. N. Slack 52, G. A. Gooch 51) & 170 (G. A. Gooch 51) by 240 runs.

1985-86: England to West Indies

Batting Averages

	M	I	NO	R	HS	Avge	100	c/s
M. W. Gatting (Middx)	5	9	0	317	80	35.22	0	4
A. J. Lamb (Northts)	8	16	1	438	78	29.20	0	5
D. I. Gower (Leics)	8	16	0	447	90	27.93	0	4
G. A. Gooch (Essex)	9	18	0	443	53	24.61	0	10
I. T. Botham (Som)	8	16	0	379	70	23.68	0	6
D. M. Smith (Worcs)	5	10	1	195	47	21.66	0	1
R. T. Robinson (Notts)	9	18	0	359	76	19.94	0	4
W. N. Slack (Middx)	4	8	1	134	52	19.14	0	3
P. Willey (Leics)	7	14	0	259	71	18.50	0	3
R. M. Ellison (Kent)	6	11	0	183	45	16.63	0	1
J. E. Emburey (Middx)	7	12	2	165	38	16.50	0	4
P. H. Edmonds (Middx)	7	12	4	118	20	14.75	0	2
P. R. Downton (Middx)	8	16	3	134	26	10.30	0	10/5
J. G. Thomas (Glam)	6	12	6	57	31*	9.50	0	5
N. A. Foster (Essex)	7	12	2	60	14	6.00	0	2
L. B. Taylor (Leics)	4	6	3	14	9	4.66	0	2
B. N. French (Notts)	2	3	0	9	9	3.00	0	5/1

Bowling Averages

	O	M	R	W	Avge	BB	5i
L. B. Taylor	93.3	17	259	13	19.92	3-27	0
P. Willey	81.4	17	162	8	20.25	2-38	0
N. A. Foster	180.3	33	583	23	25.34	6-54	2
R. M. Ellison	162.3	32	513	18	28.50	5-78	1
J. E. Emburey	239.2	56	648	21	30.85	5-78	1
P. H. Edmonds	233.4	43	590	18	32.77	4-38	0
J. G. Thomas	135	19	547	14	39.07	4-70	0
I. T. Botham	180.5	26	671	15	44.73	5-71	1

Also bowled: M. W. Gatting 3-0-15-1; G. A. Gooch 17-6-56-1; A. J. Lamb 0.0-0-1-0.

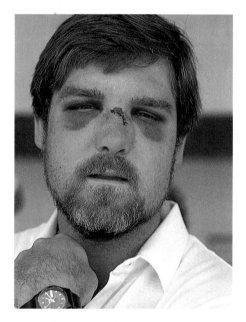

Mike Gatting had his nose broken by Malcolm Marshall during the first one-day international at Kingston, Jamaica.

The English tourists to the West Indies, 1985-6. The side lost all four Tests by a considerable margin.

1986-87: England to Australia and Sharjah

England proved the stronger of the two sides in Australia and won the series with an innings victory in the fourth Test. Australia then gained some consolation by winning the final match, achieving victory in the last over.

The England team was M. W. Gatting (capt), B. C. Broad, D. I. Gower, C. J. Richards, J. E. Emburey, C. W. J. Athey, I. T. Botham, P. A. J. DeFreitas, A. J. Lamb, G. C. Small, P. H. Edmonds, G. R. Dilley, J. J. Whitaker, N. A. Foster, B. N. French, W. N. Slack, with P. Lush and M. J. Stewart as managers.

Broad earned himself the title 'International Player of the Season', scoring three hundreds in successive Tests. Athey, who opened with Broad, also had a good tour, as did Gower, after a poor start. Dilley, Small and DeFreitas all bowled well and there was good wicketkeeping from both Richards and French.

England beat Australia in the finals of the Benson & Hedges World Series Cup and were also successful in the Perth Challenge Cup, beating Pakistan by 5 wickets.

The main criticism of the tour was of the itinerary, which was extremely gruelling due to the long programme of one-day internationals. The tour ended on 11 February, after which there was a break and the England team with some changes went to Sharjah for yet another set of one-day internationals, which England won on run rate, Pakistan, India and Australia being the other competitors.

Above Chris Broad on his way at Perth to the first of the centuries he scored in three successive Tests against Australia.

Below The England side celebrates after the Test at Melbourne.

1986-87: England to Australia

1st Match: v Queensland Country XI (Bundaberg)   Oct 18, 19, 20.
England 491-4 dec (M. W. Gatting 171, B. C. Broad 97, C. W. J. Athey 73, W. N. Slack 70, I. T. Botham 52*) & 129-3 (B. N. French 63*) drew with Queensland Country XI 160 (L. Shutle 78*).*

2nd Match: v South East Queensland Country XI (Lawes) (Limited Over)   Oct 22.
England 245-9 (A. J. Lamb 111) beat S.E. Queensland Country XI 187-6 by 58 runs.*

3rd Match: v Queensland (Brisbane)   Oct 24, 25, 26, 27.
England 135 & 339 (I. T. Botham 86, N. A. Foster 74*, A. J. Lamb 65) lost to Queensland 311-7 dec (R. B. Kerr 95, B. A. Courtice 70) & 164-5 (G. M. Ritchie 52) by 5 wkts.

4th Match: v South Australian Country XI (Wudinna) (Limited Over)   Oct 29.
S.A. Country XI 131-9 (J. Mitchell 68) lost to England 135-1 (B. C. Broad 59, W. N. Slack 54) by 9 wkts.*

5th Match: v South Australia (Adelaide)   Oct 31, Nov 1, 2, 3.
S. Australia 305-8 dec (W. B. Phillips 116, G. A. Bishop 67, P. R. Sleep 66*) & 269 (D. W. Hookes 104, W. B. Phillips 70, J. E. Emburey 6-102) lost to England 407 (J. J. Whitaker 108, A. J. Lamb 105, I. T. Botham 70, S. D. H. Parkinson 5-87) & 169-5 (B. C. Broad 63, A. J. Lamb 55) by 5 wkts.

6th Match: v Western Australian Country XI (Kalgoorlie) (Limited Over)   Nov 5.
England 293-5 (C. W. J. Athey 124) beat W.A. Country XI 176-9 by 117 runs.

7th Match: v Western Australia (Perth)   Nov 7, 8, 9, 10.
W. Australia 275 (G. R. Marsh 124, C. D. Matthews 56) & 207-8 dec (G. R. Marsh 63, G. M. Wood 53) drew with England 152 & 153-6 (A. J. Lamb 63).

8th Match: v Australia (Brisbane)   Nov 14, 15, 16, 18, 19.
England 456 (I. T. Botham 138, C. W. J. Athey 76, M. W. Gatting 61, D. I. Gower 51) & 77-3 beat Australia 248 (G. R. J. Matthews 56*, G. R. Marsh 56, G. R. Dilley 5-68) & 282 (G. R. Marsh 110, J. E. Emburey 5-80) by 7 wkts.

9th Match: v New South Wales (Newcastle)   Nov 21, 22, 23.
England 197 & 82 (M. R. Whitney 5-39) lost to N.S.W. 181 & 99-2 by 8 wkts.

10th Match: v Australia (Perth)   Nov 28, 29, 30, Dec 2, 3.
England 592-8 dec (B. C. Broad 162, D. I. Gower 136, C. J. Richards 133, C. W. J. Athey 96) & 199-8 dec (M. W. Gatting 70, S. R. Waugh 5-69) drew with Australia 401 (A. R. Border 125, S. R. Waugh 71) & 197-4 (D. M. Jones 69).

11th Match: v Victoria (Melbourne)   Dec 6, 7, 8, 9.
Victoria 101 & 345 (P. A. Hibbert 91, S. P. O'Donnell 77, G. C. Small 5-81) lost to England 263 (C. W. J. Athey 58, B. N. French 58) & 184-5 by 5 wkts.

12th Match: v Australia (Adelaide)   Dec 12, 13, 14, 15, 16.
Australia 514-5 dec (D. C. Boon 103, D. M. Jones 93, S. R. Waugh 79*, G. R. J. Matthews 73*, A. R. Border 70) & 201-3 dec (A. R. Border 100*) drew with England 455 (B. C. Broad 116, M. W. Gatting 100, C. W. J. Athey 55) & 39-2.

13th Match: v Tasmania (Hobart)   Dec 18, 19, 20, 21.
Tasmania 79 & 167 lost to England 342-9 dec (W. N. Slack 89) by an innings and 96 runs.

14th Match: v Prime Minister's XI (Canberra) (Limited Over)   Dec 23.
Prime Minister's XI 240-5 (M. R. J. Veletta 75) lost to England 241-6 (D. I. Gower 68) by 4 wkts.

15th Match: v Australia (Melbourne)   Dec 26, 27, 28.
Australia 141 (D. M. Jones 59, I. T. Botham 5-41, G. C. Small 5-48) & 194 (G. R. Marsh 60) lost to England 349 (B. C. Broad 112) by an innings and 14 runs.

16th Match: v Australia (Perth) (Limited Over)   Jan 1.
England 272-6 (B. C. Broad 76, I. T. Botham 68, A. J. Lamb 66) beat Australia 235 (D. M. Jones 104) by 37 runs.

17th Match: v West Indies (Perth) (Limited Over)   Jan 3.
England 228-9 (A. J. Lamb 71, C. J. Richards 50, J. Garner 5-47) beat West Indies 209 (A. L. Logie 51) by 19 runs.

18th Match: v Pakistan (Perth) (Limited Over)   Jan 5.
Pakistan 229-5 (Shoaib Mohammad 66, Javed Miandad 59) lost to England 232-7 (B. C. Broad 97).

19th Match: v Pakistan (Perth) (Limited Over)   Jan 7.
Pakistan 166-9 (Javed Miandad 77) lost to England 167-5 by 5 wkts.*

20th Match: v Australia (Sydney)   Jan 10, 11, 12, 14, 15.
Australia 343 (D. M. Jones 184*, G. C. Small 5-75) & 251 (S. R. Waugh 73, J. E. Emburey 7-78) beat England 275 (D. I. Gower 72, J. E. Emburey 69, P. L. Taylor 6-78) & 264 (M. W. Gatting 96, P. R. Sleep 5-72) by 55 runs.

21st Match: v West Indies (Brisbane) (Limited Over)   Jan 17.
West Indies 154 lost to England 156-4 by 6 wkts.

22nd Match: v Australia (Brisbane) (Limited Over)   Jan 18.
Australia 261-4 (D. M. Jones 101, G. R. Marsh 93) beat England 250-9 (C. W. J. Athey 111) by 11 runs.

23rd Match: v Australia (Sydney) (Limited Over)   Jan 22.
Australia 233-8 (D. M. Wellham 97) lost to England 234-7 (A. J. Lamb 77, D. I. Gower 50) by 3 wkts.*

24th Match: v West Indies (Adelaide) (Limited Over)   Jan 24.
England 252-6 (C. W. J. Athey 64, B. C. Broad 55) beat West Indies 163 by 89 runs.

25th Match: v Australia (Adelaide) (Limited Over)   Jan 26.
Australia 225-6 (A. R. Border 91, S. R. Waugh 83) beat England 192 by 33 runs.*

26th Match: v West Indies (Melbourne) (Limited Over)   Jan 30.
England 147 lost to West Indies 148-4 (I. V. A. Richards 58) by 6 wkts.

27th Match: v Australia (Melbourne) (Limited Over)   Feb 1.
Australia 248-5 (D. M. Jones 93) beat England 139 by 109 runs.

28th Match: West Indies (Devonport) (Limited Over)   Feb 3.
England 177-9 (B. C. Broad 76) beat West Indies 148 by 29 runs.

29th Match: v Australia (Melbourne) (Limited Over)   Feb 8.
Australia 171-8 (D. M. Jones 67) beat England 172-4 (I. T. Botham 71) by 6 wkts.

30th Match: v Australia (Sydney) (Limited Over)   Feb 11.
England 187-9 (B. C. Broad 53) beat Australia 179-8 by 8 runs.

1986-87: England to Australia and Sharjah

Batting Averages		M	I	NO	R	HS	Avge	100	c/s
N. A. Foster	(Essex)	4	6	2	172	74*	43.00	0	4
B. C. Broad	(Notts)	10	18	2	679	162	42.43	3	7
I. T. Botham	(Som)	8	14	2	481	138	40.08	1	11
B. N. French	(Notts)	3	5	2	113	58	37.66	0	9/1
D. I. Gower	(Leics)	9	16	2	508	136	36.28	1	4
A. J. Lamb	(Northts)	10	18	1	534	105	31.41	1	11
J. J. Whitaker	(Leics)	5	7	0	214	108	30.57	1	2
M. W. Gatting	(Middx)	10	18	0	520	100	28.88	1	11
C. W. J. Athey	(Gloucs)	9	16	1	422	96	28.13	0	7
C. J. Richards	(Surrey)	9	14	1	335	133	25.76	1	25/3
J. E. Emburey	(Middx)	9	14	3	279	69	25.36	0	6
W. N. Slack	(Middx)	5	9	0	184	89	20.44	0	5
P. A. J. DeFreitas	(Leics)	7	10	2	130	40	16.25	0	1
G. R. Dilley	(Kent)	6	6	3	39	32	13.00	0	1
G. C. Small	(Warwicks)	8	11	3	100	26	12.50	0	4
P. H. Edmonds	(Middx)	9	10	2	95	27	11.87	0	7

Bowling Averages	O	M	R	W	Avge	BB	5i
G. C. Small	258.4	72	626	33	18.96	5-48	1
M. W. Gatting	92	27	195	9	21.66	4-31	0
N. A. Foster	149	40	352	16	22.00	4-20	0
I. T. Botham	182.1	41	496	18	27.55	5-41	2
G. R. Dilley	231.1	44	685	21	32.61	5-68	1
J. E. Emburey	463.5	131	1023	31	33.00	7-78	1
P. A. J. DeFreitas	239	43	754	22	34.27	4-44	0
P. H. Edmonds	428.4	122	929	25	37.16	3-37	0

Also bowled: C. W. J. Athey 4-0-25-0; A. J. Lamb 1-1-0-0

The following took part in the matches in Sharjah only: G. A. Gooch, R. T. Robinson, N. H. Fairbrother, D. J. Capel, R. J. Bailey.

1986-87: England to Sharjah

1st Match: v India (Sharjah) (Limited Over) Apr 2.
England 211-7 (B. C. Broad 57) lost to India 214-7 (R. N. Kapil Dev 64, K. Srikkanth 56) by 3 wkts.

2nd Match: v Pakistan (Sharjah) (Limited Over) Apr 7.
Pakistan 217-9 (Javed Miandad 60) lost to England 220-5 (R. T. Robinson 83, B. C. Broad 65) by 5 wkts.

3rd Match: v Australia (Sharjah) (Limited Over) Apr 9.
England 230-6 (G. A. Gooch 86) beat Australia 219-9 (A. R. Border 84, D. C. Boon 73) by 11 runs.

1986-87: Yorkshire to West Indies

The side consisted of P. Carrick (capt), M. D. Moxon, A. A. Metcalfe, R. J. Blakey, K. Sharp, J. D. Love, D. L. Bairstow, A. Sidebottom, P. J. Hartley, P. W. Jarvis, S. J. Dennis, S. N. Hartley, P. E. Robinson and S. D. Fletcher. The Yorkshire team spent three weeks in St Lucia and Barbados before the 1987 English season. The team lost only two of their matches and managed to beat Barbadoes in a 50-overs game, as well as draw the only first-class match, against the Windward Islands.

1986-87: Yorkshire to West Indies

1st Match: v Windward Is (Castries) March 24, 25, 26
Yorkshire 213 (M. D. Moxon 75) & 260-5 dec (M. D. Moxon 105, R. J. Blakey 71) drew with Windward Is 226 & 140-5.

2nd Match: v Windward Is (Castries) (Limited Overs) March 28.
Windward Is 228-3 (L. D. John 103*, D. Joseph 63) beat Yorkshire 210 (J. D. Love 51, K. Sharp 50) by 18 runs.

3rd Match: v Police (Weymouth) (Limited Overs) March 31.
Police 111 lost to Yorkshire 113-5 (A. A. Metcalfe 55*) by 5 wkts.

4th Match: v Empire (Bank Hall) (Limited Overs) April 1
Yorkshire 186-7 beat Empire 127 by 59 runs.

5th Match: v Wanderers (Dayrells Road) April 3
Wanderers 170-7 (M. J. Sealy 73) lost to Yorkshire 171-5 (K. Sharp 58) by 5 wkts.

6th Match: v Barbados (Bridgetown) (Limited Overs) April 6.
Yorkshire 211-6 beat Barbados 201 by 10 runs.

7th Match: v Barbados Cricket League (Blenheim) (Limited Overs) April 7.
Barbados C.L. 181 beat Yorkshire 179-8 by runs.

8th Match: v Carlton (Black Rock) (Limited Overs) April 8.
Yorkshire 176-7 beat Carlton 120 by 59 runs.

9th Match: v Spartan (Queen's Park) (Limited Overs) April 10.
Yorkshire 198-8 beat Spartan 104 by 94 runs.

1986-87: Lancashire to Jamaica

The Lancashire players were D. P. Hughes (capt), C. H. Lloyd, G. D. Mendis, M. R. Chadwick, D. W. Varey, N. J. Speak, A. N. Hayhurst, P. J. W. Allott, W. K. Hegg, I. Folley, I. C. Davidson, A. J. Murphy, J. Simmons. Their brief tour of Jamaica was not very successful in that all three matches were lost, but the tour gave Jamaican players some good practice for the Shell Shield matches.

1986-87: Lancashire to Jamaica

1st Match: v Southern Parishes (Mandeville) (Limited Overs) March 25.
Lancashire 97 lost to Southern Parishes 99-4 by 6 wkts.

2nd Match: v Jamaica (Sabina Park) (Limited Overs) March 27.
Lancashire 189-6 (C. H. Lloyd 52*) lost to Jamaica 190-5 (M. C. Neita 65) by 5 wkts.

3rd Match: v Jamaica (Sabina Park) March 28, 29, 30.
Lancashire 97 & 201 (D. M. Varey 66, N. O. Perry 5-39) lost to Jamaica 264-9 dec (C. A. Davidson 73, J. C. Adams 58) & 39-1 by 9 wkts.

England's captain Mike Gatting and Pakistani umpire Shakoor Rana during their unsavoury altercation on the second day of the Second Test. The argument led to the third day being abandoned while an apology was sought from Gatting.

1987-88: England to Pakistan, India, New Zealand and Australia

The England selectors chose three squads of players to tour on the three legs of the winter programme – the World Cup held in India and Pakistan, the Test tour of Pakistan and the Test tour of New Zealand. All three squads were under the captaincy of M. W. Gatting (Middx) with J. E. Emburey (Middx) as vice-captain. The following were selected in all three squads: C. W. J. Athey (Gloucs), B. C. Broad (Notts), P. A. J. DeFreitas (Leics), G. R. Dilley (Worcs), N. A. Foster (Essex), E. E. Hemmings (Notts), R. T. Robinson (Notts), P. R. Downton (Middx), A. J. Lamb (Northants), D. R. Pringle (Essex) and G. C. Small (Warwicks) were selected for the World Cup only; D. J. Capel (Northants), N. H. Fairbrother (Lancs), B. N. French (Notts) and P. W. Jarvis (Yorks) were selected for both Test tours; N. G. B. Cook (Northants) & R. C. Russell (Gloucs) were selected for Pakistan Tests only and C. J. Richards (Surrey) and M. D. Moxon (Yorks) were selected for New Zealand only. Dilley failed a fitness test and was replaced in the World Cup squad by P. W. Jarvis. P. Lush and M. J. Stewart were managers of the three legs of the tour.

In the World Cup, which ran from 8 October to 8 November, England came second in Group B with four wins from six matches and thus qualified for the semi-finals against India. A century from Gooch enabled them to win by 35 runs and England then met Australia in the final at Calcutta. England were beaten by 7 runs, D. C. Boon with 75 winning the Man of the Match award.

England then began their tour of Pakistan. It was an arrangement which was ill-conceived, since England had played Pakistan, not only in the World Cup, but also a few months previously in England. The Test series was completely overshadowed by the acrimonious argument between the England captain and the umpire, Shakoor Rana, on the second day of the Faisalabad Test. The third day's play was abandoned while a written apology was extracted from the England captain. The remainder of the tour was completed amidst a mounting tide of newspaper comment. The fact that the T.C.C.B. awarded the England players a cash bonus for their behaviour on the tour added fuel to the press coverage. England lost the series one match to nil.

The players came home for Christmas and then flew to New Zealand for the series there, plus a mini-series in Australia. All three Tests in New Zealand were drawn and there were further problems with the unsportsmanlike actions of some players. Most cricket lovers were relieved when the winter programme ended.

1987-88: England in the World Cup

1st Match: v West Indies (Gujranwala) (Limited Over) Oct 9.
West Indies 243-7 (R. B. Richardson 53) lost to England 246-8 (A. J. Lamb 67) by 2 wkts.*

2nd Match: v Pakistan (Rawalpindi) (Limited Over) Oct 12, 13.
Pakistan 239-7 (Salim Malik 65, Ijaz Ahmed 59) beat England 221 by 18 runs.

3rd Match: v Sri Lanka (Peshawar) (Limited Over) Oct 17.
England 296-4 (G. A. Gooch 84, A. J. Lamb 76, M. W. Gatting 58) beat Sri Lanka 158-8 on faster scoring rate.

4th Match: v Pakistan (Karachi) (Limited Over) Oct 20.
England 244-9 (C. W. J. Athey 86, M. W. Gatting 60) lost to Pakistan 247-3 (Rameez Raja 113, Salim Malik 88) by 7 wkts.

5th Match: v West Indies (Jaipur) (Limited Over) Oct 26.
England 269-5 (G. A. Gooch 92) beat West Indies 235 (R. B. Richardson 93, I. V. A. Richards 51) by 34 runs.

6th Match: v Sri Lanka (Pune) (Limited Over) Oct 30.
Sri Lanka 218-7 (R. L. Dias 80) lost to England 219-2 (G. A. Gooch 61, R. T. Robinson 55) by 8 wkts.

7th Match: v India (Bombay) (Limited Over) Nov 5.
England 254-6 (G. A. Gooch 115, M. W. Gatting 56) beat India 219 (M. Azharuddin 64) by 35 runs.

8th Match: v Australia (Calcutta) (Limited Over) Nov 8.
Australia 253-5 (D. C. Boon 75) beat England 246-8 (C. W. J. Athey 58) by 7 runs.

1987-88: England to Pakistan

1st Match: v Pakistan President's XI (Rawalpindi) Nov 14, 15, 16.
England 385 (R. T. Robinson 118, C. W. J. Athey 101 ret hurt, D. J. Capel 67) drew with Pakistan President's XI 318-8 (Asif Mujtaba 157, Asif Mohammad 56).

2nd Match: v Pakistan (Lahore) (Limited Over) Nov 18.
Pakistan 166 lost to England 167-8 by 2 wkts.

3rd Match: v Pakistan (Karachi) (Limited Over) Nov 20.
England 263-6 (G. A. Gooch 142, D. J. Capel 50) beat Pakistan 240-8 (Rameez Raja 99) by 23 runs.*

4th Match: v Pakistan (Peshawar) (Limited Over) Nov 22.
England 236-8 (B. C. Broad 66, G. A. Gooch 57, M. W. Gatting 53) beat Pakistan 138 (Salim Malik 52) by 98 runs.

5th Match: v Pakistan (Lahore) Nov 25, 26, 27, 28.
England 175 (Abdul Qadir 9-56) & 130 lost to Pakistan 392 (Mudassar Nazar 120, Javed Miandad 65) by an innings and 87 runs.

6th Match: v Punjab Chief Minister's XI (Sahiwal) Dec 2, 3, 4.
England 279 (R. T. Robinson 51, Mushtaq Ahmed 6-81) & 222-5 dec (R. T. Robinson 76, N. H. Fairbrother 66) drew with Punjab Chief Minister's XI 215 (Zahoor Elahi 62) & 21-3.

7th Match: v Pakistan (Faisalabad) Dec 7, 8, 9, 11, 12.
England 292 (B. C. Broad 116, M. W. Gatting 79, Iqbal Qasim 5-83) & 137-6 (G. A. Gooch 65) drew with Pakistan 191 (Salim Malik 60) & 51-1.

8th Match: v Pakistan (Karachi) Dec 16, 17, 18, 20, 21.
England 294 (D. J. Capel 98, J. E. Emburey 70, Abdul Qadir 5-88) & 258-9 (G. A. Gooch 93, J. E. Emburey 74*, Abdul Qadir 5-98) drew with Pakistan 353 (Aamer Malik 98*, Abdul Qadir 61, Salim Malik 55, Rameez Raja 50, P. A. J. DeFreitas 5-86).

1987-88 England to New Zealand and Australia

1st Match: v Wellington (Wellington) Jan 18, 19, 20.
Wellington 188-6 dec (G. P. Burnett 87*) drew with England 310-3 (B. C. Broad 100 ret hurt, M. D. Moxon 62, M. W. Gatting 82).

2nd Match: v Wellington (Wellington) (Limited Over) Jan 21.
Wellington 202 (G. P. Burnett 63) lost to England 203-2 (M. D. Moxon 59, C. W. J. Athey 50) by 8 wkts.*

3rd Match: v Northern Districts (Hamilton) Jan 23, 24, 25.
Northern Districts 242-4 dec (D. J. White 64, B. G. Cooper 116*) & 254-4 dec (D. J. White 80, G. A. Hick 146) lost to England 203-2 dec (B. C. Broad 75, M. W. Gatting 54*) & 299-3 (R. T. Robinson 166, C. W. J. Athey 60) by 7 wkts.

4th Match: v Australia (Sydney) Jan 29, 30, 31, Feb 1, 2.
England 425 (B. C. Broad 139) drew with Australia 214 (D. M. Jones 56) & 328-2 (D. C. Boon 184*, G. R. Marsh 56).

5th Match: v Australia (Melbourne) (Limited Over) Feb 4. (day/night)
Australia 235-6 (G. R. Marsh 87) beat England 213-8 by 22 runs.

6th Match: v Shell XI (New Plymouth) Feb 7, 8, 9.
England 243-6 dec (R. T. Robinson 74) & 165-9 dec lost to Shell XI 139 & 271-5 (A. H. Jones 72) by 5 wkts.

7th Match: v New Zealand (Christchurch) Feb 12, 13, 14, 16, 17.
England 319 (B. C. Broad 114, M. D. Moxon 70, D. K. Morrison 5-69) & 152 drew with New Zealand 168 (G. R. Dilley 6-38) & 130-4 (A. H. Jones 54*).

8th Match: v President's XI (Dunedin) Feb 19, 20, 21.
President's XI 181-7 dec (K. R. Rutherford 57) & 214-7 dec (R. T. Latham 58*) lost to England 236-7 dec (M. D. Moxon 117*) and 163-2 (M. W. Gatting 97*) by 8 wkts.

9th Match: v New Zealand (Auckland) Feb 25, 26, 27, 28, 29.
New Zealand 301 (J. G. Wright 103, G. R. Dilley 5-60) & 350-7 dec (M. J. Greatbatch 107*, T. J. Franklin 62) drew with England 323 (M. D. Moxon 99, R. T. Robinson 54).

10th Match: v New Zealand (Wellington) Mar 3, 4, 5, 6, 7.
New Zealand 512-6 dec (M. D. Crowe 143, K. R. Rutherford 107*, M. J. Greatbatch 68, J. G. Bracewell 54) drew with England 183-2 (M. D. Moxon 81*, B. C. Broad 61).

11th Match: v New Zealand (Dunedin) (Limited Over) Mar 9.
New Zealand 204 (J. G. Wright 70) lost to England 207-5 (N. H. Fairbrother 50) by 5 wkts.*

12th Match: v New Zealand (Christchurch) (Limited Over) Mar 12.
New Zealand 186-8 lost to England 188-4 (B. C. Broad 56) by 6 wkts.

13th Match: v New Zealand (Napier) (Limited Over) Mar 16.
England 219 (B. C. Broad 106) lost to New Zealand 223-3 (J. G. Wright 101, M. J. Greatbatch 64) by 7 wkts.*

14th Match: v New Zealand (Auckland) (Limited Over) Mar 19.
England 208 (N. H. Fairbrother 54) lost to New Zealand 211-6 (A. H. Jones 90) by 4 wkts.

1987-88: England to Pakistan, India, New Zealand and Australia

Batting Averages

	M	I	NO	R	HS	Avge	100	c/s
M. D. Moxon (Yorks)	8	10	2	482	117*	60.25	1	7
R. T. Robinson (Notts)	11	18	2	750	166	46.87	2	3
B. C. Broad (Notts)	12	18	1	788	139	46.35	4	2
J. E. Emburey (Middx)	10	13	4	409	74*	45.44	0	5
M. W. Gatting (Middx)	11	16	3	505	97*	38.84	0	2
P. W. Jarvis (Yorks)	6	6	3	93	36*	31.00	0	1
C. W. J. Athey (Gloucs)	11	18	1	456	101*	26.82	1	6
B. N. French (Notts)	10	12	3	235	47	26.11	0	26/1
N. H. Fairbrother (Lancs)	8	11	2	202	66	22.44	0	5
E. E. Hemmings (Notts)	7	4	2	43	34	21.50	0	0
D. J. Capel (Northts)	12	15	1	295	98	21.07	0	4
N. A. Foster (Essex)	5	6	1	86	39	17.20	0	3
N. V. Radford (Worcs)	4	2	0	31	23	15.50	0	3
C. J. Richards (Surrey)	2	3	1	30	20*	15.00	0	4
G. R. Dilley (Worcs)	10	9	6	36	23	12.00	0	3
N. G. B. Cook (Northants)	5	7	1	72	32	12.00	0	0
P. A. J. DeFreitas (Leics)	7	11	0	143	41	13.00	0	2
R. C. Russell (Gloucs)	1	1	0	4	4	4.00	0	0

Bowling Averages

	O	M	R	W	Avge	BB	5i
G. R. Dilley	251.1	56	712	27	26.37	6-38	2
N. A. Foster	130	33	330	12	27.50	4-42	0
N. G. B. Cook	129.2	46	277	10	27.70	3-37	0
N. V. Radford	134	32	351	11	31.90	4-24	0
M. W. Gatting	36.2	8	99	3	33.00	1-17	0
P. A. J. DeFreitas	214.2	54	578	17	34.00	5-86	1
D. J. Capel	241.2	52	648	19	34.10	3-50	0
P. W. Jarvis	176	45	461	13	35.46	4-24	0
J. E. Emburey	373.2	123	783	15	52.20	3-49	0
E. E. Hemmings	226.1	60	579	11	52.63	4-70	0

Also bowled: B. C. Broad 1-0-4-0; G. A. Gooch 2-1-4-0; C. W. J. Athey 4-0-25-0; N. H. Fairbrother 2-0-9-0; M. D. Moxon 4-0-8-0.

The following appeared in the World Cup only and in no first-class matches: A. J. Lamb, D. R. Pringle, P. R. Downton, G. C. Small.

Australian captain Alan Border and his team celebrate after beating England by 7 runs at Calcutta to win the final of the 1987 Reliance World Cup.

TOURS TO ENGLAND

◆

A Record of All Important Cricket Tours to England,
with Accounts, Results and Statistics,
from the Australian Aboriginal Tour of 1868
to the Second Aboriginal Tour of 1988

Introduction

The first overseas cricket tour was by the English side which visited North America in 1859; it was a success both financially and socially. In the early 1860s two English teams travelled to Australia and were equally successful.

Cricket tours to England did not emulate this initial triumph. The first tourists came in 1868–they had arranged to come in 1867, but misfortune overtook them even before they left home and the proposed trip was almost cancelled completely. The 1868 team were more of a curiosity than a serious cricketing outfit, composed of Australian Aborigines who gave exhibitions of spear-throwing and other similar demonstrations between their cricketing matches. Six years later the next tourists were in fact American baseball players trying to persuade the British public to take up the game and played cricket only as a sideline.

So it was not until 1878, 19 years after the first English team went abroad, that a serious cricket team landed in England interested only in playing the game at a first-class standard. This 1878 Australian side drew enormous crowds and went home with huge profits. The prospects for future visitors seemed assured. In 1880 the Canadians came; the tour was an utter failure and due to lack of money collapsed in mid-season. The Australians also tried a second visit the same summer. The organisers made a complete mess of the fixtures and nearly all the matches for the first half of the summer were little more than exhibition games against teams of 18. Luckily the team was very successful and late in the season some first-class matches were added, plus the First Test in England–these games enabled the side to make a fair profit and Australian teams began to visit England biennially.

The Australian visitors always attracted the public and were virtually certain of financial success, but, at least until after the Second World War, none of the other major cricketing countries could tour England with any certainty that the receipts at the

Left *Michael Holding leaps into his delivery stride past umpire 'Dicky' Bird during the final Test at the Oval in 1976. He annihilated England, taking 8-92 in their first innings and 6-57 in their second.*

Right *Greg Chappell was Australia's greatest batsman of the 1970s. Here he drives through the covers in the Old Trafford Test of 1977, when in the second innings he made 112 out of Australia's total of 218. Rival skipper Tony Greig is at short leg.*

turnstiles would cover costs. The teams were almost entirely composed of amateurs, many of whom sacrificed a great deal to spend four months playing cricket in England.

Recent years have seen a fundamental change in this established pattern. The principal players from all the leading overseas countries have become as professional as the English county players—in fact many of them are English county players! This levelling of standards has meant a keener edge to all Test Matches staged in England, but in contrast the county matches against the tourists have been turned, first by the tourists and now by many countries, into little more than practice matches—as the 1983 New Zealand manager pointed out. The public have therefore largely deserted these mock contests. Can anything be done to save them? One drastic remedy might be to count the matches as part of the County Championship. This would at least force the county teams to play seriously and so create some return of public interest. Having spent many hours reading through the reports of the multitude of exciting matches played between the counties and the tourists, it seems a great pity for these gems to sink into farce.

A second change of recent vintage is the introduction of the twin-tour, which has been a mixed blessing. It allows the Australians and West Indians to visit more frequently and since both make very substantial profits, seems to be quite sensible; on the other hand the country coming first in a twin-tour year has a very good chance of a thoroughly miserable experience. The most recent season, that of 1984, has provided cricket lovers with an ideal tourists' summer—beautiful weather allied to a very strong West Indian team, a combination which brought the crowds back to all the international matches and on a few occasions even to the county fixtures.

Since 1878 the visit of a touring team to England has been the highlight of the cricket season and international competition has done a great deal to raise the standard of cricket; without the development of cricket overseas the game would have either changed radically or fossilised: English cricket owes quite a debt to the pioneers of the touring team.

Scope of work
This volume contains every tour to England on which first-class

203

Kapil Dev was India's outstanding bat and bowler on the 1982 tour. Here he cuts a ball in the Second Test at Old Trafford. Bob Taylor is behind the stumps.

matches have been played. In addition certain other tours which the author considers of historical importance have been included. Regrettably the volume could not include all cricket tours to England, but especially since the development of international airlines, the numbers of sides coming to England has increased enormously. The other tours which have been excluded are ones

from the continent of Europe, as in the companion volume *England on Tour*, because they are felt to be not only too numerous, but also of a minor nature.

Definition of a first-class match

The potted scores of all the tourists' matches are given with Test Match details in **bold type** and non-first-class match information in *italics*. The averages are compiled from first-class matches only. The list of first-class is in accordance with the details set out in *A Guide to First Class Cricket Matches Played in the British*

Isles, published by the Association of Cricket Statisticians,

Acknowledgements

The great majority of tours detailed in this work have been the subject of individual books and in some cases several books have appeared on a single tour. In addition many leading cricketers have written about the tours in their autobiographies, and although it is impracticable to list all these references, the author acknowledges his debt to them. He also wishes to acknowledge the use made of the principal cricketing annuals and magazines, namely *Wisden's Cricketers' Almanack, Lillywhite's Cricketers' Annual, Lillywhite's Cricketers' Companion, Playfair Cricket Annual*, the weekly magazine *Cricket, Playfair Cricket Monthly, Wisden Cricket Monthly, The Cricketer, Haygarth's Scores and Biographies, Cricket Almanack of New Zealand, South African Cricket Annual, Indian Cricket, Test Tours of the West Indies* and *Cricket Quarterly*.

Despite the volume of literature on cricket tours, it is surprising that some matches played by major touring teams to England have not been covered in print other than in newspapers, even in potted form. Even the 1981 Australians played a match which is not mentioned in *Wisden's Almanack* or contemporary cricket magazines. The author acknowledges with his thanks the research done by the following in an effort to ensure that all matches are included in this volume: D. A. Lambert, C. J. Clynes, C. J. Slagter, J. Stockwell, K. Warsop, S. S. Perera, P. R. Thorn, and M. P. Ronayne.

Grateful thanks are due to Philip Bailey for his meticulous checking of the tour averages and the proofs in general, to Leigh Scaife for her general assistance and to Peter Arnold for his advice and guidance.

Peter Wynne-Thomas

Summary of Tours

t tied match   *tour included Test Match(es)

Matches abandoned due to rain are included as draws, but cancelled matches are not included. Fill-in matches played when official games ended early on the final day are not included.

	Tourists	Captain	Manager	Results All matches M	W	L	D	First class M	W	L	D
1868	Australian Aborigines	C. Lawrence	W. R. Hayman	47	14	14	19				
1874	American Baseball	A. G. Spalding		7	4	0	3				
1878	1st Australians	D. W. Gregory	J. Conway	37	18	7	12	15	7	4	4
1878	Proposed Parsis			Cancelled							
1880	1st Canadians	T. Jordan		17	5	6	6				
*1880	2nd Australians	W. L. Murdoch	G. Alexander	37	21	4	12	9	4	2	3
*1882	3rd Australians	W. L. Murdoch	C. W. Beal	38	23	4	11	33	18	4	11
*1884	4th Australians	W. L. Murdoch	G. Alexander	32	18	7	7	31	17	7	7
1883	1st Philadelphians	R. S. Newhall		18	8	5	5				
*1886	5th Australians	H. J. H. Scott	B. J. Wardill	40	9	8	23	38	9	7	22
1886	1st Parsis	D. H. Patel		27	1	17	9				
1887	2nd Canadians	E. R. Ogden	G. G. S. Lindsay	19	5	5	9				
*1888	6th Australians	P. S. McDonnell	C. W. Beal	40	19	14	7	37	17	13	7
1888	2nd Parsis	P. D. Kanga		31	8	11	12				
*1890	7th Australians	W. L. Murdoch	H. F. Boyle	39	13	16	10	35	10	16	9
*1893	8th Australians	J. McC. Blackham	V. Cohen	36	18	10	8	31	14	10	7
1894	1st South Africans	H. H. Castens	W. V. Simkins	24	12	5	7				
*1896	9th Australians	G. H. S. Trott	H. A. Musgrove	34	19	6	9	34	19	6	9
1897	3rd Philadelphians	G. S. Patterson	M. C. Work	15	2	9	4	15	2	9	4
*1899	10th Australians	C. Hill	B. J. Wardill	35	16	3	16	35	16	3	16
1900	1st West Indians	R. S. A. Warner	W. C. Nock	17	5	8	4				
1901	2nd South Africans	M. Bisset	G. A. Lohmann	25	13	9	2t	15	5	9	0t
*1902	11th Australians	J. Darling	B. J. Wardill	39	23	2	14	37	21	2	14
1903	4th Philadelphians	J. A. Lester		17	7	6	4	15	6	6	3
1903	Proposed Fijians			Cancelled							
1904	Proposed Indians	M. E. Pavri		Cancelled							
1904	3rd South Africans	F. Mitchell	G. Allsop	26	13	3	9t	22	10	2	9t
*1905	12th Australians	J. Darling	F. Laver	38	16	3	19	35	15	3	17
1906	2nd West Indians	H. B. G. Austin		20	7	10	3	13	3	8	2
*1907	4th South Africans	P. W. Sherwell	G. Allsop	31	12	4	6	27	17	4	6
1907	Proposed Indians	K. S. Ranjitsinhji									
1908	5th Philadelphians	J. A. Lester	E. M. Cregar	16	7	6	3	10	4	6	0
1909	13th Australians	M. A. Noble	F. Laver	41	14	4	23	37	11	4	22
1911	1st Indians	H. H. Maharajah of Patiala	J. M. Divecha	23	6	15	2	14	2	10	2
*1912	14th Australians	S. E. Gregory	G. S. Crouch	38	9	8	21	37	9	8	20
*1912	5th South Africans	F. Mitchell	G. Allsop	37	13	8	16	37	13	8	16
1919	A.I.F.	C. Kelleway H. L. Collins		32	13	4	15	28	12	4	12

	Tourists	Captain	Manager	All matches				First class			
				M	W	L	D	M	W	L	D
*1921	15th Australians	W. W. Armstrong	S. Smith	39	23	2	14	34	21	2	11
1922	3rd Canadians	N. Seagram	H. Dean	11	0	4	7				
1923	3rd West Indians	H. B. G. Austin	R. H. Mallett	28	13	7	8	20	6	7	7
*1924	6th South Africans	H. W. Taylor	G. Allsop	38	8	9	21	35	8	9	19
*1926	16th Australians	H. L. Collins	S. Smith	40	12	1	27	33	9	1	23
1927	1st New Zealanders	T. C. Lowry	T. D. B. Hay	38	13	5	20	26	7	5	14
*1928	4th West Indians	R. K. Nunes	R. H. Mallett	41	7	12	22	30	5	12	13
*1929	7th South Africans	H. G. Deane	H. O. Frielinghaus	39	11	7	21	34	9	7	18
*1930	17th Australians	W. M. Woodfull	W. L. Kelly	34	12	1	20t	31	11	1	18t
*1931	2nd New Zealanders	T. C. Lowry	T. C. Lowry	37	7	3	27	32	6	3	23
*1932	2nd Indians	Maharaja of Porbander C. K. Nayudu		39	14	9	16	26	9	8	9
1932	South Americans	C. H. Gibson	E. W. S. Thomson	18	2	5	11	6	2	3	1
*1933	5th West Indians	G. C. Grant	J. M. Kidney	44	9	9	26	30	5	9	16
*1934	18th Australians	W. M. Woodfull	H. Bushby	34	15	1	18	30	13	1	16
*1935	8th South Africans	H. F. Wade	S. J. Snooke	41	23	2	16	31	17	2	12
*1936	3rd Indians	Maharaj Kumar of Vizianagram	Major Brittain Jones	32	5	13	14	28	4	12	12
1936	4th Canadians	W. E. N. Bell	H. Dean	15	7	1	7				
*1937	3rd New Zealanders	M. L. Page	T. C. Lowry	38	13	9	16	32	9	9	14
*1938	19th Australians	D. G. Bradman	W. H. Jeanes	36	20	2	14	30	15	2	13
*1939	6th West Indians	R. S. Grant	J. M. Kidney	35	10	6	19	25	8	6	11
1940	Proposed South Africans	A. Melville		Cancelled							
1945	Australian Services	A. L. Hassett	K. Johnson	20	7	6	7	6	3	2	1
1945	New Zealand Services	K. C. James		20	3	8	9	1	0	1	0
*1946	4th Indians	Nawab of Pataudi	P. Gupta	33	13	4	16	29	11	4	14
*1947	9th South Africans	A. Melville	A. S. Frames	34	16	6	12	28	14	5	9
*1948	20th Australians	D. G. Bradman	K. Johnson	34	25	0	9	31	23	0	8
*1949	4th New Zealanders	W. A. Hadlee	J. H. Phillips	36	15	1	20	32	13	1	18
*1950	7th West Indians	J. D. C. Goddard	J. M. Kidney	38	19	3	16	31	17	3	11
*1951	10th South Africans	A. D. Nourse	S. J. Pegler	39	10	5	24	30	5	5	20
*1952	5th Indians	V. S. Hazare	P. Gupta	34	6	5	23	29	4	5	29
*1953	21st Australians	A. L. Hassett	G. A. Davies	37	18	1	18	33	16	1	16
1953	1st Pakistan Eaglets	Details unknown									
*1954	1st Pakistanis	A. H. Kardar	F. Hussain	33	10	3	20	30	9	3	18
1954	5th Canadians	H. B. Robinson	L. J. H. Gunn	18	4	3	11	4	0	2	2
*1955	11th South Africans	J. E. Cheetham	K. G. Viljoen	31	16	4	11	28	15	4	9
*1956	22nd Australians	I. W. Johnson	W. J. Dowling	36	12	3	21	31	9	3	19
*1957	8th West Indians	J. D. C. Goddard	N. Pierce C. deCaires	35	16	3	16	31	14	3	14
*1958	5th New Zealanders	J. R. Reid	J. H. Phillips	39	8	6	25t	31	7	6	17t
*1959	6th Indians	D. K. Gaekwad	Maharaja of Baroda	37	7	11	19	33	6	11	16
*1960	12th South Africans	D. J. McGlew	A. D. Nourse	32	15	5	12	31	14	5	12
*1961	23rd Australians	R. Benaud	S. G. Webb	37	14	2	21	32	13	1	18
1961	S. A. Fezelas	R. A. McLean		21	14	0	7	3	3	0	0
*1962	2nd Pakistanis	Javed Burki	R. G. Hyder	36	6	8	22	29	4	8	17
*1963	9th West Indians	F. M. M. Worrell	B. M. Gaskin	38	19	3	16	30	15	2	13
1963	2nd Pakistan Eaglets	Wazir Mohammad		21	11	2	8	8	2	2	4
*1964	24th Australians	R. B. Simpson	R. C. Steele	36	14	4	18	30	11	3	16
*1965	6th New Zealanders	J. R. Reid	W. A. Hadlee	22	4	6	12	19	3	6	10
*1965	13th South Africans	P. L. van der Merwe	J. B. Plimsoll	20	5	3	12	18	5	2	11
*1966	10th West Indians	G. St A. Sobers	J. B. Stollmeyer	34	13	5	16	27	8	4	15
1966	1st Wilfred Isaacs	W. Isaacs	R. Eriksen	21	13	0	8				
*1967	7th Indians	Nawab of Pataudi	K. K. Tarapor	21	4	7	10	18	2	7	9
*1967	3rd Pakistanis	Hanif Mohammad	J. A. Khan	22	3	6	13	17	3	3	11
1967	S.A. Universities	W. McAdam	S. F. Burke	21	10	1	10	2	1	0	1
*1968	25th Australians	W. M. Lawry	R. J. Parish	30	10	3	17	26	8	3	15
1968	USA	A. W. M. Cooper	J. I. Marder	21	2	6	13				
1968	Proposed Ceylon			Cancelled							
*1969	11th West Indians	G. St A. Sobers	C. L. Walcott	23	3	4	16	20	2	3	15
*1969	7th New Zealanders	G. T. Dowling	G. C. Burgess	20	5	3	12	18	4	3	11
1969	2nd Wilfred Isaacs	W. Isaacs	R. Eriksen	16	9	1	6				
1969	Barbados	S. M. Nurse	R. C. Brancker	7	3	3	1	2	0	1	1

				Results							
				All matches				First class			
	Tourists	Captain	Manager	M	W	L	D	M	W	L	D
1970	Rest of World	G. St A. Sobers	F. R. Brown	5	4	1	0	5	4	1	0
1970	Jamaicans	E. D. A. St J. McMorris		12	2	2	8	4	1	0	3
1970	Proposed South Africans	A. Bacher	J. B. Plimsoll	Cancelled							
*1971	4th Pakistanis	Intikhab Alam	Salah-ud-din	19	5	4	10	19	5	4	10
*1971	8th Indians	A. L. Wadekar	H. R. Adhikhari	19	7	1	11	19	7	1	11
*1972	26th Australians	I. M. Chappell	R. C. Steele	37	14	10	13	26	11	5	10
1972	East Africans	J. Shah	H. Collins	21	5	5	11				
1972	Argentine	F. A. Forresters	I. MacGowan	7	4	2	1				
*1973	8th New Zealanders	B. E. Congdon	J. L. Saunders	23	4	3	16	19	3	2	14
*1973	12th West Indians	R. B. Kanhai	E. S. M. Kentish	23	10	2	11	17	6	1	10
*1974	9th Indians	A. L. Wadekar	H. R. Adhikari	22	5	5	12	18	4	3	11
*1974	5th Pakistanis	Intikhab Alam	O. Qureshi	23	15	0	8	17	9	0	8
1975	Proposed South Africans			Cancelled							
1975	Prudential World Cup		Final: West Indies beat Australia								
*1975	27th Australians	I. M. Chappell	F. E. Bennett	21	12	4	5	15	8	2	5
*1976	13th West Indians	C. H. Lloyd	C. L. Walcott	35	26	2	7	26	18	2	6
*1977	28th Australians	G. S. Chappell	L. V. Maddocks	32	8	8	16	23	5	4	14
*1978	6th Pakistanis	Wasim Bari	Mahmood Hussain	17	1	4	12	14	1	2	11
*1978	9th New Zealanders	M. G. Burgess	B. J. Paterson	21	5	8	8	16	5	4	7
1979	1st Sri Lankans	A. P. B. Tennekoon	R. Heyn	18	6	3	9	9	1	1	7
*1979	10th Indians	S. Venkataraghavan	C. D. Gopinath	19	1	6	12	16	1	3	12
1979	Prudential World Cup		Final: West Indies beat England								
*1980	14th West Indians	C. H. Lloyd	C. L. Walcott	30	16	3	11	16	8	0	8
*1980	29th Australians	G. S. Chappell	P. L. Riding	8	1	4	3	5	1	2	2
*1981	30th Australians	K. J. Hughes	F. W. Bennett	28	7	7	14	17	3	3	11
1981	2nd Sri Lankans	B. Warnapura		17	5	1	11	13	1	1	11
*1982	11th Indians	S. M. Gavaskar	Raj Singh	18	2	4	12	12	1	1	10
*1982	7th Pakistanis	Imran Khan	Intikhab Alam	21	7	6	8	15	6	3	6
1982	Zimbabweans	D. A. G. Fletcher	D. Ellman-Brown	13	7	2	4	2	0	0	2
*1983	10th New Zealanders	G. P. Howarth	Sir Allan Wright	21	9	6	6	13	7	3	3
1983	Prudential World Cup		Final: India beat West Indies								
*1984	15th West Indians	C. H. Lloyd	J. L. Hendriks	24	12	2	10	14	8	0	6
*1984	3rd Sri Lankans	L. R. D. Mendis	N. Chanmugam	10	1	1	8	9	0	1	8
*1985	31st Australians	A. W. Border	R. F. Merriman	30	9	5	15	20	4	3	13
1985	2nd Zimbabweans	A. J. Pycroft	D. A. Ellman-Brown	12	4	3	5	6	0	1	5
*1986	11th New Zealanders	J. V. Coney	Glenn Turner	18	5	1	12	15	4	0	11
*1986	12th Indians	Kapil Dev	Raj Singh	22	10	2	10	11	3	0	8
*1987	8th Pakistanis	Imran Khan	Haseeb Ahsan	27	6	4	15	17	2	1	14
*1988	16th West Indians	I. V. A. Richards	J. L. Hendriks	24	10	3	11	19	8	0	11
*1988	4th Sri Lankans	R. S. Madugalle	Abu Fuard	14	1	2	11	9	0	1	8
1988	2nd Australian Aboriginals	J. McGuire	Mark Ella	28	15	11	1	7	0	6	1

1868: Australian Aborigines

Inspired by the financial successes of the English tours to Australia in 1861-62 and 1863-64, W. E. B. Gurnett of Sydney persuaded the managers of an Aboriginal team of cricketers, which had played in Melbourne drawing large crowds, that a lot of money could be made by taking the team on to Sydney and then to England.

This idea was put to the managers, W. R. Hayman and T. W. S.

Wills, in late December 1866 and the team travelled to Sydney in February 1867. The matches in Sydney proved disastrous, however, and, abandoned by Gurnett, the team returned to Melbourne. Wills remained in Melbourne while Hayman escorted the Aborigines back to the farming settlement at Edenhope, some 150 miles away, where he had originally founded the team.

Charles Lawrence, a former Surrey cricketer who had stayed behind in Sydney after coming with the 1861-62 side from England, felt that Gurnett's idea was still worthwhile and in July 1867 went to Edenhope and in conjunction with Hayman re-

1868 Australian Aborigines

1st Match: v Surrey Club (Kennington Oval)   May 25, 26.
Surrey Club 222 (T. W. Baggallay 68, C. Lawrence 7-91) beat Aborigines 83 (H. Frere 5-22, I. D. Walker 5-54) and 132 (Mullagh 73) by an innings and 7 runs.

2nd Match: v Mote Park (Mote Park, Maidstone)   May 29, 30
Mote Park 151 (C. Lawrence 4-68) drew with Aborigines 119-4 (C. Lawrence 57*).

3rd Match: v Gentlemen of Kent (Gravesend)   June 2, 3.
Gentlemen of Kent 298 (M. A. Troughton 80, W. Lindsay 72, Mullagh 6-132) beat Aborigines 123 (W. S. Norton 5-27) and 106 by an innings and 69 runs.

4th Match: v Richmond (Old Deer Park, Richmond)   June 5, 6.
Richmond 74 (Cuzens 5-28) and 236 (Mullagh 4-65) drew with Aborigines 97 (Laurell 4-21) and 82-3.

5th Match: v Gentlemen of Sussex (Hove)   June 8, 9.
Aborigines 171 (C. Lawrence 63, W. Napper 4-32) and 89 (H. C. Blaker 6-36) lost to Gentlemen of Sussex 151 (S. A. Leigh 50, Mullagh 5-55) and 112-1 (O. E. Winslow 71*) by 9 wkts.

6th Match: v Gentlemen of Lewisham (Ladywell)   June 10, 11.
Gentlemen of Lewisham 60 (Mullagh 7-24) and 53 (Mullagh 4-20) lost to Aborigines 42 (E. Wade 6-19) and 72-4 by 6 wkts.

7th Match: v M.C.C. (Lord's)   June 12, 13.
M.C.C. 164 (R. A. FitzGerald 50, Mullagh 5-82, Cuzens 4-52) and 121 (Cuzens 6-65) beat Aborigines 185 (Mullagh 75, C. F. Buller 6-00) and 45 (T. Smyth 5-16) by 55 runs.

8th Match: v East Hampshire (Southsea)   June 15, 16.
East Hampshire 209 (E. Money 77, Cuzens 6-71) beat Aborigines 120 (G. Howard 5-29) and 80 (G. Howard 7-39) by an innings and 9 runs.

9th Match: v Bishop Stortford (Bishop Stortford)   June 19, 20.
Bishop Stortford 136 (Mullagh 6-36) and 23-2 beat Aborigines 58 (E. Woodham 5-21, J. G. Nash 4-32) and 99 (J. G. Nash 8-52) by 8 wkts.

10th Match: v Hastings (Hastings)   June 22, 23, 24.
Aborigines 119 (H. Mawle 5-45, N. Dunk 5-43) and 185 (Mullagh 72, Bullocky 64, H. Mawle 4-46) drew with Hastings 152 and 113-4.

11th Match: v Gentlemen of Halifax (Halifax)   June 26, 27.
Gentlemen of Halifax 64 (C. Lawrence 6-36, Mullagh 4-20) and 129 (Mullagh 5-25) lost to Aborigines 166 (Mullagh 56, J. Barraclough 4-42) and 29-3 by 7 wkts.

12th Match: v East Lancashire (Blackburn)   June 29, 30.
East Lancashire 234 (A. N. Hornby 117, Mullagh 6-84) and 6-1 drew with Aborigines 144 (A. N. Hornby 4-39) and 99 (A. N. Hornby 6-41).

13th Match: v Rochdale (Rochdale)   July 2, 3, 4.
Rochdale 105 (Mullagh 7-58) and 91 (Mullagh 5-36) beat Aborigines 27 (W. H. Buckley 6-14, G. Moore 4-10) and 92 by 77 runs.

14th Match: v Gentlemen of Swansea (Swansea)   July 6, 7.
Gentlemen of Swansea 68 (Mullagh 5-17) and 92 (Mullagh 4-23, C. Lawrence 4-40) lost to Aborigines 193 (Cuzens 50, J. T. D. Llewelyn 6-64) by an innings and 33 runs.

15th Match: v Bradford (Bradford)   July 10, 11.
Bradford 154 (Cuzens 4-21) and 16-1 drew with Aborigines 40 (Scatherd 5-11) and 171 (Mullagh 55, Beardsell 5-56)

16th Match: v Gentlemen of Yorkshire (York)   July 13, 14.
Gentlemen of Yorkshire 201 (M. Prickett 84, Red Cap 7-34) beat Aborigines 92 (H. N. Churton 5-42, F. W. Jackson 4-14) and 58 (W. F. Hamilton 6-13) by an innings and 51 runs.

17th Match: v Longsight (Longsight)   July 16, 17, 18.
Aborigines 53 and 123 (H. Royle 5-48) lost to Longsight 78 (C. Lawrence 5-49, Mullagh 4-26) and 100-6 by 4 wkts.

18th Match: v Vulcan United and Bury Clubs (Bury)   July 20, 21.
Vulcan United 99 (Mullagh 5-35) and 93 (C. Lawrence 6-62, Mullagh 4-23) drew with Aborigines 53 (D. Rowland 5-26, M. Barlow 4-26) and 128-5.

19th Match: v Carrow (Lakenham, Norwich)   July 23, 24.
Carrow 82 (Mullagh 4-18, C. Lawrence 4-57) and 101 (C. Lawrence 8-50) lost to Aborigines 235 (Cuzens 87, E. H. Willett 5-47) by an innings and 52 runs.

20th match: v Keighley (Keighley)   July 27, 28.
Keighley 118 (T. Waring 64*, Red Cap 5-54) and 146 (C. Lawrence 7-54) drew with Aborigines 101 (J. Denison 5-34) and 142-8 (Cuzens 70, Denison 4-47).

21st Match: v Bootle (Bootle)   July 30, 31, Aug 1.
Bootle 110 (C. Lawrence 5-62, Red Cap 4-37) and 90 (C. Lawrence 5-26) lost to Aborigines 115 (C. Lawrence 50*, C. Randon 4-41) and 87-1 (Cuzens 54*) by 9 wkts.

22nd Match: v Nottingham Commercial (Trent Bridge)   Aug 3, 4, 5.
Nottingham Commercial 91 (Mullagh 4-26, C. Lawrence 5-57) and 372 (G. M. Royle 100*, R. Tolley 51, Cuzens 5-82) drew with Aborigines 76 and 57-4.

23rd Match: v Longsight (Longsight)   Aug 7, 8.
Aborigines 75 (J. Shawcross 5-18, G. H. Grimshaw 4-50) and 151 (Grimshaw 4-54) beat Longsight 47 (Mullagh 6-18) and 72 (C. Lawrence 8-48) by 107 runs.

24th Match: v Gentlemen of Sheffield (Bramall Lane)   Aug 10, 11.
Gentlemen of Sheffield 233 (Capt Williams 54, Mullagh 6-95, C. Lawrence 4-86) drew with Aborigines 185 (Mullagh 55).

25th Match: v Savile Club (Dewsbury)   Aug 13, 14, 15.
Savile Club 217 (T. Hirst 90, C. Lawrence 6-96) beat Aborigines 73 (O. Scatchard 6-22) and 86 (S. Smithson 5-35) by an innings and 58 runs.

26th Match: v Tynemouth (North Shields)   Aug 17, 18, 19.
Tynemouth 54 (Mullagh 4-24, C. Lawrence 4-26) and 144 (Mullagh 5-67, C. Lawrence 5-68) lost to Aborigines 35 (T. Bramwell 6-24) and 166-8 (Cuzens 59, Brooks 4-45) by 2 wkts.

27th Match: v Northumberland (Newcastle)   Aug 21, 22.
Northumberland 162 (T. Lee 69, C. Lawrence 5-89, Cuzens 4-28) drew with Aborigines 72 (N. Grace 4-35, Bramwell 6-32) and 35-3.

28th Match: Middlesbrough (Middlesbrough)   Aug 24, 25.
Middlesbrough 151 (J. Treadgold 50, Red Cap 5-32) and 78 (C. Lawrence 5-48) drew with Aborigines 74 (R. Stainsby 5-26, R. Walton 4-45) and 77-6 (R. Stainsby 5-42).

29th Match: v Scarborough (Scarborough)   Aug 27, 28, 29.
Scarborough 90 (Cuzens 4-23) and 109 (C. Lawrence 6-54) lost to Aborigines 148 (Red Cap 56, G. Dipple 6-51) and 53-0 by 10 wkts.

30th Match: v Hunslet (Hunslet)   Aug 31, Sept 1.
Hunslet 71 (Mullagh 5-27, C. Lawrence 4-10) and 18 (C. Lawrence 5-10, Mullagh 4-7) lost to Aborigines 64 (H. Lee 5-20) and 26-3.

31st Match: v South Derbyshire (Derby)   Sept 2, 3.
South Derbyshire 121 (C. Lawrence 6-67) and 125 (J. Smith 57, Mullagh 4-40) beat Aborigines 76 (J. Smith 5-28) and 31 (J. Smith 6-16, F. Davenport 4-15) by 139 runs.

32nd Match: v Lincoln (Nettleham Rd, Lincoln)   Sept 4, 5.
Lincoln 44 (Mullagh 6-23, C. Lawrence 4-20) and 100 (C. E. Booth 54, Mullagh 5-42, Cuzens 4-30) beat Aborigines 78 (G. H. Nicholls 8-33) and 56 (G. H. Nicholls 6-20) by 10 runs.

33rd Match: v Burton-on-Trent (Burton-on-Trent)   Sept 7, 8.
Aborigines 139 (G. Nadin 4-40) and 101 (H. Bass 5-46) beat Burton-on-Trent 72 (C. Lawrence 5-29, Cuzens 4-18) and 99 (C. Lawrence 7-47) by 69 runs.

34th Match: v Bootle (Bootle)   Sept 10, 11, 12.
Aborigines 148 (Mullagh 51, T. Benson 4-19) and 156 (Mullagh 78, S. Sharpe 7-48) beat Bootle 91 (Mullagh 7-32) and 59 (Mullagh 5-17, C. Lawrence 5-37) by 154 runs.

35th Match: v Witham (Witham, Essex)   Sept 14, 15.
Aborigines 184 (Cuzens 64) beat Witham 82 (Mullagh 5-27) and 59 (C. Lawrence 7-33) by an innings and 43 runs.

36th Match: v Gentlemen of Sussex (Hove)   Sept 17, 18.
Aborigines 96 (C. Lawrence 55, S. Beard 6-53) and 113-7 drew with Gentlemen of Sussex 74 (C. Lawrence 6-33).

37th Match: v Blackheath (Westcombe Park, Blackheath)   Sept 21, 22.
Blackheath 121 and 75 beat Aborigines 67 (E. Wade 7-21) and 116 by 13 runs.

38th Match: v Gentlemen of Middlesex (so called) (Islington)   Sept 23, 24.
Gentlemen of Middlesex 105 (Mullagh 6-45) and 173 (C. Lawrence 5-62) drew with Aborigines 163 (Cuzens 66).

39th Match: v Gentlemen of the Surrey Club (Kennington Oval)   Sept 25, 26.
Gentlemen of the Surrey Club 173 (W. B. Money 68, C. Lawrence 5-72) drew with Aborigines 24-3.

40th Match: v The Press (Mote Park, Maidstone)   Sept 28, 29.
The Press 101 (C. Lawrence 6-45) and 74 (Cuzens 4-16) drew with Aborigines 82 (R. Bush 7-37).

41st Match: v Eastbourne (Eastbourne)   Sept 30, Oct 1.
Eastbourne 67 (Cuzens 6-19, Red Cap 4-10) and 94 (Red Cap 5-34) drew with Aborigines 70.

42nd Match: v Turnham Green (Hammersmith)   Oct 2, 3.
Turnham Green 62 (Mullagh 5-26) drew with Aborigines 48 (Alderton 6-10)

43rd Match: v East Hampshire (Southsea)   Oct 5, 6.
East Hampshire 51 (Twopenny 9-9) and 22 (Twopenny 6-7) lost to Aborigines 144 (G. Carter 4-30) by an innings and 71 runs.

44th Match: v Gentlemen of Hampshire (Southampton)   Oct 7, 8.
Gentlemen of Hampshire 53 (Twopenny 9-17) and 152 (C. Lawrence 4-58) drew with Aborigines 78 (A. C. Faulkner 6-31) and 49-3.

45th Match: v Reading (Reading)   Oct 9, 10.
Reading 32 (Mullagh 7-9) and 34 (Red Cap 5-10, C. Lawrence 5-23) lost to Aborigines 284 (Mullagh 94, Cuzens 66, B. Nicholson 5-25).

46th Match: v Godalming (Godalming)   Oct 12, 13, 14.
Godalming 37 (C. Lawrence 6-18) and 128 (N. W. Wallace 55, C. Lawrence 4-52) drew with Aborigines 79 and 25-5.

47th Match: v Gentlemen of the Surrey Club (Kennington Oval)   Oct 15, 16, 17.
Aborigines 56 and 143 (Cuzens 63) lost to Gentlemen of the Surrey Club 173 (J. C. Gregory 121*, C. Lawrence 5-63) and 29-1 by 9 wkts.

The first cricketing tourists to England, the 1868 Australian Aborigines. They played 47 matches, and became well-known by their nicknames: Dick-a-Dick (seen with two boomerangs), Sundown (with sticks), Twopenny (holding his boomerang with two hands), Red Cap, King Cole, etc.

formed the team.

After a period of coaching the team began a second series of matches in Australia, again culminating in Sydney. George Smith, a former mayor of Sydney, and G. W. Graham both provided money for the proposed tour to England and on 8 February 1868 the team boarded the *Paramatta* in Sydney and sailed to England, landing at Gravesend on 13 May.

The team consisted of 13 Aborigines: Mullagh, Cuzens, Bullocky, Red Cap, Twopenny, King Cole, Tiger, Dick-a-Dick, Peter, Charley, Mosquito, Jim Crow and Sundown, names used in their cricket matches, but of course only nicknames. C. Lawrence was captain, W. R. Hayman manager, and George Smith business manager.

The first match in England was played at the Oval on 25 and 26 May 1868 and the full tour consisted of 47 matches, not ending until 15, 16 and 17 October, again at the Oval. The team was opposed for the most part by sides not far below first-class standard and they won 14 and lost 14 matches. Apart from playing cricket they gave exhibitions of spear- and boomerang-throwing and other sports.

Mullagh and Cuzens were very talented all-rounders: the former hit 1,698 runs, average 23, and took 245 wickets, average 10, and the latter 1,358 runs, average 19, and 114 wickets, average 11. Lawrence was also very successful and Twopenny and Red Cap bowled well at times, but the remainder achieved little.

It was a very arduous tour. King Cole died in June and two others, Sundown and Jim Crow, went home in August because of ill-health, which reduced the party with Lawrence to 11 men. W. Shepherd, who had been engaged in England as the side's umpire, was co-opted and appeared in seven matches.

Some of the tourists left Gravesend aboard the *Dunbar Castle* on 19 October, the remainder joining the ship at Plymouth, and they arrived back in Sydney on 4 February 1869.

Their matches in England proved very popular, with 5,000 spectators attending the more important games. According to Haygarth it was a very lucrative speculation.

1874: American baseball players

Under the leadership of A. G. Spalding, a team of American baseball players came to England in August 1874 to try and popularise their sport in England. The members who played in the various cricket matches were H. Wright, J. O'Rourke, R. C. Barns, W. Anson, J. D. McBride, A. J. Leonard, G. Wright, S. Wright, A. G. Spalding (captain and manager), C. A. McVey, E. B. Sutton, H. C. Schafer, M. McGeary, G. Hall, J. McMullen, T. Murnan, T. S. Beales, J. P. Kent, J. V. Battin, W. Fisler, J. Sensenderfer, C. H. Porter, T. Clapp and A. Gedney.

The team gave a series of baseball exhibitions and combined them with cricket matches. The team did not lose a single one of their cricket matches, but in addition to being given very long odds, met very poor sides.

H. Wright and G. Wright were the principal bowlers and the best batsmen were A. G. Spalding and A. J. Leonard.

1874 American baseball players

1st Match: v M.C.C. (Lord's)   Aug 3, 4.
M.C.C. 105 (G. Wright 4-43) drew with XVIII Americans 107 (F. P. U. Pickering 8-28).

2nd Match: v Prince's Club (Prince's)   Aug 6, 7.
Prince's Club 21 (H. Wright 5-13) and 39 (H. Wright 6-23) lost to XVIII Americans 110 (McIntyre 7-32) by an innings and 50 runs.

3rd Match: v XIII of Richmond (Richmond)   Aug 8.
Richmond 108 (G. Wright 6-47, H. Wright 5-39) drew with XXII Americans 45-6.

4th Match: v Surrey Club (Oval)   Aug 13, 14.
XVIII Americans 100 (E. Barratt 10-63) and 111 drew with Surrey Club 27 (H. Wright 6-8) and 2-4.

5th Match: v Sheffield (Sheffield)   Aug 15, 17.
XVIII Americans 130 beat Sheffield 43 and 45 by an innings and 42 runs.

6th Match: v Manchester (Manchester)   Aug 20, 21.
XVIII Americans 121 and 100 beat Manchester 42 and 53 by 126 runs.

7th Match: v Ireland (Dublin)   Aug 24, 25.
XIX Americans 71 and 94 beat Ireland 47 and 32 by 86 runs.

1878: 1st Australians

Following the victory of the Australian side at Melbourne in March 1877 over the English touring team, John Conway decided to arrange for an Australian team to tour England. James Lillywhite, captain of the 1876-77 English tourists, was instructed to arrange a programme of fixtures in England for the 1878 season and Conway set about selecting his cricketers. The main obstacle for most of the players was getting 12 months' leave of absence from their full-time employment, but this was granted in almost every case and the side chosen: D. W. Gregory (captain), C. Bannerman, A. C. Bannerman, T. W. Garrett, W. L. Murdoch and F. R. Spofforth of New South Wales; F. E. Allen, J. McC. Blackham, T. P. Horan and H. F. Boyle of Victoria; G. H. Bailey of Tasmania, with J. Conway as manager and W. C. Gibbes.

The two players of note not in the side were Evans and Kendall; the tourists were reinforced by W. Midwinter of Gloucestershire on their arrival, however. This team left Sydney on 29 March, travelled via San Francisco, and arrived at Liverpool on 13 May.

They lost the first match, against Nottinghamshire, by an innings, having had very little time to practise after their long journey. They quickly remedied this initial upset by successively beating M.C.C., Yorkshire and Surrey, and this set of victories established public interest in the tour—on the two days of the Surrey match the attendances were 20,000 and 15,000.

There was a major controversy at the start of the sixth match of the tour, when W. G. Grace arrived at Lord's and persuaded Midwinter to quit the Australian team and re-join Gloucestershire; much later on another dispute arose when the major English professionals refused to appear in a match against the tourists unless they were paid £20 each. This demand was not accepted and a scratch team was selected—afterwards the Australian manager paid each of the scratch eleven £20! The tourists did not play a representative English eleven during the tour.

The outstanding player in the side was Spofforth, whose clever alterations in pace combined with movement off the pitch deceived even the best English batsmen; in first-class matches he took 97 wickets, average 11.00. Boyle and Garrett both returned better first-class averages than Spofforth but took considerably fewer wickets. Boyle relied on consistency of length for his medium-pace deliveries, while Garrett bowled off-breaks. There were two other excellent bowlers: Allan, slow left-arm, and Horan. The batting was not so strong. Charles Bannerman played some excellent innings; Murdoch was the most polished; A. C. Bannerman stubborn in defence. Gregory was disappointing, though Spofforth was a resolute hitter. Behind the stumps Blackham was the equal of the best English wicketkeepers and Murdoch acted efficiently as his stand-in. The fielding was very smart and Gregory led the side ably.

Financially the venture was a great success. The side left Liverpool aboard the s.s. *City of Richmond* on 18 September, arriving in New York on 29 September. They played six matches in America before leaving for home via San Francisco, landing in Sydney on 25 November.

1878 1st Australians

1st Match: v Nottinghamshire (Trent Bridge)   May 20, 21, 22.
Australians 63 (A. Shaw 5-20, F. Morley 4-42) and 76 (A. Shaw 6-35, F. Morley 4-30) lost to Nottinghamshire 153 (J. Selby 66, T. P. Horan 5-30) by an innings and 14 runs.

2nd Match: v M.C.C. (Lord's)   May 27.
M.C.C. 33 (F. R. Spofforth 6-4) and 19 (H. F. Boyle 5-3, F. R. Spofforth 5-16) lost to Australians 41 (A. Shaw 5-10, F. Morley 5-31) and 12-1 by 9 wkts.

3rd Match: v Yorkshire (Huddersfield)   May 30, 31, June 1.
Yorkshire 72 (H. F. Boyle 5-32, F. R. Spofforth 4-30) and 73 (F. R. Spofforth 5-31) lost to Australians 118 (T. Emmett 5-23) and 28-4 by 6 wkts.

4th Match: v Surrey (Kennington Oval)   June 3, 4.
Surrey 107 (F. R. Spofforth 8-52) and 80 (W. E. Midwinter 4-14) lost to Australians 110 (E. Barratt 8-58) and 78-5 by 5 wkts.

5th Match: v XVIII of Elland (Elland)   June 6, 7, 8.
Australians 90 (E. Osborne 6-40) and 85 (E. Osborne 6-38) beat XVIII of Elland 29 (H. F. Boyle 11-12) and 66 (F. R. Spofforth 10-37) by 80 runs.

6th Match: v XVIII of Batley (Howley Hill, Batley)   June 10, 11, 12.
Australians 160 (T. P. Horan 50, A. Hill 5-44) drew with XVIII of Batley 59-10.

7th Match: v XVIII of Longsight (Longsight)   June 13, 14, 15.
Australians 67 (S. Hind 5-12) and 67 (Sully 5-8) lost to XVIII of Longsight 63 (F. R. Spofforth 8-37, H. F. Boyle 7-21) and 74-15 by 2 wkts.

8th Match: v Gentlemen of England (Prince's)   June 17, 18.
Australians 75 (W. G. Grace 4-25, A. G. Steel 4-37) and 63 (A. G. Steel 7-35) lost to Gentlemen of England 139 (H. F. Boyle 7-48) by an innings and 1 run.

9th Match: v Middlesex (Lord's)   June 20, 21, 22.
Australians 165 (R. Henderson 4-60) and 240 (F. R. Spofforth 56, R. Henderson 5-96) beat Middlesex 122 (A. J. Webbe 50, T. W. Garrett 7-38) and 185 (E. Lyttelton 113, F. E. Allan 6-76) by 98 runs.

10th Match: v XXII of Birmingham (Bournbrook)   June 24, 25, 26.
Australians 105 (Tallboys 5-37) and 116-6 drew with XXII of Birmingham 123 (F. R. Spofforth 11-60).

11th Match: v XVIII of Hunslet (Woodhouse Hill, Hunslet)   June 27, 28, 29.
Australians 205 (C. Bannerman 52, J. Blackburn 4-28) and 180 (W. Bates 5-70) drew with XVIII of Hunslet 228 (L. Hall 79, F. R. Spofforth 8-77) and 28-9 (F. E. Allan 5-9).

12th Match: v Yorkshire (Bramall Lane, Sheffield)   July 1, 2.
Australians 88 (G. Ulyett 4-14) and 104 (G. Ulyett 4-27, W. Bates 4-42) lost to Yorkshire 167 and 26-1 by 9 wkts.

13th Match: v XVIII of Stockport (Stockport)   July 4, 5, 6.
Australians 163 (T. Brown 4-51, Martin McIntyre 4-55) and 225 (T. P. Horan 70, T. Brown 4-75) beat XVIII of Stockport 105 (F. E. Allan 10-50) and 134 (F. R. Spofforth 8-30) by 149 runs.

14th Match: v Orleans Club (Twickenham)   July 8, 9.
Australians 171 (A. C. Bannerman 71, E. Barratt 5-71) and 172 (T. P. Horan 64, E. Barratt 7-70) drew with Orleans Club 132 (F. E. R. Fryer 61) and 137-2 (I. D. Walker 60*).

15th Match: v XVIII of South Wales (Swansea)   July 10, 11.
Australians 219 (F. C. Cobden 5-41) beat XVIII of South Wales 94 (F. R. Spofforth 10-35) and 88 (H. F. Boyle 8-33) by an innings and 37 runs.

16th Match: v XVIII of Werneth and Oldham (Oldham)   July 12, 13.
XVIII of Werneth and Oldham 138 (T. P. Horan 7-40) and 117 (H. F. Boyle 8-27, F. R. Spofforth 8-56) drew with Australians 125 (Hind 5-45) and 112-7.

17th Match: v Leicestershire (Aylestone Rd, Leicester)   July 15, 16, 17.
Leicestershire 193 (J. Wheeler 60, F. R. Spofforth 5-60, T. W. Garrett 4-30) and 145 (J. Wheeler 65, F. R. Spofforth 4-27) lost to Australians 130 and 210-2 (C. Bannerman 133*) by 8 wkts.

18th Match: v Hull (Hull)   July 18, 19, 20.
Hull 250 (T. Haslewood 53) and 68 (H. F. Boyle 8-30) lost to Australians 305 (F. E. Allan 78, J. McC. Blackham 53, T. P. Horan 50) and 15-0 by 10 wkts.

19th Match: v Cambridge University (Lord's)   July 22, 23.
Cambridge 285 (A. Lyttelton 72, A. G. Steel 59) beat Australians 111 (P. H. Morton 7-45) and 102 (P. H. Morton 5-45) by an innings and 72 runs.

20th Match: XXII of Crewe (Crewe)   July 26, 26, 27.
Australians 130 (Dillon 7-54) and 102 (A. Rylott 4-32) beat XXII of Crewe 54 (F. R. Spofforth 10-13) and 79 (F. R. Spofforth 10-33, H. F. Boyle 10-43) by 99 runs.

21st Match: v XVIII of Keighley (Keighley)   July 29, 30, 31.
Australians 206 (A. C. Bannerman 55, C. Bannerman 54) and 32-3 beat XVIII of Keighley 102 (F. R. Spofforth 12-58) and 133 (F. R. Spofforth 8-59) by 7 wkts.

22nd Match: v XVIII of Rochdale (Rochdale)   Aug 1, 2, 3.
Australians 159 (J. Taylor 5-32) and 72 (Buckley 5-32, J. Tye 5-33) drew with XVIII of Rochdale 124 (T. W. Garrett 10-44) and 50-6.

23rd Match: v XXII of Buxton (Buxton)   Aug 5, 6.
XXII of Buxton 77 (F. R. Spofforth 12-30) and 134 drew with Australians 97 (F. Whatmough 4-20) and 17-1.

24th Match: v XVIII of Burnley (Burnley)   Aug 7 (One day match).
XVIII of Burnley 102 (F. R. Spofforth 9-55) drew with Australians 47-9 (F. Branch 4-23).

25th Match: v XVIII of Stanley C.C. (Stanley Park, Liverpool)   Aug 8, 9.
Australians 233 (D. W. Gregory 70, H. F. Boyle 58) beat Stanley C.C. 71 (F. R. Spofforth 10-44) and 91 (F. R. Spofforth 10-54) by an innings and 71 runs.

26th Match: v XVIII of Dudley (Dudley)   Aug 12, 13, 14.
Australians 59 (G. Morley 7-43) and 230 (C. Bannerman 50) drew with XVIII of Dudley 33 (H. F. Boyle 12-19) and 40-7.

27th Match: v Lancashire (Old Trafford)   Aug 15, 16, 17.
Lancashire 97 (F. R. Spofforth 9-53) and 162 (F. R. Spofforth 4-81) drew with Australians 140 (C. Bannerman 58, R. G. Barlow 5-47) and 47-0.

28th Match: v XVIII of Yeadon (Yeadon)   Aug 19, 20, 21.
XVIII of Yeadon 91 (F. E. Allan 8-33) and 71 (F. R. Spofforth 9-30) beat Australians 54 (R. G. Barlow 5-17, E. Peate 4-24) and 84 (W. E. Bosomworth 8-24) by 24 runs.

29th Match: v XVIII of Scarborough (Scarborough)   Aug 22, 23, 24.
Australians 295 (F. R. Spofforth 64, J. McC. Blackham 55) beat XVIII of Scarborough 124 and 125 (F. R. Spofforth 7-59) by an innings and 46 runs.

30th Match: v XVIII of Hastings and District (Hastings)   Aug 26, 27.
XVIII of Hastings and District 131 (T. W. Garrett 7-35) and 82 (F. R. Spofforth 12-39) lost to Australians 260 (G. H. Bailey 106, W. L. Murdoch 73, C. M. Cunliffe 6-79) by an innings and 47 runs.

31st Match: v Sussex (Hove)   Aug 29, 30.
Sussex 80 (H. F. Boyle 5-27) and 47 (F. R. Spofforth 6-31, H. F. Boyle 4-15) lost to Australians 75 (Jas Lillywhite jun 5-25, F. F. J. Greenfield 4-39) and 53-3 by 7 wkts.

32nd Match: v Players (Kennington Oval)   Sept 2, 3.
Australians 77 (C. Bannerman 51, E. Barratt 10-43) and 89 (W. McIntyre 6-24) beat Players 82 (F. R. Spofforth 7-37) and 76 (F. R. Spofforth 5-38) by 8 runs.

33th Match: v Gloucestershire (Clifton)   Sept 5, 6.
Gloucestershire 112 (F. R. Spofforth 7-49) and 85 (F. R. Spofforth 5-41) lost to Australians 183 (R. F. Miles 5-49) and 17-0 by 10 wkts.

34th Match: v Gentlemen of England (Scarborough)   Sept 9, 10.
Australians 157 (A. G. Steel 6-80) and 249 (C. Bannerman 54) drew with Gentlemen of England 109 (F. R. Spofforth 5-44).

35th Match: v Players (Prince's)   Sept 11, 12.
Australians 236 (C. Bannerman 61, D. W. Gregory 57) drew with Players 160 (G. Ulyett 79, T. W. Garrett 7-41).

36th Match: v XII of West of Scotland (Partick)   Sept 13, 14.
Australians 268 (A. D. Dunlop 5-15) beat XII of West of Scotland 99 (T. W. Garrett 6-38) and 85 (F. R. Spofforth 8-54) by an innings and 84 runs.

37th Match: v XVIII of Sunderland (Sunderland)   Sept 16, 17.
XVIII of Sunderland 59 (T. W. Garrett 11-28) and 147 (F. E. Allan 10-42) beat Australians 77 (T. Emmett 8-41) and 58 (T. Emmett 5-25) by 71 runs.

1878 1st Australians

Batting Averages

	M	I	NO	R	HS	Avge	100	c/s
C. Bannerman	15	28	1	566	61	20.96	0	14
W. E. Midwinter	5	10	2	124	32	15.50	0	4
G. H. Bailey	12	21	4	254	40	14.94	0	5
J. McC. Blackham	13	20	8	179	30	14.91	0	8/3
W. L. Murdoch	15	25	4	274	49	13.05	0	11/7
F. R. Spofforth	15	25	1	304	56	12.66	0	7
A. C. Bannerman	15	26	3	263	71*	11.43	0	8
T. W. Garrett	15	25	1	265	43	11.04	0	5
T. P. Horan	15	27	1	285	64	10.96	0	2
D. W.Gregory	15	22	1	214	57	10.19	0	11
F. E. Allan	15	24	6	129	33	7.16	0	7
H. F. Boyle	14	21	5	98	18	6.12	0	11

Also batted: H. N. Tennent (1 match) 2 and 1.

Bowling Averages

	O	M	R	W	Avge	BB	5i
W. E. Midwinter	65.2	33	58	8	7.25	4-14	0
H. F. Boyle	361.3	144	483	51	9.49	7-48	4
T. W. Garrett	260.2	131	318	32	9.93	7-38	2
F. R. Spofforth	658.1	250	1068	97	11.00	9-53	10
T. P. Horan	35.3	7	100	7	14.29	5-30	1
G. H. Bailey	10	2	17	1	17.00	1-9	0
F. E. Allan	348.3	159	513	25	20.52	6-76	1
W. L. Murdoch	22	6	46	2	23.00	2-46	0

Played in non-first-class matches only: H. L. Butler, J. Conway, H. H. Hyslop, W. Tobin and W. C. Wilkinson.

1880: 1st Canadians

1st Match: v West of Scotland C.C. (Partick)   May 21, 22.
West of Scotland 69 and 170 lost to Canadians 182 and 79-5 by 5 wkts.

2nd Match: v Greenock (Greenock)   May 26, 27.
Canadians 136 and 149-9 drew with Greenock 186.

3rd Match: v Royal High School F.P. (Edinburgh)   May 28, 29.
Canadians 89 and 108 lost to Royal High School F.P. 196 and 2-0 by 10 wkts.

4th Match: v Hunslet (Hunslet)   May 31, June 1.
Canadians 71 lost to Hunslet 128 and 43-1 on first innings.

5th Match: v Leicestershire (Leicester)   June 2, 3.
Leicestershire 168 drew with Canadians 64 and 49-5.

6th Match: v M.C.C. (Lord's)   June 10.
M.C.C. 192 beat XV Canadians 33 and 36 by an innings and 123 runs.

7th Match: v Crystal Palace (Crystal Palace)   June 14, 15.
Canadians 83 and 235 drew with Crystal Palace 78 and 47-4.

8th Match: v Stockport (Stockport)   June 18, 19.
Canadians 90 and 101 lost to Stockport 196 by an innings and 5 runs.

9th Match: v Cheltenham (Cheltenham)   June 22, 23 (12-a-side).
Canadians 78 and 62 drew with Cheltenham 46 and 38-2.

10th Match: v Surrey Club & Ground (Oval)   June 24 and 25.
XV Canadians 41 and 171 beat Surrey C & G 67 and 35 by 110 runs.

11th Match: v XV of Wallsden (Wallsden)   June 26.
XII Canadians 120 and 18-1 beat XV of Wallsden 62 by 58 runs on first innings.

12th Match: v Halifax (Halifax)   June 28, 29.
Halifax 114 and 76 drew with Canadians 75 and 7-3.

13th Match: v Orleans Club (Twickenham)   June 30 (XIII-a-side).
Canadians 57 and 90 lost to Orleans Club 171 by an innings and 24 runs.

14th Match: v Longsight (Longsight)   July 2, 3 (XII-a-side).
Canadians 156-8 drew with Longsight did not bat.

15th Match: v Gentlemen of Derbyshire (Derby)   July 5, 6.
Gentlemen of Derbyshire 473 (W. Curgenven 102) beat XII Canadians 140 and 104 by an innings and 229 runs.

16th Match: v Wavertree Club (Liverpool)   July 9, 10 (12-a-side).
Canadians 98 and 35 beat Wavertree 28 and 69 by 26 runs.

17th Match: v Stourbridge (Stourbridge)   July 12, 13.
Canadians 82 and 105 beat Stourbridge 93 and 68 by 26 runs.

Note: Two other matches–June 4 v Swansea and June 7 v Cardiff were abandoned due to Jordan's arrest.

1878: Proposed Parsis tour

In the autumn of 1877 the Parsis Cricket Club of Bombay arranged a programme of fixtures between June and September 1878 for an English tour. The principal players intended for the tour were J. M. Patel, R. J. Kapadia, B. Bhikaji, S. Benjoni, B. Bhirnji, E. N. Johnson, A. R. Libuwalla, P. J. Master, F. B. Sacklat, R. F. Kartruck and D. E. Dharwar.

In the spring of 1878 the tour was unexpectedly postponed until 1879 and later it was cancelled. The first Parsis tour did not take place until 1886.

1880: 1st Canadians

The team sailed from Canada on 1 May and landed at Glasgow on 14 May. The original side was T. Jordan (captain), J. Dewhurst, J. S. Gillean, F. F. Hall, J. L. Hardman, H. W. Hibberd, J. Howard, C. Kearney, A. H. Lemmon, H. Miller, W. Pinckney, D. J. Smith and A. S. Treloar. Four of the side had represented Canada against the United States and thus the team was hardly representative.

The initial visit by the Canadians turned out to be a disaster, mainly because of the tourists' captain, T. Jordan. Just after the 5th match of the programme, he was arrested on suspicion of being T. Dale, a military deserter. This suspicion was proved and Jordan (or Dale) was sent to prison. The Rev T. D. Phillips was sent from Canada to replace Jordan, but did not arrive until the end of June, by which time the tour had more or less collapsed in failure.

The best player was probably Gillean, an effective fast bowler. Smith, Pinckney and Lemmon were all useful batsmen. In England the tourists engaged Walter Wright, the Notts professional, and he appeared in some matches, but he was only at the start of his county career and not the bowler of quality that he later became.

The visit came to rather an abrupt end in mid-July for lack of money; at not one of the matches did the gate receipts cover the expenses.

At various times the side co-opted several local players: Dunn, W. Gilbert, T. Dutton, Hodgson and F. Henry.

1880: 2nd Australians

A definite decision to come to England in 1880 was not made until all the major fixtures for the 1880 English season had been arranged and the tourists arrived in London on 3 May to discover that only five county matches were on their fixture list and two of these were against a Yorkshire team not under the control of the county committee. In addition the side lacked Evans, Horan and Garrett and so on paper did not represent the full strength of Australia. The team was W. L. Murdoch (captain), F. R. Spofforth, A. C. Bannerman and G. J. Bonnor of New South Wales; J. McC. Blackham, H. F. Boyle, P. S. McDonnell, G. E. Palmer, T. U. Groube, G. Alexander (player-manager), J. Slight and W. H. Moule of Victoria and A. H. Jarvis of South Australia.

The team offered to play England for the benefit of the Cricketers' Fund, but this was rejected; an attempt by W. G. Grace to organise a match at Lord's between England and Australia also came to nothing. The tour proceeded, mainly against clubs in the north of England, with 18 men facing 11. The Australians were highly successful and it was the middle of August before they were defeated for the first time.

Public interest grew and Lord Harris was asked by the Surrey Club to chose a representative England eleven to play the Australians at the Oval. The Sussex County Committee agreed to postpone their fixture with the tourists to accommodate the match. England won the game by five wickets, after Australia had fought back from being 271 behind on their first innings. The crowds flocked to the match, with about 20,000 present on both first and second days. The match is regarded as the first Test Match ever staged in England.

Three additional first-class matches–two v Players and one v Nottinghamshire–were also added to the September programme,

1880: 2nd Australians

1st Match: XVIII of St Luke's Club (Southampton)   May 13, 14.
Australians 250 (W. L. Murdoch 97, H. F. Boyle 50) beat XVIII of St Luke's Club 115 (G. F. Grace 45*) and 113 (G. F. Grace 46) by an innings and 22 runs.

2nd Match: v Derbyshire (Derby)   May 17, 18.
Australians 129 (G. Hay 5-49, W. Mycroft 4-56) and 42-2 beat Derbyshire 45 (G. E. Palmer 5-16, F. R. Spofforth 5-24) and 125 (F. R. Spofforth 8-61) by 8 wkts.

3rd Match: v XVIII of Longsight (Longsight)   May 20, 21, 22.
XVIII of Longsight 118 and 106 lost to Australians 214 (J. McC. Blackham 81, G. J. Bonnor 73) and 12-0 by 10 wkts.

4th Match: v XVIII of Rochdale (Rochdale)   May 27, 28, 29.
Australians 212 (P. S. McDonnell 51) beat XVIII of Rochdale 92 and 94 by an innings and 26 runs.

5th Match: v XVIII of Keighley (Keighley)   May 31, June 1, 2.
XVIII of Keighley 102 and 53 drew with Australians 98 and 32-2.

6th Match: v XVIII of Burnley (Burnley)   June 3, 4.
Australians 148 (W. L. Murdoch 56) beat XVIII of Burnley 45 (F. R. Spofforth 12-10) and 76 by an innings and 27 runs.

7th Match: v XVIII of Malton (Malton)   June 7, 8, 9.
Australians 45 and 88-6 beat XVIII of Malton 45 and 95 by 4 wkts.

8th Match: v Yorkshire (Dewsbury)   June 10, 11, 12.
Yorkshire 55 (G. E. Palmer 5-22, F. R. Spofforth 5-31) and 100 (F. R. Spofforth 6-45, G. E. Palmer 4-36) lost to Australians 65 (W. Bates 6-41, E. Peate 4-20) and 91-5 by 5 wkts.

9th Match: v XVIII of North of Ireland (Belfast)   June 14, 15, 16.
Australians 102 and 131-1 (W. L. Murdoch 72) beat XVIII of North of Ireland 102 and 130 by 9 wkts.

10th Match: v XVIII of Dublin University (Dublin)   June 17, 18, 19.
Australians 170 (J. Slight 56) and 156 (A. C. Bannerman 69) drew with XVIII of Dublin University 98 and 86-7.

11th Match: v XVIII of Birmingham (Birmingham)   June 21, 22, 23.
Australians 179 beat XVIII of Birmingham 68 and 102 by an innings and 9 runs.

12th Match: v XVIII of Northampton (Northampton)   June 24, 25, 26.
Australians 86 and 63-2 beat XVIII of Northampton 86 and 48 by 8 wkts.

13th Match: v XVIII of Harrogate (Harrogate)   June 28, 29.
Australians 138 (G. J. Bonnor 59*) and 3-0 beat XVIII of Harrogate 85 and 53 by 10 wkts.

14th Match: v XVIII of Newcastle-on-Tyne (Newcastle)   July 1, 2, 3.
Australians 222 (W. L. Murdoch 117) and 58-4 drew with Newcastle 115 and 201.

15th Match: v XVIII of Middlesbrough (Middlesbrough)   July 5, 6.
Australians 207 beat XVIII of Middlesbrough 108 and 73 by an innings and 26 runs.

16th Match: v XVIII of Broughton (Manchester)   July 8, 9, 10.
Australians 107 and 98 drew with XVIII of Broughton 106 and 51-11.

17th Match: v Leicestershire (Leicester)   July 12, 13, 14.
Australians 142 (A. Rylott 4-40) and 200-7 (W. L. Murdoch 73) drew with Leicestershire 95 (F. R. Spofforth 6-60, G. E. Palmer 4-18).

18th Match: v XVIII of Werneth (Oldham)   July 16, 17.
Australians 119 (P. S. McDonnell 53) beat XVIII of Werneth 38 and 60 by an innings and 21 runs.

19th Match: v XVIII of Crystal Palace (Crystal Palace)   July 19, 20.
Australians 155 and 4-0 beat Crystal Palace 59 and 97 by 10 wkts.

20th Match: v Yorkshire (Huddersfield)   July 22, 23, 24.
Yorkshire 78 (G. E. Palmer 5-31, F. R. Spofforth 5-45) drew with Australians 229-6 (T. U. Groube 61).

21st Match: v XVIII of Hull Town (Hull)   July 26, 27, 28.
Australians 94 and 2-1 drew with XVIII of Hull Town 72 and 37.

22nd Match: v XVIII of Crewe (Crewe)   July 29, 30, 31.
Australians 257 drew with XVIII of Crewe 45 and 29-8.

23rd Match: v Gloucestershire (Clifton)   Aug 2, 3, 4.
Australians 110 (W. G. Grace 6-44) and 246 (P. S. McDonnell 79, W. G. Grace 5-90) beat Gloucestershire 191 (E. M. Grace 65, G. E. Palmer 6-77, F. R. Spofforth 4-76) and 97 (F. R. Spofforth 7-54) by 68 runs.

24th Match: v XVIII of Hunslet (Hunslet)   Aug 5, 6, 7.
Hunslet 75 and 93 lost to Australians 65 and 107-2 (A. C. Bannerman 55) by 8 wkts.

25th Match: v XVIII of Bradford (Bradford)   Aug 9, 10.
XVIII of Bradford 66 and 69 lost to Australians 95 and 41-0 by 10 wkts.

26th Match: v XVIII of Sunderland (Sunderland)   Aug 12, 13.
Australians 171 (J. McC. Blackham 52, G. J. Bonner 52) beat XVIII of Sunderland 79 and 54 by an innings and 38 runs.

27th Match: v XVIII of Scarborough (Scarborough)   Aug 19, 20, 21.
XVIII of Scarborough 170 and 98 beat Australians 96 and 80 by 90 runs.

28th Match: v XVIII of Yeadon (Yeadon)   Aug 2-3, 24, 25.
Australians 217 (A. C. Bannerman 58) beat XVIII of Yeadon 105 and 47 by an innings and 65 runs.

29th Match: v XVIII of Stockport (Stockport)   Aug 26, 27, 28.
XVIII of Stockport 132 and 156 beat Australians 70 and 118 by 100 runs.

30th Match: v XVIII of Hastings (Hastings)   Aug 30, 31, Sept 1.
XVIII of Hastings 245 (W. W. Reeve 61) and 176 (E. J. McCormick 35) drew with Australians 186 (W. L. Murdoch 86) and 60-3.

31st Match: v England (Oval)   Sept 6, 7, 8.
England 420 (W. G. Grace 152, A. P. Lucas 55, Lord Harris 52) and 57-5 beat Australia 149 (F. Morley 5-56) and 327 (W. L. Murdoch 153) by 5 wkts.

32nd Match: v XVIII of Clydesdale C.C. (Glasgow)   Sept 10, 11.
Australians 111 and 47-1 drew with XVIII of Clydesdale C.C. 234 (J. G. Walker 85).

33rd Match: v Sussex (Hove)   Sept 13, 14, 15.
Sussex 107 (G. E. Palmer 7-44) and 156-2 (M. P. Lucas 66, R. T. Ellis 58*) drew with Australians 154 (W. A. Humphreys 5-32).

34th Match: v Gentlemen of Scotland (Edinburgh)   Sept 16, 17, 18.
Scotland 143 (G. E. Palmer 5-47, H. F. Boyle 4-67) and 130 (G. E. Palmer 5-53, H. F. Boyle 4-46) lost to Australians 142 (J. Craig 6-60) and 132-4 by 6 wkts.

35th Match: v Players of England (Bradford)   Sept 20, 21, 22.
Australians 183 (H. F. Boyle 69, F. Morley 4-65) drew with Players 96 (G. E. Palmer 6-54, H. F. Boyle 4-35) and 195-9 (H. F. Boyle 6-70).
(Australians played with only ten men).

36th Match: v Nottinghamshire (Trent Bridge)   Sept 23, 24, 25.
Australians 141 (A. Shaw 5-64, F. Morley 4-38) and 77 (A. Shaw 7-31) lost to Nottinghamshire 88 (H. F. Boyle 5-37, G. E. Palmer 5-46) and 131-9 (A. Shrewsbury 66*) by 1 wkt.

37th Match: v Players of England (Crystal Palace)   Sept 27, 28, 29.
Players 90 (G. E. Palmer 5-45, H. F. Boyle 4-42) and 82 (G. E. Palmer 6-44) lost to Australians 133 (W. Mycroft 5-47) and 40-8 (W. Mycroft 5-17) by 2 wkts.

1880: 2nd Australians

Batting Averages

	M	I	NO	R	HS	Avge	100	c/s
P. S. McDonnell	9	15	1	391	79	27.93	0	4
W. L. Murdoch	9	15	1	339	153*	24.21	1	10
F. R. Spofforth	5	7	1	115	44	19.16	0	6
A. C. Bannerman	6	10	1	165	38	18.33	0	3
H. F. Boyle	9	14	3	157	69	14.27	0	13
J. McC. Blackham	9	14	2	168	42*	14.00	0	5/6
G. E. Palmer	9	11	5	81	23	13.50	0	2
G. Alexander	9	12	1	130	40	11.81	0	7
W. H. Moule	5	8	2	73	34	12.16	0	4
A. H. Jarvis	6	7	0	82	38	11.71	0	2/4
T. U. Groube	9	15	2	129	61	9.92	0	1
G. J. Bonnor	9	14	1	123	35	9.46	0	5
J. Slight	3	5	0	41	21	8.20	0	1

Bowling Averages

	O	M	R	W	Avge	BB	5i
F. R. Spofforth	207	74	336	40	8.40	8-61	6
G. E. Palmer	595.3	278	772	66	11.69	7-44	9
H. F. Boyle	422.1	197	493	31	15.90	6-70	3
W. H. Moule	39.3	15	66	4	16.50	3-23	0
G. Alexander	121	58	162	5	32.40	2-18	0
A. C. Bannerman	58	13	126	3	42.00	3-111	0

Also bowled: P. S. McDonnell 28-12-73-0; A. H. Jarvis 3-0-5-0.

Played in one non-first-class match: W. A. Giles and J. Macdonald.

so that what had appeared likely to be a financial failure ended in a modest success.

It was unfortunate for the tourists that their match-winning bowler through the major part of the tour, Spofforth, was absent through injury during September, which probably tipped the balance in the Test Match; over all matches Spofforth took 391 wickets, average 5.63. The other two bowlers were Boyle and Palmer, both of whom took over 250 wickets in all. Murdoch and McDonnell were the outstanding batsmen, each making over 1,000 runs over all matches. Bannerman remained completely dependable and Blackham kept wicket as well as in 1878. Bonnor was a tremendous hitter, but did little in the important matches. Slight was very often absent through illness, so that Alexander found himself playing very often to make up the side.

The Lord Mayor of London gave a banquet in honour of the team at the end of the tour and they left England on 5 October.

1882: 3rd Australians

Described as one long triumphal march, the tour of the 3rd Australians is regarded as the most successful of the 19th-century visits to England. The team consisted of W. L. Murdoch (captain), H. H. Massie, T. W. Garrett, F. R. Spofforth, A. C. Bannerman, G. J. Bonnor and S. P. Jones, all of New South Wales, plus J. M. Blackham, T. P. Horan, P. S. McDonnell, G. E. Palmer and H. F. Boyle from Victoria and G. Giffen of South Australia, with C. W. Beal as manager. They arrived in Plymouth aboard s.s. *Assam* on 3 May. McDonnell, who had sunstroke, had to be carried on board at the start of the voyage and though he seemed to have recovered by the time he landed in England, his batting was not as vibrant as in 1880.

The team had a productive fortnight's practice before the first match and began in great form—Massie hit a double century in the opening game and Murdoch 286 not out in the second. The tourists won a great match at the Oval against England, though as it was played throughout on a difficult wicket it possibly did not give each side a chance to display their best cricket—Spofforth's bowling was the deciding factor. Throughout the year the weather was unusually cold and play was frequently interrupted by rain and the Australians deserve great credit for winning as many as 23 matches in such alien conditions.

Of the Australian bowling, Spofforth was as deadly as ever; Boyle's deliveries looked deceptively easy; Garrett was tho-

roughly consistent and very dangerous if the wicket suited him; Palmer began in fine fettle, but an accident forced him to miss some of the later matches and Giffen's slows were not as effective as expected. Although the batsmen were not as stylish as their English counterparts, they proved difficult to remove. Murdoch was brilliant and the equal of anyone in England. Massie batted up to his Australian reputation and occasionally attacked the bowling savagery. Bannerman was as careful as ever and Bonnor and McDonnell both hit hard. Giffen and Jones did not quite come off as batsmen. The fielding, except for Horan's was magnificent, with Blackham proving himself better than any wicketkeeper in England. Murdoch captained the side well and Beal was an excellent manager—there were several small incidents, notably in connection with some umpiring decisions that seemed to go against the tourists, which might have marred

---

1882: 3rd Australians

1st Match: v Oxford University (Oxford) May 15, 16, 17.
Australians 362 (H. H. Massie 206) and 64-1 beat Oxford University 189 (E. D. Shaw 78*) and 234 (C. F. H. Leslie 56, A. O. Whiting 55, G. Giffen 7-78) by 9 wkts.

2nd Match: v Sussex (Hove) May 17, 18, 19.
Sussex 95 (G. E. Palmer 8-48) and 193 (H. Whitfeld 54*, R. T. Ellis 52, G. E. Palmer 6-62) lost to Australians 643 (W. L. Murdoch 286, G. Giffen 74, A. C. Bannerman 60, T. P. Horan 51, W. Blackman 4-159) by an innings and 355 runs.

3rd Match: v Orleans Club (Twickenham) May 22, 23.
Orleans Club 271 (A. P. Lucas 87*, G. E. Palmer 6-99) drew with Australians 75 (W. G. Grace 5-27, A. G. Steel 4-26) and 240 (W. L. Murdoch 107*, A. G. Steel 4-91).

4th Match: v Surrey (Oval) May 25, 26, 27.
Surrey 170 (H. F. Boyle 7-52) and 48 (T. W. Garrett 6-30, H. F. Boyle 4-16) lost to Australians 100 (G. G. Jones 5-31, E. Barratt 4-53) and 119-4 by 6 wkts.

5th Match: v Cambridge University (Cambridge) May 29, 30, 31.
Australians 139 (A. C. Bannerman 50, R. C. Ramsay 5-61, C. T. Studd 5-64) and 291 (G. Giffen 59, T. P. Horan 51, R. C. Ramsay 7-118) lost to Cambridge University 266 (C. T. Studd 118, G. E. Palmer 6-65) and 168-4 (J. E. K. Studd 66) by 6 wkts.

6th Match: Lancashire (Old Trafford) June 1, 2, 3.
Australians 259 (W. L. Murdoch 65, A. G. Steel 5-96, J. Crossland 4-39) and 129-6 beat Lancashire 118 (F. R. Spofforth 6-48) and 269 (R. G. Barlow 66*, A. G. Steel 50, F. R. Spofforth 6-109) by 4 wkts.

7th Match: v Yorkshire (Bradford) June 5, 6, 7.
Australians 128 (W. Bates 4-58) and 135 (E. Peate 5-75) drew with Yorkshire 146 (E. Lockwood 66, H. F. Boyle 5-30, F. R. Spofforth 5-78) and 30-3.

8th Match: v Nottinghamshire (Trent Bridge) June 8, 9, 10.
Australians 142 (J. McC. Blackham 56*) and 106 (A. Shaw 4-18) drew with Nottinghamshire 110 (T. W. Garrett 5-41, G. E. Palmer 4-38) and 12-1.

9th Match: v Derbyshire (Derby) June 12, 13, 14.
Derbyshire 106 (F. R. Spofforth 5-38, G. E. Palmer 5-59) and 77 (F. R. Spofforth 5-19) lost to Australians 292 (H. H. Massie 66, J. McC. Blackham 52) by an innings and 109 runs.

10th Match: v Yorkshire (Bramall Lane) June 19, 20, 21.
Yorkshire 92 (G. Giffen 5-16, T. W. Garrett 4-27) and 153 (G. E. Palmer 4-31, T. W. Garrett 4-37) lost to Australians 148 (W. L. Murdoch 54, E. Peate 7-51) and 99-4 by 6 wkts.

11th Match: Gentlemen (Oval) June 22, 23, 24.
Australians 334 (A. C. Bannerman 50, G. J. Bonnor 74, W. L. Murdoch 57, W. G. Grace 4-45) beat Gentlemen 182 (W. G. Grace 61, G. Giffen 8-49).

12th Match: v United Eleven (Chichester) June 26, 27, 28.
Australians 501 (T. P. Horan 112, A. C. Bannerman 88, H. H. Massie 60) beat United Eleven 166 (J. M. Read 90, F. R. Spofforth 4-51) and 72 (F. R. Spofforth 4-31, G. E. Palmer 4-36) by an innings and 263 runs.

13th Match: v Leicestershire (Leicester) June 29, 30.
Australians 106 (J. Parnham 9-68) and 116 (J. Parnham 6-61) beat Leicestershire 43 (G. E. Palmer 5-15, F. R. Spofforth 5-24) and 105 (F. R. Spofforth 7-54) by 74 runs.

14th Match: v Northants (Northampton) July 3, 4.
Northants 122 (T. W. Garrett 4-27) and 68 (G. E. Palmer 6-22) lost to Australians 270 (G. J. Bonnor 58, G. Giffen 51) by an innings and 80 runs.

15th Match: v Middlesex (Lord's) July 6, 7.
Middlesex 104 (T. W. Garrett 5-24, F. R. Spofforth 5-27) and 91 (F. R. Spofforth 4-35) lost to Australians 136 (W. L. Murdoch 51, C. T. Studd 6-73) and 61-2 by 8 wkts.

16th Match: v M.C.C. (Lord's) July 10, 11, 12.
M.C.C. 302 (C. T. Studd 114, T. W. Garrett 7-89) drew with Australians 138 (C. T. Studd 4-26).

17th Match: v Yorkshire (Dewsbury) July 13, 14, 15.
Yorkshire 129 (E. Lockwood 61, T. W. Garrett 7-50) and 64-1 drew with Australians 141 (T. Emmett 6-41).

18th Match: v Yorkshire (Bradford) July 17, 18, 19.
Australians 132 (T. Emmett 5-10) and 67 (T. Emmett 6-22) beat Yorkshire 68 and 84 (H. F. Boyle 6-39) by 47 runs.

19th Match: v Yorkshire (Middlesbrough) July 20, 21, 22.
Australians 222 (P. S. McDonnell 82, G. Ulyett 5-42) and 49-3 beat Yorkshire 129 (T. W. Garrett 7-49) and 140 (G. E. Palmer 5-42) by 7 wkts.

20th Match: v Northumberland (Newcastle) July 24, 25.
Australians 193 (T. P. Horan 76*, D. Bookless 7-109) beat Northumberland 63 (G. E. Palmer 6-21, H. F. Boyle 4-35) and 35 (G. E. Palmer 5-6, T. W. Garrett 5-20) by an innings and 95 runs.

21st Match: v Gentlemen of Scotland (Edinburgh) July 27, 28.
Australians 159 (W. L. Murdoch 58, P. Thompson 7-47) beat Gentlemen of Scotland 67 (G. E. Palmer 6-27, H. F. Boyle 4-32) and 74 (H. F. Boyle 6-17, G. E. Palmer 4-39) by an innings and 18 runs.

22nd Match: v Liverpool C.C. (Liverpool) July 31, Aug 1, 2.
Australians 240 (G. Giffen 81, T. P. Horan 70, J. Crossland 7-72) and 6-1 drew with Liverpool 112 (H. F. Boyle 5-51, G. E. Palmer 5-60) and 137 (H. F. Boyle 6-56, G. E. Palmer 4-73).

23rd Match: v Gloucestershire (Clifton) Aug 3, 4, 5.
Gloucestershire 108 (T. W. Garrett 6-58) and 183 (W. G. Grace 77, G. E. Palmer 4-61) lost to Australians 450 (T. P. Horan 141, P. S. McDonnell 70, W. E. Midwinter 4-119) by an innings and 159 runs.

24th Match: v Kent (Canterbury) Aug 7, 8, 9.
Australians 307 (J. McC. Blackham 62, S. P. Jones 59, H. H. Massie 54) and 81-3 beat Kent 222 (E. F. S. Tylecote 100*, C. W. Wilson 57, T. W. Garrett 6-62) and 165 (T. W. Garrett 6-58, G. E. Palmer 4-44) by 7 wkts.

25th Match: v Players (Oval) Aug 10, 11, 12.
Players 322 (J. M. Read 130, W. Barnes 87) beat Australians 150 (F. Morley 4-39) and 138 by an innings and 34 runs.

26th Match: v An Eleven of England (Derby) Aug 14, 15, 16.
An Eleven of England 230 (E. F. S. Tylecote 56, F. R. Spofforth 5-78) and 78 (F. R. Spofforth 4-37) drew with Australians 180 (W. L. Murdoch 70, W. Barnes 7-82) and 91-5.

27th Match: v Cambridge U, Past & Present (Portsmouth) Aug 17, 18, 19.
Cambridge U 196 (F. R. Spofforth 4-42) and 152 (A. Lyttelton 60, F. R. Spofforth 5-42, H. F. Boyle 5-63) beat Australians 141 (C. A. Smith 4-16) and 187 (G. J. Bonnor 66, C. H. Allcock 4-51, A. G. Steel 5-24) by 20 runs.

28th Match: v Somerset (Taunton) Aug 21, 22, 23.
Australians 245 (A. C. Bannerman 50) beat Somerset 96 (F. R. Spofforth 9-51) and 130 (H. F. Boyle 6-64, F. R. Spofforth 4-62) by an innings and 19 runs.

29th Match: v Gloucestershire (Clifton) Aug 25, 26.
Australians 190 (W. G. Grace 8-93) and 98-6 (H. H. Massie 55*) drew with Gloucestershire 131 (F. R. Spofforth 5-60).

30th Match: v England (Oval) Aug 28, 29.
Australia 63 (R. G. Barlow 5-19, E. Peate 4-31) and 122 (H. H. Massie 55, E. Peate 4-40) beat England 101 (F. R. Spofforth 7-46) and 77 (F. R. Spofforth 7-44) by 7 runs.

31st Match: v United Eleven (Tunbridge Wells) Aug 31, Sept 1, 2.
Australians 182 (J. Parnham 5-101, F. Lipscomb 4-22) and 49 (J. Parnham 7-25) drew with United Eleven 126 (H. F. Boyle 5-19).

32nd Match: v Nottinghamshire (Trent Bridge) Sept 4, 5, 6.
Australians 131 (W. L. Murdoch 72, A. Shaw 5-48) and 212 (P. S. McDonnell 63, F. Morley 5-74, W. Wright 4-54) beat Nottinghamshire 111 (F. R. Spofforth 6-46, T. W. Garrett 4-35) and 48 (F. R. Spofforth 5-18, H. F. Boyle 5-27) by 164 runs.

33rd Match: v I Zingari (Scarborough) Sept 7, 8, 9.
Australians 153 (H. H. Massie 51, W. Forbes 6-32) and 423-5 (G. J. Bonnor 122*, A. C. Bannerman 120*, W. L. Murdoch 53) drew with I Zingari 279 (G. B. Studd 86, H. F. Boyle 6-97, F. R. Spofforth 4-106).

34th Match: v A. Shaw's XI (Holbeck) Sept 11, 12.
Australians 79 (T. Emmett 6-30, W. E. Midwinter 4-34) and 126 (T. Emmett 5-35) beat A. Shaw's XI 79 (H. F. Boyle 7-32) and 37 (F. R. Spofforth 5-15, H. F. Boyle 5-20) by 89 runs.

35th Match: v North of England (Old Trafford) Sept 14, 15, 16.
North 245 (E. Lockwood 53, T. W. Garrett 4-60) and 30-0 beat Australians 110 (E. Peate 5-54, J. Crossland 4-39) and 162 (E. Peate 5-51, J. Crossland 4-49) by 10 wkts.

36th Match: v A. Shaw's XI (Oval) Sept 18, 19, 20.
Shaw's XI 129 (F. R. Spofforth 6-57) and 190-6 (R. G. Barlow 56) drew with Australians 87 (E. Peate 6-43).

37th Match: v Scotland (Glasgow) Sept 21, 22.
Scotland 32 (F. R. Spofforth 8-11) and 100 (F. R. Spofforth 6-47) lost to Australians 155 (J. Buchanan 5-56) by an innings and 23 runs.

38th Match: v An Eleven of England (Harrogate) Sept 23, 25, 26.
An Eleven of England 72 (H. F. Boyle 5-41, F. R. Spofforth 4-29) and 165 (T. W. Garrett 5-43) lost to Australians 134 (E. Peate 4-64) and 105-6 (E. Peate 4-48) by 4 wkts.

the visit, but they were not allowed to grow out of proportion.

From England the team travelled to the USA aboard the s.s. *Alaska*, leaving Liverpool on 29 September.

1882: 3rd Australians

Batting Averages

	M	I	NO	R	HS	Avge	100	c/s
W. L. Murdoch	32	55	5	1582	286*	31.64	2	30/3
H. H. Massie	33	57	4	1360	206	25.66	1	16
T. F. Horan	28	46	4	986	141*	23.23	2	8
A. C. Bannerman	31	52	2	1144	120*	22.88	1	27
G. J. Bonnor	25	41	7	749	122*	22.02	1	23/1
G. Giffen	30	46	4	799	81	19.02	0	12
J. McC. Blackham	27	38	6	577	62	18.03	0	27/12
P. S. McDonnell	30	49	3	794	82	17.26	0	16
S. P. Jones	18	28	1	341	59	12.62	0	16
G. E. Palmer	21	27	5	224	35	10.18	0	21
T. W. Garrett	30	42	5	368	41	9.94	0	13
H. F. Boyle	27	42	13	283	39*	9.75	0	28
F. R. Spofforth	30	41	11	263	37	8.76	0	17

Also batted: C. W. Beal (1 match) 5.

Bowling

	O	M	R	W	Avge	BB	5i
H. F. Boyle	1101.2	488	1523	125	12.18	7-32	13
F. R. Spofforth	1470	646	2079	157	13.24	9-51	16
T. W. Garrett	1167.3	474	1694	118	14.35	7-49	10
G. E. Palmer	1032.3	440	1535	100	15.35	8-48	7
G. Giffen	365.3	113	697	32	21.78	8-49	3
A. C. Bannerman	67	26	112	4	28.00	2-20	0
P. S. McDonnell	36	11	60	2	30.00	1-7	0
W. L. Murdoch	16	3	47	1	47.00	1-22	0
S. P. Jones	40	10	85	1	85.00	1-22	0

Also bowled: H. H. Massie 6-1-18-0.

F. R. Spofforth, the Demon Bowler, whose bowling ensured Australia's first Test Match victory in England, at the Oval in 1882, inspiring the famous Ashes obituary.

1884: 4th Australians

The victory of the Australian team against England at the Oval in 1882 meant that, unlike on the previous tours, there was no difficulty in arranging a strong fixture list for the 1884 visit and the programme was much more rigorous than on the three earlier visits. In contrast to the previous tours, most of the 1884 games were played out on hard, fast wickets which were supposedly not in favour of the tourists.

The team consisted of nine Victorians: H. J. H. Scott, W. H. Cooper, G. Alexander (manager), P. S. McDonnell, J. M. Blackham, G. J. Bonnor, W. E. Midwinter, G. E. Palmer and H. F. Boyle; three from New South Wales: W. L. Murdoch (captain), A. C. Bannerman and F. R. Spofforth; and G. Giffen of South Australia. There was some criticism of the composition of the side, mainly from those who felt that the cricket authorities from the colonies ought to have acted as selectors, rather than the choice being left to the promoters, the principal of whom was Alexander.

After eight matches in Australia, the side left Adelaide aboard *Sutlej* on 13 March and landed in Plymouth on 28 April, except for three members who travelled overland from Brindisi, arriving in London a week earlier.

Although England won the only Test Match to reach a definite conclusion, the Australians held the advantage in both the drawn matches: the one at Old Trafford was ruined by rain and the match at the Oval was very high scoring. The main reason for the success of the tour was the extraordinary bowling of F. R. Spofforth. His 207 wickets cost 12.57 runs each, whereas the next best figures, G. E. Palmer's, were 132, average 16.43. Giffen had some good days with the ball, but tended to be expensive and Boyle, though the wickets were rarely favourable to him, proved useful. Cooper had been injured on the journey, and was all but useless. Of the batsmen, Murdoch played a great innings of 211 at the Oval, but took a long time to find his form; McDonnell hit exceptionally well and his defence was markedly better than on his previous visit. Scott proved to be the most sound batsman, even if his style was awkward. Bannerman, Bonnor and Midwinter hardly came up to expectations, though all had days of success. Blackham established himself as the most accomplished wicketkeeper in England, but otherwise the fielding did not reach the high standard of previous tours.

The team left Gravesend in the *Mirzahpore* on 25 September.

1884: 4th Australians

Batting Averages

	M	I	NO	R	HS	Avge	100	c/s
W. L. Murdoch	30	49	5	1377	211	31.29	2	22/4
P. S. McDonnell	31	52	1	1190	103	23.33	1	22
H. J. H. Scott	31	50	8	966	102	23.00	1	24
G. Giffen	31	50	1	1036	113	21.14	1	21
A. C. Bannerman	31	51	2	959	94	19.57	0	24
G. J. Bonnor	31	50	2	905	95*	18.85	0	31
W. E. Midwinter	30	45	4	748	67	18.24	0	10
J. McC. Blackham	28	43	4	690	69	17.25	0	23/16
G. E. Palmer	30	46	10	483	68*	13.40	0	23
F. R. Spofforth	31	45	6	464	54	11.89	0	16
H. F. Boyle	27	37	14	243	48	10.56	0	28
W. H. Cooper	5	8	5	28	8*	9.33	0	3
G. Alexander	5	5	1	20	10*	5.00	0	1

Bowling Averages

	O	M	R	W	Avge	BB	5i
G. Alexander	18	7	24	2	12.00	2-24	0
F. R. Spofforth	1538	646	2564	205	12.50	8-62	22
A. C. Bannerman	22	10	32	2	16.00	2-15	0
G. E. Palmer	1213.1	446	2099	130	16.14	7-31	13
H. F. Boyle	709.1	283	1118	62	18.03	6-42	4
G. Giffen	816	282	1588	81	19.60	7-69	6
W. E. Midwinter	268.2	116	440	15	29.33	4-41	0
G. J. Bonnor	95	25	229	6	38.16	3-34	0
W. H. Cooper	130	26	309	6	51.50	2-59	0
H. J. H. Scott	56	9	157	3	52.33	1-10	0

Also bowled: P. S. McDonnell 10-4-27-0; W. L. Murdoch 5-0-25-0; J. McC. Blackham 3-0-8-1.

1884: 4th Australians

1st Match: v Lord Sheffield's XI (Sheffield Park) May 12, 13.
Lord Sheffield's XI 86 (G. Giffen 6-50, G. E. Palmer 4-34) and 120 (G. E. Palmer 6-38, G. Giffen 4-71) lost to Australians 212 (A. C. Bannerman 94, W. G. Grace 6-72) by an innings and 8 runs.

2nd Match: v Oxford University (Oxford) May 15, 16, 17.
Australians 148 (H. O. Whitby 8-82) and 168 (E. W. Bastard 5-44) lost to Oxford University 209 (T. C. O'Brien 92) and 110-3 (M. C. Kemp 63*) by 7 wkts.

3rd Match: v Surrey (Oval) May 19, 20.
Australians 195 (H. J. H. Scott 71, E. Barratt 5-93) and 48-2 beat Surrey 97 (H. F. Boyle 4-15, F. R. Spofforth 4-23) and 144 (F. R. Spofforth 5-72) by 8 wkts.

4th Match: v M.C.C. (Lord's) May 22, 23.
M.C.C. 481 (A. G. Steel 134, W. Barnes 105*, W. G. Grace 101, T. C. O'Brien 72, F. R. Spofforth 4-98) beat Australians 184 (P. S. McDonnell 64, C. T. Studd 6-96) and 182 (W. L. Murdoch 58*, W. G. Grace 4-61) by an innings and 115 runs.

5th Match: v An Eleven of England (Edgbaston) May 26.
Eleven of England 82 (F. R. Spofforth 7-34) and 26 (F. R. Spofforth 7-3) lost to Australians 76 (R. G. Barlow 7-31) and 33-6 (S. Christopherson 4-10) by 4 wkts.

6th Match: v Gentlemen of England (Lord's) May 29, 30, 31.
Gentlemen of England 277 (A. W.Ridley 68, G. F. Vernon 58, G. E. Palmer 6-82) and 129-6 (G. E. Palmer 4-59) beat Australians 135 (C. T. Studd 4-61) and 269 (H. J. H. Scott 82*) by 4 wkts.

7th Match: v Derbyshire (Derby) June 2, 3.
Australians 273 (G. E. Palmer 57*, W. Chatterton 4-66) beat Derbyshire 106 (F. H. Sugg 52, F. R. Spofforth 7-31) and 127 (G. Giffen 5-50, F. R. Spofforth 5-52) by an innings and 40 runs.

8th Match: v Lancashire (Old Trafford) June 5, 6, 7.
Australians 174 (A. Watson 4-39, J. Crossland 4-81) and 315-8 (G. Giffen 113, W. L. Murdoch 64, A. Watson 4-75) drew with Lancashire 195 (G. Giffen 6-55, F. R. Spofforth 4-82).

9th Match: v Yorkshire (Bradford) June 9, 10.
Yorkshire 55 (G. E. Palmer 5-25, F. R. Spofforth 5-29) and 72 (G. E. Palmer 6-29, F. R. Spofforth 4-32) lost to Australians 60 (T. Emmett 6-27, E. Peate 4-29) and 68-7 (E. Peate 6-33) by 3 wkts.

10th Match: v Nottinghamshire (Trent Bridge) June 12, 13, 14.
Nottinghamshire 170 (G. Giffen 7-69) and 138 (G. E. Palmer 6-70) lost to Australians 131 (W. Barnes 4-59) and 179-7 by 3 wkts.

11th Match: v Cambridge University (Cambridge) June 16, 17, 18.
Cambridge University 204 (H. W. Bainbridge 61, J. E. K. Studd 59, G. E. Palmer 6-84, F. R. Spofforth 4-45) and 93 (G. E. Palmer 5-49, F. R. Spofforth 4-39) lost to Australians 378 (W. L. Murdoch 132, G. E. Palmer 68*, H. G. Topham 5-74) by an innings and 81 runs.

12th Match: v North of England (Old Trafford) June 19, 20.
Australians 91 (E. Peate 5-28, G. Ulyett 4-35) and 107 (E. Peate 5-23) lost to North of England 220 (A. N. Hornby 94, W. Barnes 67, G. E. Palmer 5-70, Spofforth 4-70) by an innings and 22 runs.

13th Match: v Liverpool & District (Liverpool) June 23, 24.
Liverpool & District 213 (A. G. Steel 72, H. F. Boyle 5-33) and 54 (H. F. Boyle 5-24, G. E. Palmer 5-29) lost to Australians 140 (J. Crossland 5-50) and 128-9 (J. Crossland 6-20) by 1 wkt.

14th Match: v Gentlemen of England (Oval) June 26, 27, 28.
Australians 229 (J. McC. Blackham 69, W. E. Midwinter 60*, S. Christopherson 8-78) and 219 beat Gentlemen of England 261 (W. G. Grace 107, G. Giffen 4-60, F. R. Spofforth 4-94) and 141 (F. R. Spofforth 7-68) by 46 runs.

15th Match: v Players of England (Sheffield) June 30, July 1, 2.
Players of England 230 (G. Ulyett 76, F. R. Spofforth 6-80) and 134 (L. Hall 51, F. R. Spofforth 7-43) lost to Australians 189 (G. J. Bonnor 70, T. Emmett 5-41) and 178-4 (G. J. Bonnor 95*, E. Peate 4-56) by 6 wkts.

16th Match: v Eleven of England (Huddersfield) July 3, 4, 5.
Australians 175 (W. Attewell 6-39) and 124-7 (H. J. H. Scott 50, W. Attewell 4-32) drew with Eleven of England 453 (W. H. Scotton 134, W. Attewell 84, I. Grimshaw 77, E. T. Hirst 71)

17th Match: v England (Old Trafford) July 10, 11, 12.
England 95 (H. F. Boyle 6-42, F. R. Spofforth 4-42) and 180-9 (G. E. Palmer 4-47) drew with Australia 182.

18th Match: v Leicestershire (Leicester) July 14, 15.
Leicestershire 143 (F. R. Spofforth 6-50) and 64 (H. F. Boyle 5-21, F. R. Spofforth 5-28) lost to Australians 175 (W. E. Midwinter 52, A. Rylott 6-75) and 33-0 by 10 wkts.

19th Match: v Middlesex (Lord's) July 17, 18.
Middlesex 53 (F. R. Spofforth 7-16) and 106 (F. R. Spofforth 5-27, G. E. Palmer 4-54) lost to Australians 188 (W. L. Murdoch 64*, C. E. Cottrell 5-68, G. Burton 4-75) by an innings and 29 runs.

20th Match: v England (Lord's) July 21, 22, 23.
Australia 229 (H.J.H. Scott 75, G. Giffen 63, E. Peate 6-85) and 145 (G. Ulyett 7-36) lost to England 379 (A. G. Steel 148, G. E. Palmer 6-111) by an innings and 5 runs.

21st Match: v Sussex (Hove) July 24, 25, 26.
Sussex 396 (G. N. Wyatt 112, H. Phillips 111, G. E. Palmer 4-80, F. R. Spofforth 4-93) and 25-4 drew with Australians 309 (W. L. Murdoch 87, W. E. Midwinter 67, W. A. Humphreys 6-97) and 144 (W. A. Humphreys 5-69).

22nd Match: v Players of England (Oval) July 31, Aug 1.
Players of England 107 (F. R. Spofforth 8-62) and 71 (F. R. Spofforth 6-34) lost to Australians 151 (G. J. Bonnor 68, E. Peate 5-55) and 28-1 by 9 wkts.

23rd Match: v Kent (Canterbury) Aug 4, 5, 6.
Kent 169 (G. E. Palmer 4-52) and 213 (Lord Harris 60, G. E. Palmer 7-74) beat Australians 177 (P. S. McDonnell 80, A. Hearne 5-36, J. Wootton 4-72) and 109 by 96 runs.

24th Match: v Gloucestershire (Clifton College) Aug 7, 8, 9.
Gloucestershire 301 (W. G. Grace 116*, W. R. Gilbert 57, W. E. Midwinter 4-41) and 230-2 (J. H. Brain 108, W. W. F. Pullen 68*) drew with Australians 314 (H. J. H. Scott 79, P. S. McDonnell 62, W. A. Woof 6-82).

25th Match: v England (Oval) Aug 11, 12, 13.
Australia 551 (W. L. Murdoch 211, P. S. McDonnell 103, H. J. H. Scott 102, A. Lyttelton 4-19) drew with England 346 (W. W. Read 117, W. H. Scotton 90, G. E. Palmer 4-90) and 85-2.

26th Match: v Gloucestershire (Cheltenham) Aug 18, 19, 20.
Gloucestershire 183 (E. M. Grace 56, G. Giffen 6-58) and 83 (G. E. Palmer 7-31) lost to Australians 402 (G. Giffen 91, W. L. Murdoch 89, H. J. H. Scott 65, G. J. Bonnor 53, W. A. Woof 5-138) by an innings and 136 runs.

27th Match: v Nottinghamshire (Trent Bridge) Aug 21, 22, 23.
Australians 265 (F. R. Spofforth 54, W. E. Midwinter 51, W. Attewell 5-83) and 141 (W. Wright 4-58) drew with Nottinghamshire 273 (W. Flowers 69, W. Gunn 68, G. Giffen 5-86) and 15-1.

28th Match: v Cambridge University, Past and Present (Hove) Aug 25, 26, 27.
Australians 190 (A. F. J. Ford 6-64) and 180 (P. H. Morton 5-55) beat Cambridge University, Past and Present 135 (F. R. Spofforth 6-52) and 93 (F. R. Spofforth 7-33) by 142 runs.

29th Match: v South of England (Gravesend) Aug 28, 29.
Australians 358 (P. S. McDonnell 66, W. L. Murdoch 59, J. McC. Blackham 58*) beat South of England 178 (F. R. Spofforth 6-105) and 73 (F. R. Spofforth 6-23, G. Giffen 4-30) by an innings and 107 runs.

30th Match: v North of England (Trent Bridge) Sept 1, 2, 3.
North of England 91 (H. F. Boyle 5-32, F. R. Spofforth 5-40) and 255 (R. G. Barlow 101, W. Flowers 90) beat Australians 100 (W. Attewell 5-18, R. G. Barlow 4-6) and 76 (R. G. Barlow 6-42, W. Attewell 4-32) by 170 runs.

31st Match: v I Zingari (Scarborough) Sept 4, 5, 6.
I Zingari 229 (W. F. Forbes 80, F. R. Spofforth 7-114) and 140 (F. R. Spofforth 7-71) lost to Australians 233 (C. E. Cottrell 5-72, A. G. Steel 5-76) and 139-2 (P. S. McDonnell 67) by 8 wkts.

32nd Match: v South of England (Oval) Sept 11, 12.
South of England 56 (G. E. Palmer 5-10, F. R. Spofforth 5-34) and 102 (F. R. Spofforth 7-43) lost to Australians 163 (C. E. Horner 4-19, A. F. J. Ford 4-38) by an innings and 5 runs.

The team intended to play fixtures in India on the homeward voyage, but hopes of a match in Bombay did not materialise and the party arrived home on 9 November.

1884: 1st Philadelphians

Having raised a guarantee of 8,000 dollars, the Philadelphian cricket authorities chose the following for their pioneering visit to England: R. S. Newhall (captain), F. E. Brewster, W. Brockie, H. Brown, E. W. Clark, J. M. Fox, S. Law, W. C. Lowry, H. MacNutt, W. C. Morgan, C. A. Newhall, J. A. Scott, D. P. Stoever, and J. B. Thayer. The only notable absentee was D. S. Newhall, who could not obtain leave of absence from his employer. The team consisted entirely of amateurs and all the fixtures were arranged against amateur sides.

The team spent a fortnight practising on the Young America Ground before going to New York for a three-day match and on 17 May left that city on s.s. *City of Rome* for Liverpool.

The most important match of the visit was against a strong M.C.C. eleven and although they were beaten easily in this contest, the tourists had the satisfaction of beating, among others, a Gloucester team which included both E. M. and the great W. G. Grace.

There was little to choose between the three leading batsmen, J. A. Scott, R. S. Newhall and J. B. Thayer; each of them hit more than 800 runs at an average around 30. The outstanding player, however, was W. C. Lowry, whose slow left-arm bowling captured 110 wickets at an average of 12.72. No other bowler managed to reach 50 wickets.

The Americans learnt a great deal from the tour and socially were a great success. Total receipts from the gate amounted to £284, but as it was entirely an amateur venture, the lack of public interest was not considered significant. The majority of the team arrived back in New York aboard s.s. *Austral* on 17 August, having completed the return journey in 7 days and 3 hours. The immediate effect of the visit was the 1885 tour to Philadelphia by the side of E. J. Sanders.

1886: 5th Australians

It was hoped that the three leading cricket associations in Australia would select and promote this fifth team to England, but owing to differences of opinion, the job eventually fell to the Melbourne Club. Most critics felt that at least this was an improvement on the private speculations of the previous tours. The selected team was H. J. H. Scott (captain), F. R. Spofforth, G. J. Bonnor, J. M. Blackham, G. E. Palmer, J. W. Trumble, W. Bruce and J. McIlwraith, all from Victoria; T. W. Garrett, S. P. Jones and E. Evans of New South Wales; G. Giffen and A. H. Jarvis of South Australia, with B. J. Wardill of Victoria as manager. The absence of Murdoch, McDonnell and A. C. Bannerman was severely criticised.

1st Match: v Lord Sheffield's XI (Sheffield Park)   May 13, 14, 15.
Australians 98 (W. G. Grace 4-50) and 70 (W. Barnes 7-26) lost to Lord Sheffield's XI 105 (T. W. Garrett 6-22) and 64-2 by 8 wkts.

2nd Match: v Nottinghamshire (Trent Bridge)   May 18, 19.
Australians 109 (A. Shaw 4-37) and 12-2 drew with Nottinghamshire 104 (F. R. Spofforth 6-58, G. Giffen 4-31).

3rd Match: v Surrey (Oval)   May 20, 21, 22.
Surrey 171 and 87-7 beat Australians 82 (G. E. Lohmann 6-36) and 172 (G. Giffen 54*, G. G. Jones 5-34) by 3 wkts.

4th Match: v M.C.C. (Lord's)   May 24, 25, 26.
Match Abandoned–no play due to rain.

5th Match: v Oxford University (Oxford)   May 27, 28.
Australians 70 (H. O. Whitby 4-19) and 38 (H. O. Whitby 5-16, A. H. J. Cochrane 5-19) beat Oxford University 45 (F. R. Spofforth 9-18) and 38 (F. R. Spofforth 6-18, T. W. Garrett 4-13) by 25 runs.

6th Match: v North of England (Old Trafford)   May 31, June 1, 2.
Australians 45 (E. Peate 8-23) and 43 (A. Watson 6-12, E. Peate 4-27) drew with North of England 34 (F. R. Spofforth 7-19) and 15-1.

7th Match: v Gentlemen of England (Lord's)   June 3, 4.
Gentlemen of England 89 (T. W. Garrett 4-16, G. E. Palmer 4-37) and 136 (G. Giffen 6-71) lost to Australians 150 (C. W. Rock 5-51) and 86-3 by 7 wkts.

8th Match: v Derbyshire (Derby)   June 7, 8.
Derbyshire 95 (G. Giffen 7-41) and 144 (G. Giffen 9-60) lost to Australians 191 (W. Cropper 4-29) and 49-4 (W. Cropper 4-14) by 6 wkts.

9th Match: v Cambridge University (Cambridge)   June 10, 11, 12.
Australians 222 (W. Bruce 54, A. W. Dorman 4-66, C. W. Rock 4-79) and 326-5 (A. H. Jarvis 96*, H. J. H. Scott 57) drew with Cambridge University 143 (F. Marchant 51, G. Giffen 8-56).

10th Match: v Lancashire (Old Trafford)   June 14, 15, 16.
Australians 145 (S. P. Jones 54, A. Watson 5-53) beat Lancashire 46 (G. Giffen 8-23) and 87 (G. Giffen 8-42) by an innings and 12 runs.

11th Match: v Gentlemen of England (Oval)   June 17, 18, 19.
Gentlemen of England 471 (W. G. Grace 148, G. M. Kemp 83, W. E. Roller 63, M. B. Hawke 56, T. W. Garrett 6-131) and 105 (T. W. Garrett 5-38) drew with Australians 488 (S. P. Jones 151, A. H. Jarvis 71, C. E. Horner 4-153).

12th Match: v Players of England (Trent Bridge)   June 21, 22, 23.
Players of England 334 (R. G. Barlow 93, G. Giffen 4-91, G. E. Palmer 4-101) drew with Australians 205 (G. Giffen 72, R. G. Barlow 5-51) and 236-6 (G. Giffen 78)

13th Match: v Middlesex (Lord's)   June 24, 25, 26.
Middlesex 259 (G. Spillman 87, J. G. Walker 67, E. Evans 5-36) and 217 (S. W. Scott 68, A. J. Webbe 61, G. E. Palmer 7-84) lost to Australians 354 (H. J. H. Scott 123, G. Giffen 77, S. P. Jones 76, G. Burton 8-136) and 123-9 (G. Giffen 52, G. Burton 6-56) by 1 wkt.

14th Match: v Lord March's XI (Chichester)   June 28, 29.
Lord's March's XI 140 (F. R. Spofforth 6-72) and 63 (G. Giffen 7-21) lost to Australians 173 (J. Wootton 6-78) and 31-2 by 8 wkts.

15th Match: v C. I. Thornton's XI (Chiswick Park)   July 2, 3.
Australians 345 (W. Bruce 106, G. Giffen 59) drew with C. I. Thornton's XI 157 (G. Giffen 6-82, T. W. Garrett 4-29) and 130 (G. E. Palmer 4-68).

16th Match: v England (Old Trafford)   July 5, 6, 7.
Australia 205 (S. P. Jones 87, G. Ulyett 4-46) and 123 (R. G. Barlow 7-44) lost to England 223 (W. W. Read 51, F. R. Spofforth 4-82) and 107-6 by 4 wkts.

17th Match: v Nottinghamshire (Trent Bridge)   July 8, 9, 10.
Nottinghamshire 197 (A. Shrewsbury 72, F. R. Spofforth 4-51) and 157 (E. Evans 4-34, T. W. Garrett 4-53) drew with Australians 175 (G. E. Palmer 59, A. Shaw 4-19, W. H. Lockwood 4-69) and 122-4 (W. Attewell 4-18).

18th Match: v Yorkshire (Sheffield)   July 12, 13, 14.
Australians 275 (G. E. Palmer 94) and 136-4 (H. J. H. Scott 67*) beat Yorkshire 158 (W. Bates 57, T. W. Garrett 6-46, G. E. Palmer 4-33) and 249 by 6 wkts.

19th Match: v Liverpool and District (Liverpool)   July 16, 17.
Australians 152 (A. G. Steel 4-46) and 141 (H. J. H. Scott 80) drew with Liverpool and District 204 (A. G. Steel 55)

20th Match: v England (Lord's)   July 19, 20, 21.
England 353 (A. Shrewsbury 164, W. Barnes 58, F. R. Spofforth 4-73) beat Australia 121 (J. Briggs 5-29) and 126 (J. Briggs 6-45) by an innings and 106 runs.

21st Match: v Yorkshire (Huddersfield)   July 22, 23, 24.
Yorkshire 258 (F. Lee 59, R. Peel 52, G. Giffen 6-88) drew with Australians 169 (E. Peate 4-35) and 24-1.

22nd Match: v An England Eleven (Stoke-on-Trent)   July 26, 27, 28.
Australians 248 (J. McC. Blackham 71, G. Giffen 53, J. Briggs 4-65) drew with An England Eleven 119 (G. Giffen 7-46) and 148 (G. Giffen 5-45).

23rd Match: v Surrey (Oval)   July 29, 30, 31.
Australians 185 (G. Giffen 59, T. Bowley 7-64) and 107 (G. A. Lohmann 6-58) lost to Surrey 501 (J. M. Read 186, R. Abel 144, W. W. Read 80, G. Giffen 6-106) by an innings and 209 runs.

24th Match: v Kent (Canterbury)   Aug 2, 3, 4.
Kent 171 (G. G. Hearne 53*, T. W. Garrett 4-26, G. Giffen 4-74) and 35-0 beat Australians 79 (J. Wootton 4-33) and 123 (J. Wootton 5-60) by 10 wkts.

25th Match: v Gloucestershire (Clifton)   Aug 5, 6, 7.
Gloucestershire 220 (J. H. Brain 60, W. O. Moberly 60, G. E. Palmer 5-73, G. Giffen 5-86) and 358 (W. G. Grace 110, J. H. Brain 70, H. V. Page 66, G. Giffen 4-126) drew with Australians 211 (S. P. Jones 67, J. McC. Blackham 60, W. G. Grace 7-67) and 173-4 (H. J. H. Scott 75).

26th Match: v Warwickshire (Edgbaston)   Aug 9, 10, 11.
Australians 107 (J. E. Shilton 5-32, C. W. Rock 4-60) and 35-3 drew with Warwickshire 70 (G. E. Palmer 5-22, G. Giffen 5-38).

27th Match: v England (Oval)   Aug 12, 13, 14.
England 434 (W. G. Grace 170, W. W. Read 94, J. Briggs 53, F. R. Spofforth 4-65) beat Australia 68 (G. A. Lohmann 7-36) and 149 (G. A. Lohmann 5-68) by an innings and 217 runs.

28th Match: v Gloucestershire (Cheltenham)   Aug 16, 17, 18.
Australians 119 (H. V. Page 4-33) and 114 (W. A. Woof 7-32) beat Gloucestershire 74 (F. R. Spofforth 5-37, T. W. Garrett 4-11) and 133 (E. M. Grace 50, F. R. Spofforth 5-69) by 26 runs.

29th Match: v G. N. Wyatt's XI (Portsmouth)   Aug 19, 20, 21.
G. N. Wyatt's XI 183 (R. T. Thornton 51, F. R. Spofforth 4-75) and 187 (W. A. Humphreys 51*, G. E. Palmer 7-85) lost to Australians 236 (J. McC. Blackham 61, W. Bruce 56, C. A. Smith 4-49) and 135-3 (H. J. H. Scott 66*) by 7 wkts.

30th Match: v Cambridge University, Past and Present (Leyton)   Aug 23, 24, 25.
Cambridge University, Past and Present 349 (C. W. Rock 75, C. D. Buxton 57, F. R. Spofforth 4-55) and 149-4 drew with Australians 379 (G. Giffen 119, E. Evans 74*, S. P. Jones 52, A. F. J. Ford 5-76).

31st Match: v Sussex (Hove)   Aug 26, 27, 28.
Australians 200 (G. Giffen 73, W. A. Humphreys 4-86) and 300-7 (G. E. Palmer 84, J. W. Trumble 52*) drew with Sussex 352 (F. M. Lucas 93, G. Brann 104, G. E. Palmer 7-102).

32nd Match: v South of England (Gravesend)   Aug 30, 31, Sept 1.
Australians 299 (G. E. Palmer 93, G. A. Lohmann 4-84) drew with South of England 170 (G. E. Palmer 6-61) and 450 (F. Hearne 111, J. M. Read 109, W. W. Read 87, T. W. Garrett 4-101, F. R. Spofforth 4-112).

33rd Match: v Lord Londesborough's XI (Scarborough)   Sept 2, 3, 4.
Lord Londesborough's XI 558 (W. G. Grace 92, W. Flowers 82, W. H. Scotton 71, W. E. W. Collins 56*, W. Bates 53) drew with Australians 231 (W. Barnes 4-29) and 192-1 (S. P. Jones 108*, G. E. Palmer 75).

34th Match: v Players of England (Bradford)   Sept 6, 7, 8.
Australians 247 (H. J. H. Scott 72) and 226 (S. P. Jones 50, A. D. Pougher 6-62) drew with Players of England 238 (T. W. Garrett 7-82).

35th Match: v South of England (Hove)   Sept 9, 10, 11.
Australians 219 (G. Giffen 52, A. H. Jarvis 51*, G. A. Lohmann 4-66) drew with South of England 136 (T. W. Garrett 4-63) and 245-6 (W. W. Read 102*).

36th Match: v An Eleven of England (Lord's)   Sept 13, 14, 15.
An Eleven of England 319 (W. G. Grace 74, O. G. Radcliffe 57, G. Giffen 4-69) and 196 (R. Abel 52*, G. E. Palmer 6-69) drew with Australians 296 (A. H. Jarvis 84, S. P. Jones 67, W. Barnes 4-43) and 13-2.

37th Match: v South of England (Hastings)   Sept 16, 17, 18.
South of England 200 (R. Abel 75, J. W. Trumble 5-56, T. W. Garrett 4-60) and 230 (H. Pigg 59, J. W. Trumble 6-90) drew with Australians 194 (H. Pigg 4-57) and 202-6 (J. McIlwraith 62*, H. Pigg 4-68).

38th Match: v XVI of Skegness and Visitors (Skegness)   Sept 20, 21, 22.
Australians 103 (R. J. Mee 5-45, T. Emmett 4-43) and 148 (W. Bruce 54, R. J. Mee 5-55, T. Emmett 4-41) lost to XVI of Skegness and Visitors 181 (S. P. Jones 5-30) and 74-6 by 9 wkts.

39th Match: v An Eleven of England (Edgbaston)   Sept 24, 25.
Australians 186 (S. P. Jones 52, H. O. Whitby 4-42) and 56-2 drew with An Eleven of England 208 (W. W. Read 97, G. Giffen 4-68).

40th Match: v An Eleven of England (Harrogate)   Sept 27, 28.
An Eleven of England 139 and 117-3 (E. J. Diver 53) drew with Australians 121 (J. M. Preston 5-29).

The team sailed from Adelaide on 22 March aboard the *Austral* and arrived in England in the first week of May, some taking the overland route from Naples. Before leaving Australia, the tourists played a match against a Combined Fifteen in Adelaide, after a match against the Rest of Australia had fallen through over a financial dispute.

Compared with the 1884 visit 1886's results were disappointing–only 9 wins from 39 games, as opposed to 18 wins from 32.

The 1886 Australian touring party. Excluding the men at each end of the photograph, the party is, from left, back: McIlwraith, Trumble, Jarvis, Bruce, Jones, Palmer, Spofforth. Seated: Wardill (manager), Blackham, Evans, Scott (captain), Bonnor, Garrett, Giffen.

The tourists lost all three Test matches, two of them by an innings. A major factor in this lack of success was the lack of Spofforth, who dislocated a finger on his bowling hand in the 6th match, missed the next six matches and when he reappeared was never again as formidable as he had been in 1884.

Giffen proved very effective with the ball during the early part of the summer, but latterly found the wickets too good for him. Palmer could not match the figures he returned on earlier visits. Of the rest Garrett, Evans, Trumble and Jones were rarely more than ordinary bowlers. In the batting, which really needed the skills of Murdoch, Giffen, Jones and Scott proved best. Giffen was the most consistent and taking his bowling into consideration was the man of the tour. Jarvis was unreliable and Bonnor was unfortunately injured and so of little use in August–his resolute hitting might have inspired his colleagues with confidence during the later matches. Scott came in for considerable criticism – his captaincy was not up to the standard of Murdoch and at times there was a lack of discipline among the players. This was reflected in the out cricket, with even Blackham not as sound as of old and his understudy, Jarvis, unimpressive. The captain was also censured for his reluctance to bowl Evans, who was regarded in Australia as one of the best bowlers.

Despite the relative lack of success large crowds attended most of the matches and the programme was carried through with good feeling on both sides. The team travelled back to Australia via New Zealand, where they played six matches during late November and early December.

1886: 5th Australians

Batting Averages

	M	I	NO	R	HS	Avge	100	c/s
G. Giffen	35	61	8	1424	119	26.86	1	20
S. P. Jones	35	62	2	1497	151	24.95	2	23
H. J. H. Scott	36	63	5	1278	123	22.03	1	21
J. W. Trumble	34	51	8	823	56*	19.73	0	17
G. E. Palmer	33	54	4	972	94	19.44	0	30
G. J. Bonnor	20	34	3	581	49	18.74	0	17
A. H. Jarvis	33	50	6	780	96*	17.81	0	22/8
J. McC. Blackham	32	49	5	728	71	16.54	0	27/15
J. McIlwraith	27	37	5	520	62*	16.25	0	13
W. Bruce	33	47	3	704	106	16.00	0	26
R. J. Pope	4	6	4	30	12	15.00	0	1
T. W. Garrett	34	47	8	550	49*	14.20	0	11
E. Evans	28	40	15	336	74*	13.44	0	19
F. R. Spofforth	20	28	7	166	37*	7.90	0	8

Also batted: In one match: H. H. Hyslop 1 (1ct); J. Hardie O; B. J. Wardill 17 (1ct).

Bowling

	O	M	R	W	Avge	BB	5i
F. R. Spofforth	930.3	372	1527	89	17.15	9-18	7
G. Giffen	1673.2	710	2674	154	17.36	9-60	13
T. W. Garrett	1654.1	778	2221	123	18.05	7-82	5
E. Evans	490.2	246	588	28	21.00	5-36	1
G. E. Palmer	1393	552	2305	101	22.82	7-84	6
J. W.Trumble	483.3	182	803	30	26.76	6-90	2
S. P. Jones	149	52	297	7	42.42	3-47	0
W. Bruce	325	113	621	13	47.76	3-27	0

Also bowled: A. H. Jarvis 9-2-24-1; H. J. H. Scott 9-4-12-1; J. McC. Blackham 21-9-36-0.

1886: 1st Parsis

The Parsi community of Bombay began to play serious cricket in about 1850 and a number of Parsi cricket clubs were formed in the city over the next 30 years. In 1878 plans were made to take a Parsi team to England, but internal squabbles led to a libel suit and the tour did not materalise. In 1886, thanks to the work of B. B. Baria, a team was chosen and arrangements made for the inaugural tour. The team consisted of D. H. Patel (captain), P. D. Dastur, A. C. Major, J. M. Morenas, P. B. Balla, D. D. Khambata, S. Harver, M. Banaji, M. Framji, B. B. Baria, J. Ponchkhanawalla, M. Bejonji, S. N. Bhedwar, P. C. Major and A. Libuwalla. R. Henderson, a Surrey cricketer, was brought out from England to coach the team for three weeks before leaving India.

Sailing in the s.s. *Clyde* they arrived at Plymouth on 18 May and should have started their first match on 24 May, but rain prevented play on the first day at Sheffield Park.

The Parsis won only one match on the tour, but as the captain pointed out at the end of the visit, the object of the tour was to learn and so the results themselves were not important.

The most successful bowlers of the party were Bhedwar, a fast underarm bowler who took 59 wickets at 19 runs each; the fast left-arm bowler Khambata, who had 75 at 22 runs each and Framji, who bowled fast round arm and took 79 wickets at 26 runs each. Of the batsmen, not one attained an average over 20. A. C. Major hit 616 runs, average 15, P. D. Dastur 587, average 18 and J. M. Morenas 516 average 14.

The tourists left England on the voyage home to India on 12 August.

1886: 1st Parsis

1st Match: v Lord Sheffield's XV (Sheffield Park) May 24, 25.
Lord Sheffield's XV 142 drew with Parsees 46 and 53-4.

2nd Match: v M.C.C. (Lord's) May 27, 28.
M.C.C. 313 (W. Lindsay 74, W. G. Grace 65, I. D. Walker 51) beat Parsees 23 (W. G. Grace 7-18) and 66 (I. D. Walker 5-28) by an innings and 224 runs.

3rd Match: v Surrey C & G (Oval) May 31, June 1.
Surrey C & G 314 (J. C. Crawford 90, W. Lindsay 81, E. A. Bush 63, A. Major 9-119) beat Parsees 35 (C. L. Morgan 5-1) and 115 (G. G. Jones 5-12) by an innings and 164 runs.

4th Match: v Prince's C & G (Battersea) June 2, 3.
Prince's 71 (D. D. Khambatta 5-) and 229 (O. G. Radcliffe 66, H. St J. Mildmay 61, D. D. Khambatta 6-) beat Parsees 146 (A. Major 64, O. G. Radcliffe 6-) and 78 (O. G. Radcliffe 5-) by 75 runs.

5th Match: v Chiswick Park (Chiswick Park) June 4, 5.
Parsees 74 (C. M. Tuke 7-) and 89 lost to Chiswick Park 95 (S. H. Bhedwar 6-) and 71-3 by 7 wkts.

6th Match: v Essex C & G (Leyton) June 8, 9.
Parsees 69 (H. Ward 6-) and 106 lost to Essex C & G 514 (Davies 115, D. Womersley 66, C. H. Escott 53) by an innings and 339 runs.

7th Match: v Harrogate (Harrogate) June 9, 10.
Harrogate 211 (Wilkinson 65) beat Parsees 85 and 113 by an innings and 13 runs.

8th Match: v Ashton-under-Lyne (Ashton-under-Lyne) June 11, 12.
Parsees 71 and 71-7 drew with Ashton-under-Lyne 176.

9th Match: v Derbyshire C & G (Derby) June 14, 15.
Derbyshire C & G 340 (W. L. Shipston 113) drew with Parsees 62 and 12-3.

10th Match: Gentlemen of Leics (Leicester) June 16, 17.
Parsees 59 and 56 lost to Gentlemen of Leics 239 (W. H. Hay 122) by an innings and 24 runs.

11th Match: v Elland (Elland) June 18, 19.
Elland 162 and 125 drew with Parsees 109 and ?-3.

12th Match: v Hull (Hull) June 21, 22.
Parsees 56 and 107 lost to Hull 129 (D. D. Khambatta 6-41) and 35-3 by 7 wkts.

13th Match: v North Riding (Middlesbrough) June 23, 24.
North Riding 583 (A. Worsley 135) drew with Parsees 212.

14th Match: v Scarborough (Scarborough) June 25, 26.
Parsees 145 drew with Scarborough 497 (W. T. Graburn 142, H. Leadbetter 124).

15th Match: v Werneth (Oldham) July 2, 3.
Parsees 91 and 19 lost to Werneth 190 by an innings and 80 runs.

16th Match: v Liverpool C & G (Liverpool) July 5, 6.
Parsees 89 and 157 lost to Liverpool 482 (Lake 141) by an innings and 236 runs.

17th Match: v Warwickshire C & G (Edgbaston) July 7, 8.
Parsees 64 and 109 lost to Warwickshire 333 (D. Docker 120) by an innings and 169 runs.

18th Match: v Huddersfield (Huddersfield) July 9, 10.
Huddersfield 302 drew with Parsees 75 and 59-2.

19th Match: v Gentlemen of Notts (Trent Bridge) July 12, 13.
Gentlemen of Notts 248 (D. D. Khambatta 4-67) drew with Parsees 105 (F. H. Oates 5-26) and 71-4.

20th Match: v Hampshire C & G (Southampton) July 14, 15.
Hampshire 288 (G. F. Gerds 119) beat Parsees 107 and 145 by an innings and 36 runs.

21st Match: v United Services (Portsmouth) July 16, 17.
United Services 577 (H. B. Bethune 102, Lt. Hornby 122) drew with Parsees 212 (A. C. Major 97).

22nd Match: v Hastings (Hastings) July 19, 20.
Hastings 234 (J. Phillips 79, F. G. Langham 55, M. Framjee 5-) beat Parsees 96 (T. Kidman 5-) and 115 (T. Kidman 7-) by an innings and 23 runs.

23rd Match: v Normanhurst (Normanhurst) July 22.
Parsees 126 beat Normanhurst 81 by 45 runs.

24th Match: v Gentlemen of North Kent (Gravesend) July 23, 24.
Gentlemen of North Kent 340 beat Parsees 133 and 132 by an innings and 75 runs.

25th Match: v Manchester C & G (Manchester) July 26, 27.
Scores unknown.

26th Match: v Gentlemen of Northants (Northampton) July 30, 31.
Gentlemen of Northants 263 beat Parsees 25 and 176 by an innings and 62 runs.

27th Match: v Sussex (Hove) Aug 2, 3.
Sussex 360 (W. G. Heasman 100) beat Parsees 94 and 97 by an innings and 169 runs.

28th Match: v Prince Christian Victor's XII (Cumberland Lodge) Aug 7.
Prince's XII 90 and 95-2 drew with Parsees XII 33.

1887: 2nd Canadians

George Lindsay conceived the idea of this second tour to England and was responsible for the selection and organising of the team. The side comprised Dr E. R. Ogden (captain), D. W. Saunders, W. A. Henry, A. C. Allan, G. W. Jones, W. C. Little, A. Gillespie, W. W. Jones, C. J. Annand, W. W. Vickers, R. B. Ferries, G. G. S. Lindsay (manager) and W. J. Fleury. The team also included an umpire, C. N. Shanley, and a scorer, R. C. Dickson, both from

Toronto. The team made their way to New York, where they played a two-day fixture against All New York and then left for Dublin for the first match on this side of the Atlantic. The captain had come to England a fortnight before and travelled to meet the side in Dublin from London.

Though they won five matches, the Canadians' best performance was an honourable draw against a strong M.C.C. team at Lord's.

The best batsman was D. W. Saunders, who scored 613 runs, average 23.58, but the average palm goes to W. A. Henry, a hard-hitting cricketer whose 879 runs averaged 25.85. Henry was also a brilliant field in the deep. A. C. Allan was a stylish left-hander who looked most promising and he kept wicket well in several games, when Saunders, the principal keeper, was injured. The captain proved to be the outstanding all-rounder. His medium-pace right arm deliveries picked up 91 wickets at 16.70 runs each and he also scored 701 runs, average 23.37, including the side's only century.

After the last match the side broke up and several of the team went to tour the continent, while others remained longer in England. It was hoped that the tour would have beneficial effects on cricket in Canada and the major lessons learnt were running

between the wickets, instead of 'ambling', keeping strictly to the appointed times and general field placings in relation to the type of bowling. It was noted that 'long-stops' were no longer used in England.

1888: 6th Australians

Lacking such famous players as G. Giffen, F. R. Spofforth, W. Bruce, H. C. Moses and H. Trumble, all of whom were invited but declined, the combination gathered together under the managership of C. W. Beal was regarded as the weakest yet to leave Australia. The side was P. S. McDonnell (captain), C. T. B. Turner, J. J. Ferris, S. P. Jones and A. C. Bannerman, all of New South Wales; J. M. Blackham, H. F. Boyle, G. J. Bonnor, G. H. S. Trott and J. Worrall of Victoria and A. H. Jarvis and J. J. Lyons of South Australia. The side was defeated in all three of the matches they played before sailing, which simply emphasised their frailty. Travelling aboard the s.s. *Oceanien*, the team left Adelaide on 24 March and on 25 April arrived in Marseilles, from where half the members took the overland route. The whole party reassembled in London on 28 April.

When the team won each of their first five matches in England, however, Australian hopes of a successful tour were at last raised. During the 8th match S. P. Jones developed smallpox and the fact that his life was in danger for some time undoubtedly had an adverse effect on the tourists.

The soft wickets prevalent during most of the summer did assist the Australian bowlers, however, especially Turner and Ferris. The former had quite a remarkable record and was, by the end of the tour, regarded as the equal of any bowler. Ferris, the youngest of the tourists, kept an excellent length and had just enough turn to deceive most batsmen. Of the other bowlers, Trott's leg breaks were expensive and Worrall's action was most awkward, but he took some useful wickets. Neither Edwards or Lyons made much impression. S. M. J. Woods, an undergraduate at Cambridge and Australian by birth, was co-opted into the side, but did not achieve figures equal to his university cricketing.

Bonnor and McDonnell were the most attractive batsmen, though in the later stages of the visit neither showed to advantage often. Trott was sound and reliable, but the others only occasionally played good innings.

The out cricket was not always up to standard except for

Blackham who continued to demonstrate his superiority behind the stumps. In contrast with Scott in 1886, McDonnell led the team well both on and off the field and relations with the English players were most cordial.

To the surprise of many the overall record of the 1888 side was better than that of 1886. In the First Test the Australians, thanks to Turner and Ferris, won by 61 runs, but poor batting in the other two matches let them down.

The team returned to Australia in the s.s. *Cuzco*, landing in Adelaide on 27 November.

Opposite page left *The 1888 Australian party. Back: Ferris, Jones, Jarvis, Worrall, Beal (manager), Lyons, Blackham, Boyle, Edwards. Seated: Bonnor, Turner, McDonnell (captain), Trott, A. C. Bannerman.*

Opposite page, right *S. M. J. Woods was an Australian at Cambridge University who joined the 1886 tourists and played in the Tests. He did not achieve a lot, but was to become one of the few to have played cricket for both Australia and England.*

1888: 6th Australians

1st Match: v C. I. Thornton's XI (Norbury Park, Surrey) May 7, 8.
C. I. Thornton's XI 144 (J. J. Ferris 5-44, C. T. B. Turner 5-58) and 63 (J. J. Ferris 6-27, C. T. B. Turner 4-32) lost to Australians 133 (W. G. Grace 5-51, J. Wootton 4-49) and 76-4 by 6 wkts.

2nd Match: v Warwickshire (Edgbaston) May 11, 12.
Australians 346 (J. McC. Blackham 96, G. H. S. Trott 83, H. J. Pallett 4-84, J. E. Shilton 4-112) beat Warwickshire 67 (J. J. Ferris 5-25, C. T. B. Turner 5-34) and 129 (J. J. Ferris 5-59) by an innings and 150 runs.

3rd Match: v Surrey (Oval) May 14, 15.
Australians 363 (C. T. B. Turner 103, P. S. McDonnell 56, T. Bowley 4-77) beat Surrey 89 (C. T. B. Turner 6-44, J. J. Ferris 4-45) and 120 by an innings and 154 runs.

4th Match: v Oxford University (Oxford) May 17, 18, 19.
Oxford University 102 (J. J. Ferris 6-46, C. T. B. Turner 4-47) and 87 (S. P. Jones 4-19) lost to Australians 208 (P. S. McDonnell 105, H. Bassett 4-62) by an innings and 19 runs.

5th Match: v Yorkshire (Sheffield) May 21, 22.
Yorkshire 125 (J. J. Ferris 5-69, C. T. B. Turner 4-37) and 103 (C. T. B. Turner 4-34, J. J. Ferris 4-46) lost to Australians 292 (G. J. Bonnor 94, R. Peel 4-65, J. M. Preston 4-75) by an innings and 64 runs.

6th Match: v Lancashire (Old Trafford) May 24, 25.
Lancashire 98 (J. J. Ferris 8-41) and 154 (C. T. B. Turner 6-67) beat Australians 163 (S. P. Jones 57, J. Briggs 4-34) and 66 (J. Briggs 5-15, J. R. Napier 4-48) by 23 runs.

7th Match: v Gentlemen of England (Lord's) May 28, 29.
Australians 179 (S. P. Jones 61, C. A. Smith 4-45) and 213-1 (G. J. Bonnor 119, S. P. Jones 51*) drew with Gentlemen of England 490 (W. G. Grace 165, W. W. Read 109, J. Shuter 71, C. T. B. Turner 6-161, J. J. Ferris 4-131).

8th Match: v Players of England (Oval) May 31, June 1.
Players of England 231 (C. T. B. Turner 4-94) and 12-0 beat Australians 127 and 114 (W. Barnes 6-54, G. A. Lohmann 4-41) by 10 wkts.

9th Match: v Nottinghamshire (Trent Bridge) June 4, 5.
Nottinghamshire 215 (J. A. Dixon 83) and 38-0 beat Australians 76 (W. Attewell 5-33, W. Barnes 4-39) and 175 (W. Attewell 5-49, W. Barnes 4-68) by 10 wkts.

10th Match: v Cambridge University (Cambridge) June 7, 8, 9.
Cambridge University 332 (H. J. Mordaunt 78, G. M. Kemp 64, J. J. Ferris 5-79) and 232 (G. M. Kemp 56, J. J. Ferris 5-89) drew with Australians 266 (P. S. McDonnell 66, F. G. J. Ford 5-77) and 104-2.

11th Match: v Oxford University, Past and Present (Leyton) June 11, 12, 13.
Australians 176 (G. J. Bonnor 65, W. E. W. Collins 6-35) and 292 (J. D. Edwards 50*, E. A. Nepean 5-83) beat Oxford University, Past and Present 248 (A. C. M. Croome 66, C. F. H. Leslie 62, J. J. Ferris 4-51) and 146 (C. T. B. Turner 6-59) by 74 runs.

12th Match: v Middlesex (Lord's) June 14, 15, 16.
Middlesex 68 (C. T. B. Turner 4-30, J. J. Ferris 4-35) and 62 (C. T. B. Turner 7-29) lost to Australians 97 (G. Burton 6-39) and 35-2 by 8 wkts.

13th Match: v Eleven of England (Edgbaston) June 18, 19, 20.
Eleven of England (O. G. Radcliffe 71, C. T. B. Turner 4-60) and 99 (C. T. B. Turner 5-44, J. J. Ferris 5-46) lost to Australians 297 (G. J. Bonnor 73, P. S. McDonnell 67, W. G. Grace 6-74) and 8-0 by 10 wkts.

14th Match: v M.C.C. (Lord's) June 21, 22, 23.
Australians 130 (W. Barnes 5-72) and 96 (W. Attewell 4-29) beat M.C.C. 102 (Ferris 5-42) and 110 (C. T. B. Turner 6-52) by 14 runs.

15th Match: v Yorkshire (Bradford) June 25, 26, 27.
Australians 367 (G. J. Bonnor 115, A. C. Bannerman 65, W. Middlebrook 4-68, J. M. Preston 4-81) drew with Yorkshire 228 (F. Lee 83, L. Hall 67, G. H. S. Trott 5-74) and 344-7 (E. Wainwright 105, E. T. Hirst 87*).

16th Match: v North of England (Old Trafford) June 28, 29, 30.
North of England 93 (J. J. Ferris 5-38, C. T. B. Turner 4-35) and 96 (C. T. B. Turner 8-29) lost to Australians 89 (W. Attewell 4-25) and 101-5 (P. S. McDonnell 82) by 5 wkts.

17th Match: v Liverpool and District (Liverpool) July 2, 3, 4.
Australians 119 (T. Smith 4-39) and 150 (H. Richardson 7-46) beat Liverpool and District 70 (J. Worrall 5-20, C. T. B. Turner 5-40) and 69 (C. T. B. Turner 6-36) by 130 runs.

18th Match: v Leicestershire (Leicester) July 5, 6.
Leicestershire 119 (C. T. B. Turner 6-44) and 50 (C. T. B. Turner 5-20, J. J. Ferris 4-27) beat Australians 62 (H. T. Arnall-Thompson 6-31, A. D. Pougher 4-31) and 87 (A. D. Pougher 6-40) by 20 runs.

19th Match: v Derbyshire (Derby) July 9, 10.
Derbyshire 45 (C. T. B. Turner 6-20, J. J. Ferris 4-25) and 57 (C. T. B. Turner 7-26) lost to Australians 181 (W. Cropper 6-43) by an innings and 79 runs.

20th Match: v An Eleven of England (Stoke-on-Trent) July 12, 13.
Australians 242 (P. S. McDonnell 52, W. Flowers 4-52, A. D. Pougher 4-84) beat An Eleven of England 28 (C. T. B. Turner 9-15) and 79 (J. J. Ferris 6-35, C. T. B. Turner 4-33) by an innings and 135 runs.

21st Match: v Australia (Lord's) July 16, 17.
Australia 116 (R. Peel 4-36, G. A. Lohmann 4-33) beat England 53 (C. T. B. Turner 5-27) and 60 (R. Peel 4-14, G. A. Lohmann 4-33) and 62 (J. J. Ferris 5-26, C. T. B. Turner 5-36) by 61 runs.

22nd Match: v Sussex (Hove) July 19, 20, 21.
Sussex 98 (C. T. B. Turner 5-36, G. H. S. Trott 4-28) and 116 (C. T. B. Turner 5-35, J. J. Ferris 4-47) beat Australians 68 (W. A. Humphreys 5-21, A. B. Hide 4-21) and 88 (W. A. Humphreys 4-19, A. B. Hide 4-23) by 58 runs.

23rd Match: v Cambridge University, Past and Present (Leyton) July 23, 24, 25.
Cambridge University, Past and Present 137 (A. P. Lucas 50, J. J. Ferris 4-52, C. T. B. Turner 4-56) and 22-0 drew with Australians 319 (A. C. Bannerman 93*, G. J. Bonnor 78).

24th Match: v Yorkshire (Huddersfield) July 26, 27, 28.
Yorkshire 107 (C. T. B. Turner 5-23) and 49 (C. T. B. Turner 5-23, J. J. Ferris 4-16) drew with Australians 48 (R. Peel 6-19).

25th Match: v Surrey (Oval) July 30, 31, Aug 1.
Surrey 135 (C. T. B. Turner 5-52, S. M. J. Woods 4-44) drew with Australians 52 (G. A. Lohmann 5-24) and 33-2.

26th Match: v An Eleven of England (Hastings) Aug 2, 3, 4.
Australians 168 beat An Eleven of England 53 (C. T. B. Turner 8-13) and 88 (C. T. B. Turner 9-37) by an innings and 27 runs.

27th Match: v Kent (Canterbury) Aug 6, 7, 8.
Australians 116 (W. Wright 6-54, W. Hearne 4-49) and 152 (F. Martin 5-41) beat Kent 107 (J. J. Ferris 5-44, C. T. B. Turner 4-41) and 80 (C. T. B. Turner 6-28, J. J. Ferris 4-42) by 81 runs.

28th Match: v Gloucestershire (Clifton) Aug 9, 10, 11.
Gloucestershire 214 (F. Townsend 64) and 312 (O. G. Radcliffe 99, F. Townsend 92, W. G. Grace 52, J. J. Ferris 4-64, J. J. Lyons 4-97) beat Australians 143 (G. H. S. Trott 59, W. G. Grace 4-27) and 126 (F. G. Roberts 5-45) by 257 runs.

29th Match: v England (Oval) Aug 13, 14.
Australia 80 (J. Briggs 5-25) and 100 (W. Barnes 5-32, R. Peel 4-49) lost to England 317 (R. Abel 70, W. Barnes 62, G. A. Lohmann 62*, C. T. B. Turner 6-112) by an innings and 137 runs.

30th Match: v Nottinghamshire (Trent Bridge) Aug 16, 17, 18.
Nottinghamshire 441 (W. Gunn 91, W. Barnes 90, W. Flowers 62, J. J. Ferris 4-106) beat Australians 95 (W. Attewell 8-48) and 147 (J. A. Dixon 4-41, W. Attewell 4-48) by an innings and 199 runs.

31st Match: v Gloucestershire (Cheltenham) Aug 20, 21, 22.
Australians 118 (F. G. Roberts 6-51) and 151 (O. G. Radcliffe 4-24) lost to Gloucestershire 209 (W. G. Grace 92, J. J. Ferris 6-93, C. T. B. Turner 4-82) and 61-2 by 8 wkts.

32nd Match: v An Eleven of England (Crystal Palace) Aug 23, 24, 25.
An Eleven of England 108 (C. T. B. Turner 6-56) and 98 (A. M. Sutthery 54, C. T. B. Turner 4-42, J. J. Ferris 4-49) beat Australians 47 (J. J. Hulme 7-14) and 81 (J. Phillips 5-25) by 78 runs.

33rd Match: v Oxford and Cambridge Universities, Past and Present (Portsmouth) Aug 27, 28, 29.
Universities 243 (W. H. Patterson 84, Lord Harris 52, C. T. B. Turner 6-85) and 54-5 drew with Australians 298 (A. C. Bannerman 76, P. S. McDonnell 69, C. T. B. Turner 60).

34th Match: v England (Old Trafford) Aug 30, 31.
England 172 (C. T. B. Turner 5-86) beat Australia 81 (R. Peel 7-31) and 70 (R. Peel 4-37) by an innings and 21 runs.

35th Match: v An Eleven of England (Harrogate) Sept 3, 4.
Australians 70 (J. Briggs 5-43, W. Attewell 4-27) and 168 (W. Attewell 4-36) beat An Eleven of England 111 (C. T. B. Turner 5-63) and 71 (C. T. B. Turner 5-51, J. J. Ferris 4-18) by 56 runs.

36th Match: v Lord Londesborough's XI (Scarborough) Sept 6, 7, 8.
Lord Londesborough's XI 163 (C. T. B. Turner 4-48) and 145 (C. T. B. Turner 8-74) beat Australians 96 (J. Briggs 6-18) and 57 (J. Briggs 7-22) by 155 runs.

37th Match: v A. Shrewsbury's Team (Holbeck, Leeds) Sept 10, 11, 12.
Australians 86 (G. A. Lohmann 5-37) and 119 (J. Briggs 4-30, G. A. Lohmann 4-62) lost to A. Shrewsbury's Team 142 (J. J. Ferris 5-38) and 64-6 by 4 wkts.

38th Match: v A. Shrewsbury's Team (Old Trafford) Sept 13, 14, 15.
A. Shrewsbury's Team 195 (C. T. B. Turner 6-72) and 34-1 beat Australians 35 (J. Briggs 6-17) and 192 (G. H. S. Trott 73, J. Briggs 4-63) by 9 wkts.

39th Match: v South of England (Hastings) Sept 17, 18, 19.
Australians 291 (J. J. Lyons 84, G. H. S. Trott 50, G. A. Lohmann 4-93) and 62-1 beat South of England 174 (G. H. S. Trott 4-53, C. T. B. Turner 4-59) and 175 (W. G. Grace 53, J. J. Ferris 5-49, C. T. B. Turner 4-42) by 9 wkts.

40th Match: v Surrey (Oval) Sept 20, 21, 22.
Australians 259 (G. J. Bonnor 87, T. Bowley 5-44) and 123 (G. A. Lohmann 5-43) beat Surrey 211 (J. M. Read 57, H. Wood 55*, J. J. Ferris 4-69) and 137 (J. J. Ferris 5-60, C. T. B. Turner 4-42) by 34 runs.

1888: 2nd Parsis

Organised by P. D. Kanga, J. M. Divecha and D. C. Pandole, the team which represented the 2nd Parsis was much stronger than the 1886 side, only two of which were included in this second combination. The side was P. D. Kanga (captain), R. D. Cooper, D. F. Dubash, N. C. Bapasola, M. E. Pavri, J. M. Morenas, M. D. Kanga, S. H. Harvar, A. D. Vatcha, K. R. Eranee, D. S. Mehta, D. C. Pandole, B. D. Mody, D. N. Writer and J. M. Divecha. They left Bombay aboard the steamer *Poseidon* on 7 May and arrived in London on 31 May.

The team were far better than the side of 1886, though they

could point to only eight wins. Their best performance was perhaps against a good Gentleman of Surrey side at the Oval, when they lost by just nine runs.

R. D. Cooper was the best batsman, hitting 952 runs, average 18.16, but the great feature of the tour was the bowling of M. E. Pavri: fast round-arm, he took 170 wickets at 11 runs each. Curiously enough P. D. Kanga, bowling fast underarm, came second to Pavri in the averages with 71 wickets at 12 runs each. Pandole took 86 wickets at 16 and the team was considerably weakened in the last part of the tour because he had to return to India.

The main body of the team left England by train on September 14 and joined the s.s. *Poseidon* at Trieste for the voyage to Bombay.

1889: 2nd Philadelphians

There were four notable absentees: R. S. Newhall, J. A. Scott, W. C. Lowry and W. Brockie, in the party which was composed of D. S. Newhall (captain), F. E. Brewster, H. I. Brown, R. D. Brown, E. W. Clark, N. Etting, W. C. Morgan, C. R. Palmer, G. S. Patterson, J. W. Sharp, D. P. Stoever, W. Scott and A. G. Thomson, plus H. P. Baily and G. B. Warder who were late additions. Leaving New York aboard the s.s. *City of Chicago* on 19 June, the Gentlemen of Philadelphia opened their programme with two matches in Ireland.

Cricket in the United States had made considerable strides since the 1884 visit, and so it was a pity that the full strength of Philadelphia could not be represented on this second tour. The

---

1889: 2nd Philadelphians

1st Match: v Trinity College L.V.C. (Dublin) July 2, 3.
Trinity College 289 (D. N. Trotter 85, F. H. Browning 52) drew with Philadelphians 177 (C. A. Palmer 55, C. L. Johnson 6-) and 379-6 (D. P. Stoever 115*, R. D. Brown 111, A. D. Thomson 59).

2nd Match: v Gentlemen of Ireland (Dublin) July 4, 5.
Gentlemen of Ireland 206 (E. Fitzgerald 59, G. S. Patterson 6-) and 300-7 dec (F. H. Browning 87, M. C. A. Hamilton 62, E. Fitzgerald 60, G. S. Patterson 4-) drew with Philadelphians 213 (E. Clarke 52, R. L. Pike 5-) and 198-5 (R. D. Brown 81, E. Clarke 63, R. L. Pike 4-).

3rd Match: v Gentlemen of Scotland (Edinburgh) July 8, 9.
Gentlemen of Scotland 66 (E. W. Clark 5-32, G. S. Patterson 4-27) and 340 (C. T. Mannes 110, H. S. Walker 72) drew with Philadelphians 308 (G. S. Patterson 62) and 100-0 (D. P. Stoever 65*).

4th Match: v Gentlemen of Liverpool (Liverpool) July 11, 12.
Philadelphians 445 (W. Scott 125, R. D. Brown 102, W. Morgan 63, E. C. Hornby 5-86) beat Gentlemen of Liverpool 123 (G. S. Patterson 8-) and 170 (E. C. Hornby 64, W. Scott 5-) by an innings and 152 runs.

5th Match: v Gentlemen of Gloucestershire (Bristol) July 15, 16, 17.
Gentlemen of Gloucestershire 311 and 112-2 beat Philadelphians 173 (W. G. Grace 5-57) and 249 (W. G. Grace 6-73) by 8 wkts.

6th Match: v Gentlemen of Surrey (Oval) July 18, 19, 20.
Gentlemen of Surrey 294 (W. W. Read 105, W. Scott 7-91) and 355 (W. W. Read 130, J. Shuter 71, E. W. Clark 5-82, W. Scott 5-139) drew with Philadelphians 458 (W. Scott 142, W. C. Morgan 98, C. E. Horner 4-99) and 43-3.

7th Match: v Gentlemen of M.C.C. (Lord's) July 22, 23, 24.
M.C.C. 383 (R. T. Thornton 111, C. C. Clarke 80, C. I. Thornton 73, E. W. Clark 4-111) beat Philadelphians 235 (G. S. Patterson 52) and 64 (E. A. Nepean 5-30, W. G. Grace 4-32) by an innings and 84 runs.

8th Match: v Gentlemen of Kent (Town Malling) July 25, 26.
Philadelphians 177 (D. S. Newhall 51*, J. Fellowes 4-) and 101 lost to Gentlemen of Kent 209 (W. B. Hawkins 67, E. W. Clark 4-) and 70-4 by 6 wkts.

9th Match: v Gentlemen of Hampshire (Southampton) July 29, 30, 31.
Philadelphians 91 (H. W. Forster 5-35) and 229 (G. S. Patterson 106*, H. B. Bethune 4-25) beat Gentlemen of Hampshire 108 (E. W. Clark 6-30) and 210 (C. J. R. Richards 53, E. W. Clark 5-91) by 2 runs.

10th Match: v United Services (Portsmouth) Aug 2, 3.
United Services 428 (L. A. Hamilton 203, C. S. M. Jelfkins 96, R. D. Brown 5-) drew with Philadelphians 15-1.

11th Match: v Gentlemen of Sussex (Hove) Aug 5, 6.
Philadelphians 157 (W. Scott 66, G. R. Burge 7-) and 241-6 dec drew with Gentlemen of Sussex 109 (G. S. Patterson 5-) and 235-6 (M. P. Lucas 77, J. Brown 69).

12th Match: v Cambridge University L.V.C. (Cambridge) Aug 8, 9, 10.
Philadelphians 307 (E. W. Clark 88, H. B. Bolus 5-40) beat Cambridge University L.V.C. 151 (C. A. Trouncer 83*, H. P. Baily 7-33) and 144 (C. A. Trouncer 53, H. P. Baily 6-54) by an innings and 12 runs.

---

batting showed a great improvement with G. S. Patterson, W. Scott and E. W. Clark all having good innings. The bowling lacked bite and Lowry was badly missed. A summary of results does not compare favourably with 1884, but this time the standard of the opposition was higher.

When the visit ended most of the side did not return directly to the United States, but took the opportunity of visiting France to see the Paris Exhibition. As on the previous visit the team was entirely amateur and this time gave all the gate receipts due to them to the Cricketers' Fund.

1890: 7th Australians

Despite the exertions of H. F. Boyle, who was given the task of selecting the 1890 team, there were several disappointments. G. Giffen, A. C. Bannerman and G. J. Bonnor all agreed to travel and then withdrew at the last moment. Moses and McLeod also declined offers and the eventual party consisted of W. L. Murdoch (captain), S. P. Jones, C. T. B. Turner, J. J. Ferris, P.

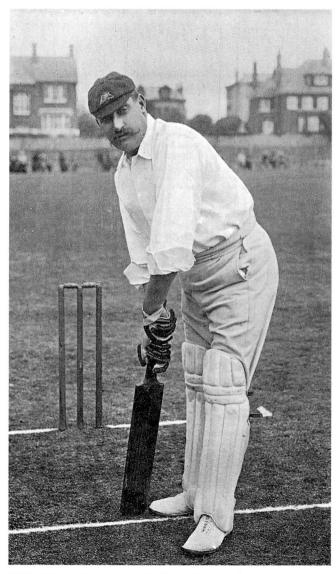

W. L. Murdoch captained the Australian tourists in 1880, 1882, 1884 and, after a break, in 1890. In 1891-92 he played for England in South Africa. He died from apoplexy while watching Australia play South Africa in 1911.

C. Charlton, S. E. Gregory, all of New South Wales; J. M. Blackham, G. H. S. Trott, F. H. Walters, H. Trumble, J. E. Barrett and H. F. Boyle (manager) of Victoria; J. J. Lyons of South Australia and E. J. K. Burn of Tasmania. The team left Melbourne in the s.s. *Liguria* on 14 March and arrived at Plymouth on 25 April, except Murdoch who came on a few weeks ahead with his wife.

A long injury list told against the tourists. S. P. Jones became a virtual passenger and Murdoch, Trott, Ferris and Barrett all reported indisposed at various times. S. M. J. Woods was invited to join the side but declined and R. J. Pope was co-opted once or twice but with no success. The team began in fine form, but a black June, with not a single win, seemed to overwhelm the side and in the end they became the first Australian visitors to lose more matches than they won.

Murdoch had virtually retired from first-class cricket five years before and some critics were doubtful about his current form—in the event he hit most runs on the tour at the highest average and his captaincy was generally approved. Of the other batsmen Barrett proved to be another Scotton; Lyons improved on his 1888 visit and Trott, following a poor start, played well in July and August. Burn and Walters failed, as did Gregory, though he fielded quite brilliantly. It was the batting that let the side down, for the bowling in the hands of Turner and Ferris was generally formidable, both these famous players enhancing the reputations which they made in 1888. The various change bowlers were not needed much and all together they could not muster half the wickets taken by Turner and Ferris. The fielding was hardly up to scratch and dropped catches lost them the Oval Test.

The Australians had been going to tour South Africa after

1890: 7th Australians

1st Match: v Lord Sheffield's XI (Sheffield Park) May 8, 9, 10.
Australians 191 (W. L. Murdoch 93, J. Briggs 4-47) beat Lord Sheffield's XI 27 (J. J. Ferris 5-18, C. T. B. Turner 4-9) and 130 (J. J. Ferris 7-70) by an innings and 34 runs.

2nd Match: v Warwickshire (Edgbaston) May 13, 14.
Australians 89 (H. J. Pallett 7-38) and 132 (H. J. Pallett 4-54) beat Warwickshire 38 (C. T. B. Turner 6-17) and 51 (C. T. B. Turner 6-17, J. J. Ferris 4-26) by 132 runs.

3rd Match: v W. H. Laverton's XI (Westbury, Wiltshire) May 15, 16, 17.
W. H. Laverton's XI 141 (J. J. Ferris 6-57, C. T. B. Turner 4-80) and 223 (O. G. Radcliffe 93, W. G. Grace 64, J. J. Ferris 6-68, C. T. B. Turner 4-82) beat Australians 67 (J. Briggs 7-33) and 116 (G. A. Lohmann 4-44, J. Briggs 4-59) by 181 runs.

4th Match: v Oxford University (Oxford) May 20, 21.
Australians 234 (C. T. B. Turner 59, G. F. H. Berkeley 8-70) beat Oxford University 120 (C. T. B. Turner 5-58) and 53 (P. C. Charlton 5-28) by an innings and 61 runs.

5th Match: v Surrey (Oval) May 23, 24, 25.
Surrey 200 (W. W. Read 87, J. J. Ferris 4-59) and 156 (J. J. Lyons 5-50, J. J. Ferris 4-65) lost to Australians 278 (J. McC. Blackham 75, F. H. Walters 53*, J. W. Sharpe 5-62) and 79-2 by 8 wkts.

6th Match: v Yorkshire (Sheffield) May 26, 27.
Australians 87 (R. Peel 6-34, G. Ulyett 4-49) and 125 (R. Peel 6-35) lost to Yorkshire 161 (C. T. B. Turner 5-59) and 53-3 by 7 wkts.

7th Match: v Lancashire (Old Trafford) May 29, 30.
Australians 316 (G. H. S. Trott 61, S. E. Gregory 59) beat Lancashire 78 (C. T. B. Turner 6-23) and 83 (C. T. B. Turner 5-40, H. Trumble 4-13) by an innings and 155 runs.

8th Match: v M.C.C. (Lord's) June 2, 3.
Australians 124 (F. Martin 4-55) and 180 (G. H. S. Trott 61, F. Martin 5-61) lost to M.C.C. 194 (J. J. Ferris 4-76) and 111-3 by 7 wkts.

9th Match: v Cambridge University (Cambridge) June 5, 6, 7.
Cambridge University 189 (G. MacGregor 73*, J. J. Ferris 4-68) and 357 (E. C. Streatfeild 74*, R. N. Douglas 57) drew with Australians 351 (J. E. Barrett 76, W. L. Murdoch 73, F. S. Jackson 4-69).

10th Match: v Middlesex (Lord's) June 9, 10, 11.
Australians 135 (J. T. Hearne 5-42, E. A. Nepean 5-63) and 176 (S. E. Gregory 53*) drew with Middlesex 113 (C. T. B. Turner 4-52).

11th Match: v Nottinghamshire (Trent Bridge) June 12, 13, 14.
Nottinghamshire 215 (A. Shrewsbury 61, C. T. B. Turner 6-75) beat Australians 62 (F. J. Shacklock 6-38, W. Attewell 4-21) and 127 (W. Attewell 4-21) by an innings and 26 runs.

12th Match: v South of England (Oval) June 16, 17, 18.
South of England 163 (W. W. Read 90, J. J. Ferris 6-88) and 121 (C. T. B. Turner 7-50) beat Australians 113 (G. A. Lohmann 4-38, F. Martin 4-44) and 74 (F. Martin 6-40, G. A. Lohmann 4-25) by 97 runs.

13th Match: v Players of England (Lord's) June 19, 20, 21.
Players of England 526 (W. Gunn 228, W. Barnes 67, J. J. Lyons 4-123) beat Australians 156 (J. J. Lyons 50, G. A. Lohmann 5-61) and 107 (J. Briggs 5-51, G. A. Lohmann 4-53) by an innings and 263 runs.

14th Match: v Yorkshire (Bradford) June 23, 24, 25.
Australians 177 (J. E. Barrett 61, G. Ulyett 4-40) and 141 (C. T. B. Turner 53, G. Ulyett 6-45) lost to Yorkshire 171 (R. Peel 73, L. Hall 64, J. J. Ferris 6-50) and 148-2 (F. Lee 67*) by 8 wkts.

15th Match: v North of England (Old Trafford) June 26, 27, 28.
Australians 216 (W. L. Murdoch 74, R. Peel 4-45) and 58-5 drew with North of England 148 (J. J. Ferris 5-31, C. T. B. Turner 5-78).

16th Match: v Derbyshire (Derby) June 30, July 1, 2.
Australians 108 (W. Sugg 4-38) and 75-9 dec (F. R. Spofforth 6-42) drew with Derbyshire 54 (C. T. B. Turner 6-16, J. J. Ferris 4-30).

17th Match: v Staffordshire's Eleven (Stoke-on-Trent) July 3, 4.
Australians 60 (W. Flowers 5-23) and 139 (W. Flowers 6-65) beat Staffordshire's Eleven 60 (J. J. Ferris 7-16) and 51 (C. T. B. Turner 7-23) by 88 runs.

18th Match: v Leicestershire (Leicester) July 7, 8, 9.
Leicestershire 166 (C. T. B. Turner 6-54) and 46 (J. J. Ferris 6-19) lost to Australians 276 (P. C. Charlton 75, J. McC. Blackham 58, A. D. Pougher 4-69) by an innings and 64 runs.

19th Match: v Gloucestershire (Bristol) July 10, 11, 12.
Gloucestershire 94 (J. J. Ferris 5-45, C. T. B. Turner 4-32) and 140-6 drew with Australians 408 (G. H. S. Trott 102, S. P. Jones 98, J. J. Lyons 68, W. G. Grace 4-125).

20th Match: v Players of England (Sheffield) July 14, 15.
Players of England 221 (A. Shrewsbury 65, J. J. Lyons 5-42) and 32-1 beat Australians 91 (G. A. Lohmann 4-45) and 161 by 9 wkts.

21st Match: v Surrey (Oval) July 17, 18, 19.
Australians 199 (J. E. Barrett 54, W. L. Murdoch 50, G. A. Lohmann 5-64, W. H. Lockwood 4-27) and 93-6 drew with 277 (W. W.Read 57, H. Trumble 5-77).

22nd Match: v England (Lord's) July 21, 22, 23.
Australia 132 (J. J. Lyons 55, W. Attewell 4-42) and 176 (J. E. Barrett 67*) lost to England 173 (G. Ulyett 74*, J. J. Lyons 5-30) and 137-3 (W. G. Grace 75*) by 7 wkts.

23rd Match: v Sussex (Hove) July 24, 25, 26.
Australians 363 (W. L. Murdoch 158, J. E. Barrett 83, C. A. Smith 4-83) beat Sussex 91 (J. J. Lyons 6-38, H. Trumble 4-45) and 227 (G. Bean 100, P. C. Charlton 5-27) by an innings and 45 runs.

24th Match: v Kent (Maidstone) July 28, 29.
Australians 189 (F. Martin 4-47) and 64-1 beat Kent 77 (C. T. B. Turner 4-7) and 174 (L. A. Hamilton 56, C. T. B. Turner 4-43, J. J. Ferris 4-55) by 9 wkts.

25th Match: v Lyric Club (Barnes) July 31, Aug 1, 2.
Lyric Club 106 (C. T. B. Turner 6-61, J. J. Ferris 4-41) and 278 (T. C. O'Brien 87, G. Ulyett 70) beat Australians 154 (G. A. Lohmann 6-23) and 134 (J. E. Barrett 61*, A. W. Mold 9-43) by 96 runs.

26th Match: v Kent (Canterbury) Aug 4, 5, 6.
Kent 145 (C. T. B. Turner 5-55) and 205 (L. A. Hamilton 117*, C. T. B. Turner 5-53, J. J. Ferris 5-101) beat Australians 114 (F. Martin 6-60, W. Wright 4-42) and 128 (A. Daffen 4-5) by 108 runs.

27th Match: v Cambridge University Past and Present (Leyton) Aug 7, 8, 9.
Cambridge University, Past and Present 389 (E. C. Streatfeild 145, C. A. Smith 58*, P. C. Charlton 4-116) and 78-8 (H. Trumble 5-38) drew with Australians 218 (J. McC. Blackham 66*, E. C. Streatfeild 5-47) and 355-6 dec (G. H. S. Trott 186, W. L. Murdoch 129)

28th Match: v England (Oval) Aug 11, 12.
Australia 92 (F. Martin 6-50) and 102 (F. Martin 6-52) lost to England 100 (J. J. Ferris 4-25) and 95-8 (J. J. Ferris 5-49) by 2 wkts.

29th Match: v Oxford and Cambridge Universities, Past and Present (Portsmouth) Aug 14, 15, 16.
Universities 233 (G. MacGregor 53) and 112-2 drew with Australians 131 (H. W. Forster 5-52, E. Smith 5-59) and 300-5 dec (J. E. Smith 4-96, W. L. Murdoch 69).

30th Match: v Nottinghamshire (Trent Bridge) Aug 18, 19, 20.
Nottinghamshire 145 (J. J. Ferris 4-61, C. T. B. Turner 4-66) and 138 (W. Gunn 50, J. J. Ferris 4-55) beat Australians 148 (F. J. Shacklock 5-44) and 115 (W. Flowers 6-38, W. Attewell 4-51) by 20 runs.

31st Match: v Gloucestershire (Cheltenham) Aug 21, 22, 23.
Australians 184 (J. J. Ferris 54*, W. A. Woof 6-81, F. G. Roberts 4-40) and 25-2 beat Gloucestershire 77 (C. T. B. Turner 42-6, J. J. Ferris 4-30) and 130 (J. J. Ferris 6-35) by 8 wkts.

32nd Match: v England (Old Trafford) Aug 25, 26, 27.
Match Abandoned: no play due to rain.

33rd Match: v Staffordshire (Stoke-on-Trent) Aug 29, 30.
Australians 144 (H. Shaw 5-45) beat Staffordshire 57 (J. J. Ferris 8-33) and 59 (C. T. B. Turner 7-33) by an innings and 28 runs.

34th Match: v North of England (Headingley) Sept 1, 2, 3.
Australians 134 (J. Briggs 7-44) and 195 (J. Briggs 5-71) beat North of England 75 (J. J. Ferris 7-35) and 94 (C. T. B. Turner 6-38) by 160 runs.

35th Match: v Lord Londesborough's XI (Scarborough) Sept 4, 5, 6.
Australians 77 (J. Briggs 9-31) and 60 (J. Briggs 6-26) beat Lord Londesborough's XI 39 (C. T. B. Turner 6-11) and 90 (C. T. B. Turner 7-46) by 8 runs.

36th Match: v M.C.C. (Lord's) Sept 8, 9, 10.
M.C.C. 372 (W. Gunn 118, T. C. O'Brien 105, W. Chatterton 51, C. T. B. Turner 5-111, J. J. Ferris 5-120) and 44-6 (J. J. Ferris 4-22) beat Australians 291 (J. J. Lyons 99, F. Martin 5-76, W. Attewell 4-60) and 124 (F. Martin 5-35, F. R. Spofforth 4-35) by 4 wkts.

37th Match: v Hurst Park Club (Hurst Park) Sept 11, 12.
Hurst Park Club 99 (H. Trumble 6-57) and 138 (P. C. Charlton 5-49) beat Australians 101 (A. W. Mold 6-57, G. A. Davidson 4-31) and 102 (A. W. Mold 4-53) by 34 runs.

38th Match: v South of England (Hastings) Sept 15, 16, 17.
South of England 262 (W. G. Grace 84, R. Abel 80, J. E. Barrett 6-68) and 22-0 beat Australians 138 (G. A. Lohmann 5-59, J. W.Sharpe 4-38) and 142 (J. W. Sharpe 6-66) by 10 wkts.

39th Match: v Eleven of England (Old Trafford) Sept 18, 19, 20.
Australians 234 (J. E. Barrett 97, W. L. Murdoch 57, W. Attewell 4-28) and 186-4 (J. E. Barrett 73*, J. J. Lyons 56) drew with Eleven of England 167 (R. Peel 55*, J. J. Ferris 6-78, C. T. B. Turner 4-83).

1890: 7th Australians

Batting Averages

	M	I	NO	R	HS	Avge	100	c/s
W. L. Murdoch	33	59	2	1394	158*	24.45	2	21/2
J. E. Barrett	32	58	7	1226	97	24.03	0	9
G. H. S. Trott	33	59	1	1211	186	20.87	2	30
J. J. Lyons	33	59	1	1029	99	17.74	0	9
J. J. Ferris	30	50	13	613	54*	16.57	0	14
C. T. B. Turner	31	54	0	854	59	15.81	0	22
J. McC. Blackham	28	47	5	655	75	15.35	0	38/27
P. C. Charlton	26	43	9	450	41	13.23	0	22
S. E. Gregory	33	55	13	501	59*	11.92	0	20
S. P. Jones	19	30	1	328	98	11.31	0	4
E. J. K. Burn	21	37	4	344	35*	10.43	0	14
F. H. Walters	23	38	3	351	53*	10.02	0	15
H. Trumble	28	44	10	288	34*	8.46	0	50
R. J. Pope	3	4	0	6	6	1.50	0	4

Also batted: (1 match) H. F. Boyle 3.

Bowling Averages

	O	M	R	W	Avge	BB	5i
C. T. B. Turner	1501.1	655	2544	179	14.21	7-23	16
J. J. Ferris	1545.1	628	2657	186	14.28	7-16	15
J. E. Barrett	38	15	89	6	14.83	6-68	1
P. C. Charlton	395.3	144	772	42	18.38	5-27	3
H. Trumble	483.4	166	1131	52	21.75	5-38	3
J. J. Lyons	404.4	112	979	43	22.76	6-38	4
G. H. S. Trott	188	34	578	20	28.90	3-20	0

Also bowled: H. F. Boyle 10-4-17-0; R. J. Pope 2-0-19-0; S. P. Jones 2-0-16-0; J. McC. Blackham 16-4-37-0; S. E. Gregory 3-0-21-0.

leaving England, but this plan and the tentative idea of a match in Bombay both fell to the ground, the team returning directly to Australia.

Despite the lack of success in England the public still flocked to watch the tourists' matches and the visit was financially a success.

1893: 8th Australians

Since the 1890 visit to England, 'The Australasian Cricket Council' had been set up with headquarters in Sydney and for the first time the English authorities received an official communication about the coming touring team. This historic document read:

Dear Sir,
It is my pleasure to inform you that the Council approved of the

following cricketers constituting 'The Australian Team' to visit England in 1893. Messrs G. Giffen, W. F. Giffen, A. H. Jarvis, J. J. Lyons (South Australia); J. M. Blackham, W. Bruce, H. Graham, R. McLeod, H. Trott, H. Trumble (Victoria); A. C. Bannerman, A. Coningham, S. E. Gregory, C. T. B. Turner (N.S.W.). Excepting Mr H. Moses of New South Wales, all Australian cricketers were available for selection. The team, accompanied by Mr Victor Cohen the manager

1893: 8th Australians

1st Match: v Lord Sheffield's XI (Sheffield Park)   May 8, 9, 10.
Lord Sheffield's XI 258 (W. G. Grace 63, A. Shrewsbury 62, W. Gunn 56, A. Coningham 5-74) and 56-2 beat Australians 138 (W. H. Lockwood 4-45, J. Briggs 4-52) and 173 (W. H. Lockwood 5-81) by 8 wkts.

2nd Match: v Warwickshire (Edgbaston)   May 11, 12.
Warwickshire 159 (G. Giffen 7-60) and 153 (W. Quaife 56, G. Giffen 6-81) lost to Australians 286 (J. J. Lyons 71, H. Graham 55, J. E. Shilton 6-115) and 28-0 by 10 wkts.

3rd Match: v Gloucestershire (Bristol)   May 15, 16, 17.
Australians 503 (G. Giffen 180, G. H. S. Trott 68, H. Graham 59) drew with Gloucestershire 41 (G. Giffen 7-11).

4th Match: v M.C.C. (Lord's)   May 18, 19, 20.
M.C.C. 424 (W. Flowers 130, F. Marchant 103, A. E. Stoddart 58) and 153-9 (R. W. McLeod 5-29) drew with Australians 243 (J. T. Hearne 4-59) and 347 (J. J. Lyons 149, A. C. Bannerman 75, J. T. Hearne 6-74).

5th Match: v Yorkshire (Bramall Lane)   May 22, 23.
Yorkshire 137 (H. Trumble 7-50) and 71 (H. Trumble 5-31, W. Bruce 4-27) beat Australians 84 (E. Wainwright 5-36) and 60 (R. Peel 6-38, E. Wainwright 4-21) by 64 runs.

6th Match: v Lancashire (Old Trafford)   May 25, 26.
Lancashire 97 (G. Giffen 5-50) and 111 (G. Giffen 6-41) lost to Australians 222 (J. Briggs 6-114) by an innings and 14 runs.

7th Match: v Surrey (Oval)   May 29, 30.
Surrey 181 (G. Giffen 5-63, C. T. B. Turner 5-73) and 113 (H. Trumble 5-40) beat Australians 156 (S. E. Gregory 66*, T. Richardson 5-57) and 80 (T. Richardson 6-38) by 58 runs.

8th Match: v Oxford University (Oxford)   June 1, 2, 3.
Australians 200 (H. Graham 64, L. C. V. Bathurst 5-40, H. A. Arkwright 5-30) and 182 (T. S. B. Wilson 4-50) beat Oxford University 208 (H. D. G. Leveson-Gower 59, R. W. McLeod 4-39) and 155 (G. Giffen 8-98) by 19 runs.

9th Match: v Yorkshire (Bradford)   June 5, 6, 7.
Australians 470 (G. Giffen 171, H. Graham 67, H. Trumble 55, R. Peel 7-116) drew with Yorkshire 220 (A. Sellers 53, G. Giffen 5-89) and 196-6 (E. Wainwright 62, R. Moorhouse 57*).

10th Match: v Cambridge University (Cambridge)   June 8, 9, 10.
Cambridge University 290 (K. S. Ranjitsinhji 58, J. Douglas 55) and 108 (C. T. B. Turner 5-45) lost to Australians 196 (C. M. Wells 4-52) and 319 (G. H. S. Trott 71, J. J. Lyons 65, J. Douglas 5-45) by 117 runs.

11th Match: v M.C.C. (Lord's)   June 12, 13, 14.
Australians 231 (J. J. Lyons 83, G. H. S. Trott 56) and 179 (C. J. Kortright 5-72) lost to M.C.C. 236 (W. G. Grace 75, C. T. B. Turner 7-86) and 178-3 (A. E. Stoddart 74) by 3 wkts.

12th Match: v South of England (Oval)   June 15, 16.
South of England 242 (A. Hearne 120, W. G. Grace 66) and 8-0 beat Australians 142 (T. Richardson 6-85) and 169 (W. Bruce 53) by 10 wkts.

13th Match: v Players (Lord's)   June 19, 20.
Australians 189 (E. J. Tyler 6-33) and 76-4 beat Players 89 (H. Trumble 7-31) and 173 (H. Trumble 7-85) by 6 wkts.

14th Match: v Kent (Gravesend)   June 22, 23.
Australians 194 (W. Bruce 77, S. E. Gregory 59, A. Hearne 6-49) beat Kent 104 (H. Trumble 5-40) and 89 (H. Trumble 7-44) by an innings and 1 run.

15th Match: v Shrewsbury's England XI (Trent Bridge)   June 26, 27, 28.
England 416 (A. E. Stoddart 94, L. C. H. Palairet 71, W. Gunn 64, A. Shrewsbury 52*, G. Giffen 4-118) beat Australians 120 (R. Peel 6-65) and 143 (S. E. Gregory 51, R. Peel 5-45) by an innings and 153 runs.

16th Match: v North of England (Old Trafford)   June 29, 30, July 1.
North 271 (A. Ward 93, A. C. MacLaren 66, C. T. B. Turner 8-95) and 259 (A. Ward 59, J. Briggs 55, G. Giffen 4-88) lost to Australians 256 (G. H. S. Trott 96, S. E. Gregory 87) and 276-7 (J. J. Lyons 75, W. Attewell 4-75) by 3 wkts.

17th Match: v Derbyshire (Derby)   July 3, 4, 5.
Derbyshire 199 (L. G. Wright 56, G. H. S. Trott 4-27) and 224 (L. G. Wright 51, G. H. S. Trott 5-54) lost to Australians 494-9 dec (H. Graham 219, A. C. Bannerman 105) by an innings and 71 runs.

18th Match: v Leicestershire (Grace Rd, Leicester)   July 6, 7.
Australians 386 (G. H. S. Trott 100, S. E. Gregory 89, W. Finney 6-67) beat Leicestershire 67 (G. Giffen 5-36, G. H. S. Trott 5-29) and 163 (A. D. Pougher 50, G. H. S. Trott 6-58) by an innings and 51 runs.*

19th Match: v Yorkshire (Headingley)   July 10, 11.
Australians 142 (R. Peel 4-36) and 146 (R. Peel 5-47) beat Yorkshire 95 (C. T. B. Turner 6-36) and 48 (W. Bruce 6-29) by 145 runs.

20th Match: v Sussex (Hove)   July 13, 14.
Sussex 107 (G. H. S. Trott 5-27) and 114 (C. T. B. Turner 5-35, G. H. S. Trott 4-56) lost to Australians 154 (W. A. Humphreys 6-49) and 68-2 by 8 wkts.

21st Match: v England (Lord's)   July 17, 18, 19.
England 334 (A. Shrewsbury 106, F. S. Jackson 91, C. T. B. Turner 6-67) and 234-8 dec (A. Shrewsbury 81, W. Gunn 77, G. Giffen 5-43) drew with Australia 269 (H. Graham 107, S. E. Gregory 57, W. H. Lockwood 6-101).

22nd Match: v Somerset (Taunton)   July 20, 21, 22.
Somerset 119 (C. T. B. Turner 4-43) and 64 (C. T. B. Turner 7-26) lost to Australians 107 (S. M. J. Woods 6-26) and 78-4 by 6 wkts.

23rd Match: v Middlesex (Lord's)   July 24, 25.
Australians 147 (H. Trumble 61, J. T. Hearne 7-58) and 457 (G. H. S. Trott 145, S. E. Gregory 112, C. T. B. Turner 65*) beat Middlesex 78 (C. T. B. Turner 6-30, H. Trumble 4-37) and 136 (G. H. S. Trott 5-33) by 390 runs.

24th Match: v Surrey (Oval)   July 27, 28, 29.
Australians 162 (W. Bruce 60, W. Brockwell 5-61, T. Richardson 5-64) and 308 (G. Giffen 82, J. W. Sharpe 4-74) lost to Surrey 356 (W. Brockwell 67, R. Henderson 60*, C. Baldwin 54, T. W. Hayward 53, A. E. Street 51, H. Trumble 4-77, C. T. B. Turner 4-79) and 118-8 (C. T. B. Turner 6-54) by 2 wkts.

25th Match: v Oxford and Cambridge Past and Present (Portsmouth)   July 31, Aug 1, 2.
Australians 843 (W. Bruce 191, A. C. Bannerman 133, H. Trumble 105, H. Graham 83, C. T. B. Turner 66, W. F. Giffen 62, G. H. S. Trott 61, J. J. Lyons 51) drew with Oxford and Cambridge 191 (C. T. B. Turner 5-54, G. Giffen 4-61) and 82-1.

26th Match: v Essex (Leyton)   Aug 3, 4, 5.
Australians 250 (W. Bruce 56, W. Mead 9-136) and 141 (W. Mead 8-69) drew with Essex 237 (H. Trumble 6-87) and 32-1.

27th Match: v Kent (Canterbury)   Aug 7, 8, 9.
Australians 229 (S. E. Gregory 51, W. Wright 5-109) and 60 (A. Hearne 5-35, W. Wright 4-24) lost to Kent 127 and 198 (W. H. Patterson 51, C. T. B. Turner 6-27) by 36 runs.

28th Match: v Liverpool and District (Liverpool)   Aug 10, 11.
Australians 195 (G. H. S. Trott 56, W. Oakley 5-50) beat Liverpool and District 85 (R. W. McLeod 7-24) and 76 (A. Coningham 6-41) by an innings and 34 runs.

29th Match: v England (Oval)   Aug 14, 15, 16.
England 483 (F. S. Jackson 103, A. E. Stoddart 83, W. G. Grace 68, A. Shrewsbury 66, A. Ward 55, W. Read 52, G. Giffen 7-128) beat Australia 91 (J. Briggs 5-34, W. H. Lockwood 4-37) and 349 (G. H. S. Trott 92, A. C. Bannerman 55, G. Giffen 53, J. Briggs 5-114, W. H. Lockwood 4-96) by an innings and 43 runs.

30th Match: v Gloucestershire (Cheltenham)   Aug 17, 18.
Australians 207 (C. L. Townsend 5-70) and 37-2 beat Gloucestershire 109 (G. Giffen 7-41) and 131 (C. T. B. Turner 6-25) by 8 wkts.

31st Match: v Second Class Counties (Edgbaston)   Aug 21, 22, 23.
Second Class Counties 147 (G. Giffen 7-53) and 154 lost to Australians 143 (J. Hulme 4-57) and 159-6 (J. J. Lyons 64) by 4 wkts.

32nd Match: v England (Old Trafford)   Aug 24, 25, 26.
Australia 204 (W. Bruce 68, T. Richardson 5-49, J. Briggs 4-81) and 236 (A. C. Bannerman 60, T. Richardson 5-107) drew with England 243 (W. Gunn 102*, G. Giffen 4-113) and 118-4.

33rd Match: v XVI of Blackpool & District (Blackpool)   Aug 28, 29, 30.
Australians 205 (J. J. Lyons 62, R. G. Barlow 4-23) and 140 (W. Hall 5-28) beat XVI of Blackpool 174 (G. Giffen 4-34, C. T. B. Turner 4-50) and 92 (C. T. B. Turner 5-28) by 79 runs.

34th Match: v Nottinghamshire (Trent Bridge)   Aug 31, Sept 1, 2.
Australians 343 (S. E. Gregory 90, J. J. Lyons 60, W. Bruce 56, W. Flowers 5-105) beat Nottinghamshire 63 (C. T. B. Turner 6-28) and 126 (C. T. B. Turner 7-24) by an innings and 154 runs.

35th Match: v C. I. Thornton's XI (Scarborough)   Sept 4, 5, 6.
C. I. Thornton's XI 345 (A. E. Stoddart 127, F. S. Jackson 62, W. Newham 52, H. Trumble 5-87) and 230-8 dec (F. S. Jackson 68, G. Giffen 6-88) drew with Australians 391 (H. Graham 95, A. C. Bannerman 74, H. Trumble 62) and 87-5.

36th Match: v South of England (Hastings)   Sept 7, 8, 9.
Australians 64 (W. H. Lockwood 6-43, T. Richardson 4-20) and 193 (J. J. Lyons 75, T. Richardson 7-86) lost to South 147 (H. T. Hewett 58, C. T. B. Turner 5-43, H. Trumble 5-60) and 112-4 by 6 wkts.

will leave Sydney by the R.M.S.S. 'Orizaba' on the 11th of March ensuing.

Yours faithfully,
John Porteus, Hon Sec. the A.C.C.

In fact Bruce and Trumble travelled by an earlier boat, arriving in England a fortnight before the main party, which stopped at Colombo for a one-day match against Ceylon, and eventually landed at Tilbury on 2 April. The pre-season criticism of the team, which was captained by Blackham, was a lack of variety in the bowling, but in general there was little to complain about.

The side faced an immediate problem in that Turner caught flu before the matches began and although he played regularly, seemed to suffer the after-effects nearly all season, which meant that the team had no fast bowler of any substance. The weakness in the bowling was not helped by a general slovenliness in the field and an epidemic of dropped catches. Blackham's captaincy came

in for considerable criticism. He certainly failed to get the best out of his men, being in no way as good as Murdoch. Admittedly he had to contend with Turner's illness and a leg injury to Giffen. A curious feature of his captaincy was a reluctance to bowl Coningham, whose style ought to have added variety.

England won the only Test which was brought to a definite conclusion, by an innings, and Shrewsbury's England side also won by an innings. The best that could be said for the tourists was that they had a better record than the 1890 side, but there was not much to choose between the two.

The batting was the strong feature of the team. Seven of the side completed 1,000 runs in all matches with little to separate the first four – Graham, Lyons, Trott and Bannerman. Giffen was not as successful with the bat as expected, however, being vulnerable against the faster bowlers. McLeod was a great disappointment, rarely scoring runs and with an unattractive style.

Except for Turner, the team sailed aboard s.s. *Germanic* for the United States on 20 September. The team won high praise for their conduct in the USA, but there were many press stories about their conduct while in England and if true, this disagreeable behaviour perhaps affected the overall results.

1893: 8th Australians

Batting Averages

	M	I	NO	R	HS	Avge	100	c/s
J. J. Lyons	29	50	1	1377	149	28.10	1	14
W. Bruce	31	53	4	1227	191	25.04	1	24
H. Graham	29	48	3	1119	107	24.93	1	25
G. H. S. Trott	31	54	2	1269	145	24.40	1	15
S. E. Gregory	29	48	4	1022	112	23.22	1	21
G. Giffen	29	50	1	1133	180	23.12	2	27
A. C. Bannerman	27	47	1	1061	133	23.06	1	7
H. Trumble	29	46	11	774	105	22.11	1	52
R. W. McLeod	27	44	11	593	47*	17.96	0	15
J. McC. Blackham	21	31	12	283	42	14.89	0	26/16
A. Coningham	12	18	2	213	46	13.31	0	5
C. T. B. Turner	26	40	4	475	66	13.19	0	9
W. F. Giffen	10	15	1	170	62	12.14	0	4
A. H. Jarvis	11	16	4	47	10	3.91	0	11/8

Bowling Averages

	O	M	R	W	Avge	BB	5i
C. T. B. Turner	1079	413	2018	148	13.63	8-95	16
H. Trumble	834.1	274	1794	108	16.61	7-31	9
A. Coningham	208.1	65	497	27	18.41	6-41	2
G. Giffen	906.4	257	2247	118	19.04	8-98	12
W. Bruce	288.4	79	718	33	21.75	6-29	1
G. H. S. Trott	296.3	64	907	38	23.86	5-27	2
R. W. McLeod	510.1	197	1031	43	23.97	7-24	2
S. E. Gregory	9	1	40	1	40.00	1-17	0

Also bowled: J. J. Lyons 17-3-61-0; H. Graham 4-0-22-0.

1894: 1st South Africans

The team for this first South African visit to England was originally to be drawn from Cape Province, but at a meeting of the South African Cricket Association it was agreed by a majority that the side should represent all South Africa. J. D. Logan immediately promised £500 towards the cost of the tour, but withdrew this when his nominee as manager, a Mr Cadwallader, was not chosen. However, there was little difficulty in raising a guarantee fund of £3,000–the Prime Minister, Cecil Rhodes, giving £500–and the selection of the side went ahead. The team consisted of H. H. Castens (captain), F. Hearne, A. W. Seccull, C. Mills, J. Middleton, G. A. Rowe and G. Cripps, all of Western Province; D. C. Parkin of Eastern Province; C. O. H. Sewell and D. C. Davey of Natal; E. A. Halliwell, T. Routledge, C. L. Johnson and G. S. Kempis of Transvaal and G. Glover of Griqualand West, with W. V. Simkins as manager. The two most notable absentees from the tourists' party were A. B. Tancred and the fast bowler H. M. Taberer. The majority of the side sailed from Cape Town aboard the s.s. *Tartar*, arriving in Southampton on 29 April.

A major disadvantage for the tourists was adapting to grass wickets. Their programme of matches did not begin until 22 May so that they could spend three weeks in practice, which they did mainly on the Private Banks ground at Catford.

Although losing two of the first four matches, the team then won a splendid victory over a fair M.C.C. eleven and afterwards showed good form against the rather moderate opposition in its programme–the tourists were rather disappointed that they met only seven first-class counties and that these counties generally fielded a weak eleven. The main result of this was minimal public interest and by the time the side arrived in Dublin for their 19th match, no money was left. The manager was forced to canvass various South Africans living in England, who subscribed enough for the team to complete the tour. Total receipts at the gate for the whole tour did not reach £500.

1894 was a wet summer and the batsmen found runs difficult to come by, but Rowe and Middleton, the two slow bowlers were

1894: 1st South Africans

1st Match: v Lord Sheffield's XI (Sheffield Park) May 22, 23.
Lord Sheffield's XI 233 (G. A. Rowe 8-52) and 6-0 beat South Africans 127 (T. Routledge 50, W. A. Humphreys 5-36) and 110 (J. Briggs 5-39) by 10 wkts.

2nd Match: v Hampshire (Southampton) May 25, 26.
Hampshire 408 (A. J. L. Hill 109, C. Robson 76, V. A. Barton 74, C. O. H. Sewell 4-46) drew with South Africans 275 (C. Mills 64, T. Soar 4-50) and 85-3.

3rd Match: v Oxford University (Oxford) May 28, 29, 30.
South Africans 145 (T. Routledge 65, L. C. V. Bathurst 8-40) and 73-1 drew with Oxford University 189 (G. J. Mordaunt 75, J. Middleton 4-51).

4th Match: v Surrey (Oval) June 1, 2.
South Africans 52 (D. L. A. Jephson 5-18) and 146 (H. H. Castens 58, A. E. Street 7-40) lost to Surrey 204 (C. Baldwin 68, J. Middleton 7-45) by an innings and 6 runs.

5th Match: v M.C.C. (Lord's) June 4, 5.
South Africans 126 (W. G. Grace 6-37) and 60 (W. G. Grace 6-37, W. Mead 4-22) beat M.C.C. 103 (J. Middleton 6-48, G. A. Rowe 4-10) and 72 (J. Middleton 6-35) by 11 runs.

6th Match: v Leicestershire (Leicester) June 11, 12.
Leicestershire 52 (G. A. Rowe 4-25, J. Middleton 4-26) and 46 (G. A. Rowe 5-22, J. Middleton 4-22) lost to South Africans 56 (A. D. Pougher 7-17) and 43-3 by 7 wkts.

7th Match: v Chatham and District (Chatham) June 18, 19.
South Africans 122 (P. Northcote 6-58) and 87 (T. Routledge 52, P. Northcote 6-23) beat Chatham and District 104 (J. Middleton 7-60) and 100 (C. Mills 5-28, J. Middleton 4-44) by 5 runs.

8th Match: v Glamorgan (Cardiff) June 22, 23.
South Africans 238 (A. W. Seccull 63, G. Cripps 51*, Eldridge 4-61) and 32-0 beat Glamorgan 139 (R. B. Sweet-Escott 50*, G. A. Rowe 5-50) and 128 (G. A. Rowe 7-56) by 10 wkts.

9th Match: v Somerset (Taunton) June 25, 26, 27.
Somerset 319 (G. Fowler 77, L. C. H. Palairet 69, A. E. Clapp 66) and 238-1 (A. E. Clapp 84*, L. C. H. Palairet 82, H. T. Stanley 61*) beat South Africans 176 (G. B. Nichols 4-34, E. J. Tyler 4-57) and 380 (C. O. H. Sewell 170, G. Cripps 54, G. B. Nichols 4-102) by 9 wkts.

10th Match: v Gloucestershire (Bristol) June 28, 29, 30.
South Africans 185 (F. Hearne 56, W. G. Grace sen 9-71) and 262 (E. A. Halliwell 110, F. Hearne 104, F. G. Roberts 4-38) lost to Gloucestershire 301 (W. G. Grace sen 129*, H. Wrathall 95, G. A. Rowe 4-95, D. C. Parkin 4-108) and 147-5 by 5 wkts.

11th Match: v Sussex (Hove) July 2, 3, 4.
Sussex 278 (F. W. Marlow 75, G. Bean 54, C. L. Johnson 4-62) and 4-1 beat South Africans 71 (W. A. Humphreys 6-34) and 210 (C. O. H. Sewell 52, W. A. Humphreys 5-86, F. H. Guttridge 4-37) by 9 wkts.

12th Match: v C. W. Wright's XI (Portsmouth) July 5, 6.
C. W. Wright's XI 241 (N. F. Druce 54, K. S. Ranjitsinhji 53) and 284-7 (K. S. Ranjitsinhji 146*) drew with South Africans 281 (T. Routledge 152, W. Morgan 5-67).

13th Match: v Warwickshire (Edgbaston) July 9, 10, 11.
Warwickshire 252 (A. F. A. Lilley 60) drew with South Africans 147 (H. J. Pallett 5-25, J. E. Shilton 4-53) and 88-4.

14th Match: v Scotland (Edinburgh) July 13, 14.
Scotland 189 (C. T. Mannes 65, G. A. Rowe 4-46) and 118 (G. Glover 6-39) lost to South Africans 214 (C. Mills 53, H. J. Stevenson 4-50) and 96-1 by 9 wkts.

15th Match: v Glasgow and District (Glasgow) July 16, 17, 18.
Glasgow and District 74 (G. A. Rowe 6-25, G. Glover 4-34) and 63 (G. A. Rowe 7-27) lost to South Africans 169 (C. O. H. Sewell 79, Davies 7-34) by an innings and 32 runs.

16th Match: v Liverpool and District (Liverpool) July 19, 20.
Liverpool and District 110 (G. A. Rowe 5-52, J. Middleton 4-22) and 207 (G. A. Rowe 4-88) lost to South Africans 287 (C. L. Johnson 112, D. C. Davey 50*, T. Smith 4-53) and 31-3 by 7 wkts.

17th Match: v Derbyshire (Derby) July 26, 27, 28.
Derbyshire 325 (W. Sugg 121, W. Chatterton 53, G. Glover 4-58) and 197 (W. Chatterton 58*, G. Glover 4-65) drew with South Africans 300 (C. O. H. Sewell 128, J. J. Hulme 4-76, G. A. Davidson 4-80) and 48-3.

18th Match: v Gentlemen of Ireland (Dublin) July 30, 31.
Gentlemen of Ireland 153 (W. D. Hamilton 68) and 181 (A. P. Gwynn 62, G. A. Rowe 7-77) lost to South Africans 250 (C. O. H. Sewell 73, R. H. Lambert 5-37) and 87-1 (T. Routledge 53*) by 9 wkts.

19th Match: v Dublin University (Dublin) Aug 1, 2.
South Africans 123 (E. A. Halliwell 62) and 52-1 beat Dublin University 107 (G. A. Rowe 4-41) and 69 (C. L. Johnson 6-33, G. A. Rowe 4-32) by 9 wkts.

20th Match: v North of Ireland (Belfast) Aug 3, 4.
South Africans 113 (Baines 8-41) and 169-8 dec (F. Hearne 50) drew with North of Ireland 109 (Hamilton 53, G. A. Rowe 7-32) and 137-9 (G. A. Rowe 6-54).

21st Match: v Leeds and District (Leeds) Aug 8, 9.
Leeds and District 125 (J. Middleton 5-30) and 66 (J. Middleton 5-32, G. A. Rowe 4-28) lost to South Africans 93 (W. Fletcher 4-29) and 99-5 by 5 wkts.

22nd Match: v Scarborough and District (Scarborough) Aug 9, 10, 11.
South Africans 124 (H. Hayley 4-40) and 96 (H. Hayley 8-39) beat Scarborough and District 90 (G. A. Rowe 6-39) and 123 (C. L. Johnson 5-17, G. A. Rowe 4-32) by 7 runs.

23rd Match: v Lord Cantelupe's XI (Bexhill-on-Sea) Aug 13, 14.
Lord Cantelupe's XI 92 (G. Glover 5-36, C. L. Johnson 4-27) and 121 (G. Glover 4-43) lost to South Africans 172 (E. A. Halliwell 65*, F. Martin 4-72) and 43-6 (A. Hearne 5-7) by 4 wkts.

24th Match: v Warwickshire (Edgbaston) Aug 16, 17.
Warwickshire 144 (C. L. Johnson 6-44) and 185-5 dec (E. J. Diver 68, W. Quaife 58) drew with South Africans 138 (S. J. Whitehead 5-38, H. J. Pallett 4-52) and 111-5.

most effective. Rowe took 136 wickets, average 12.89 and Middleton 83, average 15.79. Sewell completed 1,000 runs and with 1,038, average 30.52, easily topped the batting table.

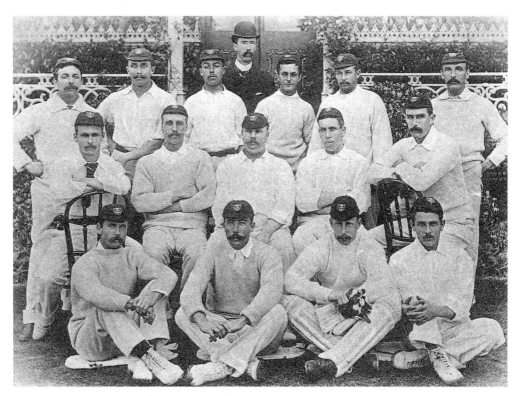

The first South African party to tour England. Back: Davey, Routledge, Sewell, Simkins (manager), Rowe, Glover, Mills. Centre: Kempis, Cripps, Castens (captain), Johnson, Seccull. Front: Hearne, Middleton, Halliwell, Parkin.

Halliwell was highly praised for his wicket-keeping, as well as hitting 759 runs, average 26.17.

The visit proved valuable experience for the South African players and, if financially unsuccessful, proved that the best South African side was little below first-class standard. The team did not travel home in one party, but broke up soon after the final game. C. O. H. Sewell decided to remain in England to qualify for Gloucestershire.

1896: 9th Australians

Critics were rather sceptical about the ability of the side chosen to represent the 9th Australians. The absence of C. T. B. Turner, J. J. Lyons and W. Bruce meant the side was not the strongest available and it was felt unlikely that it would be successful. In the event the team, favoured by fine weather and a modicum of luck, played better than any of its immediate predecessors. The side which left Adelaide aboard s.s. *Cuzco* on 14 March consisted of G. H. S. Trott (captain), H. Trumble, H. Graham and A. E. Johns, all from Victoria; S. E. Gregory, F. A. Iredale, H. Donnan, J. J. Kelly and T. R. McKibbin of New South Wales; J. Darling, C. Hill, G. Giffen and E. Jones of South Australia and C. J. Eady of Tasmania, with H. Musgrove as manager. For the first time the Australian party stopped at Colombo long enough to play a one-day game against Ceylon on 1 April and arrived in England during the third week of April.

Up until the second week of June the tourists had played nine matches, won seven and drawn two. Then they were badly beaten by M.C.C., being dismissed in their first innings for 18, but the wicket was very difficult and Giffen was unable to bat, so there were extenuating circumstances. Shortly afterwards they were defeated by a Midland Counties Eleven and by England in the First Test. This was the lowest point of the tour and after that fortune was restored, except for a defeat in the third and final Test.

An unexpected bonus was the success of all four of the batsmen who were visiting England for the first time. Darling, Iredale, Hill and Donnan all reached 1,000 runs in total with respectable averages. The most consistent bat was Gregory, whose fielding at cover-point was also quite exceptional. Trott was invaluable in a crisis, as befits the captain, and the success of the side was to a large extent due to his leadership both on and off the field. Of the bowlers Trumble was the busiest and keeping an excellent length, was successful on all types of wicket. Jones was a formidable fast bowler – very fast, but sometimes rather short. Giffen again proved himself accurate and McKibbin, whom many critics wrote off, gave English batsmen a difficult time in the later stages of the tour.

When the team left England for New York on 8 September it was reported that they had been the most popular Australian side to visit England – a fine tribute to Musgrove and Trott. After playing several matches in America the team crossed the Pacific and took part in five matches in New Zealand before finally arriving home.

1896: 9th Australians

Batting Averages

	M	I	NO	R	HS	Avge	100	c/s
S. E. Gregory	31	48	2	1464	154	31.82	3	11
J. Darling	32	53	1	1555	194	29.90	3	13
C. Hill	31	46	3	1196	130	27.81	2	14/1
F. A. Iredale	32	51	3	1328	171	27.66	4	34
G. H. S. Trott	33	54	5	1297	143	26.47	3	20
G. Giffen	32	49	1	1208	130	25.16	2	20
H. Donnan	28	44	1	1009	167	23.46	1	12
H. Trumble	30	43	11	628	45*	19.62	0	39
H. Graham	20	32	2	547	96	18.23	0	10
J. J. Kelly	25	38	8	490	45	16.33	0	37/22
A. E. Johns	10	12	6	84	31*	14.00	0	17/7
C. J. Eady	17	24	3	290	42	13.80	0	18
E. Jones	29	41	6	482	40	13.77	0	18
T. R. McKibbin	22	34	11	175	28*	7.60	0	13

Also batted: (2 matches) H. A. Musgrove 2, 0, 2 (2ct).

Bowling Averages

	O	M	R	W	Avge	BB	5i
T. R. McKibbin	647.1	198	1441	101	14.26	7/11	8
H. Trumble	1140.1	380	2340	148	15.81	7/67	12
E. Jones	887.3	282	1940	121	16.03	8/39	8
G. Giffen	864.2	219	2257	117	19.29	8/30	7
G. H. S. Trott	339.4	66	928	44	21.09	5/66	1
C. J. Eady	201	74	408	16	25.50	3/58	0
H. Donnan	100	35	231	5	46.20	2/56	0

Also bowled: J. Darling 7-2-28-1; F. A. Iredale 5-0-18-0; H. Graham 4-2-19-1; C. Hill 2-0-4-0; H. A. Musgrove 4-0-18-0.

1896: 9th Australians

1st Match: v Lord Sheffield's XI (Sheffield Park)   May 11, 12, 13.
Australians 257 (J. Darling 67, A. W. Mold 4-61) and 194 (G. H. S. Trott 59) drew with Lord Sheffield's XI 195 (K. S. Ranjitsinhji 79, E. Jones 7-84) and 180-4 (F. S. Jackson 95*).

2nd Match: v Essex (Leyton)   May 14, 15, 16.
Essex 166 (H. Trumble 4-46) and 149 (H. Carpenter 51, H. Trumble 6-62) lost to Australians 223 (C. Hill 73, W. Mead 5-68) and 93-3 by 7 wkts.

3rd Match: v C. E. de Trafford's XI (Crystal Palace)   May 18, 19.
C. E. de Trafford's XI 114 (E. Jones 8-39) and 39 (G. Giffen 7-15) lost to Australians 374 (S. E. Gregory 154, H. Donnon 54, A. D. Pougher 5-100) by an innings and 221 runs.

4th Match: Eleven of the South (Eastbourne)   May 21, 22, 23.
Australians 328-6 dec (J. Darling 115, G. Giffen 115) drew with Eleven of the South 134-5.

5th Match: v Yorkshire (Sheffield)   May 25, 26.
Australians 262 (G. H. S. Trott 61, J. Darling 57, S. E. Gregory 54) beat Yorkshire 118 (G. Giffen 6-49) and 136 (E. Jones 6-74) by an innings and 8 runs.

6th Match: v Lancashire (Old Trafford)   May 28, 29, 30.
Australians 281 (F. A. Iredale 67) and 139 (S. E. Gregory 54, J. Briggs 4-36, A. W. Mold 4-54) beat Lancashire 168 (H. Trumble 4-24, E. Jones 4-69) and 98 by 154 runs.

7th Match: v Oxford University (Oxford)   June 1, 2, 3.
Oxford University 237 (H. D. G. Leveson-Gower 93, H. K. Foster 66, E. Jones 5-47) and 129 (H. Trumble 6-17) lost to Australians 308 (G. Giffen 76, S. E. Gregory 68, F. H. E. Cunliffe 4-98) and 59-3 by 7 wkts.

8th Match: v Gloucestershire (Bristol)   June 4, 5, 6.
Gloucestershire 110 (H. Trumble 5-46, G. Giffen 4-42) and 181 (W. G. Grace 66, H. Trumble 6-81) lost to Australians 382 (H. Donnan 87, S. E. Gregory 64) by an innings and 91 runs.

9th Match: v Wembley Park (Wembley Park)   June 8, 9.
Australians 106 (F. R. Spofforth 6-49) and 131 (F. R. Spofforth 5-51) beat Wembley Park 65 (G. Giffen 6-20, H. Trumble 4-28) and 37 (G. H. S. Trott 4-18) by 135 runs.

10th Match: v M.C.C. (Lord's)   June 11, 12.
M.C.C. 219 (A. E. Stoddart 54, F. S. Jackson 51, H. Trumble 6-84) beat Australians 18 (A. D. Pougher 5-0, J. T. Hearne 4-4) and 183 (J. Darling 76, J. T. Hearne 9-73) by an innings and 18 runs.

11th Match: v Yorkshire (Headingley)   June 15, 16, 17.
Australians 144 (S. E. Gregory 59, G. H. Hirst 5-40) and 31-1 drew with Yorkshire 108 (E. Jones 7-36).

12th Match: v Midland Counties Eleven (Edgbaston)   June 18, 19, 20.
Australians 138 (J. J. Hulme 6-54) and 254 (C. Hill 98, J. J. Hulme 4-69, W. Attewell 4-73) lost to Midland Counties Eleven 267 (W. Gunn 69, W. Quaife 68, T. R. McKibbin 4-94) and 126-6 by 4 wkts.

13th Match: v England (Lord's)   June 22, 23, 24.
Australia 53 (T. Richardson 6-39) and 347 (G. H. S. Trott 143, S. E. Gregory 103, J. T. Hearne 5-76, T. Richardson 5-134) lost to England 292 (R. Abel 94, W. G. Grace 66) and 111-4 by 6 wkts.

14th Match: v Nottinghamshire (Trent Bridge)
Nottinghamshire 269 (G. Giffen 4-92) and 146 (G. Giffen 4-29, E. Jones 4-49) lost to Australians 246 (H. Graham 96) and 170-4 (F. A. Iredale 94*) by 6 wkts.

15th Match: v Yorkshire (Bradford)   June 29, 30, July 1.
Australians 224 (H. Graham 67, G. H. Hirst 5-79) and 251 (F. A. Iredale 114, S. Haigh 8-78) beat Yorkshire 145 (T. R. McKibbin 7-23) and 190 (J. Tunnicliffe 59, E. Jones 4-40) by 140 runs.

16th Match: v North of England (Old Trafford)   July 2, 3, 4.
Australians 195 (S. E. Gregory 71, A. D. Pougher 4-54) and 119 (J. Briggs 6-41, A. W. Mold 4-38) beat North of England 123 (H. Trumble 6-69) and 149 (A. F. A. Lilley 61, E. Jones 5-56, H. Trumble 4-46) by 42 runs.

17th Match: v Hampshire (Southampton)   July 6, 7.
Hampshire 134 (T. R. McKibbin 5-41, C. J. Eady 4-6) and 203 (E. G. Wynyard 68, G. H. S. Trott 5-66) lost to Australians 462 (G. Giffen 130, F. A. Iredale 106, H. Graham 66) by an innings and 125 runs.

18th Match: v Players of England (Leyton)   July 9, 10, 11.
Australians 454 (F. A. Iredale 171, G. H. S. Trott 64) beat Players of England 197 (W. Storer 62, E. Jones 4-47, G. Giffen 4-56) and 120 (E. Jones 4-27) by an innings and 137 runs.

19th Match: v Leicestershire (Leicester)   July 13, 14, 15.
Australians 584 (J. Darling 194, S. E. Gregory 102, G. Giffen 67, H. Donnan 66, A. D. Pougher 5-114) beat Leicestershire 87 (G. Giffen 8-30) and 180 (F. Geeson 53*, G. Giffen 6-89) by an innings and 317 runs.

20th Match: v England (Old Trafford)   July 16, 17, 18.
Australia 412 (F. A. Iredale 108, G. Giffen 80, G. H. S. Trott 53, T. Richardson 7-168) and 125-7 (T. Richardson 6-76) beat England 231 (A. F. A. Lilley 65*, K. S. Ranjitsinhji 62) and 305 (K. S. Ranjitsinhji 154*) by 3 wkts.

21st Match: v Derbyshire (Derby)   July 20, 21, 22.
Australians 625 (H. Donnan 167, G. H. S. Trott 141, C. Hill 130, F. A. Iredale 73, G. Giffen 63, W. Sugg 4-61) drew with Derbyshire 292 (L. G. Wright 81, G. A. Davidson 60, G. Giffen 5-123) and 61-2.

22nd Match: v M.C.C. (Lord's)   July 23, 24, 25.
Australians 202 (G. H. S. Trott 103, A. Woodcock 5-74) and 331 (C. Hill 65, G. H. S. Trott 62, F. A. Iredale 62) drew with M.C.C. 367 (A. E. Stoddart 61, E. G. Wynyard 58, W. Gunn 56, A. D. Pougher 51*, H. Trumble 4-89) and 99-3.

23rd Match: v Surrey (Oval)   July 27, 28, 29.
Surrey 283 (R. Abel 116, H. D. G. Leveson-Gower 59, T. R. McKibbin 7-80) and 147 (R. Abel 63, T. W. Hayward 51, E. Jones 4-13) lost to Australians 367 (C. Hill 118*, S. E. Gregory 60, J. Darling 51, T. W. Hayward 5-112) and 65-3 by 7 wkts.

24th Match: v Earl De La Warr's XI (Bexhill-on-Sea)   July 30, 31.
Australians 80 (J. T. Hearne 6-38, A. D. Pougher 4-38) and 138 (J. T. Hearne 7-69) lost to Earl De La Warr's XI 102 (T. R. McKibbin 5-35, G. H. S. Trott 4-36) and 117-6 (J. Douglas 68, G. Giffen 4-35) by 4 wkts.

25th Match: v Warwickshire (Edgbaston)   Aug 3, 4.
Australians 339 (J. Darling 105, S. E. Gregory 59*, G. Giffen 51, W. Quaife 5-62) beat Warwickshire 127 (E. J. Diver 54, E. Jones 6-33) and 152 (H. Trumble 5-61) by an innings and 60 runs.

26th Match: v Kent (Canterbury)   Aug 6, 7, 8.
Australians 310 (C. Hill 74) and 203 (G. H. S. Trott 61, W. Wright 4-56) beat Kent 196 (C. J. Burnup 101, E. Jones 5-53) and 141 (H. Trumble 7-67) by 176 runs.

27th Match: v England (Oval)   Aug 10, 11, 12.
England 145 (H. Trumble 6-59) and 84 (H. Trumble 6-30) beat Australia 119 (J. T. Hearne 6-41) and 44 (R. Peel 6-23, J. T. Hearne 4-19) by 66 runs.

28th Match: v Sussex (Hove)   Aug 13, 14, 15.
Sussex 221 (E. H. Killick 54, G. H. S. Trott 4-61, H. Trumble 4-75) and 248 (C. B. Fry 92, K. S. Ranjitsinhji 74, H. Trumble 6-69) lost to Australians 352 (G. Giffen 84, H. Graham 60, G. H. S. Trott 52, H. Donnan 51, E. H. Killick 5-71) and 119-4 by 6 wkts.

29th Match: v Surrey (Oval)   Aug 17, 18, 19.
Surrey 295 (T. W. Hayward 84, R. Abel 71, E. G. Hayes 62, G. Giffen 7-81) and 90-4 dec (R. Abel 50*) drew with Australians 224 (T. Richardson 6-78).

30th Match: v Gloucestershire (Cheltenham)   Aug 20, 21, 22.
Gloucestershire 133 (T. R. McKibbin 6-48) and 17 (H. Trumble 6-8, T. R. McKibbin 4-7) lost to Australians 204 (S. E. Gregory 71*, C. L. Townsend 8-79) by an innings and 54 runs.

31st Match: v Somerset (Taunton)   Aug 24, 25, 26.
Somerset 219 (H. Trumble 4-78) and 49-6 drew with Australians 129 (E. Robson 6-22).

32nd Match: v Lancashire (Liverpool)   Aug 27, 28, 29.
Australians 124 (J. Briggs 7-63) and 183 (S. E. Gregory 53, J. Briggs 5-73, A. W. Hallam 5-74) beat Lancashire 62 (T. R. McKibbin 6-27, H. Trumble 4-34) and 28 (T. R. McKibbin 7-11) by 217 runs.

33rd Match: v C. I. Thornton's XI (Scarborough)   Aug 31, Sept 1, 2.
C. I. Thornton's XI 294 (L. C. H. Palairet 71, F. S. Jackson 67, T. C. O'Brien 65, E. Jones 4-72, T. R. McKibbin 4-84) beat Australians 116 (R. Peel 7-53) and 140 (R. Peel 5-43) by an innings and 38 runs.

34th Match: v South of England (Hastings)   Sept 3, 4, 5.
Australians 222 (C. Hill 65, G. A. Lohmann 4-63) and 63 (J. T. Hearne 6-8) drew with South of England 192 (W. G. Grace 53, T. R. McTibbin 6-65, G. Giffen 4-83) and 45-2.

1897: 3rd Philadelphians

This tour was very much more ambitious than the two previous Philadelphian visits, being confined entirely to first-class matches. It was unfortunate therefore that the team lacked three notable all-rounders in Noble, F. W. Clark and Walter Scott and that G. S. Patterson, their best batsman, was injured during the visit and so missed several matches.

The party which sailed into Southampton aboard s.s. *St Paul's* on 2 June consisted of G. S. Patterson (captain), F. W. Ralston jun, F. H. Bohlen, P. H. Clark, A. M. Wood, J. B. King, Crawford Coates, E. M. Cregar, Lynford A. Biddle, H. L. Clark, H. P. Baily, H. C. Thayer, J. A. Lester and F. H. Bates, with M. C. Work as manager. J. H. Scattergood joined the team late in the tour as a wicketkeeper when Ralston was injured. The Associated Cricket Clubs of Philadelphia raised 8,000 dollars to finance the tour, but it was hoped to recover most of it from gate receipts. The players were all amateur and did not receive any money for their losses in salary while on tour.

In Philadelphia there were at most only 250 active cricketers and to be able to raise a team of first-class players from such a small base was very creditable. As it was the team beat both Warwickshire and Sussex (in spite of Ranji's presence at Hove) by a good margin.

On the whole the batting was quite adequate, with Lester very consistent, Wood scoring well and Patterson when fit showing good form. J. B. King proved easily the best bowler and grew in stature as the tour proceeded. The weakness in the team was the lack of any really good assistance for King. Baily, Cregar and P. H. Clark were useful club men, but not good enough to worry county batsmen on placid wickets. The fielding let the side down, though several hand injuries meant that players were at times at a disadvantage.

The majority of the team left England aboard s.s. *City of Paris* on 7 August, but five took advantage of being in Europe to tour the continent after the cricket had ended.

1st Match: v Oxford University (Oxford)   June 7, 8, 9.
Oxford University 363 (E. C. Wright 83, F. H. B. Champain 63) drew with Philadelphians 163-7 (F. H. E. Cunliffe 4-59).

2nd Match: v Lancashire (Old Trafford)   June 10, 11.
Philadelphians 123 (W. R. Cuttell 5-26, J. Briggs 5-77) and 86 (W. R. Cuttell 5-39, A. W. Hallam 4-15) lost to Lancashire 149 (H. P. Baily 6-51) and 64-3 by 7 wkts.

3rd Match: v Cambridge University (Cambridge)   June 14, 15.
Philadelphians 149 (A. M. Wood 73*, C. E. M. Wilson 6-48, G. L. Jessop 4-60) lost to Cambridge University 412 (G. L. Jessop 140, N. F. Druce 109, J. B. King 4-139) by an innings and 163 runs.

4th Match: v Sussex (Hove)   June 17, 18.
Philadelphians 216 (J. A. Lester 92, J. B. King 58, F. W. Tate 7-84) and 83-2 beat Sussex 46 (J. B. King 7-13) and 252 (K. S. Ranjitsinghji 74, W. Newham 67, J. B. King 6-102) by 8 wkts.

5th Match: v Middlesex (Lord's)   June 21 and 23.
Middlesex 234 (T. C. O'Brien 59, H. P. Baily 4-44, J. B. King 4-80) and 154-3 (F. G. J. Ford 112) beat Philadelphians 117 (A. E. Stoddart 4-12) and 270 (A. M. Wood 80, J. T. Rawlin 4-56, J. T. Hearne 4-80) by 7 wkts.

6th Match: v Oxford University, Past and Present (Oval)   June 24, 25, 26.
Oxford University, Past and Present 261 (J. B. King 4-83) and 84-3 beat Philadelphians 120 (F. W. Stocks 7-35) and 221 (C. Coates 84, G. F. H. Berkeley 5-77, F. W. Stocks 4-98) by 7 wkts.

7th Match: v Yorkshire (Sheffield)   June 28, 29, 30.
Philadelphians 225 (A. M. Wood 52, E. M. Cregar 50, R. Peel 4-46) drew with Yorkshire 104-4.

8th Match: v Hampshire (Bournemouth)   July 1, 2, 3.
Philadelphians 292 (G. S. Patterson 88, J. A. Lester 60, W. Andrew 4-36) and 163 (F. H. Bohlen 50, Bower 4-43) lost to Hampshire 281 (J. Spens 118*) and 178-5 (V. A. Barton 93*) by 5 wkts.

9th Match: v Warwickshire (Edgbaston)   July 8, 9, 10.
Warwickshire 296 (A. Law 72, A. F. A. Lilley 70, J. B. King 5-95) and 201 (J. B. King 7-72) lost to Philadelphians 269 (F. H. Bohlen 56*, S. Santall 6-58) and 230-5 (J. A. Lester 67, E. M. Cregar 57) by 5 wkts.

10th Match: v Nottinghamshire (Trent Bridge)   July 12, 13, 14.
Philadelphians 421 (G. S. Patterson 162, A. M. Wood 100, F. H. Bohlen 61) drew with Nottinghamshire 244 (H. B. Daft 57, P. Mason 51, P. H. Clark 4-69) and 249-8 (J. R. Gunn 107).

11th Match: v Gloucestershire (Bristol)   July 15, 16, 17.
Gloucestershire 363 (W. G. Grace 113, G. L. Jessop 101) beat Philadelphians 181 (G. S. Patterson 59*) and 153 (J. A. Lester 62, G. S. Patterson 53, F. G. Roberts 6-32, W. G. Grace 4-47) by an innings and 29 runs.

12th Match: v Somerset (Bath)   July 19, 20, 21.
Somerset 200 (R. C. N. Palairet 66, J. A. Lester 4-47) drew with Philadelphians 171-5 (A. M. Wood 57, G. S. Patterson 52).

13th Match: v M.C.C. (Lord's)   July 23, 24, 25.
M.C.C. 278 (F. Mitchell 133, P. H. Clark 5-63) and 280-8 dec (J. T. Rawlin 73, F. Mitchell 58, J. B. King 4-72) beat Philadelphians 179 (G. S. Patterson 64, A. E. Trott 7-83) and 152 (J. A. Lester 71, A. E. Trott 6-87) by 227 runs.

14th Match: v Kent (Maidstone)   July 26, 27, 28.
Kent 454 (G. J. V. Weigall 138, J. R. Mason 92, J. Easby 73, J. A. Lester 4-94) beat Philadelphians 168 (J. A. Lester 66, E. B. Shine 5-43, W. Wright 4-58) and 277 (J. A. Lester 69) by an innings and 9 runs.

15th Match: v Surrey (Oval)   July 29, 30, 31.
Surrey 263 (H. B. Chinnery 66, N. F. Druce 51*) and 372 (T. W. Hayward 85, K. J. Key 82) beat Philadelphians 273 (H. C. Thayer 59, E. H. L. Nice 4-44) and 258 (E. H. L. Nice 4-44) by 154 runs.

1897: 3rd Philadelphians

Batting Averages

	M	I	NO	R	HS	Avge	100	c/s
J. A. Lester	15	26	2	891	92	37.12	0	4
G. S. Patterson	11	17	1	540	162	33.75	1	5
A. M. Wood	15	26	1	702	100	28.08	1	12
F. H. Bohlen	12	21	2	408	61	21.47	0	4
J. B. King	15	25	3	441	58	20.04	0	15
H. C. Thayer	11	18	0	293	59	16.27	0	2
C. Coates	10	15	0	243	84	16.20	0	6
E. M. Cregar	14	22	2	320	57	16.00	0	4
P. H. Clark	15	22	10	191	29	15.91	0	6
L. A. Biddle	8	14	3	149	30*	13.54	0	8
H. L. Clark	6	9	0	91	22	10.11	0	2
F. W. Ralston	10	16	3	122	40	9.38	0	13
H. P. Baily	13	20	1	177	40	9.31	0	2
F. H. Bates	6	11	0	91	22	8.27	0	3
J. H. Scattergood	4	6	2	31	13	7.75	0	4/2

Bowling Averages

	O	M	R	W	Avge	BB	5i
J. B. King	655.4	153	1730	72	24.01	7-13	4
E. M. Cregar	185	32	624	23	27.13	3-30	0
J. A. Lester	133.1	31	408	15	27.20	4-47	0
H. P. Baily	361.3	91	1028	35	29.37	6-51	1
F. H. Bates	64	11	221	7	31.57	2-17	0
P. H. Clark	348.4	72	1051	33	31.84	5-63	1
G. S. Patterson	129.2	32	322	8	40.25	1-4	0

Also bowled: C. Coates 12-3-25-0; A. M. Wood 9-0-43-0; F. H. Bohlen 2-0-6-0; L. A. Biddle 2-0-7-0.

1899: 10th Australians

Even before the 1899 tourists left Australia, they were being hailed as the strongest team ever to come to England and in the opinon of many critics they proved to be just that. The team, which left Adelaide aboard the s.s. *Ormuz* on 22 March, was J. Darling (captain), C. Hill and E. Jones of South Australia; S. E. Gregory, J. J. Kelly, M. A. Noble, F. A. Iredale, W. P. Howell and V. T. Trumper from New South Wales; J. Worrall, H. Trumble, C. E. McLeod, F. Laver and A. E. Johns of Victoria with B. J. Wardill as manager. The team arrived on 21 April at Naples, where Noble, Iredale and Laver disembarked. Johns, Kelly, Gregory, Darling, Hill and Jones left the ship at Marseilles, but the remainder continued by sea to England. The main point about the side was that they were a team and were not reliant on one or two star batsmen or bowlers. None of the bowlers was in the class of Spofforth, Palmer or Turner and none of the

The 1899 Australian party. Back: Trumper, Laver, Trumble, Howell, McLeod, Noble. Centre: Johns, Jones, Darling (captain), Kelly, Worrall, Iredale. Front: Hill, Gregory.

batsmen equalled Murdoch, nor was there a hitter of the calibre of Massie or Bonnor. Although the team lacked the individual star quality and their batting was not as attractive to the eye as the purists would have liked, the all-round play meant that they lost only three matches and that Australia won the Ashes.

For the Test Matches there were two innovations: for the first time in England five Tests were played and the English teams were chosen by a selection committee appointed by the Board of Control, which had been set up a few months previously.

The tourists were beaten in their second match (v Essex), but this proved only a slight hiccup in their progress and they played another 21 matches before being defeated again, winning the only Test Match (at Lord's) to have a definite result.

The best batsman was undoubtedly Hill but due to illness he missed the second half of the tour. Darling, with the aid of nine not outs headed the averages, and with nearly 2,000 runs rarely failed. Gregory, Kelly, Iredale and Trumper also had good tours. Trumper, who was a last-minute choice, was the most attractive batsman, while Noble batted well if rather tediously. The bowling devolved mainly on the trio of Trumble, Howell and Jones. Jones proved almost as fast as in 1896 and any doubts about the legality of his delivery were not sustained. Howell could bowl for hours without tiring and Trumble used his height to great advantage. Noble was the best all-round man and perhaps the most disappointing was McLeod, whose batting was very moderate, though his bowling improved greatly in the latter half of the tour. There was slight criticism of the fielding which at times looked ragged. The player most affected by injury was Worrall, who was hampered by a bad leg for the whole tour.

The team travelled home in two groups, the first aboard s.s. *Oruba* leaving Tilbury on 15 September, the others remaining three more weeks in England.

1899: 10th Australians

1st Match: v South of England (Crystal Palace)   May 8, 9, 10.
South of England 246 (C. B. Fry 81, T. W. Hayward 51, E. Jones 4-78) and 222 (K. S. Ranjitsinhji 63, E. Jones 5-78) drew with Australians 375 (S. E. Gregory 124, M. A. Noble 116, C. L. Townsend 5-112) and 7-1.

2nd Match: v Essex (Leyton)   May 11, 12, 13.
Essex 199 (H. Trumble 8-79) and 144 (A. J. Turner 54, C. E. McLeod 4-32, H. Trumble 4-52) beat Australians 144 (H. I. Young 4-42) and 73 (H. I. Young 7-32) by 126 runs.

3rd Match: v Surrey (Oval)   May 15, 16, 17.
Surrey 114 (W. P. Howell 10-28) and 64 (W. P. Howell 5-29, H. Trumble 5-34) lost to Australians 249 (J. J. Kelly 50*) by an innings and 71 runs.

4th Match: v An England XI (Eastbourne)   May 18, 19, 20.
Australians 222 (E. Jones 54) and 227-8 dec (V. T. Trumper 64, W. Attewell 4-48) beat An England XI 171 (W. Gunn 52*, H. Trumble 4-35) and 106 (W. P. Howell 7-37) by 172 runs.

5th Match: v Yorkshire (Sheffield)   May 22, 23, 24.
Yorkshire 83-3 drew with Australians.

6th Match: v Lancashire (Old Trafford)   May 25, 26.
Australians 267 (V. T. Trumper 82, H. Trumble 51, W. R. Cuttell 6-83) beat Lancashire 102 (J. T. Tyldesley 52, M. A. Noble 4-18) and 81 (H. Trumble 5-20) by an innings and 84 runs.

7th Match: v Oxford University (Oxford)   May 29, 30, 31.
Australians 303 (M. A. Noble 86, F. A. Iredale 77, B. J. T. Bosanquet 6-83) and 360-4 (J. Darling 106*, M. A. Noble 100*, J. Worrall 53) drew with Oxford University 341 (F. H. B. Champain 120, R. E. Foster 80, B. J. T. Bosanquet 51, M. A. Noble 5-70).

8th Match: v England (Trent Bridge)   June 1, 2, 3.
Australia 252 (C. Hill 52, W. Rhodes 4-58, J. T. Hearne 4-71) and 230-8 dec (C. Hill 80) drew with England 193 (C. B. Fry 50, E. Jones 5-88) and 155-7 (K. S. Ranjitsinhji 93*).

9th Match: v M.C.C. (Lord's)   June 5, 6, 7.
M.C.C. 245 (J. H. Board 59, E. Jones 5-72) and 230 (C. L. Townsend 78, E. Jones 5-65) lost to Australians 352 (C. Hill 132, J. Darling 71) and 125-2 (J. Darling 53, J. Worrall 52*) by 8 wkts.

10th Match: v Cambridge University (Cambridge)   June 8, 9, 10.
Cambridge University 436 (L. J. Moon 138, T. L. Taylor 110, W. P. Howell 4-91, M. A. Noble 4-105) and 122 (W. P. Howell 6-61) lost to Australians 436 (C. Hill 160, S. E. Gregory 102, G. L. Jessop 6-142) and 124-0 (J. Darling 60*, J. Worrall 53*) by 10 wkts.

11th Match: v Yorkshire (Bradford)   June 12, 13, 14.
Australians 141 (S. E. Gregory 54, G. H. Hirst 8-48) and 415 (J. Worrall 104, M. A. Noble 83, F. Laver 67*, G. H. Hirst 5-101) drew with Yorkshire 235 (J. T. Brown 84, M. A. Noble 6-83) and 278-9 (J. T. Brown 167, M. A. Noble 6-86).

12th Match: v England (Lord's)   June 15, 16, 17.
England 206 (F. S. Jackson 73, G. L. Jessop 51, E. Jones 7-88) and 240 (A. C. MacLaren 88*, T. W. Hayward 77) lost to Australia 421 (C. Hill 135, V. T. Trumper 135*) and 28-0 by 10 wkts.

13th Match: v Oxford University, Past and Present (Portsmouth)   June 19, 20, 21.
Oxford University, Past and Present 251 (H. D. G. Leveson-Gower 59, E. Jones 4-80) and 135 (C. B. Fry 54, C. E. McLeod 5-29, F. Laver 4-27) lost to Australians 373-8 dec (J. J. Kelly 89, F. Laver 79, V. T. Trumper 55, D. H. Forbes 6-100) and 16-0 by 10 wkts.

14th Match: v Leicestershire (Leicester)   June 22, 23, 24.
Australians 194 (S. E. Gregory 66*, F. Geeson 6-65) and 177-3 dec (J. Worrall 100*) beat Leicestershire 95 (H. Trumble 4-31) and 28 (M. A. Noble 7-15) by 248 runs.

15th Match: v Derbyshire (Derby)   June 26, 27, 28.
Derbyshire 123 (M. A. Noble 4-42) and 161 (W. Storer 54*, C. E. McLeod 6-89) lost to Australians 533 (M. A. Noble 156, J. Darling 134*, H. Trumble 100, E. Jones 55, W. Storer 4-112) by an innings and 249 runs.

16th Match: v England (Headingley)   June 29, 30, July 1.
Australia 172 (J. Worrall 76, H. I. Young 4-30) and 224 (H. Trumble 56, J. T. Hearne 4-50) drew with England 220 (A. F. A. Lilley 55, H. Trumble 5-60) and 19-0.

17th Match: v Nottinghamshire (Trent Bridge)   July 3, 4, 5.
Nottinghamshire 188 (A. Shrewsbury 51, H. Trumble 5-82, W. P. Howell 4-21) and 132-6 dec (W. B. Goodacre 51*, H. Trumble 4-53) drew with Australians 234-7 dec (V. T. Trumper 85, M. A. Noble 84) and 38-5 (T. G. Wass 4-11).

18th Match: v An England Eleven (Truro)   July 7, 8.
Australians 214 (J. Darling 55, T. Richardson 4-66, R. Peel 4-95) and 69-2 beat An England Eleven 87 (E. Jones 7-31) and 192 (L. C. Braund 63, W. P. Howell 6-36) by 8 wkts.

19th Match: v Midland Counties Eleven (Edgbaston)   July 10, 11, 12.
Australians 192 (H. Trumble 50, E. G. Arnold 4-50, G. A. Wilson 4-85) and 234 (M. A. Noble 63) beat Midland Counties Eleven 185 (H. Trumble 4-41, E. Jones 4-73) and 197 (A. O. Jones 90) by 44 runs.

20th Match: v Gloucestershire (Bristol)   July 13, 14, 15.
Australians 377 (V. T. Trumper 104, F. Laver 77, F. G. Roberts 4-84, A. J. Paish 4-100) and 28-4 beat Gloucestershire 240 (H. Wrathall 52, C. L. Townsend 50, H. Trumble 6-82) and 164 by 6 wkts.

21st Match: v England (Old Trafford)   July 17, 18, 19.
England 372 (T. W. Hayward 130, A. F. A. Lilley 58) and 94-3 drew with Australia 196 (M. A. Noble 60*, W. M. Bradley 5-67, H. I. Young 4-79) and 346-7 dec (M. A. Noble 89, V. T. Trumper 63, J. Worrall 53).

22nd Match: v W. G. Grace's Team (Crystal Palace)   July 20, 21, 22.
W. G. Grace's Team 431 (A. Hearne 168, L. C. Braund 125, M. A. Noble 4-57) drew with Australians 301 (F. A. Iredale 115, W. Quaife 4-28) and 113-3.

23rd Match: v Surrey (Oval)   July 24, 25, 26.
Surrey 112 (H. Trumble 8-35) and 350 (E. G. Hayes 131, R. Abel 56, H. Trumble 5-137) beat Australians 165 (W. H. Lockwood 5-53) and 194 (V. T. Trumper 68, T. Richardson 4-49) by 104 runs.

24th Match: v Sussex (Hove)   July 27, 28, 29.
Sussex 414 (C. B. Fry 181, E. H. Killick 106, C. E. McLeod 5-91, H. Trumble 4-75) and 143-4 (E. H. Killick 57) drew with Australians 624-4 dec (V. T. Trumper 300*, J. Worrall 128, S. E. Gregory 73, J. Darling 56*).

25th Match: v M.C.C. (Lord's)   July 31, Aug 1, 2.
M.C.C. 258 (K. S. Ranjitsinhji 92, E. Jones 5-98) and 151 (C. L. Townsend 69*, W. P. Howell 4-35, M. A. Noble 4-53) lost to Australians 319 (J. Darling 128, E. Jones 51, W. Mead 4-31) and 92-1 by 9 wkts.

26th Match: v Hampshire (Southampton)   Aug 3, 4, 5.
Hampshire 393 (E. G. Wynyard 79, C. B. Llewellyn 72, A. J. L. Hill 60) and 212-6 dec (R. M. Poore 71, E. G. Wynyard 51) drew with Australians 360 (H. Trumble 83, F. A. Iredale 69, C. B. Llewellyn 8-132) and 92-3.

27th Match: v Warwickshire (Edgbaston)   Aug 7, 8, 9.
Warwickshire 135 (H. Trumble 5-62, W. P. Howell 5-67) and 226 (E. J. Diver 66, C. E. McLeod 6-89) lost to Australians 312 (J. J. Kelly 103, E. F. Field 5-79) and 50-1 by 9 wkts.

28th Match: v Kent (Canterbury)   Aug 10, 11, 12.
Australians 227 (V. T. Trumper 50, W. M. Bradley 4-39) and 94 (C. J. Burnup 5-44, W. M. Bradley 4-42) lost to Kent 184 (H. C. Stewart 71, C. E. McLeod 7-87) and 141-8 by 2 wkts.

29th Match: v England (Oval)   Aug 14, 15, 16.
England 576 (T. W. Hayward 137, F. S. Jackson 118, C. B. Fry 60, K. S. Ranjitsinhji 54, E. Jones 4-164) drew with Australia 352 (S. E. Gregory 117, J. Darling 71, J. Worrall 55, W. H. Lockwood 7-71) and 254-5 (J. Worrall 75, M. A. Noble 69*).

30th Match: v Gloucestershire (Cheltenham)   Aug 17, 18, 19.
Gloucestershire 203 (G. L. Jessop 57, F. H. B. Champain 51) and 300 (C. L. Townsend 135*, W. Troup 51) drew with Australians 228 (M. A. Noble 77) and 175-5 (F. A. Iredale 54*).

31st Match: v Middlesex (Lord's)   Aug 21, 22.
Australians 445 (J. Darling 111, F. A. Iredale 111, V. T. Trumper 62, A. E. Trott 4-107) beat Middlesex 105 (C. E. McLeod 7-57) and 110 (E. Jones 7-40) by an innings and 230 runs.

32nd Match: v Somerset (Taunton)   Aug 24, 25, 26.
Somerset 376 (C. A. Bernard 94, L. C. Braund 82, E. Robson 76, S. M. J. Woods 68, E. Jones 4-95) and 232 (C. A. Bernard 56) drew with Australians 532 (F. Laver 143, J. Darling 96, F. A. Iredale 53, V. T. Trumper 51, E. J. Tyler 4-150).

33rd Match: v Lancashire (Liverpool)   Aug 28, 29, 30.
Lancashire 184 (C. E. McLeod 4-28) and 67-0 dec drew with Australians 140 (J. Darling 58, J. I'Anson 7-31) and 36-1.

34th Match: v C. I. Thornton's XI (Scarborough)   Aug 31, Sept 1, 2.
Australians 233 (H. Trumble 60, E. G. Wynyard 4-30, E. Smith 4-94) and 83 (W. Rhodes 9-24) drew with Australians 185 (E. Wainwright 54*, H. Trumble 6-70) and 81-7 (E. Jones 5-35).

35th Match: v South of England (Hastings)   Sept 4, 5, 6.
Australians 148 (G. L. Jessop 4-30, W. M. Bradley 4-41) and 352-7 dec (J. Darling 167, F. Laver 60) beat South of England 183 (W. P. Howell 7-57) and 207 (F. G. J. Ford 52, E. Jones 7-101) by 110 runs.

1899: 10th Australians

Batting Averages

	M	I	NO	R	HS	Avge	100	c/s
J. Darling	35	56	9	1941	167	41.29	5	32
C. Hill	17	23	1	879	160	39.95	3	11
M. A. Noble	33	50	7	1608	156	37.39	3	23
J. Worrall	24	39	5	1202	128	35.35	3	12
V. T. Trumper	33	48	3	1556	300*	34.57	3	15
F. Laver	27	38	10	859	143	30.67	1	12
F. A. Iredale	27	38	3	1039	115	29.68	2	20
H. Trumble	32	51	8	1183	100	27.51	1	49
S. E. Gregory	32	49	6	1181	124	27.46	3	9
J. J. Kelly	30	39	6	768	103	23.27	1	39/3
E. Jones	28	35	4	552	55	17.80	0	24
C. E. McLeod	28	38	7	544	77	17.54	0	14
W. P. Howell	32	40	11	307	49*	10.58	0	19
A. E. Johns	8	8	3	50	27*	10.00	0	5/1

Bowling Averages

	O	M	R	W	Avge	BB	5i
H. Trumble	1249.1	431	2618	142	18.43	8-35	11
W. P. Howell	1120.4	426	2381	117	20.35	10-28	6
E. Jones	1164.1	331	2849	135	21.10	7-31	10
M. A. Noble	765.3	254	1878	82	22.90	7-15	4
C. E. McLeod	776.3	270	1860	81	22.96	7-57	6
F. Laver	243.2	79	619	23	26.91	4-27	0
V. T. Trumper	7	1	29	1	29.00	1-10	0
J. Worrall	31	2	104	1	104.00	1-59	0

Also bowled: S. E. Gregory 19-3-73-0; J. J. Kelly 3-0-16-0; F. A. Iredale 6-1-11-1; J. Darling 3-0-10-0; C. Hill 5-0-16-1.

1900: 1st West Indians

Lord Hawke, who had taken one of two English teams out to the West Indies in 1896-97, in July 1899 invited the West Indies to send a representative team to England. A selection committee representing all the West Indies met in Trinidad in January 1900 and chose R. S. A. Warner of Trinidad as captain; S. W. Sproston, G. C. Learmond and W. J. Burton of Demerara; P. J. Cox, W. Bowring, P. A. Goodman and F. Hinds from Barbados; L. S. d'Ade and S. Woods of Trinidad; M. M. Kerr and G. L. Livingstone from Jamaica; W. H. Mignon of Grenada and C. A. Ollivierre from St Vincent, with W. C. Nock of Trinidad as manager. H. B. G. Austin, H. A. Cole and Cumberbach were not available, but otherwise the team was the strongest possible. They sailed from Barbados aboard R.M.S. *Trent* on 29 May and landed at Southampton on 5 June.

After two days' practice on the Hampshire County ground, the programme arranged by Lord Hawke began on 11 June. The tour got off to a wretched start, the visitors finding the English conditions vastly different from those at home, but during the last few matches every member of the team demonstrated what he had learnt and the team showed a great improvement. An attack of malaria meant Warner missed the second half of the tour and Sproston led the side in his place.

Burton was regarded as the best bowler, closely followed by Woods. The former took 78 wickets, average 21.55, and the latter 72, average 21.54. Ollivierre proved the outstanding batsman and stayed in England to qualify for Derbyshire. Constantine, Cox, Goodman and Sproston also batted well. Ollivierre's record was 883 runs, average 32.70. The chief deficiency in the side was the lack of a good wicketkeeper and the other main problem was the appalling running and calling by the batsmen.

The English public and press took little interest in the visit and little was made in gate money. The team left Southampton aboard R.M.S. *Don* on 23 August.

1901: 2nd South Africans

As the team left South Africa aboard the s.s. *Briton* on 17 April, the local newspapers attacked the chosen party, saying that it could not, or should not be, designated 'the South African Team', since it was not selected by the South African Cricket Union and was a private venture organised by J. D. Logan and that only six of the 14 players would have the ghost of a chance of playing for South Africa in a representative match.

The team, which landed at Southampton on 3 May was M. Bisset (captain), A. Reid, A. V. C. Bisset, C. F. H. Prince, R. Graham, J. D. Logan jun, J. J. Kotze and G. A. Rowe, all of Western Province, C. M. H. Hathorn, L. J. Tancred, E. A. Halliwell, J. H. Sinclair all from Transvaal; W. A. Shalders of Griqualand West and B. C. Cooley of Natal with G. A. Lohmann as manager.

In England Conan Doyle attacked the tourists on a different issue, stating that they ought to be fighting the Boers, not coming to England to play cricket.

Unlike the 1894 team, this side was given first-class status and

1900: 1st West Indians

1st Match: v London County (Crystal Palace)   June 11, 12, 13.
London County 538 (J. R. Mason 126, H. R. Parkes 106*, W. G. Grace 71, J. Gilman 63, E. H. S. Berridge 50) beat West Indians 237 (P. A. Goodman 74, P. J. Cox 53, J. R. Mason 5-50) and 103 (J. R. Mason 5-43, W. G. Grace 5-52) by an innings and 198 runs.

2nd Match: v Worcestershire (Worcester)   June 14, 15, 16.
Worcestershire 307 (H. K. Foster 79, F. Bowley 63, S. Woods 5-77) and 257 (F. A. Pearson 88*, C. A. Ollivierre 4-37) beat West Indians 187 (S. W. Sproston 54, F. A. Pearson 6-73, A. F. Bannister 4-44) and 162 (F. A. Pearson 4-25) by 215 runs.

3rd Match: v Warwickshire (Edgbaston)   June 18, 19, 20.
Warwickshire 466 (J. E. Hill 145, A. A. Lilley 56) beat West Indians 233 (P. J. Cox 79) and 122 (A. E. M. Whittle 4-17, W. Ward 4-54) by an innings and 111 runs.

4th Match: v Gentlemen of M.C.C. (Lord's)   June 21, 22, 23.
M.C.C. 379 (A. W. F. Somerset 118, S. Woods 4-109) and 107-5 (E. C. Mordaunt 51*) beat West Indians 190 (G. C. Learmond 52, W. G. Grace 5-56) and 295 (L. S. Constantine 113, W. J. Burton 64*, A. E. Stoddart 7-92) by 5 wkts.

5th Match: v Minor Counties (Northampton)   June 25, 26, 27.
West Indians 206 (C. A. Ollivierre 69, G. J. Thompson 7-84) and 170 (F. Hinds 68, S. Lowe 5-50) beat Minor Counties 261 (G. J. Thompson 58, W. J. Burton 6-55) and 54 (S. Woods 4-31) by 61 runs.

6th Match: v Gloucestershire (Bristol)   June 28, 29, 30.
Gloucestershire 619 (G. L. Jessop 157, C. L. Townsend 140, H. Wrathall 123, W. S. A. Brown 60, T. Langdon 50, W. J. Burton 5-68) beat West Indians 96 (F. G. Roberts 5-39, C. L. Townsend 4-53) and 307 (L. S. Constantine 65) by an innings and 216 runs.

7th Match: v Leicestershire (Leicester)   July 2, 3, 4.
West Indians 386 (C. A. Ollivierre 159, P. F. Warner 113) beat Leicestershire 80 (S. Woods 5-39, W. J. Burton 4-39) and 219 (C. J. B. Wood 77, W. J. Burton 4-63) by an innings and 87 runs.

8th Match: v Nottinghamshire (Trent Bridge)   July 9, 10, 11.
Nottinghamshire 501 (W. Gunn 161, J. Iremonger 101, A. E. Hind 60, W. J. Burton 5-159) beat West Indians 209 (P. J. Cox 55, R. S. A. Warner 53*) and 265 (S. W. Sproston 72, C. A. Ollivierre 50, G. C. Learmond 50, W. Gunn 4-88) by an innings and 27 runs.

9th Match: v Wiltshire (Swindon)   July 12, 13, 14.
Wiltshire 313 (H. S. Snell 71, O. G. Radcliffe 68, A. M. Miller 62) beat West Indians 120 (W. Overton 7-33) and 93 (F. H. Humphreys 4-17) by an innings and 100 runs.

10th Match: v Lancashire (Old Trafford)   July 16, 17.
Lancashire 187 (H. Cudworth 102, W. H. Mignon 6-44) and 182 (J. Briggs 64, W. H. Mignon 4-73) beat West Indians 174 (S. Webb 5-67) and 138 (C. A. Ollivierre 60, J. Briggs 7-43) by 57 runs.

11th Match: v Derbyshire (Derby)   July 19, 20, 21.
Derbyshire 234 (W. Storer 65, L. G. Wright 58, P. J. Cox 5-61, W. J. Burton 4-78) and 182-7 dec (W. Storer 57*) drew with West Indians 300 (P. A. Goodman 104, L. S. Constantine 62, J. J. Hulme 6-76) and 45-2.

12th Match: v Staffordshire (Stoke-on-Trent)   July 23, 24.
Staffordshire 256 (Hollowood 103, W. J. Burton 7-100) and 110-4 dec drew with West Indians 228 (F. Hindle 79, A. E. Fernie 4-70) and 53-3.

13th Match: v Hampshire (Southampton)   July 26, 27, 28.
West Indians 370 (S. W. Sproston 86, W. Bowring 63, P. J. Cox 63, P. A. Goodman 52, C. B. Llewellyn 7-153) and 112 (C. B. Llewellyn 6-34) beat Hampshire 249 (C. B. Llewellyn 93, V. A. Barton 59, S. Woods 6-93) and 145 (W. J. Burton 5-50, S. Woods 4-55) by 88 runs.

14th Match: v Surrey (Oval)   July 30, 31.
West Indians 328 (P. J. Cox 142, C. A. Ollivierre 94, L. Walker 8-72) beat Surrey 117 (S. Woods 7-48) and 177 (S. Woods 5-68, W. J. Burton 4-67) by an innings and 34 runs.

15th Match: v Liverpool and District (Liverpool)
West Indians 265 (S. W. Sproston 118, P. J. Cox 76, Gregory 5-111, R. J. Burrough 4-60) and 124-5 dec (R. J. Burrough 4-42) drew with Liverpool and District 218 (C. Holden 86, P. J. Cox 5-64, W. J. Burton 5-98) and 100-0 (C. Holden 68*).

16th Match: v Yorkshire (Bradford)   Aug 6, 7, 8.
Yorkshire 23-0 drew with West Indians.

17th Match: v Norfolk (Norwich)   Aug 10, 11.
Norfolk 117 (S. Woods 5-38) and 32 (W. J. Burton 8-9) lost to West Indians 165 (L. S. d'Ade 68*, C. Shore 5-64) by an innings and 16 runs.

1901: 2nd South Africans

1st Match: v Hampshire (Southampton) May 16, 17, 18.
Hampshire 538 (C. B. Llewellyn 216, J. G. Greig 119, A. J. L. Hill 120, J. H. Sinclair 4-170) beat South Africans 346 (C. M. H. Hathorn 103, A. V. C. Bisset 94) and 141 (C. B. Llewellyn 4-6) by an innings and 51 runs.

2nd Match: v London County (Crystal Palace) May 20, 21, 22.
South Africans 262 (E. A. Halliwell 79, C. M. H. Hathorn 74*, L. C. Braund 5-117) and 316 (C. B. Llewellyn 88, C. M. H. Hathorn 86) beat London County 316 (L. Walker 114, L. C. Braund 63, C. B. Llewellyn 6-140) and 201 (C. B. Llewellyn 7-101) by 61 runs.

3rd Match: v Kent (Beckenham) May 23, 24.
South Africans 225 (A. Reid 77*) and 139 (C. Blythe 6-53) lost to Kent 227 (E. Humphreys 60, C. J. Burnup 50, J. J. Kotze 4-46, J. H. Sinclair 4-58) and 139-3 (C. J. Burnup 70) by 7 wkts.

4th Match: v Leicestershire (Leicester) May 27, 28.
South Africans 132 (F. Geeson 7-33) and 191 (R. Graham 63*, R. T. Crawford 4-33) lost to Leicestershire 286 (A. E. Knight 68, G. A. Rowe 5-121) and 38-1 by 9 wkts.

5th Match: v Warwickshire (Edgbaston) May 30, 31.
South Africans 74 (S. Hargeave 5-39, S. Santall 5-35) and 135 (L. J. Tancred 50, E. F. Field 4-22, S. Santall 4-32) lost to Warwickshire 278 (S. Kinneir 71, A. F. A. Lilley 70, J. J. Kotze 5-63) by an innings and 69 runs.

6th Match: v M.C.C. (Lord's) June 3, 4.
M.C.C. 168 (G. A. Rowe 5-68) and 170 (G. A. Rowe 5-81) beat South Africans 150 (W. A. Shalders 62) and 135 (M. Bisset 55, W. Mead 8-53) by 53 runs.

7th Match: v Derbyshire (Derby) June 6, 7, 8.
Derbyshire 305 (W. Storer 64, L. G. Wright 64, E. Needham 57, R. Graham 6-84) and 170 (C. A. Ollivierre 54, R. Graham 5-47) lost to South Africans 392 (M. Bisset 184, E. A. Halliwell 53) and 84-1 by 9 wkts.

8th Match: v Cambridge University (Cambridge) June 10, 11, 12.
South Africans 692 (C. M. H. Hathorn 239, B. C. Cooley 126*, W. A. Shalders 69, E. M. Dowson 5-191) beat Cambridge University 223 (A. E. Hind 53, G. A. Rowe 7-65) and 254 (W. P. Robertson 57, G. A. Rowe 6-90) by an innings and 215 runs.

9th Match: v Somerset (Taunton) June 13, 14, 15.
Somerset 313 (L. C. H. Palairet 72, A. E. Lewis 52*, G. A. Rowe 4-80) and 440-9 dec (A. E. Lewis 100*, G. C. Gill 85, L. C. H. Palairet 52) beat South Africans 124 (G. C. Gill 5-24, B. Cranfield 4-55) and 288 (W. A. Shalders 103, E. A. Halliwell 92, L. C. Braund 4-83) by 341 runs.

10th Match: v Gentlemen of Ireland (Dublin) June 18, 19.
Gentlemen of Ireland 177 (A. D. Comyn 58, J. H. Sinclair 6-72) and 137 (L. H. Gwynn 68, G. A. Rowe 7-53) lost to South Africans 209 (T. C. Ross 5-47) and 107-5 (L. J. Tancred 58) by 5 wkts.

11th Match: v Dublin University (Dublin) June 20, 21.
Dublin University 144 (J. J. Kotze 4-28, G. A. Rowe 4-53) and 116 (W. S. Caldwell 56, R. Graham 4-41) lost to South Africans 302 (A. Reid 61, E. A. Halliwell 51) by an innings and 42 runs.

12th Match: v Liverpool and District (Liverpool) June 24, 25.
Liverpool and District 141 (C. B. Llewellyn 6-51) and 189 (T. Ainscough 53, C. B. Llewellyn 6-79) lost to South Africans 127 (C. B. Llewellyn 51, E. E. Steel 4-37, Kitchener 4-37) and 204-5 (L. J. Tancred 56, C. M. H. Hathorn 55) by 5 wkts.

13th Match: v Durham (Darlington) June 27, 28, 29.
South Africans 225 (W. A. Shalders 61, C. M. H. Hathorn 52, Turnbull 4-75) and 502-9 dec (A. V. C. Bisset 151, E. A. Halliwell 97, C. M. H. Hathorn 81) beat Durham 188 (J. H. Sinclair 5-76, G. A. Rowe 4-52) and 93 (G. A. Rowe 6-30, J. H. Sinclair 4-50) by 446 runs.

14th Match: v Lancashire (Old Trafford) July 1, 2, 3.
South Africans 155 (S. Webb 4-33) and 141 (A. W. Mold 4-39, S. Webb 4-57) lost to Lancashire 125 (J. H. Sinclair 5-72) and 172-2 (E. E. Steel 69*) by 8 wkts.

15th Match: v Surrey (Oval) July 8, 9, 10.
Surrey 184 (W. Brockwell 51, J. H. Sinclair 6-55) and 251 (H. S. Bush 92, L. Walker 64, J. H. Sinclair 7-98) beat South Africans 129 (T. Richardson 6-50) and 247 (W. A. Shalders 63, L. J. Tancred 56, T. Richardson 5-75) by 59 runs.

16th Match: v Nottinghamshire (Trent Bridge) July 11, 12, 13.
South Africans 165 (A. W. Hallam 4-55) and 278 (W. A. Shalders 51, A. W. Hallam 4-86, T. G. Wass 4-94) beat Nottinghamshire 96 (J. J. Kotze 7-31) and 253 (A. Shrewsbury 85) by 94 runs.

17th Match: v Worcestershire (Worcester) July 15, 16, 17.
South Africans 293 (C. M. H. Hathorn 90, G. A. Wilson 5-123) and 140 (G. A. Wilson 5-39) tied with Worcestershire 224 (J. J. Kotze 6-82) and 209 (G. H. Simpson-Hayward 52, R. Graham 8-90).

18th Match: v Northamptonshire (Northampton) July 18, 19, 20.
Northamptonshire 163 (J. J. Kotze 7-48) and 246 (T. Horton 102*, G. J. Thompson 60) lost to South Africans 238 (M. Bisset 88*, J. H. Sinclair 51) and 173-5 (J. H. Sinclair 77*) by 5 wkts.

19th Match: v Staffordshire (Stoke-on-Trent) July 22, 23, 24.
South Africans 164 (A. Reid 75, Grimshaw 5-58) and 318 (C. M. H. Hathorn 99, C. F. H. Prince 95, Grimshaw 5-97) drew with Staffordshire 125 (G. A. Rowe 6-30) and 43-3.

20th Match: v Wiltshire (Swindon) July 26, 27.
Wiltshire 123 (J. E. Stevens 53, G. A. Rowe 5-52, J. H. Sinclair 4-31) drew with Wiltshire 72-6.

21st Match: v Yorkshire (Harrogate) Aug 1, 2, 3.
Yorkshire 215 (J. H. Sinclair 7-54) and 369 (E. Wainwright 116, D. Denton 83, J. H. Sinclair 7-54) beat South Africans 193 (J. H. Sinclair 80, E. Smith 6-98) and 240 (L. J. Tancred 65, E. Smith 4-55) by 151 runs.

22nd Match: v East of Scotland (Edinburgh) Aug 5, 6, 7.
East of Scotland 125 (J. J. Kotze 5-27) and 170 (G. L. D. Hole 52, R. Graham 7-40) lost to South Africans 337 (L. J. Tancred 165, H. J. Stevenson 7-106) by an innings and 42 runs.

23rd Match: v West of Scotland (Glasgow) Aug 8, 9, 10.
South Africans 170 (A. Burnett 5-16) and 172 (B. C. Cooley 57, W. W. Henson 4-34) beat West of Scotland (G. A. Rowe 5-32, J. H. Sinclair 4-47) and 51 (J. H. Sinclair 7-18) by 180 runs.

24th Match: v Gloucestershire (Clifton) Aug 15, 16.
South Africans 234 (W. A. Shalders 90, A. E. Paish 6-84) beat Gloucestershire 40 (J. H. Sinclair 7-20) and 89 (J. H. Sinclair 6-53, G. A. Rowe 4-34) by an innings and 105 runs.

25th Match: v Glamorgan (Cardiff) Aug 19, 20.
South Africans 228 (L. J. Tancred 91, S. Lowe 7-77) and 202-9 dec (M. Bisset 67*, Russell 7-77) beat Glamorgan 168 (J. Bancroft 50, G. A. Rowe 4-54) and 130 (G. A. Rowe 6-42) by 132 runs.

1901: 2nd South Africans

Batting Averages

	M	I	NO	R	HS	Avge	100	c/s
C. M. H. Hathorn	14	25	2	827	239	35.95	2	3
W. A. Shalders	14	26	0	782	103	30.07	1	7
M. Bisset	15	27	0	653	184	24.18	1	22/7
E. A. Halliwell	14	25	1	552	92	23.00	0	14/7
A. Reid	11	19	1	412	77*	22.88	0	8
L. J. Tancred	15	28	1	591	65	21.88	0	17
A. V. C. Bisset	12	23	2	405	94	19.28	0	6
J. H. Sinclair	12	23	0	428	80	18.60	0	8
B. C. Cooley	7	12	1	170	126*	15.45	1	3
R. Graham	13	24	7	229	63*	13.47	0	16
C. F. H. Prince	5	8	0	101	39	12.62	0	4/3
J. D. Logan	4	8	0	100	35	12.50	0	3
J. J. Kotze	13	23	6	211	29	12.41	0	1
G. A. Rowe	15	27	8	180	21*	9.47	0	10

Also batted: C. B. Llewellyn (1 match) 4 and 88.

Bowling Averages

	O	M	R	W	Avge	BB	5i
C. B. Llewellyn	74.4	12	241	13	18.53	7-101	2
J. H. Sinclair	328	43	1211	61	19.85	7-20	6
R. Graham	282.3	40	1046	44	23.77	8-90	3
J. J. Kotze	355.5	61	1215	49	24.79	7-31	3
G. A. Rowe	585.5	128	1750	70	25.00	7-65	6
B. C. Cooley	45.5	4	181	6	30.16	2-13	0
C. M. H. Hathorn	10	1	40	1	40.00	1-16	0
E. A. Halliwell	39.3	6	127	3	42.33	2-49	0

Also bowled: W. A. Shalders 9-2-28-2; M. Bisset 1-0-14-0; J. Logan 3-0-20-0.

won five of its 15 first-class matches, but there was general agreement that the tour fixtures were badly arranged. With South Africans accustomed to matting wickets they needed time to adapt to turf and some of the early fixtures ought to have been against minor counties, rather than having a straight run of first-class games at the beginning. In the event the team lost five of the first six games, a record which not only discouraged them, but also caused the public to be apathetic.

The main obstacle to the team in the early matches was the form of the batsmen. J. H. Sinclair, their star, performed indifferently until the end of the visit. Hathorn, Shalders, Tancred, Murray Bisset and Halliwell all batted well at times. The bowling was in the hands of two good performers in Rowe and Sinclair, who both exceeded 100 wickets in all matches and Kotze and Graham backed them up efficiently. The fielding was good with Halliwell maintaining his reputation behind the wicket.

C. B. Llewellyn, the South African playing for Hampshire, had hoped to play fairly frequently, but only turned out twice, while C. O. H. Sewell, with Gloucestershire, had been billed to assist, but never did.

The visit was not a success financially and the costs were borne by J. D. Logan. After the last match several of the side had an extended holiday in Scotland and the main bulk of the players left on the s.s. *Briton* on 14 September.

1902: 11th Australians

The praises heaped on the 1899 Australians were nothing compared with those received by their successors in 1902. The team consisted of J. Darling (captain), C. Hill and E. Jones of South Australia; V. T. Trumper, M. A. Noble, R. A. Duff, A. J. Y. Hopkins, S. E. Gregory, J. J. Kelly, H. Carter and W. P. Howell from New South Wales; W. W. Armstrong, H. Trumble and J. V. Saunders of Victoria, with B. J. Wardill as manager. The s.s. *Omrah* sailing from Adelaide on 20 March carried not only the

1902: 11th Australians

1st Match: v London County (Crystal Palace) May 5, 6, 7.
Australians 117 (C. B. Llewellyn 5-52) and 213-7 (J. Darling 92, V. T. Trumper 64) drew with London County 235 (L. C. Braund 104, M. A. Noble 4-90).

2nd Match: v Nottinghamshire (Trent Bridge) May 8, 9, 10.
Nottinghamshire 287 (J. R. Gunn 80, A. Shrewsbury 73, W. P. Howell 4-74) and 183 (W. W. Armstrong 8-47) lost to Australians 474 (J. Darling 128, A. J. Y. Hopkins 80, J. J. Kelly 66, J. R. Gunn 6-174) by an innings and 4 runs.

3rd Match: v Surrey (Oval) May 12, 13, 14.
Australians 296-5 dec (V. T. Trumper 101) beat Surrey 96 (W. P. Howell 5-23, J. V. Saunders 4-26) and 122 (W. P. Howell 6-33) by an innings and 78 runs.

4th Match: Essex (Leyton) May 15, 16, 17.
Essex 178 (P. A. Perrin 63, V. T. Trumper 5-33) and 13-2 drew with Australians 249-8 dec (C. Hill 104, W. Mead 4-105).

5th Match: v Leicestershire (Leicester) May 19, 20, 21.
Leicestershire 51 (E. Jones 6-26, M. A. Noble 4-21) and 143 (M. A. Noble 8-48) lost to Australians 126 (A. Woodcock 5-54, J. H. King 5-72) and 69-3 by 7 wkts.

6th Match: v Oxford University (Oxford) May 22, 23, 24.
Oxford University 77 (M. A. Noble 5-38, W. W. Armstrong 4-9) and 183 (J. V. Saunders 7-67) lost to Australians 314-6 dec (V. T. Trumper 121, C. Hill 64) by an innings and 54 runs.

7th Match: v M.C.C. (Lord's) May 26, 27, 28.
M.C.C. 240 (K. S. Ranjitsinhji 67, W. P. Howell 4-54) and 280-8 dec (F. Mitchell 55*, P. F. Warner 50) drew with Australians 271 (V. T. Trumper 105, W. G. Grace 5-29) and 217-3 (V. T. Trumper 86).

8th Match: v England (Edgbaston) May 29, 30, 31.
England 376-9 dec (J. T. Tyldesley 138, F. S. Jackson 53, W. H. Lockwood 52*) drew with Australia 36 (W. Rhodes 7-17) and 46-2.

9th Match: v Yorkshire (Headingley) June 2, 3.
Australians 131 (F. S. Jackson 4-30, G. H. Hirst 4-35) and 23 (G. H. Hirst 5-9, F. S. Jackson 5-12) lost to Yorkshire 107 (W. P. Howell 6-53, M. A. Noble 4-30) and 50-5 by 5 wkts.

10th Match: v Lancashire (Old Trafford) June 5, 6, 7.
Australians 356-7 (W. W. Armstrong 87, J. J. Kelly 75, V. T. Trumper 70, C. Hill 54) drew with Lancashire did not bat.

11th Match: v Cambridge University (Cambridge) June 9, 10.
Cambridge University 108 (C. H. M. Ebden 53, V. T. Trumper 5-19, H. Trumble 4-33) and 46 (A. J. Y. Hopkins 7-10) lost to Australians 337 (V. T. Trumper 128, S. E. Gregory 72, E. M. Dowson 5-146, E. R. Wilson 4-107) by an innings and 183 runs.

12th Match: v England (Lord's) June 12, 13, 14.
England 102-2 (F. S. Jackson 55*) drew with Australians did not bat.

13th Match: v An England Eleven (Eastbourne) June 16, 17, 18.
Australians 154 (W. Bestwick 4-30, G. A. Wilson 4-34) and 185 (S. E. Gregory 71, G. J. Thompson 8-88) beat An England Eleven 138 (V. F. S. Crawford 57, H. Trumble 6-26) by 131 runs.

14th Match: v Derbyshire (Derby) June 19, 20, 21.
Derbyshire 152 (A. E. Lawton 50, W. P. Howell 4-8, J. V. Sanders 4-69) and 78 (J. V. Saunders 6-40) lost to Australians 218 (A. J. Y. Hopkins 68, J. Darling 65, W. Bestwick 6-82) and 13-2 by 8 wkts.

15th Match: v Yorkshire (Bradford) June 23, 24.
Australians 106 (W. Rhodes 5-49, S. Haigh 4-18) and 87 (S. Haigh 5-49, W. Rhodes 4-22) beat Yorkshire 77 (H. Trumble 6-17, J. V. Saunders 4-58) and 72 (H. Trumble 6-27) by 44 runs.

16th Match: v An England Eleven (Bradford) June 26, 27, 28.
Australians 402 (R. A. Duff 182, V. T. Trumper 113, H. J. Knutton 9-100) and 43-1 beat An England Eleven 240 (W. Quaife 68) and 203 (R. T. Crawford 90, J. V. Saunders 4-66) by 7 wkts.

17th Match: v An Eleven of Scotland (Edinburgh) June 30, July 1.
Scotland 109 (E. Jones 4-33, A. J. Y. Hopkins 4-36) and 91 lost to Australians 305 (R. A. Duff 98) by an innings and 105 runs.

18th Match: v England (Bramall Lane, Sheffield) July 3, 4, 5.
Australia 194 (S. F. Barnes 6-49) and 289 (C. Hill 119, V. T. Trumper 62, W. Rhodes 5-63) beat England 145 (J. V. Saunders 5-50, M. A. Noble 5-51) and 195 (A. C. MacLaren 63, G. L. Jessop 55, M. A. Noble 6-52, H. Trumble 4-49) by 143 runs.

19th Match: v Warwickshire (Edgbaston) July 7, 8, 9.
Warwickshire 124 (W. W. Armstrong 6-13) and 225-7 (T. S. Fishwick 68, E. Jones 4-66) drew with Australians 316 (S. E. Gregory 83, S. Hargreave 4-81).

20th Match: v Worcestershire (Worcester) July 10, 11, 12.
Australians 274 (R. A. Duff 90, M. A. Noble 56, A. Bird 6-69) and 199 (C. Hill 50, G. A. Wilson 4-35) beat Worcestershire 202 (G. W. Gaukrodger 59, M. A. Noble 4-34) and 97 (E. Jones 6-53, W. W. Armstrong 4-34) by 174 runs.

21st Match: v Gloucestershire (Bristol) July 14, 15, 16.
Gloucestershire 155 (W. W. Armstrong 4-51) and 168 lost to Australians 545-5 dec (C. Hill 123, A. J. Y. Hopkins 105*, M. A. Noble 100, V. T. Trumper 92, R. A. Duff 62) by an innings and 222 runs.

22nd Match: v Somerset (Taunton) July 17, 18, 19.
Somerset 274 (L. C. Braund 52, H. Martyn 52, J. V. Saunders 5-109) and 315 (L. C. H. Palairet 90, P. R. Johnson 62, E. Jones 4-104) drew with Australians 348 (R. A. Duff 183, M. A. Noble 53, A. J. Y. Hopkins 52, G. C. Gill 5-80) and 16-1.

23rd Match: v Surrey (Oval) July 21, 22, 23.
Surrey 296 (R. Abel 104, W. P. Howell 5-80) and 111 (J. V. Saunders 6-9) drew with Australians 313 (V. T. Trumper 85, C. Hill 90, R. A. Duff 57, H. P. Clode 4-65) and 11-1.

24th Match: v England (Old Trafford) July 24, 25, 26.
Australia 299 (V. T. Trumper 104, C. Hill 65, R. A. Duff 54, J. Darling 51, W. H. Lockwood 6-48, W. Rhodes 4-104) and 86 (W. H. Lockwood 5-28) beat England 262 (F. S. Jackson 128, L. C. Braund 65, H. Trumble 4-75) and 120 (H. Trumble 6-53, J. V. Saunders 4-52) by 3 runs.

25th Match: v Essex (Leyton) July 28, 29, 30.
Essex 345 (F. L. Fane 81, C. P. McGahey 72, C. J. Kortright 66, E. Jones 5-55) and 184-3 dec (C. P. McGahey 59, P. A. Perrin 58, A. P. Lucas 50) drew with Australians 232 (V. T. Trumper 109) and 253-6 (V. T. Trumper 119, C. Hill 59).

26th Match: v Sussex (Hove) July 31, Aug 1, 2.
Australians 580-6 dec (M. A. Noble 284, W. W. Armstrong 172*, A. E. Relf 4-142) drew with Sussex 185 (E. H. Killick 58, J. V. Saunders 4-22) and 130-1 (E. H. Killick 60*, J. Vine 50*).

27th Match: v Glamorgan and Wiltshire (Cardiff) Aug 4, 5.
Glamorgan and Wiltshire 121 (M. A. Noble 4-44) and 178 (H. E. Morgan 50, W. S. Medlicott 50, W. W. Armstrong 7-36) lost to Australians 148 (W. Overton 4-43, H. Creber 4-65) and 155-4 by 6 wkts.*

28th Match: v Hampshire (Southampton) Aug 7, 8.
Hampshire 130 (M. A. Noble 6-33) and 116 (R. M. Poore 62*, H. Trumble 6-52) lost to Australians 325 (J. Darling 116, M. A. Noble 113, C. B. Llewellyn 4-129) by an innings and 79 runs.

29th Match: v England (Oval) Aug 11, 12, 13.
Australia 324 (H. Trumble 64*, M. A. Noble 52, G. H. Hirst 5-77) and 121 (W. H. Lockwood 5-45) lost to England 183 (H. Trumble 8-65) and 263-9 (G. L. Jessop 104, G. H. Hirst 58*, J. V. Saunders 4-105, H. Trumble 4-108) by 1 wkt.

30th Match: v M.C.C. (Lord's) Aug 14, 15, 16.
M.C.C. 212 (K. S. Ranjitsinhji 60, W. P. Howell 6-105) and 181 (H. Carpenter 66, W. W. Armstrong 6-44) lost to Australians 427 (C. Hill 136, S. E. Gregory 86, M. A. Noble 70) by an innings and 34 runs.

31st Match: v Gloucestershire (Cheltenham) Aug 18, 19, 20.
Australians 312 (V. T. Trumper 125, W. W. Armstrong 56*, G. L. Jessop 7-91) beat Gloucestershire 152 (A. J. Y. Hopkins 4-11, W. W. Armstrong 4-35) and 150 (A. J. Y. Hopkins 5-65, W. W. Armstrong 4-74) by an innings and 10 runs.

32nd Match: v Kent (Canterbury) Aug 21, 22, 23.
Australians 154 (C. Blythe 4-50) and 209 (V. T. Trumper 69) beat Kent 77 (H. Trumble 8-30) and 197 (J. V. Saunders 5-43) by 89 runs.

33rd Match: v Middlesex (Lord's) Aug 25, 26, 27.
Middlesex 204 (P. F. Warner 58, H. Trumble 8-101) and 203 (G. W. Beldam 75, H. Trumble 4-48) lost to Australians 232 (V. T. Trumper 69) and 176-4 (M. A. Noble 59*) by 6 wkts.

34th Match: v Lancashire (Liverpool) Aug 28, 29, 30.
Australians 138 (G. H. Littlewood 5-49, A. Kermode 5-68) and 105 (G. H. Littlewood 7-49) beat Lancashire 120 (J. V. Saunders 6-52) and 105 (H. Trumble 5-44, J. V. Saunders 4-37) by 18 runs.

35th Match: v Players of England (Harrogate) sept 1, 2, 3.
Players of England 184 (J. V. Saunders 4-44) and 128 (J. V. Saunders 5-44) lost to Australians 359 (V. T. Trumper 127, J. Darling 67, A. J. Y. Hopkins 58) by an innings and 47 runs.

36th Match: v C. I. Thornton's XI (Scarborough) Sept 4, 5, 6.
C. I. Thornton's XI 198 (F. S. Jackson 72, H. Trumble 5-62, J. V. Saunders 5-74) and 202-9 dec (J. T. Tyldesley 88, J. V. Saunders 5-95) drew with Australians 247 (V. T. Trumper 62, W. Rhodes 4-95) and 120-4 (V. T. Trumper 55)

37th Match: v South of England (Hastings) Sept 8, 9, 10.
Australians 249 (A. J. Y. Hopkins 74, M. A. Noble 63, L. C. Braund 4-88) and 248 (V. T. Trumper 120, J. Vine 7-31) drew with South of England 403-7 dec (T. W. Hayward 106, C. J. Burnup 66, R. Abel 55, M. A. Noble 4-89) and 87-5.

38th Match: v South of England (Bournemouth) Sept 11, 12, 13.
Australians 123 (E. G. Arnold 8-57) and 91 (F. W. Tate 6-48, E. G. Arnold 4-30) beat South of England 87 (H. Trumble 9-39) and 66 (H. Trumble 6-29) by 61 runs.

39th Match: v Players of England (Oval) Sept 15, 16, 17.
Players of England 356 (T. W. Hayward 74, J. Iremonger 66, J. T. Tyldesley 56, J. V. Saunders 4-50) drew with Australians 414 (V. T. Trumper 96, C. Hill 81, H. Trumble 68, W. Rhodes 5-115).

1902 Australians but also MacLaren's English tourists of 1901-02 on their way home. Also on board were F. R. Spofforth, L. O. S. Poidevin and Dr R. J. Pope, the last of whom assisted the side in one match. The first nine Australians arrived unexpectedly in London on 21 April, having left the ship in Marseilles–they had been intending to pass a few days in Paris, but changed their minds.

Suffering only two defeats, the team improved on the record of 1899 and there is little doubt that they thoroughly earned their success. The major contrast between 1902 and 1899 was the positive batting in which Trumper played the leading role. Gone were the careful defensive tactics of the previous visit; the team went out to win every match by positive cricket and the very wet weather throughout most of the summer did not deter them. They were a trifle lucky to avoid defeat in the First Test; the Second Test was rained off; in the Third Australia won easily, while the last two provided each team with a close win. These two final Tests caught the public imagination and perhaps for the first time Test cricket completely outshone the affairs of the County Championship.

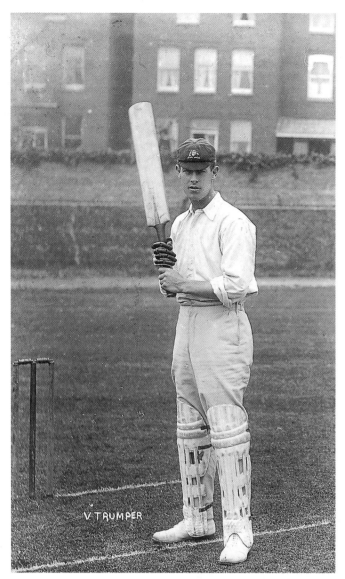

The batting of Trumper was the great talking point of the year—a glance at the averages shows why: his 2,570 runs at 48.49 were way ahead of Noble in second place. Contemporaries described him as the greatest Australian batsman to visit England and equalled only by W. G. Grace at his height. He relied very much on his wonderful eye and supreme confidence and was undeterred by the difficult wickets which were a feature of 1902. Of the other batsmen, Noble made a poor start but played well latterly. Hill had some fine innings, but was not as good as in 1899; Gregory was a disappointment; Duff had a good first tour and Armstrong and Hopkins proved useful all-round men. Trumble was the best bowler, the wickets suiting him. The left arm Saunders also bowled well but his action was criticised. Howell was disappointing, affected by the death of his father. The out fielding was quite excellent: Trumper, Hill, Duff and Hopkins were a great quartet, and Noble missed little at point. Carter looked a good prospect, but Kelly's form very much restricted his appearances behind the wicket. Darling led the side well and by

1902: 11th Australians

Batting Averages

	M	I	NO	R	HS	Avge	100	c/s
V. T. Trumper	36	53	0	2570	128	48.49	11	25
M. A. Noble	33	46	5	1357	284	33.09	3	28
C. Hill	35	49	1	1534	136	31.95	4	27
W. W. Armstrong	35	49	10	1075	172*	27.56	1	30
R. A. Duff	37	56	5	1403	183	27.50	2	22
J. Darling	35	50	5	1112	128	24.71	2	25
A. J. Y. Hopkins	37	52	6	1100	105*	23.91	1	22
S. E. Gregory	34	49	6	915	86	21.27	0	17
H. Trumble	20	28	6	389	68	17.68	0	17
J. J. Kelly	24	30	7	326	75	14.17	0	22/13
E. Jones	20	18	1	200	40	11.76	0	11
H. Carter	15	17	4	105	31	8.07	0	16/5
W. P. Howell	20	24	6	95	16	5.27	0	15
J. V. Saunders	25	32	9	82	9*	3.56	0	14

Also batted: Dr R. J. Pope (1 match) 2*.

Bowling Averages

	O	M	R	W	Avge	BB	5i
H. Trumble	912	292	1921	137	14.02	9-39	13
J. V. Saunders	710	160	2085	123	16.95	7-67	10
W. P. Howell	497	148	1215	68	17.86	6-33	5
A. J. Y. Hopkins	233.1	66	633	34	18.61	7-10	2
W. W. Armstrong	665.3	199	1361	72	18.90	8-47	3
M. A. Noble	697	203	1839	93	19.77	8-48	5
E. Jones	524.2	138	1410	66	21.36	6-26	3
V. T. Trumper	152.3	43	415	20	20.75	5-19	2

Also bowled: R. A. Duff 11-1-28-1; C. Hill 10.5-2-29-1; S. E. Gregory 4-0-21-0.

Above *Victor Trumper had a great tour in 1902, and today is widely considered to have been the greatest Australian batsman before the arrival of Bradman.*

Right *The Australian tourists of 1902, at the height of the 'Golden Age'. The series of Tests, won by Australia 2-1, was one of the most exciting of all. Back: Howell, Hill, Trumble, Wardill (manager), Armstrong, Jones, Hopkins, Duff. Centre: Trumper, Noble, Darling (captain), Saunders, Kelly. In front: Carter, Gregory.*

his example kept the whole party keen right through the summer.

A comment with present-day connotations was that Trumper had been approached to join an English county but had decided not to be bribed by money to quit Australian cricket.

The team left Southampton aboard s.s. *Dunvegan Castle* on 20 September to sail to South Africa, where they were scheduled to play three Test matches—the first such contests between the two countries.

1903: 4th Philadelphians

The major defect in the 1903 team was the absence of G. S. Patterson, who was not available. The team, which sailed from New York aboard the s.s. *Majestic* on 27 May, after a series of practice matches, was J. A. Lester (captain), F. H. Bates, F. H. Bohlen, R. D. Brown, P. H. Clark, E. M. Cregar, N. Z. Graves, H. A. Haines, T. C. Jordan, J. B. King, P. N. Le Roy, C. C.

Morris, J. H. Scattergood, F. C. Sharpless and A. M. Wood.

The team's record—seven wins to six losses—does not look particularly impressive, but the sides the tourists met were considerably stronger than on the previous visit and the results proved that Philadelphian cricket had continued to improve with the continuous exchange of teams between England and America.

The bowling, which relied so much on King in 1897, was now much better balanced. Clark partnered King and then Lester with his medium pace and Cregar's slows added effective variety. Lester was the best batsman, a talented stroke player and fully up to first-class county standard. Graves and Bohlen would also have made useful county men, while Sharpless had unlimited patience. Wood, the veteran, rarely found his form and though Morris hit the team's highest score, he did not achieve very much. An injury to Scattergood meant that the principal wicketkeeper returned home early; Jordan however filled his place adequately.

The team left England aboard s.s. *Cymric* on 14 August, Graves remaining behind in England until September.

1903: 4th Philadelphians

1st Match: v Cambridge University (Cambridge) June 8, 9, 10.
Philadelphians 209 (J. A. Lester 96, F. H. Bohlen 54, H. C. McDonnell 6-41) and 224 (F. H. Bohlen 63, J. B. King 53, E. M. Dowson 5-54, F. B. Roberts 4-44) lost to Cambridge University 379 (E. M. Dowson 71, F. B. Roberts 59, J. B. King 5-136) and 55-4 by 6 wkts.

2nd Match: v Oxford University (Oxford) June 11, 12, 13.
Philadelphians 214 (R. C. W. Burn 5-40, E. G. Whately 4-66) and 86 (R. C. W. Burn 4-24) drew with Oxford University 87 (J. B. King 8-39).

3rd Match: v Gloucestershire (Cheltenham) June 15, 16, 17.
Gloucestershire 86 (J. A. Lester 5-20) and 43 (J. A. Lester 6-13, P. H. Clark 4-25) lost to Philadelphians 155 (J. B. King 57, L. L. Cranfield 6-67, H. J. Huggins 4-46) by an innings and 26 runs.

4th Match: v Nottinghamshire (Trent Bridge) June 18, 19, 20.
Philadelphians 159 (J. A. Lester 67, F. H. Bohlen 65, T. G. Wass 6-71, J. R. Gunn 4-44) and 400-9 dec (C. C. Morris 164, N. Z. Graves 62*) beat Nottinghamshire 154 (J. R. Gunn 52, J. B. King 4-44) and 220 (J. R. Gunn 96, P. H. Clark 4-71) by 185 runs.

5th Match: v M.C.C. (Lord's) June 22, 23.
Philadelphians 65 (J. T. Hearne 6-33, W. Mead 4-31) and 93 (W. Mead 6-37) lost to M.C.C. 104 (J. B. King 7-51) and 55-5 by 5 wkts.

6th Match: v Kent (Beckenham) June 25, 26, 27.
Philadelphians 311 (J. A. Lester 70, A. Fielder 4-51) and 116 beat Kent 176 (J. Seymour 60, J. B. King 5-58, P. H. Clark 4-57) and 189 (J. B. King 4-73) by 62 runs.

7th Match: v Somerset (Taunton) June 29, 30.
Philadelphians 74 (L. C. Braund 5-23) and 219 (F. C. Sharpless 54, B. Cranfield 6-98, L. C. Braund 4-80) lost to Somerset 228 (P. H. Clark 5-54) and 67-0 by 10 wkts.

8th Match: v Lancashire (Old Trafford) July 6, 7, 8.
Lancashire 158 (A. Eccles 52, J. B. King 5-46) and 171 (J. B. King 9-62) lost to Philadelphians 187 and 143-1 (N. Z. Graves 103*) by 9 wkts.

9th Match: v Warwickshire (Coventry) July 9, 10.
Philadelphians 112 (E. F. Field 5-49, F. Moorhouse 4-30) and 191 (F. H. Bohlen 93, E. F. Field 6-82) lost to Warwickshire 153 (T. S. Fishwick 54, E. M. Cregar 8-35) and 151-3 by 7 wkts.

10th Match: v Worcestershire (Worcester) July 13, 14, 15.
Worcestershire 388 (J. A. Cuffe 91, H. K. Foster 55, P. N. Le Roy 4-62, P. H. Clark 4-148) and 205 (F. Bowley 50, P. H. Clark 8-91) beat Philadelphians 233 (P. H. Clark 67, G. H. T. Simpson-Hayward 6-78, E. G. Arnold 4-53) and 145 (P. H. Clark 52, N. Z. Graves 50, E. G. Arnold 5-40) by 215 runs.

11th Match: v Hampshire (Southampton) July 16, 17, 18.
Philadelphians 230 (J. A. Lester 67, E. M. Cregar 55, C. B. Llewellyn 6-109) drew with Hampshire 372-6 (C. B. Llewellyn 136*, A. J. L. Hill 121, E. M. Cregar 5-112).

12th Match: v P. F. Warner's XI (Oval) July 23, 24, 25.
P. F. Warner's XI 187 (J. B. King 4-64, P. H. Clark 4-89) and 274-9 dec (T. A. D. Bevington 91, B. J. T. Bosanquet 63, P. H. Clark 6-102) beat Philadelphians 82 (B. J. T. Bosanquet 5-33, F. A. Tarrant 5-40) and 183 (B. J. T. Bosanquet 7-46) by 196 runs.

13th Match: v Sussex (Hove) July 27, 28, 29.
No play due to rain.

14th Match: v Glamorgan (Cardiff) *July 30, 31.*
Glamorgan 92 (J. B. King 7-38) and 88 (J. A. Lester 5-23) lost to Philadelphians 176 (N. Z. Graves 95, A. Osborne 5-48, H. Creber 5-58) and 8-0 by 10 wkts.

15th Match: v Leicestershire (Leicester) Aug 3, 4, 5.
Philadelphians 200 (J. A. Lester 126*, J. H. King 4-72) and 287 (N. Z. Graves 67, J. A. Lester 64, G. C. Gill 4-55) beat Leicestershire 164 (J. H. King 53, H. Whitehead 53, J. B. King 5-88, P. H. Clark 4-50) and 222 (A. E. Knight 69, E. M. Cregar 5-68) by 101 runs.

16th Match: v Surrey (Oval) Aug 6, 7, 8.
Philadelphians 387 (J. B. King 98, J. A. Lester 52, A. M. Wood 50) and 251-5 dec (J. B. King 113*, F. H. Bohlen 58, E. G. Hayes 4-82) beat Surrey 241 (W. S. Lees 68, P. H. Clark 5-102) and 287 (T. W. Hayward 156*, F. Stedman 57, P. H. Clark 5-112) by 110 runs.

17th Match: v Scotland (Edinburgh) Aug 10, 11.
Philadelphians 302 (N. Z. Graves 107, F. H. Bohlen 80) drew with Scotland 145 (J. Anderson 51, J. B. King 6-49) and 83-3.

1903: 4th Philadelphians
Batting Averages

	M	I	NO	R	HS	Avge	100	c/s
J. A. Lester	13	23	3	786	126*	39.30	1	5
J. B. King	12	22	1	614	113*	29.23	1	13
F. H. Bohlen	13	24	0	639	93	26.62	0	2
N. Z. Graves	14	26	2	589	103*	24.54	1	13
C. C. Morris	12	20	1	395	164	20.78	1	9
F. C. Sharpless	10	18	1	323	54	19.00	0	6
A. M. Wood	13	23	2	358	50	17.04	0	14
P. H. Clark	14	25	4	333	67	15.85	0	9
E. M. Cregar	11	20	2	209	55	11.61	0	3
R. D. Brown	8	15	1	137	34	9.78	0	2
T. C. Jordan	10	16	7	87	22	9.66	0	15
P. N. Le Roy	6	10	2	62	25	7.75	0	7
F. H. Bates	6	11	1	70	24	7.00	0	2
H. A. Haines	8	13	1	78	20*	6.50	0	7
J. H. Scattergood	4	7	2	12	5	2.40	0	9/6

Bowling Averages

	O	M	R	W	Avge	BB	5i
J. B. King	451.3	106	1253	78	16.06	9-62	7
P. H. Clark	520.2	83	1633	79	20.67	8-91	5
J. A. Lester	158.2	31	448	21	21.33	6-13	2
E. M. Cregar	164.4	17	604	26	23.23	8-35	2
P. N. Le Roy	63.3	9	254	8	31.75	4-62	0
F. C. Sharpless	79.5	14	196	5	39.20	2-7	0
N. Z. Graves	9	0	45	1	45.00	1-13	0

Also bowled: H. A. Haines 7-0-45-0; F. H. Bates 19-5-66-0; R. D. Brown 1-0-2-0.

1903: Proposed Fijian tour

O. R. Borradaile, the secretary of Essex C.C.C., arranged a programme of matches for the 1903 Fijians, to begin at Cheltenham on 8 May against Gloucestershire Club and Ground and conclude on 10 August against Norfolk.

However, a cable in the middle of February 1903 called off the tour. No further details have been uncovered.

1904: Proposed Indian tour

The following were selected: Dr M. E. Pavri (captain), K. E. Mistri, R. P. Meherhomji and H. D. Kanga (Parsis); Ahsan-ul-Hak, Ali Hasan and Shafkat (Mohammedans) and Baloo, Jayram, Seshachari, Telang, D. D. Kanga, B. Billimoria and Bunda (Hindus). K. S. Ranjitsinhji and Singh were asked to assist the team for a few matches.

A programme of 25 matches was definitely arranged including 13 three-day matches against first-class opposition. It was hoped to arrange a further two or three games. The first fixture was against London County at Crystal Palace on 8, 9 and 10 May and the last against Yorkshire at Harrogate on 25, 26 and 27 August. A match against South Africa was fixed for Lord's on 11, 12 and 13 August.

A meeting on 26 January 1904 of the Indian Committee organising the tour voted 8 to 5 to cancel the tour on the grounds of insufficient subscriptions to finance the venture. An underlying factor in the cancellation was disagreement among the committee about the selection of the team.

1904: 3rd South Africans

The programme of the 3rd South African side was similar to its immediate predecessor's in that first-class matches were arranged but no Test Matches. The team, which landed at Southampton on 7 May, was F. Mitchell (captain), J. H. Sinclair, E. A. Halliwell, C. M. H. Hathorn, R. O. Schwarz, W. A. Shalders, L. J. Tancred, G. H. Shepstone, G. C. White and B. Wallach, all from Transvaal; J. J. Kotze, J. Middleton, S. J. Snooke and S. E. Horwood of Western Province, with G. Allsop as manager. Horwood took the place of A. Reid who withdrew at the last moment. Sir Abe Bailey guaranteed the visit financially and was considerably out of pocket as a result.

The team spent nearly three weeks in practice, mainly at Lord's, before the first fixture, which was a rain-ruined draw. Worcestershire then beat the tourists in their second match, but after this they were only beaten twice more. Their 13 wins

included one against an England eleven at Lord's, which was the highlight of the tour.

Tancred was the most consistent batsman and came out with a fine record. He opened the innings with Shalders and the pair

1904: 3rd South Africans

Batting Averages

	M	I	NO	R	HS	Avge	100	c/s
C. B. Llewellyn	6	8	2	338	81	56.33	0	3
L. J. Tancred	20	33	4	1217	113	41.96	4	12
C. M. H. Hathorn	22	33	2	1167	139	37.64	3	4
F. Mitchell	20	30	6	839	102*	34.95	1	21
G. C. White	22	30	4	773	115	29.73	1	14
R. O. Schwarz	21	27	2	692	102	27.68	1	14
W. A. Shalders	22	34	3	842	81	27.16	0	13
E. A. Halliwell	20	26	5	466	88*	22.19	0	32/13
J. H. Sinclair	21	29	0	633	103	21.82	1	14
G. H. Shepstone	6	9	0	175	64	19.44	0	3
S. J. Snooke	18	23	4	337	88*	17.73	0	8
B. Wallach	3	3	0	40	30	13.33	0	6/3
S. E. Horwood	9	11	1	103	34	10.30	0	2
J. J. Kotze	22	26	5	186	29	8.85	0	10
J. Middleton	10	12	7	22	7	4.40	0	3

Bowling Averages

	O	M	R	W	Avge	BB	5i
R. O. Schwarz	313.2	33	1187	65	18.26	6-68	4
J. J. Kotze	706.3	149	2133	104	20.50	6-58	7
J. H. Sinclair	608.3	111	2134	92	23.19	8-69	6
L. J. Tancred	41	8	151	6	25.16	4-43	0
C. B. Llewellyn	111	22	405	16	25.31	4-64	0
J. Middleton	234.2	31	766	30	25.53	4-50	0
S. J. Snooke	65	10	262	9	29.11	2-20	0
G. C. White	292	28	1121	37	30.29	5-46	1

Also bowled: G. H. Shepstone 11.2-3-37-4; E. A. Halliwell 1-0-13-0.

1904: 3rd South Africans

1st Match: v M.C.C. (Lord's)   May 30, 31, June 1.
South Africans 194 (C. B. Llewellyn 68*, B. J. T. Bosanquet 9-107) drew with M.C.C. 196-8 (E. G. Wynyard 52).

2nd Match: v Worcestershire (Worcester)   June 2, 3, 4.
Worcestershire 227 (H. K. Foster 107, G. H. T. Simpson-Hayward 58, J. Middleton 4-73) and 259 (E. G. Arnold 85, H. K. Foster 53) beat South Africans 161 (F. Mitchell 70*, E. G. Arnold 5-59) and 188 (L. J. Tancred 61, R. D. Burrows 5-43) by 107 runs.

3rd Match: v Cambridge University (Cambridge)   June 6, 7, 8.
South Africans 216 (J. H. Sinclair 50, P. R. May 4-61) and 246 (F. Mitchell 102*, H. C. McDonell 6-84) beat Cambridge University 197 (H. C. McDonell 58, J. H. Sinclair 4-45) and 195 (J. J. Kotze 5-98, J. H. Sinclair 4-61) by 70 runs.

4th Match: v Oxford University (Oxford)   June 9, 10.
Oxford University 154 (J. H. Sinclair 8-69) and 167 (R. W. Awdry 69, R. O. Schwarz 5-27) lost to South Africans 418 (F. Mitchell 82, C. M. H. Hathorn 80, G. C. White 79*, J. H. Sinclair 65, E. G. Martin 5-115) by an innings and 97 runs.

5th Match: v Gloucestershire (Bristol)   June 13, 14, 15.
South Africans 339 (L. J. Tancred 97, R. O. Schwarz 93, H. J. Huggins 4-117, E. G. Dennett 4-144) and 41-4 drew with Gloucestershire 182 (H. Wrathall 88, J. H. Sinclair 7-75) and 225 (H. Wrathall 54, G. C. White 4-54).

6th Match: v Warwickshire (Edgbaston)   June 16, 17.
Warwickshire 237 (S. Kinneir 58, J. H. Sinclair 5-99, C. B. Llewellyn 4-64) and 147 (A. C. S. Glover 73*, J. J. Kotze 6-58, R. O. Schwarz 4-29) lost to South Africans 343 (L. J. Tancred 106, S. J. Snooke 58, G. C. White 52, S. Hargreave 4-108) and 42-0 by 10 wkts.

7th Match: v Middlesex (Lord's)   June 20, 21, 22.
Middlesex 272 (B. J. T. Bosanquet 110, J. J. Kotze 5-94) and 225 (R. O. Schwarz 5-48) tied with South Africans 287 (F. Mitchell 66, W. A. Shalders 56, A. E. Trott 4-80) and 210 (L. J. Tancred 75, C. B. Llewellyn 60, A. E. Trott 6-75).

8th Match: v London County (Crystal Palace)   June 23, 24.
South Africans 332 (C. M. H. Hathorn 130, J. H. Sinclair 103) and 6-0 beat London County 168 (T. B. Nicholson 68, J. J. Kotze 6-67) and 167 (S. S. Harris 76, J. Middleton 4-59) by 10 wkts.

9th Match: v Dublin University (Dublin)   June 27, 28.
South Africans 484 (L. J. Tancred 148, G. C. White 117, J. H. Sinclair 51, E. Gibbon 5-151, S. H. Crawford 4-146) beat Dublin University 79 (R. O. Schwarz 5-16, G. C. White 5-34) and 115 (R. O. Schwarz 7-36) by an innings and 290 runs.

10th Match: v Gentlemen of Ireland (Dublin)   June 30, July 1, 2.
Gentlemen of Ireland 160 (R. O. Schwarz 5-66) and 135 (G. C. White 4-29) beat South Africans 64 (T. C. Ross 9-28) and 138 (W. Harrington 5-66) by 93 runs.

11th Match: v Hampshire (Alton)   July 7, 8.
South Africans 380 (L. J. Tancred 99, R. O. Schwarz 67, C. C. White 54, C. B. Llewellyn 5-160) beat Hampshire 168 (H. A. W. Bowell 65, J. J. Kotze 5-56) and 193 (E. M. Sprot 75, C. B. Llewellyn 60, J. Middleton 4-104) by an innings and 19 runs.

12th Match: v Somerset (Taunton)   July 11, 12.
Somerset 198 (F. M. Lee 79*, J. J. Kotze 5-82) and 154 (G. H. Shepstone 4-33) lost to South Africans 438 (R. O. Schwarz 93, W. A. Shalders 81, L. J. Tancred 73, E. A. Halliwell 72*, G. H. Shepstone 64, L. C. Braund 4-154) by an innings and 86 runs.

13th Match: v An England Eleven (Lord's)   July 14, 15, 16.
South Africans 352 (R. O. Schwarz 102, F. Mitchell 75, C. M. H. Hathorn 59) and 207 (C. M. H. Hathorn 69, E. A. Halliwell 57*, J. T. Hearne 5-90) beat An England Eleven 167 (J. H. King 55, R. O. Schwarz 4-30, J. H. Sinclair 4-55) and 203 (J. H. King 72, J. H. Sinclair 6-67, R. O. Schwarz 4-76) by 189 runs.

14th Match: v Scotland (Edinburgh)   July 18, 19.
Scotland 128 (J. H. Sinclair 5-68, J. J. Kotze 4-50) and 148 (R. M. Dickson 69, G. C. White 5-43) lost to South Africans 464-6 dec (L. J. Tancred 250, C. M. H. Hathorn 81) by an innings and 188 runs.

15th Match: v Liverpool and District (Liverpool)   July 21, 22.
South Africans 324 (F. Mitchell 87*, C. M. H. Hathorn 68, S. J. Snooke 50, Brown 4-81) beat Liverpool and District 111 (A. F. Spooner 50, R. O. Schwarz 5-40) and 118 (J. J. Kotze 6-53) by an innings and 95 runs.

16th Match: v Yorkshire (Hull)   July 28, 29, 30.
South Africans 148 (S. Haigh 4-58) and 158-8 (H. Myers 4-59) drew with Yorkshire 370 (D. Denton 66, H. Wilkinson 60, J. H. Sinclair 6-134).

17th Match: v Leicestershire (Leicester)   Aug 1, 2, 3.
Leicestershire 171 (H. Whitehead 53, J. H. Sinclair 6-65) and 292 (G. C. Gill 62, C. E. de Trafford 57, J. J. Kotze 4-98) lost to South Africans 464 (C. M. H. Hathorn 128, L. J. Tancred 109, E. A. Halliwell 88*, G. C. White 80, J. H. King 4-82, W. W. Odell 4-125) by an innings and 1 run.

18th Match: v Lancashire (Old Trafford)   Aug 4, 5, 6.
Lancashire 245 and 188 (J. S. Heap 55, J. J. Kotze 4-67) drew with South Africans 167 (J. S. Heap 5-66) and 190-2 (W. A. Shalders 79, C. M. H. Hathorn 65*).

19th Match: v Nottinghamshire (Trent Bridge)   Aug 8, 9, 10.
Nottinghamshire 320 (G. Gunn 143, R. O. Schwarz 4-60) and 242 (H. Staunton 70, J. Hardstaff 51, J. J. Kotze 5-68, J. Middleton 4-50) lost to South Africans 611 (G. C. White 115, L. J. Tancred 113, C. M. H. Hathorn 88, S. J. Snooke 88*, W. A. Shalders 77, J. H. Pennington 7-223) by an innings and 49 runs.

20th Match: v M.C.C. (Lord's)   Aug 11, 12, 13.
M.C.C. 120 (R. O. Schwarz 4-30) and 192 (F. A. Tarrant 61) lost to South Africans 223 (F. Mitchell 60*) and 90-0 by 10 wkts.

21st Match: Derbyshire (Derby)   Aug 15, 16, 17.
South Africans 120 (A. Warren 5-60) and 90-3 drew with Derbyshire 283 (E. M. Ashcroft 93, W. Storer 63).

22nd Match: v Sussex (Hove)   Aug 22, 23, 24.
Sussex 357-3 dec (K. S. Ranjitsinghi 178*, C. B. Fry 74) drew with South Africans 372-7 (C. M. H. Hathorn 139, J. H. Sinclair 79).

23rd Match: v Kent (Canterbury)   Aug 25, 26, 27.
Kent 285 (R. O'H. Livesay 78) and 196 (G. C. White 5-46) beat South Africans 188 (E. Humphreys 4-19) and 189 (C. Blythe 6-76) by 104 runs.

24th Match: v Surrey (Oval)   Aug 29, 30, 31.
Surrey 236 (E. G. Goatly 76, J. E. Raphael 56, L. J. Tancred 4-43, J. J. Kotze 4-86) and 363-7 dec (T. W. Hayward 176, E. G. Goatly 63) drew with South Africans 139 (E. H. L. Nice 5-43) and 17-0.

25th Match: v Yorkshire (Scarborough)   Sept 1, 2, 3.
South Africans 102 (G. H. Hirst 5-28, W. Rhodes 4-41) and 232-5 (L. J. Tancred 101, F. Mitchell 57*) drew with Yorkshire 387 (D. Denton 119, J. Tunnicliffe 80, R. O. Schwarz 5-101).

26th Match: v South of England (Hastings)   Sept 5, 6, 7.
South of England 237 (G. L. Jessop 159*, R. O. Schwarz 6-68) and 125-6 dec drew with South Africans 255 (C. B. Llewellyn 81, L. C. Braund 4-74) and 38-1.

turned out to be the best openers yet to come out of South Africa. Hathorn and Mitchell batted well, but Sinclair being a hitter was very variable. Predictions that the bowling would be on the weak side proved utterly false. Kotze was the fastest bowler of the season and very difficult at times – it was a pity he was such a slouch in the field. Schwarz taught himself the googly at the start of the season and was very effective, as was Sinclair, whose length was excellent. Tancred was a useful change bowler. Neither Snooke or Horwood had enough opportunities to prove themselves, and the all-rounder Shepstone could play in only a few matches because of illness. Middleton had put on a lot of weight and never looked like himself. In the field Halliwell, the vice-captain, remained magnificent behind the wicket, giving his understudy, Wallach, few chances. The fielding in general was moderate with too many passengers to hide.

The lack of public interest in the tour was blamed on very sparse publicity and the fact that several counties fielded weak teams, claiming that they were resting their best men for the County Championship games, an excuse which sounds rather familiar.

There was no doubt that in ten years South African cricket had improved very fast and most of the tourists were of first-class county standard – in fact Mitchell did play for Yorkshire and Schwarz had previously played for Middlesex. As in 1901 it was hoped that Llewellyn would play for the South Africans fairly often, but his appearances were very limited. The team did not return to South Africa as a group, but made their own ways back during September.

1905: 12th Australians

The team was J. Darling (captain), C. Hill, D. R. A. Gehrs and P. M. Newland, all of South Australia; W. W. Armstrong, C. E. McLeod and F. Laver of Victoria and from New South Wales M. A. Noble, V. T. Trumper, A. J. Y. Hopkins, R. A. Duff, S. E. Gregory, J. J. Kelly, A. Cotter and W. P. Howell, with Laver as manager.

The pattern of playing five Test Matches having been firmly established, the county and other games of the 1905 tour took another step into obscurity. Darling, the Australian captain, seemed from the beginning to have one object in view – to avoid at all costs losing the rubber against England. Armstrong, the most effective bowler, was under instructions for most of the tour to bowl negatively outside the leg stump. This safety-first policy produced very boring cricket and Darling failed in his objective since England won two Tests and the other three were drawn.

In the early part of the tour the best bowler was Laver, but in August Cotter, after being of little account, found his form and Armstrong abandoned the defensive role. Of the others Noble suffered from a spate of dropped catches and seemed to turn the ball less than on previous visits; McLeod was only steady and Howell did little. Much was expected of Hopkins, but his

1905: 12th Australians

Batting Averages

	M	I	NO	R	HS	Avge	100	c/s
W. W. Armstrong	30	45	7	1902	303*	50.05	4	34
M. A. Noble	31	46	2	2053	267	46.65	6	20
J. Darling	32	51	8	1694	117*	39.39	2	22
C. Hill	31	48	3	1722	181	38.26	4	20
V. T. Trumper	30	47	1	1667	110	36.24	2	28
R. A. Duff	28	44	0	1341	146	30.47	1	24
A. J. Y. Hopkins	28	39	5	996	154	29.29	1	16
S. E. Gregory	18	29	3	648	134	24.92	1	2
D. R. A. Gehrs	21	30	4	510	83	19.61	0	18
A. Cotter	28	40	3	673	48	18.16	0	15
J. J. Kelly	23	30	11	340	74*	17.89	0	20/7
C. E. McLeod	28	40	5	597	76	17.05	0	13
F. Laver	27	35	6	440	78	15.17	0	38
P. M. Newland	10	13	6	67	25*	9.42	0	10/3
W. P. Howell	20	27	8	179	46	9.42	0	18

Bowling Averages

	O	M	R	W	Avge	BB	5i
F. Laver	848.1	245	2092	115	18.19	8-75	8
W. W. Armstrong	1001.2	298	2221	122	18.20	8-50	10
W. P. Howell	457.5	118	1258	62	20.29	6-38	5
A. Cotter	735.1	121	2429	119	20.41	7-15	10
C. E. McLeod	731.3	208	1807	78	23.16	5-13	4
M. A. Noble	551.5	149	1464	55	26.61	6-39	1
R. A. Duff	104.5	30	312	9	34.66	2-17	0
A. J. Y. Hopkins	239	53	786	24	32.75	4-64	0

Also bowled: S. E. Gregory 2.1-1-0-12-0; C. Hill 7-1-16-0; D. R. A. Gehrs 3-0-12-0; J. Darling 2-0-10-0; V. T. Trumper 2-1-4-0.

P. M. NEWLAND.   R. A. DUFF.   C. HILL.   A. COTTER.   F. LAVER.

S. E. GREGORY.   D. R. A. GEHRS.   J. DARLING.   M. A. NOBLE.   J. J. KELLY.

W. W. ARMSTRONG.   A. J. HOPKINS.   C. E. McLEOD.   V. TRUMPER.   W. P. HOWELL.

The 1905 Australians. Top row: Newland, Duff, Hill, Cotter, Laver. Centre: Gregory, Gehrs, Darling (captain), Noble, Kelly. Bottom: Armstrong, Hopkins, McLeod, Trumper, Howell.

reputation seemed to be founded on myth. It seemed an error on the part of the selectors to include either Gregory or Howell in the party.

Trumper failed to live up to the great feats he performed in 1902, the faster wickets telling against him. Impatience cost Hill his wicket too often early on but he played well enough in August. Noble saved the side several times by his defensive play and was a very hard wicket to take. Armstrong's style had improved by leaps and bounds since 1902 and his all-round play was definitely the feature of the team. Duff had some good innings.

It must be said that Darling lost the toss in all five Tests and that the team had a most impressive record against the counties. When back in Australia, several players criticised the English umpires for making bad decisions which favoured England. Unlike the 1902 tourists the side did not travel to South Africa after leaving England, but went directly home.

1905: 12th Australians

1st Match: v Gentlemen of England (Crystal Palace) May 4, 5, 6.
Australians 270 (C. Hill 87, M. A. Noble 60, W. Brearley 5-87) and 526 (M. A. Noble 162, C. Hill 93, J. Darling 65, W. Beldam 4-207) drew with Gentlemen of England 156) A. Cotter 4-47) and 129-3.

2nd Match: v Nottinghamshire (Trent Bridge) May 8, 9, 10.
Australians 288 (W. W. Armstrong 112, M. A. Noble 62, T. G. Wass 5-85, J. R. Gunn 5-124) and 234-4 dec (V. T. Trumper 61, W. W. Armstrong 56*) drew with Nottinghamshire 219 (A. O. Jones 72, W. W. Armstrong 4-65) and 237-4 (A. O. Jones 103, G. Gunn 67).

3rd Match: v Surrey (Oval) May 11, 12, 13.
Surrey 225 (J. B. Hobbs 94) and 286 (T. W. Hayward 129*, F. Laver 5-61, M. A. Noble 4-54) drew with Australians 292 (W. W. Armstrong 86, C. E. McLeod 60, E. G. Hayes 4-56, W. S. Lees 4-124) and 199-6 (R. A. Duff 64, W. W. Armstrong 59, W. S. Lees 4-83).

4th Match: v Oxford University (Oxford) May 15, 16, 17.
Australians 241 (V. T. Trumper 77, M. A. Noble 66, E. G. Martin 4-33) and 266 (R. A. Duff 61, M. A. Noble 61, W. H. B. Evans 5-66, N. R. Udal 5-89) beat Oxford University 167 (C. N. Bruce 69, F. Laver 7-86) and 140 (F. Laver 6-47) by 200 runs.

5th Match: v Gentlemen of England (Lord's) May 18, 19, 20.
Gentlemen of England 300 (P. F. Warner 85, E. G. Wynyard 61) and 66 (F. Laver 4-13) lost to Australians 555-6 dec (W. W. Armstrong 248*, J. Darling 117*, R. A. Duff 94, W. Brearley 5-169) by an innings and 189 runs.

6th Match: v Yorkshire (Bramall Lane, Sheffield) May 22, 23, 24.
Australians 322 (V. T. Trumper 85, R. A. Duff 61, J. Darling 54, C. Hill 50) and 127 (S. Haigh 4-64) beat Yorkshire 197 (J. Tunnicliffe 52, F. Laver 8-75) and 78 (W. P. Howell 6-38, F. Laver 4-36) by 244 runs.

7th Match: v Lancashire (Old Trafford) May 25, 26, 27.
Australians 373 (C. Hill 149, W. Brearley 7-115) and 196 (M. A. Noble 52, J. Sharp 4-27, A. Kermode 4-64) beat Lancashire 221 (J. Sharp 52*, C. E. McLeod 5-49) and 104 (C. E. McLeod 5-16, F. Laver 5-44) by 244 runs.

8th Match: v England (Trent Bridge) May 29, 30, 31.
England 196 (J. T. Tyldesley 56, F. Laver 7-64) and 426-5 dec (A. C. MacLaren 140, F. S. Jackson 82*, J. T. Tyldesley 61) beat Australia 221 (C. Hill 54, M. A. Noble 50, F. S. Jackson 5-52) and 188 (S. E. Gregory 51, B. J. T. Bosanquet 8-107) by 213 runs.

9th Match: v Cambridge University (Cambridge) June 1, 2, 3.
Australians 256 (A. J. Y. Hopkins 75*, G. G. Napier 4-96) and 196 (G. G. Napier 6-85) beat Cambridge University 168 (L. G. Colbeck 52*, A. J. Y. Hopkins 4-64) and 115 (C. E. McLeod 5-13, W. W. Armstrong 4-44) by 169 runs.

10th Match: v Yorkshire (Bradford) June 5, 6, 7.
Yorkshire 324 (W. Rhodes 70, D. Denton 52) and 266-4 dec (D. Denton 153*) drew with Australians 208 (M. A. Noble 75, W. Ringrose 9-76) and 187-4 (M. A. Noble 54*).

11th Match: v M.C.C. (Lord's) June 8, 9, 10.
M.C.C. 183-8 dec (F. S. Jackson 85) drew with Australians 0-0.

12th Match: v Leicestershire (Leicester) June 12, 13, 14.
Leicestershire 286 (C. E. de Trafford 63, H. Whitehead 59, V. F. S. Crawford 52, W. P. Howell 4-87) and 218-8 dec (S. Coe 64*, M. A. Noble 4-37) drew with Australians 258 (M. A. Noble 79, T. Jayes 4-70) and 168-2 (V. T. Trumper 70).

13th Match: v England (Lord's) June 15, 16, 17.
England 282 (C. B. Fry 73, A. C. MacLaren 56) and 151-5 (A. C. MacLaren 79) drew with Australia 181 (F. S. Jackson 4-50).

14th Match: v Dublin University Past and Present (Dublin) June 19, 20, 21.
Australians 232 (D. R. A. Gehrs 52, P. A. Meldon 6-126) and 276 (V. T. Trumper 65, P. A. Meldon 4-90, T. A. Harvey 4-109) beat Dublin University Past and Present 141 (F. H. Browning 52) and 136 (F. H. Browning 54) by 231 runs.

15th Match: v Essex (Leyton) June 22, 23, 24.
Essex 118 (F. Laver 6-49) and 203 (M. A. Noble 4-66, F. Laver 4-81) beat Australians 100 (C. P. Buckenham 6-45, B. Tremlin 4-54) and 202 (A. J. Y. Hopkins 67*, C. P. Buckenham 6-92, B. Tremlin 4-81) by 19 runs.

16th Match: v Warwickshire (Edgbaston) June 26, 27, 28.
Warwickshire 161 (A. Cotter 4-76) and 168 (M. A. Noble 4-32) lost to Australians 380 (M. A. Noble 125, J. Darling 71, C. Hill 58, W. Quaife 5-66) by an innings and 51 runs.

17th Match: v Gloucestershire (Bristol) June 29, 30, July 1.
Australians 527 (V. T. Trumper 108, A. J. Y. Hopkins 93, J. J. Kelly 74*, E. G. Dennett 4-217) drew with Gloucestershire 116 (W. W. Armstrong 7-16) and 148-1 (J. H. Board 59).

18th Match: v England (Headingley) July 3, 4, 5.
England 301 (F. S. Jackson 144*) and 295-5 dec (J. T. Tyldesley 100, T. W. Hayward 60, W. W. Armstrong 5-122) drew with Australia 195 (W. W. Armstrong 66, A. Warren 5-57) and 224-7 (M. A. Noble 62).

19th Match: v Hampshire (Southampton) July 6, 7, 8.
Australians 620 (S. E. Gregory 134, C. Hill 115, M. A. Noble 101, V. T. Trumper 92, D. R. A. Gehrs 51, H. Baldwin 4-134, H. W. Persse 4-175) beat Hampshire 239 (J. G. Greig 66, A. Cotter 6-83) and 269 (J. Stone 56, H. A. W. Bowell 59, A. J. L. Hill 50, W. W. Armstrong 4-92) by an innings and 112 runs.

20th Match: v Derbyshire (Derby) July 10, 11, 12.
Australians 253 (D. R. A. Gehrs 72, V. T. Trumper 58, S. W. A. Cadman 5-94) and 250-6 dec (F. Laver 78, W. W. Armstrong 63*) beat Derbyshire 167 (W. W. Armstrong 5-29) and 231 (S. W. A. Cadman 66, L. G. Wright 58, A. Cotter 6-63) by 105 runs.

21st Match: v Somerset (Bath) July 13, 14, 15.
Australians 609-4 dec (W. W. Armstrong 303*, M. A. Noble 127, V. T. Trumper 86) drew with Somerset 228 (L. C. Braund 117, M. A. Noble 4-45, A. Cotter 4-101) and 254-4 (H. Martyn 130*, L. C. Braund 62).

22nd Match: v Scotland (Edinburgh) July 17, 18, 19.
Australians 284 (C. E. McLeod 54, J. T. Anderson 4-84) and 242 (R. A. Duff 62, V. T. Trumper 55, C. E. McLeod 52, F. G. Bull 5-58) drew with Scotland 158 (W. P. Howell 6-85, C. E. McLeod 4-20) and 211-9 (M. R. Dickson 62*, C. E. McLeod 4-30).

23rd Match: v XV of Scotland (Glasgow) July 20, 21, 22.
Australians 186 (H. Nixon 6-81) and 247-8 dec (C. Hill 79) drew with XV of Scotland 159 (C. E. McLeod 6-84, W. P. Howell 4-37) and 218-11 (G. W. Jupp 74, C. E. McLeod 5-87, W. P. Howell 4-114).

24th Match: v England (Old Trafford) July 24, 25, 26.
England 446 (T. W. Hayward 82, R. H. Spooner 52, C. E. McLeod 5-125) beat Australia 197 (J. Darling 73, W. Brearley 4-72) and 169 (R. A. Duff 60, W. Brearley 4-54) by an innings and 80 runs.

25th Match: v Surrey (Oval) July 27, 28, 29.
Australians 241 (C. Hill 89, W. C. Smith 6-27) and 271 (C. Hill 104, W. C. Smith 6-97) beat Surrey 357 (T. W. Hayward 70, F. Stedman 62, F. C. Holland 61, J. B. Hobbs 58) and 133 (T. W. Hayward 52, W. W. Armstrong 6-25) by 22 runs.

26th Match: v Sussex (Hove) July 31, Aug 1, 2.
Australians 556 (M. A. Noble 267, J. Darling 93, R. A. Duff 82, J. E. B. B. P. Q. C. Dwyer 6-178) beat Sussex 261 (C. B. Fry 70, W. W. Armstrong 5-103) and 219 (J. Vine 61, M. A. Noble 6-39).

27th Match: v Worcestershire (Worcester) Aug 3, 4, 5.
Australians 330 (M. A. Noble 113, V. T. Trumper 110, W. W. Armstrong 55, G. A. Wilson 6-80) drew with Worcestershire 78 (A. Cotter 7-15) and 51-5 (A. Cotter 5-19).

28th Match: v South Wales (Cardiff) Aug 7, 8, 9.
South Wales 132 (W. P. Howell 5-59) and 80-3 drew with Australians 361 (C. E. McLeod 103*, A. J. Y. Hopkins 92, W. W. Armstrong 59, H. Creber 4-100).

29th Match: v Middlesex (Lord's) Aug 10, 11, 12.
Australians 261 (M. A. Noble 68, W. W. Armstrong 55) and 195-9 dec (R. A. Duff 66, W. W. Armstrong 50, J. T. Hearne 5-34) beat Middlesex 145 (P. F. Warner 82, A. Cotter 4-43) and 179 (W. W. Armstrong 8-50) by 132 runs.

30th Match: v England (Oval) Aug 14, 15, 16.
England 430 (C. B. Fry 144, F. S. Jackson 76, T. W. Hayward 59, A. Cotter 7-148) and 261-6 dec (J. T. Tyldesley 112*, R. H. Spooner 79) drew with Australia 363 (R. A. Duff 146, J. Darling 57, W. Brearley 5-110) and 124-4.

31st Match: v Northamptonshire (Northampton) Aug 17, 18, 19.
Northamptonshire 149 (W. P. Howell 6-44) and 131 (W. W. Armstrong 4-64) lost to Australians 609 (A. J. Y. Hopkins 154, W. W. Armstrong 122, S. E. Gregory 96, D. R. A. Gehrs 83, V. T. Trumper 68, G. J. Thompson 5-215) by an innings and 329 runs.

32nd Match: v Lancashire (Liverpool) Aug 21, 22.
Australians 313 (V. T. Trumper 89, C. Hill 84, J. Darling 61*, W. Cook 5-103) beat Lancashire 114 (W. W. Armstrong 6-32) and 132 (W. W. Armstrong 6-60, F. Laver 4-39) by an innings and 67 runs.

33rd Match: v Kent (Canterbury) Aug 24, 25, 26.
Australians 403 (J. Darling 114, C. E. McLeod 76, M. A. Noble 70, V. T. Trumper 59, J. R. Mason 4-101) beat Kent 116 (A. Cotter 7-58) and 252 (A. Hearne 50, A. Cotter 5-124) by an innings and 35 runs.

34th Match: v Gloucestershire (Cheltenham) Aug 28, 29, 30.
Australians 195 (J. Darling 99) and 77-1 dec drew with Gloucestershire 137 (H. Wrathall 55, F. Laver 5-21, W. P. Howell 5-34) and 64-9 (A. Cotter 6-36).

35th Match: v An England Eleven (Bournemouth) Aug 31, Sept 1, 2.
An England Eleven 229 (E. G. Arnold 53, W. P. Howell 5-34, W. W. Armstrong 4-139) and 201 (E. G. Arnold 52, C. B. Llewellyn 50, W. W. Armstrong 5-69) lost to Australians 272 (V. T. Trumper 52, C. Hill 50, L. C. Braund 5-79, S. Hargreave 4-74) and 159-9 (S. Hargreave 6-76) by 1 wkt.

36th Match: v Essex (Leyton) Sept 4, 5, 6.
Australians 156 (B. Tremlin 7-72) and 319 (J. Darling 61, C. Hill 56, M. A. Noble 50, J. W. H. T. Douglas 4-73) drew with Essex 107 (C. Cotter 6-50) and 164-9 (F. L. Fane 57, W. W. Armstrong 5-62, F. Laver 4-27).

37th Match: v C. I. Thornton's England XI (Scarborough) Sept 7, 8, 9.
C. I. Thornton's England XI 282 (F. S. Jackson 123, A. Cotter 4-107) and 176-5 (R. H. Spooner 59) drew with Australians 392 (C. Hill 181, G. H. Hirst 4-70).

38th Match: v South of England 134 (M. A. Noble 4-25, C. E. McLeod 4-30) and 166-7 dec (T. W. Hayward 76, C. E. McLeod 4-50) drew with Australians 211 (A. J. Y. Hopkins 50, L. C. Braund 5-69, J. N. Crawford 4-69) and 46-2.

1906: 2nd West Indians

The West Indians were accorded first-class status for their second tour of England. The team comprised H. B. G. Austin (captain), P. A. Goodman, G. Challenor, C. K. Bancroft and O. H. Layne, all from Barbados; L. S. Constantine, G. C. Learmond, A. E. A.

Harragin, S. G. Smith and C. P. Cumberbatch of Trinidad; J. E. Parker and W. J. Burton of Demerara; R. C. Ollivierre of St Vincent and Dr J. J. Cameron and C. S. Morrison of Jamaica. They arrived aboard R.M.S. *Trent* at Southampton on 4 June.

Losing six of the first seven matches they played it became apparent that the programme arranged was too ambitious and the first-class counties did not field full strength sides against them. The public were lukewarm to the visit, which was not a financial success.

S. G. Smith was the outstanding player of the team and in all matches completed the double with 1,107 runs, average 33.54 and 116 wickets, average 19.31. Of the other players Goodman, Challenor and Ollivierre batted well at times and the last named also proved a useful bowler. Layne picked up some good wickets, but the change bowling was weak, Burton being a nonentity and Cumberbatch little better.

Smith stayed in England after the tour to qualify for Northants.

1906: 2nd West Indians

Batting Averages

	M	I	NO	R	HS	Avge	100	c/s
P. A. Goodman	11	22	3	607	107	31.94	2	15
A. E. A. Harragin	7	14	1	412	57	31.69	0	5
L. S. Constantine	13	26	0	776	92	29.84	0	18/4
G. Challenor	12	24	0	684	108	28.50	1	3
S. G. Smith	13	26	3	571	100	24.82	1	8
O. H. Layne	10	20	0	465	106	23.25	1	5
H. B. G. Austin	13	26	1	529	74	21.16	0	2
R. C. Ollivierre	12	24	0	480	67	20.00	0	12/2
W. J. Burton	2	4	2	32	19	16.00	0	3
C. K. Bancroft	11	22	5	266	53	15.64	0	11/4
G. C. Learmond	7	13	1	155	31	12.91	0	4
C. P. Cumberbatch	12	22	3	223	59*	11.73	0	20
C. S. Morrison	10	18	7	72	13	6.54	0	4
J. E. Parker	5	9	1	49	15	6.12	0	3
Dr J. J. Cameron	5	8	2	33	12	5.50	0	2

Bowling Averages

	O	M	R	W	Avge	BB	5i
R. C. Ollivierre	331.1	41	1251	58	21.56	7-23	2
O. H. Layne	261.2	39	819	34	24.08	7-26	2
S. G. Smith	492.3	72	1608	66	24.36	6-39	3
C. S. Morrison	121.2	26	371	14	26.50	4-94	0
P. A. Goodman	63	4	232	8	29.00	2-9	0
C. P. Cumberbatch	191.5	31	719	24	29.95	4-39	0
W. J. Burton	37.4	5	125	3	41.66	3-85	0
J. E. Parker	49	5	182	4	45.50	2-28	0

Also bowled: Dr J. J. Cameron 3-0-18-0; L. S. Constantine 2-0-14-0.

1907: 4th South Africans

Unlike the previous tours to England, the 1907 visit was guaranteed by the affiliated unions, the estimated cost being £2,900. The team, which sailed from Cape Town aboard the s.s. *Durham Castle* on 9 April was P. W. Sherwell (captain), J. H. Sinclair, L. J. Tancred, W. A. Shalders, C. M. H. Hathorn, R. O. Schwarz, G. C. White, G. A. Faulkner, A. E. E. Vogler and H. E. Smith, all of Transvaal; Rev C. D. Robinson and A. W. Nourse of Natal; J. J. Kotze, S. J. Snooke and S. D. Snooke of Western Province, with G. Allsop as manager. E. A. Halliwell and C. E. Floquet were originally chosen, but were unable to travel and were replaced by C. D. Robinson and S. D. Snooke. On 25 April the team stopped at Las Palmas for a one-day game, which they won by an innings, and then landed at Southampton on 30 April.

In view of the continued improvement in South African cricket, the 1907 fixtures included three Test Matches and it was hoped that the financial losses of previous visits would thereby be reversed. In the event the tourists got off to a tremendous start—of 11 games before the First Test they won eight and drew the remainder, all in their favour. Naturally this form built up public interest—well over 50,000 attended during the three days of the First Test, which was drawn. Continuing in fine style, the South Africans came to the Second Test and began by dismissing England for 76. The tourists unfortunately collapsed when

1907: 4th South Africans

1st Match: v Leicestershire (Leicester) May 20, 21, 22.
South Africans 145 (T. Jayes 4-51) and 156 (T. Jayes 4-61) beat Leicestershire 149 (R. O. Schwarz 6-55) and 54 (A. E. E. Vogler 5-37) by 98 runs.

2nd Match: v Essex (Leyton) May 23, 24, 25.
Essex 89 (J. H. Sinclair 4-23) and 167 (R. O. Schwarz 5-28) lost to South Africans 355-7 dec (G. A. Faulkner 101*, J. H. Sinclair 51) by an innings and 99 runs.

3rd Match: v M.C.C. (Lord's) May 27, 28, 29.
M.C.C. 142 (R. O. Schwarz 4-27) and 177 (F. A. Tarrant 54, A. E. E. Vogler 8-67) lost to South Africans 227 (G. C. White 74, F. A. Tarrant 6-73) and 96-7 (F. A. Tarrant 4-36) by 3 wkts.

4th Match: v Oxford University (Oxford) May 30, 31, June 1.
Oxford University 113 (R. O. Schwarz 7-41) and 16-2 drew with South Africans 182 (G. A. Faulkner 55, A. W. Nourse 54, R. G. Barnes 4-44, H. A. Gilbert 4-50).

5th Match: v Cambridge University (Cambridge) June 3, 4, 5.
South Africans 201 (G. G. Napier 6-73) and 11-1 drew with Cambridge University 103 (A. E. E. Vogler 5-42).

6th Match: v Northamptonshire (Northampton) June 6, 7, 8.
South Africans 115 (J. Thompson 6-41) and 143 (S. G. Smith 7-61) beat Northamptonshire 57 (R. O. Schwarz 6-11) and 118 (G. C. White 4-12, R. O. Schwarz 4-29) by 83 runs.

7th Match: v Middlesex (Lord's) June 10, 11, 12.
South Africans 212 (A. W. Nourse 58, F. A. Tarrant 6-97) and 404-9 dec (G. C. White 68, R. O. Schwarz 51*, E. Mignon 4-96) beat Middlesex 112 (R. O. Schwarz 6-27, J. J. Kotze 4-48) and 226 by 278 runs.

8th Match: v Hampshire (Southampton) June 13, 14, 15.
South Africans 82 (H. G. Smoker 7-35) and 329 (W. A. Shalders 105, P. W. Sherwell 74) drew with Hampshire 111 (C. B. Llewellyn 61, G. A. Faulkner 5-8).

9th Match: v Warwickshire (Edgbaston) June 17, 18, 19.
South Africans 296 (C. M. H. Hathorn 117, S. J. Snooke 57, S. Santall 7-77) and 318-6 dec (A. W. Nourse 127, G. A. Faulkner 61*) beat Warwickshire 202 (A. F. A. Lilley 63, W. Quaife 52, G. C. White 4-12) and 136 (R. O. Schwarz 5-47) by 276 runs.

10th Match: v Derbyshire (Derby) June 20, 21, 22.
Derbyshire 222 (A. Morton 72, A. E. E. Vogler 4-79) and 46 (A. E. E. Vogler 6-17, J. J. Kotze 4-23) lost to South Africans 376 (S. J. Snooke 114*, A. W. Nourse 148, C. M. H. Hathorn 54, F. Bracey 5-102) by an innings and 108 runs.

11th Match: v Kent (Catford) June 24, 25, 26.
Kent 273 (W. J. Fairservice 61, A. E. E. Vogler 4-74) and 101 (R. O. Schwarz 4-19, G. C. White 4-36) lost to South Africans 95 (C. Blythe 5-46, W. J. Fairservice 4-17) and 281 (S. J. Snooke 97, G. A. Faulkner 60, J. H. Sinclair 60, W. J. Fairservice 5-76, C. Blyth 5-114) by 2 runs.

12th Match: v England (Lord's) July 1, 2, 3.
England 428 (L. C. Braund 104, G. L. Jessop 93, J. T. Tyldesley 52, A. E. E. Vogler 7-128) drew with South Africa 140 (A. W. Nourse 62, E. G. Arnold 5-37) and 185-3 (P. W. Sherwell 115).

13th Match: v Sussex (Hove) July 4, 5, 6.
South Africans 49 (J. E. B. B. P. Q. C. Dwyer 6-25, G. R. Cox 4-21) and 327 (J. H. Sinclair 92, G. R. Cox 4-93) beat Sussex 186 and 151 by 39 runs.

14th Match: v Surrey (Oval) July 11, 12, 13.
Surrey 239 (J. N. Crawford 69, T. W. Hayward 61, A. E. E. Vogler 7-92) and 225 (T. W. Hayward 86, G. A. Faulkner 4-20) beat South Africans 162 (N. A. Knox 6-54, J. N. Crawford 4-66) and 217 (J. H. Sinclair 64, J. N. Crawford 4-79) by 85 runs.

15th Match: v Yorkshire (Bradford) July 15, 16.
Yorkshire 150 (G. C. White 4-34) and 173 (R. O. Schwarz 6-38) lost to South Africans 148 (G. H. Hirst 5-54) and 116-5 by 5 wkts.

16th Match: v Scottish Eleven (Glasgow) July 18, 19.
South Africans 573 (L. J. Tancred 119, G. A. Faulkner 107, A. W. Nourse 105, A. Broadbent 4-186) beat Scottish Eleven 68 (J. J. Kotze 7-43) and 134 (R. G. Tait 55, J. J. Kotze 5-43) by an innings and 371 runs.*

17th Match: v Scotland (Edinburgh) July 22, 23, 24.
South Africans 443 (P. W. Sherwell 109, A. E. E. Vogler 103, W. A. Shalders 80, B. L. Peel 4-123) and 28-2 beat Scotland 209 (B. L. Peel 74, R. O. Schwarz 5-58) and 258 (B. L. Peel 65, C. T. Mannes 62, R. O. Schwarz 5-18, A. E. E. Vogler 4-80) by 8 wkts.

18th Match: v Durham (Sunderland) July 25, 26.
South Africans 358 (H. E. Smith 83, W. A. Shalders 65, A. Stoner 8-100) beat Durham 125 (G. C. White 4-30, G. A. Faulkner 4-52) and 204 (E. W. Elliot 53, G. A. Faulkner 4-44, A. E. E. Vogler 4-47) by an innings and 29 runs.

19th Match: v England (Headingley) July 29, 30, 31.
England 76 (G. A. Faulkner 6-17) and 162 (C. B. Fry 54, G. C. White 4-47) beat South Africa 110 (C. Blythe 8-59) and 75 (C. Blythe 7-40) by 53 runs.

20th Match: v Lancashire (Old Trafford) Aug 1, 2.
Lancashire 169 (R. H. Spooner 57, R. O. Schwarz 6-45) and 95 (A. W. Nourse 5-44) lost to South Africans 429 (G. A. Faulkner 106*, P. W. Sherwell 69, A. E. E. Vogler 69, A. Kermode 5-94) by an innings and 165 runs.

21st Match: v Ireland (Dublin) Aug 5, 6, 7.
South Africans 218 (C. M. H. Hathorn 73*, T. C. Ross 5-99, W. Harrington 4-79) and 162 (W. Harrington 5-48) beat Ireland 153 (R. H. Lambert 51, A. E. E. Vogler 6-73) and 76 (G. A. Faulkner 6-39, R. O. Schwarz 4-20) by 151 runs.

22nd Match: v S. H. Cochrane's Team (Bray) Aug 8, 9 12-a-side.
S. H. Cochrane's Team 88 (R. O. Schwarz 6-31, A. W. Nourse 5-44) and 97 (A. E. E. Vogler 6-50, S. J. Snooke 4-38) lost to South Africans 251 (L. J. Tancred 56, W. A. Shalders 53, W. Brearley 5-113) by an innings and 66 runs.

23rd Match: v Nottinghamshire (Trent Bridge) Aug 12, 13, 14.
South Africans 258 (A. W. Nourse 66, G. A. Faulkner 51, J. R. Gunn 4-92) and 199 (T. G. Wass 5-103, J. R. Gunn 4-85) lost to Nottinghamshire 296 (J. Hardstaff 124*, A. E. E. Vogler 5-55, R. O. Schwarz 4-82) and 164-5 (J. Iremonger 92*) by 5 wkts.

24th Match: v Essex (Leyton) Aug 15, 16, 17.
South Africans 293 (G. C. White 76, A. E. E. Vogler 57, S. J. Snooke 55, W. Reeves 5-104) and 155 beat Essex 186 (A. E. E. Vogler 5-66) and 158 (G. C. White 4-44) by 104 runs.

25th Match: v England (Oval) Aug 19, 20, 21.
England 295 (C. B. Fry 129, R. E. Foster 51) and 138 (A. E. E. Vogler 4-49) drew with South Africa 178 (S. J. Snooke 63, C. Blythe 5-61) and 159-5.

26th Match: v Gloucestershire (Bristol) Aug 22, 23.
Gloucestershire 183 (J. H. Board 69, T. Langdon 54, R. O. Schwarz 5-46) and 151 (T. Langdon 78, G. A. Faulkner 4-23) lost to South Africans 372 (G. C. White 162*, R. O. Schwarz 71, E. G. Dennett 4-98) by an innings and 38 runs.

27th Match: v South Wales (Cardiff) Aug 26, 27.
South Africans 289 (S. J. Snooke 87, W. A. Shalders 62, J. Nash 6-75) beat South Wales 92 (G. C. White 6-23) and 131 (G. C. White 4-29) by an innings and 66 runs.

28th Match: v Somerset (Bath) Aug 29, 30, 31.
South Africans 233 (G. A. Faulkner 73) and 348 (S. J. Snooke 157, L. J. Tancred 67) beat Somerset 118 (R. O. Schwarz 6-46) and 105 (G. C. White 5-19) by 358 runs.

29th Match: v M.C.C. (Lord's) Sept 2, 3, 4.
M.C.C. 318 (A. E. Lawton 89, B. S. Foster 86, G. C. White 6-91) beat South Africans 135 (L. J. Tancred 61*, F. A. Tarrant 5-65) and 174 (F. A. Tarrant 5-57) by an innings and 9 runs.

30th Match: v J. Bamford's XI (Uttoxeter) Sept 5, 6.
J. Bamford's XI 92 (G. C. White 7-33) and 151 (G. C. White 4-36, G. A. Faulkner 4-44) lost to South Africans 257 (A. W. Nourse 68, G. A. Faulkner 52, E. G. Dennett 4-69) by an innings and 14 runs.

31st Match: v C. I. Thornton's England XI (Scarborough) Sept 9, 10, 11.
C. I. Thornton's England XI 397 (W. Rhodes 81, J. B. Hobbs 78, R. H. Spooner 73) and 232-2 dec (T. W. Hayward 105*, J. T. Tyldesley 99) drew with South Africans 319 (W. A. Shalders 76, A. W. Nourse 70, J. J. Kotze 60) and 192-5 (L. J. Tancred 84).

1907: 4th South Africans

Batting Averages

	M	I	NO	R	HS	Avge	100	c/s
G. A. Faulkner	25	45	6	1163	106*	29.82	2	19
S. J. Snooke	22	37	5	943	157	29.46	2	12
A. W. Nourse	25	42	1	1203	148	29.34	2	20
P. W. Sherwell	25	39	4	806	115	23.02	2	25/18
G. C. White	25	42	3	862	162*	22.10	1	14
W. A. Shalders	22	38	4	747	105	21.97	1	8
A. E. E. Vogler	25	38	4	723	103	21.26	1	20
R. O. Schwarz	26	39	8	644	71	20.77	0	17
J. H. Sinclair	24	39	1	773	92	20.34	0	6
L. J. Tancred	17	31	1	594	84	19.80	0	3
Rev C. D. Robinson	6	9	5	70	36	17.50	0	4/6
C. M. H. Hathorn	23	39	4	573	117	16.37	1	8
H. E. Smith	10	15	2	183	40*	14.07	0	1
S. D. Snooke	11	17	4	147	38*	11.30	0	7
J. J. Kotze	11	15	4	104	60	9.45	0	8

Bowling Averages

	O	M	R	W	Avge	BB	5i
R. O. Schwarz	711.3	153	1616	137	11.79	7-41	12
G. C. White	276.5	51	825	56	14.73	7-33	3
A. E. E. Vogler	592	127	1859	119	15.62	8-67	9
G. A. Faulkner	386.5	82	1013	64	15.82	6-17	3
A. W. Nourse	108	28	280	15	18.66	5-44	1
J. H. Sinclair	300.3	64	915	38	24.07	4-23	0
J. J. Kotze	190.5	32	684	25	27.36	4-23	0
S. J. Snooke	118	20	350	8	43.75	3-46	0

Also bowled: W. A. Shalders 5-1-11-0.

needing 128 for victory in the fourth innings and England won an exciting game. In the final Test the result was an even draw, so that England won the series, but South Africa had justified the elevation to Test Match status in England (the matches between English touring teams and South Africa had been called Tests since 1888-89, though hardly worthy of the name).

The great strength of the team lay in its bowlers. Schwarz and Vogler were the two principals—Schwarz relied mainly on the off-break, while Vogler used chiefly leg-breaks with the occasional googly. To back up Schwarz and Vogler were Faulkner and White, two more who bowled googlies. Faulkner was sometimes unplayable, but also could be erratic. So well did this quartet perform that Sinclair and Kotze, the main bowlers of 1904, were rarely called on. The summer was very wet, and so the batting figures were modest, but remarkable for their evenness. Nourse and Faulkner were possibly the most consistent. Hathorn, troubled by rheumatics, had a poor time, as did Tancred. The fielding was good, Sherwell kept wicket well, but the outstanding figure was White at cover-point.

The tourists ended the summer with a profit of some £1,400—thoroughly deserved. The team disbanded after the final match and went their several ways. Schwarz and S. J. Snooke in fact started a second tour—with the English team to Philadelphia.

1907: Proposed Indian tour

In November 1906 the *Bombay Gazette* printed details of a proposed 1907 Indian tour to England. A sum of 20,000 rupees had been subscribed and the following players had been invited to take part: K. S. Ranjitsinhji (captain), A. H. Mehta, K. M. Mistri, Ahsan-ul-Hak, B. Jayaram, P. Meherhomji, H. D. Kanga, P. Baloo, M. Bulsara, K. B. Mistry, S. Sechachari and M. Ali Hussain.

No firm fixture list was issued, however, and the proposed tour was abandoned. The main historical interest in the brief details is the inclusion of Ranjitsinhji in the party.

1908: 5th Philadelphians

The 1908 tour was unusual in that the fixtures did not begin until July, the two preceding visits having begun at the beginning of June. The s.s. *Umbria* sailed from New York on 20 June with the following aboard: J. A. Lester (captain), A. M. Wood, F. S. White, H. V. Hordern, N. Z. Graves, J. B. King, F. H. Bohlen, D. H. Adams, F. A. Greene, W. H. Sayen, W. P. Newhall, E. M. Cregar, T. C. Jordan and C. H. Winter. The party was completed by C. C. Morris who was already in England. Two notable omissions, both of whom were in the originally selected side, were G. S. Patterson and P. H. Clark. Cregar acted as manager.

The team relied very much on King, without whom the attack would have achieved scarcely anything, though the Australian Hordern did take some wickets with his well-disguised googlies. The biggest disappointment was Lester, whose batting on the slow wickets of 1908 was a shadow of his performance on the previous tour. The old campaigner Wood returned the best average. The fielding, especially close to the wicket, was good and Jordan kept wicket well, until he had to go home midway through the programme.

It was noticeable that no new cricketers of any real promise appeared and that Philadelphian cricket was beginning the decline from which it never recovered. As with all the previous visits, the public took little interest in their matches and the tour involved considerable expenditure by the Americans.

1908: 5th Philadelphians

1st Match: v South Wales (Cardiff)   July 6, 7, 8.
Philadelphians 108 (J. Nash 5-48, H. Creber 5-55) and 257 (C. C. Morris 62, A. M. Wood 60, H. Creber 7-97) beat South Wales 192 (A. Silverlock 61, J. B. King 5-55, H. V. Hordern 5-90) and 137 (A. Silverlock 64, J. B. King 7-39) by 36 runs.

2nd Match: v Worcestershire (Worcester)   July 9, 10, 11.
Philadelphians 138 (A. Bird 6-50) and 279 (A. M. Wood 132, R. D. Burrows 4-49) beat Worcestershire 192 (H. K. Foster 65, H. V. Hordern 6-56) and 129 (J. B. King 5-43, H. V. Hordern 5-52) by 95 runs.

3rd Match: v Hampshire (Southampton)   July 13, 14, 15.
Hampshire 463 (H. A. W. Bowell 160, W. N. White 87, A. J. L. Hill 66, C. B. Llewellyn 50, J. B. King 5-110) beat Philadelphians 275 (C. C. Morris 74, N. Z. Graves 76, J. B. King 52) and 152 (A. S. Kennedy 6-41) by an innings and 36 runs.

4th Match: v Folkestone (Folkestone)   July 17, 18.
No play owing to rain.

5th Match: v Middlesex (Lord's)   July 20.
Philadelphians 58 (F. A. Tarrant 5-19, A. E. Trott 5-31) and 55 (F. A. Tarrant 5-27, A. E. Trott 4-28) lost to Middlesex 92 (J. B. King 4-19) and 24-3 by 7 wkts.

6th Match: v Royal Artillery (Woolwich)   July 24, 25.
Royal Artillery 252 (A. J. Turner 84, Bond 57) and 111-2 drew with Philadelphians 319 (J. A. Lester 124, H. V. Hordern 55).

7th Match: v Northamptonshire (Northampton)   July 27, 28.
Philadelphians 166 (S. G. Smith 6-36) and 136 (W. Wells 5-46) lost to Northamptonshire 152 (H. V. Hordern 7-43) and 151-5 (S. G. Smith 76*) by 5 wkts.

8th Match: v Surrey (Oval)   July 30, 31, Aug 1.
Surrey 210 (A. Marshal 58, E. G. Hayes 58, J. B. King 6-47) and 251 (A. Marshal 103) beat Philadelphians 234 (W. S. Lees 6-94) and 105 (H. G. Blacklidge 4-26, W. S. Lees 4-47) by 122 runs.

9th Match: v All Ireland (Dublin)   Aug 3, 4.
All Ireland 86 (J. B. King 7-40) and 78 (J. B. King 7-23) lost to Philadelphians 171 (T. C. Ross 6-64) by an innings and 7 runs.

10th Match: v Ulster (Belfast)   Aug 7, 8.
Ulster 95 (F. O. Greene 5-60, J. B. King 4-25) and 110 (H. V. Hordern 6-44) lost to Philadelphians 319 (N. Z. Graves 62, F. H. Bohlen 56, J. B. King 53, F. S. White 52, Nutter 6-136) by an innings and 114 runs.

11th Match: v M.C.C. (Lord's)   Aug 13, 14, 15.
Philadelphians 186 (A. M. Wood 67, W. Mead 5-57) and 214 (F. S. White 62) beat M.C.C. 154 (H. V. Hordern 6-75) and 221 (H. V. Hordern 4-77, J. B. King 4-91) by 25 runs.

12th Match: v Derbyshire (Derby)   Aug 17, 18.
Derbyshire 78 (J. B. King 7-28) and 185 (J. B. King 5-88, W. H. Sayen 4-44) lost to Philadelphians 247 (F. S. White 55) and 17-1 by 9 wkts.

13th Match: v Nottinghamshire (Trent Bridge)   Aug 20, 21, 22.
Nottinghamshire 139 (J. B. King 7-76) and 206 (J. Hardstaff 77, G. Gunn 59, J. B. King 7-54) beat Philadelphians 140 (J. Iremonger 6-51) and 75 (A. W. Hallam 7-32) by 130 runs.

14th Match: v Durham (Sunderland)   Aug 24, 25.
Philadelphians 122 (D. H. Adams 56, Turnbull 4-56) and 110 (C. Adamson 6-36) beat Durham 85 (H. V. Hordern 7-37) and 41 (J. B. King 6-12, H. V. Hordern 4-28) by 106 runs.

15th Match: v Kent (Canterbury)   Aug 27, 28, 29.
Philadelphians 188 (F. E. Woolley 7-75) and 37 (W. J. Fairservice 6-12, F. E. Woolley 4-22) lost to Kent 102 (J. B. King 5-34) and 124-6 by 4 wkts.

16th Match: v XIV of Grantham and District (Grantham)   Aug 31, Sept 1.
Philadelphians 229 (J. A. Lester 101) Drew with XIV of Grantham and District 159-6 (J. B. King 5-68).

1908: 5th Philadelphians

Batting Averages

	M	I	NO	R	HS	Avge	100	c/s
A. M. Wood	9	16	0	389	132	24.31	1	8
C. C. Morris	10	18	0	347	74	19.27	0	7
F. S. White	10	18	0	346	62	19.22	0	3
W. P. Newhall	2	3	0	55	28	18.33	0	1
J. B. King	10	18	0	290	52	16.11	0	7
N. Z. Graves	10	18	1	261	76	15.35	0	1
F. A. Greene	8	15	4	160	49*	14.54	0	4
F. H. Bohlen	10	18	0	246	49	13.66	0	0
H. V. Hordern	10	18	4	180	32	12.85	0	18
J. A. Lester	10	18	0	213	40	11.83	0	4
W. H. Sayen	6	12	1	113	29	10.27	0	5
T. C. Jordan	4	8	4	36	13*	9.00	0	4/4
E. M. Cregar	3	6	1	34	10	6.80	0	2
C. H. Winter	6	11	5	24	12	4.00	0	5/7
D. H. Adams	2	4	0	8	6	2.00	0	2

Bowling Averages

	O	M	R	W	Avge	BB	5i
J. B. King	338.3	103	958	87	11.01	7-23	10
J. A. Lester	48.4	7	164	10	16.40	3-12	0
H. V. Hordern	274.1	42	930	45	20.66	7-43	4
F. A. Greene	104	13	309	13	23.76	3-61	0
W. H. Sayen	69.3	9	259	9	28.77	4-44	0
E. M. Cregar	37	3	195	0	—		

1909: 13th Australians

Australia rejected plans to stage a triangular tournament in England between Australia, South Africa and England during the 1909 season, and the season was left to the Australians alone.

The selection of the 1909 team was in the hands of the fairly new Australian Board of Control. Some leading players objected to the Board's financial stipulations and for a time it looked as if the tour would be cancelled. There were also arguments about the appointment of Laver as manager and of McAlister, who was a selector, as vice-captain. These twin problems were to erupt later, however.

The selected team was M. A. Noble (captain), W. Bardsley, S. E. Gregory, V. T. Trumper, C. G. Macartney, H. Carter, A. J. Y. Hopkins and A. Cotter of New South Wales; W. W. Armstrong, V. S. Ransford, P. A. McAlister, F. Laver and W. Carkeek of

Above *Warwick Armstrong came to England on four tours, the first in 1902 and the fourth in 1921, when he was captain and completed a run of eight successive wins over England. He is pictured in 1909. On his last tour he weighed over 20 stone and was called 'The Big Ship'.*

Below *The 1909 Australian party. Back: Whitty, Cotter, Hartigan, Ransford, Bardsley, Carter. Centre: McAlister, Trumper, Hopkins, Noble, Laver, Armstrong, O'Connor. Front: Gregory, Macartney, Carkeek.*

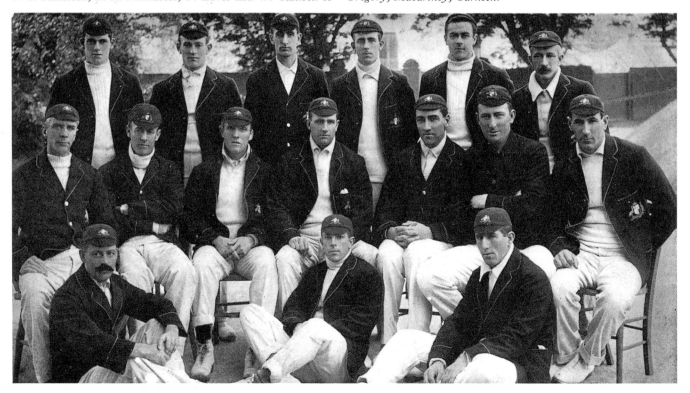

Victoria; R. J. Hartigan of Queensland and W. J. Whitty and J. D. A. O'Connor of South Australia. The only major player not on the list was C. Hill, who was not available. The team sailed aboard the s.s. *Orontes* and arrived at Naples on 23 April, from where Carter and Macartney journeyed direct and were the first to arrive in London–on 26 April. Nine of the players left the boat at Marseilles to travel overland via Paris.

Interest in the tour polarised around the five Tests and as in 1905, the county games mattered little to the tourists–in fact no fewer than 20 out of the 34 non-Test games ended as draws. To some extent the weather was to blame, but the determination of

the Australians to keep their best men fit for the Tests also played its part. In that Australia won two Tests against England's one and also had the best of the two drawn matches, the visit was a triumph for the visitors. The English press was critical of the Australians and ascribed their success to English blunders, rather than any outstanding ability by the tourists, which was rather unfair.

The batting was excellent with the two newcomers to England, Bardsley and Ransford, topping the list and mastering the soft wickets well. Armstrong proved the mainstay, with a rocklike defence. Trumper, although not repeating his feats of 1902,

1909: 13th Australians

1st Match: v Nottinghamshire (Trent Bridge)   May 6, 7, 8.
Nottinghamshire 239 (A. O. Jones 125, W. W. Armstrong 5-55) and 144 lost to Australians 389 (W. W. Armstrong 106*, V. T. Trumper 94, W. Bardsley 63, H. Carter 61, A. W. Hallam 6-144, T. G. Wass 4-107) by an innings and 6 runs.

2nd Match: v Northamptonshire (Northampton)   May 10, 11, 12.
Northamptonshire 203 (C. G. Macartney 4-40) and 235 (W. W. Armstrong 5-57) lost to Australians 319 (W. W. Armstrong 79, W. Bardsley 76, V. T. Trumper 56, S. G. Smith 5-107, G. J. Thompson 5-108) and 120-1 (W. Bardsley 63*) by 9 wkts.

3rd Match: v Essex (Leyton)   May 13, 14, 15.
Australians 609-6 dec (W. Bardsley 219, V. S. Ransford 174, V. T. Trumper 74, W. W. Armstrong 59*) drew with Essex 148 and 344-9 (F. L. Fane 115, C. P. McGahey 55, P. A. Perrin 53, A. Cotter 4-80).

4th Match: v Surrey (Oval)   May 17, 18, 19.
Surrey 191 (W. J. Whitty 5-36) and 178 (T. W. Hayward 96*, W. J. Whitty 4-28, W. W. Armstrong 4-77) beat Australians 157 (T. Rushby 6-38, W. S. Lees 4-68) and 207 (T. Rushby 4-50) by 5 runs.

5th Match: v M.C.C. (Lord's)   May 20, 21, 22.
Australians 210 (G. J. Thompson 5-26) and 175 (W. W. Armstrong 51, G. J. Thompson 5-61, A. E. Relf 4-37) lost to M.C.C. 221 (W. W. Armstrong 4-48) and 165-7 (P. F. Warner 54*, F. A. Tarrant 50) by 3 wkts.

6th Match: v Oxford University (Oxford)   May 24, 25, 26.
Australians 247 (M. A. Noble 107, S. E. Gregory 51, H. A. Gilbert 8-71) and 167-3 (V. S. Ransford 80) drew with 132 (C. G. Macartney 5-24).

7th Match: v England (Edgbaston)   May 27, 28, 29.
Australia 74 (C. Blythe 6-44, G. H. Hirst 4-28) and 151 (G. H. Hirst 5-58, C. Blythe 5-58) lost to England 121 (W. W. Armstrong 5-27) and 105-0 (J. B. Hobbs 62*) by 10 wkts.

8th Match: v Leicestershire (Leicester)   May 31, June 1, 2.
Leicestershire 272 (A. E. Knight 78, J. H. King 60, V. F. S. Crawford 74, F. Laver 6-80) and 85-5 drew with Australians 182 and 47-2.

9th Match: v Cambridge University (Cambridge)   June 3, 4, 5.
Australians 307 (V. T. Trumper 133, W. Bardsley 56, E. Olivier 5-81) drew with Cambridge University 154 (F. Laver 6-58) and 62-8 (F. Laver 4-25).

10th Match: v Hampshire (Southampton)   June 7, 8.
Hampshire 131 (F. Laver 6-53) and 83 (F. Laver 7-27) lost to Australians 83 (J. A. Newman 8-43) and 155-4 (W. W. Armstrong 72) by 6 wkts.

11th Match: v Somerset (Bath)   June 10, 11, 12.
Somerset 93 (W. J. Whitty 5-45) and 111 (L. C. Braund 51, C. G. Macartney 4-20, F. Laver 4-38) lost to Australians 139 (E. Robson 8-35) and 68-8 (W. T. Greswell 4-11, E. Robson 4-45) by 2 wkts.

12th Match: v England (Lord's)   June 14, 15, 16.
England 269 (J. H. King 60, A. Cotter 4-80) and 121 (W. W. Armstrong 6-35) lost to Australia 350 (V. S. Ransford 143, A. E. Relf 5-85) and 41-1 by 9 wkts.

13th Match: v Western Union (Glasgow)   June 17, 18, 19.
Western Union 244 (J. M. Tennent 80, J. D. A. O'Connor 6-110) and 144 (W. W. Armstrong 6-73) lost to Australians 576 (C. G. Macartney 124, R. J. Hartigan 115, W. Bardsley 108) by an innings and 188 runs.

14th Match: v Yorkshire (Bradford)   June 21, 22, 23.
Yorkshire 299 (D. Denton 106, H. Myers 53, F. Laver 5-75) drew with Australians 77-3.

15th Match: v Lancashire and Yorkshire (Old Trafford)   June 24, 25, 26.
Australians 217-6 dec (W. W. Armstrong 110*) drew with Lancashire and Yorkshire 15-2.

16th Match: v Scotland (Edinburgh)   June 28, 29.
Scotland 93 (A. J. Y. Hopkins 4-18) and 230 (R. G. Tate 52) drew with Australians 121 (W. Ringrose 5-48, A. Broadbent 4-61) and 147-7.

17th Match: v England (Headingley)   July 1, 2, 3.
Australia 188 (W. Rhodes 4-38) and 207 (S. F. Barnes 6-63) beat England 182 (J. Sharp 61, J. T. Tyldesley 55, C. G. Macartney 7-58) and 87 (A. Cotter 5-38, C. G. Macartney 4-27) by 126 runs.

18th Match: v Warwickshire (Edgbaston)   July 5, 6, 7.
Australians 456 (M. A. Noble 131, W. Bardsley 118, W. W. Armstrong 79, V. S. Ransford 66, E. F. Field 5-105) drew with Warwickshire 186 (W. Quaife 68, W. J. Whitty 5-51) and 185-8 (J. A. O'Connor 5-56).

19th Match: v Worcestershire (Worcester)   July 8, 9, 10.
Australians 389 (V. S. Ransford 138, G. H. T. Simpson-Hayward 6-132) beat Worcestershire 151 (G. H. T. Simpson-Hayward 51, W. W. Armstrong 5-49, A. Cotter 4-50) and 126 (A. J. Y. Hopkins 6-36, W. W. Armstrong 4-37) by an innings and 112 runs.

20th Match: v Gloucestershire (Bristol)   July 12, 13, 14.
Gloucestershire 230 (T. Langdon 61, J. H. Board 57, W. W. Armstrong 4-64) and 210 (T. Langdon 90, W. W. Armstrong 5-35) lost to Australians 445-8 dec (W. Bardsley 211, M. A. Noble 51*) by an innings and 5 runs.

21st Match: v Surrey (Oval)   July 15, 16, 17.
Australians 180 (M. A. Noble 65*, W. C. Smith 7-70) and 126-6 dec (V. S. Ransford 51, W. C. Smith 5-54) drew with Surrey 209 (T. W. Hayward 80, F. Laver 5-58) and 39-0.

22nd Match: v Yorkshire (Bramall Lane, Sheffield)   July 19, 20, 21.
Yorkshire 346 (W. Rhodes 108, C. H. Hardisty 72, A. Cotter 5-92, C. G. Macartney 4-32) and 172-7 dec (G. H. Hirst 50*, A. Cotter 5-44) drew with Australians 267 (W. Bardsley 90, W. W. Armstrong 70*, J. T. Newstead 5-93) and 53-0.

23rd Match: v Derbyshire (Derby)   July 22, 23, 24.
Derbyshire 116 (J. D. A. O'Connor 7-40) and 166 (W. J. Whitty 4-30) lost to Australians 264 (V. T. Trumper 113, A. J. Y. Hopkins 52, A. Morton 5-63, A. Warren 4-102) and 21-0 by 10 wkts.

24th Match: v England (Old Trafford)   July 26, 27, 28.
Australia 147 (S. F. Barnes 5-56, C. Blythe 5-63) and 279-9 dec (V. S. Ransford 54*, W. Rhodes 5-83) drew with England 119 (F. Laver 8-31) and 108-3 (R. H. Spooner 58).

25th Match: v Lancashire and Yorkshire (Hull)   July 29, 30, 31.
Lancashire and Yorkshire 261-4 (W. Rhodes 75, R. H. Spooner 66, D. Denton 55) drew with Australians did not bat.

26th Match: v South Wales (Cardiff)   Aug 2, 3, 4.
South Wales 228 (C. G. Macartney 5-39) and 107 (A. J. Y. Hopkins 4-11) lost to Australians 271 (R. J. Hartigan 88, P. A. McAlister 65) and 65-2 by 8 wkts.

27th Match: v Lancashire (Liverpool)   Aug 5, 6, 7.
Australians 87 (H. Dean 5-15) and 214 (W. W. Armstrong 72, V. T. Trumper 54, H. Dean 5-64) beat Lancashire 104 (W. W. Armstrong 4-17) and 150 (A. J. Y. Hopkins 6-15) by 47 runs.

28th Match: v England (Oval)   Aug 9, 10, 11.
Australia 325 (W. Bardsley 136, V. T. Trumper 73, C. G. Macartney 50, D. W. Carr 5-146) and 339-5 dec (W. Bardsley 130, S. E. Gregory 74, M. A. Noble 55) drew with England 352 (J. Sharp 105, W. Rhodes 66, C. B. Fry 62, A. Cotter 6-95) and 104-3 (W. Rhodes 54).

29th Match: v An England Eleven (Blackpool)   Aug 12, 13, 14.
An England Eleven 567 (A. E. Knight 163, J. W. H. T. Douglas 102, J. N. Crawford 60, J. H. King 56, J. D. A. O'Connor 6-210) drew with Australians 326 (R. J. Harrigan 88, P. A. McAlister 50, T. Jayes 4-81, C. P. Buckenham 4-103) and 390-7 (V. T. Trumper 150, P. A. McAlister 85).

30th Match: v Gloucestershire (Cheltenham)   Aug 16, 17, 18.
Australians 215 (A. J. Y. Hopkins 56*, E. G. Dennett 4-95, J. H. Huggins 4-73) and 247-8 (V. S. Ransford 121, W. Bardsley 66, E. G. Dennett 6-40) drew with Gloucestershire 411-8 dec (C. L. Townsend 129, F. B. Roberts 80, C. S. Barnett 60, J. D. A. O'Connor 4-88).

31st Match: v Kent (Canterbury)   Aug 19, 20, 21.
Kent 319 (S. H. Day 74, F. E. Woolley 68, W. J. Whitty 5-55) drew with Australians 522 (V. S. Ransford 189, W. W. Armstrong 107).

32nd Match: v Middlesex (Lord's)   Aug 23, 24, 25.
Middlesex 307-5 (P. F. Warner 127*) drew with Australians did not bat.

33rd Match: v Sussex (Hove)   Aug 26, 27, 28.
Sussex 96 (W. W. Armstrong 4-26) and 158 (W. W. Armstrong 5-68) lost to Australians 136 (A. E. Relf 6-45, J. H. Vincett 4-81) and 122-9 (J. H. Vincett 5-57) by 1 wkt.

34th Match: v M.C.C. (Lord's)   Aug 30, 31, Sept 1.
M.C.C. 189 (A. Cotter 5-80, W. W. Armstrong 4-41) and 187-1 (H. K. Foster 84, F. A. Tarrant 65*) drew with Australians 434 (V. S. Ransford 190, V. T. Trumper 80, M. A. Noble 63, C. P. Buckenham 6-98).

35th Match: v Essex (Leyton)   Sept 2, 3, 4.
Essex 263 (F. H. Gillingham 73, J. D. A. O'Connor 7-71) and 57-1 drew with Australians 278 (V. T. Trumper 71, W. Bardsley 66).

36th Match: v J. Bamford's XI (Uttoxeter)   Sept 6, 7, 8.
J. Bamford's XI 140 (J. D. A. O'Connor 6-42) drew with Australians 110-7.

37th Match: v Lord Londesborough's XI (Scarborough)   Sept 9, 10, 11.
Lord Londesborough's XI 129 (C. G. Macartney 5-53) and 276 (J. T. Tyldesley 89, K. L. Hutchings 78, W. W. Armstrong 5-48) beat Australians 113 (D. W. Carr 4-27, W. Rhodes 4-29) and 159 (D. W. Carr 4-78) by 133 runs.

38th Match: v South of England (Hastings)   Sept 13, 14, 15.
South of England 170 (W. J. Whitty 5-55, J. D. A. O'Connor 4-63) and 132 (W. W. Armstrong 6-44) drew with Australians 199 (P. A. McAlister 68, J. W. H. T. Douglas 7-75).

39th Match: v S. H. Cochrane's XI (Bray)   Sept 17, 18, 19.
Australians 271 (W. Bardsley 143, W. Quaife 4-39, S. F. Barnes 4-87) and 129 (F. A. Tarrant 5-40) drew with S. H. Cochran's XI 296 (J. B. Hobbs 56, F. A. Tarrant 52) and 99-6 (W. W. Armstrong 4-33).*

40th Match: v XIII of Northern Counties (Inverness)   Sept 27.
XIII of Northern Counties 141 lost to Australians 154 by 3 wkts.

41st Match: v West of Scotland (Titwood, Glasgow)   Oct 5.
Match abandoned: no play due to rain.

Warren Bardsley made the first of four successful tours to England in 1909 and at the Oval he became the first batsman to score a century in each innings of a Test match.

1909: 13th Australians

Batting Averages

	M	*I*	*NO*	*R*	*HS*	*Avge*	*100*	*c/s*
W. Bardsley	33	49	4	2072	219	46.04	6	11
W. W. Armstrong	29	41	8	1451	110*	43.96	3	33
V. S. Ransford	32	44	4	1736	190	43.40	6	16
V. T. Trumper	34	45	2	1435	150	33.37	3	19
P. A. McAlister	23	32	5	751	85	27.81	0	14
M. A. Noble	31	45	4	1060	131	25.85	2	16
S. E. Gregory	28	39	6	618	74	18.73	0	8
C. G. Macartney	28	37	7	503	51	16.76	0	20
A. J. Y. Hopkins	23	28	3	406	56*	16.24	0	4
H. Carter	27	33	7	408	61	15.69	0	27/18
R. J. Hartigan	19	31	1	400	88	13.33	0	18
J. D. A. O'Connor	20	27	7	217	36*	10.85	0	9
A. Cotter	26	32	0	335	37	10.45	0	12
F. Laver	17	18	4	137	17	9.78	0	7
W. Carkeek	12	15	4	101	37	9.18	0	8/2
W. J. Whitty	25	25	8	132	21	7.76	0	8

Bowling Averages

	O	*M*	*R*	*W*	*Avge*	*BB*	*5i*
F. Laver	479.5	158	999	68	14.69	8-31	7
W. W. Armstrong	858	274	1854	133	16.40	6-44	9
C. G. Macartney	480.5	139	1143	64	17.85	7-58	3
J. D. A. O'Connor	555.5	154	1433	77	18.61	7-40	6
W. J. Whitty	644	192	1551	75	20.68	5-36	4
A. J. Y. Hopkins	371.1	62	1108	51	21.74	6-15	2
V. S. Ransford	4	0	27	1	27.00	1-15	0
A. Cotter	573.2	68	1862	64	29.09	6-95	5
M. A. Noble	343.1	85	864	25	34.56	3-42	0
S. E. Gregory	15	0	84	1	84.00	1-8	0
V. T. Trumper	29	2	151	1	151.00	1-24	0

Also bowled: P. A. McAlister 0.2-0-0-1; R. J. Hartigan 1-0-4-0; W. Bardsley 2-0-7-0.

played excellently, but Noble struggled for runs. There was no one bowling star: Macartney, Cotter, Armstrong and Laver all had good days in the Tests; O'Connor's and Whitty's efforts were mainly confined to county matches and Noble seldom bowled for long. Carter kept wicket almost up to the standard of Blackham and Noble managed his fielders well and was a fine captain.

The wet weather kept down match attendances, but the team still made a handsome profit. The party split in two for the journey home–some sailing on the s.s. *Orsova* and others on the s.s. *Mongolia* which went via Singapore.

1911: 1st Indians

After several abortive attempts, including one in 1910, the first team to include the three major sections of non-European cricket in India came to England in 1911. The principal driving force

1911: 1st Indians

1st Match: v Oxford University (Oxford) June 1, 2.
Indians 193 (A. J. Evans 4-17) and 97 (A. J. Evans 5-32) lost to Oxford University 242 (I. P. F. Campbell 106, B. P. Baloo 5-87) and 49-2 by 8 wkts.

2nd Match: v South Wales (Cardiff) June 5, 6.
Indians 51 (W. S. Hacker 6-17, H. Creber 4-27) and 233 (H. F. Mulla 98, R. P. Meherhomji 75, W. S. Hacker 6-64, H. Creber 4-102) lost to South Wales 205 (G. H. Symonds 56, J. S. Warden 5-48) and 83-3 by 7 wkts.

3rd Match: v M.C.C. (Lord's) June 8, 9.
Indians 204 (K. M. Mistri 78, J. T. Hearne 5-47) and 96 (F. A. Tarrant 4-29, J. T. Hearne 4-32) lost to M.C.C. 468 (E. H. D. Sewell 129, G. J. V. Weigall 103, A. E. Lawton 75, Salamuddin 5-128, B. P. Baloo 4-96) by an innings and 168 runs.

4th Match: v Cambridge University (Cambridge) June 12, 13, 14.
Cambridge University 434 (H. G. H. Mulholland 153, D. C. Collins 111, H. E. W. Prest 50, B. P. Baloo 8-103) beat Indians 183 (K. M. Mistri 53, J. H. Bruce Lockhart 6-55) and 180 (M. Falcon 5-50, J. H. Bruce Lockhart 4-47) by an innings and 71 runs.

5th Match: v Warwickshire (Edgbaston) June 15, 16.
Indians 76 (F. R. Foster 5-31, E. F. Field 5-36) and 185 (B. P. Shivram 91, A. B. Crawford 6-36) lost to Warwickshire 199 (B. P. Baloo 4-74) and 65-0 by 10 wkts.

6th Match: v Lancashire (Old Trafford) June 19, 20.
Indians 85 (L. Cook 5-22, W. Huddleston 5-30) and 94 (H. Dean 4-41) lost to Lancashire 171 (B. P. Baloo 7-83) and 9-1 by 9 wkts.

7th Match: v Staffordshire (Stoke on Trent) June 26, 27.
Indians 74 (S. F. Barnes 5-14, Nichols 4-21) and 57 (S. F. Barnes 9-15) lost to Staffordshire 77 (B. P. Baloo 6-35, J. S. Warden 4-19) and 55-5 by 5 wkts.

8th Match: v Surrey (Oval) June 29, 30, July 1.
Indians 264 (H. D. Kanga 73, B. Jayaram 57, M. C. Bird 5-48) and 120 (M. C. Bird 5-50, E. G. Hayes 4-42) lost to Surrey 280 (E. G. Hayes 95, B. P. Baloo 4-100) and 105-4 by 6 wkts.

9th Match: v Kent (Catford) July 3, 4.
Kent 318 (E. W. Dillon 130, B. P. Baloo 5-109) and 4-1 beat Indians 145 (W. J. Fairservice 5-33, A. Fielder 4-69) and 176 (R. P. Meherhomji 84, H. J. B. Preston 4-65) by 9 wkts.

10th Match: v Northamptonshire (Northampton) July 6, 7.
Indians 133 (H. D. Kanga 65, S. G. Smith 4-15) and 149 (G. J. Thompson 4-39) lost to Northamptonshire 104 (B. P. Baloo 6-58) and 182-4 (G. A. T. Vials 54) by 6 wkts.

11th Match: v Yorkshire (Hull) July 10, 11.
Yorkshire 385 (D. Denton 118, S. Haigh 111, B. P. Baloo 4-127) beat Indians 233 (B. Jayaram 53, A. Drake 5-65, H. H. Harington 4-76) and 109 (S. Haigh 4-19) by an innings and 43 runs.

12th Match: v Leicestershire (Leicester) July 13, 14, 15.
Indians 481 (H. D. Kanga 163, R. P. Meherhomji 86, B. P. Shivram 85) and 53-3 beat Leicestershire 283 (A. E. Knight 62, Salamuddin 5-79, B. P. Baloo 5-92) and 248 (A. T. Sharp 54*, B. P. Baloo 6-93) by 7 wkts.

13th Match: v Somerset (Taunton) July 17, 18, 19.
Somerset 157 (Salamuddin 6-64, B. P. Baloo 4-48) and 303 (L. C. Braund 125) lost to Indians 196 (M. P. Bajana 108, E. Robson 6-82) and 265-9 (B. P. Shivran 113*, B. P. Baloo 55, E. Robson 5-83) by 1 wkt.

14th Match: v Lincolnshire (Sleaford) July 21, 22.
Indians 463-6 dec (B. P. Shivram 175, H. D. Kanga 81, J. S. Warden 61, N. W. Wells-Cole 4-178) beat Lincolnshire 145 (Salamuddin 6-40) and 268 (B. P. Nevile 66, G. L. Prior 59, B. P. Baloo 5-61) by an innings and 50 runs.

15th Match: v Durham (Sunderland) July 24, 25, 26.
Durham 244 and 87 (K. Salamuddin 5-45, J. S. Warden 5-42) lost to Indians 239 (K. Salamuddin 85. H. D. Kanga 78, H. Morris 6-87) and 95-2 by 8 wkts.*

16th Match: v Northumberland (Newcastle) July 27, 28, 29.
Indians 352 (R. P. Meherhomji 117, J. S. Warden 116, C. Skinner 7-126) and 102 (C. Skinner 6-46) lost to Northumberland 296 (J. Gilman 86, S. Anderson 80) and 162-9 (J. S. Warden 8-88) by 1 wkt.

17th Match: v North of Scotland (Inverness) July 31, Aug 1.
North of Scotland 158 (J. S. Warden 6-31) and 104 (M. D. Bulsara 4-46, Shafquat Hussein 5-51) lost to Indians 401-4 dec (R. P. Meherhomji 150, K. Salamuddin 129) by an innings and 139 runs.*

18th Match: v Scottish Cricket Union (Galashiels) Aug 3, 4, 5.
Indians 195 (H. F. Mulla 51, J. A. Ferguson 5-36) and 166 (D. Chapel 5-34) drew with Scottish Cricket Union 250 (T. G. Herriot 80, J. S. Warden 7-94) and 68-3.

19th Match: v Scottish Counties (Perth) Aug 7, 8, 9.
Indians 165 (R. P. Meherhomji 50, R. W. Sievewright 6-43, R. Sutton 4-80) and 218 (B. Jayaram 81, J. S. Warden 60, R. W. Sievewright 4-41, W. Webster 4-48) lost to Scottish Counties 210 (J. S. Warden 5-81) and 174-8 by 2 wkts.

20th Match: v Ulster (Belfast) Aug 11, 12.
Indians 324 (R. P. Meherhomji 96, K. Salamuddin 64, B. Jayaram 57, Littlewood 4-82) beat Ulster 26 (B. P. Baloo 5-9, K. Salamuddin 4-11) and 65 by an innings and 233 runs.

21st Match: v Woodbrook Club & Ground (Bray) Aug 14, 15, 16.
Woodbrook Club & Ground 278 (W. Pollock 72, K. Salamuddin 4-75) and 231 (G. Morrow 110, B. P. Baloo 4-50, K. Salamudin 4-72) beat Indians 255 (B. Jayaram 78, B. P. Shivram 56, J. S. Warden 53, G. A. Faulkner 5-87) and 219 (J. S. Warden 89) by 35 runs.

22nd Match: v Sussex (Hove) Aug 21, 22, 23.
Sussex 158 (M. D. Bulsara 5-30) and 149 (J. S. Warden 5-74, B. P. Baloo 4-26) beat Indians 138 (H. F. Mulla 54) and 159 (J. Vine 5-54) by 10 runs.

23rd Match: v Gloucestershire (Bristol) Aug 24, 25, 26.
Gloucestershire 252 (A. G. Dipper 56, J. S. Warden 8-91) and 379-6 dec (F. B. Roberts 154*, G. L. Jessop 79, F. M. Luce 57) drew with Indians 364 (R. P. Meherhomji 102, B. P. Shivram 88, K. Salamuddin 50, E. G. Dennett 4-106) and 74-8 (E. G. Dennett 4-29).

behind the scheme was J. M. Framjee-Patel and the team was announced by the selection committee under the presidency of Capt J. G. Greig on 2 March. The players were H. H. the Maharajah of Patiala (captain), K. Salam-ud-Din, Shafkat Hussain, Syed Hussein, B. Jayaram, P. Baloo, Dr H. D. Kanga, R. P. Meherhomji, H. F. Mulla, M. D. Pai, J. S. Warden, M. Noor Illahi, M. Bulsara, K. Sechachari, H. Manek Chand and K. M. Mistri. K. S. Ranjitsinhji was unable to make the trip. H. H. the Gaekwad of Baroda, who was at Oxford, assisted the team in some matches, as did M. P. Bajana. The duties of manager were undertaken by J. M. Divecha.

The team travelled overland from Marseilles and arrived in London on 23 May. Noor Illahi and Manek Chand were forced to drop out at the last minute and B. Shivram was included as a replacement.

A fairly ambitious programme was arranged for the team and their record was not very impressive, with only two first-class wins. The reason was to some extent misfortune, for three of the party, K. M. Mistri, B. Jayaram and M. Pai, missed many matches, the last two because of injury.

Baloo, a slow left-arm bowler, was very effective and in all matches reached over 100 wickets. J. S. Warden also bowled well at times and was the team's leading all-rounder. The fielding was haphazard, and the succession of defeats during the early days of the tour meant that there was no public interest in the matches.

The team travelled by rail to Marseilles and there boarded the s.s. *Macedonia* on 1 September bound for Bombay.

1911: 1st Indians

Batting Averages

	M	I	NO	R	HS	Avge	100	c/s
K. M. Mistri	3	6	0	188	78	31.33	0	0
P. Shivram	12	24	2	631	113*	28.68	1	4
H. D. Kanga	12	24	2	617	163	28.04	1	8
R. P. Meherhomji	14	28	0	684	102	24.42	1	3
M. P. Bajana	4	8	0	173	108	21.62	1	3
Gaekwad of Baroda	3	6	0	109	25	18.16	0	1
Maharajah of Patiala	3	6	0	107	47	17.83	0	0
B. Jaya Ram	8	16	0	283	57	17.68	0	5
J. S. Warden	14	28	0	429	47	15.32	0	16
K. Salamuddin	13	25	4	303	50	14.42	0	16
P. Baloo	14	27	0	339	55	12.55	0	5
H. F. Mulla	12	23	1	255	54	11.59	0	4
M. D. Bulsara	12	22	6	117	24*	7.31	0	6
M. Pai	4	7	0	51	24	7.28	0	4
Shafqat Hussain	8	16	3	80	21	6.15	0	1
K. Seshachari	10	18	8	47	9	4.70	0	10/6
Syed Hussein	8	16	4	52	14	4.33	0	2/2

Bowling Averages

	O	M	R	W	Avge	BB	5i
P. Baloo	504.1	77	1509	75	20.12	8-103	7
J. S. Warden	362.3	65	1126	44	25.59	8-91	3
M. D. Bulsara	218.5	45	651	23	28.30	5-30	1
K. Salamudin	326.2	48	1050	32	32.81	6-64	3
H. D. Kanga	50.5	2	224	6	37.33	2-3	0
Shafqat Hussain	62	5	282	4	70.50	2-73	0

Also bowled: K. M. Mistri 9-0-31-0; B. Jaya Ram 3-0-23-0; P. Shivram 3-0-17-0.

1912: 14th Australians

The trouble between the Australian Board of Control and the major players, which had been brewing for several years, resulted in open hostility in the winter of 1911-12 and the 'recalcitrant six', Hill, Trumper, Armstrong, Cotter, Carter and Ransford, all missed the 1912 tour. Thus the Australian Board was represented by a weak side for this inaugural Triangular Tournament summer, the brainchild of the South African, Sir Abe Bailey. The team which sailed from Australia aboard the s.s. *Otway* was S. E. Gregory (captain), R. B. Minnett, S. H. Emery, C. Kelleway, C. G. Macartney, G. R. Hazlitt, W. Bardsley, all of New South Wales; D. B. M. Smith, W. Carkeek and T. J. Matthews of Victoria; W. J. Whitty, E. R. Mayne, and H. W. Webster of South Australia; J. W. McLaren and C. B. Jennings of Queensland, with G. S. Crouch as manager. They landed at Tilbury on 29 April.

The team were beaten by Notts in their first match, but then

The Australian tourists of 1912. Back: Crouch (manager), Minnett, Hume (a visitor to the party), Kelleway, Mayne, Emery, Smith, Whitty, Webster, Hazlitt. Front: Bardsley, McLaren, Matthews, Gregory (captain), Jennings, Macartney, Carkeek.

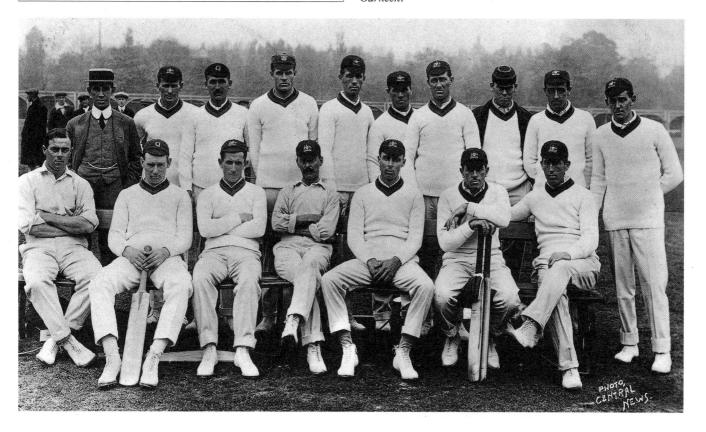

won six successive matches. In June wet weather soon exposed flaws in the side. Only three of the batsmen–Bardsley, Kelleway and Macartney–could cope with the damp conditions. What was more vital was that none of the Australian bowlers was able to exploit the same conditions. Of the 31 games after the end of May the tourists won just three.

Of the bowlers, Emery flourished only in May; Hazlitt's action was suspect, but as the season wore on he bowled with a straighter arm and in all matches reached 100 wickets, as did Whitty. Matthews achieved his famous double hat-trick, though he hardly lived up to his Australian reputation. Macartney actually topped the bowling table and was the only man capable of using the slow wickets, but because of his value as a batsman was not bowled a great deal. Bardsley and Macartney stood out as the batsmen of the team. Kelleway was an excellent man to prop up an innings and saved his best performances for the Tests. Minnett proved disappointing, as did Gregory. The fielding was generally very good, with Carkeek competent as wicketkeeper.

Off the field some of the side's behaviour was not very sensible and one critic went so far as to say that the team was socially ostracised as a result.

Ten of the team left England in mid-September to tour the United States before returning home while Bardsley, Macartney, Minnett, Hazlitt and Jennings went back on the usual route via the Suez Canal.

1912: 14th Australians

1st Match: v Nottinghamshire (Trent Bridge)   May 6, 7, 8.
Australians 248 (C. G. Macartney 84) and 166 (C. B. Jennings 51, W. Riley 6-89) lost to Nottinghamshire 202 (A. B. Crawford 51, W. J. Whitty 4-43) and 213-4 (J. R. Gunn 67*, A. O. Jones 50) by 6 wkts.

2nd Match: v Northamptonshire (Northampton)   May 9, 10.
Australians 370 (S. E. Gregory 150, C. G. Macartney 127, S. G. Smith 4-66) beat Northamptonshire 169 (G. J. Thompson 60*, S. H. Emery 5-52) and 137 (S. H. Emery 7-58) by an innings and 64 runs.

3rd Match: v Essex (Leyton)   May 13, 14, 15.
Essex 192 (J. W. H. T. Douglas 129, S. H. Emery 5-72) and 240 (F. L. Fane 61, J. W. H. T. Douglas 53) lost to Australians 564-3 dec (C. G. Macartney 208, W. Bardsley 184*, S. E. Gregory 71, E. R. Mayne 58) by an innings and 132 runs.

b4th Match: v Surrey (Oval)   May 16, 17, 18.
Surrey 139 (M. C. Bird 76, S. H. Emery 6-54, W. J. Whitty 4-43) and 205 (J. B. Hobbs 81, M. C. Bird 68, S. H. Emery 5-81) lost to Australians 292 (C. G. Macartney 123, T. J. Matthews 58, T. Rushby 5-76) and 54-3 by 7 wkts.

5th Match: v M.C.C. (Lord's)   May 20, 21, 22.
M.C.C. 169 (C. Kelleway 5-40) and 323 (C. P. Mead 61, C. Kelleway 4-64) lost to Australians 326 (W. Bardsley 137, C. G. Macartney 74, J. W. H. T. Douglas 5-95) and 169-5 (R. B. Minnett 64) by 5 wkts.

6th Match: v Oxford University (Oxford)   May 23, 24, 25.
Australians 236 (W. Bardsley 88) and 42-0 beat Oxford University 71 (W. J. Whitty 4-11, G. R. Hazlitt 4-14) and 206 (C. G. Macartney 5-44, W. J. Whitty 4-78) by 10 wkts.

7th Match: v South Africa (Old Trafford)   May 27, 28.
Australia 448 (W. Bardsley 121, C. Kelleway 114, S. J. Pegler 6-105) beat South Africa 265 (G. A. Faulkner 122*, W. J. Whitty 5-55) and 95 (C. Kelleway 5-33) by an innings and 88 runs.

8th Match: v Warwickshire (Edgbaston)   May 30, 31, June 1.
Warwickshire 275 (S. Kinneir 70, C. Charlesworth 56, S. H. Emery 4-97) and 102 (C. G. Macartney 4-22) drew with Australians 262 (C. G. Macartney 90, C. B. Jennings 68, F. R. Foster 7-94) and 43-3.

9th Match: v Middlesex (Lord's)   June 3, 4, 5.
Middlesex 67-2 drew with Australians–did not bat.

10th Match: v Cambridge University (Cambridge)   June 6, 7, 8.
Australians 255 (C. B. Jennings 62, W. Bardsley 58, H. G. H. Mulholland 5-38) drew with Cambridge University 81 (S. H. Emery 4-32).

11th Match: v Yorkshire (Bradford)   June 10, 11, 12.
Yorkshire 155 (C. G. Macartney 6-54) and 66-7 dec (G. R. Hazlitt 5-17) drew with Australians 107 (S. Haigh 5-22) and 35-6 (S. Haigh 6-14).

12th Match: v Lancashire (Old Trafford)   June 13, 14, 15.
Lancashire 146 (T. J. Matthews 5-48) and 188 (J. W. H. Makepeace 52) beat Australians 177 (C. G. Macartney 80, J. S. Heap 4-41, H. Dean 4-63) and 133.

13th Match: v Surrey (Oval)   June 17, 18, 19.
Surrey 190 (G. R. Hazlitt 5-59, T. J. Matthews 4-50) and 247 (J. B. Hobbs 76) beat Australians 109 (W. C. Smith 5-66) and 307 (D. B. M. Smith 100, C. B. Jennings 82, C. G. Macartney 51, J. W. Hitch 4-107) by 21 runs.

14th Match: v Somerset (Taunton)   June 20, 21.
Somerset 59 (R. B. Minnett 6-29, T. J. Matthews 4-25) and 204 (J. W. McLaren 4-45, S. H. Emery 4-53) lost to Australians 184 (E. Robson 7-94) and 80-0 by 10 wkts.

15th Match: v England (Lord's)   June 24, 25, 26.
England 310-7 dec (J. B. Hobbs 107, W. Rhodes 59) drew wth Australia 282-7 (C. G. Macartney 99, C. Kelleway 61).

16th Match: v Essex (Leyton)   June 27, 28, 29.
Essex 421 (J. W. H. T. Douglas 129, P. A. Perrin 104, F. L. Fane 98, G. R. Hazlitt 6-105) drew with Australians 178 (C. G. Macartney 62, H. M. Hills 5-63, W. Mead 4-63) and 320-5 (S. E. Gregory 103*, C. B. Jennings 62).

17th Match: v Yorkshire (Bramall Lane, Sheffield)   July 1, 2, 3.
Australians 299 (C. G. Macartney 87) and 3-0 drew with Yorkshire 280 (G. H. Hirst 62, D. Denton 57, B. B. Wilson 54, R. B. Minnett 4-28).

18th Match: v Lancashire (Liverpool)   July 4, 5.
Australians 183 (S. E. Gregory 58, H. Dean 6-78, W. Huddleston 4-73) and 94 (H. Dean 5-24) lost to Lancashire 163 (J. Sharp 60, W. J. Whitty 5-63) and 115-2 (R. H. Spooner 66*) by 8 wkts.

19th Match: v Scotland (Edinburgh)   July 8, 9, 10.
Australians 295 (W. Bardsley 149, C. Kelleway 64, R. W. Sievwright 7-71) and 225-4 dec (R. B. Minnett 65*) beat Scotland 172 (M. R. Dickson 98, R. B. Minnett 6-35) and 52 (W. J. Whitty 6-22) by 296 runs.

20th Match: v Scotland (Perth)   July 11, 12, 13.
Scotland 289 (W. E. Benskin 79* and 126-7 dec (G. W. Jupp 56, T. J. Matthews 7-46) drew with Australians 152 (R. W. Sievwright 4-51) and 200-3 (E. R. Mayne 85, W. Bardsley 70*).

21st Match: v South Africa (Lord's)   July 15, 16, 17.
South Africa 263 (H. W. Taylor 93, W. J. Whitty 4-68) and 173 (C. B. Llewellyn 59, T. J. Matthews 4-29) lost to Australia 390 (W. Bardsley 164, C. Kelleway 102, S. J. Pegler 4-79) and 48-0 by 10 wkts.

22nd Match: v Leicestershire (Leicester)   July 18, 19, 20.
Leicestershire 217 (C. J. B. Wood 55, S. H. Emery 4-75) and 68-3 drew with Australians 327 (C. Kelleway 87, W. Bardsley 58, J. H. King 4-130).

23rd Match: v Hampshire (Southampton)   July 22, 23, 24.
Hampshire 371 (C. P. Mead 160*, W. V. Jephson 55) and 86-2 beat Australians 197 (W. Bardsley 60, R. B. Minnett 58, A. S. Kennedy 6-90) and 256 (S. E. Gregory 85, A. S. Kennedy 5-91) by 8 wkts.

24th Match: v Sussex (Hove)   July 25, 26, 27.
Australians 398 (C. G. Macartney 142, A. E. Relf 4-159) and 338-7 dec (C. G. Macartney 121, T. J. Matthews 93, C. Kelleway 63) drew with Sussex 389 (H. H. Jam Sahib of Nawanagar 125, A. E. Relf 72, P. G. H. Fender 69) and 101-2 (R. Relf 58).

25th Match: v England (Old Trafford)   July 29, 30, 31.
England 203 (W. Rhodes 92, W. J. Whitty 4-43, G. R. Hazlitt 4-77) drew with Australia 14-0.

26th Match: v Derbyshire (Derby)   Aug 1, 2, 3.
Australians 123 (T. Forester 5-76, S. W. A. Cadman 4-43) and 137 (W. Bardsley 59*, A. Morton 5-52) drew with Derbyshire 74 (T. J. Matthews 6-23) and 82-5.

27th Match: v South Africa (Trent Bridge)   Aug 5, 6, 7.
South Africa 329 (A. W. Nourse 64, G. C. White 59*) drew with Australia 219 (W. Bardsley 56, S. J. Pegler 4-80).

28th Match: v Durham (Sunderland)   Aug 9, 10.
Durham 142 (C. Adamson 65, C. G. Macartney 5-37) drew with Australians 349 (E. B. Mayne 111, W. Bardsley 76, A. Morris 6-96).

29th Match: v Worcestershire (Dudley)   Aug 12, 13, 14.
Worcestershire 143 (G. N. Foster 62*, W. J. Whitty 6-57) drew with Australians 407 (W. Bardsley 176*, C. Kelleway 85).

30th Match: v Gloucestershire (Cheltenham)   Aug 15, 16, 17.
Australians 256 (W. Bardsley 115, E. G. Dennett 5-103) and 67-7 (E. G. Dennett 5-47*) drew with Gloucestershire 150 (G. R. Hazlitt 5-92).

31st Match: v South Wales (Cardiff)   Aug 23, 24.
Match Abandoned. No play due to rain.

32nd Match: v England (Oval)   Aug 19, 20, 21.
England 245 (J. B. Hobbs 66, F. E. Woolley 62, W. J. Whitty 4-69) and 175 (C. B. Fry 79, G. R. Hazlitt 7-25) beat Australia 111 (S. F. Barnes 5-30, F. E. Woolley 5-29) and 65 (F. E. Woolley 5-20, H. Dean 4-19) by 244 runs.

33rd Match: v An England Eleven (Norwich)   Aug 26, 27, 28.
Australians 136 (S. G. Smith 4-37, A. Morris 4-50) and 79-6 drew with An England Eleven 79 (W. J. Whitty 7-40) and 68-4 (W. J. Whitty 4-29).

34th Match: v Kent (Canterbury)   Aug 29, 30, 31.
Kent 170-6 dec (F. E. Woolley 86, G. R. Hazlitt 4-42) drew with Australians 137 (D. W. Carr 7-46).

35th Match: v Surrey and Middlesex (Oval)   Sept 2, 3, 4.
Australians 227 (W. Bardsley 111) and 182 (W. Bardsley 76, F. A. Tarrant 4-34) lost to Surrey and Middlesex 396 (M. C. Bird 112, F. A. Tarrant 61, J. B. Hobbs 57) and 15-0 by 10 wkts.

36th Match: v Lord Londesborough's XI (Scarborough)   Sept 5, 6, 7.
Lord Londesborough's XI 294 (A. E. Relf 84*, S. Haigh 56, W. Rhodes 51) and 131-5 drew with Australians 203 and 138-0 (E. R. Mayne 69*, C. Kelleway 52*).

37th Match: v South of England (Hastings)   Sept 9, 10, 11.
South of England 420 (J. Vine 107, E. L. Kidd 63, E. I. M. Barrett 51, T. J. Matthews 7-133) and 147-6 dec (E. I. M. Barrett 50*, J. W. MacLaren 4-60) drew with Australians 362 (C. G. Macartney 176, H. L. Simms 5-112) and 138-5 (C. B. Jennings 56).

38th Match: v C. B. Fry's XI (Bray)   Sept 12, 13, 14.
Australians 72 (S. F. Barnes 6-27, A. E. Relf 4-14) and 304 (C. G. Macartney 71, W. Bardsley 56, J. W. Hitch 5-85) lost to C. B. Fry's XI 280 (J. W. Hearne 95*) and 97-2 by 8 wkts.

1912: 14th Australians

Batting Averages

	M	I	NO	R	HS	Avge	100	c/s
W. Bardsley	36	52	6	2365	184*	51.41	8	22
C. G. Macartney	33	49	1	2187	208	45.56	6	19
C. Kelleway	34	48	7	1281	114	31.24	2	26
S. E. Gregory	34	47	2	1055	150	23.44	2	5
C. B. Jennings	32	50	4	1037	82	22.54	0	15
R. B. Minnett	28	41	5	722	65*	20.06	0	6
E. R. Mayne	25	43	3	766	85	19.15	0	10
T. J. Matthews	28	36	4	584	93	18.25	0	15
H. W. Webster	11	13	5	131	26	16.37	0	15/2
D. B. M. Smith	16	24	2	292	100	13.27	0	6
S. H. Emery	24	28	8	251	37*	12.55	0	14
W. J. Whitty	30	36	9	282	33	10.44	0	5
W. Carkeek	25	29	12	156	27	9.17	0	32/9
J. W. McLaren	11	16	1	132	40	8.80	0	3
G. R. Hazlitt	29	37	8	219	35*	7.55	0	13

Bowling Averages

	O	M	R	W	Avge	BB	5i
C. G. Macartney	340	110	666	38	17.52	6-54	2
W. J. Whitty	866.3	281	1971	109	18.08	7-40	5
G. R. Hazlitt	788.3	215	1890	98	19.28	7-25	5
T. J. Matthews	627.3	165	1647	85	19.37	7-46	4
J. W. McLaren	190.3	33	603	27	22.33	4-45	0
R. B. Minnett	304.2	80	966	40	24.15	6-29	2
S. H. Emery	458.1	77	1565	66	23.71	7-58	5
C. E. Kelleway	441.5	123	1130	47	24.04	5-73	2

Also bowled: E. R. Mayne 10-0-35-0; D. B. M. Smith 4-0-22-1.

1912: 5th South Africans

Batting Averages

	M	I	NO	R	HS	Avge	100	c/s
A. W. Nourse	35	55	5	1762	213*	35.24	4	24
H. W. Taylor	35	57	5	1340	96	25.76	0	5
G. P. D. Hartigan	12	18	3	372	103	24.80	1	6
G. A. Faulkner	35	51	6	1075	145*	23.88	2	32
S. J. Snooke	24	38	2	800	86	22.22	0	9
G. C. White	27	41	7	717	59*	21.08	0	7
L. J. Tancred	31	50	2	974	131	20.29	2	11
C. B. Llewellyn	6	10	0	199	75	19.90	0	1
L. A. Stricker	31	46	2	875	99	19.88	0	20/2
R. Beaumont	22	31	3	510	75	18.21	0	5
R. O. Schwarz	8	14	0	249	70	17.78	0	6
F. Mitchell	25	33	4	504	91*	17.37	0	11
S. J. Pegler	34	48	6	643	79	15.30	0	18
T. A. Ward	24	34	14	223	43	11.15	0	27/23
C. P. Carter	31	41	5	398	32	11.05	0	26
J. L. Cox	14	16	6	92	34	9.20	0	1
T. Campbell	13	17	4	115	27*	8.84	0	17/3

Bowling Averages

	O	M	R	W	Avge	BB	5i
S. J. Pegler	1286.5	352	2885	189	15.26	7-31	17
G. A. Faulkner	1015.1	207	2514	163	15.42	7-67	16
C. P. Carter	461.1	128	1116	67	16.65	5-17	4
L. A. Stricker	27	4	67	4	16.75	3-13	0
H. W. Taylor	120.1	35	292	14	20.85	4-36	0
A. W. Nourse	575.3	190	1232	50	24.64	6-33	2
G. C. White	120	15	456	18	25.33	5-21	1
S. J. Snooke	34	3	112	4	28.00	2-29	0
J. L. Cox	170.1	46	403	14	28.78	4-39	0
G. P. D. Hartigan	156	20	470	14	33.57	3-27	0
R. O. Schwarz	185.1	17	672	18	37.33	4-59	0
C. B. Llewellyn	60	6	219	4	54.75	2-71	0

1912: 5th South Africans

The team to represent South Africa in the Triangular Tournament consisted of F. Mitchell (captain), L. J. Tancred, G. A. Faulkner, S. J. Snooke, G. C. White, L. Stricker, R. Beaumont, R. O. Schwarz, S. J. Pegler, T. A. Ward and T. Campbell, all of Transvaal; H. W. Taylor, A. W. Nourse, C. B. Llewellyn, C. P. Carter and J. L. Cox from Natal and G. P. D.

The 1912 season in England saw a triangular Test series, with both Australia and South Africa touring. It was a disastrously wet summer and the experiment was not repeated. This is the South African touring party. Back: Stricker, Schwarz, Beaumont, Campbell, Hartigan, Cox. Centre: Pegler, Tancred, Mitchell (captain), Faulkner, Snooke, Nourse. Front: Taylor, Ward, Carter.

1912: 5th South Africans

1st Match: v Derbyshire (Derby) May 4, 6, 7, 8.
Derbyshire 143 (S. Cadman 53) and 129 (G. A. Faulkner 5-46, C. P. Carter 4-36) lost to South Africans 136 (A. Morton 6-52) and 138-3 by 7 wkts.

2nd Match: v Surrey (Oval) May 9, 10, 11.
South Africans 252 (R. O. Schwarz 70, J. W. Hitch 4-76) and 175 (J. W. Hitch 6-57) beat Surrey 163 (A. W. Nourse 4-44, R. O. Schwarz 4-64) and 212 (T. W. Hayward 67) by 52 runs.

3rd Match: v M.C.C. (Lord's) May 13, 14, 15.
M.C.C. 293 (F. A. Tarrant 104, A. P. Day 50, S. J. Pegler 5-75) and 221 (R. H. Spooner 72, F. A. Tarrant 52, S. J. Pegler 6-44) beat South Africans 176 (F. A. Tarrant 6-55) and 230 (S. J. Snooke 86, J. W. Hearne 4-122) by 108 runs.

4th Match: v Yorkshire (Huddersfield) May 16, 17, 18.
South Africans 170 (G. P. D. Hartigan 57, S. Haigh 5-33) and 288 (F. Mitchell 91, W. Rhodes 6-102) drew with Yorkshire 317 (D. Denton 82, G. H. Hirst 65, S. Haigh 62*, S. J. Pegler 5-77) and 10-1.

5th Match: v Oxford University (Oxford) May 20, 21, 22.
Oxford University 278 (H. H. Gaekwad of Baroda 62, A. J. Evans 56, S. J. Pegler 4-50) and 244-5 dec (A. J. Evans 107, F. H. Knott 70) drew with South Africans 179 (A. W. Nourse 94, A. J. Evans 5-73) and 138-3 (H. W. Taylor 55).

6th Match: v Worcestershire (Worcester) May 23, 24, 25.
Worcestershire 50 (S. J. Pegler 7-31) and 206 (R. O. Schwarz 4-59) lost to South Africans 298 (G. P. D. Hartigan 103, H. W. Taylor 83, G. H. T. Simpson-Hayward 5-19) by an innings and 42 runs.

7th Match: v Australia (Old Trafford) May 27, 28.
Australia 448 (W. Bardsley 121, C. E. Kelleway 114, S. J. Pegler 6-105) beat South Africa 265 (G. A. Faulkner 122*, W. J. Whitty 5-55) and 95 (C. E. Kelleway 5-33) by an innings and 88 runs.

8th Match: v Northants (Northampton) May 30, 31, June 1.
South Africans 428 (A. W. Nourse 137, R. Beaumont 75, S. J. Pegler 52*, W. Wells 4-121) drew with Northants 156 and 286 (W. H. Denton 54, R. Haywood 52, G. A. Faulkner 4-95).

9th Match: v Cambridge University (Cambridge) June 3, 4, 5.
Cambridge University 130 (R. Knight 66, C. P. Carter 5-17, G. A. Faulkner 5-53) and 132 (G. A. Faulkner 5-48) lost to South Africans 260 (L. J. Tancred 94) and 3-0 by 10 wkts.

10th Match: v Surrey (Oval) June 6, 7, 8.
Surrey 169 (A. W. Nourse 4-54, S. J. Pegler 4-74) drew with South Africans did not bat.

11th Match: v England (Lord's) June 10, 11, 12.
South Africa 58 (F. R. Foster 5-16, S. F. Barnes 5-25) and 217 (C. B. Llewellyn 75, S. F. Barnes 6-85) lost to England 337 (R. H. Spooner 119, F. E. Woolley 73, S. J. Pegler 7-65) by an innings and 62 runs.

12th Match: v Nottinghamshire (Trent Bridge) June 13, 14, 15.
Nottinghamshire 261 (J. R. Gunn 95, G. Gunn 73, S. J. Pegler 5-67) and 269-7 dec (A. O. Jones 79, J. R. Gunn 76) drew with South Africans 276 (L. A. Stricker 79, J. Iremonger 5-99) and 203-1 (L. J. Tancred 100*, H. W. Taylor 77).

13th Match: v Somerset (Bath) June 17, 18, 19.
South Africans 96 (E. Robson 5-33, W. T. Greswell 5-44) and 300-3 dec (A. W. Nourse 113, S. J. Snooke 77*, H. W. Taylor 71) drew with Somerset 127 (S. J. Pegler 6-42, C. P. Carter 4-47) and 128-7 (J. Daniell 62*).

14th Match: v South Wales (Swansea) June 20, 21, 22.
South Africans 352 (S. J. Pegler 72, L. A. Stricker 69) and 204 (S. Hacker 5-65) beat South Wales 192 (T. A. L. Whittington 57, A. W. Nourse 5-50, S. J. Pegler 5-53) and 134 (G. A. Faulkner 7-67) by 230 runs.

15th Match: v Scotland (Glasgow) June 24, 25, 26.
Scotland 136 (G. A. Faulkner 5-37, S. J. Pegler 5-53) and 93 (S. J. Pegler 4-34, J. L. Cox 4-39) lost to South Africans 326-9 dec (G. A. Faulkner 145*) by an innings and 97 runs.

16th Match: v Scotland (Edinburgh) June 27, 28, 29.
Scotland 94 (G. A. Faulkner 6-35) and 72 (G. A. Faulkner 5-32, C. P. Carter 5-37) lost to South Africans 263 (A. W. Nourse 73, R. W. Sievewright 6-121) by an innings and 97 runs.

17th Match: v Middlesex (Lord's) July 1, 2, 3.
South Africans 263 drew with Middlesex 110-7 (S. J. Pegler 5-37).

18th Match: v Warwickshire (Edgbaston) July 4, 5.
Warwickshire 92 (S. J. Pegler 4-20) and 179 (W. G. Quaife 63, C. S. Baker 50, C. P. Carter 5-43, S. J. Pegler 4-76) lost to South Africans 189 (A. W. Nourse 50, C. Charlesworth 6-56) and 86-4 by 6 wkts.

19th Match: v England (Headingley) July 8, 9, 10.
England 242 (F. E. Woolley 57, A. W. Nourse 4-52) and 238 (R. H. Spooner 82, J. B. Hobbs 55, G. A. Faulkner 4-50) beat South Africa 147 (S. F. Barnes 6-52) and 159 (S. F. Barnes 4-63) by 174 runs.

20th Match: v Australia (Lord's) July 15, 16, 17.
South Africa 263 (H. W. Taylor 93, W. J. Whitty 4-68) and 173 (C. B. Llewellyn 59, T. J. Matthews 4-29) lost to Australia 390 (W. Bardsley 164, C. E. Kelleway 102, S. J. Pegler 4-79) and 48-0 by 10 wkts.

21st Match: v Kent (Maidstone) July 18, 19, 20.
South Africans 360 (H. W. Taylor 96, L. A. Stricker 54, S. J. Snooke 52) and 152-8 dec drew with Kent 245 (E. Humphreys 62, G. A. Faulkner 6-48) and 185-4 (F. E. Woolley 59*, H. T. W. Hardinge 54, Jas Seymour 53).

22nd Match: v Woodbrook C & G (Bray) July 22, 23, 24.
South Africans 326 (L. J. Tancred 131, G. A. Faulkner 56) and 212-7 dec (H. W. Taylor 71) drew with Woodbrook C & G 290 (A. Baker 90, P. F. Quinlan 80).

23rd Match: v Ireland (Bray) July 25, 26, 27.
Ireland 108 (H. W. Taylor 4-36) and 118 (C. P. Carter 5-44, G. A. Faulkner 4-18) lost to South Africans 395 (A. W. Nourse 113, S. J. Snooke 81, L. J. Tancred 61, R. H. Lambert 5-51) by an innings and 169 runs.

24th Match: v Minor Counties (Stoke) July 29, 30, 31.
Minor Counties 127 (N. V. H. Riches 51, G. A. Faulkner 5-59) drew with South Africans 22-3.

25th Match: v Lancashire (Liverpool) Aug 1, 2, 3.
Lancashire 242 (J. Sharp 121, G. A. Faulkner 5-98) and 151 (G. A. Faulkner 5-55) beat South Africans 124 (W. Huddleston 7-42) and 44 (H. Dean 7-22) by 225 runs.

26th Match: v Australia (Trent Bridge) Aug 5, 6, 7.
South Africa 329 (A. W. Nourse 64, G. C. White 59*) drew with Australia 219 (W. Bardsley 56, S. J. Pegler 4-80).

27th Match: v Leicestershire (Leicester) Aug 8, 9.
South Africans 125 (J. H. King 5-52, H. M. Bannister 4-23) and 73 (J. H. King 7-45) beat Leicestershire 46 (G. A. Faulkner 6-21, S. J. Pegler 4-20) and 92 (G. A. Faulkner 5-38) by 60 runs.

28th Match: v England (Oval) Aug 12, 13.
South Africa 95 (S. F. Barnes 5-28, F. E. Woolley 5-41) and 93 (S. F. Barnes 8-29) lost to England 176 (G. A. Faulkner 7-84) and 14-0 by 10 wkts.

29th Match: v Sussex (Hove) Aug 15, 16, 17.
Sussex 76 (A. W. Nourse 6-33) and 220 (A. E. Relf 104, J. Vine 60, S. J. Pegler 7-55) lost to South Africans 118 (A. E. Relf 6-49) and 179-6 (G. A. Faulkner 53*) by 4 wkts.

30th Match: v Yorkshire (Bramall Lane) Aug 19, 20, 21.
South Africans 180 (L. J. Tancred 51, G. H. Hirst 4-44) and 40-1 drew with Yorkshire 149 (R. Kilner 54, S. J. Pegler 6-29).

31st Match: v Gloucestershire (Bristol) Aug 29, 30, 31.
Gloucestershire 126 (G. C. White 5-21) and 64 (S. J. Pegler 5-33, G. A. Faulkner 4-26) lost to South Africans 79 (G. Dennett 5-40, C. W. L. Parker 5-35) and 114-8 (G. L. Jessop 4-33, E. G. Dennett 4-51) by 2 wkts.

32nd Match: v Lancashire (Old Trafford) Aug 22, 23, 24.
Lancashire 170 (G. A. Faulkner 6-78) drew with South Africans 69-1.

33rd Match: v Essex (Leyton) Aug 26, 27, 28.
Essex 127 (S. J. Pegler 4-46) and 168 (W. Reeves 68, S. J. Pegler 5-42, G. A. Faulkner 5-65) drew with South Africans 166 (W. Mead 4-46) and 102-5.

34th Match: v Hampshire (Bournemouth) Sept 2, 3, 4.
South Africans 162 (L. A. Stricker 99, K. H. C. Woodroffe 5-33) and 432 (A. W. Nourse 213*, H. W. Taylor 63, H. C. McDonell 4-56) drew with Hampshire 137 (C. P. Mead 64*, S. J. Pegler 4-53) and 187-7 (C. P. Mead 77*).

35th Match: v Lionel Robinson's XI (Attleborough) Sept 5, 6, 7.
Lionel Robinson's XI 153 (S. J. Pegler 6-45) and 255 (E. H. Hendren 80, S. J. Pegler 5-75) beat South Africans 151 (M. Falcon 6-47) and 66 (F. A. Tarrant 5-8, H. L. Simms 5-24) by 191 runs.

36th Match: v Lord Londesborough's XI (Scarborough) Sept 9, 10, 11.
South Africans 100 (S. F. Barnes 6-32, G. H. Hirst 4-56) drew with Lord Londesborough's XI 63-4.

37th Match: v Gentlemen (Hastings) Sept 12, 13, 14.
Gentlemen 286 (J. W. H. T. Douglas 94, G. L. Jessop 59) and 164 (B. J. T. Bosanquet 62, G. A. Faulkner 4-43, S. J. Pegler 4-48) lost to South Africans 178 (A. W. Nourse 58, S. G. Smith 6-46) and 273-4 (H. W. Taylor 67, G. A. Faulkner 61) by 6 wkts.

Hartigan of Border, with G. Allsop as manager. The two notable omissions were A. E. E. Vogler, who was rumoured to be at loggerheads with Sir Abe Bailey, and J. W. Zulch. The side sailed in the s.s. *Balmoral Castle*, arriving in England in mid-April, except for White who left Cape Town on 24 April aboard s.s. *Walmer Castle* and missed the first few matches.

The Triangular Tournament hinged on the form of the South African side. Unfortunately the team failed to play up to the standard they reached in 1907. The famous googly bowlers of that tour achieved almost nothing in the Tests and there was no one to replace them. Schwarz and White took 36 wickets in all between them, compared with 215 in 1907. Faulkner was a success, but so much of the bowling fell to him that his batting was affected. The other success was Pegler, whose leg-breaks were highly destructive. If the bowling was not up to 1907 standard, the batting was equally poor. Nourse headed the averages, but did little in the Tests. Neither S. J. Snooke nor Tancred batted up to their South African form and the captain hardly made a run. It was unfortunate that Hartigan was ill early on and then fractured his arm, missing the last part of the tour as a result. Ward looked good behind the stumps, which was as well, for his deputy, Campbell, suffered from rheumatism in his hands.

The team in fact won 13 matches, compared with only nine Australian wins and to that extent the visit was a success. The craze for Test Match cricket completely swamped interest in the other matches, however, and so the South Africans' reputation rested solely on their failure to win a single Test Match. The very wet weather was blamed for the lack of public excitement in the Tests, but if South Africa had played up to the form of 1907 and Australia had sent over their full strength side, the weather would surely have been of secondary importance.

As it was the Triangular Tournament was marked down as a failure and not repeated until the limited-overs matches of the 1970s.

1919: Australian Imperial Forces

Soon after the First World War ended the idea of a representative Australian team touring England and playing Test Matches in 1919 was mooted. A fixture list was arranged, but at the beginning of February the proposed tour was abandoned. Then at the last moment the military authorities stepped in and agreed to finance an Australian Forces team. The proposed Test Matches were dropped, but the county fixtures retained and with a strong, young, side the team was very successful.

The players involved were C. Kelleway (captain), H. L. Collins, J. M. Taylor, C. T. Docker, E. A. Bull and E. J. Long, all of New South Wales; C. B. Willis and A. W. Lampard of Victoria; C. E. Pellew and W. S. Stirling of South Australia, plus W. A. S. Oldfield, J. M. Gregory, W. L. Trennery, J. T. Murray, S. G. Winning, H. S. B. Love and H. F. T. Heath, all of whom had not represented a state in first-class cricket up to 1919. After the first six first-class matches Kelleway left after a disagreement and the captaincy was handed over to Collins.

The team showed fine form and were not defeated until their twelfth match, when they played the Gentlemen at Lord's. They lost three more times later on, but were generally a very sound eleven. Collins was the best batsman, except for Kelleway, but the real match winner was Gregory, whose fast bowling was much quicker than any of the 1919 county bowlers' and whose batting made him a world-class all-rounder. Collins' slow left-arm deliveries put him on the top of the averages, but he did not win matches in the way Gregory did. The fielding was first-rate–the outfielders being particularly brilliant–and this added to the attraction of the side. The team played three-day matches against the counties, in contrast to the two-day championship games in vogue that summer.

1919: Australian Imperial Forces

1st Match: v Lionel Robinson's XII (Attleborough) May 14, 15, 16 (12 a side).
Lionel Robinson's XII 147 (C. T. Docker 5-34) and 362-8 dec (G. L. de Hough 87*, H. T. W. Hardinge 72) drew with A.I.F. 227 (H. L. Collins 87, S. J. Pegler 5-54) and 274-9 (J. M. Taylor 66, C. B. Willis 57, J. W. H. T. Douglas 4-80).

2nd Match: v Essex (Leyton) May 17, 19.
Essex 169 (W. M. Turner 64) and 151 (J. M. Gregory 4-47) lost to A.I.F. 434 (C. Kelleway 126, J. M. Taylor 78, J. T. Murray 77, W. S. Stirling 58*, B. Tremlin 7-171) by an innings and 114 runs.

3rd Match: v Cambridge University (Cambridge) May 21, 22, 23.
A.I.F. 650-8 dec (C. Kelleway 168, C. E. Pellew 105*, A. W. Lampard 83, H. L. Collins 69, C. T. Docker 52*) beat Cambridge University 293 (G. A. Rotherham 84*, J. H. Naumann 51, J. M. Gregory 6-68) and 118 (C. T. Docker 5-41, A. W. Lampard 4-31) by an innings and 239 runs.

4th Match: v Middlesex (Lord's) May 26, 27, 28.
A.I.F. 370 (H. L. Collins 127, J. T. Murray 91, W. S. Stirling 57) and 235 (H. L. Collins 64, C. Kelleway 52, H. W. Lee 4-48) drew with Middlesex 408 (E. H. Hendren 135, P. F. Warner 101*, A. W. Lampard 6-91) and 146-4 (E. H. Hendren 63*).

5th Match: v Oxford University (Oxford) May 29, 30.
Oxford University 152 (C. Kelleway 7-47) and 247-4 (D. J. Knight 70, F. W. Waldock 51) drew with A.I.F. 391 (J. T. Murray 133, J. M. Taylor 104, C. E. Kelleway 60, V. R. Price 6-146).

6th Match: v Surrey (Oval) May 31, June 2, 3.
A.I.F. 230 (H. L. Collins 58, C. B. Willis 52, J. W. Hitch 6-71) and 554-7 dec (A. W. Lampard 112, C. E. Pellew 106*, J. M. Taylor 96, C. Kelleway 87) drew with Surrey 344 (J. B. Hobbs 205*) and 128-5.

7th Match: v M.C.C. (Lord's) June 5, 6.
M.C.C. 133 (A. W. Lampard 5-40) and 228 (C. P. Mead 71, W. V. Jephson 63, J. M. Gregory 4-74) lost to A.I.F. 297 (J. M. Gregory 56, W. L. Trennery 55) and 66-0 by 10 wkts.

8th Match: v Sussex (Hove) June 9, 10.
Sussex 227 (R. R. Relf 64, H. L. Collins 5-45) and 241 (R. R. Relf 102, A. W. Lampard 4-52) drew with A.I.F. 289 and 77-8 (R. R. Relf 4-52).

9th Match: v Lancashire (Old Trafford) June 12, 13, 14.
A.I.F. 418 (H. L. Collins 103, W. L. Trennery 82, C. E. Pellew 55, C. B. Willis 56, J. S. Heap 4-107) beat Lancashire 125 (W. S. Stirling 5-38) and 136 (A. W. Lampard 9-42) by an innings and 157 runs.

10th Match: v Yorkshire (Bramall Lane) June 16, 17.
Yorkshire 224 (W. Rhodes 90, P. Holmes 71, J. M. Gregory 6-91) and 210 (G. H. Hirst 88, J. M. Gregory 7-79) lost to A.I.F. 265 (W. L. Trennery 54, W. Rhodes 4-69, E. Smith 4-70) and 170-9 (W. E. Blackburne 5-60) by 1 wkt.

11th Match: v Hampshire (Southampton) June 20, 21.
Hampshire 191 (C. P. Mead 91*, A. W. Lampard 4-42) and 67-1 drew with A.I.F. 136 (W. L. Trennery 56, A. S. Kennedy 6-56).

12th Match: v Gentlemen (Lord's) June 23, 24, 25.
Gentlemen 402 (F. H. Gillingham 83, A. J. Evans 68, J. W. H. T. Douglas 56, A. W. Carr 51) beat A.I.F. 85 (M. Falcon 6-41, J. W. H. T. Douglas 4-34) and 184 (J. W. White 4-38, J. W. H. T. Douglas 4-40) by an innings and 133 runs.

13th Match: v Northants (Northampton) June 26, 27, 28.
Australians 297 (J. M. Gregory 115, C. E. Pellew 70, C. N. Woolley 4-51) and 314 (W. L. Trennery 58, A. W. Lampard 51, F. Walden 4-43) beat Northants 246 (L. E. Holland 63, J. M. Gregory 4-71) and 169 (C. N. Woolley 51, H. L. Collins 5-26, J. M. Gregory 4-74) by 196 runs.

14th Match: v Western Scotland (Glasgow) June 30, July 1.
A.I.F. 733-6 dec (J. T. Murray 150*, W. S. Stiring 126*, W. L. Trennery 118, E. A. Bull 103, H. L. Collins 94, J. M. Taylor 75, Sandiford 4-148) beat Western Scotland 85 and 88 (J. M. Gregory 4-33) by an innings and 560 runs.

15th Match: v Scottish Union (Edinburgh) July 2, 3.
Scottish Union 266 (J. W. Sorrie 79, G. L. D. Hole 67, J. M. Gregory 6-89) and 79-8 (J. M. Gregory 6-38) drew with A.I.F. 350 (H. L. Collins 150, R. W. Sievewright 4-97).

16th Match: v Scotland (Glasgow) July 4, 5.
A.I.F. 357 (C. T. Docker 69, E. A. Bull 66, T. D. Watt 4-66) drew with Scotland 113.

17th Match: v Durham (West Hartlepool) July 7, 8.
A.I.F. 364 (W. L. Trennery 81, C. E. Pellew 63, C. B. Milam 4-99) and 336-8 (J. T. Murray 86, C. E. Pellew 61, C. B. Willis 57) drew with Durham 259 (T. Kinch 105, J. M. Gregory 4-61).

18th Match: v Leicestershire (Leicester) July 11, 12.
A.I.F. 551-5 dec (C. E. Pellew 187, C. B. Willis 156, H. L. Collins 121) and 28-0 drew with Leicestershire 224 (H. Whitehead 58, S. Coe 53, J. M. Gregory 4-70).

19th Match: v Derbyshire (Derby) July 14, 15.
Derbyshire 181 and 112 (J. M. Gregory 6-65, H. L. Collins 4-39) beat A.I.F. 125 (W. L. Trennery 69, J. Horsley 6-55, A. Morton 4-66) and 132 (J. T. Murray 54, J. Horsley 6-62) by 36 runs.

20th Match: v H. K. Foster's XI (Hereford) July 16, 17.
H. K. Foster's XI 224-9 dec (H. K. Foster 73, W. T. Trehawna 55, C. T. Docker 4-55) and 131-4 drew with A.I.F. 405 (J. M. Taylor 138, W. A. S. Oldfield 55, Extras 62, H. A. Gilbert 5-89).

21st Match: v Worcestershire (Worcester) July 18, 19.
Worcestershire 120 (J. M. Gregory 7-56) and 127 (A. W. Lampard 4-46, J. M. Gregory 4-49) lost to A.I.F. 450-4 dec (C. E. Pellew 195, C. B. Willis 129, W. L. Trennery 66, W. A. S. Oldfield 54) by an innings and 203 runs.

22nd Match: v Warwickshire (Edgbaston) July 21, 22.
Warwickshire 215 (E. F. Waddy 73, H. L. Collins 5-73) and 68 (W. S. Stirling 5-26, S. G. Winning 4-38) lost to A.I.F. 321 (H. L. Collins 110, C. B. Willis 52) by an innings and 38 runs.

23rd Match: v Nottinghamshire (Trent Bridge) July 24, 25, 26.
A.I.F. 371 (C. B. Willis 130, H. L. Collins 71, W. A. S. Oldfield 65, J. M. Taylor 60, W. A. Flint 5-60) and 242-5 dec (H. L. Collins 118, W. A. S. Oldfield 80*) drew with Nottinghamshire 391 (G. Gunn 131, J. Hardstaff sen 82, W. R. D. Payton 50) and 62-1.

24th Match: v Surrey (Oval) July 31, Aug 1, 2.
A.I.F. 436 (H. L. Collins 95, W. L. Trennery 78, C. B. Willis 58, A. W. Lampard 58, T. Rushby 6-77) and 260-4 dec (H. L. Collins 75, C. B. Willis 55*, J. M. Taylor 54) drew with Surrey 322 (J. N. Crawford 144*, C. T. A. Wilkinson 103, H. L. Collins 4-93, J. M. Gregory 4-109) and 121-1 (J. B. Hobbs 68*).

25th Match: v Sussex (Hove) Aug 4, 5.
Sussex 120 (J. M. Gregory 6-38, H. L. Collins 4-47) and 126 (H. L. Collins 6-27) lost to A.I.F. 300 (C. B. Willis 127) by an innings and 54 runs.

26th Match: v Kent (Canterbury) Aug 7, 8, 9.
A.I.F. 198 (J. M. Gregory 67, C. B. Willis 51, F. E. Woolley 4-37) and 419-8 dec (C. B. Willis 95, C. E. Pellew 91, W. S. Stirling 62, J. M. Gregory 56) drew with Kent 301 (J. C. Hubble 71, W. J. Fairservice 55, E. Humphreys 56, J. M. Gregory 7-100) and 172-5 (F. E. Woolley 76).

27th Match: v Essex (Southend) Aug 21, 22, 23.
A.I.F. 130 (J. W. H. T. Douglas 7-50) and 447-8 dec (J. M. Taylor 146, J. T. Murray 82, C. E. Pellew 70, J. W. H. T. Douglas 4-168) beat Essex 151 (J. M. Gregory 4-48, H. L. Collins 4-63) and 117 (J. M. Gregory 5-34) by 309 runs.

28th Match: v Gloucestershire (Clifton) Aug 27, 28.
Gloucestershire 281 (C. L. Townsend 63, A. G. Dipper 61, S. G. Winning 4-96) drew with A.I.F. 147 (J. M. Gregory 50, C. W. L. Parker 7-70) and 64-5.

29th Match: v Somerset (Taunton) Aug 29, 30.
A.I.F. 85 (E. Robson 6-45, J. C. White 4-35) and 144-4 dec (H. L. Collins 67*) beat Somerset 70 (S. G. Winning 6-30, H. L. Collins 4-38) and 64 (H. L. Collins 8-31) by 95 runs.

30th Match: v South (Hastings) Sept 1, 2, 3.
South 183 (S. G. Winning 5-57) and 280 (C. P. Mead 75, H. T. W. Hardinge 90, H. L. Collins 5-89) beat A.I.F. 162 (C. B. Willis 54, F. E. Woolley 6-74, J. C. White 4-50) and 179 (W. L. Trennery 54) by 122 runs.

31st Match: v South (Portsmouth) Sept 4, 5.
South 104 (J. M. Gregory 6-42) and 115 (S. G. Winning 5-30) lost to A.I.F. 206 (J. T. Murray 59) and 15-0 by 10 wkts.

32nd Match: v C. I. Thornton's XI (Scarborough) Sept 8, 9, 10.
A.I.F. 81 (J. W. Hitch 6-24) and 296 (C. B. Willis 96, J. M. Taylor 71, J. W. Hitch 5-102) lost to C. I. Thornton's XI 187 (J. M. Gregory 7-83) and 191-8 (J. B. Hobbs 93) by 2 wkts.

1919: Australian Imperial Forces

Batting Averages

	M	I	NO	R	HS	Avge	100	c/s
C. Kelleway	6	9	0	505	168	56.11	2	6
C. B. Willis	27	44	4	1652	156*	41.30	4	15
H. L. Collins	27	44	2	1615	127	38.45	5	19
C. E. Pellew	24	40	7	1260	195*	38.18	4	10
W. A. S. Oldfield	13	19	7	382	80*	31.83	0	16/10
J. M. Taylor	25	39	1	1187	146	31.23	3	23
J. M. Gregory	25	36	4	942	115	29.43	1	44
W. L. Trennery	24	37	3	961	82	28.26	0	11
A. W. Lampard	24	35	3	821	112	25.65	1	14
J. T. Murray	22	34	1	793	133	24.03	1	15
C. T. Docker	13	17	7	214	52*	21.40	0	12
E. A. Bull	16	23	2	395	42	18.80	0	4
W. S. Stirling	26	35	3	538	62	16.81	0	17
S. G. Winning	19	24	11	174	30	13.38	0	14
E. J. Long	16	19	9	110	14*	11.00	0	19/12

Also batted: H. S. B. Love (1 match) 0 and 2; H. F. T. Heath played one match but did not bat.

Bowling Averages

	O	M	R	W	Avge	BB	5i
H. L. Collins	728.5	164	1755	106	16.55	8-31	6
J. M. Gregory	830	124	2384	131	18.19	7-56	10
C. T. Docker	200.2	35	576	27	21.33	5-34	2
W. S. Stirling	378.5	83	963	44	21.88	5-26	2
S. G. Winning	472.4	106	1164	51	22.82	6-30	3
A. W. Lampard	519.2	72	1605	69	23.26	9-42	3
C. Kelleway	193.2	38	548	18	30.44	7-47	1
W. L. Trennery	67.4	4	221	7	31.57	2-5	0

Also bowled: E. A. Bull 7-1-27-0; C. E. Pellew 12-4-50-0; J. T. Murray 15-2-61-1; C. B. Willis 6-0-29-0; H. F. T. Heath 3-0-11-0; J. M. Taylor 2-0-8-0.

1921: 15th Australians

The team which left Fremantle aboard the s.s. *Osterley* on 22 March was W. W. Armstrong (captain), E. R. Mayne, E. A. McDonald and J. Ryder of Victoria; H. L. Collins, T. J. E. Andrews, W. Bardsley, H. Carter, J. M. Gregory, H. S. T. L. Hunter, C. G. Macartney, A. A. Mailey, J. M. Taylor and W. A. S. Oldfield and C. E. Pellew of South Australia, with S. Smith as manager. C. E. Kelleway, for business reasons, had to decline and his place was taken by Hendry. Dr R. J. Pope accompanied the side as honorary medical officer. The team took the overland route from Marseilles, except Smith and Carter, who flew from Paris.

The tour began at Leicester on the last day of April with the Australians winning by an innings. This initial success was to be repeated almost to the end. The First Test was another innings victory and Australia went on to win both the Second and Third

Tests comfortably. The last two matches against England were drawn. It appeared as if the tourists would go through the summer undefeated, but in late August an eleven selected by A. C. MacLaren unexpectedly won at Eastbourne and C. I. Thornton's side inflicted a second defeat at Scarborough and in the end the 1921 Australians had to be content with equalling the record of the 1902 side. However, in 1902 the summer had been wet, whereas in 1921 there was almost unbroken sunshine. The visitors' success was perhaps assisted by the confused decisions of the England test selectors: no fewer than 30 players were picked for the five Tests, yet the eleven employed by MacLaren to defeat the Australians at Eastbourne did not include one of them.

The strength of the Australians lay in the fast bowling partnership of Gregory and McDonald. The English batsmen were completely demoralised by them; McDonald took 27 wickets in the Tests and Gregory 19, while both topped 100 wickets in all matches. Armstrong also bowled with great success, as did Mailey, so that altogether four bowlers achieved 100 wickets. Mailey's slows looked very easy, but batsmen were soon tempted into mistakes by him. Bardsley and Macartney stood out

1921: 15th Australians

Batting Averages

	M	I	NO	R	HS	Avge	100	c/s
C. G. Macartney	31	41	2	2317	345	59.41	8	5
W. Bardsley	30	41	4	2005	209	54.18	8	9
W. W. Armstrong	30	37	8	1213	182*	41.82	3	22
J. M. Gregory	27	33	2	1135	107	36.61	3	37
J. Ryder	23	29	6	825	124*	35.86	1	13
T. J. E. Andrews	30	41	4	1212	132	32.75	1	14
E. R. Mayne	13	15	1	457	157*	32.64	1	15
J. M. Taylor	27	35	2	1019	143	30.87	1	9
H. L. Collins	24	32	0	953	162	29.78	3	17
H. S. T. L. Hendry	23	26	7	534	56*	28.10	0	28
C. E. Pellew	27	37	3	848	146	24.94	2	9
W. A. S. Oldfield	18	20	5	357	123	23.80	1	33/24
H. Carter	17	18	1	355	57	20.88	0	26/12
E. A. McDonald	26	27	6	257	36	12.23	0	10
A. A. Mailey	28	30	10	233	46*	11.65	0	34

Bowling Averages

	O	M	R	W	Avge	BB	5i
W. W. Armstrong	736.1	271	1444	100	14.44	7-55	8
E. A. McDonald	808.2	158	2284	138	16.55	8-41	10
J. M. Gregory	655.4	126	1924	116	16.58	7-52	8
A. A. Mailey	800	103	2595	134	19.36	10-66	7
H. S. T. L. Hendry	392.1	103	979	38	25.76	4-30	0
J. Ryder	193	35	492	18	27.33	4-72	0
C. G. Macartney	143	58	240	8	30.00	3-64	0
C. E. Pellew	41	13	91	2	45.50	1-4	0
H. L. Collins	76	26	184	1	184.00	1-26	0

Also bowled: J. M. Taylor 8-1-26-1; T. J. E. Andrews 26-0-136-1; E. R. Mayne 5-2-8-0; W. Bardsley 2-0-13-0.

The 1921 Australian tourists, one of the greatest of the inter-war years. Back: Bardsley, Ryder, Hendry, Gregory, Mayne, Andrews, Smith (manager). Centre: Mailey, McDonald, Collins, Armstrong (captain), Macartney, Carter, Taylor. Front: Pellew, Oldfield.

1921: 15th Australians

1st Match: v Leicestershire (Leicester)   April 30, May 2.
Leicestershire 136 (E. A. McDonald 8-41) and 142 (A. T. Sharp 56*, A. A. Mailey 5-55, E. A. McDonald 4-63) lost to Australians 430-7 dec (C. G. Macartney 177, W. Bardsley 109, J. M. Gregory 78, W. E. Benskin 4-165) by an innings and 152 runs.

2nd Match: v L. Robinson's XI (Attleborough)   May 4, 5, 6.
Australians 136 (W. W. Armstrong 51*, J. W. H. T. Douglas 6-64) and 25-1 drew with L. Robinson's XI 256-7 dec (J. B. Hobbs 85*, V. W. C. Jupp 59*, E. A. McDonald 4-62).

3rd Match: v Surrey (Oval)   May 7, 9, 10.
Australians 357-9 dec (H. L. Collins 162, C. G. Macartney 87) beat Surrey 79 (W. W. Armstrong 6-38, E. A. McDonald 4-29) and 223 (P. G. H. Fender 57, J. W. Hitch 52, W. W. Armstrong 6-39, A. A. Mailey 4-88) by an innings and 55 runs.

4th Match: v Yorkshire (Bradford)   May 11, 12, 13.
Australians 263 (J. M. Gregory 104*, W. Rhodes 5-87) and 77-3 drew with Yorkshire 224 (W. Rhodes 63, W. W. Armstrong 4-60).

5th Match: v The Services (Portsmouth)   May 14, 16, 17.
Australians 395 (W. Bardsley 132, H. L. Collins 70, C. G. Macartney 51, M. B. Burrows 4-114) and 203-5 dec (C. E. Pellew 56) beat The Services 260-9 dec (R. St L. Fowler 65, J. M. Gregory 4-94, A. A. Mailey 4-129) and 140 (C. H. B. Blount 50, J. M. Gregory 7-52) by 198 runs.

6th Match: v Essex (Leyton)   May 18, 19.
Essex 144 (E. A. McDonald 4-54) and 99 (J. M. Gregory 5-43) lost to Australians 318 (T. J. E. Andrews 60, H. S. T. L. Hendry 56*) by an innings and 75 runs.

7th Match: v M.C.C. (Lord's)   May 21, 23, 24.
M.C.C. (A. J. Evans 69*, W. W. Armstrong 4-51) and 176 (E. H. Hendren 52, A. A. Mailey 4-25) lost to Australians 191 (F. J. Durston 7-84) and 271-7 (W. Bardsley 106, F. J. Durston 4-65) by 3 wkts.

8th Match: v Oxford University (Oxford)   May 25, 26.
Oxford University 180 (H. P. Ward 50, A. A. Mailey 7-108) and 174-1 (D. R. Jardine 96*, R. L. Holdsworth 57*) drew with Australians 294 (C. G. Macartney 77, R. C. Robertson-Glasgow 4-74).

9th Match: v England (Trent Bridge)   May 28, 30.
England 112 (J. M. Gregory 6-58) and 147 (E. A. McDonald 5-32) lost to Australia 232 (W. Bardsley 66) and 30-0 by 10 wkts.

10th Match: v Cambridge University (Cambridge)   June 1, 2, 3.
Cambridge University 220 (H. Ashton 107*, E. A. McDonald 5-46) and 128 (A. A. Mailey 7-37) lost to Australians 362 (C. E. Pellew 146, T. J. E. Andrews 59) by an innings and 14 runs.

11th Match: v Middlesex (Lord's)   June 4, 6.
Middlesex 111 (W. W. Armstrong 5-15) and 90 (E. A. McDonald 5-25) lost to Australians 171 (H. W. Lee 6-53) and 32-2 by 8 wkts.

12th Match: v Gloucestershire (Bristol)   June 8, 9, 10.
Australians 533-8 dec (C. G. Macartney 149, W. Bardsley 132, E. R. Mayne 79, J. M. Gregory 78, E. G. Dennett 5-144) drew with Gloucestershire 179 (D. C. Robinson 61, J. M. Gregory 4-38) and 140-1 (A. G. Dipper 70*, C. S. Barnett 66*).

13th Match: v England (Lord's)   June 11, 13, 14.
England 187 (F. E. Woolley 95, A. A. Mailey 4-55, E. A. McDonald 4-58) and 283 (F. E. Woolley 93, L. H. Tennyson 74*, J. M. Gregory 4-76, E. A. McDonald 4-89) lost to Australia 342 (W. Bardsley 88, J. M. Gregory 52, F. J. Durston 4-102) and 131-2 (W. Bardsley 63*) by 8 wkts.

14th Match: v Hampshire (Southampton)   June 15, 16, 17.
Australians 708-7 dec (W. Bardsley 209, J. M. Taylor 143, C. G. Macartney 105, J. Ryder 76*, H. S. T. L. Hendry 53) drew with Hampshire 370 (C. P. Mead 129, C. B. Fry 59) and 135-5.

15th Match: v Surrey (Oval)   June 18, 20, 21.
Australians 213 (J. M. Gregory 101, J. W. Hitch 5-74) and 158 (J. W. Hitch 5-44, P. G. H. Fender 4-44) beat Surrey 175 and 118 (J. M. Gregory 4-45) by 78 runs.

16th Match: v Northamptonshire (Northampton)   June 22, 23.
Australians 621 (C. G. Macartney 193, J. M. Gregory 107, J. Ryder 93, J. M. Taylor 63, T. J. E. Andrews 58, J. V. Murdin 5-157) beat Northamptonshire 69 (W. W. Armstrong 6-21) and 68 (A. A. Mailey 6-46) by an innings and 484 runs.

17th Match: v Nottinghamshire (Trent Bridge)   June 25, 27.
Australians 675 (C. G. Macartney 345, C. E. Pellew 100, H. S. T. L. Hendry 51, J. M. Taylor 50, J. Hardstaff 5-133) beat Nottinghamshire 58 (J. M. Gregory 4-23) and 100 (A. A. Mailey 4-36) by an innings and 517 runs.

18th Match: v Warwickshire (Edgbaston)   June 29, 30.
Warwickshire 262 (E. F. Waddy 50, H. S. T. L. Hendry 4-64) and 118-6 drew with Australians 506 (W. W. Armstrong 117, A. A. Mailey 123, W. Bardsley 50).

19th Match: v England (Headingley)   July 2, 4, 5.
Australia 407 (C. G. Macartney 115, W. W. Armstrong 77, C. E. Pellew 52, J. M. Taylor 50, C. H. Parkin 4-106) and 273-7 dec (T. J. E. Andrews 92) beat England 259 (J. W. H. T. Douglas 75, L. H. Tennyson 63, G. Brown 57, E. A. McDonald 4-105) and 202 by 219 runs.

20th Match: v Lancashire (Old Trafford)   July 6, 7.
Lancashire 92 (J. M. Gregory 5-41, H. S. T. L. Hendry 4-30) and 184 (J. Sharp 65, J. R. Barnes 58, J. M. Gregory 5-59, A. A. Mailey 4-77) lost to Australians 284 (W. Bardsley 71, J. Ryder 56, H. S. T. L. Hendry 51, J. T. Tyldesley 5-87, C. H. Parkin 5-89) by an innings and 8 runs.

21st Match: v West of Scotland (Glasgow)   July 9, 11.
Australians 259 (J. Ryder 129, W. W. Armstrong 87, W. Bardsley 74, E. R. Mayne 69) drew with West of Scotland 227 (D. C. Stevenson 50, A. A. Mailey 4-108) and 77-3.

22nd Match: v Scotland (Perth)   July 12, 13.
Australians 422 (W. Bardsley 112, H. L. Collins 100, H. D. Mitchell 4-122, R. W. Sievewright 4-126) drew with Scotland 162 (A. A. Mailey 5-29) and 79-0 (J. Kerr 60).*

23rd Match: v Scotland (Edinburgh)   July 14, 15.
Australians 514 (T. J. E. Andrews 125, H. L. Collins 113, E. R. Mayne 80, W. W. Armstrong 61) drew with Scotland 294-8 (J. Kerr 147, G. W. A. Alexander 60).

24th Match: v Durham (Sunderland)   July 16, 18.
Durham 168 (E. A. McDonald 4-28, W. W. Armstrong 4-82) and 121 (E. A. McDonald 5-23) lost to Australians 267 (J. M. Taylor 54) and 24-0 by 10 wkts.

25th Match: v Yorkshire (Bramall Lane)   July 20, 21, 22.
Australians 251 (W. Bardsley 71, J. M. Gregory 68, A. Waddington 4-83) and 163 beat Yorkshire 126 and 113 (J. M. Gregory 4-10, A. A. Mailey 5-54) by 175 runs.

26th Match: v England (Old Trafford)   July 23, 25, 26.
England 362-4 dec (C. A. G. Russell 101, G. E. Tyldesley 78*) and 44-1 drew with Australia 175 (C. H. Parkin 5-38).

27th Match: v Essex (Southend)   July 27, 28, 29.
Essex 128 (J. M. Gregory 5-44, A. A. Mailey 4-48) and 219 (H. Ashton 90, H. S. T. L. Hendry 4-36) lost to Australians 435 (H. L. Collins 119, W. Bardsley 59, J. M. Gregory 50, G. M. Louden 7-144) by an innings and 88 runs.

28th Match: v Glamorgan (Swansea)   July 30, Aug 1, 2.
Glamorgan 213 (W. E. Bates 79, N. V. H. Riches 75, W. W. Armstrong 5-61) drew with Australians 461-8 dec (W. Bardsley 122, W. W. Armstrong 76*, J. M. Taylor 73, C. G. Macartney 63, E. R. Mayne 51).

29th Match: v Lancashire (Liverpool)   Aug 3, 4, 5.
Lancashire 100 (E. A. McDonald 8-62) and 31-2 drew with Australians 317-5 dec (W. Bardsley 124, T. J. E. Andrews 88).

30th Match: v Warwickshire (Edgbaston)   Aug 6, 8, 9.
Warwickshire 133 (C. Charlesworth 51, W. W. Armstrong 5-33) and 118 (E. A. McDonald 6-52) lost to Australians 312-7 dec (W. Bardsley 75, C. G. Macartney 72, W. W. Armstrong 50*) by an innings and 61 runs.

31st Match: v Kent (Canterbury)   Aug 10, 11, 12.
Australians 676 (E. R. Mayne 157*, C. G. Macartney 155, W. W. Armstrong 102, J. M. Gregory 78, H. S. Carter 57, G. J. Bryan 5-148) and 119-4 (H. L. Collins 56) drew with Kent 237 (A. F. Bickmore 89, H. T. W. Hardinge 74, A. A. Mailey 4-54, J. Ryder 4-72).

32nd Match: v England (Oval)   Aug 13, 15, 16.
England 403-8 dec (C. P. Mead 182*, L. H. Tennyson 51, E. A. McDonald 5-143) and 244-2 (C. A. G. Russell 102*, G. Brown 84, J. W. Hitch 51*) drew with Australia 389 (T. J. E. Andrews 94, J. M. Taylor 75, C. G. Macartney 61).

33rd Match: v Gloucestershire (Cheltenham)   Aug 20, 22, 23.
Australians 438 (W. Bardsley 127, C. G. Macartney 121, J. M. Gregory 78, C. W. L. Parker 5-148) beat Gloucestershire 127 and 175 (R. P. Keigwin 65, A. A. Mailey 10-66) by an innings and 136 runs.

34th Match: v Somerset (Taunton)   Aug 24, 25.
Australians 331 (J. Ryder 124*, H. L. Collins 101, J. J. Bridges 5-111) beat Somerset 123 (E. A. McDonald 7-31) and 150 (T. C. Lowry 56, W. W. Armstrong 7-55) by an innings and 58 runs.

35th Match: v An England XI (Eastbourne)   Aug 27, 29, 30.
An England XI 43 (W. W. Armstrong 5-15, E. A. McDonald 5-21) and 326 (G. A. Faulkner 153, H. Ashton 75, E. A. McDonald 6-98) beat Australians 174 (W. Bardsley 70, M. Falcon 6-67, G. A. Faulkner 4-50) and 167 (C. H. Gibson 6-64) by 28 runs.

36th Match: v Sussex (Hove)   Aug 31, Sept 1, 2.
Australians 209 (J. M. Taylor 72, V. W. C. Jupp 4-41, A. E. R. Gilligan 4-62) and 332-9 dec (J. Ryder 83, H. L. Collins 54, J. M. Gregory 53, M. W. Tate 4-21) beat Sussex 282 (R. A. Young 124, J. M. Gregory 6-89) and 62 (A. A. Mailey 5-13, E. A. McDonald 4-32) by 197 runs.

37th Match: v South of England (Hastings)   Sept 3, 5, 6.
Australians 444 (W. W. Armstrong 182*, T. J. E. Andrews 132, G. M. Louden 6-129) beat South of England 199 (H. Ashton 65, J. M. Gregory 5-77) and 199 (H. W. Lee 64, W. W. Armstrong 4-51, A. A. Mailey 4-97) by an innings and 46 runs.

38th Match: v C. I. Thornton's XI (Scarborough)   Sept 8, 9, 10.
C. I. Thornton's XI 280 (J. W. H. T. Douglas 61, A. Sandham 56) and 146 (A. Sandham 50, A. A. Mailey 6-56, E. A. McDonald 4-51) beat Australians 231 (W. Bardsley 55, V. W. C. Jupp 5-54) and 162 (F. E. Woolley 5-36) by 33 runs.

39th Match: v Cumberland (Whitehaven)   Sept 13.
Cumberland 201 (A. A. Mailey 4-84) lost to Australians 284-8 (J. M. Taylor 94) by 5 wkts.

as the outstanding batsmen on the tour; they were both in splendid form throughout. The latter's 345 at Trent Bridge in a single day is a record which still stands. Armstrong, owing to his bowling commitments, was content to play a supporting role. A broken thumb hampered Collins; Andrews looked a fine orthodox player; Gregory hit very hard and indeed none of the side could be described as a failure. The fielding was quite exceptional, with Bardsley and Pellew in the deep and Gregory and Hendry at slip worthy of particular praise.

The team left Southampton aboard the s.s. *Balmoral Castle* on 30 September, bound for South Africa. The tour had made a profit of £17,000.

1922: 3rd Canadians

Norman Seagram captained and organised this moderate Canadian team which arrived at Southampton on 26 July for an 11-match tour of England. Besides Seagram, the team was H. H. Humphries, C. R. Somerville, A. E. Mix, V. R. Mustard, H. S. Reid, P. E. Henderson, A. M. Inglis, S. R. Saunders, D. W. Saunders, L. M. Rathbun, T. W. Seagram, H. G. Wookey, R. D. Hague and S. E. Harper. The most interesting among the personnel was D. W. Saunders who had been a member of the

1887 Canadians 35 years before. H. Dean was the manager.

The team failed to win a single match and were quite overwhelmed in their most important fixture–the two-day game against M.C.C. at Lord's.

H. G. Wookey, the left-arm bowler, took most wickets–53 at 16.41, and C. R. Somerville made most runs: 356 at 22.25.

1922: 3rd Canadians

1st Match: v K. T. Cox's XI (Uplyme, Devon)   July 29.
K. T. Cox's XI 143 beat Canadians 90 by 53 runs.

2nd Match: v Incogniti (Wimbledon)   Aug 1, 2.
Incogniti 207 (K. A. I. Mackenzie 66, F. H. Gillingham 63) and 110-9 dec drew with 125 (H. S. Reid 52) and 61-3.

3rd Match: v Band of Brothers (Chatham Castle)   Aug 4, 5.
Band of Brothers 124 and 67-6 dec drew with Canadians 122 and 53-4.

4th Match: v Royal Navy (Chatham)   Aug 7, 8.
Royal Navy 154 and 167 (T. E. Halsey 86) drew with Canadians 88 and 29-2.

5th Match: v Free Foresters (Oval)   Aug 9, 10.
Free Foresters 252 (R. Fox 107) and 102-3 drew with Canadians 240 (C. R. Somerville 92).

6th Match: v Lords and Commons (Lord's)   Aug 11.
Lords and Commons 136 drew with Canadians 123-6.

7th Match: v Royal Artillery (Woolwich)   Aug 14, 15.
Royal Artillery 237 (H. Day 108) beat Canadians 95 and 105 by an innings and 37 runs.

8th Match: v Hampstead (Hampstead)   Aug 16.
Hampstead 174 beat Canadians 88 by 86 runs.

9th Match: v M.C.C. (Lord's)   Aug 18, 19.
M.C.C. 312 beat Canadians 175 and 126 by an innings and 11 runs.

10th Match: v Gentlemen of Essex (Brentwood)   Aug 21, 22.
Gentlemen of Essex 390 (F. L. Fane 116) drew with Canadians 221 and 151-5.

11th Match: v Royal Engineers (Chatham)   Aug 24, 25.
Royal Engineers 152 and 119-4 dec drew with Canadians 84 and 112-7.

1923: 3rd West Indies

The team which arrived in England on 30 April comprised H. B. G. Austin (captain), G. Challenor, G. N. Francis, H. W. Ince and P. H. Tarilton, all from Barbados; C. R. Browne, M. P. Fernandes and C. V. Hunter from British Guiana; L. N. Constantine, G. A. R. Dewhurst, G. John, V. S. Pascall and J. A. Small of Trinidad; and J. K. Holt, R. K. Nunes and R. L. Phillips of Jamaica, with R. H. Mallett as manager. The composition of the side was dictated by each of the four major associations in the West Indies being allowed a set number of players. The two candidates who failed to make the tour were Griffith and St Hill.

It was hoped that the side would have nearly three weeks practice before the official matches began, but rain reduced this to three or four days. The weather during the first month of the tour was cold and wet and three defeats in the first five first-class encounters meant that public interest failed to materialise–no doubt the absence of any Test Matches played its part.

Challenor was the most accomplished batsman of the team and the way he dominates the batting averages clearly shows how important he was. The principal bowlers were Francis and John, both fast, while the slow left arm of Pascall picked up some wickets without really troubling the better batsmen. The feature of the out cricket was the fielding at cover point of Constantine.

The team suffered more than its fair share of injuries, being at one time reduced to 11 men. Phillips spent most of the tour as scorer and Hunter was also absent for many matches.

1923: 3rd West Indians

1st Match: v Cambridge University (Cambridge)   May 19, 21.
West Indians 117 (P. A. Wright 6-37) and 179 (R. K. Nunes 59, H. B. G. Austin 51*, P. A. Wright 4-55) lost to Cambridge University 208 (C. T. Ashton 92, V. S. Pascall 5-67) and 89-1 (T. C. Lowry 53*) by 9 wkts.

2nd Match: v Sussex (Hove)   May 23, 24.
West Indians 213 (G. Challenor 87) and 75 (A. E. R. Gilligan 5-14) beat Sussex 190 (G. B. Street 56, G. N. Francis 4-50) and 72 (G. N. Francis 6-33, V. S. Pascall 4-24) by 26 runs.

3rd Match: v M.C.C. (Lord's)   May 26, 28, 29.
M.C.C. 228 (P. R. Johnson 103, V. S. Pascall 6-77) drew with West Indians 121-8.

4th Match: v Hampshire (Southampton)   May 30, 31.
Hampshire 143 (C. P. Mead 54, G. N. Francis 5-27) and 252-8 dec (C. P. Mead 87, A. S. Kennedy 74) beat West Indians 112 (A. S. Kennedy 6-58) and 139 (A. S. Kennedy 5-43) by 144 runs.

5th Match: v Middlesex (Lord's)   June 2, 4, 5.
Middlesex 337 (E. H. Hendren 133, R. H. Hill 71, H. W. Lee 55, G. John 4-52) and 82 (G. N. Francis 6-34, G. John 4-35) beat West Indians 264 (G. Challenor 94) and 85 (J. W. Hearne 4-22) by 70 runs.

6th Match: v Oxford University (Oxford)   June 6, 7, 8.
Oxford University 390-6 dec (G. T. S. Stevens 182, J. L. Guise 120) and 178 (G. John 4-71) lost to West Indians 388 (R. K. Nunes 89, L. N. Constantine 77, J. K. Holt 52) and 183-2 (G. Challenor 100*) by 8 wkts.

7th Match: v Essex (Ilford)   June 9, 11, 12.
Essex 148 (T. K. Dobson 49, M. P. Fernandes 50) beat Wiltshire 110 (J. K. Holt 52) lost to West Indians 289 (G. Challenor 101, R. K. Nunes 61, J. A. Small 53, L. C. Eastman 4-65, J. W. H. T. Douglas 4-113) and 93-7 (L. C. Eastman 4-39) by 3 wkts.

8th Match: v Durham (Darlington)   June 13, 14.
West Indians 125 (T. K. Dobson 4-50) and 192 (G. Challenor 53, J. K. Holt 53, L. H. Weight 4-41) beat Durham 63 (C. R. Browne 5-26) and 74 (G. N. Francis 4-21) by 180 runs.

9th Match: v Northumberland (Newcastle)   June 15, 16.
West Indians 286 (G. Challenor 105, W. Hetherton 6-92) beat Northumberland 118 (C. R. Browne 5-38) and 159 (G. N. Francis 5-53) by an innings and 9 runs.

10th Match: v Derbyshire (Buxton)   June 20, 21, 22.
West Indians 97 (L. N. Constantine 60*, S. W. A. Cadman 5-41, A. Morton 4-39) and 36-2 drew with Derbyshire 75 (C. R. Browne 4-42).

11th Match: v Northants (Northampton)   June 23, 25, 26.
West Indians 354-5 dec (P. H. Tarilton 88, M. P. Fernandes 83*, G. Challenor 67) drew with Northants 229 (A. E. Thomas 55, V. S. Pascall 4-62).

12th Match: v Lancashire (Old Trafford)   June 27, 28, 29.
Lancashire 405 (J. W. H. Makepeace 111, G. E. Tyldesley 105) and 121-5 (A. Rhodes 70, G. N. Francis 4-38) beat West Indians 215 (J. A. Small 94, R. Tyldesley 6-39) and 309 (M. P. Fernandes 73, J. A. Small 68, P. H. Tarilton 50, C. H. Parkin 4-114) by 5 wkts.

13th Match: v Cheshire (Macclesfield)   June 30, July 2, 3.
West Indians 299 (M. P. Fernandes 97, H. Dean 5-128, Dennis 4-93) and 93-5 dec beat Cheshire 162 (J. M. Beeley 60, G. John 7-59) and 90 (J. A. Small 6-18) by 140 runs.

14th Match: v Nottinghamshire (Trent Bridge)   July 4, 5, 6.
Nottinghamshire 353 (W. R. D. Payton 84, G. Gunn 65, J. A. Small 5-93) and 345 (L. Kirk 86, W. Walker 58, C. R. Browne 7-97) drew with West Indians 317 (J. A. Small 71, G. Challenor 62, G. A. R. Dewhurst 52) and 219-0 (P. H. Tarilton 109*, G. Challenor 102*).

15th Match: v Leicestershire (Leicester)   July 7, 9, 10.
West Indians 385 (M. P. Fernandes 110, G. Challenor 60, F. Bale 4-96) and 109-4 dec drew with Leicestershire 242 (W. E. Astill 62, C. R. Browne 4-54) and 179-7 (C. R. Browne 4-65).

16th Match: v. Wiltshire (Swindon)   July 11, 12.
West Indians 356-8 dec (J. A. Small 131, J. K. Holt 68, M. P. Fernandes 50) beat Wiltshire 110 (V. S. Pascall 6-51, G. John 4-43) and 212 (A. A. Bankier 69, V. S. Pascall 6-72, G. John 4-65) by an innings and 34 runs.

17th Match: v Warwickshire (Edgbaston)   July 14, 16.
Warwickshire 356 (C. R. Browne 5-76) and 104 lost to West Indians 321 (J. A. Small 85, G. Challenor 61, E. P. Hewetson 4-94) and 24-1 by 9 wkts.

18th Match: v Lord Harris's XI (Belmont)   July 20, 21.
Lord Hars's XI 117 (G. John 7-45) and 126 (G. John 7-55) lost to West Indians 80 (C. J. Capes 4-48) and 164-7 (J. A. Small 65*) by 3 wkts.

19th Match: v Dublin University (Dublin)   July 23, 24.
Dublin University 100 (G. N. Francis 5-45, C. R. Browne 4-37) and 118 (V. S. Pascall 6-24) lost to West Indians 170 and 51-2 by 8 wkts.

20th Match: v Northern Cricket Union (Belfast)   July 25, 26.
West Indians 158 (W. Pollock 5-   ) and 161 (W. Sproule 4-   ) drew with Northern Cricket Union 131 (F. Jackson 51, G. John 4-31) and 142-8 (G. John 6-60).

21st Match: v Gloucestershire (Bristol)   July 28, 30, 31.
Gloucestershire 211 (A. E. Dipper 126*, C. R. Browne 5-85) drew with West Indians 235 (G. Challenor 111*, J. A. Small 50, E. G. Dennett 4-77, W. R. Gouldsworthy 4-78).

22nd Match: v Surrey (Oval)   Aug 1, 2, 3.
Surrey 87 (G. N. Francis 5-31, C. R. Browne 4-41) and 336 (D. R. Jardine 104, W. J. Abel 63, T. F. Shepherd 53, G. N. Francis 5-45) lost to West Indians 305 (G. Challenor 155*, P. G. H. Fender 4-71) and 121-0 (G. Challenor 66*) by 10 wkts.

23rd Match: v Glamorgan (Cardiff)   Aug 4, 6, 7.
Glamorgan 115 (G. John 7-52) and 324 (J. Stone 108, F. B. Pinch 55, W. E. Bates 51) beat West Indians 201 (P. H. Tarilton 75, T. Arnott 7-40) and 195 (G. Challenor 110, J. Mercer 4-41) by 43 runs.

24th Match: v Somerset (Weston-super-Mare)   Aug 8, 9, 10.
West Indians 306 (G. Challenor 79, H. B. G. Austin 76, J. K. Holt 56, G. E. Hunt 4-55) and 134 (G. F. Earle 4-14) beat Somerset 112 (V. S. Pascall 4-35) and 130 (C. R. Browne 6-66, G. N. Francis 4-58) by 198 runs.

25th Match: v Kent (Canterbury)   Aug 18, 19, 20.
Kent 205 (B. S. Cumberlege 51, L. N. Constantine 5-48) and 250-8 dec (G. C. Collins 78, G. John 4-57) beat West Indians 154 (W. H. Ashdown 4-34, G. C. Collins 4-57) and 130 (J. A. Small 51, W. S. Cornwallis 6-37) by 171 runs.

26th Match: v Norfolk (Norwich)   Aug 22, 23, 24.
West Indians 204 (H. W. Ince 72, M. Falcon 4-61) and 206-4 dec (G. Challenor 101, H. W. Ince 60, W. A. Beadsmoore 3-45) beat Norfolk 94 (V. S. Pascall 4-27, G. John 4-37) and 85 (G. John 7-38) by 231 runs.

27th Match: v Worcestershire (Worcester)   Aug 29, 30, 31.
Worcestershire 223 (G. John 6-65) and 175-8 (H. P. Gordon 68*, C. R. Browne 4-45) drew with West Indians 145 (F. A. Pearson 6-75).

28th Match: v H. D. G. Leveson-Gower's XI (Scarborough)   Sept 3, 4, 5.
West Indians 110 and 135 (C. H. Parkin 5-36, W. Rhodes 4-37) lost to H. D. G. Leveson-Gower's XI 218 (G. E. Tyldesley 97, G. N. Francis 4-47, G. John 4-63) and 31-6 (G. N. Francis 4-12) by 4 wkts.

1923: 3rd West Indians

Batting Averages

	M	I	NO	R	HS	Avge	100	c/s
G. Challenor	20	35	5	1556	155*	51.86	6	4
M. P. Fernandes	11	19	4	523	110	34.86	1	6
J. A. Small	18	27	2	776	94	31.04	0	20
H. B. G. Austin	11	16	2	360	76	25.71	0	4
P. H. Tarilton	17	28	2	554	109*	21.30	1	2
R. K. Nunes	15	24	1	455	89	19.78	0	0
H. W. Ince	16	26	3	381	46*	16.56	0	3
L. N. Constantine	20	31	4	425	77	15.74	0	15
J. K. Holt	12	19	0	293	56	15.42	0	6
G. John	10	13	4	108	44*	12.00	0	5
G. N. Francis	15	22	4	207	41	11.50	0	15
C. R. Browne	18	26	2	258	24*	10.75	0	14
V. S. Pascall	19	28	7	222	40	10.57	0	11
G. A. R. Dewhurst	15	23	5	182	52	10.11	0	20/5

Also batted: C. V. Hunter (2 matches) 9 and 1; R. L. Phillips played once but did not bat.

Bowling Averages

	O	M	R	W	Avge	BB	5i
G. N. Francis	505.5	119	1278	82	15.58	6-33	5
G. John	363.2	84	956	49	19.51	7-52	2
L. N. Constantine	244.4	39	809	37	21.86	5-48	1
C. R. Browne	696	171	1672	75	22.29	7-97	4
V. S. Pascall	470.5	92	1263	52	24.28	6-77	2
G. Challenor	17	3	54	2	27.00	2-17	0
J. A. Small	196	28	636	19	33.47	5-93	1
J. K. Holt	25	4	80	1	80.00	1-22	0

Also bowled: R. L. Phillips 7-0-21-0.

1924: 6th South Africans

The team which arrived in Southampton on Easter Monday were H. W. Taylor (captain), A. W. Nourse, J. M. Blanckenberg and C. P. Carter of Natal; M. J. Susskind, R. H. Catterall, H. G. Deane, E. P. Nupen, T. A. Ward, D. J. Meintjes and C. D. Dixon of Transvaal, J. M. M. Commaille and P. A. M. Hands of Western Province; G. A. L. Hearne of South-Western, G. F. Bissett of Griqualand West; and S. J. Pegler, in England on holiday, but available if required. The manager was G. Allsop.

The critics were full of praise of the tourists when they arrived, but it soon became apparent that the bowling would not be good enough to beat England. Pegler was co-opted almost immediately to strengthen the attack and indeed was the principal wicket-taker in the opening matches. Just before the First Test G. M. Parker, a

1924: 6th South Africans

Batting Averages

	M	I	NO	R	HS	Avge	100	c/s
H. W. Taylor	34	53	8	1898	126	42.17	4	13
A. D. Nourse	35	54	5	1928	147*	39.34	4	21
M. J. Susskind	29	48	6	1413	137	33.64	2	22/3
R. H. Catterall	33	49	2	1329	137	28.27	3	11
J. M. M. Commaille	31	50	5	1170	85	26.00	0	7
H. G. Deane	25	33	5	621	80*	22.17	0	9
G. A. L. Hearne	13	20	1	413	68	21.73	0	5
P. A. M. Hands	19	26	5	436	64	20.76	0	6
J. M. Blanckenberg	33	45	8	768	69	20.75	0	20
E. P. Nupen	17	25	4	379	57	18.04	0	9
T. A. Ward	25	36	3	484	68	14.66	0	34/14
S. J. Pegler	29	38	7	454	50*	14.64	0	16
G. F. Bissett	7	12	3	119	28*	13.22	0	5
D. J. Meintjes	15	21	2	171	26*	9.00	0	5
C. P. Carter	23	26	7	94	19	4.94	0	12
C. D. Dixon	13	14	3	54	9	4.90	0	7
G. M. Parker	3	4	2	3	2*	1.50	0	0

Also batted: G. A. Faulkner (1 match) 25 and 12.

Bowling Averages

	O	M	R	W	Avge	BB	5i
C. P. Carter	396.5	70	1104	51	21.64	6-40	4
J. M. Blanckenberg	995	227	2666	119	22.40	8-97	10
S. J. Pegler	1041.3	289	2552	108	23.63	8-54	7
G. M. Parker	77	7	307	12	25.58	6-152	1
C. D. Dixon	358.4	92	855	32	26.71	6-39	1
G. F. Bissett	194.4	21	585	20	29.25	5-102	1
E. P. Nupen	323.4	74	857	29	29.55	4-30	0
H. W. Taylor	20	1	86	3	28.66	2-34	0
A. W. Nourse	398.3	117	954	27	35.33	3-27	0
D. J. Meintjes	374.2	64	1145	30	38.16	4-19	0
R. H. Catterall	81.5	11	265	6	44.16	3-48	0
M. J. Susskind	6	0	51	1	51.00	1-13	0

Also bowled: H. G. Deane 8-0-50-0; G. A. Faulkner 17-0-87-0; P. A. M. Hands 1.5-0-9-3; G. A. L. Hearne 8-0-28-0; T. A. Ward 2-0-11-0.

The sixth party of South Africans to tour England arrived in 1924. Back: Deane, Hands, Dixon, Susskind, Bissett, Nupen, Nourse, Allsop (manager). Centre: Blanckenberg, Commaille, Taylor (captain), Pegler, Ward. Front: Catterall, Carter, Hearne, Meintjes.

1924: 6th South Africans

1st Match: v Leicestershire (Leicester)   May 3, 5, 6.
South Africans 153 (H. W. Taylor 60*, W. E. Astill 5-70, G. Geary 4-38) and 167 (P. A. M. Hands 60, W. E. Astill 4-39, A. Skelding 4-43) drew with Leicestershire 90 (J. M. Blanckenberg 5-23) and 118-9 (E. P. Nupen 4-30).

2nd Match: v Derbyshire (Derby)   May 7, 8, 9.
South Africans 161-7 dec drew with Derbyshire 78-5.

3rd Match: v Surrey (Oval)   May 10, 12, 13.
Surrey 223 (P. G. H. Fender 107, S. J. Pegler 6-63) and 136-2 dec (J. B. Hobbs 79*) drew with South Africans 223 (A. W. Nourse 62, H. A. Peach 4-44) and 85-2.

4th Match: v Nottinghamshire (Trent Bridge)   May 14, 15, 16.
South Africans 186 (A. W. Nourse 52, F. Barratt 5-59) and 236 (A. W. Nourse 147*, S. J. Staples 5-78) lost to Nottinghamshire 185 (S. J. Pegler 5-47) and 238-7 (J. R. Gunn 89*, G. Gunn 58, S. J. Pegler 4-47) by 3 wkts.

5th Match: v Lancashire (Old Trafford)   May 17, 19, 20.
South Africans 60 (R. K. Tyldesley 7-28) and 155 (R. K. Tyldesley 5-50, C. H. Parkin 5-61) lost to Lancashire 293 (F. B. Watson 117, J. Sharp 55, S. J. Pegler 6-68) by an innings and 78 runs.

6th Match: v Gloucestershire (Bristol)   May 21, 22, 23.
South Africans 162 (A. W. Nourse 58, C. W. L. Parker 4-41) and 126-8 dec (M. J. Susskind 69*, P. T. Mills 4-54) drew with Gloucestershire 92 (J. M. Blanckenberg 4-29) and 19-1.

7th Match: v M.C.C. (Lord's)   May 24, 26, 27.
M.C.C. 145 (J. W. Hearne 59, S. J. Pegler 8-54) and 191-4 dec drew with South Africans 192 (J. W. H. T. Douglas 6-65) and 90-1 (H. W. Taylor 50*).

8th Match: v Scotland (Edinburgh)   May 29, 30.
Scotland 177 (C. P. Carter 5-51) and 163-4 dec (J. Kerr 80) drew with South Africans 186 and 59-2.*

9th Match: v Scotland (Glasgow)   May 31, June 2.
Scotland 36 (C. D. Dixon 4-14, D. J. Meintjes 4-19) and 67 (C. D. Dixon 6-39) lost to South Africans 389-5 dec (H. G. Deane 80*, R. H. Catterall 72, G. F. Hearne 63*, J. M. M. Commaille 52) by an innings and 286 runs.

10th Match: v Yorkshire (Bramall Lane)   June 4, 5, 6.
Yorkshire 236 (E. Oldroyd 67, W. Rhodes 52, J. M. Blanckenberg 4-58) and 142-3 dec (H. Sutcliffe 67*) drew with South Africans 111 (R. Kilner 4-30, G. G. Macaulay 4-47) and 141-6 (M. J. Susskind 60*).

11th Match: v Cambridge University (Cambridge)   June 7, 9, 10.
South Africans 334 (A. W. Nourse 144, R. J. O. Meyer 4-134) and 179 (R. J. O. Meyer 5-79) beat Cambridge University 191 (T. C. Lowry 67) and 197 (A. H. White 53*, C. P. Carter 5-64) by 125 runs.

12th Match: v Oxford University (Oxford)   June 11, 12, 13.
Oxford University 117-9 (G. M. Parker 4-34) drew with South Africans did not bat.

13th Match: v England (Edgbaston)   June 14, 16, 17.
England 438 (J. B. Hobs 76, E. H. Hendren 74, H. Sutcliffe 64, F. E. Woolley 64, R. Kilner 59, G. M. Parker 6-152) beat South Africans 30 (A. E. R. Gilligan 6-7, M. W. Tate 4-12) and 390 (R. H. Catterall 120, J. M. Blanckenberg 56, M. J. Susskind 51, A. E. R. Gilligan 5-83, M. W. Tate 4-103) by an innings and 18 runs.

14th Match: v Essex (Colchester)   June 18, 19, 20.
Essex 155 (S. J. Pegler 4-34) and 345-9 dec (C. A. G. Russell 108, J. O'Connor 51, F. W. H. Nicholas 50, C. P. Carter 5-70) lost to South Africans 263 (H. W. Taylor 126, G. M. Louden 6-71) and 239-9 (P. A. M. Hands 64, G. M. Louden 4-82) by 1 wkt.

15th Match: v Hampshire (Southampton)   June 21, 23, 24.
Hampshire 279 (H. L. V. Day 100, J. Newman 58, J. M. Blanckenberg 6-121) and 330 (J. Newman 60, G. Brown 59, R St L. Fowler 50, G. F. Bissett 5-102) lost to South Africa 336 (A. W. Nourse 121, J. M. Blanckenberg 69, J. M. M. Commaille 62, J. Newman 4-118) and 275-5 (H. W. Taylor 93) by 5 wkts.

16th Match: v H. D. G. Leveson-Gower's XI (Reigate)   June 25, 26, 27.
South Africans 253 (H. W. Taylor 81, W. Rhodes 6-56) and 171 (A. G. Doggart 5-58, W. Rhodes 4-39) lost to H. D. G. Leveson-Gower's XI 230 (J. M. Blanckenberg 5-53) and 196-7 (M. Leyland 53) by 3 wkts.

17th Match: v England (Lord's)   June 28, 30, July 1.
South Africa 273 (R. H. Catterall 120, M. J. Susskind 64) and 240 (M. J. Susskind 53) lost to England 531-2 dec (J. B. Hobbs 211, F. E. Woolley 134*, H. Sutcliffe 122, E. H. Hendren 50*) by an innings and 18 runs.

18th Match: v Yorkshire (Bradford)   July 2, 3, 4.
Yorkshire 285 (E. Robinson 95*, W. Rhodes 54) and 147-4 dec drew with South Africans 279 (H. W. Taylor 79, A. W. Nourse 68, G. G. Macaulay 6-66) and 64-3.

19th Match: v Northamptonshire (Northampton)   July 5, 7.
Northamptonshire 157 (V. W. C. Jupp 84, J. M. Blanckenberg 7-57) and 87 (S. J. Pegler 6-22) lost to South Africans 380 (H. W. Taylor 113, A. W. Nourse 62, E. P. Nuen 57, S. J. Pegler 50*, A. E. Thomas 8-96) by an innings and 136 runs.

20th Match: v Warwickshire (Edgbaston)   July 9, 10, 11.
South Africans 317 (H. W. Taylor 94, G. A. Jennings 5-92) and 384-8 (H. W. Taylor 116, J. M. M. Commaille 69) drew with Warwickshire 440 (F. R. Santall 102, F. S. G. Calthorpe 76, L. A. Bates 76).

21st Match: v England (Headingley)   July 12, 14, 15.
England 396 (E. H. Hendren 132, H. Sutcliffe 83, S. J. Pegler 4-116) and 60-1 beat South Africa 132 (H. W. Taylor 59, M. W. Tate 6-42) and 323 (H. W. Taylor 56, R. H. Catterall 56) by 9 wkts.

22nd Match: v Lancashire (Liverpool)   July 16, 17, 18.
Lancashire 445-6 dec (C. Hallows 124, J. L. Hopwood 105*, L. Green 79, F. B. Watson 63, J. M. Blanckenberg 4-94) drew with South Africans 259-3 (A. W. Nourse 103*, J. M. M. Commaille 85).

23rd Match: v Middlesex (Lord's)   July 19, 21, 22.
Middlesex 328 (J. W. Hearne 85, G. T. S. Stevens 81, H. L. Dales 51, J. M. Blanckenberg 5-79) drew with South Africans 139-2.

24th Match: v Durham (Sunderland)   July 23, 24.
Durham 195 (C. P. Carter 5-76) and 12-0 drew with South Africans 173 (T. K. Dobson 4-49).

25th Match: v England (Old Trafford)   July 26, 28, 29.
South Africa 116-4 (T. A. Ward 50) drew with England did not bat.

26th Match: v Sussex (Hove)   July 30, 31, Aug 1.
South Africans 337 (A. W. Nourse 73, P. A. M. Hands 58*) and 217-4 dec (M. J. Susskind 88) drew with Sussex 334 (E. H. Bowley 106, R. A. Young 53, J. M. Blanckenberg 5-102) and 96-6.

27th Match: v Glamorgan (Cardiff)   Aug 2, 4, 5.
Glamorgan 178 (J. M. Blanckenberg 8-97) drew with South Africans 15-1.

28th Match: v Surrey Oval)   Aug 6, 7, 8.
Surrey 300 (T. Shepherd 127, P. G. H. Fender 56, A. Sandham 51) and 203-4 (D. J. Knight 68) drew with South Africans 418 (M. J. Susskind 137, R. H. Catterall 63, S. Fenley 6-148).

29th Match: v Combined Services (Portsmouth)   Aug 9, 11, 12.
South Africans 182 (G. F. Hearne 68, H. W. Taylor 62, T. O. Jameson 4-33) and 420 (R. H. Catterall 137, H. W. Taylor 118, T. O. Jameson 7-152) drew with Combined Services 418 (G. J. Bryan 229, C. H. B. Blount 61, J. M. Blanckenberg 4-92) and 88-2.

30th Match: v Harlequins (Eastbourne)   Aug 13, 14.
Harlequins 73 (J. M. Blanckenberg 5-34, S. J. Pegler 5-34) and 213 (C. P. Carter 6-40) lost to South Africans 162 (H. W. Taylor 67, R. H. B. Bettington 7-52) and 125-4 (J. M. M. Commaille 68) by 6 wkts.

31st Match: v England (Oval)   Aug 16, 18, 19.
South Africa 342 (R. H. Catterall 95, M. J. Susskind 65) drew with England 421-8 (E. H. Hendren 142, F. E. Woolley 51, M. W. Tate 50).

32nd Match: v Minor Counties (Norwich)   Aug 20, 21, 22.
Minor Counties 196 (S. J. Pegler 5-46, D. J. Meintjes 4-104) and 272 (C. H. Titchmarsh 80, A. P. F. Chapman 68, J. M. Blanckenberg 4-56) beat South Africans 149 (R. J. O. Meyer 6-60) and 294 (A. W. Nourse 91, M. Falcon 5-103, W. A. Beadsmoore 4-53) by 25 runs.

33rd Match: v Kent (Canterbury)   Aug 23, 25.
Kent 418-6 dec (F. E. Woolley 176, H. T. W. Hardinge 118, C. H. Knott 63) beat South Africans 135 (C. Wright 5-39) and 194 (J. M. Blanckenberg 51*, A. P. Freeman 6-68) by an innings and 89 runs.

34th Match: v Somerset (Taunton)   Aug 27, 28.
Somerset 208 (J. C. W. MacBryan 59, J. M. Blanckenberg 6-76) and 138 (C. P. Carter 6-50) lost to South Africans 268 (R. H. Catterall 90, J. J. Bridges 6-61) and 79-1 by 9 wkts.

35th Match: v Worcestershire (Worcester)   Aug 30, Sept 1.
Worcestershire 87 (J. M. Blanckenberg 6-40, S. J. Pegler 4-41) and 161 lost to South Africans 276 (A. W. Nourse 90, C. F. Root 5-83) by an innings and 28 runs.

36th Match: v South of England (Hastings)   Sept 3, 4, 5.
South of England 312-9 dec (F. S. G. Calthorpe 127, J. B. Hobbs 56) and 218-8 dec (F. S. G. Calthorpe 52) drew with South Africans 269 (A. W. Nourse 69, T. A. Ward 68, R. R. Relf 4-24, F. E. Woolley 4-66) and 219-7 (M. J. Susskind 101).

37th Match: v North Wales (Llandudno)   Sept 8, 9.
North Wales 49 (J. M. Blanckenberg 6-12) drew with South Africans 111-7 (S. F. Barnes 5-32).

38th Match: v C. I. Thornton's XI (Scarborough)   Sept 10, 11, 12.
South Africans 143 (G. O. B. Allen 7-61) and 273 (A. W. Nourse 84) lost to C. I. Thornton's XI 461-6 dec (P. Holmes 202*, E. H. Hendren 101, W. Rhodes 56).

Bradford League professional, was brought in and was the best bowler in the opening Test, when he was bowled until he dropped. South Africa lost the Test by an innings. Parker was retained for the Second Test and G. A. Faulkner was brought out of retirement to aid the South Africans. The Second Test was lost by an innings, England losing only two wickets in making 531. The tourists did without Parker and Faulkner for the Third Test, but still lost by 9 wickets. Rain ruined the last two Tests.

The failure of the side was blamed on the matting wickets of South Africa. The lesson learnt from the visit was that South Africa had to switch to turf wickets to succeed in England.

The bowlers failed to adapt to turf. Even Blanckenberg, whose figures look impressive, could do nothing in the Tests and Nupen was also ineffectual. The young fast bowler Bissett injured his foot and was unable to play for half the tour, but even if he had been fit, it was doubtful if he would have made any material difference to the attack. The batting was reasonably successful: Taylor was occasionally brilliant but failed in the Tests whereas Catterall looked very ordinary, especially at the start of an innings, but returned an excellent Test record. Nourse was consistent except in the Tests, Susskind had an awkward style and Commaille was useful. The fielding was just ordinary, though Ward was praised for his wicketkeeping.

Despite their poor record and the wet weather, the team returned home aboard s.s. *Armadale Castle* on 26 September with a small profit.

1926: 16th Australians

The Australian selectors were severely criticised for picking the first dozen players for the tour as early as December 1925, so that whatever the form showed in the main matches of the 1925-26 season, there were only places for three or four other players. The chosen team was H. L. Collins (captain), T. J. E. Andrews, W. Bardsley, S. C. Everett, J. M. Gregory, A. A. Mailey, C. G. Macartney, W. A. S. Oldfield and J. M. Taylor of New South Wales; C. V. Grimmett and A. J. Richardson of South Australia; J. L. Ellis, H. S. T. L. Hendry, W. H. Ponsford, J. Ryder and W. M. Woodfull of Victoria. The two most notable omissions were C. Kelleway and A. F. Kippax. The manager was Sydney Smith.

The pre-season comments on the team were that the batting was strong, but the bowling, lacking as it did McDonald and Armstrong, relied too much on Gregory and Grimmett. The first 12 match results bore out this opinion: only two were won and ten drawn. The wet weather played its part, but it was obvious that the Australians were having difficulty dismissing the opposition. The pattern continued through the five-match Test series. The

---

1926: 16th Australians

1st Match: v Minor Counties (Maidenhead) April 28, 29.
Australians 179 (M. Falcon 7-42) drew with Minor Counties 115-4.

2nd Match: v Leicestershire (Leicester) May 1, 3, 4.
Australians 336 (J. M. Gregory 120*, W. H. Ponsford 56, A. Skelding 5-97) drew with Leicestershire 96 (C. G. Macartney 5-9) and 15-1.

3rd Match: v Essex (Leyton) May 5, 6, 7.
Australians 538-9 dec (W. M. Woodfull 201, C. G. Macartney 148, H. S. T. L. Hendry 71, A. B. Hipkin 5-102) drew with Essex 5-2.

4th Match: v Surrey (Oval) May 8, 10, 11.
Australians 395-9 dec (W. M. Woodfull 118, J. M. Taylor 76, H. S. T. L. Hendry 68, C. G. Macartney 53, J. H. Lockton 4-105) and 74-2 drew with Surrey 265 (A. Sandham 84, C. G. Macartney 6-63).

5th Match: v Hampshire (Southampton) May 12, 13, 14.
Australians 371 (J. M. Gregory 130*, J. M. Taylor 73, A. S. Kennedy 5-98) and 33-0 beat Hampshire 152 (A. A. Mailey 6-45) and 248 (G. Brown 78, A. A. Mailey 5-86, C. G. Macartney 4-57) by 10 wkts.

6th Match: v M.C.C. (Lord's) May 15, 17, 18.
M.C.C. 199 (G. T. S. Stevens 77, A. P. F. Chapman 51, A. J. Richardson 6-85) and 83-5 drew with Australians 383-9 dec (W. H. Ponsford 110*, C. G. Macartney 61, A. J. Richardson 50*, N. E. Haig 6-102).

7th Match: v Cambridge University (Cambridge) May 19, 20, 21.
Cambridge University 212 (H. J. Enthoven 93, E. W. Dawson 69, J. Ryder 6-74) and 81 (C. V. Grimmett 6-28, C. G. Macartney 4-21) drew with Australians 235 (W. M. Woodfull 98*, R. J. O. Meyer 6-655 and 17-2.

8th Match: v Oxford University (Oxford) May 22, 24, 25.
Oxford University 131 (A. J. Richardson 6-28) and 177 (C. H. Taylor 59, A. J. Richardson 5-36) lost to Australians 321 (T. J. E. Andrews 50) by an innings and 13 runs.

9th Match: v South of England (Bristol) May 26, 27, 28.
South of England 211 (A. P. F. Chapman 89, E. H. Hendren 62, C. G. Macartney 4-41) drew with Australians 328-6 (J. Ryder 108*, T. J. E. Andrews 74*, W. M. Woodfull 69).

10th Match: v Middlesex (Lord's) May 29, 31, June 1.
Australians 489 (T. J. E. Andrews 164, H. L. Collins 99, W. Bardsley 70, G. O. B. Allen 5-63) and 239-5 (W. M. Woodfull 100) drew with Middlesex 349 (G. T. S. Stevens 149, J. W. Hearne 59, H. R. Murrell 54, J. M. Taylor 4-73).

11th Match: v North of England (Edgbaston) June 2, 3, 4.
North of England 239 and 77-1 dec drew with Australians 105 (C. F. Root 7-42) and 110-3 (T. J. E. Andrews 68*).

12th Match: v Yorkshire (Bradford) June 5, 7, 8.
Australians 177 (G. H. Crawford 4-38) and 243-3 dec (T. J. E. Andrews 78, H. L. Collins 77*) drew with Yorkshire 155 (C. V. Grimmett 6-87) and 25-0.

13th Match: v Durham (Sunderland) June 9, 10.
Durham 125 (A. A. Mailey 8-52) and 116 (C. G. Macartney 5-22, C. V. Grimmett 4-50) lost to Australians 322-3 dec (T. J. E. Andrews 122, H. L. Collins 69, W. Bardsley 63) by an innings and 81 runs.*

14th Match: v England (Trent Bridge) June 12, 14, 15.
England 32-0 drew with Australia did not bat.

15th Match: v Yorkshire (Bramall Lane) June 16, 17, 18.
Australians 148-6 (C. G. Macartney 54) drew with Yorkshire did not bat.

16th Match: v Lancashire (Old Trafford) June 19, 21, 22.
Lancashire 149 (C. Hallows 85, A. A. Mailey 7-74) and 148 (C. G. Macartney 4-15, A. A. Mailey 4-91) lost to Australians 374 (C. G. Macartney 160, A. J. Richardson 63) by an innings and 77 runs.

17th Match: v Derbyshire (Chesterfield) June 23, 24.
Australians 373-5 dec (W. Bardsley 127, H. L. Collins 93, A. J. Richardson 58, W. M. Woodfull 53*) drew with Derbyshire 146 (C. V. Grimmett 4-53) and 55-2.

18th Match: v England (Lord's) June 26, 28, 29.
Australia 383 (W. Bardsley 193*, R. Kilner 4-70) and 194-5 (C. G. Macartney 133*) drew with England 475-3 dec (E. H. Hendren 127*, J. B. Hobbs 119, F. E. Woolley 87, H. Sutcliffe 82, A. P. F. Chapman 50*).

19th Match: v Northamptonshire (Northampton) June 30, July 1, 2.
Australians 397 (W. Bardsley 112, J. Ryder 84) beat Northamptonshire 125 (A. A. Mailey 5-29) and 125 (C. V. Grimmett 5-18, A. A. Mailey 5-58) by an innings and 147 runs.

20th Match: v Nottinghamshire (Trent Bridge) July 3, 5, 6.
Nottinghamshire 193 (W. A. Flint 79, A. A. Mailey 7-110) and 139 (A. A. Mailey 8-83) lost to Australians 468 (W. M. Woodfull 102*, T. J. E. Andrews 91, C. G. Macartney 81, W. Bardsley 87) by an innings and 136 runs.

21st Match: v Worcestershire (Worcester) July 7, 8.
Australians 197 (C. F. Root 4-61) and 182-4 dec (W. Bardsley 55, A. J. Richardson 51*) beat Worcestershire 120 (M. K. Foster 62, C. G. Macartney 5-38, C. V. Grimmett 4-2) and 83 (A. A. Mailey 4-20, C. V. Grimmett 4-31) by 176 runs.

22nd Match: v England (Headingley) July 10, 12, 13.
Australians 494 (C. G. Macartney 151, W. M. Woodfull 141, A. J. Richardson 100, M. W. Tate 4-99) drew with England 294 (G. G. Macaulay 76, C. V. Grimmett 5-88) and 254-3 (H. Sutcliffe 94, J. B. Hobbs 88).

23rd Match: v Lancashire (Liverpool) July 14, 15, 16.
Australians 468-6 dec (W. Bardsley 155, T. J. E. Andrews 95, W. M. Woodfull 65, W. H. Ponsford 50, E. A. McDonald 5-135) drew with Lancashire 235 (J. W. H. Makepeace 70, C. Hallows 59, A. A. Mailey 9-86) and 274-9 (J. W. H. Makepeace 76, J. Iddon 57, T. J. E. Andrews 6-109).

24th Match: v West of Scotland (Glasgow) July 17, 18.
West of Scotland 163 (A. J. Richardson 4-31) and 146 (S. C. Everett 4-54) lost to Australians 368-6 dec (W. H. Ponsford 109, C. G. Macartney 106) by an innings and 61 runs.

25th Match: v Eastern Districts (Perth) July 20.
Eastern Districts 120 (A. J. Richardson 4-23) lost to Australians 206-6 (J. M. Taylor 53, T. J. E. Andrews 65) by 6 wkts (Australians batted on).

26th Match: v Scotland (Edinburgh) July 21, 22.
Scotland 94 (C. V. Grimmett 7-42) and 106-4 (C. Groves 50) drew with Australians 563 (J. Ryder 105, W. M. Woodfull 94, J. M. Gregory 87, W. Bardsley 71, W. A. S. Oldfield 62).*

27th Match: v England (Old Trafford) July 24, 26, 27.
Australia 335 (W. M. Woodfull 117, C. G. Macartney 109, C. F. Root 4-84) drew with England 305-5 (G. E. Tyldesley 81, J. B. Hobbs 74, F. E. Woolley 58).

28th Match: v Surrey (Oval) July 28, 29, 30.
Australians 432-9 dec (W. M. Woodfull 156, J. Ryder 104, H. A. Peach 4-81) drew with Surrey 82-6 (C. V. Grimmett 4-30).

29th Match: v Glamorgan (Swansea) July 31, Aug 2, 3.
Australians 283 (W. H. Ponsford 143*, J. Mercer 5-74) and 200-5 dec beat Glamorgan 139 (A. A. Mailey 5-40, C. V. Grimmett 4-56) and 120 (C. V. Grimmett 4-45, A. A. Mailey 4-58) by 224 runs.

30th Match: v Warwickshire (Edgbaston) Aug 4, 5, 6.
Australians 464 (W. H. Ponsford 144, H. S. T. L. Hendry 52*, W. M. Woodfull 51, W. Quaife 4-118) drew with Warwickshire 363-9 (J. H. Parsons 80, J. M. Gregory 4-80, A. A. Mailey 4-131).

31st Match: v Gloucestershire (Cheltenham) Aug 7, 9.
Gloucestershire 144 (C. V. Grimmett 7-67) and 178 (C. V. Grimmett 4-59, A. A. Mailey 4-61) lost to Australians 287 (J. M. Taylor 95, T. J. E. Andrews 62) and 39-1 by 9 wkts.

32nd Match: v XV of Public Schools (Lord's) Aug 11, 12.
Australians 264 (W. H. Ponsford 97, W. M. Woodfull 84, W. D. S. May 6-53) drew with XV of Public Schools 114 (J. Ryder 4-9) and 105-2 (C. J. Wilson 57).*

33rd Match: v England (Oval) Aug 14, 16, 17, 18.
England 280 (H. Sutcliffe 76, A. A. Mailey 6-138) and 436 (H. Sutcliffe 161, J. B. Hobbs 100) beat Australia 302 (J. M. Gregory 73, H. L. Collins 61) and 125 (W. Rhodes 4-44) by 289 runs.

34th Match: v Somerset (Taunton) Aug 21, 23, 24.
Australians 225 (S. C. Everett 59, R. C. Robertson-Glasgow 5-78) and 229-4 dec (J. M. Taylor 75, H. L. Collins 60) beat Somerset 153 (C. V. Grimmett 5-64, A. J. Richardson 4-18) and 245 (M. D. Lyon 136) by 56 runs.

35th Match: v Kent (Canterbury) Aug 25, 26, 27.
Kent 321 (F. E. Woolley 64, J. L. Bryan 61, H. T. W. Hardinge 52, A. A. Mailey 5-133) and 219-9 dec (F. E. Woolley 88, C. H. Knott 50, J. M. Gregory 4-53) drew with Australians 386 (J. Ryder 109, H. L. Collins 86, T. J. E. Andrews 71, A. P. Freeman 6-133) and 72-4.

36th Match: v Sussex (Hove) Aug 28, 30, 31.
Australians 317 (W. Bardsley 118*, T. J. E. Andrews 70, W. M. Woodfull 52, A. E. R. Gilligan 4-67) and 153-4 dec (C. G. Macartney 65) drew with Sussex 240 (E. H. Bowley 69, C. V. Grimmett 4-63, A. A. Mailey 4-103) and 157-5 (H. W. Tate 55, C. V. Grimmett 4-42).

37th Match: v An England XI (Folkestone) Sept 1, 2, 3.
Australians 274 (H. S. T. L. Hendry 81, W. Bardsley 55, H. Larwood 7-95) drew with An England XI 199-9.

38th Match: v Civil Service (Chiswick) Sept 4, 6, 7.
Australians 454-7 dec (J. M. Taylor 201, S. C. Everett 100) drew with Civil Service 59 (H. L. Collins 6-17) and 93-3.*

39th Match: v C. I. Thornton's XI (Scarborough) Sept 8, 9, 10.
C. I. Thornton's XI 244 (J. B. Hobbs 84, P. Holmes 50, C. V. Grimmett 5-68, A. A. Mailey 4-53) and 79-3 drew with Australians 194 (V. W. C. Jupp 5-59, W. Rhodes 5-63).

40th Match: v An England XI (Blackpool) Sept 11, 13, 14.
Australians 281 (W. M. Woodfull 116, C. W. L. Parker 5-76) and 201-4 (C. G. Macartney 100*) drew with An England XI 191 (A. A. Mailey 5-58).

1926: 16th Australians

Batting Averages

	M	I	NO	R	HS	Avge	100	c/s
W. M. Woodfull	27	34	5	1672	201	57.65	8	17
C. G. Macartney	27	33	4	1561	160	53.82	6	4
W. Bardsley	27	33	3	1424	193*	47.46	5	8
W. H. Ponsford	21	26	4	901	144	40.95	3	8
H. S. T. L. Hendry	7	9	1	315	81	39.37	0	3
T. J. E. Andrews	28	37	5	1234	164	38.56	1	24
J. M. Gregory	26	30	6	843	130*	35.12	2	25
J. Ryder	28	35	7	966	109	34.50	3	8
A. J. Richardson	25	30	8	728	100	33.09	1	8
J. L. Ellis	13	15	5	322	43	32.20	0	21/23
H. L. Collins	22	27	1	779	99	29.96	0	11
J. M. Taylor	27	36	2	760	95	22.35	0	6
W. A. S. Oldfield	21	21	5	303	43*	18.93	0	21/19
C. V. Grimmett	24	21	2	263	41	13.84	0	17
S. C. Everett	13	10	1	116	59	12.88	0	8
A. A. Mailey	27	23	6	117	21	6.88	0	16

Bowling Averages

	O	M	R	W	Avge	BB	5i
C. V. Grimmett	834.3	251	1857	105	17.68	7-67	7
C. G. Macartney	559.3	242	873	49	17.81	6-63	3
A. A. Mailey	816	153	2437	126	19.34	9-86	12
A. J. Richardson	573.5	234	966	49	19.71	6-28	3
H. L. Collins	71	21	169	6	28.16	3-39	0
J. M. Gregory	423.4	77	1158	36	32.16	4-73	0
S. C. Everett	197.3	35	557	17	32.76	3-75	0
T. J. E. Andrews	80	16	240	7	34.28	6-109	1
J. Ryder	363	91	847	23	36.82	6-74	1
H. S. T. L. Hendry	49	12	117	1	117.00	1-8	0

first four were drawn, partly due to the weather, and then England won the Fifth to regain the Ashes after an interval of five years.

The team's record looked very good, with just a single defeat in 40 matches, but with all interest hinging on the Test series and that being lost, the tour could be regarded as a comparative failure.

Gregory, with a leg injury, was never able to bowl with his old fire and his figures were most disappointing. Everett, chosen at the last moment as Gregory's partner, was also injured and did not make the Test team. Richardson and Macartney both bowled usefully, though the main attack fell to Mailey and Grimmett. The latter based his skill on extreme accuracy and managed to keep even the best batsmen quiet. Mailey's leg-breaks and googlies could occasionally be expensive; this failing was more than compensated for by the days on which he was nearly unplayable and he ended with an excellent record. The batting was quite up to the best Australian standards: Macartney played superbly; Woodfull had great patience; Bardsley started feebly, then ran into fine form; only Ponsford disappointed, though he had some good innings. The fielding was not as good as in 1921 and more catches were dropped than usual. Oldfield looked worthy of his most illustrious predecessors behind the stumps.

The team boarded the s.s. *Montrose* at Liverpool for the journey across the Atlantic, arriving in Quebec on 8 October and after crossing Canada travelled in the m.s. *Aorangi* from Vancouver, via Honolulu, Suva and Auckland to Sydney, where they landed on 13 November.

1927: 1st New Zealanders

The team on this inaugural tour of England was chosen by three selectors, W. S. Brice, W. R. Patrick and F. Williams. The 14 players were T. C. Lowry (captain), E. H. L. Bernau, C. S. Dempster, M. Hendeson, K. C. James and H. M. McGirr, all of Wellington; C. F. W. Allcott, C. C. R. Dacre and J. E. Mills of Auckland; R. C. Blunt of Otago; W. H. R. Cunningham, W. E. Merritt, C. J. Oliver and M. L. Page from Canterbury. The manager was T. D. B. Hay. The two most notable omissions were J. S. Hiddleston, who could not spare the time from his business and F. T. Badcock, who withdrew at the last moment and was replaced by Bernau.

1927: 1st New Zealanders

Batting Averages

	M	I	NO	R	HS	Avge	100	c/s
C. S. Dempster	24	37	5	1430	180	44.68	3	20
R. C. Blunt	25	38	3	1540	131	44.00	2	14
T. C. Lowry	25	37	4	1277	106	38.69	4	20/5
J. E. Mills	24	39	6	1251	152	37.90	4	10
M. L. Page	25	36	3	1154	140*	34.96	2	28
C. C. R. Dacre	23	34	0	1070	176	31.47	2	11/1
C. F. W. Allcott	20	27	5	646	131	29.36	2	14
W. E. Merritt	25	33	13	538	50*	26.90	0	8
H. M. McGirr	22	31	1	737	73	24.56	0	8
K. C. James	23	31	5	411	44	15.80	0	34/31
C. J. Oliver	10	17	3	213	36	15.21	0	5
W. H. R. Cunningham	7	8	3	62	23	12.40	0	3
E. H. L. Bernau	16	20	2	203	34*	11.27	0	4
M. Henderson	14	14	5	98	30	10.88	0	5

Also batted in 1 match: E. D. Blundell 0* and 3; R. H. Fox 4 (ct1); T. D. B. Hay 2* (ct1).

Bowling Averages

	O	M	R	W	Avge	BB	5i
C. C. Dacre	50	13	133	8	16.62	5-35	1
C. S. Dempster	31	4	104	6	17.33	2-4	0
M. L. Page	182.1	52	498	23	21.65	4-10	0
W. E. Merritt	768.2	114	2530	107	23.64	6-38	5
M. Henderson	273.5	64	799	33	24.21	5-27	2
E. H. L. Bernau	276.5	55	775	32	24.21	6-35	1
C. F. W. Allcott	391.4	118	840	34	24.70	5-3	2
R. C. Blunt	610.5	100	1948	78	24.97	7-109	1
H. M. McGirr	483	117	1356	49	27.67	6-77	2
T. C. Lowry	173.2	30	450	15	30.00	3-13	0
W. Cunningham	75	13	265	5	53.00	3-34	0

Also bowled: J. E. Mills 4-0-12-1; C. Oliver 35-8-84-1; E. D. Blundell 15-2-38-0.

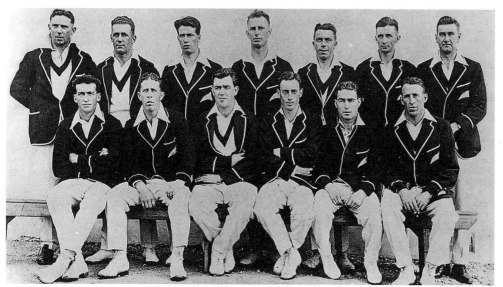

The first New Zealanders to tour in 1927 had a successful visit, improving as the summer progressed. Back: Cunningham, Oliver, Merritt, Henderson, James, Mills, Allcott. Front: Page, Dacre, Lowry (captain), Blunt, Dempster, McGirr. When the photograph was taken Bernau was absent.

1927: 1st New Zealanders

1st Match: v H. M. Martineau's XI (Holyport, Maidenhead) May 9, 10.
New Zealanders 586-9 dec (J. E. Mills 188, R. C. Blunt 119, C. C. R. Dacre 101) drew with H. M. Martineau's XI 256 (W. A. C. Wilkinson 101, E. H. L. Bernau 4-59, W. E. Merritt 4-33) and 163-6 (A. R. Tanner 72).

2nd Match: v M.C.C. (Lord's) May 11, 12, 13.
M.C.C. 392 (C. H. Titchmarsh 171, W. E. Merritt 4-104) and 426-4 dec (M. D. Lyon 110, G. O. B. Allen 104*, H. Ashton 88, C. H. Titchmarsh 71) drew with New Zealanders 460 (C. C. Dacre 107, T. C. Lowry 106, H. M. McGirr 58*, R. C. Blunt 52, G. O. B. Allen 7-120) and 224-4 (T. C. Lowry 63*, R. C. Blunt 51).

3rd Match: v Essex (Leyton) May 14, 16, 17.
New Zealanders 289 (J. E. Mills 64, T. C. Lowry 61, J. O'Connor 5-68) and 208 (C. S. Dempster 79, L. C. Eastman 5-31, J. O'Connor 5-92) lost to Essex 373 (C. A. G. Russell 76, J. O'Connor 65, M. S. Nichols 61, H. Ashton 52, H. M. McGirr 6-77) and 125-5 (R. C. Blunt 4-29) by 5 wkts.

4th Match: v Cambridge University (Cambridge) May 18, 19, 20.
New Zealanders 315 (M. L. Page 134, T. C. Longfield 4-71) and 205 (R. C. Blunt 72, T. C. Longfield 4-55) lost to Cambridge University 255 (F. J. Seabrook 106, E. W. Dawson 57, W. E. Merritt 4-77) and 267-5 (E. W. Dawson 107) by 5 wkts.

5th Match: v Middlesex (Lord's) May 21, 23, 24.
New Zealanders 234 (F. J. Durston 4-42) and 335 (H. M. McGirr 72, M. L. Page 65, C. C. R. Dacre 53, G. T. S. Stevens 5-103) lost to Middlesex 290 (E. H. Hendren 68, C. D. Gray 65, G. O. B. Allen 64) and 280-7 (G. T. S. Stevens 89, J. W. Hearne 73*) by 3 wkts.

6th Match: v Royal Navy (Portsmouth) May 25, 26, 27.
Royal Navy 144 (E. L. D. Bartley 66, R. C. Blunt 4-24) and 275 (G. S. Tuck 125, R. L. B. Cunliffe 54) drew with New Zealanders 194 (R. C. Blunt 61, C. S. Dempster 50, A. S. Cantrell 6-58) and 164-2 (J. E. Mills 76*, R. C. Blunt 76).

7th Match: v Sussex (Hove) May 28, 30, 31.
Sussex 316 (A. E. R. Gilligan 86, J. H. Parks 63, W. E. Merritt 6-92) and 191 (R. C. Blunt 4-36) lost to New Zealanders 466 (T. C. Lowry 105, R. C. Blunt 67, C. S. Dempster 57, M. L. Page 63) and 43-2 by 8 wkts.

8th Match: v Club Cricket Conference (Ealing) June 2, 3.
Club Cricket Conference 204 (R. N. Hunt 100, H. M. McGirr 5-71) and 252-6 dec (L. W. Newman 133) drew with New Zealanders 213 (K. C. James 54, W. E. Hazelton 8-83) and 183-5 (C. S. Dempster 109*).

9th Match: v Oxford University (Oxford) June 4, 6, 7.
Oxford University 337 (E. R. T. Holmes 165) and 229 (A. M. Crawley 72, M. L. Page 4-10) drew with New Zealanders 263 (J. E. Mills 54, J. W. Greenstock 5-91) and 214-6 (T. C. Lowry 69).

10th Match: v Worcestershire (Worcester) June 8, 9, 10.
New Zealanders 276 (C. C. R. Dacre 82, T. C. Lowry 74, C. V. Tarbox 6-88) and 349-5 dec (M. L. Page 140*, T. C. Lowry 106) beat Worcestershire 222 (W. V. Fox 79, W. E. Merritt 4-83) and 209 (W. V. Fox 79, H. M. McGirr 4-62, W. E. Merritt 4-75) by 194 runs.

11th Match: v Northamptonshire (Kettering) June 11, 13, 14.
Northamptonshire 237 (A. C. L. Wills 68, J. E. Timms 55, R. C. Blunt 7-109) and 260 (W. E. Merritt 4-63) beat New Zealanders 251 (R. C. Blunt 50, V. W. C. Jupp 7-92) and 164 by 82 runs.

12th Match: v Leicestershire (Leicester) June 15, 16, 17.
New Zealanders 371 (C. C. Dacre 90, M. L. Page 74, H. M. McGirr 56, H. C. Snary 5-66) and 165 (M. L. Page 65) drew with Leicestershire 242 (A. Shipman 62, M. Henderson 5-76).

13th Match: v Durham (Chester-le-Street) June 18, 20.
New Zealanders 373 (C. S. Dempster 178, M. L. Page 57, J. Cook 4-96) and 5-0 beat Durham 254 (J. Cook 106*, H. Brooks 77, M. Henderson 5-66) and 123 (M. Nichol 56, W. H. R. Cunningham 4-25) by 10 wkts.

14th Match: v Northumberland (Newcastle) June 22, 23.
New Zealanders 476 (R. C. Blunt 195, T. C. Lowry 95, G. T. Milne 4-147) beat Northumberland 272 (H. B. Pritchard 103*, C. F. Stanger-Leathes 51, W. E. Merritt 4-100) and 201 (W. E. Merritt 4-46) by an innings and 3 runs.

15th Match: v Scotland (Glasgow) June 24, 25.
Scotland 233 (A. J. Stevenson 59, M. L. Page 6-76) drew with New Zealanders 90-2.

16th Match: v Scottish Counties (Broughty Ferry) June 27, 28.
New Zealanders 304 (C. S. Dempster 154, W. Anderson 5-52) and 103-8 dec (N. M. Hailey 4-31) drew with Scottish Counties 287 (J. Haigh 115, R. A. Wood 50, W. E. Merritt 7-74) and 72-4.

17th Match: v Edinburgh Clubs (Edinburgh) June 29, 30.
Edinburgh Clubs 199 (W. E. Merritt 5-22) and 246 (D. Mackessack 94*, H. F. T. Heath 50, W. H. R. Cunningham 4-44) lost to New Zealanders 406-7 dec (C. C. R. Dacre 167, J. E. Mills 75*, C. S. Dempster 65, A. M. Gordon 4-81) and 42-0 by 10 wkts.

18th Match: v South of Scotland (Galashiels) July 1.
South of Scotland 71 (T. C. Lowry 6-25, M. L. Page 4-12) and 70-7 lost to New Zealanders 127 (R. A. Anderson 6-30) by 56 runs (One day match).

19th Match: v Yorkshire (Bradford) July 2, 4, 5.
Yorkshire 377 (P. Holmes 175*, M. Leyland 118, C. C. R. Dacre 5-35) drew with New Zealanders 133-7 (W. Rhodes 4-29).

20th Match: v Nottinghamshire (Trent Bridge) July 6, 7, 8.
New Zealanders 277 (T. C. Lowry 74, M. L. Page 71) drew with Nottinghamshire 280-6 (W, W. Whysall 82, W. Walker 50, M. L. Page 4-68).

21st Match: v East of England (Wisbech) July 9, 11.
East of England 170 and 145 (H. M. McGirr 5-21) lost to New Zealanders 243 (C. C. R. Dacre 89, W. E. Hazelton 5-68) and 76-2 by 8 wkts.

22nd Match: v Civil Service (Chiswick) July 16, 18, 19.
Civil Service 256 (E. H. Bennett 73, W. L. T. Webb 59) and 150 (E. H. Bennett 60, M. Henderson 5-27, R. C. Blunt 4-45) lost to New Zealanders 421-7 dec (J. E. Mills 104*, C. F. W. Allcott 102*, R. C. Blunt 90) by an innings and 15 runs.

23rd Match: v Army (Folkestone) July 20, 21, 22.
New Zealanders 184 (W. E. Merritt 50*, H. P. Miles 5-74) drew with Army 179-5 (E. S. B. Williams 89).

24th Match: v Warwickshire (Edgbaston) July 23, 25, 26.
Warwickshire 235 (N. Kilner 85, H. M. McGirr 4-25) and 188-7 (N. Kilner 77, W. E. Merritt 4-26) drew with New Zealanders 492-6 dec (C. S. Dempster 180, C. F. W. Allcott 131).

25th Match: v West of England (Exeter) July 27, 28, 29.
New Zealanders 230-6 dec (C. S. Dempster 58, J. E. Mills 52*) drew with West of England 93 (W. E. Merritt 6-38).

26th Match: v Glamorgan (Cardiff) July 30, Aug 1, 2.
New Zealanders 345 (C. S. Dempster 167*, R. C. Blunt 89, J. Mercer 5-82) and 205-7 dec beat Glamorgan 145 (W. E. Bates 53, E. H. L. Bernau 6-35) and 199 (J. C. Clay 115*) by 206 runs.

27th Match: v Surrey (Oval) Aug 3, 4, 5.
New Zealanders 313 (J. E. Mills 103, M. L. Page 66, R. C. Blunt 54, H. A. Peach 4-78) and 371 (C. S. Dempster 101, M. L. Page 68, H. M. McGirr 66, A. C. T. Geary 4-79) drew with Surrey 377 (J. B. Hobbs 146, A. Sandham 66, R. C. Blunt 4-128) and 284-8 (A. Ducat 100, T. H. Barling 78*, A. Sandham 50, W. E. Merritt 5-103).

28th Match: v Somerset (Weston-super-Mare) Aug 6, 8.
New Zealanders 150 (W. T. Greswell 5-41) and 128 (J. C. White 8-28) beat Somerset 117 (E. H. L. Bernau 4-27) and 67 (C. F. W. Allott 5-3) by 94 runs.

29th Match: v Gloucestershire (Cheltenham) Aug 10, 11, 12.
Gloucestershire 148 and 130-3 (A. E. Dipper 57) drew with New Zealanders 415-9 dec (T. C. Lowry 101*, J. E. Mills 86, C. C. R. Dacre 64, M. L. Page 59, C. W. L. Parker 4-142, R. A. Sinfield 4-147).

30th Match: v Derbyshire (Derby) Aug 13, 15.
Derbyshire 129 (W. E. Merritt 6-63) and 172 (J. M. Hutchinson 53, W. E. Merritt 4-67) lost to New Zealanders 541-9 dec (C. C. R. Dacre 176, J. E. Mills 100*, C. S. Dempster 81, C. F. W. Allcott 62) by an innings and 240 runs.

31st Match: v Lancashire (Old Trafford) Aug 17, 18, 19.
Lancashire 229 (G. E. Tyldesley 124, R. C. Blunt 4-53) drew with New Zealanders 57-1.

32nd Match: v Cumberland (Whitehaven) Aug 20, 22.
Cumberland 154 (W. E. Merritt 5-30) and 130 (W. E. Merritt 5-49) lost to New Zealanders 302 (C. S. Dempster 72, R. C. Blunt 71, H. O. Walmsley 5-66) by an innings and 18 runs.

33rd Match: v Bedfordshire (Bedford) Aug 24, 25.
Bedfordshire 55-5 (W. E. Merritt 5-18) drew with New Zealanders did not bat.

34th Match: v Norfolk (Norwich) Aug 26, 27.
Norfolk 104 (W. E. Merritt 6-34) and 111 (J. E. Nichols 53, C. F. W. Allott 5-16) lost to New Zealanders 312 (C. C. R. Dacre 99, R. C. Blunt 96, R. C. Rought-Rought 5-102) by an innings and 97 runs.

35th Match: v Kent (Canterbury) Aug 31, Sept 1, 2.
Kent 405 (W. H. Ashdown 84, L. E. G. Ames 84, F. E. Woolley 68, J. C. Hubble 50, W. E. Merritt 6-185) and 263-8 dec (F. E. Woolley 125, H. M. McGirr 4-84) beat New Zealanders 293 (R. C. Blunt 103, J. E. Mills 65, A. P. Freeman 5-108) and 317 (H. M. McGirr 73, C. S. Dempster 54, C. Wright 4-94) by 58 runs.

36th Match: v Wales (Llandudno) Sept 3, 5, 6.
Wales 182 (J. T. Bell 52, C. F. W. Allott 5-46) and 183-9 dec (M. Henderson 4-29) drew with New Zealanders 130 (S. F. Barnes 4-47) and 124-2 (C. S. Dempster 70).

37th Match: v Cygnets (Llandudno) Sept 7, 8.
Cygnets 250-6 dec (C. F. Walters 76*, N. V. H. Riches 64) drew with New Zealanders 195 (C. C. Dacre 61, S. T. Jagger 5-59).

38th Match: v H. D. G. Leveson-Gower's XI (Scarborough) Sept 10, 12, 13.
New Zealanders 447 (J. E. Mills 152, R. C. Blunt 131) and 103-2 (R. C. Blunt 63*) drew with H. D. G. Leveson-Gower's XI 316 (F. W. Gilligan 71, E. W. Dawson 53, W. E. Merritt 4-95).

With a long programme including 26 first-class matches, the New Zealanders were set quite an undertaking for their first English tour, but they achieved as good a record as anyone expected, beating five of the first-class counties and the majority of their defeats were in the very early stages of the tour.

The outstanding feature of their play was attacking batsmanship. Dempster and Lowry stood out in this, but Blunt and Page also did well. Dacre was sometimes too impulsive, though magnificent when he came off. Mills looked very promising. The attack lacked a penetrative fast bowler and a military medium. Henderson, the fast left-armer, failed completely, and so did Cunningham. The two slow bowlers, Merritt and Blunt, were best, but both could be wayward in length. Bernau and Allott were of occasional use. James kept wicket well. The out cricket improved with constant practice, but catches were too often grounded. Lowry led the side well and the team earned itself a good reputation both on and off the field.

1928: 4th West Indians

After three trial matches in Barbados after Christmas 1927, the following were chosen for the 1928 tour of England: R. K. Nunes (captain), F. R. Martin and E. A. Rae of Jamaica; E. L. Bartlett,

G. Challenor, G. N. Francis, H. C. Griffith and E. L. G. Hoad of Barbados; C. R. Browne, J. M. Neblett and C. V. Wight of British Guiana; L. N. Constantine, G. A. R. Dewhurst, C. A. Roach, J. A. Small and W. H. St Hill of Trinidad. Dewhurst dropped out and two additional players came into the side, O. C. Scott of Jamaica and M. P. Fernandes of British Guiana. The team was accompanied by R. H. Mallett as manager and J. E. Seheult as his assistant. The cricketers sailed from Bridgetown aboard the R.M.S. *Camito*, arriving at Avonmouth on 16 April.

They practised for three weeks before the first serious match on 5 May. In view of the form showed by the 1923 tourists the fixture list included three Tests, but the 1928 team failed to come up to its

predecessor's standard, in some respects even falling below it. They lost all three Tests by an innings and won only five matches in the whole first-class programme because of weak batting and fielding.

The fielding was generally poor—one critic estimated that 80 catches were dropped in the slips alone. The out cricket was not much better, with deep fielders throwing wildly and a number of run outs being missed in consequence. The team also missed Dewhurst behind the wicket, where Nunes was not an adequate substitute. The biggest disappointment among the batsmen was Challenor, whose average fell from 51 in 1923 to 27. Fernandes and Small's averages also dropped and this in a season that

---

1928: 4th West Indians

1st Match: v H. D. G. Leveson-Gower's XII (Pelsham)   April 26.
West Indians 224-2 dec (G. Challenor 110) drew with H. D. G. Leveson-Gower's XII 90-6.

2nd Match: v Reigate Priory (Reigate)   April 28.
West Indians 219-2 dec (C. A. Roach 116*, E. L. Bartlett 65) drew with Reigate Priory 91-6.

3rd Match: v Dulwich (Dulwich)   April 30.
Dulwich 186 (N. K. F. Porter 76) drew with West Indians 156-5.

4th Match: v Berkhamsted (Berkhamsted)   May 1.

5th Match: v H. M. Martineau's XII (Holyport)   May 2, 3.
West Indians 75 and 189-6 (M. P. Fernandes 78*) drew with H. M. Martineau's XII 200 (A. L. Hilder 61, G. N. Francis 4-28).

6th Match: v Derbyshire (Derby)   May 5, 7, 8.
Derbyshire 159 (C. R. Browne 4-44) and 177 (G. R. Jackson 63, C. R. Browne 4-37) lost to West Indians 155 (G. Challenor 75, A. G. Slater 8-24) and 185-8 by 2 wkts.

7th Match: v Essex (Leyton)   May 9, 10, 11.
Essex 369 (C. A. G. Russell 147, J. W. H. T. Douglas 53, G. N. Francis 4-73) and 259-3 (J. O'Connor 93, J. A. Cutmore 77, L. C. Eastman 58*) drew with West Indians 377 (L. N. Constantine 130, G. Challenor 62, F. R. Martin 53, M. S. Nichols 4-117, J. O'Connor 4-120).

8th Match: v Surrey (Oval)   May 12, 14, 15.
Surrey 285 (R. J. Gregory 96, D. R. Jardine 58, G. N. Francis 4-77, L. N. Constantine 4-81) and 253-0 dec (J. B. Hobbs 123*, A. Sandham 108*) drew with West Indians 318 (L. N. Constantine 50, T. Shepherd 5-103) and 118-6 (L. N. Constantine 60*, H. A. Peach 5-25).

9th Match: v Oxford University (Oxford)   May 16, 17, 18.
West Indians 324 (E. L. Bartlett 85, R. K. Nunes 76*) and 313-6 (J. A. Small 106*, L. N. Constantine 69, W. H. St Hill 58) drew with Oxford University 264 (N. M. Ford 68, A. M. Crawley 55, M. Garland-Wells 55, H. C. Griffith 4-74).

10th Match: v M.C.C. (Lord's)   May 19, 21, 22.
M.C.C. 65-1 drew with West Indians did not bat.

11th Match: v Norfolk (Norwich)   May 23, 24.
West Indians 149 (W. A. Beadsmoore 5-37) drew with Norfolk 123-9 (J. M. Neblett 5-37).

12th Match: v Cambridge University (Cambridge)   May 26, 28.
Cambridge University 141 (L. N. Constantine 5-35) and 155 (L. N. Constantine 5-51) lost to West Indians 257 (M. P. Fernandes 73, J. M. Neblett 61) and 40-1 by 9 wkts.

13th Match: v Northumberland (Newcastle)   May 30, 31.
West Indians 342 (G. Challenor 146, C. R. Browne 62, I. C. Maconachie 5-58) beat Northumberland 81 (H. C. Griffith 6-32, O. C. Scott 4-19) and 216 (J. B. Bruce 54, H. C. Griffith 4-61) by an innings and 45 runs.

14th Match: v Durham (Sunderland)   June 1, 2.
Durham 237 (T. K. Dobson 105, H. C. Griffith 4-73) and 132-9 dec (H. C. Griffith 4-25) drew with West Indians 225 (W. H. St Hill 101, A. L. Howell 4-91) and 61-3.

15th Match: v Ireland (Dublin)   June 4, 5, 6.
Ireland 173 (J. A. Small 5-67, H. C. Griffith 4-65) and 320 (T. G. McVeagh 102*, O. C. Scott 5-61) beat West Indians 142 (F. R. Martin 56) and 291 (M. P. Fernandes 73, C. A. Roach 71, E. L. Bartlett 54, T. H. Dixon 4-76) by 60 runs.

16th Match: v Middlesex (Lord's)   June 9, 10, 11.
Middlesex 352-6 dec (N. E. Haigh 119, E. H. Hendren 100*, J. W. Hearne 75) and 136 (E. H. Hendren 52, L. N. Constantine 7-57) lost to West Indians 230 (L. N. Constantine 86, F. J. Durston 4-16) and 259-7 (L. N. Constantine 103, M. P. Fernandes 54) by 3 wkts.

17th Match: v Yorkshire (Bramall Lane)   June 13, 14, 15.
Yorkshire 179 (H. C. Griffith 6-46) drew with West Indians 56-3.

18th Match: v Minor Counties (Exeter)   June 16, 18, 19.
West Indians 289 (C. A. Roach 92, F. R. Martin 81, W. E. Hazelton 4-80) and 103 (W. E. Hazelton 6-45) lost to Minor Counties 108 (H. C. Griffith 5-18) and 326 (A. Lockett 154, H. P. Miles 61) by 42 runs.

19th Match: v Civil Service (Chiswick)   June 20, 21.
Civil Service 197 (P. Ogilvie 53, J. A. Small 5-59) and 110-2 (A. E. S. Rippon 51*) drew with West Indians 330-6 dec (F. R. Martin 111, R. K. Nunes 102*).

20th Match: v England (Lord's)   June 23, 25, 26.
England 401 (G. E. Tyldesley 122, A. P. F. Chapman 50, L. N. Constantine 4-82) beat West Indies 177 (V. W. C. Jupp 4-37) and 166 (J. A. Small 52, M. W. Tate 4-37) by an innings and 58 runs.

21st Match: v Northamptonshire (Northampton)   June 27, 28.
Northamptonshire 100 (L. N. Constantine 7-45) and 208 (J. E. Timms 56, L. N. Constantine 6-67) lost to West Indians 434-9 dec (L. N. Constantine 107, G. Challenor 97, H. C. Griffith 61*, E. W. Clark 6-52) by an innings and 126 runs.

22nd Match: v Lancashire (Old Trafford)   June 30, July 2, 3.
Lancashire 235 and 144-1 dec (F. B. Watson 51) drew with West Indians 108 (J. Iddon 4-40) and 178-2 (C. A. Roach 82, F. R. Martin 77*).

23rd Match: v Yorkshire (Headingley)   July 4, 5, 6.
Yorkshire 284 (H. Sutcliffe 98, W. Barber 98, G. N. Francis 4-65) and 172-1 dec (P. Holmes 84*, A. Mitchell 51*) beat West Indians 208 (L. N. Constantine 69, F. R. Martin 60, W. Rhodes 4-37) and 58 (G. G. Macaulay 6-30) by 190 runs.

24th Match: v Nottinghamshire (Trent Bridge)   July 7, 9, 10.
Nottinghamshire 393 (A. W. Carr 100, A. Staples 84*, W. W. Whysall 80) and 246-6 dec (G. Gunn 55, F. Barratt 55*) drew with West Indians 378 (E. L. Bartlett 109, E. L. G. Hoad 73, R. K. Nunes 62, S. J. Staples 5-99) and 85-0 (L. N. Constantine 67*).

25th Match: v Staffordshire (Stoke-on-Trent)   July 11, 12.
Staffordshire 99 and 181 (H. W. Homer 64, C. R. Browne 5-67) lost to West Indians 159 (G. Challenor 71, S. F. Barnes 4-30) and 123-2 (G. Challenor 57) by 8 wkts.

26th Match: v Warwickshire (Edgbaston)   July 14, 16, 17.
West Indians 209 (L. N. Constantine 70, A. W. Speed 5-39) and 313 (G. Challenor 81, C. A. Roach 69, C. R. Browne 50*, A. W. Speed 4-60) lost to Warwickshire 384 (J. H. Parsons 161, A. J. W. Croom 69, O. C. Scott 4-104) and 139-3 by 7 wkts.

27th Match: v Worcestershire (Worcester)   July 18, 19.
West Indians 410-6 dec (G. Hoad 149*, F. R. Martin 77, O. C. Scott 75) drew with Worcestershire 439-2 (H. H. I. Gibbons 200*, M. Nichol 104, W. V. Fox 104*).

28th Match: v England (Old Trafford)   July 21, 23, 24.
West Indies 206 (C. A. Roach 50, A. P. Freeman 5-54) and 115 (A. P. Freeman 5-39) lost to England 351 (D. R. Jardine 83, W. R. Hammond 63, H. Sutcliffe 54, J. B. Hobbs 53) by an innings and 30 runs.

29th Match: v Wales (Llandudno)   July 25, 26, 27.
West Indians 198 (G. Challenor 50, S. F. Barnes 7-51) and 137 (F. P. Ryan 5-17, S. F. Barnes 5-67) lost to Wales 229 (A. Ratcliffe 71) and 107-2 (C. A. Rowland 52*) by 8 wkts.

30th Match: v Leicestershire (Leicester)   July 28, 30, 31.
Leicestershire 228 (T. E. Sidwell 59, G. L. Berry 55, H. C. Griffith 4-62, L. N. Constantine 4-75) and 198-9 dec (A. Shipman 74, N. F. Armstrong 64) drew with West Indians 271 (G. Challenor 50, L. N. Constantine 50, W. E. Astill 4-68) and 39-2.

31st Match: v Somerset (Bath)   Aug 1, 2, 3.
West Indians 130 (W. T. Greswell 4-35, J. C. White 4-50) and 230 (E. L. G. Hoad 71, W. T. Greswell 5-68, A. W. Wellard 4-59) drew with Somerset 216 (J. C. W. MacBryan 84*, J. A. Small 4-52, F. R. Martin 4-78).

32nd Match: v Glamorgan (Swansea)   Aug 4, 6, 7.
West Indians 327 (R. K. Nunes 127*, G. Challenor 55) and 164 (F. P. Ryan 7-62) drew with Glamorgan 256 (N. V. H. Riches 65, J. A. Small 5-52) and 100-3.

33rd Match: v Gloucestershire (Bristol)   Aug 8, 9, 10.
Gloucestershire 319 (F. J. Seabrook 66*, W. L. Neale 66*, O. C. Scott 4-61, L. N. Constantine 4-66) and 129-3 (A. E. Dipper 62*) drew with West Indians 399 (C. A. Roach 71, R. K. Nunes 71, O. C. Scott 66, F. R. Martin 53).

34th Match: v England (Oval)   Aug 11, 13, 14.
West Indies 238 (C. A. Roach 53, M. W. Tate 4-59) and 129 (A. P. Freeman 4-47) lost to England 438 (J. B. Hobbs 159, G. E. Tyldesley 73, H. Sutcliffe 63, M. W. Tate 54, H. C. Griffith 6-103, G. N. Francis 4-112) by an innings and 71 runs.

35th Match: v Sussex (Hove)   Aug 18, 20, 21.
West Indians 188 (J. H. Parks 5-44, A. F. Wensley 4-60) and 89 (A. F. Wensley 6-44) lost to Sussex 364 (J. G. Wagener 80, A. H. Bowley 62, W. L. Cornford 53, G. S. Grimston 52, C. R. Browne 4-81) by an innings and 87 runs.

36th Match: v Hampshire (Southampton)   Aug 22, 23, 24.
Hampshire 429 (L. H. Tennyson 217, J. A. Newman 81, L. N. Constantine 4-93) and 62-2 drew with West Indians 413 (F. R. Martin 165, C. A. Roach 84, E. L. G. Hoad 51, G. S. Boyes 5-91, J. A. Newman 4-73).

37th Match: v Kent (Canterbury)   Aug 25, 27, 28.
West Indians 282 (C. R. Browne 103, G. Challenor 64) and 216 (F. R. Martin 82, A. P. Freeman 9-104) beat Kent 127 (H. C. Griffith 6-57) and 170 (J. L. Bryan 95*, H. C. Griffith 5-61, L. N. Constantine 4-62) by 201 runs.

38th Match: v Harlequins (Eastbourne)   Aug 29, 30, 31.
West Indians 311 (J. A. Small 98, C. R. Browne 60) and 260 lost to Harlequins 676-8 dec (C. H. Knott 261*, R. H. B. Bettington 127, A. J. Evans 124, R. C. Burton 52) by an innings and 105 runs.

39th Match: v An England XI (Folkestone)   Sept 1, 3, 4.
West Indians 212 (A. P. Freeman 6-87) and 271 (L. N. Constantine 62, C. A. Roach 60, A. P. Freeman 5-109) lost to An England XI 198 (L. N. Constantine 4-66) and 288-6 (F. E. Woolley 151, R. E. S. Wyatt 75) by 4 wkts.

40th Match: v J. Cahn's XII (West Bridgford)   Sept 5, 6.
West Indians 358-9 dec (E. L. G. Hoad 145, C. V. Wight 55*) drew with J. Cahn's XII 114 (H. C. Griffith 7-46) and 63-2.

41st Match: v H. D. G. Leveson-Gower's XI (Scarborough)   Sept 8, 10, 11.
West Indians 333 (E. L. G. Hoad 124, L. N. Constantine 50) and 113 (M. W. Tate 5-28, N. E. Haig 4-33) lost to H. D. G. Leveson-Gower's XI 236 (H. Sutcliffe 64, L. N. Constantine 7-68) and 212-2 (J. B. Hobbs 119*) by 8 wkts.

Above *The fourth West Indian touring party was to play their first series of Test matches—they were heavily beaten in all three. Back: Bartlett, Martin, Rae, Small, Neblet, Francis, St Hill, Constantine. Front: Fernandes, Wright, Nunes (captain), Challenor, Browne.*

Below *A very solemn looking pair, Learie Constantine and Wilton St Hill. They were two of the biggest names in West Indian cricket, but the 35-year-old St Hill failed to do himself justice in the Tests, whereas Constantine went on to great fame.*

1928: 4th West Indians

Batting Averages

	M	I	NO	R	HS	Avge	100	c/s
E. L. G. Hoad	15	24	3	765	149*	36.42	2	5
L. N. Constantine	26	43	3	1381	130	34.52	3	33
F. R. Martin	29	46	4	1370	165	32.61	1	7
G. Challenor	24	40	1	1074	97	27.53	0	6
C. A. Roach	28	47	1	1222	92	26.56	0	13
E. L. Bartlett	15	25	1	584	109	24.33	1	1
R. K. Nunes	26	38	4	798	127*	23.47	1	14
C. V. Wight	17	26	9	343	40	20.17	0	9
O. C. Scott	12	19	3	322	75	20.12	0	4
J. A. Small	22	36	4	595	106*	18.59	1	18
M. P. Fernandes	20	33	1	581	73	18.15	0	19
C. R. Browne	21	33	2	553	103	17.83	1	10
H. C. Griffith	24	34	15	333	61*	17.52	0	8
J. M. Neblett	8	13	1	181	61	15.08	0	9
G. N. Francis	22	32	11	282	61	13.42	0	12
W. H. St. Hill	14	25	1	262	58	10.91	0	3
E. A. Rae	7	9	0	74	42	8.22	0	4

Bowling Averages

	O	M	R	W	Avge	BB	5i
L. N. Constantine	723.3	131	2456	107	22.95	7-45	6
H. C. Griffith	640.1	124	2120	76	27.89	6-46	5
J. A. Small	540.4	108	1444	50	28.88	5-52	2
G. N. Francis	599.3	118	1790	56	31.96	4-73	0
C. R. Browne	427.3	84	1111	32	34.71	4-37	0
O. C. Scott	234	20	906	25	36.24	5-61	1
F. R. Martin	335.2	83	853	19	44.89	4-78	0
J. M. Neblett	86	12	325	6	54.16	2-22	0
E. L. G. Hoad	29	2	193	2	96.50	1-31	0
C. A. Roach	48	4	194	2	97.00	1-20	0

Also bowled: G. Challenor 17.2-4-80-2; E. A. Rae 2-0-23-0.

Played in one non-first-class match: G. C. Grant.

produced endless batting records among the county players. Roach and Martin were in fact the only batsmen to have a happy tour, except Constantine whose all-round ability was brilliant: he completed the double. Inexplicably Constantine failed in the Tests, which made quite a difference. The bowling was adequate, or would have been if the fielding had supported it. Francis and Constantine were the leading bowlers, with Griffith and Small also performing well at times. Scott was the principal slow bowler, but his leg-breaks were rather expensive.

The finances of the visit were helped by the introduction of Test Matches and a profit of some £2,000 was made. The team returned home aboard the s.s. *Ingoma*, arriving back in Barbados on 13 October, except for the Jamaican contingent which sailed from Avonmouth aboard the R.M.S. *Bayano*.

1929: 7th South Africans

The South African selectors, determined to make a fresh start after the failure of the 1924 tour, made sweeping changes in the team: only three of those included in the 1929 side had travelled with the previous party. The side chosen on 4 January read H. G. Deane (captain), H. B. Cameron, J. A. J. Christy, C. L. Vincent,

1929: 7th South Africans

Batting Averages

	M	I	NO	R	HS	Avge	100	c/s
H. W. Taylor	27	46	5	1575	125	38.41	3	1
I. J. Siedle	28	46	2	1579	169*	35.88	2	13
H. G. O. Owen-Smith	22	36	3	1168	129	35.39	2	14
H. G. Deane	29	41	5	1239	133*	34.41	1	11
D. P. B. Morkel	29	48	6	1443	109	34.35	1	29
B. Mitchell	30	52	3	1615	140	32.95	3	38
H. B. Cameron	22	35	5	951	120	31.70	2	46/11
E. L. Dalton	17	29	3	820	157	31.53	3	5
R. H. Catterall	29	50	1	1411	124	28.79	2	8
Q. McMillan	25	38	10	749	86	26.75	0	16
J. A. J. Christy	18	30	1	729	148	25.13	1	11
J. P. Duminy	3	5	1	81	31	20.25	0	2
C. L. Vincent	22	32	8	349	60	14.54	0	15
N. A. Quinn	20	22	6	200	28	12.50	0	6
E. A. van der Merwe	14	18	6	139	35*	11.58	0	18/13
A. J. Bell	20	27	13	155	32*	11.07	0	7
A. L. Ochse	19	19	6	116	30	8.92	0	10

Bowling Averages

	O	M	R	W	Avge	BB	5i
N. A. Quinn	671.2	159	1553	65	23.89	6-43	6
Q. McMillan	743.4	99	2316	91	25.45	8-50	6
H. G. O. Owen-Smith	249	43	774	30	25.80	6-38	1
D. P. B. Morkel	682.1	171	1795	69	26.01	7-61	2
A. J. Bell	583	102	1698	61	27.83	6-68	2
C. L. Vincent	719.3	145	1959	69	28.39	7-36	4
R. H. Catterall	20	3	64	2	32.00	1-7	0
J. A. J. Christy	87	16	245	7	35.00	3-46	0
A. L. Ochse	592	84	1839	52	35.36	4-28	0
B. Mitchell	277.4	39	934	24	38.91	3-49	0

Also bowled: E. L. Dalton 11-1-32-0; J. P. Duminy 6.3-0-27-0; I. J. Siedle 2-0-21-0.

The South Africans of 1929. Back: Siedle, Mitchell, Ochse, Bell, Morkel, Christy, Quinn, McMillan, Dalton, Frames (secretary). Centre: Cameron, Taylor, Frelinghaus (manager), Deane (captain), Catterall, Vincent. Front: Owen-Smith, Van der Merwe.

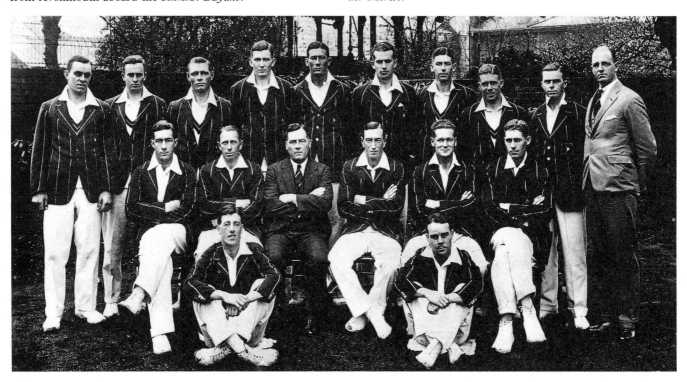

E. A. van der Merwe, Q. McMillan, B. Mitchell and H. W. Taylor of Transvaal; A. J. Bell, D. P. B. Morkel and H. G. O. Owen-Smith of Western Province; R. H. Catterall of Orange Free State, E. L. Dalton and I. J. Siedle of Natal, A. L. Ochse of Eastern Province and N. A. Quinn of Griqualand West. H. O. Frielinghaus travelled as honorary general manager and A. S. Frames as secretary. Nine of the 16 were under 24 when chosen and for the first time all the team were born and bred in South Africa.

The visitors lost two Tests and drew the others and won nine first-class matches. In bald figures the 1929 side hardly improved on the one which came in 1924, but it was apparent that the new wave of South Africans were rejuvenating cricket in their country. The team were beset during the first half of the tour with illness and injury and by the Third Test were forced to co-opt J. P. Duminy into the side.

Taylor was the leading batsman, but his two colleagues of the previous tour, Deane and Catterall, did not live up to their reputations. Siedle failed in the Tests but batted well in the ordinary matches and was usefully difficult to dismiss. Mitchell was a sound man and played a well-judged innings at Edgbaston in the Test. Morkel and Christy were fine drivers of the ball,

---

1929: 7th South Africans

1st Match: v R. Earle's XI (Godalming)   April 25.
R. Earle's XI 138 (N. A. Quinn 4-12, A. L. Ochse 4-35) drew with South Africans 129-7.

2nd Match: v P. F. Warner's XI (Bearsted).
South Africans 199-6 dec drew with P. F. Warner's XI (A. L. Ochse 5-44).

3rd Match: v Worcestershire (Worcester)   May 1, 2, 3.
South Africans 444-8 dec (H. W. Taylor 103, H. B. Cameron 102, B. Mitchell 83*) drew with Worcestershire 284 (W. V. Fox 88, M. F. S. Jewell 68, N. A. Quinn 6-75) and 262-7 (W. V. Fox 58, L. Wright 50, C. V. Tarbox 50*).

4th Match: v Leicestershire (Leicester)   May 4, 6, 7.
Leicestershire 208 (E. W. Dawson 58, A. Shipman 58) and 191-7 drew with South Africans 354-8 dec (I. J. Siedle 169*, H. G. Deane 68).

5th Match: v Surrey (Oval)   May 8, 9, 10.
Surrey 229 (P. G. H. Fender 79, C. L. Vincent 6-62) and 292-9 dec (P. G. H. Fender 98, A. Sandham 61, D. P. B. Morkel 4-121) beat South Africans 111 and 285 (D. P. B. Morkel 86, P. G. H. Fender 4-56, S. Fenley 4-68) by 125 runs.

6th Match: v Middlesex (Lord's)   May 11, 13, 14.
Middlesex 132 (D. P. B. Morkel 7-61) and 240 (E. T. Killick 111, N. E. Haig 57, N. A. Quinn 4-54, H. G. O. Owen-Smith 4-80) lost to South Africa 291 (H. G. Deane 62, B. Mitchell 51) and 85-2 by 8 wkts.

7th Match: v Oxford University (Oxford)   May 15, 16, 17.
Oxford University 152 (A. M. Crawley 79, C. L. Vincent 4-57) and 325 (A. M. Crawley 81, H. M. Garland-Wells 58, A. T. Barber 51, N. A. Quinn 6-94) lost to South Africans 298 (R. H. Catterall 67, D. P. B. Morkel 62, E. M. Wellings 4-81) and 181-6 (I. J. Siedle 90) by 4 wkts.

8th Match: v Glamorgan (Pontypridd)   May 18, 20, 21.
South Africans 212 (H. G. Deane 58, J. Mercer 8-60) and 186 (H. W. Taylor 57, J. Mercer 6-59, W. E. Jones 4-44) beat Glamorgan 113 (C. L. Vincent 7-36) and 115 (Q. McMillan 5-36, C. L. Vincent 4-53) by 170 runs.

9th Match: v Gloucestershire (Bristol)   May 22, 23, 24.
South Africans 225 (H. B. Cameron 60, T. W. J. Goddard 6-68) and 232 (J. A. J. Christy 76, C. W. L. Parker 5-56) lost to Gloucestershire 331 (R. A. Sinfield 112, A. E. Dipper 94, A. J. Bell 6-68) and 129-4 (W. R. Hammond 63*) by 6 wkts.

10th Match: v Yorkshire (Bramall Lane)   May 25, 27, 28.
South Africans 441-5 dec (I. J. Siedle 168, B. Mitchell 101, D. P. B. Morkel 59, H. B. Cameron 55*) and 277-8 (H. B. Cameron 85*, D. P. B. Morkel 68) drew Yorkshire 338 (A. Mitchell 126, H. Sutcliffe 113).

11th Match: v Cambridge University (Cambridge)   May 29, 30.
Cambridge University 98 (D. P. B. Morkel 4-13, A. L. Ochse 4-34) and 143 (E. T. Killick 77, Q. McMillan 5-45, A. L. Ochse 4-34) lost to South Africans 360 (H. B. Cameron 120, I. J. Siedle 51, P. K. Webster 4-86) by an innings and 119 runs.

12th Match: v M.C.C. (Lord's)   June 1, 3, 4.
South Africans 311 (D. P. B. Morkel 70, J. C. White 5-87) and 269-6 dec (B. Mitchell 61, I. J. Siedle 54) drew with M.C.C. 336 (K. S. Duleepsinhji 74, G. O. B. Allen 52, Q. McMillan 4-76) and 72-1.

13th Match: v Derbyshire (Derby)   June 5, 6, 7.
South Africans 166 (T. B. Mitchell 4-46, L. F. Townsend 4-62) drew with Derbyshire 208-6.

14th Match: v Lancashire (Old Trafford)   June 8, 10, 11.
South Africans 185 (F. M. Sibbles 4-31) and 150 (I. J. Siedle 75) lost to Lancashire 191 (F. B. Watson 50, A. L. Ochse 4-46) and 145-4 (T. M. Halliday 60*) by 6 wkts.

15th Match: v Minor Counties (Stoke-on-Trent)   June 12, 13, 14.
Minor Counties 201 (P. F. Remnant 62, H. G. O. Owen-Smith 6-38) and 183-6 dec (W. T. Cook 92, A. J. Bell 4-47) drew with South Africans 139 (S. F. Barnes 8-41) and 40-1.

16th Match: v England (Edgbaston)   June 15, 17, 18.
England 245 (E. H. Hendren 70, A. L. Ochse 4-79) and 308-4 dec (W. R. Hammond 138, H. Sutcliffe 114) drew with South Africa 250 (B. Mitchell 88, R. H. Catterall 67, H. Larwood 5-57) and 171-1 (R. H. Catterall 98, B. Mitchell 61*).

17th Match: v Yorkshire (Hull)   June 19, 20, 21.
South Africans 265 (H. G. Deane 60, H. G. O. Owen-Smith 52) and 260-4 dec (D. P. B. Morkel 109, H. W. Taylor 83) drew with Yorkshire 335 (W. Barber 108) and 86-2.

18th Match: v Surrey (Oval)   June 22, 24, 25.
South Africans 426-8 dec (R. H. Catterall 124, I. J. Siedle 66, H. W. Taylor 59, H. G. Deane 54) and 202-2 dec (R. H. Catterall 98) drew with Surrey 305 (T. F. Shepherd 113*, A. L. Ochse 4-103) and 111-3 (A. Ducat 62*).

19th Match: v Norfolk (Norwich)   June 26, 27.
South Africans 420 (H. W. Taylor 170, C. L. Vincent 62) beat Norfolk 126 (A. J. Bell 5-37) and 250 (F. R. Bell 69, R. H. Gladden 50) by an innings and 44 runs.

20th Match: v England (Lord's)   June 29, July 1, 2.
England 302 (H. Sutcliffe 100, M. Leyland 73, A. J. Bell 6-99, D. P. B. Morkel 4-93) and 312-8 dec (M. Leyland 102, M. W. Tate 100*, A. L. Ochse 4-99) drew with South Africa 322 (D. P. B. Morkel 88, J. A. J. Christy 70, H. G. O. Owen-Smith 52*) and 90-5.

21st Match: v Northamptonshire (Northampton)   July 3, 4, 5.
South Africans 219 (B. Mitchell 73, E. W. Clark 6-41) and 11-0 drew with Northamptonshire 268 (A. H. Bakewell 80, V. W. C. Jupp 61).

22nd Match: v Nottinghamshire (Trent Bridge)   July 6, 8, 9.
Nottinghamshire 476 (A. W. Carr 194, W. R. D. Payton 134*, W. Walker 53, D. P. B. Morkel 5-72) and 177-4 dec (W. W. Whysall 58) drew with South Africans 304 (J. A. J. Christy 148, A. Staples 4-64) and 191-6 (D. P. B. Morkel 64*, J. A. J. Christy 50).

23rd Match: v Wales (Colwyn Bay)   July 10, 11, 12.
South Africans 192 (R. H. Catterall 117, S. F. Barnes 5-28) and 239 (H. G. Deane 64, S. F. Barnes 4-62, J. Mercer 4-67) beat Wales 159 (D. E. Davies 53, A. L. Ochse 4-28, Q. McMillan 4-82) and 262 (W. E. Bates 102, J. T. Bell 68, C. L. Vincent 5-70) by 10 runs.

24th Match: v England (Headingley)   July 13, 15, 16.
South Africa 236 (R. H. Catterall 74, C. L. Vincent 60, A. P. Freeman 7-115) and 275 (H. G. O. Owen-Smith 129) lost to England 328 (F. E. Woolley 83, W. R. Hammond 65, N. A. Quinn 6-92) and 186-5 (F. E. Woolley 95) by 5 wkts.

25th Match: v Lancashire (Liverpool)   July 17, 18, 19.
Lancashire 384 (P. T. Eckersley 78*, J. L. Hopwood 65, W. Farrimond 55, C. L. Vincent 4-125) and 36-0 beat South Africans 218 (I. J. Siedle 64, J. Iddon 5-34) and 200 (R. H. Catterall 58, R. K. Tyldesley 7-52) by 10 wkts.

26th Match: v Scotland (Perth)   July 20, 22.
Scotland 148 (N. A. Quinn 6-43) and 144 (N. A. Quinn 5-33) lost to South Africans 297 (H. W. Taylor 125, I. J. Siedle 52, A. P. Baxter 4-91) by an innings and 5 runs.

27th Match: v Durham (Sunderland)   July 24, 25.
Durham 112 (Q. McMillan 5-74) and 71 (A. L. Ochse 4-18, H. G. O. Owen-Smith 4-24) lost to South Africans 243 (H. G. O. Owen-Smith 102, H. B. Cameron 63, H. Howell 5-74) by an innings and 60 runs.

28th Match: v England (Old Trafford)   July 27, 29, 30.
England 427-7 dec (F. E. Woolley 154, R. E. S. Wyatt 113, M. Leyland 55) beat South Africa 130 (D. P. B. Morkel 63, A. P. Freeman 7-71) and 265 (H. B. Cameron 83, H. W. Taylor 70, A. P. Freeman 5-100) by an innings and 32 runs.

29th Match: v Somerset (Taunton)   July 31, Aug 1, 2.
South Africans 302-4 dec (B. Mitchell 127, I. J. Siedle 59) beat Somerset 122 (Q. McMillan 8-50) and 146 by an innings and 34 runs.

30th Match: v Glamorgan (Swansea)   Aug 3, 5, 6.
Glamorgan 237 (J. T. Morgan 103*, N. A. Quinn 5-47) drew with South Africans 98-5 (J. Mercer 5-41).

31st Match: v Warwickshire (Edgbaston)   Aug 7, 8, 9.
South Africans 263 (Q. McMillan 58*, H. G. O. Owen-Smith 126, B. Mitchell 69) drew with Warwickshire 399 (A. J. W. Croom 109, L. A. Bates 94, N. Kilner 64).

32nd Match: v Essex (Leyton)   Aug 10, 12, 13.
South Africans 389-7 dec (H. W. Taylor 95, H. G. O. Owen-Smith 64, R. H. Catterall 61, H. G. Deane 58, I. J. Siedle 51) and 281-8 dec (I. J. Siedle 51, H. G. O. Owen-Smith 90, H. W. Taylor 67, H. J. Palmer 4-112) beat Essex 237 (C. A. G. Russell 90, Q. McMillan 5-81) and 106 (Q. McMillan 4-56).

33rd Match: v Hampshire (Southampton)   Aug 14, 15, 16.
South Africans 259 (Q. McMillan 53, H. G. O. Owen-Smith 51, O. W. Herman 5-76) and 408-8 dec (H. G. Deane 133*, E. L. Dalton 67) drew with Hampshire 279 (G. Brown 75, C. P. Mead 57, A. J. Bell 4-77) and 158-3 (L. Harfield 59*, C. P. Mead 50*).

34th Match: v England (Oval)   Aug 17, 19, 20.
England 258 (H. Sutcliffe 104, C. L. Vincent 5-105) and 264-1 (H. Sutcliffe 109*, W. R. Hammond 101*, J. B. Hobbs 52) drew with South Africa 492-8 dec (H. W. Taylor 121, H. G. Deane 93, D. P. B. Morkel 81, H. B. Cameron 62, Q. McMillan 50*).

35th Match: v Kent (Canterbury)   Aug 24, 26, 27.
South Africans 491-7 dec (E. L. Dalton 157, H. G. O. Owen-Smith 87, Q. McMillan 86, I. J. Siedle 73) and 287 (E. L. Dalton 59, W. H. Ashdown 5-79) drew with Kent 436 (L. E. G. Ames 145, W. H. Ashdown 87, F. E. Woolley 50, A. J. Bell 4-104) and 123-1.

36th Match: v Sussex (Hove)   Aug 28, 29, 30.
South Africans 330 (E. L. Dalton 102, H. W. Taylor 57, H. G. O. Owen-Smith 56, E. H. Bowley 5-61, M. W. Tate 4-41) and 290 (B. Mitchell 140, T. E. R. Cook 4-46) beat Sussex 239 (Jas Langridge 62, M. W. Tate 55, Q. McMillan 4-54, A. J. Bell 4-78) and 164 (Q. McMillan 5-54) by 217 runs.

37th Match: v Sir J. Cahn's XII (West Bridgford)   Aug 31, Sept 2.
South Africans 275 (D. P. B. Morkel 65, E. L. Dalton 59, T. L. Richmond 6-114) drew with Sir J. Cahn's XII 252 (F. W. H. Nicholas 55, D. P. B. Morkel 7-61).

38th Match: v C. I. Thornton's XI (Scarborough)   Sept 4, 5, 6.
C. I. Thornton's XI 388 (J. B. Hobbs 151, E. H. Hendren 114, Q. McMillan 6-106) and 130-3 dec (J. B. Hobbs 70*) drew with South Africans 211 (B. Mitchell 56, W. E. Astill 4-84) and 273-8 (J. A. J. Christy 61, E. L. Dalton 53).

39th Match: v An England XI (Folkestone)   Sept 7, 9.
South Africans 153 (H. G. O. Owen-Smith 51) and 281 (D. P. B. Morkel 59, R. H. Catterall 51, A. P. Freeman 6-135) lost to An England XI 450 (J. W. Hearne 143, F. E. Woolley 111, A. J. Bell 4-105) by an innings and 16 runs.

261

though uncertain at times; Owen-Smith, the outstanding fieldsman, batted in quite delightful vein. The main weakness was in fast bowling. Ochse headed the Test averages, but his record was a thin one. The two left-arm exponents, Quinn and Vincent, found that the dry turf wickets rarely helped them. McMillan's leg-breaks took 91 first-class wickets, but were useless in the Tests, and Morkel proved as good as anyone, his fast-medium deliveries picking up some cheap wickets—he was undoubtedly the all-rounder of the team. The out fielding was excellent and Cameron was as good as any wicketkeeper in England. The reports of the tour record approvingly that the tourists had refused several offers to turn professional and stay in England as county players. The team was not attractive to the English public and only the expenses of the tour were covered by the receipts.

1930: 17th Australians

As with the South Africans of 1929, the 1930 Australians contained a great deal of new blood, only four players having been members of the losing 1926 squad. The team announced on 30 January was W. M. Woodfull (captain), W. H. Ponsford and E. L.

1930: 17th Australians

Batting Averages

	M	I	NO	R	HS	Avge	100	c/s
D. G. Bradman	27	36	6	2960	334	98.66	10	12
A. F. Kippax	23	32	7	1451	158	58.04	4	7
W. M. Woodfull	23	26	1	1434	216	57.36	6	8
W. H. Ponsford	24	33	4	1425	220*	49.13	4	11
A. Jackson	26	35	3	1097	118	34.28	1	10
S. J. McCabe	26	33	2	1012	96	32.64	0	14
V. Y. Richardson	26	32	1	832	116	26.83	2	22/3
A. G. Fairfax	23	27	6	536	63	25.52	0	21
E. L. a'Beckett	17	21	5	397	67*	24.81	0	15
W. A. S. Oldfield	16	16	4	225	43*	18.75	0	23/11
P. M. Hornibrook	26	26	8	232	59*	12.88	0	21
C. V. Grimmett	26	23	3	237	50	11.85	0	12
A. Hurwood	20	19	1	188	61	10.44	0	12
T. W. Wall	22	19	6	107	40*	8.23	0	10
C. W. Walker	16	14	5	43	10*	4.77	0	11/14

Bowling Averages

	O	M	R	W	Avge	BB	5i
C. V. Grimmett	1015.1	262	2427	144	16.85	10-37	15
P. M. Hornibrook	819.2	240	1802	96	18.77	7-42	9
A. F. Kippax	25.3	2	91	4	22.75	3-13	0
D. G. Bradman	76	12	301	12	25.08	3-35	0
A. Hurwood	354	116	752	28	26.85	5-111	1
S. J. McCabe	281	69	723	26	27.80	4-25	0
T. W. Wall	610.2	111	1638	56	29.25	5-60	1
A. G. Fairfax	535.4	150	1218	41	29.70	6-54	1
E. L. a'Beckett	343	112	628	20	31.40	3-42	0

Also bowled: A. Jackson 5-0-8-0; W. H. Ponsford 1-0-6-0; V. Y. Richardson 1-0-8-0.

Above A young Australian on his first overseas tour going out to bat in the opening first-class match at Worcester: Don Bradman scored a century and went on to become the most successful batsman in the history of cricket.

Left The 1930 Australian touring party. Back: Kelly (manager), Jackson, Wall, a'Beckett, Hornibrook, Hurwood, Grimmett, Howard (treasurer). Centre: Fairfax, Ponsford, Richardson, Woodfull (captain), Kippax, Bradman, Walker. Front: McCabe, Oldfield.

a'Beckett of Victoria; V. Y. Richardson, C. V. Grimmett, T. W. Wall and C. W. Walker of South Australia; A. F. Kippax, D. G. Bradman, A. Jackson, S. J. McCabe, A. G. Fairfax and W. A. S. Oldfield of New South Wales; P. M. Hornibrook and A. Hurwood of Queensland, with W. L. Kelly as manager and T. Howard as treasurer.

The selectors' policy of picking a young side meant that several older players regarded as near certainties were left at home, including R. K. Oxenham, J. Ryder, J. L. Ellis and D. D. Blaikie. The team sailed to England aboard the s.s. *Orford*. Pre-season comment included the following note: 'The man whose appearance is most eagerly awaited is D. G. Bradman the dashing New South Welshman, who broke the world record individual score with his 452★ early in January.'

Bradman proved to be as prolific in England as he had been in Australia and the tour will be remembered mainly for his continuous string of successes in both Test and other first-class matches. In the five Tests he hit 974 runs at an average of 139.14

with one triple hundred, two doubles and one single. Nothing like this had ever before been seen in Test cricket. Most of his runs came from drives, but he could also hook and cut and the feature of his play was that he rarely lifted the ball, and so the chance of being caught in the outfield was minimal.

Ponsford improved on his record of 1926; Kippax could look on a fine summer; Jackson failed; McCabe was very consistent, though he never managed a high innings; Richardson was not quite on form; Woodfull led the side well and batted as the occasion demanded. There was some weakness in the tail. The bowling credits belong to Grimmett; Wall worked hard, though he had little success in the Tests; the slow left-armers of Hornibrook looked very good in the last Test and Fairfax was a capable all-rounder.

The team won the Test series two to one after losing the opening match, which was their only defeat on the visit. Eighteen games were drawn, indicating that the strong batting was not balanced by equally powerful bowling.

1930: 17th Australians

1st Match: v Worcestershire (Worcester)   April 30, May 1, 2.
Worcestershire 131 (C. V. Grimmett 4-38, A. G. Fairfax 4-36) and 196 (C. V. Grimmett 5-46) lost to Australians 492-8 dec (D. G. Bradman 236, W. M. Woodfull 133, G. W. Brook 4-148) by an innings and 165 runs.

2nd Match: v Leicestershire (Leicester)   May 3, 5, 6.
Leicestershire 148 (A. Shipman 63, G. L. Berry 50, C. V. Grimmett 7-46) drew with Australians 365-5 (D. G. Bradman 185★, V. Y. Richardson 100).

3rd Match: v Essex (Leyton)   May 7, 8, 9.
Australians 156 (A. F. Kippax 57, H. J. Palmer 5-40) and 264-6 dec (W. M. Woodfull 54, A. G. Fairfax 53★) beat Essex 67 (P. M. Hornibrook 6-11) and 146 (P. M. Hornibrook 4-29) by 207 runs.

4th Match: v Yorkshire (Bramall Lane)   May 10, 12, 13.
Yorkshire 155 (H. Sutcliffe 69, C. V. Grimmett 10-37) drew with Australians 320 (W. M. Woodfull 121, D. G. Bradman 78).

5th Match: v Lancashire (Liverpool)   May 14, 15, 16.
Lancashire 176 (P. T. Eckersley 54, C. V. Grimmett 6-57) and 165 (P. M. Hornibrook 5-38) drew with Australians 115 (J. L. Hopwood 4-13) and 137-2.

6th Match: v M.C.C. (Lord's)   May 17, 19, 20.
Australians 285 (D. G. Bradman 66, W. H. Ponsford 82★, W. M. Woodfull 52, M. J. C. Allom 5-67) and 213 (A. Jackson 64, G. O. B. Allen 4-28) drew with M.C.C. 258 (K. S. Duleepsinhji 92, A. G. Fairfax 6-54).

7th Match: v Derbyshire (Chesterfield)   May 21, 22, 23.
Derbyshire 215 (T. S. Worthington 79, H. Storer 65, P. M. Hornibrook 6-61) and 181 (P. M. Hornibrook 6-82) lost to Australians 348 (W. H. Ponsford 131, A. Jackson 63, T. S. Worthington 4-103) and 52-0 by 10 wkts.

8th Match: v Surrey (Oval)   May 24, 26, 27.
Australians 379-5 (D. G. Bradman 252★, W. M. Woodfull 50) drew with Surrey did not bat.

9th Match: v Oxford University (Oxford)   May 28, 29.
Australians 406-2 dec (W. H. Ponsford 220★, S. J. McCabe 91, A. F. Kippax 56★) beat Oxford University 124 (C. V. Grimmett 5-48) and 124 (T. W. Wall 4-29) by an innings and 158 runs.

10th Match: v Hampshire (Southampton)   May 31, June 2.
Hampshire 151 (G. Brown 56, C. V. Grimmett 7-39) and 175 (C. V. Grimmett 7-56) lost to Australians 334 (D. G. Bradman 191, S. J. McCabe 65, G. S. Boyes 6-90) by an innings and 8 runs.

11th Match: v Middlesex (Lord's)   June 4, 5, 6.
Middlesex 103 (P. M. Hornibrook 7-42) and 287 (E. H. Hendren 138, P. M. Hornibrook 4-60) lost to Australians 270 (A. F. Kippax 102, G. O. B. Allen 6-77) and 121-5 by 5 wkts.

12th Match: v Cambridge University (Cambridge)   June 7, 9, 10.
Cambridge University 145 (S. J. McCabe 4-25) and 225 (F. R. Brown 52, S. J. McCabe 4-60) lost to Australians 504-8 dec (W. M. Woodfull 216, S. J. McCabe 96) by an innings and 134 runs.

13th Match: v England (Trent Bridge)   June 13, 14, 16, 17.
England 270 (J. B. Hobbs 78, A. P. F. Chapman 52, R. W. V. Robins 50★, C. V. Grimmett 5-107) and 302 (J. B. Hobbs 74, E. H. Hendren 72, H. Sutcliffe 58, C. V. Grimmett 5-94) beat Australia 144 (A. F. Kippax 64★, R. W. V. Robins 4-51) and 335 (D. G. Bradman 131) by 93 runs.

14th Match: v Surrey (Oval)   June 18, 19, 20.
Surrey 162 (T. F. Shepherd 56, C. V. Grimmett 6-24) and 249-2 (J. B. Hobbs 146★, T. F. Shepherd 65★) drew with Australians 388-5 dec (W. M. Woodfull 141, E. L. a'Beckett 67★, T. F. Shepherd 4-65).

15th Match: v Lancashire (Old Trafford)   June 21, 23, 24.
Australians 427 (A. F. Kippax 120, A. G. Fairfax 63, A. Jackson 52) and 79-1 drew with Lancashire 259 (F. B. Watson 74, A. G. Fairfax 4-29, T. W. Wall 4-92).

16th Match: v England (Lord's)   June 27, 28, 30, July 1.
England 425 (K. S. Duleepsinhji 173, M. W. Tate 54, A. G. Fairfax 4-101) and 375 (A. P. F. Chapman 121, G. O. B. Allen 57, C. V. Grimmett 6-167) lost to Australia 729-6 dec (D. G. Bradman 254, W. M. Woodfull 155, W. H. Ponsford 81, A. F. Kippax 83) and 72-3 by 7 wkts.

17th Match: v Yorkshire (Bradford)   July 2, 3, 4.
Australians 302 (W. H. Ponsford 143) and 7-0 beat Yorkshire 146 (C. V. Grimmett 6-75) and 161 (C. V. Grimmett 5-58, A. Hurwood 4-35) by 10 wkts.

18th Match: v Nottinghamshire (Trent Bridge)   July 5, 7, 8.
Australians 296 (A. F. Kippax 93, S. J. McCabe 58, V. Y. Richardson 55, W. Voce 4-86) and 360-4 (A. F. Kippax 89, A. Jackson 79, S. J. McCabe 79, V. Y. Richardson 69) drew with Nottinghamshire 433 (W. W. Whysall 120, S. J. Staples 62, W. Walker 53, A. Hurwood 5-111).

19th Match: v England (Headingley)   July 11, 12, 14, 15.
Australia 566 (D. G. Bradman 334, A. F. Kippax 77, W. M. Woodfull 50, M. W. Tate 5-124) drew with England 391 (W. R. Hammond 113, C. V. Grimmett 5-135) and 95-3.

20th Match: v Scotland (Edinburgh)   July 16, 17, 18.
Scotland 129-3 (G. W. A. Alexander 51) drew with Australians did not bat.

21st Match: v A Scottish XI (Glasgow)   July 19, 21.
A Scottish XI 140-6 dec drew with Australians 337-9 (A. F. Kippax 140, W. M. Woodfull 65, A. Jackson 52★, A. D. Baxter 4-89).

22nd Match: v Durham (Sunderland)   July 23, 24.
No play due to rain.

23rd Match: v England (Old Trafford)   July 25, 26, 28, 29.
Australia 345 (W. H. Ponsford 83, W. M. Woodfull 54, A. F. Kippax 51, C. V. Grimmett 50) drew with England 251-8 (H. Sutcliffe 74, K. S. Duleepsinhji 54, S. J. McCabe 4-41).

24th Match: v Somerset (Taunton)   July 30, 31.
Somerset 121 and 81 (C. V. Grimmett 7-33) lost to Australians 360 (A. Jackson 118, D. G. Bradman 117, A. Young 5-70, J. C. White 4-91) by an innings and 158 runs.

25th Match: v Glamorgan (Swansea)   Aug 2, 4, 5.
Australians 245 (D. G. Bradman 58, W. H. Ponsford 53, S. J. McCabe 53, F. J. Ryan 6-76) and 71-1 drew with Glamorgan 99 (C. V. Grimmett 4-34) and 197-7 (W. E. Bates 73, M. J. L. Turnbull 52, C. V. Grimmett 4-69).

26th Match: v Warwickshire (Edgbaston)   Aug 6, 7, 8.
Warwickshire 102-3 drew with Australians did not bat.

27th Match: v Northamptonshire (Northampton)   Aug 9, 11, 12.
Northamptonshire 249 (A. H. Bakewell 84, J. E. Timms 78, P. M. Hornibrook 4-45) drew with Australians 93 (V. W. C. Jupp 6-32) and 405-8 (W. M. Woodfull 116, V. Y. Richardson 116, A. Jackson 52).

28th Match: v England (Oval)   Aug 16, 18, 19, 20, 21, 22.
England 405 (H. Sutcliffe 161, R. E. S. Wyatt 64, K. S. Duleepsinhji 50, C. V. Grimmett 4-135) and 251 (W. R. Hammond 60, H. Sutcliffe 54, P. M. Hornibrook 7-92) lost to Australia 695 (D. G. Bradman 232, W. H. Ponsford 110, A. Jackson 73, W. M. Woodfull 54, S. J. McCabe 54, A. G. Fairfax 53★, I. A. R. Peebles 6-204).

29th Match: v Gloucestershire (Bristol)   Aug 23, 25, 26.
Gloucestershire 72 (P. M. Hornibrook 4-20) and 202 (W. R. Hammond 89, P. M. Hornibrook 5-49) tied with Australians 157 (W. H. Ponsford 51, T. W. J. Goddard 5-52) and 117 (C. W. L. Parker 7-54).

30th Match: v Kent (Canterbury)   Aug 27, 28, 29.
Australians 181 (A. P. Freeman 5-78) and 320-3 dec (D. G. Bradman 205★, A. Jackson 50★) drew with Kent 227 (T. W. Wall 5-60, C. V. Grimmett 4-80) and 83-2 (F. E. Woolley 60★).

31st Match: v Sussex (Hove)   Aug 30, Sept 1, 2.
Australians 367 (A. F. Kippax 158, A. Hurwood 61, P. M. Hornibrook 59★, M. W. Tate 6-82) and 233-9 dec (A. F. Kippax 102★) drew with Sussex 269 (J. H. Parks 84, T. Cook 67★, P. M. Hornibrook 5-51) and 93-1.

32nd Match: v An England XI (Folkestone)   Sept 3, 4, 5.
An England XI 403-8 dec (L. E. G. Ames 121, W. R. Hammond 54, R. E. S. Wyatt 51, M. W. Tate 50) and 46-1 drew with Australians 432 (A. Jackson 78, W. H. Ponsford 76, D. G. Bradman 63, E. L. a'Beckett 53, M. J. C. Allom 4-94, A. P. Freeman 4-131).

33rd Match: v Club Cricket Conference (Lord's)   Sept 6, 8.
Australians 278 (D. G. Bradman 70, W. M. Woodfull 69, A. F. Kippax 63, W. T. Brindley 5-71, H. T. O. Smith 4-70) beat C.C.C. 133 (G. F. Summers 53, A. Hurwood 5-14, A. G. Fairfax 4-41) and 104 (P. M. Hornibrook 4-37) by an innings and 41 runs.

34th Match: v H. D. G. Leveson-Gower's XI (Scarborough)   Sept 10, 11, 12.
H. D. G. Leveson-Gower's XI 218-9 dec (A. Sandham 59, P. M. Hornibrook 5-69) and 247 (J. B. Hobbs 59, M. Leyland 50) drew with Australians 238 (D. G. Bradman 96, A. F. Kippax 59, W. Rhodes 5-95).

1931: 2nd New Zealanders

The New Zealanders were allotted one three-day Test Match for the 1931 tour, having not been accorded Test Match status on their first visit in 1927. The team which travelled to England aboard the R.M.S. *Rangitata* consisted of T. C. Lowry (captain and manager), C. S. Dempster and K. C. James, all of Wellington; C. F. W. Allcott, A. M. Matheson, J. E. Mills, H. G. Vivian and G. L. Weir of Auckland; R. C. Blunt of Otago and I. B. Cromb, J. L. Kerr, W. E. Merritt, M. L. Page and R. O. Talbot of Canterbury.

The team was unfortunate in that 1931 was one of the most cheerless of recent English summers and of their 32 first-class matches no fewer than 23 ended as a draw, including the single Test. This match was not rained on, however, and the New

Zealanders, who faced a first innings deficit of 230, batted brilliantly in their second innings to reach 469 for 9 declared, with Dempster and Page reaching hundreds. This success by the New Zealanders meant that in the middle of July the Board of Control decided to play two additional Tests—the matches against Surrey and Lancashire were cancelled to make way for this sudden alteration to the fixture list. In the Second Test England overwhelmed the visitors and in the Third no play was possible until the afternoon of the last day.

Dempster was the success of the tour and his being unable to play in the Second Test because of a leg injury had a great deal to do with New Zealand's defeat in that match. Mills, his opening partner, also made runs attractively. Blunt and Page had good seasons too, the latter being sounder than in 1927. Lowry was somehow capable of being captain and manager and still scoring runs. A. T. Donnelly of the New Zealand Cricket Council came to England for the second half of the tour and assisted Lowry as

---

1931: 2nd New Zealanders

1st Match: v Maori Club (Worcester Park)   May 4.
New Zealanders 183-7 dec (R. O. Talbot 53, C. S. Dempster 51) drew with Maori Club 110-7.*

2nd Match: v Essex (Leyton)   May 6, 7, 8.
New Zealanders 425 (C. S. Dempster 212, A. G. Daer 5-74) beat Essex 264 (J. O'Connor 129, W. E. Merritt 4-89) and 113 (W. E. Merritt 8-41) by an innings and 48 runs.

3rd Match: v Leicestershire (Leicester)   May 9, 11, 12.
New Zealanders 434-8 dec (M. L. Page 103, C. S. Dempster 92, J. E. Mills 67) and 90-7 (H. C. Snary 5-39) drew with Leicestershire 277 (A. Shipman 58, W. E. Astill 58, I. B. Cromb 5-62) and 273-6 dec (N. F. Armstrong 52*, A. Shipman 51, A. Coleman 55).

4th Match: v Hampshire (Southampton)   May 13, 14, 15.
New Zealanders 271 (J. L. Kerr 88, A. E. G. Baring 5-90) and 161-4 (C. S. Dempster 106*) drew with Hampshire 190 (C. P. Mead 99, A. M. Matheson 4-49, W. E. Merritt 4-79).

5th Match: v M.C.C. (Lord's)   May 16, 18, 19.
New Zealanders 302-9 dec (T. C. Lowry 101*, R. O. Talbot 66) beat M.C.C. 132 (D. R. Jardine 62*, I. B. Cromb 6-46) and 48 (W. E. Merritt 7-28) by an innings and 122 runs.

6th Match: v Worcestershire (Worcester)   May 20, 21, 22.
Worcestershire 286 (H. H. I. Gibbons 118) and 112-7 (W. E. Merritt 4-52) drew with New Zealanders 215.

7th Match: v Glamorgan (Swansea)   May 23, 25, 26.
New Zealanders 288-6 dec (C. S. Dempster 129*, I. B. Cromb 52*, W. E. Jones 6-91) and 190-4 dec (G. L. Weir 100*) drew with Glamorgan 200 (A. H. Dyson 54, W. E. Merritt 6-91) and 103-5.

8th Match: v Oxford University (Oxford)   May 27, 28, 29.
New Zealanders 488 (H. G. Vivian 135, M. L. Page 113, J. E. Mills 92, H. G. O. Owen-Smith 7-153) drew with Oxford University 129-4.

9th Match: v Middlesex (Lord's)   May 30, June 1, 2.
Middlesex 241 (E. H. Hendren 74, G. O. B. Allen 58, I. B. Cromb 8-70) and 225 (W. E. Merritt 5-77) beat New Zealanders 152 (I. A. R. Peebles 5-66) and 235 (R. C. Blunt 82, G. O. B. Allen 4-55) by 79 runs.

10th Match: v Cambridge University (Cambridge)   June 3, 4, 5.
New Zealanders 375 (R. C. Blunt 120, J. E. Mills 59) and 226-5 dec (C. S. Dempster 101*) drew with Cambridge University 305 (D. F. Surfleet 86, G. D. Kemp-Welch 61, A. H. Fabian 54, A. M. Matheson 4-76) and 200-5 (G. D. Kemp-Welch 102*, F. R. Brown 72).

11th Match: v Somerset (Bath)   June 6, 8, 9.
Somerset 244 (J. W. Lee 98, R. A. Ingle 60, R. C. Blunt 5-60) and 201 (J. L. Weir 5-57) drew with New Zealanders 255 (R. O. Talbot 60, R. C. Blunt 54).

12th Match: v Gloucestershire (Gloucester)   June 10, 11, 12.
Gloucestershire 132 (I. B. Cromb 5-42) and 86-4 dec drew with New Zealanders 89 (C. W. L. Parker 6-34, T. W. J. Goddard 4-36) and 65-6 (T. W. J. Goddard 4-21).

13th Match: v Derbyshire (Derby)   June 13, 15, 16.
Derbyshire 230 (T. S. Worthington 60*) and 91-2 drew with New Zealanders 296 (R. C. Blunt 50, T. B. Mitchell 5-97).

14th Match: v Minor Counties (Gainsborough)   June 17, 18, 19.
Minor Counties 191 (H. W. Homer 71, T. C. Lowry 4-14, W. E. Merritt 4-72) and 115-3 drew with New Zealanders 361-8 dec (J. E. Mills 150, T. C. Lowry 52, H. C. Lock 4-113).

15th Match: v Northamptonshire (Peterborough)   June 20, 22, 23.
Northamptonshire 334 (A. H. Bakewell 109, A. D. G. Matthews 51) and 166 (A. H. Bakewell 83*, W. E. Merritt 4-55) lost to New Zealanders 346 (T. C. Lowry 85, G. L. Weir 81, H. G. Vivian 73, V. W. C. Jupp 5-99) and 155-4 (J. L. Weir 73*) by 6 wkts.

16th Match: v England (Lord's)   June 27, 29, 30.
New Zealand 224 (C. S. Dempster 53, I. A. R. Peebles 5-77) and 469-9 dec (C. S. Dempster 120, M. L. Page 104, R. C. Blunt 96, I. A. R. Peebles 4-150) drew with England 454 (L. E. G. Ames 137, G. O. B. Allen 122, F. E. Woolley 80, W. E. Merritt 4-104) and 146-5.

17th Match: v Staffordshire (Stoke-on-Trent)   July 2, 3.
New Zealanders 190 and 143-5 drew with Staffordshire 301 (H. W. Homer 68, W. H. Ellerker 68, J. S. Heath 60).

18th Match: v Nottinghamshire (Trent Bridge)   July 4, 6, 7.
Nottinghamshire 332 (G. Gunn 101, A. Staples 62) drew with New Zealanders 259-8 (C. S. Dempster 65, M. L. Page 61, T. C. Lowry 51, F. Barratt 5-52).

19th Match: v Yorkshire (Harrogate)   July 8, 9, 10.
New Zealanders 303-8 dec (H. G. Vivian 101, G. L. Weir 50, H. Verity 5-101) and 123-8 dec (R. C. Blunt 52*, H. Verity 6-67) drew with Yorkshire 189 (A. Wood 62, C. F. W. Allcott 4-29, W. E. Merritt 4-79) and 192-4 (W. Barber 66*, M. Leyland 65).

20th Match: v Lancashire (Liverpool)   July 11, 13, 14.
New Zealanders 410-9 dec (G. L. Weir 101, T. C. Lowry 92, H. G. Vivian 57, G. Hodgson 5-93) and 306-8 (H. G. Vivian 83, T. C. Lowry 58*, C. S. Dempster 51, G. L. Weir 50*) drew with Lancashire 487 (C. Hallows 115, E. Paynter 102, W. Horrocks 72, G. L. Vivian 5-117).

21st Match: v Scotland (Glasgow)   July 15, 16, 17.
New Zealanders 176 (D. S. Hiddleston 4-69) and 281-7 dec (A. M. Matheson 72, R. O. Talbot 65) beat Scotland 112 (C. F. W. Allcott 5-39, G. L. Vivian 4-39) and 110 by 235 runs.

22nd Match: v Durham (Sunderland)   July 18, 20.
Durham 145 (C. F. W. Allcott 7-50) drew with New Zealanders 216-6 (I. B. Cromb 105).

23rd Match: v Combined Services (Portsmouth)   July 22, 23, 24.
Combined Services 301 (A. J. T. McGaw 52) and 301-6 dec (R. J. Shaw 119, W. A. C. Wilkinson 76) drew with New Zealanders 364 (J. L. Kerr 72, T. C. Lowry 89, K. C. James 54, R. G. W. Melsome 4-107) and 149-6.

24th Match: v Hampshire (Bournemouth)   July 25, 27, 28.
Hampshire 104 (G. L. Vivian 5-44) and 57-9 dec (C. F. W. Allcott 6-38) drew with New Zealanders 79 (A. S. Kennedy 7-29) and 51-3.

25th Match: v England (Oval)   July 29, 30, 31.
England 416-4 dec (H. Sutcliffe 117, K. S. Duleepsinhji 109, W. R. Hammond 100*) beat New Zealand 193 (T. C. Lowry 62, G. O. B. Allen 5-14) and 197 (H. G. Vivian 51, I. A. R. Peebles 4-63) by an innings and 26 runs.

26th Match: v Glamorgan (Swansea)   Aug 1, 3, 4.
Glamorgan 136 (G. L. Vivian 6-70) and 259 (J. Mercer 62*) lost to New Zealanders 363 (J. E. Mills 137, R. C. Blunt 60, H. G. Vivian 54*, J. C. Clay 4-90) and 36-1 by 9 wkts.

27th Match: v Warwickshire (Edgbaston)   Aug 5, 6, 7.
Warwickshire 401 (J. H. Parsons 190, L. A. Bates 76) drew with New Zealanders 159 and 252-6 (R. C. Blunt 87, H. G. Vivian 57, N. E. Partridge 4-64).

28th Match: v Gloucestershire (Bristol)   Aug 8, 10, 11.
Gloucestershire 123 and 109 lost to New Zealanders 257-9 dec (T. C. Lowry 96, C. S. Dempster 54, C. W. L. Parker 6-101) by an innings and 25 runs.

29th Match: v England (Old Trafford)   Aug 15, 17, 18.
England 224-3 (H. Sutcliffe 109*, K. S. Duleepsinhji 63) drew with New Zealand did not bat.

30th Match: v Norfolk (Norwich)   Aug 20, 21.
New Zealanders 225 (C. S. Dempster 93, W. G. Eagle 4-63, R. C. Rought-Rought 4-70) beat Norfolk 97 (W. E. Merritt 6-40) and 66 (A. M. Matheson 4-24) by an innings and 62 runs.

31st Match: v Essex (Southend)   Aug 22, 24, 25.
New Zealanders 412 (T. C. Lowry 129, C. S. Dempster 88, M. S. Nichols 5-75) and 59-5 (A. G. Daer 4-19) drew with Essex 150 (H. G. Vivian 4-36) and 372 (C. Bray 129, J. R. Sheffield 56, A. M. Matheson 4-72).

32nd Match: v Kent (Canterbury)   Aug 26, 27, 28.
New Zealanders 326 (J. E. Mills 163, C. S. Marriott 5-102) and 159 (C. S. Marriott 7-58) lost to Kent 437 (F. E. Woolley 224, L. E. G. Ames 115) and 49-1 by 9 wkts.

33rd Match: v Sussex (Hove)   Aug 29, 31, Sept 1.
New Zealanders 385 (C. S. Dempster 167, J. L. Kerr 59, R. O. Talbot 58, T. E. R. Cook 4-76) and 305 (R. C. Blunt 95, J. E. Mills 64, A. F. Wensley 4-58) drew with Sussex 549-9 dec (M. W. Tate 142, K. S. Duleepsinhji 103) and 18-0.

34th Match: v Gentlemen of England (Eastbourne)   Sept 2, 3, 4.
New Zealanders 377 (R. C. Blunt 225*) drew with Gentlemen of England 22-0.

35th Match: v An England XI (Folkestone)   Sept 5, 7, 8.
New Zealanders 154 (W. R. Hammond 4-42) and 349 (M. L. Page 132, A. P. Freeman 6-148) drew with An England XI 395 (A. P. F. Chapman 114, L. E. G. Ames 69, M. J. C. Allom 58*, H. G. Vivian 5-110) and 21-1.

36th Match: v H. D. G. Leveson-Gower's XI (Scarborough)   Sept 9, 10, 11.
New Zealanders 217 (G. L. Weir 58, F. R. Brown 4-41) and 370 (R. C. Blunt 127, C. S. Dempster 122) drew with H. D. G. Leveson-Gower's XI 423-4 dec (J. B. Hobbs 153, H. Sutcliffe 126, R. E. S. Wyatt 82) and 61-3.

37th Match: v Sir J. Cahn's XII (West Bridgford)   Sept 14, 15.
New Zealanders 196 (G. L. Weir 63, R. W. V. Robins 4-37, H. S. R. Critchley-Salmonson 4-42) and 129-2 drew with Sir J. Cahn's XII 312-8 dec (J. R. Gunn 101, G. F. H. Heane 53, A. M. Matheson 4-93).*

The New Zealand touring party of 1931. Back: Cromb, Kerr, James, Talbot, Weir, Merritt, Matheson. Centre: Mills, Page, Lowry (captain), Allcott, Dempster. Front: Blunt, Vivian. Only Talbot did not play in any of the three Test matches.

1932: 2nd Indians

Owing to the political situation, the proposed 1932 tour to England looked uncertain during the summer and autumn of 1931. Apart from these difficulties the selection of the team was not simple. It had been suggested that an English cricketer living in India–A. L. Hosie, C. P. Johnstone and R. B. Lagden were possibilities–should captain the side but the Indian Board

---

1931: 2nd New Zealanders

Batting Averages

	M	I	NO	R	HS	Avge	100	c/s
C. S. Dempster	23	36	6	1778	212	59.26	7	8/1
R. C. Blunt	29	42	5	1592	225*	43.02	3	18
J. E. Mills	28	43	0	1368	163	31.81	3	10
T. C. Lowry	31	44	3	1290	129	31.46	2	29/6
H. G. Vivian	25	39	6	1002	135	30.36	2	17
M. L. Page	28	41	4	990	132	26.75	4	35
G. L. Weir	29	43	3	1035	101	25.87	2	14
R. O. Talbot	24	38	6	759	66	23.71	0	16
J. L. Kerr	22	36	1	804	88	22.97	0	6
W. E. Merritt	26	37	8	545	47	18.79	0	9
A. M. Matheson	18	19	8	204	72	18.54	0	9
K. C. James	27	33	7	462	54	17.76	0	23/21
I. B. Cromb	22	33	5	448	52*	16.00	0	17
C. F. W. Allcott	20	23	7	200	26*	12.50	0	8

Bowling Averages

	O	M	R	W	Avge	BB	5i
T. C. Lowry	103	26	274	15	18.26	4-14	0
H. G. Vivian	568.3	143	1520	64	23.75	6-70	4
A. M. Matheson	388.3	71	1048	44	23.81	4-49	0
I. B. Cromb	655	175	1525	58	26.29	8-70	4
C. F. W. Allcott	437.2	155	925	35	26.42	6-38	2
W. E. Merritt	820.1	136	2622	99	26.48	8-41	4
G. L. Weir	403	129	937	27	34.70	5-57	1
R. C. Blunt	432.5	95	1182	34	34.76	5-60	1
M. L. Page	145.3	31	417	9	46.33	3-36	0
R. O. Talbot	330	90	862	17	50.70	3-33	0

Also bowled: J. L. Kerr 11-4-32-2; J. E. Mills 3-0-5-0; C. S. Dempster 1.3-0-5-0.

Played in one non-first-class match: A. E. Donnelly

1932: 2nd Indians

Batting Averages

	M	I	NO	R	HS	Avge	100	c/s
C. K. Nayudu	26	45	5	1618	162	40.45	5	20
S. Wazir Ali	23	42	4	1229	178	32.34	4	5
S. Nazir Ali	20	32	0	1020	109	31.87	1	12
Naoomal Jaoomal	26	46	4	1297	164*	30.88	2	11
N. D. Marshall	6	12	2	268	102*	26.80	1	3
S. H. M. Colah	22	36	0	900	122	25.00	1	13
L. Amar Singh	22	33	5	641	131*	22.89	2	14
P. E. Palia	16	26	4	476	53	21.63	0	6
Lall Singh	15	24	3	418	52	19.90	0	12
M. Jahangir Khan	21	34	11	448	68	19.47	0	13
Joginder Singh	8	15	4	208	79	18.90	0	5
J. G. Navle	21	39	1	600	64	15.78	0	32/9
K. S. G. of Limbdi	11	17	1	154	43	9.62	0	9
B. E. Kapadia	7	7	1	56	37	9.33	0	8/1
Ghulam Mahomed	9	10	1	80	43	8.88	0	1
S. R. Godambe	11	15	4	85	15	7.72	0	3
Mahomed Nissar	18	26	8	113	31	6.27	0	10
Maharaja of Porbander	4	3	0	2	2	0.66	0	0

Bowling Averages

	O	M	R	W	Avge	BB	5i
Mahomed Nissar	532	128	1285	71	18.09	6-32	5
L. Amar Singh	1062.2	343	2262	111	20.78	8-90	9
S. Nazir Ali	224.1	63	501	23	21.78	5-69	1
Lall Singh	6.2	1	25	1	25.00	1-9	0
C. K. Nayudu	677.4	164	1660	65	25.53	5-21	3
S. R. Godambe	205.1	47	445	16	27.81	4-47	0
M. Jahangir Khan	744.4	219	1540	53	29.05	4-48	0
Naoomal Jaoomal	155.1	11	601	17	35.35	5-68	1
P. E. Palia	303.4	79	653	17	38.41	4-46	0
S. Wazir Ali	45	10	129	3	43.00	2-3	0
Ghulam Mahomed	131	34	286	3	95.33	2-56	0

Also bowled: S. H. M. Colah 9-2-17-0; N. D. Marshall 3-0-6-0.

---

manager. Vivian was the best all-rounder, his left-arm bowling being most useful. Merritt fell away and in trying to bowl too many googlies lost control on a number of occasions. Cromb was perhaps the most effective bowler, and Allcott also had days of success. The fielding was much better than in 1927, with James an excellent wicketkeeper.

The team travelled home in the s.s. *Ruahine*, sailing from Southampton.

decided that only native-born Indians could represent India. The choice of captain was then between K. S. Duleepsinhji and the Nawab of Pataudi, but neither were available. The team was announced following a series of trials in Patiala and Lahore: the Maharajah of Patiala (captain), the K.S.G. of Limbdi, the Maharaj Kumar of Vizianagram, L. Amar Singh, S. H. M. Colah, Ghulam Mahomed, S. R. Godambe, Joginder Singh, B. E. Kapadia, Lall Singh, N. D. Marshall, Naoomal Jaoomal, J. G. Navle, C. K. Nayudu, S. Nazir Ali, Mahomed Nissar, P. E. Palia and S. Wazir Ali. The team stayed at Patiala under instruction from F. A. Tarrant for a month before sailing to England on 2 April. In the middle of March the Maharaja of Patiala and the Maharaj Kumar of Vizianagram decided they could not afford the time and the Maharaja of Porbander was brought in as captain,

with M. Jahangir Khan as the other replacement. The team was managed by Major E. W. C. Ricketts.

As with the 1931 New Zealand side the Indians were allotted a single Test. When the tour began it quickly became obvious that neither the Maharajah of Porbander nor the K.S.G. of Limbdi were able enough players for first-class cricket and C. K. Nayudu captained for the major matches.

Nayudu proved a capable leader and was also the best batsman in the team, with excellent figures for the summer. Wazir Ali, a defensive bat, hit six hundreds in all and played many good innings, while his brother Nazir Ali was much more aggressive, but often out through impatience. The other effective batsman was Jeoomal, who was similar in style to Wazir. The leading bowler, Mahomed Nissar, delivered fast in-swingers, while Amar

---

1932: 2nd Indians

1st Match: v T. Gilbert Scott's XII (Pelsham Rye)   April 29, 30.
Indians 132 (R. S. G. Scott 4-33) and 104-9 dec drew with T. Gilbert Scott's XII 157 (Ghulam Mohammad 6-42, Naoomal Jaoomal 4-42) and 52-5.

2nd Match: v Army (Aldershot)   May 2, 3.
Match Abandoned–no play due to rain.

3rd Match: v Sussex (Hove)   May 4, 5, 6.
Indians 236 (M. Naoomal Jaoomal 64, M. W. Tate 5-34, A. F. Wensley 5-72) and 247-6 dec (C. K. Nayudu 67) drew with Sussex 222 (R. S. G. Scott 58, S. Nazir Ali 5-69, L. Amar Singh 4-64) and 107-2.

4th Match: v H. M. Martineau's XI (Holyport)   May 9, 10.
H. M. Martineau's XI 88 (M. Jahangir Khan 5-47, P. E. Palia 4-16) drew with Indians 118 (R. S. Grant 4-42).

5th Match: v Blackheath XII (Blackheath)   May 12.
Indians 149 beat Blackheath XII 88 by 61 runs.

6th Match: v Glamorgan (Cardiff)   May 14, 16, 17.
Glamorgan 253 (A. H. Dyson 52, J. C. Clay 52, M. Jahangir Khan 4-48) and 197-2 dec (A. H. Dyson 100, M. J. L. Turnbull 72) drew with Indians 194 (W. E. Jones 4-38) and 184-4 (S. Wazir Ali 108).*

7th Match: v Oxford University (Oxford)   May 18, 19, 20.
Indians 324 (S. Wazir Ali 132, C. K. Nayudu 85) and 32-2 beat Oxford University 132 (Mahomed Nissar 6-32) and 219 (C. D. A. Pullan 74, P. G. Van der Bijl 73, P. E. Palia 4-46) by 8 wkts.

8th Match: v M.C.C. (Lord's)   May 21, 23, 24.
Indians 228 (C. K. Nayudu 118) drew with M.C.C. 200-7 (C. K. Nayudu 4-31).*

9th Match: v Hampshire (Southampton)   May 25, 26.
Indians 51 (J. Bailey 5-24, A. S. Kennedy 4-15) and 119 lost to Hampshire 273 (J. Arnold 113, A. S. Kennedy 50) by an innings and 103 runs.

10th Match: v Essex (Leyton)   May 28, 30, 31.
Essex 169 (L. Amar Singh 5-49) and 142-1 (L. G. Crawley 77) drew with Indians 307-7 dec (S. Nazir Ali 109, C. K. Nayudu 82).*

11th Match: v Norfolk (Norwich)   June 2, 3.
Indians 101 (A. G. Utting 4-34) and 204-9 dec (P. E. Palia 56, A. G. Utting 4-61) beat Norfolk 49 (Mahomed Nissar 6-14, S. Nazir Ali 4-26) and 128 (Mahomed Nissar 8-43) by 128 runs.

12th Match: v Northamptonshire (Kettering)   June 4, 6, 7.
Northamptonshire 155 (Mahomed Nissar 4-38, L. Amar Singh 5-45) and 151 (A. W. Snowden 51) lost to Indians 279 (C. K. Nayudu 80, S. H. M. Colah 63, V. W. C. Jupp 5-64) and 29-0 by 10 wkts.

13th Match: v Cambridge University (Cambridge)   June 8, 9, 10.
Cambridge University 92 (L. Amar Singh 5-30) and 274 (A. Ratcliffe 112, A. W. G. Hadingham 80, L. Amar Singh 6-70) lost to Indians 308 (S. H. M. Colah 96, R. C. Rought-Rought 5-71) and 59-1 by 9 wkts.*

14th Match: v Lancashire (Liverpool)   June 11, 13, 14.
Indians 493 (C. K. Nayudu 125, L. Amar Singh 131, M. Jahangir Khan 68, J. G. Navle 64, G. Hodgson 4-143) and 36-2 drew with Lancashire 399 (E. Paynter 153, G. E. Tyldesley 78).*

15th Match: v Eastern Counties (Lincoln)   June 15, 16.
Eastern Counties 122 and 173 (S. D. Rhodes 90) lost to Indians 424-5 dec (N. D. Marshall 148, K. S. G. of Limbdi 100, S. Wazir Ali 64) by an innings and 129 runs.*

16th Match: v Worcestershire (Worcester)   June 18, 20, 21.
Worcestershire 294 (Nawab of Pataudi 83, H. H. I. Gibbons 69, L. Amar Singh 4-59, M. Naoomal Jaoomal 5-68) and 210 (L. Wright 86, L. Amar Singh 7-78) lost to Indians 297 (S. Nazir Ali 58, Lall Singh 52) and 209-7 (C. K. Nayudu 61, S. Nazir Ali 56).

17th Match: v England (Lord's)   June 25, 27, 28.
England 259 (D. R. Jardine 79, L. E. G. Ames 65, Mahomed Nissar 5-93) and 275-8 dec (D. R. Jardine 85, E. Paynter 54, M. Jahangir Khan 4-60) beat India 189 (W. E. Bowes 4-49) and 187 (L. Amar Singh 51) by 158 runs.

18th Match: v Oxfordshire (Oxford)   June 29, 30.
Indians 373 (S. Wazir Ali 155, Mahomed Nissar 53, G. B. Ormerod 4-80) drew with Oxfordshire 165 (L. Amar Singh 5-50).

19th Match: v Nottinghamshire (Trent Bridge)   July 2, 4, 5.
Nottinghamshire 188 (L. Amar Singh 7-55) and 288 (C. B. Harris 67, B. Lilley 55, C. K. Nayudu 5-95, Naoomal Jaoomal 4-34) beat Indians 125 (W. Voce 5-51) and 127 (S. J. Staples 4-35) by 224 runs.

20th Match: v Staffordshire (Stoke-on-Trent)   July 6, 7.
Staffordshire 209 (L. E. Gale 66, Naoomal Jaoomal 4-39, M. Jahangir Khan 4-67) and 142-6 dec (E. Mayer 57) drew with Indians 162 (C. J. Taylor 7-61) and 94-6.*

21st Match: v Lancashire (Old Trafford)   July 9, 11, 12.
Lancashire 442-5 dec (G. E. Tyldesley 196, F. B. Watson 142) and 27-4 beat Indians 204 (S. H. M. Colah 122, H. R. W. Butterworth 6-85) and 264 (Naoomal Jaoomal 86, H. R. W. Butterworth 4-78) by 6 wkts.

22nd Match: v Durhanm (Sunderland)   July 13, 14.
Match Abandoned–no play due to rain.

23rd Match: v Yorkshire (Harrogate)   July 16, 18, 19.
Indians 160 (H. Verity 5-65) and 66 (S. Nazir Ali 52, G. G. Macaulay 8-21) lost to Yorkshire 161-8 dec (Mahomed Nissar 5-21) and 68-4 by 6 wkts.

24th Match: v Middlesex (Lord's)   July 20, 21, 22.
Indians 409-7 dec (Naoomal Jaoomal 164, C. K. Nayudu 101, S. Nazir Ali 55) and 14-2 drew with Middlesex 253 (E. H. Hendren 51, Mahomed Nissar 4-61) and 292 (J. W. Hearne 60, E. H. Hendren 58, C. K. Nayudu 5-53).*

25th Match: v Scotland (Broughty Ferry)   July 23, 25, 26.
Indians 146 (J. H. Melville 6-32) and 245 (S. Wazir Ali 126, W. Anderson 6-51) beat Scotland 81 and 110 (C. K. Nayudu 4-23) by 200 runs.*

26th Match: v Northumberland (Newcastle-on-Tyne)   July 27, 28.
Indians 101 (J. L. Allan 5-32) and 138-8 dec drew with Northumberland 143 and 45-2.

27th Match: v Glamorgan (Swansea)   July 30, Aug 1, 2.
Indians 229 (C. K. Nayudu 67, J. Mercer 5-44) and 87 (J. C. Clay 4-34) beat Glamorgan 81 (L. Amar Singh 6-38) and 181 (A. H. Howard 57) by 54 runs.

28th Match: v Warwickshire (Edgbaston)   Aug 3, 4, 5.
Indians 282 (Naoomal Jaoomal 72, L. Amar Singh 57, G. A. E. Paine 5-110) and 344-8 dec (C. K. Nayudu 162, N. D.Marshall 102, H. H. Jarrett 5-158) drew with Warwickshire 354 (R. E. S. Wyatt 83, N. Kilner 60, J. H. Parsons 53, S. R. Godambe 4-64) and 110-3.*

29th Match: v Gloucestershire (Bristol)   Aug 6, 8, 9.
Indians 236 (S. Wazir Ali 82, T. W. J. Goddard 4-58) and 390 (S. H. M. Colah 94, Joginder Singh 79, L. Amar Singh 63, T. W. J. Goddard 6-115) beat Gloucestershire 230 (B. H. Lyon 70, L. Amar Singh 8-90) and 341 (C. C. R. Dacre 95, L. Amar Singh 4-121) by 55 runs.

30th Match: v Somerset (Weston-super-Mare)   Aug 10, 11, 12.
Indians 285 (Naoomal Jaoomal 81, S. Nazir Ali 62) and 234-7 dec (C. K. Nayudu 130) beat Somerset 177 (Mahomed Nissar 6-45) and 179 (C. K. Nayudu 4-39, S. R. Godambe 4-47) by 163 runs.*

31st Match: v Surrey (Oval)   Aug 13, 15, 16.
Surrey 387-9 dec (E. W. Whitfield 101, M. J. C. Allom 60, J. F. Parker 56*, Mahomed Nissar 4-53) and 95-3 drew with Indians 204 (S. Nazir Ali 64, P. G. H. Fender 5-58) and 322-8 dec (S. Nazir Ali 84, S. Wasir Ali 82, M. J. C. Allom 4-32).*

32nd Match: v Derbyshire (Ilkeston)   Aug 17, 18, 19.
Derbyshire 248 (D. Smith 87, L. Amar Singh 4-71) and 168 (A. W. Richardson 56) beat Indians 205 (M. Naoomal Jaoomal 101, T. B. Mitchell 5-77) and 202 (T. B. Mitchell 5-77) and 202 (T. B. Mitchell 5-71, L. F. Townsend 5-78) by 9 runs.

33rd Match: v Leicestershire (Leicester)   Aug 20, 22, 23.
Indians 412-8 dec (S. Wazir Ali 178, Naoomal Jaoomal 63, P. E. Palia 53) beat Leicestershire 106 (C. K. Nayudu 5-21) and 291 (H. C. Snary 124, L. N. Amarsingh 4-61) by an innings and 15 runs.*

34th Match: v Kent (Canterbury)   Aug 24, 25, 26.
Kent 295 (A. P. F. Chapman 78, F. E. Woolley 68, Mahomed Nissar 6-92) and 154 (T. A. Pearce 65, L. N. Amarsingh 5-57) beat Indians 270 (C. K. Nayudu 99, A. E. Watt 4-53) and 121 (A. P. Freeman 6-69) by 58 runs.

35th Match: v Sir Julien Cahn's XI (West Bridgford)   Aug 27, 29.
Indians 152 (M. Jahangir Khan 63) and 164 (R. W. V. Robins 4-59) lost to Sir Julien Cahn's XI 342 (F. C. W. Newman 97, C. R. N. Maxwell 81, L. N. Amar Singh 6-107) by an innings and 26 runs.*

36th Match: v Indian Gymkhana (Osterley Park)   Aug 31, Sept 1.
Indians 343-4 dec (S. Wazir Ali 141, C. K. Nayudu 104) drew with Indian Gymkhana 320 (T. K. Contractor 80, H. S. Malik 75, D. Liversz 58, A. d'Avoine 50, C. K. Nayudu 5-81).*

37th Match: v An England XI (Folkestone)   Sept 3, 5, 6.
An England XI 282-5 dec (L. E. G. Ames 105, B. W. Hone 67) beat Indians 165 (M. S. Nichols 4-28, A. P. Freeman 4-75) and 77 (A. P. Freeman 4-39) by an innings and 40 runs.*

38th Match: v H. D. G. Leveson-Gower's XI (Scarborough)   Sept 7, 8, 9.
H. D. G. Leveson-Gower's XI 305-5 dec (H. Sutcliffe 106, M. Leyland 70) and 99-0 (A. Staples 58) drew with Indians 280 (L. Amar Singh 107, V. W. C. Jupp 5-86).*

39th Match: v North of Scotland (Elgin)   Sept 10.
Drawn.

The second Indian touring party to play in England. Back: Lall Singh, Palia, Jahangir Khan, Mahomed Nisar, Amar Singh, Kapadia, Godambe, Ghulam Mahomed, Navle. Centre: Syed Wazir Ali, Nayudu, Maharaja Porbander (captain), Limdi, Syed Nazir Ali, Joginder Singh. Front: Naoomal Jaoomal, Colah, Marshall.

Singh made the ball come very fast off the wicket and was on his day the most dangerous of the attack. Nayudu bowled slow medium and he, with Jahangir Khan, took some wickets, but the left-armer Palia met with little success.

The tourists lost the Test Match and seven other first-class games, but it was felt that the visit was more successful than had been anticipated.

1932: South Americans

The team representing South America arrived in Southampton on 16 May. The organisation of this unusual venture was mainly in the hands of E. W. S. Thomson, the honorary secretary of the Argentine Cricket Association, and he acted as manager of the party. The original invitations were sent to C. H. Gibson, D. Ayling, C. E. Ayling, J. H. Paul, F. F. Keen, A. L. Jacobs, H. W. Marshal, R. L. Stuart, J. Knox and G. Ferguson of Argentina; H. Morrissy, A. C. Grass, O. T. Cunningham and R. M. Pryor of Brazil and C. H. Sutton of Chile. Morrissy and Cunningham were unable to make the tour and J. H. Naumann of Brazil was added. The captain was C. H. Gibson. It later transpired that Naumann was unable to play and A. L. S. Jackson of Chile travelled to England a fortnight after the main group of players.

Jackson proved to be the best batsman and scored his runs in a

1932: South Americans

Batting Averages

	M	I	NO	R	HS	Avge	100	c/s
J. Knox	5	9	3	315	110*	52.50	1	3
D. Ayling	6	10	2	342	86*	42.75	0	2
R. L. Stuart	5	9	1	292	133	36.50	1	2
H. W. Marshal	5	9	1	255	153	31.87	1	5
A. C. Grass	3	6	4	60	24*	30.00	0	0
A. L. S. Jackson	5	9	0	254	78	28.22	0	1
G. W. Ferguson	6	11	0	264	85	24.00	0	2
F. F. Keen	5	7	2	81	23	16.20	0	2
R. L. Latham	5	9	1	120	58	15.00	0	6
J. H. Paul	5	8	0	90	25	11.25	0	2
C. E. Ayling	6	9	1	89	34	11.12	0	5
C. H. Gibson	6	10	0	109	50	10.90	0	6
A. L. Jacobs	2	3	0	19	10	6.33	0	3

Also batted: C. H. Sutton (1 match) 10; R. M. Pryor (1 match) 0 and 0.

Bowling Averages

	O	M	R	W	Avge	BB	5i
D. Ayling	233	80	530	33	16.06	6-49	2
J. H. Paul	54.3	14	141	7	20.14	2-23	0
C. E. Ayling	174	38	519	19	27.32	5-48	1
C. H. Gibson	204.2	53	619	19	32.57	5-113	1
F. F. Keen	154	35	448	11	40.73	3-31	0
J. Knox	20	4	75	1	75.00	1-46	0

Also bowled: R. M. Pryor 5-1-13-0; R. L. Stuart 3-0-18-0; G. W. Ferguson 1-0-1-0; C. H. Sutton 5-0-23-0.

1932: South Americans

1st Match: v Affiliated South American Banks (Teddington)   May 21.
South Americans 215-3 (H. W. Marshal 101*, R. L. Latham 68) drew with South American Banks did not bat.

2nd Match: v Richmond (Richmond)   May 26, 27.
South Americans 221 (J. H. Paul 110, J. Knox 51) drew with Richmond 141-8 (R. L. Latham 65).

3rd Match: v H. M. Martineau's XI (Holyport)   May 28.
H. M. Martineau's XI 66-2 drew with South Americans did not bat.

4th Match: v Kent 2nd XI (Canterbury)   May 30, 31.
South Americans 259 (H. W. Marshal 83, R. L. Stuart 57) and 143 (C. Lewis 4-31) lost to Kent 2nd XI 181 and 222-4 (T. A. Pearce 117*) by 6 wkts.

5th Match: v Civil Service (Chiswick)   June 2, 3.
South Americans 262 (G. W. Ferguson 95, D. Ayling 81, J. G. Heaslip 7-76) and 53-1 drew with Civil Service 136 (J. G. Heaslip 54*) and 190-5 dec (P. Ogilvie 60, J. H. Evans 88).

6th Match: v Oxford University (Oxford)   June 4, 6, 7.
Oxford University 170 (D. Ayling 4-38) and 248 (R. H. J. Brooke 119, D. Ayling 6-49) lost to South Americans 405 (H. W. Marshal 153, G. W. Ferguson 85, E. A. Barlow 5-84) and 14-0 by 10 wkts.

7th Match: v Gentlemen of Somerset (Taunton)   June 8, 9.
South Americans 216 (J. H. Paul 92, A. McDonald-Watson 5-58) and 108 (J. C. White 6-23) lost to Gentlemen of Somerset 177 (R. P. Northway 69, Cyril Ayling 4-39) and 149-2 (R. Illingworth 82*) by 8 wkts.

8th Match: v Leicestershire (Leicester)   June 11, 13, 14.
South Americans 112 (G. Geary 4-32, H. C. Snary 4-35) and 116 lost to Leicestershire 261 (C. H. Gibson 5-113) by an innings and 33 runs.

9th Match: v M.C.C. (Lord's)   June 15, 16.
M.C.C. 338-8 dec (J. W. Hearne 85, H. W. Taylor 60, W. G. L. F. Lowndes 50, Cyril Ayling 5-72) and 150-3 dec (F. J. Seabrook 67) drew with South Americans 270 (Cyril Ayling 95*, G. R. Reynolds-Brown 4-74) and 50-3.

10th Match: v Capt W. F. T. Holland's XI (Buscot's Park)   June 18.
South Americans 300-5 dec (Cyril Ayling 74*, J. Knox 76, A. L. S. Jackson 85) drew with Capt W. F. T. Holland's XI 167-7.

11th Match: v Gentlemen of Surrey (Oval)   June 20, 21.
Gentlemen of Surrey 389-6 dec (A. Jeacocke 93, H. C. Pattison 62*, E. G. Stroud 58, J. C. Christopherson 55) and 59-0 drew with South Americans 477 (C. H. Gibson 99, R. L. Latham 86, H. W. Marshal 68, G. W. Ferguson 67).

12th Match: v Army (Aldershot)   June 22, 23, 24.
South Americans 303 (R. L. Stuart 133) and 100 (M. B. Burrows 4-17) lost to Army 208 (D. Ayling 4-35, Cyril Ayling 4-54) and 196-5 (J. R. Cole 63, R. E. Hudson 59) by 5 wkts.

13th Match: v Sir J. Cahn's XI (West Bridgford)   June 25, 27, 28.
Sir J. Cahn's XI 413 (D. P. B. Morkel 251, F. C. W. Newman 85, C. H. Gibson 4-107) and 150 (D. Ayling 5-40, Cyril Ayling 5-48) lost to South Americans 338 (A. L. S. Jackson 62, D. Ayling 59, C. H. Gibson 50, T. L. Richmond 5-126) and 227-5 (D. Ayling 86*, A. L. S. Jackson 78) by 5 wkts.

14th Match: v Royal Navy (Chatham)   June 30, July 1.
Royal Navy 152 (C. H. Gibson 5-66) and 207 (T. E. Halsey 113, C. H. Sutton 4-52) drew with South Americans 119-8 (C. H. Sutton 4-52).

15th Match: v Sussex (Eastbourne)   July 2, 4, 5.
Sussex 326 (Jas Langridge 128, D. Ayling 4-85) and 142-7 dec drew with South Americans 257 (J. Knox 110*, Jas Langridge 7-87) and 113-3 (J. Knox 55*).

16th Match: v Scotland (Edinburgh)   July 7, 8, 9.
South Americans 220 (G. W. Ferguson 60, A. L. S. Jackson 56, A. D. Baxter 5-88) and 208 (R. L. Latham 58, D. Ayling 53, A. D. Baxter 6-87) lost to Scotland 345 (A. K. McTavish 109, J. F. Jones 54) and 84-2 by 8 wkts.

17th Match: v Liverpool and District (Liverpool)   July 11, 12.
South Americans 337-2 dec (D. Ayling 127, A. L. S. Jackson 123, R. L. Stuart 57*) drew with Liverpool and District 375 (Bates 111, H. N. Brown 67, H. W. Hodgson 56).

18th Match: v Sir A. D. McAlpine's XI (Marchwiel Hall)   July 13, 14.
South Americans 98-1 (A. L. S. Jackson 66*) drew with Sir A. D. McAlpine's XI did not bat.

most attractive manner. Knox looked good but did not score as heavily as was thought likely before the tour began. The Ayling brothers were the all-rounders of the team. The bowling relied on the Aylings, for Gibson was not up to his old form. Keen the left-armer was very expensive. The major fault of the side was their fielding, which made the bowling even weaker than it was and a shoal of dropped catches sapped the confidence of the tourists.

1933: 5th West Indians

As in 1928, the tourists were allotted three Tests and once again they failed to live up to the expectations of their admirers. Twenty-seven players were invited to take part in trial matches in

1933: 5th West Indians

1st Match: v A. P. Freeman's XII (Gravesend) April 24.
West Indians 231 (O. C. Da Costa 59, C. S. Marriott 4-62) drew with A. P. Freeman's XII 178-6 (F. E. Woolley 59, E. H. Hendren 57).

2nd Match: v T. Gilbert Scott's XI (Pelsham Rye) April 25, 26.
T. Gilbert Scott's XI 226-9 dec (A. M. Crawley 69, Jas Langridge 51, E. A. Martindale 4-39) drew with West Indians 145-7 (G. A. Headley 58).

3rd Match: v R. Earle's XI (Bushridge Hall) April 27.
West Indians 229-7 dec (O. C. Da Costa 68*) drew with R. Earle's XI 97-7.

4th Match: v Reigate Priory (Reigate) April 28.
West Indians 193 (F. R. Martin 63*) drew with Reigate Priory 122-9 (M. J. C. Allom 56).

5th Match: v Blackheath (Blackheath) May 1.
West Indians 235-5 dec (C. A. Roach 102*) beat Blackheath 70 (E. A. Martindale 9-27) by 165 runs.

6th Match: v G. J. V. Weigall's XI (Maidstone) May 2.
West Indians 233-6 dec (C. A. Wiles 62, G. C. Grant 59, C. A. Merry 53) drew with G. J. V. Weigall's XI 45-0.

7th Match: v Club Cricket Conference (Catford) May 3, 4.
C.C.C. 102 (R. N. Hunt 59, E. A. Martindale 5-38, E. E. Achong 4-41) and 119 lost to West Indians 233 (G. A. Headley 83, S. W. Newnham 7-62) by an innings and 12 runs.

8th Match: v Northamptonshire (Northampton) May 6, 8, 9.
Northamptonshire 288 (J. E. Timms 64, A. L. Cox 51, N. Grimshaw 54) beat West Indians 129 (G. A. Headley 52, E. W. Clark 5-32) and 97 (E. W. Clark 5-29) by an innings and 62 runs.

9th Match: v Oxford University (Oxford) May 10, 11, 12.
Oxford University 189 (H. C. Griffith 4-35) and 287-7 dec (F. G. H. Chalk 149, R. G. Stainton 89) drew with West Indians 191 (G. A. Headley 56, H. G. O. Owen-Smith 4-57) and 150-4 (F. R. Martin 67).

10th Match: v Essex (Leyton) May 13, 15, 16.
West Indians 106 (M. S. Nichols 6-31) and 370-6 dec (O. C. Da Costa 105*, C. A. Wiles 71, G. A. Headley 50) beat Essex 86 (E. A. Martindale 8-32) and 254 (J. A. Cutmore 75, L. C. Eastman 75, E. A. Martindale 4-73) by 136 runs.

11th Match: v Cambridge University (Cambridge) May 17, 18, 19.
West Indians 269 (G. A. Headley 75, G. C. Grant 61, E. Cawston 4-51) and 7-0 beat Cambridge University 104 (O. C. Da Costa 4-31, E. A. Martindale 4-34) and 171 (D. R. Wilcox 73, E. E. Achong 4-52) by 10 wkts.

12th Match: v M.C.C. (Lord's) May 20, 22, 23.
West Indians 309 (G. A. Headley 129, M. J. C. Allom 5-85, W. E. Bowes 4-72) and 268 (L. N. Constantine 51, J. C. White 4-77) beat M.C.C. 246 (A. P. F. Chapman 97, B. H. Valentine 60, E. A. Martindale 5-70, L. N. Constantine 4-88) and 179 (E. H. Hendren 61, E. E. Achong 5-49) by 152 runs.

13th Match: v Hampshire (Southampton) May 24, 25, 26.
Hampshire 306 (C. P. Mead 80, A. E. Pothecary 72, A. S. Kennedy 50) and 149 (E. A. Martindale 6-61) lost to West Indians 227 (E. L. G. Hoad 88, I. Barrow 60, A. S. Kennedy 4-45) and 232-4 (C. A. Roach 67, O. C. Da Costa 53*) by 6 wkts.

14th Match: v Surrey (Oval) May 27, 29, 30.
West Indians 460 (C. A. Roach 180, I. Barrow 60, C. A. Wiles 51, A. R. Gover 4-108) and 160-5 (O. C. Da Costa 58*) drew with Surrey 470 (J. B. Hobbs 221, F. R. Martin 4-53).

15th Match: v Worcestershire (Worcester) May 31, June 1, 2.
West Indies 239 (E. L. G. Hoad 80, M. E. White 4-73) and 257 (B. J. Sealey 103) lost to Worcestershire 215 (R. Howorth 68, H. H. I. Gibbons 61) and 284-9 (Nawab of Pataudi 162*, H. H. I. Gibbons 64) by 1 wkt.

16th Match: v Glamorgan (Cardiff) June 3, 5, 6.
West Indians 475 (G. A. Headley 129, G. C. Grant 61, B. J. Sealey 50, E. R. K. Glover 4-78) and 26-2 drew with Glamorgan 493 (A. H. Dyson 147, R. Duckfield 88, M. J. L. Turnbull 60, C. V. G. Haines 52, F. R. Martin 5-90).

17th Match: v Somerset (Taunton) June 7, 8, 9.
Somerset 272 (C. C. C. Case 86, J. C. White 58, H. C. Griffith 5-64) and 323 (E. F. Longrigg 67, W. T. Luckes 55*, E. E. Achong 4-78) drew with West Indians 482-6 dec (G. A. Headley 224*, C. A. Merry 75, I. Barrow 70).

18th Match: v Middlesex (Lord's) June 10, 12, 13.
West Indians 382 (O. C. Da Costa 67, H. C. Griffith 62, V. A. Valentine 59*, I. A. R. Peebles 4-108) and 251-5 dec (C. A. Roach 77) drew with Middlesex 178 (G. C. Newman 50, G. A. Headley 4-27) and 123-3.

19th Match: v Derbyshire (Derby) June 14, 15, 16.
West Indians 281 (G. A. Headley 58, B. J. Sealy 58, T. B. Mitchell 4-93) and 346-8 dec (G. A. Headley 200*) drew with Derbyshire 319 (G. M. Lee 78, D. Smith 67, V. A. Valentine 4-83) and 125-5 (A. F. Skinner 68).

20th Match: v Minor Counties (Lord's) June 17, 19, 20.
Minor Counties 253 (T. K. Dobson 126, E. E. Achong 6-108) and 190-5 dec (G. S. Butler 50) drew with West Indians 229 (C. A. Merry 71, F. Edwards 8-98) and 64-4.

21st Match: v England (Lord's) June 24, 26, 27.
England 296 (L. E. G. Ames 83*, C. F. Walters 51, E. A. Martindale 4-85) beat West Indies 97 (R. W. V. Robins 6-32) and 172 (G. A. Headley 50, H. Verity 4-45, G. G. Macaulay 4-57) by an innings and 27 runs.

22nd Match: v Berkhamsted XII (Berkhamsted) June 28.
Berkhamsted 211 (R. P. Nelson 81*, E. A. Martindale 5-21) drew with West Indians 162-8 (E. L. G. Hoad 57*).

23rd Match: v Sir J. Cahn's XI (West Bridgford) June 29, 30.
West Indians 155 (G. C. Grant 53, G. F. H. Heane 5-38) and 194-6 dec drew with Sir J. Cahn's XI 204 (C. R. N. Maxwell 74) and 60-1.

24th Match: v Lancashire (Liverpool) July 1, 3, 4.
West Indians 305 (I. Barrow 89, A. D. Baxter 5-80) and 240-5 (G. C. Grant 94) drew with Lancashire 393 (J. L. Hopwood 112, C. Washbrook 95, E. Paynter 54).

25th Match: v Yorkshire (Harrogate) July 5, 6, 7.
Yorkshire 240 (A. Mitchell 94*, L. N. Constantine 5-44) and 248 (H. Sutcliffe 86, A. Mitchell 67*, L. N. Constantine 4-50) beat West Indians 115 (H. Verity 7-29) and 173 (H. Verity 7-54) by 200 runs.

26th Match: v Nottinghamshire (Trent Bridge) July 8, 10, 11.
West Indians 314 (G. A. Headley 66, O. C. Da Costa 54, C. A. Merry 51) and 6-0 drew with Nottinghamshire 273 (W. Walker 70, A. Staples 50, W. Voce 64, E. A. Martindale 8-66).

27th Match: v Lancashire (Old Trafford) July 12, 13, 14.
West Indians 174-7 dec (G. A. Headley 66, A. D. Baxter 6-50) drew with Lancashire 39-2.

28th Match: v Leicestershire (Leicester) July 15, 17, 18.
West Indians 156 (G. A. Headley 60, A. Shipman 4-10) and 243-8 (C. A. Roach 66) drew with Leicestershire 295 (N. F. Armstrong 84, E. E. Achong 4-84, E. A. Martindale 4-89).

29th Match: v Staffordshire (Stoke-on-Trent) July 19, 20.
Staffordshire 122 (L. N. Constantine 7-50) and 99 (L. N. Constantine 4-22, E. E. Achong 4-31) drew with West Indians 168 (A. Lockett 4-30, E. N. Backhouse 4-58) and 55-1.

30th Match: v England (Old Trafford) July 22, 24, 25.
West Indies 375 (G. A. Headley 169, I. Barrow 105, E. W. Clark 4-99) and 225 (C. A. Roach 64, L. N. Constantine 64, Jas Langridge 7-56) drew with England 374 (D. R. Jardine 127, R. W. V. Robins 55, E. A. Martindale 5-73).

31st Match: v Northumberland (Newcastle-on-Tyne) July 27, 28.
West Indians 440 (O. C. Da Costa 91, C. A. Roach 77, E. L. G. Hoad 77, J. L. Allan 6-86) beat Northumberland 129 (V. A. Valentine 4-42, H. C. Griffith 4-49) and 128 (O. C. Da Costa 4-16, V. A. Valentine 4-44).

32nd Match: v Durham (Sunderland) July 29, 31.
Durham 256 (C. L. Adamson 93, C. Hickman 58, V. A. Valentine 5-73) drew with West Indians 140 (T. Woodhouse 5-73) and 29-3.

33rd Match: v Norfolk (Norwich) Aug 2, 3.
West Indians 496-8 dec (G. A. Headley 257*, C. A. Roach 103) and 35-2 drew with Norfolk 257 (B. W. Rought-Rought 57).

34th Match: v Glamorgan (Swansea) Aug 5, 7, 8.
Glamorgan 295 (W. G. Morgan 69, D. Davies 57, T. Every 51) and 197 (D. Davies 50) lost to West Indians 463 (B. J. Sealey 105*, G. A. Headley 89, C. A. Roach 70, D. E. Davies 4-124) and 30-0 by 10 wkts.

35th Match: v Warwickshire (Edgbaston) Aug 9, 10.
Warwickshire 367-7 dec (R. E. S. Wyatt 150*, A. J. W. Croom 86) drew with West Indians 474 (G. A. Headley 182, C. A. Merry 146, G. A. E. Paine 5-143).

36th Match: v England (Oval) Aug 12, 14, 15.
England 312 (A. H. Bakewell 107, C. J. Barnett 52, E. A. Martindale 5-93) beat West Indies 100 (C. S. Marriott 5-37) and 195 (C. A. Roach 56, C. S. Marriott 6-59) by an innings and 17 runs.

37th Match: v Sir L. Parkinson's XI (Blackpool) Aug 16, 17, 18.
West Indians 165 (E. A. McDonald 5-58) and 152 (A. J. Richardson 5-67) lost to Sir L. Parkinson's XI 116 (E. A. Martindale 8-39) and 203-3 (C. S. Dempster 76*) by 7 wkts.

38th Match: v Gloucestershire (Bristol) Aug 19, 21, 22.
Gloucestershire 570 (W. R. Hammond 264, B. H. Lyon 69, C. J. Barnett 60, H. C. Griffith 4-129) and 73-3 beat West Indians 271 (B. J. Sealey 87, R. A. Sinfield 4-54) and 371 (G. C. Grant 109, R. A. Sinfield 7-149) by 7 wkts.

39th Match: v Kent (Canterbury) Aug 23, 24.
Kent 331 (C. H. Knott 154*, L. E. G. Ames 86, E. A. Martindale 4-90) beat West Indians 73 (C. S. Marriott 5-36, A. P. Freeman 5-37) and 165 (G. C. Grant 54, C. S. Marriott 5-54, A. P. Freeman 5-85) by an innings and 93 runs.

40th Match: v Army (Aldershot) Aug 26, 28, 29.
Army 472-8 dec (R. E. H. Hudson 181, C. P. Hamilton 121) and 149-4 dec drew with West Indians 346 (B. J. Sealey 106*, E. L. G. Hoad 92, I. Barrow 52, C. P. Hamilton 5-83) and 181-4 (B. J. Sealey 62*).

41st Match: v Sussex (Hove) Aug 30, 31, Sept 1.
West Indians 431 (E. L. G. Hoad 149*, G. A. Headley 79, H. C. Griffith 84, J. H. Cornford 4-84) and 101-4 drew with Sussex 548 (John Langridge 172, A. Melville 114, T. E. R. Cook 57, H. W. Parks 81, E. A. Martindale 4-106).

42nd Match: v An England XI (Folkestone) Sept 2, 4, 5.
An England XI 362-9 dec (W. R. Hammond 133, L. E. G. Ames 58, F. E. Woolley 55) and 272-4 (F. E. Woolley 136) drew with West Indians 558 (G. A. Headley 167, G. C. Grant 115, B. J. Sealy 69, A. P. Freeman 6-208).

43rd Match: v Eastern Counties (Skegness) Sept 6, 7.
Eastern Counties 217 and 97-0 (R. E. Frearson 54*) drew with West Indians 383 (C. A. Wiles 112, G. A. Headley 95, E. L. G. Hoad 93, S. J. Staples 6-101).

44th Match: v H. D. G. Leveson-Gower's XI (Scarborough) Sept 9, 11, 12.
H. D. G. Leveson-Gower's XI 310 (R. E. S. Wyatt 108, L. F. Townsend 61, E. Paynter 50, E. A. Martindale 5-87) and 196-5 dec (R. E. S. Wyatt 83) beat West Indians 130 (H. Verity 5-20) and 251 (O. C. Da Costa 70, H. Verity 5-87, Jas Langridge 4-62) by 125 runs.

Trinidad, as a result of which G. C. Grant (captain), C. A. Roach, E. E. Achong, C. A. Wiles, B. J. Sealey, C. A. Merry and L. N. Constantine, all of Trinidad; F. R. Martin, G. A. Headley, I. Barrow, O. C. Da Costa and V. A. Valentine of Jamaica; H. C. Griffith, E. G. L. Hoad and E. A. Martindale of Barbados and C. M. Christiani of British Guiana were chosen. The manager was J. M. Kidney. A. Hunt of Bermuda and R. McGregor could consider themselves unlucky not to have been chosen, and there was some surprise that F. R. Martin was selected instead of J. E. D. Sealy.

The team sailed aboard the s.s. *Bayano* from Bridgetown on 4 April and arrived at Avonmouth on 16 April. They were blessed with fine weather almost throughout their tour–the hottest English summer since 1921, which no doubt helped to swell the large number of drawn matches, but another reason was the weakness of the West Indies bowling.

The spin attack rested solely with the left-arm Achong, who was rather expensive and the array of fast bowlers which should have been the strength of the side were most disappointing, only Martindale being really effective. Constantine was only available for some matches, being engaged in the Lancashire League, so the team also called on G. N. Francis, the old West Indian fast bowler, for one Test, but he achieved little. R. S. Grant, the captain's brother, also turned out. Headley was the success of the tour, dominating the batting and without him the side would have been in dire straits. Roach was a very exciting batsman, but his defence let him down. The batsmen in general found spin bowling very tricky, having very few slow bowlers of any class in the West Indies. Valentine and Da Costa assisted Martindale in the attack, with Da Costa the best all-rounder. The catching was not up to Test Match standard and as in previous tours the returns to the wicket tended to be on the wild side.

England won two of the Tests with ease–a splendid century by Headley earned a draw at Old Trafford.

The main party sailed from Avonmouth aboard the s.s. *Cavina* and arrived in Bridgetown on 30 September.

1933: 5th West Indians

Batting Averages

	M	I	NO	R	HS	Avge	100	c/s
G. A. Headley	23	38	3	2320	224*	66.28	7	17
B. J. Sealey	22	34	7	1072	106*	39.70	3	8
G. C. Grant	27	46	7	1195	115	30.64	2	23
C. de L. Innis	2	4	1	90	42	30.00	0	1
F. R. Martin	6	9	0	258	67	28.66	0	3
C. A. Merry	21	34	4	856	146	28.53	1	15
E. L. G. Hoad	24	43	4	1083	149*	27.76	1	3
O. C. Da Costa	27	45	6	1046	105*	26.82	1	17
C. A. Roach	28	52	2	1286	180	25.72	1	9
I. Barrow	25	45	1	1046	105	23.77	1	21/7
L. N. Constantine	5	9	0	181	64	20.11	0	5
C. A. Wiles	13	24	1	431	71	18.73	0	1
H. C. Griffith	21	28	4	415	84	17.29	0	10
V. A. Valentine	19	27	4	391	59*	17.00	0	11
E. E. Achong	27	38	13	324	25*	12.96	0	10
E. A. Martindale	25	33	10	252	25*	10.95	0	13
C. M. Christiani	13	19	1	179	40	9.94	0	27/4

Also batted: R. S. Grant (1 match) 10 and 6* (ct3); G. N. Francis (1 match) 4 and 11*.

Bowling Averages

	O	M	R	W	Avge	BB	5i
F. R. Martin	135.2	31	321	16	20.06	5-90	1
E. A. Martindale	668	109	2161	103	20.98	8-32	8
L. N. Constantine	116.3	26	310	14	22.14	5-44	1
G. C. Grant	45.5	1	246	9	27.33	3-24	0
C. A. Merry	150	25	420	13	32.30	2-5	0
O. C. Da Costa	459.1	100	1055	31	34.03	4-16	0
G. A. Headley	230.2	36	721	21	34.33	4-27	0
E. E. Achong	960.3	195	2566	71	36.14	6-138	2
H. C. Griffith	596	143	1638	44	37.22	5-64	1
B. J. Sealey	266	46	725	19	38.15	3-36	0
C. A. Roach	15	2	42	1	42.00	1-18	0
V. A. Valentine	587	126	1541	36	42.80	4-83	0
E. L. G. Hoad	28	1	150	3	50.00	2-63	0

Also bowled: I. Barrow 4-1-14-0; C. M. Christiani 1-0-6-0; G. N. Francis 18-3-52-0; R. S. Grant 7-2-11-3.

1934: 18th Australians

As a result of the controversy aroused by the 1932-33 M.C.C. tour to Australia, the Australian Board of Control cabled M.C.C. on 22 September 1933 before going ahead with arrangements for the 1934 tour to England. The cable asked M.C.C. to agree that leg-theory bowling was not in the best interests of the game. The M.C.C. replied more or ls agreeing and the Australian Board answered on 16 November that they would send a team to

The 1934 Australians. Back: Ferguson (scorer), Brown, Bromley, Wall, Bushby (manager), O'Reilly, Fleetwood-Smith, Darling, Grimmett, Bull (treasurer). Centre: Ebeling, Chipperfield, Bradman, Woodfull, Kippax, McCabe, Oldfield. Front: Barnett, Ponsford.

England in 1934. The M.C.C. at a meeting of the county captains left the matter of leg-theory bowling in the hands of the captains, 'in the complete confidence that they would not permit or countenance bowling of such a type.'

The team selected, which left Fremantle aboard the s.s. *Orford* on 26 March, was W. M. Woodfull (captain), W. H. Ponsford, L. S. Darling, B. A. Barnett, E. H. Bromley, H. I. Ebeling and L. O'B. Fleetwood-Smith, all of Victoria; D. G. Bradman, A. F. Kippax, S. J. McCabe, W. A. S. Oldfield, W. A. Brown, A. G. Chipperfield and W. J. O'Reilly from New South Wales and C. V. Grimmett and T. W. Wall of South Australia. The manager was H. Bushby and treasurer W. C. Bull.

As was now usual with Australian tours, the entire interest of the visit centred round the five Tests. The English selectors faced problems on the captaincy and the choice of fast bowlers. Jardine was diplomatically unavailable for selection and Larwood effectively put himself out of court through some newspaper articles. This eased the selectors' problems in one way, but meant that England would be without its two major players. The selectors became more muddled as the Test series continued and so Australia won by two matches to one: England's single victory was due entirely to some splendid bowling by Verity–15 for 104–on a difficult wicket at Lord's.

The 'bodyline' conflict was mainly confined to newspaper scoops until the match against Notts in late August. The success of Voce in this game, quickly followed by his mystery illness, was the cause of a great upheaval in the Notts club, but did not affect the remainder of the tour.

As in 1930, the Australians lost only one match during the entire visit and their strength revolved around a tremendous batting line-up. Even a fairly long list of illness and injury made little impression on the team's ability. The star was naturally

---

1934: 18th Australians

1st Match: v Worcestershire (Worcester)   May 2, 3.
Worcestershire 112 (C. V. Grimmett 5-53) and 95 (C. V. Grimmett 5-27, W. J. O'Reilly 4-25) lost to Australians 504 (D. G. Bradman 206, W. A. S. Oldfield 67, R. Howorth 4-135) by an innings and 297 runs.

2nd Match: v Leicestershire (Leicester)   May 5, 7, 8.
Leicestershire 152 (W. J. O'Reilly 7-39) and 263 (E. W. Dawson 91, W. E. Astill 50*, W. J. O'Reilly 4-40, L. O'B. Fleetwood-Smith 4-83) drew with Australians 368-5 dec (S. J. McCabe 108*, A. F. Kippax 89, D. G. Bradman 65).

3rd Match: v Cambridge University (Cambridge)   May 9, 10, 11.
Australians 481-5 dec (W. H. Ponsford 229*, W. A. Brown 105, L. S. Darling 98) beat Cambridge University 158 (C. V. Grimmett 9-74) and 160 (H. R. Cox 51*) by an innings and 163 runs.

4th Match: v M.C.C. (Lord's)   May 12, 14, 15.
M.C.C. 362 (E. H. Hendren 135, R. E. S. Wyatt 72, T. W. Wall 6-74) and 182-8 (R. E. S. Wyatt 102*, C. V. Grimmett 4-90) drew with Australians 559-6 dec (W. H. Ponsford 281*, S. J. McCabe 192, F. R. Brown 4-134).

5th Match: v Essex (Chelmsford)   May 16, 17, 18.
Essex 220 (M. S. Nichols 62*, W. J. O'Reilly 6-79) and 125 (C. V. Grimmett 5-54) lost to Australians 438 (A. G. Chipperfield 175, W. A. Brown 58, W. M. Woodfull 55) by an innings and 93 runs.

6th Match: v Oxford University (Oxford)   May 19, 21.
Australians 319 (L. S. Darling 100, W. H. Ponsford 75, R. G. Tindall 5-94) beat Oxford University 70 (L. O'B. Fleetwood-Smith 5-30, H. I. Ebeling 4-34) and 216 (F. C. de Saram 128, C. V. Grimmett 7-109) by an innings and 33 runs.

7th Match: v Hampshire (Southampton)   May 23, 24, 25.
Hampshire 420 (W. G. L. F. Lowndes 140, C. P. Mead 139, Lord Tennyson 56, S. J. McCabe 4-79) and 169-7 dec (J. Arnold 109*, W. J. O'Reilly 4-34) drew with Australians 433 (A. G. Chipperfield 116*, L. S. Darling 96, S. J. McCabe 79, A. E. G. Baring 5-121) and 10-1.

8th Match: v Middlesex (Lord's)   May 26, 28.
Middllsex 258 (E. H. Hendren 115, R. W. V. Robins 65) and 114 (C. V. Grimmett 5-27) lost to Australians 345 (D. G. Bradman 160, A. F. Kippax 56, H. J. Enthoven 4-59, C. I. J. Smith 4-99) and 29-0 by 10 wkts.

9th Match: v Surrey (Oval)   May 30, 31, June 1.
Surrey 475-7 dec (A. Sandham 219, R. J. Gregory 116) and 162-2 (R. J. Gregory 59*, F. R. Brown 54*) drew with Australians 629 (S. J. McCabe 240, W. H. Ponsford 125, D. G. Bradman 77, E. H. Bromley 56, A. R. Gover 5-147).

10th Match: v Lancashire (Old Trafford)   June 2, 4, 5.
Australians 367 (S. J. McCabe 142, B. A. Barnett 61*) and 338-3 (W. M. Woodfull 172*, W. A. Brown 119) drew with Lancashire 285 (G. E. Tyldesley 107, L. O'B. Fleetwood-Smith 5-107).

11th Match: v England (Trent Bridge)   June 8, 9, 11, 12.
Australia 374 (A. G. Chipperfield 99, S. J. McCabe 65, W. H. Ponsford 53, K. Farnes 5-102) and 273-8 dec (S. J. McCabe 88, W. A. Brown 73, K. Farnes 5-77) beat England 268 (E. H. Hendren 79, H. Sutcliffe 62, G. Geary 53, C. V. Grimmett 5-81, W. J. O'Reilly 4-75) and 141 (W. J. O'Reilly 7-54) by 238 runs.

12th Match: v Northamptonshire (Northampton)   June 13, 14, 15.
Australians 284 (A. G. Chipperfield 71, D. G. Bradman 65, W. H. Ponsford 56, A. D. G. Matthews 4-71) and 234 (W. A. Brown 113, A. D. G. Matthews 5-87) drew with Northamptonshire 187 (A. W. Snowden 105, L. O'B. Fleetwood-Smith 5-63) and 133-9 (A. H. Bakewell 53, J. E. Timms 50, L. O'B. Fleetwood-Smith 5-29).

13th Match: v Gentlemen (Lord's)   June 16, 18, 19.
Gentlemen 177 (C. V. Grimmett 4-76) and 287 (B. H. Lyon 67, E. R. T. Holmes 67, R. W. V. Robins 64, C. V. Grimmett 4-71) lost to Australians 230 and 235-2 (S. J. McCabe 105*, W. A. Brown 62*) by 8 wkts.

14th Match: v England (Lord's)   June 22, 23, 25.
England 440 (L. E. G. Ames 120, M. Leyland 109, C. F. Walters 82, T. W. Wall 4-108) beat Australia 284 (W. A. Brown 105, H. Verity 7-61) and 118 (H. Verity 8-43) by an innings and 38 runs.

15th Match: v Somerset (Taunton)   June 27, 28.
Somerset 116 (F. S. Lee 59*, W. J. O'Reilly 9-38) and 116 (L. O'B. Fleetwood-Smith 6-56) lost to Australians 309 (W. M. Woodfull 84, L. S. Darling 79, B. A. Barnett 51, A. W. Wellard 6-111) by an innings and 77 runs.

16th Match: v Surrey (Oval)   June 30, July 2, 3.
Surrey 175 (S. J. McCabe 4-24, C. V. Grimmett 4-64) and 184 (C. V. Grimmett 5-33) lost to Australians 251 (W. H. Ponsford 85, A. F. Kippax 50, M. J. C. Allom 4-60) and 111-4 (D. G. Bradman 61*) by 6 wkts.

17th Match: v England (Old Trafford)   July 6, 7, 9, 10.
England 627-9 dec (M. Leyland 153, E. H. Hendren 132, L. E. G. Ames 72, H. Sutcliffe 63, G. O. B. Allen 61, H. Verity 60*, C. F. Walters 52, W. J. O'Reilly 7-189) and 123-0 dec (H. Sutcliffe 69*, C. F. Walters 50*) drew with Australia 491 (S. J. McCabe 137, W. M. Woodfull 73, W. A. Brown 72, H. Verity 4-78) and 66-1.

18th Match: v Derbyshire (Chesterfield)   July 11, 12, 13.
Derbyshire 145 (H. I. Ebeling 5-28) and 139 (L. O'B. Fleetwood-Smith 5-38) lost to Australians 255 (D. G. Bradman 71, T. B. Mitchell 7-105) and 32-1 by 9 wkts.

19th Match: v Yorkshire (Bramall Lane)   July 14, 16, 17.
Yorkshire 340 (A. B. Sellers 104, C. V. Grimmett 4-113) and 157 (A. Wood 59) drew with Australians 348 (D. G. Bradman 140, W. E. Bowes 7-100) and 28-1.

20th Match: v England (Headingley)   July 20, 21, 23, 24.
England 200 (C. V. Grimmett 4-57) and 229-6 drew with Australia 584 (D. G. Bradman 304, W. H. Ponsford 181, W. E. Bowes 6-142).

21st Match: v Durham (Sunderland)   July 25, 26.
Durham 73 (L. O'B. Fleetwood-Smith 7-21) and 04-6 (C. L. Adamson 52, G. Hickman 52) drew with Australians 314-3 dec (A. F. Kippax 101, E. H. Bromley 97, W. H. Ponsford 66*).*

22nd Match: v Scotland (Edinburgh)   July 27, 28, 29.
Scotland 107 (C. S. Dempster 69, L. O'B. Fleetwood-Smith 6-45) and 116-8 drew with Australians 331-5 dec (B. A. Barnett 92, A. F. Kippax 90*, S. J. McCabe 73).

23rd Match: v Gloucestershire (Bristol)   Aug 1, 2, 3.
Australians 308-2 dec (W. M. Woodfull 131, S. J. McCabe 61*, A. F. Kippax 50*, W. H. Ponsford 54) drew with Gloucestershire 184 (W. R. Hammond 61, L. O'B. Fleetwood-Smith 7-40).

24th Match: v Glamorgan (Swansea)   Aug 4, 6, 7.
Australians 440-7 dec (W. M. Woodfull 228*, A. F. Kippax 77) drew with Glamorgan 112 (W. J. O'Reilly 7-37) and 198-5 (C. C. Smart 75, W. J. O'Reilly 4-41).

25th Match: v Warwickshire (Edgbaston)   Aug 8, 9, 10.
Australians 221 (A. J. W. Croom 4-33) and 185-4 (S. J. McCabe 77, L. S. Darling 50) drew with Warwickshire 179 (F. R. Santall 61, A. J. W. Croom 41, C. V. Grimmett 5-76).

26th Match: v Nottinghamshire (Trent Bridge)   Aug 11, 13, 14.
Australians 237 (W. M. Woodfull 81, W. Voce 8-66) and 230-2 dec (W. A. Brown 100*, S. J. McCabe 75*) drew with Nottinghamshire 183 (C. V. Grimmett 4-70) and 128-6.

27th Match: v Army (Aldershot)   Aug 15.
Army 110 lost to Australians 194-7 (D. G. Bradman 79) by 8 wkts.

28th Match: v England (Oval)   Aug 18, 20, 21, 22.
Australia 701 (W. H. Ponsford 266, D. G. Bradman 244, W. E. Bowes 4-164, G. O. B. Allen 4-170) and 327 (D. G. Bradman 77, S. J. McCabe 70, Extras 50, W. E. Bowes 55, E. W. Clark 5-98) beat England 321 (M. Leyland 110, C. F. Walters 64) and 145 (C. V. Grimmett 5-64) by 562 runs.

29th Match: v Sussex (Hove)   Aug 25, 27, 28.
Sussex 304-8 dec (J. H. Parks 60, T. E. R. Cook 60, Jas Langridge 57, L. O'B. Fleetwood-Smith 5-114) and 221 (E. H. Bowley 63, John Langridge 53, L. O'B. Fleetwood-Smith 5-87, W. J. O'Relly 4-49) lost to Australians 560 (A. F. Kippax 250, L. S. Darling 117, W. A. Brown 66) by an innings and 35 runs.

30th Match: v Kent (Canterbury)   Aug 29, 30, 31.
Kent 21-2 and 74-7 (L. O'B. Fleetwood-Smith 4-30) drew with Australians 197-1 dec (S. J. McCabe 108, W. H. Ponsford 82*).

31st Match: v An England XI (Folkestone)   Sept 1, 3, 4.
An England XI 279 (F. E. Woolley 66, W. R. Hammond 54, L. O'B. Fleetwood-Smith 5-137, W. J. O'Reilly 4-55) drew with Australians 365-4 (D. G. Bradman 149*, W. A. Brown 73, W. M. Woodfull 62*).

32nd Match: v Minor Counties (Oval)   Sept 5, 6.
Minor Counties 182 (W. E. Harbord 104) and 137-6 (H. Fisher 50*) drew with Australians 370-8 dec (B. A. Barnett 80, W. M. Woodfull 75*, L. S. Darling 59, W. A. Brown 53).*

33rd Match: v H. D. G. Leveson-Gower's XI (Scarborough)   Sept 8, 10, 11.
Australians 489 (D. G. Bradman 132, S. J. McCabe 124, W. H. Ponsford 92, K. Farnes 5-132) beat H. D. G. Leveson-Gower's XI 223 (M. S. Nichols 75, L. O'B. Fleetwood-Smith 4-111) and 218 (L. O'B. Fleetwood-Smith 6-90) by an innings and 48 runs.

34th Match: v North of Scotland (Forres)   Sept 14.
North of Scotland 48 and 98 lost to Australians 166 (I. A. R. Peebles 5-84) by an innings and 20 runs.

enough Bradman, although his figures did not quite equal those of his previous tour. Ponsford improved on 1930, being much more difficult to dismiss–both he and Bradman averaged 94 in the Tests. McCabe also improved, hitting the ball with great vigour. Brown was the best of the younger men, a most attractive batsman; Chipperfield proved useful and was a talented close fielder; Darling was too busy trying to tickle deliveries leaving him, a mistake which made Bromley lose his wicket far too often.

The bowling was in the hands of three spinners. O'Reilly, on his first tour, bowled well with a difficult off-break which was liable to jump up and have the batsman caught at forward short-leg; Grimmett devised a new grip for his googly, which batsmen found impossible to detect and he proved as deadly as in 1930. The third slow bowler was Fleetwood-Smith, a left-arm googly bowler who took over 100 wickets, yet inexplicably failed to gain a place in any of the Tests. The fast bowlers were Wall, who could not reproduce his form of 1930 and Ebeling, who only appeared in the last Test but had a good record on the tour as a whole. Oldfield kept wicket magnificently and was generally regarded as the equal of any of his predecessors. It was difficult to find a fault with the fielding.

A total of £88,313 12s 5d was taken at the gate during the five Tests and the tour as a whole was as popular and financially sound as its forerunners.

1934: 18th Australians

Batting Averages

	M	I	NO	R	HS	Avge	100	c/s
D. G. Bradman	22	27	3	2020	304	84.16	7	9
W. H. Ponsford	22	27	4	1784	281*	77.56	5	10
S. J. McCabe	26	37	7	2078	240	69.26	8	19
W. M. Woodfull	22	27	3	1268	228*	52.83	3	4
A. F. Kippax	19	23	4	961	250	50.57	1	4
A. G. Chipperfield	22	26	4	899	175	40.86	2	15
W. A. Brown	24	36	2	1308	119	38.47	5	10
L. S. Darling	25	31	1	1022	117	34.06	2	14
B. A. Barnett	18	20	6	470	92	33.57	0	18/12
W. J. O'Reilly	19	18	9	237	30*	26.33	0	7
W. A. S. Oldfield	15	16	3	295	67	22.69	0	21/19
E. H. Bromley	18	20	1	312	56	16.42	0	20
C. V. Grimmett	21	20	3	255	39	15.00	0	8
H. I. Ebeling	21	19	1	265	41	14.72	0	16
T. W. Wall	16	12	3	84	24	9.33	0	2
L. O'B. Fleetwood-Smith	20	13	6	24	7*	3.42	0	10

Bowling Averages

	O	M	R	W	Avge	BB	5i
W. J. O'Reilly	870	320	1858	109	17.04	9-38	6
L. O'B. Fleetwood-Smith	713.5	150	2036	106	19.20	7-40	12
C. V. Grimmett	985.4	308	2159	109	19.80	9-74	10
H. I. Ebeling	635	200	1290	62	20.80	5-28	1
T. W. Wall	475.2	95	1290	42	30.71	6-74	1
L. S. Darling	123.3	31	325	9	36.11	2-4	0
S. J. McCabe	305.3	71	794	21	37.80	4-79	0
E. H. Bromley	72.5	12	245	5	49.00	2-14	0
A. G. Chipperfield	197.5	46	595	12	49.58	3-91	0

Also bowled: B. A. Barnett 1-0-3-1; A. F. Kippax 5-1-13-0.

Above *Bill Ponsford, a relentless accumulator of runs, made 266 at the Oval in 1934 and shared with Bradman the highest stand in Test cricket: 451 for the second wicket.*

Right *The Australians at the 1934 Scarborough Festival. From left: Ebeling, O'Reilly (with head in hands), McCabe, (sitting back), Darling, Bradman, Fleetwood-Smith, Wall (not playing) and Woodfull.*

1935: 8th South Africans

The team selected to tour England in 1935 was H. F. Wade (captain), I. J. Siedle, E. L. Dalton, A. D. Nourse and R. J. Williams, all of Natal; H. B. Cameron, B. Mitchell, C. L. Vincent, A. B. C. Langton and E. A. B. Rowan of Transvaal; A. J. Bell and D. S. Tomlinson of Rhodesia; X. C. Balaskas and R. J. Crisp of Western Province and K. G. Viljoen of Orange Free State, with S. J. Snooke as manager. The main criticisms were the lack of a class off-spinner, the choice of Rowan instead of Briscoe and doubt about the form of Langton, who had recently had an operation.

These criticisms were decisively disproved as the side went through the summer suffering only two defeats and beating England one match to nil in the Tests—the four other

---

1935: 8th South Africans

1st Match: v Reigate Priory (Reigate) April 22.
South Africans 196-8 dec (I. J. Siedle 78) beat Reigate Priory 30 by 166 runs.

2nd Match: v R. Earle's XI (Busbridge Hall) April 25.
South Africans 156-6 dec (B. Mitchell 50) drew with R. Earle's XI did not bat.

3rd Match: v Worcestershire (Worcester) May 1, 2, 3.
Worcestershire 90 (R. J. Crisp 6-34) and 95 (A. J. Bell 5-22) lost to South Africans 351 (E. L. Dalton 91, A. D. Nourse 74, H. B. Cameron 68, C. J. Lyttelton 4-83) by an innings and 166 runs.

4th Match: v Leicestershire (Leicester) May 4, 6, 7.
South Africans 312 (E. A. B. Rowan 91, K. G. Viljoen 93, G. Geary 4-62) and 214-3 dec (E. A. B. Rowan 89, H. F. Wade 74) beat Leicestershire 123 (R. J. Crisp 5-40) and 233 (A. B. C. Langton 5-49, D. S. Tomlinson 4-63) by 170 runs.

5th Match: v Cambridge University (Cambridge) May 8, 9, 10.
Cambridge University 253 (M. Tindall 68, A. B. C. Langton 5-70) and 192 (S. C. Griffith 54, D. S. Tomlinson 4-64) lost to South Africans 485 (H. F. Wade 161, E. A. B. Rowan 103, A. D. Nourse 71, E. L. Dalton 61, J. H. Cameron 5-133, J. W. T. Grimshaw 4-104) by an innings and 40 runs.

6th Match: v Surrey (Oval) May 11, 13, 14.
South Africans 367 (A. D. Nourse 147) and 280-2 dec (A. D. Nourse 108*, I. J. Siedle 104) beat Surrey 266 (L. B. Fishlock 62, R. J. Gregory 53) and 191 (T. H. Barling 68, D. S. Tomlinson 4-62) by 190 runs.

7th Match: v Oxford University (Oxford) May 15, 16, 17.
South Africans 372 (A. D. Nourse 148, D. S. Tomlinson 70*, I. J. Siedle 52, A. R. Legard 5-114) and 369-1 (I. J. Siedle 164*, E. A. B. Rowan 104*, H. F. Wade 89) drew with Oxford University 429 (N. S. Mitchell-Innes 168, A. Benn 90, D. F. Walker 83, A. J. Bell 4-129, C. L. Vincent 4-81).

8th Match: v M.C.C. (Lord's) May 18, 20, 21.
South Africans 297 (I. J. Siedle 132*, I. A. R. Peebles 4-59) drew with M.C.C. 144 (W. F. F. Price 61, C. L. Vincent 5-47, A. B. C. Langton 4-80) and 32-3.

9th Match: v Hampshire (Southampton) May 22, 23, 24.
South Africans 304 (A. D. Nourse 75, K. G. Viljoen 66, E. L. Dalton 59) and 248 (H. B. Cameron 74, E. A. B. Rowan 63, O. W. Herman 4-53) beat Hampshire 197 (W. G. L. F. Lowndes 62, R. J. Crisp 5-59, C. L. Vincent 4-78) and 245 (J. Arnold 79, X. Balaskas 4-45) by 110 runs.

10th Match: v Middlesex (Lord's) May 25, 27, 28.
South Africans 202 (E. L. Dalton 56, H. G. O. Owen-Smith 4-55) and 163 (C. I. J. Smith 5-40) beat Middlesex 192 (A. B. C. Langton 6-53) and 151 (A. B. C. Langton 5-59, R. J. Crisp 4-45) by 22 runs.

11th Match: v Derbyshire (Ilkeston) May 29, 30, 31.
South Africans 443 (K. G. Viljoen 152, H. B. Cameron 132, T. B. Mitchell 5-167) and 200-4 dec (I. J. Siedle 98) beat Derbyshire 236 (C. L. Vincent 4-61) and 198 (D. S. Tomlinson 4-63, A. J. Bell 4-77) by 209 runs.

12th Match: v Lancashire (Old Trafford) June 1, 3, 4.
South Africans 268 (B. Mitchell 59, F. S. Booth 6-79) and 142-6 drew with Lancashire 128 (J. L. Hopwood 73*, C. L. Vincent 4-32).

13th Match: v Northamptonshire (Northampton) June 5, 6, 7.
Northamptonshire 129 (G. B. Cuthbertson 63*, R. J. Crisp 6-50) and 133 (R. J. Crisp 4-35) lost to South Africans 297 (I. J. Siedle 65, X. Balaskas 65, E. L. Dalton 58, E. W. Clark 4-78) by an innings and 35 runs.

14th Match: v Glamorgan (Cardiff) June 8, 10, 11.
South Africans 401 (E. A. B. Rowan 153, H. F. Wade 139) drew with Glamorgan 142 (D. E. Davies 75*, D. S. Tomlinson 5-72) and 245-9 (C. C. Smart 114*, W. Hughes 70*, A. B. C. Langton 6-66).

15th Match: v Club Cricket Conference (Lord's) June 12, 13.
C.C.C. 69 drew with South Africans 189-4 (E. A. B. Rowan 103).*

16th Match: v England (Trent Bridge) June 15, 17, 18.
England 384-7 dec (R. E. S. Wyatt 149, M. Leyland 69, H. Sutcliffe 61) drew with South Africa 220 (I. J. Siedle 59, H. B. Cameron 52, M. S. Nichols 6-35) and 17-1.

17th Match: v Lancashire (Liverpool) June 19, 20, 21.
Lancashire 92-6 dec drew with South Africans 153-2 (B. Mitchell 82).

18th Match: v Yorkshire (Bramall Lane) June 22, 24, 25.
South Africans 263 (I. J. Siedle 51, H. Fisher 4-52) and 301-7 dec (H. B. Cameron 103*, E. A. B. Rowan 76) beat Yorkshire 201 (A. Mitchell 61, X. Balaskas 4-55, A. J. Bell 4-65) and 235 (X. Balaskas 8-99) by 128 runs.

19th Match: v Staffordshire (Stoke-on-Trent) June 26, 27.
Staffordshire 60 (A. B. C. Langton 4-6) and 88 (A. J. Bell 4-38) lost to South Africans 190 (B. Mitchell 73, E. N. Backhouse 5-49) by an innings and 42 runs.

20th Match: v England (Lord's) June 29, July 1, 2.
South Africa 228 (H. B. Cameron 90) and 278-7 dec (B. Mitchell 164*) beat England 198 (R. E. S. Wyatt 53, X. Balaskas 5-49) and 151 (A. B. C. Langton 4-31, X. Balaskas 4-54) by 157 runs.

21st Match: v Somerset (Bath) July 3, 4, 5.
South Africans 173 (A. W. Wellard 4-61) and 284 (E. L. Dalton 78, A. D. Nourse 71, A. W. Wellard 4-92) beat Somerset 218 (F. S. Lee 86, A. B. C. Langton 6-99) and 188 (B. Mitchell 5-45, A. B. C. Langton 4-56) by 51 runs.

22nd Match: v Nottinghamshire (Trent Bridge) July 6, 8, 9.
Nottinghamshire 312 (J. Hardstaff jun 154, C. B. Harris 77, A. J. Bell 4-66) and 312-9 (G. V. Gunn 100*, G. F. H. Heane 60, B. Mitchell 6-118) drew with South Africans 512 (H. F. Wade 151, B. Mitchell 142, E. L. Dalton 77).

23rd Match: v Norfolk (Norwich) July 10, 11.
Norfolk 325 (W. J. Edrich 111, M. R. Barton 59, F. D. Cunliffe 55*, R. J. Crisp 4-65) and 59-3 drew with South Africans 367 (K. G. Viljoen 103*, I. J. Siedle 62, E. A. Rowan 57).

24th Match: v England (Headingley) July 13, 15, 16.
England 216 (W. R. Hammond 63, A. Mitchell 58, A. B. C. Langton 4-59, C. L. Vincent 4-45) and 294-7 dec (W. R. Hammond 87*, A. Mitchell 72, C. L. Vincent 4-104) drew with South Africans 171 (E. A. B. Rowan 62) and 194-5 (B. Mitchell 58).

25th Match: v Durham (Sunderland) July 17, 18.
Durham 45 (C. L. Vincent 4-12, A. B. C. Langton 4-14) and 141 (A. B. C. Langton 7-38) lost to South Africans 231 (K. G. Viljoen 85) by an innings and 45 runs.

26th Match: v Scotland (Glasgow) July 19, 20.
Scotland 91 (R. J. Crisp 7-20) and 126-6 drew with South Africans 199-5 dec (E. A. B. Rowan 71).

27th Match: v Scotland (Dundee) July 22, 23.
South Africans 252 (H. B. Cameron 67, C. L. Vincent 59*, R. A. Hollingdale 5-39) beat Scotland 80 (C. L. Vincent 6-19, D. S. Tomlinson 4-26) and 87 by an innings and 85 runs.

28th Match: v Northumberland (Newcastle) July 24, 25.
Northumberland 198 (H. C. Lee 50, R. J. Crisp 6-41) and 222 (H. C. Lee 64, A. B. C. Langton 4-44) lost to South Africans 323 (A. D. Nourse 52, E. A. B. Rowan 50, Wilson 5-103) and 101-2 by 8 wkts.

29th Match: v England (Old Trafford) July 27, 29, 30.
England 357 (R. W. V. Robins 108, A. H. Bakewell 63, M. Leyland 53, R. J. Crisp 5-99) and 231-6 dec (W. R. Hammond 63*, A. H. Bakewell 54, C. L. Vincent 4-78) drew with South Africa 318 (K. G. Viljoen 124, H. B. Cameron 53, W. E. Bowes 5-100) and 169-2 (A. D. Nourse 53*).

30th Match: v Surrey (Oval) July 31, Aug 1.
Surrey 183 (L. B. Fishlock 82, C. L. Vincent 4-53, A. B. C. Langton 4-85) and 184 (B. Mitchell 4-47, A. B. C. Langton 4-50) lost to South Africans 572 (B. Mitchell 195, E. A. B. Rowan 171, E. L. Dalton 89, A. R. Gover 4-151) by an innings and 205 runs.

31st Match: v Glamorgan (Swansea) Aug 3, 5, 6.
South Africans 309 (B. Mitchell 78, H. B. Cameron 67) and 168 (A. D. Nourse 52, J. C. Clay 6-63) beat Glamorgan 227 (R. Duckfield 63, D. S. Tomlinson 6-105) and 154 (B. Mitchell 4-13) by 96 runs.

32nd Match: v Warwickshire (Edgbaston) Aug 7, 8, 9.
South Africans 498 (A. D. Nourse 160*, E. A. Rowan 102, H. B. Cameron 73, K. Wilmot 4-115, G. A. E. Paine 4-119) beat Warwickshire 221 (W. A. Hill 83, T. Collin 53, R. J. Crisp 5-31) and 103 (R. J. Crisp 5-36) by an innings and 174 runs.

33rd Match: v Gloucestershire (Cheltenham) Aug 10, 12, 13.
Gloucestershire 279 (R. A. Sinfield 102, W. L. Neale 61, X. Balaskas 4-101) and 298 (W. R. Hammond 123, C. L. Vincent 6-90) beat South Africans 289 (K. G. Viljoen 122) and 201 (R. A. Sinfield 5-31) by 87 runs.

34th Match: v Essex (Southend) Aug 14, 15, 16.
South Africans 250 (E. L. Dalton 117, I. J. Siedle 69, J. W. A. Stephenson 7-66) and 223 (E. L. Dalton 65, M. S. Nichols 4-35) lost to Essex 302 (J. A. Cutmore 72) and 172-3 (M. S. Nichols 70, J. A. Cutmore 59*) by 7 wkts.

35th Match: v England (Oval) Aug 17, 19, 20.
South Africa 476 (B. Mitchell 128, E. L. Dalton 117, A. B. C. Langton 73*, K. G. Viljoen 60, H. D. Read 4-136) and 287-6 (E. L. Dalton 57*) drew with England 534-6 dec (M. Leyland 161, L. E. G. Ames 148*, W. R. Hammond 65).

36th Match: v Sir J. Cahn's XI (West Bridgford) Aug 22, 23.
Sir J. Cahn's XI 235 (R. C. Blunt 85, R. J. Crisp 4-66) drew with South Africans 91-0.

37th Match: v Sussex (Hove) Aug 24, 26, 27.
South Africans 218 (E. L. Dalton 51, A. B. C. Langton 51) and 156 (C. L. Vincent 51) drew with Sussex 150 (John Langridge 63).

38th Match: v Kent (Canterbury) Aug 28, 29.
South Africans 311 (E. A. B. Rowan 77, H. F. Wade 56, A. D. Nourse 51, L. J. Todd 4-70, D. V. P. Wright 4-124) beat Kent 124 (C. L. Vincent 7-48) and 49 (A. B. C. Langton 4-18, R. J. Crisp 4-21) by an innings and 138 runs.

39th Match: v An England XI (Folkestone) Aug 31, Sept 2, 3.
An England XI 96 (A. B. C. Langton 5-38, C. L. Vincent 4-32) and 106 lost to South Africans 311-5 dec (K. G. Viljoen 119*, B. Mitchell 90) by an innings and 109 runs.

40th Match: v Minor Counties (Skegness) Sept 4, 5, 6.
South Africans 394 (K. G. Viljoen 168, E. A. B. Rowan 115, H. R. W. Butterworth 5-105) and 21-2 beat Minor Counties 190 (G. S. Butler 84, R. J. Crisp 5-60) and 224 (W. J. Edrich 79, R. J. Crisp 4-60) by 8 wkts.

41st Match: v H. D. G. Leveson-Gower's XI (Scarborough) Sept 7, 9, 10.
H. D. G. Leveson-Gower's XI 457 (A. Mitchell 103, H. Sutcliffe 96, R. A. Sinfield 75, M. Leyland 55, R. J. Crisp 4-104) and 45-1 drew with South Africans 240 (E. A. B. Rowan 75, M. S. Nichols 5-55) and 382-8 dec (H. B. Cameron 160, A. D. Nourse 78, A. B. C. Langton 68).

The summer began with four successive first-class victories and from this early success the tourists never looked back. A long list of injuries did not deter them—at one point a travelling journalist acted as 12th man in the absence of any fit tourist and later the old international, Owen-Smith, was asked to stand by, although not required in the end.

The almost over-confident Rowan headed the run aggregate, his lightness of foot enabling him to perform some daring feats. Viljoen proved an excellent man in a tight corner and Mitchell also flourished. Nourse did well in the ordinary matches, but was out of touch in the Tests. Siedle began well, but as in 1929, an injury curtailed his appearances.

Cameron was as fine a wicketkeeper as ever and scored runs freely—his death just after the tour ended was a great loss. Langton took most wickets, but there was little to choose between the leading bowlers: Crisp was an awkward customer to face; Bell began well, then was out through injury, as was Balaskas.

Wade was a skilful leader and excellent fielder, but his batting was not up to his ability. The one inadequate feature of the programme was allowing only three days for each Test, which it was hoped would be remedied on the next visit.

1936: 3rd Indians

The divisions within India itself split the team that toured England in 1936. Grumbling and discontent, and once or twice open ill-discipine, caused the team to disintegrate into various factions. On 20 June, a week before the First Test, Amarnath, the best all-rounder in the side, was sent back to India for disciplinary reasons. Even this drastic step failed to right the situation and the petty quarrelling continued, though on a lesser scale. In these circumstances it is hardly surprising that the team's results were poor and that they did not manage to beat England in any of the three Tests.

H. F. Wade, the captain of the 1935 South Africans (right), inspecting the wicket at Cardiff with the Glamorgan captain M. J. Turnbull. Wade made a century in a drawn match.

internationals were drawn. This excellent record was easily the best ever achieved by South Africa and was crowned with a profit of £12,000, an amount never remotely approached by previous teams.

1935: 8th South Africans

Batting Averages

	M	I	NO	R	NS	Avge	100	c/s
K. G. Viljoen	25	35	4	1454	168	46.90	5	14
B. Mitchell	22	35	3	1451	195	45.34	4	22
E. A. B. Rowan	28	46	2	1948	171	44.27	6	12
H. B. Cameron	27	38	3	1458	160	41.65	3	28/19
A. D. Nourse	30	46	5	1681	160*	41.00	4	22
I. J. Siedle	22	37	3	1346	164*	39.58	3	7
E. L. Dalton	30	41	2	1446	117	37.07	2	19
H. F. Wade	27	39	3	1042	161	28.94	3	17
A. B. C. Langton	26	32	7	537	73*	21.48	0	23
D. S. Tomlinson	19	24	10	282	70*	20.14	0	9
R. J. Williams	7	11	0	181	46	16.45	0	10/7
R. J. Crisp	26	30	6	322	45	13.41	0	13
C. L. Vincent	25	31	4	362	51	13.40	0	17
X. Balaskas	12	16	2	146	65	10.42	0	7
A. J. Bell	15	16	8	58	24	7.25	0	12

Bowling Averages

	O	M	R	W	Avge	BB	5i
B. Mitchell	206	14	666	35	19.02	6-118	2
R. J. Crisp	690.5	105	2096	107	19.58	6-34	8
X. Balaskas	289.5	34	873	42	20.78	8-99	2
C. L. Vincent	743	187	1923	92	20.90	7-48	3
A. B. C. Langton	875.5	158	2434	115	21.16	6-53	7
A. J. Bell	413.1	77	1146	52	22.03	5-22	1
D. S. Tomlinson	361	34	1380	52	26.53	6-105	2
E. L. Dalton	122	18	384	7	54.85	2-29	0

Also bowled: K. G. Viljoen 14-4-35-0; A. D. Nourse 1-0-3-0.

1936: 3rd Indians

Batting Averages

	M	I	NO	R	HS	Avge	100	c/s
V. M. Merchant	23	40	6	1745	151	51.32	3	15
Dilawar Hussain	9	17	3	620	122	44.28	2	13/4
L. Amar Singh	7	11	1	333	77	33.30	0	3
N. B. Amarnath	12	20	1	613	130	32.26	3	5
C. Ramaswami	17	28	4	737	127*	30.70	1	5
S. Wazir Ali	16	28	5	659	155*	28.65	1	2
C. K. Nayudu	24	42	0	1102	83	26.23	0	11
S. Mushtaq Ali	24	44	1	1078	141	25.06	4	11
L. P. Jai	13	20	2	427	85	23.72	0	3
M. Baqa Jilani	11	20	3	315	113	18.52	1	3
S. S. Banerjee	17	28	8	369	47*	18.45	0	7
P. E. Palia	11	21	2	331	63	17.42	0	2
Amir Elahi	12	19	2	282	45	16.58	0	5
Maharaj of Vizianagram	26	42	5	600	60	16.21	0	9
M. J. Gopalan	7	9	2	110	25	15.71	0	3
M. Jahangir Khan	14	23	2	314	80	14.95	0	10
D. D. Hindlekar	13	23	0	333	80	14.47	0	22/10
C. S. Nayudu	12	18	3	215	58	14.33	0	6
S. Mahomed Hussain	10	17	3	169	55	12.07	0	3
Mahomed Nissar	21	31	6	195	42	7.80	0	11
K. R. Meherhomji	7	9	2	45	17	6.42	0	14/1
S. M. Hadi	2	3	0	6	5	2.00	0	0

Bowling Averages

	O	M	R	W	Avge	BB	5i
N. B. Amarnath	267.3	71	668	32	20.87	6-29	1
L. Amar Singh	293.4	94	611	26	23.50	6-35	2
Mahomed Nissar	547.5	122	1659	66	25.13	6-74	4
M. Jahangir Khan	425.5	98	1045	40	26.12	4-42	0
S. S. Banerjee	329.3	37	1177	40	29.42	4-51	0
C. K. Nayudu	499.5	66	1621	51	31.78	7-44	2
C. S. Nayudu	239.3	17	1059	33	32.09	5-91	1
V. M. Merchant	201.5	40	618	18	34.33	2-46	0
P. E. Palia	77	13	208	6	34.66	2-26	0
Maharaj of Vizianagram	18	0	116	3	38.66	1-2	0
M. Baqa Jilani	160.1	37	448	11	40.72	3-46	0
Amir Elahi	180	18	730	17	42.94	5-48	1
S. Mushtaq Ali	130	15	535	8	66.87	2-27	0
M. J. Gopalan	121	23	347	5	69.40	2-39	0

Also bowled: L. P. Jai 16-5-41-1; C. Ramaswami 8-0-22-0; S. Wazir Ali 3-0-9-0.

1936: 3rd Indians

1st Match: v A. P. Freeman's XII (Gravesend)   April 29.
Indians 185-10 dec (W. J. Edrich 4-42) drew with A. P. Freeman's XII 173-4 (W. H. Ashdown 65, F. E. Woolley 54).

2nd Match: v Worcestershire (Worcester)   May 2, 4, 5.
Indians 229 (S. H. Martin 4-42, R. T. D. Perks 4-51) and 150 (S. M. Hussain 55, R. T. D. Perks 5-37) lost to Worcestershire 248 (R. Howorth 58, Mahomed Nissar 4-89, N. B. Amarnath 4-42) and 134-7 (R. H. C. Human 68*, Mahomed Nissar 5-50) by 3 wkts.

3rd Match: v Oxford University (Oxford)   May 6, 7, 8.
Oxford University 202 (A. P. Singleton 51, N. Amarnath 4-22) and 297 (R. C. M. Kimpton 77, N. S. Mitchell-Innes 68, S. S. Banerjee 4-65) drew with Indians 352 (C. K. Nayudu 83, P. E. Palia 63, Maharaj of Vizianagram 60) and 103-5.

4th Match: v Somerset (Taunton)   May 9, 10, 11.
Somerset 496 (H. Gimblett 103, H. D. Burrough 85, L. Hawkins 79, W. F. Baldock 63*) and 89-1 beat Indians 228 (C. K. Nayudu 73, L. Hawkins 4-39) and 356 (V. M. Merchant 151, C. K. Nayudu 68, A. W. Wellard 6-52) by 9 wkts.

5th Match: v Northamptonshire (Northampton)   May 13, 14, 15.
Indians 405-9 dec (N. Amarnath 114*, C. K. Nayudu 76, V. M. Merchant 71, L. N. Amar Singh 53) drew with Northamptonshire 242 (L. N. Amar Singh 4-52) and 275-1 (A. H. Bakewell 100*, A. W. Allen 90, M. Grimshaw 73*).

6th Match: v M.C.C. (Lord's)   May 16, 18, 19.
M.C.C. 382 (J. H. Human 115, E. H. Hendren 88, R. E. S. Wyatt 65, G. O. B. Allen 54) and 36-0 beat Indians 185 and 230 (M. Jahangir Khan 80, J. M. Sims 4-68) by 10 wkts.

7th Match: v Leicestershire (Leicester)   May 20, 21, 22.
Indians 426 (M. Baqa Jilani 113, L. Amar Singh 77, F. T. Prentice 4-113) and 171-6 dec with Leicestershire 327 (C. S. Dempster 79, F. T. Prentice 72) and 47-0.

8th Match: v Middlesex (Lord's)   May 23, 25.
Indians 110 (R. W. V. Robins 5-18) and 158 lost to Middlesex 173 (J. H. A. Hulme 59, N. Amarnath 6-29) and 96-6 by 4 wkts.

9th Match: v Essex (Brentwood)   May 27, 28, 29.
Indians 184 (N. Amarnath 130) and 227 (N. Amarnath 107, T. P. B. Smith 4-46) lost to Essex 351 (J. A. Cutmore 137, T. P. B. Smith 105, N. Amarnath 4-54, S. S. Banerjee 4-115) and 61-3 by 7 wkts.

10th Match: v Cambridge University (Cambridge)   May 30, June 1, 2.
Indians 161 (S. Wazir Ali 85*, M. Jahangir Khan 4-22, J. H. Cameron 4-59) and 3-0 drew with Cambridge University 217 (A. F. T. White 82).

11th Match: v Yorkshire (Bradford)   June 6, 8.
Indians 86 (T. F. Smailes 4-26) and 115 (T. F. Smailes 6-36) lost to Yorkshire 352 (H. Verity 96*, T. F. Smailes 77, Mahomed Nissar 6-74) by an innings and 151 runs.

12th Match: v Durham (Sunderland)   June 10, 11.
Indians 174 and 203-3 dec (S. Wazir Ali 139) drew with Durham 176 (T. K. Dobson 52*, S. S. Banerjee 5-54) and 203-5 (E. Randle 85, S. S. Banerjee 5-65).*

13th Match: v Nottinghamshire (Trent Bridge)   June 13, 15, 16.
Indians 124 drew with Nottinghamshire 154-2 (J. Knowles 66*).

14th Match: v Minor Counties (Lord's)   June 17, 18, 19.
Minor Counties 286 (F. C. de Saram 86, L. N. Amar Singh 4-52, C. S. Nayudu 4-57) and 42 (L. Amar Singh 5-12, Mahomed Nissar 5-24) lost to Indians 402 (S. Mushtaw Ali 135, V. M. Merchant 95, A. Booth 5-131) by an innings and 74 runs.

15th Match: v Surrey (Oval)   June 20, 22, 23.
Indians 226 (L. P. Jai 59*, A. R. Gover 4-54) and 421-5 dec (S. Mushtaq Ali 141, L. P. Jai 85, D. D. Hindlekar 80) drew with Surrey 452 (A. Sandham 105, L. B. Fishlock 98, J. F. Parker 77*, C. K. Nayudu 4-121, C. S. Nayudu 4-121) and 52-3.

16th Match: v England (Lord's)   June 27, 29, 30.
Indians 147 (G. O. B. Allen 5-35) and 93 (G. O. B. Allen 5-43, H. Verity 4-17) lost to England 134 (M. Leyland 60, L. N. Amarnath 6-35) and 108-1 (H. Gimblett 67*) by 9 wkts.

17th Match: v Lancashire (Old Trafford)   July 4, 6, 7.
Lancashire 435-8 dec (C. Washbrook 113, N. Oldfield 107, J. L. Hopwood 55, W. H. L. Lister 50, C. S. Nayudu 4-115) and 25-1 drew with Indians 405 (C. Ramaswami 127*, V. M. Merchant 70, A. E. Nutter 6-98).

18th Match: v Ireland (Dublin)   July 9, 10, 11.
Ireland 161 and 119 (C. K. Nayudu 7-44) lost to Indians 150 (J. C. Boucher 6-30) and 131-0 (V. M. Merchant 71*) by 10 wkts.

19th Match: v Lancashire (Liverpool)   July 15, 16, 17.
Indians 271 (V. M. Merchant 135*, C. Ramaswami 78, L. W. Parkinson 4-75) and 161 (V. M. Merchant 77*, J. L. Hopwood 5-49) beat Lancashire 234 (A. E. Nutter 64*, C. Washbrook 52, Mahomed Nissar 4-53) and 114 (C. K. Nayudu 6-46) by 84 runs.

20th Match: v Derbyshire (Derby)   July 18, 20, 21.
Indians 228 (C. K. Nayudu 60, W. H. Copson 5-44) and 232-7 dec (V. M. Merchant 75) drew with Derbyshire 160 (C. S. Elliott 77, S. S. Banerjee 4-51) and 169-2 (L. F. Townsend 77, A. E. Alderman 61*).

21st Match: v England (Old Trafford)   July 25, 27, 28.
India 203 (H. Verity 4-41) and 390-5 (V. M. Merchant 114, S. Mushtaq Ali 112, C. Ramaswami 60) drew with England 571-8 dec (W. R. Hammond 167, J. Hardstaff jun 94, T. S. Worthington 87, R. W. V. Robins 76, H. Verity 66*).

22nd Match: v Glamorgan (Swansea)   Aug 1, 3, 4.
Indians 112 (J. Mercer 7-48) and 114 (J. C. Clay 8-43) lost to Glamorgan 238 (C. C. Smart 58, M. J. L. Turnbull 50, C. K. Nayudu 4-53, M. Jahangir Khan 4-63) by an innings and 12 runs.

23rd Match: v Warwickshire (Edgbaston)   Aug 5, 6, 7.
Warwickshire 181 (A. J. W. Croom 52, Amir Elahi 5-48) and 219-3 dec (A. J. W. Croom 56) drew with Indians 249 (Dilawar Hussain 101*, J. H. Mayer 4-18) and 54-3.

24th Match: v Gloucestershire (Cheltenham)   Aug 8, 10, 11.
Indians 154 (R. A. Sinfield 4-38) and 260 (M. Baqa Jilani 59, R. A. Sinfield 5-79, L. M. Cranfield 4-43) lost to Gloucestershire 313 (W. R. Hammond 81) and 104-2 by 8 wkts.

25th Match: v England (Oval)   Aug 15, 17, 18.
England 471-8 dec (W. R. Hammond 217, T. S. Worthington 128, Mahomed Nissar 5-120) and 64-1 beat India 222 (V. M. Merchant 52, S. Mushtaq Ali 52, J. M. Sims 5-73) and 312 (C. K. Nayudu 81, Dilawar Hussain 54, G. O. B. Allen 7-80) by 9 wkts.

26th Match: v Hampshire (Bournemouth)   Aug 22, 24, 25.
Indians 192 (V. M. Merchant 76, L. P. Jai 50, A. S. Kennedy 4-29, H. M. Lawson 4-55) and 199 (C. S. Nayudu 58, O. W. Herman 5-59) beat Hampshire 238 (C. G. A. Paris 74, C. P. Mead 53*, C. S. Nayudu 5-91) and 151 (C. P. Mead 53*, C. S. Nayudu 4-63) by 2 runs.

27th Match: v Kent (Canterbury)   Aug 26, 27, 28.
Indians 173 (D. V. P. Wright 4-71) and 148 (F. E. Woolley 4-22) lost to Kent 523 (A. E. Fagg 172, W. H. Ashdown 117, L. E. G. Ames 145) by an innings and 202 runs.

28th Match: v Sussex (Hove)   Aug 29, 31, Sept 1.
Indians 309 (Dilawar Hussain 122, V. M. Merchant 52) and 239 (S. Wazir Ali 67, C. Ramaswami 60, Dilawar Hussain 50, Jas Langridge 7-47) lost to Sussex (John Langridge 168, A. Melville 152, Jas Langridge 50, M. Jahangir Khan 4-103) and 71-2 by 8 wkts.

29th Match: v An England XI (Folkestone)   Sept 2, 3, 4.
An England XI 377 (B. H. Valentine 115, L. J. Todd 79, S. S. Banerjee 4-94) and 212-3 dec (L. E. G. Ames 107, F. E. Woolley 79) drew with Indians 372 (A. Wazir Ali 155*, V. M. Merchant 68, R. W. V. Robins 8-105) and 152-1 (Dilawar Hussain 69*, V. M. Merchant 64*).

30th Match: v Sir J. Cahn's XI (West Bridgford)   Sept 5, 7.
Indians 242-9 dec (S. Mushtaq Ali 83) drew with Sir J. Cahn's XI 138-6.

31st Match: v H. D. G. Leveson-Gower's XI (Scarborough)   Sept 9, 10, 11.
H. D. G. Leveson-Gower's XI 225 (H. Sutcliffe 94, M. Jahangir Khan 4-42) and 329 (C. S. Dempster 57, D. Smith 52, M. Jahangir Khan 4-92) drew with Indians 333 (S. Mushtaq Ali 140) and 146-5 (S. Mushtaq Ali 74).

32nd Match: v Indian Gymkhana (Osterley)   Sept 14, 15.
Indians 303 (L. P. Jai 100, P. E. Palia 55, F. R. de Saram 4-130) beat Indian Gymkhana 144 (C. S. Nayudu 4-21) and 83 (P. E. Palia 4-6) by an innings and 76 runs.*

The side announced on 17 February was Maharaj Kumar of Vizianagram (captain), C. K. Nayudu, S. Wazir Ali, Mohamed Nissar, N. B. Amarnath, V. M. Merchant, M. Baqa Jilani, Amir Elahi, S. Mushtaq Ali, K. R. Meherhomji, L. P. Jai, S. N. Banerjee, M. J. Gopalan, P. E. Palia, D. D. Hindlekar, S. M. Hussain and C. Ramaswami. It was agreed that L. Amar Singh, who was playing League cricket in England, and Dilawar Hussain, who was at Cambridge, would assist the side if required. C. S. Nayudu was brought over from India at the beginning of June to reinforce the team and S. M. Hadi was also co-opted in for two matches. The team was managed by Major Brittain Jones with the assistance of Major E. W. C. Ricketts.

On top of the internal strife, the tourists were hampered by several major injuries to key players—Wazir Ali could not play until the end of May due to a broken finger; Merchant missed six matches for the same reason and Jai and Hindlekar also missed matches through injury. The cold and wet weather further handicapped this beleagured band.

A big disappointment was the lack of form of C. K. Nayudu, who failed to reproduce his 1932 brilliance. Merchant proved the outstanding batsman, making his runs in a stylish manner and with an excellent hook. Mushtaq Ali was nimble footed and always in search of runs. Hindlekar also showed style, and was an agile wicketkeeper. Dilawar Hussain, who played regularly in August, was very defensive, but effective. Of the bowlers Amar Singh, when available, was the most destructive and Nissar worked very hard; Banerjee began well but completely lost his sting; C. K. Nayudu kept the runs down with his accuracy, but his brother failed completely and Jahangir Khan, another co-opted member, bowled well at the end of the tour.

1936: 4th Canadians

The Hon R. C. Matthews, a former minister in the Canadian government, organised a short tour of England at his own expense. The team was W. E. N. Bell (captain), L. C. Bell, W. G. Scott, K. H. Ross, M. I. Davies, E. F. Loney, L. A. Percival, J. G. Percival, R. C. Ripley, N. F. Pearson, E. Carlton, D. E. Carey, C. A. Seagram, J. L. Weaver and P. F. Seagram, with H. Dean as tour secretary.

The programme was against club sides and schools and the visit was intended to give the players experience of cricket in England, but in fact the tourists proved better than most of the teams they

met and the fixture card might have included some minor counties to their advantage. They easily beat the M.C.C. at Lord's, even though the premier club was represented by 11 cricketers with first-class experience, and the tourists were a great improvement on the visitors of 1922.

1936: 4th Canadians

1st Match: v Rugby School (Rugby) July 11.
Rugby School 41 (W. G. Scott 4-17) drew with Canadians 18-0.

2nd Match: v Harrow School (Harrow) July 15.
Match Abandoned due to rain.

3rd Match: v Hampstead (Hampstead) July 16.
Canadians 241-6 dec (K. H. Ross 66, E. F. Loney 50) beat Hampstead 186 (E. F. Loney 7-54) by 55 runs.

4th Match: v Harrow Wanderers (Crondall) July 17, 18.
Canadians 271 (W. E. N. Bell 65, W. G. Scott 65) beat Harrow Wanderers 53 (E. Carlton 7-25) and 126 (E. F. Loney 5-20, E. Carlton 5-48) by an innings and 92 runs.

5th Match: v Free Foreseters (Holyport) July 20, 21.
Free Foresters 196 (F. R. Brown 77, W. G. Scott 4-67) and 81 (C. A. Seagram 4-47) lost to Canadians 272 (N. F. Pearson 63, D. E. Carey 50, F. R. Brown 8-89) and 6-0 by 10 wkts.

6th Match: v M.C.C. (Lord's) July 23, 24.
Canadians 171 (J. H. Nevinson 4-22, P. G. H. Fender 4-53) beat M.C.C. 95 (E. Carlton 5-32) by 76 runs.

7th Match: v Eton College (Eton) July 25.
Canadians 169-3 (K. H. Ross 78*) drew with Eton College did not bat.

8th Match: v Ibis C.C. (Sydenham) July 27.
Canadian XII 249-10 dec (R. C. Ripley 58, L. A. Percival 50, G. E. Dewey 4-37) beat Ibis XII 66 (E. Carlton 5-9) and 40-4.

9th Match: v Royal Artillery (Woolwich) July 29, 30.
Canadians 218 (L. C. Bell 79, D. V. Hill 4-55) drew with Royal Artillery 61 (E. F. Loney 4-4) and 152-6.

10th Match: v Sir P. Lacy's XI (Bury St Edmund's) Aug 1, 2.
Canadians 155 (Lord Remnant 4-51) drew with Sir P. Lacy's XI 54 (E. Carlton 4-8) and 105-4.

11th Match: v Royal Air Force (Halton) Aug 3, 4.
Royal Air Force 172 (C. W. M. Ling 81) and 148 (E. F. Loney 5-14, E. Carlton 4-66) lost to Canadians 255-9 dec (W. G. Scott 109*) and 66-6 (M. P. Skinner 4-8) by 4 wkts.

12th Match: v Earl of Bessborough's XI (Stanstead Park) Aug 7, 8.
Canadians 175 and 5-0 beat Earl of Bessborough's XI 66 (E. Carlton 4-19) and 113 (E. Carlton 5-45) by 10 wkts.

13th Match: v Grasshoppers (Oval) Aug 12.
Grasshoppers XII 203 (L. A. Percival 6-39) beat Canadians XII 146 (B. B. Waddy 6-31, N. G. H. Bell 4-40) by 57 runs.

14th Match: v Royal Engineers (Chatham) Aug 13.
Canadian XII 297-6 dec (L. C. Bell 106*, W. E. N. Bell 78, E. F. Loney 51) drew with Royal Engineers XII 177-9 (L. F. Hancock 68).

15th Match: v Inconiti (Chatham) Aug 17, 18.
Canadians 350 (W. E. N. Bell 105, L. C. Bell 65, J. H. Palmer 5-57) and 174-7 dec (L. C. Bell 54*, J. H. Palmer 7-75) drew with Incogniti 272 (E. A. Craven 104, L. K. A. Block 72, L. A. Percival 5-57) and 207-9 (K. A. Sellar 55, A. W. G. Hadingham 53, E. Carlton 4-49).

1937: 3rd New Zealanders

The New Zealand touring party of 1937 was composed mainly of young players, only Page, Vivian and Kerr having been to England before. The full party was M. L. Page (captain), W. A. Hadlee, J. L. Kerr and A. W. Roberts of Canterbury; D. A. R.

An immaculate defensive shot from Len Hutton, on his way to a century at Old Trafford against New Zealand after making a duck at Lord's in his first Test innings. Tindall is the wicketkeeper.

Moloney, E. W. T. Tindall, J. R. Lamason, M. P. Donnelly and N. H. Gallichan of Wellington; W. N. Carson, H. G. Vivian, W. M. Wallace, J. Cowie and G. K. Weir of Auckland and J. A, Dunning of Otago, with T. C. Lowry as manager. Originally B. Griffiths of Wellington was selected, but failed a fitness test and his place was taken by Lamason.

The weather was not at all kind to the tourists during the early weeks of the season and during May and June they won only one first-class game. In the second half of the summer their form improved, however. The curious feature of the tour was how the New Zealanders played in the three Tests. Although they lost one and drew the other two, they were never outplayed and gave England a real battle, in complete contrast with their rather poor performance in some of the county games.

The chief weakness in the side was not having an adequate partner for Cowie. This fast bowler was the success of the team and caused a surprise with the speed with which he made the ball come off the pitch. He took 19 wickets in the Tests at 20.78 each, quite the most effective record. Of the other bowlers, Gallichan's left-arm slows were good when the wicket suited him; Dunning

1937: 3rd New Zealanders

1st Match: v Surrey (Oval)   May 8, 10, 11.
Surrey 149 (N. Gallichan 4-44) and 127-4 drew with New Zealanders 233 (W. N. Carson 85, A. R. Gover 6-57).

2nd Match: v M.C.C. (Lord's)   May 12, 13, 14.
New Zealanders 56-2 drew with M.C.C. did not bat.

3rd Match: v Glamorgan (Cardiff)   May 15, 17, 18.
New Zealanders 235 (E. C. Jones 4-53, J. Mercer 4-60) and 190 (D. A. R. Moloney 85, E. C. Jones 6-41) lost to Glamorgan 338 (R. Duckfield 101, C. C. Smart 63) and 90-4 by 6 wkts.

4th Match: v Oxford University (Oxford)   May 19, 20, 21.
Oxford University 251 (A. P. Singleton 75, R. C. M. Kimpton 72, E. J. H. Dixon 67, J. Cowie 6-50) and 276 (J. G. Halliday 66, E. J. H. Dixon 50) drew with New Zealanders 335 (M. W. Wallace 78, A. W. Roberts 75*) and 167-7 (D. A. R. Moloney 67).

5th Match: v Maori C.C. (Worcester Park)   May 22.
New Zealanders 167-4 (H. G. Vivian 70) drew with Maori C.C. did not bat.

6th Match: v Staffordshire (Stoke-on-Trent)   May 24, 25.
New Zealanders 119 (E. J. Wakelin 6-42) and 193-8 dec (W. A. Hadlee 60) beat Staffordshire 68 (J. A. Dunning 8-26) and 86 (G. L. Weir 4-46) by 158 runs.

7th Match: v Cambridge University (Cambridge)   May 26, 27.
Cambridge University 102 (J. A. Dunning 6-42) and 128 (J. A. R. Moloney 5-23) lost to New Zealanders 135 (M. W. Wallace 71, T. W. Fraser 5-51) and 96-2 (M. L. Page 53) by 8 wkts.

8th Match: v Lancashire (Old Trafford)   May 29, 31, June 1.
New Zealanders 282 (D. A. R. Moloney 77) and 227-6 dec (M. W. Wallace 92, W. E. Phillipson 5-50) lost to Lancashire 314 (W. E. Phillipson 70*, N. Oldfield 66, E. Paynter 51, J. Cowie 4-60) and 196-2 (J. Iddon 94*, E. Paynter 55) by 8 wkts.

9th Match: v Northamptonshire (Northampton)   June 2, 3, 4.
New Zealanders 334 (M. P. Donnelly 82, G. L. Weir 56, M. W. Wallace 50) and 280-4 dec (W. N. Carson 86, J. L. Weir 83) drew with Northamptonshire 185 (K. C. James 80, J. A. Dunning 6-80) and 308-4 (D. Brookes 102*, J. E. Timms 71, R. P. Nelson 69).

10th Match: v Derbyshire (Derby)   June 5, 7, 8.
Derbyshire 241 (J. Cowie 4-60) and 327-7 dec (A. E. Alderman 112, D. Smith 85, G. H. Pope 61*) beat New Zealanders 166 (T. B. Mitchell 5-101, G. H. Pope 4-29) and 200 (M. P. Donnelly 60*, T. B. Mitchell 5-75) by 202 runs.

11th Match: v Worcestershire (Worcester)   June 9, 10, 11.
Worcestershire 374 (V. Grimshaw 103, E. Cooper 81, J. Horton 64, A. W. Roberts 4-69, H. G. Vivian 4-70) and 208-6 dec (H. H. I. Gibbons 54, R. Howorth 53) beat New Zealanders 154 (W. A. Hadlee 58, R. T. D. Perks 4-43, R. Howorth 4-53) and 292 (G. L. Weir 134*, S. H. Martin 5-106) by 136 runs.

12th Match: v Middlesex (Lord's)   June 12, 14, 15.
New Zealanders 268 (M. L. Page 61, H. G. Vivian 56, M. W. Wallace 56) and 213 (H. G. Vivian 73, W. A. Hadlee 64, R. W. V. Robins 5-42) drew with Middlesex 212 (J. H. Human 53, J. A. Dunning 6-59) and 17-1.

13th Match: v Lancashire (Preston)   June 16, 17, 18.
New Zealanders 220 (W. E. Phillipson 4-43) and 149 (F. M. Sibbles 4-28, C. Rhodes 4-37) lost to Lancashire 443 (J. Iddon 108, N. Oldfield 101, E. Paynter 94, D. A. R. Moloney 5-107) by an innings and 74 runs.

14th Match: v Nottinghamshire (Trent Bridge)   June 19, 21, 22.
Nottinghamshire 163 (A. W. Roberts 4-61) and 454-5 (G. V. Gunn 149*, J. Hardstaff jun 110, W. W. Keeton 75, J. Knowles 57, W. Voce 52*) drew with New Zealanders 428 (M. L. Page 109, J. L. Kerr 93, T. C. Lowry 121, W. Voce 4-112).

15th Match: v Norfolk (Norwich)   June 23, 24.
Norfolk 165 (N. Gallichan 5-37) and 123 lost to New Zealanders 122 (W. S. Thompson 4-42) and 167-2 (J. L. Kerr 93) by 8 wkts.*

16th Match: v England (Lord's)   June 26, 28, 29.
England 424 (W. R. Hammond 140, J. Hardstaff jun 114, E. Paynter 74, A. W. Roberts 4-101, J. Cowie 4-118) and 226-4 dec (C. J. Barnett 83*, J. Hardstaff jun 64) drew with New Zealand 295 (A. W. Roberts 66, D. A. R. Moloney 64, M. W. Wallace 52) and 175-8 (M. W. Wallace 56).

17th Match: v Somerset (Taunton)   June 30, July 1, 2.
Somerset 254 (G. M. Bennett 50*, J. A. Dunning 4-98) and 316 (F. S. Lee 128, H. Gimblett 54, J. Cowie 5-60) lost to New Zealanders 404 (M. W. Wallace 115, J. R. Lamason 71, N. Gallichan 50, W. H. R. Andrews 6-116) and 170-3 (M. W. Wallace 77*) by 7 wkts.

18th Match: v Gloucestershire (Bristol)   July 3, 5, 6.
New Zealanders 362 (D. A. R. Moloney 65, G. L. Weir 60, J. R. Lamason 59, M. P. Donnelly 54, A. W. Roberts 50*, T. W. J. Goddard 4-96, R. A. Sinfield 4-105) and 91-4 drew with Gloucestershire 335 (W. R. Hammond 108, G. M. Emmett 50, A. W. Roberts 4-63, J. A. Dunning 4-102).

19th Match: v Leicestershire (Leicester)   July 7, 8, 9.
Leicestershire 557-4 dec (G. L. Berry 156, F. T. Prentice 123, N. F. Armstrong 121, C. S. Dempster 57*, G. S. Watson 52) drew with 285-3 (J. L. Kerr 130*, M. P. Donnelly 55*, D. A. R. Moloney 51).

20th Match: v Yorkshire (Headingley)   July 10, 12, 13.
Yorkshire 364 (L. Hutton 135, A. Mitchell 62, P. A. Gibb 52, J. A. Dunning 5-139) and 207-6 dec drew with New Zealanders 223 and 203-9 (M. P. Donnelly 97).

21st Match: v Durham (Sunderland)   July 14, 15.
New Zealanders 330 (H. G. Vivian 87, J. L. Kerr 67, J. Grigor 4-93) and 159-6 dec (M. P. Donnelly 61*, T. C. Lowry 50, F. L. Herbert 4-29) drew with Durham 270 (D. C. H. Townsend 138*, D. A. R. Moloney 5-104, N. Gallichan 4-79) and 100-4.*

22nd Match: v Scotland (Glasgow)   July 17, 19, 20.
Scotland 237 (N. S. Mitchell-Innes 87, N. Gallichan 6-46) and 154 lost to New Zealanders 214 (H. G. Vivian 75, M. W. Wallace 54, J. H. Melville 5-68) and 182-7 (M. P. Donnelly 60*, A. D. Baxter 4-87) by 3 wkts.

23rd Match: v Scotland (Dunfermline)   July 21, 22.
New Zealanders 259-8 dec (W. A. Hadlee 59, J. F. Farquhar 6-44) beat Scotland 53 and 154 (P. A. Gibb 67, N. Gallichan 7-25) by an innings and 52 runs.

24th Match: v England (Old Trafford)   July 24, 26, 27.
England 358-9 dec (L. Hutton 100, C. J. Barnett 62, J. Hardstaff jun 58, J. Cowie 4-73) and 187 (F. R. Brown 52, J. Cowie 6-67) beat New Zealand 281 (W. A. Hadlee 93, H. G. Vivian 58, A. W. Wellard 4-81) and 134 (H. G. Vivian 50, T. W. J. Goddard 6-29) by 130 runs.

25th Match: v Surrey (Oval)   July 28, 29, 30.
New Zealanders 495 (M. P. Donnelly 144, M. L. Page 90, M. W. Wallace 69, D. A. R. Moloney 51) and 198-5 dec (G. L. Weir 71) beat Surrey 277 (A. Sandham 83, E. A. Watts 85, D. A. R. Moloney 4-68) and 274 (R. J. Gregory 106) by 142 runs.

26th Match: v Glamorgan (Swansea)   July 31, Aug 2, 3.
Glamorgan 229 (D. E. Davies 58) and 340 (C. C. Smart 94, D. E. Davies 78, A. H. Dyson 77, H. G. Vivian 4-114) beat New Zealanders 127 (D. E. Davies 4-16, A. D. G. Matthews 4-49) and 110 (D. E. Davies 5-30, J. C. Clay 5-59) by 332 runs.

27th Match: v Warwickshire (Edgbaston)   Aug 4, 5, 6.
Warwickshire 259 (F. R. Santall 94) and 322-9 dec (P. Cranmer 71, J. Buckingham 68, D. A. R. Moloney 5-104) drew with New Zealanders 280 (M. P. Donnelly 94, W. A. Hadlee 76, G. A. E. Paine 4-77, W. E. Hollies 4-68) and 219-6.

28th Match: v Essex (Chelmsford)   Aug 7, 9, 10.
Essex 256 (D. R. Wilcox 116, J. A. Dunning 6-71) and 239 (D. R. Wilcox 58, B. H. Belle 51, J. Cowie 5-66, J. A. Dunning 4-99) lost to New Zealanders 368 (W. A. Hadlee 106, M. W. Wallace 88, H. G. Vivian 61, V. J. Evans 5-57) and 128-6 (G. L. Weir 50) by 4 wkts.

29th Match: v Sir J. Cahn's XI (West Bridgford)   Aug 11, 12.
Sir J. Cahn's XI 80 (J. Cowie 5-21) and 134 (J. Cowie 5-46, A. W. Roberts 4-39) lost to New Zealanders 106 and 111-1 (W. N. Carson 54) by 9 wkts.*

30th Match: v England (Oval)   Aug 14, 16, 17.
New Zealand 249 (M. P. Donnelly 58, M. L. Page 53, A. W. Roberts 50, R. W. V. Robins 4-40) and 187 (H. G. Vivian 57) drew with England 254-7 dec (J. Hardstaff jun 103, D. C. S. Compton 65) and 31-1.

31st Match: v Combined Services (Portsmouth)   Aug 18, 19.
Combined Services 180 (R. P. Borgnis 101) and 148 (J. Cowie 5-36) lost to New Zealanders 189 (H. G. Vivian 76) and 140-1 (H. G. Vivian 64*) by 9 wkts.

32nd Match: v Hampshire (Bournemouth)   Aug 21, 23, 24.
Hampshire 324 (A. E. Pothecary 130, O. W. Herman 67, W. L. Creese 61, J. Cowie 4-112) and 171-5 dec drew with New Zealanders 324 (H. G. Vivian 112, G. L. Weir 56, W. N. Carson 54, W. L. Creese 6-81) and 165-5.

33rd Match: v Kent (Canterbury)   Aug 25, 26, 27.
New Zealanders 186 (A. W. Roberts 55) and 300 (D. A. R. Moloney 75) lost to Kent 321 (F. E. Woolley 79, L. E. G. Ames 65, F. G. H. Chalk 62, J. Cowie 4-88, A. W. Roberts 4-110) and 166-9 (F. G. H. Chalk 59, A. W. Roberts 5-63) by 1 wkt.

34th Match: v Sussex (Hove)   Aug 28, 30.
Sussex 151 (J. Cowie 4-41) and 163 (Jas Langridge 91*, M. P. Donnelly 4-32) lost to New Zealanders 546 (M. W. Wallace 111, M. P. Donnelly 83, A. W. Roberts 82, D. A. R. Moloney 75, W. A. Hadlee 76, J. L. Kerr 50, M. W. Tate 4-122) by an innings and 232 runs.

35th Match: v An England XI (Folkestone)   Sept 1, 2, 3.
An England XI 464 (B. H. Valentine 102, C. J. Barnett 63, A. P. F. Chapman 61*, H. Gimblett 54, W. R. Hammond 50) and 186-9 dec (W. J. Edrich 67, W. R. Hammond 63, J. Cowie 4-57) drew with New Zealanders 431 (D. A. R. Moloney 140, J. L. Kerr 112, W. H. R. Andrews 4-69) and 182-2 (M. W. Wallace 74*).

36th Match: v Minor Counties (Gainsborough)   Sept 4, 6.
Minor Counties 310 (T. A. C. Maxwell 78, G. S. Butler 55, B. W. Rought-Rought 54, N. Gallichan 5-52, A. W. Roberts 4-35) and 76 (N. Gallichan 5-20, W. N. Carson 4-20) lost to New Zealanders 337 (J. L. Kerr 160, G. L. Weir 79, H. F. Benka 4-78) and 53-3 by 7 wkts.

37th Match: v H. D. G. Leveson-Gower's XI (Scarborough)   Sept 8, 9, 10.
H. D. G. Leveson-Gower's XI 380 (R. E. S. Wyatt 98, F. R. Brown 65, C. R. N. Maxwell 50) and 206 (J. Hardstaff jun 52, A. W. Roberts 5-47, N. Gallichan 4-56) beat New Zealanders 285 (W. A. Hadlee 68, G. L. Weir 50, A. W. Wellard 4-55) and 156 (W. A. Hadlee 55, M. S. Nichols 5-42) by 145 runs.

38th Match: v Ireland (Dublin)   Sept 11.
Ireland 79 and 30 (J. Cowie 6-3) lost to New Zealanders 64 (J. C. Boucher 7-13) and 46-2 by 8 wkts (3 day match finished in one).

1937: 3rd New Zealanders

Batting Averages

	M	I	NO	R	HS	Avge	100	c/s
M. W. Wallace	25	43	3	1641	115	41.02	2	12
M. P. Donnelly	27	44	6	1414	144	37.21	1	14
D. A. R. Moloney	26	46	4	1463	140	34.83	1	11
J. L. Kerr	23	40	2	1205	160	31.71	3	7
W. A. Hadlee	24	44	3	1225	106	29.87	1	13
H. G. Vivian	24	42	4	1118	112	29.42	1	19
T. C. Lowry	12	18	3	409	121	27.26	1	8/12
G. L. Weir	22	38	4	893	134*	26.26	1	10
A. W. Roberts	21	27	6	510	82	25.50	0	19
M. L. Page	22	37	7	666	109	22.20	1	15
W. N. Carson	20	37	4	627	86	19.00	0	17
E. W. Tindall	23	32	6	477	47	18.34	0	29/18
N. Gallichan	18	22	5	288	50	16.94	0	14
J. R. Lamason	18	28	3	395	71	15.80	0	16
J. A. Dunning	23	31	8	275	30	11.95	0	7
J. Cowie	24	30	8	149	36	6.77	0	14

Bowling Averages

	O	M	R	W	Avge	BB	5i
J. Cowie	860.1	184	2275	114	19.95	6-3	6
W. N. Carson	89	14	319	14	22.78	4-20	0
N. Gallichan	607.4	189	1413	59	23.94	6-46	3
A. W Roberts	662	172	1625	62	26.20	5-47	2
D. A. R. Moloney	407.3	33	1521	57	26.68	5-23	3
J. A. Dunning	941.3	244	2499	83	30.10	6-42	5
M. L. Page	111	13	411	12	34.25	2-36	0
H. G. Vivian	763.3	232	1809	49	36.91	4-70	0
M. P. Donnelly	214.4	38	686	16	42.87	4-32	0
J. R. Lamason	84	19	265	6	44.16	3-28	0
G. L. Weir	358	62	1027	14	73.75	2-29	0

Also bowled: W. A. Hadlee 8-1-13-0; J. L. Kerr 2-1-4-0.

and Vivian also bowled well at times and the medium-pace Roberts was hampered by injury. Wallace and Donnelly stood out in the batting line up. Donnelly attacked the bowling, but could also defend if required; Wallace hit the ball hard and had a fine cover drive. Moloney was useful and could also take wickets; Hadlee looked much better after he abandoned his defensive role and began to treat the bowling on its merits; Kerr also improved as the tour progressed but Carson, Lamason and Weir all disappointed. The fielding was first rate and Tindall was sound behind the wicket, even if he failed to reach the heights of James.

The 1938 Australians. Back: Jeanes (manager), Barnes, McCormick, O'Reilly, White, Fleetwood-Smith, Fingleton, Ferguson (scorer). Centre: Brown, Chipperfield, McCabe, Bradman, Barnett, Waite, Ward. Front: Walker, Badcock, Hassett.

1938: 19th Australians

The team of 1938 included eight of the 1934 tourists, the full side being D. G. Bradman (captain), C. L. Badcock, M. G. Waite, C. W. Walker and F. A. Ward of South Australia; S. J. McCabe, S. G. Barnes, A. G. Chipperfield, J. H. W. Fingleton, W. J. O'Reilly and E. C. S. White of New South Wales; B. A. Barnett, A. L. Hassett, E. L. McCormick and L. O'B. Fleetwood-Smith of Victoria and W. A. Brown of Queensland, with W. H. Jeanes as manager. The most criticised omission was Grimmett's, described as 'late-summer lunacy'.

The team played matches in Tasmania, Western Australia and Ceylon on their way to England aboard the s.s. *Orontes*. Barnes injured his wrist on the voyage and could not play until the end of June.

1938: 19th Australians

Batting Averages

	M	I	NO	R	HS	Avge	100	c/s
D. G. Bradman	20	26	5	2429	278	115.66	13	8
W. A. Brown	25	37	5	1854	265*	57.93	5	14
A. L. Hassett	24	32	3	1589	220*	54.79	5	18
C. L. Badcock	24	39	4	1604	198	45.82	4	14
S. G. Barnes	13	19	2	720	94	42.35	0	9/4
J. H. W. Fingleton	23	32	2	1141	124	38.03	4	17/3
S. J. McCabe	23	33	2	1124	232	36.25	2	17
C. W. Walker	9	9	4	175	42	35.00	0	7/7
B. A. Barnett	22	29	4	737	120*	29.48	1	7/23
A. G. Chipperfield	16	18	3	424	104*	28.26	1	12
M. G. Waite	24	30	3	684	77	25.33	0	4
E. S. White	19	19	7	290	52	24.16	0	11
W. J. O'Reilly	20	17	3	224	42	16.00	0	2
F. A. Ward	19	17	5	162	31	13.50	0	8
L. O'B. Fleetwood-Smith	20	20	9	99	16*	9.00	0	6
E. L. McCormick	18	15	4	49	12	4.45	0	9

Bowling Averages

	O	M	R	W	Avge	BB	5i
W. J. O'Reilly	709.4	215	1726	104	16.59	8-104	9
F. A. Ward	526.2	99	1773	92	19.27	7-51	9
L. O'B. Fleetwood-Smith	555	98	1719	88	19.53	8-98	6
E. C. S. White	375	148	708	30	23.60	3-8	0
A. G. Chipperfield	54.1	18	155	6	25.83	2-12	0
M. G. Waite	647.1	183	1454	56	25.96	7-101	4
E. L. McCormick	335	53	1136	34	33.41	6-88	1
S. J. McCabe	214	53	523	14	37.35	4-28	0
S. G. Barnes	44	4	116	2	58.00	1-32	0
A. L. Hassett	30	9	78	1	78.00	1-4	0

Also bowled: C. L. Badcock 2-0-10-0; D. G. Bradman 3-2-6-0; W. A. Brown 3-0-10-0.

1938: 19th Australians

1st Match: v Worcestershire (Worcester)   April 30, May 2, 3.
Australians 541 (D. G. Bradman 258, C. L. Badcock 67, R. T. D. Perks 4-147, R. J. Crisp 4-170) beat Worcestershire 268 (E. Cooper 61, C. J. Lyttelton 50, L. O'B. Fleetwood-Smith 8-98) and 196 (C. H. Bull 69) by an innings and 77 runs.

2nd Match: v Oxford University (Christ Church, Oxford)   May 4, 5, 6.
Australians 679-7 dec (J. H. W. Fingleton 124, S. J. McCabe 110, A. L. Hassett 146, W. A. Brown 72, D. G. Bradman 58, M. G. Waite 54, A. G. Chipperfield 53) beat Oxford University 117 (J. D. Eggar 51*, L. O'B. Fleetwood-Smith 5-28) and 75 (L. O'B. Fleetwood-Smith 4-31) by an innings and 487 runs.

3rd Match: v Leicestershire (Leicester)   May 7, 9, 10.
Leicestershire 212 (F. A. Ward 5-69) and 215 (C. S. Dempster 105, F. A. Ward 4-73) lost to Australians 590-5 dec (C. L. Badcock 198, A. L. Hassett 148, A. G. Chipperfield 104*) by an innings and 163 runs.

4th Match: v Cambridge University (Cambridge)   May 11, 12, 13.
Cambridge University 120 (N. W. D. Yardley 67, M. G. Waite 3-39, W. J. O'Reilly 5-55) and 163 (P. A. Gibb 80*, F. A. Ward 6-64) lost to Australians 708-5 dec (A. L. Hassett 220*, C. L. Badcock 186, J. H. W. Fingleton 111) by an innings and 425 runs.

5th Match: v M.C.C. (Lord's)   May 14, 16, 17.
Australians 502 (D. G. Bradman 278, A. L. Hassett 57, C. I. J. Smith 6-139) drew with M.C.C. 214 (R. E. S. Wyatt 84*, L. O'B. Fleetwood-Smith 4-69) and 87-1 (W. J. Edrich 53*).

6th Match: v Northamptonshire (Northampton)   May 18, 19, 20.
Australians 406-6 dec (W. A. Brown 194*, C. L. Badcock 72) beat Northamptonshire 194 (R. P. Nelson 74, F. A. Ward 6-75) and 135 (S. J. McCabe 4-28) by an innings and 77 runs.

7th Match: v Surrey (Oval)   May 21, 23, 24.
Australians 528 (D. G. Bradman 143, A. L. Hassett 98, W. A. Brown 96, F. R. Brown 4-147) and 232-2 dec (B. A. Barnett 120*, C. L. Badcock 95) drew with Surrey 271 (T. H. Barling 67, R. J. Gregory 60, W. J. O'Reilly 8-104) and 104-1 (L. B. Fishlock 93).

8th Match: v Hampshire (Southampton)   May 25, 26, 27.
Hampshire 157 (W. J. O'Reilly 6-65) drew with Australians 320-1 dec (D. G. Bradman 145*, J. H. W. Fingleton 123*).

9th Match: v Middlesex (Lord's)   May 28, 30, 31.
Australians 132 (J. M. Sims 4-25) and 114-2 dec drew with Middlesex 188 (D. C. S. Compton 65, E. L. McCormick 6-58, W. J. O'Reilly 4-56) and 21-0.

10th Match: v Gloucestershire (Bristol)   June 1, 2, 3.
Gloucestershire 78 (W. J. O'Reilly 6-22) and 107 (W. J. O'Reilly 5-45, L. O'B. Fleetwood-Smith 4-39) lost to Australians 164 (C. L. Badcock 51, R. A. Sinfield 8-65) and 25-0 by 10 wkts.

11th Match: v Essex (Southend)   June 4, 6.
Australians 145 (W. A. Brown 55, K. Farnes 4-43) and 153 (S. J. McCabe 50, M. S. Nichols 6-25) beat Essex 114 (F. A. Ward 7-51) and 87 (L. O'B. Fleetwood-Smith 5-28, F. A. Ward 4-26) by 97 runs.

12th Match: v England (Trent Bridge)   June 10, 11, 13, 14.
England 658-8 dec (E. Paynter 216, C. J. Barnett 126, D. C. S. Compton 102, L. Hutton 100, L. O'B. Fleetwood-Smith 4-153) drew with Australia 411 (S. J. McCabe 232, D. G. Bradman 51, K. Farnes 4-106, D. V. P. Wright 4-153) and 427-6 dec (D. G. Bradman 144*, W. A. Brown 133).

13th Match: v Gentlemen (Lord's)   June 15, 16, 17.
Australians 397 (D. G. Bradman 104, A. G. Chipperfield 51, R. J. O. Meyer 5-66) and 335-4 dec (J. H. W. Fingleton 121, C. L. Badcock 112*) beat Gentlemen 301 (F. R. Brown 88, D. R. Wilcox 50, F. A. Ward 5-108) and 149 (P. A. Gibb 67, L. O'B. Fleetwood-Smith 7-44) by 282 runs.

14th Match: v Lancashire (Old Trafford)   June 18, 20, 21.
Australians 303 (A. L. Hassett 118, C. L. Badcock 96, W. E. Phillipson 5-93) and 284-2 dec (D. G. Bradman 101*, J. H. W. Fingleton 96, W. A. Brown 70) drew with Lancashire 289 (N. Oldfield 69, W. E. Phillipson 52, E. L. McCormick 4-84) and 80-3.

15th Match: v England (Lord's)   June 24, 25, 27, 28.
England 494 (W. R. Hammond 240, E. Paynter 99, L. E. G. Ames 83, E. L. McCormick 4-101, W. J. O'Reilly 4-93) and 242-8 dec (D. C. S. Compton 76*) drew with Australia 422 (W. A. Brown 206*, A. L. Hassett 56, H. Verity 4-103) and 204-6 (D. G. Bradman 102*).

16th Match: v Derbyshire (Chesterfield)   June 29, 30.
Derbyshire 151 (T. S. Worthington 67, F. A. Ward 5-45) and 56 (M. G. Waite 5-40) lost to Australians 441-6 dec (W. A. Brown 265*, C. L. Badcock 86) by an innings and 234 runs.

17th Match: v Yorkshire (Bramall Lane)   July 2, 4, 5.
Australians 222 (A. L. Hassett 94, D. G. Bradman 59, T. F. Smailes 6-92) and 132 (T. F. Smailes 4-45) drew with Yorkshire 205 (M. G. Waite 7-101) and 83-3.

18th Match: v England (Old Trafford)   July 8, 9, 11, 12.
Match abandoned—no play due to rain.

19th Match: v Warwickshire (Edgbaston)   July 13, 14.
Warwickshire 179 (J. S. Ord 61, F. A. Ward 4-26) and 118 (W. J. O'Reilly 4-33) lost to Australians 390-8 dec (D. G. Bradman 135, W. A. Brown 101, W. E. Hollies 5-130) by an innings and 93 runs.

20th Match: v Nottinghamshire (Trent Bridge)   July 16, 18, 19.
Australians 243 (S. G. Barnes 58, D. G. Bradman 56, C. B. Harris 4-60) and 453-4 dec (D. G. Bradman 144, W. A. Brown 103, C. L. Badcock 54) beat Nottinghamshire 147 (G. V. Gunn 75, W. J. O'Reilly 5-39) and 137 (J. Hardstaff jun 67*, L. O'B. Fleetwood-Smith 5-39) by 412 runs.

21st Match: v England (Headingley)   July 22, 23, 25.
England 223 (W. R. Hammond 76, W. J. O'Reilly 5-66) and 123 (L. O'B. Fleetwood-Smith 4-34, W. J. O'Reilly 5-56) beat England 242 (D. G. Bradman 103, B. A. Barnett 57, K. Farnes 4-77) and 107-5 by 5 wkts.

22nd Match: v Somerset (Taunton)   July 27, 28, 29.
Somerset 110 and 136 (L. O'B. Fleetwood-Smith 5-30) lost to Australians 464-6 dec (D. G. Bradman 202, C. L. Badcock 110, S. J. McCabe 56*) by an innings and 218 runs.

23rd Match: v Glamorgan (Swansea)   July 30, Aug 1, 2.
Glamorgan 148-5 dec (D. E. Davies 58, M. G. Waite 4-45) drew with Australians 61-3.

24th Match: v Scotland (Broughty Ferry)   Aug 4, 5.
Australians 213 (S. J. McCabe 62, J. N. Symon 5-33) and 320 (F. A. Ward 71, J. H. W. Fingleton 69, W. D. Laidlaw 5-128) drew with Scotland 88 (L. O'B. Fleetwood-Smith 4-21) and 185-8 (F. A. Ward 4-50).

25th Match: v Scotland (Glasgow)   Aug 6.
Australians 143 beat Scotland 82 (W. J. O'Reilly 7-39) by 61 runs.

26th Match: v Durham (Sunderland)   Aug 8, 9.
Australians 380-5 dec (S. G. Barnes 140, C. L. Badcock 103*) beat Durham 105 (L. O'B. Fleetwood-Smith 6-53, W. J. O'Reilly 4-32) and 96 (W. J. O'Reilly 6-35, L. O'B. Fleetwood-Smith 4-37).*

27th Match: v Surrey (Oval)   Aug 10, 11, 12.
Australians 297 (S. J. McCabe 67, S. G. Barnes 63) drew with Surrey 105-7 (W. J. O'Reilly 4-25).

28th Match: v Kent (Canterbury)   Aug 13, 15, 16.
Australians 479 (S. G. Barnes 94, C. L. Badcock 76, D. G. Bradman 67, B. A. Barnett 54, E. S. White 52, A. E. Watt 4-102, L. J. Todd 4-145) and 7-0 beat Kent 108 (M. G. Waite 4-43) and 377 (L. E. G. Ames 139, F. E. Woolley 81, M. G. Waite 5-85) by 10 wkts.

29th Match: v Army (Aldershot)   Aug 17, 18.
Army 113 (L. O'B. Fleetwood-Smith 4-62) and 119 (W. J. O'Reilly 7-33) lost to Australians 299 (J. H. W. Fingleton 64, B. A. Barnett 58) by an innings and 67 runs.

30th Match: v England (Oval)   Aug 20, 22, 23, 24.
England 903-7 dec (L. Hutton 364, M. Leyland 187, J. Hardstaff jun 169*, W. R. Hammond 59) beat Australia 201 (W. A. Brown 69, W. E. Bowes 5-49) and 123 (K. Farnes 4-63) by an innings and 579 runs.

31st Match: v Sussex (Hove)   Aug 27, 29, 30.
Australians 336 (W. A. Brown 75, A. L. Hassett 74, D. J. Wood 4-96) and 300 (C. L. Badcock 58, A. L. Hassett 56, B. A. Barnett 53, H. E. Hammond 5-107) drew with Sussex 453 (H. T. Bartlett 157, G. Cox 76, Jas Langridge 68, R. G. Stainton 58, F. A. Ward 6-184) and 53-2.

32nd Match: v An England XI (Blackpool)   Aug 31, Sept 1.
An England XI 132 (F. A. Ward 6-44, W. J. O'Reilly 4-30) and 99 (W. J. O'Reilly 5-44, F. A. Ward 4-20) lost to Australians 174 (L. N. Amar Singh 6-84) and 58-0 by 10 wkts.

33rd Match: v An England XI (Folkestone)   Sept 3, 5, 6.
Australians 390 (S. G. Barnes 91, B. A. Barnett 82, M. G. Waite 60, L. J. Todd 4-97) and 327-7 dec (S. J. McCabe 91, J. H. W. Fingleton 51*) drew with An England XI 223 (L. E. G. Ames 78, F. A. Ward 7-112) and 38-0.

34th Match: v H. D. G. Leveson-Gower's XI (Scarborough)   Sept 10, 12, 13.
Australians 306 (S. G. Barnes 90, M. G. Waite 77, S. J. McCabe 58, M. S. Nichols 6-113) and 102 (W. E. Bowes 5-42) lost to H. D. G. Leveson-Gower's XI 363-8 dec (J. Hardstaff jun 108, L. Hutton 73, M. Leyland 51, W. J. O'Reilly 4-75) and 46-0 by 10 wkts.

35th Match: v Gentlemen of Ireland (Belfast)   Sept 15.
Australians 145 (Jas Macdonald 5-24, E. A. Ingram 4-46) beat Gentlemen of Ireland 84 (F. A. Ward 5-22) by 61 runs.

36th Match: v Gentlemen of Ireland (Dublin)   Sept 16, 17.
Gentlemen of Ireland 100 and 106 (E. D. R. Shearer 56, W. J. O'Reilly 5-39) lost to Australians 239 (S. J. McCabe 62, S. G. Barnes 53, C. L. Badcock 52, E. A. Ingram 7-83) by an innings and 33 runs.

As in 1930 and 1934, the outstanding performance of the tour was by Bradman—he managed to eclipse both his previous visits and if an ankle injury had not prevented him from playing in the final four first-class matches he might well have aggregated over 3,000 runs; as it was his average of 115.66 was a new record. In the Tests he also averaged over 100. The burden of leadership did not in any way seem to affect his batting. Brown and Hassett also batted well, though the former was rather prone to the defensive. Badcock and Fingleton came out well in the first-class games, but failed in the Tests. McCabe was a mystery; he played the innings of the tour in the Trent Bridge Test, then did little or nothing for the remainder of the visit.

The batting was Australia's strong point: its weakness lay in the bowling. McCormick was billed as one of the greatest fast bowlers in the history of the game but was continually no-balled for over-stepping the crease, which perhaps sapped his confidence. Whatever the cause he took only 34 wickets on the tour at a high cost. The attack rested almost alone on O'Reilly's shoulders. His accurate leg-breaks, bowled at almost medium pace, worried all the English batsmen at times and he headed the first-class and Test averages. Fleetwood-Smith failed to improve on his 1934 form due to his erratic length, which negated his well-disguised spin. Ward was useful at times, but nowhere near the standard of Grimmett, while the slow left arm of White was rarely seen. McCormick's efforts were not helped by the lack of an opening partner—McCabe, who opened the bowling in several Tests, was entirely ineffectual. The fielding was good and Barnett adequate behind the stumps—injury prevented the deputy wicketkeeper, Walker, from having much of a trial.

The Test rubber ended as one match each with two drawn and

the Old Trafford game washed out. There was considerable criticism about the length of the Tests, which were restricted to four days each. As with the previous visits, the public flocked to the matches and the venture was highly profitable.

1939: 6th West Indians

After some trial matches in Trinidad the following team was chosen for the tour: R. S. Grant (captain), L. N. Constantine, V. H. Stollmeyer, J. B. Stollmeyer, G. E. Gomez and T. F. Johnson of Trinidad; G. A. Headley, I. Barrow, K. H. Weekes and J. H. Cameron of Jamaica; E. A. Martindale, E. A. V. Williams, J. E. D.

Sealy and C. B. Clarke of Barbados and H. P. Bayley of British Guiana; later L. Hylton of Jamaica was added. J. M. Kidney was the manager. Among those missing C. A. Merry was the most important. The team travelled to England in two groups, the Jamaicans sailing to Liverpool from Kingston and the rest from Bridgetown to Plymouth.

After a poor start the tourists recovered to play some splendid cricket, but were beaten by England in the single Test that came to a definite conclusion—the matches were three-day ones and the other two were drawn. The eight wins from 25 matches was the best first-class record ever achieved by the West Indies in England.

This success was mainly due to Headley's batting and Constantine's bowling. Headley hit centuries in both innings of

1939: 6th West Indians

1st Match: v R. Earle's XI (Busbridge Hall)   May 1.

2nd Match: v Reigate Priory (Reigate)   May 2.

3rd Match: v L. E. G. Ames' XI (Gravesend)   May 3.
L. E. G. Ames' XI 278-6 dec (L. E. G. Ames 116, F. E. Woolley 59) drew with West Indians 225-3 (J. B. Stollmeyer 87, G. E. Gomez 54).*

4th Match: v Army (Aldershot)   May 4.
Army 130 lost to West Indians 166-8 (J. E. D. Sealy 62, J. W. J. Steele 5-64) by 3 wkts.

5th Match: v Worcestershire (Worcester)   May 6, 8.
Worcestershire 83 (E. A. Martindale 4-27) and 291 (S. H. Martin 94, E. Cooper 92) beat West Indians 142 (G. A. Headley 50, R. T. D. Perks 6-27) and 147 (R. T. D. Perks 5-48, R. Howorth 4-42) by 85 runs.

6th Match: v Lancashire (Liverpool)   May 10, 11, 12.
Lancashire 226 (C. Washbrook 64) and 256 (N. Oldfield 71, J. H. Cameron 5-23) drew with West Indians 236 (J. E. D. Sealy 67, W. E. Phillipson 5-48) and 142-3 (G. A. Headley 76*).

7th Match: v M.C.C. (Lord's)   May 13, 15, 16.
M.C.C. 435-7 (D. C. S. Compton 115, B. O. Allen 85, B. H. Valentine 73, C. R. N. Maxwell 64*) drew with West Indians did not bat.

8th Match: v Cambridge University (Cambridge)   May 17, 18, 19.
West Indians 296 (G. A. Headley 103, P. J. Dickinson 4-78, A. C. Shirreff 4-119) drew with Cambridge University 153 (T. F. Johnson 4-37, L. N. Constantine 4-44) and 192-9 (J. P. Mann 59*).

9th Match: v Surrey (Oval)   May 20, 22, 23.
West Indians 224 (J. E. D. Sealy 58, G. A. Headley 52, L. N. Constantine 52, F. R. Brown 8-94) and 191 (J. F. Parker 5-36) lost to Surrey 215 (C. B. Clarke 4-93) and 204-3 (R. J. Gregory 79, L. B. Fishlock 60) by 7 wkts.

10th Match: v Oxford University (Oxford)   May 24, 25, 26.
West Indians 480-7 dec (E. A. V. Williams 126*, J. H. Cameron 106, H. P. Bayley 104) beat Oxford University 232 and 243 (J. M. Lomas 59, E. D. R. Eagar 57) by an innings and 5 runs.

11th Match: v Glamorgan (Cardiff)   May 27, 29, 30.
Glamorgan 377 (W. Wooller 111, H. D. Davies 64, M. J. L. Turnbull 60) and 157 (L. N. Constantine 5-49) beat West Indians 253 (E. A. V. Williams 96, L. N. Constantine 63, P. F. Judge 4-57) and 208 (J. E. D. Sealy 58, W. Wooller 5-69) by 73 runs.

12th Match: v Essex (Chelmsford)   May 31, June 1.
Essex 158 (L. N. Constantine 7-49) and 194 (A. V. Avery 55, T. H. Wade 55, L. N. Constantine 6-42) lost to West Indians 219 (G. A. Headley 116*, T. P. B. Smith 4-78) and 134-8 by 2 wkts.

13th Match: v Middlesex (Lord's)   June 3, 5, 6.
West Indians 665 (G. A. Headley 227, J. E. D. Sealy 181, J. B. Stollmeyer 117) beat Middlesex 183 (W. F. Price 59*, J. H. Cameron 6-57, L. N. Constantine 4-68) and 254 (E. T. Killick 74*, W. J. Edrich 51) by an innings and 228 runs.

14th Match: v Northamptonshire (Northampton)   June 7, 8.
Northamptonshire 107 (L. G. Hylton 5-35) and 299 (D. Brookes 93, M. E. F. Dunkley 56) lost to West Indians 382 (J. H. Cameron 73, K. H. Weekes 64, G. A. Headley 63, L. G. Hylton 55) and 25-1 by 9 wkts.

15th Match: v Derbyshire (Derby)   June 10, 11, 12.
Derbyshire 309 (A. E. Alderman 90, D. Smith 64, T. D. Hounsfield 56) and 104 (L. G. Hylton 4-46) drew with West Indians 264 (G. E. Gomez 55, W. H. Copson 6-73) and 54-6 (W. H. Copson 4-19).

16th Match: v Minor Counties (Lord's)   June 14, 15, 16.
West Indians 370 (J. E. D. Sealy 79, J. B. Stollmeyer 73, K. H. Weekes 55, L. N. Constantine 55, H. Robson 4-80, C. A. Edge 4-97) and 138-4 (J. B. Stollmeyer 63) drew with Minor Counties 306 (F. Dennis 95, R. H. Parkin 55, L. N. Constantine 5-52).

17th Match: v Leicestershire (Leicester)   June 17, 19, 20.
West Indians 182 (J. B. Stollmeyer 59, G. E. Gomez 58, H. A. Smith 5-53, J. Sperry 4-42) and 314-8 (K. H. Weekes 62, J. B. Stollmeyer 50, J. Sperry 4-111) drew with Leicestershire 216 (G. L. Berry 51, E. A. Martindale 5-57).

18th Match: Lincolnshire (Scunthorpe)   June 21, 22.
Lincolnshire 120 (L. N. Constantine 8-30) and 183 lost to West Indians 363 (J. B. Stollmeyer 100, R. S. Grant 94, V. A. Hodgkinson 4-59) by an innings and 60 runs.

19th Match: v England (Lord's)   June 24, 26, 27.
West Indies 277 (G. A. Headley 106, W. H. Copson 5-85) and 225 (G. A. Headley 107, W. H. Copson 4-67) lost to England 404-5 dec (L. Hutton 196, D. C. S. Compton 120) and 100-2 by 8 wkts.

20th Match: v Norfolk (Norwich)   June 28, 29.
West Indians 369 (K. H. Weekes 123, E. A. V. Williams 78) drew with Norfolk 375-9 (H. E. Theobald 70, G. A. Edrich 53, C. B. Clarke 4-121).

21st Match: v Nottinghamshire (Trent Bridge)   July 1, 3, 4.
Nottinghamshire 149 (J. Hardstaff jun 73*, L. N. Constantine 6-50) and 267 (W. W. Keeton 82, R. J. Giles 52) lost to West Indians 510-3 dec (G. A. Headley 234*, J. E. D. Sealy 115, V. H. Stollmeyer 73*) by an innings and 94 runs.

22nd Match: v Yorkshire (Harrogate)   July 5, 6, 7.
West Indians 234 (R. S. Grant 72, G. A. Headley 61, H. Verity 4-77) and 116-6 drew with Yorkshire 114 (L. N. Constantine 5-28, C. B. Clarke 5-49).

23rd Match: v Lancashire (Old Trafford)   July 8, 10, 11.
West Indians 284 (R. S. Grant 95, G. E. Gomez 65) and 114-2 drew with Lancashire 325-4 dec (W. Place 164, J. L. Hopwood 91).

24th Match: v Northumberland (Newcastle)   July 12, 13.
West Indians 330 (V. H. Stollmeyer 84, J. B. Stollmeyer 83, E. A. V. Williams 55, G. C. Wilson 6-126) and 115-6 dec drew with Northumberland 122 (C. B. Clarke 6-51) and 251-9 (A. D. Ramsden 66, P. Vaulkard 75*, C. B. Clarke 4-68, L. N. Constantine 4-72).*

25th Match: v Durham (Sunderland)   July 15, 17.
Durham 101 (R. S. Grant 6-33, L. N. Constantine 4-35) and 42-3 drew with West Indians 203 (J. E. D. Sealy 55, F. I. Herbert 4-42).

26th Match: v Sir J. Cahn's XI (West Bridgford)   July 19, 20.
West Indians 197 (G. A. Headley 61, J. E. D. Sealy 51, J. E. Walsh 7-89) drew with Sir J. Cahn's XI 121-4.

27th Match: v England (Old Trafford)   July 22, 24, 25.
England 164-7 dec (J. Hardstaff jun 76) and 128-6 dec (L. N. Constantine 4-42) drew with West Indies 133 (G. A. Headley 51, W. E. Bowes 6-33) and 43-4.

28th Match: v Surrey (Oval)   July 26, 27, 28.
West Indians 487 (K. H. Weekes 146, G. A. Headley 93, V. H. Stollmeyer 73) and 49-3 beat Surrey 274 (J. F. Parker 100, C. B. Clarke 5-64) and 261 (H. S. Squires 58, C. B. Clarke 4-80) by 7 wkts.

29th Match: v Hampshire (Bournemouth)   July 29, 31, Aug 1.
Hampshire 106 (C. B. Clarke 6-32, R. S. Grant 4-41) and 139 (J. Bailey 70*, C. B. Clarke 7-75) lost to West Indians 222 (R. S. Grant 54) and 25-0 by 10 wkts.

30th Match: v Somerset (Taunton)   Aug 2, 3.
West Indians 84 (W. H. R. Andrews 6-40, A. W. Wellard 4-43) and 189 (K. H. Weekes 54, H. L. Hazell 4-74) lost to Somerset 345 (R. J O Meyer 78, W. T. Luckes 71*, G. M. Bennett 56, C. B. Clarke 6-138) by an innings and 72 runs.

31st Match: v Glamorgan (Swansea)   Aug 5, 7.
Glamorgan 127 (L. N. Constantine 4-33, C. B. Clarke 4-42) and 159 (H. D. Davies 58, L. N. Constantine 5-52) lost to West Indians 96 (A. D. G. Matthews 7-21) and 194-8 (J. B. Stollmeyer 57) by 2 wkts.

32nd Match: v Warwickshire (Edgbaston)   Aug 9, 10, 11.
West Indians 225 (G. E. Gomez 90, K. H. Weekes 67, J. H. Mayer 6-54) and 112-4 dec drew with Warwickshire 130 (F. R. Santall 54*, C. B. Clarke 5-57, R. S. Grant 4-43) and 100-5.

33rd Match: v Gloucestershire (Cheltenham)   Aug 12, 14, 15.
West Indians 162 (C. J. Scott 4-66) and 231-3 (G. M. Emmett 84, W. L. Neale 70) lost to Gloucestershire 152 (L. N. Constantine 5-40) by 7 wkts.

34th Match: v Wiltshire (Swindon)   Aug 16, 17.
West Indians 270 (G. E. Gomez 77, G. A. Headley 58, W. Smith 5-78) and 286-5 (J. E. D. Sealy 85, V. H. Stollmeyer 71, H. P. Bayley 63) drew with Wiltshire 333-7 dec (B. W. Hone 124, G. S. Butler 74, E. M. Nash 51, T. F. Johnson 4-61).*

35th Match: v England (Oval)   Aug 19, 21, 22.
England 352 (J. Hardstaff jun 94, N. Oldfield 80, L. Hutton 73, L. N. Constantine 5-75) and 366-3 dec (L. Hutton 165*, W. R. Hammond 138) drew with West Indies 498 (K. H. Weekes 137, V. H. Stollmeyer 96, L. N. Constantine 79, G. A. Headley 65, J. B. Stollmeyer 59, R. T. D. Perks 5-156).

36th Match: v Sussex (Hove)   Aug 26, 28, 29.
Abandoned due to war.

37th Match: v Kent (Canterbury)   Aug 30, 31, Sept 1.
Abandoned due to war.

38th Match: v W. E. Butlin's XI (Skegness)   Sept 2, 4.
Abandoned due to war.

39th Match: An England XI (Folkestone)   Sept 6, 7, 8.
Abandoned due to war.

40th Match: v H. D. G. Leveson-Gower's XI (Scarborough)   Sept 9, 11, 12.
Abandoned due to war.

41st Match: v Ireland (Dublin).
Abandoned due to war.

42nd Match: v Ireland (Belfast).
Abandoned due to war.

the Lord's Test and his figures in all first-class matches were 1,745 runs, average 72.70–no other batsman reached 1,000 runs. The other batsmen to perform well were the two Stollmeyers, though V. H. was troubled by illness, and Weekes. Grant tried to solve the problem of opening the innings by putting himself in first and was occasionally successful.

Constantine, with a mixture of fast and slow deliveries, was the only effective bowler in the Test and in all first-class matches took 103 wickets at 17.77. As he fielded brilliatly and batted vigorously, he was liable at any time to change the course of a match. Martindale, the best bowler in 1933, dropped away alarmingly and in the Tests his four wickets cost 78.50 runs each. Second to Constantine in the attack was Clarke, the leg-break and googly bowler. A damaged hand cut short Cameron's tour, but he had done little up to his injury. Hylton and Johnson were also of little use, though the latter looked worthy of a longer trial.

The Test Matches were well attended and the West Indies took £4,684 as their share–all told the finances broke about even. The worsening international situation brought the tour to an abrupt halt on 24 August. The team went by train to Glasgow the following day and on 26 August boarded the s.s. *Montrose* for Montreal, where they played a single match before making their way south.

Above *Victor Stollmeyer, like his younger brother Jeffrey, who later captained West Indies, was an opening batsman. Both were in the 1939 touring party, but Victor was troubled by illness. He played his only Test innings in the last Test played before the Second World War, and was stumped for 96.*

Right *J. E. D. Sealy, West Indies' youngest Test player on his debut in 1929-30, ended his Test career on the tour of England in 1939, when he emphasised his all-round ability by keeping wicket in the last two Tests.*

1939: 6th West Indians

Batting Averages

	M	I	NO	R	HS	Avge	100	c/s
G. A. Headley	20	30	6	1745	234*	72.70	6	10
E. A. V. Williams	11	15	3	370	126*	30.83	1	6
J. B. Stollmeyer	18	31	1	916	117	30.53	1	6
V. H. Stollmeyer	13	22	4	542	96	30.11	0	3
K. H. Weekes	19	28	1	803	146	29.74	2	6
R. S. Grant	21	32	4	785	95	28.03	0	23
J. E. D. Sealy	23	35	1	948	181	27.88	2	16/3
G. E. Gomez	19	30	2	719	90	25.67	0	10
L. N. Constantine	22	32	3	614	79	21.17	0	17
J. H. Cameron	17	23	2	438	106	20.85	1	5
H. P. Bayley	10	15	2	266	104	20.46	1	2
L. G. Hylton	15	19	4	215	55	14.33	0	10
I. Barrow	16	25	2	304	41	13.21	0	20/6
E. A. Martindale	20	30	7	286	39	12.43	0	5
C. B. Clarke	22	25	10	162	45	10.80	0	5
T. Johnson	9	9	4	30	12	6.00	0	4

Bowling Averages

	O	M	R	W	Avge	BB	5i
L. N. Constantine	488.4	67	1831	103	17.77	7-49	9
J. H. Cameron	222.6	40	664	31	21.41	6-57	2
C. B. Clarke	458.3	46	1898	87	21.81	7-75	6
R. S. Grant	211.5	33	676	25	27.04	4-41	0
L. G. Hylton	301	32	1081	39	27.71	5-35	1
G. A. Headley	10	1	30	1	30.00	1-5	0
T. Johnson	154.1	26	520	16	32.50	4-37	0
E. A. V. Williams	119.4	14	461	14	32.92	3-37	0
V. H. Stollmeyer	6	1	33	1	33.00	1-8	0
E. A. Martindale	397.7	41	1587	46	34.50	5-57	1
J. E. D. Sealy	47	4	174	5	34.80	1-8	0
J. B. Stollmeyer	34	2	182	3	60.66	2-58	0

1940: Proposed South African tour

A South African tour was scheduled for the English season of 1940, but no more than tentative arrangements had been made when the Second World War broke out in September 1939.

A report in *The Cricketer* in December 1939 suggested as near certainties for the 1940 visit A. Melville (captain), B. Mitchell, A. D. Nourse, K. G. Viljoen, E. L. Dalton, E. A. B. Rowan, A. B. C. Langton, R. J. Crisp, P. G. van der Byl, N. Gordon, R. E. Grieveson and I. J. Siedle.

1945: Australian Services

In the early months of 1945 the R.A.A.F. and the A.I.F. both arranged a programme of matches for the coming season. These programmes actually began, but after V-E Day on 8 May the match schedule was adjusted to accommodate five three-day 'Victory Tests' and other games such as a three-day match at Scarborough were added. Flight Lieutenant Keith Johnson of the Australian Board of Control flew from Australia to manage the side.

The main interest naturally centred on the Tests, which ended with two wins each and one draw. A. L. Hassett captained the Australians and W. R. Hammond led England. The leading batsman was without doubt K. R. Miller, who hit 443 runs, average 63.28, in the Tests as well as taking 10 wickets. Apart from him, the batting was rather weak and surprisingly second

---

1945: Australian Services

1st Match: v England (Lord's)   May 19, 21, 22.
England 267 (L. E. G. Ames 57, J. D. B. Robertson 53) and 294 (J. D. B. Robertson 84, W. J. Edrich 50, C. G. Pepper 4-80) lost to Australia 455 (K. R. Miller 105, A. L. Hassett 77, R. G. Williams 53, J. W. A. Stephenson 5-116) and 107-4 (C. G. Pepper 54*) by 6 wkts.

2nd Match: v England (Bramall Lane)   June 23, 25, 26.
England 286 (W. R. Hammond 100, C. Washbrook 63) and 190 beat Australia 147 (G. H. Pope 5-58) and 288 (J. A. Workman 63, R. S. Whitington 61, R. Pollard 5-76) by 41 runs.

3rd Match: v Oxford and District (Christ Church, Oxford)   July 1.
Services 142-5 dec drew with Oxford and District 104-5 (G. E. Wheatley 51*).

4th Match: v H. D. G. Leveson-Gower's XI (Eastbourne)   July 7.
H. D. G. Leveson-Gower's XI 220 (G. O. B. Allen 88, E. K. Scott 55, C. G. Pepper 4-48) drew with Services 193-6 (A. L. Hassett 55, R. S. Whitington 50).

5th Match: v Yorkshire (Bradford)   July 11, 12.
Services 204 (C. G. Pepper 51, A. Coxon 5-66, J. P. Whitehead 4-43) and 27-1 drew with Yorkshire 156 (L. Hutton 82, R. G. Williams 5-41).

6th Match: v England (Lord's)   July 14, 16, 17.
England 254 (L. Hutton 104, D. R. Cristofani 4-43) and 164 (L. Hutton 69, W. J. Edrich 58, D. R. Cristofani 5-49) lost to Australia 194 (A. L. Hassett 68, R. Pollard 6-75) and 225-6 (K. R. Miller 71, S. G. Sismey 51) by 4 wkts.

7th Match: v Gravesend Sunday Club (Gravesend)   July 15.
Services 242-4 dec (R. M. Stanford 77, A. L. Hassett 75, A. G. Cheetham 54) beat Gravesend Sunday Club 159 (G. O. B. Allen 62, C. G. Pepper 5-45) by 83 runs.

8th Match: v Yorkshire (Bramall Lane)   July 23, 24.
Services 232 (K. R. Miller 111, W. E. Bowes 4-48, A. Coxon 4-73) and 162-5 drew with Yorkshire 243 (L. Hutton 111, A. Mitchell 57, C. G. Pepper 6-69).

9th Match: v Sussex (Chichester)   July 26.
Sussex 210-5 dec (A. G. Doggart 54*) drew with Services 109-7 (Jas Langridge 5-40).

10th Match: v Metropolitan Police (Westcliff)   July 28.
Metropolitan Police 208-6 dec (J. L. Wills 57, S. Foy 53) beat Services 134 (H. Taylor 4-35, F. Allen 4-35) by 74 runs.

11th Match: v Royal Navy (Portsmouth)   Aug 1, 2.
Services 331 (A. L. Hassett 189) drew with Royal Navy 204 (K. Cranston 78, C. G. Pepper 5-57) and 139-7.

12th Match: v England (Lord's)   Aug 6, 7, 8.
Australia 388 (K. R. Miller 118, S. G. Sismey 59, C. G. Pepper 57, G. H. Pope 4-83, R. Pollard 4-145) and 140-4 drew with England 468-7 dec (C. Washbrook 112, W. R. Hammond 83, W. J. Edrich 73*, L. B. Fishlock 69).

13th Match: v Northamptonshire (Northampton)   Aug 11.
Northamptonshire 189 (J. A. R. Oliver 54, G. Carlton 4-43, C. G. Pepper 4-61) beat Services 165 (R. J. Partridge 5-43, A. L. Cox 4-54) by 24 runs.

14th Match: v North of England (Blackpool)   Aug 16, 17.
North of England 438 (N. Oldfield 171, D. Smith 109, D. R. Cristofani 4-107) beat Services 102 (A. L. Hassett 103, G. H. Pope 4-72) and 147 (R. S. Whitington 51, W. E. Hollies 5-41) by an innings and 89 runs.

15th Match: v England (Old Trafford)   Aug 20, 21, 22.
Australia 173 (K. R. Miller 77, R. Pollard 4-78) and 210 (D. R. Cristofani 110*, W. E. Phillipson 6-58) lost to England 243 (L. Hutton 64, W. R. Hammond 57, D. R. Cristofani 5-55) and 141-4 by 6 wkts.

16th Match: v Nottinghamshire (Trent Bridge)   Aug 31, Sept 1.
Services 194 (A. W. Roper 58, W. Voce 5-46) and 215 (K. R. Miller 81*, W. Voce 6-67) beat Nottinghamshire 130 (C. G. Pepper 7-40) and 176 (W. W. Keeton 52, D. R. Cristofani 6-59, C. G. Pepper 4-71) by 103 runs.

17th Match: v H. D. G. Leveson-Gower's XI (Scarborough)   Sept 5, 6, 7.
Services 506 (C. G. Pepper 168, R. S. Whitington 79, K. R. Miller 71, S. G. Sismey 78, A. D. G. Matthews 4-104) beat H. D. G. Leveson-Gower's XI 258 (L. B. Fishlock 95, R. S. Ellis 5-43) and 140 (R. S. Ellis 5-24, C. G. Pepper 4-60) by an innings and 108 runs.

18th Match: v Surrey (Kingston)   Sept 9, 10.
Services 90 (F. R. Brown 4-17) and 73 (F. R. Brown 4-16) lost to Surrey 113 (T. H. Barling 51, C. G. Pepper 4-45) and 51-7 by 3 wkts.

19th Match: v Sussex (Hove)   Sept 12.
Sussex 183-8 dec (D. R. Fell 76, R. S. Ellis 4-34) lost to Services 184-7 by 3 wkts.

20th Match: v Combined Counties (Middlesbrough)   Sept 15.
Services 268-5 dec (C. F. T. Price 120, C. Papayanni 66*) beat Combined Counties 77 (J. Pettiford 6-20) by 191 runs.

International cricket got under way again in England after the Second World War with 'Victory Test' matches between the Australian Services side and an England XI. This photograph shows the Services side enjoying tea before a large crowd at Scarborough. Stanford, Hassett and Roper have signed the picture. The services haircut in the foreground is of Keith Miller, one of Test cricket's greatest all-rounders.

and third in the Test averages were C. G. Pepper and D. R. Cristofani, both of whom were really played for their bowling. The two opening batsmen, R. S. Whitington and J. A. Workman, gave the team a good start only once. Hassett proved useful but was preoccupied with the problem of making 11

individuals into a team. R. G. Williams and D. K. Carmody came almost straight from prisoner-of-war camps into top-class cricket and too much was expected of them. S. G. Sismey kept wicket well.

The matches were played in a most pleasing spirit and watched by large crowds. It was hoped that both these facets would continue when fully representative matches returned.

1945: Australian Services

Batting Averages

	M	I	NO	R	HS	Avge	100	c/s
K. R. Miller	6	11	3	514	118	64.25	2	2
D. R. Cristofani	3	4	1	164	110*	54.66	1	0
C. G. Pepper	6	10	1	417	168	46.33	1	10
J. Pettiford	3	5	0	145	39	29.00	0	2
S. G. Sismey	6	9	0	260	78	28.88	0	10/7
A. L. Hassett	6	11	0	296	77	26.90	0	7
R. S. Whitington	6	11	0	294	79	26.72	0	4
R. M. Stanford	4	6	1	127	49	25.40	0	1
J. A. Workman	4	7	0	122	63	17.42	0	2
D. K. Carmody	3	6	0	99	42	16.50	0	3
C. F. T. Price	3	5	1	61	35	15.25	0	1
R. G. Williams	6	8	1	90	53	12.86	0	1
A. G. Cheetham	3	6	1	42	18	8.40	0	1
R. S. Ellis	6	8	5	14	9*	4.66	0	2

Also batted: A. W. Roper (1 match) 10 (ct2).

Bowling Averages

	O	M	R	W	Avge	BB	5i
C. F. T. Price	35.4	4	99	7	14.14	3-18	0
D. R. Cristofani	83.3	15	213	14	15.21	5-49	2
R. S. Ellis	323.3	60	440	23	19.13	5-24	2
J. Pettiford	39	2	139	6	23.16	3-62	0
A. G. Cheetham	75.1	11	213	7	30.42	3-47	0
K. R. Miller	137	25	306	10	30.60	3-42	0
C. G. Pepper	222.3	44	613	20	30.65	4-60	0
R. G. Williams	172	41	459	12	38.25	3-109	0

Also bowled: A. L. Hassett 0.1-0-1-0; R. S. Whitington 2-0-8-0; A. W. Roper 7-1-30-0.

Cec Pepper was a success of the Australian Services side in 1945 Later he settled in England and for 15 years was a first-class umpire.

1945: New Zealand Services

Captained by the pre-war wicketkeeper K. C. James, the New Zealand team managed to field a fairly unchanged eleven. James himself was in splendid form and in all matches during the summer reached 1,000 runs. The other leading men were C. S. Dempster, F. T. Badcock, M. P. Donnelly and R. C. Blunt, Donnelly batting brilliantly throughout. One of the best all-rounders was R. T. Morgan. T. L. Pritchard bowled well in the later games and others who looked promising were R. Hogan, F. Byerley, A. Burgess, J. D. Ridland, A. Roberts and T. M. Sharpe. The last two with Badcock were the main bowlers.

1945: New Zealand Services

1st Match: v Cambridge University (Cambridge)   May 26.
Services 153-8 dec (R. C. Blunt 70, R. Eckersley 4-38) lost to Cambridge University 157-5 (L. R. White 52) by 5 wkts.

2nd Match: v West of England (Worcester)   June 2.
West of England 91 (A. L. Roberts 4-44) lost to Services 95-5 by 5 wkts.

3rd Match: v A Lord's XI (Lord's)   June 7.
A Lord's XI 296 (L. B. Fishlock 67, F. T. Badcock 6-69) drew with Services 178-7 (R. C. Blunt 73, C. S. Dempster 69, D. B. Carr 4-51).

4th Match: v Dover Wanderers (Dover)   June 16.
Services 192-9 dec (R. T. Morgan 91, Andrae 6-62) beat Dover Wanderers 68 by 124 runs.

5th Match: v Folkestone Wanderers (Folkestone)   June 17.
Services 191-5 dec (R. T. Morgan 109*) drew with Folkestone Wanderers 125-1 (W. Neal 79*).

6th Match: v East of England (Colchester)   June 23, 24.
Services 250 (K. C. James 65) drew with East of England 184 (L. B. Fishlock 58, R. C. Blunt 6-90).

7th Match: v A.I.F. (Eastbourne)   June 30.
Services 94 (A. L. Hassett 5-31) lost to A.I.F. 279-5 (C. F. T. Price 139*, R. S. Whitington 58) by 10 wkts.

8th Match: v W. R. Hammond's XI (Edgbaston)   July 8.
Services 236-8 dec (M. P. Donnelly 100*) lost to W. R. Hammond's XI 237-3 (W. J. Edrich 132*, J. G. Dewes 54) by 7 wkts.

9th Match: v Sir P. F. Warner's XI (Lord's)   July 12.
Sir P. F. Warner's XI 266-4 dec (J. R. Bridger 136*, E. D. R. Eagar 59) beat Services 199 (M. P. Donnelly 82, A. W. H. Mallett 4-19) by 67 runs.

10th Match: v West of England (Glastonbury)   July 14.
West of England 236-3 dec (T. H. Barling 102, H. Gimblett 66, N. McCorkell 50*) drew with Services 212-7 (M. P. Donnelly 52).

11th Match: v Glamorgan (Swansea)   July 21.
Glamorgan 133-4 dec (W. G. A. Parkhouse 71, T. R. Crosskey 50*) drew with Services did not bat.

12th Match: v R.A.F. (Lord's)   July 25.
R.A.F. 236-6 dec (J. F. Parker 102*) drew with Services 154-6 (K. C. James 53).

13th Match: v East of England (Clacton)   July 28, 29.
Services 354-6 dec (K. C. James 129, M. P. Donnelly 88, R. J. Hogan 79*) drew with East of England 76 (A. C. Roberts 6-30) and 166-8 (J. Bishop 73, M. P. Donnelly 4-38).

14th Match: v Northamptonshire (Kettering)   Aug 5.
Northamptonshire 181-8 dec (R. T. Morgan 5-57) drew with Services 119-4 (K. C. James 51).

15th Match: v R. I. Scoer's XI (Edgbaston)   Aug 18.
Services 147 lost to R. I. Scorer's XI 171-2 (I. F. Bishop 72*, G. Dews 67*) by 8 wkts.

16th Match: v R. I. Scorer's XI (Edgbaston)   Aug 19.
R. I. Scorer's XI 251 (A. P. Singleton 75, G. Dews 53, F. T. Badcock 7-83) beat Services 154 (W. E. Hollies 6-55) by 97 runs.

17th Match: v H. D. G. Leveson-Gower's XI (Scarborough)   Sept 1, 2, 3.
Services 220 (M. P. Donnelly 100, A. D. G. Matthews 5-78, A. Coxon 4-39) and 312-7 dec (M. P. Donnelly 86, K. C. James 63, A. T. Burgess 61*, R. W. V. Robins 4-70) lost to H. D. G. Leveson-Gower's XI 472 (L. Hutton 188, C. Washbrook 83, A. Wood 65*, R. E. S. Wyatt 59, F. T. Badcock 6-166) and 63-2 by 8 wkts.

18th Match: v Commandos (Bognor Regis)   Sept 6.

19th Match: v Commandos (Haywards Heath)   Sept 8.

20th Match: v M. A. Crouch's XI (March)   Sept 15, 16.
M. A. Crouch's XI 178 (T. M. Sharpe 5-35) lost to Services 265-8 (R. T. Morgan 80*, T. L. Pritchard 55*, K. C. Jones 55, R. T. D. Perles 5-119) by 2 wkts.

1946: 4th Indians

The Indians travelled to England by air, the first time a Test-playing touring team had done so and in fact during the tour itself the side avoided tedious train journeys by flying to their next venue. The visit did not involve the usual long preparations, but the Indians selected a strong team for this first post-war venture: the Nawab of Pataudi (captain), V. M. Merchant, V. S. Hazare, R. S. Modi, M. H. Mankad, N. B. Amarnath, S. Mushtaq Ali, C. T. Sarwate, Gul Mahomed, Abdul Hafeez, S. S. Banerjee, S. W. Sohoni, R. B. Nimbalkar, D. D. Hindekar, C. S. Nayudu and S. G. Shinde. Punkai Gupta acted as manager.

Although the weather was rather wet and chilly, the team showed a great improvement on the efforts of 1932 and 1936. They won 11 of the 29 first-class matches and lost only four. They lost the First Test and drew the two others—all three matches were limited to three days each.

The batting was dominated by Merchant. Scoring over 2,000 runs, he was the only player to look comfortable on damp wickets.

He also captained the side in the frequent absence of the Nawab, who came out of virtual retirement to lead his country and was constantly beset with minor strains and ailments. He did little in the Tests, but occasionally demonstrated the skills he had displayed when playing for England 14 years before. Hazare came second in the batting averages and on hard pitches was very difficult to dismiss, but like most of his colleagues struggled when the ball turned.

Amarnath batted attractively, but an eye injury early on seemed to worry him for a long time. Modi began well and learnt as he went along, but rarely attacked the bowling in the way he did at home. Mushtaq Ali was always willing to take a risk, usually at the expense of his wicket.

Mankad, who performed the double, bowled his leg-breaks well and was a dogged batsman. Apart from him the only bowler to do anything in the Tests was Amarnath, whose variation of pace and spin was the downfall of some of the best England batsmen. As so often in the past the team lacked a pair of truly penetrative opening bowlers. Banerjee did not earn a place in the Test team and was only of use on hard wickets. Nayudu was very erratic and Shinde soon lost his confidence when attacked, though

---

1946: 4th Indians

1st Match: v Worcestershire (Worcester) May 4, 6, 7.
Worcestershire 191 (M. H. Mankad 4-26) and 284 (R. Howorth 105, A. P. Singleton 63, S. G. Shinde 5-50, M. H. Mankad 4-74) beat Indians 192 (R. T. D. Perks 5-53) and 267 (R. S. Modi 84, S. S. Banerjee 59, V. M. Merchant 51, R. Howorth 4-59) by 16 runs.

2nd Match: v Oxford University (Oxford) May 8, 9, 10.
Oxford University 256 (M. P. Donnelly 61, M. H. Mankad 4-58, S. G. Shinde 4-73) and 245-3 (M. P. Donnelly 116*, R. H. Maudsley 54*) drew with Indians 248 (V. S. Hazare 64, D. H. Macindoe 4-55).

3rd Match: v Surrey (Oval) May 11, 13, 14.
Indians 454 (C. T. Sarwate 124, S. S. Banerjee 121, Gul Mahomed 89, V. M. Merchant 53, A. V. Bedser 5-135) and 20-1 beat Surrey 135 (L. B. Fishlock 62) and 338 (R. J. Gregory 100, L. B. Fishlock 83, C. T. Sarwate 5-54) by 9 wkts.

4th Match: v Cambridge University (Cambridge) May 15, 16, 17.
Cambridge University 178 (V. S. Hazare 4-39) and 138 (C. T. Sarwate 5-58) lost to Indians 335-6 dec (Nawab of Pataudi 121, R. S. Modi 103, S. Mushtaq Ali 54) by an innings and 19 runs.

5th Match: v Leicestershire (Leicester) May 18, 20, 21.
Indians 198-7 dec (V. M. Merchant 111*) and 107-6 dec (V. M. Merchant 57*) drew with Leicestershire 144 (G. L. Berry 67, N. Amarnath 4-14) and 24-1.

6th Match: v Scotland (Myreside, Edinburgh) May 22, 23.
Indians 247 (V. S. Hazare 101, R. O. McKenna 6-92) beat Scotland 101 (J. Aitchison 59, C. T. Sarwate 5-30) and 90 (C. T. Sarwate 7-42) by an innings and 56 runs.

7th Match: v M.C.C. (Lord's) May 25, 27, 28.
Indians 438 (V. M. Merchant 148, V. S. Hazare 94, D. D. Hindekar 79, R. E. S. Wyatt 4-45) beat M.C.C. 139 (N. Amarnath 4-41) and 105 (M. H. Mankad 7-37) by an innings and 194 runs.

8th Match: v Indian Gymkhana Club (Osterley) May 29.
Indian Gymkhana 97 lost to Indians 149-8 (R. S. Modi 51, C. B. Clarke 5-64) by 6 wkts.

9th Match: v Hampshire (Southampton) June 1, 3, 4.
Hampshire 197 and 142 (J. Bailey 56, V. S. Hazare 4-18) lost to Indians 130 (C. J. Knott 7-36) and 212-4 by 6 wkts.

10th Match: v Glamorgan (Cardiff) June 8, 10, 11.
Indians 376-6 dec (N. Amarnath 104*, M. H. Mankad 86, V. S. Hazare 79, V. M. Merchant 52) drew with Glamorgan 149 (C. T. Sarwate 5-30, M. H. Mankad 4-68) and 73-7.

11th Match: v Combined Services (Portsmouth) June 12, 13, 14.
Combined Services 241-4 dec (J. G. Dewes 99*, J. G. W. Davies 71) and 135 (V. S. Hazare 7-66) drew with Indians 159 (V. S. Hazare 62*, J. G. W. Davies 4-37) and 116-5.

12th Match: v Nottinghamshire (Trent Bridge) June 15, 17, 18.
Indians 345-5 dec (Nawab of Pataudi 101*, V. M. Merchant 86) drew with Nottinghamshire 24-1.

13th Match: v England (Lord's) June 22, 24, 25.
India 200 (R. S. Modi 57*, A. V. Bedser 7-49) and 275 (M. H. Mankad 63, N. Amarnath 50, A. V. Bedser 4-96) lost to England 428 (J. Hardstaff jun 205*, P. A. Gibb 60, N. B. Amarnath 5-118) and 48-0 by 10 wkts.

14th Match: v Northamptonshire (Northampton) June 26, 27, 28.
Indians 328 (V. M. Merchant 110, R. S. Modi 63, N. Amarnath 52) and 171-1 (N. Amarnath 82*, V. M. Merchant 72*) drew with Northamptonshire 362 (J. E. Timms 107, D. Brookes 82, W. Barron 64, M. H. Mankad 5-99).

15th Match: v Lancashire (Liverpool) June 29, July 1, 2.
Lancashire 140 (C. Washbrook 58, S. S. Banerjee 4-32) and 185 (J. T. Ikin 55) lost to Indians 126 (R. Pollard 7-49) and 200-2 (V. M. Merchant 93*, Nawab of Pataudi 80*) by 8 wkts.

16th Match: v Yorkshire (Bradford) July 3, 4, 5.
Indians 138 (A. Booth 6-33) and 124 (E. P. Robinson 4-40, A. Booth 4-58) lost to Yorkshire 344-9 dec (L. Hutton 183*, J. V. Wilson 74, C. S. Nayudu 5-27) by an innings and 82 runs.

17th Match: v Lancashire (Old Trafford) July 6, 8, 9.
Lancashire 406 (J. T. Ikin 139, C. Washbrook 108, A. Wharton 73, S. W. Sohoni 5-82, M. H. Mankad 4-134) and 172 (M. H. Mankad 5-62) drew with Indians 456-8 dec (V. M. Merchant 242*).

18th Match: v Derbyshire (Chesterfield) July 10, 11, 12.
Indians 380-9 dec (Nawab of Pataudi 113, R. S. Modi 99, Gul Mahommad 62*, A. E. G. Rhodes 5-135) and 313-8 dec (N. B. Amarnath 89, R. S. Modi 68) beat Derbyshire 366 (E. Marsh 86, C. S. Elliott 61, M. H. Mankad 4-69, S. G. Shinde 4-109) and 209 by 118 runs.

19th Match: v Yorkshire (Bramall Lane) July 13, 15, 16.
Yorkshire 300-6 dec (P. A. Gibb 71, W. Watson 55, H. Halliday 51) and 64-0 drew with Indians 490-5 dec (V. S. Hazare 244*, M. H. Mankad 132, Nawab of Pataudi 51*).

20th Match: v Durham (Sunderland) July 17, 18.
Indians 149-5 dec (V. M. Merchant 64) drew with Durham 109-5.

21st Match: v England (Old Trafford) July 20, 22, 23.
England 294 (W. R. Hammond 69, L. Hutton 67, C. Washbrook 52, D. C. S. Compton 51, N. B. Amarnath 5-96, M. H. Mankad 5-101) and 153-5 dec (D. C. S. Compton 71*) drew with India 170 (V. M. Merchant 78, R. Pollard 5-24, A. V. Bedser 4-41) and 152-9 (A. V. Bedser 7-52).

22nd Match: v Club Cricket Conference (Guildford) July 25.
Indians 281-5 dec (V. M. Merchant 141, S. W. Sohoni 52, S. Mushtaq Ali 50) drew with C.C.C. 223-4 (K. Cranston 82*).*

23rd Match: v Sussex (Hove) July 27, 29, 30.
Indians 533-3 dec (V. M. Merchant 205, Nawab of Pataudi 110*, N. B. Amarnath 106, M. H. Mankad 105) and 148-1 (R. S. Modi 72*, V. M. Merchant 63*) beat Sussex 253 (R. G. Stainton 72, H. W. Parks 56, S. G. Shinde 4-60) and 427 (G. Cox 234*, Jas Langridge 79, M. H. Mankad 5-140) 9 wkts.

24th Match: v Somerset (Taunton) July 31, Aug 1, 2.
Indians 64 (H. T. F. Buse 5-27, W. H. R. Andrews 5-36) and 431 (V. M. Merchant 87, Nawab of Pataudi 76, C. T. Sarwate 66*) lost to Somerset 506-6 dec (M. M. Walford 141*, H. Gimblett 102, F. S. Lee 76, E. F. Longrigg 74, H. T. F. Buse 59) by an innings and 11 runs.

25th Match: v Glamorgan (Swansea) Aug 3, 5, 6.
Glamorgan 238 (E. L. James 62*, M. H. Mankad 4-81) and 237-8 dec (M. Robinson 79) lost to Indians 203 (V. M. Merchant 66, R. S. Modi 56, J. C. Clay 7-72) and 274-5 (S. Y. Mushtaq Ali 93, V. S. Hazare 59*) by 5 wkts.

26th Match: v Warwickshire (Edgbaston) Aug 7, 8, 9.
Warwickshire 375-9 dec (R. Sale 157, V. S. Hazare 4-47, M. H. Mankad 4-122) drew with Indians 197 (V. M. Merchant 86*, W. E. Hollies 5-66, T. L. Pritchard 4-46) and 21-1.

27th Match: v Gloucestershire (Cheltenham) Aug 10, 12, 13.
Gloucestershire 132-3 dec and 187 (M. H. Mankad 5-72, C. T. Sarwate 4-43) drew with Indians 135-8 dec (Nawab of Pataudi 71, T. W. J. Goddard 7-81) and 177-9 (V. S. Hazare 56, T. W. J. Goddard 4-66).

28th Match: v England (Oval) Aug 17, 19, 20.
India 331 (V. M. Merchant 128, S. Y. Mushtaq Ali 59, W. J. Edrich 4-68) drew with England 95-3.

29th Match: v Essex (Southend) Aug 24, 26, 27.
Essex 303 (T. N. Pearce 66, A. V. Avery 62, S. G. Shinde 4-69) and 201-3 dec (H. P. Crabtree 118) lost to Indians 138 (R. Smith 6-56) and 370-9 (V. M. Merchant 181, R. S. Modi 65, M. H. Mankad 52, T. P. B. Smith 5-122) by 1 wkt.

30th Match: v Kent (Canterbury) Aug 28, 29, 30.
Kent 248-3 (A. E. Fagg 109, L. E. G. Ames 78) drew with Indians did not bat.

31st Match: v Middlesex (Lord's) Aug 31, Sept 2, 3.
Indians 469-5 dec (V. S. Hazare 193*, M. H. Mankad 109*, R. S. Modi 80) beat Middlesex 124 (M. H. Mankad 5-48, V. S. Hazare 4-25) and 82 (S. S. Banerjee 4-21) by an innings and 263 runs.

32nd Match: v South of England (Hastings) Sept 4, 5, 6.
Indians 241 (V. M. Merchant 82, R. T. D. Perks 5-67) and 253-3 (S. Mushtaq Ali 66, Gul Mahommad 54*) beat South of England 218-9 dec (J. D. B. Robertson 59, N. B. Amarnath 4-57) and 266 (G. Cox 82, L. E. G. Ames 55, N. B. Amarnath 4-96) by 10 runs.

33rd Match: v H. D. G. Leveson-Gower's XI (Scarborough) Sept 7, 9, 10.
Indians 139 (R. W. V. Robins 5-42, R. Howorth 4-38) and 194-8 (Gul Mahommad 57, R. Howorth 5-34) drew with H. D. G. Leveson-Gower's XI 345 (R. Howorth 114, T. F. Smailes 79, M. H. Mankad 4-127).

at times his leg-breaks were effective.

As previously the catching made the bowlers seem even more moderate than they deserved. Despite the political upheavals in India, the team was free of all the bickering which had hampered the 1936 side and off the field matters were conducted harmoniously by both captain and manager. Despite the wet weather, a profit of £4,500 was made.

'Tich' Freeman, Frank Woolley, and the Nawab of Pataudi wearing England blazers in the 1930s. Pataudi scored a century on his debut for England in the 'bodyline' tour of Australia in 1932-33. In 1946, he led the Indian touring party to England. His son later captained India also.

1946: 4th Indians

Batting Averages

	M	I	NO	R	HS	Avge	100	c/s
V. M. Merchant	26	41	9	2385	242*	74.53	7	15
V. S. Hazare	25	33	6	1344	244*	49.77	2	9
Nawab of Pataudi	20	26	5	981	121	46.71	4	6
R. S. Modi	24	35	3	1196	103	37.37	1	7
M. H. Mankad	28	41	1	1120	132	28.00	3	21
N. B. Amarnath	24	35	3	800	106	25.00	2	9/1
S. Mushtaq Ali	21	29	1	673	93	24.03	0	11
C. T. Sarwate	19	24	8	382	124*	23.87	1	6
Gul Mahomed	18	27	6	473	89	22.52	0	9
Abdul Hafeez (Kardar)	16	24	2	384	43	17.45	0	5
S. S. Banerjee	19	19	1	295	121	16.38	1	9
S. W. Sohoni	18	24	5	293	44	15.42	0	15
R. B. Nimbalkar	8	9	1	120	30	15.00	0	12/7
D. D. Hindlekar	19	22	5	233	79	13.70	0	22/14
C. S. Nayudu	16	15	3	162	29	13.50	0	9
S. G. Shinde	18	16	9	77	21*	11.00	0	2

Bowling Averages

	O	M	R	W	Avge	BB	5i
M. H. Mankad	1160.1	301	2679	129	20.76	7-37	7
V. S. Hazare	604.1	147	1386	56	24.75	7-66	1
C. T. Sarwate	355.3	54	939	37	25.37	7-42	3
N. B. Amarnath	782	279	1503	56	26.83	5-96	2
S. G. Shinde	391	59	1174	39	30.10	5-50	1
C. S. Nayudu	257	29	800	26	30.76	5-27	1
S. S. Banerjee	322.1	42	1052	29	36.27	4-21	0
S. W. Sohoni	194.5	30	617	14	44.07	5-82	1

Also bowled: Nawab of Pataudi 2-0-12-1; Abdul Hafeez 7-1-16-0; Gul Mahomed 10-2-25-0.

1947: 9th South Africans

The team which arrived in Southampton on 18 April after a 13-day voyage from Cape Town was A. Melville (captain), B. Mitchell, K. G. Viljoen, T. A. Harris, A. M. B. Rowan, D. W. Begbie and G. M. Fullerton, all of Transvaal; L. W. Payn, D. V. Dyer, A. D. Nourse, O. C. Dawson and V. I. Smith of Natal; J. B. Plimsoll and D. M. Ovenstone of Western Province; J. D. Lindsay of North Eastern Transvaal; N. B. F. Mann of Eastern Province and L. Tuckett of Orange Free State, with A. S. Frames as manager. There were several outspoken criticisms of the team, notably the omission of R. Phillips of Border, whose supporters even offered to pay his passage to England; that E. A. B. Rowan was overlooked meant a weakness in opening batsmen. It was felt

1947: 9th South Africans

Batting Averages

	M	I	NO	R	HS	Avge	100	c/s
B. Mitchell	23	37	4	2014	189*	61.03	8	32
K. G. Viljoen	21	33	4	1441	201	49.68	6	7
A. D. Nourse	23	36	2	1453	205*	42.73	4	26
A. Melville	26	40	2	1547	189	40.71	6	27
T. A. Harris	15	20	1	701	100	36.89	1	7
O. C. Dawson	22	35	4	1002	166*	32.32	1	20
G. M. Fullerton	16	26	4	698	82	31.72	0	17/7
D. W. Begbie	15	21	1	612	132	30.60	1	8
D. V. Dyer	17	28	2	673	74	25.88	0	12
A. M. B. Rowan	22	33	9	607	100*	25.29	1	11
N. B. F. Mann	21	32	3	591	97	20.37	0	5
D. M. Ovenstone	10	14	0	184	42	13.14	0	22/7
L. W. Payn	10	10	1	102	32	11.33	0	4
L. Tuckett	18	25	4	226	40*	10.76	0	14
J. B. Plimsoll	18	18	6	127	17*	10.58	0	4
J. D. Lindsay	11	16	6	104	17	10.40	0	18·7
V. I. Smith	20	24	11	89	18*	6.84	0	11

Bowling Averages

	O	M	R	W	Avge	BB	5i
V. I. Smith	549.3	151	1344	58	23.17	7-40	4
J. B. Plimsoll	750.4	215	1586	68	23.32	7-47	4
A. M. B. Rowan	1075.4	263	2547	102	24.97	7-47	6
N. B. F. Mann	954	350	1869	74	25.25	7-95	6
L. Tuckett	724	150	1779	69	25.78	7-63	7
O. C. Dawson	601.3	146	1408	54	26.07	5-42	2
D. W. Begbie	105.3	21	322	12	26.83	3-41	0
L. W. Payn	253.4	85	571	17	33.58	3-41	0
B. Mitchell	22	3	101	2	50.50	2-53	0

Also bowled: K. G. Viljoen 1.4-0-11-1.

that N. Gordon and X. Balaskas were past their best and not capable of standing up to the long tour.

The failure of England in Australia in 1946-47 gave the tourists high hopes of beating the home side, but they failed to, and on paper the Test record of three lost and two drawn was worse than several previous South African teams'. The team found the cold and wet of May frustrating, which meant that it was some time before they found their feet.

The batting relied very much on the trio of Melville, Nourse and Mitchell with Viljoen successful in the ordinary matches but not in the Tests. Mitchell was the most consistent, but Melville and Nourse played some outstanding innings. The rest of the batting was at best moderate, with Dyer and Dawson most disappointing and the bowlers rarely making runs.

Tuckett was the most talented of the faster bowlers but a strain during the First Test seemed to affect him for the remainder of the summer. Dawson opened the bowling with Tuckett but never looked dangerous and tended to be inaccurate and Plimsoll, medium-fast, needed a helpful wicket to worry batsmen. The main attack therefore came from the spinners: Rowan with his off-breaks reached 100 wickets, but was expensive in the Tests; Mann, the slow left-armer, headed the Test averages and also managed to keep the runs down, even when bowling to Compton and Edrich, but Begbie and Payn achieved very little.

The team had three wicketkeepers in Ovenstone, Lindsay and Fullerton. The first missed many matches through a broken finger. Lindsay began as the Test keeper, but through lack of form

The 1947 South Africans arrive at Southampton. From the left they are Mann, Tuckett, Begbie, Dawson, Lindsay, Payn, Viljoen, Rowan, Nourse, Melville (captain), Plimsoll, Fullerton, Mitchell, Ovenstone, Dyer, Harris, Smith.

1947: 9th South Africans

1st Match: v Worcestershire (Worcester)   April 30, May 1, 2.
Worcestershire 202 (R. E. Bird 79, A. M. B. Rowan 5-59) and 111 (A. M. B. Rowan 5-34, N. B. F. Mann 5-36) beat South Africans 167 (R. T. D. Perks 5-66) and 107 (R. Howorth 6-38, P. F. Jackson 4-53) by 39 runs.

2nd Match: v Leicestershire (Leicester)   May 3, 5.
Leicestershire 128 (L. Tuckett 5-27) and 121 (L. Tuckett 4-32) lost to South Africans 216 (A. Melville 104, G. Lester 6-42) and 35-0 by 10 wkts.

3rd Match: v Cambridge University (Cambridge)   May 7, 8, 9.
Cambridge University 116 (J. B. Plimsoll 4-35) and 101 (V. I. Smith 7-40) lost to South Africans 370 (K. G. Viljoen 128, D. W. Begbie 80, T. E. Bailey 5-70) by an innings and 153 runs.

4th Match: v Surrey (Oval)   May 10, 12, 13.
South Africans 83 (E. A. Watts 5-31) and 311 (A. Melville 122, O. C. Dawson 75, A. V. Bedser 6-65) beat Surrey 112 (L. Tuckett 7-63) and 167 (N. B. F. Mann 4-17) by 115 runs.

5th Match: v Hampshire (Southampton)   May 14, 15, 16.
Hampshire 300-6 dec (J. Arnold 138, G. Hill 58*) and 79-7 (A. M. B. Rowan 4-31) drew with South Africans 315 (G. M. Fullerton 82, T. A. Harris 71, A. D. Nourse 54, O. W. Herman 4-46).

6th Match: v M.C.C. (Lord's)   May 17, 19, 20.
M.C.C. 230 (T. C. Dodds 80, D. Brookes 54, L. Tuckett 6-64) and 253-4 dec (D. C. S. Compton 97, D. Brookes 77) beat South Africans 127 (A. W. H. Mallett 5-55, J. W. Martin 4-55) and 198 (B. Mitchell 103*, C. Cook 6-44) by 158 runs.

7th Match: v Oxford University (Oxford)   May 21, 22, 23.
Oxford University 303-9 dec (W. G. Keighley 105) and 19-2 drew with South Africans 510-6 dec (K. G. Viljoen 110*, A. D. Nourse 101, A. Melville 84, B. Mitchell 72, T. A. Harris 68).

8th Match: v Glamorgan (Cardiff)   May 24, 26, 27.
South Africans 479-8 dec (B. Mitchell 113, A. M. B. Rowan 100*, N. B. F. Mann 97) beat Glamorgan 128 (L. Tuckett 5-48) and 220 (M. Robinson 83, A. M. B. Rowan 4-59) by an innings and 131 runs.

9th Match: v Combined Services (Portsmouth)   May 28, 29, 30.
Combined Services 182 (J. G. Dewes 68, J. B. Plimsoll 6-53) and 162 (W. F. Roberts 52, N. B. F. Mann 5-48) lost to South Africans 259 (B. Mitchell 108, O. C. Dawson 57, J. H. G. Deighton 4-88) and 86-3 by 7 wkts.

10th Match: v Middlesex (Lord's)   May 31, June 2, 3.
South Africans 424 (B. Mitchell 109, K. G. Viljoen 104, A. D. Nourse 92, J. A. Young 4-52, J. M. Sims 4-148) and 217 (T. A. Harris 76, J. M. Sims 6-89) drew with Middlesex 316-8 dec (D. C. S. Compton 154, W. J. Edrich 67, A. M. B. Rowan 4-130) and 226-6 (W. J. Edrich 133).

11th Match: v Northamptonshire (Northampton)   June 4, 5.
Northamptonshire 103 (J. B. Plimsoll 6-40, O. C. Dawson 4-37) and 184 (L. A. Smith 55, J. B. Plimsoll 5-90, O. C. Dawson 4-71) lost to South Africans 319 (T. A. Harris 67, O. C. Dawson 62, L. A. Smith 4-55) by an innings and 32 runs.

12th Match: v England (Trent Bridge)   June 7, 9, 10, 11.
South Africa 533 (A. Melville 189, A. D. Nourse 149, W. E. Hollies 5-123) and 166-1 (A. Melville 104*, K. G. Viljoen 51*) drew with England 208 (D. C. S. Compton 65, W. J. Edrich 57, L. Tuckett 5-68) and 551 (D. C. S. Compton 163, N. W. D. Yardley 99, T. G. Evans 74, C. Washbrook 59, W. J. Edrich 50, V. I. Smith 4-143).

13th Match: v Somerset (Taunton)   June 14, 16, 17.
Somerset 170 (M. Coope 64, O. C. Dawson 4-41, J. B. Plimsoll 4-70) and 155 (J. B. Plimsoll 4-41) lost to South Africans 368-8 dec (B. Mitchell 72, A. D. Nourse 65, D. W. Begbie 62, K. G. Viljoen 54*) by an innings and 43 runs.

14th Match: v England (Lord's)   June 21, 23, 24, 25.
England 554-8 dec (D. C. S. Compton 208, W. J. Edrich 189, C. Washbrook 65, L. Tuckett 5-115) and 26-0 beat South Africa 327 (A. Melville 117, A. D. Nourse 61, D. V. P. Wright 5-95) and 252 (B. Mitchell 80, A. D. Nourse 58, D. V. P. Wright 5-80) by 10 wkts.

15th Match: v Nottinghamshire (Trent Bridge)   June 28, 30, July 1.
Nottinghamshire 324 (W. W. Keeton 90, F. W. Stocks 73, J. B. Plimsoll 4-60) and 164-6 (C. B. Harris 51, R. T. Simpson 51) drew with South Africans 365 (B. Mitchell 97, D. V. Dyer 62, G. M. Fullerton 57, A. Jepson 5-115).

16th Match: v Northumberland (Newcastle)   July 2, 3.
Northumberland 172 (J. H. G. Deighton 73, J. B. Plimsoll 5-62) and 133 (J. B. Plimsoll 6-73) lost to South Africans 347 (K. G. Viljoen 130) by an innings and 32 runs.

17th Match: v England (Old Trafford)   July 5, 7, 8, 9.
South Africa 339 (K. G. Viljoen 93, B. Mitchell 80, D. V. Dyer 62, W. J. Edrich 4-95) and 267 (A. D. Nourse 115, A. Melville 59, W. J. Edrich 4-77) lost to England 478 (W. J. Edrich 191, D. C. S. Compton 115, L. Tuckett 4-148) and 130-3 by 7 wkts.

18th Match: v Gentlemen of Ireland (Dublin)   July 10, 11.
Gentlemen of Ireland 102 (A. M. B. Rowan 9-39) drew with South Africans 167-7 (A. Melville 58, E. A. Ingram 4-42).*

19th Match: v Gentlemen of Ireland (Belfast)   July 12.
Gentlemen of Ireland 32 (A. M. B. Rowan 7-10) and 61 (A. M. B. Rowan 5-14) lost to South Africans 218 (V. I. Smith 64, J. C. Boucher 4-80) by an innings and 125 runs (Two-day match finished in one).*

20th Match: v Gentlemen of Ireland (Belfast)   July 14.
South Africans 114 (J. C. Boucher 7-37) lost to Gentlemen of Ireland 202 (R. J. Barnes 57, L. Tuckett 4-23) by 6 wkts.

21st Match: v Derbyshire (Derby)   July 16, 17, 18.
Derbyshire 224 (A. C. Revill 60, C. S. Elliott 56, V. I. Smith 7-65) and 32 (V. I. Smith 6-1) lost to South Africans 172 (G. H. Pope 5-60) and 85-7 (G. H. Pope 5-36) by 3 wkts.

22nd Match: v Yorkshire (Bramall Lane)   July 19, 21, 22.
South Africans 279 (G. M. Fullerton 50, W. E. Bowes 4-36) and 147-3 drew with Yorkshire 308 (L. Hutton 137, W. G. Keighley 51, V. I. Smith 5-105, A. M. B. Rowan 4-39).

23rd Match: v Scotland (Paisley)   July 23, 24.
Scotland 177 (J. Aitchison 106) and 104-5 (L. Tuckett 4-15) drew with South Africans 278-4 dec (G. M. Fullerton 129, D. W. Begbie 74).*

24th Match: v England (Headingley)   July 26, 28, 29.
South Africa 175 (B. Mitchell 53, A. D. Nourse 51, H. J. Butler 4-34) and 184 (A. D. Nourse 57, K. Cranston 4-12) lost to England 317-7 dec (L. Hutton 100, C. Washbrook 75, N. B. F. Mann 4-68) and 47-0 by 10 wkts.

25th Match: v Glamorgan (Swansea)   Aug 2, 4, 5.
South Africans 260 (T. A. Harris 100, J. C. Clay 5-76) and 188 (J. C. Clay 6-86) beat Glamorgan 197 (A. M. B. Rowan 6-53) and 211 (A. J. Watkins 75, O. C. Dawson 5-50, A. M. B. Rowan 4-92) by 40 runs.

26th Match: v Warwickshire (Edgbaston)   Aug 6, 7, 8.
Warwickshire 330 (P. Cranmer 101, W. A. Hill 73, N. B. F. Mann 5-109, V. I. Smith 4-85) and 76 (L. Tuckett 5-30, O. C. Dawson 5-42) lost to South Africans 520-7 dec (A. D. Nourse 205*, K. G. Viljoen 113, B. Mitchell 51) by an innings and 114 runs.

27th Match: v Lancashire (Old Trafford)   Aug 9, 11, 12.
Lancashire 218 (C. Washbrook 128, L. Tuckett 4-66, O. C. Dawson 4-88) and 233-8 dec (C. Washbrook 57) drew with South Africans 338 (B. Mitchell 131, A. Melville 52, K. Cranston 5-69, W. E. Bowes 4-103) and 30-0.

28th Match: v Gloucestershire (Cheltenham)   Aug 13, 14, 15.
South Africans 225 (D. V. Dyer 74) and 248 (G. M. Fullerton 70, N. B. F. Mann 63, C. Cook 4-80) beat Gloucestershire 185 (J. F. Crapp 58, B. O. Allen 52, A. M. B. Rowan 4-40) and 155 (A. M. B. Rowan 7-47) by 133 runs.

29th Match: v England (Oval)   Aug 16, 18, 19, 20.
England 427 (L. Hutton 83, N. W. D. Yardley 59, D. C. S. Compton 53, N. B. F. Mann 4-93) and 325-6 dec (D. C. S. Compton 113) drew with South Africans 302 (B. Mitchell 120, O. C. Dawson 55) and 423-7 (B. Mitchell 189*, A. D. Nourse 97).

30th Match: v Essex (Southend)   Aug 23, 25, 26.
Essex 380 (H. P. Crabtree 117, S. J. Cray 98, D. R. Wilcox 73) and 102 (J. B. Plimsoll 7-47) lost to South Africans 400 (D. W. Begbie 132, A. Melville 84, A. M. B. Rowan 58*, T. P. B. Smith 6-158) and 85-2 by 8 wkts.

31st Match: v Kent (Canterbury)   Aug 27, 28, 29.
South Africans 410 (K. G. Viljoen 104, O. C. Dawson 87, D. V. P. Wright 5-124) and 227-7 dec (B. Mitchell 57) beat Kent 318 (J. G. W. Davies 80, T. G. Evans 61, B. H. Valentine 55, N. B. F. Mann 6-132) and 231 (N. B. F. Mann 7-95) by 88 runs.

32nd Match: v Sussex (Hove)   Aug 30, Sept 1, 2.
Sussex 415-5 dec (H. W. Parks 140, G. Cox 132, H. T. Bartlett 66*, John G. Langridge 57) and 281 (H. W. Parks 60, Jas Langridge 55) drew with South Africans 555-6 dec (K. G. Viljoen 201, A. Melville 114*, T. A. Harris 71, D. V. Dyer 54) and 45-0.

33rd Match: v South of England (Hastings)   Sept 3, 4, 5.
South Africans 510-8 dec (O. C. Dawson 166*, B. Mitchell 145, K. G. Viljoen 50) and 31-1 beat South of England 341-9 dec (D. C. S. Compton 101, W. J. Edrich 64, J. D. B. Robertson 55, A. M. B. Rowan 5-108, N. B. F. Mann 4-97) and 199 (W. J. Edrich 54, N. B. F. Mann 5-71, A. M. B. Rowan 5-83) by 9 wkts.

34th Match: v Club Cricket Conference (Guildford)   Sept 6.
South Africans 402-1 dec (T. A. Harris 229*, G. M. Fullerton 94, D. W. Begbie 59*) drew with C.C.C. 313-4 (A. C. L. Bennett 156, P. G. Wreford 50).

35th Match: v H. D. G. Leveson-Gower's XI (Scarborough)   Sept 10, 11, 12.
Cancelled due to the tourists having to leave England early because of altered shipping arrangements.

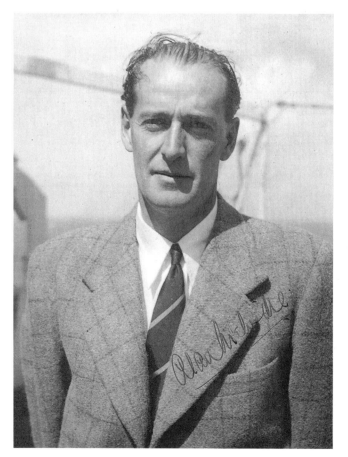

The two most successful Test batsmen among the 1947 South Africans, Bruce Mitchell (above) and captain Alan Melville (below). Both made centuries in each innings of a Test, the first two South Africans to do so. At the Oval Mitchell was on the field for all but 12 balls of the match.

lost his place to Fullerton, who also batted well on a number of occasions.

The tour was very popular with the public–no doubt partly due to Compton and Edrich's record breaking–and a profit of £10,000 was made, excluding donations the South Africans gave to Lancashire and Surrey to help the counties in their rebuilding programmes.

1948: 20th Australians

The team which left Fremantle aboard the R.M.S. *Strathaird* on 18 March was D. G. Bradman (captain), R. A. Hamence of South Australia; A. L. Hassett, I. W. Johnson, W. A. Johnston, R. N. Harvey, S. J. E. Loxton and D. T. Ring of Victoria; S. G. Barnes, K. R. Miller, R. R. Lindwall, E. R. H. Toshack, R. A. Saggers and A. R. Morris of New South Wales; W. A. Brown, C. L. McCool and D. Tallon of Queensland, with K. Johnson as manager. The selection of the team was well received and only two or three players who failed selection but deserved to go, especially Dooland and Pettiford, were mentioned.

Bradman made it clear that this tour was his farewell to first-class cricket and it proved appropriate that such a player should end in such a blaze of glory. The Test series was won by four matches to nil and for the first time an Australian side went through their first-class fixtures without a defeat.

The batting was truly formidable–in Tests seven of the side averaged about 40 and in all first-class games eight did so. Bradman did not reach 200 in any innings, but was so consistent that he averaged 89.92 and hit 11 hundreds. The team had an excellent opening pair in Barnes and Morris, both of whom bettered Bradman in the Test averages. Morris was an attractive stroke maker who could also defend well; Barnes never gave up. Hassett, though strangely quiet at times, batted well at no. 4; he was followed by the spectacular Miller and then by young Harvey, who looked a very mature batsman; Loxton hit the ball hard and was always liable to hit some sixes. This batting combination was so strong that Brown, who made eight centuries, could not get a regular place in the Test side.

1948: 20th Australians

Batting Averages

	M	I	NO	R	HS	Avge	100	c/s
D. G. Bradman	23	31	4	2428	187	89.92	11	11
A. L. Hassett	22	27	6	1563	200*	74.42	7	23
A. R. Morris	21	29	2	1922	290	71.18	7	10
W. A. Brown	22	26	1	1448	200	57.92	8	16
S. J. E. Loxton	22	22	5	973	159*	57.23	3	13
S. G. Barnes	21	27	3	1354	176	56.41	3	19
R. N. Harvey	22	27	6	1129	126	53.76	4	17
K. R. Miller	22	26	3	1088	202*	47.30	2	20
R. A. Hamence	19	22	4	582	99	32.33	0	9
I. W. Johnson	22	22	4	543	113*	30.16	1	23
D. Tallon	14	13	2	283	53	25.72	0	29/14
R. R. Lindwall	22	20	3	411	77	24.17	0	14
R. A. Saggers	17	12	3	209	104*	23.22	1	23/20
C. L. McCool	17	18	3	306	76	20.40	0	20
W. A. Johnston	21	18	8	188	29	18.80	0	9
D. T. Ring	19	14	5	150	53	16.66	0	12
E. R. H. Toshack	15	12	3	78	20*	8.66	0	2

Bowling Averages

	O	M	R	W	Avge	BB	5i
R. R. Lindwall	573.1	139	1349	86	15.68	6-14	6
W. A. Johnston	850.1	279	1675	102	16.42	6-18	6
K. R. Miller	429.4	117	985	56	17.58	6-42	3
C. L. McCool	399.2	97	1016	57	17.82	7-78	3
I. W. Johnson	667.2	228	1562	85	18.37	7-42	5
E. R. H. Toshack	502	171	1056	50	21.12	7-81	4
R. A. Hamence	56.3	13	150	7	21.42	2-13	0
S. J. E. Loxton	361.2	91	695	32	21.71	3-10	0
D. T. Ring	542.4	155	1309	60	21.81	5-45	3
A. R. Morris	35	9	91	2	45.50	1-6	0
S. G. Barnes	65.4	26	121	2	60.50	1-11	0

Also bowled: A. L. Hassett 12-0-48-0; D. G. Bradman 1-0-2-0; W. A. Brown 4.1-0-16-4; R. N. Harvey 10-3-29-1.

The 1948 Australians were considered to be one of the strongest sides ever to tour England, and they went through the tour unbeaten. Arthur Morris (above) and Sid Barnes (below) were the reliable openers, although Barnes suffered a nasty injury in the Old Trafford Test when fielding close to the bat.

Don Tallon (above) was the reliable wicket-keeper in the 1948 Australian touring side.

Ernie Toshack (below) was Australia's left-arm medium-pace bowler on the 1948 tour.

1948: 20th Australians

1st Match: v Worcestershire (Worcester)   April 28, 29, 30.
Worcestershire 233 (C. H. Palmer 85, E. Cooper 51) and 212 (L. Outschoorn 54, C. L. McCool 4-29) lost to Australians 462-8 dec (A. R. Morris 138, D. G. Bradman 107, K. R. Miller 50*, P. F. Jackson 6-135) by an innings and 17 runs.

2nd Match: v Leicestershire (Leicester)   May 1, 3, 4.
Australians 448 (K. R. Miller 202*, D. G. Bradman 81, S. G. Barnes 78, V. E. Jackson 5-91) beat Leicestershire 130 (D. T. Ring 5-45) and 147 (I. W. Johnson 7-42) by an innings and 171 runs.

3rd Match: v Yorkshire (Bradford)   May 5, 6.
Yorkshire 71 (K. R. Miller 6-42, W. A. Johnston 4-22) and 89 (W. A. Johnston 6-18) lost to Australians 101 (T. F. Smailes 6-51) and 63-6 by 4 wkts.

4th Match: v Surrey (Oval)   May 8, 10, 11.
Australians 632 (S. G. Barnes 176, D. G. Bradman 146, A. L. Hassett 110, A. R. Morris 65, D. Tallon 50*, A. V. Bedser 4-104) beat Surrey 141 (L. B. Fishlock 81*, I. W. Johnson 5-53) and 195 (H. S. Squires 54, W. A. Johnston 4-40) by an innings and 296 runs.

5th Match: v Cambridge University (Cambridge)   May 12, 13, 14.
Cambridge University 167 (K. R. Miller 5-46) and 196 (T. E. Bailey 66*, C. L. McCool 7-78) lost to Australians 414-4 dec (W. A. Brown 200, R. A. Hamence 92, A. L. Hassett 61*) by an innings and 51 runs.

6th Match: v Essex (Southend)   May 15, 17.
Australians 721 (D. G. Bradman 187, W. A. Brown 153, S. J. E. Loxton 120, R. A. Saggers 104*, S. G. Barnes 79, T. P. B. Smith 4-193) beat Essex 83 (E. R. H. Toshack 5-31) and 187 (T. N. Pearce 71, T. P. B. Smith 54, I. W. Johnson 6-37) by an innings and 451 runs.

7th Match: v Oxford University (Oxford)   May 19, 20, 21.
Australians 431 (W. A. Brown 108, S. J. E. Loxton 79*, A. R. Morris 64, D. T. Ring 53, C. L. McCool 50) beat Oxford University 185 (A. H. Kardar 54) and 156 by an innings and 90 runs.

8th Match: v M.C.C. (Lord's)   May 22, 24, 25.
Australians 552 (K. R. Miller 163, D. G. Bradman 98, S. G. Barnes 81, I. W. Johnson 80, A. L. Hassett 51, J. A. Young 4-147) beat M.C.C. 189 (L. Hutton 52, E. R. H. Toshack 6-51) and 205 (L. Hutton 64, C. L. McCool 4-35) by an innings and 158 runs.

9th Match: v Lancashire (Old Trafford)   May 26, 27, 28.
Australians 204 (M. J. Hilton 4-81) and 259-4 (R. N. Harvey 76*, S. J. E. Loxton 52) drew with Lancashire 182 (G. A. Edrich 55, W. A. Johnston 5-49).

10th Match: v Nottinghamshire (Trent Bridge)   May 29, 31, June 1.
Nottinghamshire 179 (R. T. Simpson 74, R. R. Lindwall 6-14) and 299-8 (J. Hardstaff jun 107, R. T. Simpson 70, D. T. Ring 4-104) drew with Australians 400 (W. A. Brown 122, D. G. Bradman 86, K. R. Miller 51, A. Jepson 4-109).

11th Match: v Hampshire (Southampton)   June 2, 3, 4.
Hampshire 195 (W. A. Johnston 6-74) and 103 (K. R. Miller 5-25, W. A. Johnston 5-43) lost to Australians 117 (C. J. Knott 5-57, J. Bailey 4-27) and 182-2 (W. A. Brown 81*, I. W. Johnson 74) by 8 wkts.

12th Match: v Sussex (Hove)   June 5, 7.
Sussex 86 (R. R. Lindwall 6-34) and 138 (H. W. Parks 61, R. R. Lindwall 5-25) lost to Australians 549-5 dec (A. R. Morris 184, D. G. Bradman 109, R. N. Harvey 100*, R. R. Lindwall 57) by an innings and 325 runs.

13th Match: v England (Trent Bridge)   June 10, 11, 12, 14, 15.
England 165 (J. C. Laker 63, W. A. Johnston 5-36) and 441 (D. C. S. Compton 184, L. Hutton 74, T. G. Evans 50, K. R. Miller 4-125, W. A. Johnston 4-147) lost to Australia 509 (D. G. Bradman 138, A. L. Hassett 137, S. G. Barnes 62, J. C. Laker 4-138) and 98-2 (S. G. Barnes 64*) by 8 wkts.

14th Match: v Northamptonshire (Northampton)   June 16, 17, 18.
Northamptonshire 119 and 169 (D. T. Ring 4-31, W. A. Johnston 4-49) lost to Australians 352-8 dec (A. L. Hassett 127, A. R. Hassett 60, C. L. McCool 50*, A. E. Nutter 5-57) by an innings and 64 runs.

15th Match: v Yorkshire (Bramall Lane)   June 19, 21, 22.
Australians 249 (D. G. Bradman 54, A. Coxon 4-66) and 285-5 dec (W. A. Brown 113, D. G. Bradman 86, R. N. Harvey 56) drew with Yorkshire 206 (E. R. H. Toshack 7-81) and 85-4.

16th Match: v England (Lord's)   June 24, 25, 26, 28, 29.
Australia 350 (A. R. Morris 105, D. Tallon 53, A. V. Bedser 4-100) and 460-7 dec (S. G. Barnes 141, D. G. Bradman 89, K. R. Miller 74, A. R. Morris 62) beat England 215 (D. C. S. Compton 53, R. R. Lindwall 5-70) and 186 (E. R. H. Toshack 5-40) by 409 runs.

17th Match: v Surrey (Oval)   June 30, July 1, 2.
Surrey 221 (J. F. Parker 76) and 289 (J. F. Parker 81, L. B. Fishlock 61, E. R. T. Holmes 54, C. L. McCool 6-113) lost to Australians 389 (A. L. Hassett 139, D. G. Bradman 128) and 122-0 (R. N. Harvey 73*) by 10 wkts.

18th Match: v Gloucestershire (Bristol)   July 3, 5, 6.
Australians 774-7 dec (A. R. Morris 290, S. J. E. Loxton 159*, R. N. Harvey 95, C. L. McCool 76, K. R. Miller 51) beat Gloucestershire 279 (J. F. Crapp 100*, I. W. Johnson 5-32, D. T. Ring 5-47) and 132 (I. W. Johnson 5-32, D. T. Ring 5-47) by an innings and 363 runs.

19th Match: v England (Old Trafford)   July 8, 9, 10, 12, 13.
England 363 (D. C. S. Compton 145*, R. R. Lindwall 4-99) and 174-3 dec (C. Washbrook 85*, W. J. Edrich 53) drew with Australia 221 (A. R. Morris 51, A. V. Bedser 4-81) and 92-1 (A. R. Morris 54*).

20th Match: v Middlesex (Lord's)   July 17, 19, 20.
Middlesex 203 (D. C. S. Compton 62) and 135 (J. G. Dewes 51) lost to Australians 317 (S. J. E. Loxton 123, A. R. Morris 109, J. M. Sims 6-65) and 22-0 by 10 wkts.

21st Match: v England (Headingley)   July 22, 23, 24, 26, 27.
England 496 (C. Washbrook 143, W. J. Edrich 111, L. Hutton 81, A. W. Bedser 79) and 365-8 dec (D. C. S. Compton 66, C. Washbrook 65, L. Hutton 57, W. J. Edrich 54, W. A. Johnston 4-95) lost to Australia 458 (R. N. Harvey 112, S. J. E. Loxton 93, R. R. Lindwall 77, K. R. Miller 58) and 404-3 (A. R. Morris 182, D. G. Bradman 173*) by 7 wkts.

22nd Match: v Derbyshire (Derby)   July 28, 29, 30.
Australians 456 (W. A. Brown 140, D. G. Bradman 62, K. R. Miller 57, L. Jackson 4-103) beat Derbyshire 240 (C. S. Elliott 57) and 182 (D. Smith 88, C. L. McCool 6-77) by an innings and 34 runs.

23rd Match: v Glamorgan (Swansea)   July 31, Aug 2, 3.
Glamorgan 197 drew with Australians 215-3 (K. R. Miller 84, A. L. Hassett 71*).

24th Match: v Warwickshire (Edgbaston)   Aug 4, 5, 6.
Warwickshire 138 and 155 (W. A. Johnston 4-32, C. L. McCool 4-56) lost to Australians 254 (A. L. Hassett 68, W. E. Hollies 8-107) and 41-1 by 9 wkts.

25th Match: v Lancashire (Old Trafford)   Aug 7, 9, 10.
Australians 321 (S. G. Barnes 67, W. B. Roberts 6-73) and 265-3 dec (D. G. Bradman 113*, S. G. Barnes 90) drew with Lancashire 130 and 199-7 (J. T. Ikin 99, R. R. Lindwall 4-27).

26th Match: v Durham (Sunderland)   Aug 11, 12.
Australians 282 (C. L. McCool 64, K. R. Miller 55, T. K. Jackson 5-76) drew with Durham 73-5).

27th Match: v England (Oval)   Aug 14, 16, 17, 18.
England 52 (R. R. Lindwall 6-20) and 188 (L. Hutton 64, W. A. Johnston 4-40) lost to Australia 389 (A. R. Morris 196, S. G. Barnes 61, W. E. Hollies 5-131) by an innings and 149 runs.

28th Match: v Kent (Canterbury)   Aug 21, 23.
Australians 361 (W. A. Brown 106, D. G. Bradman 65, R. N. Harvey 60, R. R. Dovey 4-90) beat Kent 51 and 124 (R. R. Lindwall 4-25) by an innings and 186 runs.

29th Match: v Gentlemen (Lord's)   Aug 25, 26, 27.
Australians 610-5 dec (A. L. Hassett 200*, D. G. Bradman 150, W. A. Brown 120, K. R. Miller 69) beat Gentlemen 245 (R. T. Simpson 106, I. W. Johnson 4-60) and 284 (W. J. Edrich 128, D. T. Ring 5-70) by an innings and 81 runs.

30th Match: v Somerset (Taunton)   Aug 28, 30.
Australians 560-5 dec (R. N. Harvey 126, I. W. Johnson 113*, A. L. Hassett 103, R. A. Hamence 99) beat Somerset 115 (C. L. McCool 4-21) and 71 (W. A. Johnston 5-34, C. L. McCool 4-23) by an innings and 374 runs.

31st Match: v South of England (Hastings)   Sept 1, 2, 3.
Australians 522-7 dec (A. L. Hassett 151, D. G. Bradman 143, R. N. Harvey 110, S. J. E. Loxton 67*) drew with South of England 298 (D. C. S. Compton 82, W. J. Edrich 52, W. A. Brown 4-16).

32nd Match: v H. D. G. Leveson-Gower's XI (Scarborough)   Sept 8, 9, 10.
H. D. G. Leveson-Gower's XI 177 (R. R. Lindwall 6-59) and 75-2 drew with Australians 489-8 dec (D. G. Bradman 153, S. G. Barnes 151, A. R. Morris 62).

33rd Match: v Scotland (Edinburgh)   Sept 13, 14.
Australians 236 (A. R. Morris 112, C. L. McCool 52, W. K. Laidlaw 5-51) beat Scotland 85 (W. A. Johnston 6-15) and 111 (A. R. Morris 5-10, D. T. Ring 4-20) by an innings and 40 runs.

34th Match: v Scotland (Aberdeen)   Sept 17, 18.
Scotland 178 and 142 (G. L. Willatt 52, D. T. Ring 4-30) lost to Australians 407-6 dec (D. G. Bradman 123*, C. L. McCool 108, I. W. Johnson 95) by an innings and 87 runs.

The bowling was headed by Lindwall, regarded as the fastest performer of the decade. He could vary his speed without a notable change in action, which worried most English batsmen. In the Tests he took 27 wickets, average 19.62. His partner Miller was noted for his bouncers and the pair ranked with any of their famous predecessors. Johnston, the left-arm fast-medium, or on occasion medium, bowler took 27 Test wickets. He alone took over 100 wickets and was the stock bowler of the side. Toshack bowled well until a knee injury in the Fourth Test. The side found little necessity for a spinner. Johnson's off-breaks were used but in the Tests cost 61 runs per wicket. McCool and Ring were mainly in the wings. The wicketkeeping of Tallon and the fielding in general was quite up to standard.

The team was watched by enormous crowds and the Australians made a record £75,000 profit. The retirement of Bradman was the end of an era.

1949: 4th New Zealanders

The team selected to tour England was W. A. Hadlee (captain), F. B. Smith and T. B. Burtt of Canterbury; W. M. Wallace, J. Cowie, B. Sutcliffe, C. Burke, V. J. Scott and J. A. Hayes of Auckland; J. R. Reid, H. B. Cave, F. L. H. Mooney and G. O. Rabone of Wellington; G. F. Cresswell of Marlborough and M. P. Donnelly, who lived in England, with J. H. Phillips as manager and W. Watts as baggage-man. There was a series of trials in the North and South Islands before this selection was made. Four player were ruled out on medical grounds: R. H. Scott, W. McD. Anderson, C. A. Snedden and G. H. Mills; of the others left out the unluckiest were A. E. Cresswell and D. D. Taylor.

Although the New Zealanders were allocated four Test

Matches, each lasted only three days, a mistaken policy which led to all the Tests being drawn. The fine weather of the summer also led to 18 draws in the tourists' programme, but they lost only one match. This record was a great advance on the three previous tours, as was the profit of about £10,000.

The two batting stars of the team were Donnelly and Sutcliffe, who both exceeded 2,000 runs. Sutcliffe, after a moderate May, overcame a weakness in his hook shot and played with increasing confidence. Donnelly was altogether more serious and his was the hardest wicket to take. Wallace began the summer in excellent form and came close to 1,000 runs in May. In June and July, however, he struggled and it was only towards the end of the tour that he looked his old self. Reid developed as the summer went on

and improved more than any of his colleagues; he was both a useful bowler and wicketkeeper–a genuine all-rounder. Hadlee played his captain's role both in the field and when batting, so that he did not score as many runs as his talent merited.

The bowling, apart from Cowie, was moderate. Burtt reached 100 wickets, but in the Tests his 17 cost 33 runs each. The proof of Cowie's ability was that the side failed to win a single match when he was absent during late July and the first half of August. The other bowlers came into the steady and reliable category and the team had great difficulty in dismissing sides when the wicket did not help the bowlers. In the field the team were always keen and the outfielding in particular was very good. Mooney kept wicket efficiently, but missed the last Test through injury.

1949: 4th New Zealanders

1st Match: v Yorkshire (Bradford) April 30, May 2, 3.
New Zealanders 370-7 dec (W. M. Wallace 82, B. Sutcliffe 72, M. P. Donnelly 69, R. Aspinall 5-80) and 224-6 dec (W. M. Wallace 126, M. P. Donnelly 52) drew with Yorkshire 346 (L. Hutton 167, E. I. Lester 50, T. B. Burtt 4-89) and 101-3.

2nd Match: v Maori C.C. (Worcester Park) May 5.
New Zealanders 159-6 dec (F. L. H. Mooney 55) beat Maori C.C. 63 by 96 runs.*

3rd Match: v Worcestershire (Worcester) May 7, 9, 10.
New Zealanders 425 (W. M. Wallace 108, V. J. Scott 103, W. A. Hadlee 97, R. O. Jenkins 4-117) and 220-5 dec (V. J. Scott 75) beat Worcestershire 279 (A. F. T. White 64, H. Yarnold 56, T. B. Burtt 4-80) and 216 (R. Howorth 62*, T. B. Burtt 7-102) by 150 runs.

4th Match: v Surrey (Oval) May 11, 12, 13.
New Zealanders 258 (B. Sutcliffe 83, J. W. McMahon 5-73) and 249-8 dec (W. A. Hadlee 119*) beat Surrey 202 (M. R. Barton 85*, G. F. Cresswell 5-73, H. B. Cave 4-56) and 156 (B. Constable 55, G. J. Whittaker 50, T. B. Burtt 6-47) by 149 runs.

5th Match: v Leicestershire (Leicester) May 14, 16, 17.
New Zealanders 430 (W. M. Wallace 171, M. P. Donnelly 146, G. Lester 4-45) drew with Leicestershire 119 (J. Cowie 6-54, H. B. Cave 4-28) and 207-1 (F. T. Prentice 104*, G. Lester 70*).

6th Match: v Cambridge University (Cambridge) May 18, 19, 20.
Cambridge University 107 and 284 (D. J. Insole 79*, G. H. G. Doggart 62, R. J. Morris 56, G. A. Rabone 5-25) lost to New Zealanders 441-5 dec (J. R. Reid 188*, W. M. Wallace 197, J. J. Warr 4-81) by an innings and 50 runs.

7th Match: v M.C.C. (Lord's) May 21, 23, 24.
M.C.C. 379 (A. J. Watkins 69, D. C. S. Compton 63, W. J. Edrich 57, R. T. Simpson 51, T. B. Burtt 6-98) and 34-1 drew with New Zealanders 313 (F. L. H. Mooney 102, G. O. Rabone 92, T. E. Bailey 5-83).

8th Match: v Oxford University (Oxford) May 25, 26, 27.
Oxford University 247 (M. B. Hofmeyr 95, C. E. Winn 58, G. A. Rabone 5-60) and 72 (T. B. Burtt 6-18) beat New Zealanders 110 (M. H. Wrigley 5-28, P. A. Whitcombe 4-45) and 126 (P. A. Whitcombe 4-65) by 83 runs.

9th Match: v Sussex (Hove) May 28, 30, 31.
Sussex 276-7 dec (John G. Langridge 154) and 130 (J. Cowie 5-22) lost to New Zealanders 160 (W. M. Wallace 62, C. Oakes 5-19) and 247-5 (M. P. Donnelly 88*, J. R. Reid 82, B. Sutcliffe 56) by 5 wkts.

10th Match: v Somerset (Taunton) June 1, 2, 3.
Somerset 191 (S. S. Rogers 54, H. Gimblett 53, T. B. Burtt 4-68) and 43-1 drew with New Zealanders 297-9 dec (F. B. Smith 93, V. J. Scott 81).

11th Match: v Glamorgan (Cardiff) June 4, 6, 7.
New Zealanders 312-8 dec (F. B. Smith 72) and 111-3 drew with Glamorgan 309 (W. Wooller 80, W. G. A. Parkhouse 61).

12th Match: v England (Headingley) June 11, 13, 14.
England 372 (D. C. S. Compton 114, L. Hutton 101, T. B. Burtt 5-97, J. Cowie 5-127) and 267-4 dec (C. Washbrook 103*, W. J. Edrich 70) drew with New Zealand 341 (F. B. Smith 96, M. P. Donnelly 64, T. E. Bailey 6-118) and 195-2 (B. Sutcliffe 82, F. B. Smith 54*).

13th Match: v Hampshire (Southampton) June 15, 16, 17.
Hampshire 129 (G. F. Cresswell 4-28) and 409 (J. Arnold 110, N. McCorkell 67, E. D. R. Eagar 82, T. B. Burtt 6-76) lost to New Zealanders 430-5 dec (V. J. Scott 129, M. P. Donnelly 100*, J. R. Reid 50) and 109-3 by 7 wkts.

14th Match: v Surrey (Oval) June 18, 20, 21.
New Zealanders 465 (B. Sutcliffe 187, V. J. Scott 96, G. O. Rabone 51, J. C. Laker 6-112) and 127-4 (G. O. Rabone 52) drew with Surrey 645-9 dec (J. F. Parker 255, G. J. Whittaker 91, E. A. Bedser 65, H. B. Cave 4-126, G. O. Rabone 4-138).

15th Match: v England (Lord's) June 25, 27, 28.
England 313-9 dec (D. C. S. Compton 116, T. E. Bailey 93, T. B. Burtt 4-102) and 306-5 (J. D. B. Robertson 121, L. Hutton 66) drew with New Zealand 484 (M. P. Donnelly 206, B. Sutcliffe 57, W. E. Hollies 5-133).

16th Match: v Combined Services (Gillingham) June 29, 30.
Combined Services 72 and 347 (J. E. Manners 123, R. G. Wilson 68, J. H. G. Deighton 59) lost to New Zealanders 469-7 dec (V. J. Scott 203, B. Sutcliffe 144, J. H. G. Deighton 4-119) by an innings and 50 runs.

17th Match: v Gloucestershire (Bristol) July 2, 4, 5.
Gloucestershire 232 (A. E. Wilson 70, T. B. Burtt 6-73) and 155 (T. B. Burtt 5-47, G. O. Rabone 5-66) lost to New Zealanders 252 (M. P. Donnelly 89, C. Cook 5-106, T. W. J. Goddard 5-131) and 138-3 (W. A. Hadlee 56) by 7 wkts.

18th Match: v Lancashire (Old Trafford) July 6, 7, 8.
Lancashire 467-5 dec (J. T. Ikin 167, K. J. Grieves 128, N. D. Howard 50) drew with New Zealanders 237 (G. A. Rabone 81, K. J. Grieves 5-64) and 204-7.

19th Match: v Derbyshire (Derby) July 9, 11, 12.
Derbyshire 121 (C. C. Burke 6-23) and 355 (A. C. Revill 145*, C. S. Elliott 104) lost to New Zealanders 371-8 dec (F. L. H. Mooney 97, T. B. Burtt 68*, J. R. Reid 50, L. Jackson 4-111) and 107-3 by 7 wkts.

20th Match: v Northamptonshire (Northampton) July 13, 14, 15.
New Zealanders 456-7 dec (J. R. Reid 107*, V. J. Scott 105, B. Sutcliffe 81, W. A. Hadlee 71) and 194-4 dec (J. R. Reid 72) drew with Northamptonshire 338 (D. W. Barrick 147*, N. Oldfield 76, T. B. Burtt 4-91) and 182-8 (D. Brookes 97, B. Sutcliffe 4-67).

21st Match: v Scotland (Glasgow) July 16, 18, 19.
New Zealanders 423 (B. Sutcliffe 183, F. B. Smith 68, W. K. Laidlaw 4-123) and 16-0 drew with Scotland 137 (T. B. Burtt 6-45, G. O. Rabone 4-65) and 299 (G. L. Willatt 101, T. R. Crosskey 81, J. Cowie 6-66) by 10 wkts.

22nd Match: v England (Old Trafford) July 23, 25, 26.
New Zealand 293 (M. P. Donnelly 75, J. R. Reid 50, T. E. Bailey 6-84) and 348-7 (B. Sutcliffe 101, M. P. Donnelly 80) drew with England 440-9 dec (R. T. Simpson 103, W. J. Edrich 78, L. Hutton 73, T. B. Burtt 6-162).

23rd Match: v Yorkshire (Bramall Lane) July 27, 28, 29.
New Zealanders 261 (B. Sutcliffe 91, J. H. Wardle 5-92) and 228 (M. P. Donnelly 95, J. H. Wardle 6-84) drew with Yorkshire 321 (N. W. D. Yardley 134*, D. B. Close 51) and 108-8 (G. F. Cresswell 5-30).

24th Match: v Glamorgan (Swansea) July 30, Aug 1, 2.
New Zealanders 378-6 dec (W. M. Wallace 169*, F. B. Smith 71) drew with Glamorgan 73 (G. F. Cresswell 6-21).

25th Match: v Warwickshire (Edgbaston) Aug 3, 4, 5.
New Zealanders 303 (M. P. Donnelly 106, B. Sutcliffe 58, T. L. Pritchard 6-96) and 280-2 (J. R. Reid 151*, G. O. Rabone 58) drew with Warwickshire 394-9 dec (H. E. Dollery 84, F. C. Gardner 70, J. S. Ord 70, A. Townsend 53, T. B. Burtt 4-122).

26th Match: v Nottinghamshire (Trent Bridge) Aug 6, 8, 9.
Nottinghamshire 323-4 dec (J. Hardstaff 123*, C. B. Harris 83, W. W. Keeton 64) and 229-4 dec (C. J. Poole 67) drew with New Zealanders 329-4 dec (J. R. Reid 155, G. O. Rabone 120*) and 105-4 (W. M. Wallace 54*).

27th Match: v Essex (Southend) Aug 10, 11, 12.
New Zealanders 420 (B. Sutcliffe 243, W. A. Hadlee 55, R. Smith 4-93, T. P. B. Smith 4-148) and 218-8 dec (B. Sutcliffe 100*, W. A. Hadlee 57) drew with Essex 304 (F. H. Vigar 89, T. C. Dodds 82, H. B. Cave 4-82) and 216-4 (S. C. Eve 69, S. J. Cray 60).

28th Match: v England (Oval) Aug 13, 15, 16.
New Zealand 345 (B. Sutcliffe 88, V. J. Scott 60, W. M. Wallace 55, A. V. Bedser 4-74) and 308-9 dec (J. R. Reid 93, W. M. Wallace 58, B. Sutcliffe 54, J. C. Laker 4-78) drew with England 482 (L. Hutton 206, W. J. Edrich 100, R. T. Simpson 68, G. F. Cresswell 6-168, J. Cowie 4-123).

29th Match: v Durham (Sunderland) Aug 18, 19.
New Zealanders 417-3 dec (F. B. Smith 106, V. J. Scott 104, F. L. H. Mooney 104*, G. O. Rabone 56) drew with Durham 171 (C. C. Burke 4-42) and 280 (H. Clarke 56, C. C. Burke 5-81).*

30th Match: v Lancashire (Liverpool) Aug 20, 22, 23.
Lancashire 318 (C. Washbrook 125, P. Greenwood 50) and 224-5 dec (C. Washbrook 68, J. T. Ikin 57, G. A. Edrich 53) lost to New Zealanders 390 (V. J. Scott 87, M. P. Donnelly 80, B. Sutcliffe 61) and 153-1 (B. Sutcliffe 79*, M. P. Donnelly 56).

31st Match: v Kent (Canterbury) Aug 24, 25, 26.
New Zealanders 358 (V. J. Scott 74, M. P. Donnelly 68, F. B. Smith 58, D. V. P. Wright 4-128) and 204-6 dec (W. M. Wallace 55) drew with Kent 184 (L. J. Todd 54, T. B. Burtt 6-56) and 250-5 (L. E. G. Ames 152*).

32nd Match: v Middlesex (Lord's) Aug 27, 29, 30.
Middlesex 315 (D. C. S. Compton 148, J. G. Dewes 92, J. Cowie 5-87) and 169 (J. G. Dewes 60, T. B. Burtt 4-50) lost to New Zealanders 328 (M. P. Donnelly 72, B. Sutcliffe 59, W. A. Hadlee 50) and 157-1 (B. Sutcliffe 110*) by 9 wkts.

33rd Match: v Club Cricket Conference (Guildford) Aug 31.
C.C.C. 217-6 dec (H. J. J. Malcolm 105) drew with New Zealanders 124-7.*

34th Match: v South of England (Hastings) Sept 3, 5, 6.
New Zealanders 367 (W. A. Hadlee 114, G. O. Rabone 78, J. R. Reid 54, T. E. Bailey 4-97) beat South of England 159 and 205 by an innings and 3 runs.

35th Match: v H. D. G. Leveson-Gower's XI (Scarborough) Sept 7, 8, 9.
H. D. G. Leveson-Gower's XI 348-5 dec (J. Hardstaff jun 123, L. Hutton 54, R. T. Simpson 54) and 202-3 dec (L. Hutton 75, R. T. Simpson 58) lost to New Zealanders 338 (M. P. Donnelly 145*, J. R. Reid 50, A. V. Bedser 5-101) and 217-4 (B. Sutcliffe 83, M. P. Donnelly 53*) by 6 wkts.

36th Match: v Combined Services (Bad Oeyhausen) Sept 13, 14.
Combined Services XII 143 and 188 (M. P. Donnelly 4-68) lost to New Zealanders 248 (W. A. Hadlee 65, J. Flood 4-59) and 87-4 by 6 wkts.*

1949: 4th New Zealanders

Batting Averages

	M	I	NO	R	HS	Avge	100	c/s
M. P. Donnelly	29	45	8	2287	206	61.81	5	24
B. Sutcliffe	29	49	5	2627	243	59.70	7	32
W. M. Wallace	27	41	6	1722	197	49.20	5	12
J. R. Reid	25	40	4	1488	188*	41.33	4	26/6
V. J. Scott	27	40	1	1572	203	40.30	4	15
W. A. Hadlee	28	44	4	1439	119*	35.97	2	24
G. O. Rabone	25	39	8	1021	120*	32.93	1	24
F. B. Smith	24	40	4	1008	96	28.00	0	10
F. L. H. Mooney	27	39	5	774	102	22.76	1	46/20
T. B. Burtt	27	31	6	436	68*	17.44	0	12
H. B. Cave	20	23	9	228	36	16.28	0	12
J. Cowie	18	17	8	131	47	14.55	0	4
C. Burke	18	17	5	171	44*	14.25	0	8
G. F. Cresswell	19	15	11	50	12*	12.50	0	6
J. A. Hayes	9	6	2	20	9*	5.00	0	2

Bowling Averages

	O	M	R	W	Avge	BB	5i
T. B. Burtt	1231	410	2929	128	22.88	4-102	11
G. F. Cresswell	692.1	184	1618	62	26.09	6-21	4
J. Cowie	615.5	129	1601	59	27.13	6-54	5
C. Burke	598.3	144	1611	54	29.83	6-23	1
J. R. Reid	127.4	20	390	13	30.00	2-7	0
J. A. Hayes	301.4	60	873	26	33.57	3-26	0
G. O. Rabone	558.4	118	1785	50	35.70	5-25	3
B. Sutcliffe	185.4	37	654	16	40.87	4-67	0
H. B. Cave	657	131	1809	42	43.07	4-28	0
M. P. Donnelly	21.3	0	130	3	43.33	1-5	0
F. B. Smith	15	5	44	1	44.00	1-6	0

Also bowled: W. A. Hadlee 5-1-30-0; F. L. H. Mooney 1-1-0-0; V. J. Scott 4-0-23-0; W. M. Wallace 3-0-11-0.

1950: 7th West Indians

The 1950 touring team was officially announced on 22 February: J. D. C. Goddard (captain), E. de C. Weekes, C. L. Walcott, C. B. Williams and R. E. Marshall of Barbados; J. B. Stollmeyer, G. E. Gomez, P. E. Jones, L. R. Pierre, K. B. Trestrail and S. Ramadhin of Trinidad; F. M. M. Worrell, A. F. Rae and A. L. Valentine of Jamaica and R. J. Christiani of British Guiana. The manager was J. M. Kidney and assistant manager the Rev Palmer-Barnes. The side was obviously very strong in batting and the leading players were unquestioned choices – Hadley was not available. Rickards, Ganteaume and Pairaudeau were the batsmen unable to find a place. Ferguson, the leg-spinner, was unlucky not to be chosen, as was Trim the fast bowler.

The main group of players arrived in Southampton on 10 April aboard the s.s. *Golfito* and spent some days in Eastbourne as guests of that town. After the farce of three-day Tests (all drawn) in 1949, the authorities allotted five days to the four Tests of 1950. The tourists' early matches gave some examples of their batting strength, but it was not until the three games preceding the First Test that the bowling and in particular the powers of Ramadhin and Valentine became apparent – the West Indies won all three matches by an innings. In the First Test Valentine took eight wickets during the first innings of his Test debut, but on a much criticised pitch Hollies and Berry bowled England to an easy win.

The West Indies' first series-winning bowlers' partnership in England was not a battery of fast men but the spinners Sonny Ramadhin (above) and Alf Valentine (left). One or other of them took at least five wickets in an innings in each of the four Tests. Ramadhin took 135 wickets in all first-class matches on the tour, Valentine 123.

The West Indies then took two more innings' victories before coming to Lord's for the Second Test. Ramadhin took 11 wickets and Valentine 7 and the West Indies won their first Test in England by a large margin. From there on the fiendish reputation of Ramadhin and Valentine gathered momentum quickly and the rest of the tour was one of almost unbroken success in which the tourists won the Test series by three to one.

The stars of the tour were the unknown spinners Valentine and Ramadhin, who took 33 and 26 wickets respectively in the Tests—no one else took more than six. The English batsmen were baffled by them, even before they arrived at the crease. The batting proved as brilliant as expected with Weekes, Worrell and Walcott all achieving a great deal, though it was Worrell who topped the Test averages with 539 runs, average 89.93. Worrell also bowled usefully, while Walcott kept wicket. Rae was the rock of the team and a most dependable opener—Gomez did well when given the opportunity. Stollmeyer batted attractively as Rae's partner. The disappointments were the fast bowlers Johnson, Jones and Pierre; Trestrail and to a lesser extent Marshall, who missed his chance of a Test place through illness.

The main section of the team left Southampton aboard the s.s. *Matina* on 23 September—their profit for the visit £30,000.

1950: 7th West Indians

1st Match: v L. C. Steven's XII (Eastbourne)   April 24, 25.
L. C. Steven's XII 191-2 dec (C. L. Walcott 58, D. V. Smith 55) drew with West Indians 231-8 (J. B. Stollmeyer 50, G. E. Gomez 67).

2nd Match: v Club Cricket Conference (Kingston-on-Thames)   April 28.
West Indians 219-5 drew with C.C.C. 107-9.

3rd Match: L. N. Constantine's XI (Motspur Park)   April 30.
West Indians 153 drew with L. N. Constantine's XI 111-8 (J. K. Holt 55).*

4th Match: v Indian Gymkhana (Osterley)   May 4.
West Indians 177-7 dec (M. H. Mankad 4-49) drew with Indian Gymkhana 78-8 (S. Ramadhin 5-9).

5th Match: v Worcestershire (Worcester)   May 6, 8, 9.
West Indians 249-4 dec (F. M. M. Worrell 85, E. de C. Weekes 54) drew with Worcestershire 134-4.

6th Match: v Yorkshire (Bradford)   May 10, 11.
Yorkshire 91 (G. E. Gomez 5-34, S. Ramadhin 4-30) and 127 (L. Hutton 67, P. E. Jones 7-29) lost to West Indians 132 (C. L. Walcott 58, K. Smales 5-44, J. H. Wardle 4-57) and 87-7 (J. H. Wardle 4-37) by 3 wkts.

7th Match: v Surrey (Oval)   May 13, 15, 16.
West Indians 537-5 dec (E. de C. Weekes 232, C. L. Walcott 128, A. F. Rae 96) and 14-1 drew with Surrey 193 (J. F. Parker 94) and 391 (L. B. Fishlock 110, M. R. Barton 99, G. E. Gomez 4-110).

8th Match: v Cambridge University (Cambridge)   May 17, 18, 19.
Cambridge University 594-4 dec (D. S. Sheppard 227, J. G. Dewes 183, G. H. G. Doggart 71, M. H. Stevenson 53) drew with West Indians 730-3 (E. de C. Weekes 304*, F. M. M. Worrell 160, R. J. Christiani 111, J. B. Stollmeyer 83, K. B. Trestrail 56*).*

9th Match: v M.C.C. (Lord's)   May 20, 22, 23.
M.C.C. 188 (W. J. Edrich 64, A. L. Valentine 5-67, J. D. C. Goddard 4-57) and 247 (R. T. Simpson 77, C. B. Williams 7-55) beat West Indians 170 (J. B. Stollmeyer 53, R. Berry 4-31, J. M. Sims 4-65) and 147 (J. M. Sims 7-65) by 118 runs.

10th Match: v Oxford University (Christ Church, Oxford)   May 24, 25, 26.
Oxford University 194 (C. E. Winn 61, S. Ramadhin 4-42) and 68-6 dec drew with West Indians 127 (R. V. Divecha 4-46) and 30-1.

11th Match: v Glamorgan (Cardiff)   May 27, 29, 30.
Glamorgan 123 (H. H. H. Johnson 5-33, A. L. Valentine 4-34) and 179 (S. Ramadhin 5-42) lost to West Indians 328 (F. M. M. Worrell 97, E. de C. Weekes 59, G. E. Gomez 55, N. G. Hever 5-85) by an innings and 26 runs.

12th Match: v Somerset (Taunton)   May 31, June 1, 2.
West Indians 267 (A. F. Rae 76, G. E. Gomez 70, A. W. Wellard 4-60) and 273-3 dec (C. L. Walcott 117, F. M. M. Worrell 104) beat Somerset 177 (H. Gimblett 77, S. Ramadhin 6-57) and 292 (J. Lawrence 67*, S. Ramadhin 5-98) by 71 runs.*

13th Match: v Lancashire (Old Trafford)   June 3, 5, 6.
West Indians 454-7 dec (A. F. Rae 114, J. B. Stollmeyer 83, C. L. Walcott 63, E. de C. Weekes 59) beat Lancashire 103 (A. L. Valentine 8-26) and 131 (A. L. Valentine 5-41, J. D. C. Goddard 4-24) by an innings and 220 runs.

14th Match: v England (Old Trafford)   June 8, 9, 10, 12.
England 312 (T. G. Evans 104, T. E. Bailey 82*, A. L. Valentine 8-104) and 288 (W. J. Edrich 71) beat West Indies 215 (E. de C. Weekes 52, R. Berry 5-63) and 183 (J. B. Stollmeyer 78, W. E. Hollies 5-63, R. Berry 4-53) by 202 runs.

15th Match: v Northumberland (Jesmond)   June 14, 15.
Northumberland 187 (C. B. Williams 6-60) and 117 (S. Ramadhin 5-51) lost to West Indians 312 (J. D. C. Goddard 53, J. M. Watson 4-87) by an innings and 8 runs.

16th Match: v Nottinghamshire (Trent Bridge)   June 17, 19, 20.
West Indians 525-5 dec (E. de C. Weekes 279, F. M. M. Worrell 83) beat Nottinghamshire 240 (F. W. Stocks 68, C. B. Williams 5-54) and 224 (R. T. Simpson 109, F. M. M. Worrell 5-57) by an innings and 61 runs.

17th Match: v Sussex (Hove)   June 21, 22, 23.
Sussex 220 (D. V. Smith 55, F. M. M. Worrell 5-27) and 114 (S. Ramadhin 5-25, G. E. Gomez 4-19) lost to West Indians 477-3 dec (J. B. Stollmeyer 198, A. F. Rae 179) by an innings and 143 runs.

18th Match: v England (Lord's)   June 24, 26, 27, 28, 29.
West Indies 326 (A. F. Rae 106, E. de C. Weekes 63, F. M. M. Worrell 52, R. O. Jenkins 5-116) and 425-6 dec (C. L. Walcott 168*, G. E. Gomez 70, F. M. M. Worrell 63, R. O. Jenkins 4-174) beat England 151 (S. Ramadhin 5-66, A. L. Valentine 4-48) and 274 (C. Washbrook 114, S. Ramadhin 6-86) by 326 runs.

19th Match: v Hampshire (Southampton)   July 1, 3, 4.
West Indians 539-4 dec (E. de C. Weekes 246, R. E. Marshall 135, C. L. Walcott 58) drew with Hampshire 268-7 (N. H. Rogers 106, N. T. McCorkell 55, S. Ramadhin 4-46).*

20th Match: v Lancashire (Liverpool)   July 5, 6, 7.
Lancashire 174 (L. R. Pierre 8-51) and 182 (A. L. Valentine 7-57) lost to West Indians 397-8 dec (F. M. M. Worrell 159, K. B. Trestrail 93) by an innings and 41 runs.

21st Match: v Northamptonshire (Northampton)   July 8, 10, 11.
West Indians 431-8 dec (R. J. Christiani 130, R. E. Marshall 99, J. B. Stollmeyer 70) drew with Northamptonshire 252 (N. Oldfield 85, D. Brookes 51, G. E. Gomez 4-51) and 206-1 (L. Livingston 81).*

22nd Match: v Leicestershire (Leicester)   July 12, 13, 14.
West Indians 682-2 dec (F. M. M. Worrell 241, E. de C. Weekes 200*, R. E. Marshall 188) beat Leicestershire 352 (G. L. Berry 121, M. Tompkin 74, S. Ramadhin 4-90, A. L. Valentine 4-101) and 81 (S. Ramadhin 6-27) by an innings and 249 runs.*

23rd Match: v Derbyshire (Chesterfield)   July 15, 17, 18.
West Indians 223 (C. L. Walcott 87, R. J. Christiani 78, C. Gladwin 6-40) and 91-4 drew with Derbyshire 111 (J. D. C. Goddard 4-38).

24th Match: v England (Trent Bridge)   July 20, 21, 22, 24, 25.
England 223 and 436 (C. Washbrook 102, R. T. Simpson 94, W. G. A. Parkhouse 69, J. G. Dewes 67, T. G. Evans 63, S. Ramadhin 5-135) lost to West Indies 558 (F. M. M. Worrell 261, E. de C. Weekes 129, A. F. Rae 68, A. V. Bedser 5-127) and 103-0 (J. B. Stollmeyer 52*) by 10 wkts.

25th Match: v Durham (Sunderland)   July 26, 27.
West Indians 375 (G. E. Gomez 114, K. B. Trestrail 105, C. B. Williams 68, T. K. Jackson 4-120) and 214-4 dec (K. B. Trestrail 100, C. L. Walcott 67) drew with Durham 163 (J. Keeler 90) and 203-4 (J. Keeler 97).*

26th Match: v Yorkshire (Bramall Lane)   July 29, 31, Aug 1.
West Indians 198 (A. Coxon 4-69) and 229 (C. L. Walcott 91, R. E. Marshall 64) beat Yorkshire 217-9 dec (L. Hutton 104, A. L. Valentine 5-57) and 175 (F. A. Lowson 60, F. M. M. Worrell 5-51) by 35 runs.

27th Match: v Surrey (Oval)   Aug 2, 3, 4.
Surrey 161 (F. M. M. Worrell 4-37) and 204 (L. B. Fishlock 97, A. L. Valentine 5-60) lost to West Indians 434 (C. L. Walcott 149, R. E. Marshall 143) by an innings and 69 runs.

28th Match: v Glamorgan (Swansea)   Aug 5, 7, 8.
West Indians 211 (K. B. Trestrail 53, R. J. Christiani 50, D. E. Davies 4-18) and 312-6 (E. de C. Weekes 147) drew with Glamorgan 322 (W. E. Jones 105, W. G. A. Parkhouse 88, S. Ramadhin 4-93).

29th Match: v Warwickshire (Edgbaston)   Aug 9, 10, 11.
West Indians 156 (C. W. Grove 8-38) and 222 (W. E. Hollies 6-57) lost to Warwickshire 284 (A. V. Wolton 89, R. T. Spooner 66, A. L. Valentine 4-57) and 96-7 (A. L. Valentine 4-36) by 3 wkts.*

30th Match: v England (Oval)   Aug 12, 14, 15, 16.
West Indies 503 (F. M. M. Worrell 138, A. F. Rae 109, G. E. Gomez 74, J. D. C. Goddard 58*, D. V. P. Wright 5-141) beat England 344 (L. Hutton 202*, J. D. C. Goddard 4-25, A. L. Valentine 4-121) and 103 (A. L. Valentine 6-39) by an innings and 56 runs.

31st Match: v Gloucestershire (Cheltenham)   Aug 19, 21.
Gloucestershire 69 (S. Ramadhin 8-15) and 97 (S. Ramadhin 5-36, A. L. Valentine 4-31) lost to West Indians 271 (C. L. Walcott 126, E. de C. Weekes 57, C. Cook 5-60) by an innings and 105 runs.

32nd Match: v Essex (Southend)   Aug 23, 24, 25.
Essex 229 (T. C. Dodds 106, A. V. Avery 52, G. E. Gomez 4-34, S. Ramadhin 4-53) and 169 (G. E. Gomez 5-79, S. Ramadhin 4-49) lost to West Indians 213 (R. J. Christiani 60, T. E. Bailey 5-44) and 186-3 (E. de C. Weekes 84, R. J. Christiani 53*) by 7 wkts.*

33rd Match: v Middlesex (Lord's)   Aug 26, 28, 29.
Middlesex 311 (J. D. B. Robertson 105, H. P. Sharp 72, A. L. Valentine 5-72) and 209-4 dec (J. G. Dewes 86) drew with West Indians 343 (R. J. Christiani 131, J. B. Stollmeyer 81, E. de C. Weekes 52) and 148-3 (R. J. Christiani 100*).*

34th Match: v Kent (Canterbury)   Aug 30, 31, Sept 1.
West Indians 265 (G. E. Gomez 149, J. W. Martin 4-75) and 170-6 dec (G. E. Gomez 88, J. W. Martin 4-72) beat Kent 146 (A. L. Valentine 4-57) and 67 (A. L. Valentine 5-6, J. D. C. Goddard 4-13) by 222 runs.

35th Match: v South of England (Hastings)   Sept 2, 4, 5.
South of England 194 (T. C. Dodds 55, S. Ramadhin 7-67) and 211 (G. H. G. Doggart 55, A. L. Valentine 4-46, S. Ramadhin 4-70) drew with West Indians 286 (C. L. Walcott 103, W. S. Surridge 5-73) and 84-2.

36th Match: v Minor Counties (Norwich)   Sept 6, 7, 8.
Minor Counties 106 (S. Ramadhin 7-33) and 312 (W. G. Keighley 92, R. V. Divecha 57, W. H. Sutcliffe 56) lost to West Indians 425-5 dec (G. E. Gomez 117, K. B. Trestrail 94, F. M. M. Worrell 62, R. E. Marshall 56) by an innings and 7 runs.*

37th Match: v H. D. G. Leveson-Gower's XI (Scarborough)   Sept 9, 11, 12.
H. D. G. Leveson-Gower's XI 190 (S. Ramadhin 6-36) and 170 (S. Ramadhin 4-49) drew with West Indians 245 (C. L. Walcott 121, A. F. Rae 51, J. E. Walsh 4-65).

38th Match: v Cumberland and Westmorland (Carlisle)   Sept 14.
West Indians 244 (R. E. Marshall 82, R. J. Newell 5-86) and 110-4 beat Cumberland and Westmorland 85 (G. E. Gomez 4-18, A. L. Valentine 4-22) by 159 runs.

1950: 7th West Indians

Batting Averages

	M	I	NO	R	HS	Avge	100	c/s
E. de C. Weekes	23	33	4	2310	304*	79.65	7	31
F. M. M. Worrell	22	31	5	1775	261	68.26	6	11
C. L. Walcott	25	36	6	1674	168*	55.80	7	30/18
R. J. Christiani	24	34	10	1094	131*	45.58	4	30/6
G. E. Gomez	27	30	4	1116	149	42.92	2	32
R. E. Marshall	20	28	0	1117	188	39.89	3	15
A. F. Rae	26	38	4	1330	179	39.11	4	15
J. B. Stollmeyer	25	37	1	1334	198	37.05	1	23
K. B. Trestrail	19	28	5	629	94	27.34	0	8
J. D. C. Goddard	22	21	5	309	58*	19.31	0	21
H. H. H. Johnson	17	16	4	184	39*	15.33	0	5
C. B. Williams	20	18	4	152	33*	10.85	0	16
P. E. Jones	17	16	4	83	20	6.91	0	14
S. Ramadhin	21	15	8	36	7*	5.14	0	3
A. L. Valentine	21	19	3	49	9*	3.06	0	7
L. R. Pierre	12	7	1	2	1	0.33	0	5

Bowling Averages

	O	M	R	W	Avge	BB	5i
S. Ramadhin	1043.4	398	2009	135	14.88	8-15	13
A. L. Valentine	1185.2	475	2207	123	17.94	8-26	10
J. D. C. Goddard	295.2	96	618	33	18.72	4-13	0
L. R. Pierre	204	39	557	24	23.20	8-51	1
F. M. M. Worrell	480.1	170	970	39	24.87	5-27	3
G. E. Gomez	680.3	221	1407	55	25.58	5-34	2
C. B. Williams	301.2	57	856	31	27.61	7-55	2
H. H. H. Johnson	435.5	102	954	34	28.05	5-33	1
P. E. Jones	388.3	82	980	33	29.69	7-29	1
R. E. Marshall	120.5	36	336	7	48.00	2-6	0
J. B. Stollmeyer	27	3	117	2	58.50	1-15	0

Also bowled: K. B. Trestrail 3-0-17-0; C. L. Walcott 12-6-22-0; E. de C. Weekes 9-0-41-2.

1951: 10th South Africans

The team chosen for the 1951 tour was A. D. Nourse (captain), C. N. McCarthy, R. A. McLean and D. J. McGlew of Natal; E. A. B. Rowan, G. M. Fullerton, A. M. B. Rowan, M. G. Melle, G. W. A. Chubb and W. R. Endean of Transvaal; J. E. Cheetham and C. B. van Ryneveld of Western Province; N. B. F. Mann and J. H. B. Waite of Eastern Province and P. N. F. Mansell of Rhodesia, with S. J. Pegler as manager. A surprise omission was H. J. Tayfield.

Although the team won one Test against England, their first-class record was abysmal, with only five wins out of 30 matches. The main factor affecting the tourists seemed to be Nourse's incapacity: he broke his thumb in the fifth match, came back to hit 208 in the First Test, but batted in severe pain and this was his

1951: 10th South Africans

Batting Averages

	M	I	NO	R	HS	Avge	100	c/s
E. A. B. Rowan	26	41	4	1852	236	50.05	5	15
J. E. Cheetham	23	33	5	1196	133*	42.71	3	14
D. J. McGlew	19	29	3	1002	114*	38.53	2	3
J. H. B. Waite	20	32	2	1011	139	33.70	3	15/5
G. M. Fullerton	26	40	4	1129	167	31.36	1	15
R. A. McLean	22	31	2	887	88	30.58	0	13
C. B. van Ryneveld	24	35	2	983	150	29.78	1	19
A. D. Nourse	18	28	2	673	208	25.88	1	11
A. M. B. Rowan	15	22	4	432	98	24.00	0	4
P. N. F. Mansell	20	27	4	504	90	21.91	0	21
W. R. Endean	20	32	3	527	72	18.17	0	22/4
H. F. Tayfield	18	22	4	304	68	16.88	0	11
N. B. F. Mann	21	26	5	316	49*	15.04	0	7
G. W. A. Chubb	22	27	8	190	24*	10.00	0	6
M. G. Melle	16	18	7	96	20	8.72	0	10
C. N. McCarthy	20	22	12	20	5	2.00	0	8

Bowling Averages

	O	M	R	W	Avge	BB	5i
M. G. Melle	358	79	1014	50	20.28	6-71	2
C. N. McCarthy	617.1	140	1414	59	23.96	8-36	3
G. W. A. Chubb	809.4	211	2005	76	26.38	6-51	4
N. B. F. Mann	647.3	246	1161	44	26.38	4-24	0
A. M. B. Rowan	566	134	1409	53	26.58	8-106	4
C. B. van Ryneveld	283	56	814	24	33.91	5-53	2
P. N. F. Mansell	408.1	80	1103	31	35.58	5-37	1
H. J. Tayfield	434.3	116	1060	29	36.55	5-84	1
G. M. Fullerton	31	12	83	2	41.50	2-41	0

Also bowled: J. E. Cheetham 1-0-3-0; D. J. McGlew 2-1-4-1; A. D. Nourse 2-0-9-0; E. A. B. Rowan 4.5-0-19-0.

Above *John Waite, who came to England three times, was the leading international wicketkeeper-batsman of the 1950s. He is playing a ball from Alec Bedser through the slips. Another outstanding wicketkeeper, Godfrey Evans, is standing up to the fast-medium Bedser.*

1951: 10th South Africans

1st Match: v D. G. Clark's XI (Maidstone)   April 25.
D. G. Clark's XI 199-4 dec (A. E. Fagg 74, G. H. G. Doggart 56) drew with South Africans 191-5 (G. M. Fullerton 118*).

2nd Match: v Union Castle (Lee)   April 27.
South Africans 177-6 dec (G. M. Fullerton 65, E. A. B. Rowan 64) drew with Union Castle 77-5.

3rd Match: v Club Cricket Conference (Luton)   April 28.
Match abandoned due to snow.

4th Match: v Worcestershire (Worcester)   May 2, 3, 4.
Worcestershire 192 (R. E. Bird 70*, A. M. B. Rowan 4-49) and 50-6 drew with South Africans 157 (R. T. D. Perks 4-36).

5th Match: v Yorkshire (Bradford)   May 5, 7, 8.
Yorkshire 214-4 dec (H. Halliday 67*, L. Hutton 58) drew with South Africans 76 (R. Appleyard 6-38) and 86-9 (F. S. Trueman 5-19, J. H. Wardle 4-32).

6th Match: v Cambridge University (Cambridge)   May 9, 10, 11.
Cambridge University 188 (D. S. Sheppard 71, C. B. van Ryneveld 5-62, N. B. F. Mann 4-34) drew with South Africans 283-4 (E. A. B. Rowan 104*, G. M. Fullerton 72, R. A. McLean 51).

7th Match: v Glamorgan (Cardiff)   May 12, 14, 15.
South Africans 330 (D. J. McGlew 110, E. A. B. Rowan 59, D. J. Shepherd 4-66) beat Glamorgan 130 (G. W. A. Chubb 5-21) and 186 (H. G. Davies 80, A. M. B. Rowan 5-42) by an innings and 14 runs.

8th Match: v Gloucestershire (Bristol)   May 16, 17, 18.
South Africans 388-9 dec (J. E. Cheetham 92, D. J. McGlew 90, J. H. B. Waite 62, G. E. E. Lambert 5-78) and 15-1 drew with Gloucestershire 207 (D. M. Young 87, C. N. McCarthy 6-56) and 322-4 dec (T. W. Graveney 93, D. M. Young 68, J. F. Crapp 64).

9th Match: v M.C.C. (Lord's)   May 19, 21, 22.
South Africans 190 (C. B. van Ryneveld 56, R. Tattersall 8-51) and 97-2 drew with M.C.C. 271 (D. C. S. Compton 147, J. D. B. Robertson 51, N. B. F. Mann 4-67).

10th Match: v Oxford University (Oxford)   May 23, 24, 25.
South Africans 300-5 dec (E. A. B. Rowan 147, J. E. Cheetham 89) and 62-0 dec drew with Oxford University 159 (M. G. Melle 5-37) and 50-0.

11th Match: v Nottinghamshire (Trent Bridge)   May 26, 28, 29.
South Africans 304 (A. M. B. Rowan 98, E. A. B. Rowan 55, H. J. Butler 5-63) and 176-2 (E. A. B. Rowan 95, G. M. Fullerton 54*) drew with Nottinghamshire 297 (J. Hardstaff 151, C. B. Harris 57, C. N. McCarthy 5-67).

12th Match: v Essex (Ilford)   May 30, 31, June 1.
South Africans 312-9 dec (J. H. B. Waite 128, H. J. Tayfield 68, K. C. Preston 4-77) and 286-5 dec (G. M. Fullerton 167, D. J. McGlew 56) drew with Essex 319-7 dec (T. C. Dodds 138, D. J. Insole 60) and 255-5 (R. Smith 147).

13th Match: v Surrey (Oval)   June 2, 4, 5.
South Africans 190 (C. B. van Ryneveld 60) and 358-8 dec (D. J. McGlew 99, W. R. Endean 72, J. E. Cheetham 68, G. A. R. Lock 4-87) drew with Surrey 246 (L. B. Fishlock 62, A. J. W. McIntyre 57, M. G. Melle 4-66) and 95-4.

14th Match: v England (Trent Bridge)   June 7, 8, 9, 11, 12.
South Africa 483-9 dec (A. D. Nourse 208, J. H. B. Waite 76, G. M. Fullerton 54) and 121 (A. V. Bedser 6-37) beat England 419-9 dec (R. T. Simpson 137, D. C. S. Compton 112, L. Hutton 63, W. Watson 57, C. N. McCarthy 4-104, G. W. A. Chubb 4-146) and 114 (A. M. B. Rowan 5-68, N. B. F. Mann 4-24) by 71 runs.

15th Match: v Northamptonshire (Northampton)   June 13, 14, 15.
Northamptonshire 426-6 dec (L. Livingston 201*, F. Jakeman 131) drew with South Africans 212 (W. R. Endean 57, G. E. Tribe 6-53) and 418-6 (E. A. B. Rowan 202*, R. A. McLean 68, G. M. Fullerton 53).

16th Match: v Lancashire (Old Trafford)   June 16, 18, 19.
South Africans 403-7 dec (J. E. Cheetham 127, J. H. B. Waite 122, E. A. B. Rowan 66) and 60-4 drew with Lancashire 412 (G. A. Edrich 121, A. Wharton 98, J. T. Ikin 64, H. J. Tayfield 5-84).

17th Match: v England (Lord's)   June 21, 22, 23.
England 311 (D. C. S. Compton 79, W. Watson 79, J. T. Ikin 51, G. W. A. Chubb 5-77, C. N. McCarthy 4-76) and 16-0 beat South Africa 115 (R. Tattersall 7-52) and 211 (G. M. Fullerton 60, J. E. Cheetham 54, R. Tattersall 5-49) by 10 wkts.

18th Match: v Combined Services (Portsmouth)   June 27, 28, 29.
South Africans 499-5 dec (J. H. B. Waite 139, J. E. Cheetham 133*, G. M. Fullerton 69, A. D. Nourse 61) drew with Combined Services 235 (D. B. Close 66, J. M. Parks 51) and 256-4 (D. B. Close 135*, J. E. Manners 75).

19th Match: v Yorkshire (Bramall Lane)   June 30, July 2, 3.
South Africans 454-8 dec (C. B. van Ryneveld 150, R. A. McLean 88, G. M. Fullerton 63, J. H. B. Waite 57, J. P. Whitehead 4-103) drew with Yorkshire 579 (L. Hutton 156, F. A. Lowson 115, J. V. Wilson 84, N. W. D. Yardley 57).

20th Match: v England (Old Trafford)   July 5, 6, 7, 9, 10.
South Africa 158 (A. V. Bedser 7-58) and 191 (E. A. B. Rowan 57, A. V. Bedser 5-54) lost to England 211 (G. W. A. Chubb 6-51) and 142-1 (L. Hutton 98*) by 9 wkts.

21st Match: v Scotland (Hamilton Crescent, Glasgow)   July 11, 12.
Scotland 115 (J. Aitchison 55, A. M. B. Rowan 4-21) drew with South Africans 110-3.

22nd Match: v Ireland (Belfast)   July 13, 14.
Ireland 159 (J. S. Pollock 58, N. B. F. Mann 4-48) and 46 (A. M. B. Rowan 7-23) lost to South Africans 145 (J. C. Boucher 4-43) and 61-2 by 8 wkts.

23rd Match: v Ireland (Dublin)   July 16, 17.
Ireland 110 (E. A. Ingram 50*, H. J. Tayfield 4-32, C. B. van Ryneveld 4-60) and 130 (S. F. Bergin 79, N. B. F. Mann 6-37) lost to South Africans 312-4 dec (R. A. McLean 107, P. N. F. Mansell 85, E. A. B. Rowan 85) by an innings and 72 runs.

24th Match: v Derbyshire (Derby)   July 18, 19, 20.
Derbyshire 258 (A. C. Revill 74, A. Hamer 65) and 205 (G. L. Willatt 50) lost to South Africans 382-9 dec (J. H. B. Waite 99, E. A. B. Rowan 74, P. N. F. Mansell 51, C. Gladwin 4-72) and 82-2 by 8 wkts.

25th Match: v Leicestershire (Leicester)   July 21, 23, 24.
Leicestershire 267 (M. Tompkin 64) and 134-6 dec lost to South Africans 235 (E. A. B. Rowan 61, C. B. van Ryneveld 61, C. H. Palmer 5-46) and 168-4 (E. A. B. Rowan 115*) by 6 wkts.

26th Match: v England (Headingley)   July 26, 27, 28, 30, 31.
South Africa 538 (E. A. B. Rowan 236, P. N. F. Mansell 90, C. B. van Ryneveld 83, R. A. McLean 67) and 87-0 (E. A. B. Rowan 60*) drew with England 505 (P. B. H. May 138, L. Hutton 100, T. E. Bailey 95, F. A. Lowson 58, A. M. B. Rowan 5-174).

27th Match: v Somerset (Taunton)   Aug 1, 2, 3.
South Africans 235 (D. J. McGlew 68, P. N. F. Mansell 62) and 180 (J. E. Cheetham 62, E. P. Robinson 5-59) beat Somerset 305 (S. S. Rogers 107*) and 86 (G. W. A. Chubb 5-21, N. B. F. Mann 4-30) by 24 runs.

28th Match: v Glamorgan (Swansea)   Aug 4, 6.
Glamorgan 111 (P. N. F. Mansell 5-37, A. M. B. Rowan 4-45) and 147 (A. M. B. Rowan 4-42, P. N. F. Mansell 4-73) beat South Africans 111 (L. B. Muncer 7-45) and 83 (J. E. McConnon 6-27, L. B. Muncer 4-16) by 64 runs.

29th Match: v Warwickshire (Edgbaston)   Aug 8, 9, 10.
Warwickshire 230 (D. D. Taylor 73, H. E. Dollery 52, A. M. B. Rowan 8-106) and 201-7 dec (D. D. Taylor 69) drew with South Africans 77 (C. W. Grove 4-31) and 290-6 (J. E. Cheetham 116*, R. A. McLean 80).

30th Match: v Sussex (Hove)   Aug 11, 13, 14.
Sussex 213 (D. S. Sheppard 100, G. H. G. Doggart 60, C. N. McCarthy 8-36) and 15-0 drew with South Africans 314 (D. J. McGlew 80, G. M. Fullerton 65).

31st Match: v England (Oval)   Aug 16, 17, 18.
South Africa 202 (E. A. B. Rowan 55, J. C. Laker 4-64) and 154 (J. C. Laker 6-55) lost to England 194 (D. C. S. Compton 73, M. G. Melle 4-9) and 164-6 by 4 wkts.

32nd Match: v Hampshire (Southampton)   Aug 22, 23, 24.
Hampshire 180 (M. G. Melle 4-39) and 243-4 dec (N. H. Rogers 118) drew with South Africans 251 (D. J. McGlew 114*) and 151-7 (C. B. van Ryneveld 65).

33rd Match: v Middlesex (Lord's)   Aug 25, 27, 28.
South Africans 297 (G. M. Fullerton 89*) drew with Middlesex 136-2 (J. D. B. Robertson 70*).

34th Match: v Kent (Canterbury)   Aug 29, 30, 31.
Kent 163 (M. C. Cowdrey 71, C. B. van Ryneveld 5-53) drew with South Africans 201-4 (J. E. Cheetham 80*, G. M. Fullerton 52*).

35th Match: v An England XI (Hastings)   Sept 1, 3, 4.
An England XI 208-9 dec (D. C. S. Compton 84, C. N. McCarthy 4-31) drew with South Africans 285 (R. A. McLean 88, G. M. Fullerton 61, J. A. Young 6-106).

36th Match: v Minor Counties (Norwich)   Sept 5, 6.
Minor Counties 182 (M. G. Melle 6-51) and 113 (P. N. F. Mansell 5-24, H. J. Tayfield 4-26) lost to South Africans 318-8 dec (J. E. Cheetham 114*, E. A. B. Rowan 73).

37th Match: v T. N. Pearce's XI (Scarborough)   Sept 8, 10, 11.
T. N. Pearce's XI 101 (G. W. A. Chubb 4-16) and 248 (L. Hutton 91, M. G. Melle 6-71) beat South Africans 95 (T. L. Pritchard 4-38) and 245 (C. B. van Ryneveld 61, A. V. Bedser 5-44) by 9 runs.

38th Match: v Dutch Team (Haarlem)   Sept 15.
Dutch Team 55 (M. G. Melle 8-18) and 60 (P. N. F. Mansell 4-24, H. J. Tayfield 4-19) lost to South Africans 154 by an innings and 39 runs.

39th Match: v Dutch Team (Haarlem)   Sept 16.
South Africans 291 (E. A. B. Rowan 106, D. J. McGlew 106) beat Dutch Team 127 (C. B. van Ryneveld 4-22) by 164 runs.

---

only innings of substance on the whole tour. Eric Rowan had to shoulder the full responsibility for the batting, which too often forced him into a defensive role which was then followed by most of his colleagues.

The young batsmen McLean, Cheetham, van Ryneveld and McGlew all gained valuable experience during the tour and with the exception of van Ryneveld, looked better batsmen at the end, but that did not really help the cause of 1951.

The main hope of success, the fast bowling partnership of

Left Tufty Mann was the leading slow bowler of the South African parties of 1947 and 1951, although his form in 1951 was affected by the illness from which he was to die the following summer.

McCarthy and Melle, never materialised. Injury meant that Melle played in only about half the matches and McCarthy lost his value through lack of both length and direction. The spin attack of Athol Rowan and Mann did a little better, but Athol's war injury meant that he had to be treated with care and after a few weeks Tayfield was flown in to reinforce the side. Tayfield achieved only modest success, however, and did not play in the Tests. The accurate medium pace of Chubb saved the side from utter ruin. He took most wickets in both Tests and first-class matches and though the oldest tourist was the only one not to be injured. The fielding was good on the whole, but some vital chances were missed. Waite kept wicket well and made some runs.

The team made a profit of £17,500, a new record for South African touring teams.

1952: 5th Indians

The team, which flew from Bombay on 21 April, was V. S. Hazare (captain), H. R. Adhikari, N. R. Chowdhury, R. V. Divecha, D. K. Gaekwad, H. G. Gaekwad, Ghulam Ahmed, C. D. Gopinath, V. L. Manjrekar, M. K. Mantri, D. G. Phadkar, G. S. Ramchand, P. Roy, C. T. Sarwate, P. Sen, S. G. Shinde and P. R. Umrigar, with P. Gupta as manager. It was agreed that M. H. Mankad would be available to play depending on his League commitments. For different reasons the three senior Indian cricketers—Merchant, Amarnath and Mushtaq Ali—did not come to England, the selectors risking all on a relatively young and inexperienced side: only three, apart from Mankad, had come over in 1946.

The policy of youth proved disastrous, not because of poor bowling, strangely, but because of feeble batting. Of course

Mankad was missed and might have provided the team's backbone. As it was he played in three Tests only and no other games.

Hazare's batting seemed to be affected by the cares of captaincy and he never appeared the fluent run getter he was in India. Umrigar scored runs in the ordinary games but in the Tests was utterly at sea against Trueman. Adhikhari was fairly consistent, but neither he nor Phadkar achieved anything when faced with the England bowlers. Roy completely lost his confidence and Gopinath could not resist the cut. Manjrekar, of the younger element, looked very promising and Dattu Gaekwad also seemed to be a good player in the making.

Ghulam Ahmed bowled well and deserved his position as chief wicket-taker in both Tests and first-class matches. Divecha began moderately, but improved as the summer went on. Hazare and Ramchand were the leading all-rounders.

Neither wicketkeeper really impressed and though the ground fielding was good, catches were missed too often.

1952: 5th Indians

1st Match: v Indian Gymkhana (Osterley)   April 30, May 1.
Indians 455 (D. G. Phadkar 158, G. S. Ramchand 62, V. S. Hazare 60, M. H. Mankad 5-140) drew with Indian Gymkhana 147-7 (B. B. Nimbalkar 80).

2nd Match: v Worcestershire (Worcester)   May 3, 5, 6.
Worcestershire 101-6 drew with Indians did not bat.

3rd Match: v Surrey (Oval)   May 7, 8, 9.
Surrey 219 (L. B. Fishlock 57, J. F. Parker 52, G. S. Ramchand 5-20) and 188 (B. Constable 57, S. G. Shinde 4-26) beat Indians 158 (J. C. Laker 6-64) and 108 (J. C. Laker 4-55) by 141 runs.

4th Match: v Leicestershire (Leicester)   May 10, 12, 13.
Leicestershire 161 (G. A. Smithson 55) and 156-8 (Ghulam Ahmed 5-52) drew with Indians 202-9 dec (V. S. Hazare 57).

5th Match: v Cambridge University (Cambridge)   May 14, 15, 16.
Indians 285 (G. S. Ramchand 134, C. N. McCarthy 5-60) and 202-8 dec (P. R. Umrigar 61, M. K. Mantri 52, J. J. Warr 5-53) drew with Cambridge University 257 (P. B. H. May 92, D. S. Sheppard 59, R. V. Divecha 4-77) and 76-2.

6th Match: v M.C.C. (Lord's)   May 17, 19, 20.
M.C.C. 383-6 dec (T. W. Graveney 158, R. T. Simpson 101, Ghulam Ahmed 4-123) and 83-2 dec drew with Indians 255 (P. Roy 62, M. J. Hilton 4-36) and 188-3 (P. R. Umrigar 91, V. L. Manjrekar 67*).*

7th Match: v Oxford University (Oxford)   May 21, 22, 23.
Oxford University 227 (M. C. Cowdrey 92, Ghulam Ahmed 8-84) and 232 (A. L. Dowding 69, M. C. Cowdrey 54, Ghulam Ahmed 5-66) lost to Indians 398-3 dec (P. R. Umrigar 229, V. S. Hazare 161*) and 62-1 by 9 wkts.*

8th Match: v Essex (Ilford)   May 24, 26, 27.
Indians 195 (H. R. Adhikari 61, R. Smith 6-36) and 368-6 dec (D. G. Phadkar 86, V. L. Manjrekar 81, D. K. Gaekwad 75, P. R. Umrigar 74) drew with Essex 410 (D. J. Insole 116, T. C. Dodds 81, T. E. Bailey 67, V. S. Hazare 4-89) and 144-9 (H. G. Gaekwad 5-44).

9th Match: v Somerset (Taunton)   May 28, 29, 30.
Somerset 330 (J. Lawrence 103, V. S. Hazare 4-53) and 188 (F. L. Angell 64, S. S. Rogers 53, P. Roy 5-53) drew with Indians 238 (D. K. Gaekwad 83, J. Lawrence 4-89) and 118-8.*

10th Match: v Glamorgan (Cardiff)   May 31, June 2, 3.
Glamorgan 164 (P. B. Clift 58, W. G. A. Parkhouse 57, G. S. Ramchand 8-33) and 170 (H. G. Gaekwad 4-32, S. G. Shinde 4-57) drew with Indians 217 (P. R. Umrigar 55, V. L. Manjrekar 55, D. J. Shepherd 4-72) and 85-8.

11th Match: v England (Headingley)   June 5, 6, 7, 9.
India 293 (V. L. Manjrekar 133, V. S. Hazare 89, J. C. Laker 4-39) and 165 (D. G. Phadkar 64, V. S. Hazare 56, F. S. Trueman 4-27, R. O. Jenkins 4-50) lost to England 334 (T. W. Graveney 71, T. G. Evans 66, Ghulam Ahmed 5-100) and 128-3 (R. T. Simpson 51) by 7 wkts.

12th Match: v Ireland (Dublin)   June 13, 14.
Indians 304 (V. L. Manjrekar 88, P. R. Umrigar 62) beat Ireland 126 and 169 (J. S. Pollock 54, E. A. Ingram 54, S. G. Shinde 5-49) by an innings and 9 runs.

13th Match: v Ireland (Belfast)   June 16, 17.
Indians 289-8 dec (D. G. Phadkar 103, M. K. Mantri 78, S. S. Huey 4-83) drew with Ireland 150 (S. G. Shinde 5-35) and 68-6.

14th Match: v England (Lord's)   June 19, 20, 21, 23, 24.
India 235 (M. H. Mankad 72, V. S. Hazare 69*, F. S. Trueman 4-72) and 378 (M. H. Mankad 184, F. S. Trueman 4-110, J. C. Laker 4-102) lost to England 537 (L. Hutton 150, T. G. Evans 10, P. B. H. May 74, T. W. Graveney 73, R. T. Simpson 53, M. H. Mankad 5-196) and 79-2 by 8 wkts.

15th Match: v Combined Services (Gillingham)   June 25, 26.
Indians 225 (B. D. Wells 5-74) and 69-1 beat Combined Services 115 (S. G. Shinde 5-60) and 178 (V. S. Hazare 4-38) by 9 wkts.

16th Match: v Lancashire (Old Trafford)   June 28, 30, July 1.
Lancashire 363 (N. D. Howard 87, W. Place 85, A. Wharton 68, Ghulam Ahmed 4-76) and 68 (G. S. Ramchand 7-27) lost to Indians 427 (P. R. Umrigar 204, R. V. Divecha 61) and 5-0 by 10 wkts.

17th Match: v Durham (Sunderland)   July 2, 3.
Durham 302-6 dec (J. Keeler 135, A. Coxon 50) drew with Indians 156 (P. R. Umrigar 61, P. K. Roy 54, R. Aspinall 6-84, A. Coxon 4-32) and 101-3.

18th Match: v Nottinghamshire (Trent Bridge)   July 5, 7, 8.
Indians 436-4 dec (P. K. Roy 163, V. S. Hazare 96, D. K. Gaekwad 70) and 16-0 drew with Nottinghamshire 468 (C. J. Poole 222*, J. Hardstaff jun 54, S. G. Shinde 5-107).

19th Match: v Derbyshire (Chesterfield)   July 9, 10, 11.
Derbyshire 162 (N. R. Chowdhury 5-30) and 296 (A. Hamer 76, D. C. Morgan 65, G. L. Willatt 63, N. R. Chowdhury 4-83) drew with Indians 86 (H. L. Jackson 6-39) and 115-3.

20th Match: v Yorkshire (Bramall Lane)   July 12, 14, 15.
Yorkshire 192 (D. B. Close 71*, R. V. Divecha 5-81, D. G. Phadkar 4-69) and 298-4 (E. I. Lester 110*, H. Halliday 77, F. A. Lowson 69) drew with Indians 377-5 dec (P. R. Umrigar 137*, H. R. Adhikari 82, M. K. Mantri 80).

21st Match: v England (Old Trafford)   July 17, 18, 19.
England 347-9 dec (L. Hutton 104, T. G. Evans 71, P. B. H. May 69) beat India 58 (F. S. Trueman 8-31) and 82 (A. V. Bedser 5-27, G. A. R. Lock 4-36) by an innings and 207 runs.

22nd Match: v Commonwealth XI (Blackpool)   July 23, 24, 25.
Indians 362 (D. G. Phadkar 94, C. D. Gopinath 79, G. Goonesena 4-76) and 213-3 dec (D. K. Gaekwad 61, M. K. Mantri 55, H. G. Gaekwad 51*) drew with Commonwealth XI 215 (A. L. Dowding 54) and 254-6 (C. J. Barnett 114).

23rd Match: v Surrey (Oval)   July 26, 28, 29.
Surrey 71 (R. V. Divecha 6-29, G. S. Ramchand 4-23) and 319 (P. B. H. May 143, Ghulam Ahmed 4-50) lost to Indians 179 (P. J. Loader 5-63) and 214-4 (H. R. Adhikari 98*, D. G. Phadkar 50*) by 6 wkts.

24th Match: v Northamptonshire (Northampton)   July 30, 31, Aug 1.
Northamptonshire 365-7 dec (D. Brookes 156) and 107-1 (D. Brookes 51*) drew with Indians 309 (V. L. Manjrekar 83, H. R. Adhikari 73, P. R. Umrigar 59).

25th Match: v Glamorgan (Swansea)   Aug 2, 4, 5.
Glamorgan 204-9 dec (J. E. Pleass 75, R. V. Divecha 8-74) and 5-0 drew with Indians 306-9 dec (G. S. Ramchand 78, P. K. Sen 75*, V. L. Manjrekar 59, D. J. Shepherd 4-112).

26th Match: v Warwickshire (Edgbaston)   Aug 6, 7, 8.
Indians 172-2 dec (H. R. Adhikari 101*) drew with Warwickshire 96-2 (N. F. Horner 57)

27th Match: v Gloucestershire (Cheltenham)   Aug 9, 11, 12.
Gloucestershire 198 (G. M. Emmett 63, T. W. Graveney 56*, Ghulam Ahmed 4-47, D. G. Phadkar 4-58) and 47-7 dec lost to Indians 138 (H. R. Adhikari 80, B. D. Wells 4-67) and 108-4 by 6 wkts.

28th Match: v England (Oval)   Aug 14, 15, 16, 18, 19.
England 326-6 dec (D. S. Sheppard 119, L. Hutton 86, J. T. Ikin 53) drew with India 98 (A. V. Bedser 5-41, F. S. Trueman 5-48).

29th Match: v Sussex (Hove)   Aug 20, 21, 22.
Indians 186 (D. K. Gaekwad 87, D. J. Wood 5-34) and 210 (V. S. Hazare 52, N. I. Thomson 5-54) lost to Sussex 220 (G. S. Ramchand 6-67) and 177-4 (John G. Langridge 80) by 6 wkts.

30th Match: v Middlesex (Lord's)   Aug 23, 25, 26.
Indians 289 (V. L. Manjrekar 104, D. K. Gaekwad 62, A. E. Moss 4-26, J. A. Young 4-74) and 294-5 dec (P. Roy 131, P. R. Umrigar 86) drew with Middlesex 255 (J. D. B. Robertson 85, V. S. Hazare 7-50) and 289-5 (W. J. Edrich 129, J. D. B. Robertson 81, D. C. S. Compton 70).

31st Match: v Kent (Canterbury)   Aug 27, 28, 29.
Kent 217 (A. E. Fagg 76, A. H. Phebey 61) and 225 (M. C. Cowdrey 101, Ghulam Ahmed 4-45, D. G. Phadkar 4-51) drew with Indians 392 (P. R. Umrigar 204, C. T. Sarwate 57) and 45-4.

32nd Match: v Hampshire (Bournemouth)   Aug 30, Sept 1, 2.
Hampshire 256 (A. C. D. Ingleby-Mackenzie 91, E. D. R. Eagar 88, D. G. Phadkar 4-60) and 206-8 dec (A. W. H. Rayment 58, J. R. Gray 55) drew with Indians 357-7 dec (P. R. Umrigar 165*, D. K. Gaekwad 69) and 100-8 (D. Shackleton 6-41).

33rd Match: v An England XI (Hastings)   Sept 3, 4, 5.
Indians 222 (D. K. Gaekwad 75, V. S. Hazare 67, F. Ridgway 6-50) and 241-7 dec (D. G. Phadkar 66, V. L. Manjrekar 60, M. K. Mantri 54) drew with An England XI 257-6 dec (D. C. S. Compton 132, R. T. Spooner 51) and 194-7 (Ghulam Ahmed 4-76).

34th Match: v Minor Counties (Norwich)   Sept 6, 8.
Indians 290 (V. L. Manjrekar 101, V. S. Hazare 63) and 168-3 (P. Roy 88, V. L. Manjrekar 55) drew with Minor Counties 200.*

35th Match: v T. N. Pearce's XI (Scarborough)   Sept 10, 11, 12.
Indians 258 (V. S. Hazare 72, P. Roy 51, T. E. Bailey 8-41) drew with T. N. Pearce's XI 68 (D. G. Phadkar 7-26) and 116-7 (G. S. Ramchand 4-54).

The Indians lost the Test series three matches to nil and won only four first-class games. The most satisfactory element of the visit was the profit of £11,000.

1952: 5th Indians

Batting Averages

	M	I	NO	R	HS	Avge	100	c/s
M. H. Mankad	3	5	0	271	184	54.20	1	0
P. R. Umrigar	25	41	6	1688	229*	48.22	5	22
V. L. Manjrekar	22	33	6	1059	133	39.22	2	8
H. R. Adhikari	22	29	3	879	101*	33.80	1	7
V. S. Hazare	27	40	5	1077	161*	30.77	1	18
D. K. Gaekwad	19	34	3	852	87	27.48	0	5
G. S. Ramchand	22	32	6	644	134	24.76	1	20
D. G. Phadkar	22	32	4	689	94	24.60	0	19
M. K. Mantri	15	27	3	550	80	22.91	0	30/9
P. Roy	23	38	2	788	163	21.88	2	6
R. V. Divecha	16	17	3	294	61	21.00	0	7
C. D. Gopinath	17	19	2	356	79	20.94	0	9
P. Sen	14	13	3	195	75*	19.50	0	21/3
S. G. Shinde	17	18	8	165	30*	16.50	0	7
H. G. Gaekwad	9	15	2	182	51*	14.00	0	4
C. T. Sarwate	14	15	1	146	57	10.42	0	4
Ghulam Ahmed	21	18	7	107	30	9.72	0	7
N. R. Chowdhury	10	10	3	21	9*	3.00	0	2

Bowling Averages

	O	M	R	W	Avge	BB	5i
P. Roy	29.2	5	82	5	16.40	5-53	1
Ghulam Ahmed	767.5	233	1754	80	21.92	8-84	4
V. S. Hazare	486.5	156	1061	44	24.11	7-50	1
G. S. Ramchand	665.5	173	1655	64	25.85	8-33	4
R. V. Divecha	484	120	1294	50	25.88	8-74	3
D. G. Phadkar	639	191	1427	53	26.92	7-26	1
H. G. Gaekwad	187.1	50	464	17	27.29	5-44	1
N. R. Chowdhury	249.1	52	744	24	31.00	5-30	1
S. G. Shinde	443.3	91	1371	39	35.15	5-107	1
C. T. Sarwate	159.1	40	459	12	38.25	3-47	0
M. H. Mankad	173	68	386	9	42.88	5-196	1
P. R. Umrigar	90	24	214	4	53.50	2-46	0

Also bowled: D. K. Gaekwad 1-0-6-0; C. D. Gopinath 1-0-1-0.

1953: 21st Australians

After some engine problems, the s.s. *Strathaird* left Fremantle on 23 March with the 1953 Australians aboard. The team was A. L. Hassett (captain), R. N. Harvey, J. C. Hill, W. A. Johnston, C. C. McDonald and D. T. Ring, all of Victoria; A. R. Morris, R. Benaud, I. D. Craig, A. K. Davidson, J. H. de Courcy, R. R. Lindwall and K. R. Miller of New South Wales; R. G. Archer and D. Tallon of Queensland; G. B. Hole and G. R. A. Langley of South Australia, with G. A. Davies as manager. Iverson, the noted spin bowler of 1950-51, had retired and instead of I. W. Johnson the selectors chose Hill; the controversial Barnes had put himself out of court by press statements and came to England in 1953 as a reporter.

Even allowing for the rather damp summer, the contrast in the Test batting figures for the 1953 and 1948 tours is astonishing. In 1953 no one averaged 40 and there were only three–Hassett,

Above *Keith Miller is trapped lbw by Trevor Bailey on the first day of the Fifth Test at the Oval. The great Australian all-rounder had made a century in the Lord's Test.*

Left *Ray Lindwall was the first great fast bowler to emerge after the Second World War. He came to England three times, in 1948, 1953 and 1956, being very effective in the first two tours, taking 86 and 85 wickets respectively.*

Harvey and Morris in the 30s—in 1948 seven of the Test batsmen had averages above 40. In addition the three with averages above 30 in 1953 were all members of the 1948 side. However, the results, on paper at least, were not quite so depressing: 16 first-class wins and only one loss, in the only one of the five Tests to be brought to a definite conclusion.

The problems began at the top: McDonald, Morris's opening partner, failed completely and Morris himself struggled against Bedser while Hole, de Courcy, Davidson and Benaud could hardly make a Test run between them.

Lindwall remained a splendid bowler and took 26 wickets in the Tests; Johnston was injured at East Molesey before the real cricket began and this injury hampered him; Miller was forced to bowl too much, which affected his batting after the first few matches. In the damp conditions the tourists lacked a top-class spinner—ironically the most prolific bowler in county cricket in 1953 was the Australian leg-spinner, Dooland, with Tribe not far behind. Of the medium-pace bowlers Archer and Davidson looked very promising. The most unfortunate player was perhaps Craig: only 17 years old and given a great write-up when he arrived in England he could do nothing right all summer.

The fielding was quite outstanding, in the best Australian tradition, and Langley, who superseded Tallon, was sound behind the stumps.

The public flocked to both Test and county matches and the tourists went away with a profit of over £100,000.

1953: 21st Australians

1st Match: v XIII of East Molesey (East Molesey) April 26.
XIII of East Molesey 244-11 dec (R. Smith 69, D. J. Insole 52, D. T. Ring 4-95) lost to Australian XIII 314-9 (A. R. Morris 103, G. B. Hole 67, G. E. Tribe 6-112) by 5 wkts.

2nd Match: v Worcestershire (Worcester) April 29, 30, May 1.
Worcestershire 333-7 dec (D. Kenyon 122, R. E. Bird 76, R. G. Broadbent 52) drew with Australians 542-7 dec (K. R. Miller 220*, G. B. Hole 112, R. G. Archer 108, J. P. Whitehead 5-89).

3rd Match: v Leicestershire (Leicester) May 2, 4.
Australians 443-8 dec (R. N. Harvey 202*, A. K. Davidson 63) beat Leicestershire 109 (D. T. Ring 4-57) and 180 (C. H. Palmer 62*, D. T. Ring 5-66, J. C. Hill 4-46) by an innings and 154 runs.

4th Match: v Yorkshire (Bradford) May 6, 7, 8.
Australians 453-6 dec (K. R. Miller 159*, R. Benaud 97, A. R. Morris 57, J. H. de Courcy 53) beat Yorkshire 145 (N. W. D. Yardley 56, R. Benaud 7-46) and 214 (L. Hutton 65, N. W. D. Yardley 56*, J. C. Hill 4-61) by an innings and 94 runs.

5th Match: v Surrey (Oval) May 9, 11.
Surrey 58 (R. G. Archer 6-26) and 122 (D. G. W. Fletcher 61, R. G. Archer 5-35) lost to Australians 256 (R. N. Harvey 66, A. V. Bedser 4-60) by an innings and 76 runs.

6th Match: v Cambridge University (Cambridge) May 13, 14.
Australians 383 (A. K. Davidson 71, R. G. Archer 63*, R. G. Marlar 5-139, T. Hare 4-73) beat Cambridge University 130 (D. T. Ring 5-19) and 147 (R. G. Archer 4-31, D. T. Ring 4-57) by innings and 106 runs.

7th Match: v M.C.C. (Lord's) May 16, 18, 19.
M.C.C. 80 (D. T. Ring 5-36) and 196 (T. E. Bailey 64*, K. R. Miller 4-47) drew with Australians 179 (R. Tattersall 4-68) and 13-2.

8th Match: v Oxford University (Oxford) May 20, 21.
Oxford University 70 and 174 (J. P. Fellows-Smith 50) lost to Australians 330 (J. H. de Courcy 142, D. K. Fasken 5-108) by an innings and 86 runs.

9th Match: v Minor Counties (Stoke-on-Trent) May 23, 25.
Australians 289 (R. N. Harvey 109, F. Taylor 5-71) beat Minor Counties 56 (R. R. Lindwall 7-20) and 62 (R. Benaud 5-13, R. G. Archer 4-25) by an innings and 171 runs.

10th Match: v Lancashire (Old Trafford) May 27, 28, 29.
Australians 298 (R. N. Harvey 103, M. J. Hilton 4-117) drew with Lancashire 232-9 dec (N. D. Howard 78*, A. Wharton 57, R. R. Lindwall 4-41).

11th Match: v Nottinghamshire (Trent Bridge) May 30, June 1.
Nottinghamshire 208 (B. Dooland 69, R. T. Simpson 65, J. C. Hill 5-62) drew with Australians 290-6 (G. B. Hole 69, A. L. Hassett 62).

12th Match: v Sussex (Hove) June 3, 4, 5.
Australians 325 (C. C. McDonald 106, R. N. Harvey 82, A. E. James 5-96) and 259-1 dec (R. B. Harvey 137*, A. L. Hassett 108*) drew with Sussex 218 (John G. Langridge 74, D. S. Sheppard 56, J. C. Hill 4-40, W. A. Johnston 4-65) and 190-9 (J. C. Hill 4-38).

13th Match: v Hampshire (Southampton) June 6, 8.
Australians 268 (R. N. Harvey 109, A. R. Morris 55, R. E. Marshall 4-69) and 169-5 dec (J. H. de Courcy 54*, A. R. Morris 50) beat Hampshire 131 (W. A. Johnston 5-75) and 148 (R. E. Marshall 71, W. A. Johnston 4-21, R. Benaud 4-38) by 158 runs.

14th Match: v England (Trent Bridge) June 11, 12, 13, 15, 16.
Australia 249 (A. L. Hassett 115, A. R. Morris 67, A. V. Bedser 7-55) and 123 (A. R. Morris 60, A. V. Bedser 7-44) drew with England 144 (R. R. Lindwall 5-57) and 120-1 (L. Hutton 60*).

15th Match: v Derbyshire (Chesterfield) June 17, 18, 19.
Australians 197 (R. Benaud 70, C. Gladwin 5-84) and 146 (G. B. Hole 73, C. C. McDonald 51, E. Smith 5-36, D. C. Morgan 4-59) drew with Derbyshire 69 (D. T. Ring 4-19) and 17-1.

16th Match: v Yorkshire (Bramall Lane) June 20, 22, 23.
Yorkshire 377 (L. Hutton 67, W. Watson 61, W. H. H. Sutcliffe 57, R. R. Lindwall 4-54) and 220-3 (L. Hutton 84, J. V. Wilson 56*) drew with Australians 323 (K. R. Miller 86, G. B. Hole 71, R. N. Harvey 69, J. H. Wardle 5-117).

17th Match: v England (Lord's) June 25, 26, 27, 29, 30.
Australia 346 (A. L. Hassett 104, A. K. Davidson 76, R. N. Harvey 59, A. V. Bedser 5-105, J. H. Wardle 4-77) and 368 (K. R. Miller 109, A. R. Morris 89, R. R. Lindwall 50, F. R. Brown 4-82) drew with England 372 (L. Hutton 145, T. W. Graveney 78, D. C. S. Compton 57, R. R. Lindwall 5-66) and 282-7 (W. Watson 109, T. E. Bailey 71).

18th Match: v Gloucestershire (Bristol) July 1, 2, 3.
Gloucestershire 137 (T. W. Graveney 52, R. R. Lindwall 4-18) and 297 (G. M. Emmett 141) lost to Australians 402-9 dec (R. N. Harvey 141, J. H. de Courcy 97, J. B. Mortimore 4-104) and 33-1.

19th Match: v Northamptonshire (Northampton) July 4, 6.
Australians 323 (R. N. Harvey 118, A. R. Morris 80, R. G. Archer 58, G. E. Tribe 5-97) beat Northamptonshire 141 (R. G. Archer 7-56) and 120 (D. T. Ring 5-46) by an innings and 62 runs.

20th Match: v England (Old Trafford) July 9, 10, 11, 13, 14.
Australia 318 (R. N. Harvey 122, G. B. Hole 66, A. V. Bedser 5-115) and 35-8 (J. H. Wardle 4-7) drew with England 276 (L. Hutton 66).

21st Match: v Dutch XI (The Hague) July 16.
Australians 279 (A. R. Morris 70, C. C. McDonald 66, E. Vriens 4-85) beat Dutch XI 122 by 157 runs.

22nd Match: v Middlesex (Lord's) July 18, 20, 21.
Middlesex 150 (R. R. Lindwall 4-40) and 112-4 (H. P. Sharp 51) drew with Australians 416 (J. H. de Courcy 74, K. R. Miller 71, R. G. Archer 58*, R. Benaud 52, A. E. Moss 4-103).

23rd Match: v England (Headingley) July 23, 24, 25, 27, 28.
England 167 (T. W. Graveney 55, R. R. Lindwall 5-54) and 275 (W. J. Edrich 64, D. C. S. Compton 61, K. R. Miller 4-63) drew with Australia 266 (R. N. Harvey 71, G. B. Hole 53, A. V. Bedser 6-95) and 147-4.

24th Match: v Surrey (Oval) July 29, 30, 31.
Surrey 209-8 dec (D. G. W. Fletcher 78, P. B. H. May 56, W. A. Johnston 4-51) drew with Australians 327-9 (R. N. Harvey 113, A. R. Morris 67, A. L. Hassett 67).

25th Match: v Glamorgan (Swansea) Aug 1, 3, 4.
Glamorgan 201 (A. J. Watkins 76, W. A. Johnston 6-63) and 188-7 (W. Wooller 71*, B. L. Muncer 56) drew with Australians 386 (R. N. Harvey 180, C. C. McDonald 56, I. D. Craig 50, J. E. McConnon 7-165).

26th Match: v Warwickshire (Edgbaston) Aug 5, 6, 7.
Warwickshire 270-8 dec (F. C. Gardner 110, N. F. Horner 61, R. R. Lindwall 4-47) and 76-3 dec drew with Australians 181 (A. L. Hassett 60, W. E. Hollies 5-45) and 53-5.

27th Match: v Lancashire (Old Trafford) Aug 8, 10, 11.
Australians 372 (A. K. Davidson 95, D. T. Ring 88, A. R. Morris 64, R. Tattersall 5-80) and 106-3 beat Lancashire 184 and 292 (K. J. Grieves 80, G. A. Edrich 59, J. T. Ikin 56) by 7 wkts.

28th Match: v Essex (Southend) Aug 12, 13.
Australians 477-7 dec (J. H. de Courcy 164, G. B. Hole 89, R. Benaud 67, A. K. Davidson 58) beat Essex 129 (D. T. Ring 5-47) and 136 (W. A. Johnston 6-39) by an innings and 212 runs.

29th Match: v England (Oval) Aug 15, 17, 18, 19.
Australia 275 (R. R. Lindwall 62, A. L. Hassett 53, F. S. Trueman 4-86) and 162 (G. A. R. Lock 5-45, J. C. Laker 4-75) lost to England 306 (L. Hutton 82, T. E. Bailey 64, R. R. Lindwall 4-70) and 132-2 (W. J. Edrich 55*) by 8 wkts.

30th Match: v Somerset (Taunton) Aug 22, 24, 25.
Australians 486 (A. L. Hassett 148, A. K. Davidson 104*, J. H. de Courcy 53) drew with Somerset 187 (R. Smith 77*, D. T. Ring 4-88) and 156-2 (P. B. Wight 109*).

31st Match: v Gentlemen (Lord's) Aug 26, 27, 28.
Gentlemen 157 (M. C. Cowdrey 50, R. Benaud 4-20) and 249 (W. J. Edrich 75, M. C. Cowdrey 57, P. B. H. May 50, R. R. Lindwall 5-68) lost to Australians 154 (R. G. Marlar 5-41) and 253-2 (A. R. Morris 126*, K. R. Miller 67) by 8 wkts.

32nd Match: v Kent (Canterbury) Aug 29, 31, Sept 1.
Kent 181 (A. H. Phebey 85, W. A. Johnston 5-35) and 108 (W. A. Johnston 6-38) lost to Australians 465-8 dec (D. Tallon 83*, G. B. Hole 78, K. R. Miller 68, J. C. Hill 51*) by an innings and 176 runs.

33rd Match: v South of England (Hastings) Sept 2, 3, 4.
South of England 198 (D. C. S. Compton 81, W. A. Johnston 6-77) and 203 (P. E. Richardson 90, J. C. Hill 4-76) lost to Australians 564-9 dec (C. C. McDonald 125, J. H. de Courcy 118, A. L. Hassett 106, A. K. Davidson 85*) by an innings and 163 runs.

34th Match: v Combined Services (Kingston) Sept 5, 7.
Australians 592-4 dec (K. R. Miller 262*, J. H. de Courcy 204, I. D. Craig 71*) beat Combined Services 161 and 170 (A. C. D. Ingleby-Mackenzie 66, J. C. Hill 6-34) by an innings and 261 runs.

35th Match: v T. N. Pearce's XI (Scarborough) Sept 9, 10, 11.
T. N. Pearce's XI 320 (R. T. Simpson 86, J. C. Hill 4-65) and 316-8 dec (L. Hutton 102, T. W. Graveney 66) lost to Australians 317 (A. L. Hassett 74, G. B. Hole 52, A. V. Bedser 4-66) and 325-8 (R. Benaud 135, A. R. Morris 70, A. V. Bedser 5-86) by 2 wkts.

36th Match: v Scotland (Paisley) Sept 15, 16.
Australians 377-9 dec (A. R. Morris 101, R. Benaud 89, G. B. Hole 56) drew with Scotland 100-3 (R. H. E. Chisholm 55).

37th Match: v Scotland (Raeburn Place, Edinburgh) Sept 18, 19.
Scotland 101 (R. R. Lindwall 4-31) and 88-2 drew with Australians 308 (R. G. Archer 63, A. K. Davidson 60, R. J. Nichol 5-99).

1953: 21st Australians

Batting Averages

	M	I	NO	R	HS	Avge	100	c/s
W. A. Johnston	16	17	16	102	28*	102.00	0	6
R. N. Harvey	25	35	4	2040	202*	65.80	10	13
K. R. Miller	24	31	3	1433	262*	51.17	4	8
A. L. Hassett	21	30	2	1236	148	44.14	5	8
J. H. de Courcy	24	31	2	1214	204	41.86	4	13
A. K. Davidson	23	30	7	944	104*	41.04	1	27
A. R. Morris	25	37	3	1302	126*	38.29	1	9
R. G. Archer	20	25	8	627	108	36.88	1	16
G. B. Hole	24	33	0	1118	112	33.87	1	22
C. C. McDonald	19	24	1	717	125	31.17	2	6
R. Benaud	22	28	1	748	135	27.70	1	18
J. C. Hill	22	19	8	220	51*	20.00	0	17
G. R. A. Langley	18	19	3	273	46	17.06	0	35/12
R. R. Lindwall	23	25	1	400	62	16.66	0	12
I. D. Craig	23	27	1	429	71*	16.50	0	18
D. T. Ring	19	20	4	252	88	15.75	0	10
D. Tallon	15	16	2	169	83*	12.07	0	20/6

Bowling Averages

	O	M	R	W	Avge	BB	5i
R. N. Harvey	22	7	43	4	10.75	3-9	0
R. R. Lindwall	639.1	178	1394	85	16.40	7-20	5
R. G. Archer	395.1	104	955	57	16.75	7-56	3
D. T. Ring	541.2	162	1353	68	19.89	5-19	5
W. A. Johnston	647	206	1541	75	20.54	6-38	6
A. K. Davidson	507	153	1048	50	20.96	3-49	0
J. C. Hill	615	223	1322	63	20.98	6-34	2
R. Benaud	444	103	1273	57	22.33	7-46	2
K. R. Miller	492.2	161	1013	45	22.51	4-47	0
A. L. Hassett	22	2	76	3	25.33	2-24	0
A. R. Morris	6.5	0	30	1	30.00	1-5	0
G. B. Hole	103	39	217	4	54.25	2-3	0

Also bowled: I. D. Craig 4-0-23-0; J. H. de Courcy 4-0-28-0; D. Tallon 7-3-28-0.

A. H. Kardar, skipper of the first official Pakistan tour of England in 1954. The tourists greatly advanced the cause of Pakistani cricket by winning the final Test, so squaring the series. Kardar previously toured with India under the name Abdul Hafeez.

1953: 1st Pakistani Eaglets

The Pakistani Eaglets visited England in 1953 mainly to blood young players for the proposed full Pakistan tour of the following summer. No details of the Eaglets tour have appeared in print, even in the English newspapers and the details of only one match–against the R.A.F. at Kingston, a two-day game which they lost–have been unearthed. The Eaglets team in that match was M. D. Aslam, Khalid Ibadulla, Nasir Ali, M. E. Z. Ghazali, Ikram Elahi, Fazal Mahmood, Zulfiqar Ahmed, Syed Ahmed, Yusuf Jafar, Ismail Gul with A. R. Gover. Most of the side were coached by Gover at his cricket school and matches were presumably confined to opponents in the London area and Home Counties. If any reader can provide further details they would be much appreciated.

1954: 1st Pakistanis

The team which represented Pakistan on this first official tour to England was A. H. Kardar (captain), Wazir Mohammad, Hanif Mohammad, Maqsood Ahmed, Waqar Hassan, Alim-ud-Din, Imtiaz Ahmed, M. E. Z. Ghazali, Mohammad Aslam, Fazal Mahmood, Ikram Elahi, Shuja-ud-Din, Khalid Wazir, Shakoor Ahmed, Khalid Hassan, Zulfiqar Ahmed, Mahmood Hussain and Khan Mohammad, with Fida Hussain as manager and Salah-ud-Din as his assistant.

A. H. Kardar had been a member of the 1946 Indian side, playing under the name of Abdul Hafeez; the remainder of the team were virtually unknown to the English public, though about a dozen of them had been to England for cricket coaching in the previous few years. Khan Mohammad was engaged in 1954 in the Lancashire League and not available for all matches.

The side's results were as good as most critics predicted, except that the team beat England in the last Test at the Oval. This came as a tremendous boost to Pakistani cricket and quite upset English

1954: 1st Pakistanis

Batting Averages

	M	I	NO	R	HS	Avge	100	c/s
Wazir Mohammad	16	22	6	628	87	39.25	0	3
Hanif Mohammad	28	48	4	1623	142*	36.88	2	9/2
Maqsood Ahmed	26	41	3	1314	133	34.57	2	14
Waqar Hassan	27	42	3	1263	123	32.38	1	9
Alim-ud-Din	20	38	3	1083	142	30.94	2	11
Imtiaz Ahmed	28	45	7	1105	105	29.07	1	65/21
A. H. Kardar	24	34	6	802	139	28.64	1	17
M. E. Z. Ghazali	19	26	5	601	64*	28.61	0	6
Mohammad Aslam	12	19	4	421	63	28.06	0	2
Fazal Mahmood	16	17	3	286	67	20.42	0	4
Shuja-ud-Din	22	28	9	366	135	19.26	1	12
Ikram Elahi	10	12	2	175	55	17.50	0	3
Khalid Wazir	16	20	5	253	53	16.86	0	10
Shakoor Ahmed	9	13	2	154	39	14.00	0	14/1
Khalid Hassan	14	11	5	76	30	12.66	0	1
Zulfiqar Ahmed	17	21	4	210	34	12.35	0	4
Mahmood Hussain	21	19	3	149	34	9.31	0	6
Khan Mohammad	5	6	2	31	13*	7.75	0	3

Bowling Averages

	O	M	R	W	Avge	BB	5i
Fazal Mahmood	665.3	246	1350	77	17.53	8-66	7
Zulfiqar Ahmed	500.2	128	1184	64	18.50	7-69	7
Mohammad Aslam	41.4	7	121	6	20.16	2-23	0
Mahmood Hussain	573.4	132	1534	72	21.30	7-61	5
Ikram Elahi	82.5	15	232	9	25.77	3-62	0
Alim-ud-Din	6.3	1	26	1	26.00	1-3	0
Khan Mohammad	161.2	23	550	20	27.50	5-61	1
Shuja-ud-Din	731	198	1933	67	28.85	5-26	2
M. E. Z. Ghazali	284.2	70	674	17	39.64	4-55	0
Khalid Hassan	273	50	913	23	39.69	3-27	0
Maqsood Ahmed	315.3	65	879	20	43.95	2-28	0
Waqar Hassan	15	3	45	1	45.00	1-9	0
Hanif Mohammad	21	1	95	2	47.50	1-15	0
A. H. Kardar	199.2	49	549	10	54.90	3-28	0
Khalid Wazir	192	47	564	9	62.66	3-82	0

Also bowled: Imtiaz Ahmed 7-0-37-0; Wazir Mohammad 5-2-5-0.

1954: 1st Pakistanis

1st Match: v Indian Gymkhana (Osterley) May 4.
Pakistanis 100-3 drew with Indian Gymkhana 66-4.

2nd Match: v Worcestershire (Worcester) May 8, 10, 11.
Pakistanis 428 (Alim-ud-Din 142, Maqsood Ahmed 111, Fazal Mahmood 67, C. W. Grove 5-88) and 37-2 beat Worcestershire 218 (P. E. Richardson 81, Fazal Mahmood 4-54) and 244 (G. Dews 70, D. Kenyon 66, Fazal Mahmood 7-48) by 8 wkts.

3rd Match: v Cambridge University (Cambridge) May 12, 13, 14.
Cambridge University 310 (D. R. W. Silk 61, M. H. Busby 57, Mahmood Hussain 4-68) and 207-5 dec (A. B. D. Parsons 66) drew with Pakistanis 311-7 dec (Fazal Mahmood 65*, Ikram Elahi 55, C. S. Smith 5-102) and 168-0 (Alim-ud-Din 100*, Hanif Mohammad 58*).

4th Match: v Leicestershire (Leicester) May 15, 17, 18.
Pakistanis 199 (Maqsood Ahmed 71, Hanif Mohammad 51, J. E. Walsh 5-70) and 321-7 dec (Maqsood Ahmed 133, Hanif Mohammad 89) drew with Leicestershire 389-8 dec (M. Tompkin 186, M. R. Hallam 61, G. A. Smithson 52, Shuja-ud-Din 5-137).

5th Match: v Oxford University (Oxford) May 19, 20, 21.
Oxford University 253 (D. K. Fasken 61, M. J. K. Smith 53, Fazal Mahmood 5-54, Khan Mohammad 4-93) and 169 (Shuja-ud-Din 4-45) lost to Pakistanis 392 (Maqsood Ahmed 79, A. H. Kardar 79, Mohammad Aslam 63) and 34-1 by 9 wkts.

6th Match: v M.C.C. (Lord's) May 22, 24, 25.
M.C.C. 307-7 dec (R. T. Simpson 126) and 210-6 dec (P. B. H. May 61, M. C. Cowdrey 60*) drew with Pakistanis 310-4 dec (Imtiaz Ahmed 95, Maqsood Ahmed 94, Alim-ud-Din 61) and 85-6.

7th Match: v Sussex (Hove) May 26, 27, 28.
Sussex 271 (G. H. G. Doggart 101, Zulfiqar Ahmed 5-81) and 171-0 (John G. Langridge 85*, D. V. Smith 78*) drew with Pakistanis 279 (A. H. Kardar 99*, Alim-ud-Din 51).

8th Match: v Hampshire (Portsmouth) May 29, 31, June 1.
Hampshire 185 (Fazal Mahmood 5-68) and 238-6 dec (H. M. Barnard 101*) drew with Pakistanis 163 (V. H. Cannings 4-33) and 86-4.

9th Match: v Devon (Torquay) June 2, 3.
Pakistanis 396-7 dec (Waqar Hassan 137, Hanif Mohammad 63, Zulfiqar Ahmed 61, Shakoor Ahmed 51, K. C. Kinnersley 4-87) drew with Devon 177 (C. B. R. Fetherstonhaugh 52) and 160-9 (Shuja-ud-Din 4-42).*

10th Match: v Glamorgan (Cardiff) June 5, 7, 8.
Pakistanis 277 (Maqsood Ahmed 75, Hanif Mohammad 58, W. Wooler 5-62) and 137-5 dec (Waqar Hassan 55, J. E. McConnon 4-29) drew with Glamorgan 204 and 28-3.

11th Match: v England (Lord's) June 10, 11, 12, 14, 15.
Pakistan 87 (J. B. Statham 4-18, J. H. Wardle 4-33) and 121-3 (Waqar Hassan 53) drew with England 117-9 dec (Khan Mohammad 5-61, Fazal Mahmood 4-54).

12th Match: v Scotland (Edinburgh) June 16, 17, 18.
Scotland 353-7 dec (W. Nichol 93, J. Aitchison 61) and 51 (Mahmood Hussain 6-17) lost to Pakistanis 295 (Waqar Hassan 72, W. Nichol 4-46, W. A. Edward 4-59) and 114-0 (Maqsood Ahmed 55*, Alim-ud-Din 53*) by 10 wkts.

13th Match: v Nottinghamshire (Trent Bridge) June 19, 21, 22.
Pakistanis 373-6 (Imtiaz Ahmed 81, M. E. Z. Ghazali 64*, A. H. Kardar 57, Hanif Mohammad 55, A. K. Walker 4-91) and 57-2 beat Nottinghamshire 155 (A. K. Walker 61, Fazal Mahmood 8-66) and 274 (F. W. Stocks 95, J. K. Kelly 51, Mahmood Hussain 5-71) by 8 wkts.

14th Match: v Combined Services (Catterick) June 23, 24, 25.
Pakistanis 267 (Hanif Mohammad 87, M. E. Z. Ghazali 58, Mohammad Aslam 50, C. T. Spencer 4-51) and 232-6 dec (Hanif Mohammad 70, P. J. Sainsbury 4-37) drew with Combined Services 319-6 dec (G. G. Tordoff 156*, J. T. Murray 71) and 78-2.

15th Match: v Yorkshire (Bramall Lane) June 26, 28, 29.
Yorkshire 433-9 dec (D. B. Close 123*, F. A. Lowson 70, J. H. Wardle 72) and 124-3 beat Pakistanis 199 (Waqar Hassan 58, D. B. Close 4-54) and 356 (A. H. Kardar 139, Waqar Hassan 75, Mohammad Aslam 57*) by 7 wkts.

16th Match: v England (Trent Bridge) July 1, 2, 3, 5.
Pakistan 157 (R. Appleyard 5-51) and 272 (Maqsood Ahmed 69, Hanif Mohammad 51) lost to England 558-6 dec (D. C. S. Compton 278, R. T. Simpson 101, T. W. Graveney 84) by an innings and 129 runs.

17th Match: v Derbyshire (Derby) July 7, 8, 9.
Pakistanis 317 (Hanif Mohammad 54, Waqar Hassan 53, Khalid Wazir 53, D. C. Morgan 4-53, R. Carter 4-82) and 124-6 dec (D. C. Morgan 5-57) drew with Derbyshire 176 (Zulfiqar Ahmed 5-53) and 191-5 (A. C. Revill 101*).

18th Match: v Lancashire (Old Trafford) July 10, 12, 13.
Lancashire 324 (G. A. Edrich 134, J. T. Ikin 53, A. Wharton 50, Mahmood Hussain 5-84, Shuja-ud-Din 4-105) and 98 (Shuja-ud-Din 5-26, Zulfiqar Ahmed 4-43) beat Lancashire 219 (Imtiaz Ahmed 87, J. B. Statham 5-52) and 206-4 (Waqar Hassan 60, Hanif Mohammad 57) by 6 wkts.

19th Match: v Northamptonshire (Northampton) July 14, 15, 16.
Northamptonshire 359-6 dec (D. W. Barrick 84*, A. P. Arnold 79, L. Livingston 75, G. E. Tribe 78) and 80-3 drew with Pakistanis 368 (Wazir Mohammad 69, Waqar Hassan 53).

20th Match: v Surrey (Oval) July 17, 19, 20.
Pakistanis 365-6 dec (Waqar Hassan 123, Wazir Mohammad 87) drew with Surrey 329-6 (M. J. Stewart 109, K. F. Barrington 102).

21st Match: v England (Old Trafford) July 22, 23, 24, 26, 27.
England 359-8 dec (D. C. S. Compton 93, T. W. Graveney 65, J. H. Wardle 54, Fazal Mahmood 4-107) drew with Pakistanis 90 (J. H. Wardle 4-19) and 25-4.

22nd Match: v Somerset (Taunton) July 28, 29, 30.
Pakistanis 287-9 dec (Hanif Mohammad 140, Wazir Mohammad 76*, M. F. Tremlett 4-99) and 263-6 dec (Shuja-ud-Din 135, A. H. Kardar 71, Yawar Saeed 4-54) drew with Somerset 255 (F. L. Angell 114, Fazal Mahmood 4-67) and 175-3 (B. G. Brocklehurst 89).

23rd Match: v Glamorgan (Swansea) July 31, Aug 2, 3.
Pakistanis 225 (Waqar Hassan 66, J. E. McConnon 4-52) and 10-1 drew with Glamorgan 202 (Fazal Mahmood 6-55).

24th Match: v Warwickshire (Edgbaston) Aug 4, 5, 6.
Warwickshire 170 (Zulfiqar Ahmed 6-49, Shuja-ud-Din 4-73) and 91-6 (Zulfiqar Ahmed 6-47) drew with Pakistanis 165 (W. E. Hollies 5-79).

25th Match: v Gloucestershire (Cheltenham) Aug 7, 9, 10.
Gloucestershire 143-9 dec (T. W. Graveney 50, Mahmood Hussain 6-50) and 42-2 drew with Pakistanis 176 (B. D. Wells 4-56).

26th Match: v England (Oval) Aug 12, 13, 14, 16, 17.
Pakistan 133 (F. H. Tyson 4-35) and 164 (J. H. Wardle 7-56) beat England 133 (D. C. S. Compton 53, Fazal Mahmood 5-53, Mahmood Hussain 4-58) and 143 (P. B. H. May 53, Fazal Mahmood 6-46) by 24 runs.

27th Match: v Canada (Lord's) Aug 18, 19.
Canada 87 (Zulfiqar Ahmed 4-25) and 82 (Zulfiqar Ahmed 5-14) lost to Pakistan 236 (M. E. Z. Ghazali 62, Wazir Mohammad 59) by an innings and 67 runs.

28th Match: v Essex (Southend) Aug 21, 23, 24.
Pakistanis 241 (Hanif Mohammad 142, T. E. Bailey 6-82) and 19-1 drew with Essex 287-7 dec (D. J. Insole 89, T. E. Bailey 52*).

29th Match: v Kent (Canterbury) Aug 25, 26, 27.
Kent 172 (Zulfiqar Ahmed 6-69) and 137 (Zulfiqar Ahmed 5-45, M. E. Z. Ghazali 4-55) lost to Pakistanis 193 (Wazir Mohammad 52, J. C. T. Page 4-70, J. Pettiford 4-87) and 120-1 by 9 wkts.

30th Match: v Middlesex (Lord's) Aug 28, 30, 31.
Pakistanis 303-7 dec (Maqsood Ahmed 76, M. E. Z. Ghazali 58*, Wazir Mohammad 55, J. A. Young 4-83) and 232-5 dec (Alim-ud-Din 85, Maqsood Ahmed 63) beat Middlesex 175 (D. Bennett 59, F. J. Titmus 54, Shuja-ud-Din 4-66) and 220 (F. J. Titmus 61, J. D. B. Robertson 59) by 140 runs.

31st Match: v Club Cricket Conference (Luton).
Pakistanis 183 (H. L. V. Griffith 4-50) beat C.C.C. 110 (Khalid Hassan 4-27) by 73 runs.

32nd Match: v An England XI (Hastings). Sept 4, 6, 7.
An England XI 182 (N. H. Rogerts 101, Mahmood Hussain 7-61) and 220-8 dec (D. W. Barr 77*) drew with Pakistanis 234 (Waqar Hassan 79, Imtiaz Ahmed 78, F. S. Trueman 5-57) and 163-4 (Waqar Hassan 82*).*

33rd Match: v T. N. Pearce's XI (Scarborough) Sept 8, 9, 10.
Pakistanis 234 (Imtiaz Ahmed 105, A. V. Bedser 4-53) and 188 (J. H. Wardle 6-67) lost to T. N. Pearce's XI 396 (E. I. Lester 100, P. B. H. May 57, J. J. Warr 54*) and 27-1 by 9 wkts.

---

calculations–with only four Tests arranged and two having been drawn, Pakistan had squared the rubber.

The star of the side was the medium-pace bowler Fazal Mahmood, who headed the averages both in the Tests and first-class games and was the architect of the Oval victory with 12 for 99. It was unfortunate that he missed several matches through injury. Mahmood Hussain opened the bowling with Fazal and following a poor start bowled very well in the closing matches of the tour. The principal spinner were Shuja-ud-Din and Zulfiqar Ahmed: the former was left-arm and bowled most overs on the tour, but did little in the Tests; Zulfiqar came second to Fazal in the first-class averages and his action was very difficult to read–he scarcely featured in the England matches, however.

Hanif Mohammad was the team's outstanding batsman; generally opening the innings he combined an excellent defence with some charming strokes. His brother Wazir broke a finger early on, but recovered and played some good innings. Maqsood began in good form, but was rather impetuous; Alim-ud-Din batted well until beset by illness; Kardar played one or two good innings, but hardly bowled at all.

The tour resulted in a modest profit.

1954: 5th Canadians

The party selected to tour England was H. B. Robinson (captain), T. L. Brierley, R. B. Bruce-Lockhart, H. G. Bullen, F. J. Cameron, B. Christen, L. J. H. Gunn, A. S. Hendy, J. H. Lucas, W. A. Percival, R. N. Quintrell, T. M. Rilstone, P. Stead, A. Wight and L. Wight, with Gunn also acting as manager. Bruce-Lockhart, who was at Cambridge, and the two Wights, formerly of the West Indies, were forced to stand down, which made a considerable difference to the team. The vacancies were filled by K. B. Trestrail, A. H. Padmore and E. H. M. Burn. T. L. Brierley was the old Glamorgan and Lancashire player, while Lucas and Cameron were West Indian players.

Though they were too weak for the four first-class fixtures, the tourists found themselves slightly above minor county standard and it was a great pity that the matches against Northumberland and Durham were completely rained off.

The leading batsman was Trestrail, who hit 751 runs, average 46.93 and only a fatal ambition to score off every ball led to his

1954: 5th Canadians

1st Match: v Hampstead (Hampstead)   July 23.
Hampstead XII 179-9 dec (C. E. Winn 75, B. Christen 5-46) lost to Canadians XII 181-4 (K. B. Trestrail 68) by 7 wkts.

2nd Match: v Lord Cornwallis XII (Maidstone)   July 24.
Canadians 224-1 dec (K. B. Trestrail 144*, R. N. Quintrell 68*) drew with Lord Cornwallis XII 192-7 (H. A. Pawson 104*, A. J. Pullen 55, T. M. Rilstone 5-83).

3rd Match: v Commonwealth XI (Slough)   July 25.
Match abandoned – no play due to rain.

4th Match: v Sandhurst Wanderers (Camberley)   July 27.
Canadians 147-4 dec (T. L. Brierley 67) drew with Sandhurst Wanderers 146-9 (J. B. H. Trennery 69, H. Padmore 4-62).

5th Match: v Combined Services (Chatham)   July 28, 29.
Combined Services 320-3 dec (A. C. Walton 103, G. G. Tordoff 79*, M. L. Y. Ainsworth 71, P. E. Richardson 53) and 150-9 dec (T. M. Rilstone 5-28) drew with Canadians 292 (K. B. Trestrail 175*) and 41-0.

6th Match: v M.C.C. (Lord's)   July 31, Aug 2.
Canadians 319-9 dec (R. N. Quintrell 77, T. L. Brierley 56, W. Voce 5-73) and 113-4 dec (K. B. Trestrail 53) beat M.C.C. 208-6 dec (D. A. Bick 66) and 211 (F. J. Cameron 4-70) by 13 runs.

7th Match: v Duke of Norfolk's XII (Arundel Castle)   Aug 1.
Duke of Norfolk's XII 163-8 dec (F. J. Cameron 4-64) drew with Canadians 133-7.

8th Match: v Essex (Clacton)   Aug 4, 5, 6.
Essex 242 (C. C. P. Williams 54, T. C. Dodds 50, T. E. Bailey 50, H. Padmore 5-47) and 272-2 dec (G. Barker 107*, P. A. Gibb 106) drew with Canadians 141 (T. E. Bailey 5-49) and 47-4.

9th Match: v Warwickshire (Edgbaston)   Aug 7, 9, 10.
Warwickshire 38-2 drew with Canadians did not bat.

10th Match: v Duke of Beaufort's XI (Badminton)   Aug 8.
Duke of Beaufort's XI 148 (G. M. Emmett 60, P. Stead 4-35) drew with Canadians 88-7.

11th Match: v Rutland and Leics (Oakham)   Aug 11, 12.
Rutland and Leics 134 (B. Christen 4-28) and 40-1 drew with Canadians 98 (K. B. Trestrail 53, J. Goodwin 5-45).

12th Match: v R. W. V. Robins' XI (Colwyn Bay)   Aug 15.
R. M. V. Robins' XI 220-8 dec (L. Outschoorn 56, A. S. Hendy 5-70) lost to Canadians 221-5 (K. B. Trestrail 69, J. H. Lucas 50*) by 5 wkts.

13th Match: v R. H. Moore's XI (Colwyn Bay)   Aug 16.
Canadians 140 (D. J. Smith 4-28) lost to R. H. Moore's XI 142-4 by 6 wkts.

14th Match: v Pakistan (Lord's)   Aug 18, 19.
Canada 87 (Zulfiqar Ahmed 4-25) and 82 (Zulfiqar Ahmed 5-14) lost to Pakistan 236 (M. E. Z. Ghazali 62, Wazir Mohammad 59) by an innings and 67 runs.

15th Match: v Northumberland (Newcastle)   Aug 21, 23.
Match abandoned – no play due to rain.

16th Match: v Durham (Sunderland)   Aug 24, 25.
Match abandoned – no play due to rain.

17th Match: v Yorkshire (Scarborough)   Aug 28, 30.
Yorkshire 265 (W. H. H. Sutcliffe 82, P. Stead 4-52) and 245-4 dec (W. H. H. Sutcliffe 88) beat Canadians 154 and 107 by 249 runs.

18th Match: v Middlesex (Lord's)   Sept 1, 2.
Canadians 154 (W. A. Percival 73, R. J. Hurst 4-19) and 243 (K. B. Trestrail 100, R. J. Hurst 4-33) beat Middlesex 198-8 dec (B. Christen 4-70) and 196 (D. Bennett 61, B. Christen 5-81) by 3 runs.

failure in the important matches. Brierley, Cameron and Quintrell managed batting averages just over 20, but the remainder achieved little.

Injury badly reduced the attack–Robinson could not bowl and Rilstone missed the second half of the tour through back injury. The invalids' list grew to such an extent that B. R. Magee was flown over from Toronto.

Percival's wicketkeeping was praised but all too often the fielders gave runs away.

1955: 11th South Africans

The team, which was the first from South Africa to fly to England, arrived on 24 April, allowing themselves 14 days before the initial county match. The side comprised J. E. Cheetham (captain) and E. R. H. Fuller, both of Western Province; D. J. McGlew, H. J. Keith, H. J. Tayfield, R. A. McLean, V. I. Smith and T. L. Goddard of Natal; N. A. T. Adcock, J. H. B. Waite, W. R. Endean and P. L. Winslow of Transvaal; P. N. F. Mansell and C. A. R. Duckworth of Rhodesia; A. R. A. Murray of Eastern Province and P. S. Heine of Orange Free State, with K. G. Viljoen as manager. The most notable omission was van Ryneveld, who was not available.

In Australia in 1952-53 the very young and inexperienced

1955: 11th South Africans

Batting Averages

	M	I	NO	R	HS	Avge	100	c/s
D. J. McGlew	22	34	2	1871	161	58.46	5	4
R. A. McLean	25	41	3	1448	151	38.10	4	18
J. E. Cheetham	19	30	8	765	112	34.77	1	13
W. R. Endean	24	40	4	1242	138*	34.50	2	16
T. L. Goddard	23	39	1	1163	121	30.60	1	21
J. H. B. Waite	24	39	3	930	113	25.83	1	55/10
P. N. F. Mansell	19	27	3	611	99	25.45	0	27
H. J. Keith	19	29	1	682	100	24.35	1	17
C. A. R. Duckworth	13	19	4	362	158	24.13	1	16/5
P. L. Winslow	22	34	2	758	108	23.68	1	15
P. S. Heine	17	25	6	361	58	19.00	0	14
A. R. A. Murray	14	20	3	275	51	16.17	0	8
H. J. Tayfield	23	35	9	392	65	15.07	0	21
E. R. H. Fuller	16	23	2	223	38	10.61	0	11
V. I. Smith	15	15	8	44	10	6.28	0	2
N. A. T. Adcock	13	11	5	18	6	3.00	0	6

Bowling Averages

	O	M	R	W	Avge	BB	5i
H. J. Tayfield	1170.5	461	2253	143	15.75	8-40	13
A. R. A. Murray	321.4	150	575	31	18.54	3-19	0
E. R. H. Fuller	486.1	145	956	49	19.51	7-60	2
P. S. Heine	653.1	175	1467	74	19.82	7-58	6
V. I. Smith	383.3	111	1030	49	21.02	5-27	3
T. L. Goddard	810	352	1314	60	21.90	5-30	3
P. N. F. Mansell	336.4	95	771	29	26.58	6-52	1
N. A. T. Adcock	364	84	914	34	26.88	3-20	0
H. J. Keith	138	60	276	8	34.50	4-60	0

Also bowled: J. E. Cheetham 1-0-3-0; W. R. Endean 1-0-1-1; D. J. McGlew 1-0-4-0; R. A. McLean 2-0-2-0.

D. J. McGlew, the most successful of the South African batsmen in 1955, headed both the Test and first-class averages of his team; he was also an outstanding fielder in the covers.

1955: 11th South Africans

1st Match: v Worcestershire (Worcester) May 7, 9, 10.
Worcestershire 260 (L. Outschoorn 80, D. Kenyon 58, H. J. Tayfield 5-93) and 209 (G. Dews 52, J. P. Whitehead 51*, H. J. Tayfield 5-81) beat South Africans 209 (R. Berry 5-60) and 143 (M. J. Horton 9-56) by 117 runs.

2nd Match: v Derbyshire (Derby) May 11, 12, 13.
Derbyshire 179 (H. J. Tayfield 4-61) and 100-4 drew with South Africans 113.

3rd Match: v Nottinghamshire (Trent Bridge) May 14, 16, 17.
South Africans 272 (D. J. McGlew 88, W. R. Endean 78, B. Dooland 5-94) and 54-0 drew with Nottinghamshire 231 (R. T. Simpson 57, F. W. Stocks 54, V. I. Smith 5-70, H. J. Tayfield 5-95).

4th Match: v Cambridge University (Cambridge) May 18, 19, 20.
South Africans 268 (D. J. McGlew 85, J. H. B. Waite 78, S. Singh 5-73) drew with Cambridge University 67 (H. J. Tayfield 4-31) and 154-8 (D. R. W. Silk 54, H. J. Tayfield 4-51).

5th Match: v M.C.C. (Lord's) May 21, 23, 24.
South Africans 185-9 dec and 184 (R. A. McLean 85, F. J. Titmus 8-43) beat M.C.C. 87 and 189 (V. I. Smith 4-76) by 93 runs.

6th Match: v Oxford University (Christ Church, Oxford) May 25, 26, 27.
South Africans 434-8 dec (T. L. Goddard 121, R. A. McLean 67, D. J. McGlew 66, P. L. Winslow 60) beat Oxford University 90 (P. S. Heine 5-31) and 207 (H. J. Keith 4-60) by an innings and 137 runs.

7th Match: v Glamorgan (Cardiff) May 28, 30, 31.
Glamorgan 234 (W. G. A. Parkhouse 62, B. Hedges 58, E. R. H. Fuller 4-46) and 73-4 drew with South Africans 156 (D. J. McGlew 53, J. E. McConnon 6-49).

8th Match: v Essex (Colchester) June 1, 2, 3.
South Africans 503-4 dec (D. J. McGlew 118, R. A. McLean 101*, P. N. F. Mansell 99, H. J. Keith 94, W. R. Endean 64) drew with Essex 350 (D. J. Insole 129, T. E. Bailey 107) and 89-5.

9th Match: v Lancashire (Old Trafford) June 4, 6, 7.
South Africans 154 (P. L. Winslow 61, A. Wharton 4-26) and 232-4 (P. N. F. Mansell 79, W. R. Endean 51) drew with Lancashire 201 (K. J. Grieves 77, H. J. Tayfield 4-27).

10th Match: v England (Trent Bridge) June 9, 10, 11, 13.
England 334 (D. Kenyon 87, P. B. H. May 83) beat South Africans 181 (D. J. McGlew 68, J. E. Cheetham 54, J. H. Wardle 4-24) and 148 (D. J. McGlew 51, F. H. Tyson 6-28) by an innings and 5 runs.

11th Match: v Somerset (Taunton) June 15, 16, 17.
Somerset 68 and 170 (P. S. Heine 7-58) lost to South Africans 270-9 dec (J. E. Cheetham 87*, Yawar Saeed 5-61, B. Lobb 4-72) by an innings and 32 runs.

12th Match: v Sussex (Hove) June 18, 20, 21.
Sussex 352-6 dec (J. M. Parks 118, D. S. Sheppard 104) and 97 (E. R. H. Fuller 7-61) lost to South Africans 308-7 dec (R. A. McLean 129, D. J. McGlew 69) and 143-1 (W. R. Endean 73*, J. H. B. Waite 53) by 9 wkts.

13th Match: v England (Lord's) June 23, 24, 25, 27.
England 133 (P. S. Heine 5-60. T. L. Goddard 4-59) and 353 (P. B. H. May 112, D. C. S. Compton 69, T. W. Graveney 60, H. J. Tayfield 5-80) beat South Africans 304 (R. A. McLean 142, H. J. Keith 57, J. H. Wardle 4-65) and 111 (J. B. Statham 7-39) by 71 runs.

14th Match: v Northamptonshire (Northampton) June 29, 30, July 1.
South Africans 409 (C. A. R. Duckworth 158, P. N. F. Mansell 88, T. L. Goddard 70, G. E. Tribe 5-81) and 80-1 drew with Northamptonshire 271 (R. Subba Row 70, D. Brookes 64, T. L. Goddard 4-20) and 133-4 (R. Subba Row 59).

15th Match: v Yorkshire (Bramall Lane) July 2, 4, 5.
South Africans 209 (D. J. McGlew 51, R. Illingworth 4-21, J. H. Wardle 4-72) and 360 (H. J. Tayfield 65, P. L. Winslow 51, J. H. Wardle 5-105) beat Yorkshire 198 (W. Watson 51, F. A. Lowson 50, H. J. Tayfield 4-94) and 178 (J. H. Wardle 74, H. J. Tayfield 4-58) by 193 runs.

16th Match: v England (Old Trafford) July 7, 8, 9, 11, 12.
England 284 (D. C. S. Compton 158) and 381 (P. B. H. May 117, D. C. S. Compton 71, M. C. Cowdrey 50, P. S. Heine 5-86) lost to South Africa 521-8 dec (J. H. B. Waite 113, P. L. Winslow 108, D. J. McGlew 104*, T. L. Goddard 62) and 145-7 (R. A. McLean 50) by 3 wkts.

17th Match: v Surrey (Oval) July 16, 18, 19.
South Africans 244 (R. A. McLean 151, P. J. Loader 4-46) and 170 (J. C. Laker 5-56) beat Surrey 140 (P. B. H. May 62, H. J. Tayfield 5-22) and 192 (T. H. Clark 58, H. J. Tayfield 8-76) by 82 runs.

18th Match: v England (Headingley) July 21, 22, 23, 25, 26.
South Africa 171 (P. J. Loader 4-52) and 500 (D. J. McGlew 133, W. R. Endean 116*, T. L. Goddard 74, H. J. Keith 73, J. H. Wardle 4-100) beat England 191 (D. C. S. Compton 61, P. S. Heine 4-70, H. J. Tayfield 4-70) and 256 (P. B. H. May 97, T. L. Goddard 5-69, H. J. Tayfield 5-94) by 224 runs.

19th Match: v Minor Counties (Stoke-on-Trent) July 27, 28.
Minor Counties 233 (K. Taylor 57, V. I. Smith 5-71, H. J. Tayfield 4-71) and 180-8 (D. E. V. Padgett 59, V. I. Smith 4-51) drew with South Africans 302 (A. R. A. Murray 100, W. R. Endean 66, F. Taylor 4-88).

20th Match: v Glamorgan (Swansea) July 30, Aug 1, 2.
South Africans 225 (H. D. Davies 5-35) and 230 (P. N. F. Mansell 61, J. S. Pressdee 4-46, A. J. Watkins 4-73) beat Glamorgan 64 (P. S. Heine 5-26) and 165 (W. E. Jones 50, H. J. Tayfield 6-35) by 226 runs.

21st Match: v Warwickshire (Edgbaston) Aug 3, 4, 5.
Warwickshire 188 (F. C. Gardner 58, E. R. H. Fuller 7-60) and 201 (P. N. F. Mansell 4-52) lost to South Africans 382-9 dec (W. R. Endean 98, D. J. McGlew 84, T. L. Goddard 71, R. A. McLean 64, W. E. Hollies 4-100) and 8-0 by 10 wkts.

22nd Match: v Gloucestershire (Cheltenham) Aug 6, 8, 9.
Gloucestershire 184 (C. A. Milton 58, V. I. Smith 5-75) and 226 (T. W. Graveney 98, E. R. H. Fuller 4-60) drew with South Africans 197 (T. L. Goddard 93, A. R. A. Murray 51, B. D. Wells 4-39, J. B. Mortimore 4-42) and 108-3 (R. A. McLean 50).

23rd Match: v Leicestershire (Leicester) Aug 10, 11, 12.
South Africans 463-6 dec (H. J. Keith 100, D. J. McGlew 161, T. L. Goddard 61, P. N. F. Mansell 53*) beat Leicestershire 208 (C. H. Palmer 68, H. J. Tayfield 5-56) and 138 (P. N. F. Mansell 6-52) by an innings and 117 runs.

24th Match: v England (Oval) Aug 13, 15, 16, 17.
England 151 (T. L. Goddard 5-31) and 204 (P. B. H. May 89, H. J. Tayfield 5-60) beat South Africa 112 (G. A. R. Lock 4-39) and 151 (J. H. B. Waite 60, J. C. Laker 5-56, G. A. R. Lock 4-62) by 92 runs.

25th Match: v Hampshire (Southampton) Aug 20, 22, 23.
South Africans 259 (D. J. McGlew 81, R. A. McLean 75, P. S. Heine 58, D. Shackleton 4-66, M. D. Burden 4-68) and 302-7 dec (P. L. Winslow 87, T. L. Goddard 77, P. S. Heine 54) beat Hampshire 166 (D. Shackleton 50, H. G. Tayfield 6-86) and 120 (H. J. Tayfield 8-40) by 275 runs.

26th Match: v Kent (Canterbury) Aug 24, 25, 26.
South Africans 467-8 dec (D. J. McGlew 161, J. E. Cheetham 112, P. L. Winslow 57, A. L. Dixon 4-122) and 25-2 beat Kent 175 (P. N. F. Mansell 4-40) and 314 (P. Hearn 79, A. E. Fagg 64, H. J. Tayfield 5-76) by 8 wkts.

27th Match: v Middlesex (Lord's) Aug 27, 29, 30.
South Africans 254 (W. R. Endean 75, T. L. Goddard 56, F. J. Titmus 6-65) and 187 (R. A. McLean 58, F. J. Titmus 5-54) beat Middlesex 108 (P. S. Heine 7-60) and 98 (V. I. Smith 5-27) by 235 runs.

28th Match: v An England XI (Hastings) Aug 31, Sept 1, 2.
South Africans 165 (H. J. Keith 60, W. Wooller 4-38) and 287-9 dec (R. A. McLean 79, J. B. Statham 4-43) drew with An England XI 218 (R. T. Spooner 50, H. J. Tayfield 4-68) and 77-7.

29th Match: v Durham (Sunderland) Sept 3, 5.
South Africans 543 (P. N. F. Mansell 148, P. L. Winslow 133, H. J. Keith 65, W. R. Endean 61, K. Williamson 4-99) beat Durham 111 (V. I. Smith 5-29) and 108 (V. I. Smith 5-44) by an innings and 324 runs.

30th Match: v T. N. Pearce's XI (Scarborough) Sept 7, 8, 9.
T. N. Pearce's XI 236 (T. L. Goddard 5-30) and 328-9 dec (T. W. Graveney 159, H. J. Tayfield 4-93) lost to South Africans 354 (W. R. Endean 138, J. E. Cheetham 52) and 211-6 (D. J. McGlew 75) by 4 wkts.

31st Match: v Cumberland and Westmorland (Carlisle) Sept 10.
South Africans 332 (R. A. McLean 83, H. J. Keith 63) drew with Cumberland and Westmorland 104-8.

The 1955 South African team at Trent Bridge.

South Africans had beaten the home side twice and virtually the same team now came to England with the same ambitions. These were realised as South Africa, though not winning the rubber, beat England at Old Trafford and Headingley, having lost the Tests at Trent Bridge and Lord's; if the weather had not been so miserable during May the South Africans might well have come into form earlier in the tour and won the series.

McGlew was the tourists' outstanding batsman, heading both Test and first-class averages–due to Cheetham's injury McGlew actually led his country to victory twice. The most attractive batsman was McLean, whose stylish stroke play delighted the English public–his best innings was 142 in the Lord's Test; Endean began badly, but improved as the tour developed; Waite gave some very sound displays and if he had not been the wicketkeeper would most probably have made well over 1,000 runs. Winslow's big hitting succeeded once or twice, though he generally disappointed. Cheetham never got going after his injury in the Lord's Test.

The team included no fewer than eight good class bowlers. Tayfield's great success was expected, but surprisingly Heine and Goddard both took over 20 Test wickets at a reasonable average.

Heine the fast bowler was always dangerous with the new ball, but his partner Adcock rarely found a length and was at last replaced by Fuller.

The fielding was outstandingly good and the equal of any previous touring party's—Mansell, Goddard, Heine and Tayfield made an excellent close quartet; McGlew saved almost hundreds of runs in the covers and McLean patrolled the outfield.

The profit from the tour amounted to about £35,000 and the total attendance was 930,000.

1956: 22nd Australians

I. W. Johnson (captain), R. N. Harvey, C. C. McDonald and L. V. Maddocks of Victoria; K. R. Miller, R. Benaud, J. W. Burke, I. D. Craig, W. P. A. Crawford and A. K. Davidson of New South Wales; G. R. A. Langley and J. W. Wilson of South Australia; R. R. Lindwall, R. G. Archer, P. J. P. Burge and K. D. Mackay of Queensland and J. W. Rutherford of Western Australia, with W. J. Dowling as manager and W. L. Rush as his assistant were the team which arrived at Tilbury aboard the liner *Himalaya* on 24 April. Of those omitted Favell, the hard hitting batsman, was the best known.

The side met a summer of damp pitches and generally grey skies, which combined with Laker and Lock to produce the worst record for an Australian team in England since 1912. The team reached the First Test on 7 June without a single win against a first-class county. This First Test was drawn due to rain, but the tourists then caused a surprise by winning the Second Test by a good margin—it was to prove the highlight of the tour.

The batting was very suspect. Much depended on Harvey, who inexplicably played only one decent innings all summer; Mackay headed the first-class averages, but could average only 12.16 in the Tests and was dropped for the final match. McDonald improved

---

1956: 22nd Australians

1st Match: v Duke of Norfolk's XI (Arundel Castle)   April 28.
Duke of Norfolk's XI 188 (D. S. Sheppard 51, R. Benaud 6-35) lost to Australians 189-7 by 3 wkts.

2nd Match: v Worcestershire (Worcester)   May 2, 3, 4.
Worcestershire 90 and 231-9 (P. E. Richardson 130*) drew with Australians 438 (R. Benaud 160, C. C. McDonald 86, L. V. Maddocks 56, K. D. Mackay 55, J. A. Flavell 4-115, G. H. Chesterton 4-131).

3rd Match: v Leicestershire (Leicester)   May 5, 7, 8.
Leicestershire 298 (G. A. Smithson 60, R. G. Archer 4-73) drew with Australians 694-6 (K. R. Miller 281*, J. W. Burke 123, P. J. P. Burge 99, R. G. Archer 88, K. D. Mackay 58).

4th Match: v Yorkshire (Bradford)   May 9, 10, 11.
Yorkshire 120-9 dec (A. K. Davidson 4-39) and 19-1 drew with Australians 94 (J. H. Wardle 5-27, R. Appleyard 4-44).

5th Match: v Nottinghamshire (Trent Bridge)   May 12, 14, 15.
Australians 547-8 dec (C. C. McDonald 195, P. J. P. Burge 131, R. Benaud 62, I. D. Craig 58) and 53-1 drew with Nottinghamshire 345 (F. W. Stocks 171, C. J. Poole 58, R. Benaud 4-88).

6th Match: v Surrey (Oval)   May 16, 17, 18.
Australians 259 (C. C. McDonald 89, K. R. Miller 57*, J. C. Laker 10-88) and 107 (G. A. R. Lock 7-49) lost to Surrey 347 (B. Constable 109, T. H. Clark 58, I. W. Johnson 6-168) and 20-0 by 10 wkts.

7th Match: v Cambridge University (Cambridge)   May 19, 21, 22.
Australians 414-7 dec (R. R. Lindwall 116*, P. J. P. Burge 61, R. G. Archer 61, R. Benaud 56) and 23-0 beat Cambridge University 155 (R. Benaud 5-55) and 281 (R. M. James 116, S. Singh 57, I. W. Johnson 4-69, R. Benaud 4-86) by 10 wkts.

8th Match: v Lancashire (Old Trafford)   May 23, 24, 25.
Lancashire 108 (W. P. A. Crawford 4-31) and 238-6 dec (A. Wharton 137) drew with Australians 160 (J. Dyson 4-17, J. B. Statham 4-34) and 90-1.

9th Match: v M.C.C. (Lord's)   May 26, 28, 29.
Australians 413 (R. N. Harvey 225, J. W. Rutherford 98, F. J. Titmus 5-130) drew with M.C.C. 203-9 (R. G. Archer 4-57).

10th Match: v Oxford University (Oxford)   May 30, 31, June 1.
Oxford University 157 (W. P. A. Crawford 4-28) and 191 (S. G. Metcalfe 64, M. A. Eagar 58, K. R. Miller 4-30) lost to Australians 234 (C. C. McDonald 112, E. S. M. Kentish 4-23, J. B. Phillips 4-69) and 171-2 (J. W. Rutherford 67*) by 8 wkts.

11th Match: v Sussex (Hove)   June 2, 4, 5.
Australians 231 (K. D. Mackay 73, R. N. Harvey 60) and 8-0 drew with Sussex 298 (D. S. Sheppard 97, R. G. Marlar 64).

12th Match: v England (Trent Bridge)   June 7, 8, 9, 11, 12.
England 217-8 dec (P. E. Richardson 81, P. B. H. May 73, K. R. Miller 4-69) and 188-3 dec (M. C. Cowdrey 81, P. E. Richardson 73) drew with Australia 148 (R. B. Harvey 64, J. C. Laker 4-58) and 120-3 (J. W. Burke 58*).

13th Match: v Northamptonshire (Northampton)   June 13, 14, 15.
Northamptonshire 339-3 dec (D. Brookes 144*, L. Livingston 85, A. P. Arnold 52) and 171 (L. Livingston 51) drew with Australians 314 (K. R. Miller 72, K. D. Mackay 64, J. W. Burke 58, R. G. Archer 51, G. E. Tribe 4-100) and 98-6.

14th Match: v Kent (Canterbury)   June 16, 18, 19.
Australians 301-4 dec (K. D. Mackay 113*, P. J. P. Burge 69*, J. W. Burke 57, R. N. Harvey 56) and 54-0 drew with Kent 210 (A. H. Phebey 67, J. W. Wilson 4-43).

15th Match: v England (Lord's)   June 21, 22, 23, 25, 26.
Australia 285 (C. C. McDonald 78, J. W. Burke 65) and 257 (R. Benaud 97, F. S. Trueman 5-90, T. E. Bailey 4-64) beat England 171 (P. B. H. May 63, K. R. Miller 5-72) and 186 (P. B. H. May 53, K. R. Miller 5-80, R. G. Archer 4-71) by 185 runs.

16th Match: v Yorkshire (Bramall Lane)   June 27, 28, 29.
Australians 306-7 dec (K. D. Mackay 122*, I. D. Craig 76) drew with Yorkshire 96-4.

17th Match: v Gloucestershire (Bristol)   June 30, July 2.
Australians 216 (R. Benaud 70, I. D. Craig 69, B. D. Wells 5-70) beat Gloucestershire 44 (J. W. Wilson 7-11) and 124 (J. W. Wilson 5-50, R. Benaud 4-51) by an innings and 48 runs.

18th Match: v Somerset (Taunton)   July 4, 5, 6.
Australians 340-5 dec (J. W. Burke 138, K. D. Mackay 71*, I. D. Craig 62) and 236-1 dec (J. W. Burke 125*, I. D. Craig 100*) drew with Somerset 275 (C. L. McCool 90, H. W. Stephenson 67, P. B. Wight 61, R. G. Archer 6-98) and 234-5 (C. L. McCool 116).

19th Match: v Hampshire (Southampton)   July 7, 9, 10.
Australians 277 (K. D. Mackay 60, P. J. P. Burge 50) and 116-3 dec drew with Hampshire 139 (R. G. Archer 4-18) and 151-4 (H. Horton 62, J. R. Gray 51).

20th Match: v England (Headingley)   July 12, 13, 14, 16, 17.
England 325 (P. B. H. May 101, C. Washbrook 98) beat Australia 143 (J. C. Laker 5-58, G. A. R. Lock 4-41) and 140 (R. N. Harvey 69, J. C. Laker 6-55) by an innings and 42 runs.

21st Match: v Club Cricket Conference (Oval)   July 20.
Match abandoned – no play due to rain.

22nd Match: v Middlesex (Lord's)   July 21, 23, 24.
Australians 207 (R. Benaud 62, F. J. Titmus 5-65) and 232-3 dec (I. D. Craig 67*, R. G. Archer 60*, C. C. McDonald 51) drew with Middlesex 198 (W. J. Edrich 84, D. C. S. Compton 61, R. R. Lindwall 4-33) and 108-5.

23rd Match: v England (Old Trafford)   July 26, 27, 28, 30, 31.
England 459 (D. S. Sheppard 113, P. E. Richardson 104, M. C. Cowdrey 80, I. W. Johnson 4-151) beat Australia 84 (J. C. Laker 9-37) and 205 (C. C. McDonald 89, J. C. Laker 10-53) by an innings and 170 runs.

24th Match: v Surrey (Oval)   Aug 1, 2, 3.
Australians 143 (J. C. Laker 4-41, E. A. Bedser 4-44) and 47-3 drew with Surrey 181-9 dec (K. R. Miller 5-84).

25th Match: v Glamorgan (Swansea)   Aug 4, 6, 7.
Australians 408-4 dec (K. D. Mackay 163*, R. G. Archer 148, P. J. P. Burge 60) beat Glamorgan 116 and 281 (W. Wooller 70, W. G. A. Parkhouse 62, J. S. Pressdee 53, J. W. Wilson 5-88) by an innings and 11 runs.

26th Match: v Warwickshire (Edgbaston)   Aug 8, 9, 10.
Warwickshire 194 (M. J. K. Smith 55, R. Benaud 5-44) and 103 (R. Benaud 6-31) lost to Australians 424-4 dec (J. W. Burke 194, R. N. Harvey 145) by an innings and 127 runs.

27th Match: v Derbyshire (Derby)   Aug 11, 13, 14.
Australians 146 (I. D. Craig 76, H. L. Jackson 4-38) and 183-3 dec (I. D. Craig 64*) beat Derbyshire 111 (R. R. Lindwall 7-40) and 161 (D. J. Green 59, K. R. Miller 5-29) by 57 runs.

28th Match: v Lancashire (Old Trafford)   Aug 15, 16, 17.
Australians 86-7 (J. B. Statham 6-27) drew with Lancashire did not bat.

29th Match: v Essex (Southend)   Aug 18, 20, 21.
Essex 154 (T. C. Dodds 58) and 183 lost to Australians 349 (C. C. McDonald 81, A. K. Davidson 75, I. D. Craig 66, K. R. Miller 50, W. T. Greensmith 4-72) by an innings and 12 runs.

30th Match: v Australia (Oval)   Aug 23, 24, 25, 27, 28.
England 247 (D. C. S. Compton 94, P. B. H. May 83*, R. G. Archer 5-53, K. R. Miller 4-91) and 182-3 dec (D. S. Sheppard 62) drew with Australia 202 (K. R. Miller 61, J. C. Laker 4-80) and 27-5.

31st Match: v Gentlemen (Lord's)   Aug 29, 30, 31.
Australians 226-8 (K. D. Mackay 67, A. K. Davidson 56, J. J. Warr 4-46) drew with Gentlemen did not bat.

32nd Match: v An England XI (Hastings)   Sept 1, 3, 4.
An England XI 222-7 dec (C. A. Milton 94, I. W. Johnson 4-47) drew with Australians 106-3.

33rd Match: v T. N. Pearce's XI (Scarborough)   Sept 5, 6, 7.
T. N. Pearce's XI 272-9 dec (T. W. Graveney 101, R. Benaud 4-103) and 200-7 dec (I. W. Johnson 5-90) lost to Australians 280-7 dec (J. W. Burke 94, R. N. Harvey 53, G. Goonesena 4-46) and 193-5 (J. W. Rutherford 78, G. Goonesena 4-81) by 5 wkts.

34th Match: v Minor Counties (Newcastle)   Sept 8, 10.
Minor Counties 144 (M. E. Scott 53) and 244 (R. W. Smithson 73, M. E. Scott 59, R. N. Harvey 5-57) lost to Australians 270 (I. D. Craig 80, L. McGibbon 4-76) and 119-3 (R. Benaud 51) by 7 wkts.*

35th Match: v Scotland (Glasgow)   Sept 12, 13.
Scotland 196 (J. Aitchison 100) drew with Australians 328 (J. W. Burke 81, D. W. Drummond 4-85).

36th Match: v Scotland (Aberdeen)   Sept 14, 15.
Scotland 111 and 81 (R. Benaud 6-34) lost to Australians 318 (K. D. Mackay 77, P. J. P. Burge 75, J. W. Burke 58) by an innings and 126 runs.

The 1956 Australian touring party. Back: Burke, Mackay, Craig, Burge, Benaud, Crawford, Archer, Rutherford, Wilson. Front: Maddocks, McDonald, Miller, Johnson (captain), Lindwall, Langley, Harvey, Davidson.

on his 1953 record and proved his ability with a great 89 against Laker at Old Trafford, when the Surrey spinner took 19 wickets. Craig, the youngest member on two successive tours, built up some fine innings; Burke's defence was sound and he was the only player to average over 30 in the Test series.

Miller headed the Test bowling table, but the wet wickets took the sting out of his deliveries; his partner Lindwall failed to make much impact against England, though he did well enough in county games; Archer, the fast bowler, was quite effective, in contrast with Crawford, who failed to live up to his reputation.

The three spinners, Johnson, Benaud and Wilson, who ought to have thrived in the wet weather, did not worry the home batsmen.

Langley and Maddocks shared the wicketkeeping and both had good tours–there was some newspaper criticism of the preparation of the Test wickets.

The tour made a profit of £60,000–less than in 1953, but the rain which caused 13 totally blank days was to blame.

Spinner Richie Benaud, on his second tour of England, failed to make the best of the wet-weather pitches so ruthlessly exploited by Laker and Lock for England.

1956: 22nd Australians

Batting Averages

	M	I	NO	R	HS	Avge	100	c/s
K. D. Mackay	20	28	7	1103	163*	52.52	3	5
J. W. Burke	21	35	7	1339	194	47.82	4	5
K. R. Miller	20	29	6	843	281*	36.65	1	12
I. D. Craig	20	29	5	872	100*	36.33	1	6
P. J. P. Burge	22	26	4	780	131	35.45	1	12
R. Benaud	23	29	4	871	160	34.84	1	14
C. C. McDonald	23	35	0	1202	195	34.34	2	3
R. N. Harvey	23	32	1	976	225	31.48	2	12
R. G. Archer	22	25	4	649	148	30.90	1	25
A. K. Davidson	15	13	3	270	75	27.00	0	12
J. W. Rutherford	22	33	5	640	98	22.85	0	17
G. R. A. Langley	16	13	8	112	41	22.40	0	38/9
R. R. Lindwall	17	18	6	260	116*	21.66	1	6
L. V. Maddocks	17	17	3	201	56	14.35	0	27/12
W. P. A. Crawford	18	15	7	101	19	12.62	0	7
I. W. Johnson	23	20	2	193	44	10.72	0	4
J. W. Wilson	19	11	3	23	8*	2.87	0	3

Bowling Averages

	O	M	R	W	Avge	BB	5i
K. R. Miller	430	97	980	50	19.60	5-29	4
R. R. Lindwall	413.3	119	924	47	19.65	7-40	1
R. G. Archer	583.4	179	1353	61	22.18	6-98	2
R. Benaud	584.5	187	1337	60	22.28	6-31	3
A. K. Davidson	241.5	79	585	26	22.50	4-39	0
J. W. Wilson	402.4	151	992	43	23.06	7-11	3
W. P. A. Crawford	343.2	79	836	31	26.96	4-28	0
I. W. Johnson	531.3	161	1348	50	26.96	6-68	2
J. W. Burke	81	34	181	6	30.16	3-5	0
K. D. Mackay	132	42	268	8	33.50	2-32	0
J. W. Rutherford	40	9	152	3	50.66	2-29	0

Also bowled: P. J. P. Burge 2-1-2-0; I. D. Craig 4-1-14-1; R. N. Harvey 6-2-24-1; G. R. A. Langley 2-1-2-0; C. C. McDonald 2-0-12-0; L. V. Maddocks 3-0-4-1.

1957: 8th West Indians

The selectors announced the party of 17 which was to tour England by hoisting the names on the scoreboard at Queen's Park in Port of Spain on 7 February. They were J. D. C. Goddard (captain), D. St E. Atkinson, W. W. Hall, G. St A. Sobers and E. de C. Weekes, all of Barbados; F. C. M. Alexander, D. T. Dewdney, R. Gilchrist, O. G. Smith, A. L. Valentine and F. M. M. Worrell of Jamaica; N. S. Asgarali, A. G. Ganteaume and S. Ramadhin of Trinidad; R. B. Kanhai, B. H. Pairaudeau and C. L. Walcott of British Guiana. The joint managers were N. Pierce and C. de Caires. A. F. Rae was not available for selection, and nor was C. B. Williams; C. C. Depeiza, one of the wicketkeepers on the 1955-56 tour, had taken a League engagement and so was not considered.

The main party of players landed in Southampton on 14 April, having sailed on the s.s. *Golfito*. For the first time the West Indies in England were allocated five five-day Tests, but unlike in 1950, when they took England by storm, they failed to win a single Test and lost the series three matches to nil. Their record against the counties was excellent, but could hardly make up for their poor showing in the Tests.

There was no doubt they missed Rae—the team rarely got off to a good opening stand, which seemed to affect the three Ws. Weekes, with a broken finger, was a pale shadow of the belligerent batsman of former years; Walcott strained a leg in the First Test and was sound but not outstanding; Worrell alone battled on and he was also required as a bowler. The three youngsters Smith,

1957: 8th West Indians

1st Match: v E. W. Swanton's XI (Eastbourne) April 25, 26.
West Indians 368-6 dec (G. St A. Sobers 110*, N. S. Asgarali 77, C. L. Walcott 60) and 69-3 drew with E. W. Swanton's XI 244-8 dec (M. J. Stewart 93).

2nd Match: v Worcestershire (Worcester) May 1, 2.
West Indians 290-9 dec (O. G. Smith 68, R. Berry 6-105) beat Worcestershire 80 (D. St E. Atkinson 5-25) and 133 (D. St E. Atkinson 5-37) by an innings and 77 runs.

3rd Match: v Northamptonshire (Northampton) May 4, 6, 7.
West Indians 328-7 dec (F. M. M. Worrell 107, N. S. Asgarali 86, E. de C. Weekes 81) and 96-6 beat Northamptonshire 91 (S. Ramadkin 5-20, A. L. Valentine 5-56) and 332 (D. W. Barrick 122, G. E. Tribe 101) by 4 wkts.

4th Match: v Oxford University (Christ Church, Oxford) May 8, 9, 10.
Oxford University 119 (A. C. Walton 64, S. Ramadhin 6-18) and 84 (S. Ramadhin 7-29) lost to West Indians 293-5 dec (G. St A. Sobers 67*, R. B. Kanhai 61, A. G. Ganteaume 60, C. L. Walcott 58, S. V. C. Clube 4-79) by an innings and 90 runs.

5th Match: v Essex (Ilford) May 11, 13, 14.
Essex 197 (B. Taylor 58, D. St E. Atkinson 8-58) and 121 (J. D. C. Goddard 5-20, D. St E. Atkinson 4-55) lost to West Indians 115 (C. L. Walcott 50, T. E. Bailey 6-37) and 204-6 (F. M. M. Worrell 61*) by 4 wkts.

6th Match: v Cambridge University (Cambridge) May 15, 16, 17.
Cambridge University 225 (G. Goonesena 55, S. Ramadhin 5-70) and 258 (G. Goonesena 69, D. J. Green 64) drew with West Indians 366-6 dec (B. H. Pairaudeau 127, C. L. Walcott 86, O. G. Smith 55*).

7th Match: v M.C.C. (Lord's) May 18, 20, 21.
West Indians 337-6 dec (C. L. Walcott 117, G. St A. Sobers 101*, A. E. Moss 4-75) and 193-3 (B. H. Pairaudeau 66) drew with M.C.C. 284 (D. B. Close 108 rt hurt, F. M. M. Worrell 6-71).

8th Match: v Yorkshire (Bramall Lane) May 22, 23, 24.
West Indians 190 (G. St A. Sobers 56, J. H. Wardle 5-46) and 272-6 dec (G. St A. Sobers 72, E. de C. Weekes 53) drew with Yorkshire 162 (J. H. Wardle 64, S. Ramadhin 6-47) and 141-8 (S. Ramadhin 4-21).

9th Match: v Nottinghamshire (Trent Bridge) May 25, 27, 28.
West Indians 489-3 dec (G. St A. Sobers 219*, C. L. Walcott 115, E. de C. Weekes 68, O. G. Smith 67*) and 298-3 (N. S. Asgarali 130*, R. B. Kanhai 95) drew with Nottinghamshire 420 (J. D. Clay 67, K. Smales 63, A. Jepson 54).

10th Match: v England (Edgbaston) May 30, 31, June 1, 3, 4.
England 186 (S. Ramadhin 7-49) and 583-4 dec (P. B. H. May 285*, M. C. Cowdrey 154) drew with West Indies 474 (O. G. Smith 161, C. L. Walcott 90, F. M. M. Worrell 81, G. St A. Sobers 53, J. C. Laker 4-119) and 72-7.

11th Match: v Gloucestershire (Bristol) June 5, 6, 7.
West Indians 241 (E. de C. Weekes 56, D. R. Smith 6-72) and 309-7 dec (D. St E. Atkinson 101*, E. de C. Weekes 73, F. C. M. Alexander 52) beat Gloucestershire 220 (D. T. Dewdney 5-69) and 176 (G. M. Emmett 91, G. St A. Sobers 5-39) by 154 runs.

12th Match: v Glamorgan (Cardiff) June 8, 10.
Glamorgan 138 (S. Ramadhin 5-31) and 77 (S. Ramadhin 6-39) lost to West Indians 119 (J. E. McConnon 6-50) and 100-5 (R. B. Kanhai 52) by 5 wkts.

13th Match: v Surrey (Oval) June 12, 13, 14.
Surrey 210 and 270-6 dec (M. J. Stewart 147*) drew with West Indians 220 (G. St A. Sobers 71, E. de C. Weekes 64, P. J. Loader 5-57, J. C. Laker 4-48) and 178-8 (O. G. Smith 84, E. A. Bedser 4-50).

14th Match: v Sussex (Hove) June 15, 17, 18.
West Indians 353-8 dec (F. M. M. Worrell 135, C. L. Walcott 67, D. L. Bates 4-53) and 284-3 dec (N. S. Asgarali 99, A. G. Ganteaume 75, G. St A. Sobers 52*, O. G. Smith 50) beat Sussex 256 (D. V. Smith 147*, A. L. Valentine 4-86) and 146 (A. L. Valentine 6-64) by 235 runs.

15th Match: v England (Lord's) June 20, 21, 22.
West Indies 127 (T. E. Bailey 7-44) and 261 (E. de C. Weekes 90, G. St A. Sobers 66, T. E. Bailey 4-54) lost to England 424 (M. C. Cowdrey 152, T. G. Evans 82, P. E. Richardson 76, R. Gilchrist 4-115) by an innings and 36 runs.

16th Match: v Derbyshire (Chesterfield) June 29, July 1, 2.
West Indians 115 (C. Gladwin 4-37) and 315 (O. G. Smith 133, A. G. Ganteaume 51, D. C. Morgan 4-47, H. L. Jackson 4-64) beat Derbyshire 140 (R. Gilchrist 5-41) and 117 (D. B. Carr 57, S. Ramadhin 4-31) by 173 runs.

17th Match: v England (Trent Bridge) July 4, 5, 6, 8, 9.
England 619-6 dec (T. W. Graveney 258, P. E. Richardson 126, P. B. H. May 104, M. C. Cowdrey 55) and 64-1 drew with West Indies 372 (F. M. M. Worrell 191*, F. S. Trueman 5-63) and 367 (O. G. Smith 168, J. D. C. Goddard 61, J. B. Statham 5-118, F. S. Trueman 4-80).

18th Match: v Ireland (Belfast) July 10, 11.
Ireland 119 (A. L. Valentine 6-38) drew with West Indians 198 (S. S. J. Huey 5-46, C. J. M. Kenny 4-68).

19th Match: v Ireland (Dublin) July 12.
West Indians 140-7 dec (F. Fee 4-61) beat Ireland 61 (G. St A. Sobers 5-43) by 79 runs.

20th Match: v Hampshire (Southampton) July 13, 15, 16.
West Indians 110 (M. Heath 4-58) and 387 (B. H. Pairaudeau 163, F. M. M. Worrell 56*, D. Shackleton 7-103) drew with Hampshire 159 (J. R. Gray 83, D. T. Dewdney 5-38) and 43-0.

21st Match: v Somerset (Taunton) July 17, 18, 19.
West Indians 78 (B. Lobb 5-37, W. E. Alley 5-38) and 254-6 dec (G. St A. Sobers 104, C. L. Walcott 61) drew with Somerset 114 (R. Gilchrist 5-33).

22nd Match: v Middlesex (Lord's) July 20, 22, 23.
Middlesex 144 (F. M. M. Worrell 5-34) and 213 (W. J. Edrich 58) drew with West Indians 176 (F. M. M. Worrell 66, D. Bennett 4-39) and 143-8 (F. M. M. Worrell 61).

23rd Match: v England (Headingley) July 25, 26, 27.
West Indies 142 (P. J. Loader 6-36) and 132 lost to England 279 (P. B. H. May 69, M. C. Cowdrey 68, D. S. Sheppard 68, F. M. M. Worrell 7-70) by an innings and 5 runs.

24th Match: v Surrey (Oval) July 31, Aug 1, 2.
Surrey 210 (M. J. Stewart 78, P. B. H. May 73, A. L. Valentine 5-47) and 199-3 dec (K. F. Barrington 103*, B. Constable 58*) lost to West Indians 140 (G. A. R. Lock 4-46) and 270-3 (F. M. M. Worrell 84*, C. L. Walcott 59, A. G. Ganteaume 53) by 7 wkts.

25th Match: v Glamorgan (Swansea) Aug 3, 5, 6.
Glamorgan 141 (L. N. Devereux 58, S. Ramadhin 4-64) and 178 (W. G. A. Parkhouse 60, S. Ramadhin 7-67) lost to West Indians 254 (A. G. Ganteaume 92, F. M. M. Worrell 69) and 66-4 (J. E. McConnon 4-20) by 6 wkts.

26th Match: v Warwickshire (Edgston) Aug 7, 8, 9.
Warwickshire 184 (N. F. Horner 98, S. Ramadhin 7-43) and 204-6 (W. J. Stewart 58, M. J. K. Smith 50) drew with West Indians 212 (R. B. Kanhai 74, W. E. Hollies 5-55).

27th Match: v Lancashire (Old Trafford) Aug 10, 12, 13.
West Indians 317-5 dec (G. St A. Sobers 86, N. S. Asgarali 84, O. G. Smith 67*, F. M. M. Worrell 59) and 91-1 beat Lancashire 79 and 327 (R. Bowman 55) by 9 wkts.

28th Match: v Yorkshire (Bradford) Aug 14, 15, 16.
Match abandoned – no play due to rain.

29th Match: v Leicestershire (Leicester) Aug 17, 19, 20.
Leicestershire 75 and 74 (A. L. Valentine 6-8) lost to West Indians 361-7 dec (R. B. Kanhai 92, F. M. M. Worrell 104, F. C. M. Alexander 83, C. H. Palmer 4-40) by an innings and 212 runs.

30th Match: v England (Oval) Aug 22, 23, 24.
England 412 (T. W. Graveney 164, P. E. Richardson 107, S. Ramadhin 4-107) beat West Indies 89 (G. A. R. Lock 5-28) and 86 (G. A. R. Lock 6-20) by an innings and 237 runs.

31st Match: v Kent (Canterbury) Aug 28, 29, 30.
Kent 355 (T. G. Evans 71, M. C. Cowdrey 54, S. Ramadhin 5-83) and 168-7 dec (S. Ramadhin 5-51) lost to West Indians 359-5 dec (C. L. Walcott 131, N. S. Asgarali 120*) and 165-3 (O. G. Smith 50*) by 7 wkts.

32nd Match: v L. E. G. Ames XI (Hastings) Aug 31, Sept 2, 3.
L. E. G. Ames' XI 322-9 dec (M. C. Cowdrey 143, B. Dooland 50, F. M. M. Worrell 4-73) and 238 (D. W. Barrick 59, S. Ramadhin 4-47) lost to West Indians 291 (O. G. Smith 79, R. B. Kanhai 71) and 270-6 (R. B. Kanhai 91, A. G. Ganteaume 60) by 4 wkts.

33rd Match: v Lancashire (Blackpool) Sept 4, 5, 6.
West Indians 174 (B. H. Pairaudeau 59, R. Tattersall 4-58) and 181-5 dec (F. M. M. Worrell 95*) drew with Lancashire 176 and 108-2 (A. Wharton 60*).

34th Match: v T. N. Pearce's XI (Scarborough) Sept 7, 9, 10.
T. N. Pearce's XI 355-9 dec (P. B. H. May 119, D. B. Close 50, N. S. Asgarali 4-72) and 186-7 dec drew with West Indians 323-7 dec (E. de C. Weekes 105, A. G. Ganteaume 75) and 151-8.

35th Match: v Minor Counties (Newcastle) Sept 14, 16.
West Indians 434 (G. St A. Sobers 151, R. B. Kanhai 146, M. Ryan 6-97) beat Minor Counties 189 (P. H. Shaw 72, S. Ramadhin 5-21) and 142 (S. Ramadhin 5-58) by an innings and 103 runs.

Everton Weekes, who broke a finger early in the tour, was not the scourge of England he had been in the 1950 series, though he made a defiant 90 in the Second Test at Lord's.

Clyde Walcott, too, was handicapped by an injury suffered in the First Test, when he scored 90 in the tourists' massive first-innings total.

1957: 8th West Indians								
Batting Averages								
	M	I	NO	R	HS	Avge	100	c/s
F. M. M. Worrell	20	34	9	1470	191*	58.80	4	10
C. L. Walcott	21	36	5	1414	131	45.61	3	28
G. St A. Sobers	25	44	6	1644	219*	43.26	3	26
O. G. Smith	26	45	9	1483	168	41.19	3	13
R. B. Kanhai	22	39	4	1093	95	31.22	0	20/5
N. S. Asgarali	21	37	3	1011	130*	29.73	2	11
E. de C. Weekes	23	40	1	1096	105	28.10	1	17
A. G. Ganteaume	19	32	3	800	92	27.58	0	11
B. H. Pairaudeau	18	33	0	781	163	23.66	2	7
F. C. M. Alexander	20	30	10	387	83	19.35	0	41/7
D. St E. Atkinson	16	23	4	324	101*	17.05	1	6
J. D. C. Goddard	17	21	4	243	61	14.29	0	12
W. W. Hall	15	16	3	178	22	13.69	0	3
R. Gilchrist	15	16	5	67	20	6.09	0	3
S. Ramadhin	20	22	4	105	28	5.83	0	2
D. T. Dewdney	16	18	7	49	22*	4.45	0	2
A. L. Valentine	16	11	6	19	7	3.80	0	4
Bowling Averages								
	O	M	R	W	Avge	BB	5i	
S. Ramadhin	937.1	361	1664	119	13.98	7-29	12	
A. L. Valentine	513	160	1180	60	19.66	6-8	4	
J. D. C. Goddard	91	31	173	8	21.62	5-20	1	
D. St E. Atkinson	605.1	201	1235	55	22.45	8-58	3	
F. M. M. Worrell	406.5	94	949	39	24.33	7-70	3	
D. T. Dewdney	317.4	45	974	36	27.05	5-38	2	
O. G. Smith	405.3	136	920	34	27.05	3-15	0	
G. St A. Sobers	477.3	145	1172	37	31.67	5-39	1	
R. Gilchrist	394.2	54	1176	37	31.78	5-33	2	
W. W. Hall	292	47	906	27	33.55	3-44	0	
N. S. Asgarali	76	24	201	5	40.20	4-72	0	

Also bowled: A. G. Ganteaume 3-0-20-0; C. L. Walcott 8-2-28-0; E. de C. Weekes 6-0-32-1.

Note: C. de Caires played in one non-first-class match.

Sobers and Kanhai all hit 1,000 runs and played in every Test; the trio looked promising but as yet could not carry the onus of the batting.

The biggest upset was the total eclipse of Valentine, whose line and length simply vanished when faced with the best batsmen; Ramadhin still bowled well in the county matches, but at Test level his 14 wickets cost 39.07 each—he was bowled to a standstill in the First Test, when in the second innings he delivered 98 overs. The three fast bowlers were Gilchrist, Hall and Dewdney—Gilchrist could deliver some vicious bumpers, but Worrell proved more effective than any of them. Of the other bowlers, Atkinson was the best until a strained shoulder forced him to miss several matches. Goddard had a poor tour and in the last Test was forced to retire with flu.

The team sailed home on 24 September from Southampton, having made a profit of £33,000.

1958: 5th New Zealanders

The New Zealand team which flew into London on 15 April was J. R. Reid (captain) of North Otago; H. B. Cave of Wanganui; J. C. Alabaster of Southland; R. W. Blair and T. Meale of Hutt Valley; J. W. d'Arcy and A. R. MacGibbon of Canterbury; N. S. Harford of Manawatu; J. A. Hayes, W. R. Playle and J. T. Sparling of Auckland; L. S. M. Miller from Wellington; A. McK.

1958: 5th New Zealanders

1st Match: v London New Zealand C.C. (Oval)   April 17.
London New Zealand C.C. 144 lost to New Zealanders 251-4 (N. S. Harford 105, L. S. M. Miller 55) by 9 wkts.

2nd Match: v Maori C.C. (Worcester Park)   April 19.
New Zealanders 187-6 drew with Maori C.C. 66-6.

3rd Match: v L. C. Steven's XI (Eastbourne)   April 24.
New Zealanders 287-8 dec (W. R. Playle 65, T. Meale 64) drew with L. C. Steven's XI 98-8 (J. W. D'Arcy 52).

DiMatch: v Duke of Norfolk's XI (Arundel Castle)   April 26.
Duke of Norfolk's XI 186-8 dec (D. V. Smith 83, H. B. Cave 4-90) drew with New Zealanders 40-0.

5th Match: v Worcestershire (Worcester)   April 30, May 1, 2.
Worcestershire 345-7 dec (P. E. Richardson 104, R. G. Broadbent 65) and 202-4 dec (D. Kenyon 102, M. J. Horton 57) drew with New Zealanders 283 (B. Sutcliffe 139) and 202-8 (T. Meale 89, R. O. Jenkins 4-59).*

6th Match: v Leicestershire (Leicester)   May 3, 5, 6.
New Zealanders 311 (W. R. Playle 96, L. S. M. Miller 68) beat Leicestershire 129 (J. C. Alabaster 6-37) and 118 (J. C. Alabaster 5-43, J. R. Reid 4-18) by an innings and 64 runs.

7th Match: v Surrey (Oval)   May 7, 8.
Surrey 288 (P. B. H. May 165, A. M. Moir 4-45) beat New Zealanders 74 (P. J. Loader 8-33) and 51 (G. A. R. Lock 5-9) by an innings and 163 runs.

8th Match: v Essex (Ilford)   May 10, 12, 13.
New Zealanders 140 (L. S. M. Miller 62) and 203 (L. H. R. Ralph 6-56) beat Essex 130 (J. A. Hayes 5-29, R. W. Blair 5-74) and 165 (T. E. Bailey 71) by 48 runs.

9th Match: v Cambridge University (Cambridge)   May 14, 15.
Cambridge University 206 (R. M. James 74, H. B. Cove 6-59) and 46 (R. W. Blair 6-19, A. R. MacGibbon 4-23) lost to New Zealanders 192 (J. R. Reid 97, A. Hurd 4-33, O. S. Wheatley 4-67) and 62-0 by 10 wkts.

10th Match: v M.C.C. (Lord's)   May 17, 19, 20.
New Zealanders 190 (L. S. M. Miller 76, N. S. Harford 52, R. Appleyard 4-36) and 266-8 dec (A. R. MacGibbon 66, L. S. M. Miller 66 N. S. Harford 59) beat M.C.C. 164 (J. A. Hayes 4-40) and 279 (M. J. K. Smith 70, J. A. Hayes 7-49) by 13 runs.*

11th Match: v Oxford University (The Parks, Oxford)   May 21, 22, 23.
New Zealanders 323-8 dec (N. S. Harford 158, J. R. Reid 91) and 45 (J. A. Bailey 6-28, D. M. Sayer 4-17) drew with Oxford University 242 (R. G. Woodcock 57, J. T. Sparling 4-41) and 68-5.

12th Match: v Glamorgan (Cardiff)   May 24, 26, 27.
Glamorgan 175-6 dec (A. J. Watkins 78, P. M. Walker 62) and 69 (H. B. Cave 4-18, A. R. MacGibbon 4-23) lost to New Zealanders 215 (J. W. D'Arcy 89, J. S. Pressdee 6-77) and 33-1 by 9 wkts.*

13th Match: v Somerset (Taunton)   May 28, 29.
Somerset 118 (A. R. MacGibbon 4-19, J. C. Alabaster 4-32) and 119 (J. A. Hayes 4-34) lost to New Zealanders 308-6 dec (J. R. Reid 161, T. Meale 64) by an innings and 71 runs.*

14th Match: v Hampshire (Southampton)   May 31, June 2, 3.
New Zealanders 249-7 dec (J. W. D'Arcy 60, J. R. Reid 55) drew with Hampshire 99 (A. M. Moir 5-27) and 98-4.

15th Match: v England (Edgbaston)   June 5, 6, 7, 9.
England 221 (P. B. H. May 84, M. C. Cowdrey 81, A. R. MacGibbon 5-64, J. C. Alabaster 4-46) and 215-6 dec (P. E. Richardson 100, M. C. Cowdrey 70) beat New Zealand 94 (F. S. Trueman 5-31) and 137 by 205 runs.

16th Match: v Derbyshire (Derby)   June 11, 12, 13.
New Zealanders 151 (J. R. Reid 51) and 70-5 dec (C. Gladwin 4-27) drew with Derbyshire 95-7 dec and 109-5.

17th Match: v Sussex (Hove)   June 14, 16, 17.
Sussex 274-9 dec (D. V. Smith 142) and 253 (D. S. Sheppard 102) drew with New Zealanders 385 (J. R. Reid 118, B. Sutcliffe 99, R. G. Marlar 4-78) and 114-8.

18th Match: v England (Lord's)   June 19, 20, 21.
England 269 (M. C. Cowdrey 65, J. A. Hayes 4-36, A. R. MacGibbon 4-86) beat New Zealand 47 (G. A. R. Lock 5-17, J. C. Laker 4-13) and 74 (G. A. R. Lock 4-12) by an innings and 148 runs.

19th Match: v Lancashire (Old Trafford)   June 25, 26, 27.
New Zealanders 144 (L. S. M. Miller 50, M. J. Hilton 8-19) drew with Lancashire 106-3.

20th Match: v Yorkshire (Bramall Lane)   June 28, 30, July 1.
Yorkshire 233-8 dec (J. V. Wilson 80) drew with New Zealanders did not bat.*

21st Match: v England (Headingley)   July 3, 4, 5, 7, 8.
New Zealand 67 (J. C. Laker 5-17, G. A. R. Lock 4-14) and 129 (G. A. R. Lock 7-51) lost to England 267-2 dec (C. A. Milton 104*, P. B. H. May 113*) by an innings and 71 runs.

22nd Match: v Scotland (Selkirk)   July 10.
Scotland 195-9 dec (J. C. Alabaster 5-31) drew with New Zealanders 119-9 (D. Barr 5-51).

23rd Match: v Scotland (Glasgow)   July 11, 12, 14.
New Zealanders 286 (B. Sutcliffe 127, J. M. Allan 4-65) beat Scotland 135 (J. T. Sparling 4-19) and 119 (J. T. Sparling 4-36) by an innings and 32 runs.

24th Match: v Ireland (Belfast)   July 16, 17.
Ireland 130 (J. T. Sparling 5-11) and 179 (R. O'Brien 52) drew with New Zealanders 208 (J. W. D'Arcy 61).

25th Match: v Ireland (Dublin)   July 18.
New Zealanders 182-4 dec (J. R. Reid 103, L. S. M. Miller 64) drew with Ireland 121-3 (P. Neville 50).*

26th Match: v Middlesex (Lord's)   July 19, 21, 22.
Middlesex 239 (J. D. B. Robertson 50, D. Bennett 56, R. W. Blair 5-74) and 174 (P. H. Parfitt 52, W. J. Edrich 51, A. M. Moir 4-30) drew with New Zealanders 289 (J. R. Reid 97, L. S. M. Miller 65, F. J. Titmus 6-86) and 3-0.

27th Match: v England (Old Trafford)   July 24, 25, 26, 28, 29.
New Zealand 267 (A. R. MacGibbon 66, J. T. Sparling 50, J. B. Statham 4-71) and 85 (G. A. R. Lock 7-35) lost to England 365-9 dec (P. B. H. May 101, P. E. Richardson 74, W. Watson 66, E. R. Dexter 52) by an innings and 13 runs.

28th Match: v Surrey (Oval)   July 30, 31.
New Zealanders 54 (D. Gibson 4-11) and 118 (N. S. Harford 54, K. F. Barrington 4-27) lost to Surrey 275 (P. B. H. May 112, M. J. Stewart 63) by an innings and 103 runs.*

29th Match: v Glamorgan (Swansea)   Aug 2, 4, 5.
New Zealanders 306-8 dec (N. S. Harford 127, J. R. Reid 69, B. Sutcliffe 55) drew with Glamorgan 104 (A. M. Moir 6-33) and 24-2.

30th Match: v Warwickshire (Edgbaston)   Aug 6, 7, 8.
Warwickshire 316-7 dec (F. C. Gardner 88, N. F. Horner 65, M. J. K. Smith 63) and 117-3 dec drew with New Zealanders 265 (T. Meale 62, J. W. D'Arcy 57, G. H. Hill 4-51) and 116-6 (J. R. Reid 56).*

31st Match: v Gloucestershire (Cheltenham)   Aug 9, 11, 12.
Gloucestershire 106 (H. B. Cave 5-39) and 160 (J. A. Hayes 4-9) drew with New Zealanders 127 (J. R. Reid 53, C. Cook 6-41, B. D. Wells 4-41) and 10-0.

32nd Match: v Northamptonshire (Northampton)   Aug 13, 14, 15.
New Zealanders 267 (J. R. Reid 114) and 232 (L. S. M. Miller 71) drew with Northamptonshire 167-3 dec and 111-2 (D. Brookes 51*).*

33rd Match: v Nottinghamshire (Trent Bridge)   Aug 16, 18, 19.
Nottinghamshire 264 (C. J. Poole 62, M. Hill 58, A. R. MacGibbon 4-80) and 175-9 dec (J. A. Hayes 4-63) drew with New Zealanders 259 (L. S. M. Miller 68, G. Goonesena 6-89) and 120-2 (J. R. Reid 73).*

34th Match: v England (Oval)   Aug 21, 22, 23, 25, 26.
New Zealand 161 and 91-3 (J. R. Reid 51*) drew with England 219-9 dec (A. R. MacGibbon 4-65).

35th Match: v Kent (Canterbury)   Aug 27, 28, 29.
Kent 140 (M. C. Cowdrey 57, H. B. Cove 5-49, R. W. Blair 4-41) and 20-0 drew with New Zealanders 136 (D. J. Halfyard 5-53).

36th Match: v A. E. R. Gilligan's XI (Hastings)   Sept 3, 4, 5.
New Zealanders 297 (N. S. Harford 80, L. S. M. Miller 51, G. E. Tribe 8-75) and 74-2 drew with A. E. R. Gilligan's XI 301-6 dec (F. M. M. Worrell 101, G. St A. Sobers 75).

37th Match: v Lancashire (Blackpool)   Sept 6, 8, 9.
Lancashire 250-4 dec (P. T. Marner 95, A. Wharton 85) and 65-2 drew with New Zealanders 253-6 dec (A. R. MacGibbon 81, T. Meale 54).

38th Match: v T. N. Pearce's XI (Scarborough)   Sept 10, 11, 12.
New Zealanders 268 (B. Sutcliffe 77, L. S. M. Miller 53, P. J. Sainsbury 4-91) and 303-8 dec (J. T. Sparling 85, B. Sutcliffe 74, N. S. Harford 56, P. J. Sainsbury 4-58) tied with T. N. Pearce's XI 313-7 dec (P. B. H. May 131, R. E. Marshall 78) and 258 (T. G. Evans 69, J. A. Hayes 5-72, J. C. Alabaster 4-71).

39th Match: v Minor Counties (Newcastle)   Sept 13, 14.
Minor Counties 305-7 dec (P. J. Sharpe 88, D. E. V. Padgett 76) drew with New Zealanders 109-7 (M. Ryan 4-28).

Moir and B. Sutcliffe of Otago; E. C. Petrie of Waikato and J. T. Ward from South Canterbury, with J. H. Phillips as manager. The side was criticised for relying too much on untried players and more especially for leaving McGregor, Guy, Chapple and Beck at home.

The team were given a full five five-day Test series–after playing four draws in 1949–but this time the arrangements seemed extravagant and if rain had not been very persistent, all five matches might well have ended within the standard first-class three days.

The New Zealanders began the tour in good form and by the First Test had won six matches and lost one. From then on disaster followed disaster and they won only one more match in 21 and lost the Test series four to nil.

The weather was dreadful for most of the summer and the batsmen, apart from Reid, found runs very hard to make. The batsmen all seemed to be on the defensive and even Sutcliffe struggled; d'Arcy opened the batting in a very determined manner–perhaps he made the bowlers look much better than they really were? In the first-class matches the bowling was very even; in the Tests MacGibbon took 20 wickets at 19.45, but no one else did much at all.

For some time the financial position of the tour looked shaky, though at the final count it made a profit of £4,000.

1958: 5th New Zealanders

Batting Averages

	M	I	NO	R	HS	Avge	100	c/s
J. R. Reid	28	39	3	1429	161	39.69	3	32/1
B. Sutcliffe	25	40	5	1085	139	31.00	2	9
L. S. M. Miller	26	42	4	1148	76	30.21	0	8
N. S. Harford	27	41	0	1067	158	26.02	2	15
T. Meale	18	27	4	502	89	21.82	0	11
A. R. MacGibbon	25	36	2	670	81	19.70	0	17
J. T. Sparling	22	33	4	513	85	17.68	0	13
J. W. D'Arcy	22	33	1	522	89	16.31	0	6
W. R. Playle	23	36	3	414	96	12.54	0	15
J. T. Ward	13	15	7	95	19	11.87	0	25/3
A. M. Moir	17	21	6	172	41*	11.46	0	5
H. B. Cave	22	29	10	216	26	11.36	0	14
E. C. Petrie	20	29	8	225	45*	10.71	0	40
J. C. Alabaster	16	22	4	176	40	9.77	0	13
J. A. Hayes	18	23	8	114	15	7.60	0	10
R. W. Blair	19	20	3	126	18	7.41	0	12

Bowling Averages

	O	M	R	W	Avge	BB	5i
J. A. Hayes	463.3	93	1253	62	20.20	7-49	3
J. T. Sparling	286.2	75	771	38	20.28	4-19	0
A. R. MacGibbon	680.2	186	1559	73	21.35	5-64	1
H. B. Cave	540.5	186	1101	50	22.02	6-59	3
J. R. Reid	366.2	107	887	39	22.74	4-18	0
R. W. Blair	475.5	116	1203	51	23.58	6-19	3
J. C. Alabaster	387.1	93	1055	43	24.53	6-37	2
A. M. Moir	300.3	87	917	35	26.20	6-33	2
B. Sutcliffe	50	6	226	7	32.28	3-67	0

Also bowled: J. W. D'Arcy 1.5-0-7-0; N. S. Harford 11-1-42-0; T. Meale 2-1-3-0; L. S. M. Miller 5-1-8-1; W. R. Playle 4-0-23-1.

Some of the fifth New Zealand touring party of 1958. Back: Miller, Meale, MacGibbon, Playle, Harford, Petrie. Front: Hayes, Cave, Reid (captain), Sutcliffe, Moir.

1959: 6th Indians

Batting Averages

	M	I	NO	R	HS	Avge	100	c/s
V. L. Manjrekar	9	14	3	755	204*	68.63	2	2
P. R. Umrigar	22	38	5	1826	252*	55.33	5	21
D. K. Gaekwad	23	38	4	1174	176	34.52	3	5
A. G. Kripal Singh	20	29	3	879	178	33.80	1	9
A. A. Baig	12	23	2	673	116	32.04	3	8
N. J. Contractor	22	40	2	1183	114	31.13	1	16
P. Roy	26	47	5	1207	155	28.73	1	12
A. L. Apte	19	34	2	881	165	27.53	3	4
C. G. Borde	26	46	7	1060	90	27.17	0	17
J. M. Ghorpade	22	37	2	833	70	23.80	0	8
R. G. Nadkarni	26	41	1	945	80	23.62	0	23
M. L. Jaisimha	22	39	4	824	83*	23.54	0	7
N. S. Tamhane	17	20	2	275	34	15.27	0	38/11
P. G. Joshi	16	29	3	336	72	12.92	0	26/11
Surendranath	25	34	13	226	27	10.76	0	11
V. M. Muddiah	12	13	6	71	46*	10.14	0	8
R. B. Desai	21	29	12	158	23	9.29	0	10
S. P. Gupte	23	31	6	176	31	7.04	0	6

Bowling Averages

	O	M	R	W	Avge	BB	5i
C. G. Borde	512.3	119	1485	72	20.62	5-33	4
S. P. Gupte	901.2	231	2526	95	26.58	8-108	4
R. G. Nadkarni	729.5	286	1563	55	28.41	4-34	0
Surendranath	901.4	274	2260	79	28.60	5-46	4
V. M. Muddiah	309.1	82	884	30	29.46	6-36	2
P. R. Umrigar	368	87	875	24	36.45	3-73	0
R. B. Desai	600.4	125	1864	45	41.42	5-89	1
M. L. Jaisimha	402.1	66	1450	29	50.00	3-54	0
A. G. Kripal Singh	193	42	568	10	56.80	3-84	0
J. M. Ghorpade	42	6	172	2	86.00	1-7	0

Also bowled: D. K. Gaekwad 2-0-11-0; P. Roy 2.2-1-12-1.

1959: 6th Indians

The team chosen for the tour was D. K. Gaekwad (captain), P. Roy, A. L. Apte, C. G. Borde, N. J. Contractor, R. B. Desai, J. M. Ghorpade, Ghulam Ahmed, S. P. Gupte, M. L. Jaisimha, P. G. Joshi, A. G. Kripal Singh, V. L. Manjrekar, R. G. Nadkarni, Surendranath and N. S. Tamhane, P. R. Umrigar with the Maharaja of Baroda as manager. Ghulam Ahmed later withdrew and V. M. Muddiah replaced him.

The Indians played five Tests and lost all five, the worst record of any Test-playing team to visit England. In 1958 the New Zealanders had the excuse that the weather was abysmal, but in

1959 the sun shone, which meant dry wickets–the type on which the Indians ought to have flourished. Surendranath, the principal seam bowler, was always trying to save runs instead of taking wickets, bowling on the leg side to a packed leg side field. The captain was criticised for the slowness of field changes and the lack of any real authority; Gaekwad seemed weighed down by his responsibilities and his batting suffered.

Manjrekar should have been the star of the batting, but was never fit and very overweight–he left the team after the Second Test and A. A. Baig, the Oxford batsman, was co-opted. He was the one bright spot in the tour and hit three hundreds in 12 games. Contractor was another slow scorer–unlike his performances at home–and combined with Roy to make a dull opening pair, a job also shared by Apte. The veteran Umrigar began in fine form, but struggled in the Tests until making a hundred at Old Trafford. Gupte, the leg spinner, took most wickets and would have obtained them cheaply if his field placings had been more appropriate to the batsmen. Borde broke a finger in the First Test and but for that might have performed the double; the other all-rounder, Kripal Singh, was unable to bowl much due to a finger injury and his batting was very moderate. Both wicketkeepers were competent but the fielding was too often slack and many runs were given away.

The side made a profit of £5,000.

1959: 6th Indians

1st Match: v Indian Gymkhana (Osterley)   April 23, 24.
Indians 268 (P. R. Umrigar 97, G. Goonesena 7-64) drew with Indian Gymkhana 136 (Surendranath 4-22) and 135-7 (K. G. Borde 4-36).

2nd Match: v Duke of Norfolk's XI (Arundel Castle)   April 25.
Match abandoned – no play due to rain.

3rd Match: v Worcestershire (Worcester)   April 29, 30, May 1.
Indians 219 (C. G. Borde 90, D. B. Pearson 4-40) and 157-3 (P. R. Umrigar 87) drew with Worcestershire 305 (G. Dews 122, R. G. Broadbent 102*, R. B. Desai 4-88).

4th Match: v Club Cricket Conference (Oval)   May 4, 5.
C.C.C. 98 (V. M. Muddiah 6-40) and 95 lost to Indians 186 (P. K. Roy 70, A. L. Apte 55, J. K. Hall 6-49) and 9-0 by 10 wkts.

5th Match: v Cambridge University (Cambridge)   May 6, 7, 8.
Cambridge University 223 (D. J. Green 80, R. G. Nadkarni 4-47) and 160 (D. J. Green 57, V. M. Muddiah 6-36) lost to Indians 436-6 dec (P. R. Umrigar 252*) by an innings and 53 runs.

6th Match: v Leicestershire (Leicester)   May 9, 11, 12.
Leicestershire 301-8 dec (M. R. Hallam 158, A. C. Revill 51) and 163-4 dec (W. Watson 85) drew with Indians 246 (D. K. Gaekwad 57, V. L. Manjrekar 51, B. S. Boshier 4-49) and 94-2.

7th Match: v Surrey (Oval)   May 13, 14, 15.
Indians 249 (V. L. Manjrekar 148, P. J. Loader 5-37) and 205-3 dec (P. R. Umrigar 83, N. J. Contractor 65) drew with Surrey 253 (B. Constable 91, K. F. Barrington 85, S. P. Gupte 6-77) and 151-2 (K. F. Barrington 59*, M. J. Stewart 50).

8th Match: v Glamorgan (Cardiff)   May 16, 18, 19.
Glamorgan 182 (J. S. Pressdee 113, C. G. Borde 4-17) and 223 (A. J. Watkins 61, J. E. McConnon 52, V. M. Muddiah 6-79) beat Indians 112 (D. J. Shepherd 4-34) and 242 (C. G. Borde 64, D. K. Gaekwad 63, J. E. McConnon 4-72) by 51 runs.

9th Match: v Essex (Ilford)   May 20, 21, 22.
Essex 285-9 dec (B. R. Knight 89, M. J. Bear 58, Surendranath 4-80) and 83-4 dec drew with Indians 188 (A. G. Kripal Singh 52, L. H. R. Ralph 5-33) and 98-2.

10th Match: v M.C.C. (Lord's)   May 23, 25, 26.
M.C.C. 374-4 dec (C. A. Milton 104, E. R. Dexter 100*, M. J. K. Smith 82) and 120-1 dec (M. J. K. Smith 64*) beat Indians 211 (C. G. Borde 88, P. R. Umrigar 82, A. E. Moss 5-41, F. H. Tyson 4-44) and 136 (R. Illingworth 5-34) by 147 runs.

11th Match: v Oxford University (Oxford)   May 27, 28, 29.
Oxford University 172 (S. P. Gupte 4-84) and 234 (J. Burki 110, S. P. Gupte 6-110) lost to Indians 459-4 dec (V. L. Manjrekar 204*, P. K. Roy 155, C. G. Borde 57*) by an innings and 53 runs.

12th Match: v Somerset (Taunton)   May 30, June 1, 2.
Indians 432-9 dec (P. R. Umrigar 203, D. K. Gaekwad 69, V. L. Manjrekar 53, B. A. Langford 4-142) and 119-8 dec (B. A. Langford 5-56) drew with Somerset 300 (C. L. McCool 91, G. G. Atkinson 60, C. G. Borde 5-42) and 52-4.

13th Match: v England (Trent Bridge)   June 4, 5, 6, 8.
England 422 (P. B. H. May 106, T. G. Evans 73, M. J. Horton 58, K. F. Barrington 56, S. P. Gupte 4-102) beat Indians 206 (P. K. Roy 54, F. S. Trueman 4-45) and 157 (J. B. Statham 5-31) by an innings and 59 runs.

14th Match: v Minor Counties (Longton)   June 10, 11, 12.
Indians 287 (D. K. Gaekwad 100, J. M. Ghorpade 67, M. L. Jaisimha 51, D. J. Laitt 4-58) and 274-7 dec (A. G. Kripal Singh 66*, J. M. Ghorpade 52) lost to Minor Counties 228 (J. T. Ikin 118) and 334-4 (P. J. Sharpe 202, F. R. Bailey 79) by 6 wkts.

15th Match: v Northamptonshire (Northampton)   June 13, 15, 16.
Northamptonshire 211 (A. Lightfoot 64, S. P. Gupte 4-84) and 208 (P. J. Watts 52, S. P. Gupte 4-95) lost to Indians 428-6 dec (P. R. Umrigar 202*, V. L. Manjrekar 55, P. K. Roy 53) by an innings and 9 runs.

16th Match: v England (Lord's)   June 18, 19, 20.
India 168 (N. J. Contractor 81, T. Greenhough 5-35) and 165 (V. L. Manjrekar 61) lost to England 226 (K. F. Barrington 80, R. B. Desai 5-89) and 108-2 (M. C. Cowdrey 63*) by 8 wkts.

17th Match: v Lancashire (Old Trafford)   June 24, 25, 26.
Lancashire 400-5 dec (G. Pullar 137, K. J. Grieves 95, J. D. Bond 66*) drew with Indians 196 (A. G. Kripal Singh 57, J. B. Statham 5-36, K. Higgs 4-66) and 87-2.

18th Match: v Derbyshire (Chesterfield)   June 27, 29, 30.
Derbyshire 241 (C. Lee 71, G. O. Dawkes 54) and 240-5 dec (D. C. Morgan 65, D. B. Carr 52) drew with Indians 323 (A. L. Apte 165, J. M. Ghorpade 70, E. Smith 5-67) and 77-2.

19th Match: v England (Headingley)   July 2, 3, 4.
India 161 (H. J. Rhodes 4-50) and 149 (D. B. Close 4-35) lost to England 483-8 dec (M. C. Cowdrey 160, K. F. Barrington 80, W. G. A. Parkhouse 78, G. Pullar 75, S. P. Gupte 4-111) by an innings and 173 runs.

20th Match: v Scotland (Paisley)   July 8, 9, 10.
Indians 293 (P. R. Umrigar 153*, D. Barr 5-43) and 210 (A. G. Kripal Singh 74) drew with Scotland 261 (F. A. Jones 88, C. G. Borde 4-57, Surendranath 4-68) and 153-8.

21st Match: v Yorkshire (Bramall Lane)   July 11, 13, 14.
Indians 381 (D. K. Gaekwad 176, P. K. Roy 87, R. G. Nadkarni 52) and 117-2 drew with Yorkshire 299 (R. Illingworth 162).

22nd Match: v Sussex (Hove)   July 15, 16, 17.
Indians 180 (C. G. Borde 50, A. E. James 5-65) and 363-5 (P. G. Joshi 72, P. K. Roy 63, P. R. Umrigar, J. M. Ghorpade 57*, C. G. Borde 58) drew with Sussex 369 (D. V. Smith 145*, L. J. Lenham 75, S. P. Gupte 4-57).

23rd Match: v Middlesex (Lord's)   July 18, 20, 21.
Indians 373-7 dec (A. A. Baig 102, N. J. Contractor 55, P. K. Roy 51, P. R. Umrigar 51, M. J. Smith 4-84) and 67-6 beat Middlesex 217 (R. W. Hooker 80, R. G. Nadkarni 4-34) and 222 (C. G. Borde 5-33, R. G. Nadkarni 4-41) by 4 wkts.

24th Match: v England (Old Trafford)   July 23, 24, 25, 27, 28.
England 490 (G. Pullar 131, M. J. K. Smith 100, K. F. Barrington 87, Surendranath 5-115) and 265-8 dec (S. P. Gupte 4-76) beat India 208 (C. G. Borde 75) and 376 (P. R. Umrigar 118, A. A. Baig 112, N. J. Contractor 56) by 171 runs.

25th Match: v Surrey (Oval)   July 29, 30, 31.
Indians 154 (P. K. Roy 95, D. A. D. Sydenham 5-42, D. Gibson 5-48) and 139 (P. R. Umrigar 56, G. A. R. Lock 5-49) drew with Surrey 214 (Surendranath 5-46) and 64-5 (Surendranath 4-28).

26th Match: v Glamorgan (Swansea)   Aug 1, 3, 4.
Indians 291 (D. K. Gaekwad 74, N. J. Contractor 50, D. J. Shepherd 5-77) and 199 (A. L. Apte 103, D. J. Shepherd 5-57) beat Glamorgan 208 (J. S. Pressdee 82, W. G. A. Parkhouse 60) and 166 (S. P. Gupte 4-51) by 114 runs.

27th Match: v Warwickshire (Edgbaston)   Aug 5, 6, 7.
Indians 284 (R. G. Nadkarni 80, R. G. Carter 4-53, R. G. Thompson 4-59) and 241-3 dec (N. J. Contractor 73, A. L. Apte 53, C. G. Borde 50*) drew with Warwickshire 356-8 dec (W. B. Bridge 56, M. J. K. Smith 52, J. G. Fox 52, F. C. Gardner 51, C. G. Borde 4-68) and 92-6.

28th Match: v Nottinghamshire (Trent Bridge)   Aug 8, 10, 11.
Indians 172 (P. R. Umrigar 80) and 255 (M. L. Jaisimha 55) lost to Nottinghamshire 284 (R. T. Simpson 100, H. M. Winfield 54, N. W. Hill 50, S. P. Gupte 8-108) and 144-2 (G. Millman 71*) by 8 wkts.

29th Match: v Yorkshire (Bradford)   Aug 12, 13, 14.
Yorkshire 146 and 159-6 drew with Indians 256 (M. L. Jaisimha 66, J. M. Ghorpade 59, R. G. Nadkarni 51, B. Stead 7-76).

30th Match: v Gloucestershire (Cheltenham)   Aug 15, 17, 18.
Gloucestershire 318-9 dec (G. M. Emmett 85, C. A. Milton 77, B. J. Meyer 63, S. P. Gupte 4-93) and 186-4 dec (C. A. Milton 57) beat Indians 179 (P. R. Umrigar 80, C. Cook 5-27) and 133 (D. R. Smith 5-32) by 192 runs.

31st Match: v England (Oval)   Aug 20, 21, 22, 24.
Indians 140 (F. S. Trueman 4-24) and 194 (R. G. Nadkarni 76) lost to England 361 (M. J. K. Smith 98, R. Subba Row 94, R. Swetman 65, R. Illingworth 50, Surendranath 5-75) by an innings and 27 runs.

32nd Match: v Hampshire (Bournemouth)   Aug 26, 27, 28.
Hampshire 360-9 dec (H. M. Barnard 128, P. J. Sainsbury 53, R. G. Nadkarni 4-89) and 147-3 dec (J. R. Gray 58, R. E. Marshall 56) drew with Indians 337 (A. A. Baig 116, A. G. Kripal Singh 64, R. G. Nadkarni 59) and 96-8.

33rd Match: v Kent (Canterbury)   Aug 29, 31, Sept 1.
Kent 258 (A. L. Dixon 76, C. G. Borde 5-44) and 147 (C. G. Borde 5-42) lost to Indians 303 (D. K. Gaekwad 116, D. J. Halfyard 4-71) and 106-2 (N. J. Contractor 51*) by 8 wkts.

34th Match: v A. E. R. Gilligan's XI (Hastings)   Sept 2, 3, 4.
A. E. R. Gilligan's XI 375 (M. R. Hallam 98, G. St A. Sobers 74) and 200-7 dec (F. M. M. Worrell 54, R. B. Desai 4-58) drew with Indians 285 (N. J. Contractor 114) and 254-6 (A. L. Apte 112, C. G. Borde 63).

35th Match: v Lancashire (Blackpool)   Sept 5, 7, 8.
Lancashire 486-7 dec (K. J. Grieves 202*, G. Pullar 78, J. D. Bond 61, G. Clayton 58) and 175-5 dec (J. D. Bond 58*) drew with Indians 448 (A. G. Kripal Singh 178, C. G. Borde 59, M. L. Jaisimha 56) and 148-3 (A. A. Baig 59, A. L. Apte 55).

36th Match: v T. N. Pearce's XI (Scarborough)   Sept 9, 10, 11.
Indians 176 (M. L. Jaisimha 83*, F. S. Trueman 4-48) and 310 (P. K. Roy 79, D. K. Gaekwad 70, A. G. Kripal Singh 62, R. Illingworth 4-61) lost to T. N. Pearce's XI 252 (Surendranath 5-52) and 235-5 (E. R. Dexter 62*, R. E. Marshall 61) by 5 wkts.

37th Match: v Durham (Sunderland)   Sept 12, 14.
Durham 267-8 dec (C. Milburn 101, D. W. Hardy 66*) and 152-7 dec (D. W. Hardy 51) drew with Indians 181 (D. K. Gaekwad 51, J. M. Watson 6-23) and 210-7 (C. G. Borde 81).

1960: 12th South Africans

The team selected for the 1960 tour were D. J. McGlew (captain), T. L. Goddard, R. A. McLean, G. M. Griffin, C. Wesley, all of Natal; J. H. B. Waite, N. A. T. Adcock, S. O'Linn, H. J. Tayfield, P. R. Carlstein and J. P. Fellows-Smith of Transvaal; A. J. Pithey and C. A. R. Duckworth of Rhodesia; A. H. McKinnon of Eastern Province and J. E. Pothecary from Western Province, with A. D. Nourse as manager. The most prominent of those not chosen was Winslow, but his current batting form was not very encouraging. The side flew into London on 17 April from Johannesburg to be greeted by a crowd of some 300 anti-apartheid demonstrators.

The main talking point before the county matches began was the suspect action of the fast bowler, Griffin, who continued to dominate the headlines until the Second Test at Lord's, when umpire Buller no-balled him for throwing and ended his bowling for the rest of the tour—he continued to play solely as a batsman.

The first-class record for the tour was only slightly worse than in 1955, but this time the visitors lost three Tests and did not win one. This poor result was because of a lack of determined batting. McGlew and Goddard both failed in the Tests—McGlew was dogged by the cares of captaincy and Goddard had his confidence shattered by Statham. The young players Carlstein, Wesley, Pithey and Duckworth made very little progress and the team had to rely on McLean, who batted well, O'Linn with his crab-like persistence and Fellows-Smith, who was used as a general stop-gap.

The bowling, limited by the absence of Griffin, did all that could be expected. Adcock bowled admirably and had the best Test record—26 wickets, average 22.57; Goddard was accuracy itself and took 17 wickets, but Tayfield bowled well in the county matches only to lose his edge in the Tests. McKinnon, left-arm slow, bowled off the wrong foot and only played in one Test, but was very effective in county matches.

Waite was an excellent wicketkeeper and headed the Test batting averages—probably the best wicketkeeper-batsman of the day. The fielding was not as sharp as in 1955.

It was a rather wet summer and financially the tour was a disaster—the first tour since the Second World War not to make a

---

1960: 12th South Africans

1st Match: v Duke of Norfolk's XI (Arundel Castle) April 30.
Duke of Norfolk's XI 220-8 dec (F. J. Titmus 56, H. J. Tayfield 5-102) lost to South Africans 224-5 (D. J. McGlew 72, R. A. McLean 54) by 5 wkts.*

2nd Match: v Worcestershire (Worcester) May 4, 5, 6.
South Africans 365-6 dec (R. A. McLean 207, A. J. Pithey 76) and 144-1 dec (D. J. McGlew 63*, T. L. Goddard 63) beat Worcestershire 235 (D. W. Richardson 72, J. E. Pothecary 4-55) and 141 (A. H. McKinnon 7-42) by 133 runs.

3rd Match: v Derbyshire (Derby) May 7, 9, 10.
Derbyshire 108 (N. A. T. Adcock 6-44) and 211 (I. W. Hall 67, N. A. T. Adcock 6-44) lost to South Africans 343-8 dec (A. J. Pithey 96, D. J. McGlew 93, S. O'Linn 73, H. L. Jackson 4-69) by an innings and 24 runs.

4th Match: v Oxford University (Oxford) May 11, 12, 13.
Oxford University 77-4 drew with South Africans did not bat.

5th Match: v Essex (Ilford) May 14, 16, 17.
Essex 98 (H. J. Tayfield 5-43) and 274 (D. J. Insole 105, G. J. Smith 50, N. A. T. Adcock 4-30) lost to South Africans 287 (J. P. Fellows-Smith 109*, T. E. Bailey 7-81) and 86-4 by 6 wkts.

6th Match: v Cambridge University (Cambridge) May 18, 19, 20.
Cambridge University 192 (R. M. Prideaux 64, A. R. Lewis 55, J. E. Pothecary 4-79) and 80 (N. A. T. Adcock 6-26) lost to South Africans 145 (J. B. Brodie 5-47) and 128-3 (D. J. McGlew 54*) by 7 wkts.

7th Match: v M.C.C. (Lord's) May 21, 23, 24.
M.C.C. 208 (P. H. Walker 57) and 137-9 dec (H. J. Tayfield 4-33) drew with South Africans 149 (J. H. B. Waite 50) and 126-7 (T. L. Goddard 56).

8th Match: v Northamptonshire (Northampton) May 25, 26, 27.
South Africans 461-3 dec (T. L. Goddard 186*, R. A. McLean 180, D. J. McGlew 52) and 101-8 dec (C. A. R. Duckworth 51*) lost to Northamptonshire 363 (R. Subba Row 108, M. E. J. C. Norman 75, H. J. Tayfield 6-123) and 203-6 by 4 wkts.

9th Match: v Nottinghamshire (Trent Bridge) May 28, 30, 31.
Nottinghamshire 280 (R. T. Simpson 63, N. W. Hill 51, T. L. Goddard 5-71) and 193-4 drew with South Africans 433 (P. R. Carlstein 80, S. O'Linn 72, D. J. McGlew 68, T. L. Goddard 68, A. J. Pithey 59, J. Cotton 5-69).

10th Match: v Minor Counties (Stoke-on-Trent) June 1, 2.
Minor Counties 220 (R. Collins 96, N. A. T. Adcock 5-37) and 170 (N. H. Moore 59, N. A. T. Adcock 5-31) lost to South Africans 373 (D. J. McGlew 124, C. Wesley 90, C. A. R. Duckworth 59, J. T. Ikin 6-79) and 20-1 by 9 wkts.

11th Match: v Glamorgan (Cardiff) June 4, 6.
Glamorgan 87 (J. P. Fellows-Smith 6-37, T. L. Goddard 4-31) and 138 (W. G. A. Parkhouse 67, H. J. Tayfield 5-44, A. H. McKinnon 4-17) lost to South Africans 358-3 dec (D. J. McGlew 151*, T. L. Goddard 146) by an innings and 133 runs.

12th Match: v England (Edgbaston) June 9, 10, 11, 13, 14.
England 292 (R. Subba Row 56, M. J. K. Smith 54, E. R. Dexter 52, N. A. T. Adcock 5-62) and 203 (H. J. Tayfield 4-62) beat South Africa 186 (J. H. B. Waite 58, F. S. Trueman 4-58) and 209 (R. A. McLean 68, J. H. B. Waite 56*) by 100 runs.

13th Match: v Somerset (Taunton) July 15, 16, 17.
South Africans 365 (D. J. McGlew 73, S. O'Linn 69, J. H. B. Waite 58) beat Somerset 122 (A. H. McKinnon 6-50) and 220 (W. E. Alley 72, A. H. McKinnon 6-69) by an innings and 23 runs.

14th Match: v Hampshire (Southampton) June 18, 20, 21.
South Africans 507 (P. R. Carlstein 151, C. Wesley 84, G. M. Griffin 65*, D. J. McGlew 62, J. P. Fellows-Smith 57, D. W. White 5-134) and 37-1 beat Hampshire 195 (D. O. Baldry 70, H. J. Tayfield 5-66) and 346 (H. Horton 117, H. M. Barnard 77, J. R. Gray 51, H. J. Tayfield 6-78) by 9 wkts.

15th Match: v England (Lord's) June 23, 24, 25, 27.
England 362-8 dec (M. J. K. Smith 99, R. Subba Row 90, E. R. Dexter 56, P. M. Walker 52, G. M. Griffin 4-87) beat South Africa 152 (J. B. Statham 6-63, A. E. Moss 4-35) and 137 (J. B. Statham 5-34) by an innings and 73 runs.

16th Match: v Gloucestershire (Bristol) June 29, 30.
South Africans 116 (J. B. Mortimore 5-52) and 49 (D. G. A'Court 6-25) lost to Gloucestershire 81 and 87-7 (N. A. T. Adcock 4-31) by 3 wkts.

17th Match: v Lancashire (Old Trafford) July 2, 4, 5.
Lancashire 351-6 dec (K. J. Grieves 104, J. D. Bond 100*, R. Collins 75) and 72-2 drew with South Africans 233 (R. A. McLean 56, J. B. Statham 4-33).

18th Match: v England (Trent Bridge) July 7, 8, 9, 11.
England 287 (K. F. Barrington 80, M. C. Cowdrey 67, T. L. Goddard 5-80) and 49-2 beat South Africa 88 (F. S. Trueman 5-27) and 247 (S. O'Linn 98, J. H. B. Waite 60, F. S. Trueman 4-77) by 8 wkts.

19th Match: v Leicestershire (Leicester) July 13, 14, 15.
Leicestershire 287-3 dec (M. R. Hallam 164, H. D. Bird 104) and 117-8 dec (T. L. Goddard 6-29) drew with South Africans 235 (C. Wesley 90) and 158-4 (P. R. Carlstein 75, R. A. McLean 53).

20th Match: v Middlesex (Lord's) July 16, 18, 19.
Middlesex 191 (P. H. Parfitt 60, R. A. White 50, N. A. T. Adcock 4-35, H. J. Tayfield 4-47) and 102-4 drew with South Africans 397-6 dec (T. L. Goddard 142, P. R. Carlstein 68, R. A. McLean 65, A. J. Pithey 57).

21st Match: v England (Old Trafford) July 21, 22, 23, 25, 26.
England 260 (K. F. Barrington 76, N. A. T. Adcock 4-66) and 153-7 dec drew with South Africa 229 (R. A. McLean 109, D. A. Allen 4-58) and 46-0.

22nd Match: v Surrey (Oval) July 27, 28, 29.
South Africans 338-6 dec (J. H. B. Waite 125, R. A. McLean 53) and 67-4 dec drew with Surrey 223-7 dec (E. A. Bedser 67*, M. J. Stewart 53, N. A. T. Adcock 5-66) and 53-2.

23rd Match: v Glamorgan (Swansea) July 30, Aug 1, 2.
Glamorgan 111 (H. J. Tayfield 7-51) and 169-9 dec (H. J. Tayfield 5-90) lost to South Africans 151 (D. J. Shepherd 8-45) and 130-1 (D. J. McGlew 76*) by 9 wkts.

24th Match: v Warwickshire (Edgbaston) Aug 3, 4, 5.
South Africans 185 (S. O'Linn 61, R. G. Thompson 4-60, J. D. Bannister 4-80) and 244-5 dec (S. O'Linn 120*, R. A. McLean 55) drew with Warwickshire 149 (H. J. Tayfield 6-66) and 135-5.

25th Match: v Yorkshire (Bramall Lane) Aug 6, 8, 9.
Yorkshire 198 (D. E. V. Padgett 63, P. J. Sharpe 53, J. E. Pothecary 4-68) and 140-9 dec (J. E. Pothecary 4-52) drew with South Africans 103 (R. Illingworth 5-26) and 91-4.

26th Match: v Sussex (Hove) Aug 10, 11, 12.
Match abandoned – no play due to rain.

27th Match: v Kent (Canterbury) Aug 13, 15, 16.
South Africans 271-9 dec (J. P. Fellows-Smith 56, T. L. Goddard 51, P. H. Jones 5-50) and 236-9 dec (J. P. Fellows-Smith 50) beat Kent 192 (P. H. Jones 71, A. H. McKinnon 7-73) and 155 (P. E. Richardson 54, A. H. McKinnon 4-62) by 160 runs.

28th Match: v England (Oval) Aug 18, 19, 20, 22, 23.
England 155 (G. Pullar 59, N. A. T. Adcock 6-65) and 479-9 dec (G. Pullar 175, M. C. Cowdrey 155) drew with South Africa 419 (T. L. Goddard 99, J. H. B. Waite 77) and 97-4.

29th Match: v Combined Services (Portsmouth) Aug 27, 29, 30.
South Africans 239 (C. Wesley 64, B. Stead 6-68) and 201-3 dec (T. L. Goddard 116, J. P. Fellows-Smith 57) beat Combined Services 103 (H. J. Tayfield 8-51) and 110 (N. A. T. Adcock 5-32) by 227 runs.

30th Match: v A. E. R. Gilligan's XI (Hastings) Aug 31, Sept 1, 2.
South Africans 238 (A. J. Pithey 70, C. Wesley 61, D. C. Morgan 4-39) and 314 (R. A. McLean 110, J. E. Pothecary 68) beat A. E. R. Gilligan's XI 261 (R. B. Kanhai 62, D. C. Morgan 59, M. E. J. C. Norman 53, H. J. Tayfield 4-107) and 178 by 113 runs.

31st Match: v Lancashire (Blackpool) Sept 3, 5.
Lancashire 90 (A. Wharton 52, T. L. Goddard 5-19) and 173 (T. L. Goddard 5-60) lost to South Africans 198 (R. A. McLean 62, C. A. R. Duckworth 50, J. B. Statham 4-25) and 66-5 by 5 wkts.

32nd Match: v T. N. Pearce's XI (Scarborough) Sept 7, 8, 9.
T. N. Pearce's XI 264 (E. R. Dexter 67, M. J. K. Smith 81, R. E. Marshall 67, C. Wesley 4-51) and 231 (M. J. K. Smith 81, R. E. Marshall 67, C. Wesley 4-51) lost to South Africans 304 (P. R. Carlstein 82, T. L. Goddard 52, D. A. Allen 5-85) and 192-6 (J. H. B. Waite 60, R. A. McLean 53) by 4 wkts.

profit; in 1955 930,000 people attended the tourists' matches, but in 1960 only 430,000 did and the expenses of £35,000 were just about covered.

1960: 12th South Africans

Batting Averages	M	I	NO	R	HS	Avge	100	c/s
D. J. McGlew	25	39	8	1327	151*	42.80	2	12
R. A. McLean	26	43	3	1516	207	37.90	4	22
T. L. Goddard	24	39	2	1377	186*	37.21	1	18
S. O'Linn	24	37	9	1014	120*	36.21	1	18
J. H. B. Waite	24	31	6	894	125	35.76	1	55/8
J. P. Fellows-Smith	23	34	7	863	109*	31.96	1	19
P. R. Carlstein	24	39	6	980	151	29.69	1	12
A. J. Pithey	18	25	3	614	96	27.90	0	10
C. Wesley	21	31	4	595	90	22.03	0	8
C. A. R. Duckworth	18	25	2	426	59	18.52	0	22/2
G. M. Griffin	18	22	2	353	65*	17.65	0	6
J. E. Pothecary	21	24	4	277	68	13.85	0	18
H. J. Tayfield	26	31	7	315	46*	13.12	0	19
A. H. McKinnon	18	14	6	70	22	8.75	0	1
N. A. T. Adcock	20	20	5	71	11	4.73	0	7

Bowling Averages	O	M	R	W	Avge	BB	5i
N. A. T. Adcock	737	196	1515	108	14.02	6-44	8
T. L. Goddard	752.2	308	1439	73	19.71	6-29	5
A. H. McKinnon	436.1	136	1107	53	20.88	7-42	4
H. J. Tayfield	1048	333	2664	123	21.65	8-51	9
G. M. Griffin	259.4	71	612	26	23.53	4-87	0
J. P. Fellows-Smith	319.4	69	829	32	25.90	6-37	1
J. E. Pothecary	632.5	163	1565	53	29.52	4-55	0
D. J. McGlew	75.1	13	264	8	33.00	2-28	0
P. R. Carlstein	36.2	3	158	4	39.50	3-37	0

Also bowled: R. A. McLean 9.2-0-28-2; J. H. B. Waite 1-0-1-0; C. Wesley 15-3-51-4.

1961: 23rd Australians

The team selected was R. Benaud (captain), R. N. Harvey, B. C. Booth, A. K. Davidson, F. M. Misson and N. C. O'Neill, all of New South Wales; P. J. P. Burge, A. T. W. Grout and K. D. Mackay of Queensland; R. A. Gaunt, L. F. Kline, W. M. Lawry, C. C. McDonald and I. W. Quick of Victoria; B. N. Jarman of South Australia and G. D. McKenzie and R. B. Simpson of Western Australia, with S. G. Webb as manager and R. C. Steele as treasurer. The main topic at the time of the selection was Australia's clutch of 'unfair' bowlers—notably Meckiff, Rourke and Burke, whose actions were akin to throwing. None of the 'doubtful' bowlers featured in the team, however, which was a relief to everyone, since it meant that there would be no repetition of the embarrassment caused by the South African Griffin's no-balling in 1960.

The team landed in England on 21 April, having sailed from Australia via Colombo where they played their customary one-day game against Ceylon. Rain prevented them having very much net practice and continued to dog the tourists for their first three county matches, all of which were drawn because of wet weather. The sun then appeared and before the First Test the tourists won four matches and lost none. The Test was a draw in favour of the Australians and three matches later they won the Second Test with a day and a half in hand. England won the Third Test due to some great bowling from Trueman. A magnificent fight back by the Australians after being 177 behind on first innings gave them victory in the Fourth Test and the final match was drawn in their favour. Thus Benaud's team beat England and provided a very interesting series. Their record in all first-class matches of 13 wins out of 32 did not look formidable, but the team played positive cricket and tried to avoid using the county games merely as match practice for the Tests.

The batting strength began with the opener, Lawry, who was very dependable and topped both Test and first-class averages; O'Neill was a disappointment only because he had come to England with a great newspaper reputation—his failing was the sweep, but he still averaged 40 in the Tests; the left-hander Harvey was the veteran of the side and he also had a good tour, playing two remarkable innings on the difficult wicket in the

Neil Harvey, the greatest Australian left-hand batsmen of the first two post-war decades, had his last England tour in 1961, batting superbly on a dreadful wicket in the Headingley Test.

1961: 23rd Australians

Batting Averages	M	I	NO	R	HS	Avge	100	c/s
W. M. Lawry	23	39	6	2019	165	61.18	9	15
N. C. O'Neill	24	37	4	1981	162	60.03	7	20
P. J. P. Burge	24	36	11	1376	181	55.04	4	16
R. B. Simpson	26	44	6	1947	160	51.23	6	23
C. C. McDonald	17	26	7	913	140	48.05	4	2
B. C. Booth	23	32	3	1279	127*	44.10	2	17
R. N. Harvey	24	35	2	1452	140	44.00	5	25
B. N. Jarman	15	14	5	354	85	39.33	0	29/14
K. D. Mackay	21	25	3	683	168	31.04	2	10
A. K. Davidson	20	25	5	607	90	30.35	0	15
R. Benaud	22	32	7	627	80*	25.08	0	18
A. T. W. Grout	17	21	3	299	49	16.61	0	51/9
F. M. Misson	19	15	3	194	33	16.16	0	20
G. D. McKenzie	21	26	8	254	48	14.11	0	8
R. A. Gaunt	17	12	6	77	30	12.83	0	5
I. W. Quick	20	18	9	108	18	12.00	0	8
L. F. Kline	19	12	2	68	22*	6.80	0	12

Bowling Averages	O	M	R	W	Avge	BB	5i
R. A. Gaunt	360.2	97	845	40	21.12	6-50	1
A. K. Davidson	634.2	182	1517	68	22.30	6-46	5
R. N. Harvey	53.3	21	93	4	23.25	4-8	0
R. Benaud	575.5	193	1436	61	23.54	6-70	5
F. M. Misson	479.3	123	1287	51	25.23	6-75	1
L. F. Kline	539.4	168	1519	54	28.12	5-16	2
K. D. Mackay	667.2	206	1479	52	28.44	5-121	1
G. D. McKenzie	569.2	156	1547	54	28.64	5-29	8
R. B. Simpson	539.4	163	1707	51	33.47	4-13	0
I. W. Quick	541.2	172	1700	50	34.00	4-107	0
N. C. O'Neill	80.5	18	269	6	44.83	2-44	0

Also bowled: B. C. Booth 12-1-37-0; W. M. Lawry 7-2-33-1; P. J. P. Burge 3-1-13-0; C. C. McDonald 3-0-14-0.

1961: 23rd Australians

1st Match: v Worcestershire (Worcester)   April 29, May 1, 2.
Australians 177 (M. J. Horton 5-46) and 141 (L. J. Coldwell 5-45) drew with Worcestershire 155 (K. D. Mackay 4-14) and 56-4.

2nd Match: v Derbyshire (Chesterfield)   May 3, 4, 5.
Australians 33-2 drew with Derbyshire did not bat.

3rd Match: v Yorkshire (Bradford)   May 6, 8, 9.
Australians 256-3 dec (N. C. O'Neill 100*, R. B. Simpson 72) drew with Yorkshire 149-8 (R. Illingworth 54).

4th Match: v Lancashire (Old Trafford)   May 10, 11, 12.
Lancashire 310-7 dec (P. T. Marner 87, J. D. Bond 68) and 204 lost to Australia.s 402-8 dec (R. N. Harvey 120, P. J. P. Burge 101*, N. C. O'Neill 74) and 114-6 (K. Higgs 4-57) by 4 wkts.

5th Match: v Surrey (Oval)   May 13, 15, 16.
Australians 341-7 dec (W. M. Lawry 165, G. A. R. Lock 4-124) and 38-0 beat Surrey 161 (P. B. H. May 58, R. B. Simpson 4-13) and 214 (M. D. Willett 55) by 10 wkts.

6th Match: v Cambridge University (Cambridge)   May 17, 18, 19.
Australians 449-3 dec (B. C. Booth 113, K. D. Mackay 106*, W. M. Lawry 100, C. C. McDonald 100) and 67-1 beat Cambridge University 230 (J. M. Brearley 73, K. D. Mackay 4-43, I. W. Quick 4-107) and 285 (J. M. Brearley 89) by 9 wkts.

7th Match: v Glamorgan (Cardiff)   May 20, 22, 23.
Australians 402 (N. C. O'Neill 124, R. N. Harvey 117, A. K. Davidson 68) and 90-0 drew with Glamorgan 235 (W. G. A. Parkhouse 70, J. S. Pressdee 54, A. K. Davidson 5-63) and 283-7 dec (J. S. Pressdee 118*).

8th Match: v Gloucestershire (Bristol)   May 24, 25, 26.
Australians 291-9 dec (A. K. Davidson 90, N. C. O'Neill 73) and 154-3 dec (R. Benaud 53*) drew with Gloucestershire 167 (R. B. Nicholls 58) and 244-8 (D. Carpenter 85).

9th Match: v M.C.C. (Lord's)   May 27, 29, 30.
Australians 381-5 dec (N. C. O'Neill 122, W. M. Lawry 104, B. C. Booth 59) and 186-0 dec (R. B. Simpson 92*, W. M. Lawry 84*) beat M.C.C. 274 (M. C. Cowdrey 115, K. F. Barrington 55, A. K. Davidson 6-46) and 230 (M. C. Cowdrey 68, M. J. K. Smith 58, R. Benaud 5-67) by 63 runs.

10th Match: v Oxford University (Oxford)   May 31, June 1, 2.
Oxford University 320-9 dec (A. A. Baig 95, C. D. Drybrough 88, F. W. Neate 78) and 235-5 (D. R. Worsley 80, A. A. Baig 73) drew with Australians 362 (R. B. Simpson 148, W. M. Lawry 72, K. D. Mackay 54, D. B. Pithey 7-47).

11th Match: v Sussex (Hove)   June 3, 5, 6.
Sussex 336 (K. G. Suttle 75, G. C. Cooper 62, N. I. Thomson 56, R. Benaud 5-83) and 189 (F. M. Misson 6-75) drew with Australians 281 (P. J. P. Burge 158) and 236-8 (C. C. McDonald 116*).

12th Match: v England (Edgbaston)   June 8, 9, 10, 12, 13.
England 195 (R. Subba Row, 59, K. D. Mackay 4-57) and 401-4 (E. R. Dexter 180, R. Subba Row 112) drew with Australia 516-9 dec (R. N. Harvey 114, N. C. O'Neill 82, R. B. Simpson 76, K. D. Mackay 64, W. M. Lawry 57).

13th Match: v Leicestershire (Leicester)   June 14, 15, 16.
Leicestershire 239 (L. R. Gardner 102, A. Wharton 74, G. D. McKenzie 5-60) and 172 (L. F. Kline 4-24) lost to Australians 356 (P. J. P. Burge 137, C. C. McDonald 105, J. van Geloven 6-98) and 56-0 by 10 wkts.

14th Match: v Kent (Canterbury)   June 17, 19, 20.
Australians 428-6 dec (N. C. O'Neill 104, W. M. Lawry 100, R. B. Simpson 65) and 202-5 dec (R. N. Harvey 66, P. H. Jones 4-41) drew with Kent 340-6 dec (M. C. Cowdrey 149, A. H. Phebey 59, S. E. Leary 51) and 284-6 (M. C. Cowdrey 121, S. E. Leary 60).

15th Match: v England (Lord's)   June 22, 23, 24, 26.
England 206 (A. K. Davidson 5-42) and 202 (K. F. Barrington 66, G. D. McKenzie 5-37) lost to Australia 340 (W. M. Lawry 130, K. D. Mackay 54, F. S. Trueman 4-118) and 71-5 by 5 wkts.

16th Match: v Somerset (Taunton)   June 28, 29, 30.
Australians 440-3 dec (C. C. McDonald 140, B. C. Booth 127*, W. M. Lawry 70) and 202-4 dec (B. N. Jarman 85) drew with Somerset 298 (W. E. Alley 134, L. F. Kline 5-89) and 230-9 (W. E. Alley 95, B. Roe 71, R. A. Gaunt 6-50).

17th Match: v Lancashire (Old Trafford)   July 1, 3, 4.
Lancashire 346 (G. Pullar 165, G. Clayton 63) and 134-2 (P. T. Marner 71*) drew with Australians 548-6 dec (N. C. O'Neill 162, W. M. Lawry 122, R. B. Simpson 103).

18th Match: v England (Headingley)   July 6, 7, 8.
Australia 237 (R. N. Harvey 73, C. C. McDonald 54, F. S. Trueman 5-58) and 120 (F. S. Trueman 6-30) lost to England 299 (M. C. Cowdrey 93, G. Pullar 53, A. K. Davidson 5-63) and 62-2 by 8 wkts.

19th Match: v Club Cricket Conference (Blackheath)   July 13.
Australians 149 (J. Melville 6-46) lost to C.C.C. 152-2 (P. J. Whitcombe 71) by 8 wkts.

20th Match: v Nottinghamshire (Trent Bridge)   July 15, 17, 18.
Australians 364-8 dec (R. N. Harvey 140, R. B. Simpson 77, B. C. Booth 59) drew with Nottinghamshire 125 (L. F. Kline 5-16, K. D. Mackay 4-36) and 222-7 (N. W. Hill 98, C. J. Poole 55, A. K. Davidson 5-32).

21st Match: v Northamptonshire (Northampton)   July 19, 20, 21.
Australians 313 (N. C. O'Neill 142) and 173 (W. M. Lawry 100) drew with Northamptonshire 289-6 dec (A. Lightfoot 80*, M. E. J. C. Norman 66, B. L. Reynolds 60) and 197-6 (M. E. J. C. Norman 84, A. Lightfoot 57*).

22nd Match: v Middlesex (Lord's)   July 22, 24, 25.
Australians 316-8 dec (K. D. Mackay 168, B. C. Booth 53, D. Bennett 5-76) and 26-0 beat Middlesex 153 (R. Benaud 4-38) and 185 (R. Benaud 5-32, R. N. Harvey 4-8) by 10 wkts.

23rd Match: v England (Old Trafford)   July 27, 28, 29, 31, Aug 1.
Australia 190 (W. M. Lawry 74, J. B. Statham 5-53) and 432 (W. M. Lawry 102, A. K. Davidson 77*, N. C. O'Neill 67, R. B. Simpson 51, D. A. Allen 4-58) beat England 367 (P. B. H. May 95, K. F. Barrington 78, G. Pullar 63, R. B. Simpson 4-23) and 201 (E. R. Dexter 76, R. Benaud 6-70) by 54 runs.

24th Match: v Surrey (Oval)   Aug 2, 3, 4.
Australians 209 (G. A. R. Lock 5-93) and 225-9 dec (R. B. Simpson 64) beat Surrey 79 (R. A. Gaunt 4-26) and 100 (K. F. Barrington 68*, L. F. Kline 4-43) by 255 runs.

25th Match: v Glamorgan (Swansea)   Aug 5, 7, 8.
Australians 192 (W. M. Lawry 66, N. C. O'Neill 63, D. J. Shepherd 5-50) and 262-4 dec (R. B. Simpson 112, R. Benaud 80*) drew with Glamorgan 149 (R. Benaud 5-71, L. F. Kline 4-60) and 124-2 (A. Jones 70*).

26th Match: v Warwickshire (Edgbaston)   Aug 9, 10, 11.
Warwickshire 251 (T. W. Cartwright 93, J. D. Bannister 66, M. J. K. Smith 53) and 183-4 dec (N. F. Horner 77) drew with Australians 296-1 dec (R. B. Simpson 132*, R. N. Harvey 115*) and 103-3 (P. J. P. Burge 51*).

27th Match: v Yorkshire (Bramall Lane)   Aug 12, 14, 15.
Australians 301-3 dec (R. B. Simpson 160, N. C. O'Neill 74*) and 180-3 dec (W. M. Lawry 84*, N. C. O'Neill 64) drew with Yorkshire 166 (L. F. Kline 4-32) and 237-7.

28th Match: v England (Oval)   Aug 17, 18, 19, 21, 22.
England 256 (P. B. H. May 71, K. F. Barrington 53, A. K. Davidson 4-83) and 370-8 (R. Subba Row 137, K. F. Barrington 83, K. D. Mackay 5-121) drew with Australia 494 (P. J. P. Burge 181, N. C. O'Neill 117, B. C. Booth 71, D. A. Allen 4-133).

29th Match: v Essex (Southend)   Aug 23, 24, 25.
Australians 198 (T. E. Bailey 4-65) and 150-2 dec (N. C. O'Neill 85*) beat Essex 154-3 dec (G. J. Smith 66*, G. Barker 56) and 139 (G. D. McKenzie 5-29) by 55 runs.

30th Match: v Hampshire (Southampton)   Aug 26, 28, 29.
Hampshire 194 (D. A. Livingstone 52) and 221 (H. Horton 58) lost to Australians 255 (B. C. Booth 79, R. N. Harvey 72, M. D. Burden 4-39) and 165-5 by 5 wkts.

31st Match: v Gentlemen (Lord's)   Aug 30, 31, Sept 1.
Gentlemen 195 (D. Kirby 60) and 325-8 (M. J. K. Smith 90, P. I. Bedford 63) drew with Australians 422 (W. M. Lawry 109, N. C. O'Neill 75, P. J. P. Burge 74, R. G. Marlar 6-184).

32nd Match: v A. E. R. Gilligan's XI (Hastings)   Sept 2, 4, 5.
A. E. R. Gilligan's XI 360 (W. E. Alley 102, M. E. J. C. Norman 84, P. B. Wight 57) and 286 (M. E. J. C. Norman 56, R. E. Hitchcock 52*) lost to Australians 364 (N. C. O'Neill 81, A. K. Davidson 65, R. B. Simpson 62, R. Benaud 50, R. E. Hitchcock 4-127) and 283-7 (B. C. Booth 73, R. N. Harvey 65, A. K. Davidson 60, G. A. R. Lock 5-110) by 3 wkts.

33rd Match: v T. N. Pearce's XI (Scarborough)   Sept 6, 7, 8.
T. N. Pearce's XI 375-8 dec (J. H. Edrich 110, P. B. H. May 100, F. S. Trueman 80*, E. R. Dexter 57) and 373-6 dec (E. R. Dexter 110, G. J. Smith 100, J. M. Parks 60, K. D. Mackay 4-110) lost to Australians 392 (B. N. Jarman 80, B. C. Booth 77, P. J. P. Burge 71, N. C. O'Neill 63, F. S. Trueman 4-59) and 359-7 (R. B. Simpson 121) by 3 wkts.

34th Match: v Minor Counties (Jesmond)   Sept 9, 11.
Minor Counties 262 (J. H. Hampshire 129, R. W. Smithson 76, L. F. Kline 7-108) and 259-6 dec (H. G. Searle 78, F. W. Neate 72, J. H. Hampshire 54) drew with Australians 263-5 dec (N. C. O'Neill 138) and 240-6 (A. K. Davidson 72, K. D. Mackay 71*).*

35th Match: v Scotland (Edinburgh)   Sept 12, 13.
Scotland 172 (F. A. Jones 52, R. Benaud 7-53) and 109-6 drew with Australians 241 (R. Benaud 77, D. Barr 4-73).

36th Match: v Ireland (Belfast)   Sept 15, 16.
Australians 209 (N. C. O'Neill 85, G. Duffy 6-29) and 155-7 dec (A. K. Davidson 50) drew with Ireland 126 (L. F. Kline 5-35) and 138-6 (H. Martin 57).

37th Match: v Ireland (Dublin)   Sept 18, 19.
Australians 291 (B. C. Booth 79, P. J. P. Burge 60, A. J. O'Riordan 5-85) and 233-6 dec (B. D. Booth 67, A. K. Davidson 59, G. Lyness 4-46) beat Ireland 76 and 166 (W. R. Hunter 50) by 282 runs.

Leeds Test. Simpson spent some time in the middle order, which did not suit him, but flourished better when taking McDonald's place as Lawry's partner. A strained wrist reduced McDonald's opportunities. Burge came second in the Test averages and gave substance in the middle, playing a particularly important innings in the last Test at the Oval.

There were no outstanding bowlers–eight players took 50 wickets each, Davidson the most with 68, and he also headed the Test table with 23, average 24.86. Unfortunately Benaud injured a shoulder early on and was never really fit afterwards. The team often relied on Mackay–he bowled most overs and was used to bottle up an end when matters seemed to be getting out of hand. Gaunt, Misson and McKenzie, the fast trio, were all youngsters

and tended to be wayward in length and direction, but all improved as the tour progressed.

Both wicketkeepers, Jarman and Grout, were highly capable and the fielding in general was of a high standard, with O'Neill in the covers and Simpson at slip outstandingly good.

The team sailed home from Tilbury with a profit of about £29,000. This was very much less than for previous post-war tours as attendances were down. There seemed no obvious reason for this drop–Benaud's team played attractive cricket, the Test series was full of interest and after a wet May, the weather was quite good. The falling gates which had been apparent in county championship matches for five or six summers had now reached even cricket's highlight, the Australian tour.

1961: South African Fezelas

E. Stanley Murphy of Durban put up about £10,000 to finance this team of young South Africans on a two-month tour of England in 1961. The side was R. A. McLean (captain), C. G. de V. Burger, M. K. Elgie and L. Morby-Smith, all of Natal; K. C. Bland and R. A. Gripper of Rhodesia; J. T. Botten and D. T. Lindsay of North Eastern Transvaal; G. S. Bunyard, E. J. Barlow and I. R. Fullerton of Transvaal; P. L. van der Merwe and C. G. Rushmere of Western Province and P. M. Pollock of Eastern Province.

The team was a great success and went through the 21-match programme without defeat, including easy victories in the three first-class fixtures. The leading bowler was Botten, who delivered fast medium with a low arm. Elgie, Barlow, Gripper and McLean all made plentiful runs and the fielding was quite superb. Lindsay kept wicket well besides providing some hurricane hitting.

At the start of the tour their opponents under-estimated the visitors' strength, but even when this was realised the team was a match for any of the opposition. The full details of matches could not be found and some of the potted scores given below are patently incorrect – the author would welcome any addenda to this tour.

1961: South African Fezelas

1st Match: v Union Castle Company.
Fezelas 293-5 dec beat Union Castle 97 by 196 runs.

2nd Match: v Col Stevens XI (Eastbourne)   June 5, 6.
Col Stevens XI 176 and 186 lost to Fezelas 326 (E. J. Barlow 120, I. R. Fullerton 88) and 37-0 by 10 wkts.

3rd Match: v Hampshire (Southampton)   June 8, 9.
Hampshire 142 and 163 lost to Fezelas 309-7 dec (C. G. de V. Burger 78) and 65-5 by 5 wkts.

4th Match: v Winchester College (Winchester)   June 10.
Fezelas 283-3 dec (R. A. Gripper 102, K. C. Bland 100) drew with Winchester 55-1.

5th Match: v Essex (Chelmsford)   June 14, 15, 16.
Essex 144 (C. G. Rushmere 4-29) and 292 (W. T. Greensmith 77) lost to Fezelas 227 (P. J. Phelan 5-74, W. T. Greensmith 4-90) and 212-4 (D. T. Lindsay 83*, C. G. de V. Burger 52) by 6 wkts.

6th Match: v B.B.C. (Chiswick)   June 17.
B.B.C. 152-6 lost to Fezelas 212-4 (M. K. Elgie 100) by 6 wkts.

7th Match: v Lincolnshire (Bourne)   June 19, 20.
Lincolnshire 91 (P. L. van der Merwe 5-26) and 135 (P. L. van der Merwe 5-41) lost to Fezelas 401 (R. A. McLean 133) by an innings and 175 runs.

8th Match: v Norfolk (Norwich)   June 21, 22.
Norfolk 98 and 201 lost to Fezelas 396-7 dec (E. J. Barlow 116, M. K. Elgie 103) by an innings and 97 runs.

9th Match: v Romany   June 24.
Romany 128 drew with Fezelas 196-5.

10th Match: v Surrey (Oval)   June 26, 27.
Surrey 167-3 dec and 248-7 (D. G. W. Fletcher 106, T. H. Clark 54) drew with Fezelas 323-3 dec (K. C. Bland 152*, C. G. de V. Burger 100).

11th Match: v Combined Services (Portsmouth)   June 28, 29, 30.
Combined Services 132 (J. T. Botten 6-36) and 129 (R. T. Virgin 51) lost to Fezelas 392-7 dec (R. A. McLean 135, I. R. Fullerton 103, M. K. Elgie 62) by an innings and 131 runs.

12th Match: v Gloucestershire (Bristol)   July 1, 3, 4.
Gloucestershire 264 (D. M. Young 104) and 123 (J. T. Botten 8-35) lost to Fezelas 452-8 dec (M. K. Elgie 117, E. J. Barlow 110, R. A. McLean 100) by an innings and 55 runs.

13th Match: v Warwickshire (Stratford-on-Avon)   July 5, 6.
Warwickshire 194 (E. J. Barlow 5-76) and 169 lost to Fezelas 366-9 dec (D. T. Lindsay 111, R. A. Gripper 79) by an innings and 1 run.

14th Match: v Lancashire (Old Trafford)   July 7, 8.
Lancashire 215-5 dec and 131-4 dec lost to Fezelas 212-4 dec (D. T. Lindsay 117*) and 196-3 by 7 wkts.

15th Match: v Cumberland (Carlisle)   July 10, 11.
Cumberland 130 and 131 lost to Fezelas 132-3 dec and 130-3 (M. K. Elgie 67) by 7 wkts.

16th Match: v West of Scotland (Glasgow)   July 12.
West of Scotland 158 lost to Fezelas 208-7 (K. C. Bland 73*) by 3 wkts.

17th Match: v Scotland (Glasgow)   July 13, 14.
Fezelas 107-0 drew with Scotland did not bat.

18th Match: v Yorkshire (Scarborough)   July 17, 18.
Yorkshire 148 and 91 lost to Fezelas 177-6 dec (E. J. Barlow 97) and 71-0 by 10 wkts.

19th Match: v Kent (Canterbury)   July 20, 21.
Kent 173 and 170-5 drew with Fezelas 311-7 dec (K. C. Bland 85).

20th Match: v R.A.F. (Hillingdon)   July 22.
R.A.F. 87 and 159-9 drew with Fezelas 276-9.

21st Match: v Dublin University (Dublin)   July 23, 24.
Dublin University 45 and 118 lost to Fezelas 291-2 dec (C. G. de V. Burger 201) by an innings and 128 runs.

1962: 2nd Pakistanis

The 1962 Pakistani side was Javed Burki (captain), Hanif Mohammad, Imtiaz Ahmed, Alim-ud-Din, Saeed Ahmed, Mushtaq Mohammad, Wallis Mathias, Ijaz Butt, Nasim-ul-Ghani, Haseeb Ahsan, Afaq Hussain, Intikhab Alam, Mohammad Farooq, Antao D'Souza, Munir Malik, Mahmood Hussain, Asif Ahmed and Shahid Mahmood with Brig R. G. Hyder as manager and Major S. A. Rahman as his assistant.

Despite having 18 players in the original party, the team had to co-opt three additional players. The off-break bowler Haseeb Ahsan injured his foot in the first county match and eventually went home and at the beginning of July Javed Akhtar was flown from Pakistan to replace him; the medium-fast bowlers Mahmood Hussain and Farooq both broke down and Fazal Mahmood, the veteran bowler, was brought in on 22 July and thrust straight into the Fourth Test; finally Shuja-ud-Din Butt was used in one match. Bringing in these players meant that several of the main team – notably Shahid Mahmood, Afaq Hussain and Asif Ahmed – were very under-used and never really had the opportunity to develop their talents. There seemed to be little forward planning during the tour and this no doubt affected the morale of some players.

The results of the visit were deeply disappointing – four Tests lost and the other drawn and only four wins in the first-class programme. The trouble began even before the arrival of the team with Hanif suffering from an old knee injury; during the entire tour this best batsman of the team was never properly fit. His brother Mushtaq flourished, however, heading the Test averages with 401 runs, average 44.55, as well as the first-class table. Burki batted occasionally though he was an uninspiring leader. The two wicketkeepers, Imtiaz and Ijaz, both scored their share of runs.

Of the bowlers, Farooq looked the most dangerous but was overbowled and broke down; Antao and Munir Malik never

---

1962: 2nd Pakistanis

Batting Averages

	M	I	NO	R	HS	Avge	100	c/s
Mushtaq Mohammad	26	47	8	1614	176	41.38	3	12
Hanif Mohammad	17	27	1	1044	191	40.15	3	6
Saeed Ahmed	24	39	2	1294	128	34.97	3	13
Javed Burki	27	43	5	1257	110*	33.07	3	19
Wallis Mathias	20	30	6	734	91	30.58	0	12
Imtiaz Ahmed	24	45	7	1140	101	30.00	1	46/5
Ijaz Butt	20	37	1	1016	129*	28.22	2	20/1
Nasim-ul-Ghani	24	33	4	769	101	26.51	1	28
Intikhab Alam	20	31	4	602	83*	22.29	0	8
Antao D'Souza	19	25	14	237	35	21.54	0	4
Alim-ud-Din	18	34	1	606	60	18.36	0	5
Shahid Mahmood	13	25	2	369	77*	16.04	0	1
Munir Malik	16	15	4	138	22	12.54	0	8
Asif Ahmed	9	14	1	155	43	11.92	0	2
Fazal Mahmood	7	8	3	56	20*	11.20	0	1
Mahmood Hussain	10	15	1	141	50	10.07	0	0
Afaq Hussain	6	6	3	26	14*	8.66	0	5
Mohammad Farooq	8	12	5	47	13	6.71	0	3
Javed Akhtar	7	6	1	30	23	6.00	0	0
Haseeb Ahsan	3	3	1	1	1	0.50	0	2

Also batted: Shuja-ud-Din Butt (1 match) 2*.

Bowling Averages

	O	M	R	W	Avge	BB	5i
Haseeb Ahsan	62.5	19	151	8	18.87	5-53	1
Mahmood Hussain	390.2	121	1032	44	23.45	6-52	2
Mohammad Farooq	250.5	46	872	33	26.42	5-76	1
Shahid Mahmood	109	27	294	11	26.72	3-55	0
Saeed Ahmed	193.1	60	508	16	31.75	3-12	0
Fazal Mahmood	282.3	79	747	22	33.95	6-69	1
Antao D'Souza	736	159	2018	58	34.79	5-67	1
Nasim-ul-Ghani	456.1	100	1506	41	36.73	5-36	1
Mushtaq Mohammad	29.3	6	111	3	37.00	1-2	0
Javed Akhtar	140	38	379	10	37.90	3-53	0
Munir Malik	669.2	165	1717	43	39.93	5-128	1
Afaq Hussain	152	27	567	13	43.61	3-150	0
Wallis Mathias	14	2	45	1	45.00	1-13	0
Intikhab Alam	474.3	105	1397	26	53.73	4-87	0
Javed Burki	111	23	323	4	80.75	2-70	0

Also bowled: Alim-ud-Din 8-0-52-0; Asif Ahmed 4-0-21-0; Shuja-ud-Din Butt 27-5-104-0.

1962: 2nd Pakistanis

1st Match: v Duke of Norfolk's XI (Arundel Castle)   April 28.
Duke of Norfolk's XI 204-6 dec (R. E. Marshall 61, Mohammad Farooq 4-42) drew with Pakistanis 173-6.

2nd Match: v Indian Gymkhana (Osterley)   April 29.
Pakistanis 250-5 dec (Hanif Mohammad 102, Saeed Ahmed 62) drew with Indian Gymkhana 169-3 (Imtiaz Ahmed 91).

3rd Match: v L. C. Steven's XI (Eastbourne)   April 30.
L. C. Steven's XI 229-7 dec (E. A. Clark 90) lost to Pakistanis 233-1 (Shahid Mahmood 105, Saeed Ahmed 90*) by 9 wkts.*

4th Match: v Worcestershire (Worcester)   May 2, 3, 4.
Worcestershire 175 (Mohammad Farooq 4-37, Haseeb Ahsan 5-53) and 245 (T. W. Graveney 117, R. G. Broadbent 52) drew with Pakistanis 113 (Mushtaq Mohammad 55, L. J. Coldwell 4-35, J. A. Flavell 4-45) and 291-9 (Javed Burki 90, Mushtaq Mohammad 86).

5th Match: v Club Cricket Conference (Ealing)   May 7, 8.
C.C.C. 236-8 dec (A. R. Day 79, J. K. Slack 58) and 113-7 dec (Antoa D'Souza 4-47) lost to Pakistanis 182 (Ijaz Butt 81, J. Melville 5-61) and 171-3 (Wallis Mathias 61, Hanif Mohammad 52*) by 7 wkts.*

6th Match: v Oxford University (The Parks, Oxford)   May 9, 10, 1.
Pakistanis 412-5 dec (Hanif Mohammad 185, Ijaz Butt 88, Imtiaz Ahmed 52) beat Oxford University 165 (D. R. Worsley 165, Mahmood Hussain 4-44) and 144 by an innings and 103 runs.*

7th Match: v Leicestershire (Leicester)   May 12, 14, 15.
Leicestershire 191 (S. Jayasinghe 60, Antoa D'Souza 5-67) and 238-6 dec (M. R. Hallam 60, J, Mitten 50) drew with Pakistanis 205 (Nasim-ul-Ghani 73, Mahmood Hussain 50) and 64-5.*

8th Match: v Cambridge University (Cambridge)   May 16, 17, 18.
Pakistanis 444-8 dec (Mushtaq Mohammad 176, Wallis Mathias 91, Hanif Mohammad 70) and 81-2 beat Cambridge University 238 (E. J. Craig 86) and 286 (E. J. Craig 67, R. H. Thomson 54, Mohammad Farooq 5-76) by 8 wkts.

9th Match: v M.C.C. (Lord's)   May 19, 21, 22.
M.C.C. 279-8 dec (E. R. Dexter 79, R. W. Barber 55, B. R. Knight 54, Mahmood Hussain 4-91) and 237-5 dec (T. W. Graveney 110) drew with Pakistanis 230 (Saeed Ahmed 61) and 152-5.

10th Match: v Sussex (Hove)   May 23, 24, 25.
Pakistanis 144 (D. L. Bates 4-13) and 260 (Javed Burki 110, E. R. Dexter 4-80) lost to Sussex 348-7 dec (E. R. Dexter 117, K. G. Suttle 55, G. C. Cooper 55) and 60-3.*

11th Match: v Lancashire (Old Trafford)   May 26, 28, 29.
Lancashire 320-6 dec (J. D. Bond 109, R. W. Barber 73) and 154-3 dec drew with Pakistanis 260 (Wallis Mathias 79, J. B. Statham 5-54) and 122-2 (Imtiaz Ahmed 64).

12th Match: v England (Edgbaston)   May 31, June 1, 2, 4.
England 544-5 dec (M. C. Cowdrey 159, P. H. Parfitt 101*, T. W. Graveney 97, E. R. Dexter 72) beat Pakistan 246 (Mushtaq 63, J. B. Statham 4-54) and 274 (Saeed Ahmed 65) by an innings and 24 runs.

13th Match: v Surrey (Oval)   June 6, 7, 8.
Pakistanis 388-6 dec (Ijaz Butt 110, Mushtaq Mohammad 89) and 237-4 dec (Saeed Butt 108) beat Surrey 348-9 dec (P. B. H. May 119, M. J. Stewart 63, R. I. Jefferson 58*) and 185 (J. H. Edrich 57, Mohammad Farooq 4-71).*

14th Match: v Glamorgan (Cardiff)   June 9, 11, 12.
Pakistanis 278 (Hanif Mohammad 109, J. B. Evans 4-66) and 158 (O. S. Wheatley 4-38) lost to Glamorgan 278-6 dec (A. Harris 101, A. Jones 92, Antoa D'Souza 4-77) and 161-3 (B. Hedges 81) by 7 wkts.*

15th Match: v Somerset (Taunton)   June 13, 14.
Pakistanis 99 (W. E. Alley 4-22) and 146 (Saeed Ahmed 70, B. Langford 6-36) lost to Somerset 331-9 dec (G. Atkinson 84, P. B. Wight 67, H. W. Stephenson 66, Mahmood Hussain 4-52) by an innings and 86 runs.*

16th Match: v Yorkshire (Bradford)   June 16, 18, 19.
Yorkshire 246 (P. J. Sharpe 136, W. B. Stott 64, Mahmood Hussain 5-57) and 137 (Mahmood Hussain 6-52, Antoa D'Souza 4-77) drew with Pakistan 285 (Nasim-ul-Ghani 63, J. B. Bolus 4-40) and 26-0.*

17th Match: v England (Lord's)   June 21, 22, 23.
Pakistan 100 (R. S. Trueman 6-31) and 355 (Javed Burki 101, Nasim-ul-Ghani 101, L. J. Coldwell 6-85) lost to England 370 (T. W. Graveney 153, E. R. Dexter 65, Mohammad Farooq 4-70) and 86-1 by 9 wkts.

18th Match: v Northamptonshire (Northampton)   June 27, 28, 29.
Northamptonshire 334-8 dec (B. L. Reynolds 79, B. S. Crump 71, P. J. Watts 68, P. D. Watts 61) and 212-6 dec (R. M. Prideaux 74, B. L. Reynolds 50) drew with Pakistanis 372 (Saeed Ahmed 112, Javed Burki 97) and 78-5.

19th Match: v Nottinghamshire (Trent Bridge)   June 30, July 2, 3.
Nottinghamshire 206 (R. T. Simpson 76, Antoa D'Souza 4-42) and 316-8 (H. M. Winfield 68, A. Gill 64, N. W. Hill 53) drew with Pakistanis 396 (Javed Burki 109, Ijaz Butt 71, Alim-ud-Din 54).*

20th Match: v England (Headingley)   July 5, 6, 7.
England 428 (P. H. Parfitt 119, M. J. Stewart 86, D. A. Allen 62, Munir Malik 5-128) beat Pakistan 131 (Alim-ud-Din 50, E. R. Dexter 4-10) and 180 (Alim-ud-Din 60, Saeed Ahmed 54, J. B. Statham 4-50) by an innings and 117 runs.

21st Match: v Lancashire (Old Trafford)   July 11, 12, 13.
Pakistan 303 (Imtiaz Ahmed 101, Shahid Mahmood 77, J. B. Statham 4-77) and 193-6 dec drew with Lancashire 161-4 dec (J. D. Bond 63*) and 126-3 (G. Pullar 50*).*

22nd Match: v Derbyshire (Burton-on-Trent)   July 14, 16, 17.
Derbyshire 217-6 dec (H. L. Johnson 84, D. B. Carr 60) and 139-6 dec (I. W. Hall 54, Munir Malik 4-70) drew with Pakistanis 168 (G. W. Richardson 4-26, H. L. Jackson 4-38) and 157-8.

23rd Match: v Hampshire (Bournemouth)   July 18, 19, 20.
Hampshire 368-2 dec (R. E. Marshall 228, D. A. Livingstone 101*) and 140-6 (H. Horton 50) drew with Pakistanis 372 (Mushtaq Mohammad 108, Hanif Mohammad 76, Shahid Mahmood 55).*

24th Match: v Middlesex (Lord's)   July 21, 23, 24.
Middlesex 294-7 dec (P. H. Parfitt 122, W. E. Russell 50, Antoa D'Souza 4-118) and 257-6 dec (P. H. Parfitt 114, E. A. Clark 75) drew with Pakistanis 352-7 dec (Hanif Mohammad 191, Alim-ud-Din 58. Saeed Ahmed 52) and 143-5.

25th Match: v England (Trent Bridge)   July 26, 27, 28, 30, 31.
England 428-5 dec (T. W. Graveney 114, P. H. Parfitt 101*, E. R. Dexter 85, D. S. Shepherd 83) drew with Pakistan 219 (Mushtaq Mohammad 55, B. R. Knight 4-38, F. S. Trueman 4-71) and 216-6 (Mushtaq Mohammad 100*, Saeed Ahmed 64).

26th Match: v Ireland (Dublin)   Aug 1, 2.
Ireland 167 (H. Martin 54, Antoa D'Souza 5-51) and 112-8 dec drew with Pakistanis 105-6 dec (Wallis Mathias 55) and 127-5 (Asif Ahmed 54*).*

27th Match: v Glamorgan (Swansea)   Aug 4, 6, 7.
Glamorgan 363-6 dec (B. Hedges 144, A. Harris 89, J. S. Pressdee 57, Intikhab Alam 4-87) drew with Glamorgan 51-1.*

28th Match: v Warwickshire (Edgbaston)   Aug 8, 9, 10.
Warwickshire 297 (K. Ibadulla 62, M. J. K. Smith 56, R. E. Hitchcock 50) drew with Pakistanis 105 (A. Wright 5-37) and 255-6 (Ijaz Butt 82, Wallis Mathias 68, W. B. Bridge 4-70).

29th Match: v Gloucestershire (Cheltenham)   Aug 11, 13, 14.
Pakistanis 233 and 30-2 drew with Gloucestershire 175-9 dec (C. A. Milton 53, Fazal Mahmood 6-69).*

30th Match: v England (Oval)   Aug 16, 17, 18, 20.
England 480-5 dec (M. C. Cowdrey 182, E. R. Dexter 172, D. S. Sheppard 57, K. F. Barrington 50*) and 27-0 beat Pakistan 183 (J. D. F. Larter 5-57) and 323 (Imtiaz Ahmed 98, Mushtaq Mohammad 72, J. D. F. Larter 4-88) by 10 wkts.

31st Match: v Kent (Canterbury)   Aug 22, 23, 24.
Pakistanis 380-7 dec (Saeed Ahmed 128, Wallis Mathias 74) and 239-3 dec (Ijaz Butt 129, Mushtaq Mohammad 75) drew with Kent 265-7 dec (R. C. Wilson 83, A. W. Catt 64) and 143-4 (P. E. Richardson 51).*

32nd Match: v Essex (Leyton)   Aug 25, 27, 28.
Pakistanis 133 (T. E. Bailey 5-47, B. R. Knight 4-66) and 223 (P. J. Phelan 6-59, B. R. Knight 4-42) lost to Essex 303 (P. A. Spicer 86, B. Taylor 58, B. R. Knight 56) and 54-1 by 9 wkts.

33rd Match: v Minor Counties (Torquay)   Aug 29, 30.
Minor Counties 60 (Antoa D'Souza 7-19) and 255-8 dec (D. H. Cole 70, G. K. Knox 51, Intikhab Alam 5-84) drew with Pakistanis 235-8 dec and 75-2.

34th Match: v A. E. R. Gilligan's XI (Hastings)   Sept 1, 3, 4.
A. E. R. Gilligan's XI 202 (E. R. Dexter 72, Antoa D'Souza 4-57) and 228-6 dec (C. A. Milton 92, E. R. Dexter 66) drew with Pakistanis 230 (Nasim-ul-Ghani 98, N. I. Thomson 6-74) and 184-8.

35th Match: v T. N. Pearce's XI (Scarborough)   Sept 5, 6, 7.
T. N. Pearce's XI 279-7 dec (A. R. Lightfoot 72, D. C. Morgan 59) and 97-1 (J. H. Edrich 51) lost to Pakistanis 162-6 dec (Wallis Mathias 56, Mushtaq Mohammad 51) and 215-5 (Intikhab Alam 83*, Nasin-ul-Ghani 51, T. E. Bailey 5-62) by 5 wkts.*

36th Match: v Durham (Sunderland)   Sept 8, 10.
Pakistan 282 (Imtiaz Ahmed 65, Javed Burki 53) and 15-0 drew with Durham 222-7 dec (D. J. Ellis 100*).*

---

troubled Test class batsmen and Fazal had lost his zip of 1954. The main reason for the failure seemed to be the very dead pitches produced in Pakistan–matting wickets were being phased out–and some radical rethinking was needed; many of the 21 players involved in the tour had talent which was being only half-used. The tourists made a profit of about £5,000.

1963: 9th West Indians

The West Indies selectors announced the side for England as early as 11 September 1962: F. M. M. Worrell (captain), L. A. King, E. D. A. St J. McMorris and A. L. Valentine, all of Jamaica; C. C. Hunte, D. W. Allan, C. C. Griffith, W. W. Hall, S. M. Nurse and G. St A. Sobers from Barbados; B. F. Butcher, L. R. Gibbs, R. B. Kanhai and J. S. Solomon of British Guiana and M. C. Carew, D. L. Murray and W. V. Rodriguez of Trinidad. Although the choice was made seven months before the team began their visit, the original side was unchanged. B. M. Gaskin acted as manager and H. L. Burnett as his assistant.

In 1960-61 the West Indies had played a great series against Australia, including the famous tied Test, and it was hoped that this almost unchanged West Indian team would revitalise Test cricket in England and pull back the crowds. The tour turned out to be the most successful ever made by the West Indies. With an ideal captain in Worrell and a hostile pair of opening bowlers–Hall and Griffith–the tourists had two ingredients of success; the third was Sobers, whose all-round ability dominated

Right *The most elegant batsman of his day and the first captain to harness fully the brilliantly individualistic talents of the West Indians, Frank Worrell led his side to a 3-1 victory in the 1963 series.*

Below *Wes Hall (left), a potent blend of athletic grace and power, and Charlie Griffith, with the awesome physique of a light-heavyweight boxer, proved a highly destructive opening attack in the 1963 series. Though never 'called' during the tour, Griffith was widely believed to have a suspect action.*

almost every game in which he played. He took 20 Test wickets and scored 302 runs, at 40.25. For once injuries to key players were negligible and the Test team was virtually unchanged for all five matches—the series being won by three to one. The side's weakness was its opening pair of batsmen and this was never properly solved, but wth Hunte, Kanhai, Butcher, Sobers and Solomon all doing well the lack of a partner for Hunte was not serious.

Kanhai looked brilliant, but made no high scores; Butcher was also reliable; Nurse was not in form early on, however, and so never won a place in the Test team; Solomon was the man for a crisis and his average was deceiving.

The main bowler after Hall and Griffith (and Sobers) was Gibbs the off-spinner, who took 26 Test wickets; Valentine did not play in the Tests. Both spinners suffered injuries and W. A. White was co-opted as a replacement. The only other major injury was to Rodriguez who strained his knee.

The tour made a profit of £30,000 after a substantial bonus to the players and the team, which had sailed to England aboard the s.s. *Golfito* to Avonmouth, flew home via New York.

1963: 9th West Indians

1st Match: v L. C. Steven's XI (Eastbourne) April 24, 25.
West Indies 188 (F. M. M. Worrell 73) and 160 (D. Baker 4-44) lost to L. C. Steven's XI 212-4 dec (G. St A. Sobers 61, C. C. Hunte 53, J. S. Solomon 50) and 140-5 (D. L. Murray 53*) by 5 wkts.

2nd Match: v Duke of Norfolk's XI (Arundel Castle) April 27.
Duke of Norfolk's XI 203 (K. F. Barrington 60, B. R. Knight 74, J. S. Solomon 8-65) Duke of Norfolk's XI 203 (K. F. Barrington 60, B. R. Knight 74, J. S. Solomon 8-65) lost to West Indians 205-7 (S. M. Nurse 70, E. D. A. St J. McNorris 52) by 3 wkts.

3rd Match: v Worcestershire (Worcester) May 1, 2, 3.
Worcestershire 119 (T. W. Graveney 75, C. C. Griffith 4-28) and 162-4 dec drew with West Indians 120-2 dec (B. F. Butcher 57*) and 57-3.

4th Match: v Gloucestershire (Bristol) May 4, 6, 7.
West Indians 89 (D. R. Smith 5-25) and 250 (J. S. Solomon 56, D. R. Smith 6-67) beat Gloucestershire 60 (C. C. Griffith 8-23) and 214 (D. M. Young 127, C. C. Griffith 5-35, G. St A. Sobers 4-75) by 65 runs.

5th Match: v Cambridge University (Cambridge) May 8, 9.
West Indians 512 (W. W. Hall 102*, R. B. Kanhai 119, C. C. Hunte 96, B. F. Butcher 82) beat Cambridge University 104 (R. C. White 55) and 205 (P. D. Briggs 57) by an innings and 203 runs.

6th Match: v Lancashire (Old Trafford) May 11, 13, 14.
West Indians 327-4 dec (M. C. Carew 93, G. St A. Sobers 70*, R. B. Kanhai 61, B. F. Butcher 55) and 59-1 drew with Lancashire 171 (K. J. Grieves 97, L. R. Gibbs 5-35) and 304 (K. J. Grieves 123, J. Dyson 63).

7th Match: v Yorkshire (Middlesbrough) May 15, 16, 17.
Yorkshire 226 (W. B. Stott 65, F. S. Trueman 55, C. C. Griffith 5-37) and 145-6 dec (F. M. M. Worrell 4-62) beat West Indies 109 (F. S. Trueman 5-38) and 151 (F. S. Trueman 5-43) by 111 runs.

8th Match: v M.C.C. (Lord's) May 18, 20, 21.
West Indians 306 (C. C. Hunte 91, B. F. Butcher 70, J. Cotton 4-49) and 79-1 beat M.C.C. 120-5 dec (J. H. Edrich 65) and 172 (G. Atkinson 63, L. R. Gibbs 4-20) by 93 runs.

9th Match: v Oxford University (The Parks, Oxford) May 22, 23, 24.
Oxford University 119 (W. W. Hall 4-27) and 219 (J. L. Cuthbertson 94, J. S. Solomon 4-34) lost to West Indians 107 (P. N. G. Mountford 7-47) and 232-4 (S. M. Nurse 116*, C. C. Hunte 63*).

10th Match: v Surrey (Oval) May 25, 27, 28.
West Indians 191 and 145-1 (M. C. Carew 74) drew with Surrey 195 (K. F. Barrington 110*, C. G. Griffith 4-42, W. W. Hall 4-42).

11th Match: v Somerset (Bath) May 29, 30, 31.
Somerset 205 (B. Roe 50, L. R. Gibbs 4-59) and 157 (C. C. Griffith 4-20) lost to West Indians 405-8 dec (B. F. Butcher 130, G. St A. Sobers 112) by an innings and 43 runs.

12th Match: v Glamorgan (Cardiff) June 1, 3, 4.
Glamorgan 163 (A. R. Lewis 52, G. St A. Sobers 4-55) and 98 (G. St A. Sobers 5-35) lost to West Indians 379 (M. C. Carew 117, R. B. Kanhai 70, D. J. Shepherd 4-86) by an innings and 118 runs.

13th Match: v England (Old Trafford) June 6, 7, 8, 10.
West Indies 501-6 dec (C. C. Hunte 182, R. B. Kanhai 90, F. M. M. Worrell 74*, G. St A. Sobers 64) and 1-0 beat England 205 (E. R. Dexter 73, L. R. Gibbs 5-59) and 296 (M. J. Stewart 87, L. R. Gibbs 5-59) by 10 wkts.

14th Match: v Ireland (Belfast) June 12.
West Indians 209-4 dec (B. F. Butcher 71*, M. C. Carew 56, E. D. A. St J. McMorris 51) drew with Ireland did not bat.

15th Match: v Ireland (Dublin) June 13.
Ireland 62 (W. A. White 4-13) and 90-7 lost to West Indians 126 (W. R. Hunter 5-36) by 5 wkts.

16th Match: v Sussex (Hove) June 15, 17, 18.
Sussex 59 and 340 (E. R. Dexter 103, A. S. M. Oakman 78) lost to West Indians 287-9 dec and 113-4 by 6 wkts.

17th Match: v England (Lord's) June 20, 21, 22, 24, 25.
West Indies 301 (R. B. Kanhai 73, J. S. Solomon 56, F. S. Trueman 6-100) and 229 (B. F. Butcher 133, F. S. Trueman 5-52, D. Shackleton 4-72) drew with England 297 (K. F. Barrington 80, E. R. Dexter 70, F. J. Titmus 52*, C. C. Griffith 5-91) and 228-9 (D. B. Close 70, K. F. Barrington 60, W. W. Hall 4-93).

18th Match: v Hampshire (Southampton) June 26, 27, 28.
Hampshire 329 (D. A. Livingstone 151, H. Horton 55, L. A. King 5-47) and 64-8 dec (G. St A. Sobers 4-29) drew with West Indians 182 (M. C. Carew 63, A. R. Wassell 4-43) and 126-9 (A. R. Wassell 4-28).

19th Match: v Essex (Southend) June 29, July 1, 2.
West Indians 205 (M. C. Carew 63, K. C. Preston 4-60) and 160-1 dec (C. C. Hunte 62*, E. D. A. St J. McMorris 56*) drew with Essex 56 (W. W. Hall 6-22) and 92-4.

20th Match: v England (Edgbaston) July 4, 5, 6, 8, 9.
England 216 (D. B. Close 55, G. St A. Sobers 5-60) and 278-9 dec (P. J. Sharpe 85*, E. R. Dexter 57, G. A. R. Lock 56, L. R. Gibbs 4-49) beat West Indies 186 (F. S. Trueman 5-75, E. R. Dexter 4-38) and 91 (F. S. Trueman 7-44) by 217 runs.

21st Match: v Minor Counties (Sunderland) July 10, 11.
Minor Counties 163 (L. A. King 6-43) and 95-5 drew with West Indians 203-8 dec (E. D. A. St J McMorris 73)

22nd Match: v Leicestershire (Leicester) July 13, 15, 16.
Leicestershire 158 (S. Jayasinghe 61, G. St A. Sobers 5-48, L. R. Gibbs 5-63) and 166-4 dec (C. C. Inman 67*) drew with West Indians 159-5 dec (M. C. Carew 61*) and 78-2 (W. V. Rodriguez 51*).

23rd Match: v Derbyshire (Chesterfield) July 17, 18, 19.
West Indians 232 (R. B. Kanhai 75, C. C. Hunte 53, H. L. Jackson 4-58, H. J. Rhodes 4-68) and 153-4 dec (B. F. Butcher 51) beat Derbyshire 112 (C. C. Griffith 4-28) and 138 by 135 runs.

24th Match: v Middlesex (Lord's) July 20, 22, 23.
Middlesex 222 (P. H. Parfitt 73, J. T. Murray 56*) and 200 (P. H. Parfitt 62, C. C. Griffith 4-29) lost to West Indians 383 (E. D. A. St J McMorris 190, C. C. Hunte 103, C. D. Drybrough 4-117) and 42-1 by 9 wkts.

25th Match: v England (Headingley) July 25, 26, 27, 29.
West Indians 397 (G. St A. Sobers 102, R. B. Kanhai 92, J. S. Solomon 62, F. S. Trueman 4-117) and 229 (B. F. Butcher 78, G. St A. Sobers 52, F. J. Titmus 4-44) beat England 174 (G. A. R. Lock 53, C. C. Griffith 6-36) and 231 (J. M. Parks 57, D. B. Close 56, L. R. Gibbs 4-76) by 221 runs.

26th Match: v Surrey (Oval) July 31, Aug 1, 2.
Surrey 311 (M. J. Stewart 81, J. H. Edrich 57) and 196-4 dec (J. H. Edrich 106*) drew with West Indians 183 (S. M. Nurse 56) and 253-8 dec (M. C. Carew 84, G. St A. Sobers 79).

27th Match: v Glamorgan (Swansea) Aug 3, 5, 6.
West Indians 237 (B. F. Butcher 99, S. M. Nurse 66, P. M. Walker 5-41) and 243-5 dec (S. M. Nurse 103*, J. S. Solomon 61, W. V. Rodriguez 51) drew with Glamorgan 207 (P. M. Walker 78, A. Rees 58, W. W. Hall 7-51) and 156-3 (A. Jones 92).

28th Match: v Warwickshire (Edgbaston) Aug 7, 8, 9.
Warwickshire 210 (R. W. Barber 113, W. W. Hall 4-50) and 187 (M. J. K. Smith 68, C. C. Griffith 6-49) lost to West Indians 270 (F. M. M. Worrell 71, D. L. Murray 67, T. W. Cartwright 4-36, R. B. Edmonds 4-61) and 133-3 (R. B. Kanhai 50*) by 7 wkts.

29th Match: v Yorkshire (Bramall Lane) Aug 10, 12, 13.
Yorkshire 260 (G. Boycott 71, D. Wilson 51) and 96 (C. C. Griffith 5-12) lost to West Indians 358-9 dec (G. St A. Sobers 100, W. V. Rodriguez 93) by an innings and 2 runs.

30th Match: v Northamptonshire (Northampton) Aug 14, 15, 16.
Northamptonshire 223 (C. Milburn 100) and 234-4 (C. Milburn 88, B. L. Reynolds 74) drew with West Indians 107 (B. S. Crump 5-36).

31st Match: v Nottinghamshire (Trent Bridge) Aug 17, 19, 20.
West Indians 314 (C. C. Hunte 89, E. D. A. St J. McMorris 87, W. A. White 68*, B. D. Wells 5-89) and 93-3 drew with Nottinghamshire 143 and 306 (A. J. Corran 75, G. Millman 60).

32nd Match: v England (Oval) Aug 22, 23, 24, 26.
England 275 (P. J. Sharpe 63, C. C. Griffith 6-71) and 223 (P. J. Sharpe 83, W. W. Hall 4-39) lost to West Indies 246 (C. C. Hunte 80, B. F. Butcher 53) and 255-2 (C. C. Hunte 108*, R. B. Kanhai 77) by 8 wkts.

33rd Match: v Kent (Canterbury) Aug 28, 29, 30.
Kent 321 (B. W. Luckhurst 96, M. H. Denness 80) and 153-6 dec (W. A. White 4-48) drew with West Indians 232 (E. D. A. St J. McMorris 100, D. L. Underwood 5-66) and 162-5.

34th Match: v A. E. R. Gilligan's XI (Hastings) Aug 31, Sept 2, 3.
A. E. R. Gilligan's XI 259-9 dec (A. Lightfoot 58) and 181-6 dec (G. J. Smith 65, M. E. J. C. Norman 51) drew with West Indians 161-3 dec (E. D. A. St J. McMorris 85*, J. S. Solomon 50) and 132-5 (G. St A. Sobers 72).

35th Match: v T. N. Pearce's XI (Scarborough) Sept 7, 9, 10.
West Indians 284 (G. St A. Sobers 101, S. M. Nurse 100, D. A. Allen 5-61) and 254-7 dec (E. D. A. St J. McMorris 64, J. S. Solomon 62) beat T. N. Pearce's XI 266-9 dec (F. S. Trueman 50) and 240 by 32 runs.

36th Match: v Sussex (Hove) Sept 12.
West Indians 177 (G. St A. Sobers 64, B. F. Butcher 57) lost to Sussex 181-6 by 4 wkts.

37th Match: v Club Cricket Conference (Gravesend) Sept 4, 5.
C.C.C. 166-2 (P. A. Whitcombe 54) drew with West Indians did not bat.

38th Match: v Sir L. N. Constantine's XII (Oval) Sept 17 (12-a-side).
West Indians 337-10 dec (F. M. M. Worrell 68, R. B. Kanhai 56) beat Sir L. N. Constantine's XII 275 (J. P. Fellows-Smith 76, T. E. Bailey 50) by 62 runs.

1963: 9th West Indians

Batting Averages

	M	I	NO	R	HS	Avge	100	c/s
G. St A. Sobers	24	34	6	1333	112	47.60	4	29
B. F. Butcher	22	34	5	1294	133	44.62	2	9
C. C. Hunte	21	37	6	1367	182	44.09	3	12
R. B. Kanhai	21	32	4	1149	119	41.03	1	12
E. D. A. St J. McMorris	17	29	5	878	190*	36.58	2	5
S. M. Nurse	17	29	2	911	116*	33.74	3	15
M. C. Carew	21	39	4	1060	117	30.28	1	7
W. V. Rodriguez	12	18	4	413	93	29.50	0	8
J. S. Solomon	23	35	6	774	62	26.68	0	9
F. M. M. Worrell	18	23	2	522	74*	24.85	0	6
A. W. White	9	14	3	228	68*	20.72	0	9
D. L. Murray	15	20	4	269	67	16.81	0	42/7
W. W. Hall	20	21	2	264	102*	13.89	1	10
L. A. King	18	22	7	202	27*	13.46	0	10
D. W. Allan	18	22	5	226	34	13.29	0	46/9
C. C. Griffith	20	23	7	164	27*	10.25	0	7
L. R. Gibbs	19	18	6	89	31	7.41	0	13
A. L. Valentine	15	11	5	10	6*	1.66	0	5

Bowling Averages

	O	M	R	W	Avge	BB	5i
C. C. Griffith	701.2	192	1527	119	12.83	8-23	8
S. M. Nurse	13	1	53	3	17.66	3.39	0
L. R. Gibbs	733	216	1564	78	20.05	6-98	4
J. S. Solomon	152.5	25	540	26	20.76	4-34	0
W. W. Hall	566.4	113	1606	74	21.70	7-31	2
C. C. Hunte	44.1	8	112	5	22.40	2-31	0
G. St A. Sobers	758.3	182	1844	82	22.48	5-35	3
A. W. White	286	83	647	28	23.10	4-48	0
M. C. Carew	32	7	99	4	24.75	2-50	0
L. A. King	493.5	100	1284	47	27.31	5-47	1
A. L. Valentine	306.3	98	822	24	34.25	3-33	0
F. M. M. Worrell	204	56	480	13	36.92	4-62	0
W. V. Rodriguez	59	6	240	4	60.00	2-19	0

Also bowled: B. F. Butcher 2.3-0-10-1; E. D. A. St J. McMorris 3-0-26-0.

1963: 2nd Pakistani Eaglets

Financed by Pakistan International Airways, the team was captained by Wazir Mohammad, and consisted of F. S. Aizazuddin, Mushtaq Mohammad, Shafqat Rana, Naushad Ali, Asif Iqbal, Salim-ud-Din, Majid J. Khan, Farooq Hamid, Mahmoodul Hasan, Intikhab Alam, Mohammad Munaf, Afaq Hussain, Sadiq Mohammad, Ijaz Hussain, Antao d'Souza, Hazeeb Ahsan, Pervez Sajjad.

1963: 2nd Pakistan Eaglets

Batting Averages

	M	I	NO	R	HS	Avge	100	c/s
F. S. Aizazuddin	4	5	0	280	187	56.00	1	0
Mushtaq Mohammad	8	12	1	593	137	53.90	2	11
Shafqat Rana	6	10	1	297	85	33.00	0	3
Naushad Ali	5	7	0	221	88	31.57	0	6
Asif Iqbal	5	8	1	208	74*	29.71	0	3
Salim-ud-Din	4	7	0	192	76	27.42	0	0
Majid J. Khan	4	6	1	125	51*	25.00	0	5
Farooq Hamid	5	6	2	94	31	23.50	0	5
Mahmoodul Hasan	6	10	1	209	50	23.22	0	0
Wazir Mohammad	8	11	0	249	66	22.63	0	3
Intikhab Alam	5	9	0	130	54	14.44	0	3
Mohammad Munaf	5	6	0	73	32	12.16	0	9
Afaq Hussain	5	7	3	40	19*	10.00	0	2
Sadiq Mohammad	4	4	0	40	23	10.00	0	1
Ijaz Hussain	3	5	0	43	19	8.60	0	3/1
Antao D'Souza	5	7	3	24	12*	6.00	0	2
Haseeb Ahsan	4	4	0	13	7	3.25	0	0

Also batted: Pervez Sajjad (2 matches) 1*, ct 1.

Bowling Averages

	O	M	R	W	Avge	BB	5i
Majid J. Khan	53	20	102	9	11.33	4-18	0
Antao D'Souza	115.5	38	221	16	13.81	5-17	2
Asif Iqbal	102.2	22	280	19	14.73	6-45	2
Mushtaq Mohammad	74.3	23	208	13	16.00	6-67	1
Pervez Sajjad	36	13	85	4	21.25	3-21	0
Intikhab Alam	142.1	29	440	19	23.15	4-43	0
Afaq Hussain	73.3	20	175	7	25.00	5-38	1
Mohammad Munaf	89.3	10	310	12	25.83	8-84	0
Farooq Hamid	91.3	14	296	9	32.88	3-56	0
Haseeb Ahsan	81	21	222	1	222.00	1-31	0

Also bowled: F. S. Aizazuddin 5-1-19-0; Mahmoodul Hasan 1-1-0-0; Salim-ud-Din 8-2-24-0; Shafqat Rana 1-0-1-0.

1963: 2nd Pakistani Eaglets

1st Match: v Oxford University (Oxford)   June 1, 3, 4.
Eaglets 212 (E. W. J. Fillery 4-38) and 343-5 dec (Mushtaq Mohammad 98, Naushad Ali 82, Salim-ud-din 59, Intikhab Alam 54) drew with Oxford University 174 (E. W. J. Fillery 75, Antao D'Souza 5-40, Intikhab Alam 4-43) and 261-5 (M. Manasseh 75, Asif Ahmed 54).

2nd Match: v Worcestershire (Worcester)   June 5, 6.
Eaglets 183 (Salim-ud-din 76, N. Gifford 5-41) and 154 lost to Worcestershire 179 (C. D. Fearnley 73, Afaq Hussain 5-38) and 162-4 (R. G. A. Headley 58) by 6 wkts.

3rd Match: v Cambridge University (Cambridge)   June 8, 10.
Cambridge U 116 (Asif Iqbal 6-45) and 192 (Mushtaq 6-67) lost to Eaglets 381 (Fakir 187, Shafqat Rana 57) by an innings and 73 runs.

4th Match: v Staffordshire (Longton)   June 12, 13.
Eaglets 283 beat Staffordshire 175 and 100 by an innings and 8 runs.

5th Match: v Lancashire (Old Trafford)   June 15.
Eaglets 260-7 dec beat Lancashire 86 by 174 runs.

6th Match: v Manchester & District C.A. (Didsbury)   June 16.
Manchester 154 lost to Eaglets 155-5 by 5 wkts.

7th Match: v Cheshire (Macclesfield)   June 17, 18.
Cheshire 187 drew with Eaglets 139-3.

8th Match: v Somerset (Taunton)   June 19, 20, 21.
Somerset 239-7 dec (C. Greetham 96, M. J. Kitchen 62) and 253-2 (P. J. Eele 103*, B. Roe 99) drew with Eaglets 303 (Mushtaq 137, Wazir 66, C. V. Lindo 8-8).

9th Match: v Kent (Dartford)   June 22, 24.
Eaglets 414-6 dec (Shafqat Rana 85, Mushtaq 56, Fakir 50, Asif Iqbal 74*, Majid Jahangir 51*) beat Kent 230 (P. E. Richardson 85, S. E. Leary 60, Munaf 8-84) and 100 (Iqbal 4-21) by an innings and 84 runs.

10th Match: v Northants (Peterborough)   June 26, 27, 28.
Eaglets 137 (B. S. Crump 5-55) and 222 (Mushtaq 108, Mahmoodul 50, M. J. Kettle 4-56) drew with Northants 113 (Majid 4-18) and 76-8 (D'Souza 5-17).

11th Match: v Scotland (Selkirk)   June 29, July 1.
Eaglets 258 (Naushad 88, D. Barr 4-64) drew with Scotland 140-5 (R. H. E. Chisholm 50).

12th Match: v Yorkshire (Harrogate)   July 3, 4.
No play due to rain.

13th Match: v Derbyshire (Derby)   July 6, 8, 9.
Eaglets 150 (Wazir 58) and 175 (A. B. Jackson 7-56) lost to Derbyshire 307 (D. C. Morgan 113, E. Smith 59, Asif 5-103) and 19-2 by 8 wkts.

14th Match: v Lincolnshire (Grimsby)   July 10, 11.
Lincolnshire 47 and 159 lost to Eaglets 254-1 dec (Shafqat 112*, Salim-ud-din 111*) by an innings and 48 runs.

15th Match: v North Wales C.A. (Colwyn Bay)   July 14.
North Wales 133-7 dec lost to Eaglets 138-3 by 7 wkts.

16th Match: v Rydal Dolphins (Colwyn Bay)   July 15.
Eaglets 186-4 dec beat Rydal Dolphins 112 by 74 runs.

17th Match: v Warwickshire (Edgbaston)   July 17, 18, 19.
Eaglets 320-8 dec drew with Warwickshire 161 and 293-4.

18th Match: v Buckinghamshire (High Wycombe)   July 21, 22.
Eaglets 279-9 dec beat Buckinghamshire 99 and 84 by an innings and 96 runs.

19th Match: v R.A.F. (Uxbridge)   July 23, 24.
R.A.F. 172 and 131 lost to Eaglets 317 by an innings and 14 runs.

20th Match: v Col. L. C. Stevens XI (Eastbourne)   July 25, 26.
Col L. C. Stevens XI 265-7 dec and 196-8 dec lost to Eaglets 233-5 dec and 229-7 by 3 wkts.

21st Match: v Indian Gymkhana (Osterley Park)   July 27, 28.
Eaglets 303-9 dec (Naushad Ali 109) and 259-3 drew with Indian Gymkhana 280.

22nd Match: v A Public Schools XI (Hornsey)   July 29, 30.
The Public Schools side did not turn up, the authorities having forgotten to organise a team!

1964: 24th Australians

The team which flew into London on 18 April was R. B. Simpson (captain), B. C. Booth, N. C. O'Neill, J. W. Martin and G. E. Corling all of New South Wales; R. M. Cowper, W. M. Lawry, I. R. Redpath, J. Potter and A. N. Connelly from Victoria; P. J. P. Burge, T. R. Veivers and A. T. W. Grout of Queensland; B. N. Jarman, R. H. D. Sellers, and N. J. N. Hawke of South Australia and G. D. McKenzie of Western Australia, with R. C. Steele as manager and J. Ledward as treasurer.

Nine of the players, including virtually all the bowlers, were on their first Test tour to England, so Simpson was in charge of a relatively inexperienced team. Two major players were missing—Benaud and Davidson, who had both retired.

Rain ruined their pre-season net practices, but May was mainly dry, so that by the time of the First Test the side had won four matches and drawn the rest. This initial meeting with England was drawn due to rain, as was the Second Test. In the Third Test

Australia won thanks to a brilliant innings from Burge; the Fourth Test was a high-scoring draw, with Simpson interested only in preventing an England win and though rain prevented any play on the final day of the last Test, it would probably have ended in a draw anyway. Thus Australia won the series one match to nil – the critics had said that Simpson led the weakest Australian side since 1912, so the captain could be pleased with his achievements, even if it involved some dull cricket along the way.

The Australian openers Lawry and Redpath both tended toward the dreary and encouraged the bowlers with their non-aggression. Booth, Burge and O'Neill were much brighter but were not reliable in the Tests, with O'Neill very disappointing. Of the trio of tyros – Cowper, Redpath and Potter – Cowper looked the best prospect. Veivers batted well and looked as if he might become a great all-rounder.

The young fast bowlers McKenzie and Hawke proved very good. McKenzie took 29 Test wickets and Hawke 18, coming first and second in the Test table as well as in the first-class one, though in reverse order. Corling was a happy cricketer, but Connolly struggled from one ailment to the next. Veivers was the best of rather a modest spin attack. Both wicketkeepers were in good form, though Grout was selected for all five Tests. The fielding was a trifle shoddy, Simpson and O'Neill of course excepted.

The tour produced a profit of some £30,000 and the team went off for a 14-day continental holiday before travelling to the Indian sub-continent for another series of Tests.

1964: 24th Australians

1st Match: v Duke of Norfolk's XI (Arundel Castle)   April 25.
Duke of Norfolk's XI 187-8 dec (M. C. Cowdrey 70, R. E. Marshall 55) lost to Australians 193-6 (N. C. O'Neill 61) by 4 wkts.

2nd Match: v Worcestershire (Worcester)   April 29, 30, May 1.
Australians 251 (R. M. Cowper 68, P. J. P. Burge 58, W. M. Lawry 50, L. J. Coldwell 7-53) and 196-4 dec (W. M. Lawry 79) drew with Worcestershire 228 (T. W. Graveney 56, G. M. McKenzie 5-47, T. R. Veivers 4-21) and 157-3 (M. J. Horton 60).

3rd Match: v Gloucestershire (Bristol)   May 2, 4, 5.
Gloucestershire 117 (A. N. Connelly 4-29) and 207 (R. B. Nicholls 76) lost to Australians 271-5 dec (W. M. Lawry 106, J. Potter 53) and 54-0 by 10 wkts.

4th Match: v Somerset (Taunton)   May 6, 7, 8.
Australians 278 (J. W. Martin 70, B. N. Jarman 63, F. E. Rumsey 4-74) and 213-1 dec (R. B. Simpson 125, I. R. Redpath 81*) beat Somerset 208-6 dec (B. Roe 64) and 111 (N. J. N. Hawke 5-25, G. D. McKenzie 4-20) by 172 runs.

5th Match: v Surrey (Oval)   May 9, 11, 12.
Australians 262 (R. B. Simpson 138, D. A. D. Sydenham 7-74) and 239-1 dec (B. C. Booth 109*, J. Potter 71*, R. B. Simpson 55) drew with Surrey 206 and 207-4 (M. J. Stewart 79, J. H. Edrich 75).

6th Match: v Nottinghamshire (Trent Bridge)   May 13, 14, 15.
Nottinghamshire 98 (N. J. N. Hawke 6-19) and 275-6 (H. I. Moore 108*, J. B. Bolus 77) drew with Australians 367-8 dec (R. M. Cowper 113, I. R. Redpath 107, B. C. Booth 64).

7th Match: v Glamorgan (Cardiff)   May 16, 18, 19.
Australians 361-7 dec (B. C. Booth 80*, I. R. Redpath 65, N. C. O'Neill 65, R. B. Simpson 57, R. M. Cowper 50, P. M. Walker 4-94) and 177-1 dec (N. C. O'Neill 109*) drew with Glamorgan 293 (G. Hughes 92, N. J. N. Hawke 5-57) and 177-3.

8th Match: v Cambridge University (Cambridge)   May 20, 21, 22.
Cambridge University 251 (M. H. Rose 66, G. D. McKenzie 4-60) and 14-0 drew with Australians 346 (R. B. Simpson 95, R. M. Cowper 63, P. J. P. Burge 50, A. R. Windows 4-72).

9th Match: v M.C.C. (Lord's)   May 23, 25, 26.
M.C.C. 229 (J. B. Bolus 72, G. Boycott 63, G. E. Corling 5-59) and 224 (J. H. Edrich 57, E. R. Dexter 55) lost to Australians 358-6 dec (N. C. O'Neill 151, R. B. Simpson 105*, I. R. Redpath 56, J. S. E. Price 4-81) and 99-1 (R. B. Simpson 52*) by 9 wkts.

10th Match: v Oxford University (The Parks, Oxford)   May 27, 28.
Oxford University 200 (J. R. A. Townsend 64) and 104 lost to Australians 424-8 dec (I. R. Redpath 162, R. M. Cowper 100) by an innings and 120 runs.

11th Match: v Lancashire (Old Trafford)   May 30, June 1, 2.
Lancashire 245 (D. M. Green 107, R. Entwistle 79, N. J. N. Hawke 5-90) drew with Australians 196 (B. C. Booth 77, S. Ramadhin 5-53).

12th Match: v England (Trent Bridge)   June 4, 5, 6, 8, 9.
England 216-8 dec and 193-9 dec (E. R. Dexter 68, G. D. McKenzie 5-53) drew with Australia 168 (R. B. Simpson 50) and 40-2.

13th Match: v Derbyshire (Derby)   June 10, 11, 12.
Derbyshire 314-5 dec (H. L. Johnson 101*, I. W. Hall 78) and 201-6 dec (C. Lee 80) drew with Australians 266-5 dec (B. C. Booth 79, W. M. Lawry 60, T. R. Veivers 52*) and 203-8 (E. Smith 4-67).

14th Match: v Yorkshire (Bramall Lane)   June 13, 15, 16.
Australians 295-8 dec (N. C. O'Neill 134, J. Potter 62, A. G. Nicholson 4-47) and 112-7 drew with Yorkshire 113 (R. H. D. Sellers 5-36) and 340-6 dec (K. Taylor 160, D. E. V. Padgett 70).

15th Match: v England (Lord's)   June 18, 19, 20, 22, 23.
Australia 176 (T. R. Veivers 54, F. S. Trueman 5-48) and 168-4 (P. J. P. Burge 59) drew with England 246 (J. H. Edrich 120, G. E. Corling 4-60).

16th Match: v Minor Counties (Bedford)   June 25, 26.
Minor Counties 148 (T. Hale 63, J. W. Martin 5-57) and 142 (R. Inglis 57, J. Potter 4-4) lost to Australians 316 (W. M. Lawry 75, B. C. Booth 57, N. M. McVicker 4-94) by an innings and 26 runs.

17th Match: v Northamptonshire (Northampton)   June 27, 29, 30.
Northamptonshire 235 (P. J. Watts 51, G. D. McKenzie 4-45) and 212 (A. Lightfoot 53, R. H. D. Sellers 4-40) lost to Australians 436 (N. C. O'Neill 90, R. M. Cowper 87, T. R. Veivers 60, R. B. Simpson 51, G. D. McKenzie 50, M. E. Scott 4-95) and 13-0 by 10 wkts.

18th Match: v England (Headingley)   July 2, 3, 4, 6.
England 268 (J. M. Parks 68, E. R. Dexter 66, G. D. McKenzie 4-74, N. J. N. Hawke 5-75) and 229 (K. F. Barrington 85) lost to Australia 389 (P. J. P. Burge 160, W. M. Lawry 78, F. J. Titmus 4-69) and 111-3 (I. R. Redpath 58*) by 7 wkts.

19th Match: v Leicestershire (Leicester)   July 8, 9, 10.
Leicestershire 311-7 dec (J. Birkenshaw 68*, G. F. Cross 53, T. R. Veivers 4-122) and 257 (C. C. Inman 93, B. J. Booth 70) drew with Australians 406 (R. B. Simpson 117, J. Potter 78) and 60-0.

20th Match: v Hampshire (Southampton)   July 11, 13, 14.
Australians 304-9 dec (W. M. Lawry 62, N. C. O'Neill 54, D. W. White 4-91) and 255-5 dec (B. C. Booth 87, R. B. Simpson 69*, R. M. Cowper 61) drew with Hampshire 251 (P. J. Sainsbury 90) and 279-8 (H. M. Barnard 123, J. R. Gray 60).

21st Match: v Sussex (Hove)   July 15, 16, 17.
Australians 330-8 dec (N. C. O'Neill 59, R. B. Simpson 52, N. I. Thomson 4-71) and 183-8 dec (R. B. Simpson 56) beat Sussex 246 (E. R. Dexter 124, M. G. Griffith 51, G. D. McKenzie 4-49, N. J. N. Hawke 4-51) and 204 (M. G. Griffith 56*, R. J. Langridge 52, N. J. N. Hawke 4-35, J. W. Martin 4-50) by 63 runs.

22nd Match: v Middlesex (Lord's)   July 18, 20, 21.
Middlesex 285-7 dec (P. H. Parfitt 121, J. T. Murray 54, R. M. Cowper 4-58) and 240-3 dec (J. M. Brearley 106*, W. E. Russell 74) drew with Australians 347-8 dec (B. C. Booth 132, P. J. P. Burge 96) and 60-2.

23rd Match: v England (Old Trafford)   July 23, 24, 25, 27, 28.
Australia 656-8 dec (R. B. Simpson 311, W. M. Lawry 106, B. C. Booth 98) and 4-0 drew with England 611 (K. F. Barrington 256, E. R. Dexter 174, J. M. Parks 60, G. Boycott 58, G. D. McKenzie 7-153).

24th Match: v Glamorgan (Swansea)   Aug 1, 3, 4.
Glamorgan 197 (T. R. Veivers 5-85) and 172 (R. B. Simpson 5-33) beat Australians 101 (T. R. Veivers 51, J. S. Pressdee 6-58, D. J. Shepherd 4-22) and 232 (W. M. Lawry 64, T. R. Veivers 54, D. J. Shepherd 5-71, J. S. Pressdee 4-65) by 36 runs.

25th Match: v Warwickshire (Edgbaston)   Aug 5, 6, 7.
Warwickshire 384 (R. W. Barber 138, R. M. Cowper 4-98) and 63-1 dec beat Australians 253-8 dec (P. J. P. Burge 100*, M. D. Mence 4-48) and 185 (J. Potter 60, B. C. Booth 53, R. B. Edmonds 5-68) by 9 wkts.

26th Match: v Yorkshire (Bradford)   Aug 8, 10, 11.
Australians 315-7 dec (B. C. Booth 193*, R. M. Cowper 52) and 229-5 dec (N. C. O'Neill 81, P. J. P. Burge 53) beat Yorkshire 222 (G. Boycott 54) and 241 (G. Boycott 122) by 81 runs.

27th Match: v England (Oval)   Aug 13, 14, 15, 17, 18.
England 182 (N. J. N. Hawke 6-47) and 381-4 (G. Boycott 113, M. C. Cowdrey 93*, K. F. Barrington 54*) drew with Australia 379 (W. M. Lawry 94, B. C. Booth 74, T. R. Veivers 67, F. S. Trueman 4-87).

28th Match: v President of M.C.C.'s XI (Lord's)   Aug 19, 20, 21.
Australians 162 (R. Harman 4-32, D. J. Brown 4-64) and 258-6 dec (B. N. Jarman 105, W. M. Lawry 80) drew with President of M.C.C.'s XI 193-9 dec (N. J. N. Hawke 4-42) and 179-7 (J. M. Brearley 67, G. Boycott 53).

29th Match: v Essex (Southend)   Aug 22, 24, 25.
Essex 425-6 dec (K. W. R. Fletcher 125, G. Barker 123, B. E. A. Edmeades 53*) and 109-4 beat Australians 218 (P. J. Phelan 5-94) and 313 (B. C. Booth 95, W. M. Lawry 52, P. J. Phelan 5-154) by 6 wkts.

30th Match: v Kent (Canterbury)   Aug 26, 27, 28.
Kent 346-6 dec (P. E. Richardson 115, M. C. Cowdrey 90) and 258-3 dec (P. E. Richardson 115, M. C. Cowdrey 50*, B. W. Luckhurst 50*) lost to Australians 354-8 dec (T. R. Veivers 79, J. Potters 75, W. M. Lawry 55, D. L. Underwood 5-100) and 252-2 (N. C. O'Neill 110, W. M. Lawry 101*) by 8 wkts.

31st Match: v Holland (The Hague)   Aug 29.
Australians 197 (N. C. O'Neill 87) lost to Holland 201-7 (R. Marseille 77, R. M. Cowper 4-69) by 3 wkts.

32nd Match: v A. E. R. Gilligan's XI (Hastings)   Sept 2, 3, 4.
A. E. R. Gilligan's XI 372 (B. L. D'Oliveira 119, E. J. Barlow 54, K. G. Suttle 53) and 251-9 dec (M. E. J. C. Norman 81, J. M. Parks 54) lost to Australians 281 (N. C. O'Neill 74, R. M. Cowper 66, J. S. Pressdee 5-83) and 346-8 (W. M. Lawry 110, B. C. Booth 69, R. M. Cowper 56) by 2 wkts.

33rd Match: v T. N. Pearce's XI (Scarborough)   Sept 5, 7, 8.
Australians 400 (W. M. Lawry 121, R. M. Cowper 110, R. B. Simpson 58) and 153-3 (R. M. Cowper 60) beat T. N. Pearce's XI 248 (J. B. Bolus 59) and 302 (P. J. Sharpe 64, B. R. Knight 55, R. H. D. Sellers 4-88) by 7 wkts.*

34th Match: v Scotland (Titwood, Glasgow)   Sept 9, 10.
Scotland 46-0 drew with Australians did not bat.

35th Match: v Scotland (Mannofield, Aberdeen)   Sept 11, 12.
Australians 296 (R. B. Simpson 84, N. C. O'Neill 64, D. Livingstone 6-93) and 117-4 (N. C. O'Neill 52) drew with Scotland 95 (J. W. Martin 4-33).

36th Match: v Sussex (Hove)   Sept 14 (50 overs match).
Australians 282-3 (P. J. P. Burge 124, B. C. Booth 79*) beat Sussex 216 (J. M. Parks 84) by 66 runs.*

The 1964 Australians. Back: James (physiotherapist), Martin, Potter, Veivers, Corling, Hawke, Connolly, McKenzie, Redpath, Cooper, Sellers, Sherwood (scorer). Front: Jarman, Burge, Booth, Steele (manager), Simpson (captain), Ledward (treasurer), Lawry, Grout, O'Neill.

1964: 24th Australians

Batting Averages

	M	I	NO	R	HS	Avge	100	c/s
R. B. Simpson	22	38	8	1714	311	57.13	5	36
B. C. Booth	23	36	8	1551	193*	55.39	3	12
R. M. Cowper	20	29	4	1286	113	51.44	3	25
N. C. O'Neill	20	34	4	1369	151	45.63	4	10
W. M. Lawry	24	41	3	1601	121	42.13	5	12
P. J. P. Burge	23	34	4	1114	160	37.13	2	18/1
T. R. Veivers	22	28	7	725	79	34.52	0	10
I. R. Redpath	22	37	4	1075	162	32.57	2	18
J. Potter	17	27	3	751	78	31.29	0	9
B. N. Jarman	12	17	2	417	105	27.80	1	26/3
R. H. D. Sellers	13	19	8	233	36	21.18	0	10
J. W. Martin	16	23	4	362	70	19.01	0	3
A. T. W. Grout	18	20	2	303	53	16.83	0	34/9
G. D. McKenzie	22	25	7	290	50	16.11	0	15
N. J. N. Hawke	22	16	6	159	37	15.90	0	12
A. N. Connolly	15	10	6	27	14	6.75	0	10
G. E. Corling	19	13	6	43	6	6.14	0	2

Bowling Averages

	O	M	R	W	Avge	BB	5i
N. J. N. Hawke	742	211	1644	83	19.80	6-19	6
G. D. McKenzie	838.1	217	1976	88	22.45	7-153	3
A. N. Connolly	323.5	74	850	28	30.35	4-29	0
R. M. Cowper	222.2	59	713	23	31.00	4-58	0
G. E. Corling	575.2	140	1381	44	31.38	5-59	1
R. B. Simpson	380.5	103	1033	32	32.28	5-33	1
J. W. Martin	361.1	86	1134	35	32.40	4-50	1
T. R. Veivers	754.3	226	1881	52	36.17	5-85	1
R. H. D. Sellers	373.5	93	1128	30	37.60	5-36	1
J. Potter	140	27	436	11	39.63	3-37	0
I. R. Redpath	30	3	147	3	49.00	2-33	0
N. C. O'Neill	108	27	356	6	59.33	2-24	0
B. C. Booth	24.3	4	106	1	106.00	1-9	0

Also bowled: P. J. P. Burge 2-0-17-0; A. T. W. Grout 2-0-22-1; B. N. Jarman 3-0-7-0; W. M. Lawry 6-0-32-0.

1965: 6th New Zealanders

The touring party for this 1965 half season programme was J. R. Reid (captain) and B. W. Sinclair from Wellington; R. W. Morgan, T. W. Jarvis and G. E. Vivian of Auckland; B. Sutcliffe of Northern Districts; B. E. Congdon, R. O. Collinge, B. W. Yuile and V. Pollard from Central Districts; G. T. Dowling, R. C. Motz, B. R. Taylor and J. T. Ward of Canterbury and F. J. Cameron of Otago, with W. A. Hadlee as manager.

In 1963 the I.C.C. had asked the M.C.C. to investigate the possibility of bringing two separate touring parties to England in some seasons, because the West Indies wanted to tour England

1965: 6th New Zealanders

Batting Averages

	M	I	NO	R	HS	Avge	100	c/s
F. J. Cameron	13	14	12	90	29*	45.00	0	1
B. W. Sinclair	15	23	1	807	130	36.68	1	2
B. E. Congdon	16	27	2	885	176*	35.40	2	10
V. Pollard	14	23	4	652	81*	34.31	0	5
J. R. Reid	16	26	1	799	165	31.96	1	8
B. Sutcliffe	10	15	3	372	102	31.00	1	7
G. T. Dowling	16	27	1	744	101*	28.61	1	6
R. W. Morgan	17	29	2	645	110	23.88	1	9
A. E. Dick	13	20	1	451	96	23.73	0	27/1
G. E. Vivian	8	9	3	138	54*	23.00	0	1
B. R. Taylor	14	22	3	433	62	22.78	0	6
R. C. Motz	14	21	3	355	95	19.72	0	0
T. W. Jarvis	10	17	1	266	84	16.62	0	6
B. W. Yuile	12	18	1	244	46	14.35	0	3
R. O. Collinge	15	18	5	136	24	10.46	0	5
J. T. Ward	6	9	6	16	8*	5.33	0	10/1

Bowling Averages

	O	M	R	W	Avge	BB	5i
R. W. Yuile	262.3	125	550	24	22.91	4-18	0
R. C. Motz	454.2	117	1241	54	22.98	6-63	4
F. J. Cameron	457	111	1148	47	24.42	6-35	4
B. R. Taylor	343.3	88	997	31	32.16	5-62	1
R. O. Collinge	432.1	104	1116	34	32.82	4-57	0
R. W. Morgan	107.5	29	341	9	37.88	3-69	0
B. E. Congdon	98	27	315	8	39.37	3-29	0
J. R. Reid	73	24	165	4	41.25	3-67	0
G. E. Vivian	98.1	18	410	7	58.57	2-19	0
V. Pollard	170.3	46	509	8	63.62	3-73	0

Also bowled: T. W. Jarvis 3-3-0-0; B. Sutcliffe 11-3-16-0; A. E. Dick 1-0-16-0; B. W. Sinclair 9-4-18-0; G. T. Dowling 13-2-58-0.

more often than in the agreed programme–their next visit after 1963 was not scheduled until 1971. In January 1964 it was announced that twin-tours were feasible and that all the countries involved agreed. The South African tour scheduled for 1966 was moved forward to the second half of 1965 and the 1965 New Zealand fixtures adjusted to suit. Each country was to play only three Tests, but both would play a Test at Lord's.

The New Zealand party left home in the middle of February and played a seven-Test tour in India and Pakistan before flying to England in late April.

Beaten three matches to nil in the Tests and with only three first-class victories in 19 matches, the tourists had a poor record. The weather, as on their last visit, was not kind and the batsmen found the variety of English wickets too difficult for them. Reid, the best batsman, injured his knee and was not fully fit; Pollard had easily the best Test record with 281 runs, average 56.20. Of the others only Dowling, the opener, put up much resistance. The veteran Sutcliffe was felled by a Trueman bouncer in the First Test and did little from then on. The best feature of the team was their pace bowling. Motz and Collinge performed well and Taylor and Cameron were useful back-ups. The spin bowling was of little use, however. Ward and Dick were both sound–A. E. Dick of Hutt Valley was not originally selected, but was flown to India

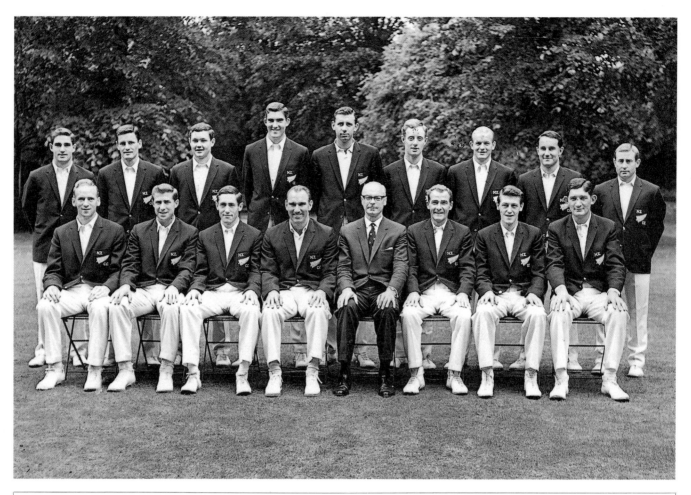

1965: 6th New Zealanders

1st Match: v London New Zealand C.C (Oval)   April 29.
London N.Z. 200-6 dec lost to New Zealanders 212-6 (B. W. Sinclair 52, R. W. Morgan 52) by 5 wkts.

2nd Match: v Duke of Norfolk's XI (Arundel Castle)   May 2.
New Zealanders 217-8 dec (N. Gifford 4-21) drew with Duke of Norfolk's XI 198-6 (E. R. Dexter 52).

3rd Match: v Worcestershire (Worcester)   May 5, 6, 7.
New Zealanders 260 (R. C. Motz 95, J. A. Flavell 8-74) and 160-5 dec (A. E. Dick 50) drew with Worcestershire 255 (T. W. Graveney 84, R. G. A. Headley 67, R. O. Collinge 4-57) and 56-1.

4th Match: v Lancashire (Old Trafford)   May 8, 10, 11.
Lancashire 225 (G. Pullar 82, R. Entwistle 57, F. J. Cameron 5-48) beat New Zealanders 115 and 104 (J. B. Statham 5-15) by an innings and 6 runs.

5th Match: v Gloucestershire (Bristol)   May 12, 13, 14.
Gloucestershire 270-7 dec (A. S. Brown 70, S. E. J. Russell 56, J. B. Mortimore 56) and 131 (R. C. Motz 5-50) lost to New Zealanders 245 (B. W. Sinclair 58, A. S. Brown 5-61) and 160-6 by 4 wkts.

6th Match: v M.C.C. (Lord's)   May 15, 17, 18.
New Zealanders 318-7 dec (B. E. Congdon 136, B. W. Sinclair 63) and 122-1 dec (B. E. Congdon 56*, B. W. Sinclair 52*) drew with M.C.C. 196 (M. C. Cowdrey 77, F. J. Cameron 4-46) and 175-3 (J. H. Hampshire 68).

7th Match: v Nottinghamshire (Trent Bridge)   May 19, 20, 21.
Nottinghamshire 172 (B. R. Taylor 4-50) and 105 (B. W. Yuile 4-18) drew with New Zealanders 122 (I. J. Davison 4-30, C. Forbes 5-31) and 118-9.

8th Match: v Cambridge University (Cambridge)   May 22, 24, 25.
Cambridge University 364-9 dec (R. C. White 151, D. L. Murray 84, R. C. Motz 5-95) drew with New Zealanders 137 (G. Hughes 4-31) and 424-8 (B. W. Sinclair 130, G. T. Dowling 87, B. E. Congdon 63).

9th Match: v England (Edgbaston)   May 27, 28, 29, 31, June 1.
England 435 (K. F. Barrington 137, M. C. Cowdrey 85, E. R. Dexter 57, R. C. Motz 5-108) and 96-1 (R. W. Barber 51) beat New Zealand 116 (F. J. Titmus 4-18) and 413 (V. Pollard 81*, B. Sutcliffe 53, R. W. Barber 4-132) by 9 wkts.

10th Match: v Yorkshire (Bradford)   June 2, 3, 4.
Yorkshire 419 (D. B. Close 115, R. A. Hutton 62, J. G. Binks 62, F. S. Trueman 60) beat New Zealanders 134, and 208 (B. E. Congdon 59, R. C. Motz 51*, D. B. Close 5-69, R. Illingworth 4-85) by an innings and 77 runs.

11th Match: v Glamorgan (Cardiff)   June 5, 7, 8.
Glamorgan 327-9 dec (A. R. Lewis 169, B. R. Taylor 5-62) and 30-1 drew with New Zealanders 279-9 dec (B. W. Sinclair 74, J. R. Reid 58).

12th Match: v Surrey (Oval)   June 9, 10, 11.
Surrey 248 (K. F. Barrington 70, M. J. Stewart 62, F. J. Cameron 5-73) and 295-4 (J. H. Edrich 139, K. F. Barrington 129*) drew with New Zealanders 422-9 dec (R. W. Morgan 110, B. W. Sinclair 88, A. E. Dick 63, B. R. Taylor 62, K. F. Barrington 5-88).

13th Match: v Somerset (Taunton)   June 12, 14, 15.
New Zealanders 155 (B. W. Sinclair 64, G. H. Hall 4-46) and 185-2 (G. T. Dowling 101*) drew with Somerset 196 (R. C. Motz 6-63).

14th Match: v England (Lord's)   June 17, 18, 19, 21, 22.
New Zealand 175 (V. Pollard 55, B. R. Taylor 51, F. E. Rumsey 4-25) and 347 (B. W. Sinclair 72, G. T. Dowling 66, V. Pollard 55) lost to England 307 (M. C. Cowdrey 119, E. R. Dexter 62, R. O. Collinge 4-85) and 218-3 (E. R. Dexter 80*, G. Boycott 76) by 7 wkts.

15th Match: v Oxford University (Oxford)   June 23, 24, 25.
New Zealanders 285 (R. W. Morgan 96, V. Pollard 68, A. G. M. Watson 4-65) drew with Oxford University 137-3 (P. J. K. Gibbs 65).

16th Match: v Kent (Maidstone)   June 26, 28, 29.
Kent 213 (M. H. Denness 86, F. J. Cameron 4-40) and 285-6 dec (M. H. Denness 82) drew with New Zealanders 360-8 dec (J. R. Reid 165, B. W. Sinclair 57) and 17-3.

17th Match: v Warwickshire (Edgbaston)   June 30, July 1, 2.
New Zealanders 297-9 dec (T. W. Jarvis 84, G. E. Vivian 54*) and 219 (J. R. Reid 84, G. T. Dowling 58, W. B. Bridge 4-56) lost to Warwickshire 319-4 dec (J. A. Jameson 137*, T. W. Cartwright 112*) and 198-1 (K. Ibadulla 93*, M. J. K. Smith 61*) by 9 wkts.

18th Match: v Northamptonshire (Northampton)   July 3, 5, 6.
Northamptonshire 282-7 dec and 188-9 drew with New Zealanders 370-9 dec (A. E. Dick 96, B. E. Congdon 86, R. W. Morgan 65).

19th Match: v England (Headingley)   July 8, 9, 10, 12, 13.
England 546-4 dec (J. H. Edrich 310*, K. F. Barrington 163) beat New Zealand 193 (J. R. Reid 54, R. Illingworth 4-42, J. D. F. Larter 4-66) and 166 (V. Pollard 53, F. J. Titmus 5-19) by an innings and 187 runs.

20th Match: v Scotland (Hamilton Crescent, Glasgow)   July 15, 16, 17.
Scotland 115 (F. J. Cameron 6-35) and 316 (J. M. Allan 99*, A. N. Gallagher 73, R. C. Motz 4-41) lost to New Zealanders 364-6 dec (B. E. Congdon 176*, J. R. Reid 70) and 71-1 by 9 wkts.

21st Match: v Ireland (Ormau, Belfast)   July 19, 20, 21.
Ireland 130 (D. Pratt 58, F. J. Cameron 5-45) and 117 lost to New Zealanders 216 (B. Sutcliffe 102, S. Huey 5-68) and 32-0 by 10 wkts.

22nd Match: v Holland (Heemmstede)   July 24, 25.
New Zealanders 361 (J. R. Reid 87, B. R. Taylor 77, Maas 5-110) drew with Holland 139 (R. C. Motz 4-28, B. R. Taylor 4-38) and 234-8 (Bakker 65, Spits 51, F. J. Cameron 4-56).

Left *The 1965 New Zealand tourists.*

Right *Vic Pollard hits to leg at Lord's in the second Test for New Zealand. He scored 55 in each innings. Jim Parks is behind the wicket and Colin Cowdrey at slip.*

when Ward was injured.

Financially the visit was not a success, losing £4,000, but the profit made in India offset this deficit.

After a match in the Netherlands the team flew to Bermuda for two games and then to Los Angeles for a match against Southern California before flying across the Pacific and home.

1965: 13th South Africans

The 1960 tour had been very disappointing and the 1965 selectors included only two of the former team in their new side. This was reduced to one when A. J. Pithey withdrew for business reasons. The team which arrived in England in the middle of June was P. L. van der Merwe (captain) and H. D. Bromfield of Western Province; R. G. Pollock, E. J. Barlow, P. M. Pollock of Eastern Province; A. Bacher, H. R. Lance and A. H. McKinnon of Transvaal; K. V. Bland of Rhodesia; D. T. Lindsay and J. T. Botten of North Eastern Transvaal; R. Dumbrill, D. Gamsy and N. S. Crookes of Natal and M. J. Macaulay of Orange Free State, with J. B. Plimsoll as manager–Lance replaced Pithey.

In South Africa it was felt that the I.C.C. had decided to relegate South Africa to a second-rate Test team by only allowing it a half-season tour, because South Africa had become a Republic and therefore been omitted from the I.C.C. The tourists were determined to prove the I.C.C. wrong and the results of the tour vindicated South Africa's opinion of its cricketers. Van der Merwe's team turned out to be one of the most attractive to visit England since the Second World War. In complete contrast to the New Zealand team which had toured during the first half of 1965, the South Africans not only beat England one nil in the Test series, but returned home with a profit of £15,000 from 17 first-class matches (New Zealand made a loss of £4,000 from 19 matches).

The team had three outstanding young cricketers in the Pollock brothers and Bland. Graeme Pollock topped both first-class and Test batting averages; Peter Pollock headed the Test and first-class bowling averages; Bland batted superbly in two Tests and his fielding was regarded as the wonder of the season–in the covers or at mid-wicket. Another bright youngster was Barlow, who opened the batting and fielded well in the slips. Lance and Lindsay were good middle-order batsmen and Lindsay also kept wicket well. The rest of the attack consisted of three useful medium-pace bowlers in Botten, Dumbrill and Macaulay, plus

The 1965 South African tourists, not the last South African party to tour England but the last representative side to play Test Matches in England.

1965: 13th South Africans

1st Match: v Derbyshire (Chesterfield) June 26, 28, 29.
South Africans 149 (E. J. Barlow 50, H. J. Rhodes 4-35) and 119 lost to Derbyshire 143 (R. Dumbrill 4-32) and 126-3 by 7 wkts.

2nd Match: v Yorkshire (Bramall Lane) June 30, July 1, 2.
South Africans 266-7 dec (J. D. Lindsay 105, D. Gamsy 54) and 140-2 (E. J. Barlow 69*) drew with Yorkshire 197 (D. B. Close 117) and 55-3.

3rd Match: v Essex (Colchester) July 3, 5, 6.
South Africans 323-6 dec (K. C. Bland 94, E. J. Barlow 78, A. Bacher 59, B. R. Knight 4-73) and 260-6 dec (R. Dumbrill 54*, J. D. Lindsay 52) drew with Essex 296 (T. E. Bailey 77, B. E. A. Edmeades 59, P. M. Pollock 5-67) and 222-9 (G. J. Saville 70, A. H. McKinnon 5-75).

4th Match: v Surrey (Oval) July 7, 8, 9.
Surrey 270-8 dec (M. J. Stewart 60, P. M. Pollock 5-50) and 193-4 dec (S. J. Storey 69*, Younis Ahmed 66) drew with South Africans 238-5 dec (E. J. Barlow 110, R. G. Pollock 60*) and 85-1.

5th Match: v Gloucestershire (Bristol) July 10, 12, 13.
Gloucestershire 279 (M. J. Procter 69, B. A. Richards 59) drew with South Africans 39-0.

6th Match: v Minor Counties (Jesmond) July 14, 15, 16.
South Africans 278-9 dec (A. Backer 121, H. R. Lance 56) and 133-4 dec beat Minor Counties 134 (A. H. McKinnon 4-40) and 74 (A. H. McKinnon 5-23, N. S. Crookes 4-24) by 203 runs.

7th Match: v Leicestershire (Leicester) July 17, 19, 20.
Leicestershire 196 (J. van Geloven 54, P. M. Pollock 4-31) and 69-3 drew with South Africans 350 (A. Bacher 119, E. J. Barlow 62, J. T. Botten 90, J. S. Savage 6-79).

8th Match: v England (Lord's) July 22, 23, 24, 26, 27.
South Africa 280 (R. G. Pollock 56) and 248 (K. C. Bland 70, E. J. Barlow 52) drew with England 338 (K. F. Barrington 91, F. J. Titmus 59, R. W. Barber 56) and 145-7 (R. Dumbrill 4-30).

9th Match: v Kent (Canterbury) July 28, 29.
South Africans 365-3 dec (R. G. Pollock 203*, K. C. Bland 61*, A. Bacher 57) beat Kent 74 (P. M. Pollock 5-28) and 144 (A. L. Dixon 53, M. J. Macaulay 4-22) by an innings and 147 runs.

10th Match: v Glamorgan (Swansea) July 31, Aug 2, 3.
Glamorgan 301 (A. R. Lewis 146*, A. H. McKinnon 4-54) drew with South Africans 144 (A. Bacher 72, J. S. Pressdee 4-11) and 198-8 (R. Dumbrill 53).

11th Match: v England (Trent Bridge) Aug 5, 6, 7, 9.
South Africa 269 (R. G. Pollock 125, T. W. Cartwright 6-94) and 289 (E. J. Barlow 76, A. Bacher 67, R. G. Pollock 59, J. D. F. Larter 5-68) beat England 240 (M. C. Cowdrey 105, P. M. Pollock 5-53) and 224 (P. H. Parfitt 86, P. M. Pollock 5-34) by 94 runs.

12th Match: v Middlesex (Lord's) Aug 11, 12, 13.
Middlesex 335-8 dec (C. T. Radley 138, F. J. Titmus 101) and 123 (N. S. Crookes 8-47) lost to South Africans 254 (R. S. Herman 4-58) and 207-5 (J. D. Lindsay 55) by 5 wkts.

13th Match: v Hampshire (Southampton) Aug 14, 16, 17.
Hampshire 286-7 dec (G. L. Keith 101*, B. S. V. Timms 80, N. S. Crookes 4-89) and 87-8 drew with South Africans 133 (A. Bacher 74, D. Shackleton 6-29) and 354-9 dec (E. J. Barlow 129, R. G. Pollock 94, A. R. Wassell 5-135).

14th Match: v Sussex (Hove) Aug 18, 19, 20.
South Africans 391 (R. G. Pollock 122, K. D. Bland 78, J. D. Lindsay 55, R. Dumbrill 50, A. Buss 4-69) and 109-5 dec drew with Sussex 238 (R. Dumbrill 5-37) and 216-7 (J. M. Parks 106).

15th Match: v Warwickshire (Edgbaston) Aug 21, 23, 24.
Warwickshire 217-7 dec (B. A. Richardson 67, R. Miller 50) and 170-9 dec (K. I. Ibadulla 52, N. S. Crookes 4-76) drew with South Africans 208-4 dec (D. Gamsy 79, A. Bacher 70).

16th Match: v England (Oval) Aug 26, 27, 28, 30, 31.
South Africa 208 (H. R. Lance 69, J. B. Statham 5-40, K. Higgs 4-47) and 392 (K. C. Bland 78, A. Bacher 70, H. R. Lance 53, K. Higgs 4-96) drew with England 202 (P. M. Pollock 5-43) and 308-4 (M. C. Cowdrey 78*, K. F. Barrington 73, W. E. Russell 70).

17th Match: v Lancashire (Old Trafford) Sept 1, 2, 3.
South Africans 273 (R. G. Pollock 75, P. M. Pollock 51*, K. Higgs 4-46) and 169 beat Lancashire 159 (N. S. Crookes 5-54) and 117 (H. D. Bromfield 5-42) by 166 runs.

18th Match: v T. N. Pearce's XI (Scarborough) Sept 4, 6.
South Africans 207 (A. Bacher 60, F. E. Rumsey 4-35) and 224 (R. Dumbrill 64, R. W. Barber 4-50) lost to T. N. Pearce's XI 241 (M. J. K. Smith 65, R. Dumbrill 4-31) and 191-2 (P. H. Parfitt 87*) by 8 wkts.

19th Match: v T. N. Pearce's XI (Scarborough) Sept 7 (40 over a side).
T. N. Pearce's XI 213-7 (M. C. Cowdrey 75) beat South Africans 200 (R. Dumbrill 53, P. L. van der Merwe 50) by 14 runs.

20th Match: v Yorkshire (Bradford) Sept 9 (60 overs a side).
Match abandoned due to rain.

1965: 13th South Africans

Batting Averages

	M	I	NO	R	HS	Avge	100	c/s
R. G. Pollock	14	24	4	1147	203*	57.35	3	6
A. Bacher	16	26	1	1008	121	40.32	2	11
E. J. Barlow	16	28	3	971	129	38.84	2	15
K. C. Bland	16	26	2	906	127	37.75	1	6
D. T. Lindsay	15	29	1	779	105	27.82	1	22/3
H. R. Lance	13	21	3	475	69	26.38	0	15
P. M. Pollock	12	13	5	182	51*	22.75	0	5
R. Dumbrill	15	22	3	429	64	22.57	0	9
D. Gamsy	11	16	1	285	79	19.00	0	22/3
J. T. Botten	12	15	3	227	90	18.91	0	4
A. H. McKinnon	11	10	6	66	14*	16.50	0	3
P. L. van der Merwe	16	24	2	363	48*	16.50	0	12
N. S. Crookes	10	10	2	90	34	11.25	0	11
M. J. Macaulay	12	12	2	111	22	11.10	0	5
H. D. Bromfield	9	11	5	36	23	6.00	0	5

Bowling Averages

	O	M	R	W	Avge	BB	5i
P. M. Pollock	371.4	108	851	50	17.02	5-28	6
N. S. Crookes	318.2	75	914	47	19.44	8-47	2
A. H. McKinnon	351.1	120	759	37	20.51	5-23	2
R. Dumbrill	287.5	75	673	31	21.70	5-37	1
J. T. Botten	340	85	818	33	24.78	3-24	0
M. J. Macaulay	329	92	739	25	29.56	4-22	0
H. R. Lance	49.3	13	120	4	30.00	3-15	0
H. D. Bromfield	266.1	88	646	20	32.30	5-42	1
E. J. Barlow	160	36	335	9	37.22	2-9	0
R. G. Pollock	123.5	31	404	8	50.50	2-25	0

Also bowled: A. Bacher 1-0-5-0; K. C. Bland 5-0-18-1.

1966: 10th West Indians

Batting Averages

	M	I	NO	R	HS	Avge	100	c/s
G. St A. Sobers	18	25	3	1349	174	61.31	4	23
B. F. Butcher	19	25	2	1105	209*	48.04	3	8
S. M. Nurse	19	26	1	1105	155	44.20	2	17
R. B. Kanhai	19	28	1	1028	192*	38.07	3	13
D. A. J. Holford	19	26	6	759	107*	37.95	2	12
C. C. Hunte	19	27	0	970	206	35.92	2	9
J. S. Solomon	17	21	4	585	104*	34.41	1	6
P. D. Lashley	18	24	2	647	78	29.40	0	15
E. D. A. St. J. McMorris	17	25	3	634	157*	28.81	2	2
M. C. Carew	18	29	1	720	132	25.71	1	9
C. C. Griffith	16	20	6	297	63*	21.21	0	5
R. C. Brancker	16	19	1	329	37	18.27	0	10
D. W. Allan	14	15	2	209	56	16.07	0	27/8
W. W. Hall	19	21	5	246	34*	15.37	0	6
J. L. Hendricks	14	16	5	144	20	13.09	0	25/10
R. A. Cohen	18	15	8	72	32*	10.28	0	9
L. R. Gibbs	17	18	8	98	19	9.80	0	9

Bowling Averages

	O	M	R	W	Avge	BB	5i
C. C. Griffith	357	86	998	49	20.36	6-59	2
G. St A. Sobers	557.2	158	1235	60	20.58	9-49	3
R. A. Cohen	283.3	59	969	40	24.22	6-71	1
L. R. Gibbs	608.4	207	1190	47	25.31	6-39	4
R. C. Brancker	330.4	81	860	33	26.06	7-77	2
D. A. J. Holford	507	117	1460	51	28.62	8-52	3
P. D. Lashley	162.2	40	407	14	29.07	3-15	0
M. C. Carew	233	78	531	17	31.23	5-80	1
W. W. Hall	439	104	1280	39	32.82	4-63	0
R. B. Kanhai	5.1	0	47	1	47.00	1-40	0
C. C. Hunte	32	8	93	1	93.00	1-10	0
J. S. Solomon	54	10	204	1	204.00	1-32	0

Also bowled: B. F. Butcher 2-0-7-0; S. M. Nurse 2-0-3-0.

the left-arm slows of McKinnon. Van der Merwe, although doing little with the bat, fielded well and built up an excellent team spirit.

There were bands of anti-apartheid demonstrators at most matches, but they did not seriously interfere with the cricket and had no effect on the South African team.

1966: 10th West Indians

The team selected was G. St A. Sobers (captain), C. C. Hunte, D. W. Allan, R. C. Brancker, W. W. Hall, D. A. J. Holford, P. D. Lashley, S. M. Nurse and C. C. Griffith, all of Barbados; B. F.

Right Gary Sobers and his team meet the Queen during the Second Test at Lord's.

Butcher, L. R. Gibbs and J. S. Solomon of British Guiana; M. C. Carew and R. B. Kanhai of Trinidad; R. A. Cohen, J. L. Hendriks and E. D. A. St J. McMorris of Jamaica, with J. B. Stollmeyer as manager. Two notable omissions were L. A. King, who had a knee injury and the wicketkeeper, D. L. Murray, who was studying at Cambridge. R. Bynoe of Barbados was strangely ignored in preference to Carew and Solomon secured a place rather than young Clive Lloyd of British Guiana.

The team arrived at London by air on 17 April. Of the eight first-class matches before the First Test, five were seriously affected by rain. This did not seem to dull the West Indian form, however, for they won the Test with an innings to spare. The Second Test was drawn, but the tourists won the Third with ease after a difficult opening and the Fourth by an innings. The England selectors made sweeping changes for the final match and the home side, captained by Close, won by an innings. Thus the West Indies won the series three to one.

The tour was a triumph for Sobers. He batted magnificently in every Test to end the series with 722 runs, average 103.14, plus 20 wickets, average 27.25. These batting and bowling figures, plus some excellent close fielding and the responsibility of captaining the side made Sobers the equal of any cricketer of any age.

The team relied heavily on his amazing talent. Solomon, McMorris and Carew, the experienced batsmen, did little to enhance their reputations and of the newcomers Lashley, Brancker and Cohen all fared indifferently.

The controversial aspect of the tour was the fast bowling of Griffith, whose action was criticised in many quarters. Griffith headed the first-class table, but the off-spinner Gibbs had the best figures in the Tests – 21 wickets, average 24.76. Griffith's partner, Hall, came into his own only in the latter half of the year. The successes among the batsmen were the consistent Nurse, Hunte as an opener (again with no effective partner), young Holford and Butcher and occasionally Kanhai. Hendriks and Allan were reliable wicketkeepers, though the former missed some matches through injury.

The Test matches proved very popular, but there was some criticism in the press about the way the tourists used the county matches simply for practice. The total profit for the tour was about £15,000 – the drop from 1963 was attributed mainly to the counter-attraction of the World Soccer Cup held in England during the summer and the wet weather, though the attitude of

---

1966: 10th West Indians

1st Match: v Duke of Norfolk's XI (Arundel Castle)   April 30.
Duke of Norfolk's XI 221-7 dec (K. F. Barrington 73, T. W. Graveney 58) lost to West Indians 223-6 (S. M. Nurse 61, P. D. Lashley 61, M. C. Carew 54) by 4 wkts.

2nd Match: v Worcestershire (Worcester)   May 4, 5, 6.
Worcestershire 206-7 (J. A. Ormrod 72) drew with West Indians did not bat.

3rd Match: v Oxford University (Oxford)   May 7, 9, 10.
Oxford University 160 (C. C. Griffith 4-35) and 211-8 (G. N. S. Ridley 50, L. R. Gibbs 5-45) drew with West Indians 381-7 dec (R. B. Kanhai 192).*

4th Match: v Nottinghamshire (Trent Bridge)   May 11, 12, 13.
West Indians 335-7 dec (G. St A. Sobers 153) and 81-3 drew with Nottinghamshire 259-6 dec (H. I. Moore 63, N. W. Hill 61, R. Swetman 57).*

5th Match: v M.C.C. (Lord's)   May 14, 16, 17.
West Indians 349-9 dec (B. F. Butcher 137) and 246-9 dec (B. F. Butcher 56) drew with West Indians 383-8 dec (M. J. K. Smith 140, J. T. Murray 100, C. Milburn 64) and 67-2.*

6th Match: v Lancashire (Old Trafford)   May 18, 19, 20.
West Indians 295-8 dec (D. A. J. Holford 107, S. M. Nurse 69, T. Greenhough 4-83) drew with Lancashire 296-4 (G. Pullar 167*, R. Entwistle 60).*

7th Match: v Cambridge University (Cambridge)   May 21, 23, 24.
West Indians 345 (G. St A. Sobers 83, P. D. Lashley 78, J. S. Solomon 73, A. B. Palfreman 4-62) and 169-6 dec (M. C. Carew 67) beat Cambridge University 220 (N. J. Cosh 98, D. A. J. Holford 4-63) and 120 (D. A. J. Holford 8-52) by 174 runs.*

8th Match: v Yorkshire (Bradford)   May 25, 26, 27.
Yorkshire 177-6 dec and 64-3 drew with West Indians 168 (C. C. Hunte 66).

9th Match: v Derbyshire (Derby)   May 28, 30, 31.
West Indians 371-2 dec (E. D. A. St J. McMorries 157, C. C. Hunte 98, S. M. Nurse 54) beat Derbyshire 105 (G. St A. Sobers 6-11) and 234 (H. L. Johnson 90) by an innings and 32 runs.*

10th Match: v England (Old Trafford)   June 2, 3, 4.
West Indies 484 (G. St A. Sobers 161, C. C. Hunte 135, F. J. Titmus 5-83) beat England 167 (L. R. Gibbs 5-37) and 277 (C. Milburn 94, M. C. Cowdrey 69, L. R. Gibbs 5-69) by an innings and 40 runs.

11th Match: v Gloucestershire (Bristol)   June 8, 9, 10.
Gloucestershire 332-9 dec (R. B. Nicholls 108, J. B. Mortimore 64, R. C. Brancker 6-101) and 103-9 dec drew, the scores being level, with West Indians 151 (A. R. Windows 8-78 dec) and 286-6 (M. C. Carew 132, A. S. Brown 4-61).

12th Match: v Sussex (Hove)   June 11, 13.
West Indians 123 (M. C. Carew 56, J. A. Snow 7-29) and 67 (J. A. Snow 4-18, A. Buss 4-18) lost to Sussex 185 (P. J. Graves 64, R. A. Cohen 6-71, C. C. Griffith 4-43) and 6-1 by 9 wkts.

13th Match: v England (Lord's)   June 16, 17, 18, 20, 21.
West Indies 269 (S. M. Nurse 64, K. Higgs 6-91) and 369-5 dec (G. St A. Sobers 163*, D. A. J. Holford 105*) drew with England 355 (T. W. Graveney 96, J. M. Parks 91, G. Boycott 60, W. W. Hall 4-106) and 197-4 (C. Milburn 126*).

14th Match: v Minor Counties (Lakenham)   June 23, 24.
Minor Counties 65 (W. W. Hall 7-31) and 211 (M. Maslin 66, W. J. Edrich 61) lost to West Indians 309-5 dec (P. D. Lashley 121, R. B. Kanhai 67, B. F. Butcher 54) by an innings and 33 runs.*

15th Match: v Essex (Southend)   June 25, 27, 28.
Essex 230 (K. W. R. Fletcher 106, W. W. Hall 4-63) and 75-4 drew with West Indians 354-6 dec (S. M. Nurse 155, J. S. Solomon 55, P. D. Lashley 54).*

16th Match: v England (Trent Bridge)   June 30, July 1, 2, 4, 5.
West Indians 235 (S. M. Nurse 93, K. Higgs 4-71, J. A. Snow 4-82) and 482-5 dec (B. F. Butcher 209*, G. St A. Sobers 94, R. B. Kanhai 63, S. M. Nurse 53) beat England 325 (T. W. Graveney 109, M. C. Cowdrey 96, B. L. d'Oliveira 76, G. St A. Sobers 4-90, W. W. Hall 4-105) and 253 (G. Boycott 71, B. L. d'Oliveira 54, C. C. Griffith 4-34) by 139 runs.

17th Match: v Middlesex (Lord's)   July 6, 7, 8.
West Indians 187-8 dec (R. W. Hooker 5-53) and 242 (C. C. Hunte 82) drew with Middlesex 243-8 dec (E. A. Clark 99, R. W. Hooker 81, C. C. Griffith 6-69) and 85-2.

18th Match: v Kent (Canterbury)   July 9, 11, 12.
West Indians 382 (E. D. A. St J. McMorris 116, D. A. J. Holford 55, A. L. Dixon 5-138) beat Kent 202 (B. W. Luckhurst 104, R. C. Brancker 7-78) and 124 (G. St A. Sobers 9-49) by an innings and 56 runs.

19th Match: v Somerset (Taunton)   July 16, 18, 19.
West Indians 445-5 dec (C. C. Hunte 206, J. S. Solomon 104, D. A. J. Holford 59*) drew with Somerset 158 (D. A. J. Holford 6-59) and 187-6 (C. R. M. Atkinson 51*).*

20th Match: v Surrey (Oval)   July 22 (60 overs a side).
Surrey 188-9 (M. J. Edwards 108) lost to West Indians 191-3 (P. D. Lashley 75, S. M. Nurse 73) by 7 wkts (Note: The original fixture was a 3-day match, July 20, 21, 22, but rain prevented any play on July 20 and 21).*

21st Match: v Northamptonshire (Northampton)   July 23, 25.
West Indians 126 and 163 (M. J. Kettle 5-58) lost to Northamptonshire 159 (C. Milburn 57, L. R. Gibbs 4-42) and 136-6 by 4 wkts.

22nd Match: v M.C.C. President's XI (Lord's)   July 27, 28, 29.
M.C.C. President's XI 164 (D. L. Amiss 69) and 182-5 drew with West Indians 227 (B. F. Butcher 74).

23rd Match: v Glamorgan (Swansea)   July 30, Aug 1, 2.
Glamorgan 337-8 dec (A. Jones 161, E. J. Lewis 56) and 53-2 dec drew with West Indians 193 and 33-2.*

24th Match: v England (Headingley)   Aug 4, 5, 6, 8.
West Indies 500-9 dec (G. St A. Sobers 174, S. M. Nurse 137, K. Higgs 4-94) beat England 240 (D. L. d'Oliveira 88, G. St A. Sobers 5-41) and 205 (R. W. Barber 55, L. R. Gibbs 6-39) by an innings and 55 runs.

25th Match: v Scotland (Hamilton Crescent, Glasgow)   Aug 11 (60 over a side).
West Indians 193 (R. B. Kanhai 68, E. R. Thompson 6-55) drew with Scotland 16-1 (Note: The original fixture was a 2-day match, Aug 10, 11, but rain prevented any play on Aug 10).

26th Match: v Warwickshire (Edgbaston)   Aug 13, 15, 16.
Warwickshire 173 and 315 (D. L. Amiss 160) lost to West Indians 441 (B. F. Butcher 128, J. S. Solomon 77, E. D. A. St J. McMorris 61, D. W. Allan 56) and 50-0 by 10 wkts.*

27th Match: v England 268 (R. B. Kanhai 104, G. St A. Sobers 81) and 225 (S. M. Nurse 70, B. F. Butcher 60) lost to England 527 (T. W. Graveney 165, J. T. Murray 112) by an innings and 34 runs.

28th Match: v Leicestershire (Leicester)   Aug 24, 25, 26.
Leicestershire 179 (J. Birkenshaw 68, C. C. Griffith 6-59) and 207 (D. A. J. Holford 6-68) lost to West Indians 234 (S. M. Nurse 66, P. D. Lashley 59, G. A. R. Lock 5-51, J. S. Savage 4-66) and 155-3 (R. B. Kanhai 62) by 7 wkts.

29th Match: v Hampshire (Southampton)   Aug 27, 29, 30.
West Indians 191 (P. D. Lashley 73, A. T. Castell 4-33) and 134-5 dec drew with Hampshire 103-2 dec and 142-2 (R. E. Marshall 54, H. Horton 54).*

30th Match: v A. E. R. Gilligan's XI (Hastings)   Aug 31, Sept 1, 2.
West Indians 351 (C. C. Griffith 63, P. D. Lashley 60, C. C. Hunte 54, D. W. Allan 51) drew with A. E. R. Gilligan's XI 70-4.*

31st Match: v T. N. Pearce's XI (Scarborough)   Sept 3, 5, 6.
West Indians 234 (D. A. J. Holford 62) and 342-8 dec (R. B. Kanhai 103, P. D. Lashley 50) lost to T. N. Pearce's XI 300-5 dec (G. Boycott 131) and 277-8 (R. M. Prideaux 72, G. Boycott 65, M. C. Carew 5-80) by 2 wkts.

32nd Match: v Warwickshire (Edgbaston)   Sept 10 (50 overs a side).
West Indians 257-4 (S. M. Nurse 102, M. C. Carew 78) beat Warwickshire 238 (D. L. Amiss 76, R. W. Barber 63, C. C. Hunte 4-38) by 19 runs.*

33rd Match: v Rest of World (Lord's)   Sept 12 (50 overs).
West Indies 254-7 (S. M. Nurse 88, C. C. Hunte 57) beat Rest of World 236-8 (R. G. Pollock 65, Hanif Mohammad 63, W. W. Hall 4-40) by 18 runs.

34th Match: v England (Lord's)   Sept 13 (50 overs a side).
England 217-7 beat West Indies 150 (S. M. Nurse 58, K. Higgs 4-50) by 67 runs.

Gary Sobers had a miraculous tour in 1966. He skippered his side to a 3-1 triuumph in the Tests, in which he averaged over 100 with the bat (he had three innings of more than 160) and took 20 wickets.

the tourists to the run of the mill county matches did not help swell the coffers.

The season ended with a new idea, the Rothman World Cup–between the West Indies, the Rest of The World and England–one-day matches limited to 50 overs each. The new competition, won by England, created considerable interest.

1966: 1st Wilfred Isaacs' South Africans

Captained by a 49-year-old opening bat, this team consisted of a blend of experience and youth: W. Isaacs (captain), R. A. McLean, D. J. McGlew, B. A. Richards and C. Wesley of Natal; N. A. T. Adcock, B. L. Irvine, D. Mackay-Coghill, H. J. Tayfield and G. L. G. Watson of Transvaal; A. Bruyns, J. McG. Cole and M. J. Procter of Western Province; J. G. Ferrant of Eastern

---

1966: Wilfred Isaacs' South Africans

1st Match: v Danish Cricket Association (Copenhagen)   July 2.
Isaacs XI 240-6 dec (B. L. Irvine 108, K. J. Funston 66*) beat Danish C.A. 176 (C. Morild 51) by 64 runs.

2nd Match: v Danish Cricket Association (Aalborg)   July 3.
Isaacs XI 201 (D. J. McGlew 61, H. Mortensen 8-84) beat Danish C.A. 106 (M. J. Procter 6-27) by 95 runs.

3rd Match: v Sidmouth (Sidmouth)   July 7.
Isaacs XI 304-6 dec (A. Bruyns 100, D. Mackay-Coghill 73) beat Sidmouth 66 (G. L. G. Watson 4-20) by 238 runs.

4th Match: v Hampshire 2nd XI (Bournemouth)   July 8, 9.
Isaacs XI 263 (D. J. McGlew 99, B. A. Richards 72, A. R. Wassell 4-82, G. L. Keith 4-36) and 133-3 dec (M. J. Procter 56) beat Hampshire 164-7 dec (G. L. Keith 51) and 159 (J. Cole 4-26) by 73 runs.

5th Match: v D. A. Allen's XI (Bristol)   July 10.
No play due to rain.

6th Match: v R. A. W. Sharp's XI (Sherborne)   July 11.
Isaacs XI 206 (M. J. Procter 55) beat R. A. W. Sharp's XI 162 (D. M. Daniels 58, H. J. Tayfield 6-77, G. Hall 4-31) by 44 runs.

7th Match: v D. R. W. Silk's XI (Marlborough)   July 12.
Isaacs XI 170-8 dec drew with D. R. W. Silk's XI 149-8.

8th Match: v Kent 2nd XI (Canterbury)   July 13.
Isaacs XI 250-6 dec (K. J. Funston 85, B. A. Richards 83) beat Kent 2nd XI 100 by 150 runs.

9th Match: v Peter West's XI (Cranbrook)   July 14.
Peter West's XI 172 (D. Mackay-Coghill 5-28) lost to Isaacs XI 173-3 (M. J. Procter 62) by 7 wkts.

10th Match: v C.C.C. (St Albans)   July 15.
C.C.C. 160-8 dec (L. G. Studds 66) drew with Isaacs XI 111-4.

11th Match: v Harlequins (Eton)   July 16.
Harlequins 189 lost to Isaacs XI 192-3 (B. A. Richards 89*) by 7 wkts.

12th Match: v P. M. Walker's XI (Cardiff)   July 17. (40 overs a side).
P. M. Walker's XI 173 (D. J. McGlew 6-50) lost to Isaacs XI 174-9 (M. J. Procter 51, D. J. Shepherd 4-40) by 1 wkt.

13th Match: v Col L. C. Stevens XI (Eastbourne)   July 18, 19.
Isaacs XI 293 (B. A. Richards 74, M. J. Procter 68, D. Mackay-Coghill 65, J. Cole 52, R. Benaud 5-73) and 199-2 dec (R. A. McLean 118) drew with Col L. C. Stevens XI 201-4 dec (R. A. Gale 84, A. H. Phebey 51) and 210-9 (R. A. Gale 92).

14th Match: v Sussex Martlets (Arundel)   July 20.
Isaacs XI 167-5 dec (A. Bruyns 81*) drew with Martlets 42-2.

15th Match: v Sussex 2nd XI (Hove)   July 21.
No play due to rain.

16th Match: v M. R. Rickett's XI (Roehampton)   July 22.
Isaacs XI 166 (B. L. Irvine 73, J. Denman 5-46) drew with M. R. Rickett's XI 100-8 (D. J. McGlew 4-15).

17th Match: v Parasites (Stoke Green)   July 23.
Parasites 156 (H. J. Tayfield 5-50, G. L. G. Watson 4-32) lost to Isaacs XI 157-3 (R. A. McLean 62*) by 7 wkts.

18th Match: v Quidnuncs (Woolwich)   July 24.
Quidnuncs 200-8 dec (J. M. Brearley 118, D. B. Carr 4-52) drew with Isaacs XI 28-1.

19th Match: v Old Johnians (Leatherhead)   July 25.
Isaacs XI 225-5 dec (A. Bruyns 101, B. L. Irvine 62, J. F. Russell 4-59) beat Old Johnians 154 by 71 runs.

20th Match: v Still-Going-Strong C.C. (Rotterdam)   July 29.

21st Match: v R. G. Ingelse XI (The Hague)   July 30.

Province; K. J. Funston and G. C. Hall of North-Eastern Transvaal; P. P. Henwood of Orange Free State, with R. Eriksen as manager. R. Benaud and D. C. S. Compton each appeared once.

The team began its tour with two matches in Denmark and ended with two in the Netherlands. In between they played 17 fixtures in England, none of which they lost. The opponents were perhaps too weak and a fixture list on the lines of the Fezelas might have been more appropriate.

1967: 7th Indians

The team which represented India in England was the Nawab of Pataudi (captain), D. N. Sardesai, A. L. Wadekar, C. G. Borde, Hanumant Singh, F. M. Engineer, R. C. Saxena, V. Subramanyam, R. F. Surti, E. A. S. Prasanna, B. S. Bedi, B. K. Kunderan, S. Venkataraghavan, S. N. Mohol, B. S. Chandrasekhar and S. Guha, with K. K. Tarapore as manager and M. Chinnaswamy as treasurer. The two players whom critics thought deserved places but who were omitted were Desai and Ranjane–the former was probably left out due to his suspect action.

Only two of the team had played first-class cricket in England before the tour and the depressingly wet weather of 1967 allied to a long injury list was altogether too much for this inexperienced party. The three new ball bowlers, Guha, Mohol and Surti, were all injured and in the Third Test, the reserve wicketkeeper, Kunderan, actually opened the bowling.

The visitors lost all three Tests and won only two of the 18 first-class matches. The Nawab headed the Test averages with 269 runs, average 44.83, followed by the left-handed Wadekar who was most reliable. The wicketkeepers Engineer and Kunderan both played some good innings and the other batsman to make an impact was Hanumant Singh.

Chandrasekhar was the only bowler to worry the England batsmen, his googlies taking 16 Test wickets, at 27.18–the other

Right The captain of the Indians, the Nawab of Pataudi batting against Hampshire at Bournemouth. His father also captained India.

Below The 1967 Indian touring party.

spinners, Bedi and Prasanna, though doing little in the Tests, had good reports against the counties. The fielding let down the bowlers.

The weather cheered up towards the end of the tour, but too late to change its course.

A profit of £7,800 was made in England and a further £1,200 during the short visit to East Africa which was made after the main tour.

1967: 3rd Pakistanis

The team to tour England during the second half of 1967 was Hanif Mohammad (captain), Majid J. Khan, Waqar Ahmed, Saeed Ahmed, Asif Iqbal, Salim Altaf, Mohammad Ilyas, Javed Burki, Arif Butt, Niaz Ahmed, Intikhab Alam, F. S. Aizazuddin, Salah-ud-din, Wasim Bari, Fasih-ud-din, Pervez Sajjad and

Ghulam Abbas, with J. A. Khan as manager and Bashir Ahmed as his assistant. In addition three players already in England and asked to play in certain matches: Mushtaq Mohammad, Nasim-ul-Ghani and Khalid Ibadulla.

Although they fared slightly better than India had done, the Pakistanis did have much better weather. England won the Test series two matches to nil, Pakistan doing well in the drawn game at Lord's.

Hanif was very defensive and this stodginess seemed to creep into even the brightest of the tourists. Saeed batted well enough when the wicket was hard; Burki was converted into an opening batsman—an experiment that failed. Majid was often brilliant in the county matches, but in the Tests his average was 6.33.

Intikhab easily topped the bowling table for first-class matches, but his four Test wickets cost 67 runs each and the only bowlers to return reasonable Test records were Mushtaq and Asif. The side suffered from many injuries, to the extent that they only just managed to produce 11 fit men for one or two fixtures.

After the two rather mundane tours of 1967 the press mooted

Hanif Mohammad batting at Lord's during the first Test on 29 July 1967. Hanif played a captain's innings of 187 not out from 329 added while he was at the wicket. It was the highest score by a Pakistani against England.

reducing the Test matches against Pakistan, India and New Zealand, when played in England, to four days.

At the end of the summer Pakistan, England and the Rest of the World competed in the Rothman World Cup–one-day matches limited to 50 overs a side which was won by the Rest of the World, captained by Sobers.

1967: 3rd Pakistanis

1st Match: v L. C. Stevens' XI (Eastbourne)   June 22, 23.
Pakistanis 251-5 dec (Saeed Ahmed 107, Hanif Mohammad 52) and 176-3 (Javed Burki 102, Hanif Mohammad 52*) drew with L. C. Stevens' XI 229-6 dec (R. B. Kanhai 97*, R. E. Marshall 51).

2nd Match: v Hampstead (Hampstead)   June 25.
Pakistanis 49-2 drew with Hampstead did not bat.

3rd Match: v Essex (Colchester)   June 28, 29, 30.
Pakistanis 251-8 dec (Ghulam Abbas 66) and 204-9 dec (Salim Altaf 53*) drew with Essex 116 (Salim Altaf 4-15) and 259-6 (G. R. Cass 81, Pervez Sajjad 4-95).

4th Match: v Kent (Canterbury)   July 1, 3, 4.
Pakistan 293 (Majid J. Khan 103, D. L. Underwood 7-78) and 151-6 drew with Kent 392-6 dec (M. C. Cowdrey 100*, S. E. Leary 78, J. N. Shepherd 73*, Niaz Ahmed 5-86).

5th Match: v Middlesex (Lord's)   July 5, 6, 7.
Pakistan 237 (Ghulam Abbas 55, Majid J. Khan 51, A. H. Latchman 7-91) and 301-4 (Javed Burki 114, Majid J. Khan 107*) drew with Middlesex 452-3 dec (W. E. Russell 167, M. J. Harris 160, J. T. Murray 53).

6th Match: v Somerset (Taunton)   July 8, 9, 10.
Somerset 502-6 dec (M. J. Kitchen 189, R. T. Virgin 162, T. I. Barwell 74*, Pervez Sajjid 5-158) drew with Pakistan 456-6 (Saeed Ahmed 129, Ghulam Abbas 116, Hanif Mohammad 107).

7th Match: v Sussex (Hove)   July 12, 13, 14.
Pakistan 245 (Majid J. Khan 112*, A. Buss 6-62) and 254-7 dec (Hanif Mohammad 63*, Ghulam Abbas 56, Salahuddin 54) drew with Sussex 338 (K. G. Suttle 78, J. M. Parks 78, G. C. Cooper 65, L. J. Lenham 51*, Pervez Sajjad 7-99) and 18-1.

8th Match: v Surrey (Oval)   July 15, 17, 18.
Pakistanis 337 (Hanif Mohammad 78, Saeed Ahmed 71, Majid J. Khan 60, Waqar Ahmed 50*) and 146-5 dec drew with Surrey 278 (I. W. Finlay 103, W. A. Smith 71) and 71-0.

9th Match: v Minor Counties (Swindon)   July 19, 20, 21.
Pakistanis 164-6 dec (Fakir Aizazuddin 74) and 218 (Niaz Ahmed 69*, Salahuddin 57, A. G. Marshall 6-53) beat Minor Counties 186 (Intikhab Alam 8-61) and 173 (M. Maslin 66*, Intikhab Alam 4-58) by 23 runs.

10th Match: v Warwickshire (Edgbaston)   July 22, 24, 25.
Warwickshire 439-6 dec (M. J. K. Smith 173*, R. N. Abberley 93, D. L. Amiss 55, J. A. Jameson 55) beat Pakistanis 216 (T. W. Cartwright 5-56) and 122 (L. R. Gibbs 4-19, T. W. Cartwright 4-43) by an innings and 101 runs.

11th Match: v England (Lord's)   July 27, 28, 29, 31, Aug 1.
England 369 (K. F. Barrington 148, T. W. Graveney 81, B. L. d'Oliveira 59) and 241-9 dec (B. L. d'Oliveira 81*) drew with Pakistan 354 (Hanif Mohammad 187*, Asif Iqbal 76) and 88-3.

12th Match: v Yorkshire (Headingley)   Aug 2, 3, 4.
Yorkshire 414-3 dec (P. J. Sharpe 197, G. Boycott 128, D. E. V. Padgett 70) drew with Pakistanis 150 (R. Illingworth 4-34) and 38-0.

13th Match: v Glamorgan (Swansea)   Aug 5, 7, 8.
Pakistanis 249-9 dec (Waqar Ahmed 79*, Asif Iqbal 75, A. E. Cordle 5-29) and 324-3 dec (Majid J. Khan 147*, Saeed Ahmed 72*, Mohammad Ilyas 63) drew with Glamorgan 250-5 dec (A. R. Lewis 128*, K. J. Lyons 51) and 72-2.

14th Match: v England (Trent Bridge)   Aug 10, 11, 12, 14, 15.
Pakistan 140 (K. Higgs 4-35) and 114 (Saeed Ahmed 68, D. L. Underwood 5-52) lost to England 252-8 dec (K. F. Barrington 109*) and 3-0 by 10 wkts.

15th Match: v Gloucestershire (Cheltenham)   Aug 16, 17, 18.
Pakistanis 176 (J. B. Mortimore 5-60, M. Bissex 5-84) and 214 (Ghulam Abbas 64, M. Bissex 5-73, J. B. Mortimore 4-42) beat Gloucestershire 208 (D. W. J. Brown 59, C. A. Milton 54, Intikhab Alam 7-52) and 133 (Pervez Sajjad 6-21, Intikhab Alam 4-51) by 49 runs.

16th Match: v Worcestershire (Worcester)   Aug 19, 21, 22.
Pakistanis 369-9 dec (Saeed Ahmed 147, Hanif Mohammad 74, B. L. d'Oliveira 4-75) and 225-5 dec (Hanif Mohammad 118, Waqar Ahmed 53) drew with Worcestershire 313 (T. W. Graveney 99, B. L. d'Oliveira 96, Saeed Ahmed 5-38) and 142-6 (R. G. A. Headley 68*).

17th Match: v England (Oval)   Aug 24, 25, 26, 28.
Pakistanis 216 (Mushtaq Mohammad 66, G. G. Arnold 5-58) and 255 (Asif Iqbal 146, Intikhab Alam 51, K. Higgs 5-58) lost to England 440 (K. F. Barrington 142, T. W. Graveney 77, F. J. Titmus 65, G. G. Arnold 59, Mushtaq Mohammad 4-80) and 34-2 by 8 wkts.

18th Match: v Lancashire (Old Trafford)   Aug 30, 31, Sept 1.
Pakistanis 208-8 dec (Ghulam Abbas 72) and 69-5 dec beat Lancashire 60-1 dec and 200 (Intikhab Alam 7-58) by 17 runs.

19th Match: v T. N. Pearce's XI (Scarborough)   Sept 2, 4, 5.
Pakistanis 365-7 dec (Ghulam Abbas 100*, Mushtaq Mohammad 77, Arif Butt 69) and 141-9 dec (F. S. Trueman 4-32, R. N. S. Hobbs 4-44) drew with T. N. Pearce's XI 310-7 dec (J. H. Edrich 81, G. Boycott 58, C. Milburn 51) and 144-6.

20th Match: v Kent (Canterbury)   Sept 9 (50 overs a side).
Kent 215-9 (S. E. Leary 80, M. C. Cowdrey 57) beat Pakistanis 142 (A. L. Dixon 5-32) by 73 runs.

21st Match: v England (Lord's)   Sept 11 (50 overs a side).
Pakistan 161-8 (Hanif Mohammad 51*) lost to England 167-4 (T. W. Graveney 77*) by 6 wkts.

22nd Match: v Rest of World (Lord's)   Sept 12 (50 overs a side).
Rest of World 223-6 (R. B. Kanhai 83, G. St A. Sobers 733*) beat Pakistan 179-9 (E. J. Barlow 4-23) by 44 runs.

Sarfraz Nawaz's successes as an opening bowler on tours to England owed much to his years with Northants.

1967: 3rd Pakistanis

Batting Averages

	M	I	NO	R	HS	Avge	100	c/s
Hanif Mohammad	14	24	5	855	187*	45.00	3	11
Majid J. Khan	14	26	3	973	147*	42.30	4	5
Waqar Ahmed	7	11	3	306	79*	38.25	0	7
Ghulam Abbas	15	28	3	871	116	34.84	2	11
Saeed Ahmed	15	28	3	845	147	33.80	2	6
Mushtaq Mohammad	4	8	1	233	77	33.28	0	2
Asif Iqbal	9	15	0	498	146	33.20	1	2
Salim Altaf	6	7	4	89	53*	29.66	0	2
Mohammad Ilyas	8	14	1	332	63	25.53	0	4
Javed Burki	15	29	2	582	114	21.55	1	4
Arif Butt	9	14	3	237	69	21.54	0	8
Niaz Ahmed	11	13	8	104	69*	20.80	0	4
Intikhab Alam	7	12	0	240	51	20.00	0	4
F. S. Aizazuddin	9	18	3	267	74	17.80	0	0
Salah-ud-din	9	15	2	212	57	16.30	0	4
Wasim Bari	12	18	3	177	27	11.80	0	23/3
Khalid Ibadulla	2	4	0	47	32	11.75	0	1
Fasih-ud-din	6	9	2	63	18*	9.00	0	8/3
Nasim-ul-Ghani	3	4	0	33	14	8.25	0	2
Pervez Sajjad	12	12	5	54	13*	7.71	0	3

Bowling Averages

	O	M	R	W	Avge	BB	5i
Intikhab Alam	241.4	47	637	35	18.20	8-61	3
Mushtaq Mohammad	77.5	19	199	9	22.11	4-80	0
Salim Altaf	171.5	42	441	15	29.40	4-15	0
Hanif Mohammad	50.2	8	147	5	29.40	3-43	0
Pervez Sajjad	352.4	72	1145	34	33.67	7-99	3
Niaz Ahmed	330	89	863	25	34.52	5-86	1
Nasim-ul-Ghani	65	12	184	5	36.80	3-32	0
Asif Iqbal	277.3	70	752	19	39.57	3-66	0
Majid J. Khan	116	22	340	8	42.50	3-35	0
Khalid Ibadulla	35	13	47	1	47.00	1-42	0
Saeed Ahmed	204.3	40	652	13	50.15	5-38	1
Arif Butt	188.4	31	654	12	54.50	3-74	0
Salah-ud-din	101	17	278	2	139.00	2-40	0

Also bowled: Ghulam Abbas 1.3-1-0-1; Mohammad Ilyas 14-0-69-0; Javed Burki 23-5-90-0; F. S. Aizazuddin 7-2-30-0; Waqar Ahmed 1-0-9-0.

1967: South African Universities

For the second successive summer a team of young South Africans toured England. The party consisted of W. McAdam (captain), R. K. Muzzell and K. Tattersall of Cape Town; R. S. Steyn, D. McCay and G. S. Hugo of Stellenbosch; A. L. Biggs, D. D. Dyer, P. P. Henwood, C. Nicholson, A. Short, A. During and P. J. D. Flanagan of Witwatersrand; P. A. Strydom of Orange Free State, with S. F. Burke as manager.

There were three three-day matches, two of which ended in

even draws and the third–v Oxford University–in an innings victory for the tourists. The other sides proved too weak for them and the only loss was against a Kent team. The best three batsmen were Smithyman, Biggs and Short, all of whom averaged over 50. Smithyman also topped the bowling averages with 51 wickets, average 14.02, but he was closely followed by Flanagan with 52 wickets, average 14.82. The fielding was exceptionally good and Traicos in the gully took 23 catches. Dyer and Strydom shared the wicketkeeping.

The cost of the tour–£11,500–was raised by raffles, dances and donations, plus personal contributions from the players.

1968: 25th Australians

The team selected was W. M. Lawry (captain), I. R. Redpath, R. M. Cowper, L. R. Joslin, and A. N. Connolly, all of Victoria; I. M. Chappell, A. P. Sheahan, E. W. Freeman, N. J. N. Hawke, A. A. Mallett and B. N. Jarman of South Australia; K. D. Walters, H. B. Taber, J. W. Gleeson and D. A. Renneberg of New South Wales; R. J. Inverarity and G. D. McKenzie of Western Australia, with R. J. Parish as manager and L. E. Truman as treasurer. Of those not chosen the most likely candidates were G. Davies, K. Stackpole and K. Cunningham, but there were no glaring omissions.

The tour made a bad start when the opening game against Worcestershire was entirely washed out–rain then badly affected the next three matches and more lost hours meant that the tourists were sadly lacking in match play by the time of the First Test. To the surprise of most critics Australia won that game by a large margin. The Second and Third Tests were both rain ruined and Australia, in the Fourth, played for and obtained a draw. This meant that the Ashes stayed with the visitors. In the final Test Underwood bowled marvellously on a tailor-made wicket to dismiss Australia for 125 and draw the series.

1968: 25th Australians

1st Match: v Duke of Norfolk's XI (Arundel Castle)   May 4.
Duke of Norfolk's XI 131-7 dec drew with Australians 37-3.

2nd Match: v Worcestershire (Worcester)   May 8, 9, 10.
Match abandoned—no play due to rain.

3rd Match: v Leicestershire (Leicester)   May 11, 13, 14.
Australians 233 (R. J. Inverarity 67, B. R. Knight 5-77) and 132-1 (W. M. Lawry 65*, R. M. Cowper 56*) drew with Leicestershire 105-9 dec.

4th Match: v Lancashire (Old Trafford)   May 15, 16, 17.
Lancashire 104-2 dec drew with Australians 29-3.

5th Match: v M.C.C. (Lord's)   May 18, 20, 21.
Australians 246-9 dec (W. M. Lawry 66, R. M. Cowper 53, I. J. Jones 4-37, D. L. Underwood 4-68) drew with M.C.C. 142 (A. N. Connolly 4-21) and 56-1.

6th Match: v Northamptonshire (Northampton)   May 22, 23, 24.
Northamptonshire 203 (C. Milburn 90, E. W. Freeman 5-78) and 192 (B. L. Reynolds 57, A. A. Mallett 7-75) lost to Australians 375 (E. W. Freeman 116, W. M. Lawry 78) and 21-0 by 10 wkts.

7th Match: v Oxford and Cambridge Universities (Cambridge)   May 25, 27, 28.
Oxford and Cambridge 108 (N. J. N. Hawke 6-26) and 135 lost to Australians 218 (I. R. Redpath 103, A. J. Khan 7-84) and 28-0 by 10 wkts.

8th Match: v Somerset (Taunton)   May 29, 30, 31.
Australians 434-3 dec (R. M. Cowper 148, I. M. Chappell 147, K. D. Walters 61*) and 182-3 (I. R. Redpath 112, L. R. Joslin 61) drew with Somerset 304 (A. Clarkson 63, R. T. Virgin 56, J. W. Gleeson 6-97) and 187 (G. D. McKenzie 4-47).

9th Match: v Surrey (Oval)   June 1, 3, 4.
Surrey 291 (M. J. Edwards 103, M. J. Stewart 76) and 137-3 (J. H. Edrich 76*) drew with Australians 362 (I. R. Redpath 106, R. M. Cowper 64, A. J. Stockley 4-74).

10th Match: v England (Old Trafford)   June 6, 7, 8, 10, 11.
Australia 357 (A. P. Sheahan 88, W. M. Lawry 81, K. D. Walters 81, I. M. Chappell 73, J. A. Snow 4-97) and 220 (K. D. Walter 86, P. I. Pocock 6-79) beat England 165 (R. M. Cowper 4-48) and 253 (B. L. d'Oliveira 87) by 159 runs.

11th Match: v Warwickshire (Edgbaston)   June 12, 13, 14.
Australians 394-7 dec (I. M. Chappell 202*, H. B. Taber 58, K. D. Walters 55) and 161-7 dec (H. B. Taber 81*, D. J. Brown 6-55) drew with Warwickshire 257 (R. B. Kanhai 60, J. A. Jameson 56, D. A. Renneberg 5-65) and 268-8 (J. A. Jameson 98, M. J. K. Smith 67*).

12th Match: v Sussex (Hove)   June 15, 16, 17.
Australians 298 (A. P. Sheahan 119, J. A. Snow 4-52, M. A. Buss 4-89) and 123-5 beat Sussex 88 (G. D. McKenzie 4-25) and 330 (M. G. Griffith 100, A. W. Greig 67, J. W. Gleeson 5-71) by 5 wkts.

13th Match: v England (Lord's)   June 20, 21, 22, 24, 25.
England 351-7 dec (C. Milburn 83, K. F. Barrington 75) drew with Australia 78 (D. J. Brown 5-42) and 127-4 (I. R. Redpath 53).

14th Match: v Essex (Southend)   June 26, 27.
Essex 140 (D. A. Renneberg 8-72) and 122 (R. M. Cowper 7-42) lost to Australians 320 (W. M. Lawry 135, I. R. Redpath 69) by an innings and 58 runs.

15th Match: v Yorkshire (Bramall Lane)   June 29, July 1, 2.
Yorkshire 355-9 dec (G. Boycott 86, R. Illingworth 69*, D. E. V. Padgett 56, G. D. McKenzie 4-73, J. W. Gleeson 4-123) beat Australians 148 (W. M. Lawry 58, R. Illingworth 4-44) and 138 (K. D. Walters 62, R. Illingworth 4-23) by an innings and 69 runs.

16th Match: v Ireland (Dublin)   July 3.
Ireland 106 (E. W. Freeman 6-15) lost to Australians 108-4 by 6 wkts.

17th Match: v Ireland (Belfast)   July 4.
Australians 213 (E. W. Freeman 70, I. R. Redpath 57, D. Goodwin 5-68) beat Ireland 92 (J. W. Gleeson 6-24) by 121 runs.

18th Match: v Nottinghamshire (Trent Bridge)   July 6, 8, 9.
Australians 357-7 dec (I. R. Redpath 84, K. D. Walters 79, R. M. Cowper 66) drew with Nottinghamshire 191 (E. W. Freeman 4-38, N. J. N. Hawke 4-51) and 41-3.

19th Match: v England (Edgbaston)   July 11, 12, 13, 15, 16.
England 409 (M. C. Cowdrey 104, T. W. Graveney 96, J. H. Edrich 88, E. W. Freeman 4-78) drew with Australia 222 (I. M. Chappell 71, R. M. Cowper 57) and 68-1.

20th Match: v Gloucestershire (Bristol)   July 17, 18, 19.
Australians 351-5 dec (I. R. Redpath 135, R. J. Inverarity 88, I. M. Chappell 73*) drew with Gloucestershire 172 (D. M. Green 50, N. J. N. Hawke 4-29) and 389-6 (C. A. Milton 155, M. J. Procter 72, D. J. Shepherd 65, D. M. Green 53).

21st Match: v Middlesex (Lord's)   July 20, 22, 23.
Middlesex 277-4 dec (P. H. Parfitt 110*, C. T. Radley 70*) and 108-8 (D. A. Renneberg 6-47) drew with Australians 227 (P. H. Parfitt 4-64).

22nd Match: v England (Headingley)   July 25, 26, 27, 29, 30.
Australia 315 (I. R. Redpath 92, I. M. Chappell 65, D. L. Underwood 4-41) and 312 (I. M. Chappell 81, K. D. Walter 56, R. Illingworth 6-87) drew with England 302 (F. M. Prideaux 64, J. H. Edrich 62, A. N. Connolly 5-72) and 230-4 (J. H. Edrich 65).

23rd Match: v Derbyshire (Chesterfield)   July 31, Aug 1, 2.
Australians 259 (K. D. Walters 95, I. R. Redpath 68, D. C. Morgan 5-83, E. Smith 4-80) and 270 (I. R. Redpath 69, R. J. Inverarity 62, I. M. Chappell 62, A. B. Jackson 4-48) beat Derbyshire 185 (E. Smith 50, A. A. Mallett 5-69) and 336 (J. F. Harvey 92, D. A. Renneberg 4-97) by 8 runs.

24th Match: v Glamorgan (Swansea)   Aug 3, 4, 5.
Glamorgan 224 (A. Jones 99, M. J. Khan 55, A. A. Mallett 4-46, J. W. Gleeson 4-73) and 250-9 dec (B. Davis 66, R. Davis 59, J. W. Gleeson 4-56) beat Australians 110 (M. A. Nash 5-28, B. Lewis 4-51) and 285 (A. P. Sheahan 137) by 79 runs.

25th Match: v Minor Counties (Torquay)   Aug 7, 8.
Minor Counties 176-4 dec and 189-7 dec (J. A. Sutton 75) drew with Australians 178-9 dec (A. G. Marshall 5-63) and 101-5.

26th Match: v Hampshire (Southampton)   Aug 10, 12, 13.
Hampshire 250 (R. E. Marshall 95, P. J. Sainsbury 54, J. W. Gleeson 4-37) and 140-9 (B. A. Richards 57, A. N. Connolly 4-14, I. M. Chappell 4-22) drew with Australians 267 (I. M. Chappell 112, D. Shackleton 5-58).

27th Match: v M.C.C. President's XI (Lord's)   Aug 14, 15, 16.
Australians 222 (I. R. Redpath 55) and 140-8 (A. P. Sheahan 54*, J. Birkenshaw 5-50) drew with M.C.C. President's XI 195-4 dec (D. L. Amiss 61).

28th Match: v Kent (Canterbury)   Aug 17, 18, 19.
Kent 210 (J. N. Shepherd 84, J. W. Gleeson 4-61) and 152 (J. W. Gleeson 5-29) lost to Australians 319 (I. M. Chappell 57, J. H. Shepherd 4-47) and 44-1 by 9 wkts.

29th Match: v England (Oval)   Aug 22, 23, 24, 26, 27.
England 494 (J. H. Edrich 164, B. L. d'Oliveira 158, T. W. Graveney 63) and 181 (A. N. Connolly 4-65) beat Australia 324 (W. M. Lawry 135, I. R. Redpath 67) and 125 (R. J. Inverarity 56, D. L. Underwood 7-50) by 226 runs.

30th Match: v Rest of the World (Lord's)   Aug 31, Sept 2, 3.
Rest of the World 219-7 dec (J. D. Lindsay 73*) and 107 lost to Australians 226 (I. R. Redpath 55, P. M. Pollock 4-41, R. Ramnarace 4-44) and 101-2 (I. R. Redpath 56*) by 8 wkts.

Right *The 1968 Australian touring party.*

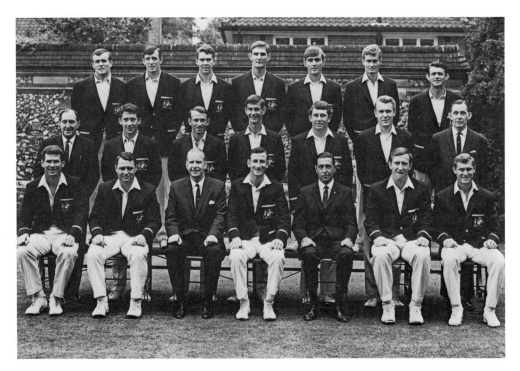

Left *Graham McKenzie, the finest Australian fast bowler of his day, found success more elusive in 1968 than on his brilliant debut tour in 1964.*

1968: 25th Australians

Batting Averages

	M	I	NO	R	HS	Avge	100	c/s
I. M. Chappell	20	30	4	1261	202*	48.50	3	20
W. M. Lawry	17	23	3	906	135	45.30	2	9
I. R. Redpath	22	37	3	1474	135	43.35	4	24
R. M. Cowper	16	24	4	744	148	37.20	1	14
K. D. Walters	21	32	2	933	95	31.10	0	13
A. P. Sheahan	22	32	3	817	137	28.17	2	17
H. B. Taber	14	16	2	365	81*	26.07	0	35/4
R. J. Inverarity	18	30	4	645	88	24.80	0	18
E. W. Freeman	13	14	0	326	116	23.28	1	8
L. R. Joslin	13	18	2	344	61	21.50	0	6
N. J. N. Hawke	14	18	5	267	47	20.53	0	11
A. A. Mallett	13	13	6	106	43*	15.14	0	4
G. D. McKenzie	16	18	2	185	50	11.56	0	11
B. N. Jarman	13	19	1	184	41	10.22	0	22/5
A. N. Connolly	15	18	8	88	22*	8.80	0	3
J. W. Gleeson	14	18	3	122	19*	8.13	0	6
D. A. Renneberg	14	12	6	27	9*	4.50	0	3

Bowling Averages

	O	M	R	W	Avge	BB	5i
A. N. Connolly	553.4	188	1116	55	20.29	5-72	1
J. W. Gleeson	538.1	198	1198	58	20.65	6-97	3
N. J. N. Hawke	323.1	90	729	35	20.82	6-26	1
R. M. Cowper	337	109	770	32	24.06	7-42	1
D. A. Renneberg	356.5	72	1010	41	24.63	8-72	3
E. W. Freeman	289.2	62	829	31	26.74	5-78	1
A. A. Mallett	428.1	115	1245	44	28.29	7-75	2
I. M. Chappell	214.1	63	529	18	29.38	4-22	0
G. D. McKenzie	523.1	145	1247	40	31.17	4-25	0
K. D. Walters	140	33	344	5	68.80	2-67	0

Also bowled: R. J. Inverarity 8-2-34-2; I. R. Redpath 3-0-16-0.

Apart from the Tests the tourists won only 7 of the 20 matches, but the weather was responsible for many of the draws. The batsmen generally had a poor time. Lawry, with a broken finger, failed to reach 1,000 runs, and so did Cowper, who missed the last five games through a broken thumb. Walters and Sheahan played some excellent innings, but generally could not cope with the wet wickets. The batting success of the tour was Ian Chappell, who had a very sound technique and headed the first-class averages as well as being second in the Test table–his young brother, Greg, was playing for Somerset. Redpath looked more mature than in 1964 and was nimble on his feet. Inverarity concentrated on defence.

A lot was expected from Hawke and McKenzie, the opening bowlers, but the best bowler turned out to be Connolly, who adapted his seamers well to the moist atmosphere. Freeman and Renneberg had occasional good days. Gleeson was easily the best spinner, sending down his leg-breaks with an unusual grip.

The fielding was a credit to the team: Sheahan, Walters and Chappell were quite remarkable–though some catches went astray in the slips.

Instead of the limited-over internationals which had been the finale to the last two seasons, Australia played the Rest of the World (excluding England) in a three-day match.

The wet May worried the Australians financially and the manager asked that all Saturday, Monday, Tuesday matches should be played Saturday, Sunday, Monday to increase revenue. In fact only Kent did this, but a good August meant that the profit from the tour was £40,000.

1968: United States of America

A national cricket association for the U.S.A. was formed in 1961 and this tour was the first one made under its auspices to England. The team was A. W. M. Cooper of California (captain); M. A. Wisdom, S. E. Dyal, S. Thackurdhin, P. A. Merrett and P. J. Hollick of New York; L. C. Mullings of Paterson, N.J.; W. A. Brook and L. F. Fernandes from Philadelphia; A. Lashkari, R. C. Severn, W. F. M. Severn and H. Durity of Los Angeles; K.

Serpanchy of San Francisco; Masood Khan and M. A. Stollmeyer of Washington; P. L. Jeffrey from St Louis, with J. I. Marder as manager. Five other players represented the side: G. Rock, P. Parry, M. A. Verity, A. Hussain and J. J. Reid.

The cost of the visit, about £6,000, was raised by donations from a variety of sources. The results on the tour were not very encouraging, but the tour's objective was educational and in that sense it was a success.

Easily the best batting records were obtained by Fernandes–581 runs, average 36.31 and Lashkari–418 runs, average 32.15. There were no outstanding bowlers. Six players obtained ten or more wickets, but none reached 20.

1968: United States of America

1st Match: v Duke of Norfolk's XI (Arundel Castle) July 20.
USA 176-8 dec drew with Duke of Norfolk's XI 117-7 (D. S. Sheppard 50, A. W. Cooper 4-19).

2nd Match: v Free Foresters (Cranbrook) July 21.
Free Foresters 170-7 dec (S. E. Dyal 4-40) beat USA 155 (A. Lashkari 53, R. M. K. Gracey 5-43) by 15 runs.

3rd Match: v Kent 2nd XI (Tunbridge Wells) July 23.
USA 119-5 dec drew with Kent 2nd XI 6-1.

4th Match: v Sussex 2nd XI (Hastings) July 24.
Sussex 2nd XI 193-4 dec (R. J. Langridge 109, A. Morgan 59) drew with USA 154-2 (P. A. Merrett 56, L. S. Fernandes 51).

5th Match: v Hertfordshire (Hitchin) July 25.
USA 172-7 dec (A. Lashkari 60, L. S. Fernandes 56, J. Iberson 5-56) beat Hertfordshire 137 (A. Lashkari 5-46) by 35 runs.

6th Match: v M.C.C. (Lord's) July 27.
USA 117 (E. A. Clark 4-20) lost to M.C.C. 118-1 (A. Day 50*) by 9 wkts.

7th Match: v Lincolnshire (Cleethorpes) July 28.
USA 160 lost to Lincolnshire 162-5 (H. Pougher 58, L. C. Mullings 4-45) by 5 wkts.

8th Match: v Nottinghamshire XI (Trent Bridge) July 31.
Nottinghamshire XI 174-7 dec (R. Bickley 50, A. W. Cooper 4-35) beat USA 77 (B. Stead 6-20) by 97 runs.

9th Match: v Northumberland (Jesmond) Aug 2.
Northumberland 267-5 dec (M. J. K. Robson 70*, I. Bell 61, J. M. Crawhall 60) drew with USA 200-9 (L. S. Fernandes 61, A. Lashkari 53).

10th Match: v Durham (Sunderland) Aug 4.
Durham 211-7 dec (J. G. Marsh 74, H. A. Durity 4-49) drew with USA 161-9 (H. J. Bailey 4-37).

11th Match: v A. J. McAlpine's XI (Marchwiel) Aug 6.
A. J. McAlpine's XI 116-1 (D. W. Richardson 71*) drew with USA did not bat.

12th Match: v Staffordshire (Stoke) Aug 7.
Match abandoned–no play due to rain.

13th Match: v Worcestershire 2nd XI (Worcester) Aug 8.
Worcestershire 2nd XI 191-5 dec (A. R. Barker 57) beat USA 116 (K. Wilkinson 4-43) by 75 runs.

14th Match: v Shropshire (Oakengates) Aug 9.
Shropshire 211-4 dec (H. M. Winfield 62, E. Marsh 60) drew with USA 191-5 (M. A. Stollmeyer 90*, P. A. Merrett 58).

15th Match: v Cheshire (Macclesfield) Aug 10, 11.
USA 288 (L. S. Fernandes 155, N. R. Halsall 4-50) and 144-5 dec lost to Cheshire 226-3 dec (S. E. Wood 87, P. D. Briggs 75) and 209-3 (S. E. Wood 83, P. D. Briggs 58) by 7 wkts.

16th Match: v Warwickshire XI (Edgbaston) Aug 12.
Warwickshire XI 221 (E. E. Hemmings 94, M. A. Khan 6-68) drew with USA 203-8 (A. Lashkari 66, L. S. Fernandes 62).

17th Match: v Lancashire 2nd XI (Old Trafford) Aug 14.
Lancashire 2nd XI 12-0 drew with USA did not bat.

18th Match: v Incogniti (Tonbridge) Aug 16.
Incogniti 240-7 dec (K. Garrard 87, S. D. Beecroft 60*, J. H. Minney 51) drew with USA did not bat.

19th Match: v Surrey XI (Oval) Aug 18.
Match abandoned–no play due to rain.

20th Match: v Cambridgeshire (Cambridge) Aug 19.
Cambridgeshire 147-6 dec (D. H. R. Fairey 54, T. S. Hale 50*) lost to USA 148-5 by 5 wkts.

21st Match: v Suffolk (Felixstowe) Aug 20.
USA 173-9 dec drew with Suffolk 145-6 (K. Serpanchy 4-29).

1968: Proposed Ceylon tour

A programme of 19 matches, including three-day games against some first-class counties, was arranged for a Ceylonese team between June and early August 1968. In February 1968 the Ceylon Government refused to make foreign exchange available for the tour and the cricket authorities had to cancel the visit.

1969: 11th West Indies

The team which toured England in 1969 was G. St A. Sobers (captain), V. A. Holder and J. N. Shepherd of Barbados; P. D. Blair, B. F. Butcher, S. G. Camacho, R. C. Fredericks, L. R. Gibbs and C. H. Lloyd of Guyana; M. C. Carew, C. A. Davis and P. Roberts of Trinidad; T. M. Findlay of St Vincent; M. L. C. Foster and J. L. Hendriks of Jamaica and G. C. Shillingford of Dominica, with C. L. Walcott as manager, P. D. B. Short as treasurer and W. F. Hoyos as secretary. Several well-known faces were omitted including the fast bowlers Hall and Griffith as well

as King and Edwards who had been their understudies on the 1968-69 tour of Australia. Batsmen R. B. Kanhai, who was injured, and S. M. Nurse, who had retired, were missing and Notts would not release the wicketkeeper D. L. Murray.

On a twin tour with New Zealand, the West Indies needed good weather in May−once more this failed to materialise and four of the first six matches were rain ruined affairs. Then, after a full game against Northants, the Warwickshire match was totally

Above *Basil Butcher made his third tour of England with the 1969 West Indians. He was successful on each, averaging 61.50 in 1969.*

1969: 11th West Indians

Batting Averages

	M	I	NO	R	HS	Avge	100	c/s
B. F. Butcher	15	20	4	984	151	61.50	3	2
C. H. Lloyd	16	21	5	904	201*	56.50	2	6
R. C. Fredericks	18	29	4	1132	168*	45.28	3	14
M. C. Carew	12	18	3	677	172*	45.13	3	8
C. A. Davis	16	25	5	848	106*	42.40	2	3
G. St A. Sobers	12	15	2	432	81	33.23	0	12
G. S. Camacho	16	25	1	746	101	31.08	1	10
M. L. C. Foster	14	19	4	396	87*	26.40	0	2
J. L. Hendriks	10	8	2	106	69*	17.66	0	11/3
P. Roberts	11	9	3	104	35*	17.33	0	2
J. N. Shepherd	13	16	2	186	32	13.28	0	6
V. A. Holder	13	11	2	104	35	11.55	0	2
T. M. Findlay	10	14	0	134	23	9.57	0	25
L. R. Gibbs	13	11	5	47	18*	7.83	0	8
G. C. Shillingford	11	8	1	32	10	4.57	0	1
P. D. Blair	9	5	3	4	4*	2.00	0	2

Bowling Averages

	O	M	R	W	Avge	BB	5i
B. F. Butcher	37	6	103	6	17.16	3-58	0
G. C. Shillingford	221.2	41	669	36	18.58	6-63	2
J. N. Shepherd	329.13	100	803	29	27.68	8-40	2
G. St A. Sobers	267.1	78	623	22	28.31	5-42	1
V. A. Holder	367.5	112	907	30	30.23	4-48	0
M. L. C. Foster	88.4	25	248	7	35.42	3-28	0
P. D. Blair	130.1	16	509	14	36.35	3-35	0
M. C. Carew	76.4	16	261	7	37.28	3-71	0
L. R. Gibbs	352.1	109	720	19	37.89	5-62	1
P. Roberts	279	84	744	16	46.50	3-59	0
C. H. Lloyd	37.5	9	106	2	53.00	1-3	0
C. A. Davis	182.2	39	479	7	68.42	2-38	0

Also bowled: G. S. Camacho 13-2-31-1; R. C. Fredericks 4-0-16-0.

Left *Butcher square cuts Basil D'Oliveira during the Second Test at Lord's.*

washed out and two of the three days of the following game, against Yorkshire, rained off. England won the Test series two matches to nil, not so much because of the tourists lack of practice as the failure of Sobers, who was worn out by continuous cricket. He hit only 150 runs in six innings in the Tests and took 11

wickets. Despite the depressing results–only two first-class wins–the visitors had some very promising players. Fredericks and Camacho formed an admirable opening partnership. Lloyd looked a wonderful prospect and Davis, who failed in Australia, improved greatly.

The best of the bowlers was Shepherd, who played for Kent. When Sobers broke down, however, he was very overbowled. Shillingford was unfortunate to pull a muscle and be idle for a month. There was a lack of spin in the attack. Hendriks was out of form behind the stumps and Findlay replaced him as the main keeper. The fielding was not a strong point, with many catches grounded.

The profit from the tour was £24,000, but there were complaints that the tourists received no part of the television fees.

1969: 11th West Indians

1st Match: v Duke of Norfolk's XI (Arundel Castle)   April 16.
Duke of Norfolk's XI 191-5 dec (J. H. Edrich 61) lost to West Indians 195-5 (C. A. Davis 68) by 5 wkts.

2nd Match: v D. H. Robins' XI (Eastbourne)   April 30, May 1, 2.
West Indians 287 (B. F. Butcher 113, D. N. F. Slade 5-45) and 319-7 dec (R. C. Fredericks 116, M. L. C. Foster 61, C. A. Davis 53*, Mushtaq Mohammad 5-121) drew with D. H. Robins' XI 262-7 dec (Mushtaq Mohammad 128*, J. S. E. Price 53*) and 337-9 (Mushtaq Mohammad 123, J. T. Murray 75).

3rd Match: v Worcestershire (Worcester)   May 3, 4, 5.
Worcestershire 235-9 dec (B. L. d'Oliveira 72, D. N. F. Slade 57*, G. C. Shillingford 6-63) and 24-0 drew with West Indians 87-6 dec.

4th Match: v Lancashire (Old Trafford)   May 7, 8, 9.
West Indians 227-5 (G. S. Camacho 101, C. A. Davis 52) drew with Lancashire did not bat.

5th Match: v Oxford and Cambridge Universities (Oxford)   May 10, 11, 12.
Oxford and Cambridge 130-3 dec (F. S. Goldstein 78) and 36-3 drew with West Indians 226-4 dec (M. C. Carew 126*).

6th Match: v Kent (Canterbury)   May 14, 15, 16.
Kent 97-2 dec (B. W. Luckhurst 59*) drew with West Indians did not bat.

7th Match: v Gloucestershire (Bristol)   May 17, 19, 20.
West Indians 171 (B. F. Butcher 68, M. J. Procter 5-48) and 143-7 dec (A. S. Brown 4-39) drew with Gloucestershire 113 (J. N. Shepherd 8-40) and 63-1.

8th Match: v Northamptonshire (Northampton)   May 21, 22, 23.
Northamptonshire 263 (R. M. Prideaux 79, G. C. Shillingford 5-79) and 182-9 dec (Mushtaq Mohammad 51) beat West Indians 146 (M. L. C. Foster 61) and 234 (G. S. Camacho 87, C. A. Davis 57, B. S. Crump 4-28) by 65 runs.

9th Match: v Warwickshire (Edgbaston)   May 24, 26, 27.
Match abandoned–no play due to rain.

10th Match: v Yorkshire (Bramall Lane)   May 28, 29, 30.
Yorkshire 181-4 dec (D. B. Close 51) drew with West Indians 25-0.

11th Match: v M.C.C. (Lord's)   May 31, June 2, 3.
M.C.C. 200 (J. H. Edrich 125, L. R. Gibbs 4-19) and 127-0 (J. H. Edrich 77*) drew with West Indians 285 (G. St A. Sobers 74, C. A. Davis 57).

12th Match: v Somerset (Taunton)   June 4, 5, 6.
West Indians 422-4 (C. H. Lloyd 128*, M. C. Carew 122, R. C. Fredericks 51, M. L. C. Foster 51) and 228-3 dec (C. A. Davis 106*, M. L. C. Foster 87*) beat Somerset 141 and 197 (G. S. Chappell 76, A. Clarkson 52, L. R. Gibbs 5-62) by 312 runs.

13th Match: v Minor Counties (Longton)   June 7, 8, 9.
Minor Counties 325-8 dec (G. J. Saville 116, F. W. Millett 102*) and 189-3 dec (P. A. Shippey 94*, G. J. Saville 55) drew with West Indians 264 (B. F. Butcher 109, R. C. Fredericks 54, S. H. Young 4-44) and 201-6 (J. L. Hendriks 69*, S. H. Young 4-48).

14th Match: v England (Old Trafford)   June 12, 13, 14, 16, 17.
England 413 (G. Boycott 128, T. W. Graveney 75, J. H. Edrich 58, B. L. d'Oliveira 57, J. N. Shepherd 5-104) and 12-0 beat West Indies 147 (D. J. Brown 4-39, J. A. Snow 4-54) and 275 (R. C. Fredericks 64) by 10 wkts.

15th Match: v Nottinghamshire (Trent Bridge)   June 18, 19, 20.
West Indians 323-5 dec (C. A. Davis 82, C. H. Lloyd 79, R. C. Fredericks 72, G. S. Camacho 51, B. Stead 4-67) and 122-5 drew with Nottinghamshire 270-5 dec (M. J. Smedley 103*).

16th Match: v Surrey (Oval)   June 21, 22, 23.
West Indians 160 (G. R. J. Roope 5-14) and 45-3 drew with Surrey 344-8 (G. R. J. Roope 97, Younis Ahmed 64, G. C. Shillingford 4-70).

17th Match: v England (Lord's)   June 26, 27, 28, 30, July 1.
West Indies 380 (C. A. Davis 103, G. S. Camacho 67, R. C. Fredericks 63, J. A. Snow 5-114) and 295-9 dec (C. H. Lloyd 70, R. C. Fredericks 60, G. St A. Sobers 50*) drew with England 344 (R. Illingworth 113, J. H. Hampshire 107, A. P. E. Knott 53) and 295-7 (G. Boycott 106, P. J. Sharpe 86).

18th Match: v Ireland (Sion Mills, Londonderry)   July 2.
West Indians 25 (D. E. Goodwin 5-6, A. J. O'Riordan 4-18) and 78-4 (B. F. Butcher 50) lost to Ireland 125-8 dec by 9 wkts.

19th Match: v Ireland (Belfast)   July 3, 4.
Ireland 126 (V. A. Holder 5-40) and 165-9 (M. C. Carew 4-42) drew with West Indians 288-5 dec (M. C. Carew 61, B. F. Butcher 61).

20th Match: v Glamorgan (Swansea)   July 5, 6, 7.
West Indians 419-5 dec (C. H. Lloyd 201*, B. F. Butcher 151) and 124-2 dec (M. C. Carew 67) drew with Glamorgan 248-6 dec (M. J. Khan 147, P. M. Walker 58) and 44-2.

21st Match: v England (Headingley)   July 10, 11, 12, 14, 15.
England 223 (J. H. Edrich 79, V. A. Holder 4-48) and 240 (G. St A. Sobers 5-42) beat West Indies 161 (B. R. Knight 4-63) and 272 (B. F. Butcher 91, G. S. Camacho 71, D. L. Underwood 4-55) by 30 runs.

22nd Match: v Leicestershire (Leicester)   July 16, 17, 18.
West Indians 385-1 dec (M. C. Carew 172*, R. C. Fredericks 168*) and 249-3 dec (R. C. Fredericks 84, B. F. Butcher 76*, C. H. Lloyd 63*) drew with Leicestershire 334 (B. Dudleston 122, C. C. Inman 68*) and 101-3.

23rd Match: v Hampshire (Southampton)   July 19, 21, 22.
Hampshire 287 (B. A. Richards 86, P. J. Sainsbury 51, D. W. White 50*) and 215-4 dec (B. A. Richards 120*) lost to West Indians 106 (R. M. H. Cottam 4-52) and 397-7 (R. C. Fredericks 129, C. H. Lloyd 84, G. St A. Sobers 81, C. A. Davis 70) by 3 wkts.

1969: 7th New Zealanders

The team which came to England for the second half of 1969 was G. T. Dowling (captain), B. F. Hastings, D. R. Hadlee, R. C. Motz and B. R. Taylor, all of Canterbury; B. W. Yuile, V. Pollard, B. E. Congdon and K. J. Wadsworth from Central Districts; B. A. G. Murray and R. O. Collinge of Wellington; G. M. Turner, B. D. Milburn of Otago; M. G. Burgess, R. S. Cunis and H. J. Howarth of Auckland, with G. C. Burgess as manager.

There were no real surprises and all the main 11 players who

Glenn Turner and Graham Dowling of the 1969 New Zealand party. Turner (left), on his first tour, was one of the leading batsmen and a future New Zealand captain; Dowling was the 1969 captain.

appeared in the Test series against the West Indies during the previous winter were chosen.

New Zealand proved themselves only a little stronger than in their tour in 1965 and again lost the Test series, without winning a match. The best batsmen were Murray, Turner and Hastings; Dowling could not find his form and Burgess only flourished in patches. Pollard was too ambitious.

The left-arm spinner Howarth had a fine record in first-class matches, but was not so sure in the Tests. Of the five pace bowlers,

Taylor topped the Test table with 10 wickets, average 15.50; Cunis improved immensely in the last few games; Hadlee was erratic and Collinge was disappointing, though he was kept from some games by illness. Motz had a back injury and did not complete the tour. The fielding was good and Wadsworth, though achieving little with the bat, kept wicket well.

From England the team flew to India and Pakistan for a series of matches and the combined finances for the whole trip showed a profit of £7,000.

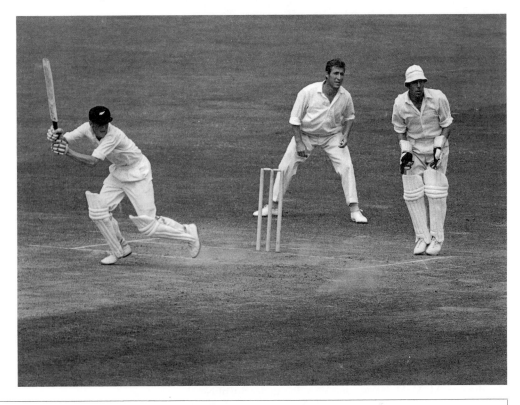

Glenn Turner, New Zealand's prolific opening batsman, clips a ball past square leg in the match against Middlesex; he finished with 124.

1969: 7th New Zealanders

1st Match: v D. H. Robins' XI (Eastbourne)   June 15, 16, 17.
D. H. Robins' XI 277-5 dec (Sadiq Mohammad 114) and 196-4 dec (R. D. V. Knight 57, M. J. K. Smith 53) drew with New Zealanders 221-3 dec (B. E. Congdon 120) and 12-0.

2nd Match: v Yorkshire (Bradford)   June 28, 30, July 1.
New Zealanders 287 (G. T. Dowling 78, G. M. Turner 53, R. A. Hutton 4-52) and 65-1 drew with Yorkshire 393-4 (D. B. Close 146, R. A. Hutton 75, C. Johnson 61*).

3rd Match: v Scotland (Glasgow)   July 2, 3, 4.
Scotland 211 (J. M. Allan 54, B. R. Taylor 4-38) and 79 lost to New Zealanders 409-8 dec (M. G. Burgess 95, B. R. Taylor 87, B. W. Yuile 81) by an innings and 119 runs.

4th Match: v Derbyshire (Chesterfield)   July 5, 7, 8.
Derbyshire 270 (I. R. Buxton 103, R. O. Collinge 4-66, R. C. Motz 4-62) and 56-4 drew with New Zealanders 283-9 dec (K. J. Wadsworth 77, M. G. Burgess 54, H. J. Rhodes 4-52).

5th Match: v Surrey (Oval)   July 9, 10, 11.
Surrey 200 and 50-2 drew with New Zealanders 330-5 dec (B. A. G. Murray 123, V. Pollard 100*).

6th Match: v Essex (Westcliff)   July 12, 13, 14.
Essex 121 (R. C. Motz 4-29) and 192 (R. E. East 58, H. J. Howarth 7-43) beat New Zealanders 201 (G. T. Dowling 65, R. E. East 6-49) and 97 (R. N. S. Hobbs 4-31) by 15 runs.

7th Match: v Middlesex (Lord's)   July 16, 17, 18.
Middlesex 325 (C. T. Radley 82, W. E. Russell 65, P. H. Parfitt 53, F. J. Titmus 52, H. J. Howarth 6-99) and 162-5 dec drew with New Zealanders 289-6 dec (G. M. Turner 124, M. G. Burgess 65, V. Pollard 56) and 182-9 (B. A. G. Murray 50).

8th Match: v Kent (Maidstone)   July 19, 21, 22.
Kent 307-8 dec (M. H. Denness 125, B. W. Luckhurst 52) and 196-4 dec drew with New Zealanders 284-9 dec (B. F. Hastings 101, V. Pollard 63) and 138-3.

9th Match: v England (Lord's)   July 24, 25, 26, 28.
England 190 (R. Illingworth 53) and 340 (J. H. Edrich 115) beat New Zealand 169 (R. Illingworth 4-37, D. L. Underwood 4-38) and 131 (D. L. Underwood 7-32) by 230 runs.

10th Match: v Minor Counties (Lincoln)   July 30, 31, Aug 1.
New Zealanders 237-6 dec (G. M. Turner 82, D. R. Hadlee 51*) and 228-4 dec (M. G. Burgess 74*, B. F. Hastings 65) beat Minor Counties 149 and 210 (J. A. Sutton 57, B. W. Yuile 5-48) by 106 runs.

11th Match: v Glamorgan (Sophia Gardens, Cardiff)   Aug 2, 3, 4.
New Zealanders 147 (B. E. Congdon 60, D. J. Shepherd 4-42) and 210 (B. A. G. Murray 77, P. M. Walker 4-51) drew with Glamorgan 193 (P. M. Walker 51, H. J. Howarth 5-79) and 107-7 (H. J. Howarth 4-34).

12th Match: v England (Trent Bridge)   Aug 7, 8, 9, 11, 12.
New Zealand 294 (B. F. Hastings 83, B. E. Congdon 66, A. Ward 4-61) and 66-1 drew with England 451-8 dec (J. H. Edrich 155, P. J. Sharpe 111, D. R. Hadlee 4-88).

13th Match: v Hampshire (Southampton)   Aug 13, 14, 15.
Hampshire 330-4 dec (B. A. Richards 132, R. M. C. Gilliat 99) drew with New Zealanders 119-2 (B. A. G. Murray 55).

14th Match: v Sussex (Hove)   Aug 16, 18, 19.
New Zealanders 273 (B. W. Yuile 72, E. J. Lewis 4-64) and 225-7 dec (B. A. G. Murray 75, V. Pollard 62, M. A. Buss 4-70) drew with Sussex 250 (P. J. Graves 104, M. G. Griffith 73, R. S. Cunis 6-54) and 121-9.

15th Match: v England (Oval)   Aug 21, 22, 23, 25, 26.
New Zealand 150 (G. M. Turner 53, D. L. Underwood 6-41) and 229 (B. F. Hastings 61, D. L. Underwood 6-60) lost to England 242 (J. H. Edrich 68, B. R. Taylor 4-47) and 138-2 (M. H. Denness 55*).

16th Match: v Worcestershire (Worcester)   Aug 27, 28, 29.
New Zealanders 263 (B. A. G. Murray 70, B. M. Brain 5-85) and 193-4 dec (B. F. Hastings 68*, B. E. Congdon 64) drew with Worcestershire 229 (B. L. d'Oliveira 88*, B. W. Yuile 4-57) and 137-5.

17th Match: v Lancashire (Old Trafford)   Aug 30, 31, Sept 1.
Lancashire 222 (C. H. Lloyd 88, J. D. Bond 54, B. R. Taylor 4-39) and 246-4 dec (C. H. Lloyd 99, J. Sullivan 62*) drew with New Zealanders 235 (R. C. Motz 73*, M. G. Burgess 61, K. Shuttleworth 7-61) and 135-5 (G. M. Turner 56*, J. S. Savage 4-46).

18th Match: v Warwickshire (Edgbaston)   Sept 3, 4, 5.
New Zealanders 193 (M. G. Burgess 74, T. W. Cartwright 5-52) and 223 (B. W. Yuile 55, D. J. Brown 4-40) beat Warwickshire 220 (J. A. Jameson 62, D. L. Amiss 54, R. S. Cunis 5-85) and 146 by 50 runs.

19th Match: v T. N. Pearce's XI (Scarborough)   Sept 6, 8, 9.
T. N. Pearce's XI 263-7 dec (P. H. Parfitt 66, M. J. Smith 62, B. W. Yuile 5-91) and 140 lost to New Zealanders 221 (G. T. Dowling 113, R. Illingworth 5-53) and 185-3 (M. G. Burgess 58*, B. A. G. Murray 53) by 7 wkts.

20th Match: v Professional Cricketers Association (Great Driffield)   Sept 7.
New Zealanders 246-9 dec (D. R. Hadlee 52) beat P.C.A. 223 (Younis Ahmed 96, M. G. Burgess 4-36) by 23 runs.*

331

1969: 7th New Zealanders

Batting Averages

	M	I	NO	R	HS	Avge	100	c/s
B. W. Yuile	10	11	5	383	81	63.83	0	5
B. A. G. Murray	12	21	1	800	123	40.00	1	8
B. F. Hastings	15	24	4	708	101	35.00	1	10
G. M. Turner	12	22	3	644	124	33.89	1	14
M. G. Burgess	16	26	5	689	95	32.80	0	7
V. Pollard	15	21	3	534	100*	29.66	1	7
G. T. Dowling	15	27	0	740	113	27.40	1	9
B. D. Milburn	8	6	5	26	17*	26.00	0	19
B. E. Congdon	16	30	3	692	66	25.62	0	18
D. R. Hadlee	10	13	4	171	51*	19.00	0	5
R. C. Motz	11	15	1	234	73*	16.71	0	2
B. R. Taylor	12	16	0	250	87	15.62	0	7
K. J. Wadsworth	14	19	0	251	77	13.21	0	27/4
R. O. Collinge	8	8	1	66	19	9.42	0	5
R. S. Cunis	12	13	4	83	19*	9.22	0	5
H. J. Howarth	12	17	8	59	11*	6.55	0	2

Bowling Averages

	O	M	R	W	Avge	BB	5i
H. J. Howarth	556.5	220	1126	57	19.75	7-43	3
B. R. Taylor	311.2	71	838	36	23.27	4-38	0
B. W. Yuile	232.2	69	621	24	25.87	5-48	2
M. G. Burgess	87.3	52	235	9	26.11	2-3	0
D. R. Hadlee	212.3	56	621	23	27.00	4-88	0
R. S. Cunis	385	100	1055	38	27.76	6-54	2
R. O. Collinge	208.3	56	498	17	29.29	4-66	0
R. C. Motz	333.2	83	809	25	32.36	4-29	0
V. Pollard	260.3	86	600	18	33.33	3-45	0
B. E. Congdon	31	6	99	2	49.50	1-20	0

Also bowled: G. T. Dowling 5-0-34-0; B. F. Hastings 1-0-1-0; B. A. G. Murray 4-1-12-1.

1969: 2nd Wilfred Isaacs' South Africans

The team for this second visit by Wilfred Isaacs was not on paper as strong as its predecessor, not having so many established players. The full side was W. Isaacs (captain); E. Chatterton, W. R. Kerr, J. P. D. Flanagan, J. H. B. Waite and D. Mackay-Coghill of Transvaal; I. R. Tayfield, R. R. Collins, P. P. Henwood, M. J. Smithyman, M. McN. Harvey and V. A. P. van der Bijl of Natal; C. I. Day of North-Eastern Transvaal; N. Rosendorff of Orange Free State; R. G. Pollock of Eastern Province and A. Bruyns of Western Province, with R. Eriksen as manager and T. Mortimer as his assistant.

The team had an excellent attack: Van der Bijl and Mackay-Coghill were a penetrative opening pair and the slow left arm of Henwood took many wickets. The batting was generally strong and went right down to almost the last man. The fielding also proved of a good standard and the side fully deserved their record of nine wins to one loss.

1969: W. Isaacs' Team

1st Match: v Essex (Basildon)   July 5, 7, 8.
W. Isaacs' XI 171 and 102-8 (A. Bruyns 56) drew with Essex 139-8 dec (G. Barker 56).

2nd Match: v Oxford University (Oxford)   July 9, 10, 11.
W. Isaacs's XI 351-7 dec (R. G. Pollock 231*) beat Oxford University 128 (A. H. Morgan 50*, V. A. P. van der Bijl 6-35) and 151 (A. H. Morgan 61, P. P. Henwood 4-18) by an innings and 72 runs.

3rd Match: v D. C. S. Compton's XI (Gerrards Cross)   July 13.
W. Isaacs' XI 242-4 dec (J. P. D. Flanagan 69, M. M. Harvey 61) beat D. C. S. Compton's XI 167 (P. P. Henwood 7-49).

4th Match: v Warwickshire 2nd XI (Edgbaston)   July 14, 15.
W. Isaacs' XI 276-6 dec (W. R. Kerr 86, C. I. Dey 59*, R. R. Collins 57) and 116-5 dec lost to Warwickshire 2nd XI 213-6 dec (B. Murray 125) and 183-5 (J. A. Jameson 58*) by 5 wkts.

5th Match: v Surrey (Oval)   July 16, 17, 18.
Surrey 230 (Intikhab Alam 73, P. P. Henwood 4-42) and 289-2 dec (Younis Ahmed 108*, M. J. Edwards 107*) drew with W. Isaacs' XI 244 (R. G. Pollock 82, C. E. Waller 4-29) and 255-9 (J. P. D. Flanagan 54, M. M. Harvey 50).

6th Match: v Ireland (Dublin)   July 19, 20, 21.
Ireland 240 and 241-7 dec (M. Reith 85, I. Anderson 56) drew with W. Isaacs' XI 242-8 dec (A. Bruyns 63) and 160-6.

7th Match: v Club Cricket Conference (South Hampstead)   July 23.
W. Isaacs' XI 225-7 dec beat C.C.C. 212 (T. M. Cordaroy 86, P. P. Henwood 5-65) by 13 runs.

Anti-apartheid demonstrators caused trouble on various occasions and at Oxford staged a sit-in on the wicket, which held up the game.

The most curious aspect of the whole visit was the ruling—several weeks after they had been played on the understanding that they were first-class—that the four three-day matches were not first-class. There was some doubt as to what jurisdiction if any the M.C.C. had over the match played in Dublin.

1969: Barbados

Ten players, to be joined by three already in England, arrived by air on 1 August. The full side was S. M. Nurse (captain), M. R. Bynoe, R. C. Brancker, P. D. Lashley, C. Blades, D. A. J. Holford, A. Bethell, D. Boxhill, R. M. Edwards, W. W. Hall, H. R. Moseley, L. Maxwell and S. Hinkson. Brancker acted as manager and the team were the guests of the International Cavaliers.

The most impressive batsman during the brief tour was Blades. Bynoe proved consistent and Nurse, Holford, Lashley and Bethel all had good innings.

Moseley was rather disappointing among the bowlers, but Hall could still produce a good head of steam and Edwards was quite dangerous.

The visit was given very little publicity, which seemed a pity in view of the attractiveness of the party.

1969: Barbados

1st Match: v Essex (Leyton)   Aug 13.
Essex 209-8 dec (K. W. R. Fletcher 51) beat Barbados 175 by 34 runs.

2nd Match: v Nottinghamshire (Trent Bridge)   Aug 20, 21, 22.
Barbados 309-9 dec (A. Bethell 84*, W. W. Hall 55, D. A. J. Holford 53, S. M. Nurse 52, B. Stead 5-96) and 232-7 dec drew with Nottinghamshire 273-6 dec (M. J. Harris 64, J. B. Bolus 64, M. J. Smedley 64) and 124-2 (J. B. Bolus 67*).

3rd Match: v International Cavaliers (Kidderminster)   Aug 24.
Barbados 252-7 dec (M. R. Bynoe 81, D. A. J. Holford 58) beat International Cavaliers 107 by 145 runs.

4th Match: v Sussex (Hove)   Aug 28, 29.
Barbados 242 (M. R. Bynoe 81) and 175-5 dec beat Sussex 143-6 dec and 188 (M. G. Griffith 71) by 86 runs.

5th Match: v International Cavaliers (Maidstone)   Aug 31.
International Cavaliers 190-7 dec (R. C. Fredericks 53) lost to Barbados 191-8 (P. D. Lashley 50) by 2 wkts.

6th Match: v International Cavaliers (Scarborough)   Sept 3, 4, 5.
International Cavaliers 340 (R. G. Pollock 101, R. Collins 58, D. A. J. Holford 4-92) and 231-9 dec (R. G. Pollock 61, R. C. Brancker 5-84) beat Barbados 271 (P. D. Swart 4-74) and 289 (M. R. Bynoe 75, P. D. Lashley 56, P. Trimborn 4-64) by 11 runs.

7th Match: v International Cavaliers (Motspur Park)   Sept 7.
International Cavaliers 217-4 dec (K. Barker 73, L. G. Rowe 54) beat Barbados 197 by 20 runs.

8th Match: v Combined Services (Portsmouth)   July 24.
Combined Services 67 (V. A. P. van der Bijl 5-20) lost to W. Isaacs' XI 68-1 by 9 wkts.

9th Match: v Standard Bank (Elmers End)   July 27.
W. Isaacs' XI 216-6 dec (M. M. Harvey 83, R. R. Collins 76) drew with Standard Bank 131-7.

10th Match: v Hampshire 2nd XI (Southampton)   July 28, 29.
Hampshire 2nd XI 160 (W. R. Kerr 4-39) and 12-2 drew with W. Isaacs' XI 63-9 dec (W. D. Buck 5-30).

11th Match: v M.C.C. (Roehampton)   July 30.
M.C.C. 156-6 dec (Richardson 78, D. Mackay-Coghill 4-30) lost to W. Isaacs' XI 157-8 by 2 wkts.

12th Match: v Gloucestershire XI (Bristol)   July 31.
Gloucestershire XI 142 (M. Bissex 52) lost to W. Isaacs' XI 145-7 by 3 wkts.

13th Match: v Cambridge Quidnuncs (Chislehurst)   Aug 3.
W. Isaacs' XI 134 (M. J. Smithyman 76) beat Cambrdige Quidnuncs 56 (V. A. P. van der Bijl 5-8) by 77 runs.

14th Match: v D. H. Robins' XI (Eastbourne)   Aug 4, 5.
D. H. Robins' XI 150 (V. A. P. van der Bijl 4-10) and 221 (D. R. Walsh 52, V. A. P. van der Bijl 5-51) lost to W. Isaacs' XI 228-5 dec (R. G. Pollock 153*) and 145-2 (R. R. Collins 69*, E. Chatterton 50) by 8 wkts.

15th Match: v Sussex Martlets (Arundel)   Aug 6.
Sussex Martlets 141 lost to W. Isaacs' XI 144-1 (A. Bruyns 85*) by 9 wkts.

16th Match: v M.C.C. Schools (Roehampton)   Aug 8.
W. Isaacs' XI 184-4 dec (E. Chatterton 62, N. Rosendorff 62) drew with M.C.C. Schools 130-9.

332

1970: Rest of the World

When the South African tour of 1970 was finally cancelled, the T.C.C.B. decided to arrange five matches between England and a Rest of the World eleven.

The Rest were managed by F. R. Brown and Sobers was appointed captain. The 14 players involved were G. St A. Sobers (captain), C. H. Lloyd, D. L. Murray, R. B. Kanhai, and L. R. Gibbs of the West Indies; M. J. Procter, E. J. Barlow, B. A. Richards, R. G. Pollock and P. M. Pollock of South Africa; Intikhab Alam and Mushtaq Mohammad of Pakistan; G. D. McKenzie of Australia and F. M. Engineer of India.

The Rest won the series four matches to one. Sobers, who had been so out of form for West Indies in 1969, topped the batting as well as taking most wickets. C. H. Lloyd also showed good all-round form, and so did Barlow.

There was little public interest in the series: only 35,000 attended over the four days of the Lord's Test and the attendance at Trent Bridge was very meagre. However, the matches were sponsored by Guinness, which paid £13,000 to the players and £7,000 in the counties.

The authorities tried to invest the matches with the title of 'Tests' and awarded the England players 'caps'. This notion did not meet with general approval and was accepted only by *Wisden's Cricketers' Almanack*, which eventually altered its opinion.

1970: Rest of the World

1st Match: v England (Lord's)   June 17, 19, 20, 22.
England 127 (R. Illingworth 63, G. St A. Sobers 6-21) and 339 (R. Illingworth 94, B. L. d'Oliveira 78, B. W. Luckhurst 67, Intikhab Alam 6-113) lost to Rest of the World 546 (G. St A. Sobers 183, E. J. Barlow 119, Intikhab Alam 61, R. G. Pollock 55, A. Ward 4-121) by an innings and 80 runs.

2nd Match: v England (Trent Bridge)   July 2, 3, 4, 6, 7.
Rest of the World 276 (C. H. Lloyd 114*, B. A. Richards 64, B. L. d'Oliveira 4-43, A. W. Greig 4-59) and 286 (E. J. Barlow 142) lost to England 279 (R. Illingworth 97, E. J. Barlow 5-66) and 284-2 (B. W. Luckhurst 113*, K. W. R. Fletcher 69*, M. C. Cowdrey 64) by 8 wkts.

3rd Match: v England (Edgbaston)   July 16, 17, 18, 20, 21.
England 294 (B. L. d'Oliveira 110, A. W. Greig 55, M. J. Procter 5-46) and 409 (B. L. d'Oliveira 81, M. C. Cowdrey 71, A. P. E. Knott 50*, G. St A. Sobers 4-89) lost to Rest of the World 563-9 dec (C. H. Lloyd 101, G. St A. Sobers 80, R. B. Kanhai 71, M. J. Procter 62, D. L. Murray 62, J. A. Snow 4-124, R. Illingworth 4-131) and 141-5 by 5 wkts.

4th Match: v England (Headingley)   July 30, 31, Aug 1, 3, 4.
England 222 (K. W. R. Fletcher 89, R. Illingworth 58, E. J. Barlow 7-64) and 376 (B. W. Luckhurst 92, G. Boycott 64, K. W. R. Fletcher 63, R. Illingworth 54, E. J. Barlow 5-78) beat Rest of the World 376-9 dec (G. St A. Sobers 114, D. L. Murray 95, A. W. Greig 4-86) and 226-8 (G. St A. Sobers 59, J. A. Snow 4-82) by 2 wkts.

5th Match: v England (Oval)   Aug 13, 14, 15, 17, 18.
England 294 (M. C. Cowdrey 73, R. Illingworth 52, A. P. E. Knott 51, G. D. McKenzie 4-51) and 344 (G. Boycott 157, K. W. R. Fletcher 63) lost to Rest of the World 355 (R. G. Pollock 114, G. St A. Sobers 79, M. J. Procter 51, P. Lever 7-83) and 287-6 (R. B. Kanhai 100, C. H. Lloyd 68, J. A. Snow 4-81) by 4 wkts.

Above *One of the best batsmen in the victorious Rest of the World side which toured England in 1970 was the West Indian Clive Lloyd, shown hooking.*

Left *South Africa's Eddie Barlow was a leading all-rounder of the Rest of the World side and is seen hitting a back-foot boundary through the covers off David Brown at Trent Bridge.*

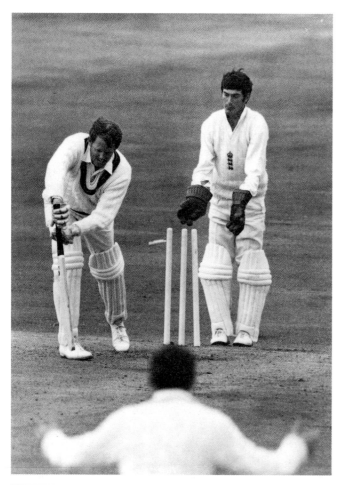

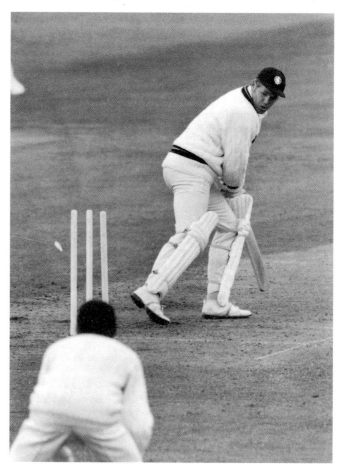

Two distinguished South African batsmen, prevented from touring England by cancellation of the 1970 tour, nevertheless played with the Rest of the World side. These pictures show them being bowled: Graeme Pollock on the left and Mike Procter below. The wicketkeeper is Alan Knott.

1970: Rest of the World

Batting Averages

	M	I	NO	R	HS	Avge	100	c/s
G. St A. Sobers	5	9	1	588	183	73.50	2	7
C. H. Lloyd	5	9	1	400	114*	50.00	2	3
M. J. Procter	5	9	3	292	62	48.66	0	2
D. L. Murray	3	4	0	172	95	43.00	0	15
E. J. Barlow	5	9	0	353	142	39.22	2	10
B. A. Richards	5	8	1	257	64	36.71	0	3
Intikhab Alam	5	8	1	240	61	34.28	0	1
R. B. Kanhai	5	9	0	284	100	31.55	1	3
R. G. Pollock	5	8	0	250	114	31.25	1	1
Mushtaq Mohammad	2	4	0	29	14	7.25	0	2
G. D. McKenzie	3	4	2	10	6*	5.00	0	0
L. R. Gibbs	4	5	3	7	3*	3.50	0	2
F. M. Engineer	2	3	0	3	2	1.00	0	8/1

Also batted: P. M. Pollock (1 match) 23*.

Bowling Averages

	O	M	R	W	Avge	BB	5i
E. J. Barlow	152	33	396	20	19.80	7-64	3
C. H. Lloyd	53	13	120	6	20.00	3-34	0
G. St A. Sobers	272.4	106	452	21	21.52	6-21	1
M. J. Procter	211.1	82	359	15	23.93	5-46	1
G. D. McKenzie	122.2	31	283	9	31.44	4-51	0
Intikhab Alam	283.5	99	637	14	45.50	6-113	1
P. M. Pollock	33	6	110	2	55.00	1-48	0
L. R. Gibbs	167	53	307	3	102.50	1-31	0
Mushtaq Mohammad	55	18	135	1	135.00	1-63	0

Also bowled: R. B. Kanhai 1-0-4-0; R. G. Pollock 0.2-0-5-0.

1970: Proposed South African tour

The team selected was A. Bacher (captain), B. L. Irvine, H. R. Lance and G. L. G. Watson of Transvaal; E. J. Barlow, M. J. Procter and G. Chevalier of Western Province; B. A. Richards, P.

H. J. Trimborn and A. Short of Natal; R. G. Pollock and P. M. Pollock of Eastern Province; J. D. Lindsay of North-Eastern Transvaal and A. J. Traicos of Rhodesia.

J. B. Plimsoll was to have been manager.

From the time the tour was announced the anti-apartheid lobby agitated for it to be cancelled. In February the Cricket Council decided to reduce the tour to 12 matches on cricket grounds where admission could be prevented if necessary to stop demonstrators causing trouble during games.

On 22 May the tour was cancelled following a formal request from the government.

1970: Jamaicans

Following the cancellation of the South African tour the Jamaican C.A., with the help of Rothmans and the Jamaican government, organised a side to visit England and take over some of the fixtures originally arranged for the South Africans.

The team was E. D. A. St J. McMorris (captain), J. L. Hendriks (player-manager), M. L. C. Foster, L. G. Rowe, R. A. Pinnock, S. A. Morgan, D. M. Lewis, A. Campbell, A. Barrett, L. Wright, L. Wellington, C. Folkes, W. Haye and O. Miles.

The tour was marred by rain, but Pinnock and Foster batted well and Miles was the outstanding bowler, his off-breaks taking 20 wickets. Of the faster bowlers Barrett, though he had little luck, and Folkes were the best.

```
1970: Jamaicans

1st Match: v Surrey (Oval)   July 13, 14.
Surrey 306-3 dec (J. H. Edrich 166, M. J. Stewart 69) drew with Jamaicans 11-4.

2nd Match: v Somerset (Taunton)   July 16, 17.
Jamaicans 219-9 dec (B. A. Langford 5-64) and 178-3 dec (L. G. Rowe 82, D. M. Lewis 53)
drew with Somerset 122-4 dec and 187-9.

3rd Match: v Worcestershire (Worcester)   July 22, 23.
Worcestershire 197-7 dec (O. Miles 4-61) and 218-5 dec (D. J. Stewart 50) drew with
Jamaicans 218-5 dec (L. G. Rowe 100*, M. L. C. Foster 71) and 108-4 (L. G. Rowe 55*).

4th Match: v Glamorgan (Swansea)   July 25, 27, 28.
Glamorgan 294-9 dec (A. Jones 109, B. Davis 52, O. Miles 4-82) drew with Jamaicans 195-6
(R. A. Pinnock 53).

5th Match: v Swansea (Swansea)   July 26 (40 overs-a-side).
Swansea beat Jamaicans.

6th Match: v South-Western Counties
Jamaicans beat South-Western Counties.

7th Match: v Glamorgan (Colwyn Bay)   Aug 1, 2.
Jamaicans 151-6 dec (S. A. Morgan 68) and 255-5 dec (M. L. C. Foster 113*) drew with
Glamorgan 175-3 dec (G. Ellis 58) and 184-8 (G. Kingston 57).

8th Match: v International Cavaliers (Southport)   Aug 5, 6.
Jamaicans 152 (S. A. Morgan 79, F. S. Trueman 5-40) and 35-2 drew with International
Cavaliers 284 (E. J. Barlow 78, R. G. Pollock 58).

9th Match: v Lancashire (Old Trafford)   Aug 8, 10, 11.
Jamaicans 296 (R. A. Pinnock 66, M. L. C. Foster 62) and 144-5 dec (S. A. Morgan 61*) drew
with Lancashire 201 (O. Miles 4-84) and 151-5 (D. Lloyd 69).

10th Match: v Sussex (Hove)   Aug 15, 16, 17.
Jamaicans 372-7 dec (R. A. Pinnock 176, M. L. C. Foster 110, J. Spencer 4-44) beat Sussex
188 (O. Miles 5-67) and 96 (C. Folkes 5-22) by an innings and 88 runs.

11th Match: v Essex (Leyton)   Aug 19, 20, 21.
Essex 107-6 dec (O. Miles 4-23) drew with Jamaicans 116-3 (L. G. Rowe 52).

12th Match: v M.C.C. (Lord's)   Aug 22 (40 overs-a-side).
M.C.C. 178-9 beat Jamaicans 138 (L. G. Rowe 59, K. D. Boyce 4-25).
```

1971: 4th Pakistanis

Political problems created uncertainty about whether the tour would take place, but happily the obstacles were overcome and the following party of players was selected: Intikhab Alam (captain), Asif Iqbal, Saeed Ahmed, Wasim Bari, Shafqat Rana, Pervez Sajjad, Naushad Ali, Saleem Altaf, Aftab Gul, Asif Masood, Sarfraz Nawaz, Sadiq Mohammad, Zaheer Abbas,

```
1971: 4th Pakistanis

Batting Averages
                        M    I   NO    R    HS    Avge   100   c/s
Zaheer Abbas           19   31    4  1508   274  55.85    4    14
Aftab Gul              16   27    2  1154   106  46.16    2     5
Mushtaq Mohammad        6    8    2   275   100  45.83    1     5
Asif Iqbal             14   20    4   709  104*  44.31    1     6
Sadiq Mohammad         17   28    1   831    91  30.85    0    13
Saeed Ahmed            14   26    4   634    97  28.81    0     9
Wasim Bari             13   18    4   336    63  24.00    0   37/3
Azmat Rana              8   12    3   192    50  21.33    0     4
Mohammad Nazir          6    8    3   106    39  21.20    0     4
Talat Ali               9   13    1   251    48  20.91    0     6
Imran Khan             11   13    4   172   36*  19.11    0     3
Salim Altaf            12   10    6    71    26  17.75    0     2
Shafqat Rana           11   16    3   228    40  17.53    0     6
Intikhab Alam          16   22    1   354    63  16.85    0    10
Sarfraz Nawaz           3    3    0    32    20  10.66    0     1
Naushad Ali             8   10    0    95    27   9.50    0  12/5
Asif Masood            12   11    3    28    14   3.50    0     1
Pervez Sajjad          12    9    6    10    9*   3.33    0     8

Also batted: Majid J. Khan (2 matches) 35, 9.

Bowling Averages
                          O      M     R    W   Avge    BB    5i
Mohammad Nazir         164.1    52   396   20  19.80   6-26    2
Intikhab Alam          647.2   157  1879   72  26.09   7-37    6
Saeed Ahmed            229.4    49   701   25  28.04   4-26    0
Pervez Sajjad          355.4   100   853   30  28.43   6-71    1
Salim Altaf            229.1    64   578   19  30.42   4-11    0
Sadiq Mohammad          58           217    7  31.00   3-66    0
Asif Iqbal             186.2    40   500   15  33.33   4-51    0
Asif Masood            326      71   909   27  33.66  5-111    1
Imran Khan             164      38   527   12  43.91   3-47    0
Mushtaq Mohammad        71      16   211    4  52.75   2-50    0
Sarfraz Nawaz           72.2    13   219    2 109.50   2-47    0

Also bowled: Majid J. Khan 14-3-31-0; Aftab Gul 1-0-4-0; Shafqat Rana 4-1-17-0; Talat Ali
6-0-25-0; Zaheer Abbas 11-0-46-0.
```

```
1971: 4th Pakistanis

1st Match: v Worcestershire (Worcester)   May 1, 3, 4.
Worcestershire 305-5 dec (G. M. Turner 179) and 251-2 dec (R. G. A. Headley 146*, G. M.
Turner 76) drew with Pakistanis 241 (Zaheer Abbas 110, Sadiq Mohammad 59) and 256-6
(Aftab Gul 80, Asif Iqbal 63*).

2nd Match: v Warwickshire (Edgbaston)   May 5, 6, 7.
Warwickshire 328-6 dec (M. J. K. Smith 127, D. L. Amiss 96) and 75-1 dec lost to Pakistanis
240-4 dec (Aftab Gul 102) and 165-3 (Aftab Gul 61) by 7 wkts.

3rd Match: v Northamptonshire (Northampton)   May 8, 10, 11.
Pakistanis 262 and 231 (Sadiq Mohammad 67) lost to Northamptonshire 336-5 dec (H. M.
Ackerman 105, Mushtaq Mohammad 76, P. J. Watts 65*) and 158-4 (G. Sharp 50*) by 6 wkts.

4th Match: v Hampshire (Portsmouth)   May 12, 13, 14.
Pakistanis 274 (Aftab Gul 66) and 272-7 dec (Aftab Gul 66, Zaheer Abbas 61, Asif Iqbal 51*,
T. E. Jesty 4-50) drew with Hampshire 269 (R. E. Marshall 122, Intikhab Alam 4-88) and
145-3 (B. A. Richards 87*).

5th Match: v Cambridge University (Cambridge)   May 15, 17, 18.
Pakistanis 126 (J. Spencer 6-40) and 235 (Zaheer Abbas 62, J. Spencer 5-58) lost to
Cambridge University 360 (M. J. Khan 94, D. R. Owen-Thomas 77, H. K. Steele 73) and 2-0 by
10 wkts.

6th Match: v Nottinghamshire (Trent Bridge)   May 19, 20, 21.
Pakistanis 283-7 dec (Zaheer Abbas 97, Sadiq Mohammad 51) and 225-5 dec (Aftab Gul 75,
Sadiq Mohammad 58) drew with Nottinghamshire 251-7 dec (M. J. Harris 85) and 234-7
(B. Hassan 125*).

7th Match: v M.C.C. (Lord's)   May 22, 24, 25.
Pakistanis 190 (P. Lever 4-28) and 47-3 drew with M.C.C. 255-5 dec (A. R. Lewis 56, D. L.
Amis 53, R. T. Virgin 50).

8th Match: v Kent (Gravesend)   May 26, 27, 28.
Pakistanis 299 (Zaheer Abbas 138, Asif Iqbal 50, B. D. Julien 4-71) drew with Kent 156-9.

9th Match: v Gloucestershire (Bristol)   May 29, 31, June 1.
Pakistanis 291 (Aftab Gul 88, Intikhab Alam 63) and 185-4 dec (Aftab Gul 106, Zaheer Abbas
58*) beat Gloucestershire 157 (M. Bissex 62, Asif Iqbal 4-51) and 215 (R. B. Nicholls 56,
Intikhab Alam 7-108) by 104 runs.

10th Match: v England (Edgbaston)   June 3, 4, 5, 7, 8.
Pakistanis 608-7 dec (Zaheer Abbas 274, Asif Iqbal 104*, Mushtaq Mohammad
100) drew with England 353 (A. P. E. Knott 116, B. L. d'Oliveira 73, Asif Masood
5-111) and 229-5 (B. W. Luckhurst 108*, Asif Masood 4-49).

11th Match: v Yorkshire (Bradford)   June 9, 10, 11.
Yorkshire 422-9 dec (R. A. Hutton 189, D. E. V. Padgett 61, Intikhab Alam 5-97) drew with
Pakistanis 140-5.

12th Match: v Oxford University (Oxford)   June 12, 14, 15.
Pakistanis 131-3 dec (Aftab Gul 65) and 83-0 (Aftab Gul 64*) drew with Oxford University
120-6 dec.

13th Match: v England (Lord's)   June 17, 18, 19, 21, 22.
England 241-2 dec (G. Boycott 121*) and 117-0 (R. A. Hutton 58*, B. W. Luckhurst
53*) drew with Pakistan 148.

14th Match: v Glamorgan (Swansea)   June 23, 24, 25.
Glamorgan 114 (Intikhab Alam 7-37) and 322 (K. J. Lyons 88, Intikhab Alam 6-99) beat
Pakistanis 158 (M. A. Nash 5-54) and 232 (Saeed Ahmed 77, Azmat Rana 50) by 46 runs.

15th Match: v Lancashire (Old Trafford)   June 26, 28, 29.
Lancashire 301-9 dec (D. Lloyd 86, D. P. Hughes 61, Salim Altaf 4-68) and 105 0 (D. Lloyd
59*) drew with Pakistanis 195-9 dec (Zaheer Abbas 100*, P. Lever 5-52).

16th Match: v Scotland (Selkirk)   June 30, July 1, 2.
Pakistanis 183-9 dec (J. M. Allan 7-54) and 181-6 (Sadiq Mohammad 70, Saeed Ahmed 56,
J. M. Allan 4-69) beat Scotland 118 (Mohmmad Nazir 5-38, Saeed Ahmed 4-26) and
92 (Mohammad Nazir 6-26, Pervez Sajjad 4-47) by 154 runs.

17th Match: v Derbyshire (Chesterfield)   July 3, 5, 6.
Derbyshire 333 (J. F. Harvey 70, C. P. Wilkins 49, J. A. Harvey-Walker 57, Intikhab Alam 5-155)
and 184 (Pervez Sajjad 6-71) lost to Pakistanis 413-7 dec (Saeed Ahmed 97, Asif Iqbal 83,
Zaheer Abbas 63, Aftab Gul 53) and 108-2 (Aftab Gul 77*) by 8 wkts.

18th Match: v England (Headingley)   July 8, 9, 10, 12, 13.
England 316 (G. Boycott 112, B. L. d'Oliveira 74) and 264 (B. L. d'Oliveira 72,, D. L.
Amiss 56, Salim Altaf 4-11) beat Pakistan 350 (Zaheer Abbas 72, Wasim Bari 63,
Mushtaq Mohammad 57) and 205 (Sadiq Mohammad 91) by 25 runs.

19th Match: v Surrey (Oval)   July 14, 15, 16.
Surrey 166 (Intikhab Alam 7-57) and 234 (M. J. Edwards 52, Nazir Mohammad 4-64) lost to
Pakistanis 268-9 dec (Zaheer Abbas 65, Asif Iqbal 52) and 133-2 by 8 wkts.
```

Azmat Rana, Talat Ali, Imran Khan, with Masud Salah-ud-din as manager. Mushtaq Mohammad was available for the Test Matches and certain other games, depending on his commitments for Northants. Majid J. Khan, who was the Cambridge captain, assisted the team in two Tests and Mohammad Nazir also played in some matches.

Zaheer Abbas was the find of the season, topping the Test batting averages with 386 runs, average 96.50 as well as the first-class table. Aftab Gul and Sadiq were the opening partnership and improved as the tour progressed, but Saeed Ahmed found the going difficult and did not strike form until the visit was almost over. Azmat Rana had an attack of malaria and missed some vital matches.

Asif Iqbal had a Test batting average of over 50 and bowled usefully at times. Asif Masood curiously achieved little in the county matches, but his swing bowling was highly effective in the Tests in which he took 13 wickets, average 26.46. Intikhab bowled easily the most overs on the tour and took most wickets, but against England was rather expensive. Imran Khan looked a very interesting prospect.

Of the three Tests, the visitors lost one and drew the other two, but Pakistan deserved to beat England at Edgbaston where Zaheer made a superlative double century and, in the final Test, the home country scraped home by just 25 runs. Pakistan could be pleased with the outcome of the visit, even if the attendances at the Tests were disappointing.

Above *One of the successes of the 1971 Pakistanis was Asif Iqbal, seen batting against Kent at Canterbury. Asif was already a Kent player, and later captained both that county and his country.*

Left *Wasim Bari was Pakistan's first-choice wicket keeper from 1967 to 1983; he was also a useful late-order batsman. Gower is the batsman.*

Below *Surrey stalwart Intikhab Alam, who skippered the 1971 Pakistanis, bowling in one of the tourists' county matches.*

1971: 8th Indians

The side which arrived in England in June for a tour during the second half of 1971 was A. L. Wadekar (captain), S. Venkataraghavan, E. D. Solkar, S. M. Gavaskar, A. V. Mankad, G. R. Viswanath, S. Abid Ali, A. A. Baig, S. M. H. Kirmani, D. N. Sardesai, D. Govindraj, K. Jayantilal, E. A. S. Prasanna, P. Krishnamurthy, B. S. Bedi and B. S. Chandrasekhar, with Col H. R. Adhikari as manager and R. P. Mehra as treasurer. F. M. Engineer, who was playing for Lancashire, was available for the Tests only.

After two drawn Test Matches, India won the Third at the Oval by four wickets and therefore took the series; it was also the first time India had beaten England in England. The Indian victory was due in the main to some inspired spin bowling by Chandrasekhar, who dismissed England in their second innings for 101, leaving his side to make 174 in the final innings.

The tourists lost only one match, making it without doubt the best ever visit by India to England.

The quartet of spinners—Chandrasekhar, Bedi, Venkatara-

1971: 8th Indians

1st Match: v Middlesex (Lord's) June 23, 24, 25.
Middlesex 233 (W. E. Russell 84, M. J. Smith 54, B. S. Chandrasekhar 5-67) and 131 (B. S. Bedi 6-29) lost to Indians 168 (G. R. Viswanath 60, J. S. E. Price 4-31) and 198-8 (S. Abid Ali 61) by 2 wkts.

2nd Match: v Essex (Colchester) June 26, 28, 29.
Indians 164 (D. N. Sardesai 53, E. D. Solkar 52, K. D. Boyce 4-33) and 231 (S. M. Gavaskar 55, A. L. Wadekar 51) lost to Essex 328-8 dec (K. W. R. Fletcher 106*, B. Ward 55) and 68-4 by 6 wkts.

3rd Match: v D. H. Robins' XI (Eastbourne) June 30, July 1, 2.
D. H. Robins' XI 288-8 dec (E. A. S. Prasanna 4-61) and 258-5 dec (H. M. Ackerman 80, P. H. Parfitt 76) drew with Indians 305-8 dec (G. R. Viswanath 100*) and 132-4 (S. M. Gavaskar 55*).

4th Match: v Kent (Canterbury) July 3, 5, 6.
Kent 394-8 dec (B. W. Luckhurst 118, J. N. Shepherd 76, M. H. Denness 59) and 176-4 dec (A. G. E. Ealham 87, D. Nicholls 57) drew with Indians 163 (A. A. Baig 58, E. D. Solkar 50*, J. N. Shepherd 4-33) and 264-7 (G. R. Viswanath 115*, A. V. Mankad 52).

5th Match: v Leicestershire (Leicester) July 7, 8, 9.
Leicestershire 198 (B. Dudleston 51, B. S. Chadrasekhar 5-63) and 168 (J. C. Balderstone 63, B. S. Chandrasekhar 6-64) lost to Indians 416-7 dec (S. M. Gavaskar 165, A. L. Wadekar 126) by an innings and 30 runs.

6th Match: v Warwickshire (Edgbaston) July 10, 12, 13.
Warwickshire 377-3 dec (J. A. Jameson 231, M. J. K. Smith 72*, J. Whitehouse 52) and 182 (R. B. Kanhai 59, B. S. Bedi 5-64, E. A. S. Prasanna 4-57) lost to Indians 562 (D. N. Sardesai 120, G. R. Viswanath 90, S. Abid Ali 93, A. L. Wadekar 77, W. Blenkiron 5-100) by an innings and 3 runs.

7th Match: v Glamorgan (Sophia Gardens, Cardiff) July 14, 15, 16.
Indians 284 (F. M. Engineer 62*, G. R. Viswanath 52, A. E. Cordle 4-49) and 245-6 dec (A. L. Wadekar 73, S. Venkataraghavan 57) beat Glamorgan 203 (M. J. Khan 78, S. Vankataraghavan 6-76) and 224 (M. A. Nash 75, A. Jones 55, B. S. Bedi 6-93) by 102 runs.

8th Match: v Hampshire (Bournemouth) July 17, 19, 20.
Hampshire 198 (R. M. C. Gilliat 50) and 271 (R. M. C. Gilliat 79, R. V. Lewis 71, S. Ventakaraghavan 9-93) lost to Indians 364 (A. V. Mankad 109, G. R. Viswanath 122, S. M. Gavaskar 53, L. R. Worrell 4-102, D. R. O'Sullivan 5-116) and 106-5 by 5 wkts.

9th Match: v England (Lord's) July 22, 23, 24, 26, 27.
England 304 (J. A. Snow 73, A. P. E. Knott 67, B. S. Bedi 4-70) and 191 (J. H. Edrich 62, S. Venkataraghavan 4-52) drew with India 313 (A. L. Wadekar 85, G. R. Viswanath 68, E. D. Solkar 67, N. Gifford 4-84) and 145-8 (S. M. Gavaskar 53, N. Gifford 4-43).

10th Match: v Minor Counties (Lakenham) July 28, 29, 30.
Minor Counties 203-5 dec (M. Maslin 61) and 199-6 dec (F. W. Millett 50) drew with Indians 252-3 dec (A. A. Baig 64, A. V. Mankad 63, S. M. Gavaskar 54) and 26-0.

11th Match: v Surrey (Oval) July 31, Aug 1, 2.
Surrey 269 (G. R. J. Roope 60, Intikhab Alam 55, Younis Ahmed 52, B. S. Bedi 7-111) and 257-4 (S. J. Storey 70*, G. R. J. Roope 56*, E. A. S. Prasanna 4-69) drew with Indians 326-8 dec (K. Jayantilal 84, A. V. Mankad 77).

12th Match: v England (Old Trafford) Aug 5, 6, 7, 9, 10.
England 386 (R. Illingworth 107, P. Lever 88, B. W. Luckhurst 78, S. Abid Ali 4-64) and 245-3 dec (B. W. Luckhurst 101, J. H. Edrich 59) drew with India 212 (S. M. Gavaskar 57, E. D. Solkar 50, P. Lever 5-70) and 65-3.

13th Match: v Yorkshire (Headingley) Aug 11, 12, 13.
Indians 145 (A. L. Wadekar 59) drew with Yorkshire 137-3 (R. G. Lamb 57*).

14th Match: v Nottinghamshire (Trent Bridge) Aug 14, 16, 17.
Indians 168-6 dec (D. N. Sardesai 57*) and 145-4 dec (A. V. Mankad 50) drew with Nottinghamshire 69-7 dec (G. Frost, B. S. Chandrasekhar 6-45).

15th Match: v England (Oval) Aug 19, 20, 21, 23, 24.
England 355 (A. P. E. Knott 90, R. A. Hutton 81, J. A. Jameson 82) and 101 (B. S. Chandrasekhar 6-38) lost to India 284 (F. M. Engineer 59, D. B. Sardesai 54, R. Illingworth 5-70) and 174-6 by 4 wkts.

16th Match: v Sussex (Hove) Aug 25, 26, 27.
Indians 220 (E. D. Solkar 90, A. W. Greig 4-78) and 276-7 (K. Jayantil 57, U. C. Joshi 5-107) drew with Sussex 386-9 dec (M. A. Buss 140, G. A. Greenidge 62, E. A. S. Prasanna 5-137).

17th Match: v Somerset (Taunton) Aug 28, 29, 30.
Indians 349-8 dec (E. D. Solkar 113, S. Abid Ali 102*, T. W. Cartwright 5-79) and 162-5 dec (A. L. Wadekar 74) drew with Somerpet 226-4 dec (D. B. Close 103*) and 127-2 (P. J. Robinson 52*).

18th Match: v Worcestershire (Worcester) Sept 1, 2, 3.
Indians 383-3 dec (S. M. Gavaskar 194, A. L. Wadekar 150) and 150-8 dec (G. R. Viswanath 53) drew with Worcestershire 248 (J. M. Parker 91, S. Venkataraghavan 4-60) and 250-5 (T. J. Yardley 104*, j. A. Ormrod 76).

19th Match: v T. N. Pearce's XI (Scarborough) Sept 4, 6, 7.
T. N. Pearce's XI 357-3 dec (R. T. Virgin 176, J. B. Bolus 75, K. W. R. Fletcher 67*) and 199-3 dec (J. B. Bolus 106*, P. H. Parfitt 63) lost to Indians 306 (A. V. Mankad 154*, E. D. Solkar 79, R. N. S. Hobbs 5-94) and 252-5 (S. M. Gavaskar 128, R. N. S. Hobbs 4-64) by 5 wkts.

The eighth Indians in 1971 were the most successful so far, and won the Test series. Their great quartet of spin bowlers was largely responsible: this is Venkataraghavan bowling against Kent.

Another of India's spin-bowling magicians was Chandrasekhar, seen in action at Canterbury; Luckhurst is the batsman, and behind him can be seen another great Indian spinner, Bishan Bedi. Chandrasekhar effectively won the Third Test (and the series) when he took 6 for 38 in England's second innings at the Oval.

ghavan and Prasanna—was perhaps the greatest set of slow bowlers ever to represent a team to England. Prasanna in fact could not make his way into the Test side and the other three more or less shared the wickets between them. The fastest bowler—Govindraj—was also not picked for the Tests and the seam attack consisted of Abid Ali.

None of the batsmen had outstanding records, but Gavaskar, Wadekar and Viswanath all played some good innings. Engineer proved vital to the Test side as a batsman. The disappointments were Baig, who attempted a comeback, Mankad and Jayantilal.

One good aspect of the tour was the vastly improved fielding, to the credit of H. R. Adhikari, who acted as much as a coach as a manager. The 1971 team was not prone to the injury and illness which had often beset Indian sides on previous visits.

1972: 26th Australians

The Australians broke fresh ground on the 1972 tour when they played England in a series of three one-day limited-overs matches sponsored by the Prudential Assurance Company. These matches did not overshadow the battle for the Ashes, but they did create considerable interest. The series was won by England, two matches to one.

The team selected for the tour was I. M. Chappell (captain), G. S. Chappell, J. R. Hammond and A. A. Mallett of South

1971: 8th Indians

Batting Averages

	M	I	NO	R	HS	Avge	100	c/s
F. M. Engineer	—	7	2	262	62*	52.40	0	8/1
E. D. Solkar	16	24	6	802	113	44.55	1	14
S. M. Gavaskar	15	27	1	1141	194	43.88	3	15
A. V. Mankad	13	22	3	795	154*	41.84	2	8
G. R. Viswanath	16	27	4	946	122	41.13	3	4
A. L. Wakekar	16	27	1	1057	150	40.65	2	23
S. Abid Ali	14	21	4	552	102*	32.47	1	11
A. A. Baig	13	21	0	526	64	25.04	0	6
S. M. H. Kirmani	7	9	4	118	37*	23.60	0	7
D. N. Sardesai	15	25	4	495	120	23.57	1	5
D. Govindraj	12	16	7	172	40*	19.11	0	5
K. Jayantilal	10	15	1	237	84	16.92	0	7
S. Venkataraghavan	14	21	1	303	57	15.15	0	12
E. A. S. Prasanna	9	7	3	33	10*	8.25	0	1
P. Krishnamurthy	9	9	2	56	32	8.00	0	16/8
B. S. Bedi	13	14	6	50	8	6.25	0	5
B. S. Chandrasekhar	13	10	4	16	6	2.66	0	9

Bowling Averages

	O	M	R	W	Avge	BB	5i
B. S. Chandrasekhar	472.5	103	1243	50	24.86	6-34	5
S. Venkataraghavan	594.2	139	1569	63	24.90	9-93	2
B. S. Bedi	603.5	171	1487	58	25.63	7-111	4
E. A. S. Prasanna	363.4	93	879	26	33.80	5-137	1
S. M. Gavaskar	46.3	5	190	4	47.50	2-8	0
E. D. Solkar	238	47	692	14	49.42	3-28	0
S. Abid Ali	303.5	53	926	16	57.87	4-64	0
A. V. Mankad	30	6	122	2	61.00	1-8	0
D. Govindraj	203	46	674	11	61.27	2-37	0

Also bowled: A. L. Wadekar 10-2-41-0; A. A. Baig 4-0-24-0; K. Jayantilal 5-0-15-0; S. M. H. Kirmani 2-0-6-0; D. N. Sardesai 5-0-14-0.

1972: 26th Australians

Batting Averages

	M	I	NO	R	HS	Avge	100	c/s
G. S. Chappell	18	28	10	1260	181	70.00	4	26
K. R. Stackpole	21	35	5	1309	154*	43.63	3	15
A. P. Sheahan	17	26	7	788	135*	41.47	1	6
K. D. Walters	19	29	5	935	154	38.95	3	7
G. D. Watson	18	27	2	915	176	36.60	2	7
R. W. Marsh	17	24	5	664	91	34.94	0	38/7
R. Edwards	18	26	3	747	170*	32.47	1	9
I. M. Chappell	20	34	2	1017	118	31.78	2	19
B. C. Francis	18	27	1	772	210	29.69	2	5
R. J. Inverarity	21	30	9	553	100*	26.33	1	13
J. R. Hammond	13	6	3	78	36*	26.00	0	4
H. B. Taber	12	11	3	180	54	22.50	0	22/5
D. J. Colley	16	16	3	268	58*	20.61	0	5
A. A. Mallett	15	13	3	146	29	14.60	0	5
J. W. Gleeson	17	12	4	88	30	11.00	0	3
D. K. Lillee	14	13	7	30	11*	5.00	0	3
R. A. L. Massie	12	10	1	45	18	5.00	0	0

Bowling Averages

	O	M	R	W	Avge	BB	5i
I. M. Chappell	43.5	14	106	10	10.60	3-1	0
R. A. Massie	381.4	115	851	50	17.02	8-53	4
D. K. Lillee	456.5	119	1197	53	22.58	6-66	3
J. W. Gleeson	354.5	106	1014	44	23.04	6-21	2
G. D. Watson	244	64	621	25	24.84	5-36	1
G. S. Chappell	206.2	51	488	19	25.68	7-58	1
R. J. Inverarity	353.5	101	983	37	26.56	5-67	1
A. A. Mallett	427	124	1165	41	28.41	5-59	3
D. J. Colley	346.4	73	946	33	28.66	5-27	2
J. R. Hammond	278	59	809	26	31.11	6-15	2
K. D. Walters	35.3	6	117	2	58.50	1-10	0
K. R. Stackpole	63	20	164	2	82.00	1-12	0

Also bowled: R. Edwards 1.2-0-15-0; B. C. Francis 2.5-0-15-1; A. P. Sheahan 4-0-19-1.

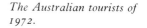

1972: 26th Australians

1st Match: v Duke of Norfolk's XI (Arundel Castle) (50 overs a side).
Duke of Norfolk's XI 241 (A. W. Greig 96, D. J. Colley 4-44) beat Australians 213-9 by 28 runs.

2nd Match: v Worcestershire (Worcester)   April 29, 30, May 1.
Worcestershire 98-2 and 99 (R. A. L. Massie 6-31) lost to Australians 68-2 and 133-4 by 6 wkts.

3rd Match: v Lancashire (Old Trafford)   May 3, 4, 5.
Australians 161-6 dec and 157 (K. Shuttleworth 4-38) drew with Lancashire 97-3 dec (B. Wood 52*) and 92-2.

4th Match: v Yorkshire (Bradford)   May 8 (50 overs a side).
Yorkshire 176-6 (G. Boycott 106) drew with Australians 58-3 off 17 overs.

5th Match: v Yorkshire (Bradford)   May 9 (50 overs a side).
Yorkshire 140 drew with Australians 27-2 off 6 overs. (Note: The original fixture was a 3 day match, May 7, 8, 9, but when rain prevented play on May 7, it was agreed to play two 50 overs matches).

6th Match: v Nottinghamshire (Trent Bridge)   May 10, 11, 12.
Nottinghamshire 176 (M. J. Harris 54, J. R. Hammond 5-46) drew with Australians 270-5 (G. S. Chappell 83*, A. P. Sheahan 69).

7th Match: v Surrey (Oval)   May 13, 15, 16.
Australians 180 (R. W. Marsh 58*) and 281-6 (I. M. Chappell 101, B. C. Francis 57) drew with Surrey 300 (J. H. Edrich 110, Intikhab Alam 59, D. J. Colley 5-72).

8th Match: v Hampshire (Southampton)   May 17, 18, 19.
Hampshire 311 (D. R. Turner 131, B. A. Richaerds 73, R. J. Inverarity 5-67) and 184-5 dec lost to Australians 191 (R. Edwards 69, R. S. Herman 4-53) and 306-1 (G. D. Watson 176, K. R. Stackpole 119*) by 9 wkts.

9th Match: v M.C.C. (Lord's)   May 20, 22, 23.
M.C.C. 208 (M. H. Denness 68, B. W. Luckhurst 50, A. A. Mallett 5-61) and 178-4 dec (B. Wood 62*, R. Illingworth 55*) lost to Australians 195-6 dec (B. C. Francis 61) and 195-6 (I. M. Chappell 57, B. C. Francis 56).

10th Match: v Gloucestershire (Bristol)   May 24, 25, 26.
Gloucestershire 121-8 dec (D. J. Colley 5-27) drew with Gloucestershire 44-1.

11th Match: v Glamorgan (Swansea)   May 27, 28, 29.
Australians 191 (D. L. Williams 5-31) and 158-3 dec (G. D. Watson 54) drew with Glamorgan 93-5 dec and 6-0.

12th Match: v Derbyshire (Chesterfield)   May 31, June 1, 2.
Australians 384-9 dec (B. C. Francis 117, K. D. Walters 109, A. P. Sheahan 80) drew with Derbyshire 257-4 (C. P. Wilkins 100*).

13th Match: v Warwickshire (Edgbaston)   June 3, 5, 6.
Australians 330 (K. D. Walters 154, K. R. Stackpole 50, S. J. Rouse 4-46) and 212-5 dec (I. M. Chappell 75) drew with Warwickshire 207-9 dec (A. I. Kallicharran 62) and 228-5 (M. J. K. Smith 78*).

14th Match: v England (Old Trafford)   June 8, 9, 10, 12, 13.
England 249 (A. W. Greig 57) and 234 (A. W. Greig 62, D. K. Lillee 6-66) beat Australia 142 (K. R. Stackpole 53, J. A. Snow 4-41, G. G. Arnold 4-62) and 252 (R. W. Marsh 91, K. R. Stackpole 67, A. W. Greig 4-53, J. A. Snow 4-87) by 89 runs.

15th Match: v Oxford and Cambridge Universities (Oxford)   June 14, 15, 16.
Oxford and Cambridge 277 (J. W. Ward 56, M. J. Khan 55) and 202 (M. J. Khan 85, P. D. Johnson 58*) lost to Australians 478-8 dec (B. C. Francis 210, R. Edwards 75, D. J. Colley 58) and 2-0 by 10 wkts.

16th Match: v Essex (Ilford)   June 17, 19, 20.
Essex 238 (B. Ward 59, K. D. Boyce 58, B. Taylor 50, J. W. Gleeson 4-60) and 193-6 (B. Taylor 68*, K. W.R. Fletcher 52) drew with Australians 435-9 dec (G. S. Chappell 181, I. M. Chappell 88, R. W. Marsh 68).

17th Match: v England (Lord's)   June 22, 23, 24, 26.
England 272 (A. W. Greig 54, R. A. L. Massie 8-84) and 116 (R. A. L. Massie 8-53) lost to Australia 308 (G. S. Chappell 131, I. M. Chappell 56, R. W. Marsh 50, J. A. Snow 5-57) and 81-2 by 8 wkts.

18th Match: v Cricketers' Association (Trent Bridge)   June 29 (50 overs a side).
Cricketers' Association 219 (B. L. d'Oliveira 75) beat Australians 162-5 (A. P. Sheahan 50) by 57 runs.

19th Match: v Somerset (Bath)   July 1, 2, 3.
Somerset 169 (A. A. Mallett 5-59) and 160-7 dec (D. B. Close 59) drew with Australians 171-4 dec and 130-4 (K. R. Stackpole 57).

20th Match: v Leicestershire (Leicester)   July 5, 6, 7.
Australians 324-7 dec (A. P. Sheahan 135, R. J. Inverarity 54) beat Leicestershire 58 (R. A. L. Massie 6-30) and 220 (B. F. Davison 58, J. W. Gleeson 5-75, R. A. L. Massie 4-33) by an innings and 46 runs.

21st Match: v Middlesex (Lord's)   July 8, 10, 11.
Middlesex 192-2 dec (P. H. Parfitt 68*, M. J. Smith 65) and 207-7 dec (C. T. Radley 91*, J. T. Murray 68) lost to Australians 167-3 dec and 233-5 (G. D. Watson 84) by 5 wkts.

22nd Match: v England (Trent Bridge)   July 13, 14, 15, 17, 18.
Australia 315 (K. R. Stackpole 114, D. J. Colley 54, J. A. Snow 5-92) and 324-4 dec (R. Edwards 170*, G. S. Chappell 72, I. M. Chappell 50) drew with England 290-4 (B. W. Luckhurst 96, B. L. d'Oliveira 50*).

23rd Match: v Minor Counties (Longton)   July 19, 20.
Australians 325-5 dec (R. J. Inverarity 100*, G. D. Watson 95, A. P. Sheahan 67) beat Minor Counties 161 (J. R. Hammond 6-15) and 138 (A. A. Mallett 4-13) by an innings and 26 runs.

24th Match: v Sussex (Hove)   July 22, 24, 25.
Australians 294 (I. M. Chappell 58, R. W. Marsh 54, M. A. Buss 5-69) and 262-2 dec (K. R. Stackpole 154*, A. P. Sheahan 50) lost to Sussex 296-5 dec (G. A. Greenidge 99, R. M. Prideaux 55) and 261-5 (G. A. Greenidge 125*) by 5 wkts.

25th Match: v Sussex (Hove)   July 23 (40 overs a side).
Sussex 61-2 drew with Australians did not bat.

26th Match: v England (Headingley)   July 27, 28, 29.
Australia 146 (K. R. Stackpole 52, D. L. Underwood 4-37) and 136 (D. L. Underwood 6-45) lost to England 263 (R. Illingworth 57, A. A. Mallett 5-114) and 21-1 by 9 wkts.

27th Match: v Scotland (Perth)   Aug 2, 3.
Scotland 159 (R. Ellis 56) and 78 (J. W. Gleeson 4-26) lost to Australians 142-8 dec (B. C. Francis 58, K. M. Hardie 5-21) and 96-4 by 6 wkts.*

28th Match: v Northamptonshire (Northampton)   Aug 5, 7, 8.
Australians 191 (B. S. Bedi 5-57) and 143 (G. D. Watson 52, B. S. Bedi 4-53) lost to Northamptonshire 210 (Mushtaq Mohammad 88, G. Cook 62, G. D. Watson 5-36) and 125-3 (D. S. Steele 60*) by 7 wkts.

29th Match: v England (Oval)   Aug 10, 11, 12, 14, 15, 16.
England 284 (A. P. E. Knott 92, P. H. Parfitt 51, D. K. Lillee 5-58) and 356- (B. Wood 90, A. P. E. Knott 63, D. K. Lillee 5-123) lost to Australia 399 (I. M. Chappell 118, G. S. Chappell 113, R. Edwards 79, D. L. Underwood 4-90) and 242-5 (K. R. Stackpole 79) by 5 wkts.

30th Match: v Kent (Canterbury)   Aug 19, 21, 22.
Australians 330-4 dec (K. D. Walters 150, G. S. Chappell 141*) and 90-1 beat Kent 139 (D. Nicholls 50, J. W. Gleeson 5-21) and 278 (A. G. E. Ealham 68, M. C. Cowdrey 64, G. S. Chappell 4-24) by 9 wkts.

31st Match: v England (Old Trafford)   Aug 24 (55 overs a side).
Australia 222-8 (R. Edwards 57, I. M. Chappell 53) lost to England 226-4 (D. L. Amiss 103, K. W. R. Fletcher 60) by 6 wkts.

32nd Match: v England (Lord's)   Aug 26 (55 overs a side).
England 236-9 (A. P. E. Knott 50) lost to Australia 240-5 (K. R. Stackpole 52, A. P. Sheahan 50) by 5 wkts.

33rd Match: v England (Edgbaston)   Aug 28 (55 overs a side).
Australia 179-9 (K. R. Stackpole 61, G. G. Arnold 4-27) lost to England 180-8 by 2 wkts.

34th Match: v Lancashire (Old Trafford)   Aug 30, 31.
Australians 208 (H. B. Taber 54) and 154 lost to Lancashire 200-5 dec (B. Wood 58*) and 165-1 (H. Pilling 61*) by 9 wkts.

35th Match: v T. N. Pearce's XI (Scarborough)   Sept 2, 4.
T. N. Pearce's XI 254 (G. R. J. Roope 60) and 148 (D. B. Close 51*, G. S. Chappell 7-58) lost to Australians 265-4 dec (G. D. Watson 157) and 139-4 (G. S. Chappell 67*) by 6 wkts.

36th Match: v T. N. Pearce's XI (Scarborough)   Sept 3 (40 overs a side).
T. N. Pearce's XI 199-9 (Mushtaq Mohammad 74) beat Australians 186 (G. D. Watson 56, G. G. Arnold 5-15) by 13 runs.

37th Match: v T. N. Pearce's XI (Scarborough)   Sept 5 (35 overs a side).
T. N. Pearce's XI 236 lost to Australians 239-4 (A. P. Sheahan 105, R. Edwards 90) by 6 wkts.*

Bob Massie bowling at Lord's in the 1972 Test Match. Massie, moving the ball prodigiously in the air, achieved the best debut of any bowler in Test history with 16 wickets in the match. The non-striker is Ray Illingworth, the England captain.

Australia; K. R. Stackpole and A. P. Sheahan of Victoria; K. D. Walters, B. C. Frances, H. B. Taber, D. J. Colley and J. W. Gleeson of New South Wales; G. D. Watson, R. W. Marsh, R. Edwards, R. J. Inverarity, D. K. Lillee and R. A. L. Massie of Western Australia, with R. Steele as manager and F. Bennett as his assistant. Surprise omissions were McKenzie, O'Keeffe and Redpath—in an effort to find a pair of fast bowlers, the selectors chose Hammond to partner Lillee. The side was very young and it was hoped that this relatively unknown team would put Australia back on the cricketing map.

In England the side made a poor start, being very badly served by the weather and neither the batsmen nor the fast bowlers really settled down until mid-June.

England won the First Test, played mainly in exceptionally cold weather, but in the Second Test Australia brought the series level with an easy victory. After a drawn game at Trent Bridge England took the lead in the Fourth Match, only to see Australia win the final game by five wickets. The public showed increasing interest in the contests and in the match at the Oval there was a full house on three days.

Lillee took 31 wickets in the Test series—a new record—and in combination with the accurate Massie dominated the attack; Massie took 23 wickets and both bowlers averaged 17 runs per victim. The most reliable of the batsmen was Stackpole who hit 485 Test runs, average 53.88; he was closely followed by Greg Chappell. The weakness in the batting was the lack of sound openers: Edwards was tried but preferred No. 6 and Francis and Watson were also disappointing. Marsh, an excellent wicket-keeper, proved a very useful batsmen late in the order. Of the spin bowlers Gleeson, the leg-spinner, was ineffective and the main burden was left to Mallett's off-breaks. Hammond, suffering an injured back, did not play in the Tests.

Apart from some misses in the slips the fielding was good and Ian Chappell, besides batting well, proved an adventurous captain.

1972: East Africans

The first East African side to tour England flew into London on 1 June. The side was J. Shah (captain), K. Vasapi, Zulfiqar Ahmed, C. Sharma, A. Lakhani, M. Queraishy, Rhaguvir, N. Thakker, H. Shah, P. Mehta, V. Tapu, P. Papel, L. Fernandes, Kibaya, U.

Patel and Walusimbi, with Major Hugh Collins as manager.

The tourists won five and lost five matches in all. The highlight of the tour was a one-day match at Lord's in which C. Sharma hit 44, but the M.C.C. team, which was composed of ten players who had appeared in first-class cricket, won by 86 runs.

The leading batsmen were J. Shah and C. Sharma, who both hit 725 runs, and H. Shah who scored 680 and also took 22 wickets. The best bowler was Zulfiqar Ahmed who captured 49 wickets at a cost of 308 runs.

1972: East Africans

It has been possible to track down the scores of only nine of the 21 fixtures, namely:

1st Match: v M.C.C. (Lord's)   June 17.
M.C.C. 249-4 dec (A. R. Day 67, D. L. Hays 64) beat East Africans 163 by 86 runs.

2nd Match: v Cambridge U. (Cambridge)   June 18, 19, 20.
Cambridge U. 360 (M. J. Khan 220, Zulfiqar Ahmed 5-76) and 169 (L. Fernandes 7-40) lost to East Africans 278 (A. Lakhani 110) and 258-6 (Jagoo 85, Jawahir Shah 72) by 4 wkts.

3rd Match: v UAU (Coventry)   July 4.
UAU 104 lost to East Africans 105-3 by 7 wkts.

4th Match: v Nottinghamshire (Trent Bridge)   July 5.
Nottinghamshire 254-8 dec (M. J. Smedley 72, B. Hassan 67, K. Vasani 5-57) lost to East Africans 255-9 (H. Shah 83, N. Tapu 52*) by 1 wkt.

5th Match: v Derbyshire II (Derby)   July 6, 7.
Derbyshire II 259-4 dec (H. Cartwright 103*, A. Hill 72, A. J. Harvey-Walker 50) and 134-8 dec (H. Cartwright 53) drew with East Africans 244-6 dec (Zulfiqar Ahmed 69) and 118-9.

6th Match: v Warwickshire (Edgbaston)   July 15, 17, 18.
Warwickshire 376 (E. E. Hemmings 72, J. Whitehouse 64, J. A. Jameson 57, K. Ibadulla 69, W. Blenkiron 54) and 195 (A. I. Kallicharran 113, U. Patel 5-66) beat East Africans 175 (A. Lakhani 79) and 100 (S. J. Rouse 6-34) by 296 runs.

7th Match: v Surrey II (Oval).
Surrey II 238 (L. E. Skinner 53, R. Ward 51, K. Vasani 5-56) and 251 (B. Howarth 71, L. Fernandes 5-40) drew with East Africans 227-7 dec (H. Shah 60, C. Sharma 56) and 133-4.

8th Match: v Club Cricket Conference (New Malden).
East Africans 255-6 dec (Jawahir Shah 91, A. Lakhani 66) and 151 (M. T. Dunn 4-22) drew with C.C.C. 227-5 dec (N. Virk 64, D. J. Evans*) and 144-8.

9th Match: v v Lancashire II (Blackburn).
Lancashire II 194-8 dec drew with East Africans 36-1.

1972: Argentinian tour

On 23 June the first team from Argentina began a 12-match tour of England. The team was F. A. Forrester (captain), C. G. Nino, D. A. Annand, R. P. Daly, J. G. A. Ferguson, P. F. Hastrup, P. Sidersky, R. J. Villamil all of Belgrano; D. Drewery and J. S. Sylvester of BACRC; R. C. Gibson, M. G. Pellens, R. J. M. Lord, A. G. Raffo, M. J. Rodman, M. E. Ryan of Lomas with I.

MacGowan as manager.

Ferguson was the best batsman with 739 runs, average 52.7; Hastrup, who opened with Ferguson also batted well, as did Raffo and Ryan. The weakness of the side was its pace attack which relied mainly on Lord who took 14 wickets, average 24.2. The spinners were Ferguson, Drewery and Forrester.

Good fielding was a feature of the team's cricket and Raffo kept wicket with panache.

The principal match of the tour was against M.C.C. at Lord's, where due to some good batting by P. E. Richardson, the tourists were defeated; their record of four wins against two defeats however was very creditable.

1973: 8th New Zealanders

The team chosen to tour England in the first half of 1973 was B. E. Congdon (captain), D. R. Hadlee, R. J. Hadlee, B. F. Hastings, V. Pollard and K. J. Wadsworth of Canterbury; G. M. Turner and R. W. Anderson of Otago; M. G. Burgess, H. J. Howarth and R. E. Redmond of Auckland; R. O. Collinge and B. R. Taylor of Wellington; E. K. Gillott and J. M. Parker of Northern Districts, with J. C. Saunders as manager. P. G. Coman, regarded as the personality of the 1972-73 domestic season, and the old internationals Vivian and Jarvis were omitted. There was an optimistic air about the side, which had two regular county players in Turner and Parker, with valuable experience of English conditions.

Though England won the Test series by two matches to nil, New Zealand had the best of the drawn game and came near to beating England at Trent Bridge—needing 479 for victory, they made 440. Curiously Turner and Parker, who opened in each Test, both failed and it was left to Pollard, Congdon and Burgess to score runs against England. All three had excellent tours.

1973: 8th New Zealanders

Batting Averages

	M	I	NO	R	HS	Avge	100	c/s
G. M. Turner	17	28	6	1380	153*	62.72	5	14
B. E. Congdon	16	22	4	1081	176	60.05	3	7
M. G. Burgess	16	20	3	836	141	49.17	3	13
V. Pollard	15	18	5	629	116	48.38	2	2
B. F. Hastings	17	24	7	662	86	38.94	0	12
J. M. Parker	15	25	3	648	106	29.45	1	12/2
R. E. Redmond	10	18	1	483	79	28.41	0	5
K. J. Wadsworth	18	18	4	372	67	26.57	0	42/4
R. W. Anderson	11	16	3	316	52	24.30	0	5
H. J. Howarth	11	7	4	69	17	23.00	0	13
B. R. Taylor	12	14	2	254	53	21.16	0	7
R. J. Hadlee	12	7	2	74	30	14.80	0	0
D. R. Hadlee	14	11	3	110	34	13.75	0	5
R. O. Collinge	15	9	2	57	17	8.14	0	2
E. K. Gillott	10	2	1	2	1*	2.00	0	2

Bowling Averages

	O	M	R	W	Avge	BB	5i
R. O. Collinge	449.2	114	1118	51	21.92	6-52	2
D. R. Hadlee	332.4	58	980	38	25.78	5-35	1
R. J. Hadlee	355.1	72	1058	38	27.84	5-56	1
B. R. Taylor	361	80	1003	34	29.50	5-37	1
B. E. Congdon	234.2	57	610	20	30.50	3-26	0
H. J. Howarth	454.3	134	1139	31	36.74	5-70	2
E. K. Gillott	136.5	24	422	10	42.20	4-46	0
V. Pollard	202	54	514	10	51.40	2-24	0

Also bowled: R. W. Anderson 1.4-0-6-0; M. G. Burgess 4-1-21-0; B. F. Hastings 4-1-11-0; J. M. Parker 2-0-13-0; R. E. Redmond 5-1-16-0.

Burgess played some most attractive innings and Congdon's 176 at Trent Bridge was the best single effort on the whole tour. Redmond and Anderson had a moderate time, the former having problems with contact lenses.

Of the bowlers, Collinge, an accurate left-arm seamer, headed both Test and first-class averages. Richard Hadlee appeared a very promising prospect among the faster bowlers, but the spinners achieved little.

The determined effort made by New Zealand in the First Test whetted the public's appetite and for once there was a great deal of interest in the tour which was reflected at the turnstiles.

1973: 8th New Zealanders

1st Match: v London New Zealand C.C. (Oval) April 19 (55 overs a side).
New Zealanders 246-6 (J. M. Parker 71) beat London N.Z. 184 (R. Hutchinson 52, R. O. Collinge 5-35) by 61 runs.

2nd Match: v D. H. Robins' XI (Eastbourne) April 24, 25, 26.
New Zealanders 250 (R. E. Redmond 65, J. N. Graham 4-25) and 299-2 dec (G. M. Turner 151*, B. E. Congdon 77, R. E. Redmond 57) drew with D. H. Robins' XI 223 (B. A. Richards 102, R. O. Collinge 4-41) and 298-9 (D. R. Turner 103, M. J. Smith 66, R. J. Hadlee 4-96).

3rd Match: v Worcestershire (Worcester) April 28, 29, 30.
New Zealanders 369-3 dec (G. M. Turner 143, B. E. Congdon 93, R. E. Redmond 79) and 26-0 drew with Worcestershire 230 (D. E. R. Stewart 69, R. O. Collinge 6-52).

4th Match: v Hampshire (Bournemouth) May 2, 3, 4.
Hampshire 223 (B. A. Richards 87, H. J. Howarth 4-63) drew with 182-4 (G. M. Turner 85).

5th Match: v Kent (Canterbury) May 5, 7, 8.
Kent 201-8 dec (M. H. Dennes 78*) and 185-5 (M. C. Cowdrey 96) drew with New Zealanders 155 (R. B. Elms 4-46).

6th Match: v Gloucestershire (Bristol) May 9, 10, 11.
Gloucestershire 355-5 dec (Sadiq Mohammad 184, M. J. Procter 85) and 126-3 dec drew with New Zealanders 284 (K. J. Wadsworth 67, B. R. Taylor 53, D. A. Graveney 4-79) and 32-1.

7th Match: v Somerset (Taunton) May 12, 13, 14.
New Zealanders 335-4 dec (J. M. Parker 106, B. F. Hastings 85*, G. M. Turner 81) and 130-4 drew with Somerset 251 (P. W. Denning 85*, J. M. Parks 68, B. R. Taylor 5-37, E. K. Gillott 4-46).

8th Match: v Glamorgan (Sophia Gardens, Cardiff) May 16, 17, 18.
Glamorgan 315-5 dec (R. C. Fredericks 98, M. J. Khan 60) and 217-3 dec (R. C. Fredericks 106, A. R. Lewis 56*) lost to New Zealanders 341-7 dec (M. G. Burgess 124*, B. E. Congdon 79, G. M. Turner 53) and 194-7 by 3 wkts.

9th Match: v M.C.C. (Lord's) May 19, 21, 22.
New Zealanders 259-1 dec (G. M. Turner 153*, J. M. Parker 88) and 63-4 dec drew with M.C.C. 146-2 dec (D. Lloyd 66*) and 37-2.

10th Match: v Derbyshire (Derby) May 23, 24, 25.
New Zealanders 144-4 dec (J. M. Parker 51) and 109-2 dec (G. M. Turner 66*) drew with Derbyshire 48-4 dec and 98-2.

11th Match: v Leicestershire (Leicester) May 26, 28, 29.
New Zealanders 283-3 dec (B. E. Congdon 134*) and 30-3 drew with Leicestershire 214-4 dec (R. Illingworth 63*).

12th Match: v Northamptonshire (Northampton) May 30, 31, June 1.
New Zealanders 247-6 dec (G. M. Turner 111, B. E. Congdon 72, B. S. Bedi 4-70) and 151-2 dec (J. M. Parker 69*) drew with Northamptonshire 163 (R. T. Virgin 50, B. R. Taylor 4-28) and 139-4 (D. S. Steele 64*).

13th Match: v Lancashire (Old Trafford) June 2, 4, 5.
Lancashire 116 (R. O. Collinge 4-44) and 164 (C. H. Lloyd 56, J. Sullivan 54, R. J. Hadlee 5-56) lost to New Zealanders 221 (B. F. Hastings 60, P. G. Lee 4-58, K. Shuttleworth 4-80) and 63-1 by 9 wkts.

14th Match: v England (Trent Bridge) June 7, 8, 9, 11, 12.
England 250 (G. Boycott 51, D. R. Hadlee 4-42, B. R. Taylor 4-53) and 325-8 dec (A. W. Greig 139, D. L. Amiss 138*) beat New Zealand 97 (A. W. Greig 4-33) and 440 (B. E. Congdon 176, V. Pollard 116, G. G. Arnold 5-131) by 38 runs.

15th Match: v Oxford and Cambridge Universities (Cambridge) June 13, 14, 15.
New Zealanders 250 (M. G. Burgess 73, Imran Khan 4-81) and 259-7 dec (R. E. Redmond 61, R. W. Anderson 52) drew with Oxford and Cambridge 299 (Imran Khan 73, H. J. Howarth 5-70) and 207-9 (Imran Khan 88, A. K. C. Jones 60, H. J. Howarth 5-75).

16th Match: v Warwickshire (Edgbaston) June 16, 18, 19.
Warwickshire 306-9 dec (M. J. K. Smith 95, R. N. Abberley 56, D. R. Hadlee 5-35) and 112-5 drew with New Zealanders 356 (V. Pollard 72, G. M. Turner 67, E. E. Hemmings 4-83).

17th Match: v England (Lord's) June 21, 22, 23, 25, 26.
England 253 (A. W. Greig 63, G. Boycott 61, G. R. J. Roope 56) and 463-9 (K. W. R. Fletcher 178, G. Boycott 92, G. R. J. Roope 51, H. J. Howarth 4-144) drew with New Zealand 551-9 dec (B. E. Congdon 175, M. G. Burgess 105, V. Pollard 105*, B. F. Hastings 86, C. M. Old 5-113).

18th Match: v Surrey (Oval) June 30, July 1, 2.
Surrey 199 (D. R. Owen-Thomas 59, D. R. Hadlee 4-37, R. O. Collinge 4-53) and 336-4 dec (Younis Ahmed 141*, D. R. Owen-Thomas 76) drew with New Zealanders 320-4 dec (G. M. Turner 121*) and 100-4.

19th Match: v England (Headingley) July 5, 6, 7, 9, 10.
New Zealand 276 (M. G. Burgess 87, V. Pollard 62, C. M. Old 4-71) and 142 (G. M. Turner 81, G. G. Arnold 5-27) lost to England 419 (G. Boycott 115, K. W. R. Fletcher 81, R. Illingworth 65, R. O. Collinge 5-74) by an innings and 1 run.

20th Match: v Scotland (Forthill, Dundee) July 11, 12.
New Zealanders 243-8 dec (J. M. Parker 69, B. E. Congdon 69) drew with Scotland 89 (H. J. Howarth 5-38) and 159-7.

21st Match: v Essex (Westcliff) July 14, 16, 17.
New Zealanders 358-7 dec (M. G. Burgess 141, V. Pollard 73, B. F. Hastings 67) beat Essex 181 (R. J. Hadlee 4-44) and 159 (B. R. Taylor 4-39) by an innings and 18 runs.

22nd Match: v England (Swansea) July 18 (55 overs a side).
New Zealand 158 (V. Pollard 55, J. A. Snow 4-32) lost to England 159-3 (D. L. Amiss 100) by 7 wkts.

23rd Match: v England (Old Trafford) July 20 (55 overs a side).
England 167-8 drew with New Zealand did not bat.

Richard Collinge bowling for New Zealand in the Second Test at Lord's during the 1973 tour. Collinge headed both Test and tour averages for the visitors.

1973: 12th West Indies

The team to tour England during the second half of 1973 was R. B. Kanhai (captain), S. G. Camacho, R. C. Fredericks, L. R. Gibbs, A. I. Kallicharran and C. H. Lloyd, all of Guyana; Inshan Ali, B. D. Julien and D. L. Murray from Trinidad; K. D. Boyce, V. A. Holder and D. A. Murray of Barbados; M. L. C. Foster and L. G. Rowe of Jamaica; G. C. Shillingford from the Windward Islands; E. T. Willett of the Leeward Islands, with E. S. M. Kentish as manager and G. L. Gibbs as his assistant. G. St A. Sobers stated that he would be available, if required for the Test

1973: 12th West Indians

Batting Averages

	M	I	NO	R	HS	Avge	100	c/s
G. St A. Sobers	3	5	1	306	150*	76.50	1	7
M. L. C. Foster	15	20	7	828	127	63.69	1	4
C. H. Lloyd	15	23	4	1128	174	59.36	3	7
R. B. Kanhai	12	16	3	653	157	50.23	2	6
R. C. Fredericks	14	25	2	1091	150	47.43	2	7
A. I. Kallicharran	13	20	1	889	135	46.78	3	13
B. D. Julien	11	13	0	521	127	40.07	2	6
D. A. Murray	10	13	5	285	107*	35.62	1	28/8
G. S. Camacho	2	4	1	97	63	32.33	0	0
E. T. Willett	11	9	5	115	56	28.75	0	8
L. G. Rowe	8	13	1	344	84	28.66	0	6
K. D. Boyce	11	13	1	312	87	26.00	0	5
R. G. A. Headley	7	13	0	292	62	22.46	0	5
D. L. Murray	12	15	3	260	53*	21.66	0	26/5
G. C. Shillingford	11	8	5	65	35*	21.66	0	1
Inshan Ali	11	8	1	123	63	17.57	0	5
V. A. Holder	11	11	1	111	23*	11.10	0	5
L. R. Gibbs	10	7	5	14	4*	7.00	0	6

Bowling Averages

	O	M	R	W	Avge	BB	5i
C. H. Lloyd	56	12	133	6	22.16	2-26	0
K. D. Boyce	294	52	921	41	22.46	6-77	3
E. T. Willett	251.4	77	694	30	23.13	8-73	2
V. A. Holder	318	87	724	28	25.85	4-28	0
B. D. Julien	253	52	722	27	26.74	5-53	2
Inshan Ali	352.2	87	1020	38	26.84	6-55	1
M. L. C. Foster	84	28	191	7	27.28	2-48	0
L. R. Gibbs	332.4	105	676	24	28.16	3-26	0
G. St A. Sobers	82.1	24	169	6	28.16	3-27	0
G. C. Shillingford	224.5	46	720	22	32.72	4-33	0
R. B. Kanhai	13.3	1	58	1	58.00	1-12	0
R. C. Fredericks	25	2	120	1	120.00	1-25	0

Also bowled: D. A. Murray 1-0-10-0.

Matches, and was selected to play in all three.

The alteration in the rules governing the registration of overseas players for county cricket was quite dramatically apparent in this 1973 side—no fewer than 11 of the team (including Sobers) were playing in English county cricket in

<table>
<tr><td>

1973: 12th West Indians

1st Match: v Essex (Chelmsford)   June 20, 21, 22.
West Indians 130-3 dec (G. S. Camacho 63) and 137-9 dec (D. L. Acfield 4-28) drew with Essex 59-3 dec and 153-9 (V. A. Holder 4-28).

2nd Match: v Hampshire (Southampton)   June 23, 25, 26.
West Indians 354-3 dec (R. C. Fredericks 122, R. B. Kanhai 119*, C. H. Lloyd 81) and 203-3 dec (C. H. Lloyd 86*) beat Hampshire 256 (R. V. Lewis 98, B. D. Julien 5-89, Inshan Ali 4-48) and 127 (B. D. Julien 4-41) by 174 runs.

3rd Match: v D. H. Robins' XI (Eastbourne)   June 27, 28, 29.
West Indians 328 (A. I. Kallicharran 113, B. D. Julien 55) and 159 (Intikhab Alam 5-53) lost to D. H. Robins' XI 316-8 dec (G. Boycott 114, Mushtaq Mohammad 55) and 172-0 (D. L. Amiss 95*, G. Boycott 74*) by 10 wkts.

4th Match: v Nottinghamshire (Trent Bridge)   June 30, July 2, 3.
Nottinghamshire 223 (M. J. Harris 106) and 292 (M. J. Smedley 110, R. A. White 80, K. D. Boyce 4-47) lost to West Indians 351-6 dec (A. I. Kallicharran 124, M. L. C. Foster 81*) and 166-1 (L. G. Rowe 84, R. C. Fredericks 82*) by 9 wkts.

5th Match: v Middlesex (Lord's)   July 4, 5, 6.
Middlesex 305-8 dec (J. M. Brearley 87, N. G. Featherstone 55) and 155-3 (J. M. Brearley 70*) drew with West Indians 341-5 dec (M. L. C. Foster 95, C. H. Lloyd 78, A. I. Kallicharran 60).

6th Match: v Glamorgan (Swansea)   July 7, 9, 10.
Glamorgan 255 (A. Jones 90, E. T. Willett 8-73) and 171 (A. Jones 60) lost to West Indians 437-7 dec (A. I. Kallicharran 135, R. C. Fredericks 91, C. H. Lloyd 55) by an innings and 11 runs.

7th Match: v Glamorgan (Swansea)   July 8 (39 overs a side).
West Indians 247-9 (B. D. Julien 104, C. H. Lloyd 55) beat Glamorgan 239-5 (R. C. Davis 101, A. Jones 63) by 8 runs.

8th Match: v Combined Services (Portsmouth)   July 12, 13.
Combined Services 113 (Inshan Ali 4-27) and 75 (L. R. Gibbs 5-8, Inshan Ali 4-38) lost to West Indians 266-7 dec (K. D. Boyce 96, R. B. Kanhai 66) by an innings and 78 runs.

9th Match: v Sussex (Hove)   July 14, 16, 17.
Sussex 205 (B. D. Julien 5-53) and 32-2 drew with West Indians 292-8 dec (C. H. Lloyd 102*, R. B. Kanhai 64, L. G. Rowe 54).

10th Match: v Kent (Canterbury)   July 18, 19, 20.
West Indians 336-6 dec (M. L. C. Foster 127, D. A. Murray 107*) and 236-4 dec (R. C. Fredericks 97, C. H. Lloyd 85) drew with Kent 300-5 dec (Asif Iqbal 113*, M. C. Cowdrey 59*) and 136-5.

11th Match: v Young England (Old Trafford)   July 21, 23, 24.
West Indians 137-3 dec (R. B. Kanhai 59*) and 55-1 drew with Young England 150-6 dec (D. L. Bairstow 57*, G. C. Shillingford 4-33).

12th Match: v England (Oval)   July 26, 27, 28, 30, 31.
West Indians 415 (C. H. Lloyd 132, A. I. Kallicharran 80, K. D. Boyce 72, G. G. Arnold 5-113) and 255 (A. I. Kallicharran 80, G. St A. Sobers 51) beat England 257 (G. Boycott 97, K. D. Boyce 5-70) and 255 (F. C. Hayes 106*, K. D. Boyce 6-77) by 158 runs.

13th Match: v Minor Counties (Torquay)   Aug 1, 2, 3.
Minor Counties 300-8 dec (A. G. Warrington 92) and 242-6 dec (S. Greensword 84*) drew with West Indians 294-8 dec (M. L. C. Foster 83, Inshan Ali 63) and 202-8 (M. L. C. Foster 79, P. Bradley 4-57).

14th Match: v Gloucestershire (Cheltenham)   Aug 4, 6, 7.
Gloucestershire 213-9 dec (Zaheer Abbas 81, K. D. Boyce 5-45) and 93-7 dec (E. T. Willett 5-35) drew with West Indians 197 (K. D. Boyce 87, R. G. A. Headley 62) and 104-6.

15th Match: v England (Edgbaston)   Aug 9, 10, 11, 13, 14.
West Indians 327 (R. C. Fredericks 150, B. D. Julien 54) and 302 (C. H. Lloyd 94, G. St A. Sobers 74, R. B. Kanhai 54, G. G. Arnold 4-43) drew with England 305 (G. Boycott 56*, D. L. Amiss 56, K. W. R. Fletcher 52) and 182-2 (D. L. Amiss 86*).

16th Match: v Yorkshire League (Harrogate)   Aug 16 (45 overs a side).
West Indians 186 (D. A. Murray 54) lost to Yorkshire League 187-4 (P. J. Squires 84) by 6 wkts.

17th Match: v Yorkshire (Scarborough)   Aug 18, 20, 21.
Yorkshire 312-5 dec (R. G. Lumb 103, G. Boycott 93, P. J. Sharpe 61) and 71-0 drew with West Indians 307 (R. B. Kanhai 73, E. T. Willett 56, D. A. Murray 50*).

18th Match: v England (Lord's)   Aug 23, 24, 25, 27, 28.
West Indians 652-8 dec (R. B. Kanhai 157, G. St A. Sobers 150*, B. D. Julien 121, C. H. Loyd 63, R. C. Fredericks 51, R. G. D. Willis 4-118) beat England 233 (K. W. R. Fletcher 68, K. D. Boyce 4-50, V. A. Holder 4-56) and 193 (K. W. R. Fletcher 86*, K. D. Boyce 4-49) by an innings and 226 runs.

19th Match: v Derbyshire (Chesterfield)   Aug 29, 30, 31.
West Indians 350-4 dec (C. H. Lloyd 174, M. L. C. Foster 73*, R. G. A. Headley 59) and 154-2 dec (R. C. Fredericks 88*) beat Derbyshire 203-9 dec (A. Hill 73, S. Venkataraghavan 51*) and 138 (J. B. Bolus 51, Inshan Ali 6-55) by 163 runs.

20th Match: v T. N. Pearce's XI (Scarborough)   Sept 1, 3, 4.
West Indians 274 (B. D. Julien 127, R. A. Woolmer 4-41) and 177-7 dec (M. L. C. Foster 60*) drew with T. N. Pearce's XI 219-7 dec (Mushtaq Mohammad 55) and 93-5.

21st Match: v T. N. Pearce's XI (Scarborough)   Sept 2 (40 overs a side).
T. N. Pearce's XI 211-8 (Asif Iqbal 60) lost to West Indians 213-4 (R. C. Fredericks 71) by 6 wkts.

22nd Match: v England (Headingley)   Sept 5 (55 overs a side).
West Indies 181 (R. B. Kanhai 55) lost to England 182-9 (M. H. Denness 66) by 1 wkt.

23rd Match: v England (Oval)   Sept 7 (55 overs a side).
England 189-9 (K. W. R. Fletcher 63) lost to West Indies 190-2 (R. C. Fredericks 105, A. I. Kallicharran 53).*

</td></tr>
</table>

1973. Warwickshire alone had four of the tourists—Kanhai, Kallicharran, Murray and Gibbs. Of the team that represented the West Indies in the First Test of 1973, ten were in fact English county players. The mystique of a group of cricketers, mostly unknown to the English public, travelling thousands of miles to challenge the home team had gone. Would the public turn out to watch the 'tourists', when the same cricketers could be seen daily in county cricket? In the event the interest in matches between the counties and the tourists was minimal, but the Test Matches and one-day internationals still commanded attention.

The visitors confounded predictions that they would struggle against England by winning the Test series two matches to nil, although they only drew the one-day games, one match each. The batting was exceptionally strong. Sobers topped the Test table with 306 runs, average 76.50, and five others—Lloyd, Fredericks, Kanhai, Julien and Kallicharran—all averaged above 40. The attack was dominated by the fast bowling of Boyce, whose 19 Test wickets cost 15.47 each; Holder provided useful support for Boyce and the leading spinner was Gibbs. Sobers and Julien completed the Test line up.

Early in the tour both Camacho and Rowe had to leave the team due to injury and R. G. A. Headley of Jamaica and Worcestershire was co-opted into the side. He played in two Tests without achieving a great deal.

The fielding, with Lloyd and Kallicharran the stars, was excellent and the two Murrays kept wicket well, though D. L. was preferred in the Tests.

Rohan Kanhai playing a typical forcing shot for the 1973 West Indians at Lord's where he made 157 in an innings victory. Knott is the wicketkeeper and Hayes the slip.

The 1973 West Indian tourists. Back row: L. Pink, Kallicharran, Inshan Ali, Julien, Boyce, Holder, Shillingford, Headley, Foster, Willett, D. A. Murray. Front row: E. Kentish (manager), D. L. Murray, Lloyd, Sobers, Kanhai (capt), L. Gibbs, Fredericks, G. Gibbs (assistant manager).

gave indications of future promise—Madan Lal as an all-rounder.

The fielding standard fell and an injured Engineer was not very effective behind the wicket.

The tour ended with two one-day internationals, both of which the Indians lost. The attendances at Old Trafford (21,175 over five days) and Edgbaston (19,900 over four days) were affected by poor weather.

1974: 9th Indians

The team of 1974 was little changed from the side that had won an historic Test victory in 1971. The 1974 members were A. L. Wadekar (captain), S. Venkataraghavan, S. Abid Ali, B. S. Bedi, G. Bose, B. S. Chandrasekhar, F. M. Engineer, S. M. Gavaskar, S. M. H. Kirmani, A. V. Mankad, Madan Lal, S. S. Naik, B. P. Patel, E. A. S. Prasanna, E. D. Solkar, G. R. Viswanath, with Lt.-Col. H. R. Adhikari as manager and B. C. Mohanty as treasurer. Gavaskar had batted in very poor form in 1973-74 and kept his place merely on his reputation. Kirmani was preferred to Krishnamurthy, who had broken a finger in Sri Lanka. A surprising omission was the young pace bowler Salgaonkar.

The spinning combination of Venkat, Chandra, Bedi and Prasanna, which had been such a factor in the success of 1971, completely failed in the Test series, which the Indians lost three matches to nil, with Abid Ali the pace bowler at the top of the table with a meagre 6 wickets, average 42.00.

The weakness in the bowling was not compensated for by the batsmen. Gavaskar did show some return to form with a century and a 50 in the First Test, but did little in the two other games; only Engineer and Viswanath proved at all reliable. No-one else managed a batting average of even 20. Patel and Madan Lal both

1974: 9th Indians

Batting Averages	M	I	NO	R	HS	Avge	100	c/s
S. M. H. Kirmani	9	10	7	144	46*	48.00	0	12/7
S. M. Gavaskar	14	26	2	993	136	41.37	3	6
S. S. Naik	11	21	3	730	135	40.55	2	3
F. M. Engineer	9	17	4	500	108	38.46	1	17/1
A. V. Mankad	13	22	6	611	66*	38.18	0	5
A. L. Wadekar	14	24	2	783	138	35.59	1	7
Madan Lal	12	18	6	399	79*	33.25	0	11
G. R. Viswanath	15	26	3	705	106	30.65	2	7
E. D. Solkar	15	27	2	709	109	28.36	1	9
B. P. Patel	14	22	3	511	107	26.89	2	6
S. Abid Ali	14	22	4	470	71	26.11	0	5
G. Bose	9	18	0	328	66	18.22	0	4
S. Ventakaraghavan	13	17	4	168	28	12.92	0	8
B. S. Bedi	13	11	3	73	19	9.12	0	6
E. A. S. Prasanna	13	13	3	52	13	5.20	0	4
B. S. Chandrasekhar	10	5	3	2	2*	1.00	0	7

Bowling Averages	O	M	R	W	Avge	BB	5i
G. Bose	15.4	1	42	4	10.50	4-23	0
S. M. Gavaskar	19	3	60	2	30.00	1-7	0
S. Abid Ali	324.4	64	965	32	30.15	6-23	2
B. S. Chandrasekhar	258.5	33	789	26	30.34	5-80	1
B. S. Bedi	604	150	1651	53	31.15	6-110	5
Madan Lal	412.4	89	1263	31	40.74	7-95	1
E. A. S. Prasanna	425.4	88	1261	28	45.03	4-59	0
E. D. Solkar	250.2	62	680	14	48.57	3-73	0
S. Ventakaraghavan	356	75	970	18	53.88	4-35	0

Also bowled: A. V. Mankad 15-1-58-1; G. R. Viswanath 3-0-26-0.

Bishan Bedi, India's slow left-arm bowler on the tour of 1974—not a successful one for the visitors, who lost all the Tests.

1974: 5th Pakistanis

The 16 players selected to tour England during the second half of 1974 were announced in April: Intikhab Alam (captain), Wasim Raja, Zaheer Abbas, Shafiq Ahmed, Majid J. Khan, Sadiq Mohammad, Mushtaq Mohammad, Asif Iqbal, Aftab Gul, Aftab Baloch, Asif Masood, Sarfraz Nawaz, Naseer Malik, Wasim Bari, Mohammad Nazir and Maazullah Khan, with Omar Qureshi as manager and Zafar Altaf as his assistant. It was agreed that Imran Khan could be co-opted after the university term, if the tour selection committee desired.

Three notable absentees were Saleem Altaf, Pervez Sajjad and Talat Ali—Pervez's omission meant the side lacked a left-arm spinner. Critics felt that the bowling was weak and the only way to overcome this deficiency was for the batsmen to score large totals fast.

The three Tests were all drawn, the first two due to rain and the last to a dead wicket which allowed the bowlers no chance. Pakistan ended the summer by winning both the one-day internationals quite convincingly, however. Majid Khan scored a brilliant hundred in the first match, then in the Second England collapsed on a wicket helping the seam bowlers, after which Zaheer hit 57 not out in 17 overs to secure victory.

The tourists were undefeated in their programme of 22 matches and the averages reflected the great batting potential. Four players averaged over 50 and two more over 40. Zaheer was in splendid form, as was Wasim Raja, Majid and the two Mohammad brothers.

The bowling was opened by Sarfaz and Asif Masood, who were

assisted by Asif Iqbal. Intikhab was the most useful of the spinners. As with the 1973 West Indies, the leading players were all English county cricketers and this experience no doubt helped to produce the strongest Pakistani side ever to tour England.

The second tourists of 1974, Pakistan, were much more successful than the first, India, thanks to their very strong batting line-up, in which Zaheer Abbas showed particularly good form. He made 240 in the Third Test at the Oval.

1974: 5th Pakistanis

1st Match: v Leicestershire (Leicester)   June 19, 20, 21.
Pakistanis 214-8 dec (Shafiq Ahmed 68, Sadiq Ahmed 68, Sadiq Mohammad 58) and 210-6 dec (Shafiq Ahmed 100*) beat Leicestershire 103 and 220 (B. F. Davison 69, J. C. Balderstone 69, Intikhab Alam 5-67) by 101 runs.

2nd Match: v Somerset (Bath)   June 22, 23, 24.
Pakistanis 311-6 dec (Mushtaq Mohammad 101, Asif Iqbal 77, Sadiq Mohammad 53) and 223-5 dec (Sadiq Mohammad 62, Shafiq Ahmed 59) beat Somerset 215 (P. W. Denning 60, Asif Iqbal 4-46) and 314 (G. I. Burgess 90, Nasir Malik 5-86) by 5 runs.

3rd Match: v Universities Athletic Union (Colwyn Bay)   June 26, 27.
Pakistanis 281-6 dec (Aftab Gul 84, Zaheer Abbas 68, Aftab Baloch 51) beat UAU 104 (Nasir Malik 5-26) and 100 (Wasim Raja 5-28) by an innings and 77 runs.

4th Match: v Middlesex (Lord's)   June 29, July 1, 2.
Pakistanis 208-6 dec (M. J. Khan 105, Asif Iqbal 64) and 113-4 (Intikhab Alam 61) beat Middlesex 77 (Asif Masood 5-35) and 242 (M. J. Smith 101, Mushtaq Mohammad 7-59) by 6 wkts.

5th Match: v Northamptonshire (Northampton)   July 3, 4, 5.
Pakistanis 145-2 (Sadiq Mohammad 69*, Zaheer Abbas 62*) drew with Northamptonshire did not bat.

6th Match: v Kent (Canterbury)   July 6, 8, 9.
Kent 294 (M. C. Cowdrey 105, D. Nicholls 77, G. W. Johnson 58, Mushtaq Mohammad 5-58) and 132 (Sarfraz Nawaz 5-44) lost to Pakistanis 298 (Sadiq Mohammad 106, Safiq Ahmed 66, G. W. Johnson 4-52) and 132-1 (M. J. Khan 53*) by 9 wkts.

7th Match: v Combined Services (Aldershot)   July 11, 12.
Combined Services 179-6 dec and 135 (M. Robinson 54, Asif Masood 5-8) lost to Pakistanis 174-4 dec (Shafiq Ahmed 74) and 142-3 (Shafiq Ahmed 73*) by 7 wkts.*

8th Match: v Warwickshire (Edgbaston)   July 13, 15, 16.
Warwickshire 416-9 dec (J. A. Jameson 88, M. J. K. Smith 81, E. E. Hemmings 74, A. I. Kallicharran 51) drew with Pakistanis 302-3 (M. J. Khan 134*, Aftab Gul 81, Mushtaq Mohammad 61*).

9th Match: v Nottinghamshire (Trent Bridge)   July 17, 18.
Nottinghamshire 51 (Sarfraz Nawaz 8-27) and 140 (B. Hassan 83*, Mushtaq Mohammad 5-30) lost to Pakistanis 240 (Intikhab Alam 57) by an innings and 49 runs.

10th Match: v Minor Counties (Jesmond)   July 20, 21, 22.
Minor Counties 290 (J. Abrahams 78, R. C. Kerslake 64, D. Bailey 60, Mushtaq Mohammad 4-47) and 194 (J. R. Turner 106) lost to Pakistanis 358-3 dec (Zaheer Abbas 137, Aftab Gul 112) and 129-5 by 5 wkts.

11th Match: v England (Headingley)   July 25, 26, 27, 29, 30.
Pakistan 285 (M. J. Khan 75, Sarfraz Nawaz 53) and 179 drew with England 183 and 238-6 (J. H. Edrich 70, K. W. R. Fletcher 67*, Sarfraz Nawaz 4-56).

12th Match: v D. H. Robins' XI (Eastbourne)   July 31, Aug 1, 2.
D. H. Robins' XI 403-5 dec (C. G. Greenidge 273*, R. N. Abberley 55, Nasir Malik 4-108) and 252-5 dec (B. A. Richards 100) lost to Pakistanis 319 (Sadiq Mohammad 104, Wasim Raja 74, R. S. Hanley 5-52) and 338-4 (M. J. Khan 114, Sadiq Mohammad 86, Mushtaq Mohammad 54) by 6 wkts.

13th Match: v Glamorgan (Swansea)   Aug 3, 4, 5.
Pakistanis 359-8 dec (Wasim Raja 139*, Zaheer Abbas 104) beat Glamorgan 107 (Sarfraz Nawaz 6-47) and 170 (Intikhab Alam 5-66) by an innings and 82 runs.

14th Match: v England (Lord's)   Aug 8, 9, 10, 12, 13.
Pakistan 130-9 dec (D. L. Underwood 5-20) and 226 (Mushtaq Mohammad 76, Wasim Raja 53, D. L. Underwood 8-51) drew with England 270 (A. P. E. Knott 83) and 27-0.

15th Match: v Lancashire (Old Trafford)   Aug 17, 19, 20.
Pakistan 282-5 dec (Mushtaq Mohammad 98, Asif Iqbal 65, M. J. Khan 61) and 232-6 dec (Sadiq Mohammad 50, Zaheer Abas 50) drew with Lancashire 213-5 dec (H. Pilling 75*) and 30-2.

16th Match: v England (Oval)   Aug 22, 23, 24, 26, 27.
Pakistan 600-7 dec (Zaheer Abbas 240, M. J. Khan 98, Mushtaq Mohammad 76) and 94-4 drew with England 545 (D. L. Amiss 183, K. W. R. Fletcher 122, C. M. Old 65, Intikhab Alam 5-116).

17th Match: v Sussex (Hove)   Aug 28, 29, 30.
Sussex 348-5 dec (J. D. Morley 85, M. J. J. Faber 58, A. W. Greig 59, G. A. Greenidge 55) and 157 (Nasir Malik 5-61) lost to Pakistanis 352-9 dec (Zaheer Abbas 117, Intikhab Alam 58, Imran Khan 56, Sadiq Mohammad 54) and 156-1 (Sadiq Mohammad 76*) by 9 wkts.

18th Match: v England (Trent Bridge)   Aug 31 (55 overs a side).
England 244-4 (D. Lloyd 116) lost to Pakistan 246-3 (M. J. Khan 109) by 7 wkts. (Note: Match reduced to 50 overs owing to rain).*

19th Match: v England (Edgbaston)   Sept 2, 3 (55 overs a side).
England 81-9 lost to Pakistan 84-2 (Zaheer Abbas 57) by 8 wkts (Note: Match reduced to 35 overs owing to rain).*

20th Match: v Worcestershire (Worcester)   Sept 4, 5, 6.
Match abandoned–no play due to rain.

21st Match: v T. N. Pearce's XI (Scarborough)   Sept 7, 9, 10.
Pakistanis 231 (M. J. Khan 87, S. Turner 5-48) and 53-4 drew with T. N. Pearce's XI 288 (N. G. Featherstone 60, Sadiq Mohammad 5-126).

22nd Match: v T. N. Pearce's XI (Scarborough)   Sept 8 (40 overs a side).
Pakistanis 130 (B. S. Bedi 7-21) beat T. N. Pearce's XI 109-9 (Asif Masood 5-23) by 21 runs. (Note: Match reduced to 27 overs owing to rain).

23rd Match: v Yorkshire League XI (Harrogate)   Sept 11.
Yorkshire League XI 79 (Asif Masood 4-10) lost to Pakistanis 80-3 by 7 wkts.

1974: 5th Pakistanis

Batting Averages

	M	I	NO	R	HS	Avge	100	c/s
Wasim Raja	11	15	6	486	139*	54.00	1	5
Zaheer Abbas	16	23	4	975	240	51.31	4	10
Shafiq Ahmed	7	12	3	451	100*	50.11	1	5
Majid J. Khan	14	23	3	1000	134*	50.00	3	13
Sadiq Mohammad	14	24	2	1007	106	45.77	2	17
Mushtaq Mohammad	14	21	3	730	101*	40.55	1	7
Asif Iqbal	12	16	2	447	77	31.92	0	6
Imran Khan	8	10	2	249	56*	31.12	0	3
Aftab Gul	6	10	0	293	112	29.30	1	1
Aftab Baloch	7	8	4	101	42*	25.25	0	4
Asif Masood	12	5	4	25	17*	25.00	0	3
Intikhab Alam	13	18	2	323	61	20.18	0	4
Sarfraz Nawaz	11	12	4	161	53	20.12	0	6
Naseer Malik	7	5	1	48	21	12.00	0	4
Wasim Bari	14	13	3	104	30*	9.45	0	35/5
Mohammad Nazir	6	4	3	9	9*	9.00	0	3
Maazullah Khan	4	2	1	1	1	1.00	0	3

Bowling Averages

	O	M	R	W	Avge	BB	5i
Mushtaq Mohammad	227.3	57	662	37	17.89	7-59	3
Asif Iqbal	78	20	200	10	20.00	4-46	0
Sarfraz Nawaz	326.4	91	774·	37	20.91	8-27	3
Asif Masood	260	64	603	29	21.00	5-35	1
Sadiq Mohammad	30.5	5	155	7	22.14	5-126	1
Intikhab Alam	328.3	75	994	44	22.59	5-66	3
Naseer Malik	127.1	14	538	20	26.90	5-61	2
Imran Khan	211	45	625	15	41.66	3-65	0
Wasim Raja	123	23	400	9	44.44	3-92	0
Aftab Baloch	21	2	106	2	53.00	2-91	0
Mohammad Nazir	118	33	366	4	91.50	2-83	0
Maazullah Khan	68	16	183	1	183.00	1-32	0

Also bowled: Majid J. Khan 3-1-10-0; Zaheer Abbas 1-0-5-0.

1975: Proposed South African tour

In September 1973 the Cricket Council announced, as had been anticipated, that the proposed 1975 tour of England by South Africa was cancelled.

1975: Prudential World Cup

On 25 and 26 July 1973 the I.C.C. approved a T.C.C.B. plan for a tournament of 60-overs-a-side matches to be played between the six Test-playing countries plus East Africa and Sri Lanka in the English season of 1975. The tournament was to be sponsored by the Prudential Assurance Company.

The players involved were as follows:

New Zealand: G. M. Turner (captain), D. R. O'Sullivan, B. J. McKechnie, R. J. Hadlee, J. F. M. Morrison, H. J. Howarth, B. L. Cairns, J. M. Parker, B. G. Hadlee, G. P. Howarth, R. O. Collinge, B. F. Hastings, D. R. Hadlee, K. J. Wadsworth and J. Heslop as manager.

Pakistan: Majid J. Khan (captain), Pervez Mir, Wasim Raja, Sarfraz Nawaz, Naseer Malik, Shafiq Ahmed, Javed Miandad, Zaheer Abbas, Wasim Bari, Asif Masood, Mushtaq Mohammad, Sadiq Mohammad, Asif Iqbal and Imran Khan.

India: S. Venkataraghavan (captain), S. M. H. Kirmani, M. Amarnath, A. D. Gaekwad, K. D. Ghavri, E. D. Solkar, P. Sharma, B. P. Patel, Madan Lal, G. R. Viswanath, S. Abid Ali, S. M. Gavaskar, F. M. Engineer, B. S. Bedi and G. S. Ramchand as manager.

East Africa: R. Shah (captain), Ramesh Sethi, Frasat Ali, Yunus Badat, Hamish McLeod, John Nagenda, Shiraz Sumar, Praful Mehta, P. G. Nana, D. Pringle, Zulfiqar Ali, S. Walusimba, Jawahir Shah, Mehmood Quaraishy and Jammer Singh as manager.

Sri Lanka: A. Tennekoon (captain), B. Warnapura, L. Kaluperuma, A. Opatha, D. Chanmugam, A. de Silva, A. Ranasinghe, D. Mendis, D. de Silva, M. Pieris, M. Tissera, D. Heyn, S. Wettimuny and E. R. Fernando.

West Indies: C. H. Lloyd (captain), C. G. Greenidge, M. L. C. Foster, I. V. A. Richards, K. D. Boyce, V. A. Holder, A. M. E. Roberts, C. L. King, B. D. Julien, A. I. Kallicharran, R. B. Kanhai, D. L. Murray, L. R. Gibbs, R. C. Fredericks, with C. L. Walcott as manager.

Australia: see following entry on 1975 tour.

Played in beautiful weather and with a number of highly interesting contests, this new venture proved very popular. The overall receipts were about £200,000 and about 158,000 people attended. The final at Lord's was an excellent game lasting late into the evening. Chappell put the West Indies in to bat, but was thwarted by Lloyd's masterly innings.

Australia's 1975 World Cup squad. Back row: Mallett, Gilmour, Lillee, Thomson, Hurst, Walker, McCosker, Turner. Front row: Edwards, Walters, I. Chappell (capt), G. Chappell, Marsh, Laird.

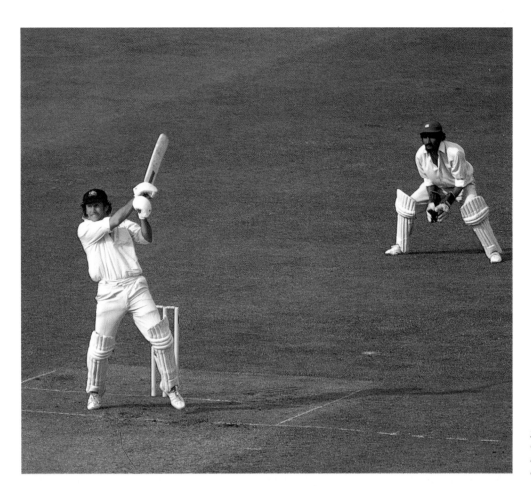

Left *Ian Chappell, captain of the 1975 Australian tourists, also led his team to the final of the Prudential World Cup, in which they lost to the powerful West Indians.*

The decisive innings of the 1975 World Cup final was the powerfully authoritative century by Clive Lloyd, seen here thrashing the ball past backward point.

1975: 27th Australians

The Australian authorities agreed to a Test Match series of four (originally three) games to be played after the World Cup Tournament. The Australian team was I. M. Chappell (captain) and A. A. Mallett of South Australia; K. D. Walters, R. B. McCosker, G. J. Gilmour and A. Turner of New South Wales; G. S. Chappell and J. R. Thomson from Queensland; R. Edwards, B. M. Laird, R W. Marsh and D. K. Lillee of Western Australia; R. D. Robinson, M. H. N. Walker, A. G. Hurst and J. D. Higgs of Victoria, with F. Bennett as manager. The team was a very youthful one and included a phalanx of fast bowlers in Lillee and Thomson, a formidable pair who had destroyed England's tourists the previous winter, Walker, Gilmour and Hurst.

Australia won the First Test, after being put in to bat, by an innings and with a day and a half in hand; Lillee and Thomson destroyed England. The Second Test was a high-scoring draw and then at Headingley vandals sabotaged the wicket by pouring oil on it. In the last Test Australia gained an enormous first innings lead, but England fought back to force a draw on a very placid pitch, so Australia won the series one match to nil.

Lillee took 21 Test wickets at an average of 21.90 and was the most effective bowler in the series. Thomson obtained 16 Test wickets, but tended to have periods of wildness. Gilmour looked a very good all-rounder, though he was selected to play in only one Test.

The best of the batsmen were Ian Chappell and McCosker. In the Tests McCosker headed the averages with 414 runs, average 82.80, but he was closely followed by Ian Chappell; brother Greg had a very poor series, though he did well enough in the county matches. Walters was another who had a good first-class record and a poor Test one and Australia relied very much on Edwards to steady the boat. The fielding was excellent, especially in the slips

and gully. Marsh coped well with the erratic Thomson and was also a useful lower order batsman.

As usual, the crowds came by the thousand to the Tests, though interest in county games continued to decline.

1975: 27th Australians

Batting Averages

	M	I	NO	R	HS	Avge	100	c/s
K. D. Walters	12	18	5	784	103*	60.30	3	13
R. B. McCosker	11	20	2	1078	127	59.88	4	3
I. M. Chappell	11	19	0	1022	192	53.78	4	4
G. S. Chappell	12	20	3	762	144	44.82	2	17
G. J. Gilmour	10	14	5	389	102	43.22	1	10
R. Edwards	12	20	4	675	101	42.18	1	3
R. D. Robinson	7	9	3	223	41	37.16	0	23/7
A. Turner	11	20	1	654	156	34.42	2	6
B. M. Laird	9	17	2	488	127	32.53	1	3
R. W. Marsh	12	17	2	469	65*	31.26	0	26/2
J. R. Thomson	10	10	4	186	49	31.00	0	5
D. K. Lillee	9	9	4	154	73*	30.80	0	1
A. A. Mallett	13	12	8	112	25*	28.00	0	13
M. H. N. Walker	10	12	3	134	25	14.88	0	5
A. G. Hurst	8	4	1	15	10*	5.00	0	4
J. D. Higgs	8	2	1	0	0*	0.00	0	3

Bowling Averages

	O	M	R	W	Avge	BB	5i
D. K. Lillee	345	107	886	41	21.60	7-67	2
K. D. Walters	47.5	9	169	7	24.14	4-34	0
G. J. Gilmour	225.1	47	789	28	28.17	6-85	1
M. H. N. Walker	374.1	94	1076	36	29.88	5-48	1
G. S. Chappell	48	16	150	5	30.00	2-22	0
I. M. Chappell	64.3	18	183	6	30.50	2-30	0
J. R. Thomson	338.1	88	1059	34	31.14	5-38	1
A. G. Hurst	197.4	49	659	21	31.38	3-8	0
J. D. Higgs	209.1	44	889	27	32.92	5-96	1
A. A. Mallett	400.5	118	1225	31	39.51	4-70	0

Also bowled: R. Edwards 5-0-27-0; B. M. Laird 2-0-7-0.

Jeff Thomson's menacing field in the First Test between England and Australia at Edgbaston. Thomson is bowling to Knott with a ring of six from slip to gully. Australia won by an innings.

1975: 27th Australians

1st Match: v Middlesex (Lord's)   June 1 (35 overs a side).
Australians 217-8 (G. S. Chappell 105) beat Middlesex 193-5 (J. M. Brearley 87) by 24 runs.

2nd Match to 6th Match: see Prudential Cup details.

7th Match: v Kent (Canterbury)   June 25, 26, 27.
Australians 415-8 dec (A. Turner 156, R. B. McCosker 58, K. D. Walters 50) and 140-3 dec (B. M. Laird 63) lost to Kent 202 (J. D. Higgs 4-49) and 354-6 (M. C. Cowdrey 151, R. A. Woolmer 71*) by 4 wkts.

8th Match: v Hampshire (Southampton)   June 28, 30, July 1.
Hampshire 351-7 dec (B. A. Richards 96, D. R. Turner 87, T. E. Jesty 79) and 247-3 dec (C. G. Greenidge 74, B. A. Richards 69*) lost to Australians 344-6 dec (G. S. Chappell 86, R. Edwards 74*) and 256-6 (I. M. Chappell 127) by 4 wkts.

9th Match: v M.C.C. (Lord's)   July 2, 3, 4.
M.C.C. 242 (G. A. Gooch 75, R. A. Woolmer 55, J. D. Higgs 4-36) and 190 (R. A. Woolmer 85, D. K. Lillee 7-67) lost to Australians 163 (B. M. Laird 55, R. A. Woolmer 4-45) and 270-3 (K. D. Walters 103*, G. S. Chappell 86*) by 7 wkts.

10th Match: v Glamorgan (Swansea)   July 5, 6, 7.
Glamorgan 302-8 dec (M. J. Khan 110, A. Jones 68, A. L. Jones 55) and 239 (R. C. Davis 87) lost to Australians 386 (G. S. Chappell 144, R. W. Marsh 64, M. A. Nash 4-86) and 157-3 by 7 wkts.

11th Match: v England (Edgbaston)   July 10, 11, 12, 14.
Australia 359 (R. W. Marsh 61, R. B. McCosker 59, R. Edwards 56, I. M. Chappell 52) beat England 101 (D. K. Lillee 5-15,.M. H. N. Walker 5-48) and 173 (K. W. R. Fletcher 51, J. R. Thomson 5-38) by an innings and 85 runs.

12th Match: v Sussex (Hove)   July 16, 17, 18.
Australians 402-7 dec (G. S. Chappell 126, R. B. McCosker 111, G. J. Gilmour 102, C. E. Waller 4-140) and 334-5 (R. B. McCosker 115, K. D. Walters 78) drew with Sussex 401-6 dec (A. E. W. Parsons 141, A. W. Greig 129*).

13th Match: v Derbyshire (Chesterfield)   July 19, 21, 22.
Australians 398-9 dec (I. M. Chappell 114, A. Turner 82) beat Derbyshire 184 (J. R. Thomson 4-54) and 176 by an innings and 38 runs.

14th Match: v Lancashire (Old Trafford)   July 23, 24, 25.
Lancashire 189 and 140-1 dec (B. Wood 84*) drew with Australians 105-7 dec (P. G. Lee 4-42) and 101-4.

15th Match: v Leicestershire (Leicester)   July 26, 28, 29.
Leicestershire 370 (B. F. Davison 189) and 217-2 dec (J. F. Steele 87*, B. Dudleston 80) beat Australians 313-4 dec (R. B. McCosker 120, I. M. Chappell 69) and 243 (K. D. Walters 102*, G. J. Gilmour 59) by 31 runs.

16th Match: v England (Lord's)   July 31, Aug 1, 2, 4, 5.
England 315 (A. W. Greig 96, A. P. E. Knott 69, D. S. Steele 50, D. K. Lillee 4-84) and 436-7 dec (J. H. Edrich 175, B. Wood 52) drew with Australia 268 (R. Edwards 99, J. A. Snow 4-66) and 329-3 (I. M. Chappell 86, R. B. McCosker 79, G. S. Chappell 73*, R. Edwards 52*).

17th Match: v Somerset (Taunton)   Aug 6, 7, 8.
Australians 331-7 dec (K. D. Walters 103, R. Edwards 56) and 57-1 (G. J. Gilmour 51*) beat Somerset 106 and 281 (B. C. Rose 68, D. B. Close 52, J. D. Higgs 5-96, A. A. Mallett 4-70) by 9 wkts.

18th Match: v Northamptonshire (Northampton)   Aug 9, 11, 12.
Northamptonshire 210 (J. R. Thomson 4-64) and 317 (D. S. Steele 102, Mushtaq Mohammad 85, M. H. N. Walker 4-52) lost to Australians 210 (B. S. Bedi 4-51) and 318-5 (I. M. Chappell 116, R. W. Marsh 65*, G. S. Chappell 58) by 5 wkts.

19th Match: v England (Headingley)   Aug 14, 15, 16, 18, 19.
England 288 (D. S. Steele 73, J. H. Edrich 62, A. W. Greig 51, G. J. Gilmour 6-85) and 291 (D. S. Steele 92) drew with Australia 135 (P. H. Edmonds 5-28) and 220-3 (R. B. McCosker 95*, I. M. Chappell 62). (Note: The pitch was sabotaged on the night of the 18th/19th and the game abandoned as a draw in consequence).

20th Match: v Essex (Chelmsford)   Aug 23, 25, 26.
Australians 365-6 dec (B. M. Laird 127, R. Edwards 101) and 325-4 dec (A. Turner 118, B. M. Laird 79, K. D. Walters 61*) beat Essex 338-8 dec (K. S. McEwan 71, K. D. Boyce 79, G. A. Gooch 68) and 254 (R. N. S. Hobbs 100, B. R. Hardie 88*) by 98 runs.

21st Match: v England (Oval)   Aug 28, 29, 30, Sept 1, 2.
Australia 532-9 dec (I. M. Chappell 192, R. B. McCosker 127, K. D. Walters 65) and 40-2 drew with England 191 (J. R. Thomson 4-50, M. H. N. Walker 4-63) and 538 (R. A. Woolmer 149, J. H. Edrich 96, G. R. J. Roope 77, D. S. Steele 66, A. P. E. Knott 64, K. D. Walters 4-34).

1976: 13th West Indies

The team, which was not announced until 26 April, was C. H. Lloyd (captain), R. C. Fredericks and A. I. Kallicharran of Guyana; W. W. Daniel, C. G. Greenidge, V. A. Holder, C. L. King and A. L. Padmore of Barbados; T. M. Findlay of the Windward Islands; H. A. Gomes, B. D. Julien, R. R. Jumadeen and D. L. Murray of Trinidad; M. A. Holding and L. G. Rowe of Jamaica; I. V. A. Richards and A. M. E. Roberts of the Leeward Islands, with C. L. Walcott as manager and F. L. Thomas as his assistant.

The very late selection was because the last Test of the West Indies v India series in the West Indies did not finish until 25 April and thus the West Indies side flew, virtually without a break in their international cricket commitments, to England to begin their tour. Any idea that this non-stop cricket would make them

The 1976 West Indians were very strong in fast bowling. Michael Holding had an exceptional match at the Oval in the Fifth Test, taking 14 wickets, including bowling Balderstone.

stale was soon dispelled: they won the Test series against England three matches to nil and at the end of it all slaughtered England three-nil in the one-day internationals, never being in danger of defeat. Their overall first-class record of 18 victories was the best ever by a West Indian side in England.

In the splendid fast attack of Holding, Roberts, Holder and Daniel, the visitors had an ideal combination for the dry wickets of 1976 and in fact the four took 84 of the 91 Test wickets to fall, the spinners, Jumadeen and Padmore being superfluous. There was considerable criticism of the many bouncers used by the West Indian bowlers, intimidation which was unnecessary as the England batsmen were already subdued.

As for the batting, Richards proved himself to be the equal of any of his contemporaries, in the Tests hitting 829 runs, average 118.42. If he had not been absent injured for one Test, the great batsman might well have become the first player to exceed a 1,000 runs in a single Test series.

Greenidge had not been a regular member of the West Indies team before the tour, but his experience with Hampshire proved invaluable and he scored 592 runs in the Tests, average 65.77. Fredericks also played an important part in the matches against England; his fluent stroke play at the start of the innings seemed to blunt the edge of the England attack. Lloyd batted dependably, but was rarely needed; Kallicharran injured a shoulder and missed many matches; King and Rowe both played some good innings.

The tour was a great success and 383,000 people watched the five Tests.

1976: 13th West Indians

1st Match: v Lavinia, Duchess of Norfolk's XI (Arundel Castle) May 8.
Duchess of Norfolk's XI 202-7 dec lost to West Indians 205-3 (C. G. Greenidge 84, A. I. Kallicharran 68) by 7 wkts.

2nd Match: v National Cricket Association XI (Oval) May 9.
West Indians 183-7 dec (I. V. A. Richards 52) drew with NCA 116-8.

3rd Match: v Surrey (Oval) May 12, 13, 14.
Surrey 303-5 dec (J. H. Edrich 118, A. R. Butcher 83, C. J. Aworth 55*) and 252 (A. R. Butcher 59) drew with West Indians 316-5 dec (C. H. Lloyd 152*, H. A. Gomes 85) and 97-3.

4th Match: v Hampshire (Southampton) May 15, 16, 17.
Hampshire 152 (V. A. Holder 5-44) and 131 (T. E. Jesty 55, A. L. Padmore 5-49) lost to West Indians 371-6 dec (I. V. A. Richards 176, H. A. Gomes 56) by an innings and 88 runs.

5th Match: v Kent (Canterbury) May 19, 20, 21.
West Indians 267-5 dec (A. I. Kallicharran 83, B. D. Julien 62*, H. A. Gomes 61) and 171-5 dec beat Kent 192-4 dec (R. A. Woolmer 114*) and 94 (B. D. Julien 5-33, W. W. Daniel 4-33) by 152 runs.

6th Match: v M.C.C. (Lord's) May 22, 24, 25.
West Indians 251-9 dec (C. G. Greenidge 82, C. H. Lloyd 60, A. Ward 4-60) and 248-3 dec (I. V. A. Richards 113, H. A. Gomes 101*) beat M.C.C. 197 (R. M. C. Gilliat 66, M. A. Holding 4-44) and 83 (V. A. Holder 5-23) by 219 runs.

7th Match: v Somerset (Taunton) May 26, 27, 28.
West Indians 389-8 dec (C. L. King 105*, C. H. Lloyd 70, I. V. A. Richards 51) and 261-1 dec (C. G. Greenidge 115, L. G. Rowe 70*, C. L. King 66*) beat Somerset 317 (D. B. Close 88, I. T. Botham 56, W. W. Daniel 5-77) and 192 (B. D. Julien 4-22) by 141 runs.

8th Match: v Sussex (Hove) May 29, 31, June 1.
West Indians 220 and 207-6 dec (A. I. Kallicharran 63) drew with Sussex 225 (R. D. V. Knight 55, B. D. Julien 7-78) and 85-1 (K. C. Wessels 55*).

9th Match: v England (Trent Bridge) June 3, 4, 5, 7, 8.
West Indies 494 (I. V. A. Richards 232, A. I. Kallicharran 97, D. L. Underwood 4-82) and 176-5 dec (I. V. A. Richards 63, J. A. Snow 4-53) drew with England 332 (D. S. Steele 106, R. A. Woolmer 82, W. W. Daniel 4-53) and 156-2 (J. H. Edrich 76*).

10th Match: v Oxford and Cambridge Universities (Cambridge) June 9, 10, 11.
West Indians 394-6 dec (H. A. Gomes 147, A. I. Kallicharran 104, B. D. Julien 78) and 104-2 beat Oxford and Cambridge 234 (C. J. Tavare 64, R. R. Jumadeen 5-97) and 262 (C. J. Tavare 59, V. J. Marks 52) by 8 wkts.

11th Match: v Lancashire (Old Trafford) June 12, 13, 14.
Lancashire 293 (J. Simmons 74*) and 230-2 dec (D. Lloyd 82, F. M. Engineer 62*, B. Wood 55) lost to West Indians 332-5 dec (R. C. Fredericks 97, C. G. Greenidge 72) and 193-4 (C. G. Greenidge 86) by 6 wkts.

12th Match: v England (Lord's) June 17, 18, 19, 21, 22.
England 250 (D. B. Close 60, A. M. E. Roberts 5-60) and 254 (D. S. Steele 64, A. M. E. Roberts 5-63) drew with West Indies 182 (C. G. Greenidge 84, C. H. Lloyd 50, D. L. Underwood 5-39, J. A. Snow 4-68) and 241-6 (R. C. Fredericks 138).

13th Match: v Northamptonshire (Northampton) June 23, 24, 25.
West Indians 413-3 dec (H. A. Gomes 166*, C. L. King 163) and 16-0 beat Northamptonshire 172 (G. Cook 53, R. R. Jumadeen 5-47, W. W. Daniel 4-44) and 256 (D. S. Steele 56, R. R. Jumadeen 4-79) by 10 wkts.

14th Match: v Leicestershire (Leicester) June 26, 28, 29.
Leicestershire 306-3 dec (J. C. Balderstone 125, J. F. Steele 114) and 281-3 dec (J. C. Balderstone 98, D. I. Gower 89*, J. F. Steele 56) lost to West Indians 334-8 dec (C. L. King 146) and 257-3 (R. C. Fredericks 114, C. G. Greenidge 101*) by 7 wkts.

15th Match: v Yorkshire (Abbeydale Park) June 30, July 1, 2.
West Indians 103 (C. M. Old 7-42) and 192 (A. I. Kallicharran 56) beat Yorkshire 186 (W. W. Daniel 4-40) and 90 (W. W. Daniel 6-21) by 19 runs.

16th Match: v Derbyshire (Chesterfield) July 3, 5, 6.
Derbyshire 257 (G. Miller 83, A. Hill 79) and 261 (E. J. Barlow 61, A. L. Padmore 6-101) lost to West Indians 497-6 dec (H. A. Gomes 190, L. G. Rowe 152, C. H. Lloyd 98) and 23-0 by 10 wkts.

17th Match: v England (Old Trafford) July 8, 9, 10, 12, 13.
West Indies 211 (C. G. Greenidge 134, M. W. W. Selvey 4-41) and 411-5 dec (I. V. A. Richards 135, C. G. Greenidge 101, R. C. Fredericks 50) beat England 71 (M. A. Holding 5-17) and 126 (A. M. E. Roberts 6-37) by 425 runs.

18th Match: v Ireland (Dublin) July 14, 15.
West Indians 333-7 dec (C. G. Greenidge 117, D. L. Murray 52) and 114-4 dec (C. G. Greenidge 60) beat Ireland 68 (V. A. Holder 8-22) and 175 (I. J. Anderson 79, R. R. Jumadeen 5-39) by 204 runs.*

19th Match: v Warwickshire (Edgbaston) July 17, 19, 20.
West Indians 356 (L. G. Rowe 121, I. V. A. Richards 71, C. H. Lloyd 67, R. G. D. Willis 6-55) drew with Warwickshire 152-8 (V. A. Holder 6-55).

20th Match: v England (Headingley) July 22, 23, 24, 26, 27.
West Indies 450 (C. G. Greenidge 115, R. C. Fredericks 109, I. V. A. Richards 66, L. G. Rowe 50, J. A. Snow 4-77) and 196 (C. L. King 58, R. G. D. Willis 5-42) beat England 387 (A. W. Greig 116, A. P. E. Knott 116) and 204 (A. W. Greig 76*) by 55 runs.

21st Match: v Essex (Chelmsford) July 28, 29, 30.
West Indians 190 (C. G. Greenidge 71, G. A. Gooch 5-40) and 306 (T. M. Findlay 51*) beat Essex 294-8 dec (K. S. McEwan 76, C. L. King 4-93) and 97 by 105 runs.

22nd Match: v Middlesex (Lord's) July 31, Aug 2, 3.
West Indians 222 (C. G. Greenidge 123, F. J. Titmus 5-41, M. W. W. Selvey 4-58) and 308 (C. G. Greenidge 67, A. M. E. Roberts 56*, I. V. A. Richards 53, N. G. Featherstone 4-50) lost to Middlesex 257 (M. J. Smith 95, P. H. Edmonds 53, A. L. Padmore 6-69) and 275-6 (M. J. Smith 106, J. M. Brearley 62, A. L. Padmore 4-78) by 4 wkts.

23rd Match: v Minor Counties (Torquay) Aug 4, 5, 6.
Minor Counties 123 (V. A. Holder 5-35, B. D. Julien 4-58) and 329 (D. Bailey 85, R. Entwistle 50, R. R. jumadeen 4-132) lost to West Indians 354 (C. H. Lloyd 145*, I. V. A. Richards 98, H. A. Gomes 52, R. C. Kerslake 4-103) and 100-3.

24th Match: v Glamorgan (Swansea) Aug 7, 9, 10.
Glamorgan 226 (M. A. Nash 64, A. L. Padmore 5-84) and 147 (D. A. Francis 53, B. D. Julien 6-54) lost to West Indians 554-4 dec (C. H. Lloyd 201*, I. V. A. Richards 121, C. G. Greenidge 130, L. G. Rowe 88) by an innings and 181 runs.

25th Match: v Glamorgan (Swansea) Aug 8 (40 overs a side).
West Indians 236-6 (R. C. Fredericks 54, R. C. Ontong 4-44) beat Glamorgan 130 (R. C. Ontong 69) by 106 runs.

26th Match: v England (Oval) Aug 12, 13, 14, 16, 17.
West Indies 687-8 dec (I. V. A. Richards 291, C. H. Lloyd 84, R. C. Fredericks 71, L. G. Rowe 70, C. L. King 63) and 182-0 dec (R. C. Fredericks 86*, C. G. Greenidge 85*) beat England 435 (D. L. Amiss 203, A. P. E. Knott 50, M. A. Holding 8-92) and 203 (A. P. E. Knott 57, M. A. Holding 6-57) by 231 runs.

27th Match: v Worcestershire (Worcester) Aug 18, 19, 20.
Worcestershire 358-8 dec (P. A. Neale 143, B. L. d'Oliveira 60, D. N. Patel 51) and 86 lost to West Indians 408 (C. L. King 109, C. H. Lloyd 73, I. V. A. Richards 57, R. C. Fredericks 53, B. L. d'Oliveira 4-71) and 38-2.

28th Match: v Gloucestershire (Bristol) Aug 21, 23, 24.
West Indians 349-8 dec (C. L. King 103, B. D. Julien 89) and 242-7 dec (H. A. Gomes 111, D. L. Murray 55, D. A. Graveney 4-76) drew with Gloucestershire 265-9 dec (A. J. Hignell 119) and 282-9 (M. J. Procter 97, A. W. Stovold 65, A. L. Padmore 4-71).

29th Match: v England (Scarborough) Aug 26 (55 overs a side).
England 202-8 (G. D. Barlow 80, A. M. E. Roberts 4-32) lost to West Indies 207-3 (I. V. A. Richards 119) by 7 wkts.*

30th Match: v England (Lord's) Aug 28, 29 (55 overs a side).
West Indies 221 (I. V. A. Richards 97) beat England 185 (D. W. Randall 88, A. M. E. Roberts 4-27) by 36 runs.

31st Match: v England (Edgbaston) Aug 30, 31 (55 overs a side).
West Indies 223-9 (C. H. Lloyd 79) beat England 173 (V. A. Holder 5-50) by 50 runs. (Note: Match reduced to 32 overs a side due to rain.)

32nd Match: v Nottinghamshire (Trent Bridge) Sept 1, 2, 3.
Nottinghamshire 244 (D. W. Randall 85, P. A. Todd 59, R. R. Jumadeen 4-30) and 146 (R. R. Jumadeen 6-40) lost to West Indians 81 (W. K. Watson 4-23) and 313-5 (C. G. Greenidge 122, C. L. King 111) by 5 wkts.

33rd Match: v T. N. Pearce's XI (Scarborough) Sept 4, 6, 7.
West Indians 256 (C. G. Greenidge 89, C. L. King 61, P. H. Edmonds 6-67) and 173 (M. W. W. Selvey 4-55) lost to T. N. Pearce's XI 293 (P. H. Edmonds 103, G. D. Barlow 90, R. R. Jumadeen 4-95, A. L. Padmore 4-103) and 139-8 (R. O. Butcher 54*, R. R. Jumadeen 4-35) by 2 wkts.*

34th Match: v T. N. Pearce's XI (Scarborough) Sept 5 (40 overs a side).
T. N. Pearce's XI 162-8 (M. J. Smith 100) lost to West Indians 164-3 (R. C. Fredericks 79, L. G. Rowe 53) by 7 wkts.

35th Match: v Northern Leagues XI (Harrogate) Sept 8 (50 overs a side).
West Indians 280 (L. G. Rowe 106, I. V. A. Richards 60, D. Wilson 4-76) beat Northern Leagues XI 236-7 (J. P. G. Chadwick 52) by 44 runs.

1976: 13th West Indians

Batting Averages

	M	I	NO	R	HS	Avge	100	c/s
I. V. A. Richards	16	25	1	1724	291	71.83	6	17/1
C. H. Lloyd	19	26	4	1363	201*	61.95	3	23
C. G. Greenidge	20	38	3	1952	134	55.77	8	28
C. L. King	21	34	10	1320	163	55.00	6	27
H. A. Gomes	21	35	6	1393	190	48.03	5	5
L. G. Rowe	17	27	1	971	152	37.34	2	11
R. C. Fredericks	21	38	3	1250	138	35.71	3	19
A. I. Kallicharran	12	21	2	678	104	35.68	1	5
D. L. Murray	18	25	9	397	55	24.81	0	37/1
B. D. Julien	18	26	3	549	89	23.86	0	9
V. A. Holder	13	14	6	173	42*	21.62	0	2
T. M. Findlay	18	21	7	276	51*	19.71	0	36/8
A. M. E. Roberts	12	10	2	135	56*	16.87	0	5
M. A. Holding	12	13	1	152	42	12.66	0	5
A. L. Padmore	16	16	6	99	26*	9.90	0	4
W. W. Daniel	15	10	3	62	30	8.85	0	5
R. R. Jumadeen	17	12	4	49	21	6.12	0	14

Bowling Averages

	O	M	R	W	Avge	BB	5i
M. A. Holding	339.3	111	791	55	14.38	8-92	3
V. A. Holder	387.1	109	1004	52	19.30	6-55	4
W. W. Daniel	371.3	88	1106	52	21.26	6-21	2
A. L. Padmore	497.3	128	1381	59	23.40	6-69	4
A. M. E. Roberts	411.1	109	1089	44	24.75	6-37	3
B. D. Julien	468.4	126	1339	51	26.25	7-78	3
C. H. Lloyd	39	13	90	3	30.00	2-24	0
R. R. Jumadeen	584	140	1740	58	30.00	6-40	3
H. A. Gomes	157.3	41	434	14	31.00	2-5	0
R. C. Fredericks	124.4	26	401	12	33.41	3-10	0
C. L. King	348.4	91	928	27	34.37	4-93	0
I. V. A. Richards	31	12	56	1	56.00	1-11	0

Also bowled: D. L. Murray 5-2-12-0; A. I. Kallicharran 10-3-18-0.

1977: 28th Australians

At the end of the Centenary Test at Melbourne in March 1977 the following were announced as the team to represent the 28th Australians: G. S. Chappell (captain), G. Dymock and J. R. Thomson of Queensland; R. W. Marsh, K. J. Hughes, M. F. Malone and C. J. Serjeant of Western Australia; R. J. Bright, R. D. Robinson and M. H. N. Walker of Victoria; G. J. Cosier and D. W. Hookes of South Australia; I. C. Davies, R. B. McCosker, K. J. O'Keefe, L. S. Pascoe and K. D. Walters of New South Wales, with L. V. Maddocks as manager and N. T. McMahon as treasurer. Three major players were absent: Ian Chappell who had retired, Lillee who was not available and Edwards. Ten of the players selected were touring England for the first time with a Test team.

The tour began in terrible weather, with the first five first-class matches all rain affected and one totally washed out. In the middle of the deluge the story broke about 13 of the tourists signing lucrative contracts to play matches in a competition set up in rivalry to the Australian Board of Control–Kerry Packer's World Series Cricket.

It is debatable how much effect this conspiracy (Packer had negotiated with the players in secret some two months before) had on the general performance of the 1977 team, but it seemed that the majority of the players had very little interest in a successful outcome of the tour. In the event England won the Test series three matches to nil and the one-day internationals two to one. The tourists won only five first-class games during the summer–the worst record in the history of Australian touring teams.

Of the batsmen, Greg Chappell was easily the best, with 371 Test runs, average 41.22; Hookes came second, the only other to average 30 in the Tests. The rest did little and so the bowlers never had many runs to play with. Thomson, considering his injury problems, did well to secure 23 Test wickets at 25.34. Walker, Pascoe and Malone all had their moments of glory and the team's results would have been better if the catching had not failed so often.

A smiling Greg Chappell leads the 1977 Australians off the plane at Heathrow at the start of the 1977 tour. The visitors had an unsuccessful campaign, losing three and drawing one of the four Tests.

1977: 28th Australians

Batting Averages

	M	I	NO	R	HS	Avge	100	c/s
G. S. Chappell	16	25	5	1182	161*	59.10	5	18
K. J. O'Keeffe	13	19	12	355	48*	50.71	0	5
R. D. Robinson	14	23	4	715	137*	37.63	1	31/3
C. S. Serjeant	15	22	2	663	159	33.15	1	2
D. W. Hookes	17	26	1	804	108	32.16	1	4
G. J. Cosier	12	20	1	587	100	30.89	1	7
I. C. Davis	13	20	0	608	83	30.40	0	5
K. J. Hughes	14	19	0	540	95	28.42	0	10
K. D. Walters	17	26	1	663	88	26.52	0	8
R. J. Bright	14	19	8	287	53*	26.09	0	5
R. B. McCosker	18	32	1	737	107	23.77	1	20
R. W. Marsh	17	24	2	477	124	21.68	1	30/2
M. H. N. Walker	15	17	2	250	78*	16.66	0	2
G. Dymock	10	6	5	16	8*	16.00	0	2
M. F. Malone	10	10	3	95	46	13.57	0	4
J. R. Thomson	16	17	1	130	25	8.12	0	3
L. S. Pascoe	11	9	3	44	20	7.33	0	0

Bowling Averages

	O	M	R	W	Avge	BB	5i
R. J. Bright	333.5	114	794	39	20.35	5-67	2
L. S. Pascoe	323.4	79	893	41	21.78	6-68	1
M. H. N. Walker	514	154	1184	53	22.33	7-19	3
M. F. Malone	327	95	837	32	26.15	5-63	1
J. R. Thomson	385.2	84	1207	43	28.06	4-41	0
K. J. O'Keeffe	335.4	112	1035	36	28.75	4-21	0
G. Dymock	192	54	468	15	31.20	3-30	0
G. S. Chappell	106	28	304	6	50.66	3-45	0

Also bowled: G. J. Cosier 16-3-36-0; D. W. Hookes 4-0-18-1; R. B. McCosker 2-1-5-0; R. W. Marsh 1-0-6-0; K. D. Walters 17-5-30-0.

With the newspapers more interested in the affairs of Packer and the outcome of the pending court hearing, the Test series was rather dwarfed by these off the field activities. Altogether it was the most miserable season since the 1912 fiasco when the leading Australian players were at loggerheads with the Board.

Greg Chappell was one of the few Australian tourists to score consistently in 1977, making a fine century (out of his side's 218) in the Second Test and averaging almost 60 in all the first-class matches.

1977: 28th Australians

1st Match: v Lavinia, Duchess of Norfolk's XI (Arundel Castle)   April 27 (45 overs a side).
Australians 186-5 (C. S. Serjeant 65) beat Duchess of Norfolk's XI 166 (P. Willey 50, G. J. Cosier 4-18) by 20 runs.

2nd Match: v Surrey (Oval)   April 30, May 2, 3.
Surrey 327-8 (G. R. J. Roope 107*, J. H. Edrich 70) drew with Australians did not bat.

3rd Match: v Kent (Canterbury)   May 4, 5, 6.
Australians 240-7 dec (K. J. Hughes 80, C. S. Serjeant 55) drew with Kent 33-2.

4th Match: v Sussex (Hove)   May 7, 9, 10.
Australians 111-1 (C. S. Serjeant 55*) drew with Sussex did not bat.

5th Match: v Hampshire (Southampton)   May 11, 12, 13.
Match abandoned—no play due to rain.

6th Match: v Glamorgan (Swansea)   May 14, 15, 16.
Glamorgan 172 (A. Jones 59) and 164-4 dec (J. A. Hopkins 66, R. J. Bright 4-53) drew with Australians 153-6 dec (G. J. Cosier 56, M. A. Nash 4-71) and 86-6 (M. A. Nash 5-32).

7th Match: v Somerset (Bath)   May 18, 19, 20.
Australians 232 (G. S. Chappell 113, G. I. Burgess 5-25, J. Garner 4-66) and 289 (D. W. Hookes 108, C. S. Serjeant 50, I. T. Botham 4-98) lost to Somerset 340-5 dec (B. C. Rose 110*, I. T. Botham 59, P. A. Slocombe 55*) and 182-3 (I. V. A. Richards 53) by 7 wkts.

8th Match: v Gloucestershire (Bristol)   May 21, 23.
Australians 154 (R. J. Bright 53*, B. M. Brain 7-51) and 251 (G. S. Chappell 102, D. A. Graveney 5-70) beat Gloucestershire 63 (M. H. N. Walker 7-19) and 169 (L. S. Pascoe 4-36, R. J. Bright 4-63) bq 173 runs.

9th Match: v Gloucestershire (Bristol)   May 24 (45 overs a side).
Gloucestershire 195 (M. J. Procter 52) lost to Australians 196-4 (K. D. Walters 52*, K. J. Hughes 51) by 6 wkts.

10th Match: v M.C.C. (Lord's)   May 25, 26, 27.
Australians 194 (K. J. Hughes 60, M. Hendrick 4-28) and 235 (R. B. McCosker 73, M. Hendrick 4-32) beat M.C.C. 136 (D. W. Randall 50) and 214 (G. D. Barlow 54, D. W. Randall 51, K. J. O'Keeffe 4-56) by 79 runs.

11th Match: v Worcestershire (Worcester)   May 28, 29, 30.
Australians 358 (G. S. Chappell 100*, I. C. Davis 83) and 210-7 dec (N. Gifford 4-65) drew with Worcestershire 243 (J. A. Ormrod 73, G. M. Turner 69, R. J. Bright 5-91, L. S. Pascoe 4-40).

12th Match: v England (Old Trafford)   June 2 (55 overs a side).
Australia 169-9 lost to England 173-8 by 2 wkts.

13th Match: v England (Edgbaston)   June 4 (55 overs a side).
England 171 (G. S. Chappell 5-20) beat Australia 70 (J. K. Lever 4-29) by 101 runs.

14th Match: v England (Oval)   June 6 (55 overs a side).
England 242 (D. L. Amiss 108, J. M. Brearley 78) lost to Australia 246-8 (G. S. Chappell 125*, R. D. Robinson 70) by 2 wkts.

15th Match: v Ireland (Dublin)   June 9, 10.
Australians 291 (C. S. Serjeant 63, D. W. Hookes 58, J. M. Monteith 6-97) and 95-5 dec drew with Ireland 200-4 dec (J. F. Short 80*, B. A. O'Brien 51) and 104-3.

16th Match: v Essex (Chelmsford)   June 11, 12, 13.
Australians 274 (R. W. Marsh 124, G. A. Gooch 4-60, K. D. Boyce 4-90) and 206-4 dec (D. W. Hookes 69*, C. S. Serjeant 59) drew with Essex 170-2 dec (K. S. McEwan 100*) and 59-4.

17th Match: v England (Lord's)   June 16, 17, 18, 20, 21.
England 216 (R. A. Woolmer 79, D. W. Randall 53, J. R. Thomson 4-41) and 305 (R. A. Woolmer 120, A. W. Greig 91, J. R. Thomson 4-86) drew with Australia 296 (C. S. Serjeant 81, G. S. Chappell 66, K. D. Walters 53, R. G. D. Willis 7-78) and 114-6 (D. W. Hookes 50).

18th Match: v Oxford and Cambridge Universities (Oxford)   June 23, 24.
Oxford and Cambridge 130 and 240-8 dec (P. M. Roebuck 77, C. J. Tavare 60*, V. J. Marks 58) drew with Australians 188-4 dec (D. W. Hookes 74, I. C. Davis 55*) and 150-5 (K. J. Hughes 54, R. Le Q. Savage 4-52).

19th Match: v Nottinghamshire (Trent Bridge)   June 25, 26, 27.
Nottinghamshire 210 (M. F. Malone 4-62) and 223 (C. E. B. Rice 59) lost to Australians 531 (C. S. Serjeant 159, G. J. Cosier 100, K. J. Hughes 95, I. C. Davis 72, R. A. White 4-77, D. R. Doshi 4-135) by an innings and 98 runs.

20th Match: v Derbyshire (Chesterfield)   June 29, 30, July 1.
Derbyshire 126 (K. J. O'Keefe 4-21, L. S. Pascoe 4-23) and 136-4 (A. Hill 59*) drew with Australians 380 (K. J. Hughes 92, R. D. Robinson 77, I. C. Davis 53).

21st Match: v Yorkshire (Scarborough)   July 2, 3, 4.
Australians 186 (R. D. Robinson 54) and 215-7 dec (D. W. Hookes 67, C. S. Serjeant 55) drew with Yorkshire 75 (M. H. N. Walker 5-29, M. F. Malone 4-38) and 233-5 (G. Boycott 103, J. D. Love 59).

22nd Match: v England (Old Trafford)   July 7, 8, 9, 11, 12.
Australia 297 (K. D. Walters 88) and 218 (G. S. Chappell 112, D. L. Underwood 6-66) lost to England 437 (R. A. Woolmer 137, D. W. Randall 79, A. W. Greig 76) and 82-1 by 9 wkts.

23rd Match: v Northamptonshire (Northampton)   July 16, 18, 19.
Australians 328-6 dec (G. S. Chappell 161*, D. W. Hookes 53) and 238-4 dec (I. C. Davis 68, G. J. Cosier 54*) drew with Northamptonshire 236 (L. S. Pascoe 6-68) and 115-1 (R. T. Virgin 66*).

24th Match: v Warwickshire (Edgbaston)   July 20, 21, 22.
Australians 260-6 dec (R. B. McCosker 77, R. D. Robinson 70*) and 320-6 dec (R. D. Robinson 137*, G. J. Cosier 56, K. D. Walters 53) beat Warwickshire 260-5 dec (J. Whitehouse 114, R. N. Abberley 72) and 190 (A. I. Kallicharran 80, M. H. N. Walker 4-36, J. R. Thomson 4-61) by 130 runs.

25th Match: v Leicestershire (Leicester)   July 23, 24, 25.
Australians 229 (D. W. Hookes 59, P. Booth 4-42) and 148-1 (I. C. Davis 65, R. B. McCosker 59*) drew with Leicestershire 178 (M. H. N. Walker 7-45).

26th Match: v England (Trent Bridge)   July 28, 29, 30, Aug 1, 2.
Australia 243 (R. B. McCosker 51, I. T. Botham 5-74) and 309 (R. B. McCosker 107, R. G. D. Willis 5-88) lost to England 364 (A. P. E. Knott 135, G. Boycott 107, L. S. Pascoe 4-80) and 189-3 (J. M. Brearley 81, G. Boycott 80*) by 7 wkts.

27th Match: v Minor Counties (Sunderland)   Aug 4, 5.
Australians 170 (B. G. Collins 4-42, J. S. Wilkinson 4-49) and 169-6 dec (I. C. Davis 55, D. W. Hookes 51) lost to Minor Counties 133-4 dec and 207-4 (P. N. Gill 92) by 6 wkts.

28th Match: v Lancashire (Old Trafford)   Aug 6, 7, 8.
Lancashire 215 and 202 (B. Wood 80, R. J. Bright 5-67) lost to Australians 251-5 dec (K. J. Hughes 89) and 167-3 (G. J. Cosier 66) by 7 wkts.

29th Match: v England (Headingley)   Aug 11, 12, 13, 15.
England 436 (G. Boycott 191, A. P. E. Knott 57, L. S. Pascoe 4-91) beat Australia 103 (I. T. Botham 5-21, M. Hendrick 4-41) and 248 (R. W. Marsh 63, M. Hendrick 4-54) by an innings and 85 runs.

30th Match: v Rest of the World (Arundel Castle)   Aug 18 (50 overs a side).
Australians 106 (R. G. D. Willis 4-19) lost to Rest of the World 110-7 by 3 wkts.

31st Match: v Middlesex (Lord's)   Aug 20, 21, 22.
Middlesex 207 and 18-0 drew with Australians 149 (W. W. Daniel 4-27).

32nd Match: v England (Oval)   Aug 25, 26, 27, 29, 30.
England 214 (M. F. Malone 5-63, J. R. Thomson 4-87) and 57-2 drew with Australia 385 (D. W. Hookes 85, M. H. N. Walker 78*, R. W. Marsh 57, R. G. D. Willis 5-102).

1978: 6th Pakistanis

With the Test cricketers of the world split into two camps by the Kerry Packer controversy, the Pakistan selectors did not choose their leading cricketers, Zaheer Abbas, Asif Iqbal, Mushtaq Mohammad, Imran Khan and Majid J. Khan, all of whom were under contract to World Series Cricket. The team announced in March was Wasim Bari (captain), Wasim Raja, Aamer Hameed, Abdul Qadir, Arshad Pervez, Haroon Rashid, Iqbal Qasim, Javed Miandad, Liaqat Ali, Masood Iqbal, Mohsin Khan, Mudassar Nazar, Naeem Ahmed, Sadiq Mohammad, Sarfraz Nawaz, Sikander Bakht, Talat Ali with Mahmood Hussain as manager and two associate managers, Imtiaz Ahmed and Zafar Altaf. Soon after the team's announcement the press reported extensively that Javed Miandad and Haroon Rashid had signed for Packer, which was denied.

The tourists suffered from extremely bad weather and did not play without interruption from the rain until their seventh match. The weak side could not afford this lack of practice and lost the two one-day internationals before the Test series by a large margin. England won the First Test with an innings and more than a day to spare, but the Pakistan manager quite rightly complained about the fast short pitched deliveries bowled against tail-end batsmen by Willis. In the Second Test Pakistan had to take the field without their only pace bowler, Sarfraz, who was

injured, and again lost by an innings. The last Test was a rain ruined draw. England thus won the series two matches to nil.

Only Sadiq Mohammad of the batsmen came out of the visit with much credit; Sarfraz, when fit, bowled well; Wasim Bari kept wicket in good form.

The Tests were not very popular and receipts compared with the first three Tests of 1977 were down by £230,000, the sponsorship by Cornhill saving the finances of the series.

1978: 6th Pakistanis

Batting Averages

	M	I	NO	R	HS	Avge	100	c/s
Sadiq Mohammad	13	20	2	675	161	37.50	1	6
Mudassar Nazar	13	21	1	677	107	33.85	1	5
Wasim Raja	12	17	5	324	56*	27.00	0	3
Talat Ali	8	14	3	278	60	25.27	0	1
Javed Miandad	13	20	4	397	59	24.81	0	5
Mohsin Khan	11	16	0	386	79	24.12	0	4
Sarfraz Nawaz	8	8	4	90	32*	22.50	0	3
Haroon Rashid	10	15	0	268	78	17.86	0	2
Wasim Bari	12	11	2	123	38*	13.66	0	13
Aamer Hameed	6	3	1	26	13	13.00	0	0
Arshad Pervez	3	5	0	59	30	11.80	0	1
Liaqat Ali	8	7	5	18	9	9.00	0	0
Abdul Qadir	7	6	0	16	9	2.66	0	4
Iqbal Qasim	9	9	2	16	8*	2.28	0	4
Sikander Bakht	6	6	1	11	4	2.20	0	0

Also batted: Masood Iqbal (1 match) (ct3) 8; Naeem Ahmed (2 matches) 2; Hasan Jamal (1 match) 7, 2*.

Bowling Averages

	O	M	R	W	Avge	BB	5i
Sarfraz Nawaz	147.3	35	330	18	18.33	5-39	1
Sadiq Mohammad	12	4	25	1	25.00	1-13	0
Liaqat Ali	188	45	510	18	28.33	3-26	0
Mudassar Nazar	100.1	23	253	8	31.62	2-28	0
Wasim Raja	89.2	15	258	8	32.25	2-15	0
Sikander Bakht	149	31	450	12	37.50	4-132	0
Hasan Jamil	24	3	77	2	38.50	2-32	0
Aamer Hameed	95	28	237	6	39.50	3-71	0
Iqbal Qasim	115.4	34	310	7	44.28	3-101	0
Abdul Qadir	123	22	396	6	66.00	2-29	0
Naeem Ahmed	47	7	136	2	68.00	1-45	0
Javed Miandad	43	4	137	2	68.50	1-14	0

1978: 6th Pakistanis

1st Match: v Worcestershire (Worcester) April 25, 26, 27.
Pakistan 31-0 drew with Worcestershire did not bat.

2nd Match: v Leicestershire (Leicester) April 29, May 1, 2.
Leicestershire 269 (J. F. Steele 62) drew with Pakistanis 90-4.

3rd Match: v Nottinghamshire (Trent Bridge) May 3, 4, 5.
Pakistanis 212-5 (Wasim Raja 56*) drew with Nottinghamshire did not bat.

4th Match: v Yorkshire (Bradford) May 6, 7, 8.
Match abandoned–no play due to rain.

5th Match: v Northamptonshire (Northampton) May 10, 11, 12.
Pakistanis 190 (Mudassar Nazar 80) and 217-9 drew with Northamptonshire 205-8 dec (D. S. Steele 86).

6th Match: v Essex (Chelmsford) May 13, 15, 16.
Pakistan 80 (N. Phillip 6-33) drew with Essex did not bat.

7th Match : v M.C.C. (Lord's) May 17, 18, 19.
M.C.C. 193 (Sarfraz Nawaz 4-44) and 149-6 dec (D. I. Gower 71) drew with Pakistanis 149-9 dec (C. M. Old 6-36) and 74-4.

8th Match: v Derbyshire (Chesterfield) May 20, 21, 22.
Derbyshire 333-3 dec (J. G. Wright 164, A. Hill 58, P. N. Kirsten 58) and 101-5 dec drew with Pakistanis 182 (Mudassar Nazar 78) and 115-3.

9th Match: v England (Old Trafford) May 24, 25 (55 overs a side).
England 217-7 (C. T. Radley 79) beat Pakistan 85 (R. G. D. Willis 4-15) by 132 runs.

10th Match: v England (Oval) May 26 (55 overs a side).
England 248-6 (D. I. Gower 114*) beat Pakistan 154-8 (Mudassar Nazar 56) by 94 runs.

11th Match: v Kent (Canterbury) May 27, 28, 29.
Pakistanis 420-7 dec (Sadiq Mohammad 161, Talat Ali 60, Javed Miandad 59, Wasim Raja 56*) and 245-7 (Mudassar Nazar 68) drew with Kent 342-7 dec (A. G. E. Ealham 95, C. J. Tavare 90, C. J. Rowe 85).

12th Match: v England (Edgbaston) June 1, 2, 3, 5.
Pakistan 164 (C. M. Old 7-50) and 231 (Sadiq Mohammad 79, P. H. Edmonds 4-44) lost to England 452-8 dec (C. T. Radley 106, I. T. Botham 100, D. I. Gower 58, Sikander Bakht 4-132) by an innings and 57 runs.

13th Match: v Hampshire (Southampton) June 10, 11, 12.
Hampshire 246 (T. E. Jesty 77, J. M. Rice 55) and 307-3 dec (D. R. Turner 111, T. E. Jesty 102* C. G. Greenidge 60) drew with Pakistanis 258 (Sandiq Mohammad 56, M. N. S. Taylor 5-67) and 217-5 (Mudassar Nazar 107, Mohsin Khan 79).

14th Match: v England (Lord's) June 15, 16, 17, 19.
England 364 (I. T. Botham 108, G. R. J. Roope 69, D. I. Gower 56, G. A. Gooch 54) beat Pakistan 105 (R. G. D. Willis 5-47, P. H. Edmonds 4-6) and 139 (I. T. Botham 8-34) by an innings and 120 runs.

15th Match: v Oxford and Cambridge Universities (Cambridge) June 22, 23.
Pakistanis 78-2 dec and 16-0 drew with Oxford and Cambridge 0-0 dec.

16th Match: v Surrey (Oval) June 24, 26, 27.
Surrey 178-3 dec (M. A. Lynch 101, G. R. J. Roope 64*) and 97-5 dec lost to Pakistanis 158-6 dec (Haroon Rashid 78, D. J. Thomas 4-47) and 121-3 (Javed Miandad 55*) by 7 wkts.

17th Match: v England (Headingley) June 29, 30, July 1, 3, 4.
Pakistan 201 (Sadiq Mohammad 97, C. M. Old 4-41, I. T. Botham 4-59) drew with England 119-7 (Sarfraz Nawaz 5-39).

1978: 9th New Zealanders

Unlike the Pakistan team, with whom they shared the 1978 summer, New Zealand did not suffer from their leading players being engaged to World Series Cricket. The team selected to tour

1978: 9th New Zealanders

Batting Averages

	M	I	NO	R	HS	Avge	100	c/s
G. P. Howarth	12	20	2	816	123	45.33	1	
B. A. Edgar	15	24	2	823	113	37.40	1	20
J. M. Parker	12	17	2	549	104*	36.60	2	7/1
R. W. Anderson	14	24	3	739	155	35.19	2	6
B. E. Congdon	13	21	5	556	110*	34.75	1	10
J. G. Wright	14	24	3	675	111	32.14	1	6
M. G. Burgess	15	24	1	552	68	24.00	0	8
R. O. Collinge	6	5	1	91	63*	22.75	0	0
G. N. Edwards	14	21	3	401	83	22.27	0	22/1
B. L. Cairns	11	16	2	239	41	17.07	0	7
J. M. McIntyre	9	9	4	85	24*	17.00	0	3
S. L. Boock	13	14	10	57	14*	14.25	0	5
G. B. Thomson	7	3	2	13	9	13.00	0	2
R. J. Hadlee	10	13	0	149	40	11.46	0	9
B. P. Bracewell	9	10	3	18	10*	2.57	0	4

Also batted: D. R. Hadlee (1 match) 8, G. B. Troup (1 match) 19 (ct1).

Bowling Averages

	O	M	R	W	Avge	BB	5i
R. J. Hadlee	280.4	72	714	41	17.41	7-77	2
S. L. Boock	386.3	156	865	39	22.17	5-9	1
B. L. Cairns	370	101	882	35	25.20	5-51	2
B. E. Congdon	279.2	84	623	23	27.08	5-40	1
B. P. Bracewell	221.2	38	694	24	28.91	3-38	0
G. B. Thomson	188	50	521	15	34.73	4-42	0
R. O. Collinge	158	35	455	13	35.00	3-43	0
J. M. McIntyre	213.4	72	573	14	40.92	3-40	0
G. B. Troup	37	6	108	2	54.00	1-37	0
D. R. Hadlee	16	0	70	1	70.00	1-70	0

Also bowled: G. P. Howarth 12-2-47-3; J. M. Parker 5-1-30-1.

England was M. G. Burgess (captain) and J. M. McIntyre of Auckland; G. P. Howarth, J. M. Parker and J. G. Wright, of Northern Districts; B. A. Edgar, Wellington; B. E. Congdon, S. L. Boock, R. J. Hadlee and D. R. Hadlee of Canterbury; B. L. Cairns and G. B. Thomson of Otago; R. W. Anderson, G. N. Edwards and B. P. Bracewell of Central Districts, with B. J. Paterson as manager.

The only notable omission was Turner, who preferred to play for Worcestershire. The tour got off to a poor start when Dayle Hadlee broke down in the first match and was unable to play again – later on G. B. Troup was co-opted for one match. Collinge was flown in as a permanent replacement for Hadlee.

The tourists were outplayed by England, losing all three Tests and the two one-day internationals. They had two outstanding players, G. P. Howarth, who hit 296 Test runs at an average of 74.00 and R. J. Hadlee, whose 13 Test wickets cost 20.76 runs each. Against England no-one else proved very effective. In the county matches Edgar, Parker and Anderson all scored well and the young Boock took wickets with his spinners.

The lack of a specialist wicketkeeper in the touring party had a detrimental effect on the bowlers, neither Edwards nor Edgar being up to the job.

Altogether the tour was not very satisfactory, but it provided experience for a number of the younger players.

The outstanding batsman for the 1979 New Zealanders was Geoff Howarth, seen here off-driving in the one-day international at Old Trafford.

1978: 9th New Zealanders

1st Match: v Lavinia, Duchess of Norfolk's XI (Arundel Castle)   June 18.
Duchess of Norfolk's XI 188-6 dec (J. E. Emburey 51*) beat New Zealanders 187 by 1 run.

2nd Match: v D. H. Robins' XI (Eastbourne)   June 21, 22, 23.
New Zealanders 269 (B. A. Edgar 56, M. G. Burgess 50, D. J. Thomas 4-64) and 32-1 drew with D. H. Robins' XI 184-6 dec (G. A. Gooch 57).

3rd Match: v Sussex (Hove)   June 24, 26, 27.
New Zealanders 266 (G. N. Edwards 83, G. P. Howarth 78) and 236-5 dec (B. A. Edgar 74, J. G. Wright 63, B. E. Congdon 51) beat Sussex 167 (C. P. Phillipson 60, B. E. Congdon 5-40, B. L. Cairns 4-16) and 267 (C. P. Phillipson 62, B. E. Congdon 4-35, S. L. Boock 4-75) by 68 runs.

4th Match: v Gloucestershire (Bristol)   June 28, 29, 30.
Gloucestershire 227 (Zaheer Abbas 83, S. L. Boock 4-35) and 207-3 dec (Zaheer Abbas 121*, D. R. Shepherd 53*) drew with New Zealanders 179-6 dec (G. P. Howarth 69, M. G. Burgess 56, B. M. Brain 5-48) and 253-6 (R. W. Anderson 122, B. A. Edgar 50).

5th Match: v Somerset (Taunton)   July 1, 2, 3.
Somerset 349-5 dec (P. M. Roebuck 131*, D Breakwell 100*) and 144-6 dec drew with New Zealanders 218-8 dec (B. A. Edgar 81) and 93-0 (B. A. Edgar 54*).

6th Match: v Glamorgan (Swansea)   July 5, 6, 7.
Glamorgan 198 (J. A. Hopkins 82, B. L. Cairns 5-51) and 263-8 dec (J. A. Hopkins 85, M. J. Llewellyn 80, B. L. Cairns 5-87) drew with New Zealanders 235-8 dec (B. A. Edgar 61) and 98-7.

7th Match: v Middlesex (Lord's)   July 8, 10, 11.
Middlesex 133 (R. J. Hadlee 4-37) and 82 (S. L. Boock 5-9, B. L. Cairns 4-17) lost to New Zealanders 225 (J. M. Parker 50, M. W. W. Selvey 4-72) by an innings and 10 runs.

8th Match: v Warwickshire (Edgbaston)   July 12, 13, 14.
Warwickshire 177 (G. W. Humpage 55, R. J. Hadlee 4-39) and 185 (R. N. Abberley 56, R. J. Hadlee 7-77) lost to New Zealanders 414-4 dec (B. E. Congdon 110*, J. M. Parker 100*, G. P. Howarth 83, J. G. Wright 61) by an innings and 52 runs.

9th Match: v England (Scarborough)   July 15 (55 overs a side).
England 206-8 (G. A. Gooch 94, B. L. Cairns 5-28) beat New Zealand 187-8 by 19 runs.

10th Match: v England (Old Trafford)   July 17 (55 overs a side).
England 278-5 (C. T. Radley 117*, D. I. Gower 50) beat New Zealand 152 (B. L. Cairns 60) by 126 runs.

11th Match: v Scotland (Broughty Ferry, Dundee)   July 19, 20, 21.
Scotland 190 (J. Ker 50, G. B. Thomson 4-42) and 125 lost to New Zealanders 472-8 dec (R. W. Anderson 155, B. A. Edgar 113, R. O. Collinge 63*, T. I. McPherson 4-110) by an innings and 157 runs.

12th Match: v Yorkshire (Headingley)   July 22, 24, 25.
New Zealanders 263-4 dec (B. A. Edgar 92, G. P. Howarth 67) and 249-9 dec (J. G. Wright 111, C. M. Old 4-49) drew with Yorkshire 281-5 dec (G. Boycott 103*, J. H. Hampshire 90) and 75-2.

13th Match: v England (Oval)   July 27, 28, 29, 31, Aug 1.
New Zealand 234 (G. P. Howarth 94, J. G. Wright 62, R. G. D. Willis 5-42) and 182 (P. H. Edmonds 4-20) lost to England 279 (D. I. Gower 111) and 138-3 (G. A. Gooch 91*) by 7 wkts.

14th Match: v Minor Counties (Torquay)   Aug 2, 3.
New Zealanders 117-3 dec (R. W. Anderson 55) and 175-3 dec lost to Minor Counties 82-2 dec and 214-7 by 3 wkts.

15th Match: v Lancashire (Old Trafford)   Aug 5, 7, 8.
New Zealanders 241-5 dec (J. M. Parker 104*, R. W. Anderson 59) drew with Lancashire 95-1 (A. Kennedy 53*).

16th Match: v England (Trent Bridge)   Aug 10, 11, 12, 14.
England 429 (G. Boycott 131, C. T. Radley 59, G. A. Gooch 55, J. M. Brearley 50, R. J. Hadlee 4-94) beat New Zealand 120 (I. T. Botham 6-34) and 190 (B. A. Edgar 60, P. H. Edmonds 4-44) by an innings and 119 runs.

17th Match: v Young England (Leicester)   Aug 16, 17, 18.
Young England 272-8 dec (D. I. Gower 108, M. W. Gatting 88, R. J. Hadlee 4-40) and 235-6 dec (C. J. Tavare 83) drew with New Zealanders 240 (B. E. Congdon 58) and 132-1 (R. W. Anderson 58*).

18th Match: v Worcestershire (Worcester)   Aug 19, 20, 21.
Worcestershire 193 (S. L. Boock 4-36) and 252 (C. N. Boyns 71, S. L. Boock 4-60) lost to New Zealanders 319 (J. G. Wright 65, G. N. Edwards 57, N. Gifford 6-68) and 127-3 (M. G. Burgess 55*) by 7 wkts.

19th Match: v England (Lord's)   Aug 24, 25, 26, 28.
New Zealand 339 (G. P. Howarth 123, M. G. Burgess 68, I. T. Botham 6-101) and 67 (I. T. Botham 5-39, R. G. D. Willis 4-16) lost to England 289 (C. T. Radley 77, D. I. Gower 71, R. J. Hadlee 5-84) and 118-3 by 7 wkts.

20th Match: v T. N. Pearce's XI (Scarborough)   Sept 2, 4, 5.
T. N. Pearce's XI 274-5 dec (B. Dudleston 90, C. E. B. Rice 90*, D. W. Randall 61) and 238-6 dec (B. Dudleston 64, C. E. B. Rice 54*) beat New Zealanders 246-9 dec (G. N. Edwards 50, P. Willey 5-65) and 228 (P. Willey 7-73) by 38 runs.

21st Match: v T. N. Pearce's XI (Scarborough)   Sept 3 (40 overs a side).
Match abandoned – no play due to rain.

1979: 1st Sri Lankans

Coming to England to compete in the I.C.C. Trophy with the other non-Test playing members of the I.C.C., Sri Lanka arranged a short tour of nine first-class matches. The team was A. P. B. Tennekoon (captain), D. S. de Silva, B. Warnapura, R. S. A. Jayasekera, R. L. Dias, L. R. D. Mendis, S. P. Pasqual, S. A. Jayasinghe, R. S. Magugalle, S. R. D. Wettimuny, R. G. C. E. Wijesuriya, A. R. M. Opatha, F. R. M. D. Gunatilleke, G. R. A. de Silva, D. L. S. de Silva and S. Jeganathan with Major-Genral Russell Heyn as manager.

Although they won only one first-class match the side produced some very useful performances at times. Tennekoon was the leading batsman and was ably assisted by D. S. de Silva, who also topped the bowling averages with his spinners. The left-arm slows of G. R. A. de Silva also commanded respect. The team lacked a good opening pair of bowlers, who would have made the world of difference to their results.

Very little publicity was given to the matches, which were generally not well attended.

1979: 1st Sri Lankans

1st Match: v Nottinghamshire (Trent Bridge)   May 12, 14, 15.
Sri Lankans 286 (D. R. de S. Wettimuny 83, R. D. Mendis 73, B. Warnapura 52, H. T. Tunnicliffe 4-30, M. K. Bore 4-45) and 129 (S. A. Jayasinghe 55*, C. E. B. Rice 5-29) lost to Nottinghamshire 408-9 dec (P. A. Todd 176, C. E. B. Rice 68, H. T. Tunnicliffe 50, S. Jeganathan 4-92) and 10-0 by 10 wkts.

2nd Match: v USA (Northampton Saints)   May 24 (60 overs a side).
USA 168 lost to Sri Lanka 170-4 (R. L. Dias 76*) by 4 wkts.

3rd Match: v Wales (Hinckley Town)   May 29, 30.
Match Abandoned–rain.

4th Match: v Holland (Moseley)   May 31, June 1 (60 overs a side).
Sri Lankans 212-8 (R. D. Mendis 51) beat Holland 167-8 (A. Bakker 74) by 45 runs.

5th Match: v Israel (Kenilworth)   June 4.
Israel won by walk-over. Sri Lanka refused to play.

6th Match: v Denmark (Mitchell & Butler, Birmingham)   June 6.
Sri Lanka 318-8 (R. L. Dias 88, R. D. Mendis 68) beat Denmark 110 by 208 runs.

7th Match: v Canada (Worcester)   June 21.
Sri Lanka 324-5 (R. D. Mendis 66, S. A. Jayasinghe 64) beat Canada 264-5 (J. C. B. Vaughan 80*) by 60 runs.

8th Match: v New Zealand (Trent Bridge)   June 9.
Sri Lanka 189 (A. P. B. Tennekoon 59) lost to New Zealand 190-1 (G. M. Turner 83*, G. P. Howarth 63*) by 9 wkts.

9th Match: v West Indies (Oval)   June 13, 14, 15.
Match abandoned–rain.

10th Match: v India (Old Trafford)   June 16, 18.
Sri Lanka 238-5 (S. R. S. Wettimuny 67, R. D. Mendis 64) beat India 191 by 47 runs.

11th Match: v Oxford University (Guildford)   June 24, 25.
Oxford University 63 (G. R. A. de Silva 6-30, D. S. de Silva 4-13) and 146 (D. S. de Silva 8-46) lost to Sri Lankans 295-8 dec (B. Warnapura 73, R. L. Dias 84*, A. P. B. Tennekoon 63, J. P. Pearce 4-94) by an innings and 86 runs.

12th Match: v Derbyshire (Derby)   June 27, 28, 29.
Derbyshire 264-7 dec (A. Hill 63, K. J. Barnett 61) and 250 (A. Hill 75) drew with Sri Lankans 300 (S. A. Jayasinghe 64, R. S. Madugalle 86).

13th Match: v Kent (Canterbury)   June 30, July 2, 3.
Kent 261-6 dec (N. R. Taylor 110, R. A. Woolmer 60, D. S. de Silva 4-82) and 201-7 (R. A. Woolmer 101*) drew with Sri Lankans 400-9 dec (A. P. B. Tennekoon 112, R. S. Madugalle 88, D. S. de Silva 76).

14th Match: v Ireland (Eglinton)   July 7, 8, 9.
Ireland 186-5 dec (I. J. Anderson 110) and 155-2 (J. F. Short 56) drew with Sri Lankans 288-6 dec (S. P. Pasqual 101*, R. D. Mendis 82).

15th Match: v Worcestershire (Worcester)   July 11, 12, 13.
Worcestershire 317-6 dec (B. L. d'Oliveira 112, D. J. Humphries 68) and 226-5 dec (D. N. Patel 118*) drew with Sri Lankans 264 (B. Warnapura 68) and 166-1 (R. S. A. Jayasekera 79*, A. P. B. Tennekoon 77*).

16th Match: v Glamorgan (Swansea)   July 14, 15, 16.
Sri Lankans 309-9 dec (D. S. de Silva 76*) and 260-6 dec (R. D. Mendis 57, R. S. A. Jayasekera 55, G. C. Holmes 4-78) drew with Glamorgan 272-8 dec (C. L. Smith 67, P. D. Swart 54) and 145-3 (J. A. Hopkins 64).

17th Match: v Scotland (Shawfield, Glasgow)   July 18, 19, 20.
Scotland 120 (G. R. A. de Silva 4-28) and 73-3 drew with Sri Lankans 114 (F. Robertson 5-35, J. Clark 4-53).

18th Match: v Sussex (Horsham)   July 25, 26, 27.
Sussex 180 (D. S. de Silva 5-57, G. R. A. de Silva 4-67) and 283-8 dec (J. R. T. Barclay 102*, K. C. Wessels 66, D. S. de Silva 5-131) drew with Sri Lankans 248 (R. L. Dias 51, J. R. T. Barclay 6-61) and 106-2 (A. P. B. Tennekoon 50).

1979: 1st Sri Lankans

Batting Averages

	M	I	NO	R	HS	Avge	100	c/s
A. P. B. Tennekoon	7	11	1	491	112	49.10	1	5
D. S. de Silva	6	7	1	291	76*	48.50	0	3
B. Warnapura	5	7	1	232	73	38.66	0	1
R. S. A. Jayasekera	5	7	1	230	79*	38.33	0	5/2
R. L. Dias	8	10	2	306	84*	38.25	0	2
L. R. D. Mendis	7	10	1	329	82	36.55	0	2
S. P. Pasqual	7	9	2	250	101*	35.71	1	3
S. A. Jayasinghe	6	7	1	183	64	30.50	0	10/4
R. S. Madugalle	7	8	0	242	88	30.25	0	8
S. R. D. Wettimuny	7	11	0	182	83	16.54	0	8
R. G. C. E. Wijesuriya	5	4	2	38	25	19.00	0	6
A. R. M. Opatha	7	8	1	101	24	14.42	0	5
F. R. M. Gunatilleke	6	5	1	41	24*	10.25	0	0
G. R. A. de Silva	7	5	1	23	16	5.75	0	2
D. L. S. de Silva	4	3	1	11	7	5.50	0	2
S. Jeganathan	5	6	1	21	8	4.20	0	2

Bowling Averages

	O	M	R	W	Avge	BB	5i
D. S. de Silva	298.1	89	781	35	22.31	8-46	3
G. R. A. de Silva	291.3	85	699	30	23.30	6-30	1
B. Warnapura	20.5	6	54	2	27.00	1-12	0
D. L. S. de Silva	79	23	199	6	33.16	2-28	0
A. R. M. Opatha	141	32	443	12	36.91	3-27	0
R. G. C. E. Wijesuriya	153	41	377	10	37.70	3-13	0
S. Jeganathan	87	25	265	7	37.85	4-92	0
F. R. M. Gunatilleke	125	34	360	7	51.42	3-32	0
S. P. Pasqual	42.1	12	144	2	72.00	1-22	0

Also bowled: S. R. D. Wettimuny 1.3-0-10-1; R. S. Madugalle 9-0-32-0; R. L. Dias 1-0-3-0.

1979: 10th Indians

After the Prudential World Cup Tournament in June 1979 the Indian side remained in England for a programme of first-class matches and a series of four Tests. The team was S. Venkataraghavan (captain), Yashpal Sharma, S. M. Gavaskar, G. R. Vishwanath, M. Amarnath, D. B. Vengsarkar, Yajurvindra Singh, A. D. Gaekwad, C. P. S. Chauhan, B. P. Patel, K. D. Ghavri, Kapil Dev, S. C. Khanna, B. Reddy, B. S. Bedi and B. S. Chandrasekhar, with C. D. Gopinath as manager and G. G. Desai as treasurer.

The team had had a very poor time in the World Cup, losing all three matches, a lack of form which continued during the second half of the 1979 season. The famous quartet of spin bowlers, Venkat, Chandra, Bedi and Prasanna, no longer commanded the

---

1979: 10th Indians

Batting Averages

	M	I	NO	R	HS	Avge	100	c/s
Yashpal Sharma	12	21	6	884	111	58.93	3	6/1
S. M. Gavaskar	13	20	1	1062	221	55.89	3	15
G. R. Viswanath	13	17	2	757	113	50.46	3	4
M. Amarnath	11	16	3	592	123	45.53	1	2
D. B. Vengsarkar	12	19	1	751	138	41.72	3	12
Yajurvindra Singh	9	14	6	293	59	36.62	0	10
A. D. Gaekwad	12	20	2	574	109	31.88	2	4
C. P. S. Chauhan	13	22	2	561	108	28.05	1	4
B. P. Patel	7	10	4	137	36*	22.83	0	1
K. D. Ghavri	12	12	5	143	33*	20.42	0	1
Kapil Dev	13	15	0	287	102	19.13	1	4
S. C. Khanns	6	4	1	41	20	13.66	0	6/4
B. Reddy	10	12	2	101	23	10.10	0	21/2
S. Venkataraghavan	13	10	0	101	28	10.10	0	3
B. S. Bedi	11	7	4	28	20	9.33	0	5
B. S. Chandrasekhar	9	5	3	2	1*	0.50	0	0

Bowling Averages

	O	M	R	W	Avge	BB	5i
B. S. Bedi	377.5	113	847	33	25.66	6-28	2
Yajurvindra Singh	138	26	437	15	29.13	5-75	1
S. Venkataraghavan	391.5	96	1065	34	31.32	5-33	1
C. P. S. Chauhan	38.3	15	132	4	33.00	1-7	0
M. Amarnath	194.5	47	533	14	38.07	4-88	0
Yashpal Sharma	31.1	3	123	3	41.00	1-13	0
K. D. Ghavri	345.5	68	1122	27	41.55	5-23	1
Kapil Dev	422	96	1327	31	42.80	5-146	1
B. S. Chandrasekhar	204.2	32	655	14	46.77	4-30	0
A. D. Gaekwad	13	4	55	1	55.00	1-10	0

Also bowled: S. M. Gavaskar 8-1-23-0.

Sunil Gavaskar delighted his supporters with a magnificent Test double-century in the second innings at the Oval which nearly won the match for India. Here he gets a ball past Hendrick while Botham and wicketkeeper Bairstow watch.

respect of the England batting—Prasanna was not even selected for the tour; Chandra missed matches through injury and Venkat was burdened by the captaincy. The principal attack lay in the hands of the faster bowlers, Kapil Dev and Ghavri; the former

had success in the Tests taking 16 wickets, average 30.93. The England attack was also rather weak and the result was three drawn Tests and one win for England.

The batting was fairly strong, led by the maestro Gavaskar, who hit 542 Test runs, average 77.42, including a splendid double century; Viswanath and Vengsarkar also averaged over 40 in the Tests and both were thoroughly competent players.

The weakness of the bowling was not helped by some fielding errors and neither wicketkeeper–Reddy and Khanna–was up to international standard.

The team went home having won just one match and drawn 12 of the 16 games played, a clear demonstration of their weakness.

1979: Prudential World Cup

Following the pattern set in 1975, the second World Cup was staged in England in June 1979. In 1979 the non-Test playing countries competed in a preliminary competition for the two final places in the World Cup, whereas in 1975 the places had been given to Sri Lanka and East Africa.

The visiting players involved in the World Cup series were:
West Indies: C. H. Lloyd (captain), C. G. Greenidge, D. L. Haynes, I. V. A. Richards, A. I. Kallicharran, C. L. King, D. L. Murray, A. M. E. Roberts, J. Garner, M. A. Holding and C. E. H. Croft.
Australia: K. J. Hughes (captain), A. M. J. Hilditch, W. M. Darling, A. R. Border, G. N. Yallop, G. J. Cosier, T. J. Laughlin, K. J. Wright, G. Dymock, R. M. Hogg, A. G. Hurst, J. K. Moss and G. D. Porter.

Above *Gordon Greenidge is run out in the 1979 World Cup final against England.*

Left *Collis King, who enlivened the Cup with his immense hitting, drives Graham Gooch into the covers in the final. His partner here is Viv Richards, who took the Man of the Match award with a superlative century.*

Pakistan: Asif Iqbal (captain), Majid J. Khan, Sadiq Mohammad, Zaheer Abbas, Haroon Rashid, Javed Miandad, Mudassar Nazar, Imran Khan, Sarfraz Nawaz, Wasim Bari and Sikander Bakht.
Canada: B. M. Mauricette (captain), S. Baksh, C. J. D. Chappell, G. R. Sealy, F. A. Dennis, M. P. Stead, C. A. Marshall, J. C. B. Vaughan, Tariq Javed, J. M. Patel, C. C. Henry, J. N. Valentine and R. G. Callender.
New Zealand: M. G. Burgess (captain), G. M. Turner, J. G. Wright, G. P. Howarth, J. V. Coney, W. K. Lees, B. J. McKecknie, B. L. Cairns, R. J. Hadlee, L. W. Stott, G. B. Troup, J. F. M. Morrison, B. A. Edgar and E. J. Chatfield.

Details of the Sri Lankan and Indian teams can be found under separate headings.

The competition again proved highly successful with gate receipts of £359,700, although the attendance dropped from 160,000 in 1975 to 132,000 in 1979, mainly due to wet weather. The sponsors, Prudential Assurance, provided £250,000 and the total surplus after expenses was £350,000.

The final between England and the West Indies, staged at Lord's, was easily won by the West Indies, who dismissed England with 9 overs in hand and 92 in arrears. Richards was Man of the Match with an excellent innings of 138 not out.

1980: 14th West Indians

The West Indies team returned from their tour of Australia and New Zealand in early March 1980 to begin the home series of Shell Shield matches on 21 March, ending on 28 April, after which the first match of their England 1980 tour was programmed for 8 May. This tight schedule ruined the climax of the West Indian domestic one-day competition, since the leading players were on their way to England when the final was being played.

The team selected for England was C. H. Lloyd (captain), S. F. A. F. Bacchus, C. E. H. Croft and A. I. Kallicharran of Guyana; I. V. A. Richards, D. R. Parry and A. M. E. Roberts of the Leeward Islands; J. Garner, C. G. Greenidge, D. L. Haynes, C. L. King,

Joel Garner, the tall West Indian, had a very successful tour in 1980, topping the Test bowling averages.

1980: 14th West Indians

Batting Averages

	M	I	NO	R	HS	Avge	100	c/s
I. V. A. Richards	13	17	1	911	145	56.93	4	13
C. H. Lloyd	12	12	2	487	116	48.70	3	7
D. L. Haynes	14	22	3	874	184	46.00	1	2
A. I. Kallicharran	15	19	1	653	90	36.27	0	14
C. G. Greenidge	13	18	2	577	165	36.06	1	6
S. F. A. F. Bacchus	15	23	2	710	164*	33.80	1	14
D. A. Murray	6	8	2	161	49	26.83	0	16/1
D. L. Murray	12	14	2	315	64	26.25	0	33/2
M. D. Marshall	12	12	2	211	52	21.10	0	2
J. Garner	11	10	0	206	104	20.60	1	8
D. R. Parry	11	13	8	103	26*	20.60	0	2
M. A. Holding	11	11	6	99	35	19.80	0	2
A. M. E. Roberts	9	10	1	114	31	12.66	0	0
C. L. King	9	11	2	86	26*	9.55	0	4
C. E. H. Croft	9	4	3	8	7*	8.00	0	0
L. G. Rowe	3	2	0	13	13	6.50	0	2

Played in one match: Timur Mohamed 2, 45.

Bowling Averages

	O	M	R	W	Avge	BB	5i
J. Garner	351	123	683	49	13.93	5-22	1
M. D. Marshall	336.3	86	864	49	17.63	7-56	2
D. R. Parry	303.1	93	800	40	20.00	5-83	1
A. M. E. Roberts	234.2	57	657	27	24.33	5-72	1
M. A. Holding	392.1	96	1096	44	24.90	6-67	2
A. I. Kallicharran	15	3	55	2	27.50	1-1	0
C. E. H. Croft	230.3	54	690	25	27.60	6-80	1
C. L. King	98	24	301	7	43.00	4-46	0
I. V. A. Richards	68	21	177	1	177.00	1-37	0

Also bowled: S. F. A. F. Bacchus 2-0-11-0; C. G. Greenidge 6-3-6-0; D. L. Haynes 1-0-2-0; C. H. Lloyd 1-0-1-0; D. A. Murray 1-0-1-0.

1980: 14th West Indians

1st Match: v Lavinia, Duchess of Norfolk's XI (Arundel Castle) May 8 (45 overs a side).
West Indians 243-4 (C. G. Greenidge 67, S. F. A. Bacchus 60, C. L. King 60*) beat Duchess of Norfolk's XI 122-9 (B. L. d'Oliveira 55*) by 121 runs.

2nd Match: v Worcestershire (Worcester) May 10, 11, 12.
Worcestershire 252 (D. R. Parry 4-55) and 144 (M. D. Marshall 7-56) lost to West Indians 266 (A. I. Kallicharran 89, M. D. Marshall 52, H. L. Alleyne 4-83) and 134-3 (C. G. Greenidge 60) by 7 wkts.

3rd Match: v Leicestershire (Leicester) May 14, 15.
Leicestershire 99 (J. Garner 5-22) and 214 (D. I. Gower 57, B. F. Davison 54, M. A. Holding 5-57) lost to West Indians 334 (C. G. Greenidge 165, S. F. A. Bacchus 60) by an innings and 21 runs.

4th Match: v Northamptonshire (Milton Keynes) May 17, 18, 19.
Northamptonshire 260 (R. G. Williams 122, D. R. Parry 5-83) and 166 (A. J. Lamb 58, D. R. Parry 4-49) lost to West Indians 369 (C. H. Lloyd 116, I. V. A. Richards 131, T. M. Lamb 4-73) and 60-4 by 6 wkts.

5th Match: v Middlesex (Lord's) May 20 (50 overs a side).
Match abandoned–no play due to rain.

6th Match: v Middlesex (Lord's) May 21 (50 overs a side).
Middlesex 124 lost to West Indians 125-1 (D. L. Haynes 52*) by 9 wkts.

7th Match: v Essex (Chelmsford) May 22 (50 overs a side).
West Indians 149 (K. R. Pont 4-36) lost to Essex 153-5 (M. H. Denness 63) by 5 wkts.

8th Match: v Essex (Chelmsford) May 23 (50 overs a side).
West Indians 290 (I. V. A. Richards 122, D. L. Haynes 88, J. K. Lever 5-42) beat Essex 149-4 (K. S. McEwan 50) by 141 runs.

9th Match: v Derbyshire (Chesterfield) May 24, 25, 26.
Derbyshire 229 (J. G. Wright 96, M. D. Marshall 4-52) and 68 (J. Garner 4-16, A. M. E. Roberts 4-28) lost to West Indians 290 (A. I. Kallicharran 88, S. F. A. Bacchus 62, M. Hendrick 5-59) and 11-1 by 9 wkts.

10th Match: v England (Headingley) May 28, 29 (55 overs a side).
West Indies 198 (C. G. Greenidge 78) beat England 174 (C. J. Tavare 82) by 24 runs.

11th Match: v England (Lord's) May 30 (55 overs a side).
West Indies 235-9 (D. L. Haynes 50) lost to England 236-7 (G. Boycott 70, P. Willey 56) by 3 wkts.

12th Match: v Kent (Canterbury) May 31, June 1, 2.
Kent 130-4 dec (C. S. Cowdrey 51*) and 84 (D. R. Parry 4-28) lost to West Indians 113-1 dec (D. L. Haynes 50*) and 103-5 by 5 wkts.

13th Match: v England (Trent Bridge) June 5, 6, 7, 9, 10.
England 263 (I. T. Botham 57, A. M. E. Roberts 5-72) and 252 (G. Boycott 75, J. Garner 4-30) lost to West Indies 308 (I. V. A. Richards 64, D. L. Murray 64, C. G. Greenidge 53, R. G. D. Willis 4-82) and 209-8 (D. L. Haynes 62, R. G. D. Willis 5-65) by 2 wkts.

14th Match: v Oxford & Cambridge Universities (Cambridge) June 12, 13.
Oxford & Cambridge 208-4 dec (A. M. Mubarak 86, D. R. Pringle 50*) and 68 (D. R. Parry 5-22) lost to West Indians 218-2 dec (S. F. A. Bacchus 79*, L. G. Rowe 53*) and 59-0 by 10 wkts.

15th Match: v Sussex (Hove) June 14, 15, 16.
Sussex 143 (Imran Khan 50, D. R. Parry 4-29) and 191-4 (T. D. Booth Jones 55, Imran Khan 54*) drew with West Indians 227-8 dec (I. V. A. Richards 55).

16th Match: v England (Lord's) June 19, 20, 21, 23, 24.
England 269 (G. A. Gooch 123, M. A. Holding 6-67, J. Garner 4-36) and 133-2 drew with West Indies 518 (D. L. Haynes 184, I. V. A. Richards 145, C. H. Lloyd 56).

17th Match: v Ireland (Dublin) June 25 (50 overs a side).
West Indians 105-2 (S. F. A. Bacchus 50) drew with Ireland 39-5.

18th Match: v Ireland (Dublin) June 26 (55 overs a side).
West Indians 284-7 (S. F. A. Bacchus 163) beat Ireland 82-1 on run rate.

19th Match: v Glamorgan (Swansea) June 28, 30, July 1.
West Indians 327-5 dec (I. V. A. Richards 100, D. L. Haynes 82, A. I. Kallicharran 58) and 60-0 drew with Glamorgan 242 (N. G. Featherstone 76, M. D. Marshall 6-54*).

20th Match: v Glamorgan (Swansea) June 29 (40 overs a side).
Glamorgan 209-5 (Javed Miandad 101*) lost to West Indians 211-5 (S. F. A. Bacchus 79, D. L. Haynes 71) by 5 wkts.

21st Match: v Gloucestershire (Bristol) July 2, 3, 4.
West Indians 278 (J. Garner 104, D. L. Murray 64, A. H. Wilkins 4-51) and 161 (S. F. A. Bacchus 69, D. A. Graveney 4-12) beat Gloucestershire 183 (Sadiq Mohammad 76, D. A. Graveney 50, C. L. King 4-46) and 198 (J. Garner 4-31) by 58 runs.

22nd Match: v Somerset (Taunton) July 5, 6, 7.
West Indians 400-7 dec (I. V. A. Richards 103, C. H. Lloyd 102, D. L. Haynes 53) drew with Somerset 77-0.

23rd Match: v England (Old Trafford) July 10, 11, 12, 14, 15.
England 150 (B. C. Rose 70) and 391-7 (G. Boycott 86, P. Willey 62*, M. W. Gatting 56) drew with West Indies 260 (C. H. Lloyd 101, I. V. A. Richards 65).

24th Match: v Scotland (Broughty Ferry) July 18 (50 overs a side).
West Indians 233 (I. V. A. Richards 69, A. I. Kallicharran 55, W. A. Donald 4-78) beat Scotland 153-7 (C. J. Warner 57*) by 80 runs.

25th Match: v Yorkshire (Headingley) July 19, 20, 21.
West Indians 342-3 dec (S. F. A. Bacchus 164*, A. I. Kallicharran 90) and 119-1 dec (D. L. Haynes 69*) beat Yorkshire 194-5 dec (J. D. Love 55, G. Boycott 53) and 209 (R. G. Lumb 54, S. N. Hartley 51, C. E. H. Croft 6-80) by 58 runs.

26th Match: v England (Oval) July 24, 25, 26, 28, 29.
England 370 (G. A. Gooch 83, G. Boycott 53, B. C. Rose 50) and 209-9 dec (M. W. Gatting 100*, M. A. Holding 4-79) drew with West Indies 265 (S. F. A. Bacchus 61, G. R. Dilley 4-57).

27th Match: v Minor Counties (Jesmond) July 31, Aug 1.
West Indians 383-7 dec (Timur Mohamed 119, A. I. Kallicharran 109, D. A. Murray 50*) and 104-3 dec (D. R. Parry 54*) drew with Minor Counties 204 (J. G. Tolchard 86, D. R. Parry 5-88) and 0-0.

28th Match: v Warwickshire (Edgbaston) Aug 2, 3, 4.
West Indians 315 (A. I. Kallicharran 75, D. L. Haynes 62, I. V. A. Richards 62) and 227-7 dec drew with Warwickshire 223 (G. W. Humpage 62, P. R. Oliver 57) and 180-3 (K. D. Smith 86).

29th Match: v England (Headingley) Aug 7, 8, 9, 11, 12.
England 143 and 227-6 (G. A. Gooch 55) drew with West Indies 245 (G. R. Dilley 4-79).

30th Match: v Essex (Stamford Bridge, London) Aug 14 (Floodlit, 40 overs).
West Indians 257-9 (S. F. A. Bacchus 87, C. L. King 56, I. V. A. Richards 53, J. K. Lever 4-41) lost to Essex 192-1 (G. A. Gooch 111*, K. S. McEwan 67*) on run rate.

M. D. Marshall and D. A. Murray of Barbados; M. A. Holding and L. G. Rowe of Jamaica; D. L. Murray of Trinidad, with C. L. Walcott as manager, and C. W. Smith as his assistant. There were no surprises in the side and no notable players were omitted.

The tour began with three convincing first-class victories, but there was an unexpected loss in a one-day game against Essex; the tourists then drew the one-day international series with England one match each–though the Cup went to the visitors on a higher scoring rate. Four of the five Test Matches were drawn due to bad weather and West Indies won the other one by 2 wickets.

As in the previous tour the West Indies attack was confined almost entirely to their fast bowlers–Croft, Garner, Holding, Marshall and Roberts–and only towards the end of the visit, when injuries handicapped Garner, Croft and Roberts, did the England batsmen flourish. Garner topped the Test bowling table with 26 wickets, average 14.26.

Richards was the dominant batsman and hit 379 runs, average 63.16, in the Tests as well as heading the first-class averages; Lloyd and Haynes also batted well and in fact the overall batting strength was quite exceptional, though both Lloyd and Rowe missed matches through injury and Rowe returned home early, to be replaced by Timur Mohamed.

The out cricket was good, but D. L. Murray had a poor season as wicketkeeper and perhaps his namesake D. A. Murray should have taken precedence in the Tests.

Total receipts from the five match Test series was £993,000, though this huge sum was mainly accounted for by increased admission charges, the wet weather reducing the actual attendances.

1980: 29th Australians

This tour was to celebrate the centenary of Test cricket in England and the Australian side did not fly to England until August. The schedule consisted of the single Centenary Test

1980: 29th Australians

Batting Averages

	M	I	NO	R	HS	Avge	100	c/s
A. R. Border	4	7	3	321	95	80.25	0	3
R. W. Marsh	5	7	4	172	56	57.33	0	11
G. S. Chappell	4	6	0	303	101	50.50	1	4
G. M. Wood	4	7	1	282	112	47.00	1	4
G. Dymock	2	1	0	37	37	37.00	0	0
K. J. Hughes	5	9	1	249	117	31.12	1	3
B. M. Laird	5	9	1	240	85	30.00	0	3
D. K. Lillee	4	4	1	81	33	27.00	0	0
A. A. Mallett	4	3	1	49	30*	24.50	0	0
R. J. Bright	3	1	0	21	21	21.00	0	1
G. N. Yallop	5	7	1	108	45	18.00	0	5
J. Dyson	3	6	1	66	33	13.20	0	0
J. R. Thomson	3	4	0	42	33	10.50	0	3
L. S. Pascoe	4	3	1	8	6	4.00	0	1

Bowling Averages

	O	M	R	W	Avge	BB	5i
D. K. Lillee	116.2	25	391	20	19.55	6-133	1
G. S. Chappell	16	4	51	2	25.50	2-32	0
L. S. Pascoe	114.1	14	445	17	26.17	5-59	2
R. J. Bright	105.1	40	292	7	41.71	3-20	0
J. R. Thomson	68	15	265	6	44.16	2-45	0
A. A. Mallett	77.2	16	282	5	56.40	2-69	0
G. Dymock	42	6	184	2	92.00	1-35	0

Dennis Lillee bowling in the Centenary Test at Lord's in 1980. Boycott is the non-striker. Lillee was the most successful bowler on a short, rain-spoiled tour.

Match and a handful of 'warm-up' games, plus two one-day internationals.

With the Packer series ended amicably, the Australian Board were in a position to select a representative side once more. The team was G. S. Chappell (captain), J. R. Thomson and G. Dymock of Queensland; A. R. Border, J. Dyson and L. S. Pascoe of New South Wales; R. W. Marsh, G. M. Wood, K. J. Hughes, B. M. Laird and D. K. Lillee of Western Australia; A. A. Mallett of South Australia; G. N. Yallop and R. J. Bright of Victoria, with P. L. Riding as manager.

The team had very little success: of the four first-class county matches they lost two, against Surrey and Notts and lost both the one-day internationals; the much publicised Centenary Test was not only rain affected, but ended in an anti-climax – England were set six hours to score the necessary runs for victory at the rate of about one per minute and never approached the target, though Australia did not look likely to dismiss the home batsmen. To make more money the Centenary Match was staged at Lord's instead of being played on the ground of the original match in 1880 – Kennington Oval.

Apart from the financial side – the receipts for the Test were £360,850 – the tour was not very successful. The two outstanding players were Border as a batsman and Lillee as a bowler.

1981: 30th Australians

The 30th Australians were K. J. Hughes (captain), G. M. Wood, T. M. Alderman, D. K. Lillee and R. W. Marsh of Western Australia; A. R. Border and M. F. Kent of Queensland; J. Dyson, D. M. Wellham, G. R. Beard, T. M. Chappell, G. F. Lawson and S. J. Rixon of New South Wales; G. N. Yallop and R. J. Bright of Victoria; R. M. Hogg of South Australia, with F. W. Bennett as manager and P. I. Philpott as cricket-manager, a new post derived from the English use of Barrington as assistant manager. The main alteration from the 1980 team was the absence of Greg Chappell, who was unavailable for the tour.

Though the tour schedule included six Test Matches for the first time, the number of first-class matches was reduced considerably by pruning the traditional programme at both ends. The matches did not start until mid-May and finished on 1 September, an acknowledgement that public interest in county matches had dwindled to a point where they made little money.

This meant that the tourists met England for the First Test after only two first-class matches uninterrupted by rain; though they had the bonus of quite unexpectedly beating England two to one in the one-day internationals.

The critics came in for another upset when Australia beat England in the First Test. The Second Test at Lord's, which

Terry Alderman getting Paul Downton lbw in the first Test at Trent Bridge in 1981. Alderman took a record 42 Test wickets on the tour for the 30th Australians.

1981: 30th Australians

1st Match: v Lavinia, Duchess of Norfolk's XI (Arundel Castle) May 16 (45 overs a side).
Australians 106 lost to Duchesss of Norfolk's XI 107-7 by 3 wkts.

2nd Match: v Hampshire (Southampton) May 20, 21, 22.
Hampshire 176-3 dec (M. C. J. Nicholas 58) drew with Australians 237-7 (R. W. Marsh 72*, J. Dyson 60).

3rd Match: v Somerset (Taunton) May 23, 24, 25.
Australians 232-8 dec drew with Somerset 25-0.

4th Match: v Glamorgan (Swansea) May 27, 28, 29.
Australians 147 (E. A. Moseley 6-23) drew with Glamorgan 84-4.

5th Match: v Gloucestershire (Bristol) May 30, 31.
Match abandoned–no play due to rain.

6th Match: v Gloucestershire (Bristol) June 1, 2.
Australians 278-7 dec (T. M. Chappell 91, G. M. Wood 81) drew with Gloucestershire 80-2 (Zaheer Abbas 60*). (Note: The original match was a 3 day game, May 30, 31, June 1, when the first two days were washed out, a new 2 day match was arranged on June 1, 2).

7th Match: v England (Lord's) June 4 (55 overs a side).
Australia 210-7 (A. R. Border 73) lost to England 212-4 (G. Boycott 75*, G. A. Gooch 53) by 6 wkts.

8th Match: v England (Edgbaston) June 6 (55 overs a side).
Australia 249-8 (G. N. Yallop 63, G. M. Wood 55) beat England 247 (M. W. Gatting 96) by 2 runs.

9th Match: v England (Headingley) June 8 (55 overs a side).
Australia 236-8 (G. W. Wood 108) beat England 165 (R. M. Hogg 4-29) by 71 runs.

10th Match: v Derbyshire (Derby) June 10, 11, 12.
Derbyshire 218-9 dec (J. G. Wright 144, T. M. Alderman 4-38) and 163-5 dec drew with Australians 190-8 dec (J. Dyson 61).

11th Match: v Middlesex (Lord's) June 13, 14, 15.
Middlesex 150 (D. K. Lillee 5-41) and 261-5 dec (J. M. Brearley 132*, M. W. Gatting 75) drew with Australians 146 and 144-4 (G. N. Yallop 52*).

12th Match: v England (Trent Bridge) June 18, 19, 20, 21.
England 185 (M. W. Gatting 52, T. M. Alderman 4-68) and 125 (D. K. Lillee 5-46, T. M. Alderman 5-62) lost to Australia 179 (A. R. Border 63) and 132-6 by 4 wkts.

13th Match: v Lancashire (Old Trafford) June 24 (55 overs a side).
Lancashire 275-3 (A. Kennedy 115*, D. Lloyd 63, C. H. Lloyd 58) beat Australians 197-4 (G. M. Wood 50) on faster scoring rate, rain intervening.

14th Match: v Kent (Canterbury) June 27, 28, 29.
Kent 147-6 dec (G. F. Lawson 5-72) drew with Australians 283-6 dec (K. J. Hughes 61).

15th Match: v England (Lord's) July 2, 3, 4, 6, 7.
England 311 (P. Willey 82, M. W. Gatting 59, G. F. Lawson 7-81) and 265-8 dec (D. I. Gower 89, G. Boycott 60) drew with Australia 345 (A. R. Border 64) and 90-4 (G. M. Wood 62*).

16th Match: v Warwickshire (Edgbaston) July 9 (55 overs a side).
Warwickshire 127-8 drew with Australians did not bat.

17th Match: v Northamptonshire (Northampton) July 11, 12, 13.
Northamptonshire 252 (R. M. Hogg 6-87) and 167-7 (R. J. Bright 5-57) drew with Australians 415-8 dec (D. M. Wellham 135*, T. M. Chappell 71, K. J. Hughes 51).

18th Match: v England (Headingley) July 16, 17, 18, 20, 21.
Australia 401-9 dec (J. Dyson 102, K. J. Hughes 89, G. N. Yallop 58, I. T. Botham 6-95) and 111 (R. G. D. Willis 8-43) lost to England 174 (I. T. Botham 50, D. K. Lillee 4-49) and 356 (I. T. Botham 149*, G. R. Dilley 56, T. M. Alderman 6-135) by 18 runs.

19th Match: v Scotland (Glasgow) July 23 (30 overs a side).
Australians 135-9 (J. Clark 4-28) beat Scotland 125-9 by 10 runs.

20th Match: v Worcestershire (Worcester) July 25, 26, 27.
Worcestershire 189 and 344-8 dec (P. A. Neale 145*, J. Birkenshaw 54) lost to Australians 293 (A. R. Border 115, M. F. Kent 92, J. Cumbes 4-62) and 241-3 (A. R. Border 70*, G. M. Wood 59, D. M. Wellham 54*) by 7 wkts.

21st Match: v England (Edgbaston) July 30, 31, Aug 1, 2.
England 189 (T. M. Alderman 5-42) and 219 (R. J. Bright 5-68) beat Australia 258 (J. E. Emburey 4-43) and 121 (I. T. Botham 5-11) by 29 runs.

22nd Match: v Surrey (Oval) Aug 6 (55 overs a side).
Match abandoned–no play due to rain.

23rd Match: v Essex (Chelmsford) Aug 8, 9, 10.
Essex 216-7 dec (G. A. Gooch 86, G. N. Yallop 4-63) and 270-8 dec (A. W. Lilley 64, K. S. McEwan 50, G. R. Beard 4-92) drew with Australians 240-5 dec and 237-8 (G. M. Wood 60, G. N. Yallop 59).

24th Match: v England (Old Trafford) Aug 13, 14, 15, 16, 17.
England 231 (C. J. Tavare 69, P. J. W. Allott 52*, D. K. Lillee 4-55, T. M. Alderman 4-88) and 404 (I. T. Botham 118, C. J. Tavare 78, A. P. E. Knott 59, J. E. Emburey 57, T. M. Alderman 5-109) beat Australia 130 (M. F. Kent 52, R. G. D. Willis 4-63) and 402 (A. R. Border 123*, G. N. Yallop 114) by 103 runs.

25th Match: v Leicestershire (Leicester) Aug 20 (55 overs a side).
Australians 213-8 (T. M. Chappell 63, J. P. Agnew 4-58) beat Leicestershire 145 by 68 runs.

26th Match: v Sussex (Hove) Aug 22, 23, 24.
Sussex 150 (M. R. Whitney 5-60) and 261 (J. R. P. Heath 56, T. J. Head 52*, R. M. Hogg 4-83) lost to Australians 236 (K. J. Hughes 52, A. N. Jones 4-68, I. A. Greig 4-76) and 176-3 (K. J. Hughes 70*, J. Dyson 65*) by 7 wkts.

27th Match: v England (Oval) Aug 27, 28, 29, 31, Sept 1.
Australia 352 (A. R. Border 106*, G. M. Wood 66, M. F. Kent 54, I. T. Botham 6-125, R. G. D. Willis 4-91) and 344-9 dec (D. M. Wellham 103, A. R. Border 84, R. W. Marsh 52, M. Hendrick 4-82, I. T. Botham 4-128) drew with England 314 (G. Boycott 137, M. W. Gatting 53, D. K. Lillee 7-89) and 261-7 (A. P. E. Knott 70*, M. W. Gatting 56, J. M. Brearley 51, D. K. Lillee 4-70).

28th Match: v Gloucestershire (Prince of Wales, Cheltenham) Sept 2 (40 overs, floodlit match).
Gloucestershire 177-8 beat Australians 105 by 72 runs.

Veteran Australian keeper Rodney Marsh works the ball to off in the Sixth Test of the 1981 series. Alan Knott is behind the stumps.

included Botham's resignation as England's captain and a rumpus among M.C.C. members, ended in a fairly miserable draw. A combination of some magnificent bowling by Willis (8 for 43) and batting by Botham (149 not out) gave England a famous victory in the Headingley Test, after Australia's first-innings lead of 227. The Fourth Test at Edgbaston produced an inspired bowling spell by Botham that again brought England victory from the jaws of defeat and Botham excelled himself in the Fifth Test with another hundred to win the Ashes for England. The final Test was drawn. This great Test series gave cricket a tremendous boost and despite Australia's poor record of three wins in 17 first-class matches, they came out of the tour with considerable credit.

Border, who hit 533 Test runs at an average of 59.22, was easily the outstanding batsman of the summer, and Wellham hit a century on his Test debut and had a good tour. Lillee and Alderman with 39 and 42 Test wickets took the bowling honours. Lawson looked useful, but broke down and Whitney was co-opted in his place.

Marsh continued to keep wicket in fine form, but rarely scored runs; the fielding, especially close to the wicket, was good.

1981: 2nd Sri Lankans

The team, which arrived in England in June, was B. Warnapura (captain), L. R. D. Mendis, S. Wettimuny, R. L. Dias, D. S. de Silva, Y. Goonasekera, N. D. P. Hettiaratchy, A. N. Ransasinghe, H. H. Devapriya, A. L. F. de Mel, R. S. Madugallo, L. W. Kaluperuma, H. M. Goonatilleke, J. R. Ratnayeke, R. G. C. E. Wijesuriya, G. R. A. de Silva and L. J. Fernando.

The most important match of the tour was against the T.C.C.B. XI at Trent Bridge; the tourists won, but it was rather a hollow victory, engineered by declarations after rain interrupted play. A combination of high scoring and bad weather meant that 11 of the 13 first-class matches were drawn.

The batting was generally sound, but the seam bowling in particular very weak and a great deal depended on the spin attack

1981: 2nd Sri Lankans

Batting Averages

	M	I	NO	R	HS	Avge	100	c/s
L. R. D. Mendis	11	14	2	545	99	45.41	0	7
S. Wettimuny	10	14	2	527	95*	43.91	0	3
R. L. Dias	11	17	2	607	127	40.46	1	6
D. S. de Silva	6	6	1	186	97	37.20	0	2
Y. Goonasekera	6	7	1	216	63	36.00	0	3
N. D. P. Hettiaratchy	10	13	1	400	80	33.33	0	11
B. Warnapura	10	16	1	408	75*	27.20	0	0
A. N. Ranasinghe	10	14	1	340	54*	26.15	0	4
H. Devapriya	5	10	0	247	68	24.70	0	9/3
A. L. F. de Mel	10	13	1	229	94	19.08	0	3
R. S. Madugalle	11	13	0	247	47	19.00	0	8
L. W. Kaluperuma	11	14	4	189	40	18.90	0	6
H. M. Goonatilleke	9	10	4	78	24	13.00	0	11/8
J. R. Ratnayeke	6	7	4	28	10	9.33	0	1
R. G. C. E. Wijesuriya	5	3	1	14	6*	7.00	0	3
G. R. A. de Silva	8	9	2	35	11	5.00	0	4
L. J. Fernando	4	1	1	7	7*	—	0	2

Bowling Averages

	O	M	R	W	Avge	BB	5i
G. R. A. de Silva	301	106	646	26	24.84	4-41	
D. S. de Silva	262	73	681	25	27.24	7-55	2
R. G. C. E. Wijesuriya	194	57	467	15	31.13	5-35	1
L. W. Kaluperuma	393.3	88	1045	31	33.70	5-34	1
A. N. Ranasinghe	228	58	624	17	36.70	5-65	1
B. Warnapura	63.2	17	215	5	43.00	2-33	0
J. R. Ratnayeke	111	22	388	9	43.11	3-38	0
A. L. F. de Mel	245	42	816	15	54.40	3-37	0
L. J. Fernando	71	11	234	1	234.00	1-37	0

Also bowled: R. L. Dias 1-0-3-0; Y. Goonasekera 1-0-5-0; S. Wettimuny 10-5-18-1.

of D. S. de Silva and Kaluperuma.

There was little public interest in the visit and the important match at Trent Bridge was not given much publicity and had only a light sprinkling of spectators.

1982: 11th Indians

Having just beaten England at home, the Indians travelled to England for a tour during the first half of the 1982 season. The touring team included the major players of the 1981-82 season, the full side being S. M. Gavaskar (captain), G. R. Viswanath, Madan Lal, D. B. Vengsarkar, Yashpal Sharma, Kapil Dev, S. V. Nayak, G. A. Parker, A. Malhotra, S. M. H. Kirmani, R. J. Shastri, S. M. Patil, P. Roy, D. R. Doshi, N. S. Yadav and Randhir Singh, with Raj Singh as manager and C. Nagaraj as his assistant.

The weather was relatively kind during May, but most of the early matches were drawn due to high scoring and it became obvious that the Indian attack was not very strong. England won both the one-day internationals with little difficulty and also the First Test, though Kapil Dev put in a splendid all-round

1982: 11th Indians

Batting Averages

	M	I	NO	R	HS	Avge	100	c/s
G. R. Viswanath	9	12	3	561	106*	62.33	2	8
Madan Lal	9	15	10	309	58*	61.80	0	1
D. B. Vengsarkar	9	13	2	610	157	55.45	1	9
S. M. Gavaskar	8	10	0	438	172	43.80	1	3
Yashpal Sharma	9	15	5	418	77*	41.80	0	6
Kapil Dev	8	11	0	438	97	39.81	0	5
S. V. Nayak	10	13	6	253	67*	36.14	0	3
G. A. Parkar	7	14	2	433	146	36.08	1	7/1
A. Malhotra	8	15	1	462	154*	33.00	1	5
S. M. H. Kirmani	9	12	3	265	65	29.44	0	11/4
R. J. Shastri	9	15	2	359	74	27.61	0	6
S. M. Patil	9	16	1	390	129*	26.00	1	1
P. Roy	7	12	0	174	51	14.50	0	1
D. R. Doshi	9	4	2	11	5*	5.50	0	0
N. S. Yadav	7	2	1	1	1*	1.00	0	0
Randhir Singh	5	3	0	0	0	0.00	0	0

Bowling Averages

	O	M	R	W	Avge	BB	5i
Madan Lal	246.1	49	763	22	34.68	4-28	0
S. M. Patil	60	9	155	4	38.75	2-26	0
D. R. Doshi	345.3	78	1003	25	40.12	6-102	1
Kapil Dev	255.4	45	810	20	40.50	5-39	1
R. J. Shastri	269.5	69	634	15	42.26	3-109	0
S. V. Nayak	205.3	39	645	14	46.07	5-54	1
Randhir Singh	131	24	418	7	59.71	2-50	0
N. S. Yadav	195	33	604	7	86.28	3-77	0

Also bowled: S. M. Gavaskar 5-0-23-0; A. Malhotra 9-1-37-1; P. Roy 1-0-14-0; D. B. Vengsarkar 0.2-0-2-0; Yashpal Sharma 10-2-32-0.

The all-rounder Kapil Dev was the outstanding Indian tourist in 1982. He is seen bowling in the First Test at Lord's with England's all-rounder Ian Botham backing up.

performance. Bad weather ruined the Second Test, in which even the first innings was not completed. The final Test was a high-scoring draw with the last day of academic interest only. Kapil Dev was again the Indian star–Gavaskar was injured while fielding and unable to bat. Thus the tour ended with just a single first-class victory.

The main Indian batsmen all flourished, but the bowling–the leading Test bowler was Doshi with 13 wickets, average 35.00–was not up to dismissing England twice, or even some of the leading counties. Too much depended on Kapil Dev, as the spinners, Doshi and Yadav, were ineffective on English wickets.

1982: 11th Indians

1st Match: v Lavinia, Duchess of Norfolk's XI (Arundel Castle)   May 5 (45 overs a side).
Indians 201-5 (Yashpal Sharma 66, A. Malhotra 54) lost to Duchess of Norfolk's XI 202-0 (Sadiq Mohammad 107*, A. W. Stovold 90*) by 10 wkts.*

2nd Match: v Warwickshire (Edgbaston)   May 9, 10, 11.
Indians 243 (D. B. Vengsarkar 72, G. R. Viswanath 67) and 351-5 (S. M. Gavaskar 172, A. Malhotra 79, D. B. Vengsarkar 57*) drew with Warwickshire 447-7 dec (A. M. Ferreira 112, Asif Din 91, T. A. Lloyd 87, R. G. D. Willis 72).

3rd Match: v Nottinghamshire (Trent Bridge)   May 12, 13, 14.
Nottinghamshire 141 (Kapil Dev 5-39) and 251-4 dec (R. T. Robinson 52, D. W. Randall 51) drew with Indians 259 (P. P. Roy 51, K. Saxelby 4-47, M. K. Bore 4-52) and 97-6.

4th Match: v Yorkshire (Bradford)   May 15, 17, 18.
Indians 376-5 dec (G. A. Parkar 146, S. M. Gavaskar 79) and 171-5 dec drew with Yorkshire 260-3 dec (K. Sharp 115, C. W. J. Athey 61*, R. G. Lumb 52) and 35-0.

5th Match: v M.C.C. (Lord's)   May 19, 20, 21.
M.C.C. 319-4 dec (D. W. Randall 130*, C. J. Tavare 99, D. I. Gower 55) and 126-2 dec drew with Indians 180 (D. B. Vengsarkar 96, G. R. Dilley 5-69) and 143-4 (G. A. Parkar 92).

6th Match: v Kent (Canterbury)   May 22, 23, 24.
Kent 302-7 dec (L. Potter 96, N. R. Taylor 62) and 248-4 dec (L. Potter 118) drew with Indians 282-3 dec (A. Malhotra 154*, Yashpal Sharma 77*) and 68-3.

7th Match: v Ireland (Belfast)   May 26 (50 overs a side).
Indians 179-2 (P. P. Roy 84) drew with Ireland did not bat.

8th Match: v Ireland (Belfast)   May 27 (50 overs a side).
Ireland 134-9 (E. A. McDermott 50, D. R. Doshi 4-11) lost to Indians 137-5 by 5 wkts.

9th Match: v Hampshire (Southampton)   May 29, 30, 31.
Hampshire 336-6 dec (T. E. Jesty 164*, M. C. J. Nicholas 72) and 236-2 dec (C. G. Greenidge 156, M. C. J. Nicholas 54*) lost to Indians 277-6 dec (G. R. Viswanath 100, S. M. H. Kirmani 65) and 298-7 (D. B. Vengsarkar 86) by 3 wkts.

10th Match: v England (Headingley)   June 2 (55 overs a side).
India 193 (Kapil Dev 60, I. T. Botham 4-56) lost to England 194-1 (B. Wood 78, C. J. Tavare 66*) by 9 wkts.*

11th Match: v England (Oval)   June 4 (55 overs a side).
England 276-9 (A. J. Lamb 99, D. I. Gower 76) beat Indians 162-8 (Madan Lal 53) by 114 runs.*

12th Match: v Northamptonshire (Northampton)   June 5, 6, 7.
Indians 203-5 dec (G. R. Viswanath 106*) and 197-4 (S. V. Nayak 67*, Yashpal Sharma 56) drew with Northamptonshire 204 (R. M. Carter 79, S. V. Nayak 5-54).

13th Match: v England (Lord's)   June 10, 11, 12, 14, 15.
England 433 (D. W. Randall 126, P. H. Edmonds 64, Kapil Dev 5-125) and 67-3 beat Indian 128 (I. T. Botham 5-46) and 369 (D. B. Vengsarkar 157, Kapil Dev 89, R. G. D. Willis 6-101) by 7 wkts.

14th Match: v Oxford and Cambridge Universities (Cambridge)   June 17, 18.
Oxford and Cambridge 288-7 dec (R. G. P. Ellis 90, R. J. Boyd-Moss 63, N. S. Yadav 5-107) and 234-7 dec (K. A. Hayes 62, D. R. Pringle 51) drew with Indians 354-6 dec (S. M. Gavaskar 120, R. J. Shastri 93, Yashpal Sharma 55) and 51-1.

15th Match: v Gloucestershire (Bristol)   June 19, 20, 21.
Indians 245-5 dec (R. J. Shastri 51, Madan Lal 51, Yashpal Sharma 50) and 200-4 dec (Madan Lal 58*) drew with Gloucestershire 200-6 dec (B. C. Broad 73, P. Bainbridge 61) and 39-4 (Madan Lal 4-28).

16th Match: v England (Old Trafford)   June 24, 25, 26, 27, 28.
England 425 (I. T. Botham 128, G. Miller 98, G. Cook 66, C. J. Tavare 57, D. R. Doshi 6-102) drew with India 379-8 (S. M. Patil 129*, S. M. H. Kirmani 58, G. R. Viswanath 54, Kapil Dev 65).

17th Match: v Essex (Chelmsford)   July 3, 4, 5.
Essex 336 (B. R. Hardie 161, N. Phillip 79) and 175-4 dec (K. R. Pont 58*, K. S. McEwan 52) drew with Indians 258-7 dec (A. Malhotra 85, G. A. Parkar 60*, D. R. Pringle 5-59) and 171-5 (R. J. Shastri 74, R. E. East 4-49).

18th Match: v England (Oval)   July 8, 9, 10, 12, 13.
England 594 (I. T. Botham 208, A. J. Lamb 107, D. W. Randall 95, G. Cook 50, D. R. Doshi 4-175) and 191-3 (C. J. Tavare 75*) drew with India 410 (Kapil Dev 97, R. J. Shastri 66, S. M. Patil 62, G. R. Viswanath 56) and 111-3 (G. R. Viswanath 75*).

1982: 7th Pakistanis

During the winter of 1981-82 there were ructions in Pakistani cricket. The eight leading Test players were dropped for refusing to play under Javed Miandad, and, as on some previous occasions the rebels' spokesman was the controversial Sarfraz. Happily the problem was resolved by the time the team flew to England for the second half of the 1982 season. The side was Imran Khan (captain), Mudassar Nazar, Zaheer Abbas, Mohsin Khan, Javed Miandad, Mansoor Akhtar, Haroon Rashid, Wasim Bari, Majid

J. Khan, Wasim Raja, Tahir Naqqash, Abdul Qadir, Saleem Yousuf, Salim Malik, Sarfraz Nawaz, Sikander Bakht and Iqbal Qasim, with Intikhab Alam as manager.

Although Pakistan lost the one-day internationals two matches to nil and the Test series by one match to two, the touring team was undoubtedly the strongest which Pakistan had sent to England. With five players with a first-class batting average above 60 and four effective bowlers in Mudassar, Imran, Abdul Qadir and Sarfraz, the side was well equipped, especially as a number of the players were familiar with English conditions.

1982: 7th Pakistanis

1st Match: v Middlesex (Lord's)   June 23, 24, 25.
Middlesex 144-9 dec (W. N. Slack 64) and 30-4 (Imran Khan 4-10) drew with Pakistanis 31-1 dec.

2nd Match: v Sussex (Hove)   June 26, 27, 28.
Pakistanis 450-2 dec (Mudassar Nazar 211*, Mohson Khan 151) beat Sussex 209 (Abdul Qadir 7-44) and 228 (G. D. Mendis 114, C. M. Wells 59, Abdul Qadir 6-78) by an innings and 13 runs.

3rd Match: v Hampshire (Bournemouth)   June 30, July 1, 2.
Pakistanis 300-9 dec (Mansoor Akhtar 87, J. W. Southern 4-88) and 101-2 dec lost to Hampshire 85-4 dec and 319-4 (T. E. Jesty 133, M. C. J. Nicholas 107*) by 6 wkts.

4th Match: v Glamorgan (Swansea)   July 3, 5.
Pakistanis 356-4 dec (Mudassar Nazar 168*, Majid J. Khan 88, Wasim Raja 50*) beat Glamorgan 155 (Abdul Qadir 5-31) and 128 (Abdul Qadir 4-20) by an innings and 73 runs.

5th Match: v Glamorgan (Swansea)   July 4 (40 overs a side).
Pakistanis 74-4 drew with Glamorgan did not bat, rain.

6th Match: v Somerset (Taunton)   July 7, 8, 9.
Pakistanis 344-5 dec (Mansoor Akhtar 153, Mohsin Khan 85) and 218-3 dec (Javed Miandad 105*) drew with Somerset 300-7 dec (I. V. A. Richards 181*) and 54-3.

7th Match: v Worcestershire (Worcester)   July 10, 11, 12.
Worcestershire 188 (P. A. Neale 68, Abdul Qadir 4-30) and 186 (M. J. Weston 93, P. A. Neale 59, Iqbal Qasim 5-52, Abdul Qadir 4-75) lost to Pakistanis 467-4 dec (Mohsin Khan 165*, Zaheer Abbas 147, Mudassar Nazar 75) by an innings and 93 runs.

8th Match: v Scotland (Glasgow)   July 14, 15.
Pakistanis 351-4 dec (Wasim Raja 174, Javed Miandad 54) drew with Scotland 111-5 (W. A. Donald 53*, Imran Khan 5-24).*

9th Match: v England (Trent Bridge)   July 17 (55 overs a side).
Pakistan 250-6 (Zaheer Abbas 53, Mudassar Nazar 51) lost to England 252-3 (A. J. Lamb 118) by 7 wkts.

10th Match: v England (Old Trafford)   July 19 (55 overs a side).
England 295-8 (M. W. Gatting 76) beat Pakistan 222 (Wasim Raja 60) by 73 runs.

11th Match: v Leicestershire (Leicester)   July 21, 22, 23.
Leicestershire 354-3 dec (D. I. Gower 176*, I. P. Butcher 71*) and 241-9 dec (T. J. Boon 90, R. W. Tolchard 61, Abdul Qadir 6-71) drew with Pakistanis 351-3 dec (Mohsin Khan 203*, Mansoor Akhtar 65) and 61-2.

12th Match: v Derbyshire (Chesterfield)   July 24, 25, 26.
Pakistanis 260-9 dec (Zaheer Abbas 51) and 299-2 dec (Zaheer Abbas 148*, Mudassar Nazar 100*) beat Derbyshire 257-6 dec (G. Miller 72*) and 162 (Imran Khan 4-27, Sikander Bakht 4-68) by 140 runs.

13th Match: v England (Edgbaston)   July 29, 30, 31, Aug 1.
England 272 (D. I. Gower 74, C. J. Tavare 54, Imran Khan 7-52) and 291 (D. W. Randall 105, R. W. Taylor 54, Tahir Naqqash 5-40) beat Pakistan 251 (Mansoor Akhtar 58, I. A. Greig 4-53) and 199 (Imran Khan 65, I. T. Botham 4-70) by 113 runs.

14th Match: v Minor Counties (Slough)   Aug 5, 6.
Minor Counties 114-5 dec and 179 (M. S. A. McEvoy 61, Iqbal Qasim 4-36) lost to Pakistanis 140-1 dec (Mansoor Akhtar 83) and 154-3 (Mansoor Akhtar 51) by 7 wkts.*

15th Match: v Surrey (Oval)   Aug 7, 8, 9.
Pakistanis 239-4 dec (Mohsin Khan 79, Zaheer Abbas 60*) and 218-4 dec (Haroon Rashid 90, Zaheer Abbas 50*) drew with Surrey 154-8 dec and 291-9 (R. D. V. Knight 111, Sarfraz Nawaz 6-92).

16th Match: v England (Lord's)   Aug 12, 13, 14, 15, 16.
Pakistanis 428-8 dec (Mohsin Khan 200, Zaheer Abbas 75, Mansoor Akhtar 57, R. B. Jackman 4-110) and 77-0 beat England 227 (Abdul Qadir 4-39) and 276 (C. J. Tavare 82, I. T. Botham 69, Mudassar Nazar 6-32) by 10 wkts.

17th Match: v England B (Leicester)   Aug 18, 19, 20.
Pakistanis 132-7 dec (K. St J. D. Emery 4-46) and 191-4 dec (Mudassar Nazar 103*) drew with England B 131-3 dec and 74-3.

18th Match: v Lancashire (Old Trafford)   Aug 21, 22, 23.
Lancashire 120-3 dec (D. Lloyd 55) drew with Pakistanis 93-1 (Mansoor Akhtar 53*).

19th Match: v England (Headingley)   Aug 26, 27, 28, 30, 31.
Pakistan 275 (Imran Khan 67*, Mudassar Nazar 65, Javed Miandad 54, I. T. Botham 4-70) and 199 (Javed Miandad 52, I. T. Botham 5-74) lost to England 256 (D. I. Gower 74, I. T. Botham 57, Imran Khan 5-49) and 219-7 (G. Fowler 86, Mudassar Nazar 4-55) by 3 wkts.

20th Match: v D. B. Close's XI (Scarborough)   Sept 1, 2.
Pakistanis 177 (Mohsin Khan 52, Haroon Rashid 50, F. D. Stephenson 5-64) and 134 (Mohsin Khan 85, N. Gifford 4-24) lost to D. B. Close's XI 357-8 dec (M. D. Crowe 104, F. D. Stephenson 63, Abdul Qadir 4-106) by an innings and 46 runs.

21st Match: v D. B. Close's XI (Scarborough)   Sept 3 (40 overs a side).
Pakistanis 264-5 (Mansoor Akhtar 88, Mohsin Khan 76, Javed Miandad 52) beat D. B. Close's XI 181 by 83 runs.

Left *Mohsin Khan batting for Pakistan in the Second Test at Lord's in 1982, when he scored a double century, the first in a Test at Lord's since New Zealander Martin Donnelly's in 1949.*

Below *Abdul Qadir took 57 wickets on tour.*

earlier the same season–apart from the relative strengths of the two teams, there was a great advantage in touring during the second half of the summer.

1982: 7th Pakistanis

Batting Averages

	M	I	NO	R	HS	Avge	100	c/s
Mudassar Nazar	11	16	6	825	211*	82.50	4	4
Zaheer Abbas	9	12	3	664	148*	73.77	2	2
Mohsin Khan	13	20	3	1248	203*	73.41	4	5
Imran Khan	9	8	4	291	67*	72.75	0	0
Javed Miandad	10	13	6	450	105*	64.28	1	14
Mansoor Akhtar	11	17	2	595	153	39.66	1	5
Haroon Rashid	10	13	3	331	90	33.10	0	8
Wasim Bari	11	7	2	162	45	32.40	0	22/7
Majid J. Khan	11	17	3	403	88	28.78	0	8
Wasim Raja	12	12	2	247	50*	24.70	0	5
Tahir Naqqash	6	4	0	65	39	16.25	0	3
Abdul Qadir	12	9	3	93	21*	15.50	0	3
Salim Yousuf	4	4	1	38	15*	12.66	0	5/2
Salim Malik	5	7	1	68	25*	11.33	0	4
Sarfraz Nawaz	6	1	0	7	7	7.00	0	1
Sikander Bakht	12	7	2	29	9	5.80	0	3
Iqbal Qasim	7	4	1	9	5	3.00	0	2

Also batted: Ehtesham-ud-Din (1 match) 0, 0*; Intikhab Alam (1 match) 0, 4; Jalal-ud-Din (3 matches) 10, 0.

Bowling Averages

	O	M	R	W	Avge	BB	5i
Mudassar Nazar	139	35	368	21	17.52	6-32	1
Imran Khan	290.3	76	621	35	17.74	7-52	2
Abdul Qadir	452.4	123	1187	57	20.82	7-44	4
Sarfraz Nawaz	127	24	351	16	21.93	6-92	1
Jalal-ud-Din	56	19	123	4	30.75	1-16	0
Sikander Bakht	326	86	959	27	35.51	4-68	0
Tahir Naqqash	160	44	537	15	35.80	5-40	1
Iqbal Qasim	161.1	36	434	12	36.16	5-52	1
Wasim Raja	117.4	30	346	9	38.44	3-34	0

Also bowled: Ehtesham-ud-Din 28-9-81-1; Intikhab Alam 6-0-17-1; Javed Miandad 3-0-16-0; Majid J. Khan 22-9-57-2; Mansoor Akhtar 16.3-6-43-1; Mohsin Khan 5-0-32-1; Salim Malik 1-0-5-0; Zaheer Abbas 0.1-0-0-0.

Imran led the side with enormous zest and bowled with great enthusiasm in the Tests, which perhaps resulted in a falling off in his batting. Abdul Qadir, with his leg-breaks and googlies, took 10 wickets, average 40.60, in the Tests, but his value was much higher than that. He continually beat the bat only to be thwarted by pads and the Pakistanis complained bitterly about some umpiring decisions in relation to this. Sarfraz, now the veteran, bowled well at Lord's to assist in Pakistan's victory. Mudassar concentrated on line and length without much guile and his medium-pace deliveries reaped a nice harvest.

Owing to injuries the team co-opted two additional players, excluding the manager, Ehtesham-ud-din and Jalal-ud-din, but neither achieved much.

The attendances were much higher than during the Indian tour

1982: 1st Zimbabweans

While in England for the 1982 I.C.C. Trophy the Zimbabwe team also played a couple of first-class matches. The team, which in fact won the I.C.C. Trophy, was D. A. G. Fletcher (captain), D. L. Houghton, A. T. Hodgson, I. P. Butchart, G. Scott, E. J. Hough, P. W. E. Rawson, Mohammad Dudhia, K. M. Curran, G. C. Wallace, A. J. Pycroft, J. G. Heron, A. J. Traicos, R. D. Brown and V. R. Hogg, with D. Ellman-Brown as manager and L. Watson as his assistant.

Houghton, Heron, Pycroft and Curran were the leading batsmen and Hogg and Hough the principal seam bowlers, with the old South African Test player Traicos as a spinner.

1982: 1st Zimbabweans

1st Match: v Worcestershire (Worcester)   June 2, 3, 4.
Worcestershire 222-9 dec (M. J. Weston 63, Younis Ahmed 63, A. J. Traicos 5-56) and 181-7 dec (Younis Ahmed 75*, P. W. E. Rawson 5-42) drew with Zimbabweans 156-3 dec (A. J. Pycroft 62*, D. A. G. Fletcher 56*) and 52-2.

2nd Match: v Leicestershire (Leicester)   June 5, 7, 8.
Zimbabweans 249-9 dec (I. P. Butchart 54, R. D. Brown 51) and 286-9 dec (J. G. Heron 83, A. J. Pycroft 50) drew with Leicestershire 284-7 dec (R. A. Cobb 64, J. F. Steele 63) and 78-5.

3rd Match: v Nottinghamshire (Trent Bridge)   June 9 (44 overs a side).
Nottinghamshire 218-3 (C. E. B. Rice 60, J. D. Birch 58*) beat Zimbabweans 142 by 76 runs.

4th Match: v Yorkshire (Abbeydale Park)   June 10 (60 overs a side).
Zimbabweans 202 (D. A. G. Fletcher 53) lost to Yorkshire 203-7 (G. Boycott 98*) by 3 wkts.

5th Match: v USA (Moseley)   June 16 (60 overs a side).
Zimbabwe 332-4 (D. L. Houghton 135, K. M. Curran 126*) beat USA 141 by 191 runs.

6th Match: v Kenya (Wolverhampton)   June 18 (25 overs a side).
Zimbabwe 192-4 (D. L. Houghton 73, J. G. Heson 50) beat Kenya 71-4 on faster run rate.

7th Match: v Gibraltar (Brewood)   June 21 (60 overs a side).
Match abandoned–rain.

8th Match: v Canada (Leamington)   June 25 (60 overs a side).
Canada 9-0 drew with Zimbabwe did not bat.

9th Match: v Israel (Bloxwich)   June 28 (60 overs a side).
Israel 65 (A. J. Traicos 4-21) lost to Zimbabwe 66-1 by 9 wkts.

10th Match: v Papua New Guinea (Wombourne)   June 30 (60 overs a side).
Papua New Guinea 94 lost to Zimbabwe 96-1 by 9 wkts.

11th Match: v Hong Kong (Bewdley)   July 5 (60 overs a side).
Hong Kong 192-4 (A. A. Lorimer 72*) lost to Zimbabwe 196-3 (A. J. Pycroft 83*, J. G. Heron 51) by 7 wkts.

12th Match: v Bangladesh (West Bromwich, Dartmouth)   July 7 (60 overs a side).
Bangladesh 124 (K. M. Curran 4-31) lost to Zimbabwe 126-2 (J. G. Heron 63*) by 8 wkts.

13th Match: v Bermuda (Leicester)   July 10 (60 overs a side).
Bermuda 231-8 lost to Zimbabwe 232-5 (A. J. Pycroft 82, C. A. T. Hodgson 57*) by 5 wkts.

1983: 10th New Zealanders

After the 1983 Prudential World Cup the New Zealand team remained in England for a programme of first-class matches and a series of four Test Matches. The team was G. P. Howarth (captain), J. G. Wright and B. L. Cairns of Northern Districts; J. J. Crowe, J. G. Bracewell, M. D. Crowe, M. C. Snedden and T. J. Franklin of Auckland; R. J. Hadlee of Canterbury; B. A. Edgar,

E. J. Chatfield, J. V. Coney and E. J. Gray of Wellington; W. K. Lees of Otago; I. D. S. Smith of Central Districts, with Sir Allan Wright as manager and P. A. Borrie as doctor. G. M. Turner played only in the World Cup and then by prior arrangement returned home. S. R. Tracy was co-opted for two first-class matches.

John Wright, the New Zealand opening batsman, sends the ball to long leg past Allan Lamb in the Oval Test of 1983.

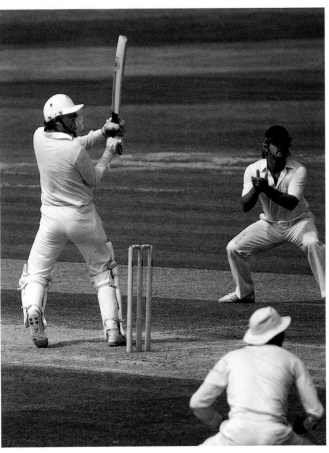

1983: 10th New Zealanders

1st Match: v England (Oval) June 9 (60 overs a side).
England 322-6 (A. J. Lamb 102) beat New Zealand 216 (M. D. Crowe 97) by 106 runs.

2nd Match: v Pakistan (Edgbaston) June 11, 12 (60 overs a side).
New Zealand 238-9 (Abdul Qadir 4-21) beat Pakistan 186 by 52 runs.

3rd Match: v Sri Lanka (Bristol) June 13 (60 overs a side).
Sri Lanka 206 (R. S. Madugalle 60, R. J. Hadlee 5-25) lost to New Zealand 209-5 (G. P. Howarth 76, G. M. Turner 50) by 5 wkts.

4th Match: v England (Edgbaston) June 15 (60 overs a side).
England 234 (D. I. Gower 92, G. Fowler 69) lost to New Zealand 238-8 (J. V. Coney 66, G. P. Howarth 60) by 2 wkts.

5th Match: v Sri Lanka (Derby) June 18 (60 overs a side).
New Zealand 181 (A. L. F. de Mel 5-32) lost to Sri Lanka 184-7 (R. L. Dias 64*, B. Kuruppa 62) by 3 wkts.

6th Match: v Pakistan (Trent Bridge) June 20 (60 overs a side).
Pakistan 261-3 (Zaheer Abbas 103*, Imran Khan 79*) beat New Zealand 250 (J. V. Coney 51*) by 11 runs.

7th Match: v Combined Services (Portsmouth) June 30, July 1.
Combined Services 100-5 dec and 105-9 (J. G. Bracewell 4-31) drew with New Zealanders 221-5 dec (T. J. Franklin 108, E. J. Gray 61*).

8th Match: v Somerset (Taunton) July 2, 3, 4.
New Zealanders 544-9 dec (G. P. Howarth 88, J. G. Wright 85, R. J. Hadlee 82, E. J. Gray 72, B. L. Cairns 60, P. H. L. Wilson 4-109) and 46-0 dec drew with Somerset 267 (J. W. Lloyds 84, P. A. Slocombe 66, E. J. Gray 4-24, J. G. Bracewell 4-91) and 221-9 (P. W. Denning 99, J. G. Bracewell 5-73).

9th Match: v Gloucestershire (Bristol) July 6, 7, 8.
Gloucestershire 120 (A. W. Stovold 58, E. J. Chatfield 6-40) and 305-8 (P. Bainbridge 146) drew with New Zealanders 338-6 dec (J. G. Wright 136, M. D. Crowe 61*, G. P. Howarth 60).

10th Match: v Middlesex (Lord's) July 9, 10, 11.
Middlesex 386-4 dec (M. W. Gatting 216, C. T. Radley 119) drew with New Zealanders 234 (G. P. Howarth 72, P. H. Edmonds 6-93) and 302-5 (M. D. Crowe 134*).

11th Match: v England (Oval) July 14, 15, 16, 17, 18.
England 209 (D. W. Randall 75*, R. J. Hadlee 6-53) and 446-6 dec (C. J. Tavare 109, G. Fowler 105, A. J. Lamb 102*) beat New Zealand 196 (R. J. Hadlee 84, R. G. D. Willis 4-43, I. T. Botham 4-62) and 270 (J. G. Wright 88, G. P. Howarth 67) by 189 runs.

12th Match: v Worcestershire (Worcester) July 20, 21, 22.
New Zealanders 246 (R. J. Hadlee 68, M. D. Crowe 65, J. D. Inchmore 5-82) and 210-6 dec beat Worcestershire 200 (D. B. d'Oliveira 77, M. S. A. McEvoy 54) and 156 (R. J. Hadlee 4-42) by 100 runs.

13th Match: v Warwickshire (Edgbaston) July 23, 25, 26.
New Zealanders 335-6 dec (J. V. Coney 68, J. J. Crowe 63, G. P. Howarth 55) and 158-3 dec (J. J. Crowe 79) beat Warwickshire 195-5 dec (D. L. Amiss 78, A. M. Ferreira 55*) and 126 (B. L. Cairns 7-46) by 172 runs.

14th Match: v England (Headingley) July 28, 29, 30, Aug 1.
England 225 (C. J. Tavare 69, A. J. Lamb 58, B. L. Cairns 7-74) and 252 (D. I. Gower 112*, E. J. Chatfield 5-95) lost to New Zealand 377 (J. G. Wright 93, B. A. Edgar 84, R. J. Hadlee 75, R. G. D. Willis 4-57) and 103-5 (R. G. D. Willis 5-35) by 5 wkts.

15th Match: v Surrey (Oval) Aug 4 (60 overs a side).
New Zealanders 222-9 (J. V. Coney 51) beat Surrey 166 by 56 runs.

16th Match: v Hampshire (Bournemouth) Aug 6, 7, 8.
Hampshire 149 & 154 lost to New Zealanders 244 (M. D. Crowe 70) and 60-1 by 9 wkts.

17th Match: v England (Lord's) Aug 11, 12, 13, 15.
England 326 (D. I. Gower 108, M. W. Gatting 81, C. J. Tavare 51, R. J. Hadlee 5-93) and 211 (I. T. Botham 61) beat New Zealand 191 (B. A. Edgar 70, N. G. B. Cook 5-35, I. T. Botham 4-50) and 219 (J. V. Coney 68) by 127 runs.

18th Match: v Essex (Chelmsford) Aug 17, 18, 19.
New Zealanders 321-4 dec (G. P. Howarth 144, M. D. Crowe 116) and 220 (M. G. Hughes 4-71) drew with Essex 233 (K. R. Pont 81, M. C. Snedden 5-68) and 260 (C. Gladwin 89, G. A. Gooch 54, J. G. Bracewell 6-111).

19th Match: v Leicestershire (Leicester) Aug 20, 21, 22.
Leicestershire 281-5 dec (B. F. Davison 123*, N. E. Briers 57, J. P. Addison 51) and 198 (J. G. Bracewell 5-80) lost to New Zealanders 265-8 dec (T. J. Franklin 61, B. A. Edgar 54, P. B. Clift 4-35) and 216-2 (T. J. Franklin 98*, J. V. Coney 50*) by 8 wkts.

20th Match: v England (Trent Bridge) Aug 25, 26, 27, 28, 29.
England 420 (I. T. Botham 103, D. W. Randall 83, D. I. Gower 72, J. G. Bracewell 4-108) and 297 (A. J. Lamb 137*, R. J. Hadlee 4-85) beat New Zealand 207 (B. A. Edgar 62, N. G. B. Cook 5-63) and 345 (R. J. Hadlee 92*, B. A. Edgar 76, J. V. Coney 68, N. G. B. Cook 4-87) by 165 runs.

21st Match: v D. B. Close's XI (Scarborough) Aug 31, Sept 1, 2.
New Zealanders 292 (B. A. Edgar 100) and 247-6 dec (M. D. Crowe 110*, J. J. Crowe 65) beat D. B. Close's XI 155 (D. B. Close 51, S. R. Tracey 5-29, M. C. Snedden 4-41) and 265 (J. H. Hampshire 85, Mushtaq Mohammad 60*) by 119 runs.

1983: 10th New Zealanders

Batting Averages

	M	I	NO	R	HS	Avge	100	c/s
M. D. Crowe	11	19	5	819	1347	58.50	3	13
R. J. Hadlee	8	11	2	477	92*	53.00	0	3
J. G. Wright	7	10	0	498	136	49.80	1	6
G. P. Howarth	11	18	1	697	144	41.00	1	12
B. A. Edgar	11	21	2	742	100	39.05	1	6
T. J. Franklin	9	18	3	539	98*	35.93	0	6
J. V. Coney	9	17	3	437	68	31.21	0	14
J. J. Crowe	11	19	2	470	79	27.64	0	13
W. K. Lees	6	9	4	136	42*	27.20	0	12
E. J. Gray	9	15	3	280	72	23.33	0	7
B. L. Cairns	11	14	2	254	60	21.16	0	6
M. C. Snedden	10	9	0	154	35	17.11	0	0
J. G. Bracewell	11	16	3	183	38	14.07	0	10
I. D. S. Smith	8	12	3	104	32*	11.55	0	18/2
E. J. Chatfield	9	8	4	45	13*	11.25	0	1
S. R. Tracy	2	2	0	4	4	2.00	0	0

Bowling Averages

	O	M	R	W	Avge	BB	5i
S. R. Tracy	33.1	5	115	8	14.37	5-29	1
M. D. Crowe	76	12	284	12	23.66	3-21	0
R. J. Hadlee	345.1	95	855	36	23.75	6-53	2
J. V. Coney	124.5	40	339	14	24.21	3-19	0
E. J. Gray	143	40	398	16	24.87	4-24	0
J. G. Bracewell	325.5	73	1095	41	26.70	6-111	3
B. L. Cairns	341.1	101	877	32	27.40	7-46	2
M. C. Snedden	236.2	37	845	30	28.16	5-68	1
E. J. Chatfield	303.3	79	818	28	29.21	6-40	2

Also bowled: B. A. Edgar 5-0-17-1; G. P. Howarth 17-4-41-1.

Played in non-first-class matches only: G. M. Turner.

The tour provided New Zealand with their first Test victory in England–in the Second Test at Lord's–but they lost the other three Tests. They won seven out of 13 first-class fixtures.

A great deal depended on the talents of Hadlee, who not only took most Test wickets–21, average 26.61–but also topped the Test batting table with 301 runs, average 50.16. Of the other batsmen Edgar was the most consistent; Wright scored runs, many of which he forfeited by faulty calling which ran out his partner; Coney batted well and could bowl some useful deliveries.

Gray and Bracewell, the principal spin bowlers, were of good county class, but hardly Test Match standard. Although the Crowe brothers achieved little in the Tests, they looked very promising cricketers.

The captain, Howarth, had some ill-luck with the bat. At the end of the tour he was outspoken about the feeble teams which the counties fielded against the tourists, but this can be blamed on touring teams since the mid-1950s mainly treating the county matches as little more than practice games. The public, by not attending, have shown long ago what they felt on this matter.

1983: Prudential World Cup

The third Prudential World Cup was staged in England in June 1983. The countries involved were the seven Test-playing nations and Zimbabwe, which had won the I.C.C. Trophy in 1982.

The visiting players involved were:

Pakistan: Imran Khan (captain), Mudassar Nazar, Mohsin Khan, Zaheer Abbas, Javed Miandad, Ijaz Faqih, Tahir Naqqash, Wasim Bari, Rashid Khan, Shahid Mahboob, Sarfraz Nawaz, Abdul Qadir, Mansoor Akhtar and Wasim Raja.

Sri Lanka: L. R. D. Mendis (captain), S. Wettimuny, B. Kuruppu, R. L. Dias, A. Ranatunga, M. A. R. Samarasekera, D. S. de Silva, A. L. F. de Mel, R. G. de Alwis, R. J. Ratnayake, V. B. John and R. S. Madugalle.

Australia: K. J. Hughes (captain), G. M. Wood, K. C. Wessels, D. W. Hookes, G. N. Yallop. A. R. Border, R. W. Marsh, G. F. Lawson, R. M. Hogg, D. K. Lillee, J. R. Thomson, K. H. MacLeay, T. M. Chappell and T. G. Hogan.

Zimbabwe: D. A. G. Fletcher (captain), A. H. Shah, G. A. Paterson, J. G. Heron, A. J. Pycroft, D. L. Houghton, K. M. Curran, I. P. Butchart, P. W. E. Rawson, A. J. Traicos, V. R. Hogg, R. D. Brown and G. E. Peckover.

India: Kapil Dev (captain), S. M. Gavaskar, K. Srikkanth, M. Amarnath, S. M. Patil, Yashpal Sharma, R. M. H. Binny, Madan Lal, S. M. H. Kirmani, R. J. Shastri, B. S. Sandhu, D. B. Vengsarkar and K. B. J. Azad.

West Indies: C. H. Lloyd (captain), C. G. Greenidge, D. L. Haynes, I. V. A. Richards, S. F. Bacchus, P. J. Dujon, H. A. Gomes, M. D. Marshall, A. M. E. Roberts, M. A. Holding, J. Garner, W. W. Daniel, W. W. David and A. L. Logie.

Above *Kapil Dev, India's great all-rounder and captain, holds the Prudential Cup after his team had unexpectedly outplayed the West Indies in the 1983 final.*

Left *A critical moment in the final: Viv Richards holes out to Kapil Dev at mid-wicket off Madan Lal's bowling.*

New Zealand: see under separate heading.

The teams played each of the other sides in their group twice, as opposed to once in 1979, a change made both to increase the gate receipts and to prevent teams getting through to the finals by accident of the weather. In fact the weather was very benevolent and the Cup was unexpectedly won by India, who beat the West Indies in the final. The Indian side owed their success mainly to Kapil Dev, Amarnath and Binny.

The total receipts were £1,195,712 and total attendance 232,081 in 27 matches, a large fall in average per match from both 1979 and 1975.

1984: 15th West Indians

The team announced on 16 April was C. H. Lloyd (captain) and R. A. Harper of Guyana; I. V. A. Richards, R. B. Richardson and E. A. E. Baptiste of the Leeward Islands; C. G. Greenidge, D. L. Haynes, T. R. O. Payne, M. D. Marshall and J. Garner from Barbados; A. L. Logie and H. A. Gomes of Trinidad; P. J. Dujon, M. A. Holding, C. A. Walsh and M. A. Small from Jamaica, with J. L. Hendriks as manager.

Croft, Clarke, Kallicharran, Rowe and King were all banned, having been on the West Indian 'rebel' tour to South Africa. The

Gordon Greenidge had an impressive record on the 1984 West Indian tour and gave an enthralling performance at Lord's, where his 214 not out in the fourth innings helped win the match by nine wickets. Here he sweeps Miller.

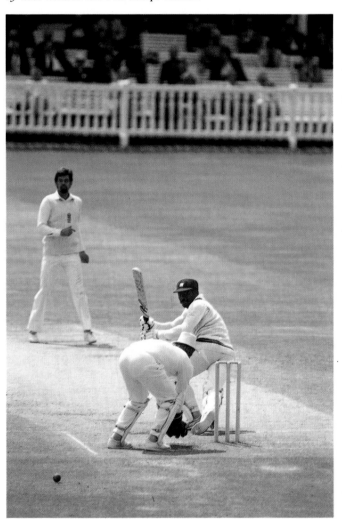

final Test against Australia in the 1983-84 season did not finish until 2 May, so that the side to England only arrived in London on 14 May and the first fixture did not begin until 19 May.

As most of the players were familiar with English conditions, the very brief preliminaries before the one-day internationals

---

1984: 15th West Indians

1st Match: v Worcestershire (Worcester)   May 19, 20, 21.
West Indians 412-9 dec (C. G. Greenidge 138, D. L. Haynes 89, P. J. Dujon 52*) drew with Worcestershire 124-1 (T. S. Curtis 82*).

2nd Match: v Somerset (Taunton)   May 23, 24, 25.
Somerset 116 (R. A. Harper 5-32) and 125 (M. D. Marshall 5-31) lost to West Indians 342 (R. A. Harper 73, H. A. Gomes 72, C. H. Lloyd 72, R. B. Richardson 50) by an innings and 101 runs.

3rd Match: v Glamorgan (Swansea)   May 26, 27, 28.
Glamorgan 175 (A. L. Jones 50, J. Garner 5-19) and 88 (E. A. E. Baptiste 4-17) lost to West Indians 489-6 dec (I. V. A. Richards 170, R. B. Richardson 111, H. A. Gomes 73, A. L. Logie 71) by an innings and 226 runs.

4th Match: v Lancashire (Liverpool)   May 29 (55 overs a side).
West Indians 297-6 (C. G. Greenidge 186, H. A. Gomes 87) beat Lancashire 241-7 (G. Fowler 94) by 56 runs.

5th Match: v England (Old Trafford)   May 31 (55 overs a side).
West Indians 272 (I. V. A. Richards 189*) beat England 168 (A. J. Lamb 75) by 104 runs.

6th Match: v England (Trent Bridge)   June 2 (55 overs a side).
West Indians 179 (C. H. Lloyd 52) lost to England 180-7 by 3 wkts.

7th Match: v England (Lord's)   June 4 (55 overs a side).
England 196-9 lost to West Indians 197-2 (I. V. A. Richards 84*, H. A. Gomes 56*) by 8 wkts.

8th Match: v Duchess of Norfolk's XI (Arundel Castle)   June 6 (50 overs a side).
West Indians 140 (C. H. Lloyd 53) beat Duchess of Norfolk's XI 76 by 64 runs.

9th Match: v Oxford and Cambridge Universities (Oxford)   June 7, 8.
West Indians 341-7 dec (D. L. Haynes 100, A. L. Logie 96, R. B. Richardson 88) drew with Oxford and Cambridge 78 and 120-2 (A. J. T. Miller 56).

10th Match: v Northants (Milton Keynes)   June 9, 10, 11.
Northants 220 (R. J. Bailey 95, D. J. Capel 63, M. D. Marshall 4-36, M. A. Small 4-52) and 220-5 dec drew with West Indians 268 (H. A. Gomes 109) and 50-0.

11th Match: v England (Edgbaston)   June 14, 15, 16, 18.
England 191 (I. T. Botham 64, J. Garner 4-53) and 235 (J. Garner 5-55) lost to West Indies 606 (H. A. Gomes 143, I. V. A. Richards 117, E. A. E. Baptiste 87*, C. H. Lloyd 71, M. A. Holding 69, D. R. Pringle 5-108) by an innings and 180 runs.

12th Match: v Ireland (Dublin)   June 21, 22.
West Indians 584-6 dec (H. A. Gomes 153, A. L. Logie 129, R. B. Richardson 78, T. R. O. Payne 73*, R. A. Harper 64, C. G. Greenidge 54) drew with Ireland 187 (R. A. Harper 4-58).

13th Match: v Essex (Chelmsford)   June 23, 24, 25.
West Indians 322-5 dec (P. J. Dujon 107, A. L. Logie 85, C. G. Greenidge 77, N. A. Foster 4-46) and 277-8 dec (C. G. Greenidge 62, I. V. A. Richards 60) drew with Essex 267 (G. A. Gooch 101, R. A. Harper 6-85) and 164-6 (D. R. Pringle 53*).

14th Match: v England (Lord's)   June 28, 29, 30, July 2.
England 286 (G. Fowler 106, B. C. Broad 55, M. D. Marshall 6-85) and 300-9 dec (A. J. Lamb 110, I. T. Botham 81) lost to West Indies 245 (I. V. A. Richards 72, I. T. Botham 8-103) and 344-1 (C. G. Greenidge 214*, H. A. Gomes 92*) by 9 wkts.

15th Match: v League Cricket Conference (Colwyn Bay)   July 5, 6.
West Indians 401 (C. G. Greenidge 93, P. J. Dujon 71, E. A. E. Baptiste 65, C. H. Lloyd 59) and 275-2 dec (R. B. Richardson 149*, T. R. O. Payne 71*) drew with League C.C. 136 (R. A. Harper 4-23) and 76-8 (C. A. Walsh 6-26).

16th Match: v Leicestershire (Leicester)   July 7, 8, 9.
Leicestershire 283 (I. P. Butcher 118, P. B. Clift 54) and 136-5 drew with West Indians 506-5 dec (H. A. Gomes 143, A. L. Logie 141, C. G. Greenidge 56*, D. L. Haynes 50).

17th Match: v England (Headingley)   July 12, 13, 14, 16.
England 270 (A. J. Lamb 100, M. A. Holding 4-70) and 159 (G. Fowler 50, M. D. Marshall 7-53) lost to West Indies 302 (H. A. Gomes 104*, P. J. W. Allott 6-61) and 131-2 by 8 wkts.

18th Match: v Minor Counties (West Bromwich)   July 19, 20.
West Indians 556-7 dec (D. L. Haynes 169, T. R. O. Payne 120, I. V. A. Richards 109, P. J. Dujon 77) and 9-0 drew with Minor Counties 240 (S. R. Atkinson 76).

19th Match: v Derbyshire (Derby)   July 21, 22.
West Indians 459 (C. G. Greenidge 113, D. L. Haynes 83, P. J. Dujon 57) beat Derbyshire 89 (W. W. Davis 5-39) and 201 (G. Miller 74*, W. W. Davis 5-32, R. A. Harper 4-41) by an innings and 169 runs.

20th Match: v England (Old Trafford)   July 26, 27, 28, 30, 31.
West Indies 500 (C. G. Greenidge 223, P. J. Dujon 101, W. W. Davis 77, P. I. Pocock 4-121) beat England 280 (A. J. Lamb 100*, J. Garner 4-51) and 156 (D. I. Gower 57*, R. A. Harper 6-57) by an innings and 64 runs.

21st Match: v Nottinghamshire (Trent Bridge)   Aug 1, 2, 3.
West Indians 361-4 (A. L. Logie 122*, I. V. A. Richards 81, D. L. Haynes 69) drew with Nottinghamshire did not bat.

22nd Match: v Middlesex (Lord's)   Aug 4, 5, 6.
West Indians 211 (R. A. Harper 58, N. G. Cowans 4-52) and 224-6 dec (A. L. Logie 84*, D. L. Haynes 62) drew with Middlesex 177-4 dec (M. W. Gatting 50*) and 87-2.

23rd Match: v England (Oval)   Aug 9, 10, 11, 13.
West Indies 190 (C. H. Lloyd 60*, I. T. Botham 5-72) and 346 (D. L. Haynes 125) beat England 162 (M. D. Marshall 5-35) and 202 (M. A. Holding 5-43, J. Garner 4-51) by 172 runs.

24th Match: v Somerset (Taunton)   Aug 17 (50 overs a side).
West Indians 210-6 (R. B. Richardson 69, I. V. A. Richards 61) lost to Somerset 213-6 (P. B. Roebuck 59, I. T. Botham 56) by 4 wkts.

1984: 15th West Indians

Batting Averages

	M	I	NO	R	HS	Avge	100	c/s
C. G. Greenidge	11	16	3	1069	223	82.23	4	5
A. L. Logie	8	10	2	585	141	73.12	2	3
H. A. Gomes	12	17	5	841	143	70.08	4	2
C. H. Lloyd	9	9	2	364	72	52.00	0	12
I. V. A. Richards	12	15	1	625	170	44.64	2	12
P. J. Dujon	12	15	2	558	107	42.92	2	27
D. L. Haynes	12	17	1	632	125	39.50	1	9
T. R. O. Payne	7	8	3	191	44	38.20	0	4/1
W. W. Davis	4	4	1	112	77	37.33	0	1
R. B. Richardson	8	10	0	335	111	33.50	1	3
R. A. Harper	13	12	2	328	73	32.80	0	14
M. A. Holding	7	7	0	189	69	27.00	0	3
E. A. E. Baptiste	10	9	1	196	87*	24.50	0	1
M. D. Marshall	8	9	0	103	34	11.44	0	3
J. Garner	8	8	1	61	29	8.71	0	4
M. A. Small	5	3	2	6	3*	6.00	0	1
C. A. Walsh	8	5	2	2	2*	0.66	0	1

Bowling Averages

	O	M	R	W	Avge	BB	5i
W. W. Davis	66	13	199	14	14.21	5-32	2
J. Garner	270.5	81	624	39	16.00	5-19	2
M. D. Marshall	260.4	75	646	40	16.15	7-53	4
R. A. Harper	302.1	106	632	37	17.08	6-57	3
M. A. Holding	178.5	42	486	21	23.14	5-43	1
M. A. Small	100	17	321	13	24.69	4-52	0
E. A. E. Baptiste	221.2	64	517	19	27.21	4-17	0
C. A. Walsh	156.1	32	557	14	39.78	3-33	0
H. A. Gomes	44	15	81	2	40.50	1-2	0
I. V. A. Richards	74	20	185	3	61.66	2-60	0

Also bowled: C. G. Greenidge 9-6-11-1.

were sufficient to acclimatise the team, who beat England by two matches to one. Despite the five missing rebels the 1984 West Indies were strong enough to tackle England and in one of the most one-sided Test series ever staged in England won all five games.

The England batsmen never came to terms with the fast attack of Marshall, Garner, and Holding, only A. J. Lamb putting up sustained resistance. When the tour began it was expected that the batting combination led by Richards would overwhelm the England bowlers. After a very powerful beginning Richards did not in fact live up to his great reputation and the batting honours were stolen by Greenidge and Gomes, both of whose Test averages were over 80. Greenidge played some very exciting innings; Gomes quietly and efficiently built up his runs. In the background was Lloyd, who came to the rescue on the odd occasions when the earlier batsmen failed. The wicketkeeper Dujon also proved a most useful batsman and indeed most of the lower order could score runs if needed. The least successful was Haynes, though he played in all five Tests. Richardson and Payne had relatively few opportunities. Owing to an injury to Marshall, W. W. Davis was co-opted into the side on 10 July as a bowler and surprised himself by scoring 77 in his one Test innings.

The Tests and one-day internationals were well attended and the tour was blessed with exceptionally fine weather. In these circumstances it was a pity that England could not field a stronger opposition.

1984: 3rd Sri Lankans

The newest recruits to the ranks of Test cricket were allocated one Test Match on their third visit to England, the match being staged at Lord's after England had been beaten five nil by the West Indies.

The team was L. R. D. Mendis (captain), S. A. R. Silva, S. Wettimuny, R. S. Madugalle, A. Ranatunga, P. A. de Silva, D. M. Vonhagt, J. R. Ratnayeke, A. L. F. De Mel, R. L. Dias, D. S. de Silva, A. D. A. Samaranayake, S. D. Anurasiri, D. S. B. P. Kuruppu, V. B. John, M. M. Yusuf, R. G. de Alwis and N. Chanmugam as manager.

Several members were struck down with food poisoning during

the first match, but this problem was soon left behind as the batsmen began to prosper on the English wickets; the bowlers meanwhile struggled and the team had great difficulty in dismissing their opponents.

The Test Match was the eighth game of this brief tour and the pundits predicted an overwhelming defeat for the newcomers, England being keen to exonerate themselves after the press's harsh criticism earlier in the year. Gower put the visitors in and at the end of the second day they were still batting with well over 400 on the board. The match then gently drifted to a draw, England's bowlers proving as feeble as those of Sri Lanka and the home country struggled through its most embarrassing Test.

Sri Lanka possessed a useful array of batsmen in S. A. R. Silva,

1984: 3rd Sri Lankans

1st Match: v Nottinghamshire (Cleethorpes)   July 25, 26, 27.
Nottinghamshire 311-8 dec (P. Johnson 80, J. D. Birch 80, D. W. Randall 52) and 210-6 dec (R. T. Robinson 115) drew with Sri Lankans 199 (E. E. Hemmings 7-47) and 123-2.

2nd Match: v Surrey (Oval)   July 28, 29, 30.
Surrey 250-9 dec (G. P. Howarth 77, A. Needham 54) and 208-8 dec (V. B. John 5-89) beat Sri mankans 194 (L. R. D. Mendis 67*) and 105 by 159 runs.

3rd Match: v Gloucestershire (Cheltenham)   Aug 4, 6, 7.
Gloucestershire 278-4 dec (S. H. Wootton 97, P. W. Romaines 83, E. J. Cunningham 61*) and 116-6 (V. B. John 6-58) drew with Sri Lankans 286-1 dec (S. Wettimuny 123*, S. A. R. Silva 91, R. S. Madugalle 57*).

4th Match: v Hampshire (Southampton)   Aug 8, 9, 10.
Hampshire 312-6 dec (R. A. Smith 132) and 291-4 dec (C. L. Smith 103*, R. A. Smith 97) drew with Sri Lankans 336-9 dec (P. A. de Silva 75, A. Ranatunga 50) and 102-3.

5th Match: v Kent (Canterbury)   Aug 11, 12, 13.
Sri Lankans 340-7 dec (A. Ranatunga 118, P. A. de Silva 59) drew with Kent 182 (D. S. de Silva 5-39, V. B. John 5-50) and 420-5 dec (D. G. Aslett 221*, M. R. Benson 65, G. W. Johnson 52*).

6th Match: v Duchess of Norfolk's XI (Arundel Castle)   Aug 16 (50 overs a side).
Duchess of Norfolk's XI 212-6 (C. Gladwin 57, D. S. de Silva 4-31) lost to Sri Lankans 216-9 (D. S. B. P. Kuruppa 58) by 1 wkt.

7th Match: v Sussex (Hove)   Aug 18, 19, 20.
Sri Lankans 193 (S. Wettimuny 73, P. A. de Silva 62, A. P. Wells 4-50) and 235 (J. R. Ratnayeke 66) drew with Sussex 345-6 dec (P. W. G. Parker 181, I. A. Greig 50).

8th Match: v England (Lord's)   Aug 23, 24, 25, 27, 28.
Sri Lanka 491-7 dec (S. Wettimuny 190, L. R. D. Mendis 111, R. L. Dias 84) and 294-7 dec (S. A. R. Silva 102, L. R. D. Mendis 94, I. T. Botham 6-90) drew with England 370 (A. J. Lamb 107, B. C. Broad 86, D. I. Gower 55, A. L. F. De Mel 4-110, V. B. John 4-98).

9th Match: v Warwickshire (Edgbaston)   Aug 29, 30, 31.
Sri Lankans 301-7 dec (S. A. R. Silva 161*) and 276-5 dec (S. A. R. Silva 70, D. M. Vonhagt 75, R. S. Madugalle 51) drew with Warwickshire 242-3 dec (R. I. H. B. Dyer 80, A. I. Kallicharran 79*) and 246-7 dec (R. I. H. B. Dyer 60, K. D. Smith 54, J. R. Ratnayeke 4-93).

10th Match: v D. B. Close's XI (Scarborough)   Sept 2, 3, 4.
D. B. Close's XI 308-5 dec (D. L. Haynes 111, G. Fowler 61) drew with Sri Lankans 216-4 (R. S. Madugalle 87, A. Ranatunga 73*).

1984: 3rd Sri Lankans

Batting Averages

	M	I	NO	R	HS	Avge	100	c/s
S. A. R. Silva	7	12	3	558	161*	62.00	2	12
L. R. D. Mendis	7	10	2	442	111	55.25	1	1
S. Wettimuny	7	11	1	505	190	50.50	2	2
R. S. Madugalle	7	12	4	336	87*	42.00	0	3
A. Ranatunga	8	11	1	419	118	41.90	1	5
P. A. de Silva	7	8	0	236	75	29.50	0	3
D. M. Vonhagt	5	9	0	251	75	27.88	0	2
J. R. Ratnayeke	8	11	5	163	66	27.16	0	5
A. L. F. De Mel	6	7	1	117	37	19.50	0	3
R. L. Dias	9	12	0	224	38	18.66	0	5
D. S. de Silva	5	4	1	55	37*	18.33	0	2
A. D. A. Samaranayake	5	2	1	14	9*	14.00	0	3
S. D. Anurasiri	4	3	1	5	5	2.50	0	2
D. S. B. P. Kuruppu	3	4	0	38	25	9.50	0	4/1
V. B. John	5	3	1	4	4	2.00	0	1

Also batted: (4 matches) M. M. Yusuf 2*; (2 matches) R. G. de Alwis 74 (3 ct).

Bowling Averages

	O	M	R	W	Avge	BB	5i
V. B. John	190.3	46	603	26	23.19	6-58	0
A. L. F. De Mel	153.2	31	470	19	24.73	4-110	0
R. S. Madugalle	31	6	75	2	37.50	1-18	0
A. Ranatunga	69	12	227	6	37.83	2-44	0
D. S. de Silva	216	62	532	13	40.92	5-39	1
J. R. Ratnayeke	227.2	43	730	16	45.62	4-93	0
A. D. A. Samaranayake	143.2	24	499	9	55.44	4-142	0
M. M. Yusuf	74	10	282	1	282.00	1-25	0
S. D. Anurasiri	89.5	21	336	1	336.00	1-65	0

Also bowled: P. A. de Silva 4-0-19-0; R. L. Dias 6-3-18-1; L. R. D. Mendis 1-0-2-0; S. Wettimuny 5-1-7-1.

Sri Lanka's 1984 tourists at Lord's. Back row: P. A. de Silva, S. A. R. Silva, Ranatunga, Mumtas Yusuf, John, Ratnayeke, de Alwis, De Mel, Samaranayake, Vonhagt, Anurasiri. Front row: N. Chanmugam (manager), Wettimuny, Dias, Mendis (capt), D. S. de Silva, Madugalle, R. Fernando (asst manager).

S. Wettimuny and L. R. D. Mendis. John was the main seam bowler, but tended to overpitch the ball and the veteran D. S. de Silva was the best of the spinners.

The public showed little interest in the tour and the five-day Test mustered only 28,000 spectators.

1985: 31st Australians

The team was A. R. Border (captain), R. B. Phillips, G. M. Ritchie, D. R. Gilbert, C. J. McDermott, S. P. O'Donnell, M. J. Bennett, R. G. Holland, G. R. J. Matthews, D. M. Wellham, G. M. Wood, K. C. Wessels, J. R. Thomson, A. M. J. Hilditch, G. F. Lawson, W. B. Phillips and D. C. Boon, with R. F. Merriman as the manager and G. Dymock his assistant.

Lacking the services of Alderman, Hogg, Maguire and Rackemann, all of whom were rejected because of their tour to South Africa, the Australian bowling looked and was threadbare. Only McDermott was effective in the Tests–except for the one match-winning effort by Holland–and thus England won the Test series by three matches to one. Of the 20 first-class games Australia won only four. Four-day matches were arranged against several counties, but the unusual amount of rain in 1985 still meant many drawn matches.

Border had a splendid summer with the bat, Hilditch began the

tour well, but then the bowlers found his weakness for the hook. The England bowlers also discovered Wessels' flaws and he was nothing like the batsman of previous years.

Wellham came second to Border in the first-class averages, but failed twice in his only Test. Ritchie on the other hand proved a useful find and played some elegant innings.

1985: 31st Australians

Batting Averages

	M	I	NO	R	HS	Avge	100	c/s
A. R. Border	14	21	2	1355	196	71.31	8	13
D. M. Wellham	10	16	4	669	125*	55.75	2	1
D. C. Boon	15	20	5	832	206*	55.46	3	13
G. M. Ritchie	16	23	3	1097	155	54.85	4	7
W. B. Phillips	14	22	3	899	128	47.31	1	20/1
S. P. O'Donnell	11	16	5	448	100*	40.72	1	5
K. C. Wessels	16	26	1	905	156	36.20	1	9
G. M. Wood	16	25	3	691	172	31.40	2	6
A. M. J. Hilditch	17	27	0	829	119	30.70	1	7
R. B. Phillips	7	7	2	130	39	26.00	0	17/3
G. R. J. Matthews	10	12	3	216	51*	24.00	0	3
C. J. McDermott	16	14	3	183	53*	16.63	0	2
J. R. Thomson	11	11	6	82	28*	16.40	0	2
M. J. Bennett	11	10	3	111	23	15.85	0	6
G. F. Lawson	13	13	2	154	53	14.00	0	1
D. R. Gilbert	10	8	3	39	12	7.80	0	2
R. G. Holland	13	10	1	59	35	6.55	0	5

Bowling Averages

	O	M	R	W	Avge	BB	5i
C. J. McDermott	421.5	49	1609	51	31.54	8-141	3
J. R. Thomson	241.3	33	988	29	34.06	6-44	2
R. G. Holland	376	94	1017	29	35.06	5-51	2
G. F. Lawson	347	61	1165	31	37.58	5-103	1
D. R. Gilbert	253.2	42	885	21	42.14	4-41	0
G. R. J. Matthews	159.4	34	521	12	43.41	3-76	0
M. J. Bennett	266.4	62	766	16	47.87	4-39	0
S. P. O'Donnell	242.4	47	819	12	68.25	3-37	0

Also bowled: D. C. Boon 6-0-33-0; A. R. Border 13-2-38-0; A. M. J. Hilditch 7-2-29-0; G. M. Ritchie 6.3-0-33-1; K. C. Wessels 32-9-79-0.

1985: 31st Australians

1st Match: v Lavinia, Duchess of Norfolk's XI (Arundel) May 5.
Australians 261-6 dec (A. R. Border 65) drew with Norfolk's XI 145-5 (R. D. V. Knight 63*).

2nd Match: v Somerset (Taunton) May 8, 9, 10.
Australians 356-4 dec (A. R. Border 106, D. M. Wellham 64, D. C. Boon 62*, W. B. Phillips 56*) and 316-6 dec (K. C. Wessels 156) beat Somerset 314 (B. C. Rose 81*, I. T. Botham 65, V. J. Marks 50) and 125 (J. R. Thomson 6-44) by 233 runs.

3rd Match: v Worcestershire (Worcester) May 11, 12, 13.
Worcestershire 303-6 dec (P. A. Neale 108, T. S. Curtis 76) and 93-4 drew with Australians 364-5 dec (A. R. Border 135, D. C. Boon 73*).

4th Match: v Nottinghamshire (Trent Bridge) May 14 (Limited Overs).
Abandoned due to rain.

5th Match: v Surrey (The Oval) May 16 (Limited Overs).
Australians 216-7 (W. B. Phillips 66*) lost to Surrey 217-4 (G. S. Clinton 86, A. R. Butcher 64) by 6 wkts.

6th Match: v Sussex (Hove) May 18, 19, 20, 21.
Australians 321 (D. C. Boon 119, K. C. Wessels 56) and 275-6 dec (G. M. Ritchie 100*, W. B. Phillips 91) drew with Sussex 262 (G. D. Mendis 81) and 153-9.

7th Match: v M.C.C. (Lord's) May 22, 23, 24.
Australians 377-6 dec (A. R. Border 125, S. P. O'Donnell 100*, K. C. Wessels 60) and 222-3 (D. M. Wellham 81*) drew with M.C.C. 291-2 dec (M. C. J. Nicholas 115*, A. J. Lamb 122*).

8th Match: v Derbyshire (Derby) May 25, 26, 27.
Australians 278-5 (A. R. Border 100, D. M. Wellham 77, A. M. J. Hilditch 60) drew with Derbyshire did not bat.

9th Match: v Derbyshire (Derby) May 28 (Limited Overs).
Derbyshire 188-9 (K. J. Barnett 54) lost to Australians 192-4 (K. C. Wessels 64) by 6 wkts.

10th Match: v England (Old Trafford) May 30 (Limited Overs).
England 219 (I. T. Botham 72, G. A. Gooch 57) lost to Australia 220-7 (A. R. Border 59) by 3 wkts.

11th Match: v England (Edgbaston) June 1 (Limited Overs).
England 231-7 (G. A. Gooch 115) lost to Australia 233-6 (A. R. Border 85*, K. C. Wessels 57) by 4 wkts.

12th Match: v England (Lord's) June 3 (Limited Overs).
Australia 254-5 (G. M. Wood 114*) lost to England 257-2 (G. A. Gooch 117*, D. I. Gower 102) by 8 wkts.

13th Match: v Yorkshire (Headingley) June 5, 6, 7.
Australians 195-2 dec (G. M. Wood 102*, G. M. Ritchie 58*) drew with Yorkshire 124-2 (G. Boycott 52*).

14th Match: v Leicestershire (Leicester) June 8, 9, 10, 11.
Leicestershire 454 (D. I. Gower 135, J. C. Balderstone 134, J. R. Thomson 5-103) and 28-0 drew with 466 (W. B. Phillips 128, G. M. Ritchie 115, A. M. J. Hilditch 56, C. J. McDermott 53*).

15th Match: v England (Headingley) June 13, 14, 15, 17, 18.
Australia 331 (A. M. J. Hilditch 119) and 324 (W. B. Phillips 91, A. M. J. Hilditch 80, K. C. Wessels 64, J. E. Emburey 5-82) lost to England 533 (R. T. Robinson 175, I. T. Botham 60, P. R. Downton 54, M. W. Gatting 53) and 123-5 by 5 wkts.

16th Match: v Oxford and Cambridge Universities (Cambridge) June 20 (Limited Overs).
Australians 265-8 (D. C. Boon 108) beat Oxford and Cambridge 186-6 (P. G. P. Roebuck 75*) by 79 runs.

17th Match: v Hampshire (Southampton) June 22, 23, 24, 25.
Hampshire 221 (V. P. Terry 60, R. G. Holland 5-51) and 64-1 dec drew with Australians 76 (K. D. James 6-22) and 154-7 (G. M. Ritchie 62).

18th Match: v England (Lord's) June 27, 28, 29, July 1, 2.
England 290 (D. I. Gower 86, C. J. McDermott 6-70) and 261 (I. T. Botham 85, M. W. Gatting 75*, R. G. Holland 5-68) lost to Australia 425 (A. R. Border 196, G. M. Ritchie 94, I. T. Botham 5-109) and 127-6 by 4 wkts.

19th Match: v Essex (Chelmsford) July 6, 7, 8, 9.
Australians 279 (A. M. J. Hilditch 80) and 333 (D. C. Boon 138, D. M. Wellham 63) drew with Essex 409 (B. R. Hardie 113*, G. A. Gooch 68, N. Phillip 50) and 169-8.

20th Match: v England (Trent Bridge) July 11, 12, 13, 15, 16.
England 456 (D. I. Gower 166, G. A. Gooch 70, G. F. Lawson 5-103) and 196-2 (R. T. Robinson 77*) drew with Australia 539 (G. W. Wood 172, G. M. Ritchie 146).

21st Match: v Minor Counties (Jesmond) July 18 (Limited Overs).
Australians 331-2 (D. M. Wellman 107*, D. C. Boon 84*, G. M. Wood 83) beat Minor Counties 206-7 (G. R. J. Roope 76) by 125 runs.

22nd Match: v Glamorgan (Neath) July 20, 21, 22.
Glamorgan 409-3 dec (Javed Miandad 200*, Younis Ahmed 118*) drew with Australians 105-1.

23rd Match: v Gloucestershire (Bristol) July 24, 25, 26.
Australians 146 (K. M. Curran 5-35) and 410-3 dec (A. R. Border 130, D. M. Wellham 105, K. C. Wessels 61*) beat Gloucestershire 181 (J. W. Lloyds 71) and 205 (C. W. J. Athey 83, K. M. Curran 58) by 170 runs.

24th Match: v Northamptonshire (Northampton) July 27, 28, 29, 30.
Australians 404-5 dec (D. C. Boon 206*, W. B. Phillips 55, G. R. J. Matthews 51*) drew with Northants 258-3 (R. J. Bailey 107*).

25th Match: v England (Old Trafford) Aug 1, 2, 3, 5, 6.
Australia 257 (D. C. Boon 61) and 340-5 (A. R. Border 146*, K. C. Wessels 50) drew with England 482-9 dec (M. W. Gatting 160, G. A. Gooch 74, A. J. Lamb 67, C. J. McDermott 8-141).

26th Match: v Ireland (Downpatrick) Aug 8.
Australia 151-4 (A. R. Border 91) drew with Ireland did not bat.

27th Match: v Middlesex (Lord's) Aug 10, 11, 12, 13.
Middlesex 397-4 dec (W. N. Slack 201*, K. R. Brown 102) drew with Australians 396-6 dec (D. M. Wellham 125*, W. B. Phillips 73, K. C. Wessels 56).

28th Match: v England (Edgbaston) Aug 15, 16, 17, 19, 20.
Australia 335 (K. C. Wessels 83, G. F. Lawson 53, R. M. Ellison 6-77) and 142 (W. B. Phillips 59) lost to England 595-5 dec (D. I. Gower 215, R. T. Robinson 148, M. W. Gatting 100*) by an innings and 118 runs.

29th Match: v Kent (Canterbury) Aug 24, 25, 26, 27.
Kent 333 (L. Potter 58) and 126 (C. J. McDermott 5-18) lost to Australians 364 (G. M. Ritchie 155, A. R. Border 103, K. C. Wessels 51) and 99-3 by 7 wkts.

30th Match: v England (The Oval) Aug 29, 30, 31, Sept 2.
England 464 (G. A. Gooch 196, D. I. Gower 157) beat Australia 241 (G. M. Ritchie 64*) and 129 (A. R. Border 58, R. M. Ellison 5-46) by an innings and 94 runs.

The captain of the Australian tourists in 1985, Allan Border, batting at Lord's, where he scored 196 in a four-wicket victory. Downton is the wicket-keeper, and Gatting, Emburey and Gower the fielders.

1985: 2nd Zimbabweans

The tour was organised to give the players some experience in England before the 1986 I.C.C. Trophy. The team was A. J. Pycroft (captain), A. J. Traicos (vice-captain), D. L. Houghton, M. P. Jarvis, E. A. Brandes, A. C. Waller, A. H. Shah, K. G. Duers, L. L. de Grandhomme, K. G. Walton, D. H. Streak, G. A. Hick, I. P. Butchart, R. D. Brown and G. A. Paterson, with D. A. Ellman-Brown as manager.

Rain marred the trip, causing five of the first-class matches to be drawn, but Zimbabwe won all their one-day matches.

The team lacked both Rawson and Curran, which weakened

the bowling. With Hick at No. 3, however, the batting had few problems; his 230 against Oxford has only been exceeded twice in first-class matches for Rhodesia/Zimbabwe. Butchart was the best all-rounder and easily the leading bowler.

1986: 11th New Zealanders

The New Zealand side which toured England in the second half of the 1986 season was the first to win a Test series in England. The team was managed by R. A. Vance, but owing to illness he returned to New Zealand and the post was filled by Glenn Turner, officially the cricket manager. The team was J. V. Coney (captain), K. R. Rutherford, E. J. Gray, W. Watson, T. J. Franklin, B. J. Barrett, D. A. Stirling, J. G. Bracewell, T. E. Blain, M. D. Crowe, E. J. Chatfield, J. G. Wright, J. J. Crowe, B. A. Edgar and I. D. S. Smith. The tourists owed a great deal to Hadlee, who appeared only in the Tests and one-day

---

1985: 2nd Zimbabweans

1st Match: v Oxford University (The Parks) June 8, 10, 11.
Oxford University 262-7 dec (D. A. Thorne 124) and 149-5 (R. S. Rutnagur 57) drew with Zimbabwe 440 (G. A. Hick 230, D. L. Houghton 104, R. S. Rutnagur 5-112).

2nd Match: v Combined Services (Aldershot) June 14.
Combined Services 70 lost to Zimbabwe 71-2 by 8 wkts.

3rd Match: v Somerset (Bath) June 15 (Limited Overs).
Somerset 191-9 (R. J. Harden 56, K. G. Duers 5-26) lost to Zimbabwe 195-6 by 4 wkts.

4th Match: v Glamorgan (Swansea) June 19, 20, 21.
Glamorgan 214 (A. L. Jones 80, I. P. Butchart 5-65) and 187-4 (S. P. Henderson 52*) drew with Zimbabwe 364 (G. A. Hick 192, G. A. Paterson 69).

5th Match: v Warwickshire (Edgbaston) June 22, 24, 25.
Warwickshire 308-2 dec (R. I. H. B. Dyer 109*, D. L. Amiss 86, T. A. Lloyd 57) and 139-5 dec (G. W. Humpage 76) drew with Zimbabwe 159-5 dec (A. C. Waller 56*) and 231-6 (G. A. Hick 65).

6th Match: v Minor Counties (Cleethorpes) June 29, 30, July 1.
Zimbabwe 214 (L. L. de Grandhomme 59, K. A. Arnold 5-57) and 293-7 dec (A. J. Pycroft 110*, I. P. Butchart 82) drew with Minor Counties 293-8 dec (S. R. Atkinson 63, G. R. J. Roope 61).

7th Match: v Wales (Builth Wells) July 8, 9.
Wales 179 (I. P. Butchart 5-45) and 320 (G. Edwards 79, D. Harris 70, L. L. de Grandhomme 5-11) beat Zimbabwe 240 (D. L. Houghton 70, A. J. Pycroft 52, R. D. Brown 50) and 192 (I. P. Butchart 96) by 67 runs.

8th Match: v League Cricket Conference (Middleton) July 10, 11.
L.C.C. 264-7 dec (D. Borthwick 65) and 83-3 beat Zimbabwe 163 (D. L. Houghton 52, A. Merricck 6-37) and 182 (D. L. Houghton 52) by 7 wkts.

9th Match: v Sussex (Hove) July 13 (Limited Overs).
Sussex 237-8 dec (A. P. Wells 80, N. J. Lenham 76) lost to Zimbabwe 238-5 (G. A. Paterson 95, A. H. Shah 52) by 5 wkts.

10th Match: v Lavinia, Duchess of Norfolk's XI (Arundel) July 14.
Norfolk's XI 217-8 dec (N. J. Lenham 74) lost to Zimbabwe 220-3 (G. A. Paterson 88, K. G. Walton 78*) by 7 wkts.

11th Match: v Surrey (The Oval) July 17, 18, 19.
Surrey 343-5 dec (A. Needham 124, T. E. Jesty 100*) and 220-4 (A. J. Stewart 88*, T. E. Jesty 54) drew with Zimbabwe 226.

12th Match: v Gloucestershire (Bristol) July 20, 22, 23.
Zimbabwe 156 and 205-4 dec (G. A. Paterson 92) lost to Gloucestershire 65-2 dec and 299-3 (P. W.Romaines 114*, B. F. Davison 53*) by 7 wkts.

1985: 2nd Zimbabweans

Batting Averages

	M	I	NO	R	HS	Avge	100	c/s
G. A. Hick	6	9	0	598	230	66.44	2	6
A. J. Pycroft	4	6	2	245	110*	61.25	1	2
D. H. Streak	3	3	1	72	29	36.00	0	1
G. A. Paterson	6	9	0	320	92	35.55	0	0
A. C. Waller	2	3	1	69	56*	34.50	0	2
D. L. Houghton	6	8	1	231	104	33.00	1	3
L. L. de Grandhomme	5	6	1	157	59	31.40	0	2
I. P. Butchart	6	8	1	134	82	19.14	0	1
A. H. Shah	4	6	1	95	40	19.00	0	1
A. J. Traicos	6	5	2	57	27*	19.00	0	7
K. G. Walton	3	5	1	57	20*	14.25	0	2
R. D. Brown	5	8	0	113	27	14.12	0	1
E. A. Brandes	3	4	1	30	19	10.00	0	0
M. P. Jarvis	4	3	1	10	6	5.00	0	1

Played in three matches: K. G. Duers 1, 0.

Bowling Averages

	O	M	R	W	Avge	BB	5i
I. P. Butchart	167	42	547	20	27.35	5-65	1
L. L. de Grandhomme	46	9	148	4	37.00	3-79	0
M. P. Jarvis	110	13	392	10	39.20	3-37	0
A. J. Traicos	167.1	48	439	8	54.87	2-33	0
K. G. Duers	66	13	235	4	58.75	3-75	0

Also bowled: E. A. Brandes 47.4-3-190-3; G. A. Hick 71-9-236-3; A. H. Shah 28-7-106-0; D. H. Streak 20.3-4-69-3.

1986: 11th New Zealanders

1st Match: v Lavinia, Duchess of Norfolk's XI (Arundel) June 22.
New Zealanders 255-6 dec (T. J. Franklin 74, M. D. Crowe 70) drew with Norfolk's XI 184-6 (T. E. Jesty 68*).

2nd Match: v Oxford and Cambridge Universities (Cambridge) June 25, 26, 27.
New Zealanders 288-3 dec (K. R. Rutherford 91*, B. A. Edgar 75, J. V. Coney 56*) and 163-1 dec (T. J. Franklin 96, E. J. Gray 56*) beat Oxford and Cambridge 158 and 154 (J. G. Bracewell 6-55) by 139 runs.

3rd Match: v Middlesex (Lord's) June 28, 29, 30.
New Zealanders 232 (J. V. Coney 93) and 239-6 (M. D. Crowe 78, E. J. Gray 53*) drew with Middlesex 436 (M. W. Gatting 135, P. R. Downton 77*, A. J. T. Miller 56).

4th Match: v Essex (Chelmsford) July 2, 3, 4.
Essex 307 (P. J. Prichard 65, J. P. Stephenson 63, J. G. Bracewell 5-110) and 207 (E. J. Gray 7-61) lost to New Zealanders 353-3 dec (M. D. Crowe 100*, J. G. Wright 96, K. R. Rutherford 63) and 165-4 by 6 wkts.

5th Match: v Sussex (Hove) July 5, 6, 7.
New Zealanders 201 and 148-4 dec (B. A. Edgar 56*) drew with Sussex 75-1 dec and 95-3.

6th Match: v Minor Counties (Lakenham) July 9, 10, 11.
Minor Counties 209 (S. G. Plumb 69, E. J. Gray 5-54) and 141 lost to New Zealanders 334-8 dec (E. J. Gray 108, J. J. Crowe 69, J. G. Wright) and 18-0 by 10 wkts.

7th Match: v Warwickshire (Edgbaston) July 12, 13, 14.
Warwicks 330-5 dec (G. W. Humpage 100*, P. A. Smith 77, B. M. McMillan 65) and 210-9 dec drew with New Zealanders 271-4 dec (M. D. Crowe 86*, J. G. Wright 66, J. V. Coney 56) and 136-2 (J. J. Crowe 65*, K. R. Rutherford 52*).

8th Match: v England (Headingley) July 16 (Limited Overs).
New Zealand 217-8 (J. J. Crowe 66) beat England 170 by 47 runs.

9th Match: v England (Old Trafford) July 18 (Limited Overs).
New Zealand 284-5 (M. D. Crowe 93*, K. R. Rutherford 63) lost to England 286-4 (C. W. J. Athey 142*, G. A. Gooch 91) by 6 wkts.

10th Match: v Nottinghamshire (Trent Bridge) July 19, 20, 21.
New Zealanders 326-8 dec (M. D. Crowe 80, J. J. Crowe 75) and 165-2 dec (M. D. Crowe 56*) drew with Nottinghamshire 227 (M. Newell 53, E. J. Gray 5-51) and 219-7 (B. C. Broad 70).

11th Match: v England (Lord's) July 24, 25, 26, 28, 29.
England 307 (M. D. Moxon 74, D. I. Gower 62, R. J. Hadlee 6-80) and 295-6 dec (G. A. Gooch 183) drew with New Zealand 342 (M. D. Crowe 106, B. A. Edgar 83, J. V. Coney 51) and 41-2.

12th Match: v Northamptonshire (Northampton) July 30, 31, Aug 1.
Northamptonshire 300-6 dec (R. J. Bailey 95, R. G. Williams 93) drew with New Zealanders 246-5 (J. G. Bracewell 100*).

13th Match: v Derbyshire (Derby) Aug 2, 3, 4.
Derbyshire 366 (B. J. M. Maher 126, G. Miller 51) drew with New Zealanders 266-5 dec (B. A. Edgar 110*, M. D. Crowe 51).

14th Match: v England (Trent Bridge) Aug 7, 8, 9, 11, 12.
England 256 (D. I. Gower 71, C. W. J. Athey 55, R. J. Hadlee 6-80) and 230 (J. E. Emburey 75) lost to New Zealand 413 (J. G. Bracewell 110, R. J. Hadlee 68, J. G. Wright 58, E. J. Gray 50) and 7-2 by 8 wkts.

15th Match: v T.C.C.B. XI (Edgbaston) Aug 13, 14, 15.
New Zealanders 218-9 dec (J. G. Wright 59, J. J. Crowe 58) and 291-6 dec (K. R. Rutherford 104, M. D. Crowe 61) drew with T.C.C.B. XI 268-6 dec (R. J. Bailey 68, A. A. Metcalfe 58) and 121-1 (A. A. Metcalfe 71*).

16th Match: v Glamorgan (Swansea) Aug 16, 17, 18.
New Zealanders 378-5 dec (J. J. Crowe 159, J. V. Coney 140*) and 71-3 drew with Glamorgan 303-5 dec (J. A. Hopkins 142, G. C. Holmes 74).

17th Match: v England (The Oval) Aug 21, 22, 23, 25, 26.
New Zealand 287 (J. G. Wright 119) and 7-0 drew with England 388-5 dec (D. I. Gower 131, M. W. Gatting 121, I. T. Botham 59*).

18th Match: v D. B. Close's XI (Scarborough) Aug 31, Sept 1, 2.
D. B. Close's XI 257 (G. Boycott 81) and 358-5 (Javed Miandad 102*, Sadiq Mohammad 77, M. A. Harper 55) drew with New Zealanders 519-7 dec (K. R. Rutherford 317, E. J. Gray 88).

Richard Hadlee in the Trent Bridge Test Match of 1986. The great all-rounder was not one of the original party but joined the team for the Tests and one-day internationals and was the series' most successful bowler.

1986: 11th New Zealanders

Batting Averages

	M	I	NO	R	HS	Avge	100	c/s
J. G. Bracewell	12	11	6	386	110	77.20	2	2
M. D. Crowe	12	18	6	787	106	65.58	2	10
J. V. Coney	13	17	5	688	140*	57.33	1	7
K. R. Rutherford	12	19	3	848	317	53.00	2	7
E. J. Gray	13	13	4	467	108	51.88	1	9
B. A. Edgar	12	19	5	590	110*	42.14	1	5
J. G. Wright	12	19	1	668	119	37.11	1	4
J. J. Crowe	13	19	2	624	159	36.70	1	11
I. D. S. Smith	9	9	3	215	48	35.83	0	17/2
R. J. Hadlee	3	3	0	93	68	31.00	0	0
D. A. Stirling	11	7	3	116	26	29.00	0	4
T. E. Blain	9	9	2	172	37	24.57	0	19/3
T. J. Franklin	7	10	0	227	96	22.70	0	5
W. Watson	12	6	3	30	10	10.00	0	3
B. J. Barrett	8	4	3	8	5*	8.00	0	1
E. J. Chatfield	7	2	1	5	5	5.00	0	3

Bowling Averages

	O	M	R	W	Avge	BB	5i
R. J. Hadlee	153.5	42	390	19	20.52	6-80	2
J. V. Coney	75	23	194	7	27.71	2-14	0
J. G. Bracewell	411	122	1042	37	28.16	6-55	2
E. J. Gray	438.2	144	1087	37	29.37	7-61	3
E. J. Chatfield	191.4	47	457	13	35.15	3-73	0
D. A. Stirling	255	36	1025	28	36.60	5-98	1
W. Watson	308.1	60	963	26	37.03	4-31	0
B. J. Barrett	157.5	18	610	15	40.66	3-32	0

Also bowled: M. D. Crowe 49.5-8-190-2; B. A. Edgar 1-0-2-0; T. J. Franklin 1-0-5-0; K. R. Rutherford 5-0-25-0; I. D. S. Smith 2-0-8-0; J. G. Wright 4-1-13-0.

internationals, otherwise appearing for his county. A broken thumb meant that Chatfield missed many matches and injury also affected Franklin and Smith.

Martin Crowe was the most successful batsman and Wright and Edgar were a very useful pair of openers. Neither Jeff Crowe nor Rutherford in the middle order was very successful; Rutherford's good average was on the strength of his 317 at Scarborough against a rather second-rate attack.

Though the bowling at Test level relied on Hadlee, the two spinners, Bracewell and the left arm Gray, had prosperous tours. Coney captained the side well, was a useful run-getter and occasionally bowled well. The fact that only one match was lost on the visit demonstrated the overall ability of the team.

1986: 12th Indians

The Indian side under the captaincy of Kapil Dev was S. M. Patil, Chetan Sharma, M. Prabhakar, R. Lamba, Maninder Singh, K. S. More, K. Srikkanth, M. Azharuddin, C. S. Pandit, R. M. H. Binny, D. B. Vengsarkar, M. Amarnath, R. J. Shastri, S. M. Gavaskar and N. S. Yadav, with Raj Singh as manager and V. B. Prabhudesai as his assistant. The principal player omitted from

1st Match: v Lavinia, Duchess of Norfolk's XI (Arundel) May 4 (Limited Overs).
Indians 217-9 lost to Norfolk's XI 181-5 (T. E. Jesty 74) by 5 wkts.

2nd Match: v Worcestershire (Worcester) May 6, 7, 8.
Worcestershire 230-9 dec (G. A. Hick 70) and 56-0 drew with Indians 297 (M. Azharuddin 76, Kapil Dev 51).

3rd Match: v Gloucestershire (Gloucester) May 10, 11, 12.
Indians 322-5 dec (D. B. Vengarskar 74, R. J. Shastri 70*, S. M. Patil 57, C. S. Pandit 50*) and 135-3 dec drew with Gloucestershire 271-5 dec (K. M. Curran 69*, P. Bainbridge 58).

4th Match: v Surrey (The Oval) May 15 (Limited Overs).
Surrey 230-8 (A. R. Butcher 140) lost to Indians 231-5 (S. M. Gavaskar 81, M. Azharuddin 55, D. B. Vengsarkar 51*) by 5 wkts.

5th Match: v Hampshire (Southampton) May 17, 18, 19.
Indians 297-6 dec (Kapil Dev 115*, R. M. H. Binny 64) and 132-5 dec (M. Azharuddin 55*) drew with Hampshire 151-1 dec (V. P. Terry 65*) and 227-6 (C. G. Greenidge 86, V. P. Terry 57).

6th Match: v Kent (Canterbury) May 21, 22, 23.
Kent 378-6 (M. R. Benson 128, N. R. Taylor 64, C. J. Tavare 58) drew with Indians did not bat.

7th Match: v England (The Oval) May 24 (Limited Overs).
England 162 lost to India 163-1 (M. Azharuddin 83*, S. M. Gavaskar 65*) by 9 wkts.

8th Match: v England (Old Trafford) May 26 (Limited Overs).
India 254-6 (K. Srittanth 67, R. J. Shastri 62*, Kapil Dev 51) lost to England 256-5 (D. I. Gower 81) by 5 wkts.

9th Match: v Ireland (Belfast) May 28 (Limited Overs).
India 57-3. Rain ended play.

10th Match: v Ireland (Downpatrick) May 29 (Limited Overs).
India 210-7 (S. M. Patil 61) beat Ireland 201-6 by 9 runs.

11th Match: v Northamptonshire (Northampton) May 31, June 1, 2.
Indians 301-5 dec (M. Amarnath 101, M. Azharuddin 100*) drew with Northants 118 (Kapil Dev 5-35) and 239-4 (R. J. Boyd-Moss 79, D. J. Capel 67*).

12th Match: v England (Lord's) June 5, 6, 7, 9, 10.
England 294 (G. A. Gooch 114, D. R. Pringle 63, Chetan Sharma 5-64) and 180 lost to India 341 (D. B. Vengsarkar 126*, M. Amarnath 69) and 136-5 by 5 wkts.

13th Match: v Oxford and Cambridge University (Oxford) June 12, 13.
Indians 348-4 dec (K. Srikkanth 113, R. Lamba 77, S. M. Patil 60) and 144-4 dec (C. S. Pandit 51) drew with Oxford and Cambridge 223-8 dec (P. A. C. Bail 52, D. A. Thorne 52) and 64-6.

14th Match: v Leicestershire (Leicester) June 14, 15, 16.
Leicestershire 269 (W. K. M. Benjamin 95*) and 244-3 dec (R. A. Cobb 80, L. Potter 65) drew with Indians 272-8 dec (M. Azharuddin 142, D. B. Vengsarkar 60) and 145-4 (K. Srikkanth 90).

15th Match: v England (Headingley) June 19, 20, 21.
India 272 (D. B. Vengsarkar 61) and 237 (D. B. Vengsarkar 102*) beat England 102 (R. H. M. Binny 5-40) and 128 by 279 runs.

16th Match: v League Cricket Conference (Chester-le-Street) June 26 (Limited Overs).
Indians 321-8 (D. B. Vengsarkar 71, S. M. Patil 61) beat L.C.C. 249-7 (C. L. Hooper 75, J. Foster 61) by 72 runs.

17th Match: v Somerset (Taunton) June 28, 29, 30.
Somerset 128 (N. S. Yadav 6-30) and 213-5 (N. A. Felton 104) drew with Indians 389-8 dec (S. M. Gavaskar 136*, R. Lamba 69, R. J. Shastri 64).

18th Match: v England (Edgbaston) July 3, 4, 5, 7, 8.
England 390 (M. W. Gatting 183*) and 235 (Chetan Sharma 6-58) drew with India 390 (M. Amarnath 79, M. Azharuddin 64) and 174-5 (S. M. Gavaskar 54).

19th Match: v Scotland (Dumfries) July 10 (Limited Overs).
Scotland 192-9 lost to India 195-7 by 3 wkts.

20th Match: v Scotland (Dumfries) July 11 (Limited Overs).
Indians 211-9 (Chetan Sharma 59, R. Lamba 53) beat Scotland 159-9 by 52 runs.

21st Match: v Yorkshire (Scarborough) July 12, 13, 14.
Yorkshire 343-7 dec (M. D. Moxon 123, A. A. Metcalfe 92) and 236-5 dec (M. D. Moxon 112*, S. N. Hartley 87) lost to Indians 325-6 dec (R. Lamba 116, C. S. Pandit 91) and 257-5 (R. Lamba 56, C. S. Pandit 56*, K. S. More 52) by 5 wkts.

22nd Match: v Pakistan (Harrogate) July 5 (Limited Overs).
Pakistan 195-5 (Salim Malik 79*) lost to India 196-9 (K. Srikkanth 58, D. B. Vengsarkar 43) by 1 wkt.

1986: 12th Indians

Batting Averages

	M	I	NO	R	HS	Avge	100	c/s
D. B. Vengsarkar	8	11	3	536	126*	67.00	2	3
Kapil Dev	6	9	4	273	115*	54.60	1	5
M. Azharuddin	10	14	3	596	142	54.12	2	12
M. Amarnath	9	13	3	473	101	47.30	1	7
R. Lamba	5	7	0	301	116	43.00	1	1
C. S. Pandit	6	8	2	252	91	42.00	0	10
K. S. More	7	8	2	228	52	38.00	0	22/1
S. M. Gavaskar	8	12	1	372	136*	33.81	1	5
R. J. Shastri	8	10	2	220	70*	27.50	0	4
Chetan Sharma	9	5	2	79	39	26.33	0	2
K. Srikkanth	9	14	0	344	90	24.57	0	5
S. M. Patil	6	8	0	188	57	23.50	0	4
R. M. H. Binny	8	9	1	182	64	22.75	0	6
M. Prabhakar	6	6	1	77	33	15.40	0	1
Maninder Singh	8	5	2	16	6*	5.33	0	3

Played in 7 matches: N. S. Yadav 13*, 9*; in 1 match: Madan Lal 20, 22.

Bowling Averages

	O	M	R	W	Avge	BB	5i
Kapil Dev	186.2	50	461	20	23.05	5-35	1
Chetan Sharma	221.3	34	736	31	23.74	6-58	2
Maninder Singh	257.1	71	612	21	29.14	4-26	0
N. S. Yadav	188.4	39	534	15	36.60	6-30	1
M. Prabhakar	119	25	353	9	39.22	3-42	0
R. M. H. Binny	182.2	29	637	16	39.81	5-40	1
R. J. Shastri	217	57	494	12	41.16	3-44	0

Also bowling: M. Amarnath 43.2-12-68-4; M. Azharuddin 20-1-68-0; R. Lamba 16-4-49-1; Madan Lal 20.5-5-48-3; C. S. Pandit 2.1-0-14-0; S. M. Patil 38-6-122-2; K. Srikkanth 20-0-91-3.

the squad was leg spinner Sivaramakrishnan, it being felt that the wickets would not be hard enough for him to be as successful as at home.

The tour was a great success, with England beaten in the Test series by two matches to nil. Vengsarkar topped both the Test and first-class batting tables and had an outstanding summer. The rest of the batting was remarkable for its depth, only Maninder Singh being an easy man to dismiss—More, the wicketkeeper, came in at no. 10 in the Tests and yet averaged 52.00.

The bowling was quite good enough to worry England: Maninder Singh, whom some forecast would fail, topped the Test table and Chetan Sharma took ten wickets in the Edgbaston Test. Madan Lal was co-opted for the Second Test when Sharma was injured and filled the gap adequately.

India also won the Texaco Trophy by dint of a faster scoring rate and this additional crown was also fully deserved.

Dilip Vengsarkar reaches his century at Headingley in 1986. Vengsarkar had earlier become the first overseas batsman to score three Test centuries at Lord's. India won the series 2-0.

1987: 8th Pakistanis

The 18-man squad which toured England consisted of Imran Khan (captain), Abdul Qadir, Asif Mujtaba, Ijaz Ahmed, Iqbal Qasim, Javed Miandad, Mansoor Akhtar, Manzoor Elahi, Mohsin Kamal, Mudassar Nazar, Ramiz Raja, Salim Jaffer, Salim Malik, Salim Yousuf, Shoaib Mohammad, Tauseef Ahmed, Wasim Akram and Zakir Khan. In addition Zulqarnain, a wicketkeeper, and Azeem Hafeez were co-opted for some matches. The manager was Haseeb Ahsan and Iqbal Qasim acted as his assistant.

The team achieved the distinction of being the first from Pakistan to win a Test series in England and for this they owed a great deal to the inspiring captaincy of Imran, as well as his all-round cricket. Javed Miandad, the outstanding batsman, missed the first few matches waiting for the birth of his child in Pakistan, but when he arrived he stamped his authority on the run-getting; bowler Wasim Akram was a good opening partner for Imran.

There was a certain amount of ill-feeling generated mainly through time-wasting and then by the English refusal to change the Test Match umpiring panel when asked by the Pakistan management, who objected to one official in particular. The Pakistan manager was often outspoken in his remarks and this gave the press plenty of copy.

1987: 8th Pakistanis

Batting Averages

	M	I	NO	R	HS	Avge	100	c/s
Javed Miandad	11	14	1	822	260	63.23	2	5
Mansoor Akhtar	16	24	3	1156	169*	55.04	4	5
Salim Malik	17	22	4	901	102	50.05	1	8
Mudassar Nasar	13	16	2	588	124	42.00	2	5
Shoaib Mohammad	16	23	5	727	121*	40.38	2	4
Imran Khan	12	13	3	349	118	34.90	1	5
Salim Yousuf	16	14	4	347	91*	34.70	0	37/2
Ramiz Raja	11	15	0	501	150	33.40	1	1
Ijaz Ahmed	11	13	1	382	69	31.83	0	9
Manzoor Elahi	4	6	0	182	74	30.33	0	4
Wasim Akram	14	11	2	245	59*	27.22	0	7
Tauseef Ahmed	8	6	4	54	16*	27.00	0	4
Zakir Khan	8	4	2	48	22*	24.00	0	4
Mohsin Kamal	12	11	6	69	28	13.80	0	5
Abdul Qadir	10	7	0	70	24	10.00	0	2
Asif Mujtaba	4	5	0	11	5	2.20	0	0

Played in one match: Zulqarnain 0*, Azeem Hafeez, Iqbal Qasim and Saleem Jaffer did not bat.

Bowling Averages

	O	M	R	W	Avge	BB	5i
Imran Khan	300.4	67	768	36	21.33	7-40	3
Wasim Akram	394	82	1095	39	28.07	6-34	2
Mohsin Kamal	288.4	47	1046	36	29.05	6-100	1
Mudassar Nazar	212	51	545	15	36.33	5-28	1
Tauseef Ahmed	212.2	66	477	13	36.69	4-51	0
Zakir Khan	165	32	554	14	39.57	4-27	0
Abdul Qadir	299.5	66	845	19	44.47	7-96	1

Also bowled: Asif Mujtaba 1-0-2-0; Azeem Hafeez 15-2-84-2; Ijaz Ahmed 4-0-21-0; Iqbal Qasim 18-6-41-1; Javed Miandad 5-2-11-0; Mansoor Akhtar 5-0-10-2; Manzoor Elahi 31.3-5-106-2; Saleem Jaffer 18-10-17-3; Salim Malik 29-6-71-2; Shoaib 18.3-3-69-2.

The captain of the eighth Pakistani tourists in 1987 was Imran Khan, an inspiring leader as well as one of the world's great all-rounders. He is walking back to his mark in the Third Test at Headingley, where his 10 wickets won the match (and series) for Pakistan.

1987: 8th Pakistanis

1st Match: v Lavinia, Duchess of Norfolk's XI (Arundel)   April 30.
Match abandoned.

2nd Match: v Surrey (The Oval)   May 2, 3, 4.
Pakistanis 195 (M. A. Feltham 5-66) and 171-3 drew with Surrey 257.

3rd Match: v Kent (Canterbury)   May 6, 7, 8.
Pakistanis 175 (Mansoor Akhtar 74, Shoaib Mohammad 50) and 171 (Ramiz Raja 50, A. P. Igglesden 5-60) lost to Kent 403-8 dec (C. J. Tavare 87, C. S. Cowdrey 75, S. G. Hinks 70, Mohsin Kamal 6-100) by an innings and 57 runs.

4th Match: v Essex (Chelmsford)   May 9, 10, 11.
Pakistanis 331-7 dec (Salim Malik 99) and 217-7 dec (Manzoor Elahi 74) beat Essex 150 (H. A. Page 60) and 188 (B. R. Hardie 83, Wasim Akram 5-40) by 210 runs.

5th Match: v Derbyshire (Derby)   May 12.
Match abandoned.

6th Match: v Somerset (Taunton)   May 14 (Limited Overs).
Somerset 217-8 (M. D. Crowe 75) beat Pakistanis 138 by 79 runs.

7th Match: v Sussex (Hove)   May 16, 17, 18.
Pakistanis 444-4 dec (Javed Miandad 211*, Salim Malik 86*) drew with Sussex 299-8 dec (N. J. Lenham 104*, A. P. Wells 55, Imran Khan 5-61).

8th Match: v England (The Oval)   May 21 (Limited Overs).
Pakistan 232-6 (Javed Miandad 113) lost to England 233-3 (B. C. Broad 99, A. J. Lamb 61) by 7 wkts.

9th Match: v England (Trent Bridge)   May 23 (Limited Overs).
England 157 (B. C. Broad 52) lost to Pakistan 158-4 (Javed Miandad 71) by 6 wkts.

10th Match: v England (Edgbaston)   May 25 (Limited Overs).
Pakistan 213-9 (Javed Miandad 68) lost to England 217-9 by 1 wkt.

11th Match: v Ireland (Dublin)   May 27 (Limited Overs).
Pakistan 276-5 (Shoaib Mohammad 101, Mansoor Akhtar 87) beat Ireland 162-9 (M. F. Cohen 53) by 114 runs.

12th Match: v Ireland (Dublin)   May 28 (Limited Overs).
Pakistan 376-7 (Manzoor Elahi 109, Salim Malik 82, Ijaz Ahmed 59) beat Ireland 144-2 (M. A. Masood 89) on faster scoring rate.

13th Match: v Middlesex (Lord's)   May 30, 31, June 1.
Pakistanis 297-9 dec (Mansoor Akhtar 135) and 342-4 dec (Salim Malik 95, Mansoor Akhtar 87, Ramiz Raja 84) drew with Middlesex 144 (Wasim Akram 6-34) and 170-1 (J. D. Carr 81*).

14th Match: v England (Old Trafford)   June 4, 5, 6, 8, 9.
England 447 (R. T. Robinson 166, B. N. French 59) drew with Pakistan 140-5 (Mansoor Akhtar 75).

15th Match: v Scotland (Glasgow)   June 11 (Limited Overs).
Pakistan 203-6 beat Scotland 128-8 by 56 runs.

16th Match: v Northants (Bletchley)   June 13, 14, 15.
Pakistanis 244 (Mudassar Nazar 72, Ramiz Raja 60) and 198-3 dec (Javed Miandad 86, Shoaib Mohammad 61*) drew with Northants 156 (R. J. Bailey 56, Mudassar Nazar 5-28) and 133-8.

17th Match: v England (Lord's)   June 18, 19, 20, 22, 23.
England 368 (C. W. J. Athey 123, B. C. Broad 55) drew with Pakistan did not bat.

18th Match: v Oxford and Cambridge Universities (Oxford)   June 24, 25, 26.
Oxford and Cambridge 201 (D. G. Price 51*) drew with Pakistanis 48-1.

19th Match: v Leicestershire (Leicester)   June 27, 28, 29.
Pakistanis 346-7 dec (Shoaib Mohammad 100, Ijaz Ahmed 60, Salim Malik 55, Javed Miandad 52) and 119-1 (Ijaz Ahmed 63*, Salim Malik 50*) drew with Leicestershire 392 (T. J. Boon 81, P. Willey 76, R. A. Coob 72).

20th Match: v England (Headingley)   July 2, 3, 4, 6.
England 136 (D. J. Capel 53) and 199 (D. I. Gower 55, Imran Khan 7-40) lost to Pakistan 353 (Salim Malik 99, Ijaz Ahmed 50, N. A. Foster 8-107) by an innings and 18 runs.

21st Match: v Minor Counties (Burton on Trent)   July 9, 10.
Pakistanis 204-8 dec (Shoaib Mohammad 90, Asif Mujtaba 62) and 233-3 dec (Ijaz Ahmed 104, Shoaib Mohammad 75) drew with Minor Counties 193-3 dec (S. P. Henderson 82, S. G. Plumb 57) and 209-5 (S. R. Atkinson 60, R. Herbert 60).*

22nd Match: v Nottinghamshire (Trent Bridge)   July 11, 13, 14.
Pakistanis 412-9 dec (Mansoor Akhtar 137, Mudassar Nazar 100) and 186-6 dec (Mudassar Nazar 61*) drew with Notts 188 and 174-5 (J. D. Birch 71*).

23rd Match: v Glamorgan (Cardiff)   July 15, 16, 17.
Pakistanis 166-5 dec (Shoaib Mohammad 63) drew with Glamorgan 187-6 (P. A. Todd 90, M. P. Maynard 66*).

24th Match: v Worcestershire (Worcester)   July 18, 19, 20.
Pakistanis 304-1 dec (Mansoor Akhtar 169*, Shoaib Mohammad 121*) drew with Worcestershire (D. B. d'Oliveira 131*, P. A. Neale 69*).

25th Match: v England (Edgbaston)   July 23, 24, 25, 27, 28.
Pakistan 439 (Mudassar Nazar 124, Salim Yousuf 91*, Javed Miandad 75, G. R. Dilley 5-92) and 205 (Shoaib Mohammad 50) drew with England 521 (M. W. Gatting 124, R. T. Robinson 80, J. E. Emburey 58, B. C. Broad 54, Imran Khan 6-129) and 109-7.

26th Match: v Hampshire (Southampton)   Aug 1, 2, 3.
Pakistanis 363 (Ramiz Raja 150) and 210-5 dec (Mansoor Akhtar 127) drew with Hampshire 256-4 dec (V. P. Terry 119*, D. R. Turner 71) and 109-1 (C. L. Smith 58*).

27th Match: v England (The Oval)   Aug 6, 7, 8, 10, 11.
Pakistan 708 (Javed Miandad 260, Imran Khan 118, Salim Malik 102, Mudassar Nasar 73, Ijaz Ahmed 69) drew with England 232 (M. W. Gatting 61, J. E. Emburey 53, Abdul Qadir 7-96) and 315-4 (M. W. Gatting 150*, I. T. Botham 51*).

1988: 17th West Indians

The team which arrived in England at the beginning of May consisted of I. V. A. Richards (Capt), C. G. Greenidge, D. L. Haynes, P. J. L. Dujon, R. B. Richardson, M. D. Marshall, A. L. Logie, R. A. Harper, C. L. Hooper, C. A. Walsh, P. V. Simmons, B. P. Patterson, W. K. M. Benjamin, C. E. L. Ambrose, K. L. T. Arthurton, I. R. Bishop, and D. Williams. J. L. Hendriks acted as manager, C. Wilkin as his assistant and C. Samuels as physiotherapist.

The main change compared with the previous West Indian tour was that Clive Lloyd was no longer in charge; this fact seemed to offer some hope to the England side, who had been thoroughly trounced in the West Indies as well as in England by Lloyd's recent sides. The One Day Internationals were staged prior to the Tests, and when England won all three of these games, it appeared that the West Indian stranglehold had been broken.

The First Test Match saw England trailing on first innings, but Gooch and Gower prevented a second innings collapse and the game was easily saved. After that England's hopes were systematically extinguished. The other four Tests were all West Indian victories and the home selectors were ridiculed by press and public as they chopped and changed the England eleven in a vain effort to regain the upper hand. Once again, West Indian fast bowlers, led by Marshall, proved too much for the English batsmen.

A typical leg-side shot from Vivian Richards, the captain of the West Indian tourists of 1988 which won the Test series 4-0. Richards had been the world's leading batsman since the early 1980s.

The West Indians' touring party, 1988. Back row: J. Hendriks (manager), Williams, Arthurton, Hooper, Benjamin, Simmons, Bishop, Ambrose, Walsh, Harper, Patterson, Logie, C. Wilkin (asst manager). Front row: Haynes, Marshall, Richards (capt), Greenidge, Dujon, Richardson.

1988: 17th West Indians

1st Match: v C. H. Lloyd's XI (Uxbridge)   May 5 (50 overs).
C. H. Lloyd's XI 228-4 lost to West Indians 229-1 by 9 wkts.

2nd Match: v Sussex (Hove)   May 7, 9, 10.
West Indies 561-9 dec (R. A. Hooper 217*, I. V. A. Richards 128, C. E. L. Ambrose 59, R. A. Bunting 5-161) and 305-5 dec (D. L. Haynes 158, R. B. Richardson 82) drew with Sussex 252 (P. W. G. Parker 89, I. R. Bishop 4-55).

3rd Match: v Duchess of Norfolk's XI (Arundel)   May 8 (40 overs).
West Indies 201-5 (A. L. Logie 53, C. L. Hooper 52, D. L. Haynes 50) beat Duchess of Norfolk's XI 135-5 (Imran Khan 56) by 66 runs.*

4th Match: v Hampshire (Southampton)   May 12 (50 overs).
West Indies 279-5 (C. G. Greenidge 103, C. L. Hooper 56, P. V. Simmons 55) beat Hampshire 186-6 by 93 runs.

5th Match: v Somerset (Taunton)   May 14, 15.
Somerset 113 (C. E. L. Ambrose 4-27, W. K. M. Benjamin 4-34) and 146 lost to West Indies 251 (C. L. Hooper 54, R. A. Harper 53*, D. L. Haynes 50, M. W. Cleal 4-41) and 12-0 by 10 wkts.

6th Match: v England (Edgbaston)   Magy 19 (55 overs).
West Indies 217 (A. L. Logie 51, C. L. Hooper 51, G. C. Small 4-31) lost to England 219-4 (M. W. Gatting 82*) by 6 wkts.

7th Match: v England (Headingley)   May 21 (55 overs).
England 186-8 beat West Indies 139 by 47 runs.

8th Match: v England (Lord's)   May 23, 24 (55 overs).
West Indies 178-7 lost to England 180-3 by 7 wkts.

9th Match: v Gloucestershire (Bristol)   May 25, 26, 27.
West Indies 257 (P. V. Simmons 53*, V. S. Greene 5-53) and 233 (I. V. A. Richards 63) drew with Gloucestershire 140 (B. P. Patterson 5-39, M. D. Marshall 4-14) and 98-1 (A. J. Wright 50*).

10th Match: v Worcestershire (Worcester)   May 28, 29, 30.
Worcestershire 321-3 dec (G. A. Hick 172, T. S. Curtis 82) drew with West Indies 170-5 (D. L. Haynes 71, I. V. A. Richards 50).

11th Match: v England (Trent Bridge)   June 2, 3, 4, 6, 7.
England 245 (G. A. Gooch 73, B. C. Broad 54, M. D. Marshall 6-96, C. E. L. Ambrose 4-53) and 301-3 (G. A. Gooch 146, D. I. Gower 88*) drew with West Indies 448-9 dec (C. L. Hooper 84, I. V. A. Richards 80, M. D. Marshall 72, D. L. Haynes 60).

12th Match: v Lancashire (Old Trafford)   June 8, 9, 10.
West Indies 287-5 dec (D. L. Haynes 93, C. G. Greenidge 67, K. L. T. Arthurton 60) drew with Lancashire 238-6 (G. D. Mendis 59).

13th Match: v Northants (Northampton)   June 11, 12, 13.
West Indies 288 (D. L. Haynes 72) and 345-8 dec (K. L. T. Arthurton 121, C. L. Hooper 74, D. Williams 51) drew with Northants 232 (N. A. Stanley 55, C. A. Walsh 5-49).

14th Match: v England (Lord's)   June 16, 17, 18, 20, 21.
West Indies 209 (A. L. Logie 81, P. J. L. Dujon 53, G. R. Dilley 5-55, G. C. Small 4-64) and 397 (C. G. Greenidge 103, A. L. Logie 95*, I. V. A. Richards 72, P. J. L. Dujon 52, G. R. Dilley 4-73, P. W. Jarvis 4-107) beat England 165 (M. D. Marshall 6-32) and 307 (A. J. Lamb 113, M. D. Marshall 4-60) by 134 runs.

15th Match: v Oxbridge (Fenner's)   June 23, 24.
West Indies 355-9 dec (D. Williams 84, K. L. T. Arthurton 70, A. L. Logie 57, C. L. Hooper 51, J. N. Perry 4-82) beat Oxbridge 38 (I. L. Bishop 4-12) and 145 (W. K. M. Benjamin 4-18) by an innings and 172 runs.

16th Match: v Kent (Canterbury)   June 25, 26.
West Indies 275 (C. L. Hooper 87, R. A. Harper 56*) beat Kent 81 (R. A. Harper 4-10) and 151 (D. J. M. Kelleher 51, I. L. Bishop 6-39) by an innings and 43 runs.

17th Match: v England (Old Trafford)   June 30, July 1, 2, 4, 5.
England 135 (C. A. Walsh 4-46) and 93 (M. D. Marshall 7-22) lost to West Indies 384-7 dec (R. A. Harper 74, P. J. L. Dujon 67, G. R. Dilley 4-99) by an innings and 156 runs.

18th Match: v Minor Counties (Trowbridge)   July 9, 10.
West Indies 358-5 dec (C. L. Hooper 140, A. L. Logie 100) drew with Minor Counties 18-1.*

19th Match: v Glamorgan (Swansea)   July 13, 14, 15.
West Indies 302-3 dec (P. J. L. Dujon 141) and 67-1 drew with Glamorgan 180-5 dec (J. A. Hopkins 87).

20th Match: v Leicestershire (Leicester)   July 16, 17, 18.
West Indies 370 (C. G. Greenidge 75, C. L. Hooper 62, P. J. L. Dujon 51) drew with Leicestershire 90 (B. P. Patterson 4-44, W. K. M. Benjamin 4-20) and 103-6.

21st Match: v England (Headingley)   July 21, 22, 23, 25, 26.
England 201 (A. J. Lamb 64*, C. E. L. Ambrose 4-48) and 138 (G. A. Gooch 50) lost to West Indies 275 (R. A. Hooper 56, D. L. Haynes 54, D. R. Pringle 5-95) and 67-0 by 10 wkts.

22nd Match: v Nottinghamshire (Trent Bridge)   July 27, 28, 29.
West Indies 362 (C. G. Greenidge 101, I. V. A. Richards 75, A. L. Logie 53, C. L. Cairns 4-82) and 17-0 drew with Notts 247 (C. W. Scott 63, F. D. Stephenson 56).

23rd Match: v Essex (Chelmsford)   July 30, 31, Aug 1.
West Indies 378 (K. L. T. Arthurton 101*, C. G. Greenidge 81, M. D. Marshall 76) and 280-3 dec (C. G. Greenidge 111, K. L. T. Arthurton 78*) drew with Essex 250-9 dec (A. W. Lilley 68, G. A. Gooch 56, P. J. Prichard 52*, I. R. Bishop 5-49) and 113-5 (G. A. Gooch 67*).

24th Match: v England (The Oval)   Aug 4, 5, 6, 8.
England 205 (R. A. Smith 57) and 202 (G. A. Gooch 84, W. K. M. Benjamin 4-52) lost to West Indies 183 (P. J. L. Dujon 64, N. A. Foster 5-64) and 226-2 (C. G. Greenidge 77, D. L. Haynes 77) by 8 wkts.

1988: 17th West Indians

Batting Averages

	M	I	NO	R	HS	Avge	100	c/s
R. A. Harper	12	13	5	622	217*	77.75	1	21
C. G. Greenidge	11	16	1	762	111	50.80	3	6
P. J. L. Dujon	12	16	4	601	141	50.08	1	31/2
K. L. T. Arthurton	10	13	3	499	121	49.90	2	8
D. L. Haynes	14	23	4	903	158	47.52	1	7
A. L. Logie	13	18	4	586	95*	41.85	0	9
I. V. A. Richards	13	16	1	624	128	41.60	1	10
C. L. Hooper	14	20	1	625	87	32.89	0	9
M. D. Marshall	9	10	1	289	76	32.11	0	3
D. Williams	8	10	1	182	51	20.22	0	11/1
R. B. Richardson	10	14	0	279	82	19.92	0	8
C. E. L. Ambrose	13	15	3	278	59*	23.16	0	1
W. K. M. Benjamin	10	10	4	102	21*	17.00	0	6
I. R. Bishop	8	6	2	56	23	14.00	0	1
B. P. Patterson	9	7	2	60	23*	12.00	0	1
C. A. Walsh	9	7	3	31	9*	7.75	0	0

Also batted: P. V. Simmons 53*.

Bowling Averages

	O	M	R	W	Avge	BB	5i
M. D. Marshall	245.4	56	553	42	13.16	7-22	3
W. K. M. Benjamin	183.1	44	467	33	14.15	4-20	0
I. R. Bishop	142	30	406	21	19.33	6-39	2
C. E. L. Ambrose	329.1	76	733	35	20.94	4-27	0
B. P. Patterson	196	30	632	25	25.28	5-39	1
K. L. T. Arthurton	27.1	8	80	3	26.66	2-1	0
R. A. Harper	219.3	18	509	19	25.78	4-10	0
C. L. Hooper	104.1	18	315	11	28.63	3-61	0
C. A. Walsh	232.2	55	622	18	34.55	5-49	2
I. V. A. Richards	45.4	10	122	3	40.66	2-1	0

Also bowled: R. B. Richardson 4-0-22-0.

1988: 4th Sri Lankans

Very much in the shadow of the West Indian tourists, the Sri Lankan party consisted of R. S. Madugalle (Capt), A. Ranatunga, F. S. Ahangama, S. D. Anurasiri, P. A. de Silva, D. S. B. P. Kuruppu, G. F. Labrooy, R. Madurusinghe, R. S. Mahanama, L. R. D. Mendis, B. E. A. Rajadurai, C. P. Ramanayake, J. R. Ratnayeke, M. A. R. Samarasekera, S. A. R. Silva, H. P. Tillekeratne. The manager was Abu Fuard, with L. R. Fernando his assistant.

The team had a strong batting contingent, with P. A. de Silva, Kuruppu and Mendis all making runs, but the bowling was weak. The result was a long series of drawn matches. Unfortunately their batting failed in the first innings of their only Test and though they fought back in the second, they were unable to save the game. England also won the single One-Day International.

1988: 4th Sri Lankans

Batting Averages

	M	I	NO	R	HS	Avge	100	c/s
J. R. Ratnayeke	8	10	5	311	60*	62.20	0	1
P. A. de Silva	6	9	3	333	117*	55.50	1	3
D. S. B. P. Kuruppu	6	10	1	438	158	48.66	1	1/1
R. S. Madugalle	8	11	2	403	97	44.77	0	4
L. R. D. Mendis	9	12	2	362	124	36.20	1	2
A. Ranatunga	8	9	1	271	84	33.87	0	3
S. A. R. Samarasekera	9	15	2	401	104	30.84	1	5
R. S. Mahanama	5	8	2	179	46*	29.83	0	1
S. A. R. Silva	8	14	1	338	112	26.00	1	15
G. F. Labrooy	7	4	1	73	42	24.33	0	2
H. P. Tillekeratne	5	6	1	121	50*	24.20	0	4
A. W. R. Madurasinghe	6	7	2	75	30	15.00	0	2
C. P. H. Ramanayake	4	3	0	20	18	6.66	0	0

Also played (in 5 matches) F. S. Ahangama 3*, 0*; (in 3 matches) S. D. Anurasiri 4*; (in 2 matches) B. E. A. Rajadurai did not bat.

Bowling Averages

	O	M	R	W	Avge	BB	5i
F. S. Ahangama	99.2	22	321	12	26.75	4-51	0
G. F. Labrooy	201.5	30	665	20	33.25	6.61	1
S. A. R. Samarasekera	127.4	14	406	10	40.60	3-31	0
C. P. H. Ramanayake	87.2	11	315	7	45.00	2-36	0
J. R. Ratnayeke	231.5	36	687	15	45.80	3-47	0
A. W. R. Madurasinghe	144.4	35	376	6	62.66	3-50	0

Also bowled: H. P. Tillekeratne 9-1-35-1; P. A. de Silva 14-5-42-1; B. E. A. Rajadurai 20-3-65-1; A. Ranatunga 50.4-11-153-2; S. D. Anurasiri 62-16-175-2.

1988: 4th Sri Lankans

1st Match: v League Cricket Conference (Oxton)   July 20, 21.
League Cricket Conference 147-8 dec and 120-4 drew with Sri Lanka 138-3 dec.

2nd Match: v Warwickshire (Edgbaston)   July 23, 24, 25.
Warwickshire 212-7 dec (D. A. Banks 61, Asif Din 59) drew with Sri Lanka 225-3 (P. A. de Silva 117*, S. A. R. Silva 62).

3rd Match: v Indian Gymkhana (Osterley)   July 27.
Indian Gymkhana 88 lost to Sri Lanka 89-1 by 9 wkts.

4th Match: v Duchess of Norfolk's XI (Arundel)   July 29.
Duchess of Norfolk's XI 214-3 dec (G. S. Clinton 107, P. W. G. Parker 50) drew with Sri Lanka 23-0.

5th Match: v Middlesex (Lord's)   July 30, Aug 1, 2.
Middlesex 224 (J. F. Sykes 88) and 185-2 dec (K. R. Brown 107*) drew with Sri Lanka 265 (A. Ranatunga 84) and 80-3.

6th Match: v Minor Counties (Sleaford)   Aug 4, 5.
Sri Lanka 224-4 dec (A. Silva 76, D. S. B. P. Kuruppu 52) and 240-4 dec (R. Mahanama 92, A. Silva 53) drew with Minor Counties 184-5 dec (S. G. Plumb 59) and 234-7 (S. G. Plumb 108, C. P. Ramanayake 4-80).

7th Match: v Nottinghamshire (Trent Bridge)   Aug 6, 7, 8.
Sri Lanka 307-7 dec (D. S. B. P. Kuruppu 158, R. S. Madugalle 72) and 244-7 dec (R. S. Madugalle 77) drew with Nottinghamshire 250-5 dec (B. C. Broad 73, R. J. Evans 50*) and 101-0 (P. R. Pollard 62*).

8th Match: v Yorkshire (Headingley)   Aug 10, 11, 12.
Yorkshire 297-5 dec (M. D. Moxon 132, K. Sharp 128, F. S. Ahangama 4-51) and 152 (R. J. Blakey 85*, G. F. Labrooy 6-61) drew with Sri Lanka 287-5 dec (S. A. R. Silva 112) and 7-1.

9th Match: v Surrey (The Oval)   Aug 13, 14, 15.
Sri Lanka 219 (A. Samarasekera 104) and 300-6 dec (L. R. D. Mendis 124, D. S. B. P. Kuruppu 87) drew with Surrey 242 (C. K. Bullen 59*, K. T. Medlycott 51, G. F. Labrooy 4-86).

10th Match: v Gloucestershire (Bristol)   Aug 17, 18, 19.
Sri Lanka 285-6 dec (J. R. Ratnayeke 60*, M. A. R. Samarasekera 53, H. P. Tillekeratne 50*) and 112-0 (P. A. de Silva 65*) drew with Gloucestershire 246-3 dec (A. J. Wright 137, P. W. Romaines 62).

11th Match: v Hampshire (Southampton)   Aug 20, 21, 22.
Hampshire 368-3 dec (V. P. Terry 190, R. A. Smith 104*, M. C. J. Nicholas 57) and 185-2 (R. J. Scott 107*) drew with Sri Lanka 280 (R. S. Madugalle 97, K. D. James 5-80) and 106-1.

12th Match: v England (Lord's)   Aug 25, 26, 27, 29, 30.
Sri Lanka 194 (J. R. Ratnayeke 59*) and 331 (A. Ranatunga 78, M. A. R. Samarasekera 57, L. R. D. Mendis 56, P. J. Newport 4-87) lost to England 429 (R. C. Russell 94, G. A. Gooch 75, K. J. Barnett 66, A. J. Lamb 63, G. F. Labrooy 4-119) and 100-3 by 7 wkts.

13th Match: v Derbyshire (Derby)   Aug 31, Sept 1, 2.
Sri Lanka 297-6 dec (P. A. de Silva 76, L. R. D. Mendis 55, D. S. B. P. Kuruppu 55) drew with Derbyshire 247-7 dec (S. C. Goldsmith 60, B. J. M. Maher 54).

14th Match: v England (The Oval)   Sept 4 (55 overs).
Sri Lanka 242-7 (L. R. D. Mendis 60) lost to England 245-5 (K. J. Barnett 84, A. J. Lamb 66) by 5 wkts.

Duleep Mendis batting at Lord's in 1988 for the fourth Sri Lankan tourists. He was a leading batsman of all the islanders' tours so far, having made a century at Lord's in 1984.

1988: 2nd Australian Aboriginals

A team of Aborigines arrived in London on May 11 to repeat the tour of 1868–the first-ever tour of the British Isles by an overseas side. The 1988 side consisted of J. McGuire (capt), N. Bulger, N. Fry, D. Monaghan, B. Pearce, D. Gardner, D. Thompson, P. Bagshaw, M. Mainhardt, M. Williams, P. Gregory, L. Marks, D. Breckenridge, J. Marsh, G. James, S. Appoo, E. G. Vanderbyl.

The manager was Mark Ella.

McGuire and Bulger, the two most experienced of the side, played some very valuable innings, and the two teenage cricketers, Appoo and Marsh were impressive. The main match against MCC was unfortunately badly affected by rain. Matches were, however, also played against several counties, whose teams included some first eleven players. All the matches were one-day fixtures, which was a little disappointing.

The second Australian Aborogine party in 1988. The Aborigines had been the first cricketing tourists to England in 1868, the second party arriving 120 years later.

1988: 2nd Australian Aboriginals

1st Match: v Surrey (Oval)   May 14.
Aboriginals 171 (K. Medlycott 6-49) lost to Surrey 173-1 (D. J. Bicknell 101*) by 9 wkts.

2nd Match: v Kent (Canterbury)   May 16.
Kent 118-6 beat Aboriginals 75-7 by 43 runs.

3rd Match: v Richmond (Richmond)   May 18.
Richmond 253-4 (D. Waugh 104, B. MacNamara 93) beat Aboriginals 217 (R. Cameron 5-31) by 36 runs.

4th Match: v Australia House (Motspur Park)   May 19.
Australia House 200-9 beat Aboriginals 199-7 by 1 run.

5th Match: v Middlesex Clubs (Uxbridge)   May 20.
Aboriginals 288-9 (S. Appoo 71, E. G. Vanderbyl 70) beat Middlesex Clubs 159 by 129 runs.

6th Match: v Indian Gymkhana (Osterley)   May 21.
Indian Gymkhana 156 lost to Aboriginals 157-5 (S. Appoo 57) by 5 wkts.

7th Match: v Sussex (Hove)   May 23.
Aboriginals 240-4 (S. Appoo 83) lost to Sussex 242-4 by 6 wkts.

8th Match: v Guildford President's XI (Guildford)   May 24.
Aboriginals 241-6 (S. Appoo 73, J. McGuire 56) beat Guildford President's XI 179-8 by 62 runs.

9th Match: v The Mote CC (Maidstone)   May 25.
Aboriginals 222-4 (N. Bulger 58, M. Williams 53*) beat The Mote 125-9 by 97 runs.

10th Match: v Farnham (Farnham)   May 27.
Aboriginals 218 (J. McGuire 110) beat Farnham 195-7 by 23 runs.

11th Match: v Sport Aid XI (Southampton)   May 28.
Sport Aid XI 178 (C. H. Lloyd 73) lost to Aboriginals 184-5 (E. G. Vanderbyl 99*) by 6 runs.

12th Match: v Alderney (Alderney)   May 30.
Aboriginals 252-3 (P. Bagshaw 79*, J. Marsh 79, N. Fry 76) beat Alderney 78-9 by 174 runs.

13th Match: v Hampshire (Southampton)   May 31.
Hampshire 196-7 beat Aboriginals 160 (N. Bulger 50, P. J. Bakker 4-22) by 36 runs.

14th Match: v Hants Clubs (Portsmouth)   June 1.
Hants Clubs 141-9 lost to Aboriginals 142-5 by 5 wkts.

15th Match: v Sutton, Cheam, Banstead & Mitcham (Sutton)   June 2.
Aboriginals 149 (J. McGuire 80, M. Roberts 4-19) beat Combined Clubs 119 (S. Appoo 6-16) by 30 runs.

16th Match: v Bath Schools (Monkton Coombe)   June 4.
Aboriginals 231-6 (D. Breckenridge 75) lost to Bath Schools 87 (D. Monaghan 5-20) by 144 runs.

17th Match: v Glamorgan (Swansea)   June 6.
Glamorgan 236-5 (P. A. Cottey 80, P. G. P. Roebuck 78) beat Aboriginals 174 (J. McGuire 58, S. Appoo 51) by 62 runs.

18th Match: v Birmingham & District (Mitchell & Butler's Grd)   June 9.
No play: rain.

19th Match: v T. Hudson's XI (Birtles Bowl)   June 10.
T. Hudson's XI 331 (T. Moody 121, R. Haynes 53, S. Appoo 4-48) beat Aboriginals 217 (D. Breckenridge 86) by 114 runs.

20th Match: v Middlesbrough Select XI (Middlesbrough)   June 11.
Aboriginals 191-6 (J. McGuire 75, T. Mahmood 4-27) lost to Middlesbrough 197-2 (G. Ireland 100) by 6 runs.

21st Match: v Lancashire (Old Trafford)   June 13.
Lancashire 211-6 (G. Fowler 50) beat Aboriginals 203 by 8 runs.

22nd Match: v Chatsworth House (Chatsworth)   June 17.
Aboriginals 251-5 (J. Marsh 74*, N. Bulger 73) beat Chatsworth House 78 (B. Pearce 4-0) by 173 runs.

23rd Match: v Humberside (Cleethorpes)   June 18.
Aboriginals 283-5 (J. Marsh 84*, N. Bulger 50) beat Humberside 61 by 222 runs.

24th Match: v Lincolnshire (Lincoln)   June 19.
Aboriginals 223-6 (J. Marsh 90*, P. Bagshaw 54) beat Lincolnshire 109 by 114 runs.

25th Match: v Oxford University (Oxford)   June 22.
Aboriginals 195-7 (P. Bagshaw 56, G. James 51) beat Oxford University 155 by 40 runs.

26th Match: v Combined Services (Uxbridge)   June 25.
Aboriginals 228-7 (J. Marsh 100) beat Combined Services 152 (P. Gregory 5-34, D. Gardner 4-27) by 76 runs.

27th Match: v C. H. Lloyd's XI (Hackney)   June 26.
Aboriginals 192-9 (D. Breckenridge 56, N. Bulger 55) beat C. H. Lloyd's XI 185-8 (S. Baruah 87) by 7 runs.

28th Match: v M.C.C. (Lord's)   June 29.
M.C.C. 72-2 drew with Aboriginals: rain.

INDEXES OF PLAYERS

◆

Touring Cricketers from England

Touring Cricketers to England

Index of touring cricketers from England

A complete list follows of the cricketers involved in the tours included in this book. Players selected for the tour to India in 1939-40 are included although the War prevented the tour taking place. The principal destination of each tour is shown in brackets after the season. The abbreviations are as follows:

A	Australia
AA	Africa and Asia
Ar	Argentine
B	Bermuda
Ba	Barbados
Bg	Bangladesh
C	Canada
Ce	Ceylon
E	Egypt
EA	East Africa
FE	Far East
I	India
J	Jamaica
K	Kenya
M	Malaysia
NA	North America
NZ	New Zealand
P	Pakistan
R	Rhodesia
SA	South Africa
SAm	South America
SL	Sri Lanka
US	United States
W	West Indies
WA	West Africa
Wo	World Tour
Z	Zimbabwe
Za	Zmbia

★ denotes played in emergency.

Abberley, R. N. 1966-67(P); 1967-68(EA)
Abel, R. 1887-88(A); 1888-89(SA); 1891-92(A)
Absolom, C. A. 1878-79(A)
A'Court, D. G. 1962(B)
Agnew, J. P. 1980-81(Z); 1985-86(SL)
Ainsworth, J. L. 1898(NA)
Akers-Douglas, I. S. 1929(E)
Albertini, W. R. 1937-38(Am)
Alexander, G. 1882-83(A)★
Allan, J. M. 1967-68(EA)
Allen, D. A. 1959-60(W); 1960-61(NZ); 1961-62(I); 1962(B); 1962-63(A); 1964-65(SA); 1965-66(A)
Allen, G. O. B. 1926-27(SAm); 1932-33(A); 1936-37(A); 1947-48(W)
Allerton, J. W. O. 1973-74(Ba)
Alley, W. E. 1961-62(EA)
Allom, M. J. C. 1927-28(J); 1929-30(NZ); 1930-31(SA)

Allott P. J. W. 1981-82(I); 1984-85(I)
Ames, L. E. G. 1928-29(A); 1929-30(W); 1932-33(A); 1934-35(W); 1936-37(A); 1938-39(SA)
Amiss, D. L. 1966-67(P); 1967-68(AA); 1967-68(EA); 1972-73(I); 1973-74(W); 1974-75(A); 1981-82(SA)
Anderson, G. 1863-64(A)
Anderson, J. O. 1911-12(Ar)★
Andrew, F. J. 1962(B)
Andrew, K. V. 1954-55(A); 1959-60(W)
Appleby, A. 1872(NA)
Appleyard, R. 1954-44(A)
Arbuthnot, L. G. 1901-02(W)
Arkwright, H. A. 1895(NA)
Archer, A. G. 1898-99(SA)
Armitage, E. L. 1935(E)
Armitage, T. 1876-77(A)
Arnold, E. G. 1903-04(A)
Arnold, G. G. 1966-67(P); 1967-68(AA); 1969-70(FE); 1972-73(I); 1973-74(W); 1974-75(A)
Arnott, T. 1924(US); 1926-27(I); 1927-28(J); 2929-30(Ar); 1934-35(W)★
Arundell, E. R. 1968-69(SA)
Asif Din 1980-81(Bg)
Aspinall, J. B. 1902-03(I)
Astill, W. E. 1924-25(SA); 1925-26(W); 1926-27(I); 1927-28(SA); 1928-29(J); 1929-30(W); 1931-32(J); 1938-39(NZ)
Athey, C. W. J. 1979-80(A); 1980-81(W); 1985-86(SL); 1986-87(A); 1987-88(NZ)
Atkinson-Clark, J. C. 1936(E)
Attewell, W. 1884-85(A); 1887-88(A); 1891-92(A)
Awdry, C. E. 1932(E); 1933(E)
Ayres, G. W. 1891-92(SA)

Bailey, D. 1977-78(K)
Bailey, J. A. 1957-58(EA); 1958-59(SAm); 1959(NA); 1981-82(FE)
Bailey, T. E. 1959-51(A); 1953-54(W); 1954-55(A); 1956-57(SA); 1958-59(A); 1963-64(J); 1964-65(W)
Bainbridge, H. W. 1886(NA)
Bainbridge, P. 1984-85(Z)
Bagnall, H. F. 1931-32(J)
Baird, H. H. C. 1911-12(Ar)
Bairstow, D. L. 1974-75(W); 1978-79(A); 1979-80(A); 1980-81(W); 1986-87(W)
Baker, H. Z. 1930(NA)
Baker, W. W. 1938(E)★
Bakewell, A. H. 1933-34(I)
Balderstone, J. C. 1980-81(Z)
Balding, I. A. 1972-73(Ba)
Ball, D. C. S. 1938(E)
Barber, R. W. 1959(NA); 1960-61(NZ); 1961-62(I); 1964-65(SA); 1965-66(A); 1975-76(WA)

Barber, W. 1935-36(NZ)
Barclay, J. R. T. 1973-74(Ba); 1975-76(WA); 1976-77(Bg)
Bardswell, G. R. 1894(NA); 1896-97(W)
Barker, A. H. 1966-67(Ba)
Barker, M. M. 1894-95(W)
Barlow, G. D. 1976-77(I)
Barlow, R. G. 1881-82(A); 1882-83(A); 1886-87(A)
Barnes, S. F. 1901-02(A); 1907-08(A); 1911-12(A); 1913-14(SA)
Barnes, W. 1879(NA); 1882-83(A); 1884-85(A); 1886-87(A)
Barnett, C. J. 1933-34(I); 1936-37(A)
Barnett, K. J. 1979-80(A); 1985-86(SL)
Barratt, F. 1929-30(NZ)
Barrick, D. 1956-57(J)
Barrington, K. F. 1955-56(P); 1959-60(R); 1959-60(W); 1961-62(I); 1962-63(A); 1963-64(I); 1964-65(SA); 1965-66(A); 1967-68(W)
Bartlett, H. T. 1938-39(SA); 1939-40(I)
Bartlett, J. N. 1951(C)
Bartley, E. L. D. 1924-25(SA)
Barton, V. A. 1891-92(SA)
Bateman-Chapman, H. F. 1889-90(I)★
Bates, K. C. 1961(B)
Bates, W. 1879(NA); 1881-82(A); 1882-83(A); 1884-85(A); 1886-87(A); 1887-88(A)
Bathurst, L. C. V. 1894(NA)
Baxter, A. D. 1935-36(NZ)
Bean, G. 1891-92(A)
Bear, M. J. 1958-59(SAm); 1960-61(NZ)★
Beaumont, J. 1887-88(A)
Beaty, M. 1977-78(K)
Bedford, P. I. 1958-59(SAm); 1959(NA); 1964-65(SAm)
Bedser, A. V. 1946-47(A); 1948-49(SA); 1959-51(A); 1954-55(A); 1956-57(I); 1959-60(R); 1962-63(A)
Bedser, E. A. 1950-51(A); 1959-60(R)
Beeson, N. W. 1938-39(J)
Beldam, C. A. 1896-97(W)
Bell, J. 1968-69(SA)
Bell, R. M. 1909(E)
Bell, T. M. 1961-62(EA)★
Bellamy, – 1904-05(W)★
Belle, B. H. 1938-39(J)
Benka, H. F. 1938(E)
Bennett, C. T. 1925-26(W)
Bennett, G. 1861-62(A)
Bennett, R. A. 1897(NA); 1901-02(W)
Benson, E. T. 1929-30(NZ)
Berens, R. 1894-95(W); 1896-97(W); 1898(NA)
Berry, R. 1950-51(A)
Beton, S. 1904-05(W)★
Biggs, L. M. 1902-03(I)★
Binks, J. G. 1961-62(I); 1963-64(I); 1964(NA)

Bird, M. C. 1909-10(SA); 1911-12(Ar); 1913-14(SA)

Birkenshaw, J. 1967-68(AA); 1969-70(W); 1972-73(I); 1973-74(W); 1974-75(W)

Bissex, M. 1966-67(P)

Blake, D. E. 1955-56(W); 1956-57(J)

Blaker, R. N. R. 1901-02(W)

Blakey, R. J. 1986-87(W)

Blenkiron, W. 1969-70(FE)

Bligh, Hon Ivo F. W. 1882-83(A)

Block, S. A. 1929(E)

Blofeld, H. C. 1966-67(Ba)

Blois, J. D. 1938(E)*

Blunt, R. C. 1933(NA)

Blythe, C. 1907-08(A); 1909-10(SA); 1901-02(A); 1903(NA); 1905-06(SA)

Board, J. H. 1897-98(A); 1898-99(SA); 1905-06(SA)

Bohlen, F. H. 1907(NA)*

Bolitho, W. E. T. 1885(NA)

Bolton, L. H. 1938(E)*

Bolus, J. B. 1963-64(I)

Bond, F. 1922-23(SA)*

Bonham-Carter, H., 1889-90(I)*

Bonnor, R. E. 1907(NA)

Boon, T. J. 1980-81(Z)

Booth, M. W. 1913-14(SA)

Booth, P. 1980-81(Z)

Booth, R. 1964-65(Wo); 1965-66(J)

Bosanquet, B. J. T. 1898(NA); 1899(NA); 1901)NA); 1901-02(W); 1902-03(NZ); 1903-04(A)

Botham, I. T. 1977-78(P); 1978-79(A); 1979-80(A); 1980-81(W); 1981-82(I); 1982-83(A); 1983-84(NZ); 1985-86(W); 1986-87(A)

Boult, F. H. 1873-74(A)

Bourke, Capt the Hon M. A. 1896-97(W)*

Bowden, M. P. 1887-88(A); 1888-89(SA)

Bowes, W. E. 1932-33(A); 1935-36(J)

Bowley E. H. 1924-25(SA); 1929-30(NZ); 1931-32(J)

Boyce, K. D. 1972-73(W)

Boycott, G. 1964(NA); 1964-65(?); 1965-66(A); 1967-68(W); 1969-70(FE); 1970-71(A); 1973-74(W); 1977-78(P); 1978-79(A); 1979-80(A); 1980-81(W); 1982-82(I); 1981-82(SA)

Boyes, G. S. 1926-27(I)

Brackley, Lord 1904-05(W); ???

Bradley, W. M. 1902-03(NA)

Brain, B. M. 1964-65(Wo); 1965-66(J)

Brand, Hon. D. F. 1922-23(NZ)

Brann, G. 1887-88(A); 1891-92(?); 1899(NA)

Branston, G. T. 1906-07(NZ); 1907(NA); 1909(E)

Braund, L. C. 1901-02(A); 1903-04(A); 1907-08(A)

Bray, E. H. 1898(NA)

Brearley, J. M. 1964-65(SA); 1966-67(P); 1972-73(W); 1976-77(I); 1977-78(P); 1978-79(A); 1979-80(A); 1980-81(?)

Brennan, D. V. 1952-52(I)

Briers, N. E. 1980-81(Z); 1981-82(FE)

Briggs, J. 1884-85(A); 1886-87(?); 1887-88(A); 1888-89(SA); 1891-92(A); 1894-95(A); 1897-98(A)

Brinckman, Sir T. E. W. 1937-38(SAm)

Broad, B. C. 1984-85(Z); 1986-87(A); 1987-88(NZ)

Brocklebank, J. M. 1937(C); 1939-40(I)

Brocklebank, T. A. L. 1920(NA); 1924(US)

Brockwell, W. 1891-92(SA); 1894-95(A)

Brodhurst, A. H. 1938-39(J); 1951(C)

Bromley-Davenport, H. R. 1894-95(W); 1895-96(SA); 1896-97(W); 1898-99(SA)

Brooke, R. H. J. 1933(E)

Brookes, D. 1947-48(W)

Brooks, R. C. 1920(NA)

Brown, A. 1961-62(I)

Brown, A. S. 1962(B); 1971-72(Z); 1972-73(SA)

Brown, D. J. 1964-65(SA); 1965-66(A); 1966-67(P); 1967-68(W); 1967-68(EA); 1968-69(P); 1972-73(SA)

Brown, F. R. 1932-33(A); 1934(B); 1936(E); 1939(E); 1950-51(A); 1956-57(SA); 1957-58(EA); 1961-62(EA)

Brown, G. 1910-11(W); 1922-23(SA); 1926-27(I); 1931-32(J)

Brown, J. T. 1894-95(A)

Browning, F. H. 1907(NA)

Bruen, H. 1885(NA)

Bryan, J. L. 1924-25(A)

Buckenham, C. P. 1909-10(SA)

Buckland, E. H. 1886(NA)

Buckley, C. F. S. 1936(E)

Bull, F. G. 1897(NA)

Burn, R. C. W. 1904-05(W); 1905(NA)

Burnham, G. Le Roy 1923(C)

Burns, W. B. 1906-07(NZ)

Burnup, C. J. 1898(NA); 1902-03(NZ); 1903(NA)

Burrows, M. B. 1920(NA)

Burton, D. C. F. 1910-11(W); 1912-13(W)

Burton, D. S. G. 1910-11(W)

Bush, F. W. 1894-95(W); 1896-97(W)

Bush, J. A. 1873-74(A)

Bushby, M. H. 1958-59(SAm); 1959(NA)

Buss, M. A. 1966-67(P)

Butcher, R. O. 1974-75(W); 1980-81(W); 1980-82(Z)

Butler, H. J. 1947-48(W)

Butt, H. R. 1895-96(SA)

Butterworth, R. E. C. 1936-37(Ce)

Caesar, J. 1859(NA); 1863-64(A)

Caffyn, W. 1859(NA); 1861-62(A); 1863-64(A)

Cahn, Sir J. 1928-29(J); 1929-30(Ar); 1933(NA); 1936-37(Ce); 1938-39(NZ)

Campbell, I. P. (1951(C)

Cameron, J. H. 1938-39(J)

Capel, D. J. 1987-88(NZ)

Carpenter, D. 1962(B)

Carpenter, R. 1859(NA); 1863-64(A)

Carr, A. W. 1922-23(SA)

Carr, D. B. 1951-52(I); 1955-56(P); 1958-59(SAm)

Carrick, P. 1975-76(SA); 1977-78(FE); 1986-87(W)

Cartwright, G. H. M. 1920(NA)

Cartwright, T. W. 1963-64(EA); 1964-65(SA); 1967-68(EA)

Castell, A. T. 1963-64(J)

Cawley, A. 1938-39(J)*

Cawston, E. 1934(E); 1936(E)

Chadwick, M. R. 1986-87(J)

Champniss, L. J. 1975-76(WA)

Chapman, A. P. F. 1922-23(NZ); 1924-25(A); 1928-29(A); 1930-31(SA); 1932-32(J); 1938(E)

Chappell, T. M. 1975-76(SA)

Charleston, – 1887-88(A)*

Charlwood, H. R. J. 1868(NA); 1876-77(A)

Chatterton, W. 1891-92(SA)

Chester, F. 1937-38(SAm)(ump)

Chesterton, G. H. 1951(C)

Chichester-Constable, R. C. J. 1926-27(I)

Childs-Clarke, A. W. 1936(E); 1937(E); 1938(E); 1939(E)

Chinnery, H. B. 1897(NA); 1902-03(I)

Clark, E. A. 1975-76(WA); 1976-77(Bg); 1978-79(Bg); 1987-88(FE)

Clark, E. W. 1927-28(J); 1933-34(I)

Clark, T. H. 1959-60(R)

Clarke, A. 1863-64(I)

Clarke, J. 1886-87(A)*

Clayton, F. G. H. 1902-03(I)

Close, D. B. 1950-51(A); 1955-56(P); 1964(NA); 1973-74(SA); 1974-75(SA)

Cobb, A. R. 1885(NA); 1886(NA)

Cobb, R. A. 1980-81(Z)

Cobbett, M. R. 1882-83(A)*

Coen, S. K. 1927-28(SA)*

Coghlan, T. B. L. 1968-69(SA)

Coldwell, L. J. 1962-63(A); 1964-65(Wo); 1965-66(J)

Cole, T. G. O. 1904-05(W)

Collins, B. G. 1977-78(K)

Collins, G. C. 1925-26(W)

Collins, L. G. A. 1907(NA)

Collins, L. P. 1907(NA)

Collins, P. 1913(US)

Colman, G. R. R. 1913(US)

Compton, D. C. S. 1946-47(A); 1948-49(SA); 1950-51(A); 1953-54(W); 1954-55(A); 1956-57(SA); 1963-64(J)

Constable, B. 1959-60(R)

Cook, C. 1962(B)

Cook, G. 1981-82(I); 1982-83(A)

Cook, G. W. 1957-58(EA)

Cook, N. G. B. 1979-80(A); 1980-81(Z); 1981-82(FE); 1982(US); 1983-84(NZ); 1984-85(Z); 1985-86(SL); 1987-88(NZ)

Cooper, K. E. 1979-80(A)

Cope, G. A. 1975-76(SA); 1976-77(I); 1977-78(P)

Copson, W. H. 1936-37(A)

Cordaroy, T. M. 1975-76(WA)

Cordle, A. E. 1969-70(W)

Corlett, S. C. 1972-73(M)

Cornford, W. L. 1929-30(NZ)

Cornwallis, O. W. 1923(C)

Cottam, R. M. H. 1968-69(P); 1972-73(I); 1974-75(W)

Cottenham, Earl of 1969-70(W); 1973-74(Ba)

Cottrell, C. E. 1886(NA)

Coventry, Hon. C. J. 1888-89(SA)

Covington, F. E. 1937-38(SAm)

Cowan, M. J. 1955-56(P)

Cowans, N. G. 1980-81(Z); 1982-83(A); 1983-84(NZ); 1984-85(I); 1985-86(SL)

Cowdrey, C. S. 1977-78(FE); 1979-80(A); 1984-85(I)

Cowdrey, M. C. 1954-55(A); 1955-56(W); 1956-57(SA); 1958-59(A); 1959-60(W); 1962-63(A); 1963-64(I); 1964-65(W); 1965-66(A); 1967-68(W); 1968-69(P); 1969-70(W); 1970-71(A); 1972-73(W); 1974-75(A); 1975-76(WA)

Cranston, K. 1947-48(W); 1961(B)

Crapp, J. F. 1948-49(SA)

Crawford, J. N. 1905-06(SA); 1907-08(A)

Crawford, V. F. S. 1901(NA)

Crawley, L.G. 1925-26(W)

Creese, W. H. 1913-14(E)

Crisp, R. J. 1936-37(Ce)

Critchley-Salmonson, H. R. S. 1929-30(Ar)

Crouch, H. R. 1939(E)

Cumbes, J. 1985(C)

Curwen, C. A. F. 1938(E)

Curwen, W. J. H. 1906-07(NZ); 1911-12(A)*

Curzon, Hon. A. M. 1889-90(I)

Cuthbertson, G. B. 1924(US)

Cuttell, W. R. 1898-99(SA)

Dacre, C. C. R. 1931-32(J)

Daft, R. 1879(NA)

Dales, H. L. 1925-26(W)

Dalmeny, Lord 1931(E)

Daniel, R. C. 1973-74(Ba)

Dashwood, T. H. K. 1901-02(W)

Davenport, J. A. 1901-02(W)

Davey, J. 1972-72(Za)

Davidson, H. K. 1938-39(J)*

Davidson, I. C. 1986-87(J)

Davies, Emrys 3939-40(I)

Davis, B. A. 1969-70(W)

Davis, M. R. 1984-85(Z)

Davis, R. C. 1969-70(W); 1971-72(Za)

Dawson, D. W. 1961-62(EA)

Dawson, E. W. 1927-28(SA); 1928-29(J); 1929-30(NZ); 1932(E); 1933(E)

Dawson, J. M. 1894-95(W); 1896-97(W)

DeFreitas, P. A. J. 1986-87(A); 1987-88(NZ)

Delisle, G. P. S. 1961(B); 1966-67(Ba)

de Little, E. R. 1889-90(I)

Dempster, C. S. 1936-37(Ce); 1938-39(NZ)

Denness, M. H. 1967-68(AA); 1969-70(W); 1972-73(I); 1973-74(W); 1974-75(A); 1977-78(FE); 1981-82(FE)

Dennis, S. J. 1982(US); 1986-87(W)

Denton, D. 1905-06(SA); 1909-10(SA)

de Soysa, G. R. J. 1938-39(J)

de Trafford, C. E. 1894(NA); 1906-07(NZ); 1911-12(Ar)

Dewes, J. G. 1950-51(A)

Dexter, E. R. 1958-59(A); 1959-60(W); 1961-62(I); 1962-63(A); 1963-64(J); 1964-65(SA)

Difford, I. D. 1905-06(SA)*; 1913-14(SA)*

Dilley, G. R. 1979-80(A); 1980-81(W); 1982-82(I); 1982-83(NZ); 1986-87(A); 1987-88(NZ)

Dillon, E. W. 1901-02(W); 1903(NA)

Dindar, A. 1962(B)

Diver, A. J. D. 1859(NA)

Dixon, E. J. H. 1938-39(J)

Dobson, B. P. 1909(E); 1912-13(W); 1913(US)

Docker, G. A. M. 1912-13(W)

Docker, L. C. 1887-88(A)

Dods, H. W. 1937-38(SAm)

Doggart, G. H. G. 1955-56(W); 1957-58(EA); 1958-59(SAm)

d'Oliveira, B. L. 1964-65(Wo); 1965-66(J); 1967-68(W); 1968-69(P); 1970-71(A)

d'Oliveira, D. B. 1984-85(Z)

Doll, M. H. C. 1912-13(W)

Dollery, H. E. 1939-40(I)

Dolphin, A. 1920-21(A); 1926-27(I)*

Dooland, B. 1956-57(I)

Douglas, J. R. 1975-76(SA)

Douglas, J. W. H. T. 1906-07(NZ); 1907(NA); 1911-12(A); 1913-14(SA); 1920-21(A); 1924-25(A)

Downton, P. R. 1977-78(P); 1980-81(W); 1980-81(Z); 1984-85(I); 1985-86(W); 1987-88(I)

Dowson, E. M. 1901(NA); 1901-02(W); 1902-03(NZ)

Druce, N. F. 1895(NA); 1897-98(A)

Drummond, A. V. 1909(E)

Drummond, G. H. 1903-04(A)*; 1904-05(W)

Ducat, A. 1929-30(NZ)*

Duckworth, G. 1928-29(A); 1930-31(SA); 1932-33(A); 1936-37(A)

Dudleston, B. 1974-75(W)

Duff, A. R. 1964-65(SAm); 1966-67(Ba); 1976-77(Bg); 1978-79(Bg)

Duleepsinhji, K. S. 1929-30(NZ)

Durlacher, E. O. 1927-28(W)*

Durston, F. J. 1928-29(J); 1937-38(SAm)

Dyson, A. H. 1938-39(NZ)

Dyson, S. 1978-79(Bg)

Eagar, E. D. R. 1956-57(J)

Ealham, A. G. E. 1972-73(W)

Earle, G. F. 1924(US); 1926-27(I); 1929-30(NZ); 1932(E); 1933(E); 1934(E)

East, R. E. 1973-74(SA); 1974-75(W)

Eastman, L. C. 1937-38(SAm)

Ebden, C. H. M. 1904-05(W); 1909(E)

Eckersley, P. T. 1926-27(I); 1927-28(J); 1929-30(Ar)

Edmonds, P. H. 1972-73(M); 1974-75(W); 1977-78(P); 1978-79(A); 1984-85(I); 1985-86(W); 1986-87(A)

Edmonds, R. B. 1967-68(EA)

Edrich, J. H. 1959-60(R); 1963-64(I); 1965-66(A); 1967-68(W); 1968-69(P); 1970-71(A); 1973-74(SA); 1974-75(A)

Edrich, W. J. 1937-38(I); 1946-47(A); 1954-55(A); 1956-57(I)

Edwards, M. J. 1969-70(W)

Eiloart, C. H. 1913(US)

Elliott, G. 1896-97(W)

Elliott, H. 1927-28(SA); 1933-34(I)

Ellison, R. M. 1984-85(I); 1985-86(W)

Elms, R. B. 1972-73(W)

Emburey, J. E. 1977-78(FE); 1978-79(A); 1979-80(A); 1980-81(W); 1981-81(Z); 1981-82(I); 1981-82(SA); 1985-86(W); 1986-87(A); 1987-88(NZ)

Emmett, T. 1876-77(A); 1878-79(A); 1879(NA); 1881-82(A)

Enthoven, H. J. 1937(C)

Entwistle, R. 1977-78(K)

Evans, R. E. 1938(E)

Evans, T. G. 1946-47(A); 1947-48(W); 1948-49(SA); 1950-51(A); 1953-54(W); 1954-55(A); 1956-57(SA); 1958-59(A); 1963-64(J); 1964-65(W)

Eyre, C. H. 1905(NA)

Faber, M. J. J. 1972-73(M); 1973-74(Ba)

Fabian, A. H. 1938-39(J)

Fagg, A. E. 1936-37(A)

Fairbairn, S. G. 1912-13(W)

Fairbrother, N. H. 1987-88(P, I, NZ, A)

Falcon, M. (1913(US)

Fane, F. L. 1901-02(W); 1902-03(NZ); 1905-06(SA); 1907-08(A); 1909-10(W)

Farnes, K. 1934-35(W); 1936-37(A); 1938-39(SA)

Farrimond, W. 1930-31(SA); 1934-35(W)

Featherstonhaugh, C. B. R. 1961(B)

Fender, P. G. H. 1920-21(A); 1922-23(SA); 1926-27(J)

Ferris, J. J. 1891-92(SA)

Fielder, A. 1903-04(A); 1907-08(A)

Findlay, W. 1911-12(Ar)

Fisher, H. 1935-36(J)

Fishlock, L. B. 1936-37(A); 1946-47(A)

Fitzgerald, R. A. 1872(NA)

Flavell, J. A. 1964-65(Wo); 1965-66(J)

Fletcher, D. G. W. 1959-60(R)

Fletcher, K. W. R. 1964-65(W); 1966-67(P); 1967-68(AA); 1968-69(P); 1969-70(FE); 1970-71(A); 1972-73(I); 1973-74(W); 1974-75(A); 1976-77(I); 1981-82(I)

Fletcher, S. D. 1986-87(W)

Flood, C. W. 1929-30(Ar)

Flower, R. W. 1982-83(EA)

Flowers, W. 1884-85(A); 1886-87(A)

Foat, J. C. 1971-72(Za)
Foley, C. P. 1904-05(W)
Foljambe, G. A. T. 1892-93(I)
Folley, I. 1986-87(J)
Forbes, D. W. A. W. 1937(C)
Ford, C. G. 1934(E); 1935(E)
Ford, F. G. J. 1894-95(A)
Ford, N. M. 1937(C)
Forster, G. 1980-81(Z)
Fortescue, Rev. A. T. 1886(NA)
Foster, F. R. 1911-12(A)
Foster, N. A. 1983-84(NZ); 1984-85(I); 1985-86(W); 1986-87(A); 1987-88(P, I, NZ, A)
Foster, R. E. 1903-04(A)
Fothergill, A. I. 1889-90(SA)
Fowler, G. 1982-83(A); 1983-84(NZ); 1984-85(I)
Fowler, R. St. L. L. 1920(NA); 1923(C)
Fox, R. H. 1906-07(NZ)
Frames, A. S. 1924-25(SA)*
Francis, B. C. 1973-74(SA); 1974-75(SA)
Francis, C. K. 1872(NA)
Francke, F. M. 1974-75(SA)
Franklin, H. W. F. 1931(E)
Frazer, J. E. 1923(C)
Freeman, A. P. 1922-23(NZ); 1924-25(A); 1927-28(SA); 1928-29(A)
Freeman, G. 1868(NA)
Freeman, G. 1868(NA)
French, B. N. 1984-85(I); 1985-86(W); 1986-87(A); 1987-88(NZ)
Fry, C. A. 1966-67(Ba); 1973-74(Ba); 1978-79(Bg)
Fry, C. B. 1896-97(SA)
Fulcher, E. J. 1911-12(Ar)

Gale, R. A. 1966-62(EA); 1964-65(SAm); 1968-69(SA)
Gardom, W. D. 1926-27(SAm)*
Garnett, H. G. 1901-02(A)
Gatting, M. W. 1977-78(P); 1980-81(W); 1980-81(Z); 1981-82(I); 1983-84(NZ); 1984-85(I); 1985-86(W); 1986-87(A); 1987-88(NZ, A, I, P)
Gaussen, H. L. 1910-11(W)
Gay, L. H. 1894-95(A)
Geary, G. 1924-25(SA); 1926-27(I); 1927-28(SA); 1928-29(A); 1931-32(J)
Gemmell, I. J. 1982-83(EA)
Gibb, P. A. 1933(NA); 1935-36(J); 1937-38(I); 1938-39(SA); 1946-47(A)
Gibbs, J. A. 1892-93(I)
Gibbs, L. R. 1967-68(EA)
Gibson, A. B. E. 1889-90(I); 1892-93(I)
Gibson, C. 1964-65(SAm)
Gibson, C. H. 1922-23(NZ)
Gibson, K. L. 1909(E)
Gifford, N. 1964-65(W); 1965-66(J); 1972-73(I); 1985-86(SL)
Gilbert, W. R. 1873-74(A)
Gill, P. N. 1977-78(K)
Gillespie, J. V. 1937(E)
Gilliat, R. M. C. 1969-70(FE)
Gilligan, A. E. R. 1922-23(SA); 1924-25(A); 1926-27(I)

Gilligan, A. H. H. 1924(US); 1924-25(SA); 1929-30(NZ)
Gillingham, Rev F. H. 1926-27(J)
Gimblett, H. 1939-40(I)
Gladwin, C. 1948-49(SA)
Gleeson, J. W. 1973-74(SA)
Goddard, G. F. 1975-76(WA)
Goddard, T. W. J. 1930-31(SA); 1938-39(SA)
Godsell, R. T. 1905(NA)
Goldie, C. F. E. 1982(US)
Goldie, K. O. 1907(NA)
Goldney, G. H. H. 1889-90(I)
Gomes, S. A. 1974-75(W)
Gooch, G. A. 1978-79(A); 1979-80(A); 1980-81(W); 1981-82(I); 1982-82(SA); 1985-86(W)
Good, A. J. 1975-76(WA)
Goodway, C. C. 1936-37(Ce); 1938-39(NZ)
Goonesena, G. 1955-56(W); 1964-65(W); 1967-68(AA)
Gough-Calthorpe, F. S. 1922-23(NZ); 1925-26(W); 1929-30(W)
Gould, I. J. 1980-81(Z); 1982-83(A)
Gover, A. V. 1937-38(I)
Gover, J. C. L. 1961(B)
Gower, D. I. 1977-78(FE); 1978-79(A); 1979-80(A); 1980-81(W); 1981-82(I); 1982-83(A); 1983-84(NZ); 1984-85(I); 1985-86(P); 1986-87(A)
Grace, E. M. 1863-64(A)
Grace, G. F. 1873-74(A)
Grace, W. G. 1872(NA); 1873-74(A); 1891-92(A)
Graham, J. N. 1972-73(W)
Graveney, T. W. 1951-52(I); 1953-54(W); 1954-55(A); 1955-56(W); 1956-57(J); 1956-57(I); 1958-59(A); 1961(B); 1962-63(A); 1963-64(J); 1964-65(Wo); 1967-68(W); 1968-69(P)
Green, D. J. 1959(NA)
Green, L. 1926-27(J); 1929-30(Ar)
Green, S. V. 1901-02(A)*
Greenhough, T. 1956-57(J); 1959-60(W)
Greenidge, G. A. 1974-75(SA)
Greenway, C. E. 1913(US)
Greenwood, A. 1873-74(A); 1876-77(A)
Gregory, R. J. 1933-34(I)
Greig, A. W. 1967-68(AA); 1969-70(W); 1972-73(I); 1973-74(W); 1974-75(A); 1974-75(SA); 1976-77(I)
Grell, E. L. G. N. 1910-11(W)*
Grieve, B. A. F. 1888-89(SA)
Griffith, G. 1861-62(A); 1868(NA)
Griffith, M. G. 1964-65(SAm); 1969-70(W)
Griffith, S. C. 1935-36(NZ); 1939-40(I); 1947-48(W); 1948-49(SA); 1957-58(EA)
Griffiths, A. 1982-83(EA)
Grundy, J. 1859(NA)
Guise, J. L. 1934(E)
Gunn, G. 1907-08(A); 1911-12(A); 1929-30(W)
Gunn, J. R. 1901-02(A); 1929-30(Ar)
Gunn, W. 1886-87(A)
Gurr, D. R. 1977-78(FE)

Hadingham, A. W. G. 1935(E)
Hadley, R. J. 1972-73(M)
Hadow, W. H. 1872(NA)
Haig, N. 1929-30(W)
Haigh, S. 1898-99(SA); 1905-06(SA)
Hall, J. B. 1936-37(Ce)
Hall, J. K. 1961(B); 1961-62(EA)
Hamblin, C. B. 1972-73(M); 1978-79(Bg)
Hammond, W. R. 1925-26(W); 1927-28(SA); 1928-29(A); 1930-31(SA); 1932-33(A); 1934-35(W); 1936-37(A); 1938-39(SA); 1946-47(A)
Hampshire, J. H. 1964(NA); 1964-65(W); 1969-70(FE); 1970-71(A); 1972-73(SA); 1974-75(W); 1974-75(SA); 1980-81(Z); 1980-81(Bg)
Handfield-Jones, R. M. 1930(E)
Handford, S. 1886(NA)*
Handley, F. L. Q. 1982-83(EA); 1985(C)
Hann, L. H. 1938(E)*
Harbord, W. E. 1934(E)*
Harbord, W. E. 1934(E); 1934-35(W)
Hardstaff, J., sen 1907-08(A); 1929-30(W)ump
Hardstaff, J., jun 1935-36(NZ); 1936-37(A); 1937-38(I); 1938-39(NZ); 1946-47(A); 1947-48(W)
Hargreaves, S. 1902-03(NZ)
Hargreaves, H. 1924(US)
Harris, Lord 1872(NA); 1878-79(A)
Harris, M. J. 1974-75(W)
Harrison, W. E. 1901(NA)
Harrison, W. P. 1906-07(NZ)
Hartley, J. C. 1895(NA); 1905-06(SA); 1922-23(NZ); 1923(C)
Hartley, P. J. 1986-87(W)
Hartley, S. N. 1986-87(W)
Hatfeild, C. E. 1911-12(Ar); 1913(US)
Hawke, Lord 1887-88(A); 1889-90(I)*; 1891(NA); 1892-93(I); 1894(NA); 1895-96(SA); 1896-97(W); 1898-99(SA); 1911-12(Ar)
Hayes, E. G. 1904-05(W); 1905-06(SA); 1907-08(A)
Hayes, F. C. 1972-73(SA); 1973-74(W); 1974-75(W); 1974-75(SA); 1975-76(SA)
Hayhurst, A. N. 1986-87(J)
Hayward, D. L. 1961(B)*
Hayward, T. 1859(NA); 1863-64(A)
Hayward, T. W. 1895-96(SA); 1897-98(A); 1901-02(A); 1903-04(A)
Hazel, N. L. 1961(B)*
Hazlerigg, A. G. 1935(E)
Head, J. R. 1896-97(W)
Headlam, C., 1902-03(I)
Headley, R. G. A. 1964-65(Wo); 1964-65(W); 1965-66(J)
Heal, M. G. 1972-73(M)
Heane, G. F. G. 1929-30(Ar); 1933(NA); 1938-39(NZ)
Hearne, A. 1891-92(SA); 1903(US)
Hearne, F. 1888-89(SA)
Hearne, G. F. 1884-85(A)*
Hearne, G. G. 1891-92(SA)
Hearne, J. T. 1891-92(SA); 1897-98(A)
Hearne, J. W. 1910-11(W); 1911-12(A); 1913-14(SA); 1920-21(A); 1924-25(A)
Heatrne, T. 1861-62(A)
Heath, L. 1910-11(W)*

Hegg, W. K. 1986-87(J)
Hemingway, W. McG. 1895(NA); 1897(NA)
Hemmings, E. E. 1974-75(SA); 1982-83(A); 1987-88(NZ)
Henderson, R. 1884-85(A)*
Henderson, S. P. 1982(US); 1985(C)
Hendren, E. H. 1920-21(A); 1924-25(A); 1928-29(A); 1929-30(W); 1930-31(SA); 1934-35(W)
Hendrick, M. 1973-74(W); 1974-75(A); 1975-76(SA); 1977-78(P); 1978-79(A); 1979-80(A); 1981-82(SA)
Henley, F. A. H. 1905(NA)
Hermon, J. V. 1932(E)
Heseltine, C., 1892-93(I); 1895-96(SA); 1896-97(W)
Hesketh-Pritchard, H. V. 1904-05(W); 1907(NA)
Hewett, H. T. 1891(NA); 1895-96(SA)
Hickson, G. A. S. 1924(US)
Higgs, K. 1965-66(A); 1967-68(W)
Hilder, A. L. 1926-27(J); 1927-28(J); 1928-29(J); 1932(E)
Hill, A. 1876-77(A)
Hill, A. E. L., 1923(C); 1932(E)
Hill, A. J. L. 1892-93(I); 1894(NA); 1896-97(SA); 1911-12(Ar)
Hill, M. Ll. 1926-27(I)
Hill, V. T. 1895(NA); 1898(NA)
Hilliard, H. 1889-90(I)*
Hill-Wood, C. K. H. 1929(E); 1930(E)
Hill-Wood, P. D. 1966-67(Ba)
Hill-Wood, W. W. H. 1922-23(NZ)
Hillyard, G. W. 1891(NA); 1894(NA)
Hilton, M. J. 1951-52(I)
Hine-Haycock, T. R. 1885(NA); 1886(NA)
Hirst, G. H. 1897-98(A); 1903-04(A)
Hitch, J. W. 1911-12(A); 1920-21(A)
Hobbs, J. B. 1907-08(A); 1909-10(SA); 1911-12(A); 1913-14(SA); 1920-21(A); 1924-25(A); 1928-29(A)
Hobbs, R. N. S. 1963-64(EA); 1963-64(J); 1964-65(SA); 1966-67(P); 1967-68(W); 1968-69(P); 1969-70(W); 1972-73(SA)
Hodgson, R. P. 1982(US)
Hodson, P. 1972-73(M)
Hollies, W. E. 1934-35(W); 1950-51(A)
Hollins, A. M. 1901(NA)
Hollins, F. H. 1901-02(W); 1902-03(I); 1923(C)
Holloway, B. H. 1910-11(W)
Holmes, A. J. 1938-39(SA); 1939-40(I)
Holmes, E. R. T. 1926-27(J); 1934-35(W); 1935-36(NZ)
Holmes, P. 1924-25(SA); 1925-26(W); 2927-28(SA)
Hone, L. 1878-79(A)
Hooper, J. M. M. 1973-74(Ba); 1975-76(WA); 1976-77(Bg)
Hopley, F. J. V. 1905(NA)
Hopper, T. J. 1985(C)
Hornby, A. H. 1902-03(I)
Hornby, A. N. 1872(NA); 1878-79(A)
Horner, C. E. 1885(NA)
Hornsby, J. H. J. 1889-90(I); 1891(NA); 1892-93(I)
Horton, M. J. 1964-65(Wo); 1965-66(J)

Hosie, A. L. 1937-38(I)*
Howard, C. G. 1954-55(A)
Howard, N. D. 1951-52(I)
Howard, R. 1936-37(A)*
Howarth, G. P. 1975-76(SA); 1977-78(FE)
Howell, H. 1920-21(A); 1924-25(A)
Howlett, R. F. 1982-83(EA)
Howorth, R. 1947-48(W)
Howland, C. B. 1958-59(Am); 1959(NA)
Hubble, J. C. 1927-28(SA)*
Huggins, R. D. P. 1982-83(EA)
Hughes, D. P. 1972-73(SA); 1974-75(W); 1986-87(J)
Hughes, J. S. 1923(C)
Hughes, S. P. 1980-81(Z)
Hughes, – 1889-90(I)*
Huish, F. H. 1903(NA)
Human, J. H. 1933-34(I); 1935-36(NZ)
Human, R. H. C. 1939-40(I)
Humpage, G. W. 1981-82(SA)
Humphrey, R. 1873-74(A)
Humphrey, T. 1868(NA)
Humphreys, E. 1912-13(W)
Humphreys, W. A. 1894-95(A)
Humphries, J. 1907-08(A)
Hunte, C. C. 1978-79(Bg)
Hunter, J. 1884-85(A)
Hunter, K. O. 1905(NA)
Hurn, J. 1968-69(SA)
Huskinson, G. N. B. 1933(E)
Hutchings, K. L. 1930(NA); 1907-08(A)
Hutton, L. 1935-36(J); 1938-39(SA); 1946-47(A); 1947-48(W); 1948-49(SA); 1950-51(A); 1953-54(W); 1954-55(A)
Hutton, R. A. 1964(NA); 1964-65(SAm); 1966-67(P); 1973-74(Ba); 1980-81(Bg)

Ibadulla, K. 1967-68(AA); 1967-68(EA)
Iddison, R. 1861-62(A)
Iddon, J. 1928-29(J); 1934-35(W)
Ikin, J. T. 1946-47(A); 1947-48(W)
Ikin, M. J. 1977-78(K)
Illingworth, R. 1959-60(W); 1962-63(A); 1964(NA); 1970-71(A)
Ingleby-Mackenzie, A. C. D. 1955-56(W); 1956-57(J); 1957-58(EA); 1958-59(SAm); 1961-62(EA); 1963-64(J); 1964-65(W); 1966-67(Ba); 1981-82(FE)
Insole, D. J. 1956-57(SA)
Intikhab Alam 1977-78(FE)
Iremonger, J. 1911-12(A)
Irwin, P. H. 1924(US)
Isaacs, W. J. H. 1937(E)
Isherwood, L. C. R. 1926-27(SAm); 1929(E)

Jackman, R. D. 1972-73(SA); 1980-81(W); 1982-83(A)
Jackson, F. S. 1892-93(I)

Jackson, G. R. 1926-27(SAm); 1927-28(SA)
Jackson, J. 1859(NA); 1863-64(A)
Jackson, V. E. 1938-39(NZ)
Jameson, J. A. 1967-68(EA); 1973-74(W); 1974-75((W); 1974-75(W); 1978-79(Bg); 1980-81(Bg); 1982(US)
Jameson, T. O. 1924-25(SA); 1925-26(W); 1926-27(SAm); 1937-38(I)
Jaques, A. 1912-13(W)
Jardine, D. R. 1920(NAm); 1928-29(A); 1932-33(A); 1933-34(I)
Jarvis, K. B. S. 1977-78(FE)
Javis, P. W. 1986-87(W); 1987-88(NZ)
Jefferson, R. I. 1961-62(EA); 1964-65(SAm)
Jenkins, R. O. 1948-49(SA)
Jenner, T. J. 1974-75(SA)
Jessop, G. L. 1897(NA); 1899(NA); 1901-02(A)
Jewell, M. F. S. 1926-27(SAm)
John, A. 1889-90(I)*
Johnson, G. W. 1972-73(W); 1973-74(SA); 1974-75(W)
Johnson, L. A. 1961-62(EA); 1963-64(EA)
Johnson, P. D. 1972-73(M); 1982-83(EA)
Johnson, P. R. 1901(NA); 1902-03(NZ); 1906-07(NZ)
Johnston, A. C. 1929(E); 1930(E)
Jones, A. 1969-70(W); 1969-70(FE)
Jones, A. K. C. 1972-73(M)
Jones, A. L. 1979-80(A)
Jones, A. O. 1901-02(A); 1907-08(A)
Jones, E. W. 1969-70(W)
Jones, I. J. 1963-64(EA); 1963-64(I); 1965-66(A); 1967-68(W)
Jones, K. V. 1977-78(K)
Jones, P. C. H. 1972-73(M)
Jones, P. H. 1977-78(K)
Judd, A. K. 1927-28(J); 1933(E); 1935(E)
Julian, R. 1975-76(WA)
Jupp, H. 1868(NA); 1873-74(A); 1876-77(A)
Jupp, V. W. C. 1922-23(SA)

Kaye, M. A. C. P. 1938-39(J)
Keighley, W. G. 1951(C)
Kemp, N. J. 1985(C)
Kemp-Welch, G. D. 1927-28(J); 1931(E); 1931-32(J)
Kendall, M. P. 1972-73(M)
Kennedy, A. S. 1922-23(SA); 1924-25(SA)
Kenny, C. J. M. 1957-58(EA)
Kenyon, D. 1951-52(I); 1964-65(Wo); 1965-66(J)
Kerr, F. W. 1889-90(I)
Kershaw, F. 1902-03(I)
Kerslake, R. C. 1964-65(SAm)
Key, K. J. 1886(NA); 1891(NA); 1902-03(I)
Kilner, R. 1924-25(A); 1925-26(W)
Kimpton, R. C. M. 1938-39(J); 1955-56(W)
Kingston, G. C. 1969-70(W)

Kinkead-Weekes, R. C. 1973-74(Ba); 1976-77(Bg)

Kinneir, S. 1911-12(A)

Kippax, P. J. 1977-78(K); 1981-82(FE); 1985(C)

Kirk, H. 1898(NA)

Knight, A. E. 1903-04(A)

Knight, B. R. 1961-62(I); 1962-63(A); 1963-64(I); 1964-65(W); 1965-66(A)

Knight, R. D. V. 1972-73(SA); 1975-66(WA)

Knott, A. P. E. 1964-65(W); 1966-67(P); 1967-68(W); 1968-69(P); 1970-71(A); 1972-73(I); 1973-74(W); 1974-75(A); 1976-77(I); 1981-82(SA)

Knott, C. H. 1929(E); 1930(E); 1931(E); 1933(E); 1934(E); 1936(E)

Lagden, Sir G. Y. 1905-06(SA)*

Laker, J. C. 1947-48(W); 1953-54(W); 1956-57(SA); 1958-59(A); 1963-64(J); 1964-65(W)

Lamb, A. J. 1982-83(A); 1983-84(NZ); 1984-85(I); 1985-86(W); 1986-87(NZ); 1987-88(I)

Lanchbury, R. J. 1985(C)

Landale, F. B. 1924(US)

Lane-Fox, E. J. 1968-69(SA)

Langridge, Jas. 1933-34(I); 1935-36(NZ); 1937-38(I); 1946-47(A)

Langridge, John R. 1939-40(I)

Langridge, R. J. 1963-64(EA)

Larkins, W. 1979-80(A); 1981-82(SA)

Larter, J. D. F. 1960-61(NZ); 1962-63(A); 1963-64(EA); 1963-64(I); 1965-66(A)

Larwood, H. 1928-29(A); 1932-33(A)

Latchman, H. 1967-68(AA)

Lawrence, C. 1861-62(A)

Lawrence, D. V. 1985-86(SL)

Lawson, M. P. L. 1937(E)*

Lawson-Smith, E. M. 1889-90(I)

Laycock, D. A. 1972-73(W)

Leadbeater, B. 1969-70(W)

Leadbeater, E. 1952-52(I)

Leaney, E. 1891-92(SA)

Leatham, A. E. 1889-90(I); 1892-93(I); 1896-97(W); 1902-03(NZ)

Lee, E. C. 1898(NA); 1901-02(W); 1920(NA)

Lee, G. M. 1927-28(J)

Lee, H. W. 1930-31(SA)*

Lee, P. G. 1973-74(SA); 1974-75(W); 1975-76(SA)

Lees, W. S. 1905-06(SA)

Legard, A. R. 1935(E)

Legge, G. B. 1927-28(SA); 1929-30(NZ)

Leigh, R. 1896-97(W)

Leigh-Barratt, R. 1894-95(W); 1896-97(W)

Leslie, C. F. H. 1882-83(A)

Lever, J. K. 1972-73(SA); 1973-74(SA); 1974-75(W); 1976-77(I); 1977-78(P); 1977-78(FE); 1978-79(A); 1979-80(A); 1981-82(I); 1982-82(SA)

Lever, P. 1970-71(A); 1974-75(A)

Leveson-Gower, H. D. G. 1896-97(W); 1897(NA); 1905-06(SA); 1909-10(SA)

Carlton Levick, T. H. 1926-27(SAm)

Levett, W. H. V. 1933-34(I)

Lewington, P. J. 1972-73(SA); 1978-79(Bg); 1985(C)

Lewis, A. R. 1964-65(SAm); 1969-70(W); 1969-70(FE); 1972-73(I); 1973-74(Ba); 1982(US)

Lewis, D. W. 1969-70(W)

Lewis, R. P. 1969-70(W)

Lewis, R. V. 1980-81(Bg); 1985(C)

Leyland, M. 1926-27(I)–; 1928-29(A); 1930-31(SA); 1932-33(A); 1934-35(W); 1935-36(J); 1936-37(A)

Liddelow, G. 1910-11(W)*

Lilley, A. F. A. 1901-02(A); 1903-04(A)

Lilley, B. 1928-29(J)

Lillywhite, Jas. jun 1868(NA); 1873-74(A); 1876-77(A); 1881-82(A); 1884-85(A); 1886-87(A)

Lillywhite, John 1859(NA)

Lindsay, W. O'B. 1931(E)

Lines, S. 1982-83(EA)

Livington, L. 1956-57(I)

Livock, G. E. 1934(E)

Livsey, W. H. 1922-23(SA)

Llewellyn, G. C. B. 1899(NA)

Lloyd, C. H. 1986-87(J)

Lloyd, D. 1974-75(A); 1975-76(SA)

Lloyd, F. O. G. 1929(E); 1930(E)

Lloyd, T. A. 1984-85(Z)

Loader, P. J. 1954-55(A); 1956-57(SA); 1958-59(A); 1959-60(R); 1961-62(EA)

Lock, G. A. R. 1953-54(W); 1955-56(P); 1956-57(SA); 1958-59(A); 1959-60(R); 1961-62(I); 1967-68(W)

Lock, H. C. 1926-27(J)

Lockwood, E. 1879(NA)

Lockwood, W. 1894-95(A)

Lockyer, T. 1859(NA); 1863-64(A)

Lofting, J. G. 1975-76(WA); 1976-77(Bg)

Lohmann, G. A. 1886-87(A); 1877-88(A); 1891-92(A); 1895-96(SA)

Lomax, I. R. 1961(B); 1966-67(Ba); 1968-69(SA)

Long, A. 1972-73(SA)

Love, J. D. 1986-87(W)

Lowndes, W. G. L. F. 1930(E); 1931(E); 1932(E)

Lowe, W. W. 1895(NA)

Lowry, T. C. 1920(NA); 1922-23(NZ); 1924(US)

Lowson, F. A. 1951-52(I)

Lubbock, A. 1872(NA)

Lubbock, E. 1872(NA)

Lucas, A. P. 1878-79(A)

Lucas, R. S. 1894(NA); 1894-95(W)

Luckhurst, B. W. 1970-71(A); 1972-73(W); 1974-75(A)

Lumb, E. 1887-88(A)*

Lush, J. G. 1938-39(NZ)

Luther, A. C. G. 1909(E)

Lyon, B. H. 1936-37(Ce)

Lyon, J. 1974-75(SA)

Lyons, K. J. 1969-70(W)

Lyttleton, Hon. C. J. (Lord Cobham) 1935-36(NZ); 1956-57(J)

McAlpine, K. 1891(NA); 1894(NA)

McAlpine, R. J. 1968-69(SA)

McArthur, K. 1887-88(A)*; 1891-92(A)*

Macauley, G. G. 1922-23(SA)

MacBryan, J. C. W. 1924-25(SA)

McConnon, J. E. 1954-55(A)

McCool, C. L. 1956-57(I)

McCorkell, N. 1937-38(I)

McCormick, E. J. 1887-88(A)*

McCorquodale, A. 1951(C)

McDonell, H. C. 1905(NA)

McEvoy, M. S. A. 1982-83(EA)

McGahey, C. P. 1901-02(A)

MacGregor, G. 1891-92(A); 1907(NA)

McIntyre, A. J. W. 1950-51(A); 1959-60(R)

McIntyre, Martin 1873-74(A)

Mackinnon, F. A. 1878-79(A)

MacLaren, A. C. 1894-95(A); 1897-98(A); 1899(NA); 1901-02(A); 1911-12(Ar); 1922-23(NZ)

Maclean, G. A. 1896-97(W)*

MacLean, J. F. 1922-23(NZ)

Maclean, M. F. 1892-93(I)

McMaster, J. E. P. 1888-89(SA)

Magill, M. D. P. 1938-39(J)

Mailey, A. A. 1938(E)*

Makepeace, J. W. H. 1920-21(A)

Mallett, V. A. L. 1926-27(SAm)*

Mallett, A. W. H. 1951(C)

Mann, E. W. 1905(NA)

Mann, F. G. 1948-49(SA)

Mann, F. T. 1922-23(SA)

Marks, V. J. 1982-83(A); 1983-84(NZ); 1984-85(I)

Marlar, R. G. 1955-56(W)

Marley, R. C. 1938-39(J)*

Marriott, C. S. 1924-25(SA); 1933-34(I)

Marriott, H. H. 1895(NA); 1897(NA)

Marryat, G. 1901(NA)*

Marshall, G. 1863-64(A)*

Marshall, R. E. 1956-57(J); 1961-62(EA); 1963-64(J); 1964-65(W)

Marshall, R. L. 1894-95(W)

Martin, F. 1891-92(SA)

Martin, J. D. 1964-65(SAm)

Martineau, H. M. 1929(E); 1930(E); 1931(E); 1932(E); 1933(E); 1934(E); 1938(E); 1939(E)

Maru, R. J. 1980-81(Z)

Mason, J. R. 1897-98(A); 1903(NA)

Masterman, J. C. 1923(C); 1930(E); 1931(E); 1937(C)

Maul, H. C. 1878-79(A)

Maxwell, C. R. N. 1933(NA); 1936-37(Ce); 1938-39(NZ)

Maxwell, Capt– 1889-90(I)*

May, P. B. H. 1953-54(W); 1954-55(A); 1956-57(SA); 1958-59(A); 1959-60(W)

May, P. R. 1906-07(NZ)

Mayhew, J. F. N. 1930(E)

Maynard, C. 1979-80(A)

Mead, C. P. 1911-12(A); 1913-14(SA); 1922-23(SA); 1927-28(J); 1928-29(A)

Melle, B. G. von B. 1913(US)

Mence, M. D. 1975-76(WA); 1976-77(Bg); 1981-82(FE)

Mendis, C. D. 1986-87(J)

Mendl, D. F. 1934(E)

Mendl, J. F. 1937(C)

Mercer, J. 1926-27(I); 1928-29(J)

Merry, W. G. 1978-79(Bg); 1979-80(A); 1980-81(Z); 1982(US); 1985(C)

Metcalfe, E. J. 1909(E); 1913(US); 1920(NA); 1924(US)

Metcalfe, S. G. 1966-67(Bg); 1968-69(SA); 1973-74(Ba)

Meyer, B. J. 1962(B)

Midwinter, W. E. 1881-82(A)

Milburn, C. 1963-64(EA); 1967-68(W); 1968-69(P)

Miles, H. P. 1926-27(SAm)

Miller, A. M. 1895-96(SA)

Miller, G. 1976-77(I); 1977-78(P); 1978-79(A); 1979-80(A); 11980-81(W); 1982-83(A)

Milles, Hon. H. A. 1891(NAm)

Millett, F. W. 1982(US)

Milligan, F. W. 1895(NAm); 1898-99(SA)

Millman, G. 1961-62(I)

Milton, C. A. 1958-59(A); 1962(B); 1971-72(Za)

Mitchell, A. 1933-34(I); 1935-36(J)

Mitchell, F. 1895(NA); 1898(NA); 1898-99(SA); 1901(NA)

Mitchell-Innes, N. S. 1935-36(NZ)

Mitchell, T. B. 1932-33(A)

Mobey, G. S. 1939-40(I)

Monkhouse, G. 1984-85(Z)

Monteith, J. D. 1980-81(Bg)

Moon, L. J. 1905(NA); 1905-06(SA)

Moore, D. N. 1931(E)

Moorhouse, H. C. 1909(E)

Mordaunt, D. J. 1959(NA); 1964-65(SAm)

Mordaunt, G. J. 1894(NA)

More, H. K. 1978-79(Bg)

More, R. E. 1901(NA)

Morkel, D. P. B. 1933(NA); 1936-37(Ce)

Morley, F. 1879(NA); 1882-83(A)

Morris, H. M. 1926-27(J)

Morrison, J. S. F. 1920(NA)

Mortimore, J. B. 1958-59(A); 1961-62(EA); 1962(B); 1963-64(EA); 1963-64(I);

Mortimer, W. 1895(NA)

Mortlock, W. 1861-62(A)

Mottram, T. J. 1973-74(Ba)

Moss, A. E. 1953-54(W); 1955-56(P); 1956-57(J); 1956-57(I); 1959-60(W); 1968-69(SA)

Moss, J. 1904-05(W)

Moxon, M. O. 1984-85(I); 1985-86(SL); 1986-87(W); 1987-88(NZ)

Mudge, H. 1936-37(Ce); 1938-39(NZ)

Mudie, W. 1861-62(A)

Mulholland, Hon. H. G. H. 1913(US)

Munt, H. R. 1929-30(Ar); 1933(NA)

Murdoch, W. L. 1891-92(SA)

Murphy, A. 1986-87(J)

Murray, J. T. 1960-61(NZ); 1961-62(I); 1962-63(A); 1963-64(J); 1964-65(SA); 1965-66(A); 1968-69(P); 1972-73(SA); 1973-74(SA)

Murray, M. P. 1961(B)

Murray, S. L. 1889-90(I)★

Murray-Wood, W. 1938-39(J); 1961(B)

Mushtaq Mohammad 1974-75(W)

Napier, G. G. 1905(NA)

Nash, M. A. 1969-70(W)

Neame, A. R. B. 1968-69(SA)

Needham, A. 1980-81(Bg); 1984(C)

Nettlefold, E. P. 1937(E)★

Neve, J. T. 1973(C)

Newham, W. 1887-88(A)

Newman, F. C. W. 1928-29(J); 1929-30(Ar); 1933(NA)

Newman, G. C. 1937(C)

Newman, P. G. 1984-85(Z)

Newton, A. E. 1885(NA); 1887-88(A)

Nevinson, J. H. 1931(E); 1937(E)

Nicholas, F. W. H. 1924-25(SA); 1928-29(J); 1929-30(Ar)

Nicholas, M. C. J. 1980-81(Bg); 1984-85(Z); 1985-86(SL)

Nicholls, D. 1972-73(W); 1975-76(WA); 1982-83(EA)

Nicholls, R. B. 1971-72(Za)

Nichols, M. S. 1928-29(J); 1929-30(NZ); 1931-32(J); 1933-34(I); 1939-40(I)

Nicholson, A. G. 1974-75(W)

Norfolk, Duke of 1956-57(J)

Norman, M. E. J. C. 1976-77(Bg)

Nurton, M. D. 1977-78(K); 1982-83(EA)

Oakman, A. S. M. 1955-56(W); 19556-57(SA)

O'Brien, T. C. 1887-88(A); 1895-96(SA)

O'Connor, J. 1926-27(J); 1928-29(J); 1929-30(W)

Old, C. M. 1969-70(W); 1972-73(I); 1973-74(W); 1974-75(A); 1976-77(I); 1977-78(P); 1978-79(A); 1980-81(W); 1982-82(SA)

Oldfield, N. 1938-39(NZ)

Ormrod, J. A. 1965-66(J); 1966-67(P)

Osborne, M. J. 1961(B)

Oscroft, W. 1873-74(A); 1879(NA)

Ottaway, C. J. 1872(NA)

Oughton, A. T. 1962(B)★

Owen-Thomas, D. R. 1976-77(Bg)

Padgett, D. E. V. 1960-61(NZ); 1964(NA)

Page, C. C. 1906-07(NZ)

Page, R. 1935(E)

Paine, G. A. E. 1934-35(W)

Palairet, R. C. N. 1896-97(W)

Palmer, C. H. 1948-49(SA); 1953-54(W)

Palmer, K. E. 1963-64(J); 1964-65(SA)★

Parfitt, P. H. 1961-62(I); 1962-63(A); 1963-64(EA); 1963-64(I); 1964-65(SA); 1965-66(A)

Parker, C. W. L. 1924-25(SA)

Parker, J. F. 1939-40(I)

Parker, J. P. 1926-27(J)

Parker-Bowles, S. H. 1966-67(Ba)

Parkhouse, W. G. A. 1950-51(A)

Parkin, C. H. 1920-21(A)

Parkin, I. U. 1901(NA)

Parks, J. H. 1935-36(NZ); 1937-38(I)

Parks, J. M. 1955-56(P); 1956-57(SA); 1959-60(W); 1960-61(NZ); 1963-64(I); 1964-65(SA); 1965-66(A); 1967-68(W)

Parks, R. J. 1984-85(Z)

Psrr, G. 1859(NA); 1863-64(A)

Parsons, G. J. 1979-80(A); 1980-81(Z)

Parsons, J. H. 1926-27(I)

Pataudi, Nawab of 1932-33(A)

Patel, D. N. 1979-80(A)

Patiala, Maharajah of 1926-27(I)★; 1933-34(I)★

Patten, M. 1923(C)

Payne, M. W. 1905(NA)

Paynter, E. 1932-33(A); 1938-39(SA)

Peach, H. A. 1928-29(J)

Pearce, T. N. 1939(E)

Peate, E. 1881-82(A)

Preebles, L. A. R. 1927-28(SA); 1930(E); 1930-31(SA); 1932(E); 1933(NA); 1936-37(Ce); 1937-38(I)

Peel, R. 1884-85(A); 1887-88(A); 1891-92(A); 1894-95(A);

Penn, E. F. 1898(NA)

Penn, F. 1878-79(A)

Perks, R. T. D. 1938-39(SA)

Perrett, D. S. 1966-67(Ba)

Philipson, H. 1889-90(I); 1891-92(A); 1894-95(A)

Phillips, F. A. 1895(NA)

Phillips, J. 1887-88(A)★

Phillipson, W. E. 1938-39(NZ)

Piachaud, J. D. 1959(NA); 1966-67(Ba); 1976-77(Bg)

Pickering, F. P. U. 1872(NA)

Pigott, A. C. S. 1979-80(A); 1983-84(NZ)

Pilkington, T. A. 1926-27(SAm)

Pilling, H. 1977-78(FE)

Pilling, R. 1881-82(A); 1887-88(A)

Pinder, G. 1879(NA)

Place, W. 1947-48(W)

Plumb, S. G. 1980-81(Bg)

Pocock, P. I. 1966-67(P); 1967-68(W); 1968-69(P); 1969-70(FE); 1972-73(I); 1973-74(W); 1974-75(W); 1984-85(I)

Pocock, N. E. J. 1981-82(FE); 1982(US); 1985(C)

Pollard, R. 1946-47(A)

Ponsonby, R. 1909-10(SA)★

Poole, C. J. 1951-52(I)

Pooley, E. 1868(NA); 1876-77(A)

Pope, G. H. 1937-38(I); 1939-40(I)

Popplewell, N. F. M. 1976-77(Bg)

Porter, S. R. 1982-83(EA)

Pougher, A. D. 1887-88(A); 1891-92(SA)

Powell, A. G. 1935-36(NZ); 1937(E); 1937(C); 1938(E); 1939(E); 1951(C)

Powell, V. 1968-69(SA)

Powys-Keck, H. J. 1902-03(I); 1904-05(W)

Preston, J. M. 1887-88(A)

Pretlove, J. F. 1959(NA)

Price, J. S. E. 1963-64(I); 1964-65(SA)

Price, W. F. F. 1929-30(W); 1937-38(Am)

Prideaux, R. M. 1959(NA); 1960-61(NZ); 1968-69(P)

Priestley, A. 1894-95(W); 1896-97(W); 1898-98(A)★; 1899(NA); 1901(NA)

Priestley, R. J. 1973-74(Ba)
Pringle, D. R. 1982-83(A); 1985-86(SL); 1987-88(I)
Pullar, G. 1959-60(W); 1961-62(I); 1962-63(A)

Quaife, William 1901-02(A)

Radcliffe, O. G. 1891-92(A)
Radley, C. T. 1972-73(SA); 1974-75(SA); 1977-78(P); 1978-79(A); 1980-81(Z)
Radford, N. V. 1987-88(NZ)
Randall, D. W. 1974-75(W); 1975-66(SA); 1976-77(I); 1977-78(P); 1978-79(A); 1979-80(A); 1982-83(A); 1983-84(NZ); 1985-86(SA)
Ranjitsinhji, K. S. 1897-98(A); 1899(NA)
Raphael, R. H. 1902-03(NZ)*; 1902-03(I)
Rawlin, J. T. 1887-88(A)
Rawlinson, Capt – 1889-90(I)
Read, H. D. 1933(E); 1935-36(NZ)
Read, J. M. 1884-85(A); 1886-87(A); 1887-88(A); 1888-89(SA); 1891-92(A)
Read, W. W. 1882-83(A); 1887-88(A); 1891-92(SA)
Reddick, T. B. 1933(NA); 1936-37(Ce)
Reed, B. L. 1979-80(Bg)
Relf, A. E. 1903-04(A); 1905-06(SA); 1912-13(W); 1913-14(SA)
Relf, R. R. 1913-14(SA)*
Revill, A. C. 1961(B)
Rhodes, A. E. G. 1951-52(I)
Rhodes, H. J. 1967-68(AA); 1981-82(FE)
Rhodes, S. D. 1929-30(Ar); 1933(NA); 1936-37(Ce)
Rhodes, S. J. 1985-86(SA)
Rhodes, W. 1903-04(A); 1907-08(A); 1909-10(SA); 1911-12(A); 1929-30(W)
Richards, C. J. 1979-80(A); 1981-82(I); 1986-87(A); 1987-88(NZ)
Richardson, D. W. 1964-65(Wo); 1964-65(W); 1965-66(J)
Richardson, P. E. 1955-56(P); 1956-57(SA); 1957-58(EA); 1958-59(A); 1961-62(I); 1963-64(J)
Richardson, T. 1894-95(A); 1897-98(A)
Richmond, T. L. 1929-30(SAm)
Ricketts, G. W. 1891(NA)
Riddell, N. A. 1977-78(K)
Ridgway, F. 1951-52(I)
Ridley, J. N. 1902-03(I)
Rimington, Capt M. F. 1892-93(I)*
Ritchie, D. M. 1923(C)
Roberts, D. 1920(N); 1937(E)
Roberts, J. H. 1888-89(SA)
Robertson, J. D. B. 1947-48(W); 1952-52(I)
Robins, R. V. C. 1957-58(EA); 1958-59(SAm); 1968-69(SA)
Robins, R. W. V. 1929-30(Ar); 1933(NA); 1936-37(A); 1951(C)

Robinson, A. G. 1901-02(W)
Robinson, C. D. 1895(NA)
Robinson, D. C. 1927-28(J)
Robinson, E. P. 1935-36(J)
Robinson, J. S. 1892-93(I); 1894(NA)
Robinson, P. E. 1986-87(W)
Robinson, R. T. 1984-85(I); 1985-86(W); 1987-88(NZ)
Robson, C. 1899(NA); 1901-02(A)
Roebeck, St G. M. de 1896-97(W)*
Roller, W. E. 1885(NA); 1886(NA)
Rome, D. A. M. 1935(E); 1936(E); 1937(E)
Romilly, Lord 1923(C)
Roope, G. R. J. 1969-70(FE); 1972-73(I); 1973-74(SA); 1977-78(P)
Root, C. F. 1925-26(W)
Rose, B. C. 1977-78(P); 1980-81(W)
Rose, W. M. 1872(NA)
Ross, N. P. O. 1982(US)
Rotherham, H. 1886(NA)
Rought-Rought, D. C. 1938(E)
Rouse, S. J. 1974-75(SA); 1974-75(W)
Rowbotham, J. 1868(NA)
Rowland, C. A. 1929-30(Ar)
Royle, V. P. F. A. 1878-79(A)
Rudd, C. R. D. 1951(C)
Russell, C. A. G. 1920-21(A); 1922-23(SA); 1924-25(SA)
Russell, R. C. 1987-88(NZ)
Russell, W. E. 1960-61(NZ); 1961-62(I); 1965-66(A)
Ryan, M. 1964(NA)

Sadiq Mohammad 1971-72(Za)
Sainsbury, P. J. 1955-56(P); 1974-75(W)
Sanders, E. J. 1885(NA); 1886(NA)
Sandham, A. 1922-23(SA); 1924-25(A); 1926-27(I); 1928-29(J); 1929-30(W); 1930-31(SA); 1938-39(SAm)
Santall, F. R. 1937-38(SAm)
Sarel, W. G. M. 1913(US)
Sayer, D. M. 1958-59(SAm); 1960-61(NZ)
Schultz, S. S. 1878-79(A)
Schwartz, R. O. 1901(NA); 1907(NA)
Scott, E. K. 1951(C)
Scott, P. A. 1892-93(I)*
Scott, R. P. 1938(E)*
Scott, R. S. G. 1929(E); 1930(E)
Scott-Chad, G. N. 1931-32(J)
Scotton, W. H. 1881-82(A); 1884-85(A); 1886-87(A)
Seabrook, F. J. 1927-28(J)
Selby, J. 1876-77(A); 1879(NA); 1881-82(A)
Sellar, K. A. 1936(E); 1937(C)
Selvey, M. W. W. 1976-77(I); 1980-81(Z)
Sevier, W. W. 1889-90(I)*
Sewell, C. O. H. 1898(NA)
Sewell, R. P. 1894-95(W)
Sewell, T. 1861-62(A)
Seymour, J. 1903(NA)
Shackleton, D. 1951-52(I)
Shackleton, J. H. 1971-72(Za)
Shand, F. L. 1889-90(I); 1892-93(I)*

Sharp, G. 1974-75(W)
Sharp, K. 1979-80(A); 1986-87(W)
Sharpe, J. W. 1891-92(A)
Sharpe, P. J. 1963-64(I); 1964(NA); 1969-70(W)
Shaw, A. 1868(NA); 1876-77(A); 1879(NA); 1881-82(A); 1884-85(A); 1886-87(A)
Shaw, G. 1928-29(J)
Shaw, W. 1886-87(A)*
Shepherd, D. J. 1961-62(EA); 1969-70(W); 1969-70(FE); 1971-72(Za)
Shepherd, D. R. 1971-72(Za)
Shepherd, J. N. 1972-73(W); 1973-74(SA); 1974-75(SA); 1974-75(W)
Sheppard, D. S. 1950-51(A); 1962-63(A)
Shermedine, G. O. 1920(NA)
Sherring, – 1892-93(I)*
Sherwin, M. 1886-87(A)
Shrewsbury, A. 1879(NA); 1881-82(A); 1884-85(A); 1886-87(A); 1887-88(A)
Shuttleworth, K. 1970-71(A)
Sidebottom, A. 1981-82(SA); 1986-87(W)
Silk, D. R. W. 1957-58(EA); 1958-59(SAm); 1959(NA); 1960-61(NZ)
Simmons, J. 1986-87(J)
Simpson, C. 1910-11(W)*
Simpson, R. T. 1948-49(SA); 1950-51(A); 1954-55(A); 1956-57(I)
Simpson-Hayward, G. H. T. 1902-03(I); 1904-05(W); 1906-07(NZ); 1907(NA); 1909(E); 1909-10(SA)
Sims, J. M. 1935-36(NZ); 1936-37(A); 1937-38(SAm)
Singh, S. 1955-56(W)
Singleton, A. P. 1937(C); 1939(E)
Skene, R. W. 1929(E)
Skinner, A. C. 1888-89(SA)
Skinner, W. R. 1937-38(SAm)
Slack, J. K. E. 1961(B)
Slack, W. N. 1980-81(Z); 1985-86(SL); 1985-86(W); 1986-87(A)
Slade, D. N. F. 1964-65(W); 1965-66(J)
Slocombe, P. A. 1975-76(SA)
Smailes, T. F. 1935-36(J)
Small, G. C. 1979-80(A); 1986-87(A); 1987-88(I)
Smith, A. C. 1959(NA); 1962-63(A); 1964-65(SAm); 1967-68(EA); 1969-70(FE)
Smith, A. E. C. 1938(E)
Smith, C. A. 1887-88(A); 1888-89(SA)
Smith, C. I. J. 1934-35(W)
Smith, C. L. 1983-84(NZ); 1985-86(SL)
Smith, D. 1935-36(NZ)
Smith, D. M. 1985-86(W)
Smith, D. R. 1960-61(NZ); 1961-62(I); 1962(B)
Smith, D. V. 1956-57(J)
Smith, E. J. 1911-12(A); 1913-14(SA); 1925-26(W)
Smith, John (Cambs) 1868(NA)
Smith, J. 1982-83(EA)
Smith, M. J. 1972-73(SA); 1973-74(SA); 1974-75(W); 1977-78(FE)
Smith, M. J. K. 1957-58(EA); 1958-59(SAm); 1959-60(W); 1961-62(I); 1963-64(EA); 1963-64(I); 1964-65(SA); 1965-66(A); 1967-68(EA)

Smith, S. G. 1910-11(W); 1912-13(W)
Smith, T. P. B. 1937-38(I); 1938-39(NZ); 1939-40(I); 1946-47(A)
Smith, W. C. 1912-13(W)
Smithson, G. A. 1947-48(W)
Smith-Turberville, H. S. 1894-95(W)
Snooke, S. J. 1907(NA)
Snow, J. A. 1967-68(W); 1968-69(P); 1970-71(A); 1973-74(SA)
Sobers, G. St A., 1964(NA)
Solbe, E. P. 1933(NA)
Somerset, A. P. F. C. 1910-11(W); 1912-13(W)
Somerset, A. W. F. 1904-05(W); 1910-11(W); 1912-13(W)
Southerton, J. 1873-74(A); 1876-77(A)
Speak, N. J. 1986-87(J)
Spooner, R. T. 1951-52(I); 1953-54(W)
Stanley, H. T. 1896-97(W)
Stanning, J. 1902-03(NZ)
Stanyforth, R. T. 1926-27(SAm); 1927-28(SA); 1929-30(W); 1932(E)
Staples, S. J. 1927-28(SA); 1928-29(A)
Statham, J. B. 1950-51(A); 1951-52(I); 1953-54(W); 1954-55(A); 1956-57(SA); 1958-59(A); 1959-60(W); 1962-63(A)
Steel, A. G. 1882-83(A)
Steele, D. S. 1975-76(SA); 1980-81(Z)
Steele, H. K. 1972-73(M)
Steele, J. F. 1974-75(SA)
Stephenson, E. 1861-62(A)
Stephenson, H. H. 1859(NA); 1861-62(A)
Stephenson, H. W. 1955-56(P)
Stevens, B. 1939(E)
Stevens, G. T. S. 1922-23(SA); 1927-28(SA); 1929-30(W); 1931-32(J)
Stevenson, G. B. 1979-80(A); 1980-81(W)
Stewart, H. C. 1903(NA)
Stewart, M. J. 1955-56(W); 1959-60(R); 1960-61(NZ); 1963-64(EA); 1963-64(I); 1967-68(AA)
Stewart, N. J. W. 1978-79(Bg); 1980-81(Bg)
Stocks, F. W. 1897(NA)
Stoddart, A. E. 1887-88(A); 1891-92(A); 1894-95(A); 1896-97(W); 1897-98(A); 1899(NA)
Stoddart, P. L. B. 1968-69(SA)
Stone, C. C. 1896-97(W)
Storer, W. 1897-98(A)
Stow, V. A. S. 1905(NA)
Street, G. B. 1922-23(SA)
Strudwick, H. 1903-04(A); 1909-10(SA); 1911-12(A); 1913-14(SA); 1920-21(A); 1924-25(A)
Studd, C. T. 1882-83(A)
Studd, G. B. 1882-83(A)
Studd, R. A. 1895(NA)
Sturdy, R. G. 1938-39(J)
Sturt, M. O. C. 1968-69(SA); 1981-82(FE)
Style, N. 1968-69(SA)
Subba Row, R. 1958-59(A); 1959-60(W)
Sullivan, D. 1926-27(J); 1927-28(J)
Sullivan, J. P. 1971-72(Za)
Summers, G. F. 1933(NA); 1936-37(Ce)
Surridge, S. S. 1980-81(Bg)
Surridge, W. S. 1959-60(R); 1961(B)

Sutcliffe, H. 1924-25(A); 1927-28(SA); 1928-29(A); 1932-33(A); 1935-36(J)
Sutcliffe, W. H. H. 1955-56(P)
Suttle, K. G. 1953-54(W); 1967-68(AA)
Swan, H. D. 1922-23(NZ); 1929-30(Ar)
Swanton, E. W. 1933(NA); 1955-56(W)
Swetman, R. 1955-56(P); 1958-59(A); 1959-60(R); 1959-60(W)

Tapling, T. K. 1889-90(I)
Tarrant, G. 1863-64(A); 1868(NA)
Tate, M. W. 1924-25(A); 1926-27(I); 1928-29(A); 1930-31(SA); 1932-33(A); 1937-38(SAm)
Tattersall, R. 1950-51(A); 1951-52(I)
Tavaré, C. J. 1981-82(I); 1982-83(A); 1983-84(NZ)
Taylor, B. 1956-57(SA); 1976-77(Bg)
Taylor, C. H. 1937(C); 1939(E)
Taylor, C. R. V. 1972-73(M)
Taylor, K. 1978-79(Bg)
Taylor, L. B. 1980-81(Z); 1981-82(SA); 1985-86(W)
Taylor, R. W. 1969-70(FE); 1970-71(A); 1973-74(W); 1974-75(A); 1977-78(P); 1978-79(A); 1979-80(A); 1981-82(I); 1982-83(A); 1983-84(NZ)
Taylor, T. L. 1902-03(NZ)
Tennyson, A. 1926-27(J)*
Tennyson, Hon L. H. 1913-14(SA); 1924-25(SA); 1925-26(W); 1926-27(J); 1927-28(J); 1928-29(J); 1931-32(J); 1937-38(I)
Terry, V. P. 1984-85(Z)
Thomas, E. 1889-90(I)
Thomas, J. C. 1985-86(W)
Thompson, C. E. 1923(C)
Thompson, G. J. 1902-03(NZ); 1904-05(W); 1909-10(SA)
Thompson, J. R. 1951(C); 1959(NA)
Thomson, N. I. 1955-56(P); 1964-65(SA)
Thorley, J. J. 1924(US)
Thornton, A. J. 1885(NA)
Thornton, Rev R. T. 1885(NA)
Throwley, Lord 1891(NA)
Titchener-Barrett, R. C. S. 1974-75(W)
Tinley, R. C. 1863-64(A)
Titchmarsh, C. H. 1922-23(NZ)
Titmus, F. J. 1955-56(P); 1962-63(A); 1963-64(I); 1964-65(SA); 1965-66(A); 1967-68(W); 1974-75(A); 1975-76(SA); 1981-82(FE); 1982(US)
Tolchard, R. W. 1967-68(AA); 1972-73(I); 1973-74(SA); 1974-75(SA); 1974-75(W); 1975-76(SA); 1976-77(I); 1977-78(FE); 1978-79(A); 1980-81(Z); 1985(C)
Tomkinson, J. E. 1902-03(I)
Tomlins, K. P. 1980-81(Z)
Tompkin, M. 1955-56(P)
Tonge, J. N. 1897(NA)
Toole, C. L. 1978-79(Bg)
Torrens, A. A. 1906-07(NZ)
Townsend, C. L. 1899(NA)
Townsend, D. C. H. 1934-35(W); 1936(E)

Townsend, L. F. 1929-30(W); 1933-34(I)
Tremlett, M. F. 1947-48(W); 1948-49(SA)
Tremlett, T. M. 1984-85(Z); 1985-86(SL)
Tribe, G. E. 1956-57(J); 1956-57(I)
Trott, A. E. 1898-99(SA); 1902-03(NZ)
Troughton, L. H. W. 1911-12(Ar)
Troup, G. B. 1975-76(SA)
Trueman, F. S. 1953-54(W); 1956-57(I); 1958-59(A); 1959-60(W); 1962-63(A); 1963-64(J); 1964(NA); 1964-65(W)
Trumper, J. O. 1973-74(Ba)
Tudor, C. L. St J. 1913(US)
Tufnell, N. C. 1906-07(NZ); 1909-10(SA); 1911-12(Ar)
Turnbull, M. J. L. 1929-30(NZ); 1930-31(SA)
Turner, C. 1935-36(J)
Turner, D. R. 1972-73(SA)
Turner, J. A. 1885(NA); 1886(NA)
Turner, N. F. 1937(E)
Turner, S. 1974-75(SA); 1974-75(W)
Twisleton-Wykeham-Fiennes, Hon E. E. 1898-99(SA)*
Tyldesley, G. E. 1924-25(SA); 1926-27(J); 1927-28(SA); 1928-29(A)
Tyldesley, H. 1922-23(NZ)
Tyldesley, J. T. 1898-99(SA); 1901-02(A); 1903-04(A)
Tyldesley, R. K. 1924-25(A)
Tylecote, E. F. S. 1882-83(A)
Tyler, A. W. 1933(E)
Tyler, E. J. 1895-96(SA)
Tyson, F. H. 1954-55(A); 1955-56(W); 1956-57(SA); 1958-59(A)

Ulyett, G. 1876-77(A); 1878-79(A); 1879(A); 1881-82(A); 1884-85(A); 1887-88(A); 1888-89(SA)
Underwood, D. L. 1966-67(P); 1967-68(AA); 1968-69(P); 1969-70(W); 1970-71(A); 1972-73(I); 1973-74(W); 1974-75(A); 1976-77(I); 1979-80(A); 1981-82(I); 1981-82(SA)
Unwin, F. St. G. 1938(E)

Valentine, B. H. 1931-32(J); 1933(E); 1933-34(I); 1935(E); 1938(E); 1938-39(SA)
Varey, D. W. 1986-87(J)
Vaulkhard, D. H. 1928-29(J)
Vere-Hodge, N. 1937(E)
Verity, H. 1932-33(A); 1933-34(I); 1935-36(J); 1936-37(A); 1938-39(SA)
Vernon, G. F. 1882-83(A); 1887-88(A); 1889-90(I); 1892-93(I)
Vernon, M. J. 1976-77(Bg)
Vine, J. 1911-12(A)
Vizard, R. D. 1889-90(I)*
Voce, W. 1929-30(W); 1930-31(SA); 1932-33(A); 1936-37(A); 1946-47(A)
Von Donop, Maj P. G. 1889-90(I)*

Waddington, A. 1920-21(A)
Wade, T. H. 1936-37(A)★
Wainwright, E. 1897-98(A)
Wakefield, W. H. 1894-95(W); 1896-97(W)
Walford, M. M. 1938-39(J); 1951(C)
Walker, D. F. 1939(E)
Walker, J. G. 1889-90(I)
Walker, M. H. N. 1974-75(SA)
Walker, P. M. 1961-62(EA); 1969-70(W)
Wallen, G. 1977-78(K)
Walsh, J. E. 1936-37(Ce); 1938-39(NZ)
Walters, C. F. 1931-32(J); 1933-34(I)
Walters, F. H. 1887-88(A)★
Walters, K. W. 1966-67(Ba)
Ward, A. (Derbys) 1969-70(W); 1970-71(A)
Ward, A. (Lancs) 1824-95(A)
Ward, J. M. 1972-73(M)
Wardle, J. H. 1947-48(W); 1953-54(W); 1954-55(A); 1956-57(SA)
Warner, P. F. 1896-97(W); 1897(NA); 1898(NA); 1898-99(SA); 1902-03(NZ); 1903-04(A); 1904-05(SA); 1911-12(A); 1926-27(SAm)
Warner, R. S. A. 1898(NA)
Warr, J. J. 1950-51(A); 1951(C); 1955-56(W); 1956-57(J); 1957-58(EA)
Washbrook, C. 1946-47(A); 1948-49(SA); 1950-51(A)
Waterfield, J. E. 1889-90(I)★
Watkins, A. J. 1948-49(SA); 1951-52(I); 1955-56(P)
Watkins, W. R. 1957-58(EA)
Watson, F. B. 1925-26(W)
Watson, Hon. R. B. 1905(NA)★
Watson, W. 1953-54(W); 1956-57(J); 1956-57(I); 1958-59(A); 1960-61(NZ); 1963-64(EA)
Watts, E. A. 1937-38(SAm); 1938-39(NZ)
Weatherby, J. H. 1894-95(W)
Webbe, A. J. 1878-79(A)
Weber, O. 1896-97(W)★
Weigall, G. J. V. 1930(NA); 1926-27(SAm); 1927-28(J)
Welch, W. M. 1936(E)
Wellard, A. W. 1937-38(I); 1939-40(I)
Wells, G. 1861-62(A)
Welman, F. T. 1886(NA)
Wenlock, D. A. 1980-81(Z)
Werner, R. H. 1937(E)★
Wharton, A. 1956-57(I)
Whatman, A. D. 1896-97(W); 1897(NA); 1901-02(W); 1902-03(NZ)
Whatmore, D. F. 1975-76(SA)
Wheatley, O. S. 1958-59(SAm); 1969-70(W)

Whetherly, R. E. 1938-39(J)
Whitaker, J. J. 1986-87(A)
Whitby, H. O. 1885(NAm)
Whitcombe, D. M. P. 1913(US)
White, A. H. 1924(US)
White, D. W. 1961-62(I); 1964-65(W)
White, J. C. 1926-27(SAm); 1928-29(A); 1930-31(SA)
White, R. C. 1964-65(SAm)
Whitfield, G. S. 1903-04(A)★
Whittington, T. A. L. 1910-11(W); 1912-13(W)
Whitwell, W. F. 1894(NA)
Whysall, W. W. 1924-25(A); 1928-29(J)
Wickham, R. W. 1896-97(W)
Wigan, P. 1966-67(Ba)
Wight, P. B. 1961-62(EA)
Wilcox, D. R. 1934(E); 1935(E); 1936(E); 1937(E); 1938(E)
Wilenkin, B. C. G. 1968-69(SA)
Wilkinson, W. A. C. 1922-23(NZ)
Wilkinson, L. L. 1938-39(SA)
Wilkinson, J. S. 1977-78(K)
Willey, P. 1972-73(SA); 1977-78(FE); 1979-80(A); 1980-81(W); 1981-82(SA); 1985-86(W)
Williams, D. 1961-62(EA)★
Williams, D. L. 1969-70(W)
Williams, E. S. B. 1931(E)
Williams, F. 1887-88(A)★
Williams, J. N. 1902-03(NZ)★
Williams, N. F. 1984-85(Z)
Williams, P. F. C. 1906-07(NZ)★
Williams, R. A. 1902-03(NZ)★; 1902-03(I)
Williams, R. G. 1979-80(A); 1984-85(Z)
Williams, W. 1896-97(W)
Willis, R. G. D. 1970-71(A); 1972-73(SA); 1973-74(W); 1974-75(A); 1976-77(I); 1977-78(P); 1978-79(A); 1979-80(A); 1980-81(W); 1981-82(I); 1982-83(A); 1982-83(NZ)
Wills, G. S. 1932(E)
Willsher, E. 1868(NA)
Wilson, C. E. M. 1895(NA); 1898-99(SA)
Wilson, D. 1960-61(NZ); 1963-64(I); 1964(NA); 1969-70(FE); 1970-71(A); 1985(C)
Wilson, D. C. 1938-39(J)
Wilson, E. R. 1901(NA); 1901-02(W); 1911-12(Ar); 1920-21(A)
Wilson, G. 1922-23(NZ)
Wilson, J. V. 1954-55(A)
Wilson, P. H. L. E. 1980-81(Bg); 1981-82(FE)
Wiltshire, G. G. M. 1971-72(Za)
Windows, A. R. 1966-67(P)

Wing, D. C. 1968-69(SA); 1975-76(WA); 1976-77(Bg)
Winlaw, R. de W. K. 1939(E)
Winter, G. E. 1898(NA)
Wisden, J. 1859(NA)
Wolfe, G. 1938-39(NZ)
Wood, A. 1935-36(J); 1937-38(SAm)
Wood, B. 1972-73(I); 1974-75(A); 1974-75(W)
Wood, G. E. C. 1929(E)
Wood, H. 1888-89(SA); 1891-92(SA)
Wood, R. 1886-87(A)★
Woods, S. M. J. 1891(NA); 1895-96(SA); 1896-97(W); 1899(NA); 1901-02(A)★
Woolley, F. E. 1909-10(SA); 1911-12(A); 1913-14(SA); 1920-21(A); 1922-23(SA); 1924-25(A); 1929-30(NZ)
Woolmer, R. A. 1972-73(W); 1973-74(SA); 1976-77(I); 1981-82(SA)
Worthington, T. S. 1929-30(NZ); 1936-37(A); 1937-38(I)
Wreford-Brown, C. 1891(NA)
Wright, C. W. 1891(NA; 1892-93(I); 1894(NA); 1895-96(SA)
Wright, D. V. P. 1938-39(SA); 1946-47(A); 1948-49(SA); 1950-51(A); 1956-57(J)
Wright, H. F. 1892-93(I)
Wright, J. G. 1977-78(FE)
Wyatt, R. E. S. 1926-27(I); 1927-28(SA); 1929-30(W); 1930-31(SA); 1932-33(A); 1934-35(W); 1936(E); 1936-37(A); 1937-38(SAm); 1939(E); 1939-40(I)
Wykes, N. G. 1937(C)
Wyld, H. J. 1905(NA)
Wynyard, E. G. 1904-05(W); 1905-06(SA); 1906-07(NZ); 1907(NA); 1909(E); 1909-10(SA); 1920(NA); 1923(C)

Yardley, N. W. D. 1937-38(I); 1938-39(SA); 1946-47(A)
Yeabsley, D. I. 1977-78(K)
Young, H. I. 1910-11(W)
Young, J. A. 1948-49(SA)
Young, R. A. 1907-08(A)
Younis Ahmed, 1973-74(SA); 1974-75(SA)

Zaheer Abbas 1971-72(Za)

McIlwraith, J. 1886
Mackay, K. D. 1956, 1961
McKenzie, G. D. 1961, 1964, 1968
McKibbin, T. R. 1896
McLaren, J. W. 1912
McLeod, C. E. 1899, 1905
McLeod, R. W. 1893
Maddocks, L. V. 1956
Mailey, A. A. 1921, 1920
Mallett, A. A. 1968, 1972, 1975, 1980
Malone, M. F. 1977
Marsh, R. W. 1972, 1975, 1977, 1980, 1981
Martin, J. W. 1964
Massie, H. H. 1882
Massie, R. A. L. 1972
Matthews, G. R. J. 1985
Matthews, T. J. 1912
Mayne, E. R. 1912, 1921
Midwinter, W. E. 1878, 1884
Miller, K. R. 1945, 1948, 1953, 1956
Minnett, R. B. 1912
Misson, F. M. 1961
Morris, A. R. 1948, 1953
Moule, W. H. 1880
Murdoch, W. L. 1878, 1880, 1882, 1884, 1890
Murray, J. T. 1919
Musgrove, H. A. 1896

Newland, P. M. 1905
Noble, M. A. 1899, 1902, 1905, 1909

O'Connor, J. D. A. 1909
O'Donnell, S. P. 1985
O'Keeffe, K. J. 1977
Oldfield, W. A. S. 1919, 1921, 1926, 1930, 1934
O'Neill, N. C. 1961, 1964
O'Reilly, W. J. 1934, 1938

Palmer, G. E. 1880, 1882, 1884, 1886
Pascoe, L. S. 1977, 1980
Pellew, C. E. 1919, 1921
Pepper, C. G. 1945
Phillips, R. B. 1985
Phillips, W. B. 1985
Ponsford, W. H. 1926, 1930, 1934
Pope, R. J. 1886, 1890, 1902
Potter, J. 1964
Price, C. F. T. 1945

Quick, I. W. 1961

Ransford, V. S. 1909
Redpath, I. R. 1964, 1968
Renneberg, D. A. 1968
Richardson, A. J. 1926
Richardson, V. Y. 1930
Ring, D. T. 1948, 1953
Ritchie, G. M. 1985
Rixon, S. J. 1981
Robinson, R. D. 1975, 1977
Roper, A. W. 1945
Rutherford, J. W. 1956
Ryder, J. 1921, 1926

Saggers, R. A. 1948
Saunders, J. V. 1902
Scott, H. J. H. 1884, 1886

Sellers, R. H. D. 1964
Serjeant, C. S. 1977
Sheahan, A. P. 1968, 1972
Simpson, R. B. 1961, 1964
Sismey, S. G. 1945
Slight, J. 1880
Smith, D. B. M. 1912
Spofforth, F. R. 1878, 1880, 1882, 1884, 1886
Stackpole, K. R. 1972
Stanford, R. M. 1945
Stirling, W. S. 1919

Taber, H. B. 1968, 1972
Tallon, D. 1948, 1953
Taylor, J. M. 1919, 1921, 1926
Tennent, H. M. 1878
Thomson, J. R. 1975, 1977, 1980, 1985
Tobin, W. 1878
Toshack, E. R. H. 1948
Trennery, W. L. 1919
Trott, G. H. S. 1888, 1890, 1893, 1896
Trumble, H. 1890, 1893, 1896, 1899, 1902
Trumble, J. W. 1886
Trumper, V. T. 1899, 1902, 1905, 1909
Turner, A. 1975
Turner, C. T. B. 1888, 1890, 1893

Veivers, T. R. 1964

Waite, M. G. 1938
Walker, C. W. 1930, 1938
Walker, M. H. N. 1975, 1977
Wall, T. W. 1930, 1934
Walters, K. D. 1968, 1972, 1975, 1977
Ward, F. A. 1938
Wardill, B. J. 1886
Watson, G. D. 1972
Webster, H. W. 1912
Wellham, D. M. 1981, 1985
Wessels, K. C. 1985
White, E. S. 1938
Whitney, M. R. 1981
Whitington, R. S. 1945
Whitty, W. J. 1909, 1912
Wilkinson, W. C. 1878
Williams, R. G. 1945
Willis, C. B. 1919
Wilson, J. W. 1956
Winning, S. G. 1919
Wood, G. M. 1980, 1981, 1985
Woodfull, W. M. 1926, 1930, 1934
Woods, S. M. J. 1888
Workman, J. A. 1945
Worrall, J. 1888, 1899

Yallop, G. N. 1980, 1981

CANADA

Allan, A. C. 1887
Annand, C. J. 1887

Bell, L. C. 1936
Bell, W. E. N. 1936
Brierley, T. L. 1954
Bruce-Lockhart, R. B. 1954
Bullen, H. G. 1954

Cameron, F. J. 1954
Carey, D. E. 1936
Carlton, E. 1936
Christen, B. 1954

Davies, M. I. 1936
Dewhurst, J. 1980
Dunn, – 1880
Dutton, T. 1880

Ferries, R. B. 1887
Fleury, W. J. 1887

Gilbert, W. 1880
Gillean, J. S. 1880
Gillespie, A. 1887
Gunn, L. J. H. 1954

Hague, R. D. 1922
Hall, F. F. 1880
Hardman, J. L. 1880
Harper, S. E. 1922
Hedgson, – 1880
Henderson, P. E. 1922
Hendy, F. 1954
Henry, F. 1880
Henry, W. A. 1887
Hibberd, H. W. 1880
Howard, J. 1880
Humphries, H. H. 1922

Inglis, A. M. 1922

Jones, G. W. 1887
Jones, W. W. 1887
Jordan, T. 1880

Kearney, C. 1880

Lemmon, A. H. 1880
Lindsay, G. G. S. 1887
Little, W. C. 1887
Loney, E. F. 1936
Lucas, J. H. 1954

Magee, B. R. 1954
Miller, H. 1954
Mix, A. E. 1922
Mustard, V. R. 1922

Ogden, Dr E. R. 1887

Pearson, N. F. 1936
Percival, J. G. 1936
Percival, L. A. 1936
Percival, W. A. 1954
Phillips, Rev T. D. 1880
Pinckney, W. 1880

Quintrell, R. N. 1954

Rathbun, L. M. 1922
Reid, H. S. 1922
Rilstone, T. M. 1954
Ripley, R. C. 1936
Robinson, H. B. 1954
Ross, K. H. 1936

Saunders, D. W. 1887, 1922
Saunders, S. R. 1922

Scott, W. G. 1936
Seagram, C. A. 1936
Seagram, P. F. 1936
Seagram, T. W. 1922
Smith, D. J. 1880
Somerville, C. R. 1922
Stead, P. 1954

Treloar, A. S. 1880

Vickers, W. W. 1887

Weaver, J. L. 1936
Wight, A. 1954
Wight, L. 1954
Wookey, H. G. 1922
Wright, W. 1880

INDIA
(includes Parsis)

Abid Ali, S. 1971, 1974
Abdul Hafeez, 1946
Adhikari, H. R. 1952
Amarnath, M. 1979, 1986
Amarnath, N. B. (Lala) 1936, 1946
Apte, A. L. 1959
Amar Singh, L. 1932, 1936
Azharuddin, M. 1986

Baig, A. A. 1959, 1971
Bajana, M. P. 1911
Balla, B. P. 1886
Baloo, P. 1911
Banaji, M. 1886
Banerjee, S. S. 1936, 1946
Bapasola, N. C. 1888
Baria, B. B. 1886
Baroda, Gaekwad of 1911
Bedi, B. S. 1967, 1974, 1979
Bedwar, S. N. 1886
Bejonji, M. 1886
Binny, R. M. H. 1986
Borde, C. G. 1959, 1967
Bose, G. 1974
Bulsara, M. D. 1911

Chandrasekhar, B. S. 1967, 1974, 1979
Chauhan, C. P. S. 1979
Chowdhury, N. R. 1952
Colah, S. H. M. 1932
Contractor, N. J. 1959
Cooper, R. D. 1888

Dastur, P. D. 1886
Dilawar Hussain 1936
Divecha, R. V. 1952
Doshi, D. R. 1982
Dubash, D. F. 1888

Elahi, Amir 1936
Engineer, F. M. 1967, 1971, 1974
Eranee, K. R. 1888

Framji, M. 1886

Gaekwad, A. D. 1979

Gaekwad, D. K. 1952, 1959
Gaekwad, H. G. 1952
Gavaskar, S. M. 1971, 1974, 1979, 1982, 1986
Ghavri, K. D. 1979
Ghorpade, J. M. 1959
Ghulam Ahmed 1952
Ghulam Mahomed 1932
Godambe, S. R. 1932
Gopalan, M. J. 1936
Gopinath, C. D. 1952
Govindraj, D. 1971
Guha, S. 1967
Gul Mahomed 1946

Hadi, S. M. 1936
Hanumant Singh 1967
Harver, S. 1886, 1888
Hazare, V. S. 1946, 1952
Hindlekar, D. D. 1936, 1946
Hussein, Syd 1911

Jai, L. P. 1936
Jaisimha, M. L. 1959
Jayantilal, K. 1971
Jaya Ram, B. 1911
Jilani, M. Baqa 1936
Joginder Singh 1932
Joshi, P. G. 1959

Kanga, H. D. 1911
Kanga, M. D. 1888
Kanga, P. D. 1888
Kapadia, B. E. 1932
Kapil Dev 1979, 1982, 1986
Khambata, D. D. 1886
Khan, M. Jahangir 1932, 1936
Khanna, S. C. 1979
Kirmani, S. M. H. 1971, 1974, 1982
Kripal Singh, A. G. 1959
Kunderan, B. K. 1967

Lall Singh 1932
Lamba, R. 1986
Libuwalla, A. 1886
Limbdi, K. S. G. of 1932

Madan Lal, S. 1974, 1982, 1986
Mahomed Hussein, S. 1936
Mahomed Nissar 1932, 1936
Major, A. C. 1886
Major, P. C. 1886
Malhotra, A. 1982
Maninder, Singh 1986
Manjrekar, V. L. 1952, 1959
Mankad, A. V. 1971, 1974
Mankad, M. H. 1946, 1952
Mantri, M. K. 1952
Marshall, N. D. 1932
Meherhomji, K. R. 1936
Meherhomji, R. P. 1911
Mehta, D. H. 1888
Merchant, V. M. 1936, 1946
Mistri, K. M. 1911
Modi, R. S. 1946
Mody, B. D. 1888
Mohol, S. N. 1967
More, K. S. 1986
Morenas, J. M. 1886, 1888

Mulla, H. F. 1911
Mushtaq Ali, S. 1936, 1946

Nadkarni, R. G. 1959
Naik, S. S. 1974
Naoomal Jeoomal 1932
Navle, J. G. 1932
Nayak, S. V. 1982
Nayudu, C. K. 1932, 1936
Nayudu, C. S. 1936, 1946
Nazir Ali, S. 1932
Nimbalkar, R. B. 1946

Pai, M. 1911
Palia, P. E. 1932, 1936
Pandit, C. S. 1986
Pandole, D. C. 1888
Parkar, G. A. 1982
Pataudi, Nawab of, Snr 1946
Pataudi, Nawab of, Jnr 1967
Patel, B. P. 1974, 1979
Patel, D. H. 1986
Patiala, Maharajah of 1911
Patil, S. M. 1982, 1986
Pavri, M. E. 1888
Phadkar, D. G. 1952
Ponchlchanawalla, J. 1886
Porbander, Maharaja of 1932
Prabhakar, M. 1986
Prasanna, E. A. S. 1967, 1971, 1974

Ramaswami, C. 1936
Ramchand, G. S. 1952
Randhir Singh 1982
Reddy, B. 1979
Roy, Pankaj 1952, 1959
Roy, Pranab 1982

Salamudin, K. 1911
Sarwate, C. T. 1946, 1952
Saxema, R. C. 1967
Sardesai, D. N. 1967, 1971
Sen, P. 1952
Seshachari, K. 1911
Shafqat Hussain 1911
Sharma, Chetan 1986
Shastri, R. J. 1982, 1986
Shinde, S. G. 1946, 1952
Shivram, P. 1911
Sohoni, S. W. 1946
Solkar, E. D. 1971, 1974
Srikkanth, K. 1986
Subramanyam, V. 1967
Surendranath, W. 1959
Surti, R. F. 1967

Tamhane, N. S. 1959

Umrigar, P. R. 1952, 1959

Vatcha, A. D. 1888
Vengsarkar, D. B. 1979, 1982, 1986
Venkataraghavan, S. 1967, 1971, 1974, 1979
Vizianagram, Maharaj of 1936

Wadekar, A. L. 1967, 1971, 1974
Warden, J. S. 1911
Wazir Ali, S. 1932, 1936
Writer, D. N. 1888

Yadav, N. S. 1982, 1986
Yajurvindra Singh 1979
Yashpal Sharma 1979, 1982

NEW ZEALAND
(including New Zealand Services in 1945)

Alabaster, J. C. 1958
Allcott, C. F. W. 1927, 1931
Anderson, R. W. 1973, 1978

Badcock, F. T. 1945
Barrett, B. J. 1986
Bernau, E. H. L. 1927
Blain, T. E. 1986
Blair, R. W. 1958
Blundell, E. D. 1927
Blunt, R. C. 1927, 1931, 1945
Boock, S. L. 1978
Bracewell, B. P. 1978
Bracewell, J. G. 1983, 1986
Burgess, A. T. 1945
Burgess, M. G. 1969, 1973, 1978
Burke, C. 1949
Burtt, T. B. 1949
Byerley, F. 1945

Cairns, B. L. 1978, 1983
Cameron, F. J. 1965
Carson, W. N. 1937
Cave, H. B. 1949, 1958
Chatfield, E. J. 1983, 986
Collinge, R. O. 1965, 1969, 1973, 1978
Coney, J. V. 1983, 1986
Congdon, B. E. 1965, 1969, 1973, 1978
Cowie, J. 1937, 1949
Cresswell, G. F. 1949
Cromb, I. B. 1931
Crowe, J. J. 1983, 1986
Crowe, M. D. 1983, 1986
Cunis, R. S. 1969
Cunningham, W. H. R. 1927

Dacre, C. C. R. 1927
D'Arcy, J. W. 1958
Dempster, C. S. 1927, 1931, 1945
Dowling, G. T. 1965, 1969
Dunning, J. A. 1937
Donnelly, M. P. 1937, 1945, 1949

Edgar, B. A. 1978, 1983, 1986
Edwards, G. N. 1978

Fox, R. H. 1927
Franklin, T. J. 1983, 1986

Gallichan, N. 1937
Gillott, E. K. 1973
Gray, E. J. 1983, 1986

Hadlee, D. R. 1969, 1973, 1978
Hadlee, R. J. 1973, 1978, 1983, 1986
Hadlee, W. A. 1937, 1949
Harford, N. S. 1958
Hastings, B. F. 1969, 1973
Hay, T. D. B. 1927
Hayes, J. A. 1949, 1958
Henderson, M. 1927

Hogan, R. 1945
Howarth, G. P. 1978, 1983
Howarth, H. J. 1969, 1973

James, K. C. 1927, 1931, 1945
Jarvis, T. W. 1965

Kerr, J. L. 1931, 1937

Lamason, J. R. 1937
Lees, W. K. 1983
Lowry, T. C. 1927, 1931, 1937

MacGibbon, A. R. 1958
McGirr, H. M. 1927
McIntyre, J. M. 1978
Matheson, A. M. 1931
Meale, T. 1958
Merritt, W. E. 1927, 1931
Milburn, B. D. 1969
Miller, L. S. M. 1958
Mills, J. E. 1927, 1931
Moir, A. M. 1958
Moloney, D. A. R. 1937
Mooney, F. L. H. 1949
Morgan, R. T. 1945
Morgan, R. W. 1965
Motz, R. C. 1965, 1969
Murray, B. A. G. 1969

Oliver, C. J. 1927

Page, M. L. 1927, 1931, 1937
Parker, J. M. 1973, 1978
Petrie, E. C. 1958
Playle, W. R. 1958
Pollard, V. 1965, 1969, 1973
Pritchard, T. L. 1945

Rabone, G. O. 1949
Redmond, R. E. 1973
Reid, J. R. 1949, 1958, 1965
Ridland, J. D. 1945
Roberts, A. C. 1945
Roberts, A. W. 1937
Rutherford, K. R. 1986

Scott, V. J. 1949
Sharpe, T. M. 1945
Sinclair, B. W. 1965
Smith, F. B. 1949
Smith, I. D. S. 1983, 1986
Snedden, M. C. 1983
Sparling, J. T. 1958
Stirling, D. A. 1986
Sutcliffe, B. 1949, 1958, 1965

Talbot, R. O. 1931
Taylor, B. R. 1965, 1969, 1973
Thomson, G. B. 1978
Tindall, E. W. 1937
Tracy, S. R. 1983
Troup, G. B. 1978
Turner, G. M. 1969, 1973

Vivian, G. E. 1965
Vivian, H. G. 1931, 1937

Wadsworth, K. J. 1969, 1973
Wallace, W. M. 1937, 1949
Ward, J. T. 1958, 1965
Watson, W. 1986
Weir, G. L. 1931, 1937
Wright, J. G. 1978, 1983, 1986

Yuile, B. W. 1965, 1969

PAKISTAN *(includes Eaglets)*

Amer Hameed 1978
Abdul Qadir 1978, 1982, 1987
Afaq Hussain 1962, 1963
Aftab Baloch 1974
Aftab Gul 1971, 1974
Aizazuddin, F. S. 1963, 1967
Alim-ud-Din 1954, 1962
Arif Butt 1967
Arshad Pervez 1978
Asif Ahmed 1962
Asif Iqbal 1963, 1967, 1971, 1974
Asif Masood 1971, 1974
Asif Mujtaba 1987
Azeem Hafeez 1987
Azmat Rana 1971

Burki, Javed 1962, 1967

D'Souza, Antao 1962, 1963

Ehtesham-ud-Din 1982

Farooq Hamid 1963
Fasih-ud-Din 1967
Fazal Mahmood 1954, 1962

Ghazali, M. E. Z. 1954
Ghulam Abbas 1967

Hanif Mohammad 1954, 1962, 1967
Haroon Rashid 1978, 1982
Hasan Jamal 1978
Haseeb Ahsan 1962, 1963

Ibadulla, Khalid 1967
Ijaz Ahmed 1987
Ijaz Butt 1962
Ijaz Hussain 1963
Ikram Elahi 1954
Imran Khan 1971, 1974, 1982, 1987
Imtiaz Ahmed 1954, 1962
Intikhab Alam 1962, 1963, 1967, 1971, 1974, 1982
Iqbal Qasim 1978, 1982, 1987

Jalal-ud-Din 1982
Javed Akhtar 1962
Javed Miandad 1978, 1982, 1987

Kardar, A. H. 1954
Khalid Hassan 1954
Khalid Wazir 1954
Khan Mohammad 1954

Liaqat Ali 1978

Maazullah Khan 1974

Mahmood Hussain 1954, 1962
Majid J. Khan 1963, 1967, 1971, 1974,
  1982
Mansoor Akhtar 1982, 1987
Mansoor Elahi 1987
Maqsood Ahmed 1954
Masood Iqbal 1978
Mathias, Wallis 1962
Mohammad Aslam 1954
Mohammad Farooq 1962
Mohammad Ilyas 1967
Mohammad Munaf 1963
Mohammad Nazir 1971, 1974
Mohsin Kamal 1987
Mohsin Khan 1978, 1982
Mudassar Nazar 1978, 1982, 1987
Munir Malik 1962
Mushtaq Mohammad 1962, 1963, 1967,
  1971, 1974

Naeem Ahmed 1978
Naseer Malik 1974
Nasim-ul-Ghani 1962, 1967
Naushad Ali 1963, 1971
Niaz Ahmed 1967

Pervez Sajjad 1963, 1967, 1971

Ramiz Raja 1987

Sadiq Mohammad 1963, 1971, 1974,
  1978
Saeed Ahmed 1962, 1967, 1971
Salah-ud-Din 1967
Saleem Jaffer 1987
Salim Altaf 1967, 1971
Salim Malik 1982, 1987
Salim-ud-Din 1963
Salim Yousuf 1982, 1987
Sarfraz Nawaz 1971, 1974, 1978,
  1982
Shahid Mahmood 1962
Shafiq Ahmed 1974
Shafqat Rana 1963, 1971
Shakoor Ahmed 1954
Shoaib Mohammad 1987
Shuja-ud-Din 1984
Shuja-ud-Din Butt 1962
Sikander Bakht 1978, 1982

Tahir Naqqash 1982
Talat Ali 1971, 1978
Tauseef Ahmed 1987

Waqar Ahmed 1954, 1967
Wasim Akram 1987
Wasim Bari 1967, 1971, 1974, 1978,
  1982
Wasim Raja 1974, 1978, 1982
Wazir Mohammad 1954, 1963

Zaheer Abbas 1971, 1974, 1982
Zakir Khan 1987
Zulfiqar Ahmed 1954

PHILADELPHIA AND UNITED STATES

Adams, D. H. 1908

Baily, H. P. 1889, 1897
Bates, F. H. 1897, 1903
Biddle, L. A. 1897
Bohlen, F. H. 1897, 1903, 1908
Brewster, F. E. 1884, 1889
Brockie, W. 1884
Brook, W. 1968
Brown, H. I. 1884, 1889
Brown, R. D. 1889, 1903

Clark, E. W. 1884, 1889
Clark, H. L. 1897
Clark, P. H. 1897, 1903
Coates, C. 1897
Cooper, A. W. M. 1968
Cregar, E. M. 1897, 1903, 1908

Durity, H. 1968
Dyal, S. E. 1968

Ettling, N. 1889

Fernandes, L. F. 1968
Fox, J. M. 1884

Graves, N. Z. 1903, 1908
Greene, F. A. 1908

Haines, H. A. 1903
Hollick, P. J. 1968
Hordern, H. V. 1908
Hussain, A. 1968

Jeffrey, P. L. 1968
Jordan, T. C. 1903, 1908

King, J. B. 1897, 1903, 1908

Lashkari, A. 1968
Law, S. 1884
Le Roy, P. N. 1903
Lester, J. A. 1897, 1903, 1908
Lowry, W. C. 1884

MacNutt, H. 1884
Masood Khan 1968
Merrett, P. A. 1968
Morgan, W. C. 1884, 1889
Morris, C. C. 1903, 1908
Mullings, L. C. 1968

Newhall, C. A. 1884
Newhall, D. S. 1889
Newhall, R. S. 1884
Newhall, W. P. 1908

Palmer, C. R. 1889
Parry, P. 1968
Patterson, G. S. 1889, 1897

Ralston, F. W. 1897
Reid, J. J. 1968
Rock, G. 1968

Sayen, W. H. 1908
Scattergood, J. H. 1897, 1903
Scott, J. A. 1884
Scott, W. 1889
Serpanchy, K. 1968
Severn, R. C. 1968

Severn, W. F. M. 1968
Sharp, J. W. 1889
Sharpless, F. C. 1903
Stoever, D. P. 1884, 1889
Stollmeyer, M. A. 1968

Thackurdhin, S. 1968
Thayer, H. C. 1897
Thayer, J. B. 1884
Thomson, A. G. 1889

Verity, M. A. 1968

Warder, G. B. 1889
WWite, F. S. 1908
Winter, C. H. 1908
Wisdom, M. A. 1968
Wood, A. M. 1897, 1903, 1908

SOUTH AFRICA
(includes W. Isaacs' Tours)

Adcock, N. A. T. 1955, 1960, 1966

Bacher, A. 1965
Balaskas, X. 1935
Barlow, E. J. 1961, 1965
Beaumont, R. 1912
Begbie, D. W. 1947
Bell, A. J. 1929, 1935
Benaud, R. 1966
Bisset, A. V. C. 1901
Bisset, G. F. 1924
Bisset, M. 1901
Blanckenberg, J. M. 1924
Bland, K. C. 1961, 1965
Botten, J. T. 1961, 1965
Bromfield, H. D. 1965
Bruyns, A. 1966, 1969
Bunyard, G. S. 1961
Burger, C. G. de V. 1961

Cameron, H. B. 1929, 1935
Campbell, T. 1912
Carlstein, P. R. 1960
Carter, C. P. 1912, 1924
Castens, H. H. 1894
Catterall, R. H. 1924, 1929
Chatterton, E. 1969
Cheetham, J. E. 1951, 1955
Christy, J. A. J. 1929
Chubb, G. W. A. 1951
Cole, J. McG. 1966
Collins, R. R. 1969
Commaille, J. M. M. 1924
Compton, D. C. S. 1966
Cooley, B. C. 1901
Cox, J. L. 1912
Cripps, G. 1894
Crisp, R. J. 1935
Crookes, N. S. 1965

Dalton, E. L. 1929, 1935
Davey, D. C. 1894
Dawson, O. C. 1947
Day, C. I. 1969
Deane, H. G. 1924, 1929
Dixon, C. D. 1924

Duckworth, C. A. R. 1955, 1960
Dumbrill, R. 1965
Duminy, J. P. 1929
Dyer, D. V. 1947

Elgie, M. K. 1961
Endean, W. R. 1951, 1955
Eriksen, R. 1966

Faulkner, G. A. 1907, 1912, 1924
Fellows-Smith, J. P. 1960
Ferrant, J. G. 1966
Flanagan, J. P. D. 1969
Fuller, E. R. H. 1955
Fullerton, G. M. 1947, 1951
Fullerton, I. R. 1961
Funston, K. J. 1966

Gamsy, D. 1965
Glover, G. 1894
Goddard, T. L. 1955, 1960
Graham, R. 1901
Griffin, G. M. 1960
Gripper, R. A. 1961

Hall, G. C. 1966
Halliwell, E. A. 1894, 1901, 1904
Harris, T. A. 1947
Hartigan, G. P. D. 1912
Harvey, M. McN. 1969
Hathorn, C. M. H. 1901, 1904, 1907
Hearne, F. 1894
Hearne, G. A. L. 1924
Heine, P. S. 1955
Hands, P. A. M. 1924
Henwood, P. P. 1966, 1969
Horwood, S. E. 1904

Irvine, B. L. 1966
Isaacs, W. 1966, 1969

Johnson, C. L. 1894

Keith, H. J. 1955
Kempis, G. S. 1894
Kerr, W. R. 1969
Kotze, J. J. 1901, 1904, 1907

Lance, H. R. 1965
Langton, A. B. C. 1935
Lindsay, D. T. 1961, 1965
Lindsay, J. D. 1947
Llewellyn, C. B. 1901, 1904, 1912
Logan, J. D. 1901

Macaulay, M. J. 1965
McCarthy, C. N. 1951
Mackay-Coghill, D. 1966, 1969
McGlew, D. J. 1951, 1955, 1960, 1966
McKinnon, A. H. 1960, 1965
McLean, R. A. 1951, 1955, 1960, 1961, 1966
McMillan, Q. 1929
Mann, N. B. F. 1947, 1951
Mansell, P. N. F. 1951, 1955
Meintjes, D. J. 1924
Melle, M. G. 1951
Melville, A. 1947
Middleton, J. 1894, 1901
Mills, C. 1894

Mitchell, B. 1929, 1935, 1947
Mitchell, F. 1904, 1912
Morbey-Smith, L. 1961
Morkel, D. P. B. 1929
Murray, A. R. A. 1955

Nourse, A. D. 1935, 1947, 1951
Nourse, A. W. 1907, 1912, 1924
Nupen, E. P. 1924

Ochse, A. L. 1929
Overstone, D. M. 1947
Owen-Smith, H. G. O. 1929

Parker, G. M. 1924
Parkin, D. C. 1894
Payn, L. W. 1947
Pegler, S. J. 1912, 1924
Pithey, A. J. 1960
Plimsoll, J. B. 1947
Prince, C. F. H. 1901
Pollock, P. M. 1961, 1965
Pollock, R. G. 1965, 1969
Pothecary, J. E. 1960
Procter, M. J. 1966

Quinn, N. A. 1929

Reid, A. 1901
Richards, B. A. 1966
Robinson, C. D. 1907
Rosendorff, N. 1969
Routledge, T. 1894
Rowan, A. M. B. 1947, 1951
Rowan, E. A. B. 1935, 1951
Rowe, G. A. 1894, 1901
Rushmore, C. G. 1961

Schwartz, R. O. 1904, 1907, 1912
Seccull, A. W. 1894
Seidle, I. J. 1929, 1935
Sewell, C. O. H. 1894
Shalders, W. A. 1901, 1904, 1907
Shepstone, G. H. 1904
Sherwell, P. W. 1907
Sinclair, J. H. 1901, 1904, 1907
Smith, H. E. 1901
Smith, V. I. 1947, 1955
Smithyman, M. J. 1969
Snooke, S. D. 1907
Snooke, S. J. 1904, 1907, 1912
Stricker, L. A. 1912
Susskind, M. J. 1924

Tancred, L. J. 1901, 1904, 1907, 1912
Tayfield, H. J. 1951, 1955, 1960, 1966
Tayfield, I. R. 1969
Taylor, H. W. 1912, 1924, 1929
Tomlinson, D. S. 1935
Tuckett, L. 1947

van der Bijl, V. A. P. 1969
van der Merwe, E. A. 1929
van der Merwe, P. L. 1961, 1965
van Ryneveld, C. B. 1951
Viljoen, K. J. 1935, 1947
Vincent, C. L. 1929, 1935
Vogler, A. E. E. 1907

Wade, H. F. 1935
Waite, J. H. B. 1951, 1955, 1960, 1969

Wallach, B. 1904
Ward, I. A. 1912, 1924
Watson, G. L. G. 1966
Wesley, C. 1960, 1966
White, G. C. 1904, 1907, 1912
Williams, R. J. 1935
Winslow, P. L. 1955

SRI LANKA

Ahangama, F. S. 1988
Anurasiri, S. D. 1984, 1988

de Alwis, R. G. 1984
de Mel, A. L. F. 1981, 1984
de Silva, D. L. S. 1979
de Silva, D. S. 1979, 1981
de Silva, G. R. A. 1979, 1981
de Silva, P. A. 1984, 1988
Devapriya, H. 1981
Dias, R. L. 1979, 1981, 1984

Fernando, L. J. 1981

Goonatillake, H. M. 1981
Gunasekera, Y. 1981
Gunatilleke, F. R. M. 1979

Hettiaratehy, N. D. P. 1981

Jayasekera, R. S. A. 1979
Jayasinghe, S. A. 1979
Jeganathan, S. 1979
John, V. B. 1984

Kaluperuma, L. W. 1981
Kuruppu, D. S. B. P. 1984, 1988

Labrooy, G. F. 1988

Madugalle, R. S. 1979, 1981, 1984, 1988
Madurasinghe, A. W. R. 1988
Mahanama, R. S. 1988
Mendis, L. R. D. 1979, 1981, 1984, 1988

Opatha, A. R. M. 1979

Pasqual, S. P. 1979

Rajadurai, B. E. A. 1988
Ramanayake, C. P. H. 1988
Ranasinghe, A. N. 1981
Ranatunga, A. 1984, 1988
Ratnayeke, J. R. 1981, 1984, 1988

Samaranayake, A. D. A. 1984
Samarasekera, S. A. R. 1988
Silva, S. A. R. 1984, 1988

Tennekoon, A. P. B. 1979
Tillekeratne 1988

Vonhagt, D. M. 1984

Warnapura, B. 1979, 1981
Wettimuny, S. R. D. 1979, 1981, 1984
Wijesuriya, R. G. C. E. 1979, 1981

Yusuf, M. M. 1984

ACKNOWLEDGEMENTS

*The publishers would like to thank the following
organisations and individuals for their kind permission
to reproduce the photographs in this book:*

AllSport/Gray Mortimore 380; AllSport/Adrian Murrell
190, 377; Colorsport 325; Patrick Eagar Title spread,
168, 169, 173, 174, 177, 179, 180, 181, 182, 183, 185,
188, 191, 193, 196r, 197t, 200, 203, 204, 323t, 329t,
336c&b, 337, 338, 340, 342, 343, 344, 346, 347, 348,
349, 350, 353, 355, 356, 358, 359, 361, 362, 363, 364,
366, 367, 368l, 369, 371, 372, 374, 375, 376, 378, 379;
Mary Evans Picture Library 14, 16b, 47; Hulton Deutsch
Picture Company 45, 67, 74, 77, 78, 82, 83, 86b, 87, 94,
96b, 98b, 101, 103, 105b, 107b, 114, 116b, 117, 118,
121t, 122, 125, 127, 129, 131, 133, 136, 139, 144, 149,
152, 155, 158, 164, 166, 290, 295, 297, 299, 302b, 304,
309, 313; Graham Morris 196l, 197b, 198; Sport and
General 121b, 202, 317, 319t, 320, 322, 324, 326, 329b,
330, 331, 336t, 345, 352; Trent Bridge Cricket Ground,
Nottingham 63, 86t, 91t, 96t, 98t, 107t, 209, 214, 216,
221, 222, 224, 227, 229, 234, 237, 241, 242, 244, 245,
247, 250, 253, 256, 259, 260, 262, 265, 267, 269, 271,
273, 274, 275, 277, 280, 281, 282, 284, 285, 286, 287,
292, 300, 302t, 306, 318, 319b, 323b, 327, 333, 334,
339; Trent Bridge Cricket Ground/Octopus Picture Library 13, 15, 16t, 17, 20, 22, 24, 25, 26, 29, 31, 32, 36, 41,
43, 44, 46, 50, 56, 60, 61, 69, 88, 91b, 105t, 109.